# international marketing

## twelfth edition

philip R. cateora

FELLOW, ACADEMY OF INTERNATIONAL BUSINESS
UNIVERSITY OF COLORADO

john L. Graham

UNIVERSITY OF CALIFORNIA, IRVINE

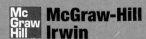

**McGraw-Hill**
**Irwin**

Boston   Burr Ridge, IL   Dubuque, IA   Madison, WI   New York   San Francisco   St. Louis
Bangkok   Bogotá   Caracas   Kuala Lumpur   Lisbon   London   Madrid   Mexico City
Milan   Montreal   New Delhi   Santiago   Seoul   Singapore   Sydney   Taipei   Toronto

## INTERNATIONAL MARKETING

Published by McGraw-Hill/Irwin, a business unit of The McGraw-Hill Companies, Inc., 1221 Avenue of the Americas, New York, NY, 10020.

ISBN 0-07-283371-8

Editorial director: *John E. Biernat*
Sponsoring editor: *Barrett Koger*
Developmental editor I: *Anna M. Chan*
Marketing manager: *Ellen Cleary*
Media producer: *Craig Atkins*
Project manager: *Susanne Riedell*
Production supervisor: *Gina Hangos*
Cover and interior designer: *Kami Carter*
Photo research coordinator: *Judy Kausal*
Photo researcher: *Charlotte Goldman*
Supplement producer: *Betty Hadala*
Senior digital content specialist: *Brian Nacik*
Cover image: © *Matt Wuerker*
Typeface: *10/12 Times New Roman*
Compositor: *GTS–Los Angeles, CA Campus*
Printer: *Von Hoffmann Corporation*

**PHOTO CREDITS** *For Table of Contents:* p. xxiii ©AFP/CORBIS; p. xxvi ©AFP/CORBIS; p. xxxiv ©Photodisc. *For Chapter/Cases Openers:* p. 2 ©Photodisc; p. 26 ©AFP/CORBIS; p. 56 ©Dave G. Houser/CORBIS; p. 156 ©Reuters NewMedia Inc./CORBIS; p. 178 AP/Wide World Photos; p. 242 ©AFP/CORBIS; p. 276 ©AFP/CORBIS; p. 398 ©AFP/CORBIS; p. 434 AP/Wide World Photos; p. 466 ©AFP/CORBIS; p. 500 ©Roger Ressmeyer/CORBIS; p. 528 AP/Wide World Photos; p. 562 Copyrighted and used by permission of KARRASS, LTD. Beverly Hills, California; p. 619 AP/Wide World Photos.

### Library of Congress Cataloging-in-Publication Data

Cateora, Philip R.
    International marketing / Philip R. Cateora, John L. Graham. --12th ed.
        p. cm. -- (The McGraw-Hill/Irwin series in marketing)
    Includes bibliographical references and index.
    ISBN 0-07-283371-8 (alk. paper)
    1. Export marketing. 2. International business enterprises. I. Graham, John L. II. Title.
III. Series.
HF1416.C375 2005
658.8'4--dc22

                                                                                2003064164

www.mhhe.com

# international marketing

# McGraw–Hill/Irwin Series in Marketing

# PREFACE

At the start of the last millennium the Chinese were the preeminent international traders. Although a truly global trading system would not evolve until some 500 years later, Chinese silk was then available in Europe.

At the start of the last century the British military, merchants, and manufacturers dominated the seas and international commerce. Literally, the sun did not set on the British Empire.

At the start of the last decade Japan's economic successes had rendered the military competition between the United States and the Soviet Union obsolete. Pundits circa 1990 predicted a Pacific Century wherein trans-Pacific trade would surpass trans-Atlantic trade. Other Asian economies would follow the lead of Japan. No one then foresaw the ascendancy and impact of the American-created information technology revolution.

What surprises do the new decade, century, and millennium hold in store for all of us? The globalization of markets has certainly accelerated through almost universal acceptance of the democratic free enterprise model and new communication technologies, including satellites and the Internet. Which will prove the better, Chinese gradualism or the Russian big-bang approach to economic and political reform? Will the information technology boom of the previous decade be followed by a demographics bust when American baby boomers try to retire in 2010? Or will NAFTA and the young folks in Mexico provide a much needed demographic balance? Ten years out the debate about global warming should be settled—more data and better science will yield the answers. What unforeseen advances or disasters will the biological sciences bring us? Will we conquer AIDS/HIV in Africa? Will weapons and warfare become obsolete?

International marketing will play a key role in providing positive answers to all these questions. We know that trade causes peace and prosperity by promoting creativity, mutual understanding, and interdependence. Markets are burgeoning in emerging economies in Eastern Europe, the Commonwealth of Independent States, China, Indonesia, Korea, India, Mexico, Chile, Brazil, and Argentina—in short, globally. These emerging economies hold the promise of huge markets in the future. In the more mature markets of the industrialized world, opportunity and challenge also abound as consumers' tastes become more sophisticated and complex and as increases in purchasing power provide consumers with new means of satisfying new demands.

Opportunities in today's global markets are on a par with the global economic expansion that existed after World War II. Today, however, the competitive environment within which these opportunities exist is vastly different from that earlier period when United States' multinationals dominated world markets. From the late 1940s through the 1960s, multinational corporations (MNCs) from the United States had little competition; today, companies from almost all the world's nations vie for global markets.

There is no better illustration of the changes that have occurred in the competition for global markets in the last quarter century than that experienced by General Electric Lighting (GEL). GEL, begun in 1887, dominated the U.S. lighting market until traditional rival Westinghouse sold its lamp operations to Philips Electronics of Holland in 1983. "Suddenly," reflected GEL's chief, "we have bigger, stronger competition. They're coming to our market, but we're not in theirs. So we're on the defensive." Not long after, GEL acquired Tungsram, a Hungarian lighting company, and Thorn EMI in Britain, and then moved into Asia via a joint venture with Hitachi. As recently as 1988, GE Lighting got less than 20 percent of its sales from outside the United States; in 2000, more than half came from abroad. What happened at GE Lighting occurred over and over again to MNCs in the United States, Europe, and Asia. The companies that succeed in the twenty-first century will be those capable of adapting to constant change and adjusting to new challenges.

The economic, political, and social changes that have occurred over the last decade have dramatically altered the landscape of global business. Consider the present and future impact of the following:

- The ever-present threat of global terrorism as represented by the September 11 attacks
- Major armed conflicts in sub-Sahara Africa and the Middle East
- The looming global recession
- The emerging markets in Eastern Europe, Asia, and Latin America, where more than 75 percent of the growth in world trade over the next 20 years is expected to occur
- The reunification of Hong Kong, Macau, and China, which finally puts all of Asia under the control of Asians for the first time in over a century
- The European Monetary Union and the successful switch from local-country currencies to one monetary unit for Europe, the euro
- The rapid move away from traditional distribution structures in Japan, Europe, and many emerging markets
- The growth of middle-income households the world over
- The continued strengthening and creation of regional market groups such as the European Union (EU), the North American Free Trade Area (NAFTA), ASEAN Free Trade Area (AFTA), the Free Trade Area of the Americas (FTAA), the Southern Cone Free Trade Area (Mercosur), and the Asian-Pacific Economic Cooperation (APEC)
- The successful completion of the Uruguay Round of the General Agreement on Tariffs and Trade (GATT) and the creation of the World Trade Organization (WTO), the last now including China and Taiwan
- The restructuring, reorganizing, and refocusing of companies in telecommunications, entertainment, and biotechnology, as well as in traditional smokestack industries around the world
- The continuing integration of the Internet into all aspects of companies' operations and consumers' lives

These are not simply news reports. These changes affect the practice of business worldwide, and they mean that companies will have to constantly examine the way they do business and remain flexible enough to react rapidly to changing global trends to be competitive.

As global economic growth occurs, understanding marketing in all cultures is increasingly important. *International Marketing* addresses global issues and describes concepts relevant to all international marketers, regardless of the extent of their international involvement. Not all firms engaged in overseas marketing have a global perspective, nor do they need to. Some companies' foreign marketing is limited to one country; others market in a number of countries, treating each as a separate market; and still others, the global enterprises, look for market segments with common needs and wants across political and economic boundaries. All, however, are affected by competitive activity in the global marketplace. It is with this future that the twelfth edition of *International Marketing* is concerned.

Emphasis is on the strategic implications of competition in different country markets. An environmental/cultural approach to international marketing permits a truly global orientation. The reader's horizons are not limited to any specific nation or to the particular ways of doing business in a single nation. Instead, the book provides an approach and framework for identifying and analyzing the important cultural and environmental uniqueness of any nation or global region. Thus, when surveying the tasks of marketing in a foreign milieu, the reader will not overlook the impact of crucial cultural issues.

The text is designed to stimulate curiosity about management practices of companies, large and small, seeking market opportunities outside the home country and to raise the reader's consciousness about the importance of viewing international marketing management strategies from a global perspective.

Although this revised edition is infused throughout with a global orientation, export marketing and the operations of smaller companies are not overlooked. Issues specific to exporting are discussed where strategies applicable to exporting arise, and examples of marketing practices of smaller companies are examined.

## New and Expanded Topics in This Edition

The new and expanded topics in this twelfth edition reflect issues in competition, changing marketing structures, ethics and social responsibility, negotiations, and the development of the manager for the twenty-first century. Competition is raising the global standards for quality, increasing the demand for advanced technology and innovation, and increasing the value of customer satisfaction. The global market is swiftly changing from a seller's market to a buyer's market. This is a period of profound social, economic, and political change. To remain competitive globally, companies must be aware of all aspects of the emerging global economic order.

Additionally, the evolution of global communications and its known and unknown impact on how international business is conducted cannot be minimized. In the third millennium people in the "global village" will grow closer than ever, and will hear and see each other as a matter of course. An executive in Germany will be able to routinely pick up his or her videophone to hear and see his or her counterpart in an Australian company or anywhere else in the world. In many respects, geographic distance is becoming irrelevant.

Telecommunications, videophones, facsimile machines, the Internet, and satellites are helping companies optimize their planning, production, and procurement processes. Information—and, in its wake, the flow of goods—is moving around the globe at lightning speed. Increasingly powerful networks spanning the globe enable the delivery of services that reach far beyond national and continental boundaries, fueling and fostering international trade. The connections of global communications bring people all around the world together in new and better forms of dialogue and understanding.

This dynamic nature of the international marketplace is reflected in the number of substantially improved and expanded topics in this twelfth edition, including the following:

- A deeper look at the causes of cultural differences
- The Internet and its expanding role in international marketing
- Negotiations with customers, partners, and regulators
- Big emerging markets (BEMs)
- Evolving global middle-income households
- World Trade Organization
- North American Free Trade Agreement
- ASEAN Free Trade Area
- Asia-Pacific Economic Cooperation
- Multicultural research
- Qualitative and quantitative research
- Country-of-origin effect and global brands
- Industrial trade shows
- A growing emphasis on both consumer and industrial services
- Trends in channel structures in Europe, Japan, and developing countries
- Ethics and socially responsible decisions
- Green marketing
- Changing profiles of global managers

# Structure of the Text

The text is divided into six parts. The first two chapters, Part 1, introduce the reader to the environmental/cultural approach to international marketing and to three international marketing management concepts: domestic market expansion, multidomestic marketing, and global marketing. As companies restructure for the global competitive rigors of the twenty-first century, so too must tomorrow's managers. The successful manager must be globally aware and have a frame of reference that goes beyond a country, or even a region, and encompasses the world. What global awareness means and how it is acquired is discussed early in the text; it is at the foundation of global marketing.

Chapter 2 focuses on the dynamic environment of international trade and the competitive challenges and opportunities confronting today's international marketer. The importance of the creation of the World Trade Organization, the successor to GATT, is fully explored. The growing importance of the Internet in conducting international business is considered, creating a foundation on which specific applications in subsequent chapters are presented.

The five chapters in Part 2 deal with the cultural environment of global marketing. A global orientation requires the recognition of cultural differences and the critical decision of whether or not it is necessary to accommodate them.

History and geography (Chapter 3) are included as important dimensions in understanding cultural and market differences among countries. Not to be overlooked is concern for the deterioration of the global ecological environment and the multinational company's critical responsibility to protect it.

Chapter 4 presents a broad review of culture and its impact on human behavior as it relates to international marketing. Specific attention is paid to Geert Hofstede's study of cultural values and behavior. The elements of culture reviewed in Chapter 4 set the stage for the in-depth analyses in Chapters 5, 6, and 7 of business customs and the political and legal environments. Ethics and social responsibility are presented in the context of the dilemma that often confronts the international manager, that is, balancing corporate profits against the social and ethical consequences of his or her decisions.

The three chapters in Part 3 are concerned with assessing global market opportunities. As markets expand, segments grow within markets; as market segments across country markets evolve, marketers are forced to understand market behavior within and across different cultural contexts. Multicultural research, qualitative and quantitative research, and the Internet as a tool in the research task are explored in Chapter 8.

Chapters 9 and 10 in Part 3 explore the impact of the three important trends in global marketing: the growth and expansion of the world's big emerging markets; the rapid growth of middle-income market segments; and the steady creation of regional market groups that include NAFTA, the European Union, AFTA, APEC, and the evolving Free Trade Area of the Americas (FTAA). Also discussed is the growing number of trade agreements that have been executed by the European Union and Japan with the FTAA and some Latin American countries.

The strategic implications of the dissolution of the USSR, the emergence of new independent republics, the shift from socialist-based to market-based economies in Eastern Europe, and the return of South Africa and Vietnam to international commerce are examined. Attention is also given to the efforts of the governments of India and many Latin American countries to reduce or eliminate barriers to trade, open their countries to foreign investment, and privatize state-owned enterprises.

These political, social, and economic changes that are sweeping the world are creating new markets and opportunities, making some markets more accessible while creating the potential for greater protectionism in others.

In Part 4, Developing Global Marketing Strategies, planning and organizing for global marketing is the subject of Chapter 11. The discussion of collaborative relationships, including strategic alliances, recognizes the importance of relational collaborations among firms, suppliers, and customers in the success of the global marketer. Many multinational companies realize that to fully capitalize on opportunities offered by global markets, they must have strengths that often exceed their capabilities. Collaborative relationships can provide technology, innovations, productivity, capital, and market access that strengthen a company's competitive position.

Chapters 12 and 13 focus on product and services management, reflecting the differences in strategies between consumer and industrial offerings and the growing importance in world markets for both consumer and business services. Additionally, the discussion on the development of global offerings stresses the importance of approaching the adaptation issue from the viewpoint of building a standardized product/service platform that can be adapted to reflect cultural differences. The competitive importance in today's global market for quality, innovation, and technology as the keys to marketing success is explored.

Chapter 14 takes the reader through the distribution process, from home country to the consumer in the target country market. The structural impediments to market entry imposed by a country's distribution system are examined in the framework of a detailed presentation of the Japanese distribution system. Additionally, the rapid changes in channel structure that are occurring in Japan, as well as in other countries, and the emergence of the World Wide Web as a distribution channel are presented.

In Chapter 15, the special issues involved in moving a product from one country market to another, and the accompanying mechanics of exporting, are addressed. The importance of the Internet in assisting the exporter to wade through the details of exporting is discussed in the context of the revised export regulations.

Chapter 16 covers advertising and addresses the promotional element of the international marketing mix. Included in the discussion of global market segmentation are recognition of the rapid growth of market segments across country markets and the importance of market segmentation as a strategic competitive tool in creating an effective promotional message. Chapter 17 discusses personal selling and sales management and the critical nature of training, evaluating, and controlling sales representatives.

Price escalation and ways it can be lessened, countertrade practices, and price strategies to employ when the dollar is strong or weak relative to foreign currencies are concepts presented in Chapter 18.

In Part 5, Chapter 19 is a thorough presentation of negotiating with customers, partners, and regulators. The discussion stresses the varying negotiation styles found among cultures and the importance of recognizing these differences at the negotiation table.

## Pedagogical Features of the Text
The text portion of the book provides a thorough coverage of its subject, with subject emphasis on the planning and strategic problems confronting companies that market across cultural boundaries.

The use of the Internet as a tool of international marketing is stressed throughout the text. On all occasions where data used in the text originated from an Internet source, the Web address is given. Problems that require the student to access the Internet are included with end-of-chapter questions. Internet-related problems are designed to familiarize the student with the power of the Internet in his or her research, to illustrate data available on the Internet, and to challenge the reader to solve problems using the Internet. Many of the examples, illustrations, and exhibits found in the text can be explored in more detail by accessing the Web addresses that are included.

Current, pithy, sometimes humorous, and always relevant examples are used to stimulate interest and increase understanding of the ideas, concepts and strategies presented in emphasizing the importance of understanding cultural uniqueness and relevant business practices and strategies.

Each chapter is introduced with a Global Perspective, a real-life example of company experiences that illustrates salient issues discussed in the chapter. Companies featured in the Global Perspectives range from exporters to global enterprises.

The boxed "Crossing Borders," an innovation of the first edition of *International Marketing,* have always been popular with students. This twelfth edition includes more than 30 new incidents that provide insightful examples of cultural differences while illustrating concepts presented in the text. They reflect contemporary issues in international marketing and can be used to illustrate real-life situations and as the basis for class discussion. They are selected to be unique, humorous, and of general interest to the reader.

The book is now presented in full color allowing for maps that allow easier depiction of geographical, cultural, and political boundaries and features. Color also allows us to better communicate through that medium the intricacies of international symbols and meanings in marketing communications. New photographs of current and relevant international marketing events are found throughout the text—all in color.

"The Country Notebook—A Guide for Developing a Marketing Plan," found in Part 6, Supplementary Material, is a detailed outline that provides both a format for a complete cultural and economic analysis of a country, and guidelines for developing a marketing plan.

In addition to "The Country Notebook," Part 6 comprises a selection of short and long cases. The short cases focus on a single problem, serving as the basis for discussion of a specific concept or issue. The longer, more integrated cases are broader in scope and focus on more than one marketing management problem. More than two-thirds of the cases are new or revised. New cases focus on healthcare marketing, negotiations, using the Internet, services and industrial marketing, and marketing research. The cases can be analyzed by using the information provided. They also lend themselves to more in-depth analysis, requiring the student to engage in additional research and data collection.

## Supplements

We have taken great care to offer new features and improvements to every part of the teaching aid package. Following is a list of specific features:

- **Instructor's Manual and Test Bank.** The Instructor's Manual, prepared by the authors, contains lecture notes or teaching suggestions for each chapter. A section called "Changes to This Edition" is included to help instructors adapt their teaching notes to the twelfth edition. A case correlation grid at the beginning of the case notes offers alternative uses for the cases.

  The Test Bank, prepared by John R. Brooks, Jr., of Houston Baptist University, is bound with the Instructor's Manual for ease of use. The Test Bank contains over 2,000 questions, including true/false, critical thinking, and essay formats. Computerized testing software with an online testing feature is also available on the instructor's CD-ROM.

- **Videos.** The video program has been revised for the twelfth edition and contains new footage of companies, topics videos, and unique training materials for international negotiations. Teaching notes and questions relevant to each chapter in the text are available at the *International Marketing* website at www.mhhe.com/cateora05.

- **PowerPoint slides.** The PowerPoint presentation that accompanies *International Marketing,* twelfth edition, contains approximately 150 exhibits from the text and other sources. All of the maps from the text are included as well. PowerPoint slides were prepared by Dr. Rajiv Mehta of the New Jersey Institute of Technology.

- **Instructor's CD-ROM.** This presentation manager, available to adopters of the textbook, contains the Instructor's Manual, Test Bank, PowerPoint, video clips, and an interactive version of the Country Notebook. Instructors have the ability to customize their lectures with this powerful tool.

- **World Wide Web Home Page.** The website is at www.mhhe.com/cateora05. Included on the site are instructor resources such as downloadable files for the complete Instructor's Manual, PowerPoint slides, video clips, and links to current events and additional resources for the classroom. Instructors can also link to McGraw-Hill's site from this location in order to create their own course website and access the complete Test Bank. For students, our site provides updates on information given in the text, links to websites, and an interactive version of the Country Notebook.

## Acknowledgments  The success of a text depends on the contributions of many people, especially those who take the time to share their thoughtful criticisms and suggestions to improve the text.

We would especially like to thank the following reviewers who gave us valuable insights into this revision.

David Amponsah
*Troy State University*

Anna Kwong
*Santa Barbara City College*

Turina Bakken
*MATC (Madison Area Technical College)*

Judith Powell
*Virginia Union University*

Charles Hermans
*Southwest Missouri State University*

Hugh Sloan
*University of Mississippi*

We appreciate the help of all the many students and professors who have shared their opinions of past editions, and we welcome their comments and suggestions on this and future editions of *International Marketing.*

A very special thanks to Barrett Koger, Anna Chan, Susanne Riedell, Gina Hangos, Kami Carter, Judy Kausal, Charlotte Goldman, Elizabeth Hadala, and Natalie Giboney at McGraw-Hill/Irwin, whose enthusiasm, creativity, constructive criticisms, and commitment to excellence have made this edition possible.

**Philip R. Cateora**
**John L. Graham**

# WALKTHROUGH
## A quick look at the new edition

**International Marketing** by Cateora and Graham has always been a pioneer in the field of international marketing. The authors continue to set the standard in this edition with new and expanded topics that reflect the swift changes of an expanding competitive global market as well as an increased coverage of technology's impact on the international market arena.

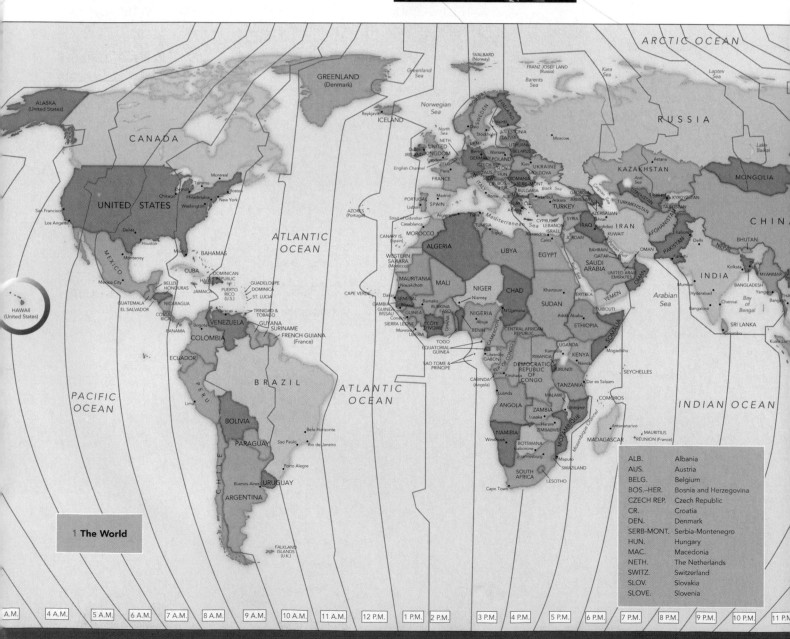

1 **The World**

| | |
|---|---|
| ALB. | Albania |
| AUS. | Austria |
| BELG. | Belgium |
| BOS.–HER. | Bosnia and Herzegovina |
| CZECH REP. | Czech Republic |
| CR. | Croatia |
| DEN. | Denmark |
| SERB-MONT. | Serbia-Montenegro |
| HUN. | Hungary |
| MAC. | Macedonia |
| NETH. | The Netherlands |
| SWITZ. | Switzerland |
| SLOV. | Slovakia |
| SLOVE. | Slovenia |

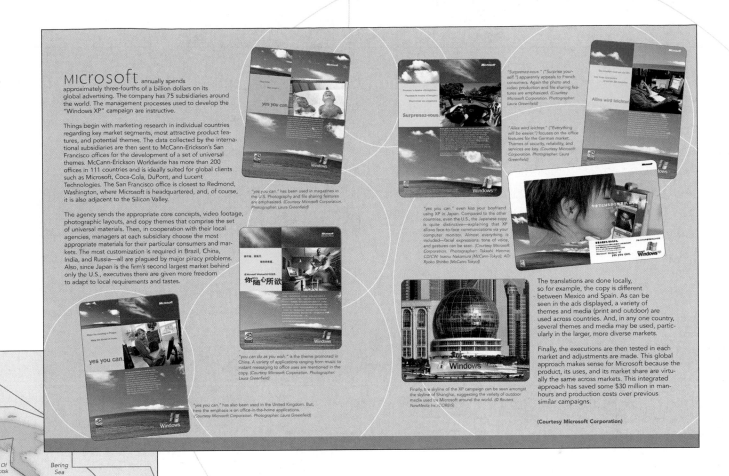

## NEW 4-Color Design

The 12th edition introduces a brand new 4-color design for the first time. New color maps and exhibits allow for improved pedagogy and a clearer presentation of international symbols and cultural meanings in marketing and advertising. In addition, photos that depend on full color for maximum impact easily bring many global examples to life. This visually stimulating combination works together to make the text material reader-friendly and accessible for both instructors and students.

# Chapter Openers

Chapter Outline provides students an at-a-glance overview of chapter topics, while Chapter Objectives summarize the chapter's goals and focus. Each chapter is introduced with a Global Perspective, a real-life example of company experiences that illustrates significant issues discussed in the chapter. Companies featured in the Global Perspective vignettes range from exporters to global enterprises.

---

## the political Environment:
### A CRITICAL CONCERN

**CHAPTER 6**

### CHAPTER OUTLINE

Global Perspective: Chiquita Bananas and Prosciutto di Parma, Louis Vuitton Handbags, Scented Bath Oils and Soaps, and Batteries—Strange Bedfellows from the World of Politics

The Sovereignty of Nations

Stability of Government Policies
  Political Parties
  Nationalism

Political Risks of Global Business
  Confiscation, Expropriation, and Domestication
  Economic Risks
  Political Sanctions
  Political and Social Activists
  Violence and Terrorism
  Cyberterrorism

Assessing Political Vulnerability
  Politically Sensitive Products and Issues
  Forecasting Political Risk

Reducing Political Vulnerability
  Joint Ventures
  Expanding the Investment Base
  Licensing
  Planned Domestication
  Political Payoffs

Government Encouragement

### CHAPTER LEARNING OBJECTIVES

What you should learn from Chapter 6:

- What the sovereignty of nations means and how it affects the stability of government policies, political parties, and nationalism
- The political risks of global business and the factors that affect stability
- The importance of the political system to international marketing and its effect on foreign investments
- The impact of political and social activists, violence, and terrorism on international business
- Assessing and reducing the effect of political vulnerability
- How and why governments encourage foreign investment

### Global Perspective

CHIQUITA BANANAS AND PROSCIUTTO DI PARMA, LOUIS VUITTON HANDBAGS, SCENTED BATH OILS AND SOAPS, AND BATTERIES—STRANGE BEDFELLOWS FROM THE WORLD OF POLITICS

As the old saying goes, "Politics makes strange bedfellows," but in this case the only one making out is Miss Chiquita Banana. Prosciutto di Parma ham from Italy, handbags from France, bath oils and soaps from Germany, and a host of other imported products from Europe were all slapped with a 100 percent import tariff as retaliation by the U.S. government against European Union (EU) banana-import rules that favor Caribbean bananas over Latin American bananas. Keep in mind that no bananas are exported from the United States, yet the United States has been engaged in a trade war over the last seven years that has cost numerous small businesses on both sides of the Atlantic millions of dollars. But how can this be, you ask? Politics, that's how!

A retailer of decorative prints has stopped selling one of the store's most popular and profitable items, English lithographs produced for him by a London art dealer. Action Battery, which sells and installs industrial batteries, has lost a quarter-million dollar account and faces the prospect of more losses. The same issue, a 100 percent tariff placed on all their imported products, has affected all these businesses; one directive from the U.S. government doubled the cost of their imported goods.

Reha Enterprises, for example, sells bath oil, soap, and other supplies imported from Germany. The tariff on its most popular product, an herbal foam bath, was raised from 5 percent to 100 percent. The customs bill for six months spiraled to $37,783 from just $1,851—a 1,941 percent tax increase. For a small business whose gross sales are less than $1 million annually, it is crippling. When the owner heard of the impending "banana war" he called everyone—his Congressman, his Senator, the United States Trade Representative (USTR). When he described his plight to a U.S. trade representative, the official expressed amazement. "They were surprised I was still importing," because they thought the tariff would cut off the industry entirely. That was their intention, which, of course, would have meant killing Reha Enterprises as well.

In effect, he was told it was his fault that he got caught up in the trade war. He should have attended the hearings in Washington just like Gillette and Mattel, and maybe his products would have been dropped from the targeted list just as theirs were. Scores of European products, from clothing to stoves to glass Christmas ornaments, dolls, and ballpoint pens that were originally targeted for the retaliatory tariffs escaped the tariff. Aggressive lobbying by large corporations, trade groups, and members of Congress got most of the threatened imported products off the list. The USTR had published a list of the targeted imports in the *Federal Register* inviting affected companies to testify. Unfortunately, the *Federal Register* is not on the owner's reading list.

In that case, he was told, he should have hired a lobbyist in Washington to keep him briefed. Good advice—but it doesn't make much sense to a company that grosses less than $1 million a year. Other advice received from an official of the USTR included the off-the-record suggestion that he might want to change the custom number on the invoice so it would appear that he was importing goods not subject to the tariff, a decision that could, if he were caught, result in a hefty fine or jail for the owner. Smaller businesses in Europe are facing similar problems as their export business dries up because of the tariffs.

How did this banana war start? The EU imposed a quota and tariffs that favored imports from ex-colonies in the Caribbean and Africa, distributed by European firms, over Latin American bananas, distributed by U.S. firms. Chiquita Brands International and Dole Food Company, contending that the EU's "illegal trade barriers" were costing $520 million annually in lost sales to Europe, asked the U.S. government for help. The government agreed that unfair trade barriers were damaging their business, and 100 percent tariffs on selected European imports were levied. Coincidentally, Chiquita Brands' annual campaign contributions increased from barely over $40,000 in 1991 to $1.3 million in 1998.

The European Union complained about the proposed U.S. tariffs and took a grievance to the World Trade Organization (WTO), which ruled in favor of the United States. The EU ignored the WTO and continued the banana tariffs, and the United States continued with its high tariffs—the banana war continued. The EU did little to comply with WTO rulings against European restrictions on importing bananas, and the war heated up. Because of lack of compliance, the USTR imposed a "carousel" provision that allows it to rotate, every six months, products that will be targeted for the 100 percent tariffs. Like all trade disputes, this one was ultimately settled, but at what cost to those caught in the middle between two nations and a giant MNC? The biggest losers were the African and Caribbean countries that Europe

---

## History and Geography:
### THE FOUNDATIONS OF CULTURE

**CHAPTER 3**

### CHAPTER OUTLINE

Global Perspective: Birth of a Nation—Panama in 67 Hours

Historical Perspective in Global Business
  History and Contemporary Behavior
  History Is Subjective
  Manifest Destiny and the Monroe Doctrine

Geography and Global Markets
  Climate and Topography
  Geography, Nature, and Economic Growth
  Social Responsibility and Environmental Management
  Resources

Dynamics of Global Population Trends
  Controlling Population Growth
  Rural/Urban Migration
  Population Decline and Aging
  Worker Shortage and Immigration

World Trade Routes

Communication Links

### CHAPTER LEARNING OBJECTIVES

What you should learn from Chapter 3:

- The importance of history and geography in the understanding of international markets
- The effects of history on a country's culture
- How culture interprets events through its own eyes
- How the United States moved West and its effect on attitudes
- Effect of geographic diversity on economic profiles of a country
- Marketers need to be responsive to geography of a country
- Economic effects of controlling population growth versus aging population
- Communications are an integral part of international commerce

### Global Perspective

BIRTH OF A NATION—PANAMA IN 67 HOURS

#### The Stage Is Set

June 1902  United States offers to buy the Panama Canal Zone from Colombia for $10 million.

August 1903  The Colombian Senate refuses the offer. Theodore Roosevelt, angered by the refusal, referred to the Colombian Senate as "those contemptible little creatures in Bogotá." Roosevelt agrees to a plot, led by a secessionist, Dr. Manuel Amador, to assist a group planning to secede from Colombia.

October 17  Panamanian dissidents travel to Washington and agree to stage a U.S.-backed revolution. The date of revolution is set for November 3 at 6 P.M.

October 18  Flag, constitution, and declaration of independence are created over the weekend. Panama's first flag was designed and sewn by hand in Highland Falls, New York, using fabric bought at Macy's.

Bunau-Varilla, a French engineer associated with the bankrupt French-Panama canal construction company and not a permanent resident in Panama, is named Panama's ambassador to the United States.

#### A Country Is Born

Tuesday,  Precisely at 6 P.M. bribes are paid to the
November 3  Colombian garrison to lay down their arms. The revolution begins, the U.S.S. *Nashville* steams into Colón harbor, and the junta proclaims Panama's independence.

Friday,  By 1:00 P.M. the United States
November 6  recognizes the sovereign state of Panama.

Saturday,  The new government sends an official
November 7  delegation from Panama to the United States to instruct the Panamanian ambassador to the United States on provisions of the Panama Canal Treaty.

Wednesday,  6:40 P.M. The Panamanian ambassador
November 18  signs the Panama Canal Treaty. At 11:30 P.M., the official Panamanian delegation arrives at a Washington, D.C., railroad station and is met by their ambassador, who informs them that the treaty was signed just hours earlier.

#### The Present

1977  United States agrees to relinquish control of Panama Canal Zone on December 31, 1999.

1997  Autoridad del Canal de Panama, the canal authority that will assume control from the U.S. Panama Canal Commission, is created.

1998  Panama gives a Chinese company the right to build new port facilities on both the Pacific and Atlantic sides, to control anchorages, to hire new pilots to guide ships through the canal, and to block all passage that interferes with the company's business.

January 1,  "The canal is ours" is jubilant cry in
2000  Panama.

January 17,  Pentagon sees potential Chinese threat to
2000  Panama Canal.

July 2002  China pressures Panama to extend diplomatic recognition to China and drop recognition of Taiwan.

2004  The saga continues.

This story is a good illustration of how history and geography can affect public and political attitudes in the present and far into the future. To the Panamanian and much of Latin America, the Panama Canal is but one example of the many U.S. intrusions during the early twentieth century that have tainted U.S.–Latin American relations. For the United States, the geographical importance of the Panama Canal for trade (shipping between the two coasts via the Canal is cut by 8,000 miles) makes control of the canal a sensitive issue, especially if that control could be potentially hostile. That a Chinese-owned company has

# Crossing Borders Boxes

These invaluable boxes offer anecdotal company examples. These entertaining examples are designed to encourage critical thinking and guide students through topics ranging from ethical to cultural to global issues facing marketers today.

**CROSSING BORDERS 3.6** Garbage without a Country

We have all read or heard the story of "the man without a country," who is sentenced to remain at sea for his entire life, aimlessly wandering the world. Of course, that is just fiction. In real life, however, there is a barge-load of garbage that aimlessly wanders the globe looking for a country that will accept it in its landfills.

Orange rinds, beer bottles, newspapers, and chicken bones—it was trash, like all trash, taken to an incinerator in Philadelphia for incineration. The ashes, like all ashes, were to be taken away to a landfill somewhere in Philadelphia. Joseph Paolino & Sons had a $6 million contract to remove the ash but kept having doors slammed in its face.

Paolino hired Amalgamated Shipping—operator of the Khian Sea, a 17-year-old, 466-foot rust bucket registered in Liberia—to dump the ash in the Bahamas, where Amalgamated was based. The Bahamian government rejected the ash, and the Khian Sea began its 14-year journey as the Flying Dutchman of debris.

Briefly returning to the United States, it then took off for Puerto Rico, Bermuda, the Dominican Republic, Honduras, Guinea-Bissau, and the Netherlands Antilles. It was turned away again and again. To make the cargo more appealing, the ash was described as "topsoil fertilizer" and the Haitian government agreed to accept the ash. Four thousand tons of ash had been already unloaded when Greenpeace and local activists protested. The Haitian government then ordered the crew to reload the ash, but the ship departed without the ash.

The ship returned to Philadelphia hoping to find a place for the remaining ash. It sailed to Senegal and ... again seeking a resting place ... ..., Indonesia, and the Philippines, ... Years later, the ship's cap... the remaining ash had been ... Indian oceans.

... the 4,000 tons of ash had ... Greenpeace found out what was ... been carried off by wind and ... ats were dying.

After a 16-year odyssey on the cargo ship Khian Sea, 2,500 tons of ash from Philadelphia incinerators is on its way back to a final resting place in Pennsylvania where it began its journey. *(AP/Wide World Photos)*

Enter an unlikely hero: New York City. In 1996, to end mob involvement in the city's garbage industry, Mayor Rudolph Giuliani established a Trade Waste commission to oversee the awarding of trash removal. When Eastern Environmental Services applied to do business in New York, the Trade Waste Commission issued an ultimatum: If Eastern wanted to haul trash in New York, it had to deal with the Khian Sea ash.

Eastern agreed to find a place in its landfills, and what was left of the ash was loaded on a barge and departed Haiti. Finally, after a 16-year odyssey, Philadelphia agreed to give the ash a final resting place.

Sources: "Wandering Waste's 14-year Journey," *Toronto Star,* May 3, 2000; Molly Hennessy-Fiske, "Unwanted Ash Transferred to One Large, Covered Barge," *Palm Beach Post,* April 30, 2000, p. 1B; Jerry Schwartz, "They Took Out the Garbage, It Keeps Coming Back," *Oregonian,* September 3, 2000, p. A6; William M. Hartnett, "2,000 Tons of Ash Await Next Leg of 14-Year Odyssey," *Palm Beach Post,* January 7, 2001, p. 1B and "Toxic Waste Returns," *Earth Island Journal,* Winter 2002–2003, p. 12.

**CROSSING BORDERS 5.1** Don't Beat Your Mother-in-Law!

The crowding and collectivism of Chinese culture provide fertile ground for hierarchy. Add in a little Confucian advice and status relationships become central for understanding Chinese business systems. Confucius' teachings were the foundation for Chinese education for 2000 years, until 1911. He defined five cardinal relationships: between ruler and ruled, husband and wife, parents and children, older and younger brothers, and between friends. Except for the last, all relationships were hierarchical. The ruled, wives, children, and younger brothers were all counseled to trade obedience and loyalty for the benevolence of their ruler, husband, parents, and older brothers, respectively. Strict adherence to these vertical relations yielded social harmony, that being the antidote for the violence and civil war of his time.

Obedience and deference to one's superiors remains a strong value in Chinese culture. The story of the Cheng family illustrates the historical salience of social hierarchy and high power distance.

In October 1865, Cheng Han-cheng's wife had the insolence to beat her mother-in-law. This was regarded as such a heinous crime that the following punishment was meted out. Cheng and his wife were both skinned alive, in front of the mother; their skin displayed at city gates in various towns and their bones burned to ashes. Cheng's granduncle, the eldest of his close relatives, was beheaded; his uncle and two brothers, and the head of the Cheng

clan, were hanged. The wife's mother, her face tattooed with the words "neglected the daughter's education," was paraded through seven provinces. Her father was beaten 80 strokes and banished to a distance of 3000 li. The heads of the family in the houses to the right and left of Cheng's were beaten 80 strokes and banished to Heilung-kiang. The educational officer in town was beaten 60 strokes and banished to a distance of 1000 li. Cheng's nine-month-old boy was given a new name and put in the county magistrate's care. Cheng's land was to be left in waste "forever." All this was recorded on a stone stele and rubbings of the inscriptions were distributed throughout the empire.

We recommend you have your children read this story! But seriously, notice the authorities held responsible the entire social network for the woman's breach of hierarchy. Status is no joke among Chinese. Age and rank of executives and other status markers must be taken into account during business negotiations with Chinese. American informality and egalitarianism will not play well on the western side of the Pacific.

Sources: Hsu, Dau-lin, "The myth of the 'Five Human Relations' of Confucius," *Monumenta Sinica,* 1970, pp. 29, 31 as quoted in Gary G. Hamilton, "Patriarchalism in Imperial China and Western Europe: a Revision of Weber's Sociology of Domination," *Theory and Society,* 13, pp. 393–425, and Mark Lam and John L. Graham, *Red China, Green China* (Boulder, CO: Rowman & Littlefield, 2003).

decision making predominates there. Despite the emphasis on rank and hierarchy in Japanese social structure, business emphasizes group participation, group harmony, and group decision making—but at the top management level.

The demands of these three types of authority systems on a marketer's ingenuity and adaptability are evident. In the case of the authoritative and delegated societies, the chief problem is to identify the individual with authority. In the committee decision setup, it is necessary that every committee member be convinced of the merits of the proposition or product in question. The marketing approach to each of these situations differs.

**Management Objectives and Aspirations**

The training and background (i.e., cultural environment) of managers significantly affect their personal and business outlooks. Society as a whole establishes the social rank or status of management, and cultural background dictates patterns of aspirations and objectives among businesspeople. These cultural influences affect the attitude of managers toward innovation, new products, and conducting business with foreigners. To fully understand another's management style, one must appreciate an individual's values, which are usually reflected in the goals of the business organization and in the practices that prevail within the company. In dealing with foreign business, a marketer must be particularly aware of the varying objectives and aspirations of management.

The availability of minerals and the ability to generate energy are the foundations of modern technology. The locations of the earth's resources, as well as the available sources of energy, are geographic accidents. The world's nations are not equally endowed, nor does a nation's demand for a particular mineral or energy source necessarily coincide with domestic supply.

In much of the underdeveloped world, human labor provides the preponderance of energy. The principal supplements to human energy are animals, wood, fossil fuel, nuclear power, and to a lesser and more experimental extent, the ocean's tides, geothermal power,

**PART SIX**

## cases 2
### THE CULTURAL ENVIRONMENT OF GLOBAL MARKETING

**OUTLINE OF CASES**

2-1 The Not-So-Wonderful World of EuroDisney—Things Are Better Now at Paris Disneyland

2-2 Cultural Norms, Fair and Lovely, and Advertising

2-3 Starnes-Brenner Machine Tool Company: To Bribe or Not to Bribe?

2-4 Ethics and Airbus

2-5 Coping with Corruption in Trading with China

2-6 When International Buyers and Sellers Disagree

# NEW Cases

New cases, both in the book and on video, accompany the new edition, enlivening the material in the book and class discussions while broadening a student's critical thinking skills. These cases bring forth many of the topics discussed in the chapters and demonstrate how these concepts are dealt with in the real world.

**CASE 2–5** Coping with Corruption in Trading with China

Corruption is on the rise in China, where the country's press frequently has detailed cases of corruption and of campaigns to crack down on it. The articles primarily have focused on domestic economic crimes among Chinese citizens, and on local officials who have been fired or assessed other penalties. Indeed, China has been rated by Transparency International as number 59 of the 102 countries the German organization rates on its "Corruption Perception Index." Finland is rated the least corrupt at number 1, the United States at 16, and Bangladesh the most corrupt at number 102.

Corruption's long arm now is reaching out to touch China's foreign business community. Traders, trade consultants, and analysts have said that foreign firms are vulnerable to a variety of corrupt practices. Although some of these firms said they had no experience with corruption in the People's Republic of China (PRC), the majority said they increasingly were asked to make payments to improve business, engage in black-market trade of import and export licenses, bribe officials to push goods through customs or the Commodity Inspection Bureau, or pay bribes in collusion to beat the system. The Hong Kong Independent Commission Against Corruption reports that outright bribes as well as gifts or payment to establish guanxi, or "connections," average 3 to 5 percent of operating costs in the PRC, or $3 billion to $5 billion of the $100 billion of foreign investments that have been made there. The most common corrupt practices confronting foreign companies in China are examined here.

**PAYING TO IMPROVE BUSINESS**

Foreign traders make several types of payments to facilitate sales in China. The most common methods used are trips abroad. Chinese officials, who rarely have a chance to visit overseas, often prefer foreign travel to cash or gifts. (This was especially true when few PRC officials had been abroad.) As a result, traders report that dangling foreign trips in front of PRC clients has become a regular part of negotiating large trade deals that involve products with a technological component. "Foreign travel is always the first inducement we offer," said an executive involved in machinery trade. In most cases, traders build these costs into the product's sale price. Some trips are "reasonable and bona fide expenditures directly related to the promotion, demonstration, or explanation of products and services, or the execution of a contract with a foreign government agency." But other trips, often officials on foreign junkets are offered large per diems and aren't invited specifically to gain technical knowledge, may be another matter.

Foreign travel isn't always an inducement—it also can be extorted. In one case, a PRC bank branch refused to issue a letter of credit for a machinery import deal. The Chinese customer suggested that the foreign trader invite the bank official on an overseas inspection tour. Once the invitation was extended, the bank issued the letter of credit.

**ANGLING FOR CASH**

MNCs also are asked sometimes to sponsor overseas education for children of trading officials. One person told a Chinese source that an MNC paid for that individual's U.S. $1,500-a-month apartment, as well as a car, university education, and expenses.

Firms find direct requests for cash payments—undeniably illegal—the most difficult. One well-placed source said that a major trader, eager for buyers in the face of an international market glut, had fallen into regularly paying large kickbacks into the Honduran, U.S., and Swiss accounts of officials at a PRC foreign trade corporation.

Refusing to make payments may not only hurt sales, it can also be terrifying. A U.S. firm was one of several bidders for a large sale; a Chinese official demanded the MNC pay a 3 percent kickback. When the company representatives refused, the official threatened: "You had better not say anything about this. You still have to do business in China, and stay in hotels here." Not surprisingly, the U.S. company lost the deal.

Traders of certain commodities may be tempted to purchase on the black market those import and export licenses that are difficult to obtain legally. A fairly disorganized underground market, for instance, exists for licenses to export China-made garments to the United States.

Some branches of the Commodity Inspection Bureau (CIB) also have posed problems for some traders. Abuses have emerged in the CIB since it started inspecting imports in 1987. A Japanese company, for instance, informed CIB officials of its intention to bring heavy industrial items into China—items that had met Japanese and U.S. standards. The officials responded that they planned to dismantle the products on arrival for inspection purposes. The problem was resolved only after the firm invited the officials to visit Japan.

Some traders get around such problems by purchasing inspection certificates on the black market. According to press accounts, these forms, complete with signatures and seals, can be bought for roughly U.S. $200.

Some claim that, for the appropriate compensation, customs officials in a southern province are very willing to reduce the dutiable value of imports as much as 50 percent. Because the savings can far exceed transport costs, some importers that would logically enter China through a northern port are redirected through the southern province.

**QUESTIONS**

1. List all the different types of bribes, payments, or favors represented in this case and say why each is either legal or illegal.

2. For those practices that you say are illegal, classify each as lubrication, extortion, or subornation, and tell why.

3. Which of the payments, favors, or bribes are illegal under the Foreign Corrupt Practices Act (FCPA)?

4. Assuming that the FCPA did not exist, what is the ethical response to each of the payments, favors, or bribes you have

# A Wealth of Supplements

## NEW Student CD-ROM

For the first time, a Student CD is available with the text, featuring a new interactive expansion of the popular Country Notebook. Live links via an interactive map allow students to conduct online research to perform a complete cultural and economic analysis of a country and provide guidelines for developing an international marketing plan.

## NEW Video Segment

In a new segment produced by author John Graham, the video takes a look at JL Design, a U.S. based manufacturer of athletic apparel. This segment examines how a small business grew to marketing their products internationally and how it has managed its growth within a global market.

# Online Learning Center

Numerous resources available for both Instructors and Students are online at www.mhhe.com/cateora05. Instructor resources include downloadable versions of the Instructor's Manual, PowerPoint presentation, and Instructor Notes to accompany the videos. Student study tools include Chapter Quizzes, International Resource Links, and the Country Notebook Online with an interactive component so students can complete this popular marketing plan project online.

Instructors and students will also have access to **PowerWeb for International Marketing** through the site. PowerWeb content includes daily news feeds, current articles, and related links.

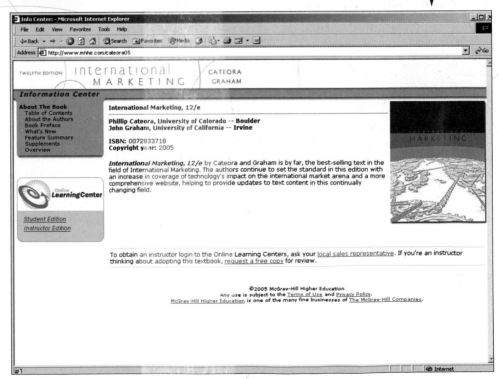

# BRIEF CONTENTS

# PART ONE

# AN OVERVIEW

# PART TWO

# THE CULTURAL ENVIRONMENT OF GLOBAL MARKETS

# PART THREE

# ASSESSING GLOBAL MARKET OPPORTUNITIES

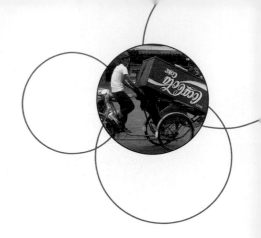

# PART FOUR

# DEVELOPING GLOBAL MARKETING STRATEGIES

# PART FIVE

# IMPLEMENTING GLOBAL MARKETING STRATEGIES

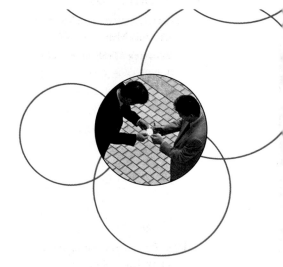

# PART SIX

# SUPPLEMENTARY MATERIAL

# LIST OF "CROSSING BORDERS" BOXES

# international marketing

**CHAPTER 1**

# The scope and challenge of international marketing

## CHAPTER LEARNING OBJECTIVES

What you should learn from Chapter 1:

- The internationalization of U.S. business

- The scope of the international marketing task

- The importance of the self-reference criterion (SRC) in international marketing

- The progression of becoming a global marketer

- The increasing importance of global awareness

# Global Perspective

## GLOBAL COMMERCE CAUSES PEACE

Global commerce thrives during peacetime. The economic boom in North America during the late 1990s was in large part due to the end of the Cold War and the opening of the formerly communist countries to the world trading system. However, we should also understand the important role that trade and international marketing play in actually producing peace.

Boeing Company, America's largest exporter, is perhaps the most prominent example. Although many would argue that Boeing's military sales (aircraft and missiles) do not exactly promote peace, over the years that business has constituted only about 20 percent of the company's commercial activity. Up until last year, of Boeing's some $60 billion in annual revenues, about 65 percent came from sales of commercial jets around the world and another 15 percent from space and communications technologies. Unfortunately, these historical numbers are being skewed by American military spending and the damage done to tourism by terrorism. Even so, the company still counts customers in 145 countries, and its 164,000 employees work in 70 countries. Its 11,000 commercial jets in service around the world carry about one billion travelers per year. Its space division is the lead contractor in the construction of the 16-country International Space Station, first manned by an American and two Russians in the fall of 2000. The space division also produces and launches communications satellites affecting people in every country.

All the activity associated with the development, production, and marketing of commercial aircraft and space vehicles requires millions of people from around the world to work together. Moreover, no company does more to enable people from all countries to meet face to face for both recreation and commerce. All this interaction yields not just the mutual gain associated with business relationships but also personal relationships and mutual understanding. The latter are the foundation of global peace and prosperity.

Individuals and small companies also make a difference, perhaps a subtler one than large multinational companies, but one just as important in the aggregate. Our favorite example is Daniel Lubetzky's company PeaceWorks. Mr. Lubetzky used a fellowship at Stanford Law School to study how to foster joint ventures between Arabs and Israelis. Then, following his own advice, he created a company that combines basil pesto from Israel with other raw materials and glass jars supplied by an Arab partner to produce the first product in a line he calls Moshe & Ali's Gourmet Foods. The company now sells some 60 products in 3,000 stores in the United States and has its headquarters on Park Avenue in New York and divisions in both Israel and Mexico. Again, beyond the measurable commercial benefits of cooperation between the involved Arabs and Israelis is the longer-lasting and more fundamental appreciation for one another's circumstances and character.

International marketing is hard work. Making sales calls is no vacation even in Paris when you've been there ten times before. But international marketing is important work. It can enrich you, your family, your company, and your country. And ultimately, when international marketing is done well,[1] by large companies or small, the needs and wants of customers in other lands are well understood, and prosperity and peace are promoted along the way.

Sources: www.boeing.com and www.peaceworks.com—both are worth a visit.

---

[1] Neil Bruce Holbert describes how international marketers can have negative influences if they take an imperialistic approach to global markets. See "Worldwide Marketing Must Not Assume Imperialistic Air," *Marketing News*, February 14, 2000, p. 20.

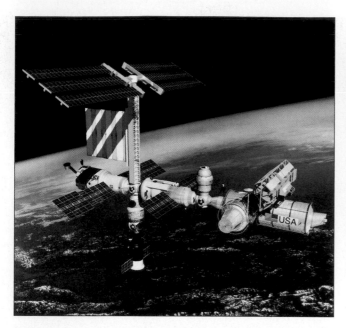

The high point of international trade at the beginning of the second millennium: Boeing is the prime contractor for the international Space Station. The project involves the cooperation of people and companies from around the world and particularly the governments of 16 countries. It also represents an important step beyond global marketing—that is, products are now being designed and delivered specifically for people residing off the globe! (© CORBIS)

Aside from the tragic loss of life resulting from the terrorism of September 11, the event also represents a direct attack on the world trading system. Hopefully, the destruction of the New York City World Trade Center will be the low point for global commerce and peace as the remainder of the second millennium unfolds. (© Reuters NewMedia Inc./CORBIS)

"Never before in American history have U.S. businesses, large and small, been so deeply involved in and affected by international business. A global economic boom, unprecedented in modern economic history, has been under way as the drive for efficiency, productivity, and open, unregulated markets sweeps the world. Powerful economic, technological, industrial, political, and demographic forces are converging to build the foundation of a new global economic order on which the structure of a one-world economic and market system will be built."

When we wrote those words three years ago to open the previous edition of this book the world was a very different place. The nation was still mesmerized by the information technology boom of the late 1990s. Most did not visualize the high-tech bust of 2001 or the associated Enron and WorldCom scandals. No one could have imagined the September 11 disasters, not even the perpetrators. Wars in Afghanistan and Iraq were not on the horizon. The major international conflict grabbing headlines then was the series of diplomatic dustups among China, Taiwan, and the United States. Who could have predicted the disruptions associated with the 2003 SARS outbreak in Asia?[2] We wrote about the promise of the space program[3] and the international space station whose future was dramatically jeopardized by the Columbia shuttle tragedy.

Through all these major events American consumers continued to spend, keeping the world economy afloat. Layoffs at industrial icons such as United Airlines and Boeing and a generally tough job market didn't slow the booming American housing market. Lower government interest rates meant a refinancing stampede, throwing the cash that fueled

---

[2]"How Big a Dent in the Economy, China Counts the Costs of SARS," *The Economist*, May 17, 2003, p. 66.

[3]Ralph Vartabedian and Peter Pae, "Shuttle Pioneer Calls for End to Manned Flights," *Los Angeles Times*, May 16, 2003, p. A28.

**CROSSING BORDERS 1.1** What Do French Farmers, Chinese Fishermen, and Russian Hackers Have in Common?

They can all disrupt American firms' international marketing efforts.

Thousands of supporters and activists gathered recently to show support for a French sheep farmer on trial for vandalizing a local McDonald's. Jose Bove has become an international legend of antiglobalization. Leader of the French Peasant Confederation, he has demonized the fast-food chain as the symbol of American trade "hegemony" and economic globalization. He and nine other farmers served six weeks in jail and paid fines for partially destroying the restaurant. Most recently, Bove has been thrown in jail again, this time for ten months, for damaging fields of genetically modified rice and corn.

Local fishermen have demanded suspension of reclamation and dredging of a bay near Hong Kong where Disney plans to build Hong Kong Disneyland. The fishermen claim that the work has plunged water quality near the site to levels much worse than predicted, killing huge numbers of fish. The spokesman for the fishermen claims they have lost some $30 million between July and September because of depleted and diseased fish stocks.

St. Petersburg has become the capital of Russian computer hackers. These are the same folks that are reputed to have invaded Microsoft's internal network. Russia's science city has become the natural hub for high-tech computer crime. Dozens of students, teachers, and computer specialists hack into computers, seeing themselves as members of an exciting subculture that has flourished since the fall of communism. Before *glasnost* and *perestroika*, those who were dissatisfied with official Soviet culture turned to samizdat literature and bootleg tapes of Western pop music. But the Gorbachev era left little to rebel against. Today Russia's hackers, who even have their own magazine titled *Khacker*, have created a new underground culture that perhaps offers more excitement than passing around banned poetry. The city also benefits from being near the Baltic States. Computer programs are copied on the black market: The latest Windows pirated software always arrives in Russia months before it appears in the West. Fines and prison terms are consequences if caught, but the black market flourishes because computers are so accessible at universities and increasingly in homes.

Sources: "Crowd Rallies for French Farmers on Trial in Attack," *Associated Press*, July 1, 2000; Agnes Lam, "Disney Dredging Killing Fish," *South China Morning Post*, November 5, 2000, p. 4; Alice Lagnado, "Russians Turn to Hacking as the New Subversion," *The Times of London*, October 28, 2000, p. 4; and John Tagliabue, "Activist Jailed in Attack on Modified Crops," *New York Times*, February 27, 2003, p. 6.

the consumer spending. Today, seeing into the future is harder than ever. Most experts expect global terrorism[4] to increase and perhaps increased armed conflicts[5] as well. Many fear a housing price collapse and the associated economic disruptions.[6]

International marketing is affected by and affects all these things. For the first time in history McDonald's is pulling out of international markets in both Latin America and the Middle East.[7] Slow economies, increasing competition, and anti-Americanism have impacted their sales in both regions. Moreover, recall that the September 11 attacks were on the *World Trade* Center in New York City. Indeed, the salient lesson for those involved in international commerce at the turn of the twenty-first century is to expect the unexpected. Any executive experienced in international business will verify that things never go as planned in global commerce. You still have to plan and forecast, but markets, particularly international ones, are ultimately unpredictable. The

---

[4]Dore Gold, "The Kingdom of Incitement," *Wall Street Journal*, April 14, 2003, p. A18.

[5]Joseph Kahn, "China Offers Its Help in U.S.–North Korea Nuclear Talks," *New York Times*, April 24, 2003, p. A3.

[6]Greg Ip, "Housing Booms Tend to Collapse—Study Finds More Harm from Home-Price Busts than Bursted Stock Bubbles," *Wall Street Journal*, April 4, 2003, p. A2.

[7]"McDonald's Posts Its First Loss and Lowers Outlook for Growth," *New York Times*, January 24, 2003, p. C18.

natural fluctuations in markets are best managed through building strong interpersonal and commercial relationships and broad portfolios of businesses. Flexibility means survival.

Perhaps now, more than ever, whether or not a U.S. company wants to participate directly in international business, it cannot escape the effects of the ever-increasing number of North American firms exporting, importing, and manufacturing abroad. Nor can it ignore the number of foreign-based firms operating in U.S. markets, the growth of regional trade areas, the rapid growth of world markets, and the increasing number of competitors for global markets.

Of all the events and trends affecting global business today, four stand out as the most dynamic, the ones that will influence the shape of international business beyond today's bumpy roads and far into the future: (1) the rapid growth of the World Trade Organization[8] and regional free trade areas such as the North American Free Trade Area and the European Union, (2) the trend toward the acceptance of the free market system among developing countries in Latin America,[9] Asia, and Eastern Europe, (3) the burgeoning impact of the Internet[10] and other global media on the dissolution of national borders, and (4) the mandate to properly manage the resources[11] and global environment for the generations to come.[12]

Today most business activities are global in scope. Technology, research, capital investment, production, and marketing, distribution, and communications networks all have global dimensions. Every business must be prepared to compete in an increasingly interdependent global economic and physical environment, and all businesspeople must be aware of the effects of these trends when managing a domestic company that exports or a multinational conglomerate. As one international expert noted, every American company is international, at least to the extent that its business performance is conditioned in part by events that occur abroad. Even companies that do not operate in the international arena are affected to some degree by the success of the European Union, the export-led growth in South Korea, the revitalized Mexican economy, the economic changes taking place in China, military conflicts in the Middle East, and global warming.

It is less and less possible for businesses to avoid the influence of the internationalization of the U.S. economy, the globalization of the world's markets, and the growth of emerging markets. As competition for world markets intensifies, the number of companies operating solely in domestic markets will decrease. Or, to put it another way, it is increasingly true that the business of American business is international business.

The challenge of international marketing is to develop strategic plans that are competitive in the intensifying global markets. For a growing number of companies, being international is no longer a luxury but a necessity for economic survival. These and other issues affecting the world economy, trade, markets, and competition will be discussed throughout this text.

## The Internationalization of U.S. Business

Current interest in international marketing can be explained by changing competitive structures coupled with shifts in demand characteristics in markets throughout the world. With the increasing globalization of markets, companies find they are unavoidably enmeshed with foreign customers, competitors, and suppliers, even within their own borders. They face competition on all fronts—from domestic firms

---

[8]Robert Guy Matthews, "U.S. Steel Tariffs Likely to Stay Despite WTO-Sanctions Threat," *Wall Street Journal*, March 31, 2003, p. A2.

[9]Craig Karmin, "Latin America Is Back in Favor with Investors," *Wall Street Journal*, April 23, 2003, p. C1.

[10]S. Subba Rao, Glenn Metts, and Carlo A. Mora Monge, "Electronic Commerce Development in Small and Medium Sized Enterprises," *Business Process Management Journal*, 2003, 1, pp. 11–32.

[11]Kenneth R. Weiss, "Seas Being Stripped of Big Fish, Study Finds," *Los Angeles Times*, May 15, 2003, p. A1.

[12]Gary Polakovic, "Airborne Soot Is Significant Factor in Global Warming," *Los Angeles Times*, May 15, 2003, p. A30.

**Exhibit 1.1**
Foreign Acquisitions of
U.S. Companies

Sources: Adapted from Kurt
Badenhausen, "Name Game,"
*Forbes*, July 24, 2000; and Denise M.
Bonilla, "Latino Market Arrives with
Giant Aspirations," *Los Angeles
Times*, May 7, 2003, p. B6.

| U.S. Companies | Foreign Owner |
| --- | --- |
| Firestone (tires) | Japan |
| Ben & Jerry's (ice cream) | U.K. |
| Alpo (pet food) | Swiss |
| Pillsbury (foods) | U.K. |
| Burger King (fast food) | U.K. |
| Random House (publishing) | Germany |
| Chrysler (autos) | Germany |
| TV Guide (magazine) | Australia |
| New York Post (newspaper) | Australia |
| CompUSA (retailing) | Mexico |
| Seagram (alcoholic beverages) | France |
| Oroweat (breads) | Mexico |
| Smith and Wesson (guns) | U.K. |

and from foreign firms. A significant portion of all CD players, computers, apparel, and dinnerware sold in the United States is foreign made. Sony, Laura Ashley, Norelco, Samsung,[13] Toyota, and Nescafé are familiar brands in the United States, and for U.S. industry they are formidable opponents in a competitive struggle for U.S. and world markets.

Many familiar U.S. companies are now foreign controlled.[14] When you drop in at a 7-Eleven convenience store or buy Firestone tires, you are buying directly from a Japanese company. Some well-known brands no longer owned by U.S. companies are Carnation (Swiss), Chrysler (German), and the all-American Smith and Wesson handgun that won the U.S. West, which is owned by a British firm. The last U.S.-owned company to manufacture TV sets was Zenith, but even it was acquired by South Korea's LG Electronics, Inc., which manufactures Goldstar TVs and other products. Pearle Vision, Universal Studios, and many more are currently owned or controlled by foreign multinational businesses (see Exhibit 1.1). Foreign investment in the United States is in excess

---

[13]James Brooke, "As Profit Falls, Samsung Turns More Aggressive," *New York Times*, April 26, 2003, p. C4.

[14]Acquisitions of American firms slowed during the economic doldrums immediately following the high-tech bust. See Avital Louria Hahn, "HABC/Household Bucks a Trend, Foreign Acquisitions of U.S. Companies at Near-Decade Low," *Investment Dealers' Digest*, November 18, 2002, pp. 10–11.

Along with NAFTA have come two of Mexico's most prominent brand names. Gigante, one of Mexico's largest supermarket chains, now has several stores in southern California including this one in Anaheim. On store shelves are a variety of Bimbo bakery products. Grupo Bimbo, a growing Mexican multinational, has recently purchased American brand-named firms such as Oroweat, Webers, and Mrs. Baird's breads.

## CROSSING BORDERS 1.2 *Blanca Nieves, La Cenicienta Y Bimbo* (Snow White, Cinderella, and Bimbo)

Bimbo is a wonderful brand name. It demonstrates so well the difficulties of marketing across borders. Of course, to North America "bimbo" is slang for a dumb blonde. Even in *Webster's Dictionary* it's defined as "a term of disparagement, a tramp."

Meanwhile in Spain, Mexico, and other Spanish-speaking countries, the word bimbo has no pejorative meaning. Indeed, it is often simply associated with the little white bear logo of Bimbo brand bread. Bimbo is the most popular brand of bread in Mexico, and with NAFTA it is stretching its corporate arms north. For example, the Mexican firm most recently acquired Mrs. Baird's Bread, the most popular local brand in Dallas, Texas. You can now see 18-wheel trucks pulling loads of Bimbo products north on Interstate 5 toward Latino neighborhoods in Southern California.

Perhaps Bimbo is the reason the city fathers in Anaheim so feared Gigante's entrance into their city? Gigante, the Mexican-owned supermarket chain, features Bimbo buns, tomatillos, cactus pears, and other Latino favorites. Gigante already has three stores in Los Angeles County, but it was denied the city's permission to open a new market near the "happiest place on Earth." One has to wonder if Disneyland, Anaheim's biggest employer, may have fretted over the juxtaposition of the Bimbo brand and their key characters, blonde little all-American Alice and her cinema sisters?

Actually, the better case can be made that the Gigante/Anaheim imbroglio was more a matter of a mix of nationalism, xenophobia, and even racism. And, the city council eventually was forced to allow Gigante to open. American firms have often run into similar problems as they expanded around the world.

Consider French nationalism. Their farmers are famous for their protests—throwing lamb chops at their trade ministers and such. Or better yet, consider culture minister Jack Lang's comments about the U.S. Cartoon Network, "We must fight back against this American aggression. It is intolerable that certain North American audiovisual groups shamelessly colonize our countries."

Or, consider our own fear and loathing of "Japanese colonization" in both the 1920s and the 1980s. This apparent xenophobia turned to racism when Americans stoned Toyotas and Hondas, but not Volkswagens and BMWs; when we decried Japanese takeovers of American firms and ignored Germany's recent gorging on the likes of Bankers Trust, Random House, and Chrysler.

A cruel irony regarding Gigante's problems in Anaheim is well revealed by a quick drive around Tijuana. During the last decade the change in Tijuana's retail facade has been remarkable. In this border town, after the North American Free Trade Agreement (NAFTA), Blockbuster Video, Burger King, COSTCO, Smart & Final, and other American brands now dominate the signage.

Sources: John L. Graham, "*Blanca Nieves, La Cenicienta, Y Bimbo,*" (translated from the Spanish) *La Opinion*, February 22, 2002, p. C1; and Denise M. Bonilla, "Latino Market Arrives with Giant Aspirations," *Los Angeles Times*, May 7, 2003, p. B6.

---

of $1.5 trillion. Companies from the United Kingdom lead the group of investors, with companies from the Netherlands, Japan, Germany, and Switzerland following in that order.[15]

Other foreign companies that entered the U.S. market through exporting their products into the United States realized sufficient market share to justify building and buying manufacturing plants in the United States.[16] Fuji Photo Film invested more than $300 million in a plant to service its 12 percent share of the U.S. film market. Honda, BMW, and Mercedes are all manufacturing in the United States. Investments go the other way as well. Ford bought Jaguar; PacifiCorp acquired Energy Group, the United Kingdom's largest electricity supplier and second-largest gas distributor; and Wisconsin Central Transportation, a medium-sized U.S. railroad, controls all U.K. rail freight business and runs the queen's private train via its English, Welsh & Scottish Railway unit. It has also acquired the company that runs rail shuttles through the Channel Tunnel. Investments by

---

[15]Some U.S. investments turn into disasters such as Bertelsmann's loan to Napster: Joseph Menn, "Piracy Battle Shifts to Bertelsmann," *Los Angeles Times*, February 20, 2003, p. C1.

[16]Denise M. Bonilla, "Latino Market Arrives with Giant Aspirations," *Los Angeles Times*, May 7, 2003, p. B6.

**Exhibit 1.2**
Top 10 U.S. Players in the Global Game

Sources: Adapted from Brian Zajac, "Global Giants," *Forbes*, July 24, 2000; and Wal-Mart Stores Annual Report 2003.

| Company | Foreign Revenues ($ Mil) | Foreign Revenues (Percent of Total) | Foreign Profits (Percent of Total) | Foreign Assets (Percent of Total) |
|---|---|---|---|---|
| ExxonMobil | 115,464 | 71.8 | 62.7 | 63.9 |
| IBM | 50,377 | 57.5 | 49.6 | 43.7 |
| Ford Motor | 50,138 | 30.8 | N/A | 44.2 |
| General Motors | 46,485 | 26.3 | 55.3 | 38.0 |
| Wal-Mart Stores | 40,794 | 16.7 | 14.7 | 32.4 |
| General Electric | 35,350 | 31.7 | 22.8 | 47.4 |
| Texaco | 32,700 | 77.1 | 54.1 | 45.2 |
| Citigroup | 28,749 | 35.1 | N/A | 41.0 |
| Hewlett-Packard | 23,398 | 55.2 | 58.0 | 51.5 |
| Compaq Computer | 21,174 | 55.0 | 101.4 | 28.2 |

U.S. multinationals abroad are nothing new. They have been roaming the world en masse since the end of World War II, buying companies and investing in manufacturing plants. What is relatively new for U.S. companies is having their global competitors competing with them in their own market, the United States.

Once the private domain of domestic businesses, the vast U.S. market that provided an opportunity for continued growth must now be shared with a variety of foreign companies and products. Companies with only domestic markets have found it increasingly difficult to sustain customary rates of growth, and many are seeking foreign markets in which to expand. Companies with foreign operations find that foreign earnings are making an important overall contribution to total corporate profits. A four-year Conference Board study of 1,250 U.S. manufacturing companies found that multinationals of all sizes and in all industries outperformed their strictly domestic U.S. counterparts. They grew twice as fast in sales and earned significantly higher returns on equity and assets. Further, the U.S. multinationals reduced their manufacturing employment, both at home and abroad, more than domestic companies.

Exhibit 1.2 illustrates how important profit generated on investments abroad is to U.S. companies. In many cases, foreign sales are more profitable than U.S. sales, and foreign returns on assets are better than in the United States—all important reasons for going international.

Companies that never ventured abroad until recently are now seeking foreign markets. Companies with existing foreign operations realize they must be more competitive to succeed against foreign multinationals. They have found it necessary to spend more money and time improving their marketing positions abroad because competition for these growing markets is intensifying. For the firm venturing into international marketing for the first time and for those already experienced, the requirement is generally the same: a thorough and complete commitment to foreign markets and, for many, new ways of operating.

## International Marketing Defined

**International marketing** is the performance of business activities designed to plan, price, promote, and direct the flow of a company's goods and services to consumers or users in more than one nation for a profit. The only difference between the definitions of domestic marketing and international marketing is that in the latter case marketing activities take place in more than one country. This apparently minor difference, "in more than one country," accounts for the complexity and diversity found in international marketing operations. Marketing concepts, processes, and principles are universally applicable, and the marketer's task is the same whether doing business in Dimebox, Texas, or Dar es Salaam, Tanzania. Business's goal is to make a profit by promoting, pricing, and distributing products for which there is a market. If this is the case, what is the difference between domestic and international marketing?

The answer lies not with different concepts of marketing but with the environment within which marketing plans must be implemented. The uniqueness of foreign marketing comes from the range of unfamiliar problems and the variety of strategies necessary to cope with different levels of uncertainty encountered in foreign markets.

Competition, legal restraints, government controls, weather, fickle consumers, and any number of other **uncontrollable elements** can, and frequently do, affect the profitable outcome of good, sound marketing plans. Generally speaking, the marketer cannot control or influence these uncontrollable elements, but instead must adjust or adapt to them in a manner consistent with a successful outcome. What makes marketing interesting is the challenge of molding the **controllable elements** of marketing decisions (product, price, promotion, distribution, and research) within the framework of the uncontrollable elements of the marketplace (competition, politics, laws, consumer behavior, level of technology, and so forth) in such a way that marketing objectives are achieved. Even though marketing principles and concepts are universally applicable, the environment within which the marketer must implement marketing plans can change dramatically from country to country or region to region. The difficulties created by different environments are the international marketer's primary concern.

## The International Marketing Task

The international marketer's task is more complicated than that of the domestic marketer because the international marketer must deal with at least two levels of uncontrollable uncertainty instead of one. Uncertainty is created by the uncontrollable elements of all business environments, but each foreign country in which a company operates adds its own unique set of uncontrollable factors.

Exhibit 1.3 illustrates the total environment of an international marketer. The inner circle depicts the domestic controllable elements that constitute a marketer's decision area, the second circle encompasses those environmental elements at home that have

**Exhibit 1.3**
The International Marketing Task

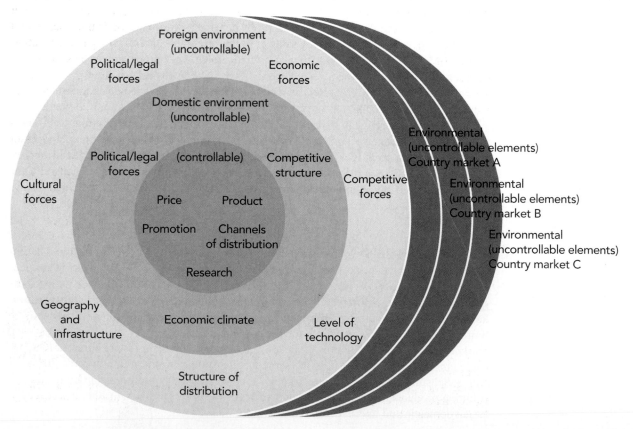

some effect on foreign-operation decisions, and the outer circles represent the elements of the foreign environment for each foreign market within which the marketer operates.[17] As the outer circles illustrate, each foreign market in which the company does business can (and usually does) present separate problems involving some or all of the uncontrollable elements. Thus the more foreign markets in which a company operates, the greater the possible variety of foreign environmental factors with which to contend. Frequently, a solution to a problem in country market A is not applicable to a problem in country market B.

## Marketing Decision Factors

The successful manager constructs a marketing program designed for optimal adjustment to the uncertainty of the business climate. The inner circle in Exhibit 1.3 represents the area under control of the marketing manager. Assuming the necessary overall corporate resources, the marketing manager blends price, product, promotion, and channels-of-distribution activities to capitalize on anticipated demand. The controllable elements can be altered in the long run and, usually, in the short run to adjust to changing market conditions, consumer tastes, or corporate objectives.

The outer circles surrounding the marketing decision factors represent the levels of uncertainty that are created by the domestic and foreign environments. Although the marketer can blend a marketing mix from the controllable elements, the uncontrollable factors are precisely that; there must be active evaluation and, if needed, adaptation. That effort, the adaptation of the marketing mix to these environmental factors, determines the ultimate outcome of the marketing enterprise.[18]

## Aspects of the Domestic Environment

The second circle in Exhibit 1.3 represents the aspects of the **domestic environment uncontrollables** that are often beyond the control of companies. These include home-country elements that can have a direct effect on the success of a foreign venture: political and legal forces, economic climate, and competition.

A political decision involving domestic foreign policy can have a direct effect on a firm's international marketing success. For example, the U.S. government placed a total ban on trade with Libya to condemn Libyan support for terrorist attacks, imposed restrictions on trade with South Africa to protest apartheid, and placed a total ban on trade with Iraq, whose actions constituted a threat to the national security of the United States and its allies. In each case, the international marketing programs of U.S. companies, whether it was IBM, Exxon, or Hawg Heaven Bait Company, were restricted by these political decisions. The U.S. government has the constitutional right to restrict foreign trade when such trade adversely affects the security or economy of the country, or when such trade is in conflict with U.S. foreign policy.

Conversely, positive effects occur when there are changes in foreign policy and countries are given favored treatment. Such were the cases when South Africa abolished apartheid and the embargo was lifted, and when the U.S. government decided to uncouple human rights issues from foreign trade policy and grant permanently normalized trade relations (PNTR) status to China, paving the way for entry into the World Trade Organization (WTO). In both cases, opportunities were created for U.S. companies. Finally, it should also be recognized that on occasion companies actually can exercise some degree of influence over such legislation in the United States. Indeed, in the case of PNTR for China, companies with substantial interests there, such as Boeing and Motorola, lobbied hard for the easing of trade restrictions.

The domestic economic climate is another important home-based uncontrollable variable with far-reaching effects on a company's competitive position in foreign markets. The capacity to invest in plants and facilities, either in domestic or foreign markets, is to

---

[17]Peter S. Davis, Ashay B. Desai, and John D. Francis, "Mode of International Entry: An Isomorphism Perspective," *Journal of International Business Studies*, 2000, 31(2), pp. 239–258.

[18]Lance Eliot Brouthers, Steve Werner, and Erika Matulich, "The Influence of Triad Nations' Environments on Price-Quality Product Strategies and MNC Performance," *Journal of International Business Studies*, 2000, 31(1), pp. 39–62.

a large extent a function of domestic economic vitality. It is generally true that capital tends to flow toward optimum use; however, capital must be generated before it can have mobility. Furthermore, if internal economic conditions deteriorate, restrictions against foreign investment and purchasing may be imposed to strengthen the domestic economy.

Competition within the home country can also have a profound effect on the international marketer's task. Until recently, Eastman Kodak dominated the U.S. film market and could depend on achieving profit goals that provided capital to invest in foreign markets. Without having to worry about the company's lucrative base, management had the time and resources to devise aggressive international marketing programs. However, the competitive structure changed when Fuji Photo Film became a formidable competitor by lowering film prices in the United States, opening a $300 million plant, and gaining 12 percent of the U.S. market. As a result, Kodak had to direct energy and resources back to the United States. Competition within its home country affects a company's domestic as well as international plans. Inextricably entwined with the effects of the domestic environment are the constraints imposed by the environment of each foreign country.

## Aspects of the Foreign Environment

In addition to uncontrollable domestic elements, a significant source of uncertainty is the number of factors in the **foreign environment uncontrollables** (depicted in Exhibit 1.3 by the outer circles). A business operating in its home country undoubtedly feels comfortable in forecasting the business climate and adjusting business decisions to these elements. The process of evaluating the uncontrollable elements in an international marketing program, however, often involves substantial doses of cultural, political, and economic shock.

A business operating in a number of foreign countries might find polar extremes in political stability, class structure, and economic climate—critical elements in business decisions. The dynamic upheavals in some countries further illustrate the problems of dramatic change in cultural, political, and economic climates over relatively short periods of time. A case in point is China, which has moved from a communist legal system in which all business was done with the state to a transitional period while a commercial legal system is developing. In this transitional phase, new laws are passed but left to be interpreted by local authorities, where confusion prevails as to what rules are still in force and what rules are no longer applicable.

For example, commercial contracts can be entered into with a Chinese company or individual only if they are considered a "legal person." To be a legal person in China, the company or person must have registered as such with the Chinese government. To complicate matters further, binding negotiations may only take place with "legal representatives" of the "legal person." So if your company enters into negotiations with a Chinese company or person, you must ask for signed legal documents establishing the right to do business. The formalities of the signature must also be considered. Will a signature on a contract be binding or is it necessary to place a traditional Chinese seal on the document? Even when all is done properly, the government still might change its mind. Coca-Cola had won approval for its plan to build a new facility to produce product for its increasing Chinese market share, but before construction began the Chinese parliament objected that Coca-Cola appeared to be too successful in China, so negotiations continue. Such are the uncertainties of the uncontrollable political and legal factors of international business.

The more significant elements in the uncontrollable international environment, shown in the outer circles of Exhibit 1.3, include political/legal forces; economic forces; competitive forces; level of technology; structure of distribution; geography and infrastructure; and cultural forces. These constitute the principal elements of uncertainty an international marketer must cope with in designing a marketing program. Although each will be discussed in depth in subsequent chapters, consider the level of technology and political/legal forces as illustrations of the uncontrollable nature of the foreign environment.

The *level of technology* is an uncontrollable element that can often be misread because of the vast differences that may exist between developed and undeveloped countries. A marketer cannot assume that the understanding of the concept of preventive maintenance

**CROSSING BORDERS 1.3** Even the Old Technology and a Telemarketer Can Save Your Life

Usually, outbound telemarketers are left out in the cold, saleswise. But, Maria del Pilar Basto, a telemarketing agent for Bell South, reached a customer with one of her calls in late May who was himself out in the cold—Colombian hiker Leonardo Diaz, trapped in an Andes mountain blizzard at an altitude above 12,500 feet.

Diaz, stuck in the storm for 24 hours, had tried to call out on his cell phone, but discovered that his prepaid minutes had run out. Basto's well-timed call initially was simply to offer to sell him more minutes. Once on the phone, though, she and her coworkers kept Diaz talking, to keep him awake and help stave off hypothermia, until rescuers arrived.

Imagine if Senor Diaz had packed along some of the new stuff available in Japan? How about Sanyo's picture phone with voice dialing (he wouldn't have had to take his hands out of his gloves), an electronic organizer (maybe he wouldn't have gotten lost in the first place),

and a built-in answering machine (Senorita del Pilar's call would have gone through even if he was frozen solid). How about a wearable PC with a headband-mounted display? Even in a blizzard that would be entertaining. Pokemon at 12,000 feet! A MiniDisc player? That would have provided some music with which to while away the time, or a method of leaving a final message for his relatives. There is also the Dick Tracy voice-activated watch/phone combination, with headphones. Perhaps Mr. Diaz might have kept better track of his minutes with that gadget.

Too bad Sanyo, Sony, or Samsung hadn't already come up with a combination compass/radar/hand warmer for Senor Diaz. Maybe next year?

Sources: Lisa M. Keefe, "Strange But True, Nice Save," *Marketing News,* December 9, 2002, p. 16; and Janice Brand, "Beyond Pokemon, Hot Products," *CIO,* January 1, 2003, p. 62.

for machinery is the same in other countries as in the United States. Technical expertise may not be available at a level necessary for product support, and the general population may not have an adequate level of technical knowledge to properly maintain equipment. In such situations, a marketer will have to take extra steps to make sure that the importance of routine maintenance is understood and carried out. Further, if technical support is not readily available, local people will have to be specially trained or the company will have to provide the support.

*Political and legal issues* face a business whether it operates at home or in a foreign country. However, the issues abroad are often amplified by the "alien status" of the company, which increases the difficulty of properly assessing and forecasting the dynamic international business climate. There are two dimensions to the *alien status* of a foreign business: It is alien in that foreigners control the business, and alien in that the culture of the host country is alien to management. The alien status of a business means that, when viewed as an outsider, it can be seen as an exploiter and receive prejudiced or unfair treatment at the hands of politicians or legal authorities, or both. Political activists can rally support by advocating the expulsion of the "foreign exploiters," often with open or tacit approval of authorities. The Indian government, for example, gave Coca-Cola the choice of either revealing its secret formula or leaving the country. The company chose to leave. When it was welcomed back several years later, it faced harassment and constant interference with its operations from political activists, inspired by competing soft drink companies.

Furthermore, in a domestic situation political details and the ramifications of political and legal events are often more transparent than they are in some foreign countries. For instance, whereas in the United States there are established legal procedures and due process to which each party in a dispute has access, legal systems in many other countries are still evolving. In many foreign countries corruption may prevail, foreigners may receive unfair treatment, or the laws may be so different from those in the home country that they are misinterpreted. The point is that a foreign company is foreign and thus always subject to the political whims of the local government to a greater degree than a domestic firm.

Japanese consumers have been faster to adopt both vending-machine and cell-phone technologies. This is so despite a wide variance in views about the importance of tradition as represented by these two views of Japanese women's dress. *(left: © Paul Chesley/Network Aspen; right: © Thomas Hoepker/Magnum Photos)*

Political/legal forces and the level of technology are only two of the uncontrollable aspects of the foreign environment that will be discussed in subsequent chapters. The uncertainty of different foreign business environments creates the need for a close study of the uncontrollable elements within each new country. Thus a strategy successful in one country can be rendered ineffective in another by differences in political climate, stages of economic development, level of technology, or other cultural variation.

## Environmental Adaptation Needed

To adjust and adapt a marketing program to foreign markets, marketers must be able to effectively interpret the influence and impact of each of the uncontrollable environmental elements on the marketing plan for each foreign market in which they hope to do business. In a broad sense, the uncontrollable elements constitute the culture; the difficulty facing the marketer in adjusting to the culture lies in recognizing their impact. In a domestic market the reaction to much of the environment's (cultural) impact on the marketer's activities is automatic; the various cultural influences that fill our lives are simply a part of our socialization, and we react in a manner acceptable to our society without thinking about it because we are culturally responsive to our environment. The experiences we have gained throughout life have become second nature and serve as the basis for our behavior.

The task of cultural adjustment, however, is the most challenging and important one confronting international marketers; they must adjust their marketing efforts to cultures to which they are not attuned. In dealing with unfamiliar markets, marketers must be aware of the frames of reference they are using in making their decisions or evaluating the potential of a market, because judgments are derived from experience that is the result of acculturation in the home country. After a frame of reference is established, it becomes an important factor in determining or modifying a marketer's reaction to situations—social and even nonsocial.

For example, a Westerner must learn that white is a symbol of mourning in parts of Asia, which is quite different from Western culture's use of white for bridal gowns. Also, time-conscious Americans are not culturally prepared to understand the meaning of time to Latin Americans. These differences must be learned to avoid misunderstandings that can lead to marketing failures. Such a failure actually occurred in one situation when ignorance led to ineffective advertising on the part of an American firm; and a second misunderstanding resulted in lost sales when a "long waiting period" in the outer office of a Latin American customer was misinterpreted by an American sales executive. Cross-cultural misunderstandings can also occur when a simple hand gesture has a number of different meanings in different parts of the world. When wanting to signify something is OK, most people in the United States raise a hand and make a circle with the thumb and forefinger. However, this same hand gesture means "zero" or "worthless" to the French, "money" to the Japanese, and a general sexual insult in Sardinia and Greece. A U.S. president sent an unintentional message to some Australian protesters when he held up his first two fingers with the back of his hand to the protesters. Meaning to give the "victory" sign, he was unaware that in Australia the same hand gesture is equivalent to holding up the middle finger in the United States.

Cultural conditioning is like an iceberg—we are not aware of nine-tenths of it. In any study of the market systems of different peoples, their political and economic structures, religions, and other elements of culture, foreign marketers must constantly guard against measuring and assessing the markets against the fixed values and assumptions of their own cultures. They must take specific steps to make themselves aware of the home-cultural reference in their analyses and decision making.

## The Self-Reference Criterion and Ethnocentrism: Major Obstacles

The key to successful international marketing is adaptation to the environmental differences from one market to another. Adaptation is a conscious effort on the part of the international marketer to anticipate the influences of both the foreign and domestic uncontrollable factors on a marketing mix and then to adjust the marketing mix to minimize the effects.

The primary obstacles to success in international marketing are a person's **self-reference criterion (SRC)** and an associated ethnocentrism. SRC is an unconscious reference to one's own cultural values, experiences, and knowledge as a basis for decisions. Closely connected is *ethnocentrism,* that is, the notion that one's own culture or company knows best how to do things. Ethnocentrism is particularly a problem for American managers at the beginning of the twenty-first century because of America's dominance in the world economy during the late 1990s. Ethnocentrism is generally a problem when managers from affluent countries work with managers and markets in less-affluent countries. Both the SRC and ethnocentrism impede the ability to assess a foreign market in its true light.

When confronted with a set of facts, we react spontaneously on the basis of knowledge assimilated over a lifetime—knowledge that is a product of the history of our culture. We seldom stop to think about a reaction; we simply react. Thus when faced with a problem in another culture, the tendency is to react instinctively and refer to our SRC for a solution. Our reaction, however, is based on meanings, values, symbols, and behavior relevant to our own culture and usually different from those of the foreign culture. Such decisions are often not good ones.

To illustrate the impact of the SRC, consider misunderstandings that can occur about personal space between people of different cultures. In the United States, unrelated individuals keep a certain physical distance between themselves and others when talking or in groups. We do not consciously think about that distance; we just know what feels right without thinking. When someone is too close or too far away, we feel uncomfortable and either move farther away or get closer to correct the distance. In doing so, we are relying on our SRC. In some cultures the acceptable distance between individuals is substantially less than that which is comfortable for Americans. When someone from another culture approaches an American too closely, the American, unaware of that culture's acceptable distance, unconsciously reacts by backing away to restore the proper distance (i.e., proper by American standards), and confusion results for both parties. Americans assume foreigners are pushy, while foreigners assume Americans are unfriendly and literally "standoffish." Both react according to the values of their own SRCs, making both victims of a cultural misunderstanding.

Your self-reference criterion can prevent you from being aware that there are cultural differences or from recognizing the importance of those differences. Thus you might fail to recognize the need to take action, you might discount the cultural differences that exist among countries, or you might react to a situation in a way offensive to your hosts. A common mistake made by Americans is to refuse food or drink when offered. In the United States, a polite refusal is certainly acceptable, but in Asia or the Middle East, a host is offended if you refuse hospitality. Although you do not have to eat or drink much, you do have to accept the offering of hospitality. Understanding and dealing with the self-reference criterion are two of the more important facets of international marketing.

Ethnocentrism and the SRC can influence an evaluation of the appropriateness of a domestically designed marketing mix for a foreign market. If U.S. marketers are not aware, they might evaluate a marketing mix based on U.S. experiences (i.e., their SRC) without fully appreciating the cultural differences that require adaptation. Esso, the brand name of a gasoline, was a successful name in the United States and would seem harmless enough for foreign countries; however, in Japan the name phonetically means "stalled car," an undesirable image for gasoline. Another example is "Pet" in Pet Milk. The name has been used for decades, yet in France the word *pet* means, among other things, "flatulence"—again, not the desired image for canned milk. Both of these examples were real mistakes made by major companies stemming from reliance on their SRC in making a decision. In U.S. culture, a person's SRC would not reveal a problem with either Esso or Pet, but in international marketing, relying on one's SRC could produce an inadequately adapted marketing program that ends in failure.

When marketers take the time to look beyond their own self-reference criteria the results are more positive. A British manufacturer of chocolate biscuits (cookies in American English), ignoring its SRC, knows that it must package its biscuits differently to accommodate the Japanese market. Thus in Japan, McVitie's chocolate biscuits are wrapped individually, packed in presentation cardboard boxes, and priced about three times higher than in the United Kingdom—the cookies are used as gifts in Japan and thus must look and be perceived as special. Unilever, appreciating the uniqueness of its markets, repackaged and reformulated its detergent for Brazil. One reason was that the lack of washing machines among poorer Brazilians made a simpler soap formula necessary. Also, since people wash their clothes in rivers, the powder was packaged in plastic rather than paper so it would not get soggy. Finally, because the Brazilian poor are price conscious and buy in small quantities, the soap was packaged in small, low-priced packages. Even McDonald's modifies its traditional Big Mac in India, where it is known as the Maharaja Mac. This burger features two mutton patties because most Indians consider cows sacred and don't eat beef. In each of these examples, had the marketers' own self-reference criteria been the basis for decisions, none of the changes would have been readily apparent based on home-market experience.

The most effective way to control the influence of ethnocentrism and the SRC is to recognize their effects on our behavior. Although it is almost impossible for someone to learn every culture in depth and to be aware of every important difference, an awareness of the need to be sensitive to differences and to ask questions when doing business in another culture can help one avoid many of the mistakes possible in international marketing. Asking the appropriate question helped the Vicks Company avoid making a mistake in Germany. It discovered that in German "Vicks" sounds like the crudest slang equivalent of "intercourse," so they changed the name to "Wicks" before introducing the product.

Be aware, also, that not every activity within a marketing program is different from one country to another; indeed, there probably are more similarities than differences. For example, the McVitie's chocolate biscuits mentioned earlier are sold in the United States in the same package as in the United Kingdom. Such similarities, however, may lull the marketer into a false sense of apparent sameness. This apparent sameness, coupled with the self-reference criterion, is often the cause of international marketing problems. Undetected similarities do not cause problems; however, the one difference that goes undetected can create a marketing failure.

**CROSSING BORDERS 1.4** Napster Lost the Battle, But the War over Intellectual Property Rights Rages on Worldwide

Perhaps the worst loan ever made was the $50 million loaned to Shawn Fanning and Napster in 2000 by Thomas Middlehoff, the charismatic but recently fired CEO of Germany's Bertelsmann (BMG Entertainment is their music division). Three years later Bertelsmann was being sued for $17 billion by recording artists and BMG's competitors, arguing that the loan allowed Napster to continue ripping them off. Of course, Napster itself is bankrupt.

In 2003 Rock 'n' rap band Linkin Park and their *Meteora* album brought a new weapon into the war. Super new prerelease security measures worked, and so did interviews disguised as songs from the album promulgated over the net designed to inoculate the net against the likes of Kazaa and the other second-generation Napsters. The innovative intellectual property protection strategies led to sales of 810,000 copies in the first week of release, easily yielding Linkin Park both a top spot on the pop charts and fat wallets as well. We assume the music was excellent, too.

Similar battles are being fought in China and sub-Sahara Africa. The intellectual property is more likely to be computer software in China and pharmaceutical products in Africa. But the war involves the same institutions—multinational companies trying to protect their ideas from the piracy of the public. China's entry into the World Trade Organization means more enforcement of copyright laws in that country. But it will be at least a decade before the Chinese develop enough of their own proprietary technology to make the transition from software pirates to copyright policemen.

Finally, the AIDS/HIV epidemic in Africa is forcing American and European pharmaceutical companies to lower prices for drugs they've developed to fight the disease. Protests, shareholder lobbying, and social responsibility have all started a general relaxation of an intellectual property rights regime that many said was killing millions of people.

Sources: Joseph Menn, "Piracy Battle Shifts to Bertelsmann," *Los Angeles Times*, February 20, 2003, p. C1; Jeff Leeds, "Unheard-Of Security, With a Massive Lockdown, Warner Bros. Records and Linkin Park All But Stop Early Leaks of the Album 'Meteora,'" *Los Angeles Times*, April 2, 2003, p. C1; and Ginger Thompson, "In the Grip of Aids, South Africa Cries for Equity," *New York Times*, May 10, 2003, p. 4.

To avoid errors in business decisions, it is necessary to conduct a cross-cultural analysis that isolates the SRC influences and to maintain a vigilance regarding ethnocentrism. The following steps are suggested as a framework for such an analysis.

1. Define the business problem or goal in home-country cultural traits, habits, or norms.
2. Define the business problem or goal in foreign-country cultural traits, habits, or norms through consultation with natives of the target country. Make no value judgments.
3. Isolate the SRC influence in the problem and examine it carefully to see how it complicates the problem.
4. Redefine the problem without the SRC influence and solve for the optimum business goal situation.

An American sales manager newly posted to Japan decided that his Japanese sales representatives did not need to come into the office every day for an early morning meeting before beginning calls on clients in Tokyo. After all, that was how things were done in the United States. However, the new policy, based on both the American's SRC and a modicum of ethnocentrism, produced a precipitous decline in sales performance. In his subsequent discussions with his Japanese staff he determined that Japanese sales representatives are motivated mostly by peer pressure. Fortunately he was able to recognize that his SRC and his American "business acumen" did not apply in this case in Tokyo. A return to the proven system of daily meetings brought sales performance back to previous levels.

The *cross-cultural analysis* approach requires an understanding of the culture of the foreign market as well as one's own culture. Surprisingly, understanding one's own culture may require additional study because much of the cultural influence on market behavior remains at a subconscious level and is not clearly defined.

## Developing a Global Awareness

Opportunities in global business abound for those who are prepared to confront myriad obstacles with optimism and a willingness to continue learning new ways. The successful businessperson in the twenty-first century will have **global awareness** and a frame of reference that goes beyond a region or even a country and encompasses the world. To be globally aware is to have (1) tolerance of cultural differences, and (2) knowledge of cultures, history, world market potential, and global economic, social, and political trends.

To be globally aware is to have *tolerance for cultural differences.* Tolerance is understanding cultural differences and accepting and working with others whose behaviors may be different from yours. You do not have to accept as your own the cultural ways of another, but you must allow others to be different and equal. For example, the fact that punctuality is less important in some cultures does not make them less productive, only different. The tolerant person understands the differences that may exist between cultures and uses that knowledge to relate effectively.

A globally aware person is knowledgeable about cultures and history. Knowledge of cultures is important in understanding behavior in the marketplace or in the boardroom. Knowledge of history is important because the way people think and act is influenced by their history. Some Latin Americans' reluctance about foreign investment or Chinese reluctance to open completely to outsiders can be understood better if you have a historical perspective.

Global awareness also involves knowledge of world market potentials and global economic, social, and political trends. Over the next few decades there will be enormous changes in market potentials in almost every region of the world, all of which a globally aware person must continuously monitor. Finally, a globally aware person will keep abreast of the global economic, social, and political trends because a country's prospects can change as these trends shift direction or accelerate. The former republics of the Soviet Union, along with Russia, Eastern Europe, China, India, Africa, and Latin America, are undergoing economic, social, and political changes that have already altered the course of trade and defined new economic powers. The knowledgeable marketer will identify opportunity long before it becomes evident to others. It is the authors' goal in this text to guide the reader toward acquiring a global awareness.

Global awareness can and should be built in organizations using several approaches. The obvious strategy is to select individual managers specifically for their demonstrated global awareness. Global awareness can also be obtained through personal relationships in other countries. Indeed, market entry is very often facilitated through previously established social ties. Certainly, successful long-term business relationships with foreign customers often result in an organizational global awareness based on the series of interactions required by commerce. Foreign agents and partners can also help directly in this regard. But perhaps the most effective approach is to have a culturally diverse senior executive staff or board of directors. Unfortunately, American managers seem to see relatively less value in this last approach than managers in most other countries.

## Stages of International Marketing Involvement

After a company decides to go international, it must decide the degree of marketing involvement and commitment it is prepared to make. These decisions should reflect considerable study and analysis of market potential and company capabilities—a process not always followed. Many companies begin tentatively in international marketing, growing as they gain experience and gradually changing strategy and tactics as they become more committed. Others enter international marketing after much research and with fully developed long-range plans, prepared to make investments to acquire a market position.

Regardless of the means employed to gain entry into a foreign market, a company may make little or no actual market investment—that is, its marketing involvement may be limited to selling a product with little or no thought given to development of market control. Alternatively, a company may become totally involved and invest large sums of money and effort to capture and maintain a permanent, specific position in the market. In general, one of five (sometimes overlapping) stages can describe the international marketing involvement of a company.[19] Although the stages of international marketing involvement are presented here in a linear order, the reader should not infer that a firm progresses from one stage to another; quite to the contrary, a firm may begin its international involvement at any one stage or be in more than one stage simultaneously. For example, because of a short product life cycle and a thin but widespread market for many technology products, many high-tech companies large and small see the entire world, including their home market, as a single market and strive to reach all possible customers as rapidly as possible.

## No Direct Foreign Marketing

A company in this stage does not actively cultivate customers outside national boundaries; however, this company's products may reach foreign markets. Sales may be made to trading companies as well as foreign customers who come directly to the firm. Or products may reach foreign markets via domestic wholesalers or distributors who sell abroad without explicit encouragement or even knowledge of the producer. As companies develop websites on the Internet, many receive orders from international Web surfers. Often an unsolicited order from a foreign buyer is what piques the interest of a company to seek additional international sales.

## Infrequent Foreign Marketing

Temporary surpluses caused by variations in production levels or demand may result in infrequent marketing overseas. The surpluses are characterized by their temporary nature; therefore, sales to foreign markets are made as goods are available, with little or no intention of maintaining continuous market representation. As domestic demand increases and absorbs surpluses, foreign sales activity is withdrawn. In this stage, there is little or no change in company organization or product lines. However, few companies today fit this model because customers around the world increasingly seek long-term commercial relationships.

## Regular Foreign Marketing

At this level, the firm has permanent productive capacity devoted to the production of goods to be marketed in foreign markets.[20] A firm may employ foreign or domestic overseas middlemen or it may have its own sales force or sales subsidiaries in important foreign markets. The primary focus of operations and production is to service domestic market needs. However, as overseas demand grows, production is allocated for foreign markets, and products may be adapted to meet the needs of individual foreign markets. Profit expectations from foreign markets move from being seen as a bonus to regular domestic profits to a position in which the company depends on foreign sales and profits to meet its goals.

Meter-Man, a small company (25 employees) in southern Minnesota that manufactures agricultural measuring devices, is a good example of a company in this stage.[21] In 1989, the 35-year-old company began exploring the idea of exporting; by 1992 the company was shipping product to Europe. Today, a third of Meter-Man's sales are in 35 countries, and soon the company expects international sales to account for about half of its business. "When you start exporting, you say to yourself, this will be icing on the cake," says the director of sales and marketing. "But now I say going international has become critical to our existence."

---

[19]Alan M. Rugman and Alain Verbeke, "Extending the Theory of the Multinational Enterprise: Internationalization and Strategic Management Perspectives," *Journal of International Business Studies*, 2003(3), pp. 125–137.

[20]George S. Yip, Javier Gomez Biscarri, and Joseph A. Monti, "The Role of Internationalization Process in the Performance of Newly Internationalizing Firms," *Journal of International Marketing*, 2000, 8(3), pp. 10–35.

[21]See www.meter-man.com for their product line and other details.

**International Marketing**

Companies in this stage are fully committed and involved in international marketing activities. Such companies seek markets all over the world and sell products that are a result of planned production for markets in various countries. This generally entails not only the marketing but also the production of goods outside the home market. At this point a company becomes an international or multinational marketing firm.

The experience of Fedders, a manufacturer of room air conditioners, typifies that of a company that begins its international business at this stage.[22] Even though it is the largest manufacturer of air conditioners in the United States, the firm faced constraints in its domestic market. Its sales were growing steadily, but air conditioner sales (the company's only product) are seasonal and thus there are times when domestic sales do not even cover fixed costs. Furthermore, the U.S. market is mature, with most customers buying only replacement units. Any growth would have to come from a rival's market share, and the rivals, Whirlpool and Matsushita, are formidable. Fedders decided that the only way to grow was to venture abroad.

Fedders decided that Asia, with its steamy climate and expanding middle class, offered the best opportunity. China, India, and Indonesia were seen as the best prospects. China was selected because sales of room air conditioners had grown from 500,000 units to over 4 million in five years, which still accounted for only 12 percent of the homes in cities like Beijing, Shanghai, and Guangzhou. The company saw China as a market with terrific growth potential. After careful study, Fedders entered a joint venture with a small Chinese air conditioner company that was looking for a partner; a new company, Fedders Xinle, was formed. They immediately found that they needed to redesign their product for this market. In China, air conditioners are a major purchase seen as a status symbol, not as a box to keep a room cool as in the United States. The Chinese also prefer a split-type air conditioner, with the unit containing the fan inside the room and the heat exchanger mounted on a wall outside. Since Fedders did not manufacture split models, it designed a new product that is lightweight, energy efficient, and packed with features such as a remote control and an automatic air-sweeping mechanism.

The joint venture appears to be successful, and the company is exploring the possibility of marketing to other Asian markets and Japan and maybe even back to the United States with the new product that it developed for the Chinese market. As Fedders expands into other markets and makes other commitments internationally, it continues to evolve as an international or multinational company. The company may remain in this stage, as most companies do, or go through a change in orientation and become a global company.

North of Beijing, China, the new development is marketed as Orange County, China. The gardens and stucco and tile exteriors are all intended to replicate the Mediterranean look and feel of homes in Newport Beach, CA. (© AFP/Getty Images)

**Global Marketing**

At the **global marketing** level, the most profound change is the orientation of the company toward markets and associated planning activities. At this stage, companies treat the world, including their home market, as one market. Market segmentation decisions are no longer focused on national borders. Instead, market segments are defined by income levels, usage patterns, or other factors that often span countries and regions.[23] Often this transition from international marketing to global marketing is catalyzed by a company's crossing the threshold of more than half its sales revenues coming from abroad. The best people in the company begin to seek international assignments, and the entire operation—organizational structure, sources of finance, production, marketing, and so forth—begins to take on a global perspective.[24]

---

[22]See www.fedders.com for details about the company.

[23]Frenkel Ter Hofstede, Jan-Benedict E. M. Steenkamp, and Michel Wedel, "International Market Segmentation Based on Consumer-Product Relations," *Journal of Marketing Research*, February 1999, 36, pp. 1–17.

[24]One author argues for a middle ground on the issue of global markets: Pankaj Ghemawat, "Semiglobalization and International Business Strategy," *Journal of International Business Studies*, 2003(34), pp. 139–152.

## CROSSING BORDERS 1.5 Orange County, CA, Travels East and West

For $500,000 you can now buy a four-bedroom house in Orange County—in China!

The homes are designed by Southern California architects and built with American features, but are located in a new development an hour's drive north of Beijing. The country road can be icy and is lined by fields and populated by trucks and sheep. The landscape is a far cry from palm-ringed golf courses and "Surfin' USA." A bit after Sun City, another half-built gated community, the tidy homes of Orange County come into view. Finally you drive through a stone portal, past advertisements that show men fly-fishing in cowboy hats and such, pulling up before the impressive mansions of Watermark Longbeach, the epicenter of *faux* L.A. in China. "I liked it immediately—it is just like a house in California," says homeowner Nasha Wei, a former army doctor turned businesswoman.

And apparently in France, the waves can actually be better than in California. Check out the 60-footers at Belharra Reef off St. Jean de Luz. Or hang ten along the surf-wear shops nearby in the hamlet of Hossegor in southwest France. They're all there: Roxy, Rip Curl Girl, Billabong, and Quicksilver Boardriders Club. And the kids in the neighborhoods and sidewalk cafes are decked out in Volcom sweatshirts, Vans sneakers, and jeans.

The $4.5-billion surf-wear industry, rooted in Orange County, CA, has established a beachhead in Europe. So many U.S. surf-wear companies have international headquarters, subsidiaries, and stores in Pays Basque that it has a new nickname: *la petite Californie.* "This is the best place to observe the market," says Petra Holtschneider, who is organizing the first Action Sports Retailer trade show in the area this summer. "So if you're not here, you're not getting it."

Sources: Elisabeth Rosenthal, "North of Beijing, California Dreams Come True," *New York Times*, February 3, 2003, p. A3; and Leslie Earnest, "Riding a French New Wave," *Los Angeles Times*, May 11, 2003, p. C1.

The example of Coca-Cola's transition from international to global is instructive. Coca-Cola had actually been a global company for years; the mid-1990s organizational change was the last step in recognizing the changes that had already occurred. Initially, all international divisions reported to an executive vice president in charge of international operations, who, along with the vice president of U.S. operations, reported to the president. The new organization consists of six international divisions—five Coca-Cola

Orange County has also come to France in the form of the southern California surfing culture and clothiers. OC's Quiksilver opened its European headquarters in southwest France in 1984. Last year European sales amounted to almost $300 million. Part of the firm's success in Europe can be attributed to hiring local nationals in key marketing positions. Maritxu Darrigrand, former French women's surfing champion with board under arm, is now Quiksilver's marketing director for Europe. (© AFP/Getty Images)

divisions and one Coca-Cola Foods division. The U.S. business unit accounts for about 20 percent of profits and has been downgraded to just part of one of the six international business units in the company's global geographic regions. The new structure does not reduce the importance of the company's North American business; it just puts other areas on an equal footing. However, it is recognition that future growth is going to come from emerging markets outside the United States.

International operations of businesses in global marketing reflect the heightened competitiveness brought about by the globalization of markets, interdependence of the world's economies, and the growing number of competing firms from developed and developing countries vying for the world's markets. *Global companies* and *global marketing* are terms frequently used to describe the scope of operations and marketing management orientation of companies in this stage.

## Strategic Orientation

The stages of international marketing involvement described above do not necessarily coincide with managers' thinking and strategic orientations. Often companies are led into international and even global markets by burgeoning consumer or customer demands, and strategic thinking is secondary to "filling the next order." But putting strategic thinking on the back burner has resulted in marketing failures for even the largest companies.

The consensus of the researchers and authors[25] in the area reveals three relatively distinctive approaches that dominate strategic thinking in firms involved in international markets:

1. Domestic market extension concept
2. Multidomestic market concept
3. Global marketing concept

It is to be expected that differences in the complexity and sophistication of a company's marketing activity depend on which orientation guides its operations. The ideas expressed in each strategic orientation reflect the philosophical orientation that also should be associated with successive stages in the evolution of the international operations in a company.

### Domestic Market Extension Orientation

The domestic company seeking sales extension of its domestic products into foreign markets illustrates this orientation to international marketing. It views its international operations as secondary to and an extension of its domestic operations; the primary motive is to market excess domestic production. Domestic business is its priority, and foreign sales are seen as a profitable extension of domestic operations. Even though foreign markets may be vigorously pursued, the firm's orientation remains basically domestic. Its attitude toward international sales is typified by the belief that if it sells in St. Louis it will sell anywhere else in the world. Minimal, if any, efforts are made to adapt the marketing mix to foreign markets; the firm's orientation is to market to foreign customers in the same manner in which the company markets to domestic customers. It seeks markets where demand is similar to the home market and its domestic product will be acceptable. This domestic market extension strategy can be very profitable; large and small exporting companies approach international marketing from this perspective. Firms with this marketing approach are ethnocentric. Meter-Man, discussed earlier, could be said to follow this orientation.

---

[25] A seminal paper in this genre was Yorum Wind, Susan P. Douglas, and Howard V. Perlmutter, "Guidelines for Developing International Marketing Strategy," *Journal of Marketing*, April 1973, pp. 14–23; also important is Anne-Wil Harzing, "An Empirical Analysis and Extension of the Bartlett and Ghoshal Typology of Multinational Companies," *Journal of International Business Studies*, 2000, 31(1), pp. 101–120.

## Multidomestic Market Orientation

When a company recognizes the importance of differences in overseas markets and the importance of offshore business to the organization, its orientation toward international business may shift to a multidomestic market strategy. A company guided by this concept has a strong sense that country markets are vastly different (and they may be, depending on the product) and that market success requires an almost independent program for each country. Firms with this orientation market on a country-by-country basis, with separate marketing strategies for each country.

Subsidiaries operate independently of one another in establishing marketing objectives and plans, and the domestic market and each of the country markets have separate marketing mixes with little interaction among them. Products are adapted for each market with little coordination with other country markets; advertising campaigns are localized, as are the pricing and distribution decisions. A company with this concept does not look for similarity among elements of the marketing mix that might respond to standardization; rather, it aims for adaptation to local country markets. Control is typically decentralized to reflect the belief that the uniqueness of each market requires local marketing input and control. Firms with this orientation are polycentric. Fedders, as it progresses in its plans, fits this orientation.

## Global Marketing Orientation

A company guided by the global marketing orientation or philosophy is generally referred to as a global company; its marketing activity is global, and its market coverage is the world. A company employing a global marketing strategy strives for efficiencies of scale by developing a standardized marketing mix applicable across national boundaries. Markets are still segmented, but country or region are considered side by side with a variety of other segmentation variables, such as consumer characteristics (age, income, language group), usage patterns, legal constraints, and so on. The world as a whole is viewed as the market, and the firm develops a global marketing strategy. The global marketing company is geocentric. Coca-Cola Company, Ford Motor Company, and Intel are among the companies that can be described as global companies.

The **global marketing concept** views an entire set of country markets (whether the home market and only 1 other country, or the home market and 100 other countries) as a unit, identifying groups of prospective buyers with similar needs as a global market segment and developing a marketing plan that strives for standardization wherever it is cost and culturally effective. This might mean a company's global marketing plan has a standardized product but country-specific advertising, or has a standardized theme in all countries with country- or cultural-specific appeals to a unique market characteristic, or has a standardized brand or image but has adapted products to meet specific country needs, and so on. In other words, the marketing planning and marketing mix are approached from a global perspective, and where feasible in the marketing mix, efficiencies of standardization are sought. Wherever cultural uniqueness dictates the need for adaptation of the product, its image, and so on, it is accommodated. For example, McDonald's standardizes its processes, logo, most of its advertising, and store decor and layouts whenever and wherever possible. However, you will find wine on the menu in France and beer in Germany, a Filipino-style spicy burger in Manila, and pork burgers in Thailand—all to accommodate local tastes and customs. The point is, being global is a mindset, a way of looking at the market for commonalities that can be standardized across regions or country-market sets.

As the competitive environment facing U.S. businesses becomes more internationalized—and it surely will—the most effective orientation for many firms involved in marketing into another country will be a **global orientation**. This means operating as if all the country markets in a company's scope of operations (including the domestic market) were approachable as a single global market and standardizing the marketing mix where culturally feasible and cost effective. This does not, however, mean a slavish adherence to one strategic orientation. Depending on the product and market, other orientations may make more marketing sense. For example, Procter & Gamble may pursue a global strategy for disposable diapers, but a multidomestic strategy in Asian markets for detergents.

## The Orientation of *International Marketing*

Most problems encountered by the foreign marketer result from the strangeness of the environment within which marketing programs must be implemented. Success hinges, in part, on the ability to assess and adjust properly to the impact of a strange environment. The successful international marketer possesses the best qualities of the anthropologist, sociologist, psychologist, diplomat, lawyer, prophet, and businessperson.

In light of all the variables involved, with what should a text in foreign marketing be concerned? It is the opinion of the authors that a study of foreign marketing environments and cultures[26] and their influences on the total marketing process is of primary concern and is the most effective approach to a meaningful presentation. Consequently, the orientation of this text can best be described as an environmental/cultural approach to international strategic marketing.[27] By no means is it intended to present principles of marketing; rather, it is intended to demonstrate the unique problems of international marketing. It attempts to relate the foreign environment to the marketing process and to illustrate the many ways in which culture can influence the marketing task. Although marketing principles are universally applicable, the cultural environment within which the marketer must implement marketing plans can change dramatically from country to country. It is with the difficulties created by different environments that this text is primarily concerned.

The text is concerned with any company marketing in or into any other country or groups of countries, however slight the involvement or the method of involvement. Hence, this discussion of international marketing ranges from the marketing and business practices of small exporters, such as a Colorado-based company that generates more than 50 percent of its $40,000 annual sales of fish-egg sorters in Canada, Germany, and Australia, to the practices of global companies such as Motorola, Avon, and Johnson & Johnson, all of which generate more than 50 percent of their annual profits from the sales of multiple products to multiple country-market segments all over the world.

The first section of *International Marketing* offers an overview of international marketing, including a brief discussion of the global business environment confronting the marketer. The next section deals exclusively with the uncontrollable elements of the environment and their assessment, followed by chapters on assessing global market opportunities. Then, management issues in developing global marketing strategies are discussed. In each chapter, the impact of the environment on the marketing process is illustrated.

Space prohibits an encyclopedic approach to all the issues of international marketing; nevertheless, the authors have tried to present sufficient detail so that readers will appreciate the real need to make a thorough analysis whenever the challenge arises. The text provides a framework for this task.

## Summary

The internationalization of American business is proceeding with increasing pace. The globalization of markets and competition necessitates all managers to pay attention to the global environment. International marketing is defined as the performance of business activities including pricing, promotion, product, and distribution decisions across national borders. The international marketing task is made more daunting because environmental factors such as laws, customs, and cultures vary from country to country. These environmental differences must be taken into account if firms are to market products and services at a profit in other countries.

Key obstacles facing international marketers are not limited to environmental issues. Just as important are difficulties associated

---

[26] A multiyear survey of high-tech executives in the southern California area has continuously mentioned cultural differences as one of the most prominent obstacles to international commerce. See Dennis J. Aigner, *The 2004 Orange County Executive Survey*, annually published from 1986 to 2004, Graduate School of Management, University of California, Irvine.

[27] Lawrence E. Harrison and Samuel P. Huntington (eds.), *Culture Matters* (New York: Basic Books, 2000).

with the marketer's own self-reference criteria and ethnocentrism. Both limit the international marketer's abilities to understand and adapt to differences prevalent in foreign markets. A global awareness and sensitivity are the best solutions to these problems, and these should be nurtured in international marketing organizations.

Three different strategic orientations are found among managers of international marketing operations. Some see international marketing as ancillary to the domestic operations. A second kind of company sees international marketing as a crucial aspect of sales revenue generation, but each market is treated as a separate entity. Finally, a global orientation views the globe as the marketplace and market segments are no longer based solely on national borders—common consumer characteristics and behaviors come into play as key segmentation variables applied across countries.

## Questions

1. Define:

| | |
|---|---|
| international marketing, 9 | self-reference criterion |
| uncontrollable elements, 10 | (SRC), 15 |
| controllable elements, 10 | global awareness, 18 |
| domestic environment | global marketing, 20 |
| uncontrollables, 11 | global marketing concept, 23 |
| foreign environment | global orientation, 23 |
| uncontrollables, 12 | |

2. "The marketer's task is the same whether applied in Dimebox, Texas, or Dar es Salaam, Tanzania." Discuss.

3. How can the increased interest in international marketing on the part of U.S. firms be explained?

4. Discuss the four phases of international marketing involvement.

5. Discuss the conditions that have led to the development of global markets.

6. Differentiate between a global company and a multinational company.

7. Differentiate among the three international marketing concepts.

8. Prepare your lifelong plan to be globally aware.

9. Discuss the three factors necessary to achieve global awareness.

10. Define and discuss the idea of global orientation.

11. Visit the Bureau of Economic Analysis homepage (www.bea.doc.gov). Select the section, International articles, and find the most recent information on Foreign Direct Investments in the United States. Which country has the highest dollar amount of investment in the United States? Second highest?

**CHAPTER 2**

# The Dynamic Environment of International Trade

## CHAPTER LEARNING OBJECTIVES

What you should learn from Chapter 2:

- The basis for the reestablishment of world trade following World War II

- The importance of balance-of-payment figures to a country's economy

- The effects of protectionism on world trade

- The seven types of trade barriers

- The provisions of the Omnibus Trade and Competitiveness Act

- The importance of GATT and the World Trade Organization

- The emergence of the International Monetary Fund and the World Bank Group

# Global Perspective

## TRADE BARRIERS—AN INTERNATIONAL MARKETER'S MINEFIELD

We all know the story about our trade disputes with Japan. Japan has so many trade barriers and high tariffs that U.S. manufacturers are unable to sell in Japan as much as Japanese companies sell in the United States. The Japanese claim that "unique" Japanese snow requires skis made in Japan, and U.S. baseballs are not good enough for Japanese baseball. Even when Japan opened their rice market, the popular California rice had to be mixed and sold with inferior grades of Japanese rice.

However, the Japanese are not alone; it seems every country takes advantage of the open U.S. market while putting barriers in the way of U.S. exports. The French, for example, protect their film and broadcast industry from foreign competition by limiting the number of American shows that can appear on television, the percentage of American songs broadcast on radio, and the proportion of U.S. movies that can be shown in French theaters. Most recently France is preparing to launch its own "French" version of CNN with strong government financial support. Not only do these barriers and high tariffs limit how much U.S. companies can sell; they also raise prices for imported products much higher than they sell for in the United States.

Consider the fiscal hazards facing international marketing managers at a company like Neutrogena[1] that is contemplating exporting its products to Russia. Upon arrival there the firm's products might be classified by Russian customs officers into any one of three separate categories for the purposes of assigning tariffs: pharmaceuticals at a 5 percent duty, soap at 15 percent, or cosmetics at 20 percent. Of course, Neutrogena managers would argue for the lowest tariff by pointing out that their hypoallergenic soaps are recommended by dermatologists. And as long as shipments remain relatively small, the customs officers might not argue. However, as exports to Russia grow from cartons to container loads, the product classification receives more scrutiny. Simple statements on packaging such as, "Pure Neutrogena skin and hair care products are available at drug stores and *cosmetic counters*," would give the Russians reason to claim the highest duty of 20 percent.

Barriers to trade, both tariff and nontariff, are one of the major issues confronting international marketers. Fortunately, tariffs generally have been reduced to record lows and substantial progress has been made on eliminating nontariff barriers. However, nations continue to use trade barriers for a variety of reasons, some rational and some not so rational.

Sources: Adapted from Todd G. Buchholz, "Free Trade Keeps Prices Down," *The Consumers' Research Magazine*, October 1995, p. 22; Tomas Kellner, "What Gaul!" *Forbes*, April 28, 2003, p. 52; and www.neutrogena.com.

---

[1]Neutrogena has been a division of Johnson & Johnson since 1994. See "Performance Rankings of the S&P 500," *Business Week*, March 25, 2003, pp. 61–84 in which J&J is ranked number four.

**Exhibit 2.1**
Top Ten 2002 U.S. Trading
Partners ($ billions,
merchandise trade)

Source: www.census.gov/
foreign-trade/top

| Country | Total Trade | Exports | Imports | Balance |
|---|---|---|---|---|
| Canada | 371.4 | 160.8 | 210.6 | −49.8 |
| Mexico | 232.3 | 97.5 | 134.7 | −37.2 |
| Japan | 172.9 | 51.4 | 121.5 | −70.1 |
| China | 147.2 | 22.1 | 125.2 | −103.1 |
| Germany | 89.1 | 26.6 | 62.5 | −35.9 |
| United Kingdom | 74.1 | 33.3 | 40.9 | −7.6 |
| South Korea | 58.2 | 22.6 | 35.6 | −13.0 |
| Taiwan | 50.6 | 18.4 | 32.2 | −13.8 |
| France | 47.4 | 19.0 | 28.4 | −9.4 |
| Italy | 34.4 | 10.1 | 24.3 | −14.2 |

Yesterday's competitive market battles were fought in Western Europe, Japan, and the United States; tomorrow's competitive battles will extend to Latin America, Eastern Europe, Russia, India, Asia, and Africa as these emerging markets continue to open to trade. More of the world's people, from the richest to the poorest, will participate in the world's wealth through global trade. The emerging global economy in which we live brings us into worldwide competition with significant advantages for both marketers and consumers. Marketers benefit from new markets opening and smaller markets growing large enough to become viable business opportunities. Consumers benefit by being able to select from the widest range of goods produced anywhere in the world at the lowest prices.

Bound together by satellite communications and global companies, consumers in every corner of the world are demanding an ever-expanding variety of goods. As Exhibit 2.1 illustrates, world trade is an important economic activity. Because of this importance, the inclination is for countries to control international trade to their own advantage. As competition intensifies, the tendency toward protectionism gains momentum. If the benefits of the social, political, and economic changes now taking place are to be fully realized, free trade must prevail throughout the global marketplace. The creation of the World Trade Organization (WTO) is one of the biggest victories for free trade in decades.

This chapter includes a brief survey of the United States' past and present role in global trade and some concepts important in understanding the relationship between international trade and national economic policy. A discussion of the logic and illogic of protectionism, the major impediment to trade, is followed by a review of the General Agreement on Tariffs and Trade (GATT) and its successor, the World Trade Organization (WTO), two multinational agreements designed to advance free trade.

**1000** First millenium ends; Y1K problem overblown—widespread fear of the end of the world proved unfounded
**1000** Vikings first settle Newfoundland
**1004** Chinese unity crumbles with treaty between the Song and the Liao giving the Liao full autonomy; China remains fractured until the Mongol invasion in the thirteenth century (see 1206)
**1025** Navy of Cholas in Southern India crushes the empire of Srivijaya in modern Myanmar to protect their trade with China

**1054** Italy and Egypt formalize commercial relations
**1066** William the Conqueror is victorious over Harold II in the Battle of Hastings, establishing Norman rule in England and forever linking the country with the continent
**1081** Venice and Byzantium conclude a commercial treaty (renewed in 1126)
**1095** First of the crusades begins; Pope Urban II calls on Europe's noblemen to help the Byzantines repel the Turks; the crusaders' travel, stories, and goods acquired along the way help increase trade across

Europe and with the Mediterranean and Asia; eighth major crusade ends, Syria expels the Christians
**1100** Japan begins to isolate itself from the rest of the world, not really opening up again until the mid-nineteenth century (see 1858)
**1100** China invents the mariner's compass and becomes a force in trade; widespread use of paper money also helps increase trade and prosperity
**1100** Inca Empire in the Andes begins to develop, eventually encompassing about 12

million people until its destruction by the Spanish in 1553; cities specialize in certain farming and trade with others for what they don't make
**1132** Corporate towns in France granted charters by Henry I to protect commerce
**1189** German merchants conclude treaty with Novgorod in Russia
**1200** Islam is introduced to Southeast Asia by spice traders
**1200** More than 60,000 Italian merchants work and live in Constantinople
**1206** Genghis Khan becomes the Great Khan, controlling

## The Twentieth to the Twenty-first Century

At no time in modern economic history have countries been more economically interdependent, have greater opportunities for international trade existed, or has the potential for increased demand existed than now, at the opening of the twenty-first century. In the preceding 100 years, world economic development has been erratic.

Bicycles and websites are both part of marketing in China.
(© AFP/CORBIS)

The first half of the twentieth century was marred by a major worldwide economic depression that occurred between two world wars and that all but destroyed most of the industrialized world. The last half of the century, while free of a world war, was marred by struggles between countries espousing the socialist Marxist approach and those following a democratic capitalist approach to economic development. As a result of this ideological split, traditional trade patterns were disrupted.

After World War II, as a means to dampen the spread of communism, the United States set out to infuse the ideal of capitalism throughout as much of the world as possible. The Marshall Plan to assist in rebuilding Europe, financial and industrial development assistance to rebuild Japan, and funds channeled through the Agency for International Development and other groups designed to foster economic growth in the underdeveloped world were used to help create a strong world economy. The dissolution of colonial powers created scores of new countries in Asia and Africa. With the striving of these countries to gain economic independence and the financial assistance offered by the United States, most of the noncommunist world's economies grew and new markets were created.

The benefits from the foreign economic assistance given by the United States flowed both ways. For every dollar the United States invested in the economic development and rebuilding of other countries after World War II, hundreds of dollars more returned in the form of purchases of U.S. agricultural products, manufactured goods, and services. This overseas demand created by the Marshall Plan and other programs[2] was important to the United States economy since

---

[2]The Organization for Economic Cooperation and Development (OECD) was a direct result of the Marshall Plan. See Timothy Bainbridge, "A Brief History of the OECD," *OECD Observer,* Summer 2000, pp. 111–113.

---

most of northern China; after his death in 1227, the Khan clan conquers much of Asia by mid-century and promotes trade and commerce, reviving the ancient Silk Road that linked Chinese and Western traders
**1215**   Magna Carta, a pact between the English king and his subjects, is signed by King John, who becomes subject to the rule of law
**1229**   German merchants sign trade treaty with the Prince of Smolensk in Russia
**1252**   First gold coins issued in the West since the fall of Rome, in Florence

**1269**   England institutes toll roads
**1270**   Venetian Marco Polo and his father travel through Asia and the Middle East, becoming the first European traders to establish extensive links with the region
**1279**   Kublai Khan unites China and creates the Yuan (Origin) dynasty; by the time he dies in 1294, he has created a unified Mongul Empire extending from China to eastern Europe
**1300**   The early stirrings of the Renaissance begin in Europe as people are exposed to other

cultures, primarily through merchants and trade
**1300**   Trade fairs are held in numerous European cities
**1315**   A great famine hits Europe, lasting two years, more widespread and longer than any before
**1348**   The plague (the Black Death) kills one-fourth to one-third of the population in Europe (25 million people) in just three years, disrupting trade as cities try to prevent the spread of the disease by restricting visitors; it likely started in Asia in the 1320s; massive inflation took hold, since goods could

only be obtained locally; serfs were in high demand and began moving to higher wage payers, forever altering Europe's labor landscape
**1358**   German Hanseatic league officially formed by the Hansa companies of merchants for trade and mutual protection, eventually encompassing more than 70 cities and lasting nearly 300 years
**1375**   Timur Lang the Turk conquers lands from Moscow to Delhi
**1381**   English rioters kill foreign Flemish traders as part of the 100,000-strong peasant

the vast manufacturing base built to supply World War II and the swelling labor supply of returning military personnel created a production capacity well beyond domestic needs. The major economic boom and increased standard of living the United States experienced after World War II was fueled by fulfilling pent-up demand in the United States and demand created by the rebuilding of war-torn countries of Europe and Asia. In short, the United States helped to make the world's economies stronger, which enabled them to buy more from us.

In addition to U.S. economic assistance, a move toward international cooperation among trading nations was manifest in the negotiation of the General Agreement on Tariffs and Trade (GATT).[3] International trade had ground to a halt following World War I when nations followed the example set by the U.S. enactment of the Smoot-Hawley Act (1930), which raised average U.S. tariffs on more than 20,000 imported goods to levels in excess of 60 percent. In retaliation, 60 countries erected high tariff walls and international trade was stalled, along with most economies. A major worldwide recession catapulted the world's economies into the Great Depression when trade all but dried up after tariffs and other trade barriers were raised to intolerable heights.[4]

Determined not to repeat the economic disaster following World War I, world leaders created GATT, a forum for member countries to negotiate a reduction of tariffs and other barriers to trade. The forum proved successful in reaching those objectives. With the ratification of the Uruguay Round agreements, the GATT became part of the World Trade Organization (WTO) and its 117 original members moved into a new era of free trade.

## World Trade and U.S. Multinationals

The rapid growth of war-torn economies and previously underdeveloped countries, coupled with large-scale economic cooperation and assistance, led to new global marketing opportunities. Rising standards of living and broad-based consumer and industrial markets abroad created opportunities for American companies to expand exports and investment worldwide. During the 1950s, many U.S. companies that had never before marketed outside the United States began to export, and others made significant investments in marketing and production facilities overseas.

At the close of the 1960s, U.S. multinational corporations (MNCs) were facing major challenges on two fronts: resistance to direct investment and increasing competition in export markets. Large investments by U.S. businesses in Europe and Latin America heightened the concern of these countries about the growing domination of U.S. multinationals. The reaction in Latin American countries was to expropriate direct U.S. investments or to force companies to sell controlling interests to nationals. In Europe, apprehension

---

[3]Michael H. Hunt, "Free Trade, Free World: the Advent of GATT," *Business History Review,* summer 2000, 74(2), pp. 350–352.

[4]Thomas A. Bailey and David M. Kennedy, *The American Pageant* (13th edition, Boston: Houghton Mifflin, 2004).

rebellion against Richard II, which was led by Wat Tyler in a failed attempt to throw off the yoke of feudalism
**1392** England prohibits foreigners from retailing goods in the country
**1400** Koreans develop movable-type printing (see 1450)
**1404** Chinese prohibit private trading in foreign countries, but foreign ships may trade in China with official permission
**1415** Chinese begin significant trading with Africa through government expeditions—

some believe they sailed to North America as well in 1421
**1425** Hanseatic city of Brugge becomes the first Atlantic seaport to be a major trading center
**1427** Aztec Empire is created by Itzcotl; it encompasses about 6 million people until its destruction in 1519
**1430** Portuguese Henry the Navigator explores west African coast to promote trade
**1441** Mayan Empire collapses as the city of Mayapán is destroyed in a revolt
**1450** Renaissance takes hold in Florence, its birthplace

**1450** Gutenberg Bible is first book printed with movable type; the ability to mass-produce books creates an information revolution
**1453** Byzantine Empire is destroyed as Muhammad II sacks Constantinople (renaming it Istanbul)
**1464** French royal mail service established by Louis XI
**1470** Early trademark piracy committed by Persians, who copy mass-produced Chinese porcelain to capitalize on its popularity in foreign countries

**1479** Under the Treaty of Constantinople, in exchange for trading rights in the Black Sea, Venice agrees to pay tribute to the Ottoman Empire.
**1482** England organizes a postal system that features fresh relays of horses every 20 miles
**1488** Bartolomeu Dias sails around the coast of Africa; this, along with the voyages of Christopher Columbus, ushers in the era of sea travel
**1492** Christopher Columbus "discovers" the New World

manifested itself in strong public demand to limit foreign investment. Concern there that Britain might become a satellite where there could be manufacturing but no determination of policy led to specific guidelines for joint ventures between British and U.S. companies. In the European Community, U.S. multinationals were rebuffed in ways ranging from tight control over proposed joint ventures and regulations covering U.S. acquisitions of European firms and strong protectionism laws.

The threat felt by Europeans was best expressed in the popular book, *The American Challenge*, published in 1968, in which the French author, J. J. Servan-Schreiber, wrote:

> Fifteen years from now it is quite possible that the world's third greatest industrial power, just after the United States and Russia, will not be Europe but American Industry in Europe. Already, in the ninth year of the Common Market, this European market is basically American in organization.[5]

Servan-Schreiber's prediction did not come true for many reasons, but one of the more important reasons was that American MNCs were confronted by a resurgence of competition from all over the world. The worldwide economic growth and rebuilding after World War II was beginning to surface in competition that challenged the supremacy of American industry. Competition arose on all fronts; Japan, Germany, most of the industrialized world, and many developing countries were competing for demand in their own countries and were looking for world markets as well. Countries once classified as less developed were reclassified as newly industrialized countries (NICs). NICs such as Brazil, Mexico, South Korea, Taiwan, Singapore, and Hong Kong experienced rapid industrialization in selected industries and became aggressive world competitors in steel, shipbuilding, consumer electronics, automobiles, light aircraft, shoes, textiles, apparel, and so forth. In addition to the NICs, developing countries such as Venezuela, Chile, and Bangladesh established state-owned enterprises (SOEs) that operated in other countries. One state-owned Venezuelan company has a subsidiary in Puerto Rico that produces canvas, cosmetics, chairs, and zippers; there are also Chilean and Colombian companies in Puerto Rico; in the U.S. state of Georgia, there is a Venezuelan company in agribusiness; and Bangladesh, the sixth largest exporter of garments to the United States, also owns a mattress company in Georgia.

In short, economic power and potential became more evenly distributed among countries than was the case when Servan-Schreiber warned Europe about U.S. multinational domination. Instead, the U.S. position in world trade is now shared with other countries. For example, in 1950 the United States represented 39 percent of world gross national product (GNP) but by 2000, it represented 23 percent. In the meantime, however, the global GNP was much larger, as was the world's manufacturing output—all countries shared in a much larger economic pie. This change was reflected in the fluctuations in

---

[5]J.J. Servan-Schreiber, *The American Challenge* (New York: Atheneum Publishers, 1968), p. 3.

---

**1494**   Portugal and Spain divide the unexplored world between them with the Treaty of Tordesillas
**1500**   Rise of mercantilism, the accumulation of wealth by the state to increase power, in Western Europe; states without gold or silver mines try to control trade to maintain a surplus and accumulate gold and silver; Englishman Thomas Mun was one of the great proponents in 1600, who realized that the overall balance of trade was the important factor,

not whether each individual trade resulted in a surplus
**1500**   Slave trade becomes a major component of commerce
**1504**   Regular postal service established between Vienna, Brussels, and Madrid
**1520**   First chocolate brought from Mexico to Spain
**1521**   Mexico is conquered by Hernán Cortés after Aztec ruler Montezuma is accidentally killed
**1522**   Magellan's expedition completes its three-year sail around the world; it is the first successful circumnavigation

**1531**   Antwerp stock exchange is the first exchange to move into its own building, signifying its importance in financing commercial enterprises throughout Europe and the rising importance of private trade and commerce; Antwerp emerges as a trading capital
**1532**   Brazil is colonized by the Portuguese
**1534**   England breaks from the Catholic Church, ending its dominance of politics and trade throughout Europe, as Henry VIII creates the Church of England

**1553**   South American Incan Empire ends with conquest by Spanish; the Incas had created an extensive area of trade, complete with an infrastructure of roads and canals
**1555**   Tobacco trade begins after its introduction to Europe by Spanish and Portuguese traders
**1557**   Spanish crown suffers first of numerous bankruptcies, discouraging cross-border lending
**1561**   Dutch traders bring tulips to Europe from Near East for first time

**Exhibit 2.2**
The Nationality of the World's 100 Largest Industrial Corporations (size measured by annual revenues)

Source: For 2003 data, *2003 Global 500, Fortune,* www.fortune.com

| | 1963 | 1979 | 1984 | 1990 | 1993 | 1996 | 2000 | 2003 |
|---|---|---|---|---|---|---|---|---|
| US | 67 | 47 | 47 | 33 | 32 | 24 | 36 | 42 |
| Germany | 13 | 13 | 8 | 12 | 14 | 13 | 12 | 11 |
| Britain | 7 | 7 | 5 | 6 | 4 | 2 | 5 | 3 |
| France | 4 | 11 | 5 | 10 | 6 | 13 | 11 | 7 |
| Japan | 3 | 7 | 12 | 18 | 23 | 29 | 22 | 20 |
| Italy | 2 | 3 | 3 | 4 | 4 | 4 | 3 | 3 |
| Netherlands–United Kingdom | 2 | 2 | 2 | 2 | 2 | 2 | — | 2 |
| Netherlands | 1 | 3 | 1 | 1 | 1 | 2 | 5 | 4 |
| Switzerland | 1 | 1 | 2 | 3 | 3 | 5 | 3 | 4 |
| Argentina | — | — | 1 | — | — | — | — | — |
| Belgium | — | 1 | 1 | 1 | — | — | 1 | — |
| Brazil | — | 1 | — | 1 | 1 | — | — | — |
| Canada | — | 2 | 3 | — | — | — | — | — |
| India | — | — | 1 | — | — | — | — | — |
| Kuwait | — | — | 1 | — | — | — | — | — |
| Mexico | — | 1 | 1 | 1 | 1 | 1 | — | — |
| Venezuela | — | 1 | 1 | 1 | 1 | 1 | — | — |
| South Korea | — | — | 4 | 2 | 4 | 4 | — | — |
| Sweden | — | — | 1 | 2 | 1 | — | — | — |
| South Africa | — | — | 1 | 1 | — | — | — | — |
| Spain | — | — | — | 2 | 2 | — | — | 1 |
| Turkey | — | — | — | — | 1 | — | — | — |
| China | — | — | — | — | — | — | 2 | 3 |

growth of MNCs from other countries as well. Exhibit 2.2 shows the dramatic changes between 1963 and 2003. In 1963, the United States had 67 of the world's largest industrial corporations. By 1996, that number had dropped to a low of 24, while Japan moved from having 3 of the largest to 29 and South Korea from none to 4. And following the great economic boom in the late 1990s in the United States, 42 of the largest companies were American, only 20 Japanese, and none were Korean.

Another dimension of world economic power, the balance of merchandise trade, reflected the changing role of the United States in world trade. Between 1888 and 1971, the United States sold more to other countries than it bought from them; that is, the United States had a favorable **balance of trade**. By 1971, however, the United States had a trade deficit of $2 billion that grew steadily until it peaked at $160 billion in 1987. After that, the deficit in merchandise trade declined to $74 billion in 1991 but began increasing again and by 2002 had surpassed $400 billion.

The heightened competition for U.S. businesses during the 1980s and early 1990s raised questions similar to those heard in Europe two decades earlier: how to maintain the competitive strength of American business, to avoid the domination of U.S. markets by foreign multinationals, and to forestall the buying of America. In the 1980s, the U.S. saw its competitive position in capital goods such as computers and machinery erode sharply. From 1983 to 1987, almost 70 percent of the growth of the merchandise trade deficit was

**1564** William Shakespeare is born; many of his plays are stories of merchant traders
**1567** Typhoid fever, imported from Europe, kills two million Indians in South America
**1588** Spanish Armada defeated by Britain, heralding Britain's emergence as the world's greatest naval power; this power enables Britain to colonize many regions of the globe and leads to its becoming the

world's commercially dominant power for the next 300 years
**1596** First flush toilet is developed for Britain's Queen Elizabeth I
**1597** Holy Roman Empire expels English merchants in retaliation for English treatment of Hanseatic League
**1600** Potatoes are brought from South America to Europe where they quickly spread to the rest of world and become a

staple of agricultural production
**1600** Japan begins trading silver for foreign goods
**1600** Britain's Queen Elizabeth I grants charter to the East India Company, which dominates trade with the East until its demise in 1857
**1601** France makes postal agreements with neighboring states

**1602** Dutch charter their own East India Company, which will dominate the South Asian coffee and spice trade
**1607** British colony of Jamestown built
**1609** Dutch begin fur trade through Manhattan
**1611** Japan gives Dutch limited permission to trade
**1612** British East India Company builds its first factory in India

in capital goods and automobiles. At the time, those were America's high-wage, high-skill industries. U.S. industry got a wake-up call and responded by restructuring its industries, in essence, "getting lean and mean." By the late 1990s, the U.S. was once again holding its own in capital goods, particularly with trade surpluses in the high-tech category.

Among the more important questions raised were those concerning the ability of U.S. firms to compete in foreign markets and the fairness of international trade policies of some countries. Trade friction revolved around Japan's sales of autos and electronics in the United States and Japan's restrictive trade practices. The United States, a strong advocate of free trade, was confronted with the dilemma of how to encourage trading partners to reciprocate with open access to their markets without provoking increased protectionism. Besides successfully pressuring Japan to open its markets for some types of trade and investment, the U.S. was a driving force behind the establishment of the WTO.

By the last decade of the twentieth century profound changes in the way the world would trade were already under way. The final integration of the countries of the European Union, the creation of the North American Free Trade Agreement (NAFTA) and the ASEAN Free Trade Area (AFTA), and the rapid evolution of the Asia-Pacific Economic Cooperation (APEC) are the beginnings of global trading blocks that many experts expect to dominate trade patterns in the future. With the return of Hong Kong in 1997 and Macao in 2000 to China, all of Asia is now controlled and managed by Asians for the first time in 400 years. During the decades since World War II, the West set the patterns for trade, but increasingly Asia will be a major force, if not the leading force.

## The First Decade of the Twenty-first Century and Beyond

The unprecedented and precipitous growth of the U.S. economy in the late 1990s has slowed dramatically in the last few years. Growth in most of the rest of the world has followed suit with the exception of China. The Organization for Economic Cooperation and Development (OECD) estimates that the economies of member countries will expand an average of 3 percent annually for the next 25 years, the same rate as in the past 25 years. Conversely, the economies of the developing world will grow at faster rates—from an annual rate of 4 percent in the past quarter century to a rate of 6 percent for the next 25 years. Their share of world output will rise from about one-sixth to nearly one-third over the same period. The World Bank estimates that five countries—Brazil, China, India, Indonesia, and Russia—whose share of world trade is barely a third of that of the European Union, will by 2020 have a share 50 percent higher than that of the EU. As a consequence, there will be movement in economic power and influence away from industrialized countries—Japan, the United States, and the European Union—to countries in Latin America, Eastern Europe, Asia, and Africa.

This does not mean that markets in Europe, Japan, and the United States will cease to be important; those economies will continue to produce large, lucrative markets and the companies established in those markets will benefit. It does mean that if a company is to be a major player in the future, now is the time to begin laying the groundwork. How will these changes that are taking place in the global marketplace impact on international business? For one thing, the level and intensity of competition will change as companies focus on gaining entry into or maintaining their position in emerging markets, regional trade areas, and the established markets in Europe, Japan, and the United States.

**1620**   *Mayflower* sails for the New World
**1620**   Father of the Scientific Revolution, Francis Bacon, publishes *Novum Organum*, promoting inductive reasoning through experimentation and observation
**1625**   Dutch jurist Hugo Grotius, sometimes called the father of international law, publishes *On the Laws of War and Peace*

**1636**   Harvard University founded
**1637**   Dutch tulip craze results in history's first boom-bust market crash
**1651**   English pass first of so-called Navigation Acts to restrict Dutch trade by forcing colonies to trade only with English ships
**1654**   Spain and Germany develop hereditary land rights, a concept that will help lead to

the creation of great wealth in single families and thus to the development of private commercial empires
**1687**   Apple falling on Newton's head leads to his publication of the law of gravity
**1694**   The Bank of England is established; it offers loans to private individuals at 8 percent interest
**1698**   First steam engine is invented

**1719**   French consolidate their trade in Asia into one company, the French East India Company; rival British East India Company maintains its grip on the region's trade, however, and French revert to individual company trading 60 years later
**1725**   Rise of Physiocrats, followers of the economic philosopher François Quesnay, who believed that production, not trade, created wealth and

Companies are looking for ways to become more efficient, improve productivity, and expand their global reach while maintaining an ability to respond quickly to deliver a product that the market demands. For example, large multinational companies such as Matsushita of Japan continue to expand their global reach. Nestlé is consolidating its dominance in global consumer markets by acquiring and vigorously marketing local-country major brands. Samsung of South Korea has invested $500 million in Mexico to secure access to markets in the North American Free Trade Area. Whirlpool, the U.S. appliance manufacturer that secured first place in the global appliance business by acquiring the European division of the appliance maker, N. V. Philip's, immediately began restructuring itself into its version of a global company. These are a few examples of changes that are sweeping multinational companies as they gear up for the future.

Global companies are not the only ones aggressively seeking new market opportunities. Smaller companies are using novel approaches to marketing and seeking ways to apply their technological expertise to exporting goods and services not previously sold abroad. A small Midwestern company that manufactures and freezes bagel dough for supermarkets to bake and sell as their own saw opportunities abroad and began to export to Japan. International sales, though small initially, showed such potential that the company sold its U.S. business to concentrate on international operations. Other examples of smaller companies include Nochar Inc., which makes a fire retardant it developed a decade ago for the Indianapolis 500. The company now gets 32 percent of its sales overseas, in 29 countries. The owner of Buztronics Inc., a maker of promotional lapel buttons, heard from a friend that his buttons, with their red blinking lights, would do great in Japan. He made his first entry in exporting to Japan and after only a year, 10 percent of Buztronics sales come from overseas. While 50 of the largest exporters account for 30 percent of U.S. merchandise exports, the rest come from middle and small firms like those mentioned above. There is a flurry of activity in the business world as companies large and small adjust to the internationalization of the marketplace at home and abroad.

As is always true in business, the best-laid plans can fail or be slowed by dramatic changes in the economy. When the U.S. economy was less involved in international trade, economic upheavals abroad often went unnoticed except by the very largest companies. Today, when the stock market in Hong Kong drops precipitously as it did in 1997 and South Korea and several Southeast Asia economies faltered shortly thereafter, the U.S. stock market reacted with its largest daily drop in several years. The fear was about the potential negative impact on U.S. technology industries if the economies of Asian customers slowed. Four years later most of the world's emerging markets were on a somewhat slower but nevertheless positive growth path than before the financial crisis of 1997.

## Balance of Payments

When countries trade, financial transactions among businesses or consumers of different nations occur. Products and services are exported and imported, monetary gifts are exchanged, investments are made, cash payments are made and cash receipts received, and vacation and foreign travel occurs. In short, over a period of time there is a constant flow of money into and out of a country. The system of accounts that records a nation's international financial transactions is called its **balance of payments**.

---

that natural law should rule, which meant producers should be able to exchange goods freely; movement influenced Adam Smith's ideas promoting free trade
**1740**   Maria Theresa becomes Empress of the Holy Roman Empire (until 1780); she ends serfdom and strengthens the power of the state
**1748**   First modern, scientifically drawn map, the Carte

Géométrique de la France, comprising 182 sheets, was authorized and subsequently drawn by the French Academy; Louis XV proclaimed that the new map, with more accurate data, lost more territory than his wars of conquest had gained
**1750**   Benjamin Franklin shows that lightning is a form of electricity by conducting it through the wet string of a kite

**1750**   Industrial Revolution begins and takes off with the manufacture, in 1780, of the steam engine to drive machines; increased productivity and consumption follow (as do poor working conditions and increased hardships for workers)
**1760**   China begins strict regulation of foreign trade, to last nearly a century, when they permit Europeans to do busi-

ness only in a small area outside Canton and only with appointed Chinese traders
**1764**   British victories in India begin Britain's dominance of India, Eastern trade, and trade routes
**1764**   British begin numbering houses, making mail delivery more efficient and providing the means for the development of direct mail merchants centuries later

A nation's balance-of-payments statement records all financial transactions between its residents and those of the rest of the world during a given period of time—usually one year. Because the balance-of-payments record is maintained on a double-entry book-keeping system, it must always be in balance. As on an individual's financial statement, the assets and liabilities or the credits and debits must offset each other. And like an individual's statement, the fact that they balance does not mean a nation is in particularly good or poor financial condition. A balance of payments is a record of condition, not a determinant of condition. Each of the nation's financial transactions with other countries is reflected in its balance of payments.

A nation's balance of payments presents an overall view of its international economic position and is an important economic measure used by treasuries, central banks, and other government agencies whose responsibility is to maintain external and internal economic stability. A balance of payments represents the difference between receipts from foreign countries on one side and payments to them on the other. On the plus side of the U.S. balance of payments are merchandise export sales, money spent by foreign tourists, payments to the United States for insurance, transportation, and similar services, payments of dividends and interest on investments abroad, return on capital invested abroad, new foreign investments in the United States, and foreign government payments to the United States.

On the minus side are costs of goods imported, spending by American tourists overseas, new overseas investments, and the cost of foreign military and economic aid. A deficit results when international payments are greater than receipts. It can be reduced or eliminated by increasing a country's international receipts (i.e., gain more exports to other countries or more tourists from other countries) and/or reducing expenditures in other countries.

A balance-of-payments statement includes three accounts: the **current account**—a record of all merchandise exports, imports, and services plus unilateral transfers of funds; the **capital account**—a record of direct investment, portfolio investment, and short-term capital movements to and from countries; and the official **reserves account**—a record of exports and imports of gold, increases or decreases in foreign exchange, and increases or decreases in liabilities to foreign central banks. Of the three, the current account is of primary interest to international business.

The current account is important because it includes all international merchandise trade and service accounts, that is, accounts for the value of all merchandise and services imported and exported and all receipts and payments from investments. Exhibit 2.3 gives the current account calculations for the United States in 2002.

Since 1971 the United States has had a favorable current account balance (as a percentage of GDP) in only a few years—see Exhibit 2.4. The imbalances resulted primarily from U.S. demand for oil,[6] petroleum products, cars, consumer durables, and other merchandise. Indeed, the merchandise trade deficit for 2002 was $484 billion. Such imbalances have drastic effects on the balance of payments, and, therefore, the value of

---

[6]"Oil Imports Widen U.S. Trade Deficit," *Los Angeles Times,* May 14, 2003, p. C4.

**1773**   Boston Tea Party symbolizes start of American Revolution; impetus comes from American merchants trying to take control of distribution of goods that were being controlled exclusively by Britain
**1776**   American Declaration of Independence proclaims the colonies' rights to determine their own destiny, particularly their own economic destiny

**1776**   Theory of modern capitalism and free trade expressed by Adam Smith in *The Wealth of Nations;* he theorized that countries would only produce and export goods that they were able to produce more cheaply than could trading partners; he demonstrates that mercantilists were wrong; it is not gold or silver that will enhance the state, but the *material* that can be purchased with it

**1783**   Treaty of Paris officially ends the American Revolution following British surrender to American troops at Yorktown in 1781
**1787**   U.S. constitution approved; it becomes a model document for constitutions for at least the next two centuries; written constitutions help to stabilize many countries and encourage foreign investment and trade with them

**1789**   French Revolution begins; it alters the power structure in Europe and helps lead to the introduction of laws protecting the individual and to limited democracy in the region
**1792**   Gas lighting introduced; within three decades most major European and U.S. cities use gas lights
**1804**   Steam locomotive introduced; it becomes the dominant form of transport of

**Exhibit 2.3**
U.S. Current Account by Major Components, 2002 ($ billions)

| Exports | |
|---|---|
| Goods | 683 |
| Services | 289 |
| Income receipts | 245 |
| **Imports** | |
| Goods | −1167 |
| Services | −240 |
| Income payments | −257 |
| **Unilateral current transfers, net** | −56 |
| Current account balance | −504 |

U.S. currency in the world marketplace.[7] Factors such as these eventually require an adjustment through a change in exchange rate, prices, and/or incomes. In short, after the wealth of a country whose expenditures exceed its income has been exhausted, that country, like an individual, must reduce its standard of living. If its residents do not do so voluntarily, the rate of exchange of its money for foreign monies declines; and through the medium of the foreign exchange market, the purchasing power of foreign goods is transferred from that country to another. As can be seen in Exhibit 2.5, the U.S. dollar strengthened against most of the other major currencies during the 1990s, but has weakened recently.[8]

---

[7]Rich Miller, Peter Coy, Christine Tierney, David Fairlamb, "Good News! The Dollar is Down," *BusinessWeek,* May 26, 2003, pp. 36–39.

[8]"Super-Euro, Europe's Once Sickly Currency Is Flexing Its Muscles," *The Economist,* May 10, 2003, p. 66.

**Exhibit 2.4**    United States Current Account Balance (% of GDP)

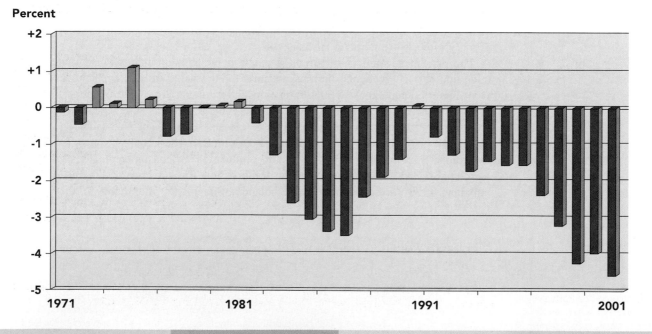

**Percent**

**Exhibit 2.5**   What Would One U.S. Dollar Buy?

|               | 1985   | 1988  | 1992  | 1993   | 1994   | 1995  | 1996   | 1997   | 1999   | 2000*  | 2003*  |
|---------------|--------|-------|-------|--------|--------|-------|--------|--------|--------|--------|--------|
| British pound | 0.86   | 0.54  | 0.56  | 0.66   | 0.68   | 0.63  | 0.64   | 0.59   | 0.62   | 0.68   | 0.61   |
| French franc  | 9.6    | 5.4   | 5.29  | 5.67   | 5.55   | 4.95  | 5.12   | 5.94   | 6.49   | 7.28   | —      |
| Japanese Yen  | 250.23 | 123.7 | 126.7 | 111.08 | 102.18 | 93.96 | 108.78 | 129.15 | 102.58 | 112.21 | 118.7  |
| Swiss franc   | 2.25   | 1.29  | 1.41  | 1.48   | 1.37   | 1.18  | 1.24   | 1.43   | 1.58   | 1.68   | 1.31   |
| EURO          |        |       |       |        |        |       |        |        | 0.99   | 1.11   | 1.17   |
| Mexico Peso   | 0.37   | 2.28  | 3.12  | 3.11   | 5.31   | 6.45  | 7.60   | 7.92   | 9.43   | 9.47   | 10.6   |

*Foreign Exchange Rates for 2000 and 2003 are the average rates of exchange in December.

Source: Euromonitor International, 2004

As the U.S. trade deficit grows, pressures should begin to push the value of the dollar to lower levels.[9] When foreign currencies can be traded for more dollars, U.S. products are less expensive for the foreign customer and exports increase, at the same time, foreign products are more expensive for the U.S. customer and the demand for imported goods is dampened.

## Protectionism

International business must face the reality that this is a world of **tariffs, quotas,** and **nontariff barriers** designed to protect a country's markets from intrusion by foreign companies. Although the General Agreement on Tariffs and Trade (GATT) has been effective in reducing tariffs, countries still resort to measures of **protectionism.** Nations utilize legal barriers,[10] exchange barriers, and psychological barriers to restrain entry of unwanted goods. Businesses work together to establish private market barriers while the market structure itself may provide formidable barriers to imported goods. The complex distribution system in Japan is a good example of a market structure creating a barrier to trade. However, as effective as it is in keeping some products out of the market, in a legal sense it cannot be viewed as a trade barrier.

### Protection Logic and Illogic

Countless reasons to maintain government restrictions on trade are espoused by protectionists, but essentially all arguments can be classified as follows: (1) protection of an infant industry, (2) protection of the home market, (3) need to keep money at home, (4) encouragement of capital accumulation, (5) maintenance of the standard of living and real wages, (6) conservation of natural resources, (7) industrialization of a low-wage nation, (8) maintenance of employment and reduction of unemployment, (9) national defense, (10) increase of business size, and (11) retaliation and bargaining. Economists in general recognize as valid only the arguments for infant industry, national defense, and industrialization of underdeveloped countries. The resource conservation argument becomes increasingly valid in an era of environmental consciousness and worldwide shortages of raw materials and agricultural commodities. There might be a case for

---

[9]"Hurray for the Trade Deficit," *Wall Street Journal,* February 24, 2003, p. A14.

[10]Matt Pottinger, "Software Firms Face Setback In China—Proposed Rules Would Force Regional Governments to Use Domestic Vendors," *Wall Street Journal,* March 7, 2003, p. B5.

---

independence for Spanish colonies in Latin America, leading to new governments in Bolivia, Colombia, Ecuador, Peru, and Venezuela
**1814**  First practical steam locomotive is built by George Stephenson in England, leading to the birth of railroad

transportation in 1825, with the first train carrying 450 passengers at 15 miles per hour
**1815**  Napoleon defeated at Battle of Waterloo and gives up throne days later
**1815**  British build roads of crushed stone, greatly

improving the quality and speed of road travel
**1817**  David Ricardo publishes *Principles of Political Economy and Taxation,* in which he proposes modern trade theory; that comparative advantage drives trade, and that countries will produce and export goods

for which they have a *comparative* advantage as opposed to Adam Smith's *absolute* advantage (see 1776)
**1821**  Britain is first to adopt gold standard to back value of its currency
**1823**  U.S. President James Monroe promulgates the

# CROSSING BORDERS 2.1 Trade Barriers, Hypocrisy, and the United States

The United States thinks of itself as the leader in free trade and frequently brings actions against nations as unfair trade partners. Section 301[11] of the Omnibus Trade and Competitiveness Act authorizes the U.S. government to investigate and retaliate against specific foreign trade barriers judged to be unfair and to impose up to 100 percent tariffs on exports to the U.S. from guilty nations unless they satisfy U.S. domestic demands. But critics say the United States is somewhat hypocritical in some of the stands taken because the United States is just as guilty of protecting its markets with trade barriers. A Japanese government study alleges that the United States engages in unfair trade practices in 10 of 12 policy areas reviewed in the study. Notably, the United States imposes quotas on imports, has high tariffs, and abuses antidumping measures. Are the critics correct? Is the U.S. being hypocritical when it comes to free trade? You be the judge.

The United States launched a Section 301 investigation of Japanese citrus quotas. "The removal of Japan's unfair barriers could cut the price of oranges for Japanese consumers by one third," said the U.S. trade representative. Coincidentally, the United States had a 40 percent tariff on Brazilian orange juice imports when the investigation was initiated.

The United States brought a 301 case against Korea for its beef import quotas even though the United States has beef import quotas that are estimated to cost U.S. consumers $873 million annually in higher prices. Another 301 case was brought against Brazil, Korea, and Taiwan for trade barriers on footwear even though the United States maintains tariffs as high as 67 percent on footwear imports.

Can you believe that we have two phone-book-sized volumes of the U.S. customs code that includes restrictions on such innocuous items as scissors, sweaters, leather, costume jewelry, tampons, pizzas, cotton swabs, ice cream from Jamaica, and even products we do not produce such as vitamin $B_{12}$? We also have restrictions on products, such as cars, supercomputers, lumber, and every type of clothing imaginable. Would-be Latin American exporters find hundreds of their most promising export products on the customs list, such as grapes, tomatoes, onions, steel, cement, asparagus, and shoes. Visit www.usitc.gov/taffairs.htm and select the Interactive Tariff Database to see some other examples.

So, is the United States as guilty as the rest or not?

Sources: Abstracted from James Bovard, "A U.S. History of Trade Hypocrisy," *The Wall Street Journal*, March 8, 1994, p. A10; "Business: Sugar Solution," *Economist*, April 22, 2000, p. 58; and Robert Guy Matthews, "U.S. Steel Tariffs Likely to Stay Despite WTO-Sanction Threat," *Wall Street Journal*, March 31, 2003, p. A2.

temporary protection of markets with excess productive capacity or excess labor when such protection could facilitate an orderly transition. Unfortunately, such protection becomes long term and contributes to industrial inefficiency while detracting from a nation's realistic adjustment to its world situation.

Most protectionists argue the need for tariffs on one of the three premises recognized by economists, whether or not these arguments are relevant to their products. Proponents are likely also to call on the maintenance-of-employment argument because it has substantial political appeal. When arguing for protection, the basic economic advantages of international trade are ignored. The fact that the consumer ultimately bears the cost

---

[11]"Section 301, a provision of U.S. trade law, enables the U.S. government to take action against countries deemed to have engaged in "unreasonable, unjustifiable, or discriminatory" practices that restrict U.S. commerce.

---

doctrine bearing his name that declares the Americas closed to colonization in an attempt to assert U.S. influence over the region
**1837** Reign of Britain's Queen Victoria begins; she oversees the growth of the British Empire and Britain's

emergence as an industrial power (she dies in 1901)
**1837** Electronic telegraph begins wide commercial use, transmitting information, including production orders, swiftly
**1839** Process for recording negative images on paper is

introduced in England, the precursor to modern film technology
**1841** Briton David Livingstone begins 30 years of exploring in Africa
**1842** Hong Kong ceded to Britain with the treaty of Nanjing following the Opium War;

the city becomes a financial and trading center for Asia
**1844** Chinese open five ports to U.S. ships
**1847** First government-backed postage stamps issued by U.S. leading to more certain and efficient communication by post

## CROSSING BORDERS 2.2  A Word for Open Market

Bastiat's century-old farcical letter to the French Chamber of Deputies points up the ultimate folly of tariffs and the advantages of utilizing the superior production advantage of others.

To the Chamber of Deputies:

We are subjected to the intolerable competition of a foreign rival, who enjoys such superior facilities for the production of light that he can inundate our national market at reduced price. This rival is no other than the sun. Our petition is to pass a law shutting up all windows, openings, and fissures through which the light of the sun is used to penetrate our dwellings, to the prejudice of the profitable manufacture we have been enabled to bestow on the country.

Signed: Candlestick Makers,
F. Bastiat

of tariffs and other protective measures is conveniently overlooked. Sugar[12] and textiles are good examples of protected industries in the United States that cannot be justified by any of the three arguments. U.S. sugar prices are artificially held higher than world prices for no sound economic reason.

To give you some idea of the cost to the consumer, consider the results of a recent study of 21 protected industries. The research showed that U.S. consumers pay about $70 billion per year in higher prices because of tariffs and other protective restrictions. On average, the cost to consumers for saving one job in these protected industries was $170,000 per year, or six times the average pay (wages and benefits) for manufacturing workers. Those figures represent the average of 21 protected industries, but the cost is much higher in selected industries. In the steel industry, for example, countervailing duties and antidumping penalties on foreign suppliers of steel since 1992 have saved the jobs of 1,239 steelworkers at a cost of $835,351 each. Unfortunately, protectionism is politically popular, but it rarely leads to renewed growth in a declining industry. And the jobs that are saved are saved at a very high cost, which constitutes a hidden tax that consumers unknowingly pay.

**Trade Barriers**   To encourage development of domestic industry and protect existing industry, governments may establish such barriers to trade as tariffs, quotas, boycotts, monetary barriers, nontariff barriers, and market barriers. Barriers are imposed against imports and against foreign businesses. While the inspiration for such barriers may be economic or political, they are encouraged by local industry. Whether or not the barriers are economically logical, the fact is they exist.

**Tariffs.**   A **tariff**, simply defined, is a tax imposed by a government on goods entering at its borders. Tariffs may be used as a revenue-generating tax or to discourage the importation of goods, or for both reasons.[13] In general, tariffs:

---

[12]"Brazil Highlights Importance of Reform for U.S. Sugar Program," *World Trade*, January 2003, p. 14.
[13]Herbert Dieter, "Free Trade and Pick-Up Trucks," *Far Eastern Economic Review*, February 6, 2003, p. 20.

**1848** John Stuart Mill publishes *Principles of Political Economy*, completing the modern theory of trade by stating that gains from trade are reflected in the strength of the *reciprocal* demand for imports and exports and that gains would come from better terms of trade (see 1817)

**1848** The Communist Manifesto, authored by Germans Karl Marx and Friedrich Engels, is issued; it becomes the basis for the communist movements of the twentieth century
**1851** First international world's fair held in London, showcasing new technology

**1856** Declaration of Paris recognizes the principle of free movement for trade, even in wartime—blockades could only extend along the enemy's coast; it also establishes the practice of allowing the accession to treaties of nations other than the original signatories

**1857** Russia and France sign trade treaty
**1858** Ansei Commercial Treaties with Japan open the formerly closed country to trade with the West (treaties follow "opening" of Japan to the West by American Matthew Perry in 1854)

| | |
|---|---|
| *Increase* | Inflationary pressures. |
| | Special interests' privileges. |
| | Government control and political considerations in economic matters. |
| | The number of tariffs (they beget other tariffs via reciprocity). |
| *Weaken* | Balance-of-payments positions. |
| | Supply-and-demand patterns. |
| | International relations (they can start trade wars). |
| *Restrict* | Manufacturers' supply sources. |
| | Choices available to consumers. |
| | Competition. |

In addition, tariffs are arbitrary, discriminatory, and require constant administration and supervision. They often are used as reprisals against protectionist moves of trading partners. In a dispute with the European Union (EU) over pasta export subsidies, the United States ordered a 40 percent increase in tariffs on European spaghetti and fancy pasta. The EU retaliated against U.S. walnuts and lemons. The pasta war raged on as Europe increased tariffs on U.S. fertilizer, paper products, and beef tallow, and the United States responded in kind. The war ended when the Europeans finally dropped pasta export subsidies. More recently the European Union and the United States have been battling a similar trade war over bananas! Most recently, less-developed countries are increasingly voicing complaints about American and European tariffs on agricultural products.[14]

Imports are restricted in a variety of ways other than tariffs. These nontariff barriers include quality standards on imported products, sanitary and health standards, quotas, embargoes, boycotts, and antidumping penalties. Exhibit 2.6 gives a complete list of non-tariff barriers.

**Quotas.**   A **quota** is a specific unit or dollar limit applied to a particular type of good. There is a limit on imported television sets in Great Britain, and there are German quotas on Japanese ball bearings, Italian restrictions on Japanese motorcycles, and U.S. quotas on sugar, textiles,[15] and, of all things, peanuts. Quotas put an absolute restriction on the quantity of a specific item that can be imported. When the Japanese first let foreign rice into their country it was on a quota basis, but since 2000 the quotas have been replaced by tariffs.[16] Even more complicated, the banana war between the United States and the European Union appears at this date to be headed to a mixed system wherein a quota of bananas is allowed into the EU with a tariff, then a second quota comes in tariff-free. Like tariffs, quotas tend to increase prices. U.S. quotas on textiles are estimated to add 50 percent to the wholesale price of clothing.

---

[14]George Pitcher, "Trade War Looms as West Faces Third World Uprising," *Marketing Week,* April 3, 2003, p. 29.

[15]"Deal Limits Vietnamese Imports," *Los Angeles Times,* April 7, 2003, p. A34.

[16]See the USA Rice Federation's website for details—www.usarice.com.

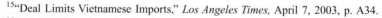

**1860**   The Cobden Treaty aims to create free trade by reducing or eliminating tariffs between Britain and France; also leads to most-favored-nation status in bilateral agreements and eventually to multilateral agreements
**1860**   Passports are introduced in the U.S. to regulate foreign travel
**1866**   The principle of the electric dynamo is found by

German Werner Siemens, who produces the first electric power transmission system
**1866**   The trans-Atlantic cable is completed, allowing nearly instant (telegraphic) communication between the U.S. and Europe
**1869**   Suez Canal completed after 11 years of construction; the canal significantly cuts the time for travel between Europe and Asia, shortening, for exam-

ple, the trip between Britain and India by 4,000 miles
**1869**   First U.S. transcontinental rail route is completed, heralding a boon for commerce; first commercially viable typewriter patented; until computer word processing becomes common more than a century later, the typewriter enables anyone to produce documents quickly and legibly

**1873**   U.S. adopts the gold standard to fix the international value of the dollar
**1875**   Universal Postal Union created in Switzerland to provide for an international mail service
**1876**   Alexander Graham Bell is granted a patent for the telephone, which revolutionizes communications
**1880**   Thomas Edison creates first electric power station, after

**Exhibit 2.6** Types of Nontariff Barriers

**Specific Limitations on Trade**
Quotas
Import licensing requirements
Proportional restrictions of foreign to domestic goods
   (local-content requirements)
Minimum import price limits
Embargoes

**Customs and Administrative Entry Procedures**
Valuation systems
Antidumping practices
Tariff classifications
Documentation requirements
Fees

**Standards**
Standards disparities
Intergovernmental acceptances of testing methods
   and standards
Packaging, labeling, marking standards

**Governmental Participation in Trade**
Government procurement policies
Export subsidies
Countervailing duties
Domestic assistance programs

**Charges on Imports**
Prior import deposit requirements
Administrative fees
Special supplementary duties
Import credit discriminations
Variable levies
Border taxes

**Others**
Voluntary export restraints
Orderly marketing agreements

Source: Reprinted from *Journal of World Business*, A. D. Cao, "Nontariff Barriers to U.S. Manufactured Exports," p. 94, copyright (1980) with permission from Elsevier.

**Voluntary Export Restraints.** Similar to quotas are the **voluntary export restraints** (VERs) or **orderly market agreements** (OMAs). Common in textiles, clothing, steel, agriculture, and automobiles, the VER is an agreement between the importing country and the exporting country for a restriction on the volume of exports. Japan has a VER on automobiles to the United States; that is, Japan has agreed to export a fixed number of automobiles annually. When televisions were still manufactured in the United States, Japan signed an OMA limiting Japanese color television exports to the United States to 1.56 million units per year. However, as a result of the OMA, Japanese companies began investing in television manufacturing in the United States and Mexico, and as a result they regained the entire market share that had been lost through the OMA, eventually dominating the entire market. A VER is called voluntary because the exporting country sets the limits; however, it is generally imposed under the threat of stiffer quotas and tariffs being set by the importing country if a VER is not established.

**Boycotts and Embargoes.** A government boycott is an absolute restriction against the purchase and importation of certain goods from other countries. An embargo is a refusal to sell to a specific country. A public boycott can be either formal or informal and may be government sponsored or sponsored by an industry. The United States uses boycotts and embargoes against countries with which there is a dispute. For example, Cuba, Iran, and Iraq had or still have sanctions imposed by the United States. There is rising concern, however, that government-sponsored sanctions cause unnecessary harm

inventing the electric light in 1878, which lights New York City and starts a revolution in culture and business—making a truly 24-hour day and paving the way for electronic machines
**1881** Zoopraxiscope, which shows pictures in motion, is developed
**1884** The basis for establishing standard time and measuring the longitude of any spot in the world is created with the

designation of Greenwich, England, as the prime meridian (0° longitude)
**1886** American Federation of Labor founded, becoming a model for workers around the world to unite against management and gain higher pay and better working conditions
**1901** Italian Guglielmo Marconi sends the first radio message; the radio could be said to spark the start of globaliza-

tion because of the speed with which information is able to be transmitted
**1903** First successful flight of an airplane, piloted by Orville Wright, takes place at Kitty Hawk, North Carolina
**1904** First vacuum tube is developed by John Fleming, allowing alternating current to become direct current and helping to create widespread use of the radio

**1913** Assembly line introduced by Henry Ford; it will revolutionize manufacturing
**1914** The first war to involve much of the world begins with the assassination of Archduke Francis Ferdinand and lasts four years; construction of Panama Canal completed, making trade faster and easier
**1917** Lenin and Trotsky lead Russian revolution, creating a living economic model that will

## CROSSING BORDERS 2.3    Crossing Borders with Monkeys in His Pants

Robert Cusack smuggled a pair of endangered pygmy monkeys into the United States—in his pants! On June 13, 2002 a U.S. Fish and Wildlife Service special agent was called to Los Angeles International Airport after Cusack was detained by U.S. Customs on arrival from Thailand. Officials soon also discovered that Cusack had four endangered birds of paradise and 50 protected orchids with him. "When one of the inspectors opened up his luggage, one of the birds flew out," tells one official. "He had to go catch the bird." After finding the other purloined birds and exotic flowers, the inspectors asked, "Do you have anything else you should tell us about?" Cusack answered, "Yes, I have monkeys in my pants." The monkeys ended up in the Los Angeles Zoo, and the smuggler ended up in jail for 57 days. He also paid a five-figure fine.

Richard Connors, a Chicago lawyer, should have known better. He was caught smuggling thousands of Cuban cigars into the United States in violation of the 40-year-old trade embargo against Castro's Cuba. Connors, who had made monthly trips to Cuba via Canada and Mexico, faces up to five years in prison for his transgressions.

Smuggling isn't just a game played by sneaky individuals. Multinational companies can also get into the act. During this past year alone, convictions were obtained for smuggling cell phones into Vietnam, cigarettes into Iraq and Canada, and platinum into China. In perhaps the biggest ever corporate case, after a nine-year lawsuit Amway Corporation agreed to pay the Canadian government $38.1 million dollars to settle charges they had avoided customs duties by undervaluing merchandise it exported from the United States to Canadian distributors over a six-year period. Indeed, as long as there have been trade barriers, smuggling has been a common response. One-hundred years ago Rudyard Kipling wrote:

Five and twenty ponies trotting through the dark—
Brandy for the Parson, 'baccy for the clerk;
Laces for a lady, letters for a spy;
And watch the wall, my darling, while the Gentlemen go by!

Sources: "Amway Pays $38 Million to Canada," *Los Angeles Times*, September 22, 1989, p. 3; "Conviction in Cigar Smuggling," *New York Times*, October 11, 2002, p. 27; Patricia Ward Biederman, "Smuggler to Pay for Pocketing Monkeys," *Los Angeles Times*, December 19, 2002, p. B1; and Barry Wain, "Two Vietnamese Brothers Fall Victim to Their Success," *Wall Street Journal*, May 15, 2003, p. A15.

for both the United States and the country being boycotted without reaching desired results. It is not unusual for the citizens of a country to boycott goods of other countries at the urging of their government or civic groups. Nestlé products were boycotted by a citizens group that considered the way Nestlé promoted baby milk formula misleading to mothers and harmful to their babies in less-developed countries.

**Monetary Barriers.**    A government can effectively regulate its international trade position by various forms of exchange-control restrictions. A government may enact such restrictions to preserve its balance-of-payments position or specifically for the advantage or encouragement of particular industries. There are three barriers to consider: blocked currency, differential exchange rates, and government approval requirements for securing foreign exchange.

Blocked currency is used as a political weapon or as a response to difficult balance-of-payments situations. In effect, blockage cuts off all importing or all importing above a certain level. Blockage is accomplished by refusing to allow importers to exchange its national currency for the sellers' currency.

affect trade (adversely) for the rest of the century
**1919**    First nonstop transAtlantic flight completed, paving the way for cargo to be transported quickly around the globe
**1920**    League of Nations created, establishing a model for

international cooperation (though it failed to keep the peace)
**1923**    Vladimir Zworykin creates first electronic television, which will eventually help integrate cultures and consumers across the world

**1929**    Great Depression starts with crash of U.S. stock market
**1930**    Hawley-Smoot Tariff passed by U.S. Senate, plunging the world deeper into the Great Depression
**1935**    Radar developed in Britain; it allows travel on ships and planes even when there is

no visibility, enabling the goods to keep to a transport schedule (eventually allowing the development of just-in-time and other cost-savings processes)
**1938**    American Chester Carlson develops dry copying process for documents (xerography) (which, among other

## CROSSING BORDERS 2.4 Jefferson's Folly—Trade Cannot Be Used as a Stick

It was 1807 when Thomas Jefferson came up with trade sanctions as an innovation in diplomacy. The donkeys he endeavored to persuade then (England and France) were quite big and quite stubborn. Jefferson's goal was to get these warring nations to leave American ships alone on the high seas. Lacking a competitive navy, our third president dreamed up the trade embargo—rather than using trade as a carrot he planned to withhold trade and use it as a stick. However, instead of changing French or English policies and behaviors, Jefferson's policy actually endangered New England traders. They complained:

> Our ships all in motion, once whiten'd the ocean;
> They sail'd and return'd with a Cargo;
> Now doom'd to decay, they are fallen a prey,
> To Jefferson, worms, and EMBARGO.

Jefferson's embargo fell apart in just 15 months. Only the War of 1812 settled the problems of English aggression at sea.

Consider the track record of trade sanctions in this past century. In 1940 the United States told the Japanese to get out of China, and the ensuing embargo of gasoline and scrap metal led directly to the Pearl Harbor attack. Since 1948 Arab countries have boycotted Israel. Given that countries trade most with their close neighbors, you have to wonder how much this lack of trade has promoted the continuing conflicts in the area. Israel is still there. In 1959 Castro took over Cuba. For 40 years the United States has boycotted sugar and cigars, and Castro is still there. OPEC's 1973 oil flow slowdown was intended to get America to stop supporting Israel. However, the dollars still flow fast to Israel and now Egypt as well.

In 1979 the United States told the Soviets to get out of Afghanistan. They refused. America boycotted the Moscow Olympics and stopped selling them grain and technology. The Soviet response was to continue to kill Afghans (as well as Soviet soldiers) for another 10 years. Moreover, in 1980 the Soviet's and their allies' athletes stayed away from the Los Angeles games. And the high-tech embargo didn't work anyway. A San Diego division of Caterpillar lost millions of dollars in service contracts for Soviet natural gas pipelines. These revenues were lost permanently, because the Soviets taught themselves how to do the maintenance and overhauls. In Moscow in 1989, despite the U.S. embargo, they had every brand of computer then available in the West, including IBMs, Apples, and the best from Taiwan and Japan as well.

Source: John L. Graham, "Trade Brings Peace," a paper delivered at a conference at Cambridge University in England on May 26, 2003 entitled "War and Reconciliation: Perspectives of the World Religions."

The differential exchange rate is a particularly ingenious method of controlling imports. It encourages the importation of goods the government deems desirable and discourages importation of goods the government does not want. The essential mechanism requires the importer to pay varying amounts of domestic currency for foreign exchange with which to purchase products in different categories. For example, the exchange rate for a desirable category of goods might be one unit of domestic money for one unit of a specific foreign currency. For a less-desirable product, the rate might be two domestic currency units for one foreign unit. For an undesirable product, the rate might be three domestic units for one foreign unit. An importer of an undesirable product has to pay three times as much for the foreign exchange as the importer of a desired product.

Government approval to secure foreign exchange is often used by countries experiencing severe shortages of foreign exchange. At one time or another, most Latin American and East European countries have required all foreign exchange transactions to be

things, enables governments to require that multiple forms be filled out to move goods)
**1939**   World War II begins with German invasion of Poland; over 50 million people die
**1943**   The first programmable computer, Colossus I, is created in England at Bletchley Park; it helps to crack German codes
**1944**   Bretton Woods Conference creates basis for economic cooperation among 44 nations and the founding of the International Monetary Fund to help stabilize exchange rates
**1945**   Atomic weapons introduced; World War II ends; United Nations founded
**1947**   General Agreement on Tariffs and Trade (GATT) signed by 23 countries to try to reduce barriers to trade around the world
**1948**   Transistor is invented; it replaces the vacuum tube, starting a technology revolution
**1949**   People's Republic of China founded by Mao Zedong, which restricts access to the largest single consumer market on the globe

Cracker Jack invented the toy-with-candy promotion back in 1912. However, the Italian chocolatier, Ferrero, took things much further. Their milk chocolate Kinder eggs contain "sopresas" that kids enjoy in 37 countries around the world. The product is unavailable in the United States because of choking hazards. The product pictured is produced in Argentina for sale in Mexico, and it includes a warning label regarding kids under three. Cracker Jack has had to eliminate many of the cool little toys it put in the packages for the same reason. Nestlé introduced a product similar to Kinder eggs in the U.S. market in the late 1990s, but had to withdraw it for safety reasons. Wonderball is the latest version of that, but it has edible chocolate figures inside. See www.ferrero.com.ar and www.crackerjack.com for more details. Toys must be larger than the diameter of the plastic tube pictured on the right to meet the U.S. safety standard. (left: © Sharon Hoogstraten; right: AP/Wide World Photos)

approved by a central minister. Thus importers who want to buy a foreign good must apply for an exchange permit, that is, permission to exchange an amount of local currency for foreign currency.

The exchange permit may also stipulate the rate of exchange, which can be an unfavorable rate depending on the desires of the government. In addition, the exchange permit may stipulate that the amount to be exchanged must be deposited in a local bank for a set period prior to the transfer of goods. For example, Brazil has at times required funds to be deposited 360 days prior to the import date. This is extremely restrictive because funds are out of circulation and subject to the ravages of inflation. Such policies cause major cash flow problems for the importer and greatly increase the price of imports. Needless to say, these currency-exchange barriers constitute a major deterrent to trade.

**Standards.**    Nontariff barriers of this category include standards to protect health, safety, and product quality. The standards are sometimes used in an unduly stringent or discriminating way to restrict trade, but the sheer volume of regulations in this category is a problem in itself.[17] A fruit content regulation for jam varies so much from country to country that one agricultural specialist says, "A jam exporter needs a computer to avoid one or another country's regulations." Different standards are one of the major disagreements between the United States and Japan. The size of knotholes in plywood shipped to Japan can determine whether or not the shipment is accepted; if a knothole is too large, the shipment is rejected because quality standards are not met.

---

[17]Sabrina Tavernise, "Russia Revokes Licenses for All Imports of Meat and Poultry," *New York Times*, February 1, 2003, p. C3.

According to the U.S. government, you can't call it a "catfish" unless it's grown in America. Vietnamese are producing filets in flooded rice paddies at about $1.80 a pound at wholesale. American fish farmers are charging about $2.80. Neither consumers nor ichthyologists can tell the difference between the Asian and American fish, but Uncle Sam has stepped in anyway. The Congressional claim on the "catfish" name has forced the U.S. to stifle its own protests about Europeans claiming exclusive rights to the name "herring." (© *Tom McHugh/Photo Researchers, Inc.*)

The United States and other countries require some products (automobiles in particular) to contain a percentage of "local content" to gain admission to their markets. The North American Free Trade Agreement (NAFTA) stipulates that all automobiles coming from member countries must have at least 62.5 percent North American content to deter foreign car makers from using one member nation as the back door to another.

Trade restrictions abound, and the United States is one of the governments using them. According to one source, approximately 45 percent of U.S. manufactured imports are subject to some form of nontariff barrier. For more than a decade, U.S. government officials have arranged "voluntary" agreements with the Japanese steel and automobile industries to limit sales to the United States. Similar negotiations with the governments of major textile producers have limited textile imports into the United States. Although countries create barriers to trade, they appreciate the growing interdependence of the world's economies and thus strive to lower barriers in a controlled and equitable manner. The General Agreement on Tariffs and Trade (GATT) and the World Trade Organization (WTO) both have as their goal the elimination of trade barriers.

**Antidumping Penalties.**   Historically tariffs and nontariff trade barriers have impeded free trade, but over the years they have been eliminated or lowered through the efforts of GATT and WTO. Now there is a new nontariff barrier: antidumping laws that have emerged as a way of keeping foreign goods out of a market.[18] Antidumping laws were designed to prevent foreign producers from using **predatory pricing**, a practice whereby a foreign producer would intentionally sell their products in the United States for less than the cost of production to undermine the competition and take control of the market. It was intended as a kind of antitrust law for international trade. Violators are assessed antidumping duties for selling below cost or are assessed countervailing duties to prevent the use of foreign government subsidies to undermine American industry. Many countries have similar laws, which are allowed under WTO rules.

Recent years have seen a staggering increase in antidumping cases in the United States. In one year, 12 U.S. steel manufacturers launched antidumping cases against 82 foreign steelmakers in 30 countries.[19] Many economists felt that there was no need for these antidumping charges because of the number of companies and countries involved; supply and demand could have been left to sort out the best producers and prices. Of course, targeted countries have complained as well.[20] Nevertheless, antidumping cases are becoming de facto trade barriers. The investigations are very costly, take a long time to resolve, and they effectively limit trade until they are resolved. Further, the threat of being hit by an antidumping charge is enough to keep some companies out of the market.

---

[18]Pascal Lamy, "Come on, America, Play by the Rules!" *Wall Street Journal,* March 3, 2003, p. A16.

[19]Robert Guy Matthews, "U.S. Steel Tariffs Likely to Stay Despite WTO-Sanction Threat," *Wall Street Journal,* March 31, 2003, p. A2.

[20]"Japan, EU Prod WTO for Reaction to U.S. Steel Duties," *Purchasing,* April 6, 2000, p. 44.

**1971**   First microprocessor produced by Intel, which leads to the personal computer; Communist China joins the UN, making it truly a global representative body

**1971**   U.S. abandons gold standard, allowing the international monetary system to base exchange rates on perceived values instead of ones fixed in relation to gold

**1973**   Arab oil embargo jolts industrial world into understanding the totally global nature of supply and demand
**1980**   CNN founded, providing instant and common information the world over, taking

another significant step in the process of globalization started by the radio in 1901
**1987**   ISO issues ISO 9000 to create a global quality standard
**1989**   Berlin Wall falls, symbolizing the opening of the

## CROSSING BORDERS 2.5   The Dumper Becomes the Dumped upon and Vice Versa

Our favorite example of the difficulties of making dumping cases stick regards two typewriter companies. One of the most contentious and longest-lasting dumping cases in history ended abruptly in 1994 when both parties realized the fight was futile. Smith Corona, a 120-year-old American firm, and Brother Industries of Japan made a joint statement agreeing to end all litigation between them: "Both of our companies are better served by concentrating on the marketplace and serving our customers."

The 14-year legal battle started with the American firm accusing the Japanese of dumping portable typewriters into the U.S. market—that is, selling them for below manufacturing costs. However, Smith Corona during the mid-1990s shifted its production from Cortland, New York, to Mexico, Singapore, and other plants outside the United States. How could the American company claim Brother's imports from Japan were hurting an American company with no domestic production?

Meanwhile, Brother began moving production capacity from Nagoya, Japan, to Bartlett, Tennessee, qualifying it as an American manufacturer. Indeed, in 1991 Brother claimed it was the firm that represented the U.S. domestic typewriter industry and not Smith Corona, which in 1989 became a public company with 48 percent British ownership. Brother filed a cross suit alleging that Smith Corona was dumping its Singapore-made typewriters in the United States. In 1993 the U.S. Commerce Department appeared to agree with Brother in a preliminary determination. At that point both firms decided to terminate their battle. After all, most consumers were dumping their typewriters in favor of computers anyway!

Source: Amal Kumar Jan, "Smith Corona, Brother Industries End 14 Years of Litigation over Dumping," *Wall Street Journal*, February 8, 1994. Copyright 1994 by Dow Jones & Co. Inc. Reproduced with permission of Dow Jones & Co. Inc. via Copyright Clearance Center. Check each company website for a listing of their current products—www.brother.com and www.smithcorona.com.

## Easing Trade Restrictions

Lowering the trade deficit has been a priority of the U.S. government for a number of years. Of the many proposals brought forward, most deal with fairness of trade with some of our trading partners instead of reducing imports or adjusting other trade policies. Many believe that too many countries are allowed to trade freely in the United States without granting equal access to U.S. products in their countries. Japan was for two decades the trading partner with which we had the largest deficit and with which there was the most concern about fairness. The Omnibus Trade and Competitiveness Act of 1988 addressed the trade fairness issue and focused on ways to improve U.S. competitiveness. At the turn of the century, China became the trade partner of most concern for the United States.

### The Omnibus Trade and Competitiveness Act

The *Omnibus Trade and Competitiveness Act of 1988* is many faceted, focusing on assisting businesses to be more competitive in world markets as well as on correcting perceived injustice in trade practices. The trade act was designed to deal with trade deficits, protectionism, and the overall fairness of our trading partners. Congressional concern centered on the issue that U.S. markets were open to most of the world but markets in Japan, Western Europe, and many Asian countries were relatively closed. The act reflected the realization that we must deal with our trading partners based on how they actually operate, not on how we want them to behave. Some see the act as a protectionist measure, but the government sees it as a means of providing stronger tools to open foreign markets and to help U.S. exporters be more competitive. The bill covers three areas considered critical in improving U.S. trade: market access, export expansion, and import relief.

East to the West for ideas and commerce
**1991**   Soviet Union formally abandons communism, as most formerly communist states move toward capitalism and the trade it fosters; Commonwealth of Independent States

(CIS) established between Russia, Ukraine, and Belarus
**1993**   NAFTA ratified by U.S. Congress; European Union created from the European Community, along with a framework for joint security and foreign policy action, by the 1991 Maas-

tricht Treaty on European Union; the EEC is renamed the EC
**1994**   The Chunnel (Channel Tunnel) is opened between France and Britain, providing a ground link for commerce between the Continent and Britain

**1995**   World Trade Organization (WTO) set up as successor to GATT; by 2000 more than 130 members account for over 90 percent of world trade
**1997**   Hong Kong, a world trading and financial capital and bastion of capitalism, is

The billboard overlooking a busy shopping district in Beijing proclaims the importance of China's space technology to all passersby. Meanwhile, Boeing and Hughes have had to pay $32 million in a settlement with the U.S. government for allegedly giving the Chinese sensitive space technology in the middle 1990s. The restrictions on technology sales have rendered American high-tech firms less competitive in international markets even beyond China such as Canada.

The issue of the openness of markets for U.S. goods is addressed as market access. There are many barriers that restrict or prohibit goods from entering a foreign market. Unnecessarily restrictive technical standards, compulsory distribution systems, customs barriers, tariffs, quotas, and restrictive licensing requirements are just a few. The act gives the U.S. president authority to restrict sales of a country's products in the U.S. market if that country imposes unfair restrictions on U.S. products. Further, if a foreign government's procurement rules discriminate against U.S. firms, the U.S. president has the authority to impose a similar ban on U.S. government procurement of goods and services from the offending nation.

Besides emphasizing market access, the act also recognizes that some problems with U.S. export competitiveness stem from impediments on trade imposed by U.S. regulations and export disincentives. Export controls, the Foreign Corrupt Practices Act (FCPA), and export promotion were specifically addressed in the export expansion section of the act. Export licenses could be obtained more easily and more quickly for products on the export control list. In addition, the act reaffirmed the government's role in being more responsive to the needs of the exporter. Two major contributions facilitating export trade were computer-based procedures to file for and track export license requests, and the creation of the National Trade Data Bank (NTDB) to improve access to trade data.

Export trade is a two-way street: We must be prepared to compete with imports in the home market if we force foreign markets to open to U.S. trade. Recognizing that foreign penetration of U.S. markets can cause serious competitive pressure, loss of market share, and, occasionally, severe financial harm, the import relief section of the Omnibus Trade and Competitiveness Act provides a menu of remedies for U.S. businesses adversely affected by imports. Companies seriously injured by fairly traded imports can petition the government for temporary relief while they adjust to import competition and regain their competitive edge.

The act has resulted in a much more flexible process for obtaining export licenses, fewer products on the export control list, and greater access to information, and has established a basis for negotiations with India, Japan, and other countries to remove or lower barriers to trade. However, since the release of a 1999 Congressional report accusing China of espionage regarding defense technology, restrictions on exports of many high-tech products have again been tightened for national security reasons.[21]

As the global marketplace evolves, trading countries have focused attention on ways of eliminating tariffs, quotas, and other barriers to trade. Four ongoing activities to support the growth of international trade are GATT, the associated World Trade Organization (WTO), the International Monetary Fund (IMF), and The World Bank Group.

---

[21]David Briscoe, "Satellite Exports Dwindle under New Rules," *Associated Press,* May 18, 2000.

returned to communist Chinese control; Pathfinder lands on Mars, and rover goes for a drive but finds no one with whom to trade
**1999**   Euro introduced in 11 European Union nations, paving the way for the creation

of a true trade union and trade bloc
**1999**   Seattle Round of WTO negotiations pits United States versus European Union; first great protest against globalization

**1999**   Control of the Panama Canal, a major trade lane, is returned to Panama
**2000**   Second millenium arrives, predicted computer problems do not occur
**2001**   September 11 terrorist attack on the World Trade Cen-

ter in New York City and the Pentagon in Washington, D.C.
**2002**   United States attacks Taliban in Afghanistan
**2003**   United States attacks regime of Saddam Hussein in Iraq

## General Agreement on Tariffs and Trade

Historically, trade treaties were negotiated on a bilateral (between two nations) basis, with little attention given to relationships with other countries. Further, there was a tendency to raise barriers rather than extend markets and restore world trade. The United States and 22 other countries signed the *General Agreement on Tariffs and Trade* (**GATT**) shortly after World War II. Although not all countries participated, this agreement paved the way for the first effective worldwide tariff agreement. The original agreement provided a process to reduce tariffs and created an agency to serve as a watchdog over world trade. GATT's agency director and staff offer nations a forum for negotiating trade and related issues. Member nations seek to resolve their trade disputes bilaterally; if that fails, special GATT panels are set up to recommend action. The panels are only advisory and have no enforcement powers.

The GATT treaty and subsequent meetings have produced agreements significantly reducing tariffs on a wide range of goods. Periodically, member nations meet to reevaluate trade barriers and establish international codes designed to foster trade among members. In general, the agreement covers these basic elements: (1) trade shall be conducted on a nondiscriminatory basis; (2) protection shall be afforded domestic industries through customs tariffs, not through such commercial measures as import quotas; and (3) consultation shall be the primary method used to solve global trade problems.

Since GATT's inception there have been eight "rounds" of intergovernmental tariff negotiations. The most recently completed was the Uruguay Round (1994), which built on the successes of the Tokyo Round (1974)—the most comprehensive and far-reaching round undertaken by GATT up to that time. The Tokyo Round resulted in tariff cuts and set out new international rules for subsidies and countervailing measures, antidumping, government procurement, technical barriers to trade (standards), customs valuation, and import licensing. Although the Tokyo Round addressed nontariff barriers, some areas were not covered, which continued to impede free trade.

In addition to market access, there were issues of trade in services, agriculture, and textiles; intellectual property rights; and investment and capital flows. The United States was especially interested in addressing services trade and intellectual property rights since neither had been well protected. Based on these concerns, the eighth set of negotiations (Uruguay Round) was begun in 1986 at a GATT trade minister's meeting in Punta del Este, Uruguay, and finally concluded in 1994. By 1995, 80 GATT members, including the United States, the European Union (and its member states), Japan, and Canada, had accepted the agreement.

The market access segment (tariff and nontariff measures) was initially considered to be of secondary importance in the negotiations, but the final outcome went well beyond the initial Uruguay Round goal of a one-third reduction in tariffs. Instead, virtually all tariffs in ten vital industrial sectors were eliminated with key trading partners. This resulted in deep cuts (ranging from 50 to 100 percent) on electronic items and scientific equipment, and the harmonization of tariffs in the chemical sector at very low rates (5.5 to 0 percent).

U.S. exporters of paper products serve as a good example of the opportunities that opened as a result of these changes. Currently, U.S. companies competing for a share of the paper products market in the European Community have to pay tariffs as high as 9 percent while European competitors enjoy duty-free access within the EU. When the Uruguay Round market-access package was implemented, these high tariffs were eliminated. Another example is Korean tariffs as high as 20 percent on scientific equipment, which were reduced to an average of 7 percent, permitting U.S. exporters to be more competitive in that market.

An important objective of the United States in the Uruguay Round was to reduce or eliminate barriers to international trade in services. The General Agreement on Trade in Services (GATS) was the first multilateral, legally enforceable agreement covering trade and investment in the services sector. It provides a legal basis for future negotiations aimed at eliminating barriers that discriminate against foreign services and deny them market access. For the first time, comprehensive multilateral disciplines and procedures covering trade and investment in services have been established. Specific market-opening

**CROSSING BORDERS 2.6** Not a Single Grain of Foreign Rice
Shall Ever Enter Japan

For Japan, rice is a near-sacred product, deeply embedded in history, culture, economics, politics, and symbolism. For the Japanese, rice is "our Christmas tree," and rice-producing land is reverently called "our holy land." In Japanese eyes, rice—far more than beef, citrus fruit, or textiles—represents the ultimate non-negotiable market-access topic. "Not a single grain of foreign rice shall ever enter Japan" was the solemn vow of Japanese politicians of all stripes, backed by public opinion, the press, the business community, academics, and the bureaucracy. Opposition to imported rice reflected a national consensus.

Small wonder that American demands in 1986 for opening the Japanese rice market were seen as a threat to Japanese culture itself. There is some irony in America criticizing Japan's inefficient rice-farming system. After all, it was the American-led occupation after World War II that had broken up existing large land holdings into the small tracts that would become the bastions of rice farmers whose votes politicians rewarded with generous subsidies perpetuating these economically inefficient plots.

Negotiations lasted some eight years. The Americans were able to include the rice issue as part of the larger GATT negotiations on farming subsidies. Japanese resistance to rice imports finally buckled under pressure from Canada, the EU, and the United States as the 1994 due date for GATT passage approached. Internally, the Japanese politicians representing the interests of the farm lobby yielded to the interests of the country's huge exporting interests in automobiles and electronics. The final agreement reached included quotas on rice imports until 2000, with tariffs being applied after that date. Now, Japan imports some $150 million worth of rice from California and Lousiana every year—much more than a single grain. Even so, the price paid for rice by Japanese consumers is raised by a whopping 490 percent tariff on imports.

Source: One of the single best cases written on the Japanese style of negotiation is Michael Blaker's, "Negotiating on Rice: 'No, No, a Thousand Times No'" in Peter Berton, Hiroshi Kimura, and I. William Zartman (eds.), *International Negotiation: Actors, Structure/Process, Values* (New York: St. Martin's Press, 1999); www.usarice.com; and Ken Belson, "Global Talks on Farming Begin Friday," *New York Times*, February 13, 2002, p. W1.

concessions from a wide range of individual countries were achieved, and provision was made for continued negotiations to further liberalize telecommunications and financial services.

Equally significant were the results of negotiations in the investment sector. Trade-Related Investment Measures (TRIMs) established the basic principle that investment restrictions can be major trade barriers and therefore are included, for the first time, under GATT procedures. As a result of TRIMs, restrictions in Indonesia that prohibit foreign firms from opening their own wholesale or retail distribution channels can be challenged. So can investment restrictions in Brazil that require foreign-owned manufacturers to buy most of their components from high-cost local suppliers and that require affiliates of foreign multinationals to maintain a trade surplus in Brazil's favor by exporting more than they sell within the country.

Another objective of the United States for the Uruguay Round was achieved by an agreement on Trade-Related Aspects of Intellectual Property Rights (TRIPs). The TRIPs agreement establishes substantially higher standards of protection for a full range of intellectual property rights (patents, copyrights, trademarks, trade secrets, industrial designs, and semiconductor chip mask works) than are embodied in current international agreements, and it provides for the effective enforcement of those standards both internally and at the border.

The Uruguay Round also provided for a better integration of the agricultural and textiles areas into the overall trading system. The reductions of export subsidies, internal supports, and actual import barriers for agricultural products are included in the agreement. The Uruguay Round also includes another set of improvements in rules covering antidumping, standards, safeguards, customs valuation, rules of origin, and import licensing. In each case, rules and procedures were made more open, equitable, and predictable, thus leading to a more level playing field for trade. Perhaps the most notable achievement of the Uruguay Round was the creation of a new institution as a successor to the GATT—the World Trade Organization.[22]

## World Trade Organization (WTO)

At the signing of the Uruguay Round trade agreement in Marrakech, Morocco, in April 1994, U.S. representatives pushed for an enormous expansion of the definition of trade issues.[23] The result was the creation of the World Trade Organization, which encompasses the GATT structure and extends it to new areas not adequately covered in the past. The **WTO** is an institution, not an agreement as was GATT. It sets many rules governing trade between its 132 members, provides a panel of experts to hear and rule on trade disputes between members, and, unlike GATT, issues binding decisions. It requires, for the first time, the full participation of all members in all aspects of the current GATT and the Uruguay Round agreements, and, through its enhanced stature and scope, provides a permanent, comprehensive forum to address the trade issues of the twenty-first-century global market.

All member countries have equal representation in the WTO's ministerial conference, which meets at least every two years to vote for a director general who appoints other officials. Trade disputes, such as the one about genetically modified foods,[24] are heard by a panel of experts selected by the WTO from a list of trade experts provided by member countries. The panel hears both sides and issues a decision; the winning side will be authorized to retaliate with trade sanctions if the losing country does not change its practices. Although the WTO has no actual means of enforcement, international pressure to comply with WTO decisions from other member countries is expected to force compliance. The WTO ensures that member countries agree to the obligations of all the agreements, not just those they like.[25] For the first time, member countries, including developing countries (the fastest-growing markets of the world), are undertaking obligations to open their markets and be bound by the rules of the multilateral trading system.

There was some resistance to the World Trade Organization provision of the Uruguay Round before it was finally ratified by the three super powers, Japan, the European Union, and the United States. A legal wrangle between European Union countries centered on whether the EU's founding treaty gives the European Commission the sole right to negotiate for its members in all areas covered by the WTO.

In the United States, ratification was challenged because of concern for the possible loss of sovereignty over its trade laws to the WTO, the lack of veto power (the U.S. could have a decision imposed on it by a majority of the WTO's members), and the role the United States would assume when a conflict arises over an individual state's laws that might be challenged by a WTO member. The GATT agreement was ratified by the U.S. Congress; soon after, the EU, Japan, and more than 60 other countries followed. All 117 members of the former GATT supported the Uruguay agreement. Since its inception on January 1, 1995, the WTO's agenda has been full, with issues ranging from threats of boycotts and sanctions to the membership of China and Russia.[26] Indeed, a major event in international trade during recent years was China's 2001 entry into the WTO.[27] Instead of waiting for various rounds of negotiations to iron out problems, the WTO offers a framework for a continuous discussion and resolution of issues that retard trade.

---

[22]See www.wto.org.

[23]Jean-Emile Denis, "Making International Marketing Decisions under WTO Rules," *Thunderbird International Business Review,* 45(2), March/April 2003, pp. 185–210.

[24]Michael Schroeder and Scott Miller, "U.S. to Ask WTO to Halt EU's Ban on Modified Food," *Wall Street Journal,* May 14, 2003, p. A2.

[25]Michael Schroeder, "U.S. Trade: Olive Branch or Big Stick?" *Wall Street Journal,* May 7, 2003, A4.

[26]Kara Josephberg, Jane Pollack, Jenna Victoriano, and Oriyan Gitig, "Russia Increases Anti-piracy Efforts, Enhances Trademark Protection," *Intellectual Property & Technology Law Journal* 15(3), March 2003, pp. 22–27.

[27]Lara Wozniak, "DHL and FEDEX Race to Integrate China," *Far Eastern Economic Review,* February 27, 2003, p. 8.

The WTO has its detractors, but most indications are that it is gaining acceptance by the trading community. The number of countries that have joined and those that want to become members are good measures of its importance. Another indicator is the accomplishments since its inception: It has been the forum for successful negotiations to open markets in telecommunications and in information technology equipment, something the United States had sought for the last two rounds of GATT. It also has been active in settling trade disputes and it continues to oversee the implementation of the agreements reached in the Uruguay Round. But with its successes come other problems, namely, how to counter those countries that want all the benefits of belonging to the WTO but also want to protect their markets.

## Skirting the Spirit of GATT and the WTO

Unfortunately, as is probably true of every law or agreement, since its inception there have been those who look for loopholes and ways to get around the provisions of the WTO. For example, China was asked to become a member of the WTO, but to be accepted it had to show good faith in reducing tariffs and other restrictions on trade. To fulfill the requirements to join the WTO, China reduced tariffs on 5,000 product lines and eliminated a range of traditional nontariff barriers to trade, including quotas, licenses, and foreign exchange controls. At the same time, U.S. companies have begun to notice an increase in the number and scope of technical standards and inspection requirements. As a case in point, China recently has applied safety and quality inspection requirements on such seemingly benign imported goods as jigsaw puzzles. It also has been insisting that a long list of electrical and mechanical imports undergo an expensive certification process that requires foreign companies but not domestic companies to pay for on-site visits by Chinese inspection officials. Under WTO rules, China now must justify the decision to impose certain standards and provide a rationale for the inspection criteria. However, the foreign companies will have to request a review before the WTO will investigate. The WTO recognizes the need for standards (safety, health, and so on) although it advocates worldwide harmonization of product standards.

Antidumping duties are becoming another favorite way for nations to impose duties, under the justification that a foreign company is selling at unfair prices. Most nations have dumping laws that ostensibly are designed to keep foreign companies from dumping product, that is, selling below cost to unfairly gain a share of market and lessen competition. This law always has been difficult to interpret because "selling below cost" is difficult to measure; most countries have defined it whatever way necessary to serve their purpose. When companies are found to be dumping, the country places an extra tax on the product to offset the advantage of the lower price. If the government has subsidized the company that is found guilty of dumping, an additional countervailing duty is collected to offset the subsidy.

In an attempt to standardize the definition, the WTO defines dumping as selling at a lower price in the foreign market than in other markets or selling at below average total costs. The interpretation and calculation of average total costs creates the most difficulty in evaluating cases. Antidumping actions do not require evidence of predatory behavior, or intentions to monopolize, or of any other efforts to drive competitors out of business.

Following the example of the United States (the region's most prolific user of antidumping cases)[28] Mexico and other Latin American countries have increased their use of antidumping and countervailing duties as protectionist measures. As one Mexican official involved in antidumping cases noted, "We have learned our trade in the United States and learned it well." Despite the clever tactics used by some countries to skirt its provisions, the WTO is considered to have a positive effect on international trade.

Finally, frustrated with the slow progress of the most recent round of WTO trade negotiations,[29] several countries are negotiating bilateral trade agreements. For example, the

---

[28]Elizabeth Becker, "WTO Rules against U.S. on Steel Tariff," *New York Times,* March 27, 2003, p. C1.

[29]Ken Belson, "Global Talks on Farming Begin on Friday," *New York Times,* February 13, 2003, p. W1.

United States is currently negotiating free-trade agreements with Singapore,[30] Morocco, Australia, and the Americas. The European Union is engaged in similar activities with Albania and South American countries.[31] To the extent that the bilateral talks ultimately lead to multilateral concessions, then such activities are not inconsistent with WTO goals and aspirations.

## The International Monetary Fund and World Bank Group

The International Monetary Fund[32] (**IMF**) and the World Bank Group[33] are two global institutions created to assist nations in becoming and remaining economically viable. Each plays an important role in the environment of international trade by helping to maintain stability in the financial markets and by assisting countries that are seeking economic development and restructuring.

Inadequate monetary reserves and unstable currencies are particularly vexing problems in global trade. So long as these conditions exist, world markets cannot develop and function as effectively as they should. To overcome these particular market barriers that plagued international trading before World War II, the International Monetary Fund (IMF) was formed. Originally 29 countries signed the agreement; now there are 181 countries as members. Among the objectives of the IMF are the stabilization of foreign exchange rates and the establishment of freely convertible currencies to facilitate the expansion and balanced growth of international trade. Member countries have voluntarily joined to consult with one another in order to maintain a stable system of buying and selling their currencies so that payments in foreign money can take place between countries smoothly and without delay. The IMF also lends money to members having trouble meeting financial obligations to other members. Argentina[34] and Turkey[35] have recently received such help from the IMF, but the results have been mixed.

To cope with universally floating exchange rates, the IMF developed **special drawing rights** (SDRs), one of its more useful inventions. Because both gold and the U.S. dollar have lost their utility as the basic medium of financial exchange, most monetary statistics relate to SDRs rather than dollars. The SDR is in effect "paper gold," and represents an average base of value derived from the value of a group of major currencies. Rather than being denominated in the currency of any given country, trade contracts are frequently written in SDRs because they are much less susceptible to exchange-rate fluctuations. Even floating rates do not necessarily accurately reflect exchange relationships. Some countries permit their currencies to float cleanly without manipulation (clean float), whereas other nations systematically manipulate the value of their currency (dirty float), thus modifying the accuracy of the monetary marketplace. Although much has changed in the world's monetary system since the IMF was first established, it still plays an important role in providing short-term financing to governments struggling to pay current-account debts.

Although the International Monetary Fund has some severe critics,[36] most agree that it has performed a valuable service and at least partially achieved many of its objectives. Surely, the IMF proved its value in the financial crisis among some Asian countries in 1997. The impact of the crisis was lessened substantially as a result of actions taken by

[30]Evelyn Iritani, "Singapore Trade Deal Gives U.S. 'Full Access,'" *Los Angeles Times,* May 7, 2003, p. C1.

[31]Scott Miller, "Lamy Makes Case for WTO's Way," *Wall Street Journal,* March 20, 2003, p. B1.

[32]www.imf.org.

[33]www.worldbank.org.

[34]Larry Rohter, "Peso Policy is Overturned in Argentina," *New York Times,* March 6, 2003, p. C1.

[35]Claudia Rosett, "How the IMF Lost Turkey," *Wall Street Journal,* April 2, 2003, p. A14.

[36]Mary Locke, "Funding the IMF: The Debate in the U.S. Congress," *Finance & Development,* September 2000, 37(3), pp. 56–59; and Sadanand Dhume, "Calling the IMF," *Far Eastern Economic Review,* January 23, 2003, p. 18.

the IMF. During the financial crisis, the IMF provided loans to several countries including Thailand, Indonesia, and South Korea. Had these countries not received aid ($60 billion to Korea alone), the economic reverberations may have led to a global recession. As it was, all the major equity markets reflected substantial reductions in market prices and the rate of economic growth in some countries was slowed.

Sometimes confused with the IMF, the World Bank Group[37] is a separate institution that has as its goal the reduction of poverty and the improvement of living standards by promoting sustainable growth and investment in people. The World Bank provides loans, technical assistance, and policy guidance to developing-country members to achieve its objectives. There are five institutions in the World Bank Group, each of which performs the following services: (1) lending money to the governments of developing countries to finance development projects in education, health, and infrastructure; (2) providing assistance to governments for developmental projects to the poorest developing countries (per capita incomes of $925 or less); (3) lending directly to the private sector to help strengthen the private sector in developing countries with long-term loans, equity investments, and other financial assistance; (4) providing investors with investment guarantees against "noncommercial risk," such as expropriation and war, to create an environment in developing countries that will attract foreign investment; and (5) promoting increased flows of international investment by providing facilities for the conciliation and arbitration of disputes between governments and foreign investors. The World Bank also provides advice, carries out research, and produces publications in the area of foreign investment law. Since their inception, these institutions have played a pivotal role in the economic development of countries throughout the world and thus contributed to the expansion of international trade since World War II.

## Protests against Global Institutions

Beginning in 1999, what some are calling "anti-capitalist protestors" began to influence the workings of the major global institutions described previously.[38] The basic complaint against the WTO, IMF, and others is the amalgam of unintended consequences of globalization: environmental concerns, worker exploitation, domestic job losses,[39] cultural extinction, higher oil prices, and diminished sovereignty of nations. The antiglobalization protests first caught the attention of the world press during a WTO meeting in Seattle in November 1999. Then came the World Bank and IMF meetings in April 2000 in Washington, D.C., the World Economic Forum in Melbourne, Australia, in September 2000, and IMF/World Bank meetings in Prague, also in September 2000. Some 10,000 protestors faced some 11,000 police in Prague. The protestors have established websites associated with each event, which are labeled according to the respective dates. You might also check www.destroyIMF.org to see the ominous tone represented. The websites and the Internet have proved to be important media aiding organizational efforts. The protests and violence have continued at other meetings of world leaders regarding economic issues, such as the G-8 meetings in Evian, France, in 2003 and in individual countries affected by the IMF.[40]

The protest groups, some of them with responsible intent, have affected policy. For example, "anti-sweatshop" campaigns, mostly in America and mostly student led, have had effects beyond college campuses. A coalition of nongovernmental organizations, student groups, and UNITE, the textile workers' union, recently sued clothing importers, including Calvin Klein and Gap, over working conditions in the American commonwealth of Saipan in the Pacific. Faced with litigation and extended public campaigns against

[37]Warren Vieth, "World Bank, IMF Say Third-World Development Lags," *Los Angeles Times,* April 14, 2003, p. A17.

[38]"Anti-Capitalist Protests: Angry and Effective," *Economist,* September 23, 2000, pp. 85–87.

[39]Pete Engardio, Aaron Bernstein, and Manjeet Kripalani, "Is Your Job Next?" *BusinessWeek,* February 3, 2003, pp. 50–60

[40]"What Will the IMF Say Now? Bolivia," *The Economist,* February 22, 2003, p. 33.

Starbucks may be replacing
McDonald's as the American
brand foreigners most love to
hate. Here local police fail to stop
anti-World Trade Organization
rioters in Seattle from breaking
windows close to home.
(© AFP/CORBIS)

their brands, 17 companies settled, promising better working conditions. Similarly, a World Bank project in China, which involved moving poor ethnic Chinese into lands that were traditionally Tibetan, was abandoned after a political furor led by a relatively small group of pro-Tibetan activists. Given the apparent successes associated with these grass-roots efforts to influence policy at these global institutions we must expect more of the same in the future.

## Summary

Regardless of the theoretical approach used in defense of international trade, it is clear that the benefits from absolute or comparative advantage can accrue to any nation. Heightened competition from around the world has created increased pressure for protectionism from every region of the globe at a time when open markets are needed if world resources are to be developed and utilized in the most beneficial manner. It is true that there are circumstances when market protection may be needed and may be beneficial to national defense or the encouragement of infant industries in developing nations, but the consumer seldom benefits from such protection.

Free international markets help underdeveloped countries become self-sufficient, and because open markets provide new customers, most industrialized nations have, since World War II, cooperated in working toward freer trade. Such trade will always be partially threatened by various governmental and market barriers that exist or are created for the protection of local businesses. However, the trend has been toward freer trade. The changing economic and political realities are producing unique business structures that continue to protect certain major industries. The future of open global markets lies with the controlled and equitable reduction of trade barriers.

## Questions

1. Define:

   balance of trade, 32
   balance of payments, 34
   current account, 35
   capital account, 35
   reserves account, 35
   tariffs, 37, 39
   quotas, 37, 40
   nontariff barriers, 37
   protectionism, 37

   voluntary export restraints (VER), 41
   orderly market agreements, 41
   predatory pricing, 45
   GATT, 48
   WTO, 50
   IMF, 52
   special drawing rights, 52

2. Discuss the globalization of the U.S. economy.

3. Differentiate among the current account, balance of trade, and balance of payments.

4. Explain the role of price as a free market regulator.

5. "Theoretically, the market is an automatic, competitive, self-regulating mechanism which provides for the maximum consumer welfare and which best regulates the use of the factors of production." Explain.

6. Interview several local businesspeople to determine their attitudes toward world trade. Further, learn if they buy or sell goods produced in foreign countries. Correlate the attitudes and report on your findings.

7. What is the role of profit in international trade? Does profit replace or complement the regulatory function of pricing? Discuss.

8. Why does the balance of payments always balance even though the balance of trade does not?

9. Enumerate the ways in which a nation can overcome an unfavorable balance of trade.

10. Support or refute each of the various arguments commonly used in support of tariffs.

11. France exports about 18 percent of its gross domestic product, while neighboring Belgium exports 46 percent. What areas of economic policy are likely to be affected by such variations in exports?

12. Does widespread unemployment change the economic logic of protectionism?

13. Review the economic effects of major trade imbalances such as those caused by petroleum imports.

14. Discuss the main provisions of the Omnibus Trade and Competitiveness Act of 1988.

15. The Tokyo Round of GATT emphasized the reduction of nontariff barriers. How does the Uruguay Round differ?

16. Discuss the impact of GATS, TRIMs, and TRIPs on global trade.

17. Discuss the evolution of world trade that led to the formation of the WTO.

18. Visit www.usitc.gov/taffairs.htm (U.S. Customs tariff schedule) and look up the import duties on leather footwear. You will find a difference in the duties on shoes of different value, material composition, and quantity. Using what you have learned in this chapter, explain the reasoning behind these differences. Do the same for frozen and/or concentrated orange juice.

19. The GATT has had a long and eventful history. Visit www.wto.org/wto/about/about.htm and write a short report on the various rounds of GATT. What were the key issues addressed in each round?

# HISTORY and Geography:
## THE FOUNDATIONS OF CULTURE

**CHAPTER 3**

## CHAPTER LEARNING OBJECTIVES

What you should learn from Chapter 3:

• The importance of history and geography in the
  understanding of international markets

• The effects of history on a country's culture

• How culture interprets events through its own eyes

• How the United States moved West and its effect
  on attitudes

• Effect of geographic diversity on economic profiles
  of a country

• Marketers need to be responsive to geography
  of a country

• Economic effects of controlling population growth
  versus aging population

• Communications are an integral part of international
  commerce

# Global Perspective

## BIRTH OF A NATION—PANAMA IN 67 HOURS

### The Stage Is Set

| June 1902 | United States offers to buy the Panama Canal Zone from Colombia for $10 million. |
| August 1903 | The Colombian Senate refuses the offer. Theodore Roosevelt, angered by the refusal, referred to the Colombian Senate as "those contemptible little creatures in Bogotá." Roosevelt agrees to a plot, led by a secessionist, Dr. Manuel Amador, to assist a group planning to secede from Colombia. |
| October 17 | Panamanian dissidents travel to Washington and agree to stage a U.S.-backed revolution. The date of revolution is set for November 3 at 6 P.M. |
| October 18 | Flag, constitution, and declaration of independence are created over the weekend. Panama's first flag was designed and sewn by hand in Highland Falls, New York, using fabric bought at Macy's. |
| | Bunau-Varilla, a French engineer associated with the bankrupt French-Panama canal construction company and not a permanent resident in Panama, is named Panama's ambassador to the United States. |

### A Country Is Born

| Tuesday, November 3 | Precisely at 6 P.M. bribes are paid to the Colombian garrison to lay down their arms. The revolution begins, the U.S.S. *Nashville* steams into Colón harbor, and the junta proclaims Panama's independence. |
| Friday, November 6 | By 1:00 P.M. the United States recognizes the sovereign state of Panama. |
| Saturday, November 7 | The new government sends an official delegation from Panama to the United States to instruct the Panamanian ambassador to the United States on provisions of the Panama Canal Treaty. |

| Wednesday, November 18 | 6:40 P.M. The Panamanian ambassador signs the Panama Canal Treaty. At 11:30 P.M., the official Panamanian delegation arrives at a Washington, D.C., railroad station and is met by their ambassador, who informs them that the treaty was signed just hours earlier. |

### The Present

| 1977 | United States agrees to relinquish control of Panama Canal Zone on December 31, 1999. |
| 1997 | Autoridad del Canal de Panama, the canal authority that will assume control from the U.S. Panama Canal Commission, is created. |
| 1998 | Panama gives a Chinese company the right to build new port facilities on both the Pacific and Atlantic sides, to control anchorages, to hire new pilots to guide ships through the canal, and to block all passage that interferes with the company's business. |
| January 1, 2000 | "The canal is ours" is jubilant cry in Panama. |
| January 17, 2000 | Pentagon sees potential Chinese threat to Panama Canal. |
| July 2002 | China pressures Panama to extend diplomatic recognition to China and drop recognition of Taiwan. |
| 2004 | The saga continues. |

This story is a good illustration of how history and geography can affect public and political attitudes in the present and far into the future. To the Panamanian and much of Latin America, the Panama Canal is but one example of the many U.S. intrusions during the early twentieth century that have tainted U.S.–Latin American relations. For the United States, the geographical importance of the Panama Canal for trade (shipping between the two coasts via the Canal is cut by 8,000 miles) makes control of the canal a sensitive issue, especially if that control could be potentially hostile. That a Chinese-owned company has operational control of both the Pacific and Atlantic ports and could pose an indirect threat to the Panama Canal Zone does not sit well. Recent history of U.S. conflict with China and the past history of Western domination of parts of China creates in the minds of many an adversarial relationship between the two countries. Further, some wonder if Panama would be reluctant to ask the United States to intervene at some future date, perhaps fearing that the Americans might stay another 98 years. Although the probability of China sabotaging the canal is slim at best, historical baggage makes one wonder what would happen should U.S. relations with China deteriorate to the point that the canal was felt to be in jeopardy.

Sources: Bernard A. Weisberger, "Panama: Made in U.S.A.," *American Heritage,* November 1989, pp. 24–25; Juanita Darling, "'The Canal Is Ours' Is Jubilant Cry in Panama," *Los Angeles Times,* January 1, 2000, p. A-1; "Pentagon Sees Potential China Threat to Panama Canal," *Asian Political News,* January 17, 2000, p. 20; "Which China Card?," *Economist,* July 13, 2002, p. 34; and, "Handy Things, Canals," *Economist,* February 27, 2003.

*Culture* can be defined as a society's accepted basis for responding to external and internal events. Even though the nuances of a culture can be observed, one cannot expect to fully understand a society's actions and points of view without an appreciation for the influence of the historical events it has experienced and the geographical uniqueness to which a culture has had to adapt. If a marketer is to interpret a culture's behavior and attitudes, it is essential to have some idea of a country's history and geography.

The goal of this chapter is to introduce the reader to the impact of history and geography on the marketing process. The influence of history on behavior and attitudes toward foreign marketers and the influence of geography on markets, trade, and environmental issues are examined.

# Historical Perspective in Global Business

History helps define a nation's "mission," how it perceives its neighbors, how it sees its place in the world, and how it sees itself. Insights into the history of a country are important for understanding attitudes about the role of government and business, the relations between managers and the managed, the sources of management authority, and attitudes toward foreign corporations.

To understand, explain, and appreciate a people's image of itself and the attitudes and unconscious fears that may be reflected in its view of foreign cultures, it is necessary to study the culture as it is now as well as to understand the culture as it was—that is, a country's history.[1]

## History and Contemporary Behavior

Unless you have a historical sense of the many changes that have buffeted Japan—seven centuries under the shogun feudal system,[2] the isolation before the coming of Admiral Perry in 1853, the threat of domination by colonial powers,[3] the rise of new social classes, Western influences, the humiliation of World War II, and involvement in the international community—it is difficult to fully understand its contemporary behavior. Why do the Japanese have such strong loyalty toward their companies? Why is the loyalty found among participants in the Japanese distribution systems so difficult for an outsider to

---

[1]How can anyone understand the conflict that exists between Israel and the Palestinians without an appreciation for the long history of tension that exists there? See for example, Romesh Ratnesar, "The Dawn of Israel," *Time Atlantic,* March 31, 2003; Bernard Gilland, "Zionism, Israel and the Arabs," *Contemporary Review,* January 2003, p. 27; and "Israel and the Palestinians, It Should Have Been So Simple," *The Economist,* January 25, 2003.

[2]For an interesting discussion of aspects of Japan's political, economic, and social life that helps to explain how Japan is today and why it is like that, see Duncan McCargo, *Contemporary Japan,* (New York: Palgrave Macmillan 2nd edition, 2003).

[3]For centuries, Japan sought isolation from the rest of the world, refusing to trade or become involved in any way. When Commodore Perry sailed to the Land of the Rising Sun, Japan was opened to the West. Treaties, signed with the United States, Britain, Holland, Russia, and France, extended jurisdiction onto Japanese soil and limited the country's right to impose taxes on imports. According to one account, these unequal and humiliating treaties had much to do with shaping Japan's goal to make itself the West's industrial and military equal. For a history of the period, see Ann Graham Gaines, *Commodore Perry Opens Japan to Trade in World History,* (Berkeley Heights, NJ: Enslow Publishers, Inc., 2000).

## CROSSING BORDERS 3.1  In Paraguay, a Fantasy Is Fulfilled by a Trip to Fremont, Ohio?

As the saying goes, "History is written by the victor," which is just another way of saying that history is subjective. It may surprise you that Rutherford B. Hayes, the nineteenth president of the United States, is revered in Paraguay. He is a national hero: "He's our inspiration—our source of strength." The largest state in Paraguay is named Presidente Hayes; he is commemorated in textbooks, monuments, and folklore; and he and President John F. Kennedy are considered to be in a class above all other U.S. presidents. He is so important that a national TV program, "Tell Me A Dream," which specializes in making fantasies come true, fulfilled the dream of a 17-year-old girl who wanted to travel to the United States by giving her an all-expense-paid trip to Fremont, Ohio, President Hayes's final resting place and the site of the Rutherford B. Hayes Presidential Center.

Why such interest in a president that the United States considers at best mediocre, who is viewed as such a minor historical figure that his hometown tore down his birthplace to put up a gas station, and whose most enduring achievement was his introduction of the children's

Easter Egg Roll on the lawn of the White House? Why is he a hero in a country in which he never set foot? Because shortly after taking office, he was asked to arbitrate a bitter dispute between Paraguay and Argentina over the ownership of Chaco, a scorching and largely uninhabitable tract of grassland about the size of Colorado. There had been a disastrous war between Paraguay and the Triple Alliance of Argentina, Brazil, and Uruguay. Paraguay had lost but was negotiating for the ownership of Chaco, and Hayes's terse four-paragraph decision sided with Paraguay. No one knows whether President Hayes was really personally involved in the decision, or what the rationale was. "Perhaps they just flipped a coin," observed one historian. But that makes no difference, because in the eyes of the Paraguayans, "President Hayes obviously possessed the greatness of spirit to have seen the justness of the Paraguayan cause."

Source: Matt Moffett, "Paraguayans Knew JFK, and He Was No Rutherford B. Hayes," *Wall Street Journal*, April 10, 2000, p. A-1. Copyright 2000 by Dow Jones & Co. Inc. Reproduced with permission of Dow Jones & Co. Inc. via Copyright Clearance Center.

develop? Why are decisions made by consensus? Answers to such questions can be explained in part by Japanese history.

Loyalty to family, to country, to company, and to social groups and the strong drive to cooperate, to work together for a common cause, permeate many facets of Japanese behavior and have historical roots that date back thousands of years. Loyalty and service, a sense of responsibility, and respect for discipline, training, and artistry have been stressed since ancient times as necessary for stability and order. Confucian philosophy, taught throughout Japan's history, emphasizes the basic virtue of loyalty "of friend to friend, of wife to husband, of child to parent, of brother to brother, but, above all, of subject to lord," that is, to country. A fundamental premise of Japanese ideology reflects the importance of cooperation for the collective good. Japanese achieve consensus by agreeing that all will unite against outside pressures that threaten the collective good. A historical perspective gives the foreigner in Japan a basis on which to begin developing cultural sensitivity and a better understanding of contemporary Japanese behavior.

**History Is Subjective**   History is important in understanding why a country behaves as it does, but history from whose viewpoint? Historical events always are viewed from one's own biases and self-reference criterion (SRC), and thus what is recorded by one historian may not be what another records, especially if the historians are from different cultures.[4] Historians traditionally try to be objective, but few can help filtering events through their own cultural biases. Our perspective influences not only our view of history, but also subtly influences how we view other matters. For example, maps of the world sold in the United States

---

[4]The way in which the war in Iraq has been reported will ultimately influence the historical perspective of this event. See, for example, Dan Gilfogg, "Everybody's Watching, but Different Channels," *U.S. News and World Report*, April 7, 2003, p. 50.

The Monumento de los Niños Heroes honors six young cadets who during the Mexican-American War of 1847 chose death over surrender. The Mexican-American War is important in Mexican history and helps to explain, in part, the Mexican love-hate relationship with the United States. (© Dave G. Houser/CORBIS)

generally show the United States at the center, whereas maps in Britain show Britain at the center, and so on for other nations.[5]

A crucial element in understanding any nation's business and political culture is the subjective perception of its history. Why do Mexicans have a love-hate relationship with the United States? Why were Mexicans required to have majority ownership in most foreign investments until recently? Why did dictator General Porfirio Díaz lament, "Poor Mexico, so far from God, so near the United States"? Why, because Mexicans see the United States as a threat to their political, economic, and cultural independence.

Most citizens of the United States are mystified by such feelings. After all, the United States has always been Mexico's good neighbor. Most would agree with President John F. Kennedy's proclamation during a visit to Mexico that "Geography has made us neighbors, tradition has made us friends." North Americans may be surprised to learn that most Mexicans "felt it more accurate to say 'Geography has made us closer, tradition has made us far apart.'"[6]

Citizens of the United States feel they have been good neighbors. They see the Monroe Doctrine as protection for Latin America from European colonization and the intervention of Europe in the governments of the Western Hemisphere. Latin Americans, on the other hand, tend to see the Monroe Doctrine as an offensive expression of U.S. influence in Latin America. Or to put it another way, "Europe keep your hands off—Latin America is only for the United States," an attitude perhaps typified by former U.S. president Ulysses S. Grant, who, in a speech in Mexico in 1880, described Mexico as a "magnificent mine" that lay waiting south of the border for North American interests.

United States Marines sing with pride of their exploits "from the halls of Montezuma to the shores of Tripoli." To the Mexican, the exploit to which the "halls of Montezuma" refers is remembered as U.S. troops marching all the way to the center of Mexico City and extracting as tribute 890,000 square miles that became Arizona, California, New Mexico, and Texas (see Exhibit 3.1). A prominent monument at the entrance of Chapultepec Park recognizes *Los Niños Heroes* (the boy heroes), who resisted U.S. troops, wrapped themselves in Mexican flags, and jumped to their deaths rather than surrender.

---

[5] Professor Lyn S. Amine of St. Louis University brought this observation to our attention

[6] For an insightful review of some of the issues that have affected relations between the United States and Mexico, see John Skirius, "Railroad, Oil and Other Foreign Interest in the Mexican Revolution, 1911–1914," *Journal of Latin American Studies,* February 2003, p. 25.

**Exhibit 3.1**
Territorial Expansion of
United States From 1783

The United States expanded
westward to the Pacific by a
series of financial deals,
negotiated settlements, and
forcible annexations. The
acquisition of territory from
Mexico began with the Battle of
San Jacinto in 1836 when Texas
staged a successful revolt against
the rule of Mexico and became
The Republic of Texas—later to
join the Union in 1845. The
Mexican War (1846–1848)
resulted in Mexico ceding
California and a large part of the
West to the United States.

Source: *Oxford Atlas of the World*,
10th ed., 2002, (NY: Oxford University
Press, 2002), p. 182

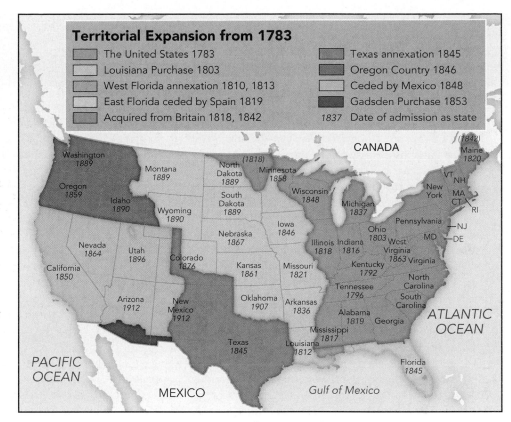

Mexicans can recount the heroism of *Los Niños Heroes* and the loss of Mexican territory to the United States. Every September 13, the president of Mexico, his cabinet, and
the diplomatic corps assemble at the Mexico City fortress to recall the defeat that led to
the *"despojo territorial"* (territorial plunder).

The Mexican Revolution, which overthrew dictator Díaz and launched the modern
Mexican state, is particularly remembered for the expulsion of foreigners, especially
North American businessmen who were the most visible of the wealthy and influential
entrepreneurs in Mexico.

**Manifest Destiny
and the Monroe
Doctrine**

Manifest Destiny and the Monroe Doctrine were accepted as the basis for U.S. foreign
policy during much of the nineteenth and twentieth centuries. **Manifest Destiny**, in its
broadest interpretation, meant that Americans were a chosen people ordained by God to
create a model society. More specifically, it referred to the territorial expansion of the
United States from the Atlantic to the Pacific. The idea of Manifest Destiny was used to
justify U.S. annexation of Texas, Oregon, New Mexico, and California and later, U.S.
involvement in Cuba, Alaska, Hawaii, and the Philippines. Exhibit 3.1 illustrates when
and by what means the present United States was acquired.

The **Monroe Doctrine**, a cornerstone of U.S. foreign policy, was enunciated by President James Monroe in a public statement proclaiming three basic dicta: no further European colonization in the New World, abstention of the United States from European political affairs, and nonintervention of European governments in the governments of the
Western Hemisphere.

After 1870, interpretation of the Monroe Doctrine became increasingly broad. In 1881,
its principles were evoked in discussing the development of a canal across the Isthmus
of Panama. Theodore Roosevelt applied the Monroe Doctrine with an extension that
became known as the **Roosevelt Corollary**.[7] The corollary stated that not only would the

---

[7]Michael Barone, "A Big Stick," *The U.S. News and World Report,* February 25, 2002, p. 52.

## CROSSING BORDERS 3.2   What Do the Mexican–American War, Ireland, and *Gringo* All Have in Common?

Revered in Mexico, honored in Ireland, and all but forgotten in the United States are the San Patricios (St. Patrick's Battalion). During the Mexican–American War the San Patricios were approximately 250 men, mostly Irish, who made up a battalion of defectors from the U.S. Army and fought for Mexico. During the two-year conflict, the immigrant deserters forged a strong alliance with the Mexicans. Most were executed by the Americans for their pains, but they became a symbol of independence and defense against imperialism.

The San Patricios fought well, but when they ended up back in American hands, 50 of them died by hanging and many others were branded on the right cheek with a two-inch letter *D* for *deserter*. When the war ended, Mexico was forced to cede half its territory to the United States.

The Mexican–American conflict that lasted from 1846 to 1848 may be dismissed as irrelevant "history" north of the border, but not south of it. Every year the

San Patricios are remembered with a ceremony in Mexico City and County Galway, Ireland, home of the brigade's commanding officer.

Now we know what Ireland and the Mexican–American War have in common, but what about the word *gringo*? According to some sources, at day's end the San Patricios would sit around their campfires singing a song called "Green Grow the Lilacs." The story goes that the Mexican soldiers began to refer to their comrades as "los greengrows." To be fair, we should share the other explanation for the derivation of *gringo*: Some historians say the word was used in Spain prior to the discovery of America and was an alteration of *griego* ("Greek") to indicate foreign gibberish or "it's Greek to me."

Source: James Callaghan, "The San Patricios," *American Heritage*, November 1995, p. 58; "The Irish Connection," *Hispanic*, March 2001, p. 20; and "Legend of Los San Patricios," *The News*, March 20, 2001.

United States prohibit non-American intervention in Latin American affairs but it would also police the area and guarantee that Latin American nations met their international obligations. The corollary sanctioning American intervention was applied in 1905 when Roosevelt forced the Dominican Republic to accept the appointment of an American economic adviser, who quickly became the financial director of the small state. It was also used in the acquisition of the Panama Canal Zone from Colombia in 1903 and the formation of a provisional government in Cuba in 1906.

The manner in which the United States acquired the land for the Panama Canal Zone typifies the Roosevelt Corollary—whatever is good for the United States is justifiable. As the Global Perspective at the beginning of this chapter illustrates, the creation of the country of Panama was a total fabrication of the United States. Today such adventures would not be condoned by the United States or its allies, yet it is also true that the United States sent troops to Panama in 1990 to bring Panama's president Noriega to trial, and in 1994, the United States sent more than 20,000 troops to occupy Haiti and return "democracy" there.[8]

According to U.S. history, these Latin American adventures were a justifiable part of our foreign policy; to Latin Americans, they were unwelcome intrusions in Latin American affairs. This perspective has been constantly reinforced by U.S. intervention in Latin America since 1945 (see Exhibit 3.2). The way historical events are recorded and interpreted in one culture can differ substantially from the way those same events are recorded and interpreted in another. From the U.S. view, each of the interventions illustrated in Exhibit 3.2 was justified. A comparison of histories goes a long way in explaining the differences in outlooks and behavior of people on both sides of the border. Many Mexicans believe that their "good neighbor" to the north is not reluctant to throw its weight around when it wants something. There are suspicions that self-interest is the primary motivation for good relations with Mexico.[9]

---

[8]An interesting discussion of the resentment that is building against U.S. foreign military interventions since World War II is found in Chalmers A. Johnson, *Blowback: The Costs and Consequences of American Empire* (New York: Holt, Henry & Company, 2000).

[9]Richard Lambert, "Misunderstanding Each Other," *Foreign Affairs*, March 1, 2003, p. 62.

Members of the San Antonio Living History Association, portraying Alamo defenders, fire a volley marking the final day of battle at the Alamo which fell after a 13-day siege in 1836. To many Texans, San Antonio is the self-proclaimed cradle of Texas freedom, and "Remember the Alamo" has the same emotional meaning as "Viva Mexico" has among many Mexicans. *(AP/Wide World Photos)*

By seeing history from a Latin American perspective, it is understandable how a national leader, under adverse economic conditions, can point a finger at the United States or a U.S. multinational corporation and evoke a special emotional, popular reaction that would divert attention away from the government in power. As a case in point, after the U.S. House of Representatives voted to censure Mexico for drug corruption, President Zedillo was under pressure to take a hard stand with Washington. He used the anniversary of Mexico's 1938 expropriation of the oil industry from foreign companies to launch a strong nationalist attack. He praised the state oil monopoly Pemex as a "symbol of our historical struggles for sovereignty." Union members cheered him on, waving a huge banner that read: "In 1938 Mexico was 'decertified' because it expropriated its oil and it won—today we were decertified for defending our dignity and sovereignty."[10]

The leader might be cheered for expropriation or confiscation of a foreign investment even though the investment was making an important contribution to the economy. To understand a country's attitudes, prejudices, and fears, it is necessary to look beyond the surface of current events to the inner subtleties of the country's entire past for clues. Comments by three Mexicans best summarize this section:

> History is taught one way in Mexico and another way in the United States . . . the U.S. robbed us but we are portrayed in U.S. textbooks as bandits who invaded Texas.

---

[10]Such attitudes continue to hamper relations between the U.S. and Mexico. See Mary Anastasia O'Grady, "Americas: Fears of Yankee Imperialism Inhibit Perimeter Security," *Wall Street Journal,* June 7, 2002, p. A11.

**Exhibit 3.2** U.S. Intervention in Latin America Since 1945

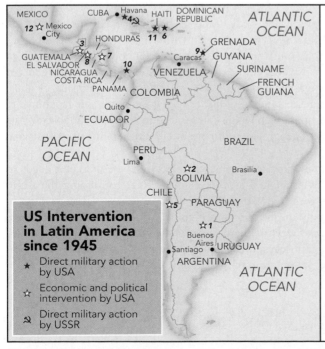

**US Intervention in Latin America since 1945**

★ Direct military action by USA

☆ Economic and political intervention by USA

⚒ Direct military action by USSR

1 USA attempts to thwart election of Perón (1946)

2 Popular Revolution neutralized by US economic pressure (1952)

3 CIA-organized invasion overthrows Arbenz (1954) following expropriation of United Fruit Company lands

4 Nationalist revolution (1959) and alliance with USSR (1960). USA declares economic embargo and CIA organizes failed Bay of Pigs invasion (1961). Cuban Missile Crisis (1962).

5 Covert intervention by USA against elected Marxist government of Popular Unity (1970–73)

6 Military intervention to suppress possible communist influence (1965)

7 Revolution (1979): USA funds counter-revolutionary movement (1980s)

8 Covert intervention by USA to defeat left wing guerrillas (1980–88)

9 US invasion to restore stable government (1983)

10 US invasion to arrest President Noriega on charges of drug trafficking (1989)

11 "Negotiated" US invasion to restore democracy (1994)

12 North American Free Trade Agreement (1994)

Source: *Oxford Atlas of the World,* 10th ed., 2002, (NY: Oxford University Press, 2002), p. 259.

## CROSSING BORDERS 3.3   Microsoft Adapts Encarta to "Local History"

Adapting your product to the local culture is an important strategy for many products. Understanding a country's history helps to achieve that goal. Microsoft has nine different editions reflecting local "history" in order to be sure that its Encarta multimedia encyclopedia on CD-ROM does not contain cultural blunders. As a consequence, it often reflects different and sometimes contradictory understandings of the same historical events. For example, who invented the telephone? In the U.S., U.K., and German editions it's Alexander Graham Bell, but ask the question in the Italian edition and you get an answer of Antonio Meucci, an Italian-American candlemaker who Italians believe beat Bell by five years. For electric lightbulbs, it is Thomas Alva Edison in the United States, but in the United Kingdom it is the British inventor Joseph Swan. Other historical events reflect local perceptions. The nationalization of the Suez Canal, for example, is described in the U.S. edition as a decisive intervention by superpowers. In the French and U.K. editions, it is summed up as a "humiliating reversal" for Britain and France—a phrase that does not appear in the U.S. edition.

Although Microsoft is on the mark by adapting these events to their local historical context, it has, on occasion, missed the boat on geography. South Korean ire was raised when the South Korean island of Ullung-do was placed within Japan's borders and when the Chon-Ji Lake, where the first Korean is said to have descended from heaven, was located in China. And finally, an embarrassed Microsoft apologized to the people of Thailand for referring to Bangkok as a commercial sex center, assuring the women's activists group that protested that the revised version would "include all the great content that best reflects its rich culture and history."

Source: Kevin J. Delaney, "Microsoft's Encarta Has Different Facts for Different Folks," *Wall Street Journal*, June 25, 1999, p. A-1; "Microsoft Apologizes for the Thailand Sex Hub Reference," *Agence France-Presse*, February 23, 2000; and Steve Young and Anand Naidoo, "Microsoft Criticized for Making Correction to Encarta Encyclopedia," *CNN International: World News*, August 22, 2000.

We may not like gringos for historical reasons, but today the world is dividing into commercial blocks, and we are handcuffed to each other for better or worse.

We always have been and we continue to be a colony of the United States.[11]

## Geography and Global Markets

Geography, the study of the earth's surface, climate, continents, countries, peoples, industries, and resources, is an element of the uncontrollable environment that confronts every marketer but which receives scant attention. The tendency is to study the aspects of geography as isolated entities rather than as important causal agents of the marketing environment. Geography is much more than memorizing countries, capitals, and rivers.[12] It also includes an understanding of how a society's culture and economy are affected as a nation struggles to supply its people's needs within the limits imposed by its physical makeup. Thus the study of geography is important in the evaluation of markets and their environment.

This section discusses the important geographic characteristics the marketer needs to consider when assessing the environmental aspects of marketing. Examining the world as a whole provides the reader with a broad view of world markets and an awareness of the effects of geographic diversity on the economic profiles of various nations. Climate and topography are examined as facets of the broader and more important elements of geography. A brief look at the earth's resources and population—the building blocks of world markets—completes the presentation on geography and global markets.

---

[11]"Amid Anti-War Feelings, U.S. Fighting War Myths in Mexico," *Dow Jones International News,* March 27, 2003.

[12]Tony Burdett, "Geographic Ignorance," *Salt Lake Tribune*, March 3, 2000, p. AA2.

**Climate and Topography**

As elements of geography, the climate and physical terrain of a country are important environmental considerations when appraising a market. The effect of these geographic features on marketing ranges from the obvious influences on product adaptation to more profound influences on the development of marketing systems.[13]

Altitude, humidity, and temperature extremes are climatic features that affect the uses and functions of products and equipment. Products that perform well in temperate zones may deteriorate rapidly or require special cooling or lubrication to function adequately in tropical zones. For example, manufacturers have found that construction equipment used in the United States requires extensive modifications to cope with the intense heat and dust of the Sahara Desert. A Taiwanese company sent a shipment of drinking glasses via ship to a buyer in the Middle East. The glasses were packed in wooden crates with hay used as dunnage to prevent breakage. The glasses arrived in shards. Why? When the crates moved to the warmer, less humid climate of the Middle East, the moisture content of the hay dropped significantly and shriveled to a point that it offered no protection.[14]

Within even a single national market, climate can be sufficiently diverse to require major adjustments. In Ghana, a product adaptable to the entire market must operate effectively in extreme desert heat and low humidity and in tropical rain forests with consistently high humidity. Climate differences in Europe caused Bosch-Siemens to alter its washing machines: Because the sun does not shine regularly in Germany or in Scandinavia, washing machines must feature a minimum spin cycle of 1,000 rpm and a maximum approaching 1,600 rpm. Clothes must be dryer coming out of the washer because users do not have the luxury of hanging them out to dry. In Italy and Spain however, clothes can be damp since the abundant sunshine is sufficient to justify a spin cycle speed of 500 rpm.

A thick sandstorm covers the seaside in downtown Beirut. The sandstorm, the worst for 30 years, blanketed the region, limiting visibility and forcing planes to land at other airports. Sandstorms are not uncommon in arid regions and are an important factor when marketing in these areas. (©*Reuters NewMedia Inc./CORBIS*)

Different seasons between the northern and southern hemispheres also affect global strategies. JCPenney had planned to open five stores in Chile as part of its expansion into countries below the equator. It wanted to capitalize on its vast bulk-buying might for its North American, Mexican, and Brazilian stores to provide low prices for its expansion into South America. After opening its first store in Chile, the company realized that the plan was not going to work—when it was buying winter merchandise in North America, it needed summer merchandise in South America. The company quickly sold its one store in Chile; its expansion into South America was limited to Brazil.[15]

South America represents an extreme but well-defined example of the importance of geography in marketing considerations. The economic and social systems there can be explained, in part, in terms of the geographical characteristics of the area. It is a continent 4,500 miles long and 3,000 miles wide at its broadest point. Two-thirds of it is comparable to Africa in its climate, 48 percent of its total area is made up of forest and jungle, and only 5 percent is arable. Mountain ranges cover South America's west coast for 4,500 miles, with an average height of 13,000 feet and a width of 300 to 400 miles. This is a natural, formidable barrier that has precluded the establishment of commercial routes between the Pacific and Atlantic coasts. South America's natural barriers inhibit national growth, trade, and communication. It is a vast land area with population concentrations on the outer periphery and an

---

[13]Peter Coy, "Geography Is Not Destiny," *BusinessWeek*, September 16, 2002, p. 18.

[14]Michael D. White, *International Marketing Blunders* (Novato, CA: World Trade Press, 2002), p. 79.

[15]Miriam Jordan, "Penney Blends Two Business Cultures," *The Wall Street Journal*, April 5, 2001.

**CROSSING BORDERS 3.4** Fog, Fog Everywhere and Water to Drink

When you live in Chungungo, Chile, one of the country's most arid regions with no nearby source of water, you drink fog. Of course! Thanks to a legend and resourceful Canadian and Chilean scientists, Chungungo now has its own supply of drinkable water after a 20-year drought. Before this new source of water, Chungungo depended on water trucks that came twice a week.

Chungungo has always been an arid area, and legend has it that the region's original inhabitants used to worship trees. They considered them sacred because a permanent flow of water sprang from the treetops, producing a constant interior rain. The legend was right—the trees produced rain! Thick fog forms along the coast. As it moves inland and is forced to rise against the hills, it changes into tiny raindrops, which are in turn retained by the tree leaves, producing the constant

source of rain. Scientists set out to take advantage of this natural phenomenon.

The nearby ancient eucalyptus forest of El Tofo hill provided the clue that scientists needed to create an ingenious water-supply system. To duplicate the water-bearing effect of the trees, they installed 86 "fog catchers" on the top of the hill—huge nets supported by 12-foot eucalyptus pillars, with water containers at their base. About 1,900 gallons of water are collected each day and then piped into town. This small-scale system is cheap (about one-fifth as expensive as having water trucked in), clean, and provides the local people with a steady supply of drinking water.

Sources: "Drinking Fog," *World Press Review*; and "Silver Lining," *Economist*, February 5, 2000, p. 75.

isolated and almost uninhabited interior. In Colombia, for example, mountain ranges are a major barrier to travel. The airtime from Bogotá to Medellín, the second-largest city in Colombia, is 30 minutes; by highway, the same trip takes 10 to 12 hours. Other regions of the world with extreme topographic and climatic variations are China, Russia, India, and Canada.

Such physical barriers can pose serious impediments to economic growth and trade. As countries seek economic opportunities and the challenges of the global marketplace, they invest in infrastructure to overcome such physical barriers. The Tunnel across the English Channel and the Oresund Link in Europe, and the Colonia Bridge in South America all reflect the respective country's attempts to ease the burden of geographic barriers.

After more than 200 years of speculation, a tunnel under the English Channel between Britain and France was officially opened in 1994. Historically, the British had resisted a tunnel; they did not trust the French or any other European country and saw the English Channel as protection. But, when they became members of the European Community economic reality meant that the channel tunnel had to be built to facilitate trade with other EU members.

Sweden and Denmark agreed to build a bridge and tunnel across the Baltic Strait to continental Europe. The 10-mile-long Oresund Link, completed in 2000, accommodates freight and high-speed passenger trains and a four-lane motorway that reduces a five-hour trip between Copenhagen and Aarhus, Denmark, to two and a half hours. Ultimately, it will be possible to drive from Lapland in northernmost Scandinavia to Calabria in southern Italy and then on to Sicily once the bridge over the Messina Strait connecting Calabria to Sicily is completed. The Messina Strait suspension bridge will be 2.2 miles long—three times the length of San Francisco's Golden Gate. It will have twelve traffic lanes and two railway lines carrying an estimated 9,000 vehicles an hour and 200 trains a day. [16] These are all tangible symbols that these nations are ending their political isolation from the rest of Europe and are linking themselves economically to the Continent's future and to membership in the European Union.

---

[16]Stephen Jewkes, "Messina Strait Project," *Europe*, October 2002, p. 26.

A commitment among Argentina, Brazil, Paraguay, and Uruguay, members of Mercosur,[17] a fledging common market, has resulted in an agreement to build the Colonia Bridge between Argentina and Uruguay. It will be the longest bridge in the world (a span of 41 km) and will decrease the overall driving distance between Buenos Aires and Montevideo from 342 miles to 154 miles, reducing shipping costs for all member countries.[18] Geographic hurdles have a direct effect on a country's economy, markets, and the related activities of communication and distribution.

## Geography, Nature, and Economic Growth

Always on the slim margin between subsistence and disaster, less-privileged countries suffer disproportionately from natural and human-assisted catastrophes. Climate and topography coupled with civil wars, poor environmental policies, and natural disasters push these countries further into economic stagnation.[19] Without irrigation and water management, droughts, floods, and soil erosion afflict them, often leading to creeping deserts that reduce the long-term fertility of the land. Population increases, deforestation, and overgrazing intensify the impact of drought and lead to malnutrition and ill health, further undermining these countries' abilities to solve their problems.[20] Cyclones cannot be prevented, nor can inadequate rainfall, but there are means to control their effects. Unfortunately, each disaster seems to push these countries further away from effective solutions. Countries that suffer the most from major calamities are among the poorest in the world. Many have neither the capital nor the technical ability to minimize the effects of natural phenomena; they are at the mercy of nature.[21]

As countries prosper, natural barriers are overcome. Tunnels are dug and bridges and dams are built in an effort to control or to adapt to climate, topography, and the recurring extremes of nature.[22] Humankind has been reasonably successful in overcoming or minimizing the effects of geographical barriers and natural disasters, but as they do so they must contend with problems of their own making. The construction of dams is a good example of how an attempt to harness nature for good has a bad side. Developing countries consider dams a cost-effective solution to a host of problems. Dams create electricity, help control floods, provide water for irrigation during dry periods, and can be a rich source of fish. However, there are side effects; dams displace people (the Three Gorges Dam in China will displace 1.2 million people),[23] and silt that ultimately clogs the reservoir is no longer carried downstream to replenish the soil and add nutrients. Similarly, the Narmada valley dam project in India will provide electricity, flood control, and irrigation, but it has already displaced tens of thousands of people, and as the benefits are measured against social and environmental costs, questions of its efficacy are being raised. In short, the need for gigantic projects such as these must be measured against their social and environmental costs.[24]

As the global rush toward industrialization and economic growth accelerates, environmental issues become more apparent. Disruption of ecosystems, relocation of people, inadequate hazardous waste management, and industrial pollution are problems that must be addressed by the industrialized world and those seeking economic development.[25] The problems are mostly by-products of processes that have contributed

---

[17]Mercosur (Southern Cone Common Market) is the common market agreement among Argentina, Brazil, Paraguay, and Uruguay. Mercosur will be discussed in depth in Chapter 10.

[18]For a comprehensive discussion of this project made by an Uruguayan student, visit www.uwc.ca/pearson/ensy/mega/mega.htm and scroll down to Maria de Marco, "Rio de la Plata Crossing.

[19]Yemris Fointuna, "Death Toll in Flores Floods, Landslides Reaches 56," *Jakarta Post*, April 6, 2003.

[20]Peter Moszynski, "Ethiopia: Can Famine Be Avoided?" *New African,* February 2003, p. 30.

[21]Naomi Lubick, "Bid Dam, Big Problem," *Science World,* January 2003, p. 5

[22]"Big Dam To Start Generating Power," *Beijing Review*, February 2, 2003, p. 9

[23]Lynn Neary, "Profile: China Largest Hydroelectric Project and the Effect It Will Have on Some of Country's Citizens," *All Things Considered,"* July 8, 2002.

[24]Donald J. Johnston, "Sustainable Development: Our Common Future," *OECD Observer,* August 29, 2002.

[25]Ian Mackinnon, "India's Big River Plan," *Newsweek (Atlantic Edition),* March 24, 2003, p. 44.

Large trucks are dwarfed by the 185-meter-high sluice gates of the Three Gorges Dam. China began filling the reservoir in a major step toward completion of the world's largest hydroelectric project. The level is expected to reach 135 meters (446 feet), inundating thousands of acres including cities and farms along the Yangtze. (AP/Wide World Photos)

A woman sits in the remains of demolished buildings below a water level marker on the bank of the Yangtze River. Many residents along the banks of the river moved their homes and farmland to higher ground, but were, nevertheless, caught by rising water, which inundated their crops even though the high water level had been announced well in advance. (AP/Wide World Photos)

significantly to economic development and improved lifestyles. During the last part of the twentieth century, there was considerable effort on the part of governments and industry to develop better ways to control nature and to allow industry to grow while protecting the environment.[26]

## Social Responsibility and Environmental Management

Nations, companies, and people reached a consensus during the close of the last decade: Environmental protection is not an optional extra—it is an essential part of the complex process of doing business. Many view the problem as a global issue rather than a national issue and as one that poses common threats to humankind and thus cannot be addressed by nations in isolation. Of special concern to governments and businesses are ways to stem the tide of pollution and to clean up decades of neglect.

Companies looking to build manufacturing plants in countries with more liberal pollution regulations than they have at home are finding that regulations everywhere have gotten stricter. Many governments are drafting new regulations and enforcing existing ones.[27] A strong motivator is the realization that pollution is on the verge of getting completely out of control.[28] An examination of rivers, lakes, and reservoirs in China revealed that toxic substances polluted 21 percent and that 16 percent of the rivers were seriously polluted with excrement.[29]

The very process of controlling industrial wastes leads to another and perhaps equally critical issue: the disposal of hazardous waste, a by-product of pollution controls. Estimates of hazardous wastes collected annually exceed 300 million tons; the critical issue is disposal that does not simply move the problem elsewhere.[30] Countries finding it more difficult to dispose of wastes at home are seeking countries willing to assume the burden

[26]Visit www.gemi.org for information on Global Environmental Management Initiative, an organization of U.S. multinational companies dedicated to environmental protection.

[27]"Impose Stiff Penalties in Toxic Waste Cases," *New Straits Times-Management News*, January 6, 2003.

[28]"Choking Future Awaits Asia's Cities," *New Scientist*, January 25, 2003, p. 13.

[29]Bjorn Lomborg, "How Healthy Is the World?" *British Medical Journal*, December 21, 2002, p. 1416.

[30]D'vora Ben Shaul, "Toxic Waste?—Not in My Backyard," *Jerusalem Post*, February 21, 1999, p. 7.

## CROSSING BORDERS 3.5  Climate and Success

A major food processing company had production problems with a pineapple cannery it built at the delta of a river in Mexico. It built the pineapple plantation upstream and planned to barge the ripe fruit downstream for canning, load them directly on ocean liners, and ship them to the company's various markets. When the pineapples were ripe, however, the company found itself in trouble: Crop maturity coincided with the flood stage of the river. The current in the river during this period was far too strong to permit the backhauling of barges upstream; the plan for transporting the fruit on barges could not be implemented. With no alternative means of transport, the company was forced to close the operation. The new equipment was sold for 5 percent of original cost to a Mexican group that immediately relocated the cannery. A seemingly simple, harmless oversight of weather and navigation conditions was the primary cause for major losses to the company.

Source: David A. Ricks, *Blunders in International Business*, 3rd edition (Cambridge, MA: Blackwell Publishers, 2000), p. 20. Reprinted by permission of Blackwell Publishing. Also found in Michael D. White, *International Marketing Blunders* (Novato, CA: World Trade Press, 2002), p. 82.

Chinese bottle collectors navigate through a trash-infested canal in Beijing. Environmental concerns are being neglected as China attempts to emerge into an industrialized nation. According to recent statistics, five of the 10 cities with the world's worst air pollution are in China, and all of China's major freshwater lakes are polluted. *(AP/Wide World Photos)*

of disposal. Waste disposal is legal in some developing countries as governments seek the revenues that are generated by offering sites for waste disposal. In other cases, illegal dumping is done clandestinely.[31] A treaty among members of the Basel Convention that required prior approval before dumping could occur was later revised to a total ban on the export of hazardous wastes by developed nations. The influence and leadership provided by this treaty are reflected in a broad awareness of pollution problems by businesses and people in general.[32]

Governments, organizations, and businesses are becoming increasingly concerned with the social responsibility and ethical issues surrounding the problem of maintaining economic growth while protecting the environment for future generations. The Organization for Economic Cooperation and Development, the United Nations, the European Union, and international activist groups are undertaking programs to strengthen environmental policies. The issue that concerns all is whether economic development and protection for the environment can coexist. **Sustainable development**, a joint approach among those (governments, businesses, environmentalists, and others) who seek economic growth with "wise resource management, equitable distribution of benefits and reduction of negative efforts on people and the environment from the process of economic growth," is the concept that guides many governments and multinational companies today. Sustainable development is not about the environment or the economy or society. It is about striking a lasting balance between all of these.[33] More and more companies are embracing the idea of sustainable development as a "win-win" opportunity.[34] Responsibility for protecting the environment does not rest solely with governments, businesses, or activist groups, however; each citizen has a social and moral responsibility to include environmental protection among his or her highest goals.[35]

[31]Craig Welch, "U.S. Government Steps Up Pursuit of Ships Illegally Dumping Sludge at Sea," *The Seattle Times*, April 7, 2003.

[32]For a comprehensive view of OECD programs including environmental issues, visit www.oecd.org.

[33]Joke Waller-Hunter, "Sustainable Development," OECD *Observer*, August 5, 2002.

[34]Visit www.oecd.org, the OECD website, for a directory to complete coverage of sustainable development.

[35]Visit www.webdirectory.com for the Amazing Environmental Organization Web Directory, a search engine with links to an extensive list of environmental subjects.

## CROSSING BORDERS 3.6   Garbage without a Country

We have all read or heard the story of "the man without a country," who is sentenced to remain at sea for his entire life, aimlessly wandering the world. Of course, that is just fiction. In real life, however, there is a barge-load of garbage that aimlessly wanders the globe looking for a country that will accept it in its landfills.

Orange rinds, beer bottles, newspapers, and chicken bones—it was trash, like all trash, taken to an incinerator in Philadelphia for incineration. The ashes, like all ashes, were to be taken away to a landfill somewhere in Philadelphia. Joseph Paolino & Sons had a $6 million contract to remove the ash but kept having doors slammed in its face.

Paolino hired Amalgamated Shipping—operator of the *Khian Sea*, a 17-year-old, 466-foot rust bucket registered in Liberia—to dump the ash in the Bahamas, where Amalgamated was based. The Bahamian government rejected the ash, and the *Khian Sea* began its 14-year journey as the Flying Dutchman of debris.

Briefly returning to the United States, it then took off for Puerto Rico, Bermuda, the Dominican Republic, Honduras, Guinea-Bissau, and the Netherlands Antilles. It was turned away again and again. To make the cargo more appealing, the ash was described as "topsoil fertilizer" and the Haitian government agreed to accept the ash. Four thousand tons of ash had been already unloaded when Greenpeace and local activists protested. The Haitian government then ordered the crew to reload the ash, but the ship departed without the ash.

The ship returned to Philadelphia hoping to find a place for the remaining ash but to no avail. They left again seeking a resting place. It sailed to Senegal and Cape Verde, Sri Lanka, Indonesia, and the Philippines, arriving in Singapore empty. Years later, the ship's captain admitted in court that the remaining ash had been dumped in the Atlantic and Indian oceans.

Meanwhile, in Haiti, where the 4,000 tons of ash had been left on the beach, Greenpeace found what was left. Most of the ash had been carried off by wind and water, and Haitians said goats were dying.

After a 16-year odyssey on the cargo ship *Khian Sea*, 2,500 tons of ash from Philadelphia incinerators is on its way back to a final resting place in Pennsylvania where it began its journey. (*AP/Wide World Photos*)

Enter an unlikely hero: New York City. In 1996, to end mob involvement in the city's garbage industry, Mayor Rudolph Giuliani established a Trade Waste commission to oversee the awarding of trash removal. When Eastern Environmental Services applied to do business in New York, the Trade Waste Commission issued an ultimatum: If Eastern wanted to haul trash in New York, it had to deal with the *Khian Sea* ash.

Eastern agreed to find a place in its landfills, and what was left of the ash was loaded on a barge and departed Haiti. Finally, after a 16-year odyssey, Philadelphia agreed to give the ash a final resting place.

Sources: "Wandering Waste's 14-year Journey," *Toronto Star*, May 3, 2000; Molly Hennessy-Fiske, "Unwanted Ash Transferred to One Large, Covered Barge," *Palm Beach Post*, April 30, 2000, p. 1B; Jerry Schwartz, "They Took Out the Garbage, but It Keeps Coming Back," *Oregonian*, September 3, 2000, p. A6; William M. Hartnett, "2,000 Tons of Ash Await Next Leg of 14-Year Odyssey," *Palm Beach Post*, January 7, 2001, p. 1B and "Toxic Waste Returns," *Earth Island Journal*, Winter 2002–2003, p. 12.

**Resources**   The availability of minerals and the ability to generate energy are the foundations of modern technology. The locations of the earth's resources, as well as the available sources of energy, are geographic accidents. The world's nations are not equally endowed, nor does a nation's demand for a particular mineral or energy source necessarily coincide with domestic supply.

In much of the underdeveloped world, human labor provides the preponderance of energy. The principal supplements to human energy are animals, wood, fossil fuel, nuclear power, and to a lesser and more experimental extent, the ocean's tides, geothermal power,

Cattle dung, which is used both as farmyard manure and, dried into cakes, as household fuel, is being carried to a local market in India. India's cattle produce enormous quantities of dung, which some studies suggest provide the equivalent of 10,000 megawatts of energy annually.

and the sun. Of all the energy sources, oil and gas contribute more than 60 percent of world energy consumption. Because of its versatility and the ease with which it is stored and transported, petroleum-related products continue to dominate energy usage. (See Exhibit 3.3.)

Many countries that were self-sufficient during much of their early economic growth have become net importers of petroleum during the past several decades and increasingly depend on foreign sources. A spectacular example is the United States, which was almost completely self-sufficient until 1942, became a major importer by 1950, and between 1973 and 2000 increased its dependency from 36 percent to over 60 percent of its annual requirements.[36] If present rates of consumption continue, predictions are that the United States will be importing over 70 percent of its needs by the mid-2000s; that is more than 17 million barrels of oil each day.[37] Exhibit 3.3 compares North American domestic energy consumption with other world regions. It is interesting to note that although North America is currently a major consumer of energy, industrializing Asia and the three industrialized areas (as shown in Exhibit 3.3) do not lag far behind.

Since World War II, concern for the limitless availability of seemingly inexhaustible supplies of petroleum has become a prominent factor. The dramatic increase in economic growth in the industrialized world and the push for industrialization in the remaining world has put tremendous pressure on the earth's energy resources. This rapid change to market-driven economies and an increasing reliance on petroleum supplies from areas of political instability in three major petroleum-exporting regions—the Middle East, the former Soviet Union, and Latin America—creates a global interdependence of energy resources. This means that political upheavals and price changes will have a profound impact on oil prices[38] and on the economies of the industrialized and industrializing countries.

The location, quality, and availability of resources will affect the pattern of world economic development and trade well into the twenty-first century. In addition to the raw materials of industrialization, there must be an available and economically feasible energy supply to successfully transform resources into usable products. As the global demand for resources intensifies and prices rise, resources will continue to increase in importance among the uncontrollable elements of the international marketer's decisions.

## Dynamics of Global Population Trends
Current population, rural/urban population shifts, rates of growth, age levels, and population control help determine today's demand for various categories of goods. Although not the only determinant, the existence of sheer numbers of people is significant in appraising potential consumer markets. Changes in the composition and distribution of population among the world's countries will profoundly affect future demand.

Recent estimates indicate there are more than 6 billion people in the world, and population is expected to grow to 9.4 billion by 2050. Further, 98 percent of the projected growth for 2050 will occur in less-developed regions.[39] Exhibit 3.4 shows that 83 percent

---

[36]Bob Davis and Bhushan Bahree, "Why the U.S. Is Still Hooked on Oil Imports," *Wall Street Journal-Eastern Edition,* March 18, 2003, A1.

[37]"U.S. Likely to Remain Dependant on Oil for Another Two Decades," *Knight Ridder Washington Bureau,* January 10, 2002.

[38]See "Oil Prices Regain Ground On Talk of Torched Fields, "*Dow Jones Newswires,* March 20, 2003 as an example of the impact of the Iraq war on oil prices.

[39]See "UNFPA State of World Population–2002" *UN Population Fund* can be found at www.unfpa.org.

**Exhibit 3.3**   World Energy Consumption*

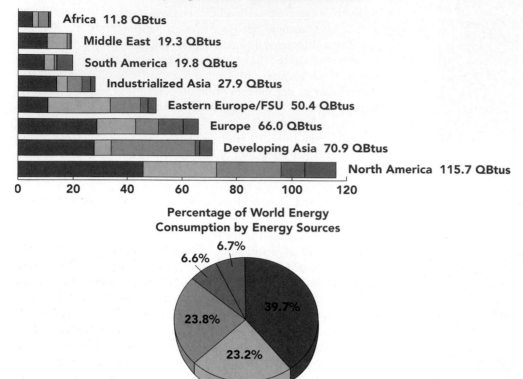

**Total World Energy Consumption
By Region and Fuel (Quadrillion Btu)**

Africa  11.8 QBtus
Middle East  19.3 QBtus
South America  19.8 QBtus
Industrialized Asia  27.9 QBtus
Eastern Europe/FSU  50.4 QBtus
Europe  66.0 QBtus
Developing Asia  70.9 QBtus
North America  115.7 QBtus

0    20    40    60    80    100    120

**Percentage of World Energy
Consumption by Energy Sources**

6.7%
6.6%
39.7%
23.8%
23.2%

■ Oil      □ Gas      ■ Coal
■ Nuclear  ■ Hydro/other

*Energy consumed by world regions, measured in quadrillion BTUs in 1999. Total world consumption was 381.8 quadrillion BTUs. The largest portion of the hydro/other category is hydro electrical energy. Fuels such as wood, peat, animal waste, wind, solar and geothermal account for less than 1.0 Quadrillion BTUs in the other portion of the *hydro/other* category.

Sources: Data compiled from: "Introduction to World Geography," *Oxford Atlas of the World*, (NY: Oxford University Press, 2002) Energy Information Administration (EIA), *International Energy Outlook 2002*, (Washington, DC, December 2001), www.eia.doe.gov/oiaf/ieo.

of the population will be concentrated in less-developed regions by 2025 and, if growth rates continue, 88 percent by 2050. The International Labor Organization estimates that 1.2 billion jobs must be created worldwide by 2025 to accommodate these new entrants. Further, most of the new jobs will need to be created in urban areas where most of the population will reside.[40]

**Controlling Population Growth**

Faced with the ominous consequences of the population explosion, it would seem logical for countries to take appropriate steps to reduce growth to manageable rates, but procreation is one of the most culturally sensitive uncontrollables. Economics, self-esteem, religion, politics, and education all play a critical role in attitudes about family size.

The prerequisites to population control are adequate incomes, higher literacy levels, education for women, universal access to health care, family planning, improved nutrition, and, perhaps most important, a change in basic cultural beliefs regarding the

[40]Peter Auer and Mariangels Fortuny, "Ageing of the Labour Force in OECD Countries; Economic and Social Consequences," Employment Paper 2000/2, International Labour Organization, www.ilo.org/public/english/employment/strat/publ/ep00-2.htm.

**Exhibit 3.4**
World Population by
Region, 2000–2050, and
Life Expectancy at
Birth,1995–2000 (millions)

Source: Compiled from "World
Population Prospects: 2002 Revision,"
United Nations Population Division,
Department of Economic and Social
Information and Policy Analysis, 2003,
www.un.org/popin/(select World
Population).

| Regions | 2000 | 2025 | 2050 | Life Expectancy at Birth 1995–2000 |
|---|---|---|---|---|
| World | 6,070 | 7,851 | 8,919 | 65 |
| More-developed regions* | 1,194 | 1,214 | 1,220 | 75 |
| Less-developed regions† | 4,877 | 6,610 | 7,699 | 63 |
| Least-developed countries‡ | 688 | 1,149 | 1,675 | 49 |
| Africa | 796 | 1,292 | 1,803 | 50 |
| Asia | 3,680 | 4,742 | 5,222 | 66 |
| Europe | 728 | 696 | 632 | 73 |
| Latin America | 520 | 687 | 768 | 69 |
| Northern America | 316 | 394 | 448 | 76 |
| Oceania | 31 | 40 | 46 | 73 |

*More-developed regions comprise all regions of Europe and Northern America, Australia–New Zealand, and Japan.
†Less-developed countries comprise all regions of Africa, Asia (excluding Japan) and Latin America, and the regions of Melanesia, Micronesia, and Polynesia.
‡Least-developed countries as defined by the United Nations General Assembly include 48 countries, of which 33 are in Africa, 9 in Asia, 1 in Latin America, and 5 in Oceania. They are included in less-developed regions.

A farmer rubs his eyes while surveying land that was deforested for agricultural use in northern Brazil. At the behest of environmentalists, the government pledged new controls to reduce deforestation of Brazil's Amazon rain forest which is home to up to 30 percent of the world's animal and plant life. (© *Reuters NewMedia Inc./CORBIS*)

importance of large families. Unfortunately, minimal progress in providing improved living conditions and changing beliefs has occurred. India serves as a good example of what is happening in much of the world. India's population was once fairly stable, but with improved health conditions leading to greater longevity and lower infant mortality, its population will exceed that of China by 2050. The government's attempts to institute change are hampered by a variety of factors, including political ineptitude and slow change in cultural norms. Nevertheless, the government continues to pass laws with the intended purpose of limiting the number of births. The most recent attempt is a law that bars those with more than two children from election to the national Parliament and state assemblies. This would mean that, based on family size, many now in office could not seek reelection.[41]

Perhaps the most important deterrent to population control is cultural attitudes about the importance of large families.[42] In many cultures, the prestige of a man, whether alive or dead, depends on the number of his progeny, and a family's only wealth is its children. Such feelings are strong. Prime Minister Indira Gandhi found out how strong when she attempted mass sterilization of males, which reportedly was the main cause of her defeat in a subsequent election. Additionally, many religions discourage or ban family planning and thus serve as a deterrent to control. Nigeria has a strong Muslim tradition in the north and a strong Roman Catholic tradition in the east, and both faiths favor large families. Most traditional religions in Africa encourage large families; in fact, the principal deity for many is the goddess of land and fertility.

Family planning and all that it entails is by far the most universal means governments use to control birthrates, but many believe that a decline in the fertility rate is a function of economic prosperity and will come only with economic development. There is ample anecdotal evidence that fertility rates decline as economies prosper. For example,

[41]VK Paghunathan, "3 Tykes and You're Out," *Straits Times,* April 11, 2003.

[42]See for example, Jianghong Li and William Lovely, "Village Context, Women's Status, and Son Preference Among Rural Chinese Women," *Rural Sociology,* March 2003, p. 87.

**Exhibit 3.5**
Rural and Urban
Population, 2001–2030
(millions)

Source: Compiled from "World
Population Prospects- The 2001
Revision—1998," United Nations
Population Division, Department of
Economic and Social Information and
Policy Analysis, 2003,
www.un.org/popin/(select World
Population).

| Regions | Urban | | Rural | | Percent Urban | |
|---|---|---|---|---|---|---|
| | 2001 | 2030 | 2001 | 2030 | 2001 | 2030 |
| World | 2,923 | 4,980 | 3,211 | 3,289 | 47.7 | 60.2 |
| More-developed regions* | 902 | 1,005 | 292 | 1,212 | 75.5 | 82.6 |
| Less-developed regions† | 2,002 | 3,976 | 2,919 | 3,078 | 40.9 | 56.4 |
| Least-developed countries‡ | 179 | 582 | 505 | 750 | 26.2 | 43.7 |
| Africa | 307 | 787 | 506 | 702 | 37.7 | 53.0 |
| Asia | 1,414 | 2,679 | 2,307 | 2,271 | 38.0 | 54.1 |
| Europe | 534 | 540 | 192 | 130 | 75.6 | 80.5 |
| Latin America | 399 | 608 | 127 | 116 | 75.8 | 83.2 |
| Northern America | 246 | 335 | 71 | 70 | 77.6 | 84.5 |
| Oceania | 23 | 32 | 8 | 8 | 74.3 | 74.3 |

*More-developed regions comprise all regions of Europe and Northern America, Australia–New Zealand, and Japan.
†Less-developed countries comprise all regions of Africa, Asia (excluding Japan) and Latin America, and the regions of Melanesia, Micronesia, and Polynesia.
‡Least-developed countries as defined by the United Nations General Assembly include 48 countries, of which 33 are in Africa, 9 in Asia, 1 in Latin America, and 5 in Oceania. They are included in less-developed regions.

before Spain's economy began its rapid growth in the 1980s, families had six or more children; now, Spain has one of the lowest birthrates in Europe, an average of 1.24 children per woman. Similar patterns have followed in other European countries as economies prospered.[43]

**Rural/Urban Migration**

Migration from rural to urban areas is largely a result of a desire for greater access to sources of education, health care, and improved job opportunities. In the early 1800s, fewer than 3.5 percent of the world's people were living in cities of 20,000 or more, and fewer than 2 percent in cities of 100,000 or more; today more than 40 percent of the world's people are urbanites, and the trend is accelerating. Once in the city, perhaps three out of four migrants achieve some economic gains. The family income of a manual worker in urban Brazil, for example, is almost five times that of a farm laborer in a rural area.

By 2025, it is estimated that more than 60 percent of the world's population will live in urban areas (see Exhibit 3.5), and at least 27 cities will have populations of 10 million or more, 23 of which will be in the less-developed regions.[44] Tokyo has already overtaken Mexico City as the largest city on Earth, with a population of 26 million, a jump of almost 8 million since 1990.

Although migrants experience some relative improvement in their living standards, intense urban growth without investment in services eventually leads to serious problems. Slums populated with unskilled workers living hand to mouth put excessive pressure on sanitation systems, water supplies,[45] and other social services. At some point, the disadvantages of unregulated urban growth begin to outweigh the advantages for all concerned.

Consider the conditions that exist in Mexico City today. Besides smog, garbage, and pollution brought about by the increased population, Mexico City faces a severe water shortage. Local water supplies are nearly exhausted and in some cases unhealthy.[46] Water

[43]Gautam Naik et.al., "Global Baby Bust," *The Wall Street Journal,* January 24, 2003, p. B1.

[44]For a comprehensive review of the growth of cities and resulting problems, see Erla Zwigle, "Cities," *National Geographic,* November 2002, p. 72.

[45]Dan Vergano, "Water Shortages Could Leave World in Dire Straits," *USA Today,* January 27, 2003.

[46]Rosario Torres Limon, "Drinking Water Source of Death in Mexico—OECD," Reuters, August 12, 2000.

consumption from all sources is about 16,000 gallons per second, but the underground aquifers are producing only 2,640 gallons per second. Water comes from hundreds of miles away and has to be pumped up to an elevation of 7,444 feet to reach Mexico City. This is a grim picture of one of the most beautiful and sophisticated cities in Latin America. Such problems are not unique to Mexico; throughout the developing world, poor sanitation and inadequate water supplies are consequences of runaway population growth.[47] An estimated 1.1 billion people are currently without access to clean drinking water, and 2.8 billion lack access to sanitation services.[48] Estimates are that 40 percent of the world's population, 2.5 billion people, will be without clean water if more is not invested in water resources.[49] Prospects for improvement are not encouraging because most of the world's urban growth will take place in the already economically strained developing countries.[50]

**Population Decline and Aging**

While the developing world faces a rapidly growing population, the industrialized world's population is in decline and rapidly aging. Birthrates in Western Europe[51] and Japan have been decreasing since the early or mid-1960s; more women are choosing careers instead of children, and many working couples are electing to remain childless. As a result of these and other contemporary factors, population growth in many countries has dropped below the rate necessary to maintain present levels. Just to keep the population from falling, a nation needs a fertility rate of about 2.1 children per woman. Not one major country has sufficient internal population growth to maintain itself, and this trend is expected to continue for the next 50 years. Europe's population could decline by as much as 88 million (from 375 million to 287 million) people if present trends continue to 2015.[52]

At the same time that population growth is declining in the industrialized world, there are more aging people today than ever before. Global life expectancy has grown more in the last 50 years than over the previous 5,000 years. Until the Industrial Revolution, no more than 2 or 3 percent of the total population were over the age of 65. Today in the developed world, the over-age-65 group will amount to 14 percent, and by 2030, this group will reach 25 percent in some 30 different countries.[53] Further, the number of "old old" will grow much faster than the "young old." The United Nations projects that by 2050, the number of people aged 65 to 84 worldwide will grow from 400 million to 1.3 billion (a threefold increase), while the number of people ages 85 and over will grow from 26 million to 175 million (a sixfold increase)—and the number aged 100 and over will increase from 135,000 to 2.2 million (a sixteenfold increase). Exhibit 3.6 illustrates the disparity in aging that is typical among lesser-developed countries (Kenya), developing countries (Brazil) and an economically developed country, the United Kingdom (U.K.). Countries like Kenya, with a high proportion of young, face high education and health cost, whereas countries like the U.K., with top-heavy population pyramids, face high pension and healthcare costs for the elderly with fewer wage earners to bear the burden.

Europe, Japan, and the United States epitomize the problems caused by an increasing percentage of elderly people who must be supported by a declining number of skilled workers. In 1998, Japan crossed a threshold anticipated with fear by the rest of the developed

[47]Yoriko Kawaguchi, "Water Is Life," *OECD Observer,* March 19, 2003.

[48]For more details of global water problems, visit www.wateryear2003.org.

[49]Alex Vass, "Over Half the World Will Face Water Shortages by 2032," *British Medical Journal,* June 2002.

[50]Rick Weiss, "Fresh Water Reserves Shrinking, U.N. Says," *LA Times-Washington Post Service,* March 6, 2003.

[51]Birthrates in Britain have dropped to a historic low with women having an average of 1.64 children. In Italy and Spain birthrates have fallen to 1.2 children per woman, in Germany the figure is 1.3, it is 1.4 in Greece, and 1.5 in Switzerland. The U.S. is 1.99, just below maintenance levels. "Birth Rate Drops to the Lowest Ever," *Daily Mail,* December 12, 2002.

[52]Mark Henderson, "Europe Shrinking As Birthrates Decline," *The Times,* March 28, 2003.

[53]Naik Gautam, "Leveraging the Age Gap," *The Wall Street Journal,* February 27, 2003, p. B1.

**Exhibit 3.6**    Age Density for World and Selected Countries

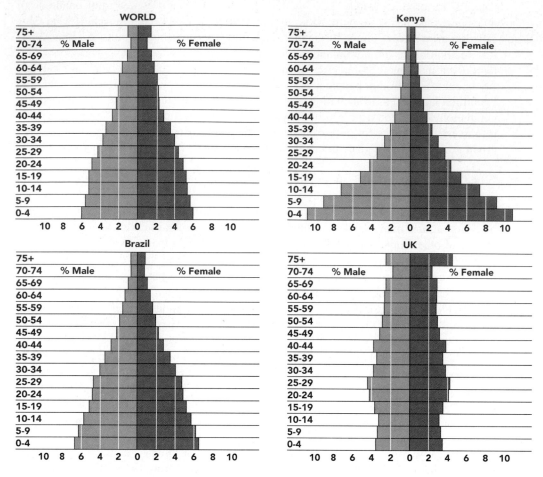

Source: *Oxford Atlas of the World*, 10th ed., 2002, (NY: Oxford University Press, 2002), p. 259.

world: the point at which there are more retirees withdrawing funds from the pension system than there are workers contributing to it.[54] The elderly require higher government outlays for health care and hospitals, special housing and nursing homes, and pension and welfare assistance, but the workforce that supports these costs is dwindling. The part of the world with the largest portion of people over age 65 is also the part of the world with the fewest number of people under age 15. This means that there will be fewer workers to support future retirees. The result will either be to place an intolerable tax burden on future workers, to force more of the over-65 group to remain in the labor force, or to create pressure to change existing laws to allow mass migration to stabilize the worker/retiree ratio. Every solution has its problems.

**Worker Shortage and Immigration**

For most countries mass immigration is not well received by the resident population. However, a recent report from the United Nations makes the strongest argument for change in immigration as a viable solution. The free flow of immigration will help to ameliorate the dual problems of explosive population expansion in less-developed countries and worker shortage in industrialized regions. Europe is the region of the world most affected by aging and thus has a steadily decreasing worker/retiree ratio. The proportion of older persons will increase from 20 percent in 1998 to 35 percent in 2050. The country with the largest share of old people will be Spain, closely followed by Italy.

---

[54]Sebastian Moffett, "Going Gray: For Ailing Japan, Longevity Begins to Take Its Toll," *The Wall Street Journal*, February 11, 2003, p. A1.

## CROSSING BORDERS 3.7  Where Have All the Women Gone?

Three converging issues in China have the potential of causing a serious gender imbalance by the early 2000s:

- China, the world's most populous country, has a strict one-child policy to curb population growth.
- Traditional values dictate male superiority and a definite parental preference for boys.
- Prenatal scanning allows women to discover the sex of their fetuses and thereby abort unwanted female fetuses.

As a consequence, Chinese statisticians have begun to forecast a big marriage gap for the generation born in the late 1980s and early 1990s. In 1990, China recorded 113.8 male births for every 100 female births, far higher than the natural ratio of 106 to 100. The result, according to the World Health Organization, is that China is short 50 million females. The first wave of children born under the policy is reaching marriageable ages and there are far too few brides to go around. So what is a desperate bachelor to do?

The shortage has prompted some parents to acquire babies as future brides for their sons. Infants are considered more appealing because they are less likely to run away, will look on their buyers as their own parents, and are cheaper than buying a teenage bride.

As a result there is trade in baby girls abducted or bought from Chinese farm families and sold to others who want a daughter, a servant, or a future bride for a son. The discovery of 28 baby girls, none older than 3 months, packed in nylon tote bags aboard a long-distance bus was a striking example of the trade. Buying a baby girl can cost as little as $100 and won't result in the fines imposed on couples who violate birth control limits, which can equal as much as six years' income.

Another alternative is to marry a relative. At age 20, with his friends already paired off, Liu found himself the odd man out. His parents, farmers in a small backwater village, could not raise the $2,000 required to attract a bride for their son. Desperate, Liu's mother asked her sister for a favor: Could she ask Hai, her daughter, to be Liu's bride? Young women like Hai are not apt to defy their parents, and so Liu and Hai were wed.

Sources: "Sex Determination Before Birth," Reuters News Service, May 3, 1994; "Seven Times as Many Men," AP News Service, March 31, 1994; Hannah Beech, "With Women So Scarce, What Can Men Do?, *Time Canada*, July 2002, p. 8; and Joe McDonald, "Chinese Trade in Baby Girls Thrives," *AP Online*, March 25, 2003.

---

Recognizing the problem Spain has changed immigration laws to open their borders to all South Americans of Spanish descent.[55] To keep the worker/retiree ratio from falling, Europe will need 1.4 billion immigrants during the next 50 years, whereas Japan and the United States will need 600 million immigrants between now and 2050. Immigration will not help to ameliorate the problem if political and cultural opposition to immigration cannot be overcome.

The trends of increasing population in the developing world with substantial shifts from rural to urban areas, declining birthrates in the industrialized world, and global population aging will have profound effects on the state of world business and world economic conditions. Unless there are successful adjustments to these trends,[56] many countries will experience slower economic growth, serious financial problems for senior retirement programs, and further deterioration of public and social services, leading to possible social unrest.[57]

## World Trade Routes

Trade routes bind the world together, minimizing distance, natural barriers, lack of resources, and the fundamental differences between peoples and economies. As long as one group of people in the world wants something that another group somewhere else has and there is a means of travel between the two, there is trade. Early trade routes were

---

[55]"Spain Opens Migrant Floodgates," *the Australian*, January 15, 2003.

[56]Will Leibfritz, Retiring Later Makes Sense," *OECD Observer*," January 13, 2003.

[57]See, for example, Zachary Zimmer and Julia Kwong, "Family Size and Support of Older Adults in Urban and Rural China: Current Effects and Future Implications," *Demography*, February 2003, p. 23.

## Exhibit 3.7
### 500 Years of Trade

U.S. negotiators seem miffed that Latin American countries didn't trip all over themselves to forge a free trade zone of the Americas pact. Indeed, the U.S. team blamed Brazil for the pact's failure to move further along.

But the United States often fails to recognize that many Latin American countries have strong relationships with Europe, Asia, and the rest of the world—and these relationships were in place long before the United States even existed.

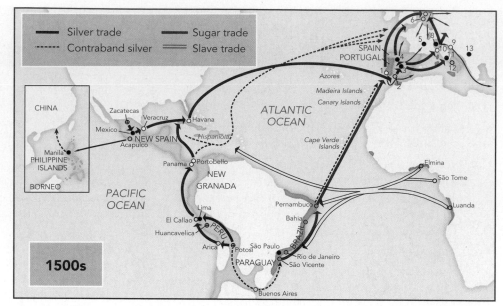

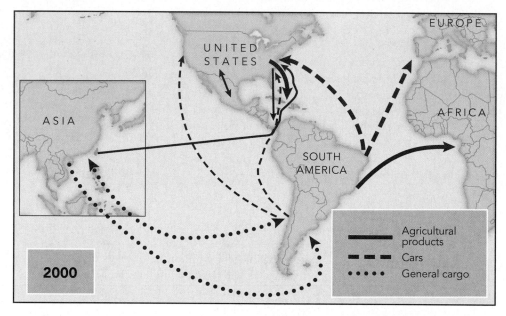

overland;[58] later came sea routes, air routes, and finally, some might say, the Internet to connect countries.[59]

As Exhibit 3.7 illustrates, trade routes among Europe, Asia, and the Americas were well established by the 1500s. The Spanish empire founded the city of Manila in the Philippines to receive its silver-laden galleons bound for China. On the return trip the ship's cargo of silk and other Chinese goods would be off-loaded in Mexico, carried overland to the Atlantic, and put on Spanish ships to Spain. What we sometimes fail to recognize is that these same trade routes remain important today and that many Latin American countries have strong relationships with Europe, Asia, and the rest of

---

[58]For a short history of the silk road, see Ann Saccomano, "The Great Trade Routes," *World Trade*, January 1, 2002.

[59]At least among some importers and exporters the Web is considered as vital a business tool as trucks, ships, planes, trains, and automobiles. See, for example, Teresa M. McAleavy, "Importers, Exporters Learn to Spin a Wide Web in Rochelle Park, N.J.," *The Record*, September 19, 2002.

A young man using a mobile phone to order a bottle of Coke from a vending machine at Sydney's Central Railway station: In the first of its kind in Australia, Telstra Corp Ltd., Australia's largest telecoms carrier, and global drinks giant Coca-Cola are testing a new service called "Dial a Coke," in which Telstra mobile customers grab a drink from a vending machine and have the A$2 (US $0.97) billed to their phones. One can only imagine the innovations that will emerge over the next few decades. (*©Reuters NewMedia Inc./CORBIS*)

the world that date back to the 1500s. The commodities traded have changed between 1500 and 2003 but trade and the trade routes continue to be important. Today, instead of off-loading goods in Mexico and carrying them on mule carts overland to the Atlantic, ships travel from the Pacific to the Atlantic via the Panama Canal. Ships that are too large for the canal off-load their containers onto a railroad that crosses the Isthmus of Panama to another container ship.[60]

Trade routes represent the attempts of countries to overcome economic and social imbalances created in part by the influence of geography. The majority of world trade occurs among the most industrialized and industrializing countries of Europe, North America, and Asia. It is no surprise that the major sea-lanes and the most developed highway and rail systems, as seen in Map 8, link these major trading areas. It is interesting to note the volume of airfreight between major industrial centers and less-developed countries. Although surface and sea dominate international freight movements, airfreight is extremely important for countries that do not have access to navigable waters and/or with inadequate surface transportation. Air transportation has made otherwise isolated parts of the world reasonably accessible.

Various means of modern transportation are vital to global trade and are critical in overcoming the impediments of geography. Moving people, goods, and services across continents, improving living standards, and spreading knowledge are directly related to transportation, whether by foot, animal, sail, or other means. As countries trade, knowledge and ideas—the basis of economic growth—are also exchanged.

## Communication Links
An underpinning of all commerce is effective communications—knowledge of where goods and services exist and where they are needed and the ability to communicate instantaneously across vast distances. Facilitating the expansion of trade have been continuous improvements in electronic communications. First came the telegraph, then the telephone, television, satellites, the computer, and the Internet. Each revolution in electronic technology has had a profound effect on human condition, economic growth, and the manner in which commerce functions. Each new communications technology has spawned new business models; some existing businesses have reinvented their practices to adapt to the new technology, while other businesses have failed to respond and thus ceased to exist.[61] The Internet revolution will be no different; it too affects human condition, economic growth, and the manner in which commerce operates. As will be discussed in subsequent chapters, the Internet is already shaping how international business is managed. However, as the Internet and other electronic technology permeate the fabric of the world's cultures, the biggest changes are yet to come!

---

[60]Larry Luxner, "New Tracks for the Panama Canal," *Americas*, September/October 2001, p. 5.

[61]For an interesting and insightful review of the impact information and communication technology will have on how business operates, see Jose de la Torre and Richard W. Moxon, "Introduction to the Symposium E-Commerce and Global Business: The Impact of the Information and Communication Technology Revolution on the Conduct of International Business," *Journal of International Business Studies*, 2001, 4th Quarter, vol. 32, no. 4, p. 617.

# Summary

One British authority admonishes foreign marketers to study world geography until "the mere mention of a town, country, or river enables it to be picked out immediately on the map." Although it may not be necessary for the student of foreign marketing to memorize the world map to that extent, a prospective international marketer should be reasonably familiar with the world, its climate, and topographic differences. Otherwise, the important marketing characteristics of geography could be completely overlooked when marketing in another country. The need for geographical and historical knowledge goes deeper than being able to locate continents and their countries. Geographic hurdles must be recognized as having a direct effect on marketing and the related activities of communications and distribution. For someone who has never been in a tropical rain forest with an annual rainfall of at least 60 inches (and sometimes more than 200 inches), it is difficult to anticipate the need for protection against high humidity. Likewise, it is hard to comprehend the difficult problems caused by dehydration in constant 100-degrees-plus heat in the Sahara region. Indirect effects from the geographical ramifications of a society and culture may be ultimately reflected in marketing activities. Many of the peculiarities of a country (i.e., peculiar to the foreigner) would be better understood and anticipated if its history and geography were studied more closely. Without a historical understanding of a culture, the attitudes within the marketplace may not be fully understood.

Aside from the simpler and more obvious ramifications of climate and topography, there are complex historical and geographical influences on the development of the general economy and society of a country. In this case, the need for studying history and geography is to provide the marketer with an understanding of why a country has developed as it has rather than as a guide for adapting marketing plans. History and geography are two of the environments of foreign marketing that should be thoroughly understood and that must be included in foreign marketing plans to a degree commensurate with their influence on marketing effort.

# Questions

1. Define the following terms:

   Manifest Destiny, 61          Roosevelt Corollary, 61
   Monroe Doctrine, 61           sustainable development, 69

2. Why study geography in international marketing? Discuss.

3. Why study a country's history? Discuss

4. How does an understanding of history help an international marketer?

5. Why is there a love-hate relationship between Mexico and the United States? Discuss.

6. Some say the global environment is a global issue rather than a national one. What does this mean? Discuss.

7. Pick a country and show how employment and topography affect marketing within the country.

8. Pick a country (other than Mexico) and show how significant historical events have affected the country's culture.

9. Discuss the bases of world trade. Give examples illustrating the different bases.

10. The marketer "should also examine the more complex effect of geography on general market characteristics, distribution systems, and the state of the economy." Comment.

11. The world population trend is shifting from rural to urban areas. Discuss the marketing ramifications.

12. Select a country with a stable population and one with a rapidly growing population. Contrast the marketing implications of these two situations.

13. "World trade routes bind the world together." Discuss.

14. Discuss how your interpretation of Manifest Destiny and the Monroe Doctrine might differ from a Latin American's.

15. The telegraph, telephone, television, satellites, computer, and the Internet have all affected how international business operates. Discuss how each of these communications innovations affects international business management.

# world maps

1 **The World**

ALASKA
(United States)

CANADA

GREENLAND
(Denmark)

Greenland
Sea

Norwegian
Sea

Reykjavik
ICELAND

North
Sea

NORW

SWED

Oslo
Sto

DEN.

Berlin

NETH.

GERM

Dublin
IRELAND

UNITED
KINGDOM

BELG.

London

SWITZ

English Channel

Paris

ITAL

FRANCE

UNITED   STATES

Montreal

Toronto

Detroit

Chicago

Philadelphia

Boston

New York

Washington

San Francisco

PORTUGAL

Madrid

SPAIN

Lisbon

Los Angeles

AZORES
(Portugal)

Strait of Gibraltar

Algiers

Tunis

Casablanca

TUN

ATLANTIC
OCEAN

Dallas

Houston

MEXICO

Monterrey

MOROCCO

CANARY IS.
(Spain)

ALGERIA

Miami

BAHAMAS

WESTERN
SAHARA
(Morocco)

Mexico City

CUBA

DOMINICAN
REPUBLIC

MAURITANIA

MALI

BELIZE

HAITI

GUADELOUPE

Nouakchott

NIO

HONDURAS

JAMAICA

DOMINICA

CAPE VERDE

Dakar

GUATEMALA

PUERTO
RICO
(U.S.)

ST. LUCIA

SENEGAL

Bamako

BURKINA
FASO

Niam

EL SALVADOR

NICARAGUA

GAMBIA

Bissau

GUINEA-
BISSAU

GUINEA

NIGE

COSTA
RICA

Caracas

TRINIDAD &
TOBAGO

SIERRA LEONE

Conakry

CÔTE
D'IVOIRE

GHANA

Ab

BENI

PANAMA

Bogota

VENEZUELA

GUYANA

Monrovia

LIBERIA

SURINAME

TOGO

COLOMBIA

FRENCH GUIANA
(France)

EQUATORIAL
GUINEA

ECUADOR

SAO TOME &
PRINCIPE

CABIN
(Ang

PERU

BRAZIL

ATLANTIC
OCEAN

PACIFIC
OCEAN

Lima

HAWAII
(United States)

BOLIVIA

Belo Horizonte

PARAGUAY

Sao Paulo

Rio de Janeiro

Porto Alegre

CHILE

Buenos Aires

URUGUAY

ARGENTINA

FALKLAND
ISLANDS
(U.K.)

| 3 A.M. | 4 A.M. | 5 A.M. | 6 A.M. | 7 A.M. | 8 A.M. | 9 A.M. | 10 A.M. | 11 A.M. | 12 P.M. | 1 P.M. | 2 P.M. | 3 |

## 2 Environment

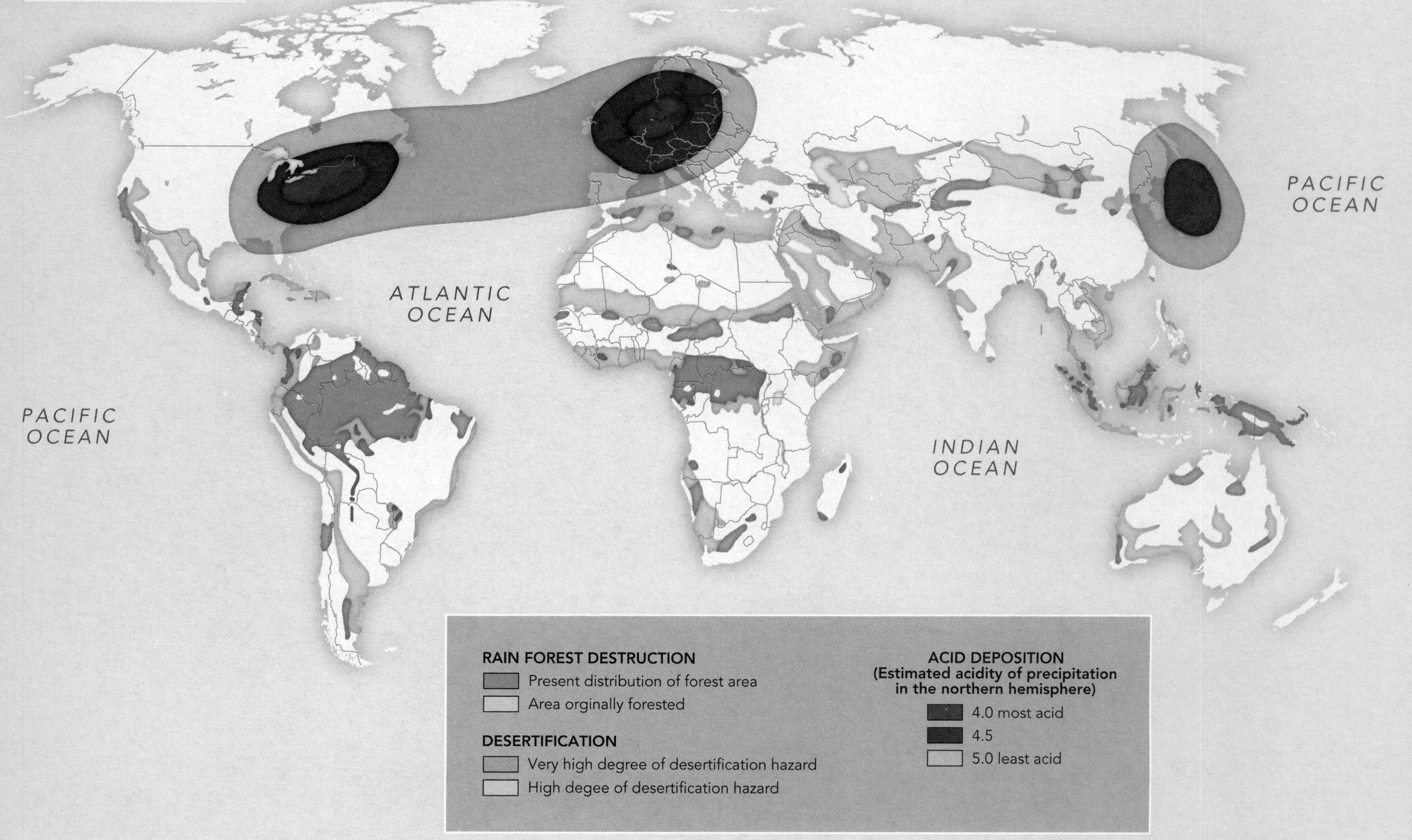
PACIFIC OCEAN
ATLANTIC OCEAN
PACIFIC OCEAN
INDIAN OCEAN
RAIN FOREST DESTRUCTION
Present distribution of forest area
Area orginally forested
DESERTIFICATION
Very high degree of desertification hazard
High degee of desertification hazard
ACID DEPOSITION
(Estimated acidity of precipitation in the northern hemisphere)
4.0 most acid
4.5
5.0 least acid

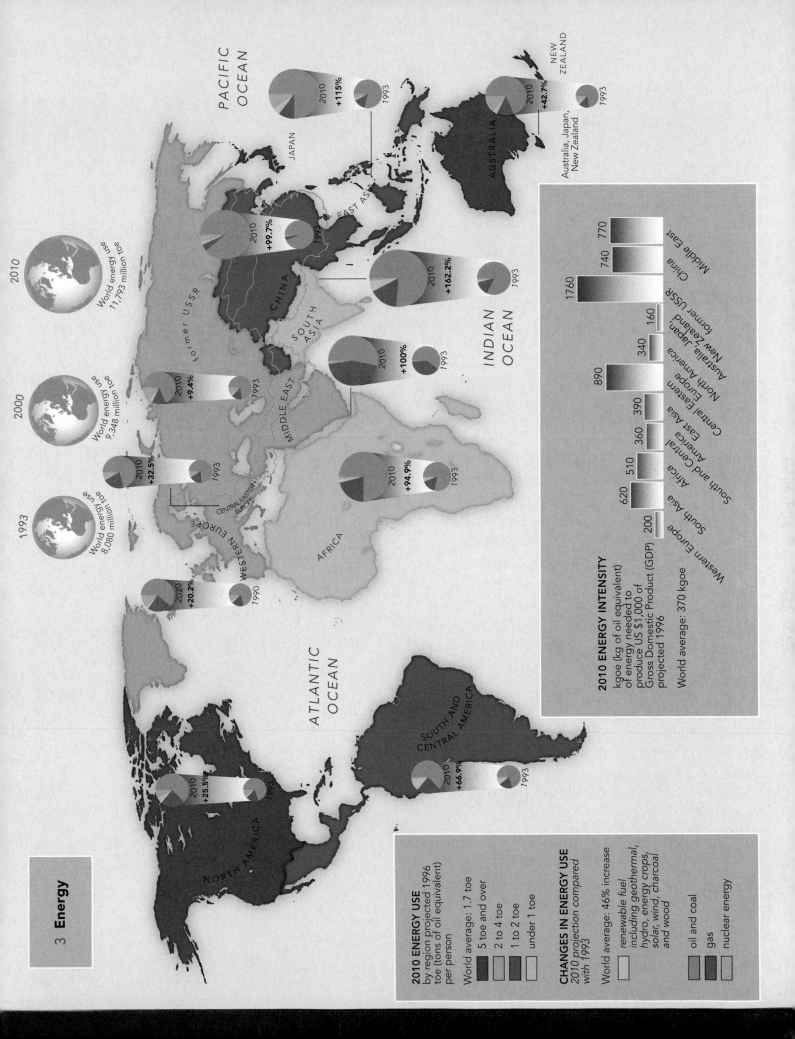

3 **Energy**

PACIFIC OCEAN

2010 — World energy use 11,793 million toe

2000 — World energy use 9,348 million toe

1993 — World energy use 8,080 million toe

JAPAN — 2010 +115% — 1993

NEW ZEALAND — 2010 +42.7% — 1993

AUSTRALIA

Australia, Japan, New Zealand

EAST ASIA

former USSR

CHINA — 2010 +99.7% — 1993

SOUTH ASIA — 2010 +162.2% — 1993

MIDDLE EAST — 2010 +100% — 1993

2010 +9.4% — 1993

CENTRAL EASTERN EUROPE — 2010 +32.5% — 1993

WESTERN EUROPE

AFRICA — 2010 +94.9% — 1993

INDIAN OCEAN

2020 +20.2% — 1990

ATLANTIC OCEAN

NORTH AMERICA — 2010 +25.5% — 1993

SOUTH AND CENTRAL AMERICA — 2010 +66.9% — 1993

**2010 ENERGY INTENSITY**

kgoe (kg of oil equivalent)
of energy needed to
produce US $1,000 of
Gross Domestic Product (GDP)
projected 1996

World average: 370 kgoe

Western Europe — 200
South Asia — 620
Africa — 510
South and Central America — 360
East Asia — 390
Central Eastern Europe — 890
North America — 340
Australia, Japan, New Zealand — 160
former USSR — 1760
China — 740
Middle East — 770

**2010 ENERGY USE**
by region projected 1996
toe (tons of oil equivalent)
per person

World average: 1.7 toe

5 toe and over
2 to 4 toe
1 to 2 toe
under 1 toe

**CHANGES IN ENERGY USE**
2010 projection compared
with 1993

World average: 46% increase

renewable fuel
including geothermal,
hydro, energy crops,
solar, wind, charcoal
and wood

oil and coal
gas
nuclear energy

# 4 Water

## THE WORLD'S WATER
1993 percentages

salt water 97.5%

fresh water 2.5%

69% glaciers and permanent snow cover

30% fresh groundwater

0.9% other, including soil moisture, ground ice and swamp water

0.3% freshwater lakes and river flows

## WATER SHORTAGES
proportion of world's population facing water shortages 1995 and 2050

**1995**
relative sufficiency 92%
stress 5%
scarcity 3%
world population 5.7 billion

**2050**
relative sufficiency 58%
stress 24%
scarcity 18%
world population 9.4 billion

## 2050 FRESH WATER
Availability per person per year cubic meters
projected 1997
borders 1998

**water scarcity:** under 1,000 cubic meters per person
chronic water shortages impede economic development and cause environmental degradation

**water stress:** 1,000–1,700 cubic meters per person
chronic and widespread water supply problems

**relative water sufficiency:** over 1,700 cubic meters per person
intermittent or localized shortages

relative sufficiency in 1995 although shortage predicted for 2050

Note: Based on UN population data 1996

CANADA
U.S.A.
MEXICO
GUATEMALA
EL SALVADOR
COSTA RICA
BELIZE
HONDURAS
NICARAGUA
PANAMA
CUBA
JAMAICA
HAITI
DOM REP
BARBADOS
COLOMBIA
ECUADOR
PERU
VENEZUELA
GUYANA
SURINAME
FRENCH GUIANA (Fr.)
BRAZIL
BOLIVIA
PARAGUAY
CHILE
ARGENTINA
URUGUAY
FALKLAND ISLANDS (U.K.)

ICELAND
IRELAND
U.K.
PORTUGAL
SPAIN
FRANCE
NORWAY
SWEDEN
FINLAND
DENMARK
NETH.
BEL.
LUX.
GERMANY
SWITZ.
ITALY
MALTA
TUNISIA
EST.
LAT.
LITH.
POLAND
BELARUS
UKRAINE
CZECH
SLOV.
AUS.
HUNG.
SLO.
CRO.
B-H.
S-M.
MACE.
ALB.
GREECE
ROMANIA
BULG.
MOL.
TURKEY
CYPRUS
SYRIA
LEB.
ISRAEL
JOR.

MOROCCO
WESTERN SAHARA (Morocco)
MAURITANIA
MALI
NIGER
CHAD
ALGERIA
LIBYA
EGYPT
SUDAN
SENEGAL
GAMBIA
GUINEA-BISSAU
CAPE VERDE
GUINEA
SIERRA LEONE
LIBERIA
COTE D'IVOIRE
BURKINA FASO
GHANA
TOGO
BENIN
NIGERIA
CAMEROON
EQ. GUINEA
GABON
CONGO
CENT. AFR. REP.
ETHIOPIA
ERITREA
DJIBOUTI
SOMALIA
KENYA
UGANDA
RWA.
BUR.
DEM. REP. OF THE CONGO
TANZANIA
ANGOLA
ZAMBIA
MALAWI
MOZAMBIQUE
ZIMB.
BOTSWANA
NAMIBIA
SWAZILAND
LESOTHO
SOUTH AFRICA
MADAGASCAR
COMOROS
MAURITIUS

RUSSIA
MONGOLIA
CHINA
KAZAKHSTAN
UZBEKISTAN
TURKMENISTAN
KYRGYSTAN
TAJ.
GEORGIA
ARM.
AZER.
IRAN
IRAQ
KUWAIT
SAUDI ARABIA
BAHRAIN
QATAR
U.A.E.
OMAN
YEMEN
AFGHANISTAN
PAKISTAN
NEPAL
INDIA
SRI LANKA

## 5 Telecommunications

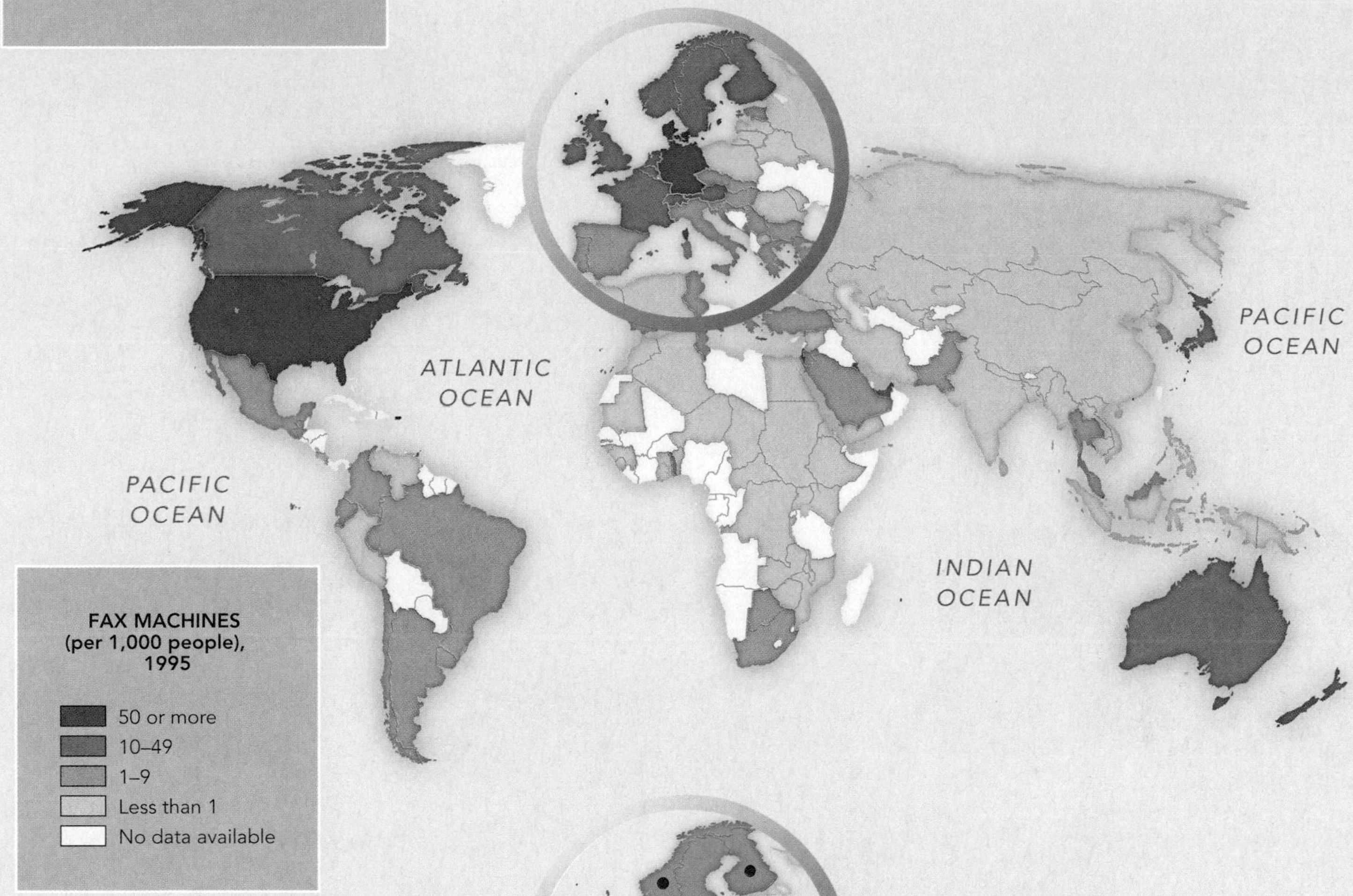

ATLANTIC OCEAN
PACIFIC OCEAN
PACIFIC OCEAN
INDIAN OCEAN
FAX MACHINES (per 1,000 people), 1995
50 or more
10–49
1–9
Less than 1
No data available

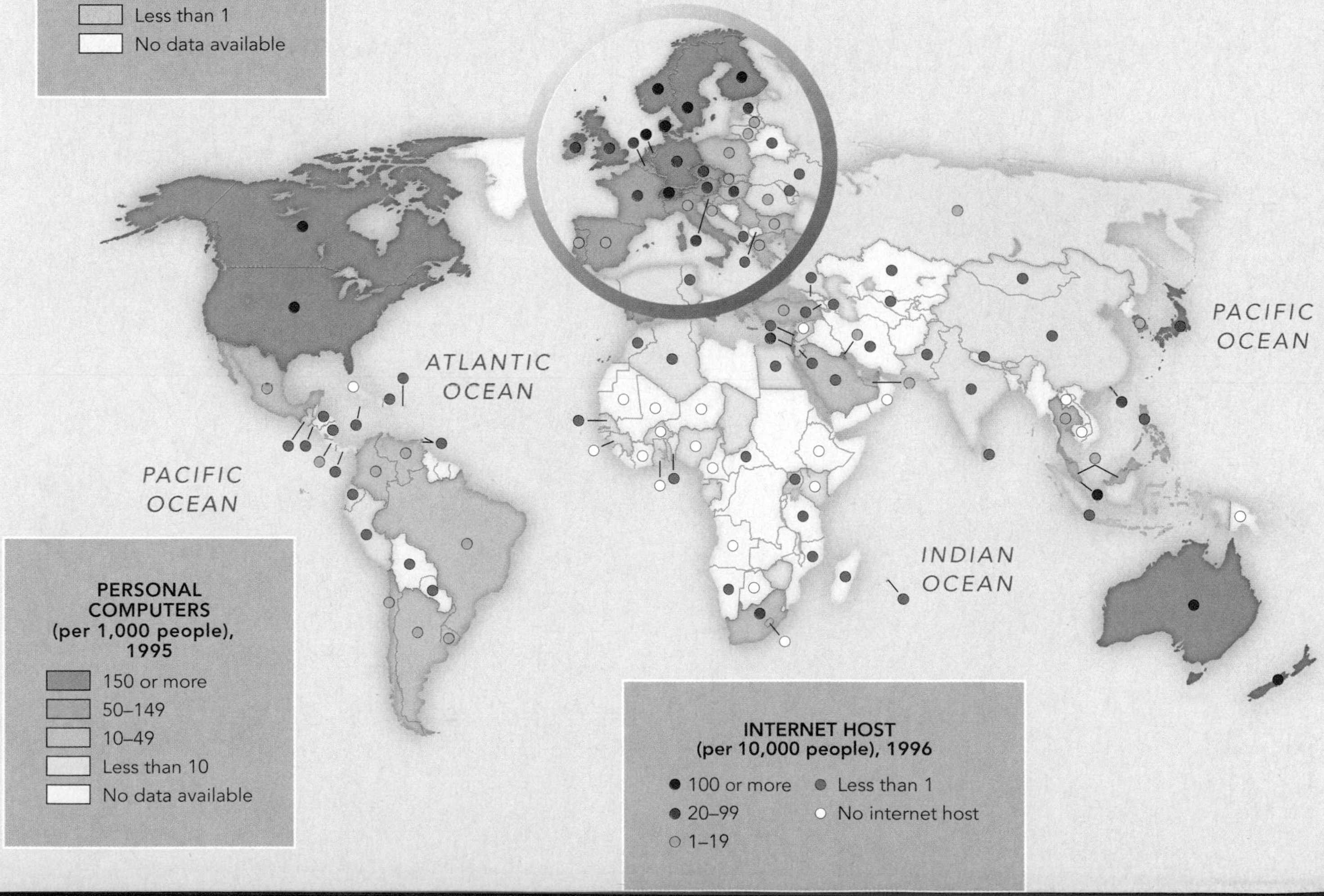

ATLANTIC OCEAN
PACIFIC OCEAN
PACIFIC OCEAN
INDIAN OCEAN
PERSONAL COMPUTERS (per 1,000 people), 1995
150 or more
50–149
10–49
Less than 10
No data available
INTERNET HOST (per 10,000 people), 1996
100 or more
20–99
1–19
Less than 1
No internet host

PACIFIC OCEAN

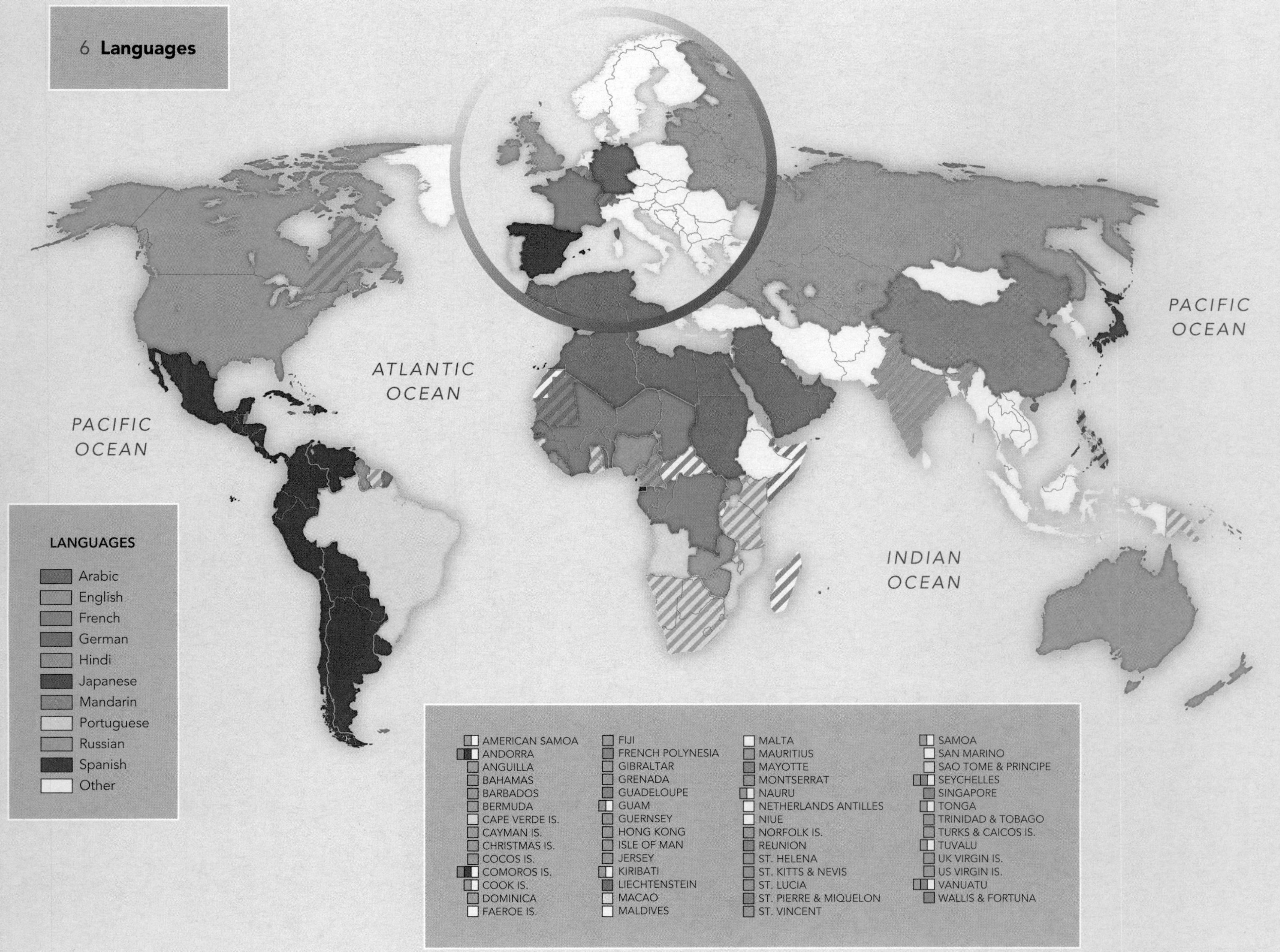

PACIFIC OCEAN

ATLANTIC OCEAN

INDIAN OCEAN

**LANGUAGES**

Arabic
English
French
German
Hindi
Japanese
Mandarin
Portuguese
Russian
Spanish
Other

AMERICAN SAMOA
ANDORRA
ANGUILLA
BAHAMAS
BARBADOS
BERMUDA
CAPE VERDE IS.
CAYMAN IS.
CHRISTMAS IS.
COCOS IS.
COMOROS IS.
COOK IS.
DOMINICA
FAEROE IS.

FIJI
FRENCH POLYNESIA
GIBRALTAR
GRENADA
GUADELOUPE
GUAM
GUERNSEY
HONG KONG
ISLE OF MAN
JERSEY
KIRIBATI
LIECHTENSTEIN
MACAO
MALDIVES

MALTA
MAURITIUS
MAYOTTE
MONTSERRAT
NAURU
NETHERLANDS ANTILLES
NIUE
NORFOLK IS.
REUNION
ST. HELENA
ST. KITTS & NEVIS
ST. LUCIA
ST. PIERRE & MIQUELON
ST. VINCENT

SAMOA
SAN MARINO
SAO TOME & PRINCIPE
SEYCHELLES
SINGAPORE
TONGA
TRINIDAD & TOBAGO
TURKS & CAICOS IS.
TUVALU
UK VIRGIN IS.
US VIRGIN IS.
VANUATU
WALLIS & FORTUNA

7 Religions

RELIGIONS

- Atheism (and Communism)
- Buddhism
- Hindu
- Muslim
- Traditional/Tribal
- Others
- Christian (Orthodox)
- Christian (no major sect)
- Christian (Protestant)
- Christian (Roman Catholic)

- Christian (no major sect), Muslim, Hindu
- Christian (no major sect), Traditional, Buddhism
- Christian (no major sect), Traditional, Hindu, Muslim
- Christian (no major sect), Christian (Roman Catholic), Hindu, Muslim, Others
- Christian (Roman Catholic), Buddhism, Others

- Christian (Roman Catholic), Muslim, Traditional
- Christian (no major sect), Muslim, Traditional
- Christian (Orthodox), Muslim, Atheism
- Christian (Roman Catholic), Muslim, Others

PACIFIC OCEAN

ATLANTIC OCEAN

INDIAN OCEAN

PACIFIC OCEAN

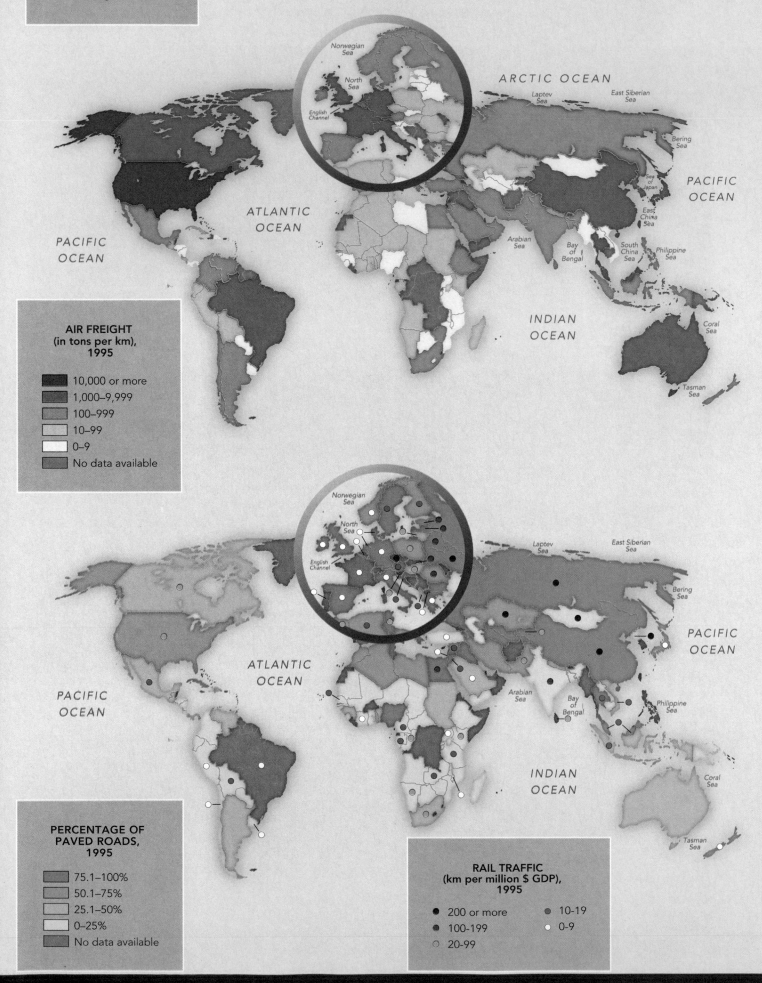

**AIR FREIGHT**
(in tons per km),
1995

- 10,000 or more
- 1,000–9,999
- 100–999
- 10–99
- 0–9
- No data available

**PERCENTAGE OF PAVED ROADS, 1995**

- 75.1–100%
- 50.1–75%
- 25.1–50%
- 0–25%
- No data available

**RAIL TRAFFIC**
(km per million $ GDP),
1995

- 200 or more
- 100-199
- 20-99
- 10-19
- 0-9

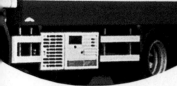

## CHAPTER 4

# cultural Dynamics in Assessing Global Markets

**CHAPTER LEARNING OBJECTIVES**

What you should learn from Chapter 4:

- The importance of culture to an international marketer

- The origins and elements of culture

- The impact of cultural borrowing

- The strategy of planned change and its consequences

# Global Perspective

## EQUITIES AND eBAY—CULTURE GETS IN THE WAY

One trillion dollars! That's about a hundred trillion yen. Either way you count, it's a lot of money. American brokerage houses such as Fidelity Investments, Goldman Sachs, and Merrill Lynch rushed new investment products and services to market in Japan to try to capture the huge capital outflow expected from ten-year time deposits held in the Japanese postal system. Liberalization of Japan's capital markets in recent years now gives Japanese more freedom of choice in their investments. Post office time deposits still yield about a 2 percent return in Japan, and bank savings yields have been around zero. By American e-trading standards, that means an electronic flood of money moving out of the post offices and into the stock markets. Right?

However, Japan is not America. There is no American-style risk-taking culture among Japanese investors. The volume of stock trading in Japan is about one-sixth that of the United States. In Japan, only 9 percent of household financial assets are directly invested in stocks and a mere 2 percent in mutual funds. In contrast, about 50 percent of U.S. households own stock. Says one analyst, "Most of the population [in Japan] doesn't know what a mutual fund is." So will the flood be just a trickle? And what about online stock trading? Internet usage in Japan has burgeoned—there are now some 75 million users in Japan. That's about the same percentage as in the United States. But the expected deluge into equities has been a dribble. Merrill Lynch and others are cutting back staff now as fast as they built it just a couple of years ago.

A French firm is trying to break through a similar aversion to both e-trading and equities in France. That is, only about 10 million adults use the Internet in France, and half that number own stocks. The French have long shied away from stock market investments, seeing them as schemes to enrich insiders while fleecing novices. Given the Enron and WorldCom scandals here, you can almost hear the chortling in the sidewalk cafes there.

eBay, the personal online auction site so successful in the United States, is running into comparable difficulties in both Japan and France. The relatively low rate of Internet usage in France is just part of the problem. For the Japanese it is embarrassing to sell castoffs to anyone, much less buy them from strangers. Garage sales are unheard of. In France, company founder Pierre Omidyar's home country, eBay runs into French laws restricting operations to a few government-certified auctioneers.

Based on a knowledge of differences in cultural values between the United States and both Japan and France, we should expect a slower diffusion of these high-tech Internet services in the latter two countries. e-trading and e-auctions have both exploded on the American scene. However, compared with those in many other countries, U.S. investors are adverse to neither the risk and uncertainties of equity investments nor the impersonal interactions of online transactions.

Sources: William D. Echikson, "Rough Crossing for eBay," *Business Week E.Biz,* February 7, 2000, p. EB48; Yukimo Ono, "Pizza Queen of Japan Turns Web Auctioneer," *Wall Street Journal,* March 6, 2000, p. B1; Brian Bremner, "A Nation of Risk-Takers?" *Business Week,* May 8, 2000, p. 68; Euromonitor (2003); and "Sayonara; Financial Centers," *The Economist,* February 1, 2003, pp. 61–62.

Culture deals with a group's design for living. It is pertinent to the study of marketing, especially international marketing. If you consider the scope of the marketing concept—the satisfaction of consumer needs and wants at a profit—it is apparent that the successful marketer must be a student of culture. For example, when a promotional message is written, symbols recognizable and meaningful to the market (the culture) must be used.

When designing a product, the style, uses, and other related marketing activities must be made culturally acceptable (i.e., acceptable to the present society) if they are to be operative and meaningful. In fact, culture is pervasive in all marketing activities—in pricing, promotion, channels of distribution, product, packaging, and styling—and the marketer's efforts actually become a part of the fabric of culture. The marketer's efforts are judged in a cultural context for acceptance, resistance, or rejection. How such efforts interact with a culture determines the degree of success or failure of the marketing effort.

The manner in which people consume, the priority of needs and the wants they attempt to satisfy, and the manner in which they satisfy them are functions of their culture that temper, mold, and dictate their style of living. **Culture** is the human-made part of human environment—the sum total of knowledge, beliefs, art, morals, laws, customs, and any other capabilities and habits acquired by humans as members of society.[1]

Markets constantly change; they are not static but evolve, expand, and contract in response to marketing effort, economic conditions, and other cultural influences. Markets and market behavior are part of a country's culture. One cannot truly understand how markets evolve or how they react to a marketer's effort without appreciating that markets are a result of culture. Markets are the result of the three-way interaction of a marketer's efforts, economic conditions, and all other elements of the culture. Marketers are constantly adjusting their efforts to cultural demands of the market, but they also are acting as *agents of change* whenever the product or idea being marketed is innovative. Whatever the degree of acceptance in whatever level of culture, the use of something new is the beginning of cultural change, and the marketer becomes a change agent.

This is the first of four chapters that focus on culture and international marketing. A discussion of the broad concept of culture as the foundation for international marketing is presented in this chapter. The next chapter, "Culture, Management Style, and Business Systems," discusses culture and how it influences business practices and the behaviors and thinking of managers. Chapters 6 and 7 examine elements of culture essential to the study of international marketing: the political environment and the legal environment.

This chapter's purpose is to heighten the reader's sensitivity to the dynamics of culture. It is neither a treatise on cultural information about a particular country nor thorough marketing science or epidemiological study of the various topics. Rather, it is designed to emphasize the importance of cultural differences to marketers and the need for study of each country's culture(s) and all its origins and elements, and to point out some relevant aspects on which to focus.

# Culture's Pervasive Impact

Culture affects every part of our lives, every day, from birth to death and everything in between. It even affects how we sleep. For example, we are told that Spaniards sleep less than other Europeans[2] and Japanese children often sleep with their parents.[3] You can clearly see cultural influences in the birthrate tables in Exhibit 4.1. Looking across the data from the three countries, the gradual birthrate decline beginning in the 1960s is evident. Birthrates decline as countries move from agricultural to industrial to service economies. Immediate causes may be government policies and birth control

---

[1]An interesting website that has information on various cultural traits, gestures, holidays, language, religions, and so forth is www.webofculture.com. To order detailed cultural information regarding most countries, see www.culturegrams.com.

[2]This seems a reasonable proposition to the authors given that the best restaurants in Madrid are still serving the main course after midnight!

[3]"Cultural Differences, You Say Tomato," *The Economist*, April 19, 2003, p. 68.

**Exhibit 4.1**
Birthrates (per 1000
women)

Source: World Bank, *World Development Indicators*, 2004. Copyright 2004 by Transaction Pubs. Reprinted with permission of Transaction Pubs via Copyright Clearance Center.

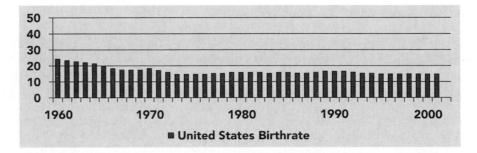

■ United States Birthrate

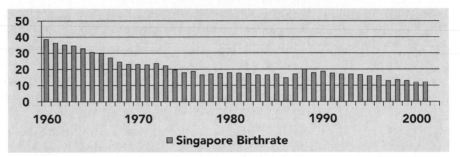

▣ Singapore Birthrate

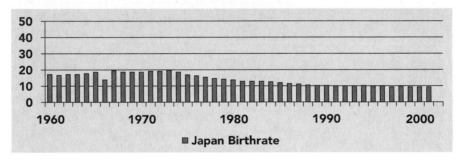

■ Japan Birthrate

technologies, but a global change in values is also occurring. Almost everywhere smaller families are becoming favored. This cultural change now leads experts to predict that the planet's population will actually begin to decline after 2050.[4]

A closer look at Exhibit 4.1 reveals even more interesting consequences of culture. Please notice the little peaks in 1976 and 1988 in the Singapore data. The same pattern can be seen in birthrate data from Taiwan. Those "extra" births are not a matter of random fluctuation. In Chinese culture, being born in the Year of the Dragon (12 animals—dogs, rats, rabbits, pigs, and so on—correspond to specific years in the calendar) is considered good luck. Such birthrate spikes have implications for sellers of diapers, toys, schools, colleges, and so forth in successive years in Singapore. However, superstitions have an even stronger influence on the birthrates in Japan, also shown in Exhibit 4.1. In 1966 there was a one-year 20 percent drop in Japanese fertility rates caused by a belief that women born in the Year of the Fire Horse, which occurs every 60 years, will lead unhappy lives and perhaps murder their husbands. This sudden and substantial decline in fertility has historically occurred every 60 years since Japan started keeping birth records, and reflects abstinence, abortions, and birth certificate fudging. This superstition has resulted in the stigmatization of women born in 1966 and has had a large impact on market potential for a wide variety of consumer goods and services in Japan. It will be interesting to see how technological innovations and culture will interact in Japan in 2026, the next Year of the Fire Horse.[5]

---

[4]Gautam Niak et al., "Global Baby Bust," *Wall Street Journal*, January 24, 2003, p. B1.

[5]Robert W. Hodge and Naohiro Ogawa, *Fertility Change in Contemporary Japan* (Chicago: University of Chicago Press, 1991).

**Exhibit 4.2**   Patterns of Consumption (annual per capita)

| Country | Cut Flowers (stems) | Chocolate (kg) | Fish (kg) | Pasta (kg) | Wine (lt) | Tobacco (sticks) |
|---|---|---|---|---|---|---|
| France | 81 | 4.3 | 8.6 | 4.6 | 30.4 | 1375 (−1)* |
| Germany | 120 | 8.7 | 5.3 | 5.1 | 21.3 | 1719 (+4) |
| Italy | 87 | 2.5 | 8.5 | **20.7** | **34.4** | 1869 (+12) |
| Netherlands | **125** | 5.0 | 6.1 | 2.5 | 17.9 | 1050 (+4) |
| Spain | 33 | 1.7 | **19.8** | 4.4 | 13.1 | **2288 (+10)** |
| United Kingdom | 48 | **10.5** | 3.0 | 2.1 | 15.7 | 973 (−16) |
| Japan | 110 | 1.8 | 59.4 | 10.9 | 6.9 | 2472 (−4) |
| United States | 75 | 5.6 | 4.9 | 3.5 | 5.9 | 1428 (−18) |

*5-year growth rate, percent.

Source: EuroMonitor International, 2004.

Culture's influence is also illustrated in the consumption data presented in Exhibit 4.2. The focus is on the six European Union (EU) countries, but data from the two other major markets of affluence in the world are also included—Japan and the United States. The products compared are those that might be included in a typical (American) romantic dinner date.

First come the flowers and candy. The Dutch are the champion consumers of cut flowers, and this particular preference for petals will be further explored in the pages to come. The British love their chocolate. Perhaps the higher consumption rate there is caused by Cadbury's[6] advertising, or perhaps the cooler temperatures have historically allowed for easier storage and better quality in the northern countries. At least among our six EU countries, per capita chocolate consumption declines with latitude.

In Europe the Spaniards are the most likely to feast on fish. Of course, they don't even come close to the Japanese preference for seafood—they even eat it raw! From the data in Exhibit 4.2 one might conclude that being surrounded by water explains the preference for seafood. However, what about the British? The flat geography in England and Scotland allows for the efficient production of beef, and a bit later in this section we consider the consequences of their strong preference for red meat. The Italians eat more pasta, which is not a surprise, but history is important. Pasta was actually invented in China and in 1270 Marco Polo brought the innovation back to Italy, where it has flourished. Proximity to China also explains the high rate of Japanese pasta (noodle) consumption.

How about alcohol and tobacco? Grapes grow best in France and Italy, and a combination of climate and soil conditions explains at least part of the pattern of wine consumption seen in the exhibit. Culture also influences the laws regarding age limits for drinking. The legal environment also has implications for the consumption of cigarettes. Indeed, current consumption numbers are not the most striking. The most interesting data are the 5-year growth rates. Demand is shrinking remarkably fast in the United States and United Kingdom. Even the Japanese are succeeding in reducing the consumption of cigarettes. But the Italians and Spaniards are losing the battle.

Any discussion of tobacco consumption leads immediately to the consequences of consumption. One might expect that a high consumption of romantic products, such as flowers, candy, and wine, might lead to a high birthrate. Reference to Exhibit 4.3 doesn't yield any clear conclusions. The Germans have some of the highest consumption levels of these products, but the lowest birthrate among the eight countries.

Perhaps the Japanese diet's[7] emphasis on fish yields them the longest life expectancy? But there is actually not much variation in length of life among the eight affluent countries represented in Exhibit 4.3. The way that people die does vary substantially across

[6]See Cadbury's website for the history of chocolate, www.cadbury.co.uk. Chocolate is also an important product in Switzerland where the consumption per capital is over 12 kg. The mountain climate is cooler and, of course, Nestle has their corporate headquarters there.

[7]Notice we are not referring to the Japanese Diet, their legislature, although fishing rights are a hugely important international issue for that body.

**Exhibit 4.3**   Consequences of Consumption

| | | | Death Rate per 100,000 | | | |
|---|---|---|---|---|---|---|
| **Country** | **Birthrate (per 100,000)** | **Life Expectancy** | **Ischemic Heart Disease** | **Chronic Liver Disease and Cirrhosis** | **Lung Cancer** | **Stomach Cancer** |
| France | **12.3** | **79** | 75 | 16 | 42 | 9 |
| Germany | 8.2 | 78 | **241** | **22** | 46 | 16 |
| Italy | 8.6 | **79** | 131 | 19 | 55 | **19** |
| Netherlands | 10.6 | 78 | 113 | 5 | 54 | 11 |
| Spain | 8.9 | 78 | 100 | 15 | **59** | 15 |
| United Kingdom | 10.6 | 77 | 162 | 9 | 57 | 12 |
| Japan | 9.2 | 81 | 59 | 11 | 42 | 41 |
| United States | 13.1 | 78 | 193 | 11 | 55 | 5 |

Source: World Health Organization (www3.who.int/whosis/menu.cfm, click on WHO Mortality Database, then Table 1), 2004.

the countries. The influence of fish versus red meat consumption on the incidence of heart problems is easy to see. Liver problems seem to be associated with greater wine consumption. Perhaps the high incidence of lung cancer in Spain is associated with their high consumption of cigarettes.

The most interesting datum in the table is the extremely high incidence of stomach cancer in Japan. The latest studies suggest two possible causes: (1) salty foods such as soy sauce, and (2) the bacterium *Helicobacter pylori*. The latter is associated with the unsanitary conditions prevalent in Japan immediately after World War II,[8] and is still hurting health in Japan today. Finally, because stomach cancer in Japan is so prevalent, they have developed the most advanced treatment for the disease. Even though the death rate is highest, the treatment success rate is likewise the highest in Japan. Whether you are in Tacoma, Toronto, or Tehran, the best medicine for stomach cancer may be a ticket to Tokyo. Indeed, this last example demonstrates well that culture not only affects consumption, it also affects production (of medical services in this case) as well!

The point is that culture matters.[9] It is imperative for foreign marketers to learn to appreciate the intricacies of cultures different from their own if they are to be effective in foreign markets.

## Definitions and Origins of Culture

There are many ways to think about culture. Dutch management professor Geert Hofstede refers to culture as the "software of the mind" and argues that it provides a guide for humans on how to think and behave; it is a problem-solving tool.[10] Anthropologist and business consultant Edward Hall provides a definition even more relevant to international marketing managers: "The people we were advising kept bumping their heads against an invisible barrier. . . . We knew that what they were up against was a completely different way of organizing life, of thinking, and of conceiving the underlying assumptions about the family and the state, the economic system, and even Man himself."[11] The salient points in Hall's comments are that cultural differences are often invisible, and that if marketers ignore them it often hurts both companies and careers. Finally, James Day

---

[8]Peter Landers, "U.S., Japan Differ on a Cancer—Japanese Focus on Stomach Cancer Produces Better Results," *Wall Street Journal,* April 16, 2002, p. D6.

[9]Lawrence E. Harrison and Samuel P. Huntington (eds.), *Culture Matters* (New York: Basic Books, 2000).

[10]Geert Hofstede, *Culture's Consequences*, 2nd edition, (Thousand Oaks, CA: Sage, 2001); Susan P. Douglas, "Exploring New Worlds: The Challenge of Global Marketing," *Journal of Marketing,* January 2001, pp. 103–109.

[11]Edward T. Hall, *The Silent Language* (New York: Doubleday, 1959), p. 26.

**Exhibit 4.4**    Origins, Elements, and Consequences of Culture

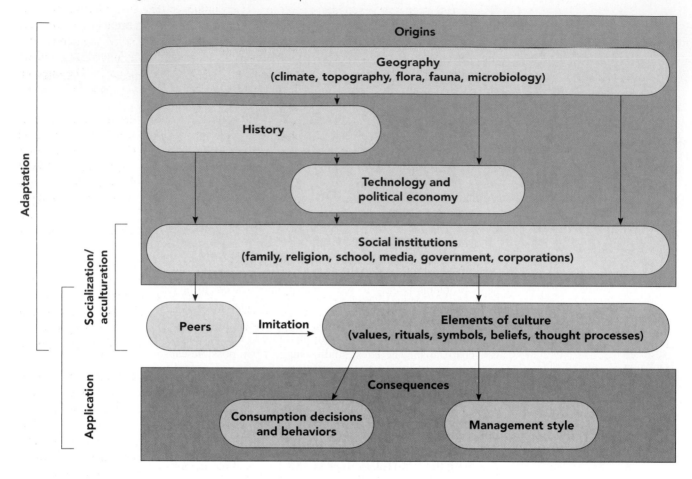

Hodgson, former U.S. ambassador to Japan, describes culture as a "thicket."[12] This last metaphor holds hope for struggling international marketers. According to the ambassador, thickets are tough to get through, but effort and patience often do lead to successes.

Most traditional definitions of culture center around the notion that culture is the sum of the *values, rituals, symbols, beliefs, and thought processes* that are *learned, shared* by a group of people, and *transmitted* from generation to generation.[13] So culture resides in the individual's mind. But the expression "a culture" recognizes that large collectives of people can be like-minded to a great degree.

The best international marketers not only appreciate the cultural differences pertinent to their businesses, they also understand the origins of these differences. Possession of the latter, deeper knowledge will help marketers notice cultural differences in new markets and foresee changes in current markets of operation. Exhibit 4.4 depicts the causal factors and social processes that determine and form cultures and cultural differences. Humans make *adaptations* to changing environments through *innovation*. Individuals learn culture from social institutions through *socialization* (growing up) and *acculturation* (adjusting to a new culture). Individuals also absorb culture through role modeling, or imitation of their peers. Finally, people make decisions about consumption and production through *application* of their culture-based knowledge.

[12]James D. Hodgson, Yoshihiro Sano, and John L. Graham, *Doing Business with the New Japan* (Boulder, CO: Rowman & Littlefield, 2000).

[13]Melvin Herskovitz, *Man and His Works* (New York: Alfred A. Knopf, 1952), p. 634. See also Chapter 10, "Culture," in Raymond Scupin and Christopher R. Decorse, *Anthropology: A Global Perspective,* 5th edition, (Engelwood Cliffs, NJ: Prentice Hall, 2004).

**Geography**  In the previous chapter we described the immediate effects of geography on consumer choice. But geography exercises a more profound influence than just affecting the sort of jacket you buy. Indeed, geography (broadly defined here to include climate, topography, flora, fauna, and microbiology) has influenced history, technology, economics, our social institutions, and yes, our ways of thinking.[14] Geographical influences manifest themselves in our deepest cultural values developed through the millennia. The ongoing cultural divide across the English Channel is also representative of geography's historical impact on human affairs.

The ideas of two researchers are particularly pertinent to any discussion of geography's influence on everything from history to present-day cultural values. First, Jared Diamond,[15] a professor of physiology, tells us that historically innovations spread faster east-to-west than north-to-south. Before the advent of transoceanic shipping, ideas flowed over the Silk Road, but not across the Sahara or the Isthmus of Panama. He uses this geographical approach to explain the dominance of Euro-Asian cultures with their superior technology and more virulent germs, over African and American cultures. Indeed, Diamond's most important contribution is his material on the influence of microbiology on world history.

Second, Philip Parker,[16] a marketing professor, explains geography's deep influence on history, economics, and consumer behavior. For example, he reports strong correlations between the latitude (climate) and the per capita gross domestic product (GDP) of countries. Like Diamond before him, he explains social phenomenon using principles of physiology. The management implications of his treatise have to do with using ambient temperature as a market segmentation variable. We will return to this issue in Chapter 8.

**History**  The impact of specific events in history can be seen reflected in technology, social institutions, cultural values, and even consumer behavior. Diamond's book is filled with examples. For instance, much of American trade policy depends on the happenstance of tobacco (that is, the technology of a new cash crop) being the original source of the Virginia colony's economic survival in the 1600s. In a like manner, the Declaration of Independence, and thereby Americans' values and institutions, were fundamentally influenced by the coincident 1776 publication of Adam Smith's *Wealth of Nations*. Also notice that the military conflicts in the Middle East in 2003 caused new cola brands to be developed, including Mecca Cola, Muslim Up, and Arab Cola.[17]

**The Political Economy**  For most of the twentieth century three approaches to governance competed for world dominance: fascism, communism, and democracy/free enterprise. Fascism fell in 1945. Communism crumbled in the 1990s.[18] One pundit even declared the "end of history."[19] Unfortunately, we have September 11 and the conflicts in the Middle East to keep the list of bad things growing. Much more detail is included in Chapters 6 and 7 on the influences of politics and the legal environment on the culture of commerce and consumption, so we will leave this important topic until then. The main point here is for you to appreciate the influence of the political economy on social institutions and cultural values and ways of thinking.

---

[14]Richard E. Nisbett, *The Geography of Thought: How Asians and Westerners Think Differently . . . and Why* (New York: Free Press, 2003).

[15]Jared Diamond, *Guns, Germs and Steel, the Fates of the Human Societies* (New York: Norton, 1999), a Pulitzer Prize winner, recipient of the Phi Beta Kappa Award in Science, and a wonderful read for anyone interested in history and/or innovation.

[16]Philip Parker, *Physioeconomics* (Cambridge, MA: MIT Press, 2000), a data-rich discussion of global economics well worth the read.

[17]John Tagliabue, "U.S. Brands Abroad Are Feeling Global Tension," *New York Times*, March 15, 2003.

[18]Some might argue that communism has survived in North Korea, Cuba, or the People's Republic of China, but at least in the last case free enterprise is on the ascendancy. The former look more like dictatorships to most.

[19]Francis Fukuyama, *The End of History and the Last Man* (New York: Free Press, 1992).

The Floriad, the biggest exhibition of flowers on earth, happens once every decade. You can go to the next one in 2012.

Outside the Aalsmeer Flower Auction—notice the jet landing at nearby Schiphol Airport which serves both Amsterdam and Aalsmeer.

The Pope in St. Peter's Square on Easter Sunday surrounded by Dutch flowers. (© Giansanti Gianni/CORBIS SYGMA)

The Amsterdam flower market—a busy place for local consumers and tourists.

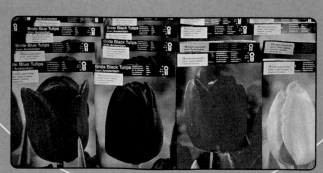

400 years later, the one-dollar black tulip is available in the Amsterdam flower market.

## we all love flowers. But, for the Dutch, flowers are more important than that. For them, it's more like a national fascination, fixation, or even a fetish for flowers. why?

The answer is an instructive story about culture and international markets, the broader subjects of this chapter. The story starts with geography, goes through the origins and elements of culture, and ends with the Dutch being the masters of the exhibition, consumption, and production of flowers.

**Geography.** The rivers and the bays make the Netherlands a great trading country. The miserable weather, rain and snow more than 200 days per year, make it a colorless place, gray nearly year round. The flying Dutchmen not only went to the Spice Islands for spice for the palate, they also went to the eastern Mediterranean for spice for the eyes. That is, the vibrant colors of tulip first came to Europe from the Ottoman Empire on a Dutch ship in 1593.

**History.** The Dutch enthusiasm for the new "visual drug" was great. Its most potent form was, ironically, the black tulip. Prices exploded, and speculators bought and sold promissory notes guaranteeing the future delivery of black tulip bulbs. This derivatives market yielded prices in today's dollars of $1 million or more for a single bulb, enough to buy a 5-story house in central Amsterdam today. Not only did the tulip mania create futures markets, it also caused the first great market bust in recorded history. Prices plummeted when the government took control in 1637. Now at the Amsterdam flower market you can buy a black tulip bulb for about a dollar!

A view of a Dutch harbor with trading ships circa 1600. (© Archivo Iconografico, S.A./CORBIS)

Inside Aalsmeer, 150 football fields of cut flowers, 20 million per day, are readied for auction.

The bidders in 4 huge auction rooms pay attention to the "clock" as high starting prices tick down. The wholesale buyer that stops the clock pays the associated price in this the archetypical "Dutch auction."

## technology and economics.

The technology in the story comes in the name of Carolus Clusius, a botanist that developed methods for manipulating the colors of the tulips in the early 1600s. This added to their appeal and value, and the tulip trade became international for the Dutch.

### social institutions.
Every Easter Sunday the Pope addresses the world at St. Peter's Square in Rome reciting, "Bedankt voor bloemen." Thus, he thanks the Dutch nation for providing the flowers for this key Catholic ritual. The Dutch government once every tenth year sponsors the largest floriculture exhibition in the world, the Floriad. You can go next in 2012. Finally, at the Aalsmeer Flower Auction near Amsterdam, the prices are set for all flowers in all markets around the world. The Dutch remain the largest exporters of flowers (60% global market share) shipping them across Europe by trucks and worldwide by air freight.

Outside again at Aalsmeer, trucks are loaded for shipments by land across Europe and airfreight worldwide.

### cultural values.
The high value the Dutch place on flowers is reflected in many ways, not the least of which is their high consumption rate as seen in Exhibit 4.2.

### aesthetics as symbols.
Rembrandt Van Rijn's paintings, including his most famous "Night Watch" (1642, Rijksmuseum, Amsterdam), reflect a dark palette. Artists generally paint in the colors of their surroundings. A quarter century later his compatriot Vincent Van Gogh used a similar bleak palette when he worked in Holland. Later, when Van Gogh went to the sunny and colorful south of France the colors begin to explode on his canvases. And, of course, there he painted flowers!

Rembrandt's "Night Watch."
(© Rijksmuseum, Amsterdam/SuperStock)

Van Gogh's "Vase with Fifteen Sunflowers" painted in the south of France in 1889, and sold to a Japanese insurance executive for some $40 million in 1987, at the time the highest price ever paid for a single work of art. The Japanese are also big flower consumers—see Exhibit 4.2! (AP/Wide World Photos)

Van Gogh's "Potato Eaters" painted in The Netherlands in 1885. (© Yves Forestier/CORBIS SYGMA)

## Technology

Sit back for a moment and consider which technological innovation you think has had the greatest impact on institutions and cultural values in the last 50 years in the United States. Seriously, stop reading, look out your window, and for a moment consider the question.

There are many good answers, but only one best one. Certainly jet aircraft, air conditioning, televisions, computers, and the Internet all make the list. But the best answer is most likely the birth control pill.[20] Birth control techniques have had a huge effect on everyday life for most Americans. Mainly, it has freed women to have careers and freed men to spend more time with kids. Before the advent of the birth control pill men's and women's roles were prescribed by reproductive responsibilities and roles. Now half the marketing majors in the United States are women. Now 10 percent of the crew on American aircraft carriers are women. Before the pill was available these facts were unimaginable.

Obviously, not everyone is happy with these new "freedoms." For example, in 1968 the Catholic church forbade use of the birth control pill. But it is undeniable that the technology of birth control has deeply affected social institutions and cultural values. Families are smaller, and government and schools are forced to address issues such as abstinence and condom distribution.

## Social Institutions

**Social institutions**, including family, religion, school, the media, government, and corporations all affect the ways in which people relate to one another, organize their activities to live in harmony with one another, teach acceptable behavior to succeeding generations, and govern themselves. The positions of men and women in society, the family, social classes, group behavior, age groups, and how societies define decency and civility are interpreted differently within every culture. In cultures where the social organizations result in close-knit family units, for example, it is usually more effective to aim a promotion campaign at the family unit than at individual family members. Travel advertising in culturally divided Canada has pictured a wife alone for the English-speaking market segment but a man and wife together for the French-speaking segments of the population because the latter are traditionally more closely bound by family ties.

The roles and status positions found within a society are influenced by the dictates of social institutions. The caste system in India is one such institution. The election of a low-caste person—formally called an "untouchable"—as president made international news because it was such a departure from traditional Indian culture. Decades ago, brushing against an untouchable or even glancing at one was considered enough to defile a Hindu of high status. Even though the caste system had been outlawed, it remains a part of the culture.

**Family.**   Family forms and functions vary substantially around the world, even around the country. Consider the Dutch executive who lives with his mother, wife, and kids in a home in Maastricht that his family has owned for the last 300 years. Then there's the common practice of the high-income folks in Cairo buying an apartment house and filling it up with the extended family—grandparents, married siblings, cousins, and kids. Or how about the Japanese mother caring for her two children pretty much by herself, often sleeping with them at night. Meanwhile her husband catches up on sleep during his four hours a day commuting via train. And there's the American family in California, both parents work like dogs to support their cars, closets, and kids in college, all the while worrying about aging grandparents halfway across the country in Texas.

All these differences lead directly to differences in how children think and behave. For example, individualism is being taught the first night the American infant is tucked into her own separate bassinette. Values for egalitarianism are learned the first time Dad washes the dishes in front of the kids or Mom heads off to work or the toddler learns that both Grandpa and little brother are properly called "you."

---

[20]Bernard Asbell, *The Pill: A Biography of the Drug that Changed the World* (New York: Random House, 1995).

In the United States, kids attend school 180 days per year; in China, they attend 251 days—that's six days a week. There's a great thirst for the written word in China—here children read books rented from a street vendor. (© Cary Wolinsky)

**Religion.**   In most cultures the first social institution infants are exposed to outside the home takes the form of a church, mosque, shrine, or temple. The impact of religion on the value systems of a society and the effect of value systems on marketing must not be underestimated. For example, Protestants believe that one's relationship with God is a personal one, and confessions are made directly through prayer. Alternatively, Catholics confess to priests, setting up a hierarchy within the Church. Thus some scholars reason that Protestantism engenders egalitarian thinking. Religion clearly does affect people's habits, their outlook on life, the products they buy, the way they buy them, and even the newspapers they read.

The influence of religion is often quite strong. So when marketers have little or no understanding of a religion, it is easy to deeply offend. One's own religion is often not a reliable guide of another's beliefs. Most people do not understand religions other than their own, and what is known about other religions is often incorrect. The Islamic religion is a good example to show our need for a basic understanding of all major religions. There are between 800 million and 1.2 billion people in the world who embrace Islam, yet major multinational companies often offend Muslims. The French fashion house of Chanel unwittingly desecrated the Koran by embroidering verses from the sacred book of Islam on several dresses shown in its summer collections. The designer said he had taken the design, which was aesthetically pleasing to him, from a book on India's Taj Mahal palace and that he was unaware of its meaning. To placate a Muslim group that felt the use of the verses desecrated the Koran, Chanel had to destroy the dresses with the offending designs, along with negatives of the photos taken of the garments. Chanel certainly had no intention of offending Muslims because some of its most important customers embrace Islam. This example shows how easy it is to offend if the marketer, in this case the designer, is not familiar with other religions.

**School.**   Education, one of the most important social institutions, affects all aspects of the culture, from economic development to consumer behavior. The literacy rate of a country is a potent force in economic development. Numerous studies indicate a direct link between the literacy rate of a country and its capability for rapid economic growth. According to the World Bank, no country has been successful economically with less than 50 percent literacy, but when countries have invested in education the economic rewards have been substantial. Literacy has a profound effect on marketing. It is much easier to communicate with a literate market than to one in which the marketer has to depend on symbols and pictures to communicate.

**The Media.**   The four social institutions that most strongly influence values and culture are schools, churches, families, and most recently, the media. In the United States during the last 30 years, women joined the workforce in growing numbers, substantially reducing the influence of family on American culture. Media time (TV and increasingly the Internet) has replaced family time—much to the detriment of American culture, some argue. Indeed, at this point in time it is hard to gauge the long-term effects of the hours spent with Bart Simpson or an EverQuest cleric-class character. Indeed, the British Prime Minister's cameo on the "Simpsons" TV program reflects its prominence around the world.[21]

---

[21]"Britian: Blair vs. Bart, Politics and Comedy," *The Economist*, April 19, 2003, p. 49.

American kids spend only 180 days per year in school. Contrast that with 251 days in China, 240 days in Japan, and 200 days in Germany. Indeed, Chinese officials are recognizing the national disadvantage of too much school—narrow minds. Likewise, Americans more and more complain about the detrimental effects of too much media.

**Government.**   Compared with the early (during childhood) and direct influences of family, religion, school, and the media during childhood, governments hold relatively little sway. Cultural values and thought patterns are pretty much set before and during adolescence. Most often governments try to influence the thinking and behaviors of adult citizens for the citizens' "own good." For example, the French government has been urging citizens to procreate since the time of Napoleon. Now they are offering a new "birth bonus" of $800 given to women in their seventh month of pregnancy— this despite France having the second highest fertility rate in the EU behind only Ireland (see Exhibit 4.3).[22]

Of course, in some countries the government owns media and regularly uses propaganda to form "favorable" public opinions. Or there may be no separation of church and state—Iran is currently ruled by religious clerics, for example. Governments also affect ways of thinking indirectly, through their support of religious organizations and schools. For example, both the Japanese and Chinese governments are currently trying to promote more creative thinking among students through mandated changes in classroom activities and hours. Finally, governments influence thinking and behavior through the passage, promulgation, promotion, and enforcement of a variety of laws affecting consumption and marketing behaviors. The Irish government is newly concerned about its citizens' consumption of Guinness and other alcohol products. Their studies suggest that excessive drinking costs the country 2 percent of GDP, so to discourage underage drinking the laws are being tightened again (see Chapter 16, page 392 for more details).[23]

**Corporations.**   Of course, corporations influence us early via the media. But more important is that most innovations are introduced to societies by companies, many times multinational companies. Indeed, merchants and traders throughout history were the primary conduit for the diffusion of innovations, whether it be over the Silk Road or via today's air freight and/or the Internet. Multinational firms have access to ideas from around the world. Through the efficient distribution of new products and services based on these new ideas, cultures are changed and new ways of thinking are stimulated. The crucial role of companies as change agents is discussed in detail in the last section of this chapter.

## Elements of Culture

Earlier we defined culture by listing its five elements: values, rituals, symbols, beliefs, and thought processes. International marketers must design products, distribution systems, and promotional programs with due consideration of each of the five elements.

### Cultural Values

Underlying the cultural diversity that exists among countries are fundamental differences in **cultural values**. The most useful information on how cultural values influence various types of business and market behavior comes from seminal work by Geert Hofstede.[24] Studying more than 90,000 people in 66 countries, he found that the cultures of the nations studied differed along four primary dimensions. Subsequently, he and hundreds of other researchers determined that a wide variety of business and consumer

---

[22]"Keep It Up: France's Government Says It Wants to Bolster the Family," *The Economist*, May 3, 2003, p. 53.

[23]"The Irish Are Hard Drinkers—Too Hard, Says Their Government," *The Economist*, May 3, 2003, p. 54.

[24]Geert Hofstede, *Culture's Consequences*, 2nd edition, (Thousand Oaks, CA: Sage, 2001).

**Exhibit 4.5**

Hofstede's Indices, Language, and Linguistic Distance

Source: Geert Hofstede, *Culture's Consequences*, 2nd edition (Thousand Oaks, CA: Sage, 2001). Used by permission of Geert Hofstede.

| Country | IDV Score | PDI Score | UAI Score | Primary Language | Distance from English |
|---|---|---|---|---|---|
| Arab countries | 38 | 80 | 68 | Arabic | 5 |
| Australia | 90 | 36 | 51 | English | 0 |
| Brazil | 38 | 69 | 76 | Portuguese | 3 |
| Canada | 80 | 39 | 48 | English (French) | 0, 3 |
| Colombia | 13 | 67 | 80 | Spanish | 3 |
| Finland | 63 | 33 | 59 | Finnish | 4 |
| France | 71 | 68 | 86 | French | 3 |
| Germany | 67 | 35 | 65 | German | 1 |
| Great Britain | 89 | 35 | 35 | English | 0 |
| Greece | 35 | 60 | 112 | Greek | 3 |
| Guatemala | 6 | 95 | 101 | Spanish | 3 |
| India | 48 | 77 | 40 | Dravidian | 3 |
| Indonesia | 14 | 78 | 48 | Bahasa | 7 |
| Iran | 41 | 58 | 59 | Farsi | 3 |
| Japan | 46 | 54 | 92 | Japanese | 4 |
| Mexico | 30 | 81 | 82 | Spanish | 3 |
| Netherlands | 80 | 38 | 53 | Dutch | 1 |
| New Zealand | 79 | 22 | 49 | English | 1 |
| Pakistan | 14 | 55 | 70 | Panjabi | 3 |
| South Korea | 18 | 60 | 85 | Korean | 4 |
| Taiwan | 17 | 58 | 69 | Taiwanese | 6 |
| Turkey | 37 | 66 | 85 | Turkish | 4 |
| United States | 91 | 40 | 46 | English | 0 |
| Uruguay | 36 | 61 | 100 | Spanish | 3 |
| Venezuela | 12 | 81 | 76 | Spanish | 3 |

behavior patterns are associated with three of those four dimensions.[25] The four[26] dimensions are as follows: the Individualism/Collectivism Index (IDV), which focuses on self-orientation; the Power Distance Index (PDI), which focuses on authority orientation; the Uncertainty Avoidance Index (UAI), which focuses on risk orientation; and the Masculinity/Femininity Index (MAS), which focuses on assertiveness and achievement. The Individualism/Collectivism dimension has proven the most useful of the four dimensions, justifying entire books on the subject.[27] Because MAS has proven least useful, we will not consider it further here. Please see Exhibit 4.5 or the Appendix for details.

**Individualism/Collectivism Index.** The Individualism/Collectivism Index refers to the preference for behavior that promotes one's self-interest. Cultures that score high in IDV reflect an "I" mentality and tend to reward and accept individual initiative, whereas those low in individualism reflect a "we" mentality and generally subjugate the individual to the group. This does not mean that individuals fail to identify with groups when a culture scores high on IDV, but rather that personal initiative and independence are accepted and endorsed. Individualism pertains to societies in which the ties between individuals are loose; everyone is expected to look after himself or herself and his or her immediate family. Collectivism, as its opposite, pertains

---

[25]Debanjan Mitra and Peter N. Golder, "Whose Culture Matters? Near-Market Knowledge and Its Impact on Foreign Market Entry Timing," *Journal of Marketing Research* 39(3), August 2002, pp. 350–365; and Boonghee Yoo and Naveen Donthu, "Culture's Consequences, a Book Review," *Journal of Marketing Research* 39(3), August 2002, pp. 388–389.

[26]In a subsequent study, a fifth dimension, Long-Term Orientation (LTO), was identified as focusing on temporal orientation. See Geert Hofstede and Michael Harris Bond, "The Confucius Connection," *Organizational Dynamics*, Spring 1988, 16(4), pp. 4–21; and Hofstede, 2002.

[27]Harry C. Triandis, *Individualism and Collectivism* (Boulder, CO: Westview Press, 1995).

to societies in which people from birth onward are integrated into strong, cohesive groups, which throughout people's lifetimes continue to protect them in exchange for unquestioning loyalty.

**Power Distance Index.**    The Power Distance Index measures the tolerance of social inequality, that is, power inequality between superiors and subordinates within a social system. Cultures with high PDI scores tend to be hierarchical, with members citing social role, manipulation, and inheritance as sources of power and social status. Those with low scores, on the other hand, tend to value equality and cite knowledge and respect as sources of power. Thus people from cultures with high PDI scores are more apt to have a general distrust of others (not in their groups) because power is seen to rest with individuals and is coercive rather than legitimate. High PDI scores tend to indicate a perception of differences between superior and subordinate and a belief that those who hold power are entitled to privileges. A low score reflects more egalitarian views.

**Uncertainty Avoidance Index.**    The Uncertainty Avoidance Index measures the tolerance of uncertainty and ambiguity among members of a society. Cultures with high UAI scores are highly intolerant of ambiguity and as a result tend to be distrustful of new ideas or behaviors. They tend to have a high level of anxiety and stress and a concern with security and rule following. Accordingly, they dogmatically stick to historically tested patterns of behavior, which in the extreme become inviolable rules. Those with very high UAI scores thus accord a high level of authority to rules as a means of avoiding risk. Cultures scoring low in uncertainty avoidance are associated with a low level of anxiety and stress, a tolerance of deviance and dissent, and a willingness to take risks. Thus those cultures low in UAI take a more empirical approach to understanding and knowledge, whereas those high in UAI seek absolute truth.

**Cultural Values and Consumer Behavior.**    Let's go back to the e-trading example that opened this chapter and see how Hofstede's notions of cultural values might help us predict the speed of diffusion of such new consumer services as equity investments and electronic auctions in Japan and France. As shown in Exhibit 4.5, the United States scores the highest of all countries on individualism, at 91, with Japan at 46 and France at 71. In America, where individualism reigns supreme, we might predict that the social activity of sitting alone at one's computer might be most acceptable. In both Japan and France, where values favor group activities, face-to-face conversations with stockbrokers and neighbors might be preferred to impersonal electronic communications.

Similarly, both Japan (92) and France (86) score quite high on Hofstede's Uncertainty Avoidance Index, and the United States scores low (46). Based on these scores, both Japanese and French investors might be expected to be less willing to take the risks of stock market investments—and indeed, the security of post office deposits or bank savings accounts is preferred there. So in both instances Hofstede's data on cultural values suggest that diffusion of these innovations will be slower in Japan and France than in the United States. Such predictions are quite consistent with recent research findings that cultures scoring higher on individualism and lower on uncertainty avoidance tend to be more innovative.[28]

Perhaps the most interesting application of cultural values and consumer behavior regards a pair of experiments done with American and Chinese students.[29] Both groups were shown print ads using other-focused emotional appeals (that is, a couple pictured having fun on the beach) versus self-focused emotional appeals (an individual having fun on the beach). The researchers predicted that the individualistic Americans would respond more favorably to the self-focused appeals, and the collectivistic Chinese to the

[28]Jan-Benedict E. M. Steenkamp, Frenkel ter Hofstede, and Micel Wedel, "A Cross-National Investigation into the Individual and National Cultural Antecedents of Consumer Innovativeness," *Journal of Marketing,* April 1999, 63, pp. 55–69.

[29]Jennifer L. Aaker and Patti Williams, "Empathy vs. Pride: The Influence of Emotional Appeals across Cultures," *Journal of Consumer Research* December 1998, 25, pp. 241–261.

# CROSSING BORDERS 4.1 It's Not the Gift That Counts, but How You Present It

Giving a gift in another country requires careful attention if it is to be done properly. Here are a few suggestions.

### Japan

Do not open a gift in front of a Japanese counterpart unless asked, and do not expect the Japanese to open your gift.

Avoid ribbons and bows as part of the gift wrapping. Bows as we know them are considered unattractive, and ribbon colors can have different meanings.

Do not offer a gift depicting a fox or badger. The fox is the symbol of fertility; the badger, cunning.

### Europe

Avoid red roses and white flowers, even numbers, and the number 13. Do not wrap flowers in paper.

Do not risk the impression of bribery by spending too much on a gift.

### Arab World

Do not give a gift when you first meet someone. It may be interpreted as a bribe.

Do not let it appear that you contrived to present the gift when the recipient is alone. It looks bad unless you know the person well. Give the gift in front of others in less-personal relationships.

### Latin America

Do not give a gift until after a somewhat personal relationship has developed unless it is given to express appreciation for hospitality.

Gifts should be given during social encounters, not in the course of business.

Avoid the colors black and purple; both are associated with the Catholic Lenten season.

### China

Never make an issue of a gift presentation—publicly or privately.

Gifts should be presented privately, with the exception of collective ceremonial gifts at banquets or after speeches.

### United States

Gifts that are too ostentatious can cause big problems.

Source: "International Business Gift-Giving Customs," available from The Parker Pen Company, n.d.; James Day Hodgson, Yoshihiro Sano, and John L. Graham, *Doing Business with the New Japan* (Boulder, CO: Rowman & Littlefield, 2000); Simon Romero and Geraldine Fabrikant, "The Rise and Fall of Global Dreams," *New York Times*, March 3, 2002, p. B.1.

other-focused appeals. However, they found the opposite. The Americans responded better to the other-focused ads, and the Chinese vice versa. Their second experiment helped explain these unexpected results. That is, in both cases what the participants liked about the ads was their *novelty* vis-à-vis their own cultures. So even in this circumstance, cultural values provide useful information for marketers. However, the complexity of human behavior, values, and culture is manifest.

**Rituals**  Life is filled with rituals, or patterns of behavior and interaction that are learned and repeated. The most obvious rituals are associated with major events in life. Marriage ceremonies and funerals are good examples. Perhaps the one most important to readers of this book is the graduation ritual, *Pomp and Circumstance*, funny hats, long speeches, and all. Very often these rituals differ across cultures. There is an entire *genre* of foreign films about weddings.[30] Perhaps best is *Monsoon Wedding*. Grooms on white horses and edible flowers are apparently part of the ceremony for high-income folks in New Delhi. We even know of at least one cross-cultural wedding in the United States that had the reception before the ceremony!

---

[30]Other excellent films in this genre are *Cousin, Cousine* (French), *Four Weddings and a Funeral* (the U.K.), *Bend It Like Beckham* (the U.K., Asian immigrants), *Wedding in Galilee* (Palestine/Israel), and *The Wedding Banquet* (Taiwan).

Every Muslim is enjoined to make the hajj, or pilgrimage, to Mecca once in his or her lifetime if physically able. Here some 2 million faithful from all over the world annually participate in what is the largest ritual meeting on earth. Meanwhile, televised rituals such as the Academy Awards and World Cup soccer draw billions in the form of virtual crowds. (© AFP/CORBIS)

Life is also filled with little rituals such as dinner at a restaurant or a visit to a department store, or even grooming before heading off to work or class in the morning. In a nice restaurant in Madrid, dessert may precede the entre, but dinner often starts at about midnight, and the entire process can be a three-hour affair. Walking into a department store in the United States often yields a search for an employee to answer questions. Not so in Japan, where the help bows at the door as you walk in. Visit a doctor in the United States and a 15-minute wait in a cold exam room with nothing on but a paper gown is typical. In Spain the exams are often done in the doctor's office. There's no waiting because you find the doctor sitting at her desk.

Rituals are important. They coordinate everyday interactions and special occasions. They let people know what to expect. In the final chapter we discuss the ritual of business negotiations, and that ritual varies across cultures as well.

**Symbols**    Anthropologist Edward T. Hall tells us that culture is communication. In his seminal article about cultural differences in business settings he talks about the "languages" of time, space, things, friendships, and agreements.[31] Learning to correctly interpret the symbols that surround us is a key part of socialization. This learning begins immediately after birth as we begin to hear the language spoken and see the facial expressions and feel the touch and taste the milk of our mothers.[32] We begin our discussion of symbolic systems with language, the most obvious part and the part that most often involves conscious communication.

**Language.**    We should mention that in some parts of the world language is itself thought of as a social institution, often with political importance. Certainly the French go to extreme lengths and expense to preserve the purity of their *Francaise*.[33] In Canada language is the focus of political disputes including secession, although things seem to have

---

[31]Edward T. Hall, "The Silent in Overseas Business," *Harvard Business Review*, May–June, 1960, pp. 87–96. A discussion of the salience of Hall's work appears in John L. Graham, "Culture and Human Resources Management," Alan M. Rugman and Thomas L. Brewer (eds.), *The Oxford Handbook of International Business* (Oxford: Oxford University Press, 2001) pp. 503–536.

[32]The spices a nursing mother consumes actually affect the flavor of the milk she produces.

[33]Mary Blume, "Sin Be Damned, French Say 'Let's Eat,'" *New York Times*, March 6, 2003, p. E1.

**CROSSING BORDERS 4.2** Ici On Parle Français

Frequently there is a conflict between a desire to borrow from another culture and the natural inclination not to pollute one's own culture by borrowing from others. France offers a good example of this conflict. On the one hand, the French accept such U.S. culture as the "Oprah Winfrey" show on television, award Sylvester "Rambo" Stallone the Order of Arts and Letters, listen to Bruce Springsteen, and dine on all-American gastronomic delights such as the Big Mac and Kentucky Fried Chicken. At the same time, there is an uneasy feeling that accepting so much from America will somehow dilute the true French culture. Thus in an attempt to somehow control cultural pollution, France embarked on a campaign to expunge examples of *"franglais"* from all walks of life, including television, billboards, and business contracts. If the culture ministry had its way, violators would be fined. Lists of correct translations included *heures de grande ecoute* for "prime time," *coussin gonflable de protection* for "airbag," *sable américain* for "cookie," and some 3,500 other expressions. Although the demand for hamburgers and U.S. television shows could not be stemmed, perhaps the language could be saved.

With a tongue-in-cheek response, an English lawmaker said he would introduce a bill in Parliament to ban the use of French words in public. Order an aperitif in a British bar or demand an encore at the end of an opera and you might be in trouble—and so go the "language wars."

Perhaps the French *should* be concerned. After years of "Law and Order"-type TV dramas seen in France, it is reported that French prisoners address a judge in a courtroom as "Your Honor," rather than the traditionally acceptable "Mr. President." They also ask to have their "*Miranda* rights read to them" and routinely demand to see a warrant when police want to search their homes. Neither is part of the French legal code.

*Postscript.* The use of foreign words in media and advertising got a last-minute reprieve when France's highest constitutional authority struck down the most controversial parts of the law, saying it only applies to public services and not to private citizens.

Sources: Maarten Huygen, "The Invasion of the American Way," *World Press Review*, November 1992, pp. 28–29; "La Guerre Franglaise," *Fortune*, June 13, 1994, p. 14; "The Internet and Linguistic Diversity," *The American Prospect*, March 27–April 10, 2000; and Mary Blume, "Sin Be Damned, French Say 'Let's Eat,'" *New York Times*, March 3, 2003, p. E1.

calmed down there most recently.[34] Unfortunately, as the number of spoken languages continues to decline worldwide, so does the interesting cultural diversity of the planet.

The importance of understanding the language of a country cannot be overestimated, particularly if you are selling your products in France! The successful international marketer must achieve expert communication, which requires a thorough understanding of the language as well as the ability to speak it. Advertising copywriters should be concerned less with obvious differences between languages and more with the idiomatic meanings expressed. For instance, it is not sufficient to say you want to translate into Spanish, because in Spanish-speaking Latin America the language vocabulary varies widely. *Tambo,* for example, means a roadside inn in Bolivia, Colombia, Ecuador, and Peru; a dairy farm in Argentina and Uruguay; and a brothel in Chile. If that gives you a problem, consider communicating with the people of Papua, New Guinea. Some 750 languages, each distinct and mutually unintelligible, are spoken there. This crucial issue of accurate translation in marketing communications will be discussed further in Chapters 8 and 16.

The relationship between language and international marketing is important in another way. Recent studies indicate that a new concept, **linguistic distance**, is proving useful to marketing researchers in market segmentation and strategic entry decisions. Linguistic distance has been shown to be an important factor in determining the amount of trade between countries.[35] The idea is that crossing "wider" language differences increases transaction costs.

[34]Clifford Krauss, "Quebec Seeking to End Its Old Cultural Divide," *New York Times*, April 13, 2003, p. A12.

[35]Pankaj Ghemawat, "Distance Still Matters, the Hard Reality of Global Expansion," *Harvard Business Review,* September 2001, pp. 137–147.

Over the years linguistics researchers have determined that languages around the world conform to family trees[36] based on the similarity of their forms and development. For example, Spanish, Italian, French, and Portuguese are all classified as Romance languages because of their common roots in Latin. Distances can be measured on these linguistic trees. If we assume English[37] to be the starting point, German is one branch away, Danish two, Spanish three, Japanese four, Hebrew five, Chinese six, and Thai seven. These "distance from English" scores are listed for various cultures in Exhibit 4.5.

Other work in the area is demonstrating a direct influence of language on cultural values and expectations. For example, as linguistic distance from English increases, individualism decreases.[38] These studies are the first in this genre, and much more work needs to be done. However, the notion of linguistic distance appears to hold promise for better understanding and prediction of cultural differences in both consumer and management values, expectations, and behaviors.

Moreover, the relationship between language spoken and cultural values holds deeper implications. That is, as English spreads around the world via school systems and the Internet, cultural values of individualism and egalitarianism will spread with it. For example, Chinese Mandarin speakers and Spanish speakers must learn two words for "you" (*ni* and *nin,* and *tu* and *usted,* respectively). The proper usage of the two depends completely on knowledge of the social context of the conversation. Respect for status is communicated by the use of *nin* and *usted.* In English there is only one form for "you." Speakers can ignore social context and status and still speak correctly. It's easier, and social status becomes less important. Française beware!

**Aesthetics As Symbols.**    Art communicates. Indeed, Confucius is reputed to have opined, "A picture is worth a thousand words." Of course, a dance or a song can be equally meaningful. As we acquire our culture we learn the meaning of this wonderful symbolic system represented in **aesthetics**, that is, the arts, folklore, music, drama, and dance. Customers everywhere respond to images, myths, and metaphors that help them define their personal and national identities and relationships within a context of culture and product benefits. The uniqueness of a culture can be spotted quickly in symbols having distinct meanings. Think about the subtle earth tones of the typical Japanese restaurant compared with the bright reds and yellows in the décor of ethnic Chinese restaurants. Similarly, a long-standing rivalry between the Scottish Clan Lindsay and Clan Donald caused McDonald's Corporation some consternation when they chose the Lindsay tartan design for new uniforms for its restaurant hosts and hostesses. Godfrey Lord Macdonald, Chief of Clan Donald, was outraged and complained that McDonald's had a "complete lack of understanding of the name." Of course, the plaid in the uniforms is now the least of the firm's worries as British consumers are becoming more concerned about health-related matters.[39]

Without a culturally correct interpretation of a country's aesthetic values, a whole host of marketing problems can arise. Product styling must be aesthetically pleasing to be successful, as must advertisements and package designs. Insensitivity to aesthetic values can offend, create a negative impression, and generally render marketing efforts ineffective. Strong symbolic meanings may be overlooked if one is not familiar with a culture's aesthetic values. The Japanese, for example, revere the crane as being very lucky because

---

[36]For the most comprehensive representation of global linguistic trees, see Jiangtian Chen, Robert R. Sokal, and Merrit Ruhlen, "Worldwide Analysis of Genetic and Linguistic Relationships of Human Populations," *Human Biology,* August 1995, 67(4), pp. 595–612.

[37]We appreciate the ethnocentricity in using English as the starting point. However, the linguistic trees can be used to measure distance from any language. For example, analyses using French or Japanese as the starting point have proven useful as well.

[38]Joel West and John L. Graham, "A Linguistics-Based Measure of Cultural Distance and Its Relationship to Managerial Values," working paper, Graduate School of Management, University of California, Irvine, 2004; and John L. Graham, 2001.

[39]"McDonald's Tartan Choice Upsets Scottish Clan," *Advertising Age,* May 12, 1997, p. 3; and Victoria Furness, "Fast-Food Giants Face an Unhealthy Future," *Marketing Week,* January 9, 2003, p. 18.

**Exhibit 4.6**

Metaphorical Journeys through 23 Nations

Source: Martin J. Gannon, *Understanding Global Cultures, Metaphorical Journeys through 23 Nations*, 2nd edition, Thousand Oaks, CA: Sage, 2001. Used by permission of Sage Publications.

| | |
|---|---|
| The Thai Kingdom | The Traditional British House |
| The Japanese Garden | The Malaysian *Balik Kampung* |
| India: The Dance of Shiva | The Nigerian Marketplace |
| Bedouin Jewelry and Saudi Arabia | The Israeli Kibbutzim and Moshavim |
| The Turkish Coffeehouse | The Italian Opera |
| The Brazilian Samba | Belgian Lace |
| The Polish Village Church | The Mexican Fiesta |
| *Kimchi* and Korea | The Russian Ballet |
| The German Symphony | The Spanish Bullfight |
| The Swedish *Stuga* | The Portuguese Bullfight |
| Irish Conversations | The Chinese Family Altar |
| American Football | |

it is said to live a thousand years; however, the use of the number four should be avoided completely because the word for four, *shi*, is also the Japanese word for death. Thus tea cups are sold in sets of five in Japan, not four.

Finally, one author has suggested that understanding different cultures' metaphors is a key doorway to success. In Exhibit 4.6 we list the metaphors Martin Gannon[40] has identified to represent cultures around the world. In the fascinating text he compares "American Football" (with its individualism, competitive specialization, huddling, and ceremonial celebration of perfection) to the "Spanish Bullfight" (with its pompous entrance parade, audience participation, and the ritual of the fight) to the "Indian Dance of the Shiva" (with its cycles of life, family, and social interaction). Any good international marketer would see fine fodder for advertising campaigns in the insightful descriptions depicted.

**Beliefs**   Of course, much of what we learn to believe comes from religious training, and it is not possible to adequately consider matters of true faith and spirituality here. Moreover, the relationship between superstition and religion is not at all clear. For example, one explanation of the origin of the Western aversion to the number 13 has to do with Jesus sitting with his 12 disciples at the Last Supper.

However, many of our beliefs are secular in nature. What Westerners often call superstition plays a large role in a society's belief system in some parts of the world. For example, in parts of Asia, ghosts, fortune telling, palmistry, blood types, head-bump reading, phases of the moon, faith healers, demons, and soothsayers can all be integral elements of society. For example, recall the Japanese concern about being born during the Year of the Fire Horse, discussed earlier.

It's called art, science, philosophy, or superstition, depending on who is talking, but the Chinese practice of *feng shui* is an important ancient belief held by Chinese, among others. Feng shui is the process that links humans and the universe to *ch'i*, the energy that sustains life and flows through our bodies and surroundings, in and around our homes and workplaces. The idea is to harness this ch'i to enhance good luck, prosperity, good health, and honor for the owner of a premise and to minimize the negative force, *sha ch'i*, and its effect. Feng shui requires engaging the services of a feng shui master to determine the positive orientation of a building in relation to either the owner's horoscope, the date of establishment of the business, or the shape of the land and building.[41] It is not a look or a style, and it is more than aesthetics: Feng shui is a strong belief in establishing a harmonious environment through the design and placement of furnishings and the avoidance of buildings facing northwest, the "devil's entrance," and southwest, the "devil's backdoor."

Too often, one person's beliefs are another person's funny story. It is a mistake to discount the importance of myths, beliefs, superstitions, or other cultural beliefs, however

---

[40]Martin J. Gannon, *Understanding Global Cultures, Metaphorical Journeys through 23 Nations* (Thousand Oaks, CA: Sage, 2001).

[41]Kirsten Lagatree, "Feng Shui: Prevent Chi from Rushing Out," *Los Angeles Times,* April 4, 2000, p. K4; and S. Irene Virbila, "Late Nights at White Lotus," *Los Angeles Times,* March 20, 2003, p. E24.

strange they may appear, because they are an important part of the cultural fabric of a society and influence all manner of behavior. For the marketer, it can be an expensive mistake to make light of superstitions in other cultures when doing business there. To make a fuss about being born in the right year under the right phase of the moon and to rely heavily on handwriting and palm-reading experts, as in Japan, can be difficult to comprehend for a Westerner who refuses to walk under a ladder, worries about the next seven years after breaking a mirror, buys a one-dollar lottery ticket, and seldom sees a thirteenth floor in a building.

## Thought Processes

We are now learning in much more detail the degree to which ways of thinking vary across cultures. Richard Nisbett, in his wonderful book, *The Geography of Thought*,[42] broadly discusses differences in "Asian and Western" thinking. He starts with Confucius and Aristotle and develops his arguments through consideration of historical and philosophical writings, as well as findings from more recent behavioral science research, including his own social-psychological experiments conducted with colleagues. Although he acknowledges the dangers surrounding generalizations about Japanese, Chinese, and Korean cultures on the one hand, and European and American cultures on the other, many of his conclusions are consistent with our own work related to international negotiations, cultural values, and linguistic distance.

A good metaphor for his views involves going back to Confucius' picture ("worth 1000 words"). Asians tend to see the whole picture and can report details about the background and foreground. Westerners alternatively focus on the foreground and can provide great detail about central figures, but see almost nothing in the background. This difference in perception—focus versus big picture—is associated with a wide variety of differences in values, preferences, and expectations about future events. Nisbett's book is essential reading for anyone marketing products and services internationally. His insights are pertinent to Japanese selling in Boston as well as Belgians selling in Beijing.

Each of the five cultural elements must be evaluated in light of how they might affect a proposed marketing program. Newer products and services and more extensive programs involving the entire cycle from product development through promotion to final selling require greater consideration of cultural factors. Moreover, the separate origins and elements of culture we have presented interact, often in synergistic ways. Therefore, the marketer must also take a step back and consider larger cultural consequences of marketing actions.

## Cultural Knowledge

There are two kinds of knowledge about cultures. One is **factual knowledge** about a culture; it is usually obvious and must be learned. Different meanings of colors, different tastes, and other traits indigenous to a culture are facts that a marketer can anticipate, study, and absorb. The other is **interpretive knowledge**—an ability to understand and to appreciate fully the nuances of different cultural traits and patterns. For example, the meaning of time, attitudes toward other people and certain objects, the understanding of one's role in society, and the meanings of life can differ considerably from one culture to another and may require more than factual knowledge to be fully appreciated. In this case, interpretive knowledge is also necessary.

## Factual versus Interpretive Knowledge

Frequently, factual knowledge[43] has meaning as a straightforward fact about a culture but assumes additional significance when interpreted within the context of the culture. For example, that Mexico is 98 percent Roman Catholic is an important bit of factual knowledge. But equally important is what it means to be a Catholic within Mexican culture versus being Catholic in Spain or Italy. Each culture practices Catholicism in a slightly different way. For example, All Soul's Day is an important celebration among some Catholic countries. In Mexico, however, the celebration receives special emphasis. The Mexican

---

[42]Richard E. Nisbett, *The Geography of Thought: How Asians and Westerners Think Differently . . . and Why* (New York: Free Press, 2003).

[43]The information provided in CultureGrams is a good example of readily available factual knowledge. See www.culturegrams.com.

**CROSSING BORDERS 4.3** Gaining Cultural Awareness in Seventeenth- and Eighteenth-Century England: The Grand Tour

Gaining cultural awareness has been a centuries-old need for anyone involved in international relations. The concept of the *Grand Tour*, a term first applied over 300 years ago in England, was, by 1706, firmly established as the ideal preparation for soldiers, diplomats, and civil servants. It was seen as the best means of imparting to young men of fortune a modicum of taste and knowledge of other countries. By the summer of 1785, there were an estimated 40,000 English on the Continent.

The Grand Tourist was expected to conduct a systematic survey of each country's language, history, geography, clothes, food, customs, politics, and laws. In particular, he was to study its most important buildings and their valuable contents, and he was encouraged to collect prints, paintings, drawings, and sculpture. All this could not be achieved in a few weeks, and several years were to lapse before some tourists saw England's shores again. Vast sums of money were spent. At times, touring was not the relatively secure affair of today. If the Grand Tourist managed to avoid the pirates of Dunkirk, he then had to run a gauntlet of highwaymen

on Dutch roads, thieves in Italy and France, marauding packs of disbanded soldiery everywhere, and the Inquisition in Spain, to say nothing of ravenous wolves and dogs.

He had to be self-contained; he carried with him not only the obligatory sword and pistols but also a box of medicines and other spices and condiments, a means of securing hotel rooms at night, and an overall to protect his clothes while in bed. At the end of these Grand Tours, many returned with as many as 800 or 900 pieces of baggage. These collections of art, sculpture, and writings can be seen today in many of the mansions throughout the British Isles.

Nowadays, more than 150,000 American college students go on their own international "road trips" in the form of study-abroad programs. This is double the number from 10 years ago. A jolly good show!

Source: Nigel Sale, *Historic Houses and Gardens of East Anglica* (Norwich, England: Jerrold Colour Publications, 1976), p. 1; Tamar Lewin, "Study Abroad, Nail-Biting at Home," *New York Times*, April 9, 2003, p. D.9.

observance is a unique combination of pagan (mostly Indian) influence and Catholic tradition. On the Day of the Dead, as All Soul's Day is called by many in Mexico, it is believed that the dead return to feast. Hence, many Mexicans visit the graves of their departed, taking the dead's favorite foods to place on the graves for them to enjoy. Prior to All Soul's Day, bakeries pile their shelves with bread shaped like bones and coffins, and candy stores sell sugar skulls and other special treats to commemorate the day. As the souls feast on the food, so do the living celebrants. Although the prayers, candles, and the idea of the soul are Catholic, the idea of the dead feasting is pre-Christian Mexican. Thus a Catholic in Mexico observes All Soul's Day quite differently from a Catholic in Spain. The interpretive as well as factual knowledge about religion in Mexico is necessary to fully understand this part of Mexican culture.

Interpretive knowledge requires a degree of insight that may best be described as a feeling. It is the kind of knowledge that depends on past experience for interpretation and is prone to misinterpretation if one's home-country frame of reference (SRC) is used. Ideally, the foreign marketer should possess both kinds of knowledge about a market. Many facts about a particular culture can be learned through research in published materials. This effort can also transmit a small degree of empathy, but to appreciate the culture fully it is necessary to live with the people for some time. Because this ideal solution is not practical for a marketer, other solutions are sought. Consultation and cooperation with bilingual nationals with marketing backgrounds is the most effective answer to the problem. This has the further advantage of helping the marketer acquire an increasing degree of empathy through association with people who understand the culture best—locals.

**Cultural Sensitivity and Tolerance**

Successful foreign marketing begins with **cultural sensitivity**—being attuned to the nuances of culture so that a new culture can be viewed objectively, evaluated, and appreciated. Cultural sensitivity, or cultural empathy, must be carefully cultivated. Perhaps the most important step is the recognition that cultures are not right or wrong, better or

**CROSSING BORDERS 4.4** Cultures Are Just Different, Not Right or Wrong, Better or Worse

We must not make value judgments as to whether or not cultural behavior is good or bad, better or worse. There is no cultural right or wrong, just difference.

People around the world feel as strongly about their cultures as we do about ours. Every country thinks its culture is the best, and for every foreign peculiarity that amuses us, there is an American peculiarity that amuses others. The Chinese tell American dog jokes, reflecting their amazement that we could feel the way we do about an animal that the Chinese consider better for

eating than petting. (Actually, with growing affluence in China, dogs are surviving as pets more frequently, and pet food sales have increased 70 percent during the last five years.) And we're surprised that the French take their dogs to the finest restaurants, where the dogs themselves might be served sitting at the table.

Sources: Lennie Copeland and Lewis Griggs, *Going International* (New York: Plume, 1997), p. 7; Cindy Sui, "In China, Not Every Dog Has His Day," *Washington Post*, May 5, 2000, p. A18; Euromonitor, 2003.

worse; they are simply different. As suggested previously, for every amusing, annoying, peculiar, or repulsive cultural trait we find in a country, there is a similarly amusing, annoying, or repulsive trait others see in our culture. For example, we bathe, perfume, and deodorize our bodies in a daily ritual that is seen in many cultures as compulsive, while we often become annoyed with those cultures less concerned with natural body odor.

Just because a culture is different does not make it wrong. Marketers must understand how their own cultures influence their assumptions about another culture. The more exotic the situation, the more sensitive, tolerant, and flexible one needs to be. Being culturally sensitive will reduce conflict and improve communications, and thereby increase success in collaborative relationships.

Besides knowledge of the origins and elements of cultures, the international marketer also should have appreciation of how cultures change and accept or reject new ideas. Because the marketer usually is trying to introduce something completely new (such as e-trading), or to improve what is already in use, how cultures change and the manner in which resistance to change occurs should be thoroughly understood.

## Cultural Change

Culture is dynamic in nature; it is a living process. But the fact that cultural change is constant seems paradoxical, because another important attribute of culture is that it is conservative and resists change. The dynamic character of culture is significant in assessing new markets even though changes face resistance. There are a variety of ways societies change. Some have change thrust on them by war (for example, the changes in Japan after World War II) or by natural disaster. More commonly, change is a result of a society seeking ways to solve the problems created by changes in its environment. One view is that culture is the accumulation of a series of the best solutions to problems faced in common by members of a given society. In other words, culture is the means used in adjusting to the environmental and historical components of human existence.

Accident has provided solutions to some problems; invention has solved many others. However, societies usually have found answers by looking to other cultures from which they can borrow ideas. **Cultural borrowing** is common to all cultures. Although each society has a few truly unique situations facing it (such as stomach cancer in Japan), most problems confronting all societies are similar in nature.

## Cultural Borrowing

Cultural borrowing is a responsible effort to learn from others' cultural ways in the quest for better solutions to a society's particular problems. Thus unique cultures are the result, in part, of imitating a diversity of others. For example, consider American (U.S.) culture and a typical U.S. citizen, who begins breakfast with an orange from the eastern Mediterranean, a cantaloupe from Persia, or perhaps a piece of African watermelon. After her fruit and first coffee she goes on to waffles, cakes made by a Scandinavian technique from wheat domesticated in Asia Minor. Over these she pours maple syrup, invented by the Indians of the Eastern U.S. woodlands. As a side dish she may have the eggs of a species of bird domesticated in Indo-China, or bacon, thin strips of the flesh of an animal domesticated in Eastern Asia, that have been salted and smoked by a process developed in northern Europe. While eating, she reads the news of the day, imprinted in characters invented by the ancient Semites on a material invented in China by a process invented in Germany. As she reads the accounts of foreign troubles, she will, if she is a good conservative citizen, thank a Hebrew deity in an Indo-European language that she is 100 percent American.[44]

Actually, this citizen is correct to assume that she is 100 percent American because each of the borrowed cultural facets has been adapted to fit her needs, molded into uniquely American habits, foods, and customs. Americans behave as they do because of the dictates of their culture. Regardless of how or where solutions are found, after a particular pattern of action is judged acceptable by society, it becomes the approved way and is passed on and taught as part of the group's cultural heritage. Cultural heritage is one of the fundamental differences between humans and other animals. Culture is learned; societies pass on to succeeding generations solutions to problems, constantly building on and expanding the culture so that a wide range of behavior is possible. The point is, of course, that although many behaviors are borrowed from other cultures, they are combined in a unique manner that becomes typical for a particular society. To the foreign marketer, this similar-but-different feature of cultures has important meaning in gaining cultural empathy.

## Similarities: An Illusion

For the inexperienced marketer, the similar-but-different aspect of culture creates illusions of similarity that usually do not exist. Several nationalities can speak the same language or have similar race and heritage, but it does not follow that similarities exist in other respects—that a product acceptable to one culture will be readily acceptable to the other, or that a promotional message that succeeds in one country will succeed in the other. Even though people start with a common idea or approach, as is the case among English-speaking Americans and the British, cultural borrowing and assimilation to meet individual needs translate over time into quite distinct cultures. A common language does not guarantee a similar interpretation of word or phrases. Both British and Americans speak English, but their cultures are sufficiently different so that a single phrase has different meanings to each and can even be completely misunderstood. In England, one asks for a lift instead of an elevator, and an American, when speaking of a bathroom, generally refers to a toilet, whereas in England a bathroom is a place to take a tub bath. Also, the English "hoover"[45] a carpet whereas Americans vacuum. The movie title *The Spy Who Shagged Me* means nothing to most Americans, but it means a lot to British consumers. Indeed, anthropologist Edward Hall warns that Americans and British have a harder time understanding each other because of *apparent* and *assumed* cultural similarities.

There is also the tendency to speak of the "European consumer" as a result of the growing economic unification of Europe. Many of the obstacles to doing business in Europe have been or will be eliminated as the EU takes shape, but marketers anxious to enter the market must not jump to the conclusion that an economically unified Europe means a common set of consumer wants and needs. Cultural differences among the members of the EU are the product of centuries of history that will take centuries to erase. The United States itself has many subcultures that even today, with mass communications and rapid travel, defy complete homogenization. It would be folly to suggest that the South is in all respects culturally the same as the Northeastern or Midwestern parts of the United States, just as it would be folly to assume that the unification of Germany has erased cultural differences after 30 years of political and social separation.

---

[44]Ralph Linton, *The Study of Man* (New York: Appleton-Century-Crofts, 1936), p. 327.

[45]This is also a good example of a brand name becoming generic, similar to asking someone to "xerox" a letter instead of asking it to be photocopied. The Hoover brand vacuum cleaner was among the first popular brands in England; thus, "hoover" the carpet.

Marketers must assess each country thoroughly in terms of the proposed products or services and never rely on the often-used axiom that if it sells in one country, it will surely sell in another. As worldwide mass communications and increased economic and social interdependence of countries grow, similarities among countries will increase and common market behaviors, wants, and needs will continue to develop. As this process occurs, the tendency will be to rely more on apparent similarities when they may not exist. A marketer is wise to remember that a culture borrows and then adapts and customizes to its own needs and idiosyncrasies; thus, what may appear to be the same on the surface may be different in its cultural meaning.

The scope of culture is broad. It covers every aspect of behavior within a society. The task of foreign marketers is to adjust marketing strategies and plans to the needs of the culture in which they plan to operate. Whether innovations develop internally through invention, experimentation, or by accident, or are introduced from outside through a process of borrowing or immigration, cultural dynamics always seem to take on both positive and negative aspects.

## Resistance to Change

A characteristic of human culture is that change occurs. That people's habits, tastes, styles, behavior, and values are not constant but are continually changing can be verified by reading 20-year-old magazines. However, this gradual cultural growth does not occur without some resistance; new methods, ideas, and products are considered suspect before they are accepted, if ever.

The degree of resistance to new patterns varies. In some situations new elements are accepted completely and rapidly; in others, resistance is so strong that acceptance is never forthcoming. One study using Hofstede's data shows that consumers' acceptance of innovations varies across cultures—innovation was associated with higher individualism (IDV), and lower power distance (PDI) and uncertainty avoidance (UAI).[46]

The picture here demonstrates the imagery and symbolism used by protest groups in the battle of genetically modified foods, or as the protestors have labeled them, "Frankenfoods." Of course, the label attempts to associate some very benign innovations in food production with the fictional monster of movie lore—an effective public relations gambit on the part of the protestors. *(Illustration by Frances Jetter. Used by permission of Frances Jetter.)*

Other studies show that the most important factors in determining what kind and how much of an innovation will be accepted is the degree of interest in the particular subject, as well as how drastically the new will change the old—that is, how disruptive the innovation will be to presently acceptable values and behavior patterns. Observations indicate that the most readily accepted innovations are those that hold the greatest interest within the society and are least disruptive. For example, rapid industrialization in parts of Europe has changed many long-honored attitudes involving time and working women. Today, there is an interest in ways to save time and make life more productive; the leisurely continental life is rapidly disappearing. With this time-consciousness has come the very rapid acceptance of many innovations that might have been resisted just a few years ago. Instant foods, labor-saving devices, and fast-food restaurants, all supportive of a changing attitude toward work and time, are rapidly gaining acceptance.

The resistance to genetically modified (GM) food (some call it "Frankenfood") has become an important and interesting example.[47] European ethnocentrism certainly entered into the equation early—they protested in the streets about the introduction of products such as tomatoes genetically designed to ripen slowly. Conversely, Asian governments labeled the foods as genetically altered and Asian consumers ate them. In America, where this revolution in biotechnology first took hold, the government didn't bother labeling food and consumers didn't care—at least not until about 2000. Now the protests have begun in the United States. Companies such

[46]Idil Sayrac Yaveroglu and Naveen Donthu, "Cultural Influences on the Diffusion of New Products," *Journal of International Consumer Marketing*, 14(4), pp. 49–63.

[47]Annelies Verdurme and Jacque Viaene, "Consumer Beliefs and Attitude toward Genetically Modified Food: Basis for Segmentation and Implications for Communication," *Agribusiness*, winter 2003, 19(1), pp. 91–113; and Lizette Alvarex, "Consumers in Europe Resist Gene-Altered Foods," *New York Times*, February 11, 2003, p. A3.

as Frito-Lay have responded by eliminating GM ingredients, and the federal government is debating new labeling laws.

Although cultures meet most newness with some resistance or rejection, that resistance can be overcome. Cultures are dynamic, and change occurs when resistance slowly yields to acceptance as the basis for resistance becomes unimportant or forgotten. Gradually there comes an awareness of the need for change, or ideas once too complex become less so because of cultural gains in understanding, or an idea is restructured in a less-complex way, and so on. After a need is recognized, it may be impossible to prevent the acceptance of a new idea. For some ideas, solutions to problems, or new products, resistance can be overcome in months; for others, approval may come only after decades or centuries.

An understanding of the process of acceptance of innovations is of crucial importance to the marketer. The marketer cannot wait centuries or even decades for acceptance but must gain acceptance within the limits of financial resources and projected profitability periods. Possible methods and insights are offered by social scientists who are concerned with the concepts of planned social change. Historically, most cultural borrowing and the resulting change have occurred without a deliberate plan, but increasingly changes are occurring in societies as a result of purposeful attempts by some acceptable institution to bring about change, that is, planned change.

## Planned and Unplanned Cultural Change

The first step in bringing about planned change in a society is to determine which cultural factors conflict with an innovation, thus creating resistance to its acceptance. The next step is an effort to change those factors from obstacles into stimulants for change. The same deliberate approaches used by the social planner to gain acceptance for hybrid grains, better sanitation methods, improved farming techniques, or protein-rich diets among the peoples of underdeveloped societies can be adopted by marketers to achieve marketing goals.[48]

Marketers have two options when introducing an innovation to a culture: They can wait, or they can cause change. The former requires hopeful waiting for eventual cultural changes that prove their innovations to be of value to the culture; the latter involves introducing an idea or product and deliberately setting about to overcome resistance and to cause change that accelerates the rate of acceptance. The folks at Fidelity Investments in Japan, for example, pitched a tent in front of Tokyo's Shinjuku train station and have showered commuters with investment brochures and demonstrations of its Japanese language WebXpress online stock trading services to cause faster changes in Japanese investor behavior. However, as mentioned earlier, the changes have not happened fast enough for most foreign firms targeting this business.[49]

Obviously not all marketing efforts require change to be accepted. In fact, much successful and highly competitive marketing is accomplished by a strategy of **cultural congruence**. Essentially this involves marketing products similar to ones already on the market in a manner as congruent as possible with existing cultural norms, thereby minimizing resistance. However, when marketing programs depend on cultural change to be successful, a company may decide to leave acceptance to a strategy of **unplanned change**— that is, introduce a product and hope for the best. Or a company may use a strategy of **planned change**—that is, deliberately set out to change those aspects of the culture offering resistance to predetermined marketing goals.

As an example of unplanned cultural change, consider how the Japanese diet has changed since the introduction of milk and bread soon after World War II. Most Japanese, who were predominantly fish eaters, have increased their intake of animal fat and protein to the point that fat and protein now exceed vegetable intake. As many McDonald's hamburgers are likely to be eaten in Japan as the traditional rice ball wrapped in edible

---

[48]Two very important books on this topic are Everett M. Rogers, *Diffusion of Innovations*, 4th ed. (New York: Free Press, 1995); and Gerald Zaltman and Robert Duncan, *Strategies for Planned Change* (New York: Wiley & Sons, 1979).

[49]"Sayonara: Financial Centers," *The Economist,* February 1, 2003, pp. 61–62.

MTV meets Mom in Mumbai (formerly Bombay), India. Culture does change—dress and even names of major cities!  Even so, a local resident tells us everyone still calls it Bombay despite the official alteration. (© Joe McNally)

seaweed, and American hamburgers are replacing many traditional Japanese foods. Burger King recently purchased Japan's homegrown Morinaga Love restaurant chain, home of the salmon burger—a patty of salmon meat, a slice of cheese, and a layer of dried seaweed, spread with mayonnaise and stuck between two cakes of sticky Japanese rice pressed into the shape of a bun—an eggplant burger, and other treats. The chain will be converted and will sell Whoppers instead of the salmon-rice burger.[50]

The Westernized diet has caused many Japanese to become overweight. To counter this, the Japanese are buying low-calorie, low-fat foods to help shed excess weight and are flocking to health clubs. All this began when U.S. occupation forces introduced bread, milk, and steak to Japanese culture. The effect on the Japanese was unintentional, but nevertheless change occurred. Had the intent been to introduce a new diet—that is, a strategy of planned change—specific steps could have been taken to identify resistance to dietary change and then to overcome these resistances, thus accelerating the process of change.

Marketing strategy is judged culturally in terms of acceptance, resistance, or rejection. How marketing efforts interact with a culture determines the degree of success or failure, but even failures leave their imprint on a culture. All too often marketers are not aware of the scope of their impact on a host culture. If a strategy of planned change is implemented, the marketer has some responsibility to determine the consequences of such action.

## Consequences of Innovation

When product diffusion (acceptance) occurs, a process of social change may also occur. One issue frequently raised concerns the consequences of the changes that happen within a social system as a result of acceptance of an innovation. The marketer seeking product diffusion and adoption may inadvertently bring about change that affects the very fabric of a social system. Consequences of diffusion of an innovation may be functional or dysfunctional, depending on whether the effects on the social system are desirable or undesirable. In most instances, the marketer's concern is with perceived functional consequences—the positive benefits of product use. In most situations innovative products for which the marketer purposely sets out to gain cultural acceptance have minimal, if any, dysfunctional consequences, but that cannot be taken for granted.

---

[50]Interestingly the articles we found did not mention this change in diet as a potential factor in the prevalence of stomach cancer in Japan. However, given that medical science does not yet completely understand the disease, one has to wonder. And the other major environmental catastrophe of the time, the atomic bombs, is not mentioned either (see Exhibit 4.3 and page 97).

One might think that the introduction of a processed feeding formula into the diet of babies in underdeveloped countries where protein deficiency is a health problem would have all the functional consequences of better nutrition and health, stronger and faster growth, and so forth. However, there is much evidence that in many situations the dysfunctional consequences far exceeded the benefits. In Nicaragua (and numerous other developing countries), as the result of the introduction of the formula, a significant number of babies were changed from breast-feeding to bottle-feeding before the age of 6 months. In the United States, with appropriate refrigeration and sanitation standards, a similar pattern exists with no apparent negative consequences. In Nicaragua, however, where sanitation methods are inadequate, a substantial increase in dysentery and diarrhea and a higher infant mortality rate resulted.

A change from breast-feeding to bottle-feeding at an early age without the users' complete understanding of purification caused dysfunctional consequences. This was the result of two factors: the impurity of the water used with the milk and the loss of the natural immunity to childhood disease that a mother's milk provides. This was a case of planned change that resulted in devastating consequences. The infant formula companies set out to purposely change traditional breast-feeding to bottle-feeding. Advertising, promotions of infant formula using testimonials from nurses and midwives, and abundant free samples were used to encourage a change in behavior. It was a very successful marketing program, but the consequences were unintentionally dysfunctional. An international boycott of infant formula products by several groups resulted in the company agreeing to alter its marketing programs to encourage breast-feeding. This problem first occurred some 30 years ago and is still causing trouble for the company. The consequences of the introduction of an innovation can be serious for society and the company held responsible, whether the act was intentional or not.[51]

Some marketers may question their responsibility beyond product safety as far as the consequences of their role as change agents are concerned. The authors' position is that the marketer has responsibility for the dysfunctional results of marketing efforts whether intentional or not. Foreign marketers may cause cultural changes that can create dysfunctional consequences. If proper analysis indicates that negative results can be anticipated from the acceptance of an innovation, it is the responsibility of the marketer to design programs not only to gain acceptance for a product but also to eliminate any negative cultural effects.

# Summary

A complete and thorough appreciation of the origins (geography, history, political economy, technology, and social institutions) and elements (cultural values, rituals, symbols, beliefs, and ways of thinking) of culture may well be the single most important gain to a foreign marketer in the preparation of marketing plans and strategies. Marketers can control the product offered to a market—its promotion, price, and eventual distribution methods—but they have only limited control over the cultural environment within which these plans must be implemented. Because they cannot control all the influences on their marketing plans, they must attempt to anticipate the eventual effect of the uncontrollable elements and plan in such a way that these elements do not preclude the achievement of marketing objectives. They can also set about to effect changes that lead to quicker acceptance of their products or marketing programs.

Planning marketing strategy in terms of the uncontrollable elements of a market is necessary in a domestic market as well, but when a company is operating internationally each new environment that is influenced by elements unfamiliar and sometimes unrecognizable to the marketer complicates the task. For these reasons, special effort and study are needed to absorb enough understanding of the foreign culture to cope with the uncontrollable features. Perhaps it is safe to generalize that of all the tools the foreign marketer must have, those that help generate empathy for another culture are the most valuable. Each of the cultural elements is explored in depth in subsequent chapters. Specific attention is given to business customs, political culture, and legal culture in the following chapters.

---

[51]See the Nestlé Infant Formula case toward the end of the book for complete details regarding the ongoing infant formula controversy.

# Questions

1. Define the following terms:

   culture, 94
   social institutions, 102
   cultural values, 104
   linguistic distance, 109
   aesthetics, 110
   factual knowledge, 112
   interpretive knowledge, 112

   cultural sensitivity, 113
   cultural borrowing, 114
   strategy of cultural
      congruence, 117
   strategy of unplanned
      change, 117
   strategy of planned change, 117

2. Which role does the marketer play as a change agent?

3. Discuss the three cultural change strategies a foreign marketer can pursue.

4. "Culture is pervasive in all marketing activities." Discuss.

5. What is the importance of cultural empathy to foreign marketers? How do they acquire cultural empathy?

6. Why should a foreign marketer be concerned with the study of culture?

7. What is the popular definition of culture? Where does culture come from?

8. It is stated that members of a society borrow from other cultures to solve problems that they face in common. What does this mean? What is the significance to marketing?

9. "For the inexperienced marketer, the 'similar-but-different' aspect of culture creates an illusion of similarity that usually does not exist." Discuss and give examples.

10. Outline the elements of culture as seen by an anthropologist. How can a marketer use this cultural scheme?

11. Social institutions affect culture and marketing in a variety of ways. Discuss, giving examples.

12. "Markets are the result of the three-way interaction of a marketer's efforts, economic conditions, and all other elements of the culture." Comment.

13. What are some particularly troublesome problems caused by language in foreign marketing? Discuss.

14. Suppose you were requested to prepare a cultural analysis for a potential market. What would you do? Outline the steps and comment briefly on each.

15. Cultures are dynamic. How do they change? Are there cases where changes are not resisted but actually preferred? Explain. What is the relevance to marketing?

16. How can resistance to cultural change influence product introduction? Are there any similarities in domestic marketing? Explain, giving examples.

17. Innovations are described as being either functional or dysfunctional. Explain and give examples of each.

18. Defend the proposition that a multinational corporation has no responsibility for the consequences of an innovation beyond the direct effects of the innovation, such as the product's safety, performance, and so forth.

19. Find a product whose introduction into a foreign culture may cause dysfunctional consequences and describe how the consequences might be eliminated and the product still profitably introduced.

# culture, management style, and business systems

## CHAPTER LEARNING OBJECTIVES

What you should learn from Chapter 5:

- The necessity for adapting to cultural differences

- How and why management styles vary around the world

- The extent and implications of gender bias in other countries

- The importance of cultural differences in business ethics

- The differences between relationship-oriented and information-oriented cultures

# Global Perspective

## DO BLONDES HAVE MORE FUN IN JAPAN?

An American executive told the following story: "My first trip to Japan was pretty much a disaster for several reasons. The meetings didn't run smoothly because every day at least 20, if not more, people came walking in and out of the room just to look at me. It is one thing to see a woman at the negotiation table, but to see a woman who is blonde, young, and very tall by Japanese standards (5′8″ with no shoes) leading the discussions was more than most of the Japanese men could handle.

"Even though I was the lead negotiator for the Ford team, the Japanese would go out of their way to avoid speaking directly to me. At the negotiation table I purposely sat in the center of my team, in the spokesperson's strategic position. Their key person would not sit across from me, but rather two places down. Also, no one would address questions and/or remarks to me—to everyone (all male) on our team—but none to me. They would never say my name or acknowledge my presence. And most disconcerting of all, they appeared to be laughing at me. We would be talking about a serious topic such as product liability, I would make a point or ask a question, and after a barrage of Japanese they would all start laughing."

However, for years Barbie dolls that were sold in Japan looked different from their U.S. counterparts. They had Asian facial features, black hair, and Japanese-inspired fashions.

Then about three years ago Mattel, Inc. conducted consumer research around the world and learned something surprising: The original Barbie, with her yellow hair and blue eyes, played as well in Hong Kong as it did in Hollywood. Girls didn't care if Barbie didn't look like them.

"It's all about fantasies and hair," says Peter Broegger, general manager of Mattel's Asian operations. "Blonde Barbie sells just as well in Asia as in the U.S."

Major toy makers are rethinking one of the basic tenets of their $55 billion global industry—that children in different countries want different playthings. The implications are significant for both kids and companies. In the past, giants such as Mattel, Hasbro Inc., and Lego Co. produced toys and gear in a variety of styles. Increasingly, they are designing and marketing one version worldwide.

Sources: James D. Hodgson, Yoshihiro Sano, and John L. Graham, *Doing Business with the New Japan* (Boulder, CO: Rowman & Littlefield, 2000); and Lisa Banon and Carlta Vitzthum, "One-Toy-Fits-All: How Industry Learned to Love the Global Kid," *Wall Street Journal*, April 29, 2003, p. A1.

Perhaps nothing causes more problems for Americans negotiating in other countries than their impatience. Everyone around the world knows that delaying tactics work well against time-conscious U.S. bargainers.

Culture, including all its elements, profoundly affects management style and overall business systems. This is not a new idea. German sociologist Max Weber made the first strong case back in 1930.[1] Culture not only establishes the criteria for day-to-day business behavior but also forms general patterns of values and motivations. Executives are largely captives of their heritages and cannot totally escape the elements of culture they learned growing up.

In the United States, for example, the historical perspective of individualism and "winning the West" seems to be manifest in individual wealth or corporate profit being dominant measures of success. Japan's lack of frontiers and natural resources and its dependence on trade have focused individual and corporate success criteria on uniformity, subordination to the group, and society's ability to maintain high levels of employment. The feudal background of southern Europe tends to emphasize maintenance of both individual and corporate power and authority while blending those feudal traits with paternalistic concern for minimal welfare for workers and other members of society. Various studies identify North Americans as individualists, Japanese as consensus oriented and committed to the group, and central and southern Europeans as elitists and rank conscious. Although these descriptions are stereotypical, they illustrate cultural differences that are often manifest in business behavior and practices.[2] Such differences also coincide quite well with Hofstede's scores listed in Exhibit 4.5 in the last chapter.[3]

A lack of empathy for and knowledge of foreign business practices can create insurmountable barriers to successful business relations. Some businesses plot their strategies with the idea that their counterparts from other business cultures are similar to themselves and are moved by similar interests, motivations, and goals—that they are "just like us." Even though that may be true in some respects, enough differences exist to cause frustration, miscommunication, and, ultimately, failed business opportunities if these differences are not understood and responded to properly.

Knowledge of the management style—that is, the business culture, management values, and business methods and behaviors—existing in a country and a willingness to accommodate the differences are important to success in an international market. Unless marketers remain flexible by accepting differences in basic patterns of thinking, local business tempo, religious practices, political structure, and family loyalty, they are hampered, if not prevented, from reaching satisfactory conclusions to business transactions. In such situations, obstacles take many forms, but it is not unusual to have one negotiator's business proposition accepted over another's simply because "that one understands us."

This chapter focuses on matters specifically related to the management style. Besides an analysis of the need for adaptation, it reviews differences in management styles and ethics, and is concluded with a discussion of culture's influence on strategic thinking.

## Required Adaptation

Adaptation is a key concept in international marketing, and willingness to adapt is a crucial attitude. Adaptation, or at least accommodation, is required on small matters as well as large ones. In fact, the small, seemingly insignificant situations are often the most crucial. More than tolerance of an alien culture is required. There is a need for affirmative

[1]Max Weber, *The Protestant Ethic and Spirit of Capitalism* (London: George Allen & Unwin, 1930, 1976).

[2]Philip Harris and Robert T. Moran, *Managing Cultural Differences,* 5th edition (Houston: Gulf Publishing, 2000).

[3]Geert Hofstede, *Culture's Consequences,* 2nd edition (Thousand Oaks, CA: Sage, 2001).

acceptance, that is, open tolerance of the concept "different but equal." Through such affirmative acceptance, adaptation becomes easier because empathy for another's point of view naturally leads to ideas for meeting cultural differences.

As a guide to adaptation, there are ten basic criteria that all who wish to deal with individuals, firms, or authorities in foreign countries should be able to meet: (1) open tolerance, (2) flexibility, (3) humility, (4) justice/fairness, (5) ability to adjust to varying tempos, (6) curiosity/interest, (7) knowledge of the country, (8) liking for others, (9) ability to command respect, and (10) ability to integrate oneself into the environment. In short, add the quality of adaptability to the qualities of a good executive for a composite of the successful international marketer. It is difficult to argue with these ten items. As one critic commented, "They border on the 12 Boy Scout laws." However, as you read this chapter you will see that it is the obvious that we sometimes overlook.

## Degree of Adaptation

Adaptation does not require business executives to forsake their ways and change to local customs; rather, executives must be aware of local customs and be willing to accommodate to those differences that can cause misunderstandings. Essential to effective adaptation is awareness of one's own culture and the recognition that differences in others can cause anxiety, frustration, and misunderstanding of the host's intentions. The self-reference criterion (SRC) is especially operative in business customs. If we do not understand our foreign counterpart's customs, we are more likely to evaluate that person's behavior in terms of what is acceptable to us.

The key to adaptation is to remain American but to develop an understanding of and willingness to accommodate the differences that exist. A successful marketer knows that in China it is important to make points without winning arguments; criticism, even if asked for, can cause a host to lose face. In Germany, it is considered discourteous to use first names unless specifically invited to do so. Instead, address a person as Herr, Frau, or Fraulein with the last name. In Brazil, do not be offended by the Brazilian inclination to touch during conversation. Such a custom is not a violation of your personal space but rather the Brazilian way of greeting, emphasizing a point, or making a gesture of goodwill and friendship. A Chinese, German, or Brazilian does not expect you to act like one of them. After all, you are American, not Chinese, German, or Brazilian, and it would be foolish for an American to give up the ways that have contributed so notably to American success. It would be equally foolish for others to give up their ways. When different cultures meet, open tolerance and a willingness to accommodate each other's differences are necessary. Once a marketer is aware of cultural differences and the probable consequences of failure to adapt or accommodate, the seemingly endless variety of customs must be assessed. Where does one begin? Which customs should be absolutely adhered to? Which others can be ignored? Fortunately, among the many obvious differences that exist between cultures, only a few are troubling.

## Imperatives, Electives, and Exclusives

Business customs can be grouped into **imperatives**, customs that must be recognized and accommodated; **electives**, customs to which adaptation is helpful, but not necessary; and **exclusives**, customs in which an outsider must not participate. An international marketer must appreciate the nuances of cultural imperatives, cultural electives, and cultural exclusives.

**Cultural Imperatives.** Cultural imperatives are the business customs and expectations that must be met and conformed to or avoided if relationships are to be successful. Successful businesspeople know the Chinese word *guanxi,* the Japanese *ningen kankei,* or the Latin American *compadre.* All refer to friendship, human relations, or attaining a level of trust. They also know there is no substitute for establishing friendship in some cultures before effective business negotiations can begin.

Informal discussions, entertaining, mutual friends, contacts, and just spending time with others are ways *guanxi, ningen kankei, compadre,* and other trusting relationships are developed. In those cultures where friendships are a key to success, the businessperson should not slight the time required for their development. Friendship motivates local

Chinese Foreign Trade Minister Shi Guangsheng (on right) toasts with U.S. Commerce Department Secretary Don Evans and U.S. Ambassador to China Clark Randt, Jr. (on left) in Beijing. Negotiators agreed on funding projects in e-commerce, renewable energy, environmental protection, and aviation. They disagreed about U.S. tariffs on steel imports. (© Reuters NewMedia Inc./CORBIS)

agents to make more sales, and friendship helps establish the right relationship with end users that leads to more sales over a longer period. Naturally, after-sales service, price, and the product must be competitive, but the marketer who has established *guanxi, ningen kankei,* or *compadre* has the edge. Establishing friendship is an imperative in many cultures. If friendship is not established, the marketer risks not earning trust and acceptance, the basic cultural prerequisites for developing and retaining effective business relationships.

The significance of establishing friendship cannot be overemphasized, especially in those countries where family relationships are close. In China, for example, the outsider is, at best, in fifth place in order of importance when deciding with whom to conduct business. The family is first, then the extended family, then neighbors from one's hometown, then former classmates, and only then, reluctantly, strangers—and the last only after a trusting relationship has been established.

In some cultures a person's demeanor is more critical than in other cultures. For example, it is probably never acceptable to lose your patience, raise your voice, or correct someone in public, no matter how frustrating the situation. In some cultures such behavior would only cast you as boorish, but in others it could end a business deal. In Asian cultures it is imperative to avoid causing your counterpart to lose face. In China, to raise your voice, to shout at a Chinese person in public, or to correct them in front of their peers causes them to lose face.

A complicating factor in cultural awareness is that what may be an imperative to avoid in one culture is an imperative to do in another. For example, in Japan prolonged eye contact is considered offensive and it is imperative that it be avoided. However, with Arab and Latin American executives it is important to make strong eye contact or you run the risk of being seen as evasive and untrustworthy.

**Cultural Electives.**   Cultural electives relate to areas of behavior or to customs that cultural aliens may wish to conform to or participate in but that are not required. In other words, it is not particularly important but it is permissible to follow the custom in question. The majority of customs fit into this category. One need not greet another man with a kiss (a custom in some countries), eat foods that disagree with the digestive system (so long as the refusal is gracious), or drink alcoholic beverages (if for health, personal, or religious reasons). On the other hand, a symbolic attempt to participate in such options is not only acceptable but also may help to establish rapport. It demonstrates that the marketer has studied the culture. Japanese do not expect a Westerner to bow and to understand the ritual of bowing among Japanese, yet a symbolic bow indicates interest and some sensitivity to their culture that is acknowledged as a gesture of goodwill. It may help pave the way to a strong, trusting relationship.

A cultural elective in one county may be an imperative in another. For example, in some cultures one can accept or tactfully and politely reject an offer of a beverage, while in other cases the offer of a beverage is a special ritual and to refuse it is an insult. In the Czech Republic an aperitif or other liqueur offered at the beginning of a business meeting, even in the morning, is a way to establish good will and trust. It is a sign that you are being welcomed as a friend. It is imperative that you accept unless you make it clear to your Czech counterpart that the refusal is because of health or religion. Chinese business negotiations often include banquets at which large quantities of alcohol are consumed in an endless series of toasts. It is imperative that you participate in the toasts with a raised glass of the offered beverage, but to drink is optional. Your Arab business associates will offer coffee as part of the important ritual of establishing a level of friendship and trust; you should accept even if you only take a ceremonial sip. Cultural electives are the most visibly different customs and thus more obvious. Often, it is compliance with the less obvious imperatives and exclusives that is more critical.

**Cultural Exclusives.**   Cultural exclusives are those customs or behavior patterns reserved exclusively for the locals and from which the foreigner is barred. For example, a Christian attempting to act like a Muslim would be repugnant to a follower of Mohammed. Equally offensive is a foreigner criticizing or joking about a country's politics, mores, and peculiarities (that is, peculiar to the foreigner) even though locals may, among themselves, criticize such issues. There is truth in the old adage, "I'll curse my brother, but if you curse him, you'll have a fight." There are few cultural traits reserved exclusively for locals, but a foreigner must carefully refrain from participating in those that are reserved.

Foreign managers need to be perceptive enough to know when they are dealing with an imperative, an elective, or an exclusive and have the adaptability to respond to each. There are not many imperatives or exclusives, but most offensive behaviors result from not recognizing them. It is not necessary to obsess over committing a faux pas. Most sensible businesspeople will make allowances for the occasional misstep. But the fewer you make the smoother the relationship will be. By the way, you can ask for help. That is, if you have a good relationship with your foreign counterparts you can always ask them to tell you when you have "misbehaved."

## The Impact of American Culture on Management Style

There are at least three reasons to briefly focus on American culture and management style. First, for American readers it is important to be aware of the elements of culture influencing decisions and behaviors. Such a self-awareness will help American readers adapt to working with associates in other cultures. Second, for readers new to American culture, it is useful to better understand your business associates from the United States. The U.S. market is the biggest export market in the world. Hopefully this knowledge will help everyone be more patient while conducting business across borders. Third, during the late 1990s American business culture was exported around the world, just as in the 1980s Japanese management practices were imitated almost everywhere. Management practices that are developed in the U.S. environment will not be appropriate and useful everywhere.[4] That is clear. So understanding their bases will help everyone make decisions about applying, adapting, or rejecting American practices. Indeed, most often Peter Drucker's advice will apply: "[D]ifferent people have to be managed differently."[5]

There are many divergent views regarding the most important ideas on which normative U.S. cultural concepts are based. Only those that occur most frequently in discussions of cross-cultural evaluations are represented by the following:

- "Master of destiny" viewpoint
- Independent enterprise as the instrument of social action
- Personnel selection and reward based on merit
- Decisions based on objective analysis
- Wide sharing in decision making
- Never-ending quest for improvement
- Competition yielding efficiency

The *"master of destiny"* philosophy is fundamental to U.S. management thought. Simply stated, people can substantially influence the future; they are in control of their own destinies. This viewpoint also reflects the attitude that although luck may influence an individual's future, on balance, persistence, hard work, a commitment to fulfill expectations, and effective use of time give people control of their destinies. In contrast, many

---

[4]See Michael Song, Jinhong Xie, and Barbara Dyer, "Antecedents and Consequences of Marketing Managers' Conflict-Handling Behaviors," *Journal of Marketing,* January 2000, 64, pp. 50–66 for an excellent discussion of differences among Chinese, Japanese, U.K., and U.S. managers.

[5]Peter F. Drucker, *Management Challenges for the 21st Century* (New York: HarperBusiness, 1999), p. 17.

cultures have a more fatalistic approach to life. They believe individual destiny is determined by a higher order and that what happens cannot be controlled.

In the United States, approaches to planning, control, supervision, commitment, motivation, scheduling, and deadlines are all influenced by the concept that individuals can control their futures. Recall from Chapter 4 that the United States scored highest on Hofstede's individualism scale.[6] In cultures with more collectivistic and fatalistic beliefs, these good business practices may be followed, but concern for the final outcome is different. After all, if one believes the future is determined by an uncontrollable higher order, then what difference does individual effort really make?

The acceptance of the idea that *independent enterprise* is an instrument for social action is the fundamental concept of U.S. corporations. A corporation is recognized as an entity that has rules and continuity of existence, and is a separate and vital social institution. This recognition can result in strong feelings of obligation to serve the company. Sometimes the company may take precedence over family, friends, or other activities that might detract from what is best for the company. This is in sharp contrast to the attitudes held by Mexicans, who feel strongly that personal relationships are more important in daily life than work and the company.[7]

Consistent with the view that individuals control their own destinies is the belief that personnel selection and reward must be made on *merit*. The selection, promotion, motivation, or dismissal of personnel by U.S. managers emphasizes the need to select the best-qualified persons for jobs, retaining them as long as their performance meets standards of expectations, and continuing the opportunity for upward mobility as long as those standards are met. In other cultures where friendship or family ties may be more important than the vitality of the organization, the criteria for selection, organization, and motivation are substantially different from those in U.S. companies.[8] In some cultures, organizations expand to accommodate the maximum number of friends and relatives. If one knows that promotions are made on the basis of personal ties and friendships rather than on merit, a fundamental motivating lever is lost. On the other hand, in many other cultures, social pressure from one's group often motivates strongly.

The very strong belief in the United States that business decisions are based on *objective analysis* and that managers strive to be scientific has a profound effect on the U.S. manager's attitudes toward objectivity in decision making and accuracy of data. While judgment and intuition are important criteria for making decisions, most U.S. managers believe decisions must be supported and based on accurate and relevant information. Thus in U.S. business great emphasis is placed on the collection and free flow of information to all levels within the organization, and on frankness of expression in the evaluation of business opinions or decisions. In other cultures, such factual and rational support for decisions is not as important; the accuracy of data and even the proper reporting of data are not prime prerequisites. Furthermore, existing data frequently are for the eyes of a select few. The frankness of expression and openness in dealing with data characteristic of U.S. businesses do not fit easily into some cultures.

Compatible with the views that one controls one's own destiny and that advancement is based on merit is the prevailing idea of *wide sharing in decision making.* Although decision making is not a democratic process in U.S. businesses, there is a strong belief that individuals in an organization require and, indeed, need the responsibility of making decisions for continued development. Thus decisions are frequently decentralized, and the ability as well as the responsibility for making decisions is pushed down to lower

---

[6]Geert Hofstede, *Culture's Consequences* (Thousand Oaks, CA: Sage, 2001).

[7]Eva S. Kras' *Management in Two Cultures: Bridging the Gap between U.S. and Mexican Managers* (Yarmouth, ME: Intercultural Press, 1995) provides a still useful description of the differences between managers' thinking in the two countries.

[8]Nini Yang, Chao C. Chen, Jaepil Choi, and Yimin Sou, "Sources of Work-Family Conflict: A Sino-U.S. Comparison of the Effects of Work and Family Demands," *Academy of Management Journal* 2000, 43(1), pp. 113–123.

ranks of management. In many cultures, decisions are highly centralized, in part because of the belief that only a few in the company have the right or the ability to make decisions. In the Middle East, for example, only top executives make decisions.

A key value underlying the American business system is reflected in the notion of a *never-ending quest for improvement*. The United States has always been a relatively activist society; in many walks of life, the prevailing question is "Can it be done better?" Thus management concepts reflect the belief that change is not only normal but also necessary, that nothing is sacred or above improvement. In fact, the merit on which one achieves advancement is frequently tied to one's ability to make improvements. Results are what count; if practices must change to achieve results, then change is in order. In other cultures, the strength and power of those in command frequently rest not on change but on the premise that the status quo demands stable structure. To suggest improvement implies that those in power have failed; for someone in a lower position to suggest change would be viewed as a threat to another's private domain rather than as the suggestion of an alert and dynamic individual.

Perhaps most fundamental to Western management practices is the notion that *competition is crucial* for efficiency, improvement, and regeneration. Gordon Gekko put it most banally in the movie *Wall Street:* "Greed is good." Adam Smith in his *Wealth of Nations* wrote one of the most important sentences in the English language: "By pursuing his own interest he frequently promotes that of the society more effectually than when he really intended to promote it."[9] This is the "invisible hand" notion that justifies competitive behavior because it improves society and its organizations. Competition among salespeople (for example, sales contests) is a good thing because it promotes better individual performance and, consequently, better corporate performance. When companies compete, society is better off, according to this reasoning. However, managers and policy makers in other cultures often do not share this "greed is good" view. Cooperation is more salient, and efficiencies are attained through reduced transaction costs. These latter views are more prevalent in collectivistic cultures such as China or Japan.

---

[9]Adam Smith, *The Wealth of Nations,* Book IV (1776; reprint, New York: Modern Library, 1994), p. 485.

What's different about Adam Smith's "By pursuing his own interests he frequently promotes that of society more effactually than when he really intended to promote it" and Gordon Gekko's "Greed is good" statements? It's the adverb. Smith didn't say "always," "most of the time," or even "often." He said "frequently." Today many on Wall Street ignore this crucial difference. *(left: © Bettmann/CORBIS; right: 20th Century Fox/The Kobal Collection)*

# Management Styles around the World

Because of the diverse structures, management values, and behaviors encountered in international business, there is considerable variation in the ways business is conducted.[10] No matter how thoroughly prepared a marketer may be when approaching a foreign market, a certain amount of cultural shock occurs when differences in the contact level, communications emphasis, tempo, and formality of foreign businesses are encountered. Ethical standards differ substantially across cultures, as do rituals such as sales interactions and negotiations. In most countries, the foreign trader is also likely to encounter a fairly high degree of government involvement. Among the four dimensions of Hofstede's cultural values discussed in Chapter 4, the Individualism/Collectivism Index (IDV) and Power Distance Index (PDI) are especially relevant in examining methods of doing business cross culturally.

## Authority and Decision Making

Business size, ownership, public accountability, and cultural values that determine the prominence of status and position (PDI) combine to influence the authority structure of business. In high-PDI countries such as Mexico and Malaysia, understanding the rank and status of clients and business partners is much more important than in more egalitarian (low PDI) societies such as Denmark and Israel. In high-PDI countries subordinates are not likely to contradict bosses, but in low-PDI countries they often do. Although the international businessperson is confronted with a variety of authority patterns, most are a variation of three typical patterns: top-level management decisions, decentralized decisions, and committee or group decisions.

Top-level management decision making is generally found in those situations where family or close ownership gives absolute control to owners and where businesses are small enough to make such centralized decision making possible. In many European businesses, such as those in France, decision-making authority is guarded jealously by a few at the top, who exercise tight control. In other countries, such as Mexico and Venezuela, where a semifeudal, land-equals-power heritage exists, management styles are characterized as autocratic and paternalistic. Decision-making participation by middle management tends to be de-emphasized; dominant family members make decisions that tend to please the family members more than to increase productivity. This is also true for government-owned companies where professional managers must follow decisions made by politicians, who generally lack any working knowledge about management. In Middle Eastern countries, the top man makes all decisions and prefers to deal only with other executives with decision-making powers. One always does business with an individual.

As businesses grow and professional management develops, there is a shift toward decentralized management decision making. Decentralized decision making allows executives at different levels of management to exercise authority over their own functions. As mentioned above, this is typical of large-scale businesses with highly developed management systems such as those found in the United States. A trader in the United States is likely to be dealing with middle management, and title or position generally takes precedence over the individual holding the job.

Committee decision making is by group or consensus. Committees may operate on a centralized or decentralized basis, but the concept of committee management implies something quite different from the individualized functioning of the top management and decentralized decision-making arrangements just discussed. Because Asian cultures and religions tend to emphasize harmony and collectivism, it is not surprising that group decision making predominates there. Despite the emphasis on rank and hierarchy in Japanese social structure, business emphasizes group participation, group harmony, and group decision making—but at the top management level.

The demands of these three types of authority systems on a marketer's ingenuity and adaptability are evident. In the case of the authoritative and delegated societies, the chief

---

[10]Websites that provide information about management styles around the world are www.culturesavvy. com, www.countrynet.com, and www.executiveplanet.com.

## CROSSING BORDERS 5.1  Don't Beat Your Mother-in-Law!

The crowding and collectivism of Chinese culture provide fertile ground for hierarchy. Add in a little Confucian advice and status relationships become central for understanding Chinese business systems. Confucius' teachings were the foundation for Chinese education for 2000 years, until 1911. He defined five cardinal relationships: between ruler and ruled, husband and wife, parents and children, older and younger brothers, and between friends. Except for the last, all relationships were hierarchical. The ruled, wives, children, and younger brothers were all counseled to trade obedience and loyalty for the benevolence of their ruler, husband, parents, and older brothers, respectively. Strict adherence to these vertical relations yielded social harmony, that being the antidote for the violence and civil war of his time.

Obedience and deference to one's superiors remains a strong value in Chinese culture. The story of the Cheng family illustrates the historical salience of social hierarchy and high power distance:

In October 1865, Cheng Han-cheng's wife had the insolence to beat her mother-in-law. This was regarded as such a heinous crime that the following punishment was meted out. Cheng and his wife were both skinned alive, in front of the mother, their skin displayed at city gates in various towns and their bones burned to ashes. Cheng's granduncle, the eldest of his close relatives, was beheaded; his uncle and two brothers, and the head of the Cheng clan, were hanged. The wife's mother, her face tattooed with the words "neglected the daughter's education," was paraded through seven provinces. Her father was beaten 80 strokes and banished to a distance of 3000 *li*. The heads of the family in the houses to the right and left of Cheng's were beaten 80 strokes and banished to Heilung-kiang. The educational officer in town was beaten 60 strokes and banished to a distance of 1000 *li*. Cheng's nine-month-old boy was given a new name and put in the county magistrate's care. Cheng's land was to be left in waste "forever." All this was recorded on a stone stele and rubbings of the inscriptions were distributed throughout the empire.

We recommend you have your children read this story! But seriously, notice the authorities held responsible the entire social network for the woman's breach of hierarchy. Status is no joke among Chinese. Age and rank of executives and other status markers must be taken into account during business negotiations with Chinese. American informality and egalitarianism will not play well on the western side of the Pacific.

Sources: Hsu, Dau-lin, "The Myth of the 'Five Human Relations' of Confucius," *Monumenta Sinica*, 1970, pp. 29, 31 as quoted in Gary G. Hamilton, "Patriarchalism in Imperial China and Western Europe: a Revision of Weber's Sociology of Domination," *Theory and Society*, 13, pp. 393–425; and Mark Lam and John L. Graham, *Red China, Green China* (Boulder, CO: Rowman & Littlefield, 2004).

problem is to identify the individual with authority. In the committee decision setup, it is necessary that every committee member be convinced of the merits of the proposition or product in question. The marketing approach to each of these situations differs.

## Management Objectives and Aspirations

The training and background (i.e., cultural environment) of managers significantly affect their personal and business outlooks. Society as a whole establishes the social rank or status of management, and cultural background dictates patterns of aspirations and objectives among businesspeople. These cultural influences affect the attitude of managers toward innovation, new products, and conducting business with foreigners. To fully understand another's management style, one must appreciate an individual's values, which are usually reflected in the goals of the business organization and in the practices that prevail within the company. In dealing with foreign business, a marketer must be particularly aware of the varying objectives and aspirations of management.

**Security and Mobility.** Personal security and job mobility relate directly to basic human motivation and therefore have widespread economic and social implications. The word *security* is somewhat ambiguous, and this very ambiguity provides some clues to managerial variation. To some, security means a big paycheck and the training and ability required for moving from company to company within the business hierarchy; for

**Exhibit 5.1**
Annual Hours Worked

Source: International Labor
Organization, 2004.

| | |
|---|---|
| Britain | 1719 |
| Canada | 1776 |
| Germany | 1480 |
| Hong Kong | 2287 |
| Japan | 1842 |
| Norway | 1399 |
| Singapore | 2307 |
| United States | 1979 |

others, it means the security of lifetime positions with their companies; to still others, it means adequate retirement plans and other welfare benefits. In European companies, particularly in the countries late in industrializing, such as France and Italy, there is a strong paternalistic orientation, and it is assumed that individuals will work for one company for the majority of their lives. For example, in Britain managers place great importance on individual achievement and autonomy, whereas French managers place great importance on competent supervision, sound company policies, fringe benefits, security, and comfortable working conditions. There is much less mobility among French managers than British.

**Personal Life.**   For many individuals, a good personal and/or family life takes priority over profit, security, or any other goal. In his worldwide study of individual aspirations, David McClelland[11] discovered that the culture of some countries stressed the virtue of a good personal life as being far more important than profit or achievement. The hedonistic outlook of ancient Greece explicitly included work as an undesirable factor that got in the way of the search for pleasure or a good personal life. Alternatively, according to Max Weber,[12] at least part of the standard of living that we enjoy in the United States today can be attributed to the hard-working Protestant ethic from which we derive much of our business heritage.

To the Japanese, personal life is company life. Many Japanese workers regard their work as the most important part of their overall lives. Metaphorically speaking, such workers may even find themselves "working in a dream." The Japanese work ethic—maintenance of a sense of purpose—derives from company loyalty and frequently results in the Japanese employee maintaining identity with the corporation. Although this notion continues to be true for the majority, there is strong evidence that the faltering Japanese economy has moved the position of the Japanese "salary man" from that of one of Japan's business elite to one of derision. Japan's business culture is gradually shifting away from the lifelong employment that led to intense company loyalty.

We can get some measure of the work–personal life tradeoff made in different cultures with reference to Exhibit 5.1. As a point of reference, 40 hours per week times 50 weeks equals 2000 hours. Americans work an average number of hours, far more than the Europeans and fewer than the Southeast Asians. Most Americans get about two weeks of paid vacation, whereas in Europe they take between 4 and 6 weeks! In Singapore and Hong Kong Saturday is a workday. However, the scariest datum isn't in the table. Although hours worked are decreasing almost everywhere, in the United States the numbers are increasing, up 36 from 1990.[13] Thank you, Max Weber!

**Affiliation and Social Acceptance.**   In some countries, acceptance by neighbors and fellow workers is a predominant goal within business. The Asian outlook is reflected in the group decision making so important in Japan, and the Japanese place high importance on fitting in with their group. Group identification is so strong in Japan that when

---

[11]David C. McClelland, *The Achieving Society* (New York: Free Press, 1985).

[12]Max Weber, *The Protestant Ethic and Spirit of Capitalism* (London: George Allen & Unwin, 1930, 1976).

[13]Steven Greenhouse, "Americans' International Lead in Hour's Worked Grew in 90s, Report Shows," *New York Times,* September 1, 2001, p. A8; and Craig S. Smith, "Shortened Workweek Shortens French Tempers," *New York Times,* January 10, 2003, p. A3.

**CROSSING BORDERS 5.2**   A Classic—Edward T. Hall's Language (Symbolism) of Space

Like time, the language of space is different wherever one goes. The American businessman, familiar with the pattern of American corporate life, has no difficulty appraising the relative importance of someone else, simply by noting the size of his office in relation to other offices around him.

One pattern calls for the president or the chairman of the board to have the biggest office. The executive vice president will have the next largest, and so on down the line until you end up in the "bull pen." More important offices are usually located at the corners of and on the upper floors. Executive suites will be on the top floor. The relative rank of vice presidents will be reflected in where they are placed along "executive row." The French, on the other hand, are much more likely to lay out space as a network of connecting points of influence, activity, or interest. The French supervisor will ordinarily be found in the middle of his subordinates where he can control them.

Americans who are crowded will often feel that their status in the organization is suffering. As one would expect in the Arab world, the location of an office and its size constitute a poor index of the importance of the man who occupies it. What we would experience as crowded, the Arabs often regard as spacious. The same is true in Spanish cultures. A Latin American official illustrated the Spanish view of this point while showing me around a plant. Opening the door to an 18-by-20-foot office in which 17 clerks and their desks were placed, he said, "See, we have nice, spacious offices. Lots of space for everyone."

In the Middle East and Latin America, the businessman is likely to feel left out in time and overcrowded in space. People get too close to him, lay their hands on him, and generally crowd his physical being. In Scandinavia and Germany, he feels more at home, but at the same time the people are a little cold and distant. It is space itself that conveys this feeling.

Source: Excerpted by permission of *Harvard Business Review*. From "The Silent Language in Overseas Business," by Edward T. Hall, May–June, 1960, pp. 87–96. Copyright © 1960 by the Harvard Business School Publishing Corporation, all rights reserved.

a worker is asked what he does for a living, he generally answers by telling you he works for Sumitomo or Mitsubishi or Matsushita, rather than that he is a chauffeur, an engineer, or a chemist.

**Power and Achievement.**   Although there is some power-seeking by business managers throughout the world, power seems to be a more important motivating force in South American countries. In these countries, many business leaders are not only profit-oriented but also use their business positions to become social and political leaders. The motivations for achievement identified by McClelland are related but different. And one way to measure achievement is by the amount of money in the bank; another is high rank. These last aspirations are particularly relevant to the United States.

**Communication Styles**

Edward T. Hall, professor of anthropology and for decades a consultant to business and government on intercultural relations, tells us that communication involves much more than just words. His article, "The **Silent Language** of Overseas Business," which appeared in the *Harvard Business Review* in 1960[14] remains as worthwhile reading. In it he describes symbolic meanings of time, space, things, friendships, and agreements, and how they vary across cultures. In 1960 Hall could not have anticipated the innovations brought on by the Internet. However, all of his ideas about cross-cultural communication apply to that medium as well.[15] We begin here with a discussion of communication in the face-to-face setting and then move to the electronic media.

---

[14]*Harvard Business Review*, May–June 1960, pp. 87–96.

[15]Some claim that the Internet is changing "offices" in a fundamental way, but we expect Hall's ideas to be worthwhile far into the future. See Brad Stone, "Designing Your Next Office," *Newsweek*, April 28, 2003, pp. 46–47.

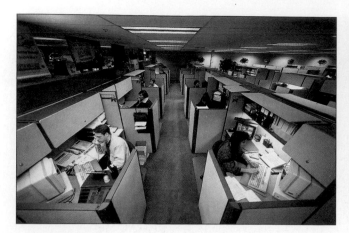 

Speaking of office space: Notice the individualism reflected in the American cubicles and the collectivism demonstrated by the Japanese office organization. *(left: © Ed Kashi/CORBIS; right: © Tom Wagner/CORBIS SABA)*

**Face-to-Face Communication.**   No language readily translates into another because the meanings of words differ widely among languages. For example, the word "marriage," even when accurately translated, can connote very different things in different languages. In one it may mean love, in another restrictions. Though it is the basic communication tool of marketers trading in foreign lands, managers, particularly from the United States, often fail to develop even a basic understanding of just one other language, much less master the linguistic nuances that reveal unspoken attitudes and information.

Verbal communication, no matter how imprecise, is at least explicit. But much business communication depends on implicit messages that are not verbalized. Edward Hall goes on to say, "In some cultures, messages are explicit; the words carry most of the information. In other cultures . . . less information is contained in the verbal part of the message since more is in the context."

Based on decades of anthropological fieldwork, Hall[16] places 11 cultures along a high-context/low-context continuum (see Exhibit 5.2). Communication in a high-context culture depends heavily on the contextual (*who* says it, *when* it is said, *how* it is said) or nonverbal aspects of communication, whereas the low-context culture depends more on explicit, verbally expressed communications.

A brief example of the high/low-context dimension of communication style regards an international marketing executive's description of a Los Angeles business entertainment event. "I picked him (a German client) up at his hotel near LAX and asked what kind of food he wanted for dinner. He said, 'Something local.' Now in LA local food is Mexican food. I'd never met anyone that hadn't had a taco before! We went to a great Mexican place in Santa Monica and had it all, guacamole, salsa, enchiladas, burritos, a real Alka-Seltzer kind of night. When we were done I asked how he liked the food. He responded rather blandly, 'It wasn't very good.'"

The American might have been taken aback by his client's honest, and perhaps too direct answer. However, the American knew well about German frankness[17] and just rolled with the "blow." Germans, being very low-context oriented, just deliver the information without any "social padding." Most Americans would soften the blow some with

---

[16]Edward T. Hall, "Learning the Arabs' Silent Language," *Psychology Today,* August 1979, pp. 45–53. Hall has several books that should be read by everyone involved in international business: *The Silent Language* (New York: Doubleday, 1959), *The Hidden Dimension* (New York: Doubleday, 1966), and *Beyond Culture* (New York: Anchor Press-Doubleday, 1976).

[17]Interestingly, the etymology of the term "frankness" has to do with the Franks, an ancient Germanic tribe that settled along the Rhine. This is not mere coincidence. It's history influencing symbols (that is, language)!

**Exhibit 5.2**
Contextual Background of
Various Countries

Note: Patterned after E. T. Hall.

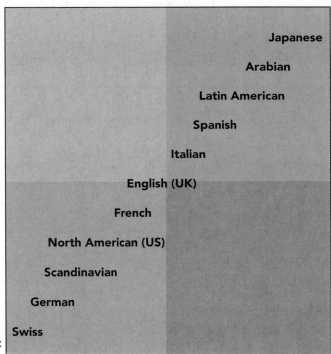

**High Context
Implicit**

Japanese

Arabian

Latin American

Spanish

Italian

English (UK)

French

North American (US)

Scandinavian

German

Swiss

**Low Context
Explicit**

an answer more like, "It was pretty good, but maybe a bit too spicy." A high-context oriented Japanese would heavily pad the response with something like, "It was very good. Thanks." But then the Japanese would never order Mexican food again.

Although an American or German might view the Japanese response as less than truthful, from the Japanese perspective, he was just preserving a harmonious relationship. The Japanese have two words for truth, *honne* (true mind) and *tatemae* (official stance).[18] The former delivers the information and the latter preserves the relationship. In high-context Japan, the latter is often more important.

**Internet Communications.**   The message on a business-to-business website is an extension of the company and should be as sensitive to business customs as any other company representative would be. After a message is posted it can be read anywhere at any time. As a consequence, the opportunity to convey an unintended message is infinite. Nothing about the Web will change the extent to which people identify with their own languages and cultures; thus language should be at the top of the list when examining the viability of a company's website.

Estimates are that 78 percent of today's website content is written in English, but an English e-mail message cannot be understood by 35 percent of all Internet users. A study of businesses on the European continent highlights the need for companies to respond to e-mail in the languages of their websites. One-third of the European senior managers surveyed said they would not tolerate English online. They do not believe that middle managers can use English well enough to transact business on the Internet. There is some support for such a belief. In a test of "perceived" versus "actual" English-language skills, 4,500 Europeans were asked to translate a series of English phrases or sentences. Less than half had an acceptable command of English, and in France, Spain, and Italy fewer than 3 percent had command of the language.

At the extreme are the French, who even ban the use of English terms. The French Ministry of Finance issued a directive that all official French civil service correspondence

---

[18]James D. Hodgson, Yoshihiro Sano, John L. Graham, *Doing Business with the New Japan* (Boulder, CO: Rowman & Littlefield, 2000).

## CROSSING BORDERS 5.3  When Yes Means No, or Maybe, or I Don't Know, or ?

Once my youngest child asked if we could go to the circus and my reply was, "Maybe." My elder child asked the younger sibling, "What did he say?" The prompt reply, "He said *no!*"

All cultures have ways to avoid saying no when they really mean no. After all, arguments can be avoided, hurt feelings postponed, and so on. In some cultures, saying no is to be avoided at all costs because to say no is rude, offensive, and disrupts harmony. When the maintenance of long-lasting, stable personal relationships is of utmost importance, as in Japan, saying no is to be avoided because of the possible damage to a relationship. As a result, the Japanese have developed numerous euphemisms and paralinguistic behaviors to express negation. To the unknowing American, who has been taught not to take no for an answer, the unwillingness to say no is often misinterpreted to mean that there is hope that the right argument or more forceful persuasion is all that is needed to get a yes. But don't be misled. The Japanese will listen politely and respond with *hai*, which means "yes," but it only means, "I hear what you are saying, keep talking," not "I agree with what you are saying."

When a Japanese avoids saying yes or no clearly, it most likely means that he or she wishes to say no. One example at the highest levels of government occurred in negotiations between the prime minister of Japan and the president of the United States. The prime minister responded to a request by the president by saying, "We'll deal with it." It was only later that the U.S. side discovered, to the frustration of all concerned, that such a response generally means no. Other euphemistic, decorative no's sometimes used by the Japanese include: "It's very difficult," "We will think about it," "I'm not sure," and "We'll give this some more thought." Or they leave the room with an apology.

Americans generally respond directly with a yes or no and then give their reasons why. The Japanese tend to embark on long explanations first, and then leave the conclusion extremely ambiguous. Etiquette dictates that Japanese may tell you what you want to hear, may not respond at all, or may be evasive. This ambiguity often leads to misunderstanding and cultural friction.

Sources: Mark Zimmerman, *How to Do Business with the Japanese* (New York: Random House, 1985), pp. 105–110; Laurie Underwood, "Topics American Chamber of Commerce in Taipei," American Chamber of Commerce in Taipei, April 1997, p. 12; and Dean Allen Foster, *The Global Etiquette Guide to Asia: Everything You Need to Know for Business and Travel Success* (New York: John Wiley & Sons, 2000).

must avoid common English-language business words such as *start-up* and *e-mail;* instead, *jeune pousse* ("a young plant") and *courier electronique* are recommended. The solution to the problem is to have country-specific websites, like those of IBM, Microsoft, and others. Dell Computer, for example, makes its Premier Pages websites, built for its business clients, available in 12 languages. There are a host of companies that specialize in website translations; in addition, there are software programs to translate the company message into another language. However, cultural and linguistic correctness can be a problem with machine translation. If not properly done, there is the likelihood that English phrases will be translated in a way that will embarrass or even damage a company. One way to avoid this is to prepare the original source material in easy-to-translate English devoid of complicated phrases, idioms, or slang. Unfortunately, no machine translation is available that can manage all the nuances of language or syntax.

It would be ideal if every representative of your company spoke fluently the language of and understood the culture of your foreign customers or business associates. But that is an impossible goal for most companies. However, there is no reason why every person who accesses a company's website should not be able to communicate in his or her own language if a company wants to be truly global.

In addition to being language friendly, a website should be examined for any symbols, icons, and other nonverbal impressions that could convey an unwanted message. Icons that are frequently used on websites can be misunderstood. For example, an icon such as a hand making a high-five sign will be offensive in Greece; an image of a thumb-to-index finger, the A-OK gesture, will infuriate visitors in Brazil; a two-fingered peace sign when turned around has a very crude meaning to the British; and AOL's "You've

## CROSSING BORDERS 5.4 You Say You Speak English?

The English speak English and North Americans speak English, but can the two communicate? It is difficult unless you understand that in England:

Newspapers are sold at *bookstalls.*

An apartment house is a *block of flats.*

A *closet* usually refers to the *W.C.*, or *water closet*, which is the toilet—where, by the way, you don't go to *tinkle* since tinkle is used as in the statement "Give me a tinkle," which means to phone someone. When one of your British friends says she is going to "spend a penny," she is going to the ladies' room.

A *ladder* is not used for climbing but refers to a run in a stocking.

A *bathing dress* or *bathing costume* is what the British call a bathing suit, and for those who want to go shopping, it is essential to know that a *tunic* is a blouse; a *stud* is a collar button, nothing more; and *suspenders* are garters and *braces* are suspenders.

After shopping, you put your packages in the *boot* of your car, not the trunk.

You will be putting your clothes not in a closet, but in a *cupboard.*

When a British gentleman tells you to "Keep your pecker up," he's telling you to "Keep your chin up" in American English.

When the desk clerk asks what time you want to be *knocked up* in the morning, he is only referring to your wake-up call.

When an American describes a colleague as *sharp*, that is, quick, intelligent, and able, it's a compliment, but in England it implies the person is devious and unprincipled.

The reason a British gentleman expresses delight when an American casually mentions that his father "was 80 years old when he died on the job" is that "on the job" is English slang for "having sex."

When you *table* something in England, you mean you want to discuss it, not postpone it as in the United States.

A *billion* means a million million (1,000,000,000,000) and not a thousand million as in the United States.

---

Got Mail" looks a lot like a loaf of bread to a European. Colors can also pose a problem; green is a sacred color in some Middle Eastern cultures and should not be used for something frivolous like a Web background.

Finally, it appears that e-mail use and usage rates by managers are also affected by culture.[19] That is, businesspeople in high-context cultures do not use the medium to the same extent as those in low-context cultures. The structure of the Japanese language has at least hindered the diffusion of Internet technologies in that country.[20] Moreover, businesspeople in Hong Kong behave less cooperatively in negotiations using e-mail than in face-to-face encounters.[21] Much of the contextual information so important in high-context cultures simply cannot be signaled via the computer.

**Formality and Tempo**

The breezy informality and haste that seem to characterize American business relationships appear to be American exclusives that businesspeople from other countries not only fail to share but also fail to appreciate. A German executive commented that he was taken aback when employees of his Indiana client called him by his first name. He noted, "In Germany you don't do that until you know someone for 10 years—and never if you are at a lower rank." This apparent informality, however, does not indicate a lack of commitment to the job. Comparing British and American business managers, an English executive commented about the American manager's compelling involvement in business, "At a cocktail party or a dinner, the American is still on duty."

Even though Northern Europeans seem to have picked up some American attitudes in recent years, do not count on them being "Americanized." As one writer says, "While using

---

[19]"IT in Japan, Watching the World Scroll By," *The Economist*, April 19, 2003, p. 55.

[20]Hodgson et al., *Doing Business in the New Japan*, 2000.

[21]Guang Yang, "The Impact of Computer-Mediated Communications on the Process and Outcomes of Buyer-Seller Negotiations," unpublished doctoral dissertation, Graduate School of Management, University of California, Irvine.

## CROSSING BORDERS 5.5  Time: A Many-Cultured Thing

Time is cultural, subjective, and variable. One of the most serious causes of frustration and friction in cross-cultural business dealings occurs when counterparts are out of sync with each other. Differences often appear with respect to the pace of time, its perceived nature, and its function. Insights into a culture's view of time may be found in its sayings and proverbs. For example:

- "Time is money." (United States)
- "Those who rush arrive first at the grave." (Spain)
- "The clock did not invent man." (Nigeria)
- "If you wait long enough, even an egg will walk." (Ethiopia)
- "Before the time, it is not yet the time; after the time, it's too late." (France)

The precision of clocks also tells a lot about a culture. In a study on how cultures keep time, the researcher found that clocks are slow or fast by an average of just 19 seconds in Switzerland. When a man in Brazil was queried about the time, however, he was more than three hours off when he said it was "exactly 2:14." When a postal employee in the central post office in Jakarta

was asked the time, he responded that he didn't know the time but to go outside and ask a street vendor.

The perception of how much one works is typically overstated among different cultures. For example, American women tend to overestimate by 26 percent, and American men tend to overestimate by 15 percent the number of hours worked per week. Contrast this with a British study that reported that university teachers misstated the amount they worked by 39 percent, and that 72 percent of the estimates by Nigerian teachers were inaccurate.

Finally, differing perceptions of time apparently can even cause major rifts in international agreements. The greatest Atlantic alliance of the last 50 years was in part jeopardized by American "impatience" regarding attacking Iraq.

Sources: Alan Zarembo, "What If There Weren't Any Clocks to Watch?" *Newsweek*, June 30, 1997; Robert Levine, *The Geography of Time* (New York: Basic Books, 1998); Glen H. Brodowsky and Beverlee B. Anderson, "A Cross-Cultural Study of Consumer Attitudes toward Time," *Journal of Global Marketing*, 2000, 13(3), p. 95; and John Tagliabue, "France and Germany Draw a Line, Against Washington," *New York Times*, January 23, 2003, p. A10.

first names in business encounters is regarded as an American vice in many countries, nowhere is it found more offensive than in France," where formality still reigns. Those who work side by side for years still address one another with formal pronouns. France is higher on Hofstede's Power Distance Index (PDI) than the United States, and such differences can lead to cultural misunderstandings. For example, the formalities of French business practices as opposed to Americans' casual manners are symbols of the French need to show rank and Americans' tendency to downplay it. Thus the French are dubbed snobbish by Americans, while the French consider Americans crude and unsophisticated.

Haste and impatience are probably the most common mistakes of North Americans attempting to trade in the Middle East. Most Arabs do not like to embark on serious business discussions until after two or three opportunities to meet the individual they are dealing with; negotiations are likely to be prolonged. Arabs may make rapid decisions once they are prepared to do so, but they do not like to be rushed and they do not like deadlines. The managing partner of the Kuwait office of KPMG Peat Marwick says of the "flying-visit" approach of many American businesspeople, "What in the West might be regarded as dynamic activity—the 'I've only got a day here' approach—may well be regarded here as merely rude."

Marketers who expect maximum success have to deal with foreign executives in ways that are acceptable to the foreigner. Latin Americans greatly depend on friendships but establish these friendships only in the South American way: slowly, over a considerable period of time. A typical Latin American is highly formal until a genuine relationship of respect and friendship is established. Even then the Latin American is slow to get down to business and will not be pushed. But, all this is more complicated than just haste versus sloth. How people perceive time helps to explain some of the differences between U.S. managers and those from other cultures.

**P-Time versus M-Time**

North Americans are a more time-bound culture than Middle Eastern and Latin cultures. Our stereotype of those cultures is "they are always late," and their view of us is "you are always prompt." Neither statement is completely true though both contain some truth. What is true, however, is that we are a very time-oriented society—time is money to us—whereas in other cultures time is to be savored, not spent.

Edward Hall defines two time systems in the world: monochronic and polychronic time. **M-time**, or *monochronic time,* typifies most North Americans, Swiss, Germans, and Scandinavians. These Western cultures tend to concentrate on one thing at a time. They divide time into small units and are concerned with promptness. M-time is used in a linear way and it is experienced as being almost tangible in that one saves time, wastes time, bides time, spends time, and loses time. Most low-context cultures operate on M-time. **P-time**, or *polychronic time,* is more dominant in high-context cultures, where the completion of a human transaction is emphasized more than holding to schedules. P-time is characterized by the simultaneous occurrence of many things and by "a great involvement with people." P-time allows for relationships to build and context to be absorbed as parts of high-context cultures.

One study comparing perceptions of punctuality in the United States and Brazil found that Brazilian timepieces were less reliable and public clocks less available than in the United States. Researchers also found that Brazilians more often described themselves as late arrivers, allowed greater flexibility in defining early and late, were less concerned about being late, and were more likely to blame external factors for their lateness than were Americans.[22] Please see comparisons of 31 countries in Exhibit 5.3.

The American desire to get straight to the point and get down to business is a manifestation of an M-time culture, as are other indications of directness. The P-time system gives rise to looser time schedules, deeper involvement with individuals, and a wait-and-see-what-develops attitude. For example, two Latin Americans conversing would likely opt to be late for their next appointments rather than abruptly terminate the conversation before it came to a natural conclusion. P-time is characterized by a much looser notion of being on time or late. Interruptions are routine; delays are expected. It is not so much putting things off until *mañana* as it is the concept that human activity is not expected to proceed like clockwork.

Most cultures offer a mix of P-time and M-time behavior, but have a tendency to be either more P-time or M-time in regard to the role time plays. Some are similar to Japan, where appointments are adhered to with the greatest M-time precision but P-time is followed after a meeting begins. The Japanese see U.S. businesspeople as too time-bound and driven by schedules and deadlines that thwart the easy development of friendships. The differences between M-time and P-time are reflected in a variety of ways throughout a culture.

When businesspeople from M-time and P-time meet, adjustments need to be made for a harmonious relationship. Often clarity can be gained by specifying tactfully, for example, whether a meeting is to be on "Mexican time" or "American time." An American who has been working successfully with the Saudis for many years says he has learned to take plenty of things to do when he travels. Others schedule appointments in their offices so they can work until their P-time friend arrives. The important thing for the U.S. manager to learn is adjustment to P-time in order to avoid the anxiety and frustration that comes from being out of synchronization with local time. As global markets expand, however, more businesspeople from P-time cultures are adapting to M-time.

**Negotiations Emphasis**

Business negotiations are perhaps the most fundamental business rituals. All the just-discussed differences in business customs and culture come into play more frequently and more obviously in the negotiating process than in any other aspect of business. The basic elements of business negotiations are the same in any country: They relate to the product, its price and terms, services associated with the product, and finally, friendship

---

[22]Robert Levine, *The Geography of Time* (New York: Basic Books, 1998).

**Exhibit 5.3**
Speed Is Relative

Rank of 31 countries for overall pace of life [combination of three measures: (1) minutes downtown pedestrians take to walk 60 feet, (2) minutes it takes a postal clerk to complete a stamp-purchase transaction, and (3) accuracy in minutes of public clocks].

Source: Robert Levine, "The Pace of Life in 31 Countries," *American Demographics*, 19/11, 1997, pp. 20–29. Copyright 1997, American Demographics, a PRIMEDIA company. All rights reserved.

| Overall Pace | Country | Walking 60 Feet | Postal Service | Public Clocks |
|---|---|---|---|---|
| 1 | Switzerland | 3 | 2 | 1 |
| 2 | Ireland | 1 | 3 | 11 |
| 3 | Germany | 5 | 1 | 8 |
| 4 | Japan | 7 | 4 | 6 |
| 5 | Italy | 10 | 12 | 2 |
| 6 | England | 4 | 9 | 13 |
| 7 | Sweden | 13 | 5 | 7 |
| 8 | Austria | 23 | 8 | 9 |
| 9 | Netherlands | 2 | 14 | 25 |
| 10 | Hong Kong | 14 | 6 | 14 |
| 11 | France | 8 | 18 | 10 |
| 12 | Poland | 12 | 15 | 8 |
| 13 | Costa Rica | 16 | 10 | 15 |
| 14 | Taiwan | 18 | 7 | 21 |
| 15 | Singapore | 25 | 11 | 4 |
| 16 | United States | 6 | 23 | 20 |
| 17 | Canada | 11 | 21 | 22 |
| 18 | South Korea | 20 | 20 | 16 |
| 19 | Hungary | 19 | 19 | 18 |
| 20 | Czech Republic | 21 | 17 | 23 |
| 21 | Greece | 14 | 13 | 29 |
| 22 | Kenya | 9 | 30 | 24 |
| 23 | China | 24 | 25 | 12 |
| 24 | Bulgaria | 27 | 22 | 17 |
| 25 | Romania | 30 | 29 | 5 |
| 26 | Jordan | 28 | 27 | 19 |
| 27 | Syria | 29 | 28 | 27 |
| 28 | El Salvador | 22 | 16 | 31 |
| 29 | Brazil | 31 | 24 | 28 |
| 30 | Indonesia | 26 | 26 | 30 |
| 31 | Mexico | 17 | 31 | 26 |

between vendors and customers. But it is important to remember that the negotiating process is complicated, and the risk of misunderstanding increases when negotiating with someone from another culture.

Attitudes brought to the negotiating table by each individual are affected by many cultural factors and customs often unknown to the other participants and perhaps unrecognized by the individuals themselves. His or her cultural background conditions each negotiator's understanding and interpretation of what transpires in negotiating sessions. The possibility of offending one another or misinterpreting each other's motives is especially high when one's self-reference criteria (SRC) is the basis for assessing a situation. One standard rule in negotiating is "know thyself" first, and second, "know your opponent." The SRC of both parties can come into play here if care is not taken. How business customs and culture influence negotiations is the focus of Chapter 19.

# Gender Bias in International Business
The gender bias[23] against women managers that exists in some countries, coupled with myths harbored by male managers, creates hesitancy among U.S. multinational companies to offer women international assignments. Although

---

[23]Gender bias is now taking on a new character that has long-term implications for the workplace. In a reversal of historical patterns, in most of the industrialized countries women are now in the majority on college campuses. Please see Michelle Colin, "The New Gender Gap," *BusinessWeek*, May 26, 2003, pp. 75–81.

women constitute nearly half of the U.S. workforce, they represent relatively small percentages of the employees who are chosen for international assignments—only 18 percent. Why? The most often cited reason, the inability of women to succeed abroad, might be more fiction than fact. As one executive was quoted as saying, "Overall, female American executives tend not to be as successful in extended foreign work assignments as are male American executives." Unfortunately, such attitudes are shared by many and probably stem from the belief that the traditional roles of women in male-dominated societies preclude women from establishing successful relationships with host-country associates. An often-asked question is whether it is appropriate to send women to conduct business with foreign customers in cultures where females are typically not in managerial positions. To some it appears logical that if women are not accepted in managerial roles within their own cultures, a foreign woman will not be any more acceptable.

It is true that in many cultures—Asian, Middle Eastern, and Latin American—women are not typically found in upper levels of management, and men and women are treated very differently. Indeed, the scariest newspaper headline ever written may have been, "Asia, Vanishing Point for as Many as 100 Million Women." The article, appearing in the *International Herald Tribune* in 1991,[24] points out that the birthrate in most countries around the world is about 105 boys for every 100 girls. However, in countries like the United States or Japan, where generally women outlive men, there are about 96 men per 100 women in the population. The current numbers[25] of men per 100 women in other Asian countries are: Korea 102, China 103, India 109, and Pakistan 106. The article describes systematic discrimination against females from birth. Now illegal everywhere, ultrasound units are still being used for making gender-specific abortion decisions, and all this prejudice against females is creating disruptive shortages of women.[26] In some provinces in China there are currently 120 men per 100 women.

Despite the substantial prejudices toward women in foreign countries, evidence suggests, however, that prejudice toward foreign women executives may be exaggerated and that the treatment local women receive in their own cultures is not necessarily an indicator of how a foreign businesswoman is treated. It would be inaccurate to suggest that there is no difference in how male and female managers are perceived in different cultures. However, this does not mean that women are not successful in foreign postings.

A key to success for either men or women often hinges on the strength of a firm's backing. When a woman manager receives training and the strong backing of her firm, she usually receives the respect commensurate with the position she holds and the firm she represents. For success, a woman needs a title that gives immediate credibility in the culture in which she is working, and a support structure and reporting relationship that will help her get the job done.[27] In short, with the power of the corporate organization behind her, resistance to her as a woman either does not materialize or is less troublesome than anticipated. Once business negotiations begin, the willingness of a business host to engage in business transactions and the respect shown to a foreign businessperson grow or diminish depending on the business skills he or she demonstrates, regardless of gender. As one executive stated, "The most difficult aspect of an international assignment is getting sent, not succeeding once sent."

The number of women in managerial positions in most European countries, with the exception of Germany, is comparable to the United States. The International Labor

[24]"Asia, Vanishing Point for As Many As 100 Million Women," *International Herald Review,* January 7, 1991, p. 2.

[25]Euromonitor, 2004.

[26]In the late 1980s, before the use of sonograms for gender-selective abortion decisions was banned in India, marketers used the cruel pitch, "Pay 500 rupees now and save 50,000 later." The latter number reflects the average-sized dowry in the area. For more depressing details see "Missing Sisters," *The Economist,* April 19, 2003, p. 68.

[27]Nancy J. Adler, "Pacific Basin Managers: A Gaijin, Not a Woman," *Human Resource Management,* 26(2), summer 1987 pp. 169–191; and Nancy J. Adler, *International Dimensions of Organizational Behavior,* 4th edition (Mason, OH: Southwestern College Publishing, 2001).

Organization notes that in the United States, 43 percent of managerial positions are held by women, in Britain 33 percent, and in Switzerland 28 percent. In Germany, however, the picture is less positive. According to one economic source, German female executives held just 9.2 percent of management jobs in 2000, and these meet stiff resistances from their male counterparts when they vie for upper-level positions. But the good news is the indication that some German businesses are attempting to remedy the situation. One step taken to help boost women farther up the executive ladder is a so-called cross-mentoring system organized by Lufthansa and seven other major corporations. High-ranking managers in one company offer advice to women managers in another firm in an effort to help them develop a similar kind of "old-boy network" that allows male managers to successfully climb the corporate ladder.

As world markets become more global and international competition intensifies, U.S. companies need to be represented by the most capable personnel available, from entry level to CEO. Research shows that global companies are requiring international experience for top executive positions. Executives who have had international experience are more likely to get promoted, have higher rewards, and have greater occupational tenure. The lack of international experience should not be a structural barrier to breaking through the glass ceiling in corporate America; it seems shortsighted to limit the talent pool simply because of gender.

So what about our female Ford executive mentioned at the start of the chapter? She was not having fun in Japan when we left her story. However, by all accounts (from peers, supervisors, and even her Japanese counterparts) that first encounter was not representative of her continuing successes with the Japanese. She attributes her subsequent effectiveness to the strong support of her male Ford team members and her own recognition of the importance of building personal relationships with the Japanese. She explains:

> My husband, also a Ford manager working with Japanese clients, and I decided to have a few of our Mazda associates over for an "All-American" dinner during their next trip to Detroit. So we started out inviting three people to our home. We thought this would be a nice intimate way to get to know one another and provide the Japanese with an honest-to-goodness homemade American meal. By the eve of the dinner word had gotten out and we had 13 for dinner. They sort of invited themselves, they changed their meetings around, and some even flew in from the Chicago Auto Show. We had a wonderful time and for the first time they saw me as a person. A mom and a wife as well as a business associate. We talked about families, some business, not particulars, but world economics and the auto industry in general. The dinner party was a key turning point in my relationships with Mazda.[28]

## Business Ethics

The moral question of what is right or appropriate poses many dilemmas for domestic marketers. Even within a country, ethical standards are frequently not defined or always clear. The problem of business ethics is infinitely more complex in the international marketplace because value judgments differ widely among culturally diverse groups. That which is commonly accepted as right in one country may be completely unacceptable in another. Giving business gifts of high value, for example, is generally condemned in the United States, but in many countries of the world gifts are not only accepted but also expected.[29]

### Corruption Defined

Consistent with the previous discussions about language, the meaning of the word corruption varies considerably around the world. In formerly communist countries where Marxism was an important part of the educational system, *profits* can be seen as a kind of corruption. What American managers view as essential others view as a sign of

[28]Hodgson et al., *Doing Business with the New Japan*, 2000.

[29]See www.ethics.org and www.business-ethics.org for more pertinent information.

Scantily clad, blonde Barbie (here in Jakarta) or *Matrix Reloaded*, an R-rated American film (here advertised on the streets of Beijing), might be seen as "corrupting" forces in many countries. Indeed, many parents in the United States would see both in such terms. Products and services directed at kids get special attention from parents and regulators around the world. *(left: © Reuters New Media Inc./CORBIS)*

exploitation. *Individualism,* so important to Americans, can also be seen as a kind of corruption. The Japanese have an expression, "The nail that sticks up gets hammered down." In India many attribute the decline in society there to the *rampant consumerism,* such as that promoted on MTV. Of course, such rampant consumerism is what kept the American economy afloat right after the turn of the century. In some countries there is no greater Satan than R-rated American movies with their sex and violence. In China missionaries and religious movements are viewed by the government as being potentially dangerous and disruptive. Many in sub-Saharan Africa view western *intellectual property laws* as a kind of exploitation that prevents treatment of AIDs for millions. During the 1997–1998 financial crisis many governmental leaders in Southeast Asia decried *currency speculators* as the worst kind of corruption.

And then there is *Barbie* having great fun in Japan these days. Recall the report at the beginning of the chapter. We hope the love affair lasts, but we are not confident it will. The article does describe the extensive marketing research Mattel did with kids. But there is no mention made about marketing research with their parents.[30] We guarantee that selling a big-busted, blonde doll to their daughters will be viewed as a kind of corruption by some Asian parents, and perhaps governmental officials as well. Particularly, if America is perceived as pursuing military and economic hegemony, a strong reaction against symbols of America will follow. Watch out Barbie, GI Joe, and your other toy store friends.

## The Western Focus on Bribery

Before the Enron and WorldCom crises, to most Americans the word corruption meant bribery. Now in the domestic context fraud has moved to the more prominent spot in the headlines. However, during the 1970s, for U.S. companies engaged in international markets bribery became a national issue with public disclosure of political payoffs to foreign recipients by U.S. firms. At the time, there were no U.S. laws against paying bribes in foreign countries, but, for publicly held corporations, the Securities and Exchange

---

[30]Lisa Bannon and Carlta Vitzthum, "One-Toy-Fits-All," *Wall Street Journal,* April 29, 2003, p. A1.

Commission's (SEC) rules required accurate public reporting of all expenditures. Because the payoffs were not properly disclosed, many executives were faced with charges of violating SEC regulations.

The issue took on proportions greater than that of nondisclosure because it focused national attention on the basic question of ethics. The business community's defense was that payoffs were a way of life throughout the world: If you didn't pay bribes, you didn't do business. Consider this situation circa 1975:

> Suppose your company makes large, high-priced generators for power plants and a foreign official promises you a big order if you slip a million dollars into his Swiss bank account. If you are an American and you agree, you have committed a felony and face up to five years in prison. If you are German, Dutch, French, or Japanese, among others, you have merely booked another corporate tax deduction—the value of the bribe—and you have the contract as well. In fact, French tax authorities actually have a sliding scale of acceptable "commissions" paid to win business in different countries. The Asian deduction is 15 percent, although that drops to between 8 percent and 11 percent in India, where apparently it costs less to buy officials. It is important to note that bribes usually violate the laws in the countries where the bribery takes place. In countries where bribes can be deducted as a business expense, the laws clearly state they apply only to transactions outside that country.

The decision to pay a bribe can be seen as creating a major conflict between what is ethical and proper and what is profitable and sometimes necessary for business. Many global competitors perceive payoffs as a necessary means of accomplishing business goals. A major complaint of U.S. businesses was that other countries did not have legislation as restrictive as does the United States. The U.S. advocacy of global antibribery laws has led to an accord by the member nations of the Organization for Economic Cooperation and Development (OECD) to force their companies to follow rules similar to those that bind U.S. firms. To date 33 of the world's largest trading nations, including the United States, have signed the OECD Convention on combating the bribery of foreign public officials in international business transactions. In Latin America, the Organization of American States (OAS) has taken a global lead in ratifying an agreement against corruption. Long considered almost a way of business life, bribery and other forms of corruption now have been criminalized.

Leaders of the region realize that democracy depends on the confidence the people have in the integrity of their government, and that corruption undermines economic liberalization. The actions of the OAS coupled with those of the OECD will obligate a majority of the world's trading nations to maintain a higher standard of ethical behavior than has existed before. Unfortunately, India, China, and other Asian and African countries are not members of either organization. The actions of the OECD and OAS reflect the growing concern among most trading countries regarding the need to bring corruption under control. International businesspeople often justify their actions in paying bribes and corrupting officials as necessary because "corruption is part of their culture," failing to appreciate that it takes two to tango—a bribe giver and a bribe taker.

An international organization called Transparency International[31] (TI) is dedicated to "curbing corruption through international and national coalitions encouraging governments to establish and implement effective laws, policies and anticorruption programs." Among its various activities, TI conducts an international survey of businesspeople, political analysts, and the general public to determine their perceptions of corruption in 102 countries. In the Corruption Perception Index (CPI), shown in part in Exhibit 5.4, Finland, with a score of 9.7 out of a maximum of 10, was perceived to be the least corrupt and Bangladesh, with a score of 1.2, as the most corrupt. TI also ranks 21 bribe-paying countries, and the ranking is reported in Exhibit 5.5 in its entirety. TI is very emphatic that its intent is not to expose villains and cast blame, but to raise public awareness that

[31] www.transparency.org.

**Exhibit 5.4**

Transparency International Corruption Perception Index

Higher numbers correspond to a lower prevalence of bribe taking. Top 20 and bottom 20 are shown; see www.transparency.org for the most complete and up-to-date listings.

Source: Corruption Perceptions Index 2002. Used by permission of Transparency International. 2003 Index available at www.transparency.org.

| Rank | Country | CPI Score | Rank | Country | CPI Score |
|------|---------|-----------|------|---------|-----------|
| 1 | Finland | 9.7 | 81 | Albania | 2.5 |
| 2 | Denmark | 9.5 | 81 | Guatemala | 2.5 |
| 2 | New Zealand | 9.5 | 81 | Nicaragua | 2.5 |
| 4 | Iceland | 9.4 | 81 | Venezuela | 2.5 |
| 5 | Singapore | 9.3 | 85 | Georgia | 2.4 |
| 5 | Sweden | 9.3 | 85 | Ukraine | 2.4 |
| 7 | Canada | 9.0 | 85 | Vietnam | 2.4 |
| 7 | Luxembourg | 9.0 | 88 | Kazakhstan | 2.3 |
| 7 | Netherlands | 9.0 | 89 | Bolivia | 2.2 |
| 10 | United Kingdom | 8.7 | 89 | Cameroon | 2.2 |
| 11 | Australia | 8.6 | 89 | Ecuador | 2.2 |
| 12 | Norway | 8.5 | 89 | Haiti | 2.2 |
| 12 | Switzerland | 8.5 | 93 | Moldova | 2.1 |
| 14 | Hong Kong | 8.2 | 93 | Uganda | 2.1 |
| 15 | Austria | 7.8 | 95 | Azerbaijan | 2.0 |
| 16 | USA | 7.7 | 96 | Indonesia | 1.9 |
| 17 | Chile | 7.5 | 96 | Kenya | 1.9 |
| 18 | Germany | 7.3 | 98 | Angola | 1.7 |
| 18 | Israel | 7.3 | 98 | Madagascar | 1.7 |
| 20 | Belgium | 7.1 | 98 | Paraguay | 1.7 |
| 20 | Japan | 7.1 | 101 | Nigeria | 1.6 |
| 20 | Spain | 7.1 | 102 | Bangladesh | 1.2 |

will lead to constructive action. As one would expect, those countries receiving low scores are not pleased; however, the effect has been to raise public ire and debates in parliaments around the world—exactly the goal of TI.

Transparency International's CPI is also proving useful in academic studies of the causes and consequences of bribery. Completely consistent with our discussion of the origins and elements of culture described in Chapter 4 (see Exhibit 4.4), higher levels of bribery have

**Exhibit 5.5**

Transparency International Bribe Payers Index*

Higher scores correspond to lower levels of bribe paying internationally.

*Based on responses to questions such as: In the business sectors with which you are most familiar, please indicate how likely companies from the following countries are to pay or offer bribes to win or retain business in this country (respondent's country of residence).

Source: www.transparency.org. Used by permission of Transparency International.

| Rank | Country | 2002 | OECD Convention (as of 14 May 2002) |
|------|---------|------|-------------------------------------|
| 1 | Australia | 8.5 | Ratified |
| 2 | Sweden | 8.4 | Ratified |
| 2 | Switzerland | 8.4 | Ratified |
| 4 | Austria | 8.2 | Ratified |
| 5 | Canada | 8.1 | Ratified |
| 6 | Belgium | 7.8 | Ratified |
| 6 | Netherlands | 7.8 | Ratified |
| 8 | United Kingdom | 6.9 | Ratified |
| 9 | Germany | 6.3 | Ratified |
| 9 | Singapore | 6.3 | Not Signed |
| 11 | Spain | 5.8 | Ratified |
| 12 | France | 5.5 | Ratified |
| 13 | Japan | 5.3 | Ratified |
| 13 | United States | 5.3 | Ratified |
| 15 | Hong Kong | 4.3 | Not Signed |
| 15 | Malaysia | 4.3 | Not Signed |
| 17 | Italy | 4.1 | Ratified |
| 18 | South Korea | 3.9 | Ratified |
| 19 | Taiwan | 3.8 | Not Signed |
| 20 | China (People's Republic) | 3.5 | Not Signed |
| 21 | Russia | 3.2 | Not signed |

## CROSSING BORDERS 5.6    Bangladesh at the Bottom of the Corruption List? Uganda Is Moving Up.

The press in India (score of 2.7 on Transparency International's Corruption Perception Index where higher numbers mean more corruption) reports on the rampant corruption in neighboring Bangladesh (score of 1.2):

DHAKA: A magazine editor arrested on extortion charges was targeted by police for highlighting the case of a missing reporter, his family alleged on Wednesday. Mahmudul Haq, editor of *Upanagar* magazine, was arrested on Tuesday night on a street in Dhaka, Bangladesh's capital, police said. The news magazine is based in Sitakund, an industrial town 215 kilometers southeast of Dhaka. Haq was visiting Dhaka to press authorities to do more to trace Atahar Khasru, a friend and reporter who has been missing since April 30. Haq's family accused police of arresting the editor to harass him for aggressively pursuing the missing reporter's case and criticizing police for failing to find him. Last month, a local political leader, Nurul Islam, submitted a complaint to police accusing Haq of extortion and intimidation of businessmen. Haq denied the allegations and said he was being targeted for writing about corrupt police and politicians. On Tuesday, Khasru's family filed a case with the police accusing Nurul Islam and three other ruling party members of kidnapping the missing reporter.

From this report in the *Times of India* (May 7, 2003) it's indeed hard to tell who's good and who's bad in Bangladesh. Everyone is accusing everyone—the press, the police, and the politicians. What a mess!

Meanwhile, things seem to be improving in Uganda: Inside the hot, stuffy hearing room, already two months into the case of forgotten bank accounts and unexplained fleets of luxury four-wheel drive vehicles, Justice Julie Sebutinde loses her temper—again. She wags her finger at the witnesses, employees of Uganda's notoriously corrupt tax authority. "Today, I am going to have your lunch and supper," she barks.

Ms. Sebutinde, a petite, fiery mother of two, is the Uganda government's weapon of choice against corruption. Her investigations of the police department, the military, and most recently the tax authority, have exposed graft that has managed to shock a country where public skimming rarely surprises anyone.

All this has made the outspoken, sometimes outrageous "Lady Justice," as she is commonly known, into a celebrity here. Her popularity illustrates the growing pressure on countries like Uganda—currently ranked (near worst) among most-corrupt nations by Transparency International—to clean up their acts. "She is our voice," says Brenda Okello, a waitress at Madonna's Restaurant in downtown Kampala, serving plates of roasted goat and steamed bananas to the lunchtime crowd.

Indeed, Uganda has improved five places in the CPI 2002, perhaps thanks to "Lady Justice."

Source: Transparency International, www.transparency.org, 2003; and Rachel Scheier, "Uganda's Answer to Corruption: Fiery 'Lady Justice,'" *Christian Science Monitor*, May 7, 2003, p. 1. Reprinted by permission of Rachel Scheier.

been found in low-income nations and nations with a communist[32] past, both aspects of the political economy. Additionally, higher levels of bribery are found in collectivistic (IDV) and high power distance (PDI) countries. Finally, higher levels of bribery and the Foreign Corrupt Practices Act have deterred American firms participation in such countries.[33] Moreover, firms seem to generally eschew investments in corrupt countries as well.[34]

**Bribery: Variations on a Theme**

Although bribery is a legal issue, it is also important to see bribery in a cultural context in order to understand different attitudes toward it. Culturally, attitudes are significantly different among different peoples. Some cultures seem to be more open about taking

[32]Wayne Sandholtz and Rein Taagerpera, "Corruption, Culture, and Communism," working paper, Center for Global Peace and Conflict Studies, University of California, Irvine, 2004.

[33]H. Rika Houston and John L. Graham, "Culture and Corruption in International Markets: Implications for Policy Makers and Managers," *Consumption, Markets, and Culture*, 4(3), 2000, pp. 315–340.

[34]Mohsin Habib and Leon Zurawicki, "Corruption and Foreign Direct Investment," *Journal of International Business Studies*, 33(2), 2000, pp. 291–307.

bribes, while others, like the United States, are publicly contemptuous of such practices. But the U.S. firms are far from virtuous—we believe the TI "grade" of a C+ (7.6) to be about right. Regardless of where the line of acceptable conduct is drawn, there is no country where the people consider it proper for those in positions of political power to enrich themselves through illicit agreements at the expense of the best interests of the nation. A first step in understanding the culture of bribery is to appreciate the limitless variations that are often grouped under the word *bribery*. The activities under this umbrella term range from extortion through subornation to lubrication.

**Bribery and Extortion.**   The distinction between bribery and extortion depends on whether the activity resulted from an offer or from a demand for payment. Voluntarily offered payment by someone seeking unlawful advantage is *bribery*. For example, it is bribery if an executive of a company offers a government official payment if the official will incorrectly classify imported goods so the shipment will be taxed at a lower rate than correct classification would require. On the other hand, it is *extortion* if payments are extracted under duress by someone in authority from a person seeking only what they are lawfully entitled to. An example of extortion would be a finance minister of a country demanding heavy payments under the threat that a contract for millions of dollars would be voided.

On the surface, extortion may seem to be less morally wrong because the excuse can be made that "if we don't pay we don't get the contract" or "the official (devil) made me do it." But even if it is not legally wrong, it is morally wrong—and in the United States it is legally wrong.

**Subornation and Lubrication.**   Another variation of bribery is the difference between lubrication and subornation. *Lubrication* involves a relatively small sum of cash, a gift, or a service given to a low-ranking official in a country where such offerings are not prohibited by law. The purpose of such a gift is to facilitate or expedite the normal, lawful performance of a duty by that official. This is a practice common in many countries of the world. A small payment made to dock workers to speed up their pace so that unloading a truck takes a few hours rather than all day is an example of lubrication.

On the other hand, **subornation** involves giving large sums of money—frequently not properly accounted for—designed to entice an official to commit an illegal act on behalf of the one offering the bribe. Lubrication payments accompany requests for a person to do a job more rapidly or more efficiently; subornation is a request for officials to turn their heads, not to do their jobs, or to break the law.

**Agent's Fees.**   A third type of payment that can appear to be a bribe but may not be is an agent's fee. When a businessperson is uncertain of a country's rules and regulations, an agent may be hired to represent the company in that country. For example, an attorney may be hired to file an appeal for a variance in a building code on the basis that the attorney will do a more efficient and thorough job than someone unfamiliar with such procedures. Although this is often a legal and useful procedure, if a part of that agent's fees is used to pay bribes, the intermediary's fees are being used unlawfully. Under U.S. law, an official who knows of an agent's intention to bribe may risk prosecution and jail time. The Foreign Corrupt Practices Act **(FCPA)** prohibits U.S. businesses from paying bribes openly or using middlemen as conduits for a bribe when the U.S. official knows that part of the middleman's payment will be used as a bribe. There are many middlemen (attorneys, agents, distributors, and so forth) who function simply as conduits for illegal payments. The process is further complicated by legal codes that vary from country to country; what is illegal in one country may be winked at in another and be legal in a third. The answer to the question of bribery is not an unqualified one. It is easy to generalize about the ethics of political payoffs and other types of payments; it is much more difficult to make the decision to withhold payment of money when the consequences of not making the payment may affect the company's ability to do business profitably or at all. With the variety of ethical standards and levels of morality that exist in different cultures, the dilemma of ethics and pragmatism that faces international business cannot be resolved until the anticorruption accords among the OECD and OAS members are fully implemented and multinational businesses refuse to pay extortion or offer bribes.

The Foreign Corrupt Practices Act has had a positive effect. According to the latest Department of Commerce figures, since 1994 American businesses have bowed out of 294 major overseas commercial contracts valued at $145 billion rather than pay a bribe. This information corroborates the academic evidences cited above. Even though there are numerous reports indicating a definite reduction in U.S. firms paying bribes, the lure of contracts is too strong for some companies. Lockheed Corporation made $22 million in questionable foreign payments during the 1970s. More recently the company pled guilty to paying $1.8 million in bribes to a member of the Egyptian national parliament, in exchange for lobbying for three air cargo planes worth $79 million to be sold to the military. Lockheed was caught and fined $25 million, and cargo plane exports by the company were banned for three years. Lockheed's actions during the 1970s were a major influence on the passing of the FCPA. The company now maintains one of the most comprehensive ethics and legal training programs of any major corporation in the United States.

It would be naïve to assume that laws and the resulting penalties alone will put an end to corruption. Change will come only from more ethically and socially responsible decisions by both buyers and sellers and by governments willing to take a stand.

## Ethically and Socially Responsible Decisions

To behave in an ethically and socially responsible way should be the hallmark of every businessperson's behavior, domestic or international. It requires little thought for most of us to know the socially responsible or ethically correct response to questions about breaking the law, harming the environment, denying someone his or her rights, taking unfair advantage, or behaving in a manner that would bring bodily harm or damage. Unfortunately, the difficult issues are not the obvious and simple right-or-wrong ones. In many countries the international marketer faces the dilemma of responding to sundry situations where there is no local law, where local practices condone a certain behavior, or where the company willing to "do what is necessary" is favored over the company that refuses to engage in practices that are not ethical. In short, being socially responsible and ethically correct are not simple tasks for the international marketer operating in countries whose cultural and social values or economic needs are different from those of the marketer.

In normal business operations there are five broad areas where difficulties arise in making decisions, establishing policies, and engaging in business operations: (1) employment practices and policies, (2) consumer protection, (3) environmental protection, (4) political payments and involvement in political affairs of the country, and (5) basic human rights and fundamental freedoms. In many countries, laws may help define the borders of minimal ethical or social responsibility, but the law is only the floor above which one's social and personal morality is tested. The statement that "there is no controlling legal authority" may mean that the behavior is not illegal but it does not mean that the behavior is morally correct or ethical. Ethical business conduct should normally exist at a level well above the minimum required by law or the "controlling legal authority." In fact, laws are the markers of past behavior that society has deemed unethical or socially irresponsible.

Perhaps the best guide to good business ethics are the examples set by ethical business leaders.[35] However, three ethical principles also provide a framework to help the marketer distinguish between right and wrong, determine what ought to be done, and properly justify his or her actions. Simply stated they are as follows.

- **Utilitarian ethics**—Does the action optimize the "common good" or benefits of all constituencies? And who are the pertinent constituencies?

- **Rights of the parties**—Does the action respect the rights of the individuals involved?

---

[35]John A. Byrne, "Goodbye to an Ethicist," *BusinessWeek,* February 10, 2003.

- **Justice or fairness**—Does the action respect the canons of justice or fairness to all parties involved?

Answers to these questions can help the marketer ascertain the degree to which decisions are beneficial or harmful, right or wrong, or whether the consequences of actions are ethically or socially responsible. Perhaps the best framework to work within is defined by asking: Is it legal? Is it right? Can it withstand disclosure to stockholders, to company officials, and to the public?[36]

Although the United States has clearly led the campaign against international bribery, European firms and institutions are apparently putting more effort and money into the promotion of what they call "corporate social responsibility."[37] For example, the watch dog group Corporate Social Responsibility (CSR) Europe, in cooperation with the INSEAD business school outside Paris, is studying the relationship between investment attractiveness and positive corporate behaviors on several dimensions. Their studies find a strong link between firms' social responsibility and European institutional investors' choices for equity investments.[38] All this is not to say that European firms do not still have their own corporate misbehaviors.[39] However, we expect more efforts in the future to focus on measuring and monitoring corporate social responsibility around the world.

## Culture's Influence on Strategic Thinking

Perhaps Lester Thurow provided the most articulate description of how culture influences managers' thinking about business strategy.[40] He distinguished between the British-American "individualistic" kind of capitalism and the "communitarian" form of capitalism in Japan and Germany. The business systems in the latter two countries are typified by cooperation among government, management, and labor, particularly in Japan. On the other hand, adversarial relationships among labor, management, and government are more the norm in the United Kingdom, and particularly in the United States. We see these cultural differences reflected in Hofstede's results—on the IDV scale the United States is 91, the United Kingdom is 89, Germany is 67, and Japan is 46.

We also find evidence of these differences in a comparison of the performance of American, German, and Japanese firms.[41] In the less individualistic cultures labor and management cooperate—in Germany labor is represented on corporate boards, and in Japan management takes responsibility for the welfare of the labor force. Because the welfare of the workforce matters to Japanese and German firms, their sales revenues are more stable over time. American-style layoffs are eschewed. The individualistic American approach to labor-management relations is adversarial—each side takes care of itself. Therefore we have damaging strikes and huge layoffs that result in more volatile performance for American firms.

At the start of this century, the American emphasis on competition seems to be the best approach. But it is important to recall that key word in Adam Smith's justification for competition—"frequently." It's worth repeating here, "By pursuing his own interest he frequently promotes that of society. . . ." Smith wrote *frequently,* not *always, most of*

[36]For a comprehensive study of social contracts and ethics, see Thomas W. Dunfee, N. Craig Smith, and William T. Ross, "Social Contracts and Marketing Ethics," *Journal of Marketing,* July 1999, p. 14.

[37]Isabelle Maignan and David A. Ralston, "Corporate Social Responsibility in Europe and the U.S.: Insights form Businesses' Self-Presentations," *Journal of International Business Studies,* 33(3), 2002, pp. 497–514.

[38]See www.csreurope.org; and Howard Stock, "Euro Funds Bank on Social Metrics," *Investor Relations Business,* April 21, 2003, p. 1.

[39]Carol Matlack, John Rossant, David Fairlamb, and Kerry Campbell, "The Year of Nasty Surprises: Suddenly the Continent Is Awash in Accounting Scandals," *BusinessWeek,* March 10, 2003, pp. 48–50.

[40]Lester Thurow, *Head to Head* (New York: William Morrow, 1992).

[41]Cathy Anterasian, John L. Graham, and R. Bruce Money, "Are U.S. Managers Superstitious about Market Share?" *Sloan Management Review* 37(4), 1996, pp. 67–77.

After a decade of stagnation in Japan, the social contract of life-time employment is softening. This is reflected in more frequent corporate layoffs, frustrating job searches, and "tent villages" in public places such as Ueno Park in Tokyo. But, even at their worst in history, Japanese jobless are just a trickle compared to the torrent of pink slips and homeless folks when the American economy heads south. *(left: © Tom Wagner/CORBIS SABA)*

*the time,* or even *often.*[42] A competitive, individualistic approach works well in the context of an economic boom. During the late 1990s American firms dominated Japanese and European ones. The latter seemed stodgy, conservative, and slow in the global information economy. However, downturns in a competitive culture can be ugly things. A review of the performance and layoffs at Boeing during the commercial aircraft busts of the late 1990s and early 2000s is instructive.

It should also be mentioned that Thurow and others writing in the area omitted a fourth kind of capitalism—that found in Chinese cultures. Its distinguishing characteristics are a more entrepreneurial approach and an emphasis on *guanxi* (one's network of personal connections)[43] as the coordinating principle among firms.[44] This fourth kind of capitalism is also predicted by culture. Chinese cultures are high on PDI and low on IDV and the strong reciprocity implied by the notion of *guanxi* fits the profile well.

## A Synthesis, Relationship-Oriented versus Information-Oriented Cultures

With increasing frequency studies are noting a strong relationship between Hall's high/low context and Hofstede's Individualism/Collective and Power Distance indices. For example, low-context American culture scores relatively low on power distance and high on individualism, while high-context Arab cultures score high on power distance and low on individualism. This is not at all surprising given that Hofstede[45] leans heavily on Hall's ideas in developing and labeling the dimensions of culture revealed via his huge database. In fact, the three dimensions, high/low context, IDV, and PDI, are correlated above the $r = 0.6$ level, suggesting that all three dimensions are largely measuring the same thing.[46] Likewise, when we compare linguistic distance (to English) and Transparency International's Corruption Perception Index to the other three we see similar levels of correlation among all five dimensions. And while metrics for other dimensions of business culture do not yet exist, a pattern is evident. Please see Exhibit 5.6.

---

[42]For more in this vein see Roger Lowenstein, "How Good Is Greed?" *Smart Money,* February 2003, pp. 56–57.

[43]Mark Lam and John L. Graham, *Red China, Green China* (Boulder, CO: Rowman & Littlefield, 2004).

[44]Steven S. Standifird and R. Scott Marshall, "Transaction Cost Advantage in Guanxi-Based Business Practice," *Journal of World Business* 35(1), pp. 212–42.

[45]Geert Hofstede, *Culture's Consequences,* 2nd edition (Thousand Oaks, CA: Sage, 2001).

[46]This continuum has also been labeled "social context salience" in H. Rika Houston and John L. Graham, 2000.

**Exhibit 5.6**
Dimensions of Culture,
A Synthesis

| **Information-Oriented (IO)** | **Relationship-Oriented (RO)** |
| --- | --- |
| Low-context | High-context |
| Individualism | Collectivism |
| Low power distance | High power distance (including gender) |
| Bribery less common | Bribery more common |
| Low distance from English | High distance from English |
| Linguistic directness | Linguistic indirectness |
| Monochronic time | Polychronic time |
| Internet | Face-to-face |
| Foreground | Background |
| Competition | Reduce transaction costs |

The pattern displayed is not definitive, only suggestive. Not every culture fits every dimension of culture in a precise way. However, the synthesis is useful in many ways. Primarily, it gives us a simple yet logical way to think about many of the cultural differences described in Chapters 4 and 5. For example, American culture is low-context, individualistic (IDV), low power distance (PDI), and obviously close to English. Bribery is less common and Americans are monochronic time oriented, linguistically direct, foreground-focused,[47] and they achieve efficiency through competition. Therefore the United States is categorized hereafter in the book as an *information-oriented culture.* Alternatively, Japanese culture is high-context, collectivistic, high power distance, far from English, bribery is more common, polychronic (in part), linguistically indirect, background-focused. Japanese culture achieves efficiency through reduction of transaction costs, and therefore is properly categorized as a *relationship culture.* All this is true even though both the United States and Japan are populous, high-income democracies. Both cultures do achieve efficiency, but through different methods. The American business system uses competition, whereas the Japanese depend more on reducing transaction costs.

The most managerially useful aspect of this synthesis of cultural differences is that it allows us to make predictions about unfamiliar cultures. Reference to the three metrics available give us some clues about how consumers and business partners will behave and think. Hofstede has provided scores for 78 countries and regions, and we have included them in the Appendix. Find a country on the list and you have some information about that market. One might expect Trinidad to be an information-oriented culture and Russia to be a relationship-oriented culture, and so on. Moreover, measures of linguistic distance (any language can be used as the focal one, not just English) are available for every country or person. Thus we would expect that someone who speaks Javanese as his or her first language is more relationship-oriented.

In closing we are quite encouraged by the publication of the important book, *Culture Matters.*[48] We obviously agree with the sentiment of the title, and hope the book will help rekindle the interest in culture's pervasive influences that Max Weber and others initiated so long ago.

---

[47]Richard E. Nisbett, *The Geography of Thought* (New York: Free Press, 2003).

[48]Lawrence I. Harrison and Samuel P. Huntington (eds.), *Culture Matters* (New York: Basic Books, 2000).

# Summary

Management styles differ around the world. Some cultures emphasize the importance of information and competition while others focus more on relationships and transaction cost reductions. However, there are no simple answers and the only safe generalization is that businesspersons working in another country must be sensitive to the business environment and must be willing to adapt when necessary. Unfortunately, it is not always easy to know when such adaptation is necessary; in some instances adaptation is optional whereas in others it is actually undesirable. Understanding the culture you are entering is the only sound basis for planning.

Business behavior is derived in large part from the basic cultural environment in which the business operates and, as such, is subject to the extreme diversity encountered among various cultures and subcultures. Environmental considerations significantly affect the attitudes, behavior, and outlook of foreign businesspeople. Motivational patterns of such businesspeople depend in part on their personal backgrounds, their business positions, their sources of authority, and their own personalities.

Varying motivational patterns inevitably affect methods of doing business in different countries. Marketers in some countries thrive on competition, while in others they do everything possible to eliminate it. The authoritarian, centralized decision-making orientation in some nations contrasts sharply with democratic decentralization in others. International variation characterizes contact level, ethical orientation, negotiation outlook, and nearly every part of doing business. The foreign marketer can take no phase of business behavior for granted.

The new breed of international businessperson emerging in recent years has a heightened sensitivity to cultural variations. However, sensitivity is not enough; the international trader must be constantly alert and prepared to adapt when necessary. One must always realize that no matter how long you are in a country, the outsider is not a local; in many countries that person may always be treated as an outsider. Finally, one must avoid the critical mistake of assuming that knowledge of one culture will provide acceptability in another.

# Questions

1. Define:

   cultural imperative, 125
   cultural elective, 125
   cultural exclusive, 125
   silent language, 133
   M-time, 139
   P-time, 139

   subornation, 147
   FCPA, 147
   principle of utilitarian ethics, 148
   principle of rights of the
      parties, 148
   principle of justice or fairness, 149

2. "More than tolerance of an alien culture is required; there is a need for affirmative acceptance of the concept 'different but equal.'" Elaborate.

3. "We should also bear in mind that in today's business-oriented world economy, the cultures themselves are being significantly affected by business activities and business practices." Comment.

4. "In dealing with foreign businesses, the marketer must be particularly aware of the varying objectives and aspirations of management." Explain.

5. Suggest ways in which persons might prepare themselves to handle unique business customs that may be encountered in a trip abroad.

6. Business customs and national customs are closely interrelated. In which ways would one expect the two areas to coincide and in which ways would they show differences? How could such areas of similarity and difference be identified?

7. Identify both local and foreign examples of cultural imperatives, electives, and exclusives. Be prepared to explain why each example fits into the category you have selected.

8. Contrast the authority roles of top management in different societies. How do the different views of authority affect marketing activities?

9. Do the same for aspirational patterns.

10. What effects on business customs might be anticipated from the recent rapid increases in the level of international business activity?

11. Interview some foreign students to determine the types of cultural shock they encountered when they first came to your country.

12. Differentiate between:

    Private ownership and family ownership
    Decentralized and committee decision making

13. In which ways does the size of a customer's business affect business behavior?

14. Compare three decision-making authority patterns in international business.

15. Explore the various ways in which business customs affect the structure of competition.

16. Why is it important that the business executive be alert to the significance of differing management styles?

17. Suggest some cautions that an individual from a relationship-oriented culture should bear in mind when dealing with someone from an information-oriented culture.

18. Political payoffs are a problem. How would you react if you faced the prospect of paying a bribe? If you knew that by not paying you would not be able to complete a $10 million contract?

19. Differentiate among the following:

    subornation            lubrication
    extortion              bribery

20. Distinguish between P-time and M-time.

21. Discuss how a P-time person reacts differently from an M-time person in keeping an appointment.

22. What is meant by "laws are the markers of past behavior that society has deemed unethical or socially irresponsible"?

23. What are the three ethical principles that provide a framework to help distinguish between right and wrong? Explain.

24. Visit Transparency International's website and check to see how the CPI Index for countries listed in Exhibits 5.4 and 5.5 have changed. Searching TI's databank, explain why the changes have occurred. The site is found at www.transparency.org.

25. Discuss the pros and cons of the statement "there is no controlling legal authority," as a basis for ethical behavior.

26. "The *company.com* page is a company's front door and that doorway should be global in scope." Discuss. Visit several websites of major multinational companies and evaluate their "front door" to the global world.

27. Visit the websites of Shell and Nike and compare their statements on corporate values. What are the major issues that each address? Do you think their statements are useful as guides to ethically and socially responsible decision making?

28. Go to your favorite web reference source and access some recent news articles on Nike and alleged human rights violations. Access the Nike statement on corporate values and write a brief statement on the alleged violations and Nike's statement of corporate values.

# Appendix: Index Scores for Countries and Regions

| Country | Power Distance | Uncertainty Avoidance | Individualism/ Collectivism | Masculinity/ Femininity | Long-Short-Term Orientation | Primary Language | Distance from English |
|---|---|---|---|---|---|---|---|
| Argentina | 49 | 86 | 46 | 56 | | Spanish | 3 |
| Australia total | 36 | 51 | 90 | 61 | 31 | English | 0 |
| Aborigines | 80 | 128 | 89 | 22 | 10 | Australian | 7 |
| Austria | 11 | 70 | 55 | 79 | 31 | German | 1 |
| Bangladesh | 80 | 60 | 20 | 55 | 40 | Bengali | 3 |
| Belgium total | 65 | 94 | 75 | 54 | 38 | Dutch | 1 |
| Dutch speakers | 61 | 97 | 78 | 43 | | Dutch | 1 |
| French speakers | 67 | 93 | 72 | 60 | | French | 3 |
| Brazil | 69 | 76 | 38 | 49 | 65 | Portuguese | 3 |
| Bulgaria | 70 | 85 | 30 | 40 | | Bulgarian | 3 |
| Canada total | 39 | 48 | 80 | 52 | 23 | English | 0 |
| French speakers | 54 | 60 | 73 | 45 | 30 | French | 3 |
| Chile | 63 | 86 | 23 | 28 | | Spanish | 3 |
| China | 80 | 30 | 20 | 66 | 118 | Mandarin | 6 |
| Colombia | 67 | 80 | 13 | 64 | | Spanish | 3 |
| Costa Rica | 35 | 86 | 15 | 21 | | Spanish | 3 |
| Czech Republic | 57 | 74 | 58 | 57 | 13 | Czech | 1 |
| Denmark | 18 | 23 | 74 | 16 | 46 | Danish | 3 |
| Ecuador | 78 | 67 | 8 | 63 | | Spanish | 3 |
| Estonia | 40 | 60 | 60 | 30 | | Estonian | 4 |
| Finland | 33 | 59 | 63 | 26 | 41 | Finnish | 4 |
| France | 68 | 86 | 71 | 43 | 39 | French | 3 |
| Germany | 35 | 65 | 67 | 66 | 31 | German | 1 |
| Great Britain | 35 | 35 | 89 | 66 | 25 | English | 0 |
| Greece | 60 | 112 | 35 | 57 | | Greek | 3 |
| Guatemala | 95 | 101 | 6 | 37 | | Spanish | 3 |
| Hong Kong | 68 | 29 | 25 | 57 | 96 | Cantonese | 6 |
| Hungary | 46 | 82 | 80 | 88 | 50 | Hungarian | 4 |
| India | 77 | 40 | 48 | 56 | 61 | Dravidian | 3 |
| Indonesia | 78 | 48 | 14 | 46 | | Bahasa | 7 |
| Iran | 58 | 59 | 41 | 43 | | Farsi | 3 |
| Ireland | 28 | 35 | 70 | 68 | 43 | English | 0 |
| Israel | 13 | 81 | 54 | 47 | | Hebrew | 5 |
| Italy | 50 | 75 | 76 | 70 | 34 | Italian | 3 |
| Jamaica | 45 | 13 | 39 | 68 | | English | 0 |
| Japan | 54 | 92 | 46 | 95 | 80 | Japanese | 4 |
| Korea (South) | 60 | 85 | 18 | 39 | 75 | Korean | 4 |
| Luxembourg | 40 | 70 | 60 | 50 | | Luxembourgish | 1 |

| Country | Power Distance | Uncertainty Avoidance | Individualism/ Collectivism | Masculinity/ Femininity | Long-Short-Term Orientation | Primary Language | Distance from English |
|---|---|---|---|---|---|---|---|
| Malaysia | 104 | 36 | 26 | 50 | | Malay | 7 |
| Malta | 56 | 96 | 59 | 47 | | Maltese | 5 |
| Mexico | 81 | 82 | 30 | 69 | | Spanish | 3 |
| Morocco | 70 | 68 | 46 | 53 | | Arabic | 5 |
| Netherlands | 38 | 53 | 80 | 14 | 44 | Dutch | 1 |
| New Zealand | 22 | 49 | 79 | 58 | 30 | English | 0 |
| Norway | 31 | 50 | 69 | 8 | 44 | Norwegian | 1 |
| Pakistan | 55 | 70 | 14 | 50 | 0 | Panjabi | 3 |
| Panama | 95 | 86 | 11 | 44 | | Spanish | 3 |
| Peru | 64 | 87 | 16 | 42 | | Spanish | 3 |
| Philippines | 94 | 44 | 32 | 64 | 19 | Tagalog | 7 |
| Poland | 68 | 93 | 60 | 64 | 32 | Polish | 3 |
| Portugal | 63 | 104 | 27 | 31 | 30 | Portuguese | 3 |
| Romania | 90 | 90 | 30 | 42 | | Romanian | 3 |
| Russia | 93 | 95 | 39 | 36 | | Russian | 3 |
| Salvador | 66 | 94 | 19 | 40 | | Spanish | 3 |
| Singapore | 74 | 8 | 20 | 48 | 48 | Mandarin | 6 |
| Slovakia | 104 | 51 | 52 | 110 | 38 | Slovak | 3 |
| South Africa | 49 | 49 | 65 | 63 | | Afrikaans | 1 |
| Spain | 57 | 86 | 51 | 42 | 19 | Spanish | 3 |
| Surinam | 85 | 92 | 47 | 37 | | Dutch | 1 |
| Sweden | 31 | 29 | 71 | 5 | 33 | Swedish | 1 |
| Switzerland total | 34 | 58 | 68 | 70 | 40 | German | 1 |
| German speakers | 26 | 56 | 69 | 72 | | German | 1 |
| French speakers | 70 | 70 | 64 | 58 | | French | 3 |
| Taiwan | 58 | 69 | 17 | 45 | 87 | Taiwanese | 6 |
| Thailand | 64 | 64 | 20 | 34 | 56 | Thai | 7 |
| Trinidad | 47 | 55 | 16 | 58 | | English | 0 |
| Turkey | 66 | 85 | 37 | 45 | | Turkish | 4 |
| United States | 40 | 46 | 91 | 62 | 29 | English | 0 |
| Uruguay | 61 | 100 | 36 | 38 | | Spanish | 3 |
| Venezuela | 81 | 76 | 12 | 73 | | Spanish | 3 |
| Vietnam | 70 | 30 | 20 | 40 | 80 | Vietnamese | 7 |
| Yugoslavia total | 76 | 88 | 27 | 21 | | Serbo-Croatian | 3 |
| Croatia (Zagreb) | 73 | 80 | 33 | 40 | | Serbo-Croatian | 3 |
| Serbia (Beograd) | 86 | 92 | 25 | 43 | | Serbo-Croatian | 3 |
| Slovenia (Ljubljana) | 71 | 88 | 27 | 19 | | Slovene | 3 |
| **Regions** | | | | | | | |
| Arab countries | 80 | 68 | 38 | 53 | | Arabic | 5 |
| East Africa | 64 | 52 | 27 | 41 | 25 | | 8 |
| West Africa | 77 | 54 | 20 | 46 | 16 | | 8 |

Source: Geert Hofstede, *Culture's Consequences*, 2nd edition (Thousand Oaks, CA: Sage, 2001).

# CHAPTER 6

# the political environment:
## A CRITICAL CONCERN

## CHAPTER LEARNING OBJECTIVES

What you should learn from Chapter 6:

- What the sovereignty of nations means and how it affects the stability of government policies, political parties, and nationalism

- The political risks of global business and the factors that affect stability

- The importance of the political system to international marketing and its effect on foreign investments

- The impact of political and social activists, violence, and terrorism on international business

- Assessing and reducing the effect of political vulnerability

- How and why governments encourage foreign investment

# Global Perspective

## CHIQUITA BANANAS AND PROSCIUTTO DI PARMA, LOUIS VUITTON HANDBAGS, SCENTED BATH OILS AND SOAPS, AND BATTERIES—STRANGE BEDFELLOWS FROM THE WORLD OF POLITICS

As the old saying goes, "Politics makes strange bedfellows," but in this case the only one making out is Miss Chiquita Banana. Prosciutto di Parma ham from Italy, handbags from France, bath oils and soaps from Germany, and a host of other imported products from Europe were all slapped with a 100 percent import tariff as retaliation by the U.S. government against European Union (EU) banana-import rules that favor Caribbean bananas over Latin American bananas. Keep in mind that no bananas are exported from the United States, yet the United States has been engaged in a trade war over the last seven years that has cost numerous small businesses on both sides of the Atlantic millions of dollars. But how can this be, you ask? Politics, that's how!

A retailer of decorative prints has stopped selling one of the store's most popular and profitable items, English lithographs produced for him by a London art dealer. Action Battery, which sells and installs industrial batteries, has lost a quarter-million dollar account and faces the prospect of more losses. The same issue, a 100 percent tariff placed on all their imported products, has affected all these businesses; one directive from the U.S. government doubled the cost of their imported goods.

Reha Enterprises, for example, sells bath oil, soap, and other supplies imported from Germany. The tariff on its most popular product, an herbal foam bath, was raised from 5 percent to 100 percent. The customs bill for six months spiraled to $37,783 from just $1,851—a 1,941 percent tax increase. For a small business whose gross sales are less than $1 million annually, it is crippling. When the owner heard of the impending "banana war" he called everyone—his Congressman, his Senator, the United States Trade Representative (USTR). When he described his plight to a U.S. trade representative, the official expressed amazement. "They were surprised I was still importing," because they thought the tariff would cut off the industry entirely. That was their intention, which, of course, would have meant killing Reha Enterprises as well.

In effect, he was told it was his fault that he got caught up in the trade war. He should have attended the hearings in Washington just like Gillette and Mattel, and maybe his products would have been dropped from the targeted list just as theirs were. Scores of European products, from clothing to stoves to glass Christmas ornaments, dolls, and ballpoint pens that were originally targeted for the retaliatory tariffs escaped the tariff. Aggressive lobbying by large corporations, trade groups, and members of Congress got most of the threatened imported products off the list. The USTR had published a list of the targeted imports in the *Federal Register* inviting affected companies to testify. Unfortunately, the *Federal Register* is not on the owner's reading list.

In that case, he was told, he should have hired a lobbyist in Washington to keep him briefed. Good advice—but it doesn't make much sense to a company that grosses less than $1 million a year. Other advice received from an official of the USTR included the off-the-record suggestion that he might want to change the custom number on the invoice so it would appear that he was importing goods not subject to the tariff, a decision that could, if he were caught, result in a hefty fine or jail for the owner. Smaller businesses in Europe are facing similar problems as their export business dries up because of the tariffs.

How did this banana war start? The EU imposed a quota and tariffs that favored imports from ex-colonies in the Caribbean and Africa, distributed by European firms, over Latin American bananas, distributed by U.S. firms. Chiquita Brands International and Dole Food Company, contending that the EU's "illegal trade barriers" were costing $520 million annually in lost sales to Europe, asked the U.S. government for help. The government agreed that unfair trade barriers were damaging their business, and 100 percent tariffs on selected European imports were levied. Coincidentally, Chiquita Brands' annual campaign contributions increased from barely over $40,000 in 1991 to $1.3 million in 1998.

The European Union complained about the proposed U.S. tariffs and took a grievance to the World Trade Organization (WTO), which ruled in favor of the United States. The EU ignored the WTO and continued the banana tariffs, and the United States continued with its high tariffs—the banana war continued. The EU did little to comply with WTO rulings against European restrictions on importing bananas, and the war heated up. Because of lack of compliance, the USTR imposed a "carousel" provision that allows it to rotate, every six months, products that will be targeted for the 100 percent tariffs. Like all trade disputes, this one was ultimately settled, but at what cost to those caught in the middle between two nations and a giant MNC? The biggest losers were the African and Caribbean countries that Europe favored in the dispute. A glut in production has driven prices down and farmers are selling fewer bananas at lower prices.

This Global Perspective epitomizes the conflicts in which companies and governments often find themselves embroiled when engaging in international business. Whether domestic or international, government actions can affect your business in ways difficult to imagine. Always hovering around is the cloud that politics can cast over your well-designed business plan. As you read this chapter, make a mental note of which of the topics apply to this Perspective.

Sources: "U.S. Sets Import Tariffs in Latest Salvo in Ongoing Battle over Banana Trade," *Minneapolis Star Tribune,* March 4, 1999; Timothy Dove, "Hit by a $200,000 Bill from the Blue," *Time,* February 7, 2000, p. 54; "How to Become a Top Banana," *Time,* February 7, 2000, p. 42; Ben Ross, "Candle Maker to Sue EC After Getting Burnt in Banana War," *Independent on Sunday,* April 22, 2001; Robert Fairburn, "Banana War Boost for Knitwear Firms," *Daily Record,* April 13, 2001; and Sarah Ryle, "Banana War Leaves the Caribbean a Casualty," *The Observer,* November 24, 2002.

No company, domestic or international, large or small, can conduct business without considering the influence of the political environment within which it operates. One of the most undeniable and crucial realities of international business is that both host and home governments are integral partners. A government reacts to its environment by initiating and pursuing policies deemed necessary to solve the problems created by its particular circumstances. Reflected in its policies and attitudes toward business are a government's ideas of how best to promote the national interest, considering its own resources and political philosophy. A government controls and restricts a company's activities by encouraging and offering support or by discouraging and banning or restricting its activities—depending on the pleasure of the government.

International law recognizes the sovereign right of a nation to grant or withhold permission to do business within its political boundaries and to control where its citizens conduct business. Thus the political environment of countries is a critical concern for the international marketer. This chapter examines some of the more salient political considerations in assessing global markets.

## The Sovereignty of Nations

In the context of international law, a *sovereign state* is independent and free from all external control; enjoys full legal equality with other states; governs its own territory; selects its own political, economic, and social systems; and has the power to enter into agreements with other nations. **Sovereignty** refers to both the powers exercised by a state in relation to other countries and the supreme powers exercised over its own members.[1] A state sets requirements for citizenship, defines geographical boundaries, and controls trade and the movement of people and goods across its borders. Additionally, a citizen is subject to the state's laws even when beyond national borders. It is with the extension of national laws beyond a country's borders that much of the conflict in international business arises.[2] This is especially true when another country considers its own sovereignty to be compromised.

Nations can and do abridge specific aspects of their sovereign rights in order to coexist with other nations. The European Union,[3] North American Free Trade Agreement (NAFTA), North Atlantic Treaty Organization (NATO), and World Trade Organization (WTO) are examples of nations voluntarily agreeing to give up some of their sovereign rights in order to participate with member nations for a common, mutually beneficial goal.[4] Even though a state often relinquishes certain of its sovereign rights in order to coexist with others, any breach of a sovereign right to which it has not consented is considered an unfriendly act.

---

[1] For those interested in learning more about the concept of sovereignty, see Stephen D. Krasner, (editor), *Problematic Sovereignty,* New York, NY: Columbia University Press, 2001.

[2] "Peace Versus Sovereignty," *Jakarta Post,* April 29, 2003, p. 6A.

[3] As the EU gains strength each year, the sovereignty of each of its members continues to be an issue. See, for example, William Pfaff, "What About National Sovereignty in Future Europe?" *International Herald Tribune,* February 18, 2000.

[4] For more on sovereignty and the EU including a discussion of future problems when Eastern European nations are admitted to the EU, see Lesile Friedman Goldstein, *Constituting Federal Sovereignty: The European Union in Comparative Context,* Baltimore, MD: Johns Hopkins University Press, 2001.

When countries agree to relinquish some of their sovereignty there often remains a nagging fear that too much has been given away. For example, the WTO is considered by some to be a threat to national sovereignty. Adherence to the WTO inevitably means loss of some degree of national sovereignty because the member nations have pledged to abide by international covenants and arbitration procedures that can override national laws and have far-reaching ramifications for citizens. Sovereignty was one of the issues at the heart of the spat between the United States and the EU over Europe's refusal to lower tariffs and quotas on bananas (see the Global Perspective).

Foreign investment can also be perceived as a threat to sovereignty and thus become a rallying cry by opposing factions. For example, Mexico badly needs privately financed electricity generating plants to meet electrical power demands and to upgrade the country's overloaded transmission network. The Mexican government entered into an agreement with a Belgian company to build a power plant that would bypass the state electricity monopoly and sell electricity directly to large Mexican manufacturers. But the Mexican Constitution limits private ownership of utilities and any exception requires a two-thirds vote of the legislature. The Institutional Revolutionary Party saw the attempt to open Mexico's protected energy industry as an assault on Mexican sovereignty and blocked the agreement.[5] This highlights the fact that national sovereignty is a critical issue in assessing the environment in which a firm operates.

## Stability of Government Policies

The ideal political climate for a multinational firm is a stable, friendly government. Unfortunately, governments are not always stable and friendly, nor do stable, friendly governments remain so. Radical shifts in government philosophy when an opposing political party ascends to power,[6] pressure from nationalist and self-interest groups, weakened economic conditions, bias against foreign investment or conflicts between governments[7] are all issues that can affect the stability of a government. Because foreign businesses are judged by standards as variable as there are nations, the stability and friendliness of the government in each country must be assessed as an ongoing business practice.[8]

At the top of the list of political issues concerning foreign businesses is the stability or instability of prevailing government policies. Governments might change or new political parties might be elected, but the concern of the multinational corporation is the continuity of the set of rules or code of behavior and the continuation of the rule of law—regardless of which government is in power.[9] A change in government, whether by election or coup, does not always mean a change in the level of political risk. In Italy, for example, there have been more than 50 different governments formed since the end of World War II. Although the political turmoil in Italy continues,[10] business goes on as usual. In contrast, India has had as many different governments since 1945 as Italy, with several in the past few years favorable to foreign investment and open markets; however, much government policy remains hostile to foreign investment. Senior civil servants who are not directly accountable to the electorate but who remain in place despite the change of the elected government continue with former policies. Even after elections of parties favoring economic reform, the bureaucracy continues to be staffed by old-style central planners.

---

[5]Elisabeth Malkin, "Mexico Turns to Investors To Add to Power Capacity," *New York Times,* March 18, 2003.

[6]Paul S. Orogun, "Crisis of Government, Ethnic Schisms, Civil War, and Regional Destabilization of the Democratic Republic of Congo," *World Affairs,* July 2002, p. 25.

[7]E. Eduardo Castillo, "Fox: Mexico's Opposition to Iraq War Damaged U.S.–Mexican Relations," *APWorldstream,* April 10, 2003.

[8]For an interesting analogy of how governments should relate to foreign investors, see Yose Rizal Damuri, "Investors Are Like Mistresses," *The Jakarta Post,* December 12, 2002.

[9]Attitudes about investing in Russia began to change when President Putin pledged that he would restore the "rule of law." Martin R. Snyder, "Doing Business in Russia Again?!" *The Moscow Times,* January 9, 2002.

[10]Steve Pagani, "New Government or Elections? Italy Awaits," *Reuters,* April, 19, 2000.

A supporter of presidential candidate Francisco Labastida of the ruling Institutional Revolutionary Party (PRI) waits for results in Mexico's general elections. Francisco Labastida was the first candidate in the PRI's 70-year rule of Mexico to win the party's nomination for president in an open election. Until then, the incumbent president handpicked the PRI's candidate. (© AFP/CORBIS)

Conversely, radical changes in policies toward foreign business can occur in the most stable governments. The same political party, the Institutional Revolutionary Party (PRI), controlled Mexico from 1929 to 2000. During that period, the political risk for foreign investors ranged from expropriation of foreign investments to Mexico's membership in NAFTA and an open door for foreign investment and trade. In recent years, the PRI created a stable political environment for foreign investment in contrast to earlier expropriations and harassment. Beginning with the elections in 2000, however, a new era in Mexican politics emerged as a result of profound changes within the PRI brought about by President Zedillo. Since 1929, the Mexican president had selected his successor, who, without effective challenge, was always elected. President Zedillo changed the process by refusing to nominate a candidate; instead he let the nomination be decided by an open primary—the first in seven decades. From a field of four candidates the PRI selected Labastida Ochoa and the opposing party, PAN,[11] selected Vicente Fox who, although considered a long shot, won the presidency. Although the PAN had gained strength for several years in the congress and among state governments, its presidential candidates never had a winning chance until the 2000 election.

Seventy-one years of uninterrupted rule by the PRI ended in 2000. It was the first time in the country's long history of ancient kingdoms, colonialism, civil war, dictatorship, and revolution that one regime has given way to another peacefully. Further, this election will go on record as the cleanest and tightest in Mexican history.

A new era in Mexico's economic and social history began when President Fox assumed office. However, the tasks facing the new president are enormous. It is too soon to tell if President Fox will be able to move the Mexican government in a direction that will overcome the economic and social problems[12] facing Mexico and at the same time maintain a stable and friendly environment for foreign investments. If this monumental shift in political power is to be successful, a government must be fashioned that will differentiate a Fox administration from his predecessors while building on the PRI's recent successes in the economic arena.[13] The economic turmoil that has erupted during past changes of government must be avoided, an entrenched bureaucracy with allegiance to an opposing political party must be won over or replaced, an escalating crime wave (estimated to cost at least 6.2 percent of Mexico's gross domestic product) must be controlled,[14] and a favorable relationship must be maintained with members of the North American Free Trade Association (NAFTA).[15]

Some African countries are unstable, with seemingly unending civil wars, boundary disputes, and oppressive military regimes. Sierra Leone has had three changes in government in five years; the most recent coup d'etat (1997) ended the country's brief experiment with

---

[11]PAN stands for Partido Action National. There are eight political parties in Mexico but PAN and PRI are the largest.

[12]"Pig Farmers Block International Bridge Between Mexico, United States," *APWorldstream,* June 11, 2002.

[13]Kieran Murray, "Analysis—Mexico's Parties Struggle In New Democracy," *Reuters,* July 19, 2001.

[14]David Luhnow, "End of Textbook Printing Scandal Is Bright Spot for Mexico's Fox," *The Wall Street Journal,* April 15, 2003.

[15]As an aftermath of the Iraq/U.S. war there were hard feelings between Mexico and the U.S. when President Fox, facing Mexican anti-war sentiment, refused to back the United States vote in the UN Security Council. The hard feelings were only temporary as both sides took steps to mend the rift. Nevertheless, this is a good illustration of how international turbulence can affect relationships among countries and create a tenuous investment environment. Hugh Dellios, "Mexico's President Makes Public Appeals to Mend Rift With U.S.," *Chicago Tribune,* April 22, 2003.

Supporters of Vicente Fox cheer after hearing election results marking a watershed in Mexican history. Vicente Fox of the National Action Party defeated Francisco Labastida of the PRI (Institutional Revolutionary Party) and ended the tenure of the longest ruling party, which had governed Mexico for 71 years. (© AFP/CORBIS)

democracy. Shortly after the coup a civil war erupted and UN peacekeeping forces had to maintain peace.[16] Central Africa,[17] where ethnic wars have embroiled seven nations, is one of the most politically unstable regions in the world.[18] Africa is trapped in a vicious cycle. For its nations to prosper they need foreign investment. But investment is leery of unstable nations, which is the status of most of Africa.[19] A recent World Bank study showed that the 47 nations of sub-Saharan Africa were attracting less than $2 billion annually in direct foreign investment—about one-tenth of what a developing nation such as Mexico attracts.

If there is potential for profit and if permitted to operate within a country, multinational companies can function under any type of government as long as there is some long-run predictability and stability. PepsiCo, for example, operated profitably in the Soviet Union when it had one of the world's most extreme political systems. Years before the disintegration of the Communist Party, PepsiCo established a very profitable business with the USSR by exchanging Pepsi syrup for Russian vodka.[20]

Socioeconomic and political environments invariably change, as they have in the USSR and Mexico. These changes are often caused by or reflected in changes in political philosophy or a surge in feelings of nationalistic pride.

## Political Parties

Particularly important to the marketer is knowledge of the philosophies of all major political parties within a country, since any one of them might become dominant and alter prevailing attitudes. In those countries where there are two strong political parties that typically succeed one another in control of the government, it is important to know the direction each party is likely to take. In Great Britain, for example, the Labour Party traditionally has tended to be more restrictive regarding foreign trade than the Conservative Party. The Labour Party, when in control, sometimes limits imports, whereas the Conservative Party tends to liberalize foreign trade when it is in power. A foreign firm in Britain can expect to seesaw between the liberal trade policies of the Conservatives and the restrictive ones of the Liberals.

Even in Mexico, where a dominant party (PRI) maintained absolute control for seven decades, knowledge of the philosophies of all political parties is important. Over the years, the doctrines of opposing parties have had an influence on the direction of Mexican policy. With the recent election of the PAN party nominee for president, it is even more essential to know the philosophy and direction of both the PRI and PAN, the two major political parties in Mexico.[21]

The election of Vladimir Putin as president of Russia has been favorably received. By all accounts Russia's economy has been stagnant for more than 20 years. Corruption, half-baked market policies, expansion of the ranks of petty civil servants, and a chaotic legal system have produced an economy that in many ways is as dysfunctional

[16]"Sierra Leone Rebel Faces War Crimes Court," The *Washington Post,* March 16, 2003.

[17]"Central African States Must Work Hard to Create Peace, U.S. Says," *African News Service,* October 30, 2002.

[18]Statement of Dr. Francois Grignon, Committee on House International Relations Subcommittee on Africa, "Conditions in The Congo," FDHC Congressional Testimony, House International Relations, April 3, 2002.

[19]Visit www.eiu.com for abstracts of the Economist Intelligence Unit's country reports of current political and economic data. Some information on this site is fee only, but other sources are free.

[20]Visit the Pepsi website in Russia for a history of Pepsi in Russia, Pepsi advertising in Russia, and other information at www.pepsi.ru.

[21]"Mexican Parties at a Glance," *AP Online,* July 2, 2000.

as the old Soviet system.[22] Mr. Putin's apparent commitment to economic reform and his statement that "the only dictatorship Russia will obey is the dictatorship of the rule of law"[23] are seen as encouraging notes that there will be reform in Russia. However, most agree that it will take time to unseat an entrenched bureaucracy and a court system infested with low-paid communist-era judges who are susceptible both to bribery and political pressure.

An astute international marketer must understand all aspects of the political landscape to be properly informed about the political environment. Unpredictable and drastic shifts in government policies deter investments, whatever the cause of the shift. In short, a current assessment of political philosophy and attitudes within a country is important in gauging the stability and attractiveness of a government in terms of market potential.

## Nationalism

Economic and cultural nationalism, which exists to some degree within all countries, is another factor important in assessing business climate. **Nationalism** can best be described as an intense feeling of national pride and unity, an awakening of a nation's people to pride in their country. This pride can take an anti-foreign business bias, and minor harassment and controls of foreign investment are supported, if not applauded. Economic nationalism has as one of its central aims the preservation of national economic autonomy in that residents identify their interests with the preservation of the sovereignty of the state in which they reside.[24] In other words, national interest and security are more important than international considerations.

Feelings of nationalism are manifested in a variety of ways, including a call to "buy our country's products only" (e.g., "Buy American"),[25] restrictions on imports, restrictive tariffs, and other barriers to trade. They may also lead to control over foreign investment, often regarded with suspicion, which then becomes the object of intensive scrutiny and control. Generally speaking, the more a country feels threatened by some outside force, the more nationalistic it becomes in protecting itself against the intrusion.[26]

During the period after World War II when many new countries were founded and many others were seeking economic independence, manifestations of militant nationalism were rampant. Expropriation of foreign companies, restrictive investment policies, and nationalization of industries were common practices in some parts of the world. This was the period when India imposed such restrictive practices on foreign investments that companies such as Coca-Cola, IBM, and many others chose to leave rather than face the uncertainty of a hostile economic climate. In many Latin American countries, similar attitudes prevailed and led to expropriations and even confiscation of foreign investments.

By the late 1980s, militant nationalism had subsided; today, the foreign investor, once feared as a dominant tyrant that threatened economic development, is often sought after as a source of needed capital investment. Nationalism comes and goes as conditions and attitudes change, and foreign companies welcomed today may be harassed tomorrow and vice versa.

India's xenophobia, rooted in its colonial past, has led to demonstrations aimed at Pepsi. Local politicians rail against the "foreign devil" and call for bottles of Pepsi to be smashed. (© Sharad Saxena/India Today)

---

[22]"Putin, Gref Discuss Administrative Reform," *Interfax,* February 21, 2003.

[23]"Putin Reaffirms Need to Protect Foreigners' Rights," *Interfax,* January 22, 2003.

[24]Following in the footsteps of the Spanish Basques, nationalism in the semiautonomous region of Spanish Catalonia manifests itself in the issue of sovereignty. "Catalan Nationalists Draft Sovereignty Bill," *New York Times,* March 25, 2003.

[25]Kent L. Granzin and John J. Painter, "Motivational Influences on "Buy Domestic" Purchasing: Marketing Management Implications from a Study of Two Nations," *Journal of International Marketing,* 9, no. 2, (2001) pp. 73–96.

[26]Richard J. Whalen, "The New Nationalism?" *Across the Board,* January/February, 2002, is a detailed review of Harold James, *The End of Globalization: Lessons From the Great Depression,* (Boston, MA: Harvard University Press, 2001). The review relates James' book to the terrorist attack on the Twin Towers, antiglobalization and the possible consequences of the new nationalism.

**CROSSING BORDERS 6.1** Coke's Back and It Still Has the Secret

For 91 years, the formula for making Coca-Cola has been a closely guarded secret. Then the government of India ordered Coca-Cola to disclose it or cease operations in that country. A secret ingredient called 7-X supposedly gives Coke its distinctive flavor. The government's minister for industry told the Indian parliament that Coca-Cola's Indian branch would have to transfer 60 percent of its equity shares to Indians and hand over its know-how by April 1978 or shut down.

Indian sales accounted for less than 1 percent of Coca-Cola's worldwide sales, but the potential market in India, a country of 800 million, was tremendous. The government refused to let the branch import the necessary ingredients, and Coca-Cola—whose products were once as abundant as the bottled drinking water sold in almost every Indian town of more than 50,000—packed up its bags and left the country. The minister for industry said that Coca-Cola's activities in India "furnish a classic example of how multinational corporations operating in a low-priority, high-profit area in a developing country attain run-away growth and . . . trifle with the weaker indigenous industry."

Sixteen years later, India's attitudes toward foreign investment changed and Coca-Cola reentered the market without having to divulge its formula. During Coke's 16-year exile, however, Pepsi-Cola came to India and captured a 26 percent market share. Not to worry; there is plenty of growth potential for both considering that India's per capita consumption is just 3 eight-ounce bottles a year, versus about 12 for Pakistan and 1,484 in Mexico. To forestall further political vulnerability, Coke sold 49 percent of its Indian bottler subsidiary to institutional investors and employees. They hope this will put to rest an issue that concerned the Indian government, which wanted Indians to own part of Coke's local operation—in other words, Coke took steps to domesticate their operations.

Sources: "Indian Government Rejects Coke's Bid to Sell Soft Drinks," *Wall Street Journal*, March 16, 1990, p. B5; and "Coke Adds Fizz to India," *Fortune*, January 10, 1994, pp. 14–15 and Manjeet Kripalani, "Finally, Coke Gets It Right," *Business Week*, February 10, 2003, p. 47.

Although militant economic nationalism has subsided, nationalistic feelings can be found even in the most economically prosperous countries.[27] When U.S. negotiators pushed Japan to import more rice to help balance the trade deficit between the two countries, nationalistic feelings rose to a new high. Deeply rooted Japanese notions of self-sufficiency, self-respect, and concern for the welfare of Japanese farmers caused Japan to resist any change for several years. It was only after a shortfall in the Japanese rice harvests that restrictions on rice imports were temporarily eased. Even then, all imported foreign rice had to be mixed with Japanese rice before it could be sold.

*The World Is Not Merchandise, Who Is Killing France? The American Strategy,* and *No Thanks Uncle Sam* are best-selling titles in France that epitomize nationalistic feeling in that country. Although such attitudes may seem odd in a country that devours U.S. movies, eats U.S. fast foods, views U.S. soap operas, and shops at U.S. Wal-Mart stores, nationalistic feelings—whatever the cause—are a critical part of the political environment. The United States is not immune to strong nationalistic feelings either. The rift between France and the United States over the Iraq/U.S. war led to hard feelings on both sides[28] and an American backlash against French wine, French cheese[29] and even products Americans thought were French. French's mustard felt compelled to issue a press release stating that it is an "American company founded by an American named 'French'".[30] It is important to appreciate that no nation-state, however secure, will

[27]John Rossant, "Suddenly Europe Fears Fortress America," *Business Week*, June 24, 2002.

[28]Melissa Eddy, "Some Europeans Boycotting American Goods," *AP Online*, April 1, 2003.

[29]Robert J. McCartney, "French Businesses Say U.S. Boycott Is Hurting Them," *The Washington Post*, April 16, 2003.

[30]Floyd Norris, "French's Has an Unmentioned British Flavor," *The New York Times*, March 28, 2003. The news release failed to mention that French's is a subsidiary of Reckitt Benckiser P.L.C., a British firm—but then, the British did support the U.S. position.

tolerate penetration by a foreign company into its market and economy if it perceives a social, cultural, economic or political threat to its well-being.

## Political Risks of Global Business

Issues of sovereignty, differing political philosophies, and nationalism are manifest in a host of governmental actions that enhance the risks of global business. Risks can range from confiscation, the harshest, to many lesser but still significant government rules and regulations such as exchange controls, import restrictions, and price controls that directly affect the performance of business activities. Although not always officially blessed, social or political activist groups can provoke governments into action that proves harmful to business. Of all the political risks, the most costly are those actions that result in a transfer of equity from the company to the government, with or without adequate compensation.

### Confiscation, Expropriation, and Domestication

The most severe political risk is **confiscation**, that is, the seizing of a company's assets without payment. The two most notable recent confiscations of U.S. property occurred when Fidel Castro became the leader in Cuba and later when the Shah of Iran was overthrown. Confiscation was most prevalent in the 1950s and 1960s when many underdeveloped countries saw confiscation, albeit ineffective, as a means of economic growth.

Less drastic, but still severe, is **expropriation**, where the government seizes an investment but some reimbursement for the assets is made. Often the expropriated investment is nationalized (i.e., it becomes a government-run entity). A third type of risk is **domestication**. It occurs when host countries gradually cause the transfer of foreign investments to national control and ownership through a series of government decrees by mandating local ownership and greater national involvement in a company's management. The ultimate goal of domestication is to force foreign investors to share more of the ownership and management with nationals than was the case before domestication.

Rather than a quick answer to economic development, expropriation and nationalization have often led to nationalized businesses that were inefficient, technologically weak, and noncompetitive in world markets. Risks of confiscation and expropriation have lessened over the last decade because experience has shown that few of the desired benefits materialize after government takeover. Today, countries often require prospective investors to agree to share ownership, use local content, enter into labor and management agreements, and share participation in export sales as a condition of entry. The company must become domesticated as a condition for investment.

Countries now view foreign investment as a means of economic growth. As the world becomes more economically interdependent, it is obvious that much of the economic success of countries such as South Korea, Singapore, and Taiwan is tied to foreign investments. Throughout the world, nations that only a few years ago restricted or forbade foreign investments are now courting foreign investors as a much-needed source of capital and technology. Additionally, they have begun to privatize[31] telecommunications, broadcasting, airlines, banks, railroads, and other nationally owned companies as a means of enhancing competition and attracting foreign capital.[32]

The benefits of privatizing are many. In Mexico, for example, privatization of the national telephone company resulted in almost immediate benefits when the government received hundreds of millions of dollars of much-needed capital from the sale and immediate investment in new telecommunications systems. A similar scenario has played out in Brazil, Argentina, India, and many Eastern European countries. Ironically, many of the businesses that were expropriated and nationalized in earlier periods are now being privatized.

---

[31]Mona Makhija, "Comparing the Resource-Based and Market-Based Views of the Firm: Empirical Evidence From Czech Privatization," *Strategic Management Journal,* May 2003, p. 19.

[32]"Uzbekistan Taking Additional Measures to Deepen Privatization," *Interfax Financial Times Information Limited,* April 18, 2003.

**Exhibit 6.1**

Exchange controls are extended to products by applying a system of multiple exchange rates to regulate trade in specific commodities classified as either necessities or luxuries. Necessary products are placed in the most favorable (low) exchange categories, whereas luxuries are heavily penalized with high foreign exchange rates. Myanmar, for example, has three exchange rates for the kyat (Kt): the official rate (Kt 6:U.S. $1); the market rate (Kt 100–125:U.S. $1); and an import duty rate (Kt 100:U.S. $1). Since the kit is not convertible—that is, not officially exchangeable for currencies that can be spent outside the country—investors are severely affected by tax liability, and their ability to send profits outside the country is diminished. Under such exchange rates, tax liability can be very high. For instance, a profit of Kt 135,000 is worth U.S. $22,500 at the official exchange rate of Kt 6 to U.S. $1, but at the market rate, the investor has earned only U.S. $1,000. The exchange rate difference means that the investor has to pay tax on U.S. $21,500 of nonexistent, unearned income.

Sources: "Myanmar's Crumbling Kit," *Asiaweek*, March 2, 2001, p. 8, and "Kyatastrophe," *Economist.com*, March 20, 2003.

## Economic Risks

Even though expropriation and confiscation are waning as risks of doing business abroad, international companies are still confronted with a variety of economic risks that can occur with little warning. Restraints on business activity may be imposed under the banner of national security to protect an infant industry, to conserve scarce foreign exchange, to raise revenue, or to retaliate against unfair trade practices, among a score of other real or imagined reasons. These economic risks are an important and recurring part of the political environment that few international companies can avoid.[33]

**Exchange Controls.**  Exchange controls stem from shortages of foreign exchange held by a country. When a nation faces shortages of foreign exchange or there is a substantial amount of capital leaving the country, controls may be levied over all movements of capital, or selectively against the most politically vulnerable companies to conserve the supply of foreign exchange for the most essential uses.[34] A recurrent problem for the foreign investor is getting profits in and out of the host country without loss of value, which can occur when a currency is devalued. Such was the case when Venezuela imposed currency controls, after a two-month-long national strike, in an attempt to stem the flow of capital from the country. The Bolivar was pegged at 1,598 to the dollar, a 53 percent loss in value from one year earlier.[35] Exhibit 6.1 illustrates how exchange controls can affect an international company's profits. Many countries maintain regulations for control of currency, and, in the event an economy should suffer an economic setback or foreign exchange reserves suffer severely, the controls on convertibility are imposed quickly, as was the case in Venezuela.[36]

**Local-Content Laws.**  In addition to restricting imports of essential supplies to force local purchase, countries often require a portion of any product sold within the country to have local content, that is, to contain locally made parts. Thailand, for example, requires that all milk products contain at least 50 percent milk from local dairy farmers.[37] Contrary to popular belief, local-content requirements are not restricted to Third World countries. The European Community has had a local-content requirement as high as 45 percent for "screwdriver operations," a name often given to foreign-owned assemblers, and NAFTA requires 62 percent local content for all cars coming from member countries.

**Import Restrictions.**  Selective restrictions on the import of raw materials, machines, and spare parts are fairly common strategies to force foreign industry to purchase more supplies within the host country and thereby create markets for local industry. Although

---

[33]Carleste Hughes, "A Lively Southern Exposure Latin America Holds Both Risk and Reward," *International Herald Tribune*, May 23, 2002.

[34]"Brazil: Forex Regulations," *Economist Intelligence Unit*, April 23, 2003.

[35]Mike Esterl, "U.S. Companies Face New Challenges in Post-Strike Venezuela," *Dow Jones International News*, February 20, 2003.

[36]Gordon Platt, "The Americas: Venezuela Imposes Currency Controls," *Global Finance*, March 2003.

[37]"Cabinet Keeps Local Milk Rule," *Nation* (Thailand), April 5, 2000.

Union workers from Daewoo Motor and its marketing arm, Daewoo Motor Sales Co., burn effigies representing General Motors and the automakers' creditors at a protest in Seoul, South Korea. The protest was against the proposed sale of South Korea's Daewoo Motors Co. to General Motors Corp. Thousands of students and workers from the hard-line Korean Confederation of Trade Unions, including dismissed Daewoo Motor union workers, clashed with police after a peaceful rally to protest against mass layoffs. (© Reuters NewMedia Inc./CORBIS)

this is done in an attempt to support the development of domestic industry, the result is often to hamstring and sometimes interrupt the operations of established industries.[38] The problem then becomes critical when there are no adequately developed sources of supply within the country.

**Tax Controls.**     Taxes must be classified as a political risk when used as a means of controlling foreign investments. In such cases, they are raised without warning and in violation of formal agreements.[39] India, for example, taxes PepsiCo and the Coca-Cola Company 40 percent on all soda bottled in India. Its most recent assault on new business is the attempt to collect $40 million in taxes on travel tickets sold online from Sabre's (the airlines reservations service) data center in Tulsa, Oklahoma. The Indian government contends that Sabre has a permanent establishment in India in the form of data flows between Sabre's Tulsa processing center and the desktop computers of travel agents in India.[40] To underdeveloped countries with economies constantly threatened with a shortage of funds, unreasonable taxation of successful foreign investments appeals to some government officials as the handiest and quickest means of finding operating funds. As the Internet grows in importance, countries will surely seize on Internet transactions as a lucrative source of revenue.

**Price Controls.**     Essential products that command considerable public interest, such as pharmaceuticals, food, gasoline, and cars, are often subjected to price controls.[41] Such controls applied during inflationary periods can be used to control the cost of living. They also may be used to force foreign companies to sell equity to local interests.[42] A side effect on the local economy can be to slow or even stop capital investment.

**Labor Problems.**     In many countries, labor unions have strong government support that they use effectively in obtaining special concessions from business.[43] Layoffs may be forbidden, profits may have to be shared, and an extraordinary number of services

---

[38]"Russia Mulls Rice Import Restrictions," *Interfax*, February 19, 2003.

[39]"CCZ Has Got It Wrong on Price Controls," *African News Service*, April 26, 2002.

[40]Glen Burkins, "U.S. Delegation to India to Address Roadblocks to Foreign Businesses," *Wall Street Journal*, March 24, 2000.

[41]Bernard Plessis, "Laws Inhibit African Expansion," *Finance Week*, January 1, 2003, p. 40.

[42]"Government Orders More Price Freezes," *African News Service*, February 7, 2003.

[43]"French Store Chain Sues M Over Redundancy Terms," *The Times*, March 26, 2003.

## CROSSING BORDERS 6.2 The Other Side of the Story

Protests against using cheap foreign labor have been waged against Nike, Levi Strauss, Kmart, Target, and others, but is there another side to the story?

To hear the antiglobalists tell it, their disruption of trade meetings and international conferences and calls for boycott of goods made in Third World countries are justified because they are speaking out for poor workers in the Third World. How cruel is it for an MNC to pay a Third World worker a meager $5 a day when the same labor would cost $16 in the United States? But is this argument really sound?

Begin with the charge that companies are exploiting foreign workers by paying them appallingly low wages. Though $5 a day seems like an outrage by U.S. standards, is it unjust for Coca-Cola, Levi Strauss, or General Electric to pay that much to workers in a country where the going wage rate is $3 a day, and where things cost much less than they do in the United States?

If this is so unjust, why are there long lines of applicants when MNCs advertise for jobs? There would be no reason for Third World workers to take those jobs unless they were the highest paying jobs available. Not only do these jobs help improve the lives of foreign employees who work for the foreign companies, they also help other families in Third World countries, because the increased

demand for labor pushes up wages even for those employed by local businesses. If this is the case, one might argue, why not do better and pay higher wages?

The obvious answer is that those companies wouldn't use Third World labor at all. Multinational companies hire foreign workers because they are much cheaper to employ than their domestic counterparts. When those jobs are lost, who makes up the difference for the families out of work?

Sometimes the workers who are being defended aren't necessarily happy about the protesters' efforts. The U.S. activists launched demonstrations at Kohl's stores across the United States to call attention to their cause—sweatshop conditions in a factory in Chentex that makes jeans sold under the store's private label and clothes for Wal-Mart, Kmart, Target, and J.C. Penney. The Nicaraguan garment factory workers protested themselves saying they want U.S. labor activists to stop slamming their employer because the bad publicity could cause the plant to close. So, which side do you stand on?

Source: Dinesh D'Souza, "Antiglobalist Hypocrisy," *Red Herring*, July 2002, and "Nicaraguan Workers Protest U.S. Boycott of Their Plant," *Dow Jones International*, January 11, 2001. Reproduced with permission of DOW JONES & CO INC in the format textbook via Copyright Clearance Center.

may have to be provided. In fact, in many countries foreign firms are considered fair game for the demands of the domestic labor supply. In France, the belief in full employment is almost religious in fervor; layoffs of any size, especially by foreign-owned companies, are regarded as national crises.[44]

### Political Sanctions

In addition to economic risks, one or a group of nations may boycott another nation, thereby stopping all trade between the countries, or may issue sanctions against the trade of specific products.[45] The United States has long-term boycotts of trade with Cuba, Iran, and Libya. The United States has been criticized for its demand for continued sanctions against Cuba and its threats of future sanctions against countries that violate human rights issues.[46]

History indicates that sanctions are often not successful in reaching desired goals. Such is the case with Cuba, North Korea,[47] and Iran, where the undesirable behavior that the sanctions were meant to change continues and the only ones who seem to be hurt are the people and companies that get caught in the middle.

### Political and Social Activists

Although not usually officially sanctioned by the government, the impact of political and social activists (**PSA**s) can also interrupt the normal flow of trade.[48] PSAs can range from those who seek to bring about peaceful change to those who resort to violence and

---

[44]Adam Sage, "How Far Will Paris Go to Save Businesses and Jobs?" *The Times*, February 7, 2003.

[45]James Dao, "U.S. to Punish 10 Businesses for Iran Sales," *New York Times*, July 7, 2002.

[46]Andrew Meadows, "Legal Trade With Cuba Gains Favor," *The Tampa Tribune*, February 28, 2003.

[47]Murray Heibert, "Punishing Kim," *Far Eastern Economic Review*, April 10, 2003.

[48]Saritha Rai, "War Protests in India Aim At Bottlers," *New York Times*, April 1, 2003.

Activists of the Bharatiya Janata Party wearing "evil" masks shout anti-government slogans near the Union Carbide plant in the central Indian city of Bhopal on the eve of World Environment Day, June 4, 2003. The activists protested on Wednesday to draw the attention of the government to chemical wastage and demanded the clean up of hazardous waste in the area. The leak from the Union Carbide pesticide plant in 1984 was one of the world's worst industrial accidents, killing 3,000 people and leaving thousands of others with lifetime illnesses. (© *Reuters NewMedia Inc./CORBIS*)

terrorism to affect change. When well organized, the actions of PSAs can be effective.

One of the most effective and best-known PSA actions was against Nestlé and the sale of baby formula in Third World markets. The worldwide boycott of Nestlé products resulted in substantial change in the company's marketing. More recently, activists of the Free Burma Campaign (FBC) have applied enough pressure to cause several U.S. garment companies to stop importing textiles from Burma (now known as Myanmar). Furthermore, activists on several U.S. college campuses boycotted Pepsi-Cola drinks and PepsiCo-owned Pizza Hut and Taco Bell stores, saying that the company contributes to abysmal human rights in Myanmar. The results of the boycott were serious enough that PepsiCo sold its stake in its joint venture in Myanmar and withdrew from that market. The concern was that potential losses in the United States outweighed potential profits in Myanmar. Holland's Heineken and Denmark's Carlsberg beer companies withdrew from Myanmar for similar reasons.

PSA groups such as Greenpeace, Consumers International, and others have been successful in raising doubts about the safety of genetically modified (GM) foods.[49] Europeans'[50] fears about "Frankenfood," as they are sometimes called, have spread throughout much of the world[51] and persuaded some famine-ridden countries in Africa to reject GM grains.[52] In some areas in Uganda an airborne fungus is decimating 80 percent of the banana plants. Bananas are staple foods there; they eat banana pancakes, banana mash, and banana bread. They season their beans with banana salt and they guzzle banana beer and sip banana gin.[53] Although a GM banana plant has been developed that is immune to the leaf fungus, because of the fear of GM foods, Uganda's legislature has not enacted laws that will permit bio-engineered banana plants into the country.

The rather broad issue of globalization is also the focus of many PSA groups.[54] The demonstrations in Seattle during a WTO meeting, in Washington, D.C., against the World Bank and the International Monetary Fund (IMF), and similar demonstrations in other countries reflect a growing concern about a global economy. Whether misguided, uninformed, or just "wackos," as they have been described, PSAs can be a potent force in rallying public opinion and are an important political force that should not be dismissed, as companies such as Nike, McDonald's, Nestlé, and others know.

**Violence and Terrorism**

Although not usually government initiated, violence is another related risk for multinational companies to consider in assessing the political vulnerability of their activities. The State Department reported 408 terrorist incidents worldwide in 2001, up from 383 in 2000. Of those, 111 were directed at U.S. businesses. Terrorism has many different goals. Multinational corporations are targeted to embarrass a government and its relationship with firms; to generate funds by kidnapping executives to finance terrorist

---

[49]"The Case for Caution," *Newsweek,* January 27, 2003.

[50]Lezette Alvarez, "Consumers in Europe Resist Gene-Altered Foods," *The New York Times,* February 11, 2003.

[51]"Protests Build Worldwide Against Genetically Modified Food," *Inter Press Service,* March 17, 2003.

[52]"Zambia Faces Hard Choices on GM Food," *Inter Press Service,* November 20, 2002.

[53]Roger Thurow, "As U.S., EU Clash on Biotech Crops, Africa Goes Hungry," *The Wall Street Journal,* February 26, 2002, p. A1.

[54]Kathleen Carr, "Students Challenge Columbia U.–Nike Contract Terms," *Columbia Daily Spectator,* November 14, 2002.

## CROSSING BORDERS 6.3  Oops—Things Don't Always Turn Out the Way You Want

There were boycotts and protests against the U.S./Iraq war worldwide—they were against the United States going to war. There were other protests against countries that did not support U.S. actions. Some made a meaningful statement, but others, well, didn't exactly come out the way expected.

As diplomatic tensions over Iraq peaked, U.S. patriotic fervor swelled. The South Carolina legislature called for a boycott of French products—because France gave aid and comfort to Saddam it made no sense to buy French products. The resolution passed the state House 90–9. As the idea gained support something happened: Someone realized that one of the companies that would

be a big loser would be Michelin tires. As it turned out, many of the Michelin tires sold in the United States are made in factories across South Carolina. A boycott against Michelin would be a boycott against American products, made in 17 U.S. factories in seven states. The legislature backpedaled and let the issue drop. "The global economy is so interconnected today, you'd be shooting yourself in the foot," said South Carolina's Commerce Secretary. "You might be putting our neighbor out of work."

Source: Glenn R. Simpson, "Multinational Firms Take Steps to Avert Boycotts Over War," *The Wall Street Journal*, April 4, 2003.

goals, and to use as pawns in political or social disputes not related to them; and to inflict terror within a country, such as the terrorist attacks on September 11 did.

September 11 has raised the cost of doing business domestically and internationally.[55] The dominance of the United States in world affairs exposes U.S. businesses to many uncertainties, from the growing danger of political violence to investment risks in emerging markets.[56] In the past 30 years, 80 percent of terrorist attacks against the United States have been aimed at American businesses.[57] Since September 11, McDonalds, Kentucky Fried Chicken, and Pizza Hut together have been bombed in more than ten countries including Turkey, Saudi Arabia, Russia, Lebanon, and China; most bombings have been linked with militant Islamic groups.[58] There are reasons to expect that terrorists will increasingly target businesses, both because they are less well defended than government targets and because of what they symbolize.[59]

**Cyberterrorism**      New on the horizon is the potential for cyberterrorism. Although in its infancy, the Internet is a vehicle for terrorist attacks by foreign and domestic antagonists wishing to inflict damage on a company with little chance of being caught. One problem in tracing a cyberterrorist is that it is hard to determine whether a cyber attack was launched by a rogue state, a terrorist, or by a hacker as a prank.[60] The "I Love You" worm, which caused an estimated $25 billion in damage, was probably just an out-of-control prank.[61] However, the Melissa virus that overloaded the websites of CNN, ZDNet, Yahoo, and Amazon.com with a flood of electronic messages that crippled them for hours, was considered to be purposeful attacks on specific targets.

[55]Thomas A. Stewart, "The World According to C.K. Prahalad," *Business 2.0,* January 2002, p. 92.

[56]"Doing Business in a Dangerous World," *Harvard Business Review,* April 2002.

[57]"Significant Terrorist Incidents, 1961–2001: A Brief Chronology," *Office of the Historian, Bureau of Public Affairs, U.S. Department of State,* September 28, 2001, www.state.gov.

[58]Dan Murphy, "U.S. Multinational Companies Wary of Backlash," *Christian Science Monitor,* April 2, 2003, p. 12.

[59]For a complete discussion of the risks businesses face today see Stuart Poole-Robb, Alan Bailey, Dan C. Pinck and John Wheeler, *Risky Business: Corruption, Fraud, Terrorism and Other Threats to Global Business* (London, England: Kogan Page Ltd., August 21, 2002).

[60]Steve Alexander, "The Cyberterror Scare," *Minneapolis Star Tribune,* February 12, 2003.

[61]Sandy Portnoy and Marcia Savage, "'I Love You' Virus Leaves Bitter Aftermath," *Computer Reseller News,* May 15, 2000, p. 3.

Each wave of viruses gets more damaging and spreads so rapidly that considerable harm is done before it can be stopped. The "Slammer,"[62] for example, brought Internet service to a crawl. It doubled its numbers every 8.5 seconds during the first minute of its attack and infected more than 75,000 hosts within 10 minutes.[63] After infecting hundreds of thousands of computers in Europe and North America the "goner worm" traveled to Australia overnight and brought down government agencies, financial and manufacturing sites, and at least 25 MNCs. This virus arrived in an e-mail message with an invitation to download a screen saver; it then infected the computer and sent the virus to everyone in the computer's address list.[64] Whether perpetrated by pranksters or hackers out to do harm, these incidents show that cyberterrorism can do considerable damage to a company, an entire industry, or a country's infrastructure.[65]

Because of mounting concern over the rash of attacks, business leaders and government officials addressed a Group of Eight[66] conference convened to discuss cybercrime, expressing an urgent need for cooperation among governments, industry, and users to combat the growing menace of cybercrime. As the Internet grows, "it's only a matter of time before every terrorist, anarchist and prankster with a PC and a phone line will be waging a virtual war and inflicting real harm." The Internet has become an effective tool of PSAs to spread the word on whatever cause they sponsor. During protest rallies against the U.S./Iraq war, organizers were able to coordinate protest demonstrations in 600 cities worldwide and to disseminate information easily. A Google search for "peace protest" during that time resulted in 788,000 entries, including news briefs, websites for peace organizations, online petitions for peace, where to show up with your placard, where to send your dollars, and how to write your congressman.[67] The Internet is a potent tool for cyberterrorism, and, unless systems are designed to safeguard it against these intrusions, the costs to governments and industry will be enormous and may prevent the Internet from reaching its full potential. Cyberterrorism is another risk that multinational companies must guard against.[68]

# Assessing Political Vulnerability

There are at least as many reasons for a company's political vulnerability as there are political philosophies, economic variations, and cultural differences. Some companies are more politically vulnerable than others because they receive special government attention. Depending on the desirability of a company, this special attention may result in positive actions toward the company or in negative attention.

Unfortunately, there are no absolute guidelines a marketer can follow to determine whether a company and its products will be subject to political attention. It is not unusual for countries seeking investments in high-priority industries to excuse companies from taxes, customs duties, quotas, exchange controls, and other impediments to investment. In a bid to attract foreign investment and increase exports, India announced a new trade policy that eases restraints and offers tax breaks for companies developing and maintaining infrastructure.[69] Conversely, firms marketing products not considered a high priority or firms that fall from favor often face unpredictable government restrictions.

[62]"Internet Worm Hits Companies Globally," *The Wall Street Journal*, January 27, 2003, p. B4.

[63]For more information, see: www.silicondefense.com.

[64]"Email Worm Makes a Meal of Business, Finance and Politics," *The Australian*, December 12, 2001.

[65]"Expert Warns Cyberterrorism Is Latest Weapon," *AP News*, February 25, 2003.

[66]The Group of Eight consists of government representatives from Britain, Canada, France, Germany, Italy, Japan, Russia, and the United States that convene periodically to examine issues that affect the group.

[67]Mary Brown Malouf, "Web Unites Peace Rallies Across Globe," *The Salt Lake Tribune*, February 18, 2003.

[68]For a report on security steps that need to be taken to protect the government and business, see "Challenges for Selected Agencies and Industry Sectors," Government Accounting Office, February 28, 2003.

[69]Saritha Rai, "India: Trade Rules Eased," *New York Times*, April 1, 2003.

As a case in point, Continental Can Company's joint venture to manufacture cans for the Chinese market faced a barrage of restrictions when the Chinese economy weakened. China decreed that canned beverages were wasteful and must be banned from all state functions and banquets. Tariffs on aluminum and other materials imported for producing cans were doubled and a new tax was imposed on canned-drink consumption. For Continental Can, an investment that had the potential for profit after a few years was rendered profitless by a change in the attitude of the Chinese government.

## Politically Sensitive Products and Issues

Although there are no specific guidelines to determine a product's vulnerability at any point, there are some generalizations that help to identify the tendency for products to be politically sensitive. Products that have or are perceived to have an effect on the environment, exchange rates, national and economic security, and the welfare of people, and that are publicly visible or subject to public debate, are more apt to be politically sensitive.

An activist group protests the use of beef products in the French fries sold at McDonald's fast food outlet in Bombay, India. The protest was staged after McDonald's admitted before a Washington court that their French fries were laced with flavors of beef products. A lawsuit against McDonald's alleged they secretly flavored the fries with beef fat and misled the customers. Beef and pork products are strictly banned in India since they may hurt the religious sentiments of majority Hindus and minority Muslims. Violation of local customs, however minor they may seem, can lead to protest by activists groups. (AP/Wide World Photos)

Fast-food restaurants, which are obviously visible, have often been lightning rods for groups opposed to foreign companies. Health authorities closed a Kentucky Fried Chicken (KFC) restaurant for health reasons (two flies were seen in the kitchen) after months of protesters arguing that foreign investment should be limited to high technology. "India does not need foreign investment in junk-food," said the leader of the protesting farmers' group. The store was later reopened by court order.

Health is often the subject of public debate, and products that affect or are affected by health issues can be sensitive to political concern. The European Union has banned hormone-treated beef for more than a decade. There is a question about whether the ban is a valid health issue or just protection for the European beef industry. The World Trade Organization concluded in 1989 that the ban had no scientific basis; nevertheless, Europe has yet to lift the ban. Reluctance to respond to the WTO directive may be the result of the recent outcry against genetically modified (GM) foods that has, for all practical purposes, caused GM foods to be banned in Europe. Public opinion against "Frankenfood" has been so strong that Unilever announced that it would stop using GM ingredients in all its products in Britain. Additionally, 11 leading restaurant chains, including McDonald's, Pizza Hut, Wimpy, and Burger King, have eliminated GM ingredients. The issue has not risen to the same level of concern in the United States as in Europe; to forestall such adverse public opinion, many U.S. companies are slowing the introduction of GM foods. Fearing a strong public reaction as in Europe, McDonald's has decided to stop using genetically modified potatoes for its French fries in its U.S. stores.

## Forecasting Political Risk

In addition to qualitative measures of political vulnerability, a number of firms are employing systematic methods of measuring political risk. Political risk assessment is an attempt to forecast political instability to help management identify and evaluate political events and their potential influence on current and future international business decisions.

Risk assessment is used to estimate the level of risk a company is assuming when making an investment and to determine the amount of risk it is prepared to accept. In the former Soviet Union and China, the risk may be too high for some companies, but stronger and better-financed companies can make long-term investments in those countries that will be profitable in the future. Early risk is accepted in exchange for being in the country when the economy begins to grow and risk subsides.

## CROSSING BORDERS 6.4  Curbing Child Labor—Boycotts, Rallies, and Demonstrations Get Attention, But Is There a Better Way?

The image from Pakistan is heartrending: Ten-year-old children bend over soccer balls, stitching seams for ten hours a day. Poor families in Brazil, Mexico, Zaire, India, and many other nations put their children to work. Look around your house. Chances are, Mexican children helped make some products found there. Wire harnesses that go into some Whirlpool, General Electric, and Amana refrigerators as well as the ribbons used to wrap boxes of Godiva chocolates, all come from these child factory workers.

These kids are doing the same work as the adults—working night shifts and even graveyard shifts. In Mexico from Matamoras to Tijuana, children, sometimes as young as 12, fill labor-intensive jobs. A bus that takes them to work is referred to as *"El Kinde"* because so many of its occupants look like they belong in kindergarten.

This isn't a scene from centuries past. According to the International Labor Organization,* there are an estimated 250 million children worldwide between the ages of 4 and 15 who, for one reason or another, are obliged to work. In many parts of the world, child labor is "still very much condoned or accepted, and is directly tied to the issue of poverty."

A study by UNICEF (www.unicef.org) across nine Latin American countries found that if a family were to lose the income from their 13- to 17-year-old children, they would face a drop in income of 10 percent to 20 percent. Their meager earnings help provide basic food and medicine for themselves and young siblings. As one official commented, "Child labor is not always exploitation, but in many cases a necessity."

The attempt to curb reported child exploitation by product boycott campaigns in developed countries falls short of attacking the root of the problem. Unfortunately, boycotts often lead to the relocation or closure

* Visit www.ilo.org and search on "child labor" for current data and studies.

of sweat-shop-style factories; without the jobs, the children are forced to look for other ways of earning money—ways that can be just as bad, if not worse, than the original factory work.

There is something well-meaning Americans, college students, religious organizations, countries, and organizations such as the World Bank can do. They can introduce and support programs that pay poor mothers to keep their children in school and out of the labor force. Mexico, Brazil, and Honduras have established such programs. This type program in Mexico, called Progresa, pays poor Mexican families a monetary stipend (close to what the children would earn if working) if schools certify that their children attend classes regularly. Most families earn about $100 a month from the program, and the increase has had a noticeable effect on their behavior.

It's not just a giveaway program: Children are required to attend school regularly and get routine, free medical checkups and mothers must attend seminars on hygiene and nutrition. The family's Progresa payments are suspended if a student misses more than 15 percent of classes.

This pioneering Mexican approach is highly successful. An evaluation shows that after only a couple of years, Progresa significantly raised the schooling of children in very poor Mexican families. It also narrowed the education gap between girls and boys and reduced the labor force participation of boys. A similar program in Brazil helped boost secondary school enrollment by more than 50 percent in just five years.

Sources: Gary S. Becker, "Bribe Third World Parents to Keep Their Kids in School," *Business Week,* November 22, 1999; "The Americas: Banana Skins; Ecuador's Economy," April 27, 2002; Nancy San Martin, "Overworked and Underage: Maquiladoras Say Hiring Minors against Policy but Hard to Halt," *Dallas Morning News,* March 5, 2000; Geri Smith, "Mexico: A Powerful Incentive to Keep Kids in School," *Business Week,* May 1, 2000; and "Child Labor," *The Independent Bangladesh,* April 30, 2003.

During the chaos that arose after the political and economic changes in the USSR, the newly formed republics were anxious to make deals with foreign investors, yet the problems and uncertainty made many investors take a wait-and-see attitude. However, as one executive commented, "If U.S. companies wait until all the problems are solved, somebody else will get the business." Certainly the many companies that are investing in the former Soviet Union or China do not expect big returns immediately; they are betting on the future. For a marketer doing business in a foreign country, a necessary part of any market analysis is an assessment of the probable political consequences of a marketing plan, since some marketing activities are more susceptible to political considerations than others. Basically, it boils down to evaluating the essential nature of the immediate activity. The following section explores additional ways in which businesses can reduce political vulnerability.

A young Mexican boy stretches leather over a shoe last with pliers in a workshop. According to the International Labor Organization (ILO), an estimated 246 million children aged 5-17 were in child labor in 2002. Child labor is found throughout the developing world—Mexican children make shoes, Pakistani children work inside embroidery shops, and children in Afghanistan weave rugs—all for a pittance even by local pay scales. For example, Afghan rug makers contract children to make rugs, paying their families roughly 8 U.S. dollars a year. To make an eighteen foot rug takes approximately one month. You do the math. (© Danny Lehman/CORBIS)

## Reducing Political Vulnerability

Even though a company cannot directly control or alter the political environment of the country within which it operates, there are measures that can reduce the degree of susceptibility of a specific business venture to politically induced risks.

Foreign investors frequently are accused of exploiting a country's wealth at the expense of the national population and for the sole benefit of the foreign investor. This attitude is best summed up in a statement made by a recent president of Peru: "We have had massive foreign investment for decades but Peru has not achieved development. Foreign capital will now have to meet government and social goals." Such charges are not wholly unsupported by past experiences.

As long as these impressions persist, the political climate for foreign investors will continue to be hostile. Companies must manage external affairs in foreign markets to ensure that the host government and the public are aware of their contributions to the economic, social, and human development of the country. Relations between governments and MNCs are generally positive if the investment (1) improves the balance of payments by increasing exports or reducing imports through import substitution; (2) uses locally produced resources; (3) transfers capital, technology, or skills; (4) creates jobs; or (5) makes tax contributions.

In addition to the economic contributions a company makes, corporate philanthropy also helps to create positive images among the general population. Many MNCs strive to benefit countries through their social programs, which polish their image as well. For example, Microsoft, recognizing that developing countries need sophisticated technical assistance, pledged more than $100 million in technology and training as part of a deal to put government services online in Mexico. Cisco Systems, the leading maker of Internet hardware, relies on nonprofit organizations to run its 10,000 networking academies, which train college and high school students to create computer networks in 150 countries. Merck, the pharmaceutical company, developed a pill to fight river blindness in Africa and Latin America. River blindness is a parasitic disease transmitted to humans thorough the bite of the black fly commonly found along the riverbanks in some African countries. The parasite infiltrates, multiplies, and spreads throughout the body for as long as 15 years, causing acute skin rashes, terrible itching, and sometimes disfigurement or blindness. The pill is taken just once a year and prevents the disease. Merck contributed millions of doses to fight the disease in developing countries.[70]

In China, Procter & Gamble is helping local schools and universities to train and educate leaders. And in Malaysia, Motorola and Intel have instituted training programs to enhance the skills of local workers. Lever Brothers has a strong commitment to corporate social responsibility with a focus toward children. It sponsors the Missionaries of Charity in Chittagong, Bangladesh. Similarly it has completely renovated the children's ward of a hospital. The company also sponsors the National Polio Day. Its Pepsodent brand plays a pivotal role in oral hygiene awareness through its Dental Health Week and School Education Program. Lifebuoy sponsors the Lifebuoy Friendship Hospital, a floating hospital aimed to provide health care facilities and health education to the poor.[71] Although these philanthropic gestures may be seen as "enlightened self-interest," any activity that improves the welfare of the population will ultimately create a stronger economy, benefiting the country as well as the MNC.[72]

Eckhard Pfeiffer, president and CEO of Compaq Computer Corporation, watches as a 12-year-old Chinese youth works on the Internet at the opening of a Compaq Internet classroom in a Beijing youth center. Compaq is opening Internet centers throughout China, and Pfeiffer is on a five-day trip to demonstrate the company's commitment. Many multinational companies make philanthropic gestures such as Compaq's. These activities make a significant contribution to the country and also benefit the company by influencing future computer users. (AP/Wide World Photos)

[70]David Shook, "Merck Is Treating the Third World," *Business Week Online,* October 10, 2002.

[71]"Company Profile: Lever Brothers," *The Independent,* June 3, 2002.

[72]Peter Baker, "This Corporate Do-Gooder Gets Dirty," *Business Week Online,* April 2, 2003.

## CROSSING BORDERS 6.5  Dodging the Bullet in Yugoslavia

During most of the 78-day air war against Yugoslavia in 1999, McDonald's kept the burgers flipping while NATO kept the bombs dropping. After only one night of air strikes, mobs of youths, whipped to patriotic fervor by the state-controlled media's attacks on the "NATO criminals and aggressors," targeted six McDonald's stores, smashing windows and scribbling insults on doors and walls. McDonald's Corporation was forced to temporarily close its 15 restaurants in Yugoslavia. Weeks later when local managers flung the doors open again, they accomplished an extraordinary comeback using an unusual marketing strategy: They put McDonald's U.S. citizenship on the back burner.

Within a week after the attacks, they had launched a campaign to identify the plight of ordinary Serbs with the Mac. "McDonald's is sharing the destiny of all people here," read a sign at one branch. A key aspect of the campaign was to present McDonald's as a Yugoslav company. Restaurants promoted the McCountry, a domestic pork burger with paprika garnish, and lowered its price. Pork is considered the most Serbian of meats.

In a national flourish to evoke Serbian identity and pride, McDonald's produced posters and lapel buttons showing the golden arches topped with a traditional Serbian cap called the *sajkaca* (pronounced shy-KACH-a). The managing director of Yugoslavia's McDonald's said they needed to get Serbs to view the company as their own. He masterminded the campaign to "Serbify" McDonald's. It was in this vein that he and his team decided to redesign the logo with the Serbian cap cocked at a haughty angle over one arch. Traditional national emblems, like the *sajkaca*, a strong, unique Serbian symbol, had undergone a revival in recent years with the rise of Serbian nationalism. "By adding this symbol of our cultural heritage, we hoped to denote our pride in being a local company."

Additionally, more than 3,000 free burgers were delivered to the participants of the Belgrade marathon, which was dominated by an anti-NATO theme. At the same time, the company announced that for every burger sold it would donate one dinar (about a nickel) to the Yugoslav Red Cross to help victims of NATO's air strikes. They also handed out free cheeseburgers at anti-NATO rallies.

When the war was over, the company basked in its success. Cash registers were ringing at prewar levels. McDonald's restaurants around the country were thronged with Serbs hungry for Big Macs and fries. And why not, asks 16-year-old Jovan Stojanovic, munching on a burger. "I don't associate McDonald's with America," he says. "Mac is ours." This is music to McDonald's ears. "We managed to save our brand."

That was no easy task. McDonald's is a global symbol of Western pop culture, Yankee know-how, and American corporate cunning; such prominence on the world stage can be a lightning rod for trouble. "We have been in Yugoslavia for years, during which time we sponsored schools, sports clubs, and children's hospitals," he says. "We're part of the community. The Belgrade McDonald's, the first in Central Europe, quickly became a source of local pride. At soccer matches in the old Yugoslavia, when teams from Belgrade met opponents from Zagreb, the Croatian capital, Belgrade fans would taunt their rivals with chants of "We have McDonald's and you don't!"

The real success of the campaign can best be illustrated by customer comments when the restaurant reopened and unveiled its new approach. "We are so happy to see the campaign to help people hurt by the war. It's very humane and the only way to justify the business of an American restaurant in Yugoslavia." Another wrote: "McDonald's is the only American who wished to become a Serb."

Source: Robert Block, "How Big Mac Kept from Becoming a Serb Archenemy," *Wall Street Journal*, September 3, 1999. Copyright 1999 by Dow Jones & Co. Inc. Reproduced with permission of Dow Jones & Co. Inc. via Copyright Clearance Center.

---

Though companies strive to become good corporate citizens in their host countries, it often serves the interests of political parties seeking publicity or scapegoats for their own failures to focus public opinion on the negative aspects of MNCs, whether fairly or not. Companies that establish deep local roots and show by example, rather than meaningless talk, that their strategies are aligned with the long-term goals of the host country stand the best chance of overcoming a less than positive image. "In times like these," says one executive, "global citizenship is perhaps more important than ever."[73] An effective defense for the multinational company is to actively participate in improving the lives of local citizens.

---

[73]Susan E. Reed, "Business; Technology Companies Take Hope in Charity," *New York Times*, March 23, 2003.

In addition to corporate activities focused on the social and economic goals of the host country and good corporate citizenship, MNCs can use other strategies to minimize political vulnerability and risk.

**Joint Ventures**

Typically less susceptible to political harassment, joint ventures can be with locals or other third-country multinational companies; in both cases, a company's financial exposure is limited. A joint venture with locals helps minimize anti-MNC feelings, and a joint venture with another MNC adds the additional bargaining power of a third country.

**Expanding the Investment Base**

Including several investors and banks in financing an investment in the host country is another strategy. This has the advantage of engaging the power of the banks whenever any kind of government takeover or harassment is threatened. This strategy becomes especially powerful if the banks have made loans to the host country; if the government threatens expropriation or other types of takeover, the financing bank has substantial power with the government.

**Licensing**

A strategy that some firms find eliminates almost all risks is to license technology for a fee. Licensing can be effective in situations where the technology is unique and the risk is high. Of course, there is some risk assumed because the licensee can refuse to pay the required fees while continuing to use the technology.

**Planned Domestication**

The strategies just discussed can be effective in forestalling or minimizing the effect of a total takeover. However, in those cases where a host country in demanding local participation, the most effective long-range solution is planned phasing out, that is, *planned domestication*. This is not the preferred business practice, but the alternative of government-initiated domestication can be as disastrous as confiscation. As a reasonable response to the potential of domestication, planned domestication can be profitable and operationally expedient for the foreign investor. Planned domestication is, in essence, a gradual process of participating with nationals in all phases of company operations.

Today, the climate for foreign investment is more positive than it was decades ago, so planned domestication may not be necessary. In fact, most developing countries demand many of the steps just outlined as conditions for market entry. However, planned domestication is a meaningful strategy to help avoid hostility toward an investment. It is better to plan to blend into a foreign market on your own terms than have the host country force domestication or, worse, employ expropriation. Despite such efforts on the part of MNCs, the reality is that political risks always loom in the background, ready to emerge at any time.

**Political Payoffs**

One approach to dealing with political vulnerability is the political payoff—an attempt to lessen political risks by paying those in power to intervene on behalf of the multinational company.[74] Political payoffs, or bribery, have been used to lessen the negative effects of a variety of problems. Paying heads of state to avoid confiscatory taxes or expulsion, paying fees to agents to ensure the acceptance of sales contracts, and providing monetary encouragement to an assortment of people whose actions can affect the effectiveness of a company's programs are decisions that frequently confront multinational managers and raise ethical questions.

Bribery poses problems for the marketer at home and abroad because it is illegal for U.S. citizens to pay a bribe even if it is a common practice in the host country. There may be short-term benefits to political payoffs, but in the long run the risks are high and bribery should be avoided.

---

[74]Abdul Quader Chowdhury, "Getting Rid of Corruption," *The Independent Bangladesh,* September 13, 2002.

## Government Encouragement

Governments, both foreign and in the United States, encourage foreign investment as well as discourage it. In fact, within the same country some foreign businesses may fall prey to politically induced harassment while others may be placed under a government umbrella of protection and receive preferential treatment. The difference lies in the evaluation of a company's contribution to the nation's interest.

The most important reason to encourage foreign investment is to accelerate the development of an economy. An increasing number of countries are encouraging foreign investment with specific guidelines aimed toward economic goals.[75] Multinational corporations may be expected to create local employment, transfer technology, generate export sales, stimulate growth and development of local industry, conserve foreign exchange, or meet a combination of these expectations as a requirement for market concessions.[76] Recent investments in China, India, and the former republics of the USSR include provisions stipulating specific contributions to economic goals of the country that must be made by foreign investors.

The U.S. government is motivated for economic as well as political reasons to encourage American firms to seek business opportunities in countries worldwide, including those that are politically risky. It seeks to create a favorable climate for overseas business by providing the assistance that helps minimize some of the more troublesome politically motivated financial risks of doing business abroad. The Department of Commerce (DOC) at www.doc.gov is the principal agency that supports U.S. business abroad. The International Trade Administration (ITA) at www.ita.gov, a bureau in the DOC, is dedicated to helping U.S. business compete in the global marketplace. Other agencies that provide assistance to U.S. companies include:

- Export Import Bank (Ex-Im Bank) underwrites trade and investments for U.S. firms. www.exim.gov
- Foreign Credit Insurance Association (FCIA) and agency of the Ex-Im Bank— provides credit insurance that minimizes nonpayment risk caused by financial, economic, or political uncertainties. It includes insurance against confiscation, civil disturbances, and the cancellation or restriction of export or import licenses. www.fcia.com
- The Agency for International Development (AID) provides aid to underdeveloped countries and has limited protection in support of "essential" projects in approved countries and for approved products. www.uaid.gov
- The Overseas Private Investment Corporation (OPIC) provides risk insurance for companies investing in less-developed countries. www.opic.gov

## Summary

Vital to every marketer's assessment of a foreign market is an appreciation for the political environment of the country within which he or she plans to operate. Government involvement in business activities abroad, especially foreign-controlled business, is generally much greater than business is accustomed to in the United States. The foreign firm must strive to make its activities politically acceptable or it may be subjected to a variety of politically condoned harassment.

In addition to the harassment that can be imposed by a government, the foreign marketer frequently faces the problem of uncertainty of continuity in government policy. As governments change political philosophies, a marketing firm accepted under one administration might find its activities undesirable under another. An unfamiliar or hostile political environment does not necessarily preclude success for a foreign marketer if the company becomes a local economic asset and responds creatively to the issues raised by political and social activists. The U.S. government may aid American business in its foreign operations, and if a company is considered vital to achieving national economic goals, the host country often provides an umbrella of protection not extended to others.

---

[75]"Tax Incentives Key to Turning Korea Into NE Asian Hub," *The Korea Times,* July 8, 2002.

[76]Matthew Mok, "Pooling Best Practices to Woo MNCs," *New Straits Times-Management Times,* September 5, 2002.

# Questions

1. Define the following terms:

   sovereignty, 158          expropriation, 164
   nationalism, 162          domestication, 164
   confiscation, 164         PSAs, 167

2. Why would a country rather domesticate than expropriate?

3. "A crucial fact when doing business in a foreign country is that permission to conduct business is controlled by the government of the host country." Comment.

4. What are the main factors to consider in assessing the dominant political climate within a country?

5. Why is a working knowledge of political party philosophy so important in a political assessment of a market? Discuss.

6. How can a change in the political party in power affect an investor? Discuss and give examples

7. What are the most common causes of instability in governments? Discuss.

8. Discuss how governmental instability can affect marketing.

9. What are the most frequently encountered political risks in foreign business? Discuss.

10. Expropriation is considered a major risk of foreign business. Discuss ways in which this particular type of risk can be minimized somewhat as a result of company activities. Explain how these risks have been minimized by the activities of the U.S. government.

11. How do exchange controls impede foreign business? Discuss.

12. How do foreign governments encourage foreign investment? Discuss.

13. How does the U.S. government encourage foreign investment?

14. What are the motives behind U.S. government encouragement for foreign investment? Explain.

15. Discuss measures a company might take to lessen its political vulnerability.

16. Select a country and analyze it politically from a marketing viewpoint.

17. The text suggests that violence is a politically motivated risk of international business. Comment.

18. There is evidence that expropriation and confiscation are less frequently encountered today than just a few years ago. Why? What other types of political risks have replaced expropriation and confiscation in importance?

19. You are an executive in a large domestic company with only minor interests in international markets; however, corporate plans call for major global expansion. Visit the home page of Control Risks Group at www.crg.com. After thoroughly familiarizing yourself with the services offered by CRG, write a brief report to management describing how its services could possibly help with your global expansion.

20. Visit the website www.politicalresources.net/ and select the Political Site of the Week. Write a brief political analysis highlighting potential problem areas for a company interested in investing in that country.

21. Search the Web for information on the activities of PSAs outside the United States and write a briefing paper for international management on potential problems.

22. Discuss ways the companies discussed in the Global Perspective could have minimized their losses in the banana wars.

23. Discuss any ethical and socially responsible issues that may be implied in the Global Perspective.

**CHAPTER 7**

# the international Legal environment:

## PLAYING BY THE RULES

CHAPTER LEARNING OBJECTIVES

What you should learn from Chapter 7:

- The four heritages of today's legal systems

- The important factors in jurisdiction of legal disputes

- Issues associated with jurisdiction of legal disputes and the various methods of dispute resolution

- The unique problems of protecting intellectual property rights internationally

- Ways to protect against piracy and counterfeiting

- The legal differences between countries and how the differences can affect international marketing plans

- The different ways U.S. laws can be applied to U.S. companies operating outside the United States

- The many issues of evolving cyberlaw

# Global Perspective

## THE PAJAMA CAPER

Six headlines illustrate the entanglements possible when U.S. law, host-country law, and a multinational company collide:

- "Wal-Mart's Cuban-Made Pajamas Defy Embargo"
- "Wal-Mart Ignites Row by Pulling Cuban Pajamas off Shelves in Canada"
- "Canada, U.S. Wager Diplomatic Capital in a High-Stakes Pajama Game"
- "Cuban Quandary: Wal-Mart in Hot Water for Yanking Pajamas"
- "Canada Probes Wal-Mart Move against Cuban Pajamas"
- "Wal-Mart Puts Cuban Goods Back on Sale"

The controversy arose over a U.S. embargo forbidding U.S. businesses to trade with Cuba, and concerned whether or not the embargo could be enforced in Canada. Wal-Mart was selling Cuban-made pajamas in Canada. When Wal-Mart officials in the United States became aware of the origin of manufacture, they issued an order to remove all the offending pajamas because it is against U.S. law (the Helms-Burton Act) for a U.S. company or any of its foreign subsidiaries to trade with Cuba. Canada was incensed at the intrusion of U.S. law on Canadian citizens. The Canadians felt they should have the choice of buying Cuban-made pajamas.

Wal-Mart was thus caught in the middle of conflicting laws in Canada and the United States and a Canada–U.S. foreign policy feud over the extraterritoriality of U.S. law. Wal-Mart Canada would be breaking U.S. law if it continued to sell the pajamas, and be subject to a million-dollar fine and possible imprisonment. However, if the company pulled the pajamas out of Canadian stores as the home office ordered, it would be subject to a $1.2 million fine under Canadian law. After discussion with Canadian authorities, Wal-Mart resumed selling the pajamas. Canada was upset with the United States for attempting to impose its laws on Canadian companies (Wal-Mart Canada is a subsidiary of Wal-Mart U.S.), and the United States said that Wal-Mart was violating its laws in not abiding by the boycott with Cuba. The situation illustrates the reality of the legal environment and international marketing—companies are subject to both home-country laws and host-country laws when doing business in another country. The federal government finally settled with Wal-Mart in 2003 and the pajama caper was finally closed.

Sources: *Boston Globe,* March 3, 1997; *St. Louis Post-Dispatch,* March 9, 1997; *Washington Post,* March 14, 1997, p. A6; *Wall Street Journal,* March 14, 1997, p. B4; John W. Boscariol, "An Anatomy of a Cuban Pajama Crisis," *Law and Policy in International Business,* Spring 1999, p. 439; and Verne Kopytoff, "U.S. Firms Face Fines/Violations of Trade Sanctions Alleged," *The San Francisco Chronicle,* April 18, 2003.

How would you like to play a game where the stakes were high; there was no standard set of rules to play by; the rules changed whenever a new player entered the game; and when a dispute arose, the referee used the other players' rules to interpret who was right? That fairly well describes the international legal environment. Because no single, uniform international commercial law governing foreign business transactions exists, the international marketer must pay particular attention to the laws of each country within which it operates. An American company doing business with a French customer has to contend with two jurisdictions (U.S. and France), two tax systems, two legal systems, and a third supranational set of European Community laws and regulations that may override French commercial law. The situation is similar when doing business in Japan, Germany, or any other country. Laws governing business activities within and between countries are an integral part of the legal environment of international business.

The legal systems of different countries are so disparate and complex that it is beyond the scope of this text to explore the laws of each country individually. There are, however, issues common to most international marketing transactions that need special attention when operating abroad. Jurisdiction, dispute resolution, intellectual property, the extraterritoriality of U.S. laws, cyberlaw, and associated problems are discussed in this chapter to provide a broad view of the international legal environment. Although space and focus limit an in-depth presentation, the material presented should be sufficient for the reader to conclude that securing expert legal advice is a wise decision when doing business in another country.[1] The foundation of a legal system profoundly affects how the law is written, interpreted, and adjudicated. The place to begin is with a discussion of the different legal systems.[2]

## Bases for Legal Systems

Three heritages form the bases for the majority of the legal systems of the world: (1) common law, derived from English law and found in England, the United States, Canada,[3] and other countries once under English influence; (2) civil or code law, derived from Roman law and found in Germany, Japan, France, and in non-Islamic and non-Marxist countries; (3) Islamic law, derived from the interpretation of the Koran and found in Pakistan, Iran, Saudi Arabia, and other Islamic states, and (4) a commercial legal system in the Marxist-socialist economies of Russia and the republics of the former Soviet Union, Eastern Europe, China, and other Marxist-socialist states whose legal system centered on the economic, political, and social policies of the state. As each country moves toward its own version of a free market system and enters the global market, a commercial legal system is also evolving from those Marxist-socialist tenets. China has announced that it will adopt a constitution-based socialist legal system with Chinese characteristics.[4]

The differences among these four systems are of more than theoretical importance because due process of law may vary considerably among and within these legal systems. Even though a country's laws may be based on the doctrine of one of the four legal systems, its individual interpretation may vary significantly—from a fundamentalist interpretation of Islamic law as found in Pakistan to a combination of several legal systems found in the United States, where both common and code law are reflected in the laws.

---

[1]Lisa Bertagnoli, "Firms Follow Multinational Clients," *Crain's Chicago Business,* July 8, 2002.

[2]Goran Therborn, "The World's Trader, the World's Lawyer: Europe and Global Business," *European Journal of Social Theory,* November 2002, p. 403.

[3]All of the provinces of Canada have a common-law system, with the exception of Quebec, which is a code-law province. All states in the United States are common law, with the exception of Louisiana, which is a code-law state.

[4]"Legal System with Chinese Characteristics Taking Form," *Xinhua News Agency,* March 10, 2003.

## CROSSING BORDERS 7.1  Patent Law: The United States versus Japan— Differences in Culture Do Matter

The goal of Western patent systems is to protect and reward individual entrepreneurs and innovative businesses, to encourage invention, and to advance practical knowledge. The intent of the Japanese patent system is to share technology, not to protect it. In fact, it serves a larger, national goal: the rapid spread of technological know-how among competitors in a manner that avoids litigation, encourages broad-scale cooperation, and promotes Japanese industry as a whole. Even Japan's legal system is tilted against the inventor. Although Japanese patent law requires firms to compensate employees for their mega-buck ideas, it doesn't specify how much. There's nothing to stop a company from giving a researcher only a few hundred dollars for a major invention.

This approach is entirely consistent with the broader characteristics of Japanese culture, which emphasizes harmony, cooperation, and hierarchy. It favors large companies over small ones, discourages Japanese entrepreneurship, and puts foreign companies that do not appreciate the true nature of the system at a substantial disadvantage. The following table compares patent laws in the United States and Japan.

| United States | Japan |
|---|---|
| Operates under "first to invent" rule | Operates under "first to register" rule |
| Protects individual inventors | Promotes technology sharing |
| Patent applications secret | Patent applications public |
| Patents granted in up to 24 months | Patents granted in 4 to 6 years |
| Patents valid for 17 years from date issued | Patents valid 20 years from application |

Sources: Donald M. Spero, "Clay Jacobson Calls It Patently Unfair," *Business Week,* August 19, 1991, p. 48; "Differences in National Patent Laws Breed Discord and Confusion," *Jane's Defense Contracts,* September 1997, p. 9; "Japan's Inventors Struggle to Stay on the Cutting Edge of Technological Innovation," *Time,* May 1, 2000; Bill Roberts, "The Muddle of Invention," *Electronic Business,* January 1, 2000, p. 72; and Yoshitaka Sonoda, "Constant Change to IP Laws Feeds Uncertainty," *Managing Intellectual Property,* September 2002, p. 72.

## Common and Code Law

The basis for **common law**[5] is tradition, past practices, and legal precedents set by the courts through interpretations of statutes, legal legislation, and past rulings.[6] Common law seeks "interpretation through the past decisions of higher courts which interpret the same statutes or apply established and customary principles of law to a similar set of facts." **Code law**,[7] on the other hand, is based on an all-inclusive system of written rules (codes) of law. Under code law, the legal system is generally divided into three separate codes: commercial, civil, and criminal.

Common law is recognized as not being all-inclusive, whereas code law is considered complete as a result of catchall provisions found in most code-law systems. For example, under the commercial code in a code-law country, the law governing contracts is made inclusive with the statement that "a person performing a contract shall do so in conformity with good faith as determined by custom and good morals." Although code law is considered all-inclusive, it is apparent from the foregoing statement that some broad interpretations are possible in order to include everything under the existing code.

Steps are being taken in common-law countries to codify commercial law even though the primary basis of commercial law is common law, that is, precedents set by court decisions. An example of the new uniformity is the acceptance of the Uniform Commercial Code by most states in the United States. Even though U.S. commercial law has been codified to some extent under the Uniform Commercial Code, the philosophy of interpretation is anchored in common law.

---

[5]Also known as English law.

[6]For an interesting discussion on the prospects of England having to give up its common-law system for European law (code law) as a result of its membership in the European Union, see Paul Craig Roberts, "England Losing Its Grip on Law," *The Washington Times,* November 30, 2001.

[7]Also known as Napoleonic Code.

As discussed later in the section on protection of intellectual property, laws governing intellectual property offer the most striking differences between common-law and code-law systems. Under common law, ownership is established by use; under code law, ownership is determined by registration. In some code-law countries, certain agreements may not be enforceable unless properly notarized or registered; in a common-law country, the same agreement may be binding so long as proof of the agreement can be established. Although every country has elements of both common and code law, the differences in interpretation between common- and code-law systems regarding contracts, sales agreements, and other legal issues are significant enough that an international marketer familiar with only one system must enlist the aid of legal counsel for the most basic legal questions.

Another illustration of where fundamental differences in the two systems can cause difficulty is in the performance of a contract. Under common law in the United States, it is fairly clear that impossibility of performance does not necessarily excuse compliance with the provisions of a contract unless it is impossible to comply for reason of an act of God, such as some extraordinary happening of nature not reasonably anticipated by either party of a contract. Hence, floods, lightning, earthquakes, and similar occurrences are generally considered acts of God. Under code law, acts of God are not limited solely to acts of nature but are extended to include "unavoidable interference with performance, whether resulting from forces of nature or unforeseeable human acts," including such things as labor strikes and riots.

Consider the following situations: A contract was entered into to deliver a specific quantity of cloth. In one case, before the seller could make delivery an earthquake caused the destruction of the cloth and compliance was then impossible. In the second case, pipes in the sprinkler system where the material was stored froze and broke, spilling water on the cloth and destroying it. In each case, loss of the merchandise was sustained and delivery could not be made. Were the parties in these cases absolved of their obligations under the contract because of the impossibility of delivery? The answer depends on the system of law invoked.

In the first situation, the earthquake would be considered an act of God under both common and code law, and impossibility of performance would excuse compliance under the contract. In the second situation, courts in common-law countries would probably rule that the bursting of the water pipes did not constitute an act of God if it happened in a climate where freezing could be expected. Therefore, impossibility of delivery would not necessarily excuse compliance with the provisions of the contract. In code-law countries, where the scope of impossibility of performance is extended considerably, the destruction might very well be ruled an act of God, and thus release from compliance with the contract could be obtained.

## Islamic Law

The basis for the *Shari'ah* (**Islamic law**) is interpretation of the Koran. It encompasses religious duties and obligations as well as the secular aspect of law regulating human acts. Broadly speaking, Islamic law defines a complete system that prescribes specific patterns of social and economic behavior for all individuals.[8] It includes issues such as property rights, economic decision making, and types of economic freedom. The overriding objective of the Islamic system is social justice.

Among the unique aspects of Islamic law is the prohibition against the payment of interest. The Islamic law of contracts states that any given transaction should be devoid of *riba,* which is defined as unlawful advantage by way of excess of deferment, that is, interest or usury. Prohibiting the receipt and payment of interest is the nucleus of the Islamic system. However, other principles of Islamic doctrine advocate risk sharing, individuals' rights and duties, property rights, and the sanctity of contracts. The Islamic system places emphasis on the ethical, moral, social, and religious dimensions to enhance equality and fairness for the good of society. Another principle of the Islamic legal system

---

[8]Veeramalla Anjaiah, "Debt Enslavement Still Exists in Society Says Mahathir," *The Jakarta Post,* November 4, 2002.

Banking in Dubai, UAE, requires an understanding of Islamic law and customs. Prohibition against the payment of interest and prohibition against investments in businesses dealing with alcohol and gambling are some of the tenets of Islamic law that affect banking. (© Derek Berwin/Getty Images)

is the prohibition against investment in those activities that violate the *Shari'ah*. For example, any investment in a business dealing with alcohol, gambling, and casinos would be prohibited.

Prohibition against the payment of interest affects banking and business practices severely. However, there are acceptable practices that adhere to Islamic law and permit the transaction of business. Mortgages for property are difficult because payment of interest is forbidden under Islamic law. Buyers of real property have to use a financier, who buys the property and then sells it to them in return for repayments of the capital. Instead of charging interest a financier either sells the property at a higher price or sells it at the same price and takes additional payments to cover what would have been interest.[9] Of the other ways to comply with Islamic law in financial transactions, trade with markup or cost-plus sale (*murabaha*) and leasing (*ijara*) are the most frequently used. In both *murabaha* and *ijara*, a mutually negotiated margin is included in the sale price or leasing payment. These practices meet the requirements of *Shari'ah* by enabling borrowers and lenders to share in the rewards as well as losses in an equitable fashion. They also ensure that the process of wealth accumulation and distribution in the economy is fair and representative of true productivity. Strict fundamentalists often frown on such an arrangement, but it is practiced and is an example of the way the strictness of Islamic law can be reconciled with the laws of non-Islamic legal systems.

Because the laws are based on interpretation of the Koran, the international marketer must have knowledge of the religion's tenets[10] and understand the way the law may be interpreted in each region. Regional courts can interpret Islamic law from the viewpoint of fundamentalists (those that adhere to a literal interpretation of the Koran) or they may use a more liberal translation. A company can find local authorities in one region willing to allow payment of interest on deferred obligations as stipulated in a contract, while in another region all interest charges may be deleted and replaced with comparable "consulting fees." In yet another, authorities may void a contract and declare any payment of interest illegal. Marketers conducting business in Islamic-law countries must be knowledgeable about this important legal system.

## Marxist-Socialist Tenets

As socialist countries become more directly involved in trade with non-Marxist countries, it has been necessary to develop a commercial legal system that permits them to engage in active international commerce.[11] The pattern for development varies among the countries because each has a different background and each is at a different stage in its development of a market-driven economy. For example, Central European countries such as the Czech Republic and Poland had comprehensive codified legal systems before communism took over, and their pre–World War II commercial legal codes have been revised and reinstituted. Consequently, they have moved toward a legal model with greater ease than some others have. Russia and most of the republics of the former USSR and China, on the other hand, have had to build from scratch an entire commercial legal system.[12] Under the premise that law, according to **Marxist-socialist tenets**, is strictly subordinate to prevailing economic conditions, such fundamental propositions as private ownership, contracts, due process, and other legal mechanisms needed to be developed.

---

[9]Mark Atherton, "Muslim Mortgages a Step Nearer," *The Times*, April 12, 2003.

[10]For an interesting discussion on Islamic beliefs about insurance and interest, see Khurshid Ahmad and Joseph A. Petrick, "The Challenge and Opportunity of Islamic Insurance," *Risk Management*, March 2003, p. 28.

[11]Davik Kotz, "A Failed Economic Model," *The St. Petersburg Times*, January 30, 2001.

[12]Alex Nicholson, "Building an Empire Based On the Rule of Law," *Moscow Times*, January 23, 2003.

China and Russia differ, however, in that each has taken a different direction in its political economic growth. Russia is moving toward a democratic system, whereas China is attempting to activate a private sector within a multicomponent or mixed economy in a socialist legal framework, that is, "perform its functions according to law and contribute to the development of socialist democracy and political civilization in China."[13]

Both countries have actively passed laws, although the process has been slow and often disjointed. China has implemented over 150 laws and regulations governing trade, yet the process is hampered by vaguely written laws, the lack of implementation mechanisms for the new laws, and an ineffective framework for dispute resolution and enforcement.[14] A good example is China's attempt to control what goes on in Chinese cyberspace by applying the States Secrets Law to the Internet. The definition of a state secret is so broad that it can cover any information not cleared for publication with the relevant authorities.

Russia's experience has been similar to China's in that vaguely worded laws have been passed without mechanisms for implementation. The situation in Russia is often described as chaotic because of the laws' lack of precision. For example, it has become a crime to illegally receive or disseminate commercial secrets, but there is no exact definition of a commercial secret. Copyright law violations that cause "great damage" are listed, but with no clear definition of how much damage constitutes "great." Both China and Russia are hampered by not having the heritage of a legal commercial code to build on as many of the Eastern European countries had.

The international marketer must be concerned with the differences among common law, code law, Islamic law, and socialist legal systems when operating between countries; the rights of the principals of a contract or some other legal document under one law may be significantly different from their rights under the other. It should be kept in mind that there could also be differences between the laws of two countries whose laws are based on the same legal system. Thus the problem of the marketer is one of anticipating the different laws regulating business, regardless of the legal system of the country.

## Jurisdiction in International Legal Disputes

Determining whose legal system has jurisdiction when a commercial dispute arises is another problem of international marketing. A frequent error is to assume that disputes between citizens of different nations are adjudicated under some supranational system of laws. Unfortunately, no judicial body exists to deal with legal commercial problems arising between citizens of different countries. Confusion probably stems from the existence of international courts such as the World Court at The Hague and the International Court of Justice, the principal judicial organ of the United Nations. These courts are operative in international disputes between sovereign nations of the world rather than between private citizens.

Legal disputes can arise in three situations: between governments, between a company and a government, and between two companies. The World Court can adjudicate disputes between governments, whereas the other two situations must be handled in the courts of the country of one of the parties involved or through arbitration. Unless a commercial dispute involves a national issue between states, the International Court of Justice or any similar world court does not handle it. Because there is no "international commercial law," the foreign marketer must look to the legal system of each country involved—the laws of the home country or the laws of the countries within which business is conducted, or both.[15]

---

[13]"Li Peng Urges People's Congress to Contribute to Political Civilization," *Xinhua News Agency (China),* March 10, 2003.

[14]"Top Legislator Vows to Boost Rule of Law In China," *Xinhua News Agency (China),* January 10, 2001.

[15]For a legal and thorough discussion of the globalization of jurisdiction, see Paul Schiff Berman, "The Globalization of Jurisdiction," *University of Pennsylvania Law Review,* December 2002, p. 311.

**CROSSING BORDERS 7.2** České Budějovice, Privatization, Trademarks, and Taste Tests—What Do They Have in Common with Anheuser-Busch? Budweiser, That's What!

Anheuser-Busch (AB) launched a massive public relations program in the small Czech town of České Budějovice, where a local brewery produces "Budweiser Budvar." Anheuser-Busch planted trees along main avenues, opened a new cultural center offering free English courses to citizens and management advice to budding entrepreneurs, and ran newspaper ads touting the possibilities of future cooperation.

Anheuser-Busch's goal was to win support for a minority stake in the Czech state-owned brewery, Budějovicky Budvar N.P., when the government privatized it. So why was AB interested in a brewery whose annual production of 500,000 barrels is the equivalent of two days' output for AB?

Part ownership is critically important to Anheuser-Busch for two reasons. They are in search of new markets in Europe, and they want to be able to market the Budweiser brand in Europe. So what's the connection? They don't have the rights to use the Budweiser brand in Europe because Budějovicky Budvar N.P owns it. Their public relations plan didn't work because many Czechs see Budvar as the "family silver." Although the Czech prime minister asked publicly for American investors to put money into the Czech Republic, Czech Budweiser was not on the government's privatization list. "I believe in the strength of American investors, but I do not believe in the quality of American beer."

Anheuser-Busch established the name Budweiser in the United States when German immigrants founded the St. Louis family brewery and began selling under the Budweiser brand in 1876, which is 19 years before the Czech brewery opened. The Czechs claim they have been using the name since before Columbus discovered the New World and that Budweiser refers to Budwis, the original name of the city where Budvar is located. That is the name commonly used to refer to beer brewed in that area hundreds of years before Anheuser-Busch started brewing Budweiser.

The Anheuser-Busch Company markets Budweiser brand beer in North America, but in Europe it markets Busch brand beer because the Czechs have the rights to the use of the name Budweiser. Diplomacy and public relations didn't work, so what next? The parties are tied up in legal wrangling over who has the rights to the Budweiser name and to derivations of it, such as Bud. More than 40 lawsuits and 40 administrative cases are pending across Europe. U.S. law protects Anheuser-Busch's rights to the Budweiser label in the United States; the Czech's sell their beer as "Czechvar."

The Czech brewery exports to 37 countries, mainly in Europe, and AB has sales in more than 70 countries around the world. Anheuser-Busch sought a court order to have the Czech company's products taken off the shelves in Hong Kong and has launched similar lawsuits in the United Kingdom and the United States. AB said the Czech brewery had imported and sold beer in the United States labeled "Budweiser Budvar" in the state of Maryland. It says the Czech brewery is mimicking its name to confuse beer drinkers and cash in on the U.S. company's success.

The Czech government petitioned the WTO to grant beer regions the same kind of labeling protection that it gives to wine regions. Just as sparkling wines made in the Champagne region of France are the only ones legally entitled to call themselves champagne, it would mean that only beers brewed in České Budějovice could call themselves Budweiser and only those brewed in Pilzen, another Czech town, could claim to be Pilsner. It seems unlikely that they will win approval since Pilsner has become a generic designation for a style of beer, and unlike the grapes that champagne comes from, the malt and the hops that go into beer do not come exclusively from České Budějovice.

The legal battle for the exclusive right to use the brand names Bud and Budweiser has spread worldwide. So far, this tactic hasn't worked too well either. Britain's high court allowed both companies to use the names Bud and Budweiser, whereas Switzerland's highest court banned Anheuser-Busch from selling beer under the Bud name.

We all know that the proof of who's best is in the tasting, right? Both lagers have legions of fans. The U.S. version lives up to its old slogan of "king of beers," at least as far as sales go: It's the top-selling beer in the world. The Czech version—nicknamed the "beer of kings" because it comes from a town that once brewed for royalty—has large followings in Germany and other parts of Europe. So the *St. Louis Post-Dispatch* hosted a blind taste test to determine which beer is better—Budvar won.

Visit the Budvar website (www.budvar.cz) for the history of Budvar and a tour of the plant, and visit the AB home page at www.anheuser-busch.com.

Sources: Stamborski, "Battle of the Buds: Taste Testers Say That Budvar Is Better," *St. Louis Post-Dispatch*, November 28, 1999, p. E1; "Prime Minister Says Budvar Will Stay Czech," *Modern Brewery*, March 2000; "Battle of the Buds Pits Small Czech Brewery Against U.S. Behemoth," *Chicago Tribune*, May 31, 2001; "Lords Nip Beer Battle in Bud," *Managing Intellectual Property*, March 2003, p. 14; and, Gregory Cancelada, "Czech Brewery Retains Right to Use 'Budweiser' and 'Bud' Trademarks," *St. Louis Dispatch*, February 17, 2003.

When international commercial disputes must be settled under the laws of one of the countries concerned, the paramount question in a dispute is: Which law governs? Jurisdiction[16] is generally determined in one of three ways: (1) on the basis of jurisdictional clauses included in contracts, (2) on the basis of where a contract was entered into, or (3) on the basis of where the provisions of the contract were performed.

The most clear-cut decision can be made when the contracts or legal documents supporting a business transaction include a jurisdictional clause. A clause similar to the following establishes jurisdiction in the event of disagreements:

> That the parties hereby agree that the agreement is made in Oregon, USA, and that any question regarding this agreement shall be governed by the law of the state of Oregon, USA.

This clause establishes that the laws of the state of Oregon would be invoked should a dispute arise. If the complaint were brought in the court of another country, it is probable that the same Oregon laws would govern the decision. Cooperation and a definite desire to be judicious in foreign legal problems have led to the practice of foreign courts judging disputes on the basis of the law of another country or state whenever applicable. Thus, if an injured party from Oregon brings suit in the courts of Mexico against a Mexican over a contract that included the preceding clause, it would not be unusual for the Mexican courts to decide on the basis of Oregon law. This is assuming, of course, it was recognized that Oregon law prevailed in this dispute either as a result of the prior agreement by the parties or on some other basis.

## International Dispute Resolution

When things go wrong in a commercial transaction—the buyer refuses to pay, the product is of inferior quality, the shipment arrives late, or any one of the myriad problems that can arise—what recourse does the international marketer have? The first step in any dispute is to try to resolve the issue informally, but if that fails the foreign marketer must resort to more resolute action. Such action can take the form of conciliation, arbitration, or as a last resort, litigation. Most international businesspeople prefer a settlement through arbitration rather than by suing a foreign company.

### Conciliation

Most disputes that arise in commercial transactions, are settled informally. When resolution is not forthcoming, however, conciliation can be an important first step in settling a dispute. **Conciliation** (also known as *mediation*) is a nonbinding agreement between parties to resolve disputes by asking a third party to mediate differences. The function of the mediator is to carefully listen to each party and to explore, clarify, and discuss the various practical options and possibilities for a solution with the intent that the parties will agree on a solution. Unlike arbitration and litigation, conciliation sessions are private and all conferences between parties and the mediator are confidential; the statements made by the parties may not be disclosed or used as evidence in any subsequent litigation or arbitration. The track record for the conciliation process is excellent, with a majority of disputes reaching settlement and leading to the resumption of business between the disputants.

Conciliation is considered to be especially effective when resolving disputes with Chinese business partners because they feel less threatened by conciliation than arbitration. The Chinese believe that when a dispute occurs, informal, friendly negotiation should be used first to solve the problem; if that fails, conciliation should be tried. In fact, some Chinese companies may avoid doing business with companies that resort first to arbitration. Conciliation can be either formal or informal. Both sides agreeing on a third party to mediate can establish informal conciliation. Formal conciliation is conducted under the auspices of some tribunal such as the Beijing Conciliation Center, which assigns one or two conciliators to mediate. If agreement is reached, a conciliation

---

[16]Lawrence W. Newman and David Zaslowsky, "International Litigation," *New York Law Journal,* April 30, 2003.

statement based on the signed agreement is recorded. Although conciliation may be the friendly route to resolving disputes in China, it is not legally binding; thus, an arbitration clause should be included in all conciliation agreements. Experience has shown that having an arbitration clause in the conciliation agreement makes it easier to move to arbitration if necessary.

## Arbitration

If conciliation is not used or an agreement cannot be reached, the next step is **arbitration**. When all else fails, arbitration rather than litigation is the preferred method for resolving international commercial disputes. The usual arbitration procedure is for the parties involved to select a disinterested and informed party or parties as referee to determine the merits of the case and make a judgment that both parties agree to honor. Although informal arbitration is workable, most arbitration is conducted under the auspices of one of the more formal domestic and international arbitration groups organized specifically to facilitate the resolution of commercial disputes. These groups have formal rules for the process and experienced arbitrators to assist. In most countries, decisions reached in formal arbitration are enforceable under the law.[17]

The popularity of arbitration has led to a proliferation of arbitral centers established by countries, organizations, and institutions. All have adopted standardized rules and procedures to administer cases, and each has its strengths and weaknesses. Some of the more active are the following:

- The Inter-American Commercial Arbitration Commission
- The Canadian-American Commercial Arbitration Commission (for disputes between Canadian and U.S. businesses)
- The London Court of Arbitration (decisions are enforceable under English law and English courts)

- The American Arbitration Association (www.adr.org/)
- The International Chamber of Commerce (www.iccwbo.org/; select Arbitration)

The procedures used by formal arbitration organizations are similar. Arbitration under the rules of the International Chamber of Commerce (ICC) affords an excellent example of how most organizations operate. When an initial request for arbitration is received, the chamber first attempts conciliation between the disputants. If this fails, the process of arbitration is started. The plaintiff and the defendant select one person each from among acceptable arbitrators to defend their case, and the ICC Court of Arbitration appoints a third member, generally chosen from a list of distinguished lawyers, jurists, and professors.

The history of ICC effectiveness in arbitration has been spectacular. An example of a case that involved arbitration by the ICC concerned a contract between an English business and a Japanese manufacturer. The English business agreed to buy 100,000 plastic dolls for 80 cents each. On the strength of the contract, the English business sold the entire lot at $1.40 per doll. Before the dolls were delivered, the Japanese manufacturer had a strike; the settlement of the strike increased costs, and the English business was informed that the delivery price of the dolls had increased from 80 cents to $1.50 each. The English business maintained that the Japanese firm had committed to make delivery at 80 cents and should deliver at that price. Each side was convinced that it was right.

The Japanese, accustomed to code law, felt that the strike was beyond control (an act of God) and thus compliance with the original provisions of the contract was excused. The English, accustomed to common law, did not accept the Japanese reasons for not complying because they considered a strike part of the normal course of doing business and not an act of God. The dispute could not be settled except through arbitration or litigation; they chose arbitration. The ICC appointed an arbitrator who heard both sides and ruled that the two parties would share proportionately in the loss. Both parties were

---

[17]"Putin Signs Arbitration Procedural Code, Law on Arbitration Courts," *Interfax,* July 25, 2002.

satisfied with the arbitration decision, and costly litigation was avoided. Most arbitration is successful, but success depends on the willingness of both parties to accept the arbitrator's rulings.

Contracts and other legal documents should include clauses specifying the use of arbitration to settle disputes.[18] Unless a provision for arbitration of any dispute is incorporated as part of a contract, the likelihood of securing agreement for arbitration after a dispute arises is reduced. A typical arbitration clause is as follows:

> Any controversy or claim arising out of or relating to this contract shall be determined by arbitration in accordance with the International Arbitration Rules of the American Arbitration Association.

It is suggested that the number of arbitrators, the place of arbitration (city and/or country), and the language of the arbitration be stated as well.[19]

Although an arbitration clause in a contract can avert problems, sometimes enforcing arbitration agreements can be difficult.[20] Arbitration clauses require agreement on two counts: (1) The parties agree to arbitrate in the case of a dispute according to the rules and procedures of some arbitration tribunal, and (2) they agree to abide by the awards resulting from the arbitration. Difficulty arises when the parties to a contract fail to honor the agreements. Companies may refuse to name arbitrators, refuse to arbitrate, or, after arbitration awards are made, they may refuse to honor the award. In most countries, arbitration clauses are recognized by the courts and are enforceable by law within those countries. More than 120 countries have ratified the Convention on the Recognition and Enforcement of Foreign Arbitral Awards, also known as the New York Convention, which binds them to uphold foreign arbitration awards. Under the New York Convention, the courts of the signatory countries automatically uphold foreign arbitral awards issued in member countries. In addition to the New York Convention, the United States is a signatory of the Inter-American Convention on International Arbitration to which many Latin American countries are party. The United States is also party to a number of bilateral agreements containing clauses providing for enforcement of arbitral awards. When all else fails, the final step to solve a dispute is **litigation**.

## Litigation

Lawsuits in public courts are avoided for many reasons. Most observers of lawsuits between citizens of different countries believe that almost all victories are spurious because the cost, frustrating delays, and extended aggravation that these cases produce are by far more oppressive than any matter of comparable size. In India, for instance, there is a backlog of more than three million cases, and litigating a breach of contract between private parties can take a decade or more. The best advice is to seek a settlement, if possible, rather than sue. Other deterrents to litigation are the following:

- Fear of creating a poor image and damaging public relations.
- Fear of unfair treatment in a foreign court. (Although not intentional, there is justifiable fear that a lawsuit can result in unfair treatment since the decision could be made by either a jury or judge not well versed in trade problems and the intricacies of international business transactions.)
- Difficulty in collecting a judgment that may otherwise have been collected in a mutually agreed settlement through arbitration.
- The relatively high cost and time required when bringing legal action. The Rheem Manufacturing Company, a billion-dollar manufacturer of heating and air conditioning systems, estimates that by using arbitration over litigation, it has reduced the time and cost of commercial-dispute resolution by half.
- Loss of confidentiality. Unlike arbitration and conciliation proceedings that are confidential, litigation is public.

---

[18]Nicolas C. Ulmer, "Bullet-Proofing Your International Arbitration," *World Trade,* July 2000, p. 70.

[19]The American Arbitration Association, www.iccwbo.org/ (select arbitration).

[20]Stephanus Haryanto, "Arbitration Can Settle Legal Disputes," *Jakarta Post,* March 29, 2000.

## CROSSING BORDERS 7.3 Counterfeit, Pirated, or the Original—Take Your Choice

Intellectual properties—trademarks, brand names, designs, manufacturing processes, formulas—are valuable company assets that U.S. officials estimate are knocked off to the tune of $300 billion a year due to counterfeiting and pirating. Some examples from China:

- *Design rip-offs.* Estimates are that nearly 7 million of the 11 million motorcycles and scooters produced in China in one year were copies bearing the Yahama name. Some state-owned factories produce copies four months after a new model is launched.

- *Product rip-offs.* Exact copies of products made by Procter & Gamble, Colgate-Palmolive, Reebok, and Nike are common throughout southern China. Exact copies of any Madonna album are available for as little as $1, as are CDs and movies. Bestfoods estimates that one-quarter of its Skippy Peanut Butter is pirated.

- *Brand name rip-offs.* Bausch & Lomb's Ray Ban sunglasses become Ran Bans. Colgate in the familiar bright red tube becomes Cologate. The familiar red rooster on Kellogg's Corn Flakes appears on Kongalu Corn Strips packages that boast of "the trustworthy sign of quality that is famous around the world." Bogus Budweiser is sold in 640-ml bottles. Yameha, Suzaki, and Hondea motorcycles are nearly identical to models of Yamaha, Suzuki, and Honda.

- *Book rip-offs.* Even the rich and powerful fall prey to pirating. Soon after *My Father, Deng Xiaoping,* a biography written by Deng Rong, daughter of Deng Xiaoping, was published, thousands of illegal copies flooded the market. The true owners also sell original versions of the products mentioned above in China.

In an attempt to control counterfeits, China passed a law that allows customers to demand a double refund for fake merchandise sold in department stores. This has led to bootleg "vigilantes" who knowingly buy knockoffs and take them back demanding the double refund for violating the law. Wang Hai claimed to have made more than $10,000 buying bogus phones and fax machines and then getting a double refund. "I couldn't believe it, every major department store was selling rip-offs," commented Wang. "If I had more money, I would have emptied out every store in Beijing." The Wang Hai phenomenon, as it is called, is spreading throughout China.

Sources: Marcus W. Brauchli, "Chinese Flagrantly Copy Trademarks of Foreigners," *The Wall Street Journal,* June 26, 1994, p. B-1; "How Heinz and Procter & Gamble Fight Counterfeiting," *Business China,* November 25, 1996, p. 6; "China's Piracy Plague," *Business Week,* June 5, 2000, p. 44; Todd Zaun and Karby Leggett, "Motorcycle Makers from Japan Discover Piracy Made in China," *The Wall Street Journal,* July 25, 2001; and Ching-Ching Ni, "Anti-Counterfeit Law Allows Chinese Consumers to Cash In," *Los Angeles Times,* September 14, 2002, p. A3.

One authority suggests that the settlement of every dispute should follow four steps: first, try to placate the injured party; if this does not work, conciliate, arbitrate, and finally, litigate. The final step is typically taken only when all other methods fail. Actually, this advice is probably wise whether one is involved in an international dispute or a domestic one.[21]

## Protection of Intellectual Property Rights: A Special Problem

Companies spend millions of dollars establishing brand names or trademarks to symbolize quality and design a host of other product features meant to entice customers to buy their brands to the exclusion of all others.[22] Millions more are spent on research to develop products, processes, designs, and formulas that provide companies with advantages over their competitors. Such intellectual or industrial properties are among the more valuable assets a

---

[21]For a technical look at international litigation, see Lawrence W. Newman and David Zaslowsky, "International Litigation," *New York Law Journal,* April 30, 2003.

[22]The International Chamber of Commerce has published two comprehensive reports on intellectual property titled "What Is Intellectual Property?" and "Roadmaps on Current and Emerging Intellectual Property Issues 2002," available at www.iccwbo.org/ (select Intellectual Property).

company may possess. Brand names such as Kodak, Coca-Cola, and Gucci, processes such as xerography, and computer software are invaluable. One financial group estimated that the Marlboro brand had a value of $33 billion, Kellogg's $9 billion, Microsoft $9.8 billion, and Levi's $5 billion; all have experienced infringement of their intellectual property rights. Normally, property rights can be legally protected to prevent other companies from infringing on such assets. Companies must, however, keep a constant vigil against piracy and counterfeiting.[23]

## Counterfeiting and Piracy

Counterfeit and pirated goods come from a wide range of industries—apparel, automotive parts, agricultural chemicals, pharmaceuticals, books, records, films, computer software, baby formula to auto parts. Estimates are that more than 10 million fake Swiss timepieces carrying famous brand names such as Cartier and Rolex are sold every year, netting illegal profits of at least $500 million. Although difficult to pinpoint, lost sales from the unauthorized use of U.S. patents, trademarks, and copyrights amount to about $60 billion annually. That translates into more than a million lost jobs.[24] Software and music are especially attractive targets for pirates because they are costly to develop but cheap to reproduce. Pirated CD music sales are estimated to exceed $5 billion annually and are growing at 6 percent per year. And unauthorized U.S. software that sells for $500 in this country can be purchased for less than $10 in the Far East. The Business Software Alliance, a trade group, estimates that software companies lost over $2.9 billion in the Asia-Pacific region, $3.4 billion in Europe, and $3.2 billion in North America in one year.

The piracy industry has grown so sophisticated that many counterfeit goods are almost impossible to distinguish from the original. Toys, a popular knockoff candidate, are often counterfeited and sold before the original ones arrive in legitimate stores;[25] copies are churned out in the same Chinese town where the originals are made. To thwart counterfeiters, Microsoft included a hologram on its software boxes and packaging, but it too has been duplicated to such perfection that the packages containing knockoff CDs of Windows NT are almost indistinguishable from the original. A genuine Chinese-language version of Windows XP comes in a shrink-wrapped box with the familiar logo and costs $245, about four months' salary for an average Chinese worker. The retail price is too much for the worker to pay "retail" but there is an alternative—a nearby stand sells illegally copied XP CDs for $5.50 a CD. It is estimated that more than 90 percent of the application software used in China comes from illegal copies.[26]

Although counterfeiting CDs, toys, and similar products costs companies billions of dollars in lost revenue and has the potential of damaging the product's brand image, the counterfeiting of pharmaceuticals can do serious physical harm. In Colombia, investigators found an illegal operation making more than 20,000 counterfeit tablets a day of the flu drug Dristan, a generic aspirin known as Dolex, and Ponstan 500, a popular painkiller made by Pfizer, Inc. The counterfeited pills contained boric acid, cement, floor wax, talcum powder, and yellow paint with high lead levels, all used to replicate the genuine medications' appearance.

Counterfeits range from copies that have the same efficacy as the original to those with few or no active ingredients, to those made of harmful substances. It is estimated by a pharmaceutical manufacturers association that two percent of the $327 billion worth

The global popularity of the Harry Potter books leads to a variety of rip-offs and fakes. "Harry Potter and Leopard Walk Up to Dragon," the title of the book pictured, was written by a anonymous Chinese author. The fake fifth book in the Harry Potter series, which bears the name of the series author J.K. Rowling, is selling for 10 Yuan (U.S. $1.20) at bookstalls in Beijing. DVD movies of "Harry Potter and the Chamber of Secrets" sell for less than U.S. $2.00. *(AP/Wide World Photos)*

[23]Robert T. Green and Tasman Smith, "Executive Insights: Countering Brand Counterfeiters," *Journal of International Marketing,* January 2002, p. 89.

[24]"Faking It," *The Economist,* February 15, 2003, p. 40.

[25]Geoffrey A. Fowler, "Copies 'R' Us" *The Wall Street Journal,* January 31, 2003, p. B1.

[26]Robyn Meredith, "Microsoft's Long March," *Forbes,* February 17, 2003, p. 78.

of drugs sold each year are counterfeit, or about $6 billion worth. In some African and Latin American nations, as much as 60 percent are counterfeit. The World Health Organization estimates that 8 percent of the bulk drugs imported into the U.S. are counterfeit, unapproved, or substandard.[27]

Another problem is collusion between the contract manufacturer and illegitimate sellers. In China, exact copies of New Balance shoes are fabricated by contract manufacturers who are or were New Balance suppliers. They flood the market with genuine shoes that are sold for as little as $20. Unilever discovered that one of its suppliers in Shanghai made extra cases of soap which were sold directly to retailers. One of Procter & Gamble's Chinese suppliers sold empty P&G shampoo bottles to another company that filled them with counterfeit shampoo.[28] Counterfeiting and piracy of intellectual property constitutes outright theft, but the possibility of legally losing the rights to intellectual property because of inadequate protection of property rights and/or a country's legal structure is another matter.

**Inadequate Protection**

A packet of a Chinese version of the sex-enhancing Viagra pills on sale at a park in the Chinese city of Shenyang. The shape and composition of the fake Viagra pills, which had been declared as "pearl calcium," were similar to real Viagra. The Chinese police raided an underground crime ring that was churning out millions of counterfeit Viagra pills to hopeful men across the country's southeast. Since the real Viagra costs more than four times as much as the fake pills, many customers bought the fake pills for use as business gifts. (© AFP/CORBIS)

The failure to protect intellectual property rights adequately in the world marketplace can lead to the legal loss of rights in potentially profitable markets. Because patents, processes, trademarks, and copyrights are valuable in all countries, some companies[29] have found their assets appropriated and profitably exploited in foreign countries without license or reimbursement. Further, they often learn not only that other firms are producing and selling their products or using their trademarks, but that the foreign companies are the rightful owners in the countries where they operate.

There have been many cases where companies have legally lost the rights to trademarks and have had to buy back these rights or pay royalties for their use. The problems of inadequate protective measures taken by the owners of valuable assets stem from a variety of causes. One of the more frequent errors is assuming that because the company has established rights in the United States, they will be protected around the world, or that rightful ownership can be established should the need arise. Such was the case with McDonald's in Japan, where enterprising Japanese registered the golden arches trademark. Only after a lengthy and costly legal action with a trip to the Japanese Supreme Court was McDonald's able to regain the exclusive right to use the trademark in Japan. After having to "buy" its trademark for an undisclosed amount, McDonald's maintains a very active program to protect its trademarks.

Similarly, a South Korean company legally uses the Coach brand on handbags and leather goods. The company registered the Coach trademark first and has the legal right to use that mark in Korea. The result is that a Coach-branded briefcase that is virtually identical to the U.S. product can be purchased for $135 in South Korea versus $320 in the United States. A U.S. attorney who practices with a South Korean firm noted that he has seen several cases in which a foreign company comes to Korea and naively starts negotiating with a Korean company for distribution or licensing agreements, only to have the Korean company register the trademark in its own name. Later, the Korean company will use that registration as leverage in negotiations or, if the negotiations fall apart, will sell the trademark back to the company. Many businesses fail to take proper steps to legally protect their intellectual property. They fail to understand that some countries do not follow the common-law principle that ownership is established by prior use or to realize that registration and legal ownership in one country does not necessarily mean ownership in another.

---

[27]Kery Capell and Suzanne Timmons, "What's In That Pill?" *Business Week,* June 18, 2001, p. 60.

[28]Gabriel Kahn, "A Sneaker Maker Says China Partner Became Its Rival," *The Wall Street Journal,* December 19, 2002, A1.

[29]"Intellectual Property: Patently Problematic," *The Economist,* September 14, 2002, p. 75.

**Prior Use versus Registration**

In the United States, a common-law country, ownership of intellectual property rights is established by **prior use versus registration**—whoever can establish first use is typically considered the rightful owner. In many code-law countries, however, ownership is established by registration rather than by prior use—the first to register a trademark or other property right is considered the rightful owner. For example, a trademark in Jordan belongs to whoever registers it first in Jordan. Thus you can find "McDonald's" restaurants, "Microsoft" software, and "Safeway" groceries all legally belonging to a Jordanian. After a lengthy court battle that went to the Spanish Supreme Court, Nike lost its right to use the "Nike" brand name for sports apparel in Spain. Cidesport of Spain had been using Nike for sports apparel since 1932 and sued to block Nike (U.S.) sportswear sales. Since Cidesport does not sell shoes under the Nike label, Nike (U.S.) is able to continue selling their brand of sports shoes in Spain. A company that believes it can always establish ownership in another country by proving it used the trademark or brand name first is wrong and risks the loss of these assets.

Besides the first-to-register issue, companies may encounter other problems with registering. China has improved intellectual property rights protection substantially and generally recognizes "first to invent."[30] However, a Chinese company can capture the patent for a product invented elsewhere; it needs only to reverse-engineer or reproduce the product from published specifications and register it in China before the original inventor. Latvia and Lithuania permit duplicate registration of trademarks and brand names. A cosmetics maker registered Nivea and Niveja cosmetics brands in the former Soviet Union in 1986 and again in Latvia in 1992, but a Latvian firm had registered and had been selling a skin cream called Niveja since 1964. Neither the Soviet[31] nor the Latvian authorities notified either firm. It is up to applicants to inform themselves about similar trademarks that are already registered. The case is being taken to the Supreme Court of Latvia. It is best to protect intellectual property rights through registration. Several international conventions provide for simultaneous registration in member countries.

**International Conventions**

Many countries participate in international conventions designed for mutual recognition and protection of intellectual property rights. There are three major international conventions:

1. The Paris Convention for the Protection of Industrial Property, commonly referred to as the Paris Convention, includes the United States and 100 other countries.

2. The Inter-American Convention includes most of the Latin American nations and the United States.

3. The Madrid Arrangement, which established the Bureau for International Registration of Trademarks, includes 26 European countries.

In addition, the World Intellectual Property Organization (WIPO) of the United Nations is responsible for the promotion of the protection of intellectual property and for the administration of the various multilateral treaties through cooperation among its member states.[32] Furthermore, two multicountry patent arrangements have streamlined patent procedures in Europe. The first, the Patent Cooperation Treaty (PCT), facilitates the process for application for patents among its member countries. It provides comprehensive coverage in that a single application filed in the United States supplies the interested party with an international search report on other patents to help evaluate whether or not to seek protection in each of the countries cooperating under the PCT. The second,

---

[30]Turgut Guvenli and Rajib Sanyal, "Perception and Management of Legal Issues in China by U.S. Firms," *Journal of Socio-Economics,* May 2003, p. 161.

[31]"Number of Counterfeit Products Growing in Russia," *Interfax,* February 26, 2003.

[32]Visit www.wipo.org, the home page of the WIPO, for detailed information on the various conventions and the activities of WIPO.

## CROSSING BORDERS 7.4   Aspirin in Russia, Bayer in the United States—It's Enough To Give You a Headache

Russia's patent office awarded the German chemical company Bayer AG the registered trademark to the word *aspirin*. If the trademark award holds, Bayer will have the exclusive right to market pain relievers under the brand name Aspirin in Russia. The word and labeling *aspirin* fell out of use in Russia in the 1970s, when the chemical name acetylsalicylic acid, aspirin's main ingredient, came into use. Bayer AG believes its trademark rights will be upheld and they will be the only company able to sell acetylsalicylic acid as Aspirin; the Russian patent office agrees. There are several reasons for granting Bayer the trademark: *Aspirin* has fallen out of popular use in Russia, Bayer was the world's first manufacturer of aspirin and marketed acetylsalicylic acid under the brand name Aspirin nearly a century ago, Bayer holds trademark rights to Aspirin in many countries, and they registered the name first.

In the United States it's a different story. Bayer AG lost the exclusive right to Aspirin when U.S. courts declared *aspirin* to be the generic term for acetylsalicylic acid. Later, Bayer AG lost the right to the name Bayer as well. Bayer AG did not sell the famous Bayer aspirin in the United States because Sterling Winthrop owned the Bayer trademark. The U.S. government confiscated the domestic assets of Bayer AG after World War I, and in 1919 sold them along with the rights to the Bayer name. Although Sterling Winthrop had the exclusive use of the name Bayer, it did not have the exclusive use of the term *aspirin* because U.S. courts ruled it to be a generic term.

Ownership changes rapidly in international business. Bayer of Germany bought Sterling Winthrop, the U.S. owner of the Bayer brand, from the Kodak Company in 1994, and now Bayer of Germany once again owns the brand Bayer worldwide. The change in ownership in the United States, however, did not affect the trademark dispute over the brand name *Aspirin*, which remains generic in the United States.

The moral to the story: Patent and trademark protection is a complicated issue for international companies, and the value of Bayer and Aspirin are worth fighting for.

Sources: Marya Fogel, "Bayer Trademarks the Word 'Aspirin' in Russia, Leaving Rivals Apoplectic," *The Wall Street Journal*, October 29, 1993, p. A-9; Andrew Wood, "Companies: Bayer Corp.; New Recognition for an Old Name," *Chemical Week*, September 10, 1997, p. 51; "Bayer Lost Rights to Painkiller in 1918, Fight over Cipro Recalls an Aspirin Headache," *The Washington Times*, October 28, 2001; and Linda Wertheimer, "Dr. Mark Plummer Talks About Bayer's History Regarding Rights to Their Drugs," *All Things Considered (NPR)*, October 19, 2001.

the European Patent Convention (EPC), established a regional patent system allowing any nationality to file a single international application for a European patent.[33] Companies have a choice between relying on national systems when they want to protect a trademark or patent in just a few member countries and applying for protection in all 15 member states. Trademark protection is valid for ten years and is renewable; however, if the mark is not used within five years, protection is forfeited. After the patent or trademark is approved, it has the same effect as a national patent or trademark in each individual country designated on the application.

The Trade-Related Aspects of Intellectual Property Rights (TRIPs)[34] agreement, a major provision of the World Trade Organization, is the most comprehensive multilateral agreement on intellectual property to date. TRIPs sets standards of protection for a full range of intellectual property rights that are embodied in current international agreements. The three main provisions of the TRIPs agreement require that participating members be in compliance with minimum standards of protection by 2006, set procedures and remedies for the enforcement of intellectual property rights, and make disputes between WTO members with respect to TRIPs obligations subject to the WTO's dispute settlement procedures.[35]

---

[33]Leo Cendrowicz, "UK Leads Anti-Piracy Declaration," *Billboard*, April 12, 2003, p. 6.

[34]For a comprehensive review of the effectiveness of TRIPs in various countries, see Stetson Sanders, "The Good, the Bad, and the Ugly," *Legal Times*, March 24, 2003.

 [35]For a discussion of TRIPs, visit www.wto.org and select Intellectual Property.

Microsoft loses millions of dollars annually from sales by street vendors who sell counterfeit goods openly. Pirated versions of Microsoft's Windows XP, selling for only 16 Yuan (two USD) each, could be found in Beijing's central computer market days before Microsoft planned its official release. *(www.adrianbradshaw.com)*

Chinese customs agents stand guard over counterfeit CD, DVDs, and CD-ROMs, readied for destruction by Chinese authorities in Zhuhai, Southern China. Sixteen million counterfeit items were destroyed during the event held in a region known both as a major export-manufacturing base and the heartland of China's piracy industry. The Chinese government is grappling with a tenacious torrent of domestically produced fake goods in a nation of appetites whetted for famous brand names on the cheap. Along with China's membership in the World Trade Organization comes access to global markets and pressure to better police product piracy. *(AP/Wide World Photos)*

After a trademark, patent, or other intellectual property right is registered, most countries require that these rights be worked and properly policed. The United States is one of the few countries in which an individual can hold a patent without the patented entity being manufactured and sold throughout the duration of the patent period. Other countries feel that in exchange for the monopoly provided by a patent, the holder must share the product with the citizens of the country. Hence, if patents are not produced within a specified period, usually from one to five years (the average is three years), the patent reverts to public domain.

This rule is also true for trademarks; products bearing the registered mark must be sold within the country or the company may forfeit its right to a particular trademark. McDonald's faced that problem in Venezuela. Even though the McDonald's trademark was properly registered in that code-law country, the company did not use it for more than two years. Under Venezuelan law, a trademark must be used within two years or it is lost. Thus, a Venezuelan-owned "Mr. McDonalds," with accompanying golden arches, is operating in Venezuela. The U.S. McDonald's Corporation faces a potentially costly legal battle if it decides to challenge the Venezuelan company.

Individual countries expect companies to actively police their intellectual property by bringing violators to court. Policing can be a difficult task, with success depending in large measure on the cooperation of the country within which the infringement or piracy takes place. A lack of cooperation in some countries may stem from cultural differences regarding how intellectual property is viewed. In the United States, the goal of protection of intellectual property is to encourage invention and to protect and reward

## CROSSING BORDERS 7.5 "My Name Is Captain Kidd, As I Sailed, As I Sailed"

We know about the piracy of music CDs, software, Levi's jeans and other products, but what about the other piracy—piracy on the high seas?

The MV *Global Mars* departed Malaysia for India with 6,000,000 tons of palm oil products but was hijacked at sea. With typical callousness, the pirates tied up and blindfolded the crew and kept them prisoners for 11 days before setting them adrift in a small boat with little food or water. A fishing vessel rescued the 18 members of the crew two days later. The *Global Mars* was not found, and a $100,000 reward for information about its location was posted. Agents believed the vessel had been repainted and given a new name so that the pirates, armed with false registration papers and bills of lading, could try to dispose of their booty.

Pirates boarded three small- to medium-sized tankers in Southeast Asian waters and a fourth in the Arabian Gulf in one week. All the vessels were carrying marine fuel oil. Crews were beaten with iron bars, tied together, gagged, and blindfolded. After transferring the cargo to another tanker, all communications and navigation equipment was smashed and the ships were set adrift. In another incident, 10 pirates in speedboats attacked an Indonesian-flagged ship on the Malaysian–Indonesian border. All communications were switched off and the crew was held at gunpoint for an hour. They left with cargo worth about $13,000.

An unknown number of buccaneers boarded the ship *Arctic Ocean* in Guayaquil, breaking open a cargo container and stealing computers, printers, and other high-tech equipment.

Yes, men like Blackbeard, Jean Lafitte, and Henry Morgan, sea robbers of the fifteenth and sixteenth centuries, still exist today in the form of modern pirates. The International Maritime Bureau (IMB) reported that pirate attacks on ships have tripled in the last decade, with 103 reported attacks in the first three months of 2003. Pirates carried guns on 53 occasions, and knives were used in 31 attacks. Modern piracy is violent, bloody, and ruthless. Piracy is such a problem that the IMB has launched a weekly report on the ICC website to alert ship owners, cargo owners, and insurance companies of incidents of piracy.

What makes piracy a tempting crime is the difficulty of effective law enforcement, and the unwillingness of many countries to prosecute pirates caught in their own territorial waters for acts of piracy committed under another country's jurisdiction. Not much has changed in three centuries.

Sources: "Tanker Hijackings on the Rise," ICC; Weekly Piracy Report, ICC, May 22, 2000; "Piracy Report Reveals Major Increase in Attacks in 1999," ICC, January 24, 2000; "Plucky Pirates," *Latin Trade*, August 2000, p. 69; Sean Yoong, "Pirate Attacks Soar Worldwide Amid Economic Downturn," *AP Worldstream*, May 9, 2002; "Japanese Owned Ships Report 16 Pirate Incidents in 2002, *Kyoto World News Service*, February 6, 2003; "Pirate Attacks Have Tripled in A Decade, IMB Report Finds," ICC, May 2003; and Jasbant Singh, "Pirates Raid Indonesian Tanker Ship," *AP Online*, March 29, 2003. For a current report on piracy visit www.iccwbo.org and select piracy.

innovative businesses. In Korea, the attitude is that the thoughts of one person should benefit all. In Japan, the intent is to share technology rather than protect it; an invention should serve a larger, national goal, with the rapid spread of technology among competitors in a manner that promotes cooperation. In light of such attitudes, the lack of enthusiasm toward protecting intellectual property is better understood. The United States is a strong advocate of protection, and at U.S. insistence many countries[36] are becoming more cooperative about policing cases of infringement and piracy. After decades of debate, European Union ministers agreed on a common continentwide system for patented inventions. Instead of being forced to submit an application in all 11 EU countries and languages, inventors can submit only one and in English, French, or German.[37]

## Commercial Law within Countries

When doing business in more than one country, a marketer must remain alert to the different legal systems. This problem is especially troublesome for

---

[36]Paul Meller, "Europe Offers Plan to Fight Counterfeit Goods," *New York Times*, January 31, 2003.

[37]"EU Agrees on a Common System for Patents," *The Wall Street Journal*, March 4, 2003, p. A-13.

the marketer who formulates a common marketing plan to be implemented in several countries. Although differences in languages and customs may be accommodated, legal differences between countries may still present problems for a marketing program.

## Marketing Laws

All countries have laws regulating marketing activities in promotion, product development, labeling, pricing, and channels of distribution. In some countries, there may be only a few laws with lax enforcement; in others, there may be detailed, complicated rules to follow that are stringently enforced. There often are vast differences in enforcement and interpretation among countries having laws covering the same activities. Laws governing sales promotions in the European Union offer good examples of such diversity.

In Austria, premium offers, free gifts, or coupons are considered as cash discounts and are prohibited. Premium offers in Finland are allowed with considerable scope as long as the word *free* is not used and consumers are not coerced into buying products. France also regulates premium offers, which are, for all practical purposes, illegal there because it is illegal to sell for less than cost price or to offer a customer a gift or premium conditional on the purchase of another product. French law does permit sales twice a year, in January and August, which can legally last for four to six weeks. This event is so popular that it is advertised on radio, TV, and even special police are required to control the crowds. One poll indicated that over 40 percent of the French set aside money during the year for sale time and 56 percent will spend less money on essentials to buy things on sale.[38]

A manufacturer or retailer cannot offer products different from the kind regularly offered (e.g., a detergent manufacturer cannot offer clothing or kitchen utensils). Until 2000, when a 1930 law prohibiting discounts, rebates, and lifetime guarantees was revoked, German law covering promotion in general was about as stringent as could be found. Building on a statute against "unfair competition," the German courts prevented businesses from offering all sorts of incentives to lure customers. For example, a German drugstore was blocked from celebrating its birthday by giving away 75-cent shopping bags showing a penguin holding a birthday cake. Since most stores charged for heavy-duty bags, the court ruled that giving them away free violated the Free Gift Act. Even donations are banned; a German retailer lost a court fight to advertise that it would contribute a small sum to the fight against AIDS for each transaction with a Visa card.[39] Most incentives that targeted particular groups of customers were illegal, as were most offers of gifts. Similarly, enterprises could not offer price cuts of more than 3 percent of a product's value.

The various product comparison laws, a natural and effective means of expression, are another major stumbling block. In Germany, comparisons in advertisements are always subject to the competitor's right to go to the courts and ask for proof of any implied or stated superiority. In Canada, the rulings are even more stringent: All claims and statements must be examined to ensure that any representation to the public is not false or misleading. Such representation cannot be made verbally in selling or be contained in or on anything that comes to the attention of the public (such as product labels, inserts in products, or any other form of advertising, including what may be expressed in a sales letter). Courts have been directed by Canadian law to take into account in determining whether a representation is false or misleading the "general impression" conveyed by the representation as well as its literal meaning. The courts are expected to apply the "credulous person standard," which means that if any reasonable person could possibly misunderstand the representation, the representation is misleading. In essence, puffery, an acceptable practice in the United States, could be interpreted in Canada as false and misleading advertising. Thus a statement such as "the strongest drive shaft in Canada" would be judged misleading unless the advertiser had absolute evidence that the drive shaft was stronger than any other drive shaft for sale in Canada.

---

[38]Elaine Sciolino, "Battle Plans Go into Action As France Copes with a Twice-Yearly Onslaught," *Oregonian,* January 9, 2003, p. A6.

[39]"German Shoppers Get Coupons," *The Wall Street Journal,* April 5, 2001, A1.

A customer looks at a display of sale watches that are indicated as being "Genuine Fake." Almost all the expensive brands of watches can be bought at bargain prices throughout Asia. At least the customer above can't claim false and misleading advertising.
(© Dave Bartruff/CORBIS)

In Puerto Rico and the Virgin Islands, the law requires that the rules for any promotion be printed in Spanish and English. During the entire time of the promotion, both versions must be printed in at least one general-circulation newspaper once a week. If the promotion includes a prize drawing, Puerto Rico requires that a notary be present when the drawing takes place. China is experimenting with a variety of laws to control how foreign companies do business. Magazines have been ordered to use a direct translation of the often-obscure name that appears on their license or use no English name at all. Thus *Cosmopolitan* would become "Trends Lady," *Woman's Day* would become "Friends of Health," and *Esquire* would become "Trends Man." Such diversity of laws among countries extends to advertising, pricing, sales agreements, and other commercial activities.

There is some hope that the European Union (EU) will soon have a common commercial code.[40] One step in that direction is the proposal to harmonize the pan-European regulation of promotions based on the conservative laws that cover promotions in Germany, Austria, and Belgium. However, this proposal is meeting with strong resistance from several groups because of its severe restriction on promotions.

Although the EU is a beautiful picture of economic cooperation, there is still the reality of dealing with 15 different countries, cultures, and languages, as well as 15 different legal systems. Even though some of Germany's complicated trade laws were revoked in 2000, there remain such groups as the Center for Combating Unfair Competition, an industry-finance organization, that continue to work to maintain the status quo. Before the German law was revoked, the Center's lawyers filed a thousand lawsuits a year, going after, for example, a grocery store that offered discount coupons or a deli that gave a free cup of coffee to a customer who had already bought ten; their efforts will surely continue.

Although the goal of full integration and a common commercial code has not been totally achieved in the EU, decisions by the European Court continue to strike down individual country laws that impede competition across borders.[41] In a recent decision, the European Court ruled that a French cosmetics company could sell its wares by mail in Germany and advertise them at a markdown from their original prices, a direct contradiction of German law. As the Single European Market Act is implemented many of the legal and trade differences that have existed for decades will vanish. Surprisingly enough, standards set by the EU for food, software, cars, and other items affect U.S. product standards as well. In many cases, the reconciliation of so many different consumer protection standards that existed in European countries prior to the EU resulted in rules more rigorous than those for many U.S. products. Consequently, many U.S. products have been redesigned to comply with European Standards. It used to be that if something was designed for U.S. standards it could be sold anywhere in the world. For many products that is no longer the case. For example, Carrier air conditioners were redesigned to comply with European recycling rules; Microsoft modified contracts with software makers; Internet service providers gave consumers a wider choice of technologies; McDonald's ceased including soft plastic toys with its Happy Meals and withdrew all genetically engineered potatoes from its restaurants worldwide. All this is because of the need to reconcile U.S. standards with those of the EU. For many U.S. products with markets in Europe it is less expensive to meet EU standards than to design products especially for Europe.[42]

---

[40]"EU Parliament Moves Again To Impose Tobacco Ad Ban," *The Wall Street Journal,* November 20, 2002.

[41]Brandon Mitchener, "Increasingly, Rules of Global Economy Are Set in Brussels," *The Wall Street Journal,* April 23, 2002.

[42]Brandon Mitchener, "Increasingly, Rules of Global Economy Are Set in Brussels," *The Wall Street Journal,* April 23, 2002, p. A1.

## Green Marketing Legislation

A Greenpeace protester peers out from inside a plastic rubbish bin in Hong Kong, where activists were calling on the government to develop a comprehensive recycling industry which they claim will create 2,000 new jobs. A recent study by Greenpeace found that only 148 out of 18,200 rubbish bins in Hong Kong have waste separation compartments. It is calling on the government to revamp its current waste management procedures to facilitate a comprehensive system to reduce, recover, and recycle. (© AFP/CORBIS)

Multinational corporations also face a growing variety of legislation designed to address environmental issues.[43] Global concern for the environment extends beyond industrial pollution, hazardous waste disposal, and rampant deforestation to include issues that focus directly on consumer products. Green marketing[44] laws focus on environmentally friendly products and on product packaging and its effect on solid waste management.

Germany has passed the most stringent green marketing laws that regulate the management and recycling of packaging waste. The new packaging laws were introduced in three phases. The first phase required all transport packaging, such as crates, drums, pallets, and Styrofoam containers, to be accepted back by the manufacturers and distributors for recycling. The second phase required manufacturers, distributors, and retailers to accept all returned secondary packaging, including corrugated boxes, blister packs, packaging designed to prevent theft, packaging for vending machine applications, and packaging for promotional purposes. The third phase requires all retailers, distributors, and manufacturers to accept returned sales packaging, including cans, plastic containers for dairy products, foil wrapping, Styrofoam packages, and folding cartons such as cereal boxes. The requirement for retailers to take back sales packaging has been suspended as long as the voluntary green dot program remains a viable substitute.[45] A green dot on a package identifies manufacturers that have agreed to ensure a regular collection of used packaging materials directly from the consumer's home or from designated local collection points.

Reclaiming recyclables extends beyond packaging to automobiles. By 2006, manufacturers based in EU nations must take back any cars they produced that no longer have resale value and pay for proper disposal. Furthermore, by 2006, 85 percent of a scrapped car's material must be recovered for future use.

Many European countries also have devised schemes to identify products that comply with certain criteria that make them more environmentally friendly than similar products. Products that meet these criteria are awarded an "eco-label" that the manufacturer can display on packaging to signal to customers that it is an environmentally friendly product. The EU is becoming more aggressive in issuing new directives and in harmonizing eco-labeling and other environmental laws across all member states.[46] Eco-labeling and EU packaging laws are discussed in more detail in the chapter on consumer products (Chapter 12).[47]

## Antitrust

With the exception of the United States, antitrust laws have been either nonexistent or not enforced in most of the world's countries for the better part of the twentieth century. However, the European Union, Japan, and many other countries have begun to actively enforce their antitrust laws patterned after those in the United States.[48] Antimonopoly, price discrimination, supply restrictions, and full-line forcing are areas in which the European Court of Justice has dealt severe penalties. For example, before Procter & Gamble

[43]"EU Eco-Label Celebrates 10th Anniversary," *European Report,* December 4, 2002.

[44]Brian Kenety, "Environment-EU: Cultivating 'Flower Power' For Green Products," *Inter Press Services,* January 11, 2002.

[45]Steve Zwick, "A Better Package Deal? Germany's Green Dot—A Symbol of Success in the Recycling Business," *Time International,* May 21, 2001, p. 55.

[46]"Environment: Ecologists Warn Against Weakening European Eco-Label Scheme," *European Reporter,* March 14, 2003.

[47]For information on the EU's environmental directives as well as other information about the EU, visit www.europa.eu.int. This address will take you to the home page where you can search for topics and visit various information sources about the EU.

[48]Mark Landler and Paul Meller, "Europe Votes to Overhaul Antitrust Regulations," *New York Times,* November 11, 2002, p. W1.

was allowed to buy VP-Schickedanz AG, a German hygiene products company, it had to agree to sell off one of the German company's divisions that produced Camelia, a brand of sanitary napkins. P&G already marketed a brand of sanitary napkins in Europe, and the Commission was concerned that allowing them to keep Camelia would give them a controlling 60 percent of the German sanitary products market and 81 percent of Spain's. In another instance, Coca-Cola was fined $1.8 million for anticompetitive practices by France's antitrust authority.

The United States also intervenes when non-U.S. companies attempt to acquire American companies. Nestlé's proposed $2.8 billion acquisition of Dreyer's Grand Ice Cream hit a roadblock as U.S.[49] antitrust officials opposed the deal on grounds that it would lead to less competition and higher prices for gourmet ice cream in the United States.[50] At times, companies are subject to antitrust charges in more than one country. Microsoft had a partial victory against antitrust charges brought in the United States[51] only to face similar anticompetitive charges against Microsoft's Windows 2000 operating system in the EU.[52] The probe is based on possible competitive benefits to European software concerns if legal limits are placed on Microsoft.[53] American companies have faced antitrust violations since the trust-busting days of President Theodore Roosevelt, but much less so in other parts of the world. Enforcement of antitrust laws in Europe was almost nonexistent until the new European Union established antitrust legislation.

Competitive methods that are illegal in the United States can be legal in another. If you go to one of the 15 Tony Roma franchises in Mexico, the only beer you can buy is Modelo brewed by Grupo Modelo SA, maker of the top-selling imported beer in the United States, Corona Extra. "We used to have 28 different kinds of beer, including American beers" says the General Manager of Tony Roma's, "but Modelo gave us money to sell only its beer." A Modelo distributor paid one town to ban stores from selling any other beer in exchange for cash, school uniforms, lighting for public parks and free beer at city parties. That kind of tie-up, illegal in the United States, is common in restaurants, corner stores, and stadiums throughout Mexico. Such tactics have given Modelo and its rival, Fomento Economico Mexicano SA, 99 percent of the market. Legal in Mexico, these tactics give Modelo and other Mexican brewers an advantage in the U.S. market where Corona accounts for 40 percent of all U.S. beer imports and has 11 percent of the overall U.S. beer market compared with just one percent of the Mexican market for U.S. beer. Ironically, Pepsi Cola and Coca-Cola dominate the Mexican soft drink market and have used similar tactics to compete with one another, that is, until a recent ruling that Coke is no longer allowed to make such tie-ins because they prevent Pepsi from competing.[54] Worldwide antitrust enforcement or lack thereof is just one more important area of law that each multinational firm must consider in its strategic decision making.

## U.S. Laws Apply in Host Countries

All governments are concerned with protecting their political and economic interests domestically and internationally; any activity or action, wherever it occurs, that adversely threatens national interests is subject to government control. As such, leaving the political boundaries of a home country does not exempt a business from home-country laws. Regardless of the nation where business is done, a U.S. citizen is

[49]"FTC Moves to Block Nestlé Deal," *Weekly Corporate Growth Report,* March 10, 2003, p. 11.

[50]William Hall, "Nestlé May Be Close to Dreyer's Deal," *The Financial Times,* May 14, 2003.

[51]James Doran and Nic Hopkins, "Victory with Strings for Microsoft," *The Times,* November 2, 2002.

[52]John R. Wilke and Brandon Mitchener, "Microsoft Rivals Allege Antitrust in New EU Case," *The Wall Street Journal,* February 2, 2003, p. A1.

[53]Paul Miller, "Microsoft's Antitrust Problems Remain Unresolved in Europe," *New York Times,* May 1, 2003, p. W1.

[54]David Luhnow, "Why Corona Is Big Here, and Miller Is So Scarce in Mexico," *The Wall Street Journal,* January 1, 2003, B1.

subject to certain laws of the United States. What is illegal for an American business at home can also be illegal by U.S. law in foreign jurisdictions for the firm, its subsidiaries, and licensees of U.S. technology.

Laws that prohibit taking a bribe, trading with the enemy,[55] participating in a commercial venture that negatively affects the U.S. economy, participating in an unauthorized boycott such as the Arab boycott, or any other activity deemed to be against the best interests of the United States apply to U.S. businesses and their subsidiaries and licensees regardless of where they operate. Thus at any given time a U.S. citizen in a foreign country must look not only at the laws of the host country, but at home law as well.[56]

The question of jurisdiction of U.S. law over acts committed outside the territorial limits of the country has been settled by the courts through application of a long-established principle of international law, the "objective theory of jurisdiction." This concept holds that even if an act is committed outside the territorial jurisdiction of U.S. courts, those courts can nevertheless have jurisdiction if the act produces effects within the home country. The only possible exception may be when the violation is the result of enforced compliance with local law.

## Foreign Corrupt Practices Act

Recall from Chapter 5 that the Foreign Corrupt Practices Act (FCPA) makes it illegal for companies to pay bribes to foreign officials, candidates, or political parties. Stiff penalties can be assessed against company officials, directors, employees, or agents found guilty of paying a bribe or of knowingly participating in or authorizing the payment of a bribe. However, also recall that bribery, which can range from lubrication to extortion, is a common business custom in many countries.[57]

The original FCPA lacked clarity, and early interpretations were extremely narrow and confusing. Subsequent amendments in the Omnibus Trade and Competitiveness Act clarified two of the most troubling issues. Corporate officers' liability was changed from having reason to know that illegal payments were made to knowing of or authorizing illegal payments. In addition, if it is customary in the culture, small (grease or lubrication) payments made to encourage officials to complete routine government actions such as processing papers, stamping visas, and scheduling inspections are not illegal per se.

The debate continues as to whether or not the FCPA puts U.S. businesses at a disadvantage. Some argue that U.S. businesses are at a disadvantage in international business transactions in those cases where bribery payments are customary, whereas others contend that it has little effect, indeed, that it helps companies to "just say no." The truth probably lies somewhere in between.[58] The consensus is that most U.S. firms are operating within the law, and several studies indicate that the FCPA has not been as detrimental to MNC interest as originally feared because exports to developed and developing countries continue to be favorable.

U.S. firms seem to be able to compete and survive without corruption in the most corrupt societies. This does not mean, however, that violations do not occur or that companies are not penalized for violations. For example, a U.S. environmental engineering firm was found to have made corrupt payments to an Egyptian government official to assist the company in gaining a contract. The company agreed not to violate the FCPA in the future and agreed to pay a civil fine of $400,000 and to reimburse the Department of Justice for the costs of the investigation. Furthermore, the company agreed to establish FCPA compliance procedures and to provide certifications of compliance annually for five years.

---

[55]Gary Mihollin, "Trading With the Enemy," *Commentary*, May 2002, p. 41.

[56]Robert Gearty, "New York Oil Consultant Arrested on Charges of Bribing President of Kazakhstan," *Daily News*, April 1, 2003.

[57]For discussions of the FCPA, updates, and other information, visit the FCPA home page at www.usdoj.gov/criminal/fraud/fcpa.html.

[58]Ronald Fink et al., "Bribery and Corruption," *CFO*, June 2002, p. 46.

**National
Security Laws**

U.S. firms, their foreign subsidiaries, or foreign firms that are licensees of U.S. technology cannot sell a product to a country in which the sale is considered by the U.S. government to affect national security. Further, responsibility extends to the final destination of the product regardless of the number of intermediaries that may be involved in the transfer of goods.

An extensive export control system was created to slow the spread of sensitive technologies to the former USSR, China, and other communist countries that were viewed as major threats to U.S. security. The control of the sale of goods considered to have a strategic and military value was extremely strict. But with the end of the Cold War, export controls were systematically dismantled, that is, until September 11, 2001. Weapons of mass destruction (WMD)[59] were the threat now facing the United States. Unfortunately, many of the products used in WMD are difficult to control because they have dual purposes; that is, they have legitimate uses as well as being important in manufacturing WMD. For example, Iraq, which was allowed to import medical equipment despite a U.N. embargo, purchased, under the pretext of medical benefits, six machines that destroy kidney stones. The manufacturer accepted the claim that Saddam Hussein was concerned about kidney stones in the Iraqi population and began shipping the machines. However, an integral component of these machines is a high-precision electronic switch that can also be used to set off the chain reaction in thermonuclear weapons. When 120 additional switches as "spare parts" were ordered, a red flag went up and the shipments were stopped. There are many dual-purpose technologies that are exported from the United States.[60] A problem with dual-purpose exports is the intent of the buyer.[61] Silicon Graphics Inc. sold computer equipment to a Russian nuclear laboratory that contended the equipment was for nonmilitary use, which would have been legal. However, the Department of Justice ruled that since they were shipped to a government-operated facility involved in both civil and noncivil activities, Silicon Graphics should have applied for the correct export license. The company paid a fine of one million dollars plus a $500,000 fine for each of the export violations. National security laws prohibit a U.S. company, its subsidiaries, joint ventures, or licensees to sell controlled products without special permission from the U.S. government.[62] The consequences of violation of the Trading with the Enemy Act can be severe: fines,[63] prison sentences, and in the case of foreign companies, economic sanctions.

Exports are controlled for the protection and promotion of human rights, as a means of enforcing foreign policy, because of national shortages, to control technology, and a host of other reasons the U.S. government deems necessary to protect its best interests. In years past, the government restricted trade with South Africa (because of human rights violations) and restricted the sale of wheat to the Soviet Union in retaliation for their invasion of Afghanistan (foreign policy). Currently, the government restricts the sale of leading-edge electronics (control of technology) and prohibits the export of pesticides that have not been approved for use in the United States (to avoid the return of residue of unauthorized pesticides in imported food and protect U.S. consumers from the so-called circle of poison). In each of these cases, U.S. law binds U.S. businesses regardless of where they operate.[64]

**Antitrust Laws**

Antitrust enforcement has two purposes in international commerce. The first is to protect American consumers by ensuring that they benefit from products and ideas produced by foreign competitors as well as by domestic competitors. Competition from foreign

---

[59]James A. Lewis, "Weapons of Mass Destruction," *FDCH Congressional Testimony,* November 7, 2002.

[60]Gary Milhollin, "Trading With The Enemy," *Commentary,* May 2002, p. 42.

[61]Richard Read, "Security Interests Clash Over Technology Exports to China," *The Oregonian,* February 2, 2003.

[62]"Canadian Convicted for Cuba Trade," *Toronto Star,* April 4, 2002.

[63]Jeff Geth, "@ Companies Pay Penalties For Improving China Rockets," *New York Times,* March 6, 2003.

[64]Export controls will be discussed in more detail in Chapter 15.

A local Egyptian fast-food restaurant does brisk business since many Egyptians have adhered to the Arab boycott on American products. Arab activists are asking people to boycott American companies because of American support for Israel. Highly visible U.S. companies in the Mideast, such as Starbucks, McDonald's, and Coca-Cola, have at one time or another experienced the results of the Arab boycott.
(© Norbert Schiller/Getty Images)

producers is important when imports are, or could be, a major source of a product or when a single firm dominates a domestic industry. This becomes relevant in many joint ventures, particularly if the joint venture creates a situation in which a U.S. firm entering a joint venture with a foreign competitor restricts competition for the U.S. parent in the U.S. market.

The second purpose of antitrust legislation is to protect American export and investment opportunities against any privately imposed restrictions. The concern is that all U.S.-based firms engaged in the export of goods, services, or capital should be allowed to compete on merit and not be shut out by restrictions imposed by bigger or less-principled competitors.

The questions of jurisdiction and how U.S. antitrust laws apply are frequently asked but only vaguely answered. The basis for determination ultimately rests with the interpretation of Sections I and II of the Sherman Act. Section I states that "every contract, combination . . . or conspiracy in restraint of trade or commerce among the several states or with foreign nations is hereby declared to be illegal"; Section II makes it a violation to "monopolize, or attempt to monopolize, or combine or conspire with any other person or persons, to monopolize any part of the trade or commerce among the several states, or with foreign nations."

The Justice Department recognizes that application of U.S. antitrust laws to overseas activities raises some difficult questions of jurisdiction. It recognizes that U.S. antitrust-law enforcement should not interfere unnecessarily with the sovereign interest of a foreign nation. At the same time, however, the Antitrust Division is committed to controlling foreign transactions at home or abroad that have a substantial and foreseeable effect on U.S. commerce. When such business practices occur, there is no question in the Antitrust Division of the Department of Justice that U.S. laws apply.

## Antiboycott Law

Under the antiboycott law,[65] U.S. companies are forbidden to participate in any unauthorized foreign boycott; further, they are required to report any request to cooperate with a boycott.[66] The antiboycott law was a response to the Arab League boycott of Israeli businesses.[67] The Arab League boycott of Israel has three levels: A primary boycott bans direct trade between Arab states and Israel, a secondary boycott bars Arab governments from doing business with companies that do business with Israel, and a tertiary boycott bans Arab governments from doing business with companies that do business with companies doing business with Israel.[68]

When companies do not comply with the Arab League's boycott directives, their names are placed on a blacklist and they are excluded from trade with members of the Arab League. U.S. companies are caught in the middle: If they trade with Israel, the Arab

---

[65]The antiboycott law only applies to those boycotts not sanctioned by the U.S. government. Sanctioned boycotts, such as the boycotts against trade with Cuba and Iran, are initiated by the U.S. and must be honored by U.S. firms.

[66]Jon Griffin, "Beware of Arabs' Boycott," *Evening Mail,* January 31, 2003.

[67]Jannie Zacharia, "U.S Seeking Stiffer Penalties for Supporters of Arab Boycott," *Jerusalem Post,* November 7, 2002.

[68]For those non-U.S. companies trading with the Arab League and complying with the boycott, each was required to include a statement on the shipping invoices. On an invoice for 10 buses to be shipped from Brazil to Kuwait, the following statement appeared: "We certify that we are the producer and supplier of the shipped goods; we are neither blacklisted by the Arab boycott of Israel nor are we the head office, branch, or subsidiary of a boycotted company. No Israeli capital is invested in this firm, no company capital or capital of its owners is invested in any Israeli company; our products are not of Israeli origin and do not contain Israeli raw material or labor."

League will not do business with them, and if they refuse to do business with Israel in order to trade with an Arab League member, they will be in violation of U.S. law.[69] One hospital supply company that had been trading with Israel was charged with closing a plant in Israel in order to have the company taken off the Arab blacklist.[70] After an investigation, the company pleaded guilty, was fined $6.6 million, and was prohibited from doing business in Syria and Saudi Arabia for two years. A less costly fine of $12,000 was paid by a freight forwarder who certified that the goods shipped for a third party were not of Israeli origin, were not shipped from Israel, and did not contain any material from Israel.

**Extraterritoriality of U.S. Laws**

The issue of the extraterritoriality of U.S.[71] laws is especially important to U.S. multinational firms because the long arm of U.S. legal jurisdiction causes anxiety for heads of state. Foreign governments fear the influence of American government policy on their economies through U.S. multinationals.

Especially troublesome are those instances when U.S. law is in conflict with host countries' economic or political goals. Conflict arises when the host government requires joint ventures to do business within the country and the U.S. Justice Department restricts or forbids such ventures because of their U.S. anticompetitive effects. Host countries see this influence as evidence of U.S. interference. When U.S. MNCs' subsidiaries are prohibited from making a sale in violation of the U.S. Trading with the Enemy Act, host governments react with hostility toward the extraterritorial application of U.S. foreign policy. This chapter's Global Perspective is a good illustration of the extraterritoriality of U.S. law and how it has an impact on a friendly neighbor as well as a major multinational company.

An interesting development for MNCs is being held liable for the human-rights abuses of foreign governments. Lawsuits are being brought in U.S. courts against U.S. MNCs charging them with doing business with oppressive regimes. Unocal Corporation is being sued for doing business with Burma's military rulers who forced peasants at gunpoint to help build a pipeline for Unocal.[72] Unocal denies the charges.[73] This case was brought under the Alien Claims Act originally intended to reassure Europe that the fledgling United States would not harbor pirates or assassins. It permits foreigners to sue in U.S. courts for violations of the "law of nations." Businesses like IBM, Citibank, and Coca-Cola worry that they may be socked with huge jury damages for the misdeeds of oppressive governments. Employment lawyers warn that multinational companies are likely to face more lawsuits from the Third World.[74]

When the intent of any kind of overseas activity is to restrain trade, there is no question about the appropriateness of applying U.S. laws. There is a question, however, when the intent is to conclude a reasonable business transaction. If the U.S. government encourages U.S. firms to become multinational, then the government needs to make provisions for resolution of differences when conflict arises between U.S. law and host government laws.

## Cyberlaw: Unresolved Issues

The Internet is by its nature a global enterprise in which no political or national boundaries are closed. Although this is its strength, it also creates problems when existing laws do not clearly address the uniqueness of the Internet and its related activities. Existing law is vague or does not completely cover such issues as the protection of

[69]For a list of current cases against firms violating the antiboycott law, see www.bxa.doc.gov and select Antiboycott Compliance and then Antiboycott Case Histories.

[70]"AJ Congress Praises Commerce Department Crackdown on Arab Boycott," *U.S. Newswire,* November 11, 2002.

[71]James H. Zrust, "Extraterritorial Income Laws and U.S. Competitiveness," *Congressional Testimony Committee on Senate Finance, United States Senate,* July 30, 2002.

[72]At the time of this writing the case was still traveling through the courts on appeal.

[73]Paul Magnusson, "Making a Federal Case Out of Overseas Abuses," *Business Week,* November 11, 2002, p. 78.

[74]"Global Lawsuits to Increase," *People Management,* March 20, 2003, p. 9.

domain names, taxes, jurisdiction in cross-border transactions, and contractual issues. The European Union, the United States, and many other countries are drafting legislation to address the myriad legal questions not clearly addressed by current law. But until these laws apply worldwide, companies must rely on individual country laws which may or may not provide protection.

**Cybersquatters**

Unfortunately, the ease with which Web names can be registered and the low cost of registering has led to thousands being registered. **Cybersquatters** (CSQ) buy and register descriptive nouns, geographic names, ethnic groups, pharmaceutical substances and other similar descriptors and hold them until they can be sold at an inflated price. For example, a cybersquatter sold www.themortgage.com for $500,000; the record price paid so far is $7.5 million for the domain name www.business.com. If a cybersquatter has registered a generic domain name that a company wants, the only recourse is to buy it.

Another ploy of CSQ is to register familiar names and known trademarks that divert traffic from intended destinations or to sell competing products. eBay, the world's largest online auction house, was embroiled in a dispute with an entrepreneur in Nova Scotia who registered www.ebay.ca, thus forcing the U.S. company to use www.ca.ebay.com for its newly launched Canadian website until it was successful in regaining the use of www.ebay.ca; both web addresses now go to the same site.

CSQ register a well-known brand or trademark that misdirects a person to the CSQ's site or to a competing company's site. For example, an adult entertainment website registered www.candyland.com. Hasbro, the toy company, markets a game for children called "Candy Land." Disturbed by the thought that customers might end up at an adult entertainment site, Hasbro wanted to have the site vacated. They had the option of suing to have it removed or to buy the domain name. Hasbro elected to sue and, although the adult website was not directly infringing on its trademark, the courts deemed it to be damaging to the reputation of Hasbro and its children's game. The Web address now takes you directly to a Hasbro site.

Other cybersquatting abuses that can pose a serious threat to business include parody sites, protest sites, and hate sites. A good example is www.walmartsucks.org, a site highly critical of Wal-Mart. This type of website may be difficult to prevent because the right to free speech is protected. The only defense Wal-Mart might have is to challenge the website's right to use a trade name to direct someone to that site.

An example of a parody website involves Kraft Foods, Inc., which sued a cartoonist who called himself King Velveeda on his website www.cheesygraphics.com. Kraft sued for trademark infringement of its "Velveeta," the processed cheese.[75] A preliminary injunction stopped the cartoonist from using the Velveeda name, which was purged from the website. However, "How I Got Krapt on by Corporate America," a diary of the case, appears on the site. The issue in the Wal-Mart complaint is not to deny the right to express an opinion but whether or not it is right to use a trademarked trade name to direct someone to the site. In the case of Kraft, the court will decide if Velveeda is an infringement but they may not be able to stop the diary on the website.[76]

A growing number of celebrity names have been hijacked. Julia Roberts had her name registered by a CSQ, www.juliaroberts.com, and so did British Prime Minister Tony Blair's baby. His name was registered, www.leoblair.com, minutes after the name was made public.[77] Julia Roberts sued under the Anticybersquatting Consumer Protection Act (ACPA), a dispute-resolution forum in the United States that facilitates action against domain name squatters if the domain name infringes on a trademark or personal name.[78]

---

[75]If you plan to access this site, please be warned that it can lead to some objectionable material. You do not have to access that material in order to see the Krapt information.

[76]"Kraft's Canned Cheese," *Marketing News,"* December 9, 2002, p. 13.

[77]"Cybersquatters Target Baby Leo," *BBC News,* May 21, 2000.

[78]Tom Carl, "Trade Mark Owners: 19. Cybersquatters: 1." *Managing Intellectual Property,* March 2002, p. 59.

Prime Minister Blair had "leoblair.com" evicted by his appeal to Nominet Dispute Resolution Service (DRS), a forum for resolving cybesquatting disputes in the United Kingdom. DRS requires the complainant to prove that it has rights in respect to a name or mark identical or similar to the respondent's domain name; and that the domain name is an abusive registration. Abusive registration is defined as a domain name which was either registered or has been used in a manner which takes unfair advantage of, or is unfairly detrimental to, the complainant's rights.[79]

In addition to CSQs hijacking trademarks, personal names, and other intellectual property, lawsuits involving libel, defamation, and product liability are creating legal quagmires for Internet users. Consider a case involving Dow Jones and an Australian industrialist over an allegedly defamatory article that appeared on one of the U.S.-based Dow Jones' publication's website. The plaintiff sued Dow Jones, the website owner, as the author of the article.[80] Dow Jones argued that the suit should be tried in a New Jersey court, where its servers, the point of publication, are located. The Australian argued that the suit should be brought in Australia because that is where his reputation had been damaged. Australian law favors plaintiffs, whereas in the United States the First Amendment Rights demand a high burden of proof in libel cases. Australian courts sided with the plaintiff.

It is easy to imagine many situations where the actions of companies or information posted on a site can lead to a lawsuit when Internet content is unlawful in one country but not in the host country. For example, an American studio that makes a movie with nude scenes could be prosecuted in a country that bans nudity in movies. Not only would the movie studio be libel but the Internet service provider could be liable for material posted on its website. Writers and publishers could face libel suits in countries with restrictive laws of free speech where weak or nonexistent free speech protections are tools to intimidate and censor.[81] Internet publishers or individual website owners fear they can be sued for defamation from any or many jurisdictions, merely because their articles can be downloaded anywhere in the world. Lawsuits involving libel, defamation, and product liability cause companies to voluntarily restrict their websites to selected countries rather than leave themselves open to legal action.[82] The Internet is not a libel-free zone.

The United States has taken a giant step in dealing with domain name pirates by passing the Anticybersquatting Consumer Protection Act (ACPA); and the World Intellectual Property Organization (WIPO) established a structure through the Internet Corporation for Assigned Names and Numbers (ICANN) in which anyone registering a domain name with complying registries must agree to dispute resolution. This is known as the Uniform Dispute Resolution Policy (UDRP). Neither the ACPA nor the UDRP provide failsafe ways of recovering a domain name after it has been cybersquatted.[83]

A study indicated that protection is needed for geographical names, ethnic groups, and pharmaceutical substances, all of which have been appropriated by CSQs. These abuses will continue unless preventive steps are taken. Agencies like the ACPA, DRS, and the World Intellectual Property Organization (WIPO)[84] are useful, but, besides being costly, they only address disputes involving sites using names that are trademarked and have commercial value or are so well known they have common law trademark rights.[85] Although protection from cybersquatters is not perfect, if a business takes steps to properly defend

[79]Elif Kaban, "UN Blow to Cybersquatters Seeking a Quick Buck," *Reuters,* June 9, 2000.

[80]Ralph Wragg, "Journalist to Test Right of Free Speech in Gutnick Case," *Australian Business News,* April 17, 2003.

[81]"Tied Up In Knots," *The Economist,* June 9, 2001, p. 67.

[82]"Australian Court's Ruling on Libel Suit Jurisdiction Might Spur Self-censorship, Filtered Content or Cutbacks In Reporting," *San Jose Mercury News,* December 27, 2002.

[83]Jonathan Robinson, "How to Prevent Cybersquatters," *Managing Internet Property,* March 2003, p. 25.

[84]The World Intellectual Property Organization (WIPO) is one of the 16 specialized agencies of the United Nations system of organizations. It administers 23 international treaties dealing with different aspects of intellectual property.

[85]Robert Evans, "UN Body Urges Stronger Rules on Cybersquatters," *Reuters,* September 3, 2001.

its brand names, trade names, or product names, and properly registers them, it greatly enhances its ability to defend against improper use of the name by a third party. Countries that recognize intellectual property generally refer to those laws to resolve disputes.

Most countries' courts are inclined to assert jurisdiction over online activity, where it originates, so long as harm is experienced locally and the sense is that the party responsible either knew or ought to have known that the harm was a likely consequence of the actions. However, most agree that the laws that are expressly designed to apply not just in a single country but worldwide are necessary to untangle the legal hassles that are occurring.[86]

Of 100 business leaders polled by the International Chamber of Commerce, more than one-third said legal uncertainty covering Internet operations affected "significant business decisions." The most immediate impact, according to the ICC, is clear: Many online merchants refuse to sell outside their home countries.[87]

## Taxes

Another thorny issue in e-commerce concerns the collection of taxes. A typical tax system relies on knowing where a particular economic activity is located. But the Internet enables individual workers to operate in many different countries while sitting at the same desk. When taxes should be collected, where they should be collected, and by whom, are all issues under consideration by countries around the world.[88] In the past, a company was deemed to have a taxable presence in a country if it had a permanent establishment there. But it is not clear whether the existence of a server or a website qualifies as such a presence. One proposal that has enthusiastic support from tax authorities is for servers to be designated as "virtual permanent establishments" and thus subject to local taxes.

It is difficult to pinpoint when and where a sale takes place in cyberspace, and, unless elusive taxpayers can be pinpointed, any tax may be difficult to collect.[89] In "bricks and mortar" sales, the retailer collects, but when the Internet site is in one country and the customer is in another, who collects? One proposal is to have shipping companies such as FedEx or credit card companies collect taxes—obviously, neither party is receiving this suggestion enthusiastically.

The EU Commission announced plans for a directive to force foreign companies to levy value-added tax (VAT) on services delivered via the Internet, television, or radio to customers in the EU.[90] Foreign companies with sales via the Internet over 100,000 euros ($95,410) inside the EU would have to register in at least one EU country and levy VAT at that country's rate, somewhere between 15 percent and 25 percent. The tax is justified on the basis of leveling the playing field. EU companies have to charge their EU customers VAT whereas foreign companies supplying the same service to the same customers are duty free. U.S. companies are protesting, calling the proposal "e-protectionism." Although the EU plan is only a proposal now, as the value of Internet transactions increases, the taxman will sooner or later get his share.[91]

## Jurisdiction of Disputes and Validity of Contracts

As countries realize that existing laws relating to commerce do not always clearly address the uniqueness of the Internet and its related activities, a body of cyberlaw is gradually being created.[92] Two of the most troubling questions are whose laws will prevail in legal disputes between parties located in different countries, and the contractual validity of

---

[86]"In Web Disputes, U.S. Law Rules the World," *Toronto Star,* February 24, 2003.

[87]Matthew Newman, "So Many Countries, So Many Laws," *The Wall Street Journal,* April 28, 2003, p. R-8.

[88]Jeanette Borzo, "Internet Commerce Seeking a Level Online Playing Field: Euro Helps Unmask Disparities," *International Herald Tribune,* May 13, 2002.

[89]Michael Geist, "Fairness Says It's Time to Tax Goods Sold Online," *The Toronto Star,* March 3, 2003.

[90]Jim Krane, "EU Plans to Tax Internet Sales," *AP Online,* May 8, 2002.

[91]For a report on a resolution on cross-border tax issues proposed by OECD, see "OECD Launches Project On Improving the Resolution of Cross-Border Tax Disputes," www.oecd.org and select taxation. The OECD proposes a variety of issues related to the Internet, all of which can be found at this site.

[92]"The 2003 World Computer and Internet Law Congress Program Is Announced," *PR Newswire,* April 16, 2003. For more information on the Internet Law Congress, visit www.cla.org.

electronic communications. The European Union is having the most difficulty in reconciling the vast differences in the laws among its member states in order to create a uniform law. For example, a draft regulation debated in Brussels and other European capitals would have required vendors to comply with 15 different, and sometimes bizarre, sets of national rules on consumer protection—ranging from dozens of restrictions on advertising to France's requirement that all contracts must be concluded in French regardless of whether businesses intend to sell goods for export to France.

The EU Commission has adopted an e-commerce directive that will permit online retailers to trade by the rules of their home country unless the seller had enticed or approached the consumer by way of advertising. In that case, any legal action takes place in the consumer's country of residence. The rationale is that if a company actively seeks customers in a given country it ought to be willing to abide by that country's consumer-protection laws. Whether the directive will be accepted by all 15 member states is still problematic.[93]

The European Commission has begun to review the entire regulatory framework for the technological infrastructure of the information society. They are working on various pieces of legislation intended to place electronic commerce on an equal footing with conventional commerce. One of the first steps was to introduce a European Union–wide computer network named EEJ-net that provides an easy way to resolve small-scale disputes out of court. Problems over deliveries, defective products, or products that do not fit their description can be dealt with by a single one-stop national contact point, or clearinghouse, in each member state. The consumer will be able to find information and support in making a claim to the out-of-court dispute-resolution system in the country where the product supplier is based.

Establishing the validity of contractual law for e-commerce is making substantial progress also. India, for example, has recently passed a law that recognizes e-mail as a valid form of communication, electronic contracts as legal and enforceable, and digital signatures as binding. Several countries are preparing, or have passed, legislation similar to the United Kingdom's that allows digital signatures to be used in the creation of online contracts that are just as legally binding as any paper-based original document.[94]

## Summary

Businesses face a multitude of problems in their efforts to develop successful marketing programs. Not the least of these problems is the varying legal systems of the world and their effect on business transactions. Just as political climate, cultural differences, local geography, different business customs, and the stage of economic development must be taken into account, so must such legal questions as jurisdictional and legal recourse in disputes, protection of intellectual property rights, extended U.S. law enforcement, and enforcement of antitrust legislation by U.S. and foreign governments. A primary marketing task is to develop a plan that will be enhanced, or at least not adversely affected, by these and other environmental elements. New to the international legal scene is the Internet, which, by its nature, creates a new set of legal entanglements, many of which have yet to be properly addressed. One thing is certain: The freedom that now exists on the World Wide Web will be only a faint memory before long. The myriad questions created by different laws and different legal systems indicate that the prudent path to follow at all stages of foreign marketing operations is one leading to competent counsel well versed in the intricacies of the international legal environment.

## Questions

1. Define the following terms:

   common law, 181
   code law, 181
   Islamic law, 182
   Marxist-socialist tenets, 183
   conciliation, 186

   arbitration, 187
   litigation, 188
   prior use versus registration, 192
   cybersquatters, 204

2. How does the international marketer determine which legal system will have jurisdiction when legal disputes arise?

3. Discuss the state of international commercial law.

4. Discuss the limitations of jurisdictional clauses in contracts.

5. What is the "objective theory of jurisdiction"? How does it apply to a firm doing business within a foreign country?

---

[93]David McGuire, "Internet Legal Borders Remain Hazy," *Newsweek Business Information, Inc.,* April 29, 2003.

[94]"USA Regulations—Top 10 Internet Law Developments in 2001," *EIU Viewswire,* March 15, 2002.

6. Discuss some of the reasons why it is probably best to seek an out-of-court settlement in international commercial legal disputes rather than to sue.

7. Illustrate the procedure generally followed in international commercial disputes when settled under the auspices of a formal arbitration tribunal.

8. What are intellectual property rights? Why should a company in international marketing take special steps to protect them?

9. In many code-law countries, registration rather than prior use establishes ownership of intellectual property rights. Comment.

10. Discuss the advantages to the international marketer arising from the existence of the various international conventions on trademarks, patents, and copyrights.

11. "The legal environment of the foreign marketer takes on an added dimension of importance since there is no single uniform international commercial law which governs foreign business transactions." Comment.

12. Why is conciliation a better way to resolve a commercial dispute than arbitration?

13. Differentiate between conciliation and arbitration.

14. Assume you are a vice president in charge of a new business-to-business e-commerce division of a well-known major international auto parts manufacturer. A cybersquatter has registered the company name as a domain Web name. What are your options to secure the domain name for your company? Discuss the steps you should take to ensure worldwide protection of your domain name.

15. Discuss the issues of a website being sued for libel for information posted on the site.

16. Discuss the motives of a cybersquatter. What recourse does a company have to defend itself against a cybersquatter?

Ford
Forschungszentrum
Aachen

# Developing a Global Vision through Marketing Research

CHAPTER **8**

## CHAPTER LEARNING OBJECTIVES

What you should learn from Chapter 8:

- The importance of problem definition in international research

- The problems of availability and use of secondary data

- Quantitative and qualitative research methods

- Multicultural sampling and its problems in less-developed countries

- Sources of secondary data

- How to analyze and use research information

# Global Perspective

## SELLING APPLES IN JAPAN CAN BE A BRUISING BUSINESS

Selling apples in Japan—whether they are of the edible or computer variety—can be a bruising business. In both cases, designing effective and competitive marketing strategies requires a deep knowledge of buyer behavior that may be distinctly different from that which marketers encounter in the United States.

It took Washington State apple growers 24 years to get their fruit past customs inspectors in Japan. The door finally opened to Red and Golden Delicious apples in 1995, and Japanese consumers immediately gobbled up nearly 8,500 tons. But in 1996, sales dropped precipitously to only 800 tons. The slide in sales can be attributed in part to the fact that U.S. apple growers did not anticipate the strength of Japanese consumers' seasonal preferences; Americans buy and eat apples year round, but Japanese consumers do not. The growers also did not anticipate the lasting effects of nationalism among many Japanese. As one older Japanese woman wrote to her sister in the United States, "Younger Japanese people simply do not have any respect. They just buy those American apples with no shame. They do not have any loyalty to the Japanese farmers. All they care about is the lower price." The late 1990s recession in Asia also hurt sales of Washington apples. More recently a World Trade Organization ruling pried open the Japanese apple market to new varieties—Braeburn, Fuji, Gala, Granny Smith, and Jona Gold. However, at least in the beginning, the American apples have moved slower than anticipated due to lower prices on domestic varieties and new competition from Tasmania.

As for apples of the computer variety, Apple Computers traditionally has been a greater success in Japan than in the States. Its market share in Japan jumped to nearly 8 percent since Steve Jobs again took the reins at Apple, and it hopes to maintain its industry-leading growth rate well into the next century. But it won't be easy to continue taking a big

bite out of the $40 billion Japanese personal computer (PC) market. Apple continues to have mixed results at home, and the losses in market share and reputation in the United States have certainly affected buyers' perceptions in Japan. During the 2001 computer bust, Apple's sales fell 47 percent in Japan compared with "only" 33 percent worldwide. Ouch!

Moreover, the Japanese PC market works differently than that in the United States. Japanese businesses are relatively slow to use PCs to boost productivity, and managers prefer to network in face-to-face settings rather than via electronic hookups. Additionally, there are few information professionals in Japan compared with the United States. Such circumstances suggest that the rate of adoption of PCs in the Japanese workplace will not parallel that in the United States, meaning Apple has a smaller market in which to operate. Indeed, its most recent successes in Japan have been in the consumer market, where its bright colors make a fashion statement. Of course, fashions come and fashions go. Let's hope these Apples don't become perishable!

Selling either kind of apple in Japan will require the best marketing research efforts of U.S. firms. The basis of a marketing budget is the all-important forecast of demand, which requires statistical analyses and macroeconomic data from Japan. But before those data are collected, consumer focus groups and surveys must be conducted. U.S. marketers must also travel across the Pacific for visits to grocery stores, consumers' homes, or office buildings to see firsthand these evolving markets at their cores.

Sources: Garry Barker, "Apple Rolls out More iThings," *The Age,* February 22, 2000, p. 1; "USDA Reports on Japan Farm Sector Developments," Dow Jones Commodities Service, March 22, 2000. For the latest information on Apple Computer, Inc.'s current performance see their latest annual report, 2004.

Microsoft's Bill Gates takes his company's old advertising slogan, "Where do you want to go today?" very seriously. While he and his ads espouse the advantages of virtual travel, his own actual international travel schedule is also quite heavy. He finds face-to-face meetings with foreign vendors, partners, customers, and regulators a crucial part of trying to understand international markets. Here he shakes hands with the first Xbox customer in Japan. (© AFP/CORBIS)

Information is the key component in developing successful marketing strategies and avoiding major marketing blunders. Information needs range from the general data required to assess market opportunities to specific market information for decisions about product, promotion, distribution, and price. Sometimes the information can be bought from trusted research vendors or supplied by internal marketing research staff. But sometimes even the highest-level executives have to "get their shoes dirty" by putting in the miles and talking to key customers and directly observing the marketplace in action.[1] As an enterprise broadens its scope of operations to include international markets, the need for current, accurate information is magnified. Indeed, some researchers maintain that entry into a fast-developing, new-to-the-firm foreign market is one of the most daunting and ambiguous strategic decisions an executive can face. A marketer must find the most accurate and reliable data possible within the limits imposed by time, cost, and the present state of the art. The measure of a competent researcher is twofold: the ability to utilize the most sophisticated and adequate techniques and methods available within these limits, and the effective communication of insights to the decision makers in the firm. The latter often requires involving senior executives directly in the research process itself.

**Marketing research** is traditionally defined as the systematic gathering, recording, and analyzing of data to provide information useful in marketing decision making. Although the research processes and methods are basically the same whether applied in Columbus, Ohio, or Colombo, Sri Lanka, **international marketing research** involves two additional complications. First, information must be communicated across cultural boundaries. That is, executives in Chicago must be able to "translate" their research questions into terms that consumers in Guangzhou, China, can understand. Then the Chinese answers must be put into terms (i.e., reports and data summaries) that American managers can comprehend. Fortunately, there are often internal staff and research agencies that are quite experienced in these kinds of cross-cultural communication tasks.

Second, the environments within which the research tools are applied are often different in foreign markets. Rather than acquire new and exotic methods of research, the international marketing researcher must develop the ability for imaginative and deft application of tried and tested techniques in sometimes totally strange milieus. The mechanical problems of implementing foreign marketing research often vary from country to country. Within a foreign environment, the frequently differing emphases on the kinds of information needed, the often limited variety of appropriate tools and techniques available, and the difficulty of implementing the research process constitute the challenges facing most international marketing researchers.

This chapter deals with the operational problems encountered in gathering information in foreign countries for use by international marketers. Emphasis is on those elements of data generation that usually prove especially troublesome when conducting research in an environment other than the United States.

---

[1]Peter Drucker's wisdom improves with age. In his *Wall Street Journal* article of May 11, 1990 (p. A15), he eloquently makes the case for direct observation of the marketplace by even the most senior executives. For the most substantive argument in that same vein, see Gerald Zaltman's description of emotional aspects of managerial decision making in "Rethinking Market Research: Putting People Back In," *Journal of Marketing Research,* November 1997, 34, pp. 424–437.

# Breadth and Scope of International Marketing Research

The basic difference between domestic and foreign market research is the broader scope needed for foreign research, necessitated by higher levels of uncertainty. Research can be divided into three types based on information needs: (1) general information about the country, area, and/or market; (2) information necessary to forecast future marketing requirements by anticipating social, economic, consumer, and industry trends within specific markets or countries; and (3) specific market information used to make product, promotion, distribution, and price decisions and to develop marketing plans. In domestic operations, most emphasis is placed on the third type, gathering specific market information, because the other data are often available from secondary sources.

A country's political stability, cultural attributes, and geographical characteristics are some of the kinds of information not ordinarily gathered by domestic marketing research departments but which are required for a sound assessment of a foreign market. This broader scope of international marketing research is reflected in Unisys Corporation's planning steps, which call for collecting and assessing the following types of information:

**1. Economic.** General data on growth of the economy, inflation, business cycle trends, and the like; profitability analysis for the division's products; specific industry economic studies; analysis of overseas economies; and key economic indicators for the United States and major foreign countries.

**2. Cultural, sociological, and political climate.** A general non-economic review of conditions affecting the division's business. In addition to the more obvious subjects, it also covers ecology, safety, and leisure time and their potential impact on the division's business.[2]

**3. Overview of market conditions.** A detailed analysis of market conditions that the division faces, by market segment, including international.

**4. Summary of the technological environment.** A summary of the state-of-the-art technology as it relates to the division's business, carefully broken down by product segments.

**5. Competitive situation.** A review of competitors' sales revenues, methods of market segmentation, products, and apparent strategies on an international scope.[3]

Such in-depth information is necessary for sound marketing decisions.[4] For the domestic marketer, most such information has been acquired after years of experience with a single market, but in foreign markets this information must be gathered for each new market.

There is a basic difference between information ideally needed and that which is collectible and/or used. Many firms engaged in foreign marketing do not make decisions with the benefit of the information listed. Cost, time, and human elements are critical variables. Some firms have neither the appreciation for information nor adequate time or money for implementation of research. As a firm becomes more committed to foreign marketing and the cost of possible failure increases, however, greater emphasis is placed on research. Marketing research expenditures reflect the size and growth of markets around the world. Please see Exhibit 8.1 for a listing of the top twenty markets for international marketing research.

---

[2]Debanjan Mitra and Peter N. Golder, "Whose Culture Matters? Near-Market Knowledge and Its Impacts on Foreign Market Entry Timing," *Journal of Marketing Research,* August 2002, 39(3), pp. 350–365.

[3]Alexander Mullen, Martin Blunck, Editha Kalbfeisch, and Hans-Georg Rohbeck, "Using Pharmaceutical Development Databases for Competitive Intelligence," *Online,* May–June 2003, pp. 44–49.

[4]Apparently governments also get into the industrial competitive intelligence game as well. See Edward Iwata,"More U.S. Trade Secrets Walk out Door with Foreign Spies," *USA Today,* February 13, 2003, p. 5A.

**Exhibit 8.1**
Top Twenty Countries
for Marketing Research
Expenditures (millions of
dollars)

Source: *Marketing News,* July 8, 2002,
pp. 16–17. Used by permission of
American Marketing Association.

| | | | |
|---|---|---|---|
| United States | $5,992 | Sweden | 228 |
| United Kingdom | 1,623 | Mexico | 213 |
| Germany | 1,290 | Brazil | 197 |
| Japan | 1,206 | China | 181 |
| France | 958 | Switzerland | 118 |
| Canada | 434 | Belgium | 114 |
| Italy | 415 | S. Korea | 106 |
| Spain | 273 | Austria | 91 |
| Australia | 273 | Argentina | 90 |
| Netherlands | 228 | Taiwan | 74 |

## The Research Process

A marketing research study is always a compromise dictated by limits of time, cost, and the present state of the art.[5] The researcher must strive for the most accurate and reliable information within existing constraints. A key to successful research is a systematic and orderly approach to the collection and analysis of data. Whether a research program is conducted in New York or New Delhi, the research process should follow these steps:

1. Define the research problem and establish research objectives.
2. Determine the sources of information to fulfill the research objectives.
3. Consider the costs and benefits of the research effort.
4. Gather the relevant data from secondary or primary sources, or both.
5. Analyze, interpret, and summarize the results.
6. Effectively communicate the results to decision makers.

Although the steps in a research program are similar for all countries, variations and problems in implementation occur because of differences in cultural and economic development. Whereas the problems of research in England or Canada may be similar to those in the United States, research in Germany, South Africa, or Mexico may offer a multitude of different and difficult distinctions. These distinctions become apparent with the first step in the research process—formulation of the problem. Subsequent text sections illustrate some frequently encountered difficulties facing the international marketing researcher.

## Defining the Problem and Establishing Research Objectives

The **research process** should begin with a definition of the research problem and the establishment of specific research objectives. The major difficulty here is converting a series of often ambiguous business problems into tightly drawn and achievable research objectives. In this initial stage, researchers often embark on the research process with only a vague grasp of the total problem. A good example of such a loosely defined problem is that of the Russian airline, Aeroflot. The company started a branding study to inform marketing decision makers regarding how to improve its longstanding reputation for poor safety standards and unreliable service. This is a tough challenge for international marketing researchers.[6]

This first, most crucial step in research is more critical in foreign markets because an unfamiliar environment tends to cloud problem definition. Researchers either fail to anticipate the influence of the local culture on the problem or fail to identify the self-reference criterion (SRC) and so treat the problem definition as if it were in the researcher's home environment.[7] In assessing some foreign business failures it is apparent that research was conducted, but the questions asked were more appropriate for the U.S. market than for

---

[5]Thomas T. Semon provides an interesting description of how problems can crop up here, see "Raw Numbers, Not Indexes, Tell Real Story," *Marketing News,* March 3, 2003, p. 11.

[6]"Aeroflot Tries to Ditch Bad Image with Rebranding," *Marketing,* January 9, 2003, p. 3.

[7]For example, see Naresh K. Malhotra and Betsy Charles Bartels, "Overcoming the Attribute Prespecification Bias in International Marketing Research by Using Non-Attribute-Based Correspondence Analysis," *International Marketing Review,* 2002, 19(1), pp. 65–79.

## THE FAR SIDE® BY GARY LARSON

**"Say ... what's a mountain goat doing way up here in a cloud bank?"**

The first step in marketing research is defining the problem. The pilots in Larson's cartoon eloquently reflect the major problem in international marketing research. Defining the problem can be much more difficult in foreign markets, and more careful preliminary qualitative work is crucial in avoiding international marketing research "collisions with mountains!" By the way, this is not an Aeroflot joke. (*The Far Side® by Gary Larson © 1983 FarWorks, Inc. All Rights Reserved. Used with permission.*)

the foreign one. For example, all of Disney's years of research and experience in keeping people happy standing in long lines could not help them anticipate the scope of the problems they would run into at EuroDisney. The firm's experience had been that the relatively homogeneous clientele at both the American parks and Tokyo Disneyland were cooperative and orderly when it came to queuing up. Actually, so are most British and Germans. But the rules about queuing in other countries such as Spain and Italy are apparently quite different, creating the potential for a new kind of intra-European "warfare" in the lines. Understanding and managing this multinational customer service problem required new ways of thinking. Isolating the SRC and asking the right questions are crucial steps in the problem formulation stage.

Other difficulties in foreign research stem from failure to establish problem limits broad enough to include all relevant variables. Information on a far greater range of factors is necessary to offset the unfamiliar cultural background of the foreign market. Consider proposed research about consumption patterns and attitudes toward hot milk-based drinks. In the United Kingdom, hot milk-based drinks are considered to have sleep-inducing, restful, and relaxing properties and are traditionally consumed prior to bedtime. People in Thailand, however, drink the same hot milk-based drinks in the morning on the way to work and see them as being invigorating, energy-giving, and stimulating. If one's only experience is the United States, the picture is further clouded since hot milk-based drinks are frequently associated with cold weather, either in the morning or the evening, and for different reasons each time of day. The market researcher must be certain the problem definition is sufficiently broad to cover the whole range of response possibilities and not be clouded by his or her self-reference criterion.

This is a problem that Mattel Inc. may run into headlong. The company conducted a coordinated global research program using focus groups of children in several countries. Based on their findings the firm is cutting back on customization and ignoring local managers' advice by globally selling an unmodified Barbie. Not only is it dangerous to ignore the advice of local managers, it is also dangerous to ignore parents' opinions involving toys. Kids may like a blonde Barbie, but parents may not. We will follow this case with great interest.[8]

After the problem is adequately defined and research objectives established, the researcher must determine the availability of the information needed. If the data are available—that is, if they have been collected already by some other agency—the researcher should then consult these **secondary data** sources.

## Problems of Availability and Use of Secondary Data
The U.S. government provides comprehensive statistics for the United States; periodic censuses of U.S. population, housing, business, and agriculture are conducted and, in some cases, have been taken for over

[8]Lisa Bannon and Carlta Vitzhum, "One-Toy-Fits-All: How Industry Learned to Love the Global Kid," *Wall Street Journal,* April 29, 2003, p. A1.

100 years. Commercial sources, trade associations, management groups, and state and local governments provide the researcher with additional sources of detailed U.S. market information. Often the problem for American marketing researchers is sorting through too much data!

Unfortunately, the quantity and quality of marketing-related data available on the United States is unmatched in other countries. The data available on and in Japan is a close second, and several European countries do a good job of data collection and reporting them. Indeed, on some dimensions the quality of data collected in these latter countries can actually exceed that in the United States. However, in many countries substantial data collection has been initiated only recently. Through the continuing efforts of organizations such as the United Nations and the Organization for Economic Cooperation and Development (OECD), improvements are being made worldwide.

In addition, with the emergence of Eastern European countries as potentially viable markets, a number of private and public groups are funding the collection of information to offset a lack of comprehensive market data. Several Japanese consumer goods manufacturers are coordinating market research on a corporate level and have funded 47 research centers throughout Eastern Europe. As market activity continues in Eastern Europe and elsewhere, market information will improve in quantity and quality. To build a database on Russian consumers, one Denver, Colorado, firm used a novel approach to conduct a survey: It ran a questionnaire in Moscow's *Komsomolskaya Pravda* newspaper asking for replies to be sent to the company. The 350,000 replies received (3,000 by registered mail) attested to the willingness of Russian consumers to respond to marketing inquiries. The problems of availability, reliability, and comparability of data and of validating secondary data are described in the following sections.

## Availability of Data

Much of the secondary data that an American marketer is accustomed to having about U.S. markets is just not available for many countries. Detailed data on the numbers of wholesalers, retailers, manufacturers, and facilitating services, for example, are unavailable for many parts of the world, as are data on population and income. Most countries simply do not have governmental agencies that collect on a regular basis the kinds of secondary data readily available in the United States. If such information is important, the marketer must initiate the research or rely on private sources of data.

Another problem relating to the availability of data is researchers' language skills. For example, although data are often copious regarding the Japanese market, being able to read Japanese is a requisite for accessing them, either online or in text. This may seem a rather innocuous problem, but those who have tried to maneuver through foreign data can appreciate the value of having a native speaker of the appropriate language on the research team.

## Reliability of Data

Available data may not have the level of reliability necessary for confident decision making for many reasons. Official statistics are sometimes too optimistic, reflecting national pride or politics rather than practical reality, while tax structures and fear of the tax collector often adversely affect data.

Although not unique to them, less-developed countries are particularly prone to being both overly optimistic and unreliable in reporting relevant economic data about their countries. China's National Statistics Enforcement Office recently acknowledged that it had uncovered about 60,000 instances of false statistical reports since beginning a crackdown on false data reporting several months earlier.[9] Seeking advantages or hiding failures, local officials, factory managers, rural enterprises, and others filed fake numbers on everything from production levels to birthrates. For example, a petrochemical plant reported one year's output to be $20 million, 50 percent higher than its actual output of $13.4 million. Finally, if you believe the statistics, until 2000 the Chinese in Hong Kong are the world-champion consumers of fresh oranges—64 pounds per year per person, twice as much as

---

[9]Mark L. Clifford, "How Fast is China Really Growing?" *BusinessWeek,* March 10, 2003, p. 65.

## CROSSING BORDERS 8.1  Headache? Take Two Aspirin and Lie Down

Such advice goes pretty far in countries such as Germany, where Bayer invented aspirin more than 100 years ago, and the United States. But people in many places around the world don't share such Western views about medicine and the causes of disease. Many Asians, including Chinese, Filipinos, Koreans, Japanese, and Southeast Asians, believe illnesses such as headaches are the result of the imbalance between *yin* and *yang*. *Yin* is the feminine, passive principle that is typified by darkness, cold, or wetness. Alternatively, *yang* is the masculine, active principle associated with light, heat, or dryness. All things result from their combination, and bad things like headaches result from too much of one or the other. Acupuncture and moxibustion (heating crushed wormwood or other herbs on the skin) are common cures for *yin* outweighing *yang*, or vice versa. Many Laotians believe pain can be caused by one of the body's 32 souls being lost or by sorcerers' spells. The exact cause is often determined by examining the yolk of a freshly broken egg. In other parts of the world, such as Mexico and Puerto Rico, illness is believed to be caused by an imbalance of one of the four body humors: "blood—hot and wet; yellow bile—hot and dry; phlegm—cold and wet; and black bile—cold and dry." Even in the high-tech United States, many people believe that pain is often a "reminder from God" to behave properly.

For companies such as Bayer, a key question to be addressed in marketing research is how and to what extent aspirin can be marketed as a supplement to the traditional remedies. That is, will little white pills mix well with phlegm and black bile?

Sources: Larry A. Samovar, Richard E. Porter, and Lisa A. Stefani, *Communication between Cultures*, 3rd edition (Belmont, CA: Wadsworth Publishing, 1998), pp. 224–225; the direct quote is from N. Dresser, *Multicultural Manners: New Rules for Etiquette for a Changing Society* (New York: John Wiley & Sons, 1996), p. 236. Also see "Bayer's Profits Rise," *New York Times*, May 8, 2003, p. 1

Americans. However, apparently about half of all the oranges imported into Hong Kong, some $30 million worth, were actually finding their way into the rest of China, where U.S. oranges were illegal. One might predict a crash in citrus sales to Hong Kong now that WTO entry for China means that American oranges can be directly shipped there.

Willful errors in the reporting of marketing data are not uncommon in the most industrialized countries, either. Often print media circulation figures are purposely overestimated even in OECD countries. The European Union (EU) tax policies can also affect the accuracy of reported data. Production statistics are frequently inaccurate because these countries collect taxes on domestic sales. Thus some companies shave their production statistics a bit to match the sales reported to tax authorities. Conversely, foreign trade statistics may be exaggerated slightly because each country in the EU grants some form of export subsidy. Knowledge of such "adjusted reporting" is critical for a marketer who relies on secondary data for forecasting or estimating market demand.

**Comparability of Data**

Comparability of available data is the third shortcoming faced by foreign marketers. In the United States, current sources of reliable and valid estimates of socioeconomic factors and business indicators are readily available. In other countries, especially those less developed, data can be many years out of date as well as having been collected on an infrequent and unpredictable schedule. Naturally, the rapid change in socioeconomic features being experienced in many of these countries makes the problem of currency a vital one. Further, even though many countries are now gathering reliable data, there are generally no historical series with which to compare the current information.

A related problem is the manner in which data are collected and reported. Too frequently, data are reported in different categories or in categories much too broad to be of specific value. The term *supermarket*, for example, has a variety of meanings around the world. In Japan a supermarket is quite different from its American counterpart. Japanese supermarkets usually occupy two- or three-story structures; they sell foodstuffs, daily necessities, and clothing on respective floors. Some even sell furniture, electric home appliances, stationery, and sporting goods, and have a restaurant. General merchandise stores, shopping centers, and department stores are different from stores of the same name in the United States.[10]

**Validating Secondary Data**

The shortcomings discussed here should be considered when using any source of information. Many countries have similarly high standards for the collection and preparation of data as those generally found in the United States, but secondary data from any source, including the United States, must be checked and interpreted carefully. As a practical matter, the following questions should be asked to effectively judge the reliability of secondary data sources:

1. Who collected the data? Would there be any reason for purposely misrepresenting the facts?
2. For what purposes were the data collected?
3. How were the data collected? (methodology)
4. Are the data internally consistent and logical in light of known data sources or market factors?

Checking the consistency of one set of secondary data with other data of known validity is an effective and often-used way of judging validity. For example, a researcher might check the sale of baby products with the number of women of childbearing age and with birthrates, or the number of patient beds in hospitals with the sale of related hospital equipment. Such correlations can also be useful in estimating demand and forecasting sales.

In general, the availability and accuracy of recorded secondary data increase as the level of economic development increases. There are exceptions; India is at a lower level of economic development than many countries but has accurate and relatively complete government-collected data.

Fortunately, interest in collecting quality statistical data rises as countries realize the value of extensive and accurate national statistics for orderly economic growth. This interest in improving the quality of national statistics has resulted in remarkable improvement in the availability of data during the last 20 years. However, where no data are available, or the secondary data sources are inadequate, it is necessary to begin the collection of primary data.

The Appendix to this chapter includes a comprehensive listing of secondary data sources, including websites on a variety of international marketing topics. Almost all secondary data available on international markets can now be discovered or acquired via the Internet. For example, the most comprehensive statistics regarding international finances, demographics, consumption, exports, and imports are accessible through a single source,  the U.S. Department of Commerce at www.stat-usa.gov. Many other governmental, institutional, and commercial sources of data can be found on the Internet as well.

# Gathering Primary Data: Quantitative and Qualitative Research

If, after seeking all reasonable secondary data sources, research questions are still not adequately answered, the market researcher must collect **primary data**—that is, data collected specifically for the particular research project at hand. The researcher may question the firm's sales representatives, distributors, middlemen, and/or customers to get appropriate market information. In most primary data collection, the researcher questions respondents to determine what they think about some topic or how they might behave under certain conditions. Marketing research methods can be grouped into two basic types: quantitative and qualitative research. In both methods, the marketer is interested in gaining knowledge about the market.

In *quantitative research,* usually a large number of respondents are asked to reply either verbally or in writing to structured questions using a specific response format (such as yes/no) or to select a response from a set of choices. Questions are designed to obtain

---

[10]Matthew B. Myers, Roger J. Calantone, Thomas J. Page, Jr., and Charles R. Taylor, "An Application of Multiple-Group Causal Models in Assessing Cross-Cultural Measurement Equivalence," *Journal of International Marketing,* 2000, 8(4), pp. 108–121.

# CROSSING BORDERS 8.2  Oops! Even the Best Companies Can Make Mistakes

Microsoft and Telefonos de Mexico are joining forces to launch a new Spanish-language Internet Portal www.T1msn.com. Microsoft is also donating some $100 million to help the Mexican government go online. However, Microsoft hasn't always gotten along so well with Mexican consumers. At one time Mexican users of the Spanish-language version of Microsoft Word were quite angry. One might also say they were mad, burning, violent, bothered, steaming, raging, stormy, furious, irate, livid, frothy, piqued, annoyed, seething, resentful, infuriated, irked, vexed, roiled, enraged, ireful, ruffled, churlish, wrathful, and irritated.

The problem was the thesaurus, or synonym dictionary, that Microsoft included with their popular word processing program. When asked to provide alternatives for the word *Indian,* the thesaurus generated suggestions that included *cannibal* and *savage.* In Mexico, where most people can claim indigenous ancestry, that just wasn't right. It wasn't kosher or politically correct for that matter, either.

Similar problems arose with the words *lesbian,* whose suggested alternatives were *pervert* and *depraved person,* and *western,* whose suggested alternatives were *Aryan, white,* and *civilized.*

Critics minced no words. "I see this as profoundly dangerous because it is a lack of respect for our dignity as Mexicans and for our indigenous roots," said Adriana Luna, a Mexican congresswoman. Another deputy called the dictionary "fascist" and "conservative."

For Microsoft that translated into "public relations disaster." Its response, however, was swift. The company said the thesaurus was created by an outside contractor, but accepted full responsibility all the same. Calling the word suggestions "offensive" and "mistaken," it "asked for forgiveness of customers who have been offended." Microsoft also promised a revised dictionary, promised to make its Spanish-language products more sensitive to different countries' usage, and provided the new version to current users free of charge.

Microsoft seemed suitably embarrassed . . . as well as ashamed, humbled, distressed, disgraced, and chastened. But under the circumstances, we suggest that all avoid using another synonym for their situation: red-faced!

Source: *Latin Trade,* September 1996, p. 16; Elliot Spagat, "WRAP: Mexico's Telemex, Microsoft Launch Spanish Portal," *Dow Jones International News,* March 21, 2000; Susan E. Reed, "Technology Companies Take Hope in Charity," *New York Times,* March 23, 2003, p. 3.

specific responses regarding aspects of the respondents' behavior, intentions, attitudes, motives, and demographic characteristics.[11] Quantitative research provides the marketer with responses that can be presented with precise estimations. The structured responses received in a survey can be summarized in percentages, averages, or other statistics. For example, 76 percent of the respondents prefer product A over product B, and so on. Survey research is generally associated with quantitative research, and the typical instrument used is the questionnaire administered by personal interview, mail, telephone, and most recently over the Internet.

Scientific studies often are conducted by engineers and chemists in product-testing laboratories around the world. There, product designs and formulas are developed and tested in consumer usage situations. Often those results are integrated with consumer opinions gathered in concurrent survey studies. One of the best examples of this kind of marketing research comes from Tokyo. You may not know it, but the Japanese are the world champions of bathroom and toilet technology. Their biggest company in that industry, Toto, has spent millions of dollars developing and testing consumer products. Thousands of people have collected data (using survey techniques) on the best features of a toilet, and at the company's "human engineering laboratory," volunteers sit in a Toto bathtub with electrodes strapped to their skulls, to measure brain waves and "the effects of bathing on the human body." Toto is now introducing one of its high-tech (actually low-tech compared with what

---

[11]A good example of this sort of study involves a cross-cultural comparison of consumer panel data: Frederik T. Schut, Stefan Gress, and Juergen Wasem, "Consumer Price Sensitivity and Social Health Insurer Choice in Germany and the Netherlands," *Journal of Health Care Finance and Economics,* June 2003, 3(2), p. 117.

they offer in Japan) toilets in the U.S. market. It's a $600 seat, lid, and control panel that attaches to the regular American bowl. It features a heated seat and deodorizing fan.

In *qualitative research,* if questions are asked they are almost always open-ended or in-depth, and unstructured responses that reflect the person's thoughts and feelings on the subject are sought. Direct observation of consumers in choice or product usage situations is another important qualitative approach to marketing research. One researcher spent two months observing birthing practices in American and Japanese hospitals to gain insights into the export of healthcare services. Nissan Motors sent a researcher to live with an American family (renting a room in their house for six weeks) to directly observe how Americans use their cars. Anderson Worldwide, Nynex, and Texas Commerce Bank have all employed anthropologists that specialize in observational and in-depth interviews in their marketing research. Qualitative research seeks to interpret what the people in the sample are like—their outlooks, their feelings, the dynamic interplay of their feelings and ideas, their attitudes and opinions, and their resulting actions.[12] The most often used form of qualitative questioning is the focus group interview.[13] However, oftentimes in-depth interviewing of individuals can be just as effective while consuming far fewer resources.

Qualitative research is used in international marketing research to formulate and define a problem more clearly and to determine relevant questions to be examined in subsequent research.[14] It is also used where interest is centered on gaining an understanding of a market,[15] rather than quantifying relevant aspects. For example, a small group of key executives at Solar Turbines International, a division of Caterpillar Tractor Company, called on key customers at their offices around the world. They discussed in great depth with both financial managers and production engineers potential applications and the demand for a new size of gas-turbine engine the company was considering developing. The data and insights gained during the interviews to a large degree confirmed the validity of the positive demand forecasts produced internally through macroeconomic modeling. The multimillion-dollar project was then implemented. Additionally, during the discussions new product features were suggested by the customer personnel that proved most useful in the development efforts.

Qualitative research is also helpful in revealing the impact of sociocultural factors on behavior patterns and in developing research hypotheses that can be tested in subsequent studies designed to quantify the concepts and relevant relationships uncovered in qualitative data collection. Procter & Gamble has been one of the pioneers of this type of research—the company has systematically gathered consumer feedback for some 70 years. It was the first company to conduct in-depth consumer research in China. In the mid-1990s P&G began working with the Chinese Ministry of Health to develop dental hygiene programs and has now reached over one million children in 28 cities. The company now offers Crest toothpaste in two flavors and toothbrushes in four colors to Chinese consumers.

Oftentimes the combination of qualitative and quantitative research proves quite useful in industrial and business-to-business marketing settings as well. In one study the number of personal referrals used in buying financial services in Japan was found to be much greater than in the United States.[16] The various comments made by the executives during the personal interviews in both countries proved invaluable in interpreting the quantitative results, suggesting implications for managers and providing ideas for further research. Likewise, the comments of sales managers in Tokyo during in-depth interviews

[12]Paul E. Green, Yoram Wind, Abba M. Krieger, and Paul Saatsoglou, "Applying Qualitative Data," *Marketing Research*, Spring 2000, 12(1), pp. 17–25.

[13]*Marketing News* provides a directory of focus group vendors including those in other countries. See the March 3, 2003 issue, p. 19.

[14]Donna C. Barson, "Quantitative and Qualitative Market Research," *Global Cosmetic Industry,* February 2003, p. 18.

[15]Ursula Wrobel, "'Not in Front of Your Mother!': Online Marketing for Pharmaceutical Products Addressing Taboo Topics," *Qualitative Market Research,* 2002, 5(1), pp. 19–27.

[16]R. Bruce Money, "Word-of-Mouth Referral Sources for Buyers of International Corporate Financial Services," *Journal of World Business,* Fall 2000, 35(3), pp. 314–329.

**CROSSING BORDERS 8.3**  China Handcuffs Marketing Researchers

China has announced that firms conducting market research must be officially licensed, and has claimed the right to halt any such projects deemed harmful to national security.

The new rules, unveiled at a government news conference, mark Beijing's most recent effort to control the country's freewheeling market-research industry. In particular, projects conducted by foreign firms are receiving renewed scrutiny. Although the demand for marketing research is huge in China, officials appear worried that some surveys are addressing politically sensitive areas such as confidence in the government and economy or are investigating regional weaknesses within the country.

"Some foreign market research has been of poor quality. At other times, the research has been used to hurt our country's national security and the greater interest of the public," Zhai Ligong, Deputy Director of China's State Statistical Bureau, said to reporters.

Under the latest set of rules, companies seeking to conduct studies for foreign companies must obtain licenses. Companies are also required to give the State Statistical Bureau a detailed list of their research projects every two months, and may on occasion be required to reveal specific findings to the government officials. Firms have also been ordered to share survey questions and findings with the government before sharing them with their clients. The specter of forced partnerships with government-affiliated rivals has also been raised.

Thus far enforcement of such regulations has been slack, but arrests for similar "crimes" are being made. Let's hope WTO membership and a growing economy will encourage the Chinese government to reconsider such efficiency-killing constraints on commerce.

Source: Karby Leggett and Leslie Chang, "China Adds Limits for Researchers, Sparking Concern at Foreign Firms," *Wall Street Journal Interactive Edition*, July 28, 2000; and Erik Eckholm, "China: Internet Operator Sentenced," *New York Times*, May 20, 2003, p. 8. Copyright 2000 by Dow Jones & Co. Inc. Reproduced with permission of Dow Jones & Co. Inc. via Copyright Clearance Center.

helped researchers understand why individual financial incentives were found not to work with Japanese sales representatives.[17]

As we shall see later in this chapter, using either research method in international marketing research is subject to a number of difficulties caused by the diversity of cultures and languages encountered.

## Problems of Gathering Primary Data

The problems of collecting primary data in foreign countries are different only in degree from those encountered in the United States. Assuming the research problem is well defined and the objectives are properly formulated, the success of primary research hinges on the ability of the researcher to get correct and truthful information that addresses the research objectives. Most problems in collecting primary data in international marketing research stem from cultural differences among countries, and range from the inability of respondents to communicate their opinions to inadequacies in questionnaire translation.

**Ability to Communicate Opinions**

The ability to express attitudes and opinions about a product or concept depends on the respondent's ability to recognize the usefulness and value of such a product or concept. It is difficult for a person to formulate needs, attitudes, and opinions about goods whose use may not be understood, that are not in common use within the community, or that have never been available. For example, it may be impossible for someone who has never had the benefits of an office computer to express accurate feelings or provide any reasonable information about purchase intentions, likes, or dislikes concerning a new computer software package. The more complex the concept, the more difficult it is to design research that will help the respondent communicate meaningful opinions and reactions. Under these circumstances, the creative capabilities of the international marketing researcher are challenged.

---

[17]R. Bruce Money and John L. Graham, "Sales Person Performance, Pay, and Job Satisfaction: Tests of a Model Using Data Collected in the U.S. and Japan," *Journal of International Business Studies*, 1999, 30(1), pp. 149–172.

No company has had more experience in trying to understand consumers with communication limitations than Gerber. Babies may be their business, but babies often can't talk, much less fill out a questionnaire. Over the years Gerber has found that talking to and observing both infants and their mothers are important in marketing research. In one study Gerber found that breast-fed babies adapted to solid food more quickly than bottle-fed babies because breast milk changes flavor depending on what the mother has eaten. For example, infants were found to suck longer and harder if their mother had recently eaten garlic. In another study, weaning practices were studied around the world. Indian babies were offered lentils served on a finger. Some Nigerian children got fermented sorghum, fed by the grandmother through the funnel of her hand. In some parts of tropical Asia mothers "food-kissed" prechewed vegetables into their babies' mouths. Hispanic mothers in the United States tend to introduce baby food much earlier than non-Hispanic mothers and continue it well beyond the first year. All this research helps the company decide which products are appropriate for which markets. For example, the Vegetable and Rabbit Meat and the Freeze-Dried Sardines and Rice flavors popular in Poland and Japan, respectively, most likely won't make it to American store shelves.

## Willingness to Respond

Cultural differences offer the best explanation for the unwillingness or the inability of many to respond to research surveys. The role of the male, the suitability of personal gender-based inquiries, and other gender-related issues can affect willingness to respond.[18]

In some countries, the husband not only earns the money but also dictates exactly how it is to be spent. Because the husband controls the spending, it is he, not the wife, who should be questioned to determine preferences and demand for many consumer goods. In some countries, women would never consent to be interviewed by a male or a stranger. A French Canadian woman does not like to be questioned and is likely to be reticent in her responses. In some societies, a man would certainly consider it beneath his dignity to discuss shaving habits or brand preference in personal clothing with anyone—most emphatically not a female interviewer.

Anyone asking questions about any topic from which tax assessment could be inferred is immediately suspected of being a tax agent. Citizens of many countries do not feel the same legal and moral obligations to pay their taxes as do U.S. citizens. Tax evasion is thus an accepted practice for many and a source of pride for the more adept. Where such an attitude exists, taxes are often seemingly arbitrarily assessed by the government, which results in much incomplete or misleading information being reported. One of the problems revealed by the government of India in a recent population census was the underreporting of tenants by landlords trying to hide the actual number of people living in houses and flats. The landlords had been subletting accommodations illegally and were concealing their activities from the tax department.

In the United States, publicly held corporations are compelled by the Securities and Exchange Commission (SEC) to disclose certain operating figures on a periodic basis. In many European countries, however, such information is seldom if ever released and then most reluctantly. Attempts to enlist the cooperation of merchants in setting up an in-store study of shelf inventory and sales information ran into strong resistance because of suspicions and a tradition of competitive secrecy. The resistance was overcome by the researcher's willingness to approach the problem step by step. As the retailer gained confidence in the researcher and realized the value of the data gathered, more and more requested information was provided. Besides the reluctance of businesses to respond to surveys, local politicians in underdeveloped countries may interfere with studies in the belief that they could be subversive and must be stopped or hindered. A few moments with local politicians can prevent days of delay.

---

[18]It should be noted that often data are collected whether or not consumers like it. Most consumers would be surprised to know to what degree hotels keep track of travelers' purchases. See Christina Binkley, "Soon, the Desk Clerk Will Know All About You—Hilton Hotels' New System Helps It Customize Service, Though Privacy May Suffer," *Wall Street Journal,* May 8, 2003, p. D4.

Midnight in New Delhi—both customer service and telephone survey research is being outsourced to lower-wage English-speaking countries. Cost savings of such outsourcing must be balanced with consumer reluctance in cross-cultural communication settings, particularly those involving voluntary responses to marketing research. (© Pablo Bartholomew/ Netphotograph.com)

Although such cultural differences may make survey research more difficult to conduct, it is possible. In some communities, locally prominent people could open otherwise closed doors; in other situations, professional people and local students have been used as interviewers because of their knowledge of the market. Less direct measurement techniques and nontraditional data analysis methods may also be more appropriate. In one study, Japanese supermarket buyers rated the nationality of brands (foreign or domestic) as relatively unimportant in making stocking decisions when asked directly; however, when an indirect, paired-comparison questioning technique was used, brand nationality proved to be the most important factor.[19]

**Sampling in Field Surveys**

The greatest problem in sampling stems from the lack of adequate demographic data and available lists from which to draw meaningful samples.[20] If current, reliable lists are not available, sampling becomes more complex and generally less reliable. In many countries, telephone directories, cross-index street directories, census tract and block data, and detailed social and economic characteristics of the population being studied are not available on a current basis, if at all. The researcher must estimate characteristics and population parameters, sometimes with little basic data on which to build an accurate estimate.

To add to the confusion, in some South American, Mexican, and Asian cities, street maps are unavailable, and in some Asian metropolitan areas, streets are not identified nor are houses numbered. In contrast, one of the positive aspects of research in Japan and Taiwan is the availability and accuracy of census data on individuals. In these countries, when a household moves it is required to submit up-to-date information to a centralized government agency before it can use communal services such as water, gas, electricity, and education.

The effectiveness of various methods of communication (mail, telephone, personal interview, and Internet) in surveys is limited. In many countries, telephone ownership is extremely low, making telephone surveys virtually worthless unless the survey is intended to cover only the wealthy. In Sri Lanka, fewer than 10 percent of the residents—only the

[19]Frank Alpert, Michael Kamins, Tomoaki Sakano, Naoto Onzo, and John L. Graham, "Retail Buyer Beliefs, Attitudes, and Behaviors toward Pioneer and Me-Too Follower Brands: A Comparative Study of Japan and the United States," *International Marketing Review,* 18(2), 2001, pp. 160–187.

[20]N.L. Reynolds, A.C. Simintiras, and A. Diamantopoulos, "Theoretical Justification of Sampling Choices in International Marketing Research: Key Issues and Guidelines for Researchers," *Journal of International Business Research,* 2003, 34, pp. 80–89.

wealthy—have telephones. Even if the respondent has a telephone, the researcher may still be unable to complete a call.

The adequacy of sampling techniques is also affected by a lack of detailed social and economic information. Without an age breakdown of the total population, for example, the researcher can never be certain of a representative sample requiring an age criterion because there is no basis of comparison for the age distribution in the sample. A lack of detailed information, however, does not prevent the use of sampling; it simply makes it more difficult. In place of probability techniques, many researchers in such situations rely on convenience samples taken in marketplaces and other public gathering places.

McDonald's got into trouble over sampling issues. The company was involved in a dispute in South Africa over the rights to its valuable brand name in that fast-emerging market. Part of the company's claim revolved around the recall of the McDonald's name among South Africans. In the two surveys the company conducted and provided as proof in the proceedings, the majority of those sampled had heard the company name and could recognize the logo. However, the Supreme Court judge hearing the case took a dim view of the evidence because the surveys were conducted in "posh, white" suburbs whereas 76 percent of the South African population is black. Based in part on these sampling errors, the judge threw out McDonald's case.

Inadequate mailing lists and poor postal service can be problems for the market researcher using mail to conduct research. In Nicaragua, delays of weeks in delivery are not unusual, and expected returns are lowered considerably because a letter can be mailed only at a post office. In addition to the potentially poor mail service within countries, the extended length of time required for delivery and return when a mail survey is conducted from another country further hampers the use of mail surveys. Although airmail reduces this time drastically, it also increases costs considerably.

The kinds of problems encountered in drawing a random sample include the following:

- No officially recognized census of population.
- No other listings that can serve as sampling frames.
- Incomplete and out-of-date telephone directories.
- No accurate maps of population centers. Thus, no cluster (area) samples can be developed.

Although all the conditions described do not exist in all countries, they illustrate why the collection of primary data requires creative applications of research techniques when firms expand into many foreign markets.

## Language and Comprehension

The most universal survey research problem in foreign countries is the language barrier. Differences in idiom and the difficulty of exact translation create problems in eliciting the specific information desired and in interpreting the respondents' answers.[21] Equivalent concepts may not exist in all languages. Family, for example, has different connotations in different countries. In the United States, it generally means only the parents and children. In Italy and many Latin countries it could mean the parents, children, grandparents, uncles, aunts, cousins, and so forth. The meaning of names for family members can have different meanings depending on the context within which they are used. In the Italian culture, the words for aunt and uncle are different for the maternal and paternal sides of the family. The concept of affection is a universal idea, but the manner in which it is manifested in each culture may differ. Kissing, an expression of affection in the West, is alien to many Eastern cultures and even taboo in some.

Literacy poses yet another problem. In some less-developed countries with low literacy rates, written questionnaires are completely useless. Within countries, too, the problem of dialects and different languages can make a national questionnaire survey impractical. In

---

[21]Shi Zhang and Bernd H. Schmitt, "Creating Local Brands in Multilingual International Markets," *Journal of Marketing Research,* August 2001, 38, pp. 313–325.

India, there are 14 official languages and considerably more unofficial ones. One researcher has used pictures of products as stimuli and pictures of faces as response criterion in a study of eastern German brand preferences to avoid some of the difficulties associated with language differences and literacy in international research. Still others have used other nonverbal kinds of response elicitation techniques such as pictures and collages.[22]

Furthermore, a researcher cannot assume that a translation into one language will suffice in all areas where that language is spoken. Such was the case when one of the authors was in Mexico and requested a translation of the word *outlet,* as in *retail outlet,* to be used in Venezuela. It was read by Venezuelans to mean an electrical outlet, an outlet of a river into an ocean, and the passageway into a patio. Needless to say, the responses were useless—although interesting. Thus it will always be necessary for a native speaker of the target country's language to take the "final cut" of any translated material.[23]

All marketing communications, including research questionnaires, must be written perfectly. If not, consumers and customers will not respond with accuracy, or even at all. The obvious solution of having questionnaires prepared or reviewed by a native speaker of the language of the country is frequently overlooked. Even excellent companies such as American Airlines bring errors into their measurement of customer satisfaction by using the same questionnaire in Spanish for their surveys of passengers on routes to Spain and Mexico. To a Spaniard orange juice is *zumo de naranja;* a Mexican would order *jugo de naranja.* These apparently subtle differences are no such things to Spanish speakers. In another case, a German respondent was asked the number of washers (washing machines) produced in Germany for a particular year; the reply reflected the production of the flat metal disk. Marketers use three different techniques, back translation, parallel translation, and decentering, to help ferret out translation errors ahead of time.

**Back Translation.**  In **back translation** the questionnaire is translated from one language to another, and then a second party translates it back into the original.[24] This process pinpoints misinterpretations and misunderstandings before they reach the public. A soft-drink company wanted to use a very successful Australian advertising theme, "Baby, it's cold inside," in Hong Kong. They had the theme translated from English into Cantonese by one translator and then retranslated by another from Cantonese into English, in which the statement came out as "Small mosquito, on the inside it is very cold." Although "small mosquito" is the colloquial expression for "small child" in Hong Kong, the intended meaning was lost in translation.

**Parallel Translation.**  Back translations may not always ensure an accurate translation because of commonly used idioms in both languages. **Parallel translation** is used to overcome this problem. In this process, more than two translators are used for the back translation; the results are compared, differences discussed, and the most appropriate translation selected.

**Decentering.**  A third alternative, known as **decentering**, is a hybrid of back translation. It is a successive process of translation and retranslation of a questionnaire, each time by a different translator. For example, an English version is translated into French and then translated back to English by a different translator. The two English versions are compared and where there are differences, the original English version is modified and the process is repeated. If there are still differences between the two English versions, the original English version of the second iteration is modified and the process of translation and back translation is repeated. The process continues to be repeated until

---

[22]Gerald Zaltman, "Rethinking Marketing Research: Putting the People Back In," *Journal of Marketing Research,* November 1997, 34, pp. 424–437.

[23]Stephen P. Iverson, "The Art of Translation," *World Trade,* April 2000, pp. 90–92; *M2 Presswire,* "iLanguage and Uniscape Partner to Power Global Websites," February 6, 2001.

[24]For example, see James P Neelankavil, Anil Mathur, and Yong Zhang, "Determinants of Managerial Performance: A Cross-Cultural Comparison of Perceptions of Middle Managers in Four Countries," *Journal of International Business Studies,* 2000, 31(1), pp. 121–140.

The complexities of the Japanese language confront second graders in Kyoto, where students write some of the 200-plus characters for the sound *shou*. The language commonly uses 15,000 kanji characters, which are borrowed from Chinese. The differences in the structure of the language from English make translation of questionnaires a most daunting task. (© Cary Wolinsky)

an English version can be translated into French and back translated, by a different translator, into the same English. In this process, the wording of the original instrument undergoes a change, and the version that is finally used and its translation have equally comprehensive and equivalent terminologies in both languages.

Regardless of the procedure used, proper translation and perfect use of the local language in a questionnaire are of critical importance to successful research design. Because of cultural and national differences, confusion can just as well be the problem of the researcher as of the respondent. The question itself may not be properly worded in the English version, or English slang or abbreviated words may be translated with a different or ambiguous meaning. Such was the case mentioned earlier with the word *outlet* for *retail outlet*. The problem was not with the translation as much as with the term used in the question to be translated. In writing questions for translation, it is important that precise terms, not colloquialisms or slang, be used in the original to be translated. One classic misunderstanding that occurred in a *Reader's Digest* study of consumer behavior in Western Europe resulted in a report that France and Germany consumed more spaghetti than did Italy. This rather curious and erroneous finding (see Exhibit 4.2, page 96) resulted from questions that asked about purchases of "packaged and branded spaghetti." Italians buy their spaghetti in bulk; the French and Germans buy branded and packaged spaghetti. Because of this crucial difference, the results underreported spaghetti purchases by Italians. Had the goal of the research been to determine how much branded and packaged spaghetti was purchased, the results would have been correct. However, because the goal was to know about total spaghetti consumption, the data were incorrect. Researchers must always verify that they are asking the right question.

Some of the problems of cross-cultural marketing research can be addressed after data are collected. For example, we know that consumers in some countries such as Japan tend to respond to rating scales more conservatively than Americans.[25] That is, on a 1 to 7 scale anchored by "extremely satisfied" and "extremely dissatisfied," Japanese may tend to answer more toward the middle (more 3s and 5s), whereas Americans' responses may tend toward the extremes (more 1s and 7s). Such a response bias can be managed through statistical standardization procedures to maximize comparability.[26] Some translation problems can also be detected and mitigated post hoc through other statistical approaches as well.

## Multicultural Research: A Special Problem

As companies become global marketers and seek to standardize various parts of the marketing mix across several countries, multicultural studies become more important.[27] A company needs to determine to what extent adaptation of the marketing mix is appropriate.[28] Thus, market characteristics across diverse cultures must be compared for similarities and differences before a company proceeds with

[25]George Fields, Hotaka Katahira, and Jerry Wind, *Leveraging Japan: Marketing to the New Asia* (San Francisco: Josey-Bass, 2000).

[26]Hans Baumgartner and Jan-Benedict E. M. Steenkamp, "Response Styles in Marketing Research: A Cross-National Investigation," *Journal of Marketing Research,* May 2001, 38, pp. 143–156.

[27]Thomas Tsu Wee Tan, and Tan Jee Lui, "Globalization and Trends in International Marketing Research in Asia," *Journal of Business Research,* October, 2002, 55(10), pp. 799–804.

[28]Erin White and Sarah Ellison, "Unilever Ads Offer a Tribute to Dirt—Campaign Signals Desire to Create Consistent Image for Global Array of Brands," *Wall Street Journal,* June 2, 2003, p. B3.

standardization on any aspect of marketing strategy. The research difficulties discussed thus far have addressed problems of conducting research within a culture. When engaging in multicultural studies, many of these same problems further complicate the difficulty of cross-cultural comparisons.[29]

**Multicultural research** involves dealing with countries that have different languages, economies, social structures, behavior, and attitude patterns. When designing multicultural studies, it is essential that these differences be taken into account. An important point to keep in mind when designing research to be applied across cultures is to ensure comparability and equivalency of results. Different methods may have varying reliabilities in different countries. It is essential that these differences be considered in the design of a multicultural survey. Such differences may mean that different research methods should be applied in individual countries.

In some cases the entire research design may be different between countries to maximize the comparability of the results. For example, Japanese, compared with American businesspeople, tend not to respond to mail surveys. This problem was handled in two recent studies by using alternative methods of questionnaire distribution and collection in Japan. In one study, attitudes of retail buyers regarding pioneer brands were sought. In the U.S. setting a sample was drawn from a national list of supermarket buyers and questionnaires were distributed and collected by mail. Alternatively, in Japan questionnaires were distributed through contact people at 16 major supermarket chains and then returned by mail directly to the Japanese researchers. The second study sought to compare the job satisfaction of American and Japanese sales representatives. The questionnaires were delivered and collected via the company mail system for the U.S. firm. For the Japanese firm, participants in a sales training program were asked to complete the questionnaires during the program. Although the authors of both studies suggest that the use of different methods of data collection in comparative studies does threaten the quality of the results, the approaches taken were the best (only) practical methods of conducting the research.

The adaptations necessary to complete these cross-national studies serve as examples of the need for resourcefulness in international marketing research. However, they also raise serious questions about the reliability of data gathered in cross-national research. There is evidence that often insufficient attention is given not only to nonsampling errors and other problems that can exist in improperly conducted multicultural studies, but also to the appropriateness of research measures that have not been tested in multicultural contexts.

---

[29]Masaski Kotabe, "Contemporary Research Trends in International Marketing," Chapter 17 in Alan Rugman and Thomas Brewer (eds.), *Oxford Handbook of International Business* (Oxford: Oxford University Press, 2001).

Marketing researchers in India have to consider the problems of language diversity in India. Here the primary 13 languages (besides English) are listed on a 20-rupee note.

# Research on the Internet: A Growing Opportunity

It is literally impossible to keep up with the worldwide growth in Internet usage. We know that at this writing there are more than 500 million users in more than 200 countries.[30] About one-third of the users are in the United States, but two-thirds of the hosts are there. International Internet usage is growing almost twice as fast as American usage. Growth in countries such as Costa Rica was dramatically spurred by the local government's decision to reclassify computers as "educational tools," thus eliminating all import tariffs on the hardware. The demographics of users worldwide are as follows: 60 percent male and 40 percent female; average age about 32; about 60 percent college educated; median income of about $60,000; usage time about 2.5 hours per week; and main activities are e-mail and finding information. The percentage of home pages by language is English, 80 percent; German, 3 percent; Japanese, 4 percent; French, 2 percent; Spanish, 1 percent; and all others less than 1 percent each.

For many companies the Internet provides a new and increasingly important medium for conducting a variety of international marketing research. Indeed, a survey of marketing research professionals suggests that the most important influences on the industry are the Internet and globalization. New product concepts and advertising copy can be tested over the Internet for immediate feedback.[31] Worldwide consumer panels[32] have been created to help test marketing programs across international samples. It has been suggested that there are at least seven different uses for the Internet in international research:

**1. Online surveys and buyer panels.** These can include incentives for participation, and they have better "branching" capabilities (asking different questions based on previous answers) than more expensive mail and phone surveys.

**2. Online focus groups.** Bulletin boards can be used for this purpose.

**3. Web visitor tracking.** Servers automatically track and time visitors' travel through websites.

**4. Advertising measurement.** Servers track links to other sites, and their usefulness can therefore be assessed.

**5. Customer identification systems.** Many companies are installing registration procedures that allow them to track visits and purchases over time, creating a "virtual panel."

**6. E-mail marketing lists.** Customers can be asked to sign up on e-mail lists to receive future direct marketing efforts via the Internet.

**7. Embedded research.** The Internet continues to automate traditional economic roles of customers, such as searching for information about products and services, comparison shopping among alternatives, interacting with service providers, and maintaining the customer brand relationship. More and more of these Internet processes look and feel like research processes themselves. The methods are often embedded directly into the actual purchase and use situations and are therefore more closely tied to actual economic behavior than traditional research methods can be. Some firms even provide the option of custom designing products online—the ultimate in applying research for product development purposes.

The city of Toronto, Canada, posts an online city guide (www.toronto.com). On it is a pop-up survey to solicit visitors' reactions and demographic information. The latter data are collected to help build visitor profiles, including browsing patterns, that can be used in promotional materials given to potential advertisers. More online research applications are reported by SurveySite (www.surveysite.com), a Toronto-based company.

---

[30]World Bank Development Indicators, 2004.

[31]Ely Dahan and V. Srinivasan, "The Predictive Power of Internet-Based Product Concept Testing Using Visual Depiction and Animation," *Journal of Product Innovation Management,* March 2000, 17(2), pp. 4–9.

[32]Information regarding worldwide Internet panels is available at www.decisionanalyst.com.

It is quite clear that as the Internet continues to grow, even more kinds of research will become feasible, and it will be quite interesting to see the extent to which new translation software impacts marketing communications and research over the Internet. Some companies now provide translation services for questionnaires, including commonly used phrases such as "rate your satisfaction level."[33] Surveys in multiple languages can be produced quite quickly given the translation libraries now available from some application service providers. Finally, as is the case in so many international marketing contexts, privacy is and will continue to be a matter of personal and legal consideration. A vexing challenge facing international marketers will be the cross-cultural concerns about privacy and the enlistment of cooperative consumer and customer groups.

The ability to conduct primary research is one of the exciting aspects about the Internet. However, there are some severe limitations because of the potential bias of a sample universe composed solely of Internet respondents.[34] Nevertheless, as more of the general population in countries gain access to the Internet, this tool will be all the more powerful and accurate for conducting primary research. Also, the Internet can be used as one of several methods of collecting data offering more flexibility across countries.[35]

Today the real power of the Internet for international marketing research is the ability to easily access volumes of secondary data. These data have been available in print form for years, but now they are much easier to access and, in many cases, are more current. Instead of leafing through reference books to find two- or three-year-old data, as is the case with most printed sources, you can often find up-to-date data on the Internet. Such Internet sites as www.stat-usa.gov provide almost all data that are published by the U.S. government. If you want to know the quantity of a specific product being shipped to a country, the import duties on a product, and whether or not an export license is required, it's all there via your computer.

In addition to government sources, there are many private websites that provide information free or for a nominal price. Visit www.exporthotline.com to find market research for 80 countries, directories of business listings, and imports and exports by product and country—just to name a few of the resources. For people interested in doing business in Japan, JETRO (www.jetro.go.jp), a Japanese trade organization, provides information ranging from how to do business in Japan to specific product studies. Likewise, many universities offer sites that have links to resources all over the world. One of the best is globaledge.msu.edu/ibrd/ibrd.asp.

There are volumes of good secondary data that can be accessed from your computer that will make international marketing research much easier and more efficient than it has ever been. Keep in mind, however, that this information must be validated, just as any secondary information should.

## Estimating Market Demand

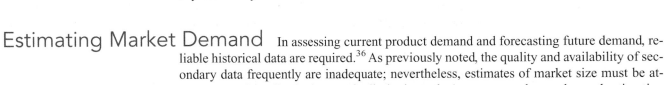

In assessing current product demand and forecasting future demand, reliable historical data are required.[36] As previously noted, the quality and availability of secondary data frequently are inadequate; nevertheless, estimates of market size must be attempted to plan effectively. Despite limitations, there are approaches to demand estimation that are usable with minimum information. The success of these approaches relies on the ability of the researcher to find meaningful substitutes or approximations for the needed

---

[33]See, for example, www.markettools.com.

[34]Arundhati Parmar, "Net Research Is Not Quite Global," *Marketing News,* March 3, 2003, pp. 51–52.

[35]Janet Ilieva, Steve Baron, and Nigel M. Healey, "Online Surveys in Marketing Research; Pros and Cons," *International Journal of Marketing Research,* 2002, 44(3), pp. 361–376.

[36]Although almost 20 years old, still the best summary of forecasting methods and their advantages, disadvantages, and appropriate applications is David M. Georgoff and Robert G. Murdick, "Manager's Guide to Forecasting," *Harvard Business Review,* January-February 1986, pp.110–120.

## CROSSING BORDERS 8.4 Forecasting the Global Healthcare Market

In 2000, Johns Hopkins Hospital in Baltimore treated more than 7,500 patients from foreign countries. That's up from just 600 in 1994. And there were no hassles with insurance companies and HMOs. In fact, many of these patients paid cash—even for $30,000 surgical procedures! The Mayo Clinic in Rochester, Minnesota, has been serving foreigners for decades. The number there has jumped by about 15 percent in five years. Similar growth is happening in places such as Mount Sinai Hospital in Miami, the University of Texas Cancer Center, and the UCLA Medical Center. The Mayo Clinic has even set up a Muslim prayer room to make patients and their families feel more comfortable. Fast growth, yes (some say exponential), but will it continue? Forecasting this demand so that decisions can be made about staffing and numbers of beds is a daunting project indeed.

Demand in Mexico and Latin America seems to be coming primarily for treatment of infectious and digestive diseases and cancer. Demand from the Middle East stems more from genetic diseases, heart diseases,

cancer, and asthma. From Asia, wealthy patients are coming mainly to California for treatment of cancer and coronary diseases. Europeans travel to the United States for mental illness services, cancer and heart disease, and AIDS treatments. Given that Japan has the world's best success rate for treating stomach cancer, one would forecast that to be a growth sector in the future.

But perhaps the strangest market to forecast is global war wounded. Recently Johns Hopkins contracted to replace limbs for soldiers involved in a border clash between Ecuador and Peru at $35,000 per patient. The description in the *Wall Street Journal* article might have been a bit overzealous: "There are wars all over the world, bombs all over the world. Casualty patients are a new and enriching market niche."

Sources: "U.S. Hospitals Attracting Patients from Abroad," *USA Today*, July 22, 1997, p. 1A; Ron Hammerle, "Healthcare Becoming a Lot Less Local," *Modern Healthcare*, March 20, 2000, p. 40; and Peter Landers, "U.S. and Japan Differ on a Cancer—Japanese Focus on Stomach Cancer Produces Better Results," *Wall Street Journal*, April 16, 2002, p. D6.

economic, geographic,[37] and demographic relationships. Some of the necessary but frequently unavailable statistics for assessing market opportunity and estimating demand for a product are current trends in market demand.

When the desired statistics are not available, a close approximation can be made using local production figures plus imports, with adjustments for exports and current inventory levels. These data are more readily available because they are commonly reported by the United Nations and other international agencies. After approximations for sales trends are established, historical series can be used as the basis for projections of growth. In any straight extrapolation, however, the estimator assumes that the trends of the immediate past will continue into the future. In a rapidly developing economy, extrapolated figures may not reflect rapid growth and must be adjusted accordingly. Given the greater uncertainties and data limitations associated with foreign markets, two methods of forecasting demand are particularly suitable for international marketers: expert opinion and analogy.

**Expert Opinion**   For many market estimation problems, particularly in foreign countries that are new to the marketer, **expert opinion** is advisable. In this method, experts are polled for their opinions about market size and growth rates. Such experts may be companies' own sales managers or outside consultants and government officials. The key in using expert opinion to help in forecasting demand is *triangulation,* that is, comparing estimates produced by different sources. One of the tricky parts is how best to combine the different opinions. Developing scenarios is useful in the most ambiguous situations, such as predicting demand for accounting services in emerging markets such as China and Russia or trying to predict the impact of SARS on tourism in Hong Kong.[38]

---

[37]For a fascinating description of the potential role of ambient temperature (and latitude) in forecasting demand, see Philip M. Parker and Nader T. Tavassoli, "Homeostasis and Consumer Behavior across Cultures," *International Journal of Research in Marketing*, March 2000, 17(1), pp. 33–53.

[38]Phillip Day, "Asians Decline Invitations to Go Out Shopping," *Wall Street Journal*, April 30, 2003, p. A15.

**Analogy**    Another technique is to estimate by **analogy**. This assumes that demand for a product develops in much the same way in all countries as comparable economic development occurs in each country. First, a relationship must be established between the item to be estimated and a measurable variable[39] in a country that is to serve as the basis for the analogy. Once a known relationship is established, the estimator then attempts to draw an analogy between the known situation and the country in question. For example, suppose a company wanted to estimate the market growth potential for a beverage in country X, for which it had inadequate sales figures, but the company had excellent beverage data for neighboring country Y. In country Y it is known that per capita consumption increases at a predictable ratio as per capita gross domestic product (GDP) increases. If per capita GDP is known for country X, per capita consumption for the beverage can be estimated using the relationships established in country Y. Caution must be used with analogy because the method assumes that factors other than the variable used (in this example GDP) are similar in both countries, such as the same tastes, taxes, prices, selling methods, availability of products, consumption patterns, and so forth. For example, the 13 million WAP (Wireless Access Protocol) users in Japan led to a serious overestimation of WAP adoptions in Europe—the actual number of 2 million was less than the 10 million forecasted for 2000. Or consider the relevance of the adoption rate of personal computers in the United States as it helps predict adoption rates in the other four countries listed in Exhibit 8.2. How might Apple Computer use the American data to help them predict demand in Japan? Despite the apparent drawbacks to analogy, it can be useful where data are limited.

All the methods for market demand estimation described in this section are no substitute for original market research when it is economically feasible and time permits. The best approach to forecasting is almost always a combination of such macroeconomic database approaches and interviews with potential and current customers. As more adequate data sources become available, as would be the situation in most of the economically developed countries, more technically advanced techniques such as multiple regression analysis or input-output analysis can be used.

Finally, it should go without saying that forecasting demand is one of the most difficult and important business activities. All business plans depend entirely on forecasts of

---

[39]These variables may be population and other demographics or usage rates or estimates, and so forth. Using combinations of such variables is also referred to as a *chain-ratio* approach to forecasting.

**Exhibit 8.2**    Personal Computer Diffusion Rate (per 1000 people)

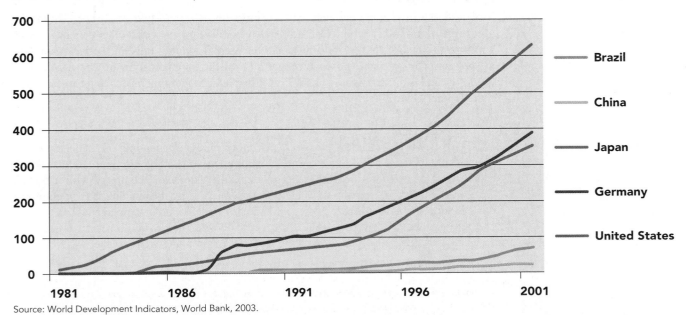

Source: World Development Indicators, World Bank, 2003.

a future that no one can see. Even the best companies make big mistakes. For example, Microsoft apparently didn't anticipate the waning interests of Japanese in video games in 2003.[40]

## Problems in Analyzing and Interpreting Research Information   After data are collected, the final steps in the research process are the analysis and interpretation of findings in light of the stated marketing problem. Both secondary and primary data collected by the market researcher are subject to the many limitations just discussed. In any final analysis, the researcher must take into consideration these factors and, despite their limitations, produce meaningful guides for management decisions.

Accepting information at face value in foreign markets is imprudent. The meanings of words, the consumer's attitude toward a product, the interviewer's attitude, or the interview situation can distort research findings. Just as culture and tradition influence the willingness to give information, so they also influence the information given. Newspaper circulation figures, readership and listenership studies, retail outlet figures, and sales volume can all be distorted through local business practice. To cope with such disparities, the foreign marketing researcher must possess three talents to generate meaningful marketing information.

First, the researcher must possess a high degree of cultural understanding of the market in which research is being conducted. In order to analyze research findings, the social customs, semantics, current attitudes, and business customs of a society or a subsegment of a society must be clearly understood. At some level it will be absolutely necessary to have a native of the target country involved in the interpretation of the results of any research conducted in a foreign market.

Second, a creative talent for adapting research methods is necessary. A researcher in foreign markets often is called on to produce results under the most difficult circumstances and short deadlines. Ingenuity and resourcefulness, willingness to use "catch as catch can" methods to get facts, patience, a sense of humor, and a willingness to be guided by original research findings even when they conflict with popular opinion or prior assumptions are all considered prime assets in foreign marketing research.

Third, a skeptical attitude in handling both primary and secondary data is helpful. For example, it might be necessary to check a newspaper pressrun over a period of time to get accurate circulation figures, or deflate or inflate reported consumer income in some areas by 25 to 50 percent on the basis of observable socioeconomic characteristics. Indeed, where data are suspect, such triangulation through the use of multiple research methods is crucial.

These essential traits suggest that an international marketing researcher should be a foreign national or should be advised by a foreign national who can accurately appraise the data collected in light of the local environment, thus validating secondary as well as primary data. Moreover, regardless of the sophistication of a research technique or analysis, there is no substitute for decision makers themselves getting into the field for personal observation.

## Responsibility for Conducting Marketing Research   Depending on the size and degree of involvement in foreign marketing, a company in need of foreign market research can rely on an outside foreign-based agency or on a domestic company with a branch within the country in question. It can conduct research using its own facilities or employ a combination of its own research force with the assistance of an outside agency.

Many companies have an executive specifically assigned to the research function in foreign operations; he or she selects the research method and works closely with foreign

---

[40]Mark Magnier, "Japanese Show Waning Interest in Video Games," *Los Angeles Times,* January 21, 2003, p. C1.

Ford keeps track of European technology and consumers at their research center in Aachen, Germany.

management, staff specialists, and outside research agencies. Other companies maintain separate research departments for foreign operations or assign a full-time research analyst to this activity. For many companies, a separate department is too costly; the diversity of markets would require a large department to provide a skilled analyst for each area or region of international business operations.

A trend toward decentralization of the research function is apparent. In terms of efficiency, it appears that local analysts are able to provide information more rapidly and accurately than a staff research department. The obvious advantage to decentralization of the research function is that control rests in hands closer to the market. Field personnel, resident managers, and customers generally have a more intimate knowledge of the subtleties of the market and an appreciation of the diversity that characterizes most foreign markets. One disadvantage of decentralized research management is possible ineffective communications with home-office executives. Another is the potential unwarranted dominance of large-market studies in decisions about global standardization. That is to say, the larger markets, particularly the United States, justify more sophisticated research procedures and larger sample sizes, and results derived via simpler approaches that are appropriate in smaller countries are often unnecessarily discounted.

A comprehensive review of the different approaches to multicountry research suggests that the ideal approach is to have local researchers in each country, with close coordination between the client company and the local research companies. This cooperation is important at all stages of the research project, from research design to data collection to final analysis. Further, two stages of analysis are necessary. At the individual country level, all issues involved in each country must be identified, and at the multicountry level, the information must be distilled into a format that addresses the client's objectives. Such recommendations are supported on the grounds that two heads are better than one and that multicultural input is essential to any understanding of multicultural data. With just one interpreter of multicultural data, there is the danger of one's self-reference criterion resulting in data being interpreted in terms of one's own cultural biases. Self-reference bias can affect the research design, questionnaire design, and interpretation of the data.

If a company wants to use a professional marketing research firm, many are available. Most major advertising agencies and many research firms have established branch offices worldwide. There also has been a healthy growth in foreign-based research and consulting firms. Of the ten largest marketing research firms in the world (based on revenues), four are based in the United States, including the largest; three are in the United Kingdom; one is in France; one is in Germany; and one is in the Netherlands. The latest count of marketing research firms in China is more than 400 and growing fast.[41] In Japan, where it is essential to understand the unique culture, the quality of professional market research firms is among the best. A recent study reports that research methods applied by Japanese firms and American firms are generally quite similar, but with notable differences in the greater emphasis of the Japanese on forecasting, distribution channels, and sales research. A listing of international marketing research firms is printed annually as an advertising supplement in the *Marketing News.*[42]

An increasingly important issue related to international marketing research is the growing potential for governmental controls on the activity. In many countries consumer privacy issues are being given new scrutiny as the Internet expands companies' capabilities to gather data on consumers' behaviors. However, perhaps the most distressing development in this area is China's recent crackdown on marketing research activities there. Please see Crossing Borders 8.3 for more details.

[41]Barton Lee, Soumya Saklani, and David Tatterson, "Top Prospects, State of the Marketing Research Industry in China," *Marketing News,* June 10, 2002, pp. 12–13.

[42]See the "Directory of International Marketing Research Firms," *Marketing News,* April 28, 2003, pp. 11–26.

**Exhibit 8.3**    Managing the Cultural Barrier in International Marketing Research

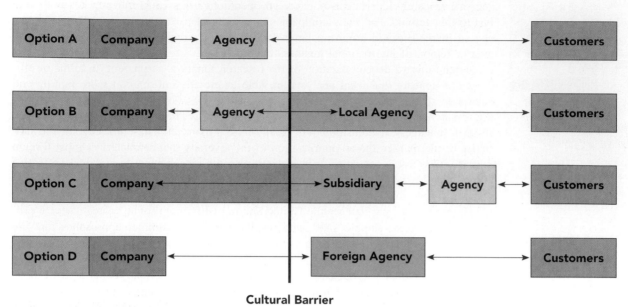

**Cultural Barrier**

## Communicating with Decision Makers
Most of the discussion in this chapter is about getting information from or about consumers, customers, and competitors. It should be clearly recognized, however, that getting the information is only half the job. That information must also be given to decision makers in a timely manner. High-quality international information systems design will be an increasingly important competitive tool as commerce continues to globalize, and resources must be invested accordingly.[43]

Decision makers, often top executives, should be directly involved not only in problem definition and question formulation, but also in the fieldwork of seeing the market and hearing the voice of the customers in the most direct ways when the occasion warrants it (as in new foreign markets). Top managers should have a "feel" for their markets that even the best marketing reports cannot provide.

Finally, international marketers face an additional obstacle to obtaining the best information about customers. At the most basic level, marketing research is mostly a matter of talking to customers. Marketing decision makers have questions about how best to serve customers, and those questions are posed and answered often through the media of questionnaires and research agencies. Even when both managers and customers speak the same language and are from the same culture, communication can become garbled in either direction. That is, customers misunderstand the questions and/or managers misunderstand the answers. Throw in a language/cultural barrier, and the chances of misinformation expand dramatically.

The four kinds of company-agency-customer relationships possible are presented in Exhibit 8.3. Options B and C are better suited for managing the cultural barrier across the chain of communication. That is, in both cases the cultural barrier is bridged *within* a company, wherein people have a common corporate culture and work together on an everyday basis. In option B the translation (in the broadest sense of the term—that is, of both questionnaires and reports) is worked out between employees of the international marketing research agency. In option C the translation is managed within the company itself. In options A and D both cultural and organizational barriers are being crossed simultaneously, thus maximizing the chances for miscommunication. These same company-agency-customer considerations are also pertinent to the other kinds of

[43]Milton Liebman, "Competitive Edge," *Medical Marketing & Media,* February 1, 2003, p. 36.

communications between companies and customers, such as advertising and distribution channel control, and this uniquely international topic is addressed again in subsequent chapters.

## Summary

The basic objective of the market research function is providing management with information for better decision making. This objective is the same for domestic and international marketing. In foreign marketing research, however, achieving that objective presents some problems not encountered on the domestic front.

Customer attitudes about providing information to a researcher are culturally conditioned. Foreign market information surveys must be carefully designed to elicit the desired data and at the same time not offend the respondent's sense of privacy. Besides the

cultural and managerial constraints involved in gathering information for primary data, many foreign markets have inadequate or unreliable sources of secondary information. Such challenges suggest three keys to successful international marketing research: (1) the inclusion of natives of the foreign culture on research teams; (2) the use of multiple methods and triangulation; and (3) the inclusion of decision makers, even top executives, who must on occasion talk directly to or directly observe customers in foreign markets.

## Questions

1. Define the following terms:

   marketing research, 212    back translation, 225
   international marketing    parallel translation, 225
      research, 212    decentering, 225
   research process, 214    multicultural research, 227
   secondary data, 215    expert opinion, 230
   primary data, 218    analogy, 231

2. Discuss how the shift from making "market entry" decisions to "continuous operations" decisions creates a need for different types of information and data.

3. Discuss the breadth and scope of international marketing research. Why is international marketing research generally broader in scope than domestic marketing research?

4. The measure of a competent researcher is the ability to utilize the most sophisticated and adequate techniques and methods available within the limits of time, cost, and the present state of the art. Comment.

5. What is the task of the international marketing researcher? How is it complicated by the foreign environment?

6. Discuss the stages of the research process in relation to the problems encountered. Give examples.

7. Why is the formulation of the research problem difficult in foreign market research?

8. Discuss the problems of gathering secondary data in foreign markets.

9. "In many cultures, personal information is inviolably private and absolutely not to be discussed with strangers." Discuss.

10. What are some problems created by language and the ability to comprehend the questions in collecting primary data? How can a foreign market researcher overcome these difficulties?

11. Discuss how decentering is used to get an accurate translation of a questionnaire.

12. Discuss when qualitative research may be more effective than quantitative research.

13. Sampling offers some major problems in market research. Discuss.

14. Select a country. From secondary sources found on the Internet compile the following information for at least a five-year period prior to the present:

    principal imports      principal exports
    gross national product      chief of state
    major cities and population      principal agricultural crop

15. "The foreign market researcher must possess three essential capabilities to generate meaningful marketing information." Discuss.

## Appendix: Sources of Secondary Data

For almost any marketing research project, an analysis of available secondary information is a useful and inexpensive first step. Although there are information gaps, particularly for detailed market information, the situation on data availability and reliability is improving. The principal agencies that collect and publish information useful in international business are presented here, with some notations regarding selected publications.

### A. Websites for International Marketing

1. www.stat-usa.gov. STAT-USA/Internet is clearly the single most important source of data on the Internet. STAT-USA, a part of the U.S. Department of Commerce's Economics and Statistics Administration, produces and distributes at a nominal subscription fee the most extensive government-sponsored business, economic, and trade information databases in the world today, including the National Trade Data Bank (see section B6 of this appendix), Economic Bulletin Board, and Global Business Procurement Opportunities.

**2.** www.ita.doc.gov. The website of the Commerce Department's International Trade Administration provides export assistance, including information about trade events, trade statistics, tariffs and taxes, marketing research, and so forth.

**3.** www.usatradeonline.gov. Provides import and export information on more than 18,000 commodities, but the user must subscribe.

**4.** www.census.gov/foreign-trade/www/. The U.S. Census Bureau provides a variety of international trade statistics.

**5.** www.odci.gov/cia/publications/pubs.html. Find the CIA *World Factbook* here, as well as other pertinent trade information.

**6.** www.customs.ustreas.gov. The U.S. Customs Service provides information regarding customs procedures and regulations.

**7.** www.opic.gov. The Overseas Private Investment Corporation (OPIC) provides information regarding its services.

**8.** www.exim.gov. The Export-Import Bank of the United States (Ex-Im Bank) provides information related to trade financing services provided by the U.S. government.

**9.** www.imf.org. The International Monetary Fund (IMF) provides information about the IMF and international banking and finance.

**10.** www.wto.org. The World Trade Organization (WTO) provides information regarding its operations.

**11.** www.oecd.org. The Organization of Economic Cooperation and Development (OECD) provides information regarding OECD policies and associated data for 29 member countries.

**12.** www.jetro.go.jp. The Japan External Trade Organization (JETRO) is the best source for data on the Japanese market.

**13.** www.euromonitor.com. Euromonitor is a company providing a variety of data and reports on international trade and marketing.

**14.** www.webofculture.com. The Web of Culture provides a variety of data on cultural dimensions such as language, gestures, and religion for a large number of countries.

**15. University-based websites.** Notable sites connected to several data sources include the Michigan State University Center for International Business Education and Research (globaledge.msu.edu/ibrd/ibrd.asp) and the University of California at Berkeley (www.lib.berkeley.edu/BUSI/bbg18.html).

**16.** www.worldchambers.com. The World Network of Chambers of Commerce and Industry provides data and addresses regarding chambers of commerce around the world.

**17.** www.ipl.org/ref/RR/static/bus4700.html. The Internet Public Library provides Internet addresses for dozens of sources of trade data worldwide.

**18.** http://iserve.wtca.org. The World Trade Centers Association provides information about services provided by the World Trade Centers in the United States, including export assistance, trade leads, training programs, and trade missions.

**19.** www.worldtrademag.com. *World Trade* magazine provides online its annual Resource Guide to products, goods, and services for international trade.

## B. U.S. Government Sources

The U.S. government actively promotes the expansion of U.S. business into international trade. In the process of keeping U.S. businesses informed of foreign opportunities, the U.S. government generates a considerable amount of general and specific market data for use by international market analysts. The principal source of information from the U.S. government is the Department of Commerce, which makes its services available to U.S. businesses in a variety of ways. First, information and assistance are available either through personal consultation in Washington, D.C., or through any of the US&FCS (U.S. and Foreign Commercial Service) district offices of the International Trade Administration of the Department of Commerce located in key cities in the United States. Second, the Department of Commerce works closely with trade associations, chambers of commerce, and other interested associations in providing information, consultation, and assistance in developing international commerce. Third, the department publishes a wide range of information available to interested persons at nominal cost.

**1. Foreign Trade Report FT410.** U.S. exports—commodity by country. The FT410 provides a statistical record of all merchandise shipped from the United States to foreign countries, including both quantity and dollar value of these exports to each country during the month covered by the report. Additionally, it contains cumulative export statistics from the first of the calendar year. You can learn which of more than 150 countries have bought any of more than 3,000 U.S. products. By checking the FT410 over a period of three or four years, you can determine which countries have the largest and most consistent markets for specific products.

**2. International Economic Indicators.** Quarterly reports providing basic data on the economy of the United States and seven other principal industrial countries. Statistics included are gross national product, industrial production, trade, prices, finance, and labor. This report measures changes in key competitive indicators and highlights economic prospects and recent trends in the eight countries.

**3. Market Share Reports.** An annual publication prepared from special computer runs shows U.S. participation in foreign markets for manufactured products during the last five-year period. The 88 reports in a country's series represent import values for the U.S. and eight other leading suppliers, and the U.S. percentage share for about 900 manufactured products.

**4. International Marketing Information Series.** Publications that focus on foreign market opportunities for U.S. suppliers. This series is designed to assemble, under a common format, a diverse group of publications and reports available to the U.S. business community. The following publications are made available on a continuing basis under this program:

*a.* Global market surveys. Extensive foreign market research is conducted on target industries and target business opportunities identified by the Commerce Department. Findings are developed into global market surveys. Each survey condenses foreign market research conducted in 15 or more nations into individual country market summaries.

*b.* Country market sectoral surveys. These in-depth reports cover the most promising U.S. export opportunities in a single foreign country. About 15 leading industrial sectors usually are included. Surveys currently available deal with Brazil, Nigeria, Venezuela, Indonesia, and Japan.

*c. Overseas Business Reports (OBR).* These reports provide basic background data for businesspeople who are evaluating various export markets or are considering entering new areas. They include both developing and industrialized countries.

*d.* Foreign economic trends and their implications in the United States. This series gives in-depth reviews of current business conditions, current and near-term prospects, and the latest available data on the gross national product, foreign trade, wage and price indexes, unemployment rates, and construction starts.

*e. Business America.* The Department of Commerce's principal periodical, a monthly news magazine, provides an up-to-date source of worldwide business activity, covering topics of general interest and new developments in world and domestic commerce.

**5. Trade Opportunities Program (TOP).** Overseas trade opportunities, private and government, are transmitted to the TOP computers through various American embassies and councils. U.S. business firms can indicate the product or products they wish to export and the types of opportunities desired (such as direct sales and representation) in countries of interest. The TOP computer matches the product interest of the foreign buyer's agent or distributor with the U.S. subscriber's interest. When a match occurs, a trade opportunity notice is mailed to the U.S. business subscriber.

**6. National Trade Data Bank (NTDB).** The Commerce Department provides a number of the data sources mentioned previously plus others in their computerized information system in the National Trade Data Bank. The NTDB is a one-step source for export promotion and international trade data collected by 17 U.S. government agencies. Updated each month and released on the Internet, the NTDB enables the reader to access more than 100,000 trade-related documents. The NTDB contains the latest census data on U.S. imports and exports by commodity and country; the complete CIA (Central Intelligence Agency) *World Factbook;* current market research reports compiled by the U.S. & Foreign Commercial Service; the complete *Foreign Traders Index,* which contains over 55,000 names and addresses of individuals and firms abroad that are interested in importing U.S. products; State Department country reports on economic policy and trade practices; the publications *Export Yellow Pages, A Basic Guide to Exporting,* and the *National Trade Estimates Report on Foreign Trade Barriers;* the *Export Promotion Calendar;* and many other data series. The NTDB is also available at over 900 federal depository libraries nationwide.

In addition, the Department of Commerce provides a host of other information services. Besides the material available through the Department of Commerce, consultation and information are available from a variety of other U.S. agencies. For example, the Department of State, Bureau of the Census, and Department of Agriculture can provide valuable assistance in the form of services and information for an American business interested in international operations.

## C. Other Sources

### 1. Bibliographies

*a. International Directory of Business Information Sources and Services.* 2d ed. London: Europa. Provides directory information on over 5,000 organizations, including details of libraries and publications.

*b.* Weekly, James K., *Information for International Marketing: An Annotated Guide to Sources* (Bibliographies and Indexes in Economics and Economic History, No. 3). Westport, CT: Greenwood. Lists and briefly annotates more than 190 government publications, databases, periodicals, and basic reference sources. Appendixes present brief directory listings for publishers, state trade contacts, U.S. foreign service offices in foreign countries, foreign embassies in the United States, the U.S. International Trade Administration, and international marketing journals.

*c. World Directory of Marketing Information Sources.* London: Euromonitor. (Also on CD-ROM.) Provides 6,000 entries, including libraries, market research companies, trade associations, trade journals, online sources, and international business contacts.

### 2. Directories

*a. American Export Register.* New York: Thomas Publishing, International Division. Annual. Includes an alphabetical product list with over 220,000 product and service listings in more than 4,200 separate categories as well as lists of U.S. and foreign embassies and consulates, chambers of commerce, world trade center clubs, U.S. and world ports, and banks.

*b.* Arpan, Jeffrey S., and David A. Ricks. *Directory of Foreign Manufacturers in the United States.* 5th enl. ed. Atlanta: Publishing Services Division, College of Business Administration, Georgia State University. Lists nearly 6,000 foreign-owned manufacturing firms in the United States.

*c. D&B Principal International Businesses Directory.* Wilton, CT: Dun's Marketing Services. Annual. (Also on CD-ROM.) Covers approximately 55,000 companies in 140 countries, listing businesses by product classification and alphabetically.

*d. Directory of American Firms Operating in Foreign Countries.* 14th ed. New York: World Trade Academy Press. Alphabetically lists U.S. firms with foreign subsidiaries and affiliates operating in over 125 countries; also lists the foreign operations grouped by countries.

*e. Directory of United States Importers and Directory of U.S. Exporters.* New York: Journal of Commerce. Annual. (Also on CD-ROM.) Contains verified business profiles on a total of 60,000 active trading companies. These annual guides also include a product index with the Harmonized Commodity Code numbers, customs information, foreign consulates, embassies, and international banks.

*f. Encyclopedia of Global Industries.* Detroit: Gale. Alphabetically covers 125 vital international industries, providing in-depth information including statistics, graphs, tables, charts, and market share.

*g. Export Yellow Pages.* Washington, DC: Venture Publishing North-America; produced in cooperation with the Office of Export Trading Company Affairs and International Trade Administration. Annual. Provides detailed information on over 12,000 export service providers and trading companies, agents, distributors, and companies outside the United States; also includes a product/service index and an alphabetical index.

*h. FINDEX: The Worldwide Directory of Market Research Reports.* London: Euromonitor. Annual. (Also on CD-ROM.) Abstracts and indexes more than 9,000 market research and company reports, spanning 12 broad product sectors.

*i. International Brands and Their Companies.* Detroit: Gale. Annual. Lists nearly 65,000 international consumer brand names attributed to 15,000 manufacturers, importers, and distributors, giving for each brand a description of the product, company name, and a code for the source from which the information was taken.

*j. International Companies and Their Brands.* 4th ed. Detroit: Gale. Lists 25,000 manufacturers, importers, and distributors and the nearly 80,000 brand names attributed to them, giving for each company the firm's address and telephone number and an alphabetical listing of its trade names.

*k. International Directory of Corporate Affiliations.* New Providence, NJ: National Register Publishing. Semiannual. Contains critical information on over 2,300 corporate parents with revenues of more than $50 million annually, 42,000 subsidiaries worldwide, and 54,000 key executives.

*l. International Tradeshow.* Frankfurt: m+a Publishers for Fairs, Exhibitions and Conventions. Semiannual. Contains detailed information on global trade fairs and exhibitions that are of national and international significance.

*m. Trade Directories of the World.* San Diego: Croner Publications. Looseleaf. Includes more than 3,000 trade, industrial, and professional directories in 1,000 categories in 175 countries.

*n. World Directory of Consumer Brands and Their Owners.* London: Euromonitor, 1996. Provides information on 17 market sectors, including consumer electronics, consumer healthcare, and leisure and entertainment.

*o. World Directory of Trade and Business Associations.* London: Euromonitor, 1995. (Also on CD-ROM.) Contains entries from a broad range of sectors, giving details of publications produced, aims and objectives of the association, and whether they provide assistance in further research.

*p. World Retail Directory and Sourcebook.* 2d ed. London: Euromonitor. (Also on CD-ROM.) Identifies over 2,000 retailers, breaking them down by country and classifying them by organization and type of product sold.

*q. Worldwide Franchise Directory.* Detroit: Gale. Irregular. Provides information concerning some 1,574 franchising companies in 16 countries, arranged by type of business in more than 80 categories.

### 3. Marketing Guides

*a. Export Market Locator.* Wilton, CT: Dun & Bradstreet. Annual. (Also on CD-ROM.) Identifies the five largest and five fastest-growing global markets for a product; software version provides statistical information on more than 5,000 product lines, allowing searching by SIC code, Harmonized Commodity Code, or keyword commodity description. Reports available for single products.

*b. Exporters Encyclopaedia.* Wilton, CT: Dun & Bradstreet. Annual. Comprehensive world marketing guide, in five sections; section two, "Export Markets," gives important market information on 220 countries (import and exchange regulations, shipping services, communications data, postal information, currency, banks, and embassies); other sections contain general export information. Also available are regional guides for Asia-Pacific, Europe, and Latin America, and export guides for single countries.

*c. International Business Handbook.* Binghamton, NY: Haworth Press. Includes a global overview as well as separate chapters on 15 countries or regions, covering such topics as consumer cultures, business customs, methods of entry, and global strategies.

*d. Reference Book for World Traders: A Guide for Exporters and Importers.* San Diego: Croner Publications. Looseleaf. Provides information required for market research and for planning and executing exports and imports to and from all foreign countries; under each country it provides a listing of services to exporters and importers, including marketing research organizations, marketing publications, and custom brokers.

*e. U.S. Custom House Guide.* Hightstown, NJ: K-III Directory Co. Annual. Provides a comprehensive guide to importing, including seven main sections: import how-to, ports sections, directory of services, tariff schedules (Harmonized Tariff Schedules of the United States), special and administrative provisions, custom regulations, and samples of import documents.

### 4. Demographic Data

*a. Consumer Europe.* London: Euromonitor. Annual. Provides demographic data on consumer products for the major countries of Europe and Eastern Europe, totals for the European Community, and comparison among the European Community, Japan, and the United States.

*b. European Marketing Data and Statistics.* London: Euromonitor, Annual. (Also on CD-ROM.) Presents data from 32 European countries on everything from economic indicators to transport infrastructure in spreadsheet form, including ten-year trend data for each country and a full list of useful information sources.

*c. International Marketing Data and Statistics.* London: Euromonitor. Annual. (Also on CD-ROM.) Presents extensive marketing data for all countries outside Europe, including ten-year trend data for most series.

*d. World Market Share Reporter.* 2d ed. Detroit: Gale. Provides market share data for hundreds of products, services, and commodities in countries of regions other than North America and Mexico.

### 5. Periodical Indexes

*a. ABI/INFORM.* Charlotte, NC: UMI/Data Courier. Weekly. (Computer file and CD-ROM.) Indexes and abstracts articles from some 1,000 business and management periodicals published worldwide. More than half the journals are indexed cover-to-cover, the others selectively. Abstracts are about 200 words long; available online on Data-Star, European Space Agency, Lexis-Nexis, Orbit Search Service, STN International, University Microfilm International, Ovid Technologies, and Knight-Ridder Information; and on CD-ROM as *ABI/INFORM Global Edition.*

*b. Predicasts F & S Index Europe.* Foster City, CA: Information Access Co. Monthly. (Print file, computer file, and CD-ROM.) Covers company, product, and industry information for the European Community (Common Market), Scandinavia, other regions in Western Europe, the former USSR, and East European countries in financial publications, business-oriented newspapers, trade magazines, and special reports; available online through Ovid Technologies, Data-Star, and Knight-Ridder Information and on CD-ROM as *Predicasts F & S Index Plus Text.* Abstracts in the computer file and on CD-ROM vary in length from 400 to 600 words and contain full text for many shorter articles.

*c. Predicasts F & S Index International.* Foster City, CA: Information Access Co. Monthly. (Print file, computer file, and CD-ROM.) Covers company, product, and industry information for Canada, Latin America, Africa, the Mideast, Asia, and Oceania in financial publications, business-oriented newspapers, trade magazines, and special reports; available online through Ovid Technologies, Data-Star, and Knight-Ridder Information and on CD-ROM as *Predicasts F & S Index Plus Text.* Abstracts in the computer file and on CD-ROM vary in length from 400 to 600 words and contain full text for many shorter articles.

### 6. Periodicals

*a.* Business Briefings. *Business Africa, Business Asia, Business China, Business Eastern Europe, Business Europe, Business Latin America, Business Middle East, Russia, India Business Intelligence, Crossborder Monitor, Ostwirtschafts-report.* New York: Business International. Biweekly or monthly. (Also on CD-ROM.) Reports issued for each title provide current news about companies, products, markets, and recent developments in laws and practices.

*b. Business Operations Report.* Eastern Europe, Middle East & Africa, Latin America, Asia. (Also on CD-ROM.) Provides hands-on operating information for setting up or operating a business, including information and commentary on new marketing and sales challenges and import and export policies.

*c. China Hand.* New York: Business International. Monthly. (Also on CD-ROM.) Provides comparative information on provinces and sites for setting up new operations and keeping up-to-date with regulatory changes and business developments.

*d. East Asian Business Intelligence.* Washington, DC: International Executive Reports. Biweekly. Provides sales and contracting opportunities for East Asian countries, including a brief description of the business opportunity, the person to contact, and the address, phone, and fax numbers.

*e. Investing Licensing and Trading Abroad.* New York: Business International. Semiannual. (Also on CD-ROM.) Directed toward companies that export directly or that have established subsidiaries, joint ventures, or licensing arrangements abroad; outlines business requirements for overcoming restrictions and other legal hurdles in 60 countries.

*f. Marketing in Europe.* New York: Economists Intelligence Unit. Monthly. Contains detailed studies of markets for consumer products in France, Germany, Italy, Belgium, and the Netherlands, including food, drink, tobacco, clothing, furniture, leisure goods, chemists? goods, household goods, and domestic appliances.

*g. Market Research International.* London: Euromonitor. Monthly. Each issue features diverse products and markets, focusing on international market review, global market trends and developments, U.S. market report, Japan market report, emerging market report, and market focus.

*h. World Commodity Forecasts: Industrial Raw Materials* and *Food, Feedstuffs and Beverages.* New York: Business International. Annual, with updates. Provide analysis of market trends, with specific price forecasts up to two years ahead for 28 commodities.

# emerging Markets

**CHAPTER 9**

## CHAPTER LEARNING OBJECTIVES

What you should learn from Chapter 9:

- The political and economic changes affecting global development

- The connection between the economic level of a country and the marketing task

- Marketing's contribution to the growth and development of a country's economy

- The growth of developing markets and their importance to regional trade

- The political and economic factors that affect stability of regional market groups

- The NIC growth factors and their role in economic development

# Global Perspective

## WAL-MART, TIDE, AND THREE-SNAKE WINE

Developing markets are experiencing rapid industrialization, growing industrial and consumer markets, and new opportunities for foreign investment. Consider the following illustration: In China, it is just a few shopping days before the advent of the Year of the Monkey and the aisles at the local Wal-Mart supercenter are jammed with bargain hunters pushing carts loaded high with food, kitchen appliances, and clothing. It could be the preholiday shopping rush in any Wal-Mart in Middle America, but the shoppers here are China's nouveau riche. Superstores have proven popular with Chinese consumers, who devote a large part of their spending on food and daily necessities. Wal-Mart has been able to tap into the Chinese sense of social status by offering membership cards that confer not only eligibility for special discounts but social status as well.

Alongside Campbell's soup and Bounty paper towels are racks of dried fish and preserved plums. One shelf is stacked high with multiple brands of *congee,* a popular southern Chinese breakfast dish, and another has *nam yue* peanuts and packets of bamboo shoots. In the liquor section in the back of the store is three-snake rice wine, complete with the dead serpents' bodies coiled together in the potent liquid. About 95 percent of what Wal-Mart sells in China is sourced locally.

At present Wal-Mart operates 1,200 units in nine foreign countries including ten in China. Revenues and profits are growing nicely for its international operations and overseas expansion is set to continue, particularly in China since its entry into the World Trade Organization. As one executive commented, "It boggles the mind to think if everybody washed their hair every day, how much shampoo you would sell [in China]."

The China market can be difficult to tap and may not be profitable for many years. Most foreign retailers are in a learning mode about the ways and tastes of the East, which are very different from those on Main Street U.S.A. Pricesmart designed its Beijing store with two huge loading docks to accommodate full-sized diesel trucks in anticipation of the big deliveries needed to keep shelves well packed. What the company found was Chinese distributors arriving with goods in car trunks, on three-wheel pedicabs, or strapped to the backs of bicycles.

Procter & Gamble offered powdered Tide detergent in large quantities, but China's oppressive summer humidity turned it into unwieldy clumps. Stocking large quantities of paper towels and disposable diapers didn't work well either—most customers didn't know what a paper towel was, and diapers were too expensive a luxury for most. Package sizes also posed a problem—small Chinese apartments could not handle the large American-sized packages.

On top of all that, foreign retailers have had to learn to deal with the uncertainty of China's complex and rapidly changing business climate, where personal connections matter more than business plans, and rules and regulations often are a matter of interpretation. "It doesn't matter what the law says," notes one retailer. "What matters is what the guy behind the desk interprets the law to say."

How do you sell $75 jeans or $150 wireless phones in a country where the per capita gross domestic product is only a couple thousand dollars a year? Marketing researchers found that extended families are showering their money on the kids, a common form of conspicuous consumption in the developing world. Even in China, the spending power of youth is nothing to discount. Studies have shown that the average 7- to 12-year-old in a large city has $182 a year in spending money—admittedly less than the $377 in France or $493 in the United States, but still a significant amount considering the huge population.

Sources: Keith B. Richburg, "Attention Shenzen Shoppers! U.S. Retail Giants Are Moving into China, and Finding the Learning Curve Formidable," *Washington Post,* February 12, 1997; David Barboza, "The Bold Struggle for China's Belly," *New York Times*, March 6, 2003, p. C1; and www.walmartstores.com.

The distribution of Coca-Cola is often one of the first signs of a country transforming from a command economy to free enterprise. Here the cyclo driver transports a promotional refrigerator in Ho Chi Minh City (formerly Saigon), Vietnam. (© AFP/CORBIS)

Not many years ago, large parts of the developing world were hostile toward foreign investment and imposed severe regulatory barriers to foreign trade. But few nations are content with the economic status quo; now, more than ever, they seek economic growth, improved standards of living, and an opportunity for the good life most people want as part of the global consumer world. China and other emerging markets throughout the world will account for 75 percent of the world's total growth in the next decade and beyond, according to U.S. Department of Commerce estimates. The transition from socialist to market-driven economies, the liberalization of trade and investment policies in developing countries, the transfer of public-sector enterprises to the private sector, and the rapid development of regional market alliances are changing the way countries will trade and prosper in the twenty-first century.

China, South Korea, Poland, Argentina, Brazil, Mexico, and India are some of the countries undergoing impressive changes in their economies and emerging as vast markets. In these and other countries there is an ever-expanding and changing demand for goods and services. As countries prosper and their people are exposed to new ideas and behavior patterns via global communications networks, old stereotypes, traditions, and habits are cast aside or tempered, and new patterns of consumer behavior emerge. Twenty-nine-inch Sony televisions in China, Avon cosmetics in South Korea, Wal-Mart discount stores in Argentina, Brazil, Mexico, China, and Thailand, McDonald's beefless Big Macs in India, Whirlpool washers and refrigerators in Eastern Europe, Sara Lee food products in Indonesia, and Amway products in the Czech Republic represent the opportunities in emerging markets.

A pattern of economic growth and global trade that will extend well into the twenty-first century appears to be emerging. It consists of three multinational market regions that comprise major trading blocs: Europe, Asia, and the Americas. Within each trading bloc are fully industrialized countries, as typified by Germany, Japan, and the United States; rapidly industrializing countries such as Mexico, Singapore, and South Korea that are close on the heels of the fully industrialized; and other countries that are achieving economic development but at more modest rates. Outside the triad of Europe, Asia, and the Americas are others at different levels of development striving to emulate their more prosperous neighbors. Indonesia, Malaysia, Thailand, and the Philippines are beginning to chase the leaders' tails, though from much lower levels of income. All four groups are creating enormous global markets. This chapter and the next explore the emerging markets and the multinational market regions and market groups that comprise the global trading blocs of the future.

## Marketing and Economic Development

The economic level of a country is the single most important environmental element to which the foreign marketer must adjust the marketing task. The stage of economic growth within a country affects the attitudes toward foreign business activity, the demand for goods, the distribution systems found within a country, and the entire marketing process. In static economies, consumption patterns become rigid, and marketing is typically nothing more than a supply effort. In a dynamic economy, consumption patterns change rapidly. Marketing is constantly faced with the challenge of detecting and providing for new levels of consumption, and marketing efforts must be matched with ever-changing market needs and wants.

Economic development presents a two-sided challenge. First, a study of the general aspects of economic development is necessary to gain empathy regarding the economic climate within developing countries. Second, the state of economic development must be studied with respect to market potential, including the present economic level and the economy's growth potential. The current level of economic development dictates the kind and degree of market potential that exists, while knowledge of the dynamism of the economy allows the marketer to prepare for economic shifts and emerging markets.

**Economic development** is generally understood to mean an increase in national production that results in an increase in the average per capita gross domestic product (GDP).[1] Besides an increase in average per capita GDP, most interpretations of the concept also imply a widespread distribution of the increased income. Economic development, as commonly defined today, tends to mean rapid economic growth and increases in consumer demand—improvements achieved "in decades rather than centuries."

**Stages of Economic Development**

The best-known model for classifying countries by **stage of economic development** is the five-stage model presented by Walt Rostow.[2] Each stage is a function of the cost of labor, the technical capability of the buyers, the scale of operations, interest rates, and the level of product sophistication. Growth is the movement from one stage to another, and countries in the first three stages are considered to be economically underdeveloped. Briefly, the stages are as follows.

**Stage 1: The traditional society.** Countries in this stage lack the capability of significantly increasing the level of productivity. There is a marked absence of systematic application of the methods of modern science and technology. Literacy is low, as are other types of social infrastructure.

**Stage 2: The preconditions for take-off.** This second stage includes those societies in the process of transition to the take-off stage. During this period, the advances of modern science are beginning to be applied in agriculture and production. The development of transportation, communications, power, education, health, and other public undertakings has begun in small but important ways.

**Stage 3: The take-off.** At this stage, countries achieve a growth pattern that becomes a normal condition. Human resources and social overhead have been developed to sustain steady development, and agricultural and industrial modernization lead to rapid expansion.

**Stage 4: The drive to maturity.** After take-off, sustained progress is maintained and the economy seeks to extend modern technology to all fronts of economic activity. The economy takes on international involvement. In this stage, an economy demonstrates that it has the technological and entrepreneurial skills to produce not everything, but rather anything it chooses to produce.

**Stage 5: The age of high mass consumption.** The age of high mass consumption leads to shifts in the leading economic sectors toward durable consumer goods and services. Real income per capita rises to the point where a very large number of people have significant amounts of discretionary income.

Although Rostow's classification has met with some criticism because of the difficulty of distinguishing among the five stages, it provides the marketer with some indication of the relationship between economic development and the types of products a country needs, and of the sophistication of its industrial infrastructure.

Alternatively, the United Nations classifies a country's stage of economic development based on its level of industrialization. It groups countries into three categories:

---

[1] Gross domestic product (GDP) and gross national product (GNP) are two measures of a country's economic activity. GDP is a measure of the market value of all goods and services produced within the boundaries of a nation, regardless of asset ownership. Unlike gross national product, GDP excludes receipts from that nation's business operations in foreign countries, as well as the share of reinvested earnings in foreign affiliates of domestic corporations.

[2] Walt W. Rostow, *The Stages of Economic Growth,* 2nd edition (London: Cambridge University Press, 1971), p. 10. See also W. W. Rostow, *The Stages of Economic Growth: A Non-Communist Manifesto* (London: Cambridge University Press, 1991).

**Exhibit 9.1**   Economic and Social Data for Selected Countries

| Country | Consumer Spending | | | | Health and Education | | |
| --- | --- | --- | --- | --- | --- | --- | --- |
| | Food ($ millions) | Percentage of Total | Clothing ($ millions) | Percentage of Total | Hospital Beds (per 1000) | Physicians (per 1000) | Literacy (%) |
| United States | 535,287 | 7.1 | 309,755 | 4.1 | 4.0 | 2.8 | 99.5 |
| Argentina | 20,249 | 24.3 | 4,475 | 5.4 | 3.3 | 2.7 | 96.9 |
| Brazil | 49,101 | 16.6 | 11,292 | 3.7 | 3.1 | 1.3 | 87.3 |
| Colombia | 14,278 | 27.2 | 1,489 | 2.1 | 1.5 | 1.2 | 91.9 |
| Mexico | 109,755 | 24.4 | 17,492 | 3.9 | 1.2 | 1.8 | 91.4 |
| Venezuela | 19,359 | 31.4 | 1,125 | 1.8 | 1.5 | 2.4 | 92.8 |

Source: Euromonitor, World Bank, 2003.

1. **MDCs (more-developed countries).** Industrialized countries with high per capita incomes, such as Canada, England, France, Germany, Japan, and the United States.

2. **LDCs (less-developed countries).** Industrially developing countries just entering world trade, many of which are in Asia and Latin America, with relatively low per capita incomes.

3. **LLDCs (least-developed countries).** Industrially underdeveloped, agrarian, sub-sistence societies with rural populations, extremely low per capita income levels, and little world trade involvement. LLDCs are found in Central Africa and parts of Asia.

The UN classification has been criticized because it no longer seems relevant in the rapidly industrializing world today. In addition, many countries that are classified as LDCs are industrializing at a very rapid rate whereas others are advancing at more traditional rates of economic development. It is interesting to note in Exhibit 9.1 the differences in consumer spending among the Latin American countries and the United States.

Countries that are experiencing rapid economic expansion and industrialization and do not exactly fit as LDCs or MDCs are more typically referred to as *newly industrialized countries* (**NICs**). These countries have shown rapid industrialization of targeted industries and have per capita incomes that exceed other developing countries. They have moved away from restrictive trade practices and instituted significant free market reforms; as a result, they attract both trade and foreign direct investment. Chile, Brazil, Mexico, South Korea, Singapore, and Taiwan are some of the countries that fit this description. NICs have become formidable exporters of many products, including steel, automobiles, machine tools, clothing, and electronics, as well as vast markets for imported products.

Brazil provides an example of the growing importance of NICs in world trade, exporting everything from alcohol to carbon steel. Brazilian orange juice, poultry, soybeans, and weapons (Brazil is the world's sixth-largest weapons exporter) compete with U.S. products for foreign markets. Embraer, a Brazilian aircraft manufacturer, sold planes to over 60 countries and provides a substantial portion of the commuter aircraft used in the United States and elsewhere. Even in automobile production, Brazil is a world player; it ships more than 200,000 cars, trucks, and buses to Third World countries annually. Volkswagen produced more than 3 million VW Beetles in Brazil and invested more than $500 million in a project to produce the Golf and Passat automobiles. The firm also recently announced a deal to sell $500 million worth of auto parts to a Chinese partner.[3] General Motors has invested $600 million to create what it calls "an industrial complex"—a collection of 17 plants occupied by suppliers such as Delphi, Lear, and Goodyear to

---

[3]Tony Smith, "Cultivating Partnership," *New York Times*, April 23, 2003, p. W1.

Another sign of Vietnam's emergence in the world economy is the dramatic effect new production there (on the left) has had on world coffee prices in recent years. World prices crashed from a high of $1.85 per pound in 1997 to about $0.50 in 2001, adversely affecting growers in Brazil (on the right) and all other countries. (© *Christopher Anderson/VII*)

deliver preassembled modules to GM's line workers. All in all, auto and auto parts makers are investing more than $2.8 billion aimed at the 200 million people in the Mercosur[4] market, the free trade group formed by Argentina, Brazil, Paraguay, and Uruguay.

Among the NICs, South Korea, Taiwan, Hong Kong, and Singapore have had such rapid growth and export performance that they are known as the "Four Tigers" of Southeast Asia. The Four Tigers have almost joined the ranks of developed economies in terms of GDP per head. These countries managed to dramatically improve their living standards by deregulating their domestic economies and opening up to global markets. From typical Third World poverty, each has achieved a standard of living equivalent to that of industrialized nations, with per capita incomes in Hong Kong and Singapore rivaling those of the wealthiest Western nations.

These four countries began their industrialization as assemblers of products for U.S. and Japanese companies. They are now major world competitors in their own right. Korea exports such high-tech goods as petrochemicals, electronics, machinery, and steel, all of which are in direct competition with Japanese and U.S.-made products. In consumer products, Hyundai, Kia, Samsung, and Lucky-Goldstar are among the familiar Korean-made brand names in automobiles, microwaves, and televisions sold in the United States. Korea is also making sizable investments outside its borders. A Korean company recently purchased 58 percent of Zenith, the last remaining TV manufacturer in the United States. At the same time, Korea depends on Japan and the United States for much of the capital equipment and components needed to run its factories.

## NIC Growth Factors

Both Rostow's and the UN's designations for stages of economic development reflect a static model in that they do not account for the dynamic changes in economic, political, and social conditions in many developing countries, especially among NICs. Why some countries have grown so rapidly and successfully while others with similar or more plentiful resources languish or have modest rates of growth is a question to which many seek answers. Is it cultural values, better climate, more energetic population, or just an "Asian Miracle"? There is ample debate as to why the NICs have grown while other underdeveloped nations have not. Some attribute their growth to cultural values, others to cheap labor, and still others to an educated and literate population. Certainly all of these factors have contributed to growth, but there are other important factors that are present in all the rapidly growing economies, many of which seem to be absent in those nations that have not enjoyed comparable economic growth.

[4]See www.guia.mercosur.com and/or www.mercosur.org.uy.

One of the paradoxes of Africa is that its people are for the most part desperately poor while its land is extraordinarily rich. East Asia is the opposite: It is a region mostly poor in resources that over the last few decades enjoyed an enormous economic boom. When several African countries in the 1950s (for example, Congo, the former Zaire) were at the same income level as many East Asian countries (for example, South Korea) and were blessed with far more natural resources, it might have seemed reasonable for the African countries to have prospered more than their Asian counterparts. Although there is no doubt that East Asia enjoyed some significant cultural and historical advantages, its economic boom relied on other factors that have been replicated elsewhere but are absent in Africa. The formula for success in East Asia was an outward-oriented, market-based economic policy coupled with an emphasis on education and health care. This is a model that most newly industrialized countries have followed in one form or another.

The factors that existed to some extent during the economic growth of NICs were as follows:

- Political stability in policies affecting their development.

- Economic and legal reforms. Poorly defined and/or weakly enforced contract and property rights are features the poorest countries have in common.

- Entrepreneurship. In all of these nations, free enterprise in the hands of the self-employed was the seed of the new economic growth.

- Planning. A central plan with observable and measurable development goals linked to specific policies was in place.

- Outward orientation. Production for the domestic market and export markets with increases in efficiencies and continual differentiation of exports from competition was the focus.

- Factors of production. If deficient in the factors of production—land (raw materials), labor, capital, management, and technology—an environment existed where these factors could easily come from outside the country and be directed to development objectives.

- Industries targeted for growth. Strategically directed industrial and international trade policies were created to identify those sectors where opportunity existed.[5] Key industries were encouraged to achieve better positions in world markets by directing resources into promising target sectors.

- Incentives to force a high domestic rate of savings and to direct capital to update the infrastructure, transportation, housing, education, and training.

- Privatization of state-owned enterprises (SOEs) that placed a drain on national budgets. Privatization released immediate capital to invest in strategic areas and gave relief from a continuing drain on future national resources. Often when industries are privatized, the new investors modernize, thus creating new economic growth.

The final factors that have been present are large, accessible markets with low tariffs. During the early growth of many of the NICs, the first large open market was the United States, later joined by Europe and now, as the fundamental principles of the World Trade Organization (WTO) are put into place, by much of the rest of the world.

Although it is customary to think of the NIC growth factors as applying only to industrial growth, the example of Chile shows that economic growth can occur with agricultural development as its economic engine. Chile's economy expanded at an average rate of 7.2 percent since 1987 and is considered one of the least risky Latin American economies for foreign investment. However, since 1976, when Chile opened up trade,

[5]Sadrudin A. Ahmed Alain d'Astous, and Jelloul Elijabri, "The Impact of Technological Complexity on Consumers' Perceptions of Products Made in Highly and Newly Industrialized Countries," *International Marketing Review*, 19(4/5), 2002, pp. 387–407.

Despite world-class scientists, the Indian pharmaceutical industry (with its ownership restrictions, price controls, and weak intellectual property restrictions) does not benefit from innovations and international investments compared to more open emerging economies such as China. (AP/Wide World Photos)

the relative size of its manufacturing sector declined from 27 percent of GDP in 1973 to 16.8 percent in 1995. Agriculture, on the other hand, did not decline. Exports of agricultural products have been the star performers. Chile went from being a small player in the global fruit market, exporting only apples in the 1960s, to one of the world's largest fruit exporters in 2000. Sophisticated production technology and management methods were applied to the production of table grapes, wine, salmon from fish farms,[6] and a variety of other processed and semiprocessed agricultural products. Salmon farming, begun in the early 1980s, has made salmon a major export item. Salmon exports to the United States are 40,000 tons annually, whereas U.S. annual production of farm-raised salmon is only 31,000 tons. Chile is also a major exporter of the fishmeal that is fed to hatchery-raised salmon.

Chile's production technology has resulted in productivity increases and higher incomes. Its experience indicates that there are ways other than manufacturing for countries to grow economically. The process is to continually adapt to changing tastes, constantly improve technology, and find new ways to prosper from natural resources. Contrast Chile today with the traditional agriculturally based economies that depend on one crop today (e.g., bananas) and will still depend on that same crop 20 years from now. This type of economic narrowness was the case with Chile a few decades ago when it depended heavily on copper. To expand its economy beyond dependency on copper, Chile began with what it did best—exporting apples. As the economy grew, the country invested in better education and infrastructure and improved technology to provide the bases to develop other economic sectors, such as grapes, wine, salmon, and tomato paste.

Regional cooperation and open markets are also crucial for economic growth. As will be discussed in Chapter 10, being a member of a multinational market region is essential if a country is to have preferential access to regional trade groups. As a step in that direction, in 2003 Chile and the United States signed a free trade agreement.[7]

## Information Technology, the Internet, and Economic Development

In addition to the growth factors previously discussed, a country's investment in information technology (IT) is an important key to economic growth. The cellular phone, the Internet, and other advances in IT open opportunities for emerging economies to catch up with richer ones. New, innovative electronic technologies can be the key to a sustainable future for developed and developing nations alike.

It is argued that because the Internet cuts transaction costs and reduces economies of scale from vertical integration, it reduces the economically optimal size for firms. Lower transaction costs make it possible for small firms in Asia or Latin America to work together to develop a global reach. Smaller firms in emerging economies can now sell into a global market. It is now easier, for instance, for a tailor in Shanghai to make a suit by hand for a lawyer in Boston, or a software designer in India to write a program for a firm in California. One of the big advantages that rich economies have is their closeness to wealthy consumers, which will be eroded as transaction costs fall.

The Internet accelerates the process of economic growth by speeding up the diffusion of new technologies to emerging economies. Unlike the decades it took before many developing countries benefited from railways, telephones, or electricity, the Internet is spreading rapidly throughout Asia, Latin America, and Eastern Europe. IT can jump-start national economies and allow them to leapfrog from high levels of illiteracy to computer literacy.

The Internet also facilitates education, a fundamental underpinning for economic development. The African Virtual University links 24 underfunded and ill-equipped

---

[6]Gene Barrett, Mauricio I. Caniggia, and Lorna Reed "There Are More Vets than Doctors in Chile," *World Development*, November 2002, 30(11), pp. 1951–1965.

[7]"Chile and U.S. Sign Accord on Free Trade," *New York Times*, June 7, 2003, p. 3.

African campuses to classrooms and libraries worldwide, and grants degrees in computer science, computer engineering, and electrical engineering. South Africa's School Net program links 1,035 schools to the Net, and the government's Distance Education program brings multimedia teaching to rural schools.

Mobile phones and other wireless technologies greatly reduce the need to lay down a costly telecom infrastructure to bring telephone service to areas not now served. In Caracas, Venezuela, for example, where half of the city's 5 million population lives in nonwired slums, cell phones with pay-as-you-go cards have provided service to many residents for the first time. The Grameen Bank, a private commercial enterprise in Bangladesh, has a program to supply phones to 300 villages. There are only four phones for every 1,000 people in Bangladesh, one of the lowest phone-penetration rates in the world. The new network will be nationwide, putting every villager within two kilometers of a cellular phone.

The Internet allows for innovative services at a relatively inexpensive cost. For example, cyber post offices in Ghana offer e-mail service for the price of a letter. Telecenters in five African countries provide public telephone, fax, computer, and Internet services where students can read online books and local entrepreneurs can seek potential business partners. Medical specialists from Belgium help train local doctors and surgeons in Senegal via video linkups between classrooms and operating centers and provide them with Internet access to medical journals and databases. It would be prohibitively expensive if they had to travel there to teach; via Internet technology, it costs practically nothing.

Substantial investments in the infrastructure to create easy access to the Internet and other aspects of IT are being made by governments and entrepreneurs. Hong Kong is investing in a $1.7 billion cyberport to house high-tech companies. If successful, it will create a new information economy and thousands of new jobs. Singapore's broadband network brings fast digital transmission capacity to homes and offices, allowing delivery of advanced multimedia services. Vietnam has entered the first stage of e-commerce development with the opening of a software zone in Hanoi and plans to spend $32.4 million to develop an information technology park.

India not only stands firmly at the center of many success stories in California's Silicon Valley (Indian engineers provide some 30 percent of the workforce there) but is also seeing Internet enthusiasm build to a frenzy on its own shores. Indian entrepreneurs and capital are creating an Indian Silicon Valley of their own. Dubbed "Cyberabad," exports are growing 50 percent annually and each worker adds $27,000 of value per year, an extraordinary figure in a country where per capita GDP is below $500. After a little more than a decade of growth, the Indian industry has an estimated 280,000 software engineers in about 1,000 companies.

Similar investments are being made in Latin America and Eastern Europe as countries see the technology revolution as a means to dramatically accelerate their economic and social development. As one economist commented, "Traditional economic reforms in the 1980s and 1990s managed to stop hyperinflation and currency crises, but further change will not produce significant new growth needed to combat poverty. Governments must work to provide public access to the Internet and other information technologies."

The IT revolution is not limited to broad, long-range economic goals; as Crossing Borders 9.1 illustrates, it can have an almost immediate impact upon the poorest inhabitants of an emerging country.

## Objectives of Developing Countries

A thorough assessment of economic development and marketing should begin with a brief review of the basic facts and objectives of economic development.

Industrialization is the fundamental objective of most developing countries. Most countries see in economic growth the achievement of social as well as economic goals. Better education, better and more effective government, elimination of many social inequities, and improvements in moral and ethical responsibilities are some of the expectations of developing countries. Thus, economic growth is not measured solely in economic goals but also in social achievements.

**CROSSING BORDERS 9.1** The Benefits of Information Technology in Village Life

Delora Begum's home office is a corrugated-metal-and-straw hut in Bangladesh with a mud floor, no toilet, and no running water. Yet in this humble setting, she reigns as the "phone lady," a successful entrepreneur and a person of standing in her community. It's all due to a sleek Nokia cell phone. Mrs. Begum acquired the handset in 1999. Her telephone "booth" is mobile: During the day, it's the stall on the village's main dirt road; at night, callers drop by her family hut to use the cell phone.

After the phone hookup was made, incomes and quality of life improved almost immediately for many villagers. For as long as he can remember, a brick factory manager had to take a two-and-a half-hour bus ride to Dhaka to order furnace oil and coal for the brick factory. Now, he avoids the biweekly trip: "I can just call if I need anything, or if I have any problems." The local carpenter uses the cell phone to check the current market price of wood, so he ensures a higher profit for the furniture he makes.

The only public telecom link to the outside world, this unit allows villagers to learn the fair value of their rice and vegetables, cutting out middlemen notorious for exploiting them. They can arrange bank transfers or consult doctors in distant cities and, in a nation where only 45 percent of the population can read and write,

the cell phone allows people to dispense with a scribe to compose a letter. It also earns some $600 a year for its owner—twice the annual per capita income in Bangladesh.

When members of the Grand Coast Fishing Operators Cooperative salt and smoke the day's catch to prepare it for market, it may seem light years away from cyberspace, but for these women the Internet is a boon. The cooperative set up a website that enables its 7,350 members to promote their produce, monitor export markets, and negotiate prices with overseas buyers before they arrive at markets in Senegal. Information technology has thus improved their economic position.

Finally, it seems that new technology can also breed new economic disputes. A disagreement over an unpaid $50 phone bill in a village 110 kilometers northeast of Dhaka, Bangladesh turned into a gunfight between two groups of villagers that left five dead and twenty-five injured.

Sources: Miriam Jordan, "It Takes a Cell Phone," *Wall Street Journal*, June 25, 1999, p. B-1; "A Great Leap: Developing Countries Are Finding Ways to Leverage Advances in Information Technology and Help Narrow the North–South Divide," *Time International*, January 31, 2000, p. 42; and "Bangladesh—Five Killed in Shootout over Telephone Bill," *Los Angeles Times*, March 31, 2003, p. A17.

Because foreign businesses are outsiders, they often are feared as having goals in conflict with those of the host country. Considered exploiters of resources, many multinational firms were expropriated in the 1950s and 1960s. Others faced excessively high tariffs and quotas, and foreign investment was forbidden or discouraged. Today, foreign investors are seen as vital partners in economic development. Experience with state-owned businesses proved to be a disappointment to most governments. Instead of being engines for accelerated economic growth, state-owned enterprises were mismanaged, inefficient drains on state treasuries. Many countries have deregulated industry, opened their doors to foreign investment, lowered trade barriers, and begun privatizing SOEs. The trend toward privatization is currently a major economic phenomenon in industrialized as well as in developing countries.

## Infrastructure and Development

One indicator of economic development is the extent of social overhead capital, or infrastructure, within the economy. **Infrastructure** represents those types of capital goods that serve the activities of many industries. Included in a country's infrastructure are paved roads, railroads, seaports, communications networks, and energy supplies—all necessary to support production and marketing. The quality of an infrastructure directly affects a country's economic growth potential and the ability of an enterprise to engage effectively in business. See Exhibit 9.2 for some comparisons of infrastructure among countries at different levels of economic development.

Infrastructure is a crucial component of the uncontrollable elements facing marketers. Without adequate transportation facilities, for example, distribution costs can increase substantially, and the ability to reach certain segments of the market is impaired. To a

**Exhibit 9.2**   Infrastructure of Selected Countries

| Country | Roads (1000 km) | Vehicles (per 1000 people) | Rail Lines (km) | Electrical Power (kwh per capita) | Mobile Phones (per 1000 people) | Personal Computers (per 1000 people) |
|---|---|---|---|---|---|---|
| United States | 6,304 | 759 | 160,000 | 12,331 | 451 | 625 |
| Brazil | 1,724 | 79 | 25,652 | 1,877 | 167 | 63 |
| China | 1,403 | 8 | 58,656 | 827 | 110 | 19 |
| Colombia | 113 | 51 | — | 788 | 76 | 42 |
| Germany | 231 | 529 | 36,652 | 5,963 | 682 | 382 |
| India | 3,319 | 7 | 62,759 | 354 | 6 | 6 |
| Japan | 1,162 | 560 | 20,165 | 7,628 | 588 | 349 |
| Kenya | 64 | 13 | 2,634 | 106 | 19 | 6 |
| Mexico | 330 | 151 | 17,697 | 1,655 | 217 | 69 |
| South Africa | 362 | 143 | 22,657 | 3,745 | 252 | 69 |
| Spain | 664 | 467 | 13,866 | 4,653 | 655 | 168 |

Source: Euromonitor, 2003.

marketer, the key issue is the impact of a country's infrastructure on a firm's ability to market effectively. Business efficiency is affected by the presence or absence of financial and commercial service infrastructure found within a country—such as advertising agencies, warehousing storage facilities, credit and banking facilities, marketing research agencies, and quality-level specialized middlemen. Generally speaking, the less developed a country is, the less adequate the infrastructure is for conducting business. Companies do market in less-developed countries but it is often necessary to modify offerings and augment existing levels of infrastructure.

Countries begin to lose economic development ground when their infrastructure cannot support an expanding population and economy. A country may have the ability to produce commodities for export but cannot export them because of an inadequate infrastructure. For example, Mexico's economy has been throttled by its archaic transport system, and some observers estimate that the system will grind to a halt if the economy grows at an expected 7 to 9 percent a year. Roads and seaports are inadequate, and the railroad system has seen little modernization since the 1910 revolution. If it were not for Mexico's highway system (although it, too, is in poor condition), the economy would have come to a halt; Mexico's highways have consistently carried more freight than its railroads. Conditions in other Latin American countries are no better. Shallow harbors and inadequate port equipment make a container filled with computers about $1,000 more expensive to ship from Miami to San Antonio, Chile (about 3,900 miles), than the same container shipped from Yokohama, Japan, to Miami (8,900 miles).

## Marketing's Contributions

How important is marketing to the achievement of a nation's goals? Unfortunately, marketing (or distribution) is not always considered meaningful to those responsible for planning. Economic planners frequently are more production oriented than marketing oriented and tend to ignore or regard distribution as an inferior economic activity. Given such attitudes, economic planners generally are more concerned with the problems of production, investment, and finance than the problems of efficiency of distribution.

There is a strongly held opinion (albeit wrong) that an economic system must first have the capacity to produce before the level of consumption and distribution becomes a problem. With this concept in mind, one developing nation invested $20 million in a fertilizer plant without making provisions for the sale and distribution of the product. After a few weeks of production, the plant accumulated a huge inventory it was unable to distribute effectively. Marketing problems had been ignored, resulting in excess inventory; the plant had to stop production, while a severe shortage of fertilizer existed in a nearby area. The country had production capability, but the product could not be distributed.

## CROSSING BORDERS 9.2 Infrastructure: India

Animals in India provide 30,000 megawatts (MW) of power, more than the 29,000 MW provided by electricity.

Because of the religious ban on the slaughter of cattle in almost all states in the country, India has the highest cattle population in the world—perhaps as many as 360 million head. Bullocks are used for plowing fields, turning waterwheels, working crushers and threshers, and above all for hauling carts. The number of bullock carts has doubled to 15 million since India's independence in 1947. Bullocks haul more tonnage than the entire railway system (though over a much shorter distance); in many parts of rural India they are the only practical means of moving things about.

As a bonus, India's cattle produce enormous quantities of dung, which is used both as farmyard manure and, when dried in cakes, as household fuel. Each animal produces an estimated average of 3 kilograms of dung per day. Some studies suggest that these forms of energy are the equivalent of another 10,000 MW.

Although Indian farmers prefer machines for plowing and hauling carts, bullocks and other draft animals are still in demand. Because it will take a long time for farmers to replace these draft animals with machines and there is concern that the better breeds may degenerate or become extinct, the government has developed an artificial insemination program to preserve the best breeds.

Sources: "Bullock Manure," *Economist*, October 17, 1981, p. 88; S. Rajendran, "India: Scheme to Preserve Local Cattle Breed on Anvil," *The Hindu*, August 9, 1997; "Not Enough Bulls to Till the Land," *Times of India*, May 9, 2000; and Tim Sullivan, "India's Leader in a Beef over Dietary Insult," *Los Angeles Times*, April 6, 2003, p. A20.

While it is difficult to compete with China's low manufacturing costs,[8] imagine marketing where there is production but little disposable income, no storage, limited transportation that goes to the wrong markets, and no middlemen and facilitating agents to activate the flow of goods from the manufacturer to the consumer. When such conditions exist in developing markets, marketing and economic progress are retarded. To some degree, this is the problem in China and many of the republics of the former Soviet Union. In China, for example, most of the 1 billion potential consumers are not accessible because of a poor or nonexistent distribution network. Indeed, the true consumer market in China is probably limited to no more than 20 percent of those who live in the more affluent cities. No distribution and channel system exists to effectively distribute products, so companies must become resourceful to make up for poor infrastructure.

For example, after nearly a decade of frustration in trying to effectively market and service its products in China, IBM took a bold step and entered a venture with the Railways Ministry that allowed IBM to set up IBM service centers dubbed the "Blue Express." The agreement created a national network of service centers in railway stations that has enabled IBM to ship computer parts via the railroad around the country within 24 hours; competitors must book cargo space weeks in advance. In addition, the ministry's staff of more than 300 computer engineers helps out by providing customer services on IBM products.

Such innovative thinking by IBM and other marketers often accelerates the development of a more efficient market system. IBM's service centers set an example of effective service before and after sales—important marketing activities. Management training for the thousands of employees of franchises such as Pizza Hut, McDonald's, and Kentucky Fried Chicken has spread expertise throughout the marketing system as the trainees move on to more advanced positions.

Marketing is an economy's arbitrator between productive capacity and consumer demand. The marketing process is the critical element in effectively utilizing production resulting from economic growth; it can create a balance between higher production and higher consumption. Although marketing may be considered a passive function, it is instrumental in laying the groundwork for effective distribution. An efficient distribution

---

[8]William M. Bulkeley and Jason Dean, "IBM Grabs Business from Asian Foundries," *Wall Street Journal*," May 8, 2003, p. B4.

and channel system and all the attendant middlemen match production capacity and resources with consumer needs, wants, and purchasing power.

## Marketing in a Developing Country

A marketer cannot superimpose a sophisticated marketing strategy on an underdeveloped economy. Marketing efforts must be keyed to each situation, custom tailored for each set of circumstances. A promotional program for a population that is 90 percent illiterate is vastly different from a program for a population that is 90 percent literate. Pricing in a subsistence market poses different problems than pricing in an affluent society. An efficient marketing program is one that provides for optimum utility given a specific set of circumstances. In evaluating the potential in a developing country, the marketer must make an assessment of the existing level of market development within the country.

### Level of Market Development

The level of market development roughly parallels the stages of economic development. Exhibit 9.3 illustrates various stages of the marketing process as it evolves in a growing economy. The table is a static model representing an idealized evolutionary process. As discussed earlier, economic cooperation and assistance, technological change, and political, social, and cultural factors can and do cause significant deviations in this evolutionary process. However, the table focuses on the logic and interdependence of marketing and economic development. The more developed an economy, the greater the variety of marketing functions demanded, and the more sophisticated and specialized the institutions become to perform marketing functions. The evolution of the channel structure illustrates the relationship between market development and the stage of economic development of a country.

As countries develop, the distribution and channel systems develop. In the retail sector, specialty stores, supermarkets, and hypermarkets emerge, and mom-and-pop stores give way to larger establishments. In short, the number of retail stores declines and the volume of sales per store increases. Additionally, a defined channel structure from manufacturer to wholesaler to retailer develops and replaces the import agent that traditionally assumed all the functions between importing and retailing.

Advertising agencies, facilities for marketing research, repair services, specialized consumer-financing agencies, and storage and warehousing facilities are facilitating agencies created to serve the particular needs of expanded markets and economies.

It is important to remember that these institutions do not come about automatically, nor does the necessary marketing institution simply appear. Part of the marketer's task when studying an economy is to determine what in the foreign environment will be useful and how much adjustment will be necessary to achieve stated objectives. In some developing countries it may be up to the marketer to institute the foundations of a modern market system.

The limitation of Exhibit 9.3 in evaluating the market system of a particular country is that the system is in a constant state of flux. To expect a neat, precise progression through each successive growth stage, as in the geological sciences, is to oversimplify the dynamic nature of marketing development. A significant factor in the acceleration of market development is that countries or areas of countries have been propelled from the eighteenth to the twenty-first century in the span of two decades by the influence of borrowed technology.

Marketing structures of many developing countries are simultaneously at many stages. It is not unusual to find traditional marketing retail outlets functioning side by side with advanced, modern markets. This is especially true in food retailing, where a large segment of the population buys food from small produce stalls while the same economy supports modern supermarkets equal to any found in the United States. On the same street as the Wal-Mart store described in the Global Perspective are mom-and-pop food stands. Exhibit 9.4 provides market indicators for selected countries.

### Demand in a Developing Country

Estimating market potential in less-developed countries involves myriad challenges. Most of the difficulty arises from **economic dualism**, that is, the coexistence of modern and traditional sectors within the economy. The modern sector is centered in the capital city

**Exhibit 9.3**  Evolution of the Marketing Process

| Stage | Substage | Example | Marketing Functions | Marketing Institutions | Channel Control | Primary Orientation | Resources Employed | Comments |
|---|---|---|---|---|---|---|---|---|
| Agricultural and raw materials | Self-sufficient | Nomadic or hunting tribes | None | None | Traditional authority | Subsistence | Labor<br>Land | Labor intensive<br>No organized markets |
|  | Surplus commodity product | Agricultural economy, such as coffee, bananas | Exchange | Small-scale merchants, traders, fairs, export-import | Traditional authority | Entrepreneurial Commercial | Labor<br>Land | Labor and land intensive<br>Product specialization<br>Local markets<br>Import oriented |
| Manufacturing | Small scale | Cottage industry | Exchange<br>Physical distribution | Merchants, wholesalers, export-import | Middlemen | Entrepreneurial Financial | Labor<br>Land<br>Technology<br>Transportation | Labor intensive<br>Product standardization and grading<br>Regional and export markets<br>Import oriented |
|  | Mass production | U.S. economy, 1885–1914 | Demand creation<br>Physical distribution | Merchants, wholesalers, traders, and specialized institutions | Producer | Production and finance | Labor<br>Land<br>Technology<br>Transportation<br>Capital | Capital intensive<br>Product differentiation<br>National, regional, and export markets |
| Marketing | Commercial—transition | U.S. economy, 1915–1929 | Demand creation<br>Physical distribution<br>Market information | Large-scale and chain retailers | Producer | Entrepreneurial Commercial | Labor<br>Land<br>Technology<br>Transportation<br>Capital<br>Communication | Capital intensive<br>Changes in structure of distribution<br>National, regional, and export markets |
|  | Mass distribution | U.S. economy, 1950 to present | Demand creation<br>Physical distribution<br>Market information<br>Market and product planning, development | Integrated channels of distribution<br>Increase in specialized middlemen | Producer<br>Retailer | Marketing | Labor<br>Land<br>Technology<br>Transportation<br>Capital<br>Communication | Capital and land intensive<br>Rapid product innovation<br>National, regional, and export markets |

# CROSSING BORDERS 9.3  Got Distribution Problems? Call Grandma or Your Local University!

It may sound trivial, but in China's teeming cities, getting cold carbonated drinks into the hands of the young can be a struggle. Fierce competitors Coca-Cola and PepsiCo rely on Grandma and hip college students with space-age coolers to slake Chinese thirst.

Coca-Cola was having problems with Shanghai's two main shopping streets, Nanjing Lu and Huaihai Lu. The area was becoming too expensive for the small stores that offered Coke. Further, traffic regulations were constantly changing, downtown deliveries required a special pass, and street vendors were banned. So how did Coca-Cola get its product to market? Enter one of the lingering remnants of the old communist regime: that bastion of the geriatric busybody, the Chinese street committee.

Initially the Chinese street committee consisted of older people whose job was to make sure all within their territory were being "good Chinese citizens." If not, they scolded scofflaws, and if that didn't work, reported them to higher authorities. To carry out their jobs committee members had privileged status. Anyone wearing the *zhi qin* (on duty) armband could pretty much go where they liked and do whatever they wanted. As the Chinese experienced more personal freedom, however, they resented being spied on and bossed around by self-important old people—the traditional role of the street committee was becoming obsolete.

The members, however, retained their privileged status, which, as Coca-Cola managers noted, meant they could push carts laden with ice-cold Coke around traffic and through street vendor–restricted areas of downtown Shanghai. So, each committee was recruited to store, chill, and sell ice-cold Coke on an exclusive basis on its turf. Coca-Cola has signed up a fleet of 150 pushcarts and 300 specially designed tricycles.

PepsiCo, facing a similar problem, recruited young, energetic, and outgoing university students to roam through the hottest and most crowded shopping areas. Toting space-age coolers strapped to their backs, the students dispense cups of cold Pepsi stored at 2 degrees Celsius. With a cup dispenser on one shoulder strap, a money belt, and a dispensing gun snaking around from behind, the student sellers are mobile vending machines—and walking, talking billboards.

The latest Coke/Pepsi contest in China is over the rights to use NBA star Yao Ming's image in ads. Even though the 7-foot-5 center for the Houston Rockets signed a deal with Pepsi and appeared in their TV ads for the Chinese market, his likeness concurrently appeared on bottles of Coke in Shanghai. It will be interesting to see how the companies decide to split the big guy—and we're sure the government will help "mediate" the dispute!

Sources: "Those Ever-Resourceful Coke Boys: Distribution Is It," *Business China*, April 28, 1997, p. 12; and Bruce Gilley, "Pepsi Gets Street Smart: In Its Campaign to Win over Young Chinese, Pepsi-Cola Is Drafting Student Ambassadors," *Far Eastern Economic Review*, June 2000, p. 37; and Peter Wonacott and Betsy McKay, "Yao is Pitchman Torn Between Two Colas," *Wall Street Journal*, May 16, 2003, p. B1.

and has jet airports, international hotels, new factories, and an expanding westernized middle class. Alongside this modern sector is a traditional sector containing the remainder of the country's population. Although the two sectors may be very close geographically, they are centuries apart in production and consumption. This dual economy affects the size of the market and, in many countries, creates two distinct economic and marketing levels. India is a good example. The eleventh largest industrial economy in the world, India has a population of approximately 1 billion, of which 200 to 250 million are considered middle class. The modern sector demands products and services similar to those available in any industrialized country; the remaining 750 million in the traditional sector, however, demand items more indigenous and basic to subsistence. As one authority on India's market observed, "A rural Indian can live a sound life without many products. Toothpaste, sugar, coffee, washing soap, bathing soap, kerosene are all bare necessities of life to those who live in semi-urban and urban areas."

In countries with dual sectors, there are at least two different market segments. Each can be profitable, but each requires its own marketing program and products appropriate for its market characteristics. Many companies market successfully to both the traditional and the modern market segments in countries with mixed economies. The traditional sector may offer the greatest potential initially, but as the transition from the

**Exhibit 9.4**   Market Indicators in Selected Countries

| Country | Population (millions) | GDP* (per capita) | Cars (per 1000 people) | TVs (per 1000 people) | Personal Computers (per 1000 people) |
|---|---|---|---|---|---|
| United States | 285.3 | $31,592 | 759 | 835 | 625 |
| Argentina | 37.5 | 7,468 | 181 | 326 | 91 |
| Australia | 19.4 | 24,203 | 601 | 731 | 516 |
| Brazil | 172.4 | 4,633 | 79 | 349 | 63 |
| Canada | 31.1 | 23,080 | 581 | 700 | 460 |
| China | 1,271.8 | 878 | 8 | 312 | 19 |
| France | 59.2 | 30,492 | 564 | 632 | 337 |
| Germany | 82.3 | 32,813 | 529 | 586 | 382 |
| India | 1,032.4 | 477 | 8 | 83 | 6 |
| Indonesia | 209.0 | 1,034 | 25 | 153 | 11 |
| Italy | 57.9 | 21,144 | 591 | 494 | 195 |
| Japan | 127.0 | 44,458 | 560 | 731 | 349 |
| Kenya | 30.7 | 325 | 13 | 26 | 6 |
| South Korea | 47.3 | 13,502 | 239 | 363 | 256 |
| Mexico | 99.4 | 3,739 | 151 | 283 | 69 |
| Poland | 38.6 | 3,716 | 286 | 401 | 85 |
| South Africa | 43.2 | 4,068 | 143 | 152 | 69 |
| Spain | 41.1 | 17,595 | 467 | 598 | 168 |
| United Kingdom | 58.8 | 22,592 | 424 | 950 | 366 |

*Constant 1995 dollars.

Source: World Bank, 2003. Copyright 2003 by TRANSACTION PUBS. Reprinted with permission of TRANSACTION PUBS via Copyright Clearance Center.

traditional to the modern takes place (i.e., as the middle-income class grows), an established marketer is better able to capitalize on the growing market.

Tomorrow's markets will include expansion in industrialized countries and the development of the traditional side of less-developed nations,[9] as well as continued expansion of the modern sectors of such countries. The traditional sector offers the greatest long-range potential, but profits only come with a willingness to invest time and effort for longer periods. Market investment today is necessary to produce profits tomorrow.

New markets also mean that the marketer must help educate the consumer. Procter & Gamble, Colgate, and Unilever[10] are all aggressively pursuing dental health education programs—from school visits to scholarships at dental universities to sponsorship of oral care research. While creating new markets for their products they are also helping to spread more healthful practices. In China, for instance, only about 20 percent of the population in rural areas brushes daily—most view brushing as purely cosmetic, rather than medicinal. P&G's efforts may change that attitude as school children frolic with Crest's giant inflatable Tooth Mascot, which appears when the mobile dental van makes a stop in the countryside. Crest's program reaches 1 million children in China each year.[11]

The companies that will benefit in the future from emerging markets in Eastern Europe, China, Latin America, and elsewhere are the ones that invest when it is difficult and initially unprofitable. In some of the less-developed countries, it may be up to the marketer to institute the very foundations of a modern market system, thereby gaining a foothold in an economy that will someday be highly profitable. The price paid for

[9]Sarah Ellison, "P&G Posts 15% Increase in Profit," *Wall Street Journal*, January 29, 2003, p. B4.

[10]Erin White and Sarah Ellison, "Unilever Ads Offer a Tribute to Dirt," *Wall Street Journal*, June 2, 2003, p. B3.

[11]"P&G in Touch with Consumer Needs," *Chain Drug Review*, June 7, 1999; and Normandy Madden, "China Warms up to P&G," *Advertising Age*, April 7, 2003, p. S5.

entering in the early stages of development may be lower initial returns on investment, but the price paid for waiting until the market becomes profitable may be a blocked market with no opportunity for entry.

## Developing Countries and Emerging Markets

The U.S. Department of Commerce estimates that over 75 percent of the expected growth in world trade over the next two decades will come from the more than 130 developing and newly industrialized countries; a small core of these countries will account for more than half of that growth.[12] Commerce researchers also predict that imports to the countries identified as big emerging markets (**BEMs**),[13] with half the world's population and accounting for 25 percent of the industrialized world's GDP today, will by 2010 be 50 percent of that of the industrialized world. With a combined GDP of over $2 trillion, the BEMs already account for as large a share of world output as Germany and the United Kingdom combined, and exports to the BEMs exceed exports to Europe and Japan combined.

Big emerging markets share a number of important traits. They

- Are all physically large
- Have significant populations
- Represent considerable markets for a wide range of products
- Have strong rates of growth or the potential for significant growth
- Have undertaken significant programs of economic reform
- Are of major political importance within their regions
- Are "regional economic drivers"
- Will engender further expansion in neighboring markets as they grow

Although these criteria are general and each country does not meet all the criteria, the Department of Commerce has identified those countries listed in Exhibit 9.5 as BEMs. Other countries such as Venezuela and Colombia may warrant inclusion in the near future. The list is fluid because some countries drop off whereas others are added as economic conditions change. Inducements for those doing business in BEMs include Export-Import Bank loans and political-risk insurance channeled into these areas.

The BEMs differ from other developing countries in that they import more than smaller markets and more than economies of similar size. As they embark on economic development, demand increases for capital goods to build their manufacturing base and develop infrastructure. Increased economic activity means more jobs and more income to spend on products not yet produced locally. Thus, as their economies expand, there is an accelerated growth in demand for goods and services, much of which must be imported. BEM merchandise imports are expected to be nearly $1 trillion ($1,000,000,000,000) higher than they were in 1990; if services are added, the amount jumps beyond the trillion-dollar mark.

Because many of these countries lack modern infrastructure, much of the expected growth will be in industrial sectors such as information technology, environmental technology, transportation, energy technology, healthcare technology, and financial services. India, for example, has less than 40 million telephone lines to serve a population of 1 billion, and Turkey's plans for improving health services will increase the demand for private hospital services and investments in new equipment.

What is occurring in the BEMs is analogous to the situation after World War II when tremendous demand was created during the reconstruction of Europe. As Europe rebuilt its infrastructure and industrial base, demand for capital goods exploded; as more money

[12]C.K. Prahalad, Allen Hammond, "Serving the World's Poor, Profitably," *Harvard Business Review*, September 2002, 80(9), pp. 24–32.

[13]For more information on emerging markets see www.library.yale.edu/socsci/emerge/bigten.html.

**Exhibit 9.5** Big Emerging Markets

| Country | Population (millions) | GDP* (billions) | GDP* (per capita) | Imports of Goods and Services (billions) | Exports of Goods and Services (billions) |
|---|---|---|---|---|---|
| **Asia** | | | | | |
| China | 1,271.8 | $1,117.2 | $ 878 | $371.4 | $457.4 |
| India | 1,032.4 | 492.5 | 477 | 80.4 | 78.0 |
| South Korea | 47.3 | 639.2 | 13,502 | 213.8 | 320.9 |
| **Latin America** | | | | | |
| Argentina | 37.5 | 280.0 | 7,468 | 32.0 | 34.7 |
| Brazil | 172.4 | 798.8 | 4,633 | 79.9 | 86.0 |
| Colombia | 43.0 | 98.0 | 2,277 | 18.4 | 18.8 |
| Mexico | 99.4 | 372.7 | 3,739 | 188.0 | 158.5 |
| Venezuela | 24.6 | 81.9 | 3,326 | 23.7 | 24.8 |
| **Europe** | | | | | |
| Poland | 38.6 | 143.6 | 3,716 | 56.5 | 54.1 |
| Turkey | 68.5 | 190.3 | 2,873 | 56.5 | 65.2 |
| **Africa** | | | | | |
| South Africa | 43.2 | 175.9 | 4,068 | 42.0 | 46.2 |

*Constant 1995 dollars.

Source: World Bank, 2003. Copyright 2003 by TRANSACTION PUBS. Reproduced with permission of TRANSACTION PUBS via Copyright Clearance Center.

was infused into its economies, consumer demand also increased rapidly. For more than a decade, Europe could not supply its increasing demand for industrial and consumer goods. During that period, the United States was the principal supplier because most of the rest of the world was rebuilding or had underdeveloped economies. Meeting this demand produced one of the largest economic booms the United States had ever experienced. As we shall see later in the chapter, consumer markets and market segments in the BEMs are already booming. Unlike the situation after World War II, however, the competition will be fierce as Japan, Europe, the NICs, and the United States vie for these big emerging markets.

**The Americas** A political and economic revolution has been taking place in the Americas (see Exhibit 9.6) over the last two decades.[14] Most of the countries have moved from military dictatorships to democratically elected governments, and sweeping economic and trade liberalization is replacing the economic model most Latin American countries followed for decades. Privatization of state-owned enterprises and other economic, monetary, and trade policy reforms show a broad shift away from the inward-looking policies of import substitution (that is, manufacturing products at home rather than importing them) and protectionism so prevalent earlier. The trend toward privatization of state-owned enterprises in the Americas followed a period in which governments dominated economic life for most of the twentieth century. State ownership was once considered the ideal engine for economic growth. Instead of economic growth, however, they ended up with inflated public-sector bureaucracies, complicated and unpredictable regulatory environments, the outright exclusion of foreign and domestic private ownership, and inefficient public companies.

Today many Latin American countries are at roughly the same stage of liberalization that launched the dynamic growth in Asia during the 1980s and 1990s. In a positive response to these reforms, investors have invested billions of dollars in manufacturing plants, airlines, banks, public works, and telecommunications systems. Because of its size and resource base, the Latin American market has always been considered to have great economic and market possibilities. The population of nearly 460 million

[14] There are several websites for information on countries in the Americas: www.enterweb.org/latin.htm, www.oas.org, and www.lanic.utexas.edu.

**CROSSING BORDERS 9.4**  Marketing in the Third World: Teaching, Pricing, and Community Usage

Much of the marketing challenge in the developing world, which is not accustomed to consumer products, is to get consumers to use the product and to offer it in the right sizes. For example, because many Latin American consumers can't afford a 7-ounce bottle of shampoo, Gillette sells it in half-ounce plastic bottles. And in Brazil, the company sells Right Guard in plastic squeeze bottles instead of metal cans.

But the toughest task for Gillette is convincing Third World men to shave. Portable theaters called mobile propaganda units are sent into villages to show movies and commercials that tout daily shaving. In South African and Indonesian versions, a bewildered bearded man enters a locker room where clean-shaven friends show him how to shave. In the Mexican film, a handsome sheriff is tracking bandits who have kidnapped a woman. He pauses on the trail and snaps a double-edged blade into his razor and lathers his face to shave. In the end, of course, the smooth-faced sheriff gets the woman. From packaging blades so that they can be sold one at a time to educating the unshaven about the joys of a smooth face, Gillette is pursuing a growth strategy in the developing world.

What Gillette does for shaving, Colgate-Palmolive does for oral hygiene. Video vans sent into rural India show an infomercial designed to teach the benefits of toothpaste and the proper method of brushing one's teeth. "If they saw the toothpaste tube, they wouldn't know what to do with it," says the company's Indian marketing manager. The people need to be educated about the need for toothpaste and then how to use the product. Toothpaste consumption has doubled in rural India in a six-year period.

Educating people to use a product and offering it at an affordable price are important tactics in emerging markets. So is making unaffordable products available through "community usage." The idea is that to increase usage of a product or service, a consumer need not own it but need only have access to it. Private telephones, for example, did not produce the income newly privatized companies anticipated. India's 20 million private phones averaged only $229 of revenue per year. The average revenue per pay phone (called public call offices), by contrast, exceeds $6,870. Community usage provided an unanticipated opportunity, and companies have shifted emphasis to expanding a network of pay phones.

There are over 6 million PC computers in Indian households and some 8 million Internet users. Several companies are seeking to tap into this opportunity with community usage. One U.K.-based company has a contract with the state of Tamil Nadu to set up 13,000 community Internet cafes and are in discussions for similar installations with other state governments.

Source: David Wessel, "Gillette Keys Sales to Third World Taste," *Wall Street Journal,* January 23, 1986, p. 30; "Selling to India," *Economist,* May 1, 2000; and Raja Ramachandran, "Understanding the Market Environment of India," *Business Horizons,* January/February 2000, p. 44; and World Bank, 2003.

is one-half greater than that of the United States and 100 million more than the European Community.

The strength of these reforms has been tested during the last decade, a turbulent period both economically and politically for some countries. Argentina, Brazil, and Mexico, the three BEMs in Latin America, were affected by the economic meltdown in Asia and the continuing financial crisis in Russia. The Russian devaluation and debt default caused a rapid deterioration in Brazil's financial situation; capital began to flee the country, and Brazil[15] devalued its currency. Economic recession in Brazil—coupled with the sharp devaluation of the real—reduced Argentine exports, and Argentina's economic growth slowed.[16] Mexico was able to weather the Russian debt default partly because of debt restructuring and other changes after the major devaluation and recession in the early 1990s. Other Latin American countries suffered economic downturns that led to devaluations and in some cases political instability. Nevertheless, Latin America is still working toward economic reform.

---

[15]*The Economist* provides an in-depth study of the Brazilian economy—see "Make or Break, A Survey of Brazil," February 22, 2003, pp. 1–16.

[16]Stephan Richter, "Ford's Debt Trap," *Chief Executive,* March 2003, p. 26.

**Exhibit 9.6**
The Americas

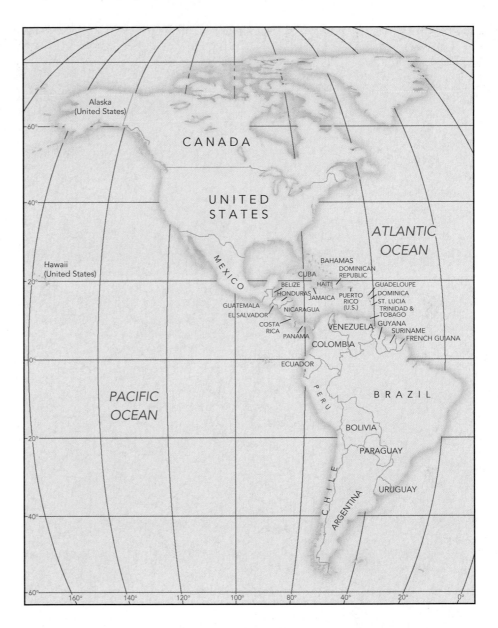

**Eastern Europe and the Baltic States**

Eastern Europe and the Baltic states (see Exhibit 9.7), satellite nations of the former USSR, have moved steadily toward establishing postcommunist market reforms.[17] New business opportunities are emerging almost daily, and the region is described as anywhere from chaotic with big risks to an exciting place with untold opportunities. Both descriptions fit as countries continue to adjust to the political, social, and economic realities of changing from the restrictions of a Marxist-socialist system to some version of free markets and capitalism. However, not all of the countries have made the same progress, nor have they had the same success in economic reform and growth.

A little more than a decade after the fall of the Berlin Wall, five countries in Central Europe are fully integrated with the world economy and likely to join the European Union, while some countries in the former Soviet Union and the Balkans are struggling. For example, Poland's economic output has continued at a steady pace upward since 1990, whereas Ukraine's has shrunk by half. And while Russian businesses struggle to raise cash at any price, companies in Hungary borrow at rates close to Western European levels.

[17]For detailed information on each of the Eastern European countries (indeed, on any country), visit www.stat-usa.gov and click on Globus & NTDB, then click on the Country Commercial Guide.

**Exhibit 9.7**
Eastern Europe and the
Baltic States

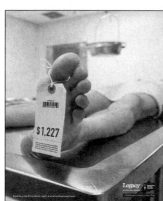

As demand for tobacco declines in the more developed countries, manufacturers direct more marketing efforts in the direction of emerging economies. Indeed, recently Philip Morris published a report estimating the cost savings for the Czech government every time a smoker dies, that is, $1,227. Apparently, they did not think through the public relations implications of this grisly bit of research. (*Courtesy American Legacy Foundation, American Cancer Society, and Campaign for Tobacco Free Kids*)

The differences can be explained in part by factors ranging from religion and culture to the political complexion of the countries' first post-1998 governments. However, a consensus is emerging that while these factors were important, the decisive factor has been sweeping economic change. Those countries that rapidly instituted the broadest free market policies and implemented the most radical reforms (such as extensive privatization of small and medium-size enterprises and banking reforms) prospered most in the long run. Rapid liberalization of trade combined with their macroeconomic stabilization policies and broad institutional reforms created a supportive environment for the expansion and reorientation of their trade. Since the early 1990s Eastern European countries' trade has been redirected away from dependence on former socialist countries and toward the more affluent Western European markets, thus resulting in trade patterns that are more in tune with both historical (pre–World War II) and current market realities.

**Eastern Europe.**    It is dangerous to generalize beyond a few points about Eastern Europe because each of the countries has its own economic problems and is at a different stage in its evolution from a socialist to a market-driven economy (see Exhibit 9.8). Most Eastern European countries are privatizing state-owned enterprises, establishing

**Exhibit 9.8**   Eastern European Markets

| Country | Population (millions) | GDP* (billions) | GDP* (per capita) | Imports of Goods and Services (billions) | Exports of Goods and Services (billions) |
|---|---|---|---|---|---|
| Albania | 3.2 | $ 3.3 | $ 1,032 | $ 1.2 | $ 0.5 |
| Bosnia/Herzegovina | 4.1 | 6.4 | 1,584 | 3.5 | 1.7 |
| Bulgaria | 7.9 | 13.1 | 1,630 | 10.8 | 8.5 |
| Croatia | 4.4 | 23.5 | 5,355 | 13.1 | 10.6 |
| Czech Republic | 10.2 | 57.1 | 5,583 | 51.1 | 46.1 |
| Hungary | 10.2 | 56.4 | 5,540 | 38.0 | 36.6 |
| Macedonia | 2.0 | 4.9 | 2,417 | 2.6 | 2.0 |
| Poland | 38.6 | 143.6 | 3,716 | 56.5 | 54.1 |
| Romania | 22.4 | 31.2 | 1,393 | 20.0 | 14.5 |
| Slovak Republic | 5.4 | 23.8 | 4,405 | 19.6 | 18.6 |
| Slovenia | 2.0 | 23.9 | 11,984 | 15.5 | 14.6 |

*Constant 1994 dollars.

Source: World Bank, 2003. Copyright 2003 by TRANSACTION PUBS. Reproduced with permission of TRANSACTION PUBS via Copyright Clearance Center.

free market pricing systems, relaxing import controls, and wrestling with inflation. The very different paths taken toward market economies have resulted in different levels of progress. Countries such as the Czech Republic, which moved quickly to introduce major changes, seem to have fared better than countries such as Hungary, Poland, and Romania, which held off privatizing until the government restructured internally. Moving quickly allows the transformation to be guided mainly by the spontaneity of innovative market forces rather than by government planners or technocrats. Those countries that took the slow road permitted the bureaucrats from communist days to organize effectively to delay and even derail the transition to a market economy.

Yugoslavia has been plagued with internal strife over ethnic divisions, and four of its republics (Croatia, Slovenia, Macedonia, and Bosnia/Herzegovina) seceded from the federation, leaving Serbia and Montenegro in the reduced Federal Republic of Yugoslavia. Soon after seceding, a devastating ethnic war broke out in Croatia and Bosnia/Herzegovina that decimated their economies. A tentative peace, maintained by United Nations peacekeepers, now exists, but for all practical purposes the economies of Croatia and Bosnia are worse now than ever before.

Nevertheless, most countries in the region continue to make progress in building market-oriented institutions and adopting legislation that conforms to that of advanced market economies.[18] The Czech Republic, Hungary, the Slovak Republic, and Poland have become members of the OECD.[19] Joining the OECD means they accept the obligations of the OECD to modernize their economies and to maintain sound macroeconomic policies and market-oriented structural reforms. These four countries are on the fast track to become members of the European Union,[20] but the initial target date of 2003 has been moved back to 2006, which to some EU member states[21] is a more realistic target date. This delay is causing some consternation on the part of the first tier of applicants because they have been making the internal changes necessary for membership. Delay can be harmful economically and politically. These countries are eager to stabilize their developing democracies and their westward tilt in foreign and security policies. Postponing membership means they have to wait longer without free access to the EU's single markets. As a consequence, reforms, encouraged by the prospect of membership, may be slowed or reversed.

[18]Claudia H. Deutsch, "In a Dull Economy, Avon Finds a Hidden Gloss," *New York Times*, June 1, 2003, p. B4.

[19]www.oecd.org.

[20]James Mehring, "High Hurdles for New EU Members to Clear," *BusinessWeek*, May 5, 2003, p. 26.

[21]See the EU website at europa.eu.int.

**Exhibit 9.9**
Asia

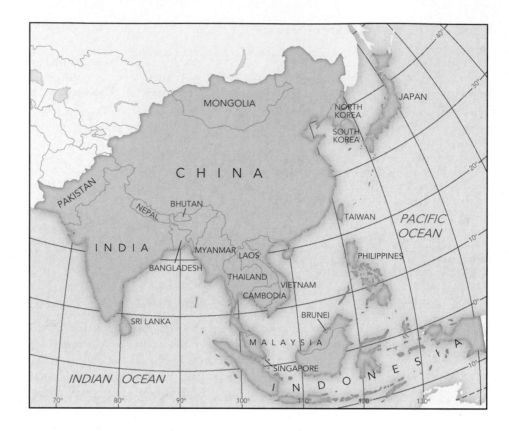

**The Baltic States.**   The Baltic states—Estonia, Latvia, and Lithuania—are a good example of the difference that the right policies can make. All three countries started off with roughly the same legacy of inefficient industry and Soviet-style command economies. Estonia quickly seized the lead by dropping the ruble, privatizing companies and land, letting struggling banks fail, and adopting one of the freest trading regimes of the three countries. Its economic growth has handily outpaced Latvia's and Lithuania's. Since regaining independence in 1991, Estonia's economic reform policy has led to a liberalized, nearly tariff-free, open-market economy.

Although there has been steady progress in Latvia and Lithuania, government bureaucracy, corruption, and organized crime—common problems found in the countries of the former Soviet Union—continue. These represent the most significant hurdles to U.S. trade and investment. Although the governments and all major political parties support a free market system, there are still visible traces of the Soviet methodology and regulatory traditions at the lower levels of bureaucracy.

All three Baltic countries are WTO members and all are seeking membership in the EU and currently enjoy candidate's status.[22]

**Asia**   Asia (see Exhibit 9.9) has been the fastest-growing area in the world for the past three decades, and the prospects for continued economic growth over the long run are excellent.[23] Beginning in 1996, the leading economies of Asia (Japan, Hong Kong, South Korea, Singapore, and Taiwan) experienced a serious financial crisis, which culminated in the meltdown of the Asian stock market. A tight monetary policy, an appreciating dollar, and a deceleration of exports all contributed to the downturn. Despite this economic adjustment, the 1993 estimates by the International Monetary Fund (IMF) that Asian economies would have 29 percent of the global output by the year 2000 were on target.

[22]Poul Funder Larson, "For Latvians, Decision on EU is Daunting and Mysterious," *Wall Street Journal*, January 8, 2003, p. C3.

[23]Visit *Asia Week* for current information on Asian countries: www.asiaweek.com.

**Exhibit 9.10**   Asian Markets—Selected Countries

| Country | Population (millions) | GDP* (billions) | GDP* (per capita) | Imports of Goods and Services (billions) | Exports of Goods and Services (billions) |
|---|---|---|---|---|---|
| Australia | 19.4 | $ 469.2 | $24,203 | $105.1 | $100.5 |
| China | 1,271.8 | 1,117.2 | 878 | 371.4 | 457.4 |
| Hong Kong | 6.7 | 164.8 | 24,505 | 260.1 | 268.5 |
| India | 1,032.4 | 492.5 | 477 | 80.4 | 78.0 |
| Indonesia | 209.0 | 216.2 | 1,034 | 50.4 | 60.3 |
| Japan | 127.0 | 5,647.7 | 44,458 | 487.6 | 591.9 |
| South Korea | 47.3 | 639.2 | 13,502 | 213.8 | 320.9 |
| Taiwan | 22.7 | 282.2 | 12,261 | 108.1 | 125.6 |

*Constant 1995 dollars.

Source: World Bank, Euromonitor 2003. Copyright 2003 by TRANSACTION PUBS. Reproduced with permission of TRANSACTION PUBS via Copyright Clearance Center.

Both as sources of new products and technology and as vast consumer markets, the countries of Asia—particularly those along the Pacific Rim—are just beginning to gain their stride (see Exhibit 9.10).

**Asian-Pacific Rim.**   The most rapidly growing economies in this region are the group sometimes referred to as the Four Tigers (or Four Dragons): Hong Kong, South Korea, Singapore, and Taiwan. Often described as the "East Asian miracle," they were the first countries in Asia, besides Japan, to move from a status of developing countries to newly industrialized countries. They have grown from suppliers of component parts and assemblers of Western products to become major global competitors in electronics, shipbuilding, heavy machinery, and a multitude of other products. In addition, each has become a major influence in trade and development in the economies of the other countries within their spheres of influence. The rapid economic growth and regional influence of the member countries of the Association of Southeast Nations (ASEAN) over the last decade has prompted the U.S. Trade Representative to discuss free-trade agreements—Singapore has already signed up.[24] They are vast markets for industrial goods and, as will be discussed later, important emerging consumer markets.

The Four Tigers are rapidly industrializing and extending their trading activity to other parts of Asia. Japan was once the dominant investment leader in the area and was a key player in the economic development of China, Taiwan, Hong Kong, South Korea, and other countries of the region, but as the economies of other Asian countries have strengthened and industrialized, they are becoming more important as economic leaders. For example, South Korea is the center of trade links with north China and the Asian republics of the former Soviet Union. South Korea's sphere of influence and trade extends to Guangdong and Fujian, two of the most productive Chinese Special Economic Zones, and is becoming more important in interregional investment as well.

**China.**   The economic and social changes occurring in China since it began actively seeking economic ties with the industrialized world have been dramatic. China's dual economic system, embracing socialism along with many tenets of capitalism, produced an economic boom with expanded opportunity for foreign investment that has resulted in annual GNP growth averaging nearly 10 percent since 1970. Most analysts predict that an 8 percent to 10 percent average for the next 10 to 15 years is possible. At that rate China's GNP should equal that of the United States by 2015. All of this growth depends on China's ability to deregulate industry, import modern technology, privatize overstaffed, inefficient SOEs, and continue to attract foreign investment. The prospects look good.

[24]Trish Saywell and Murray Hiebert, "Engaging the U.S. with Trade," *Far Eastern Economic Review,* May 22, 2003, pp. 18–19.

A vendor delivers a Christmas tree in Beijing. Since China's reforms and loosening of controls on religion at the end of the 1970s, the number of Christians has risen from two million to 50 million. There continue to be restrictions on freedom of religion, but as economic freedom grows so do political freedoms. (© AFP/CORBIS)

Two major events that occurred in 2000 are having a profound effect on China's economy: admission to the World Trade Organization and the United States' granting China normal trade relations (NTR) on a permanent basis (PNTR). PNTR and China's entry to the WTO cuts import barriers currently imposed on American products and services. The United States is obligated to maintain the market access policies that it already applies to China, and has for over 20 years, and to make its normal trade relation status permanent. After years of procrastination, China has gotten serious about doing what is necessary to join the WTO and has made a wholehearted and irrevocable commitment to creating a market economy that is tied to the world at large.

An issue that concerns many is whether China will follow WTO rules when it has to lower its formidable barriers to imported goods. Enforcement of the agreement will not just happen. Experience with many past agreements has shown that it is often next to impossible to get compliance on some issues. Some of China's concessions are repeats of unfulfilled agreements extending back to 1979. The United States has learned from its experience with Japan that the toughest work is yet to come. A promise to open markets to U.S. exports can be just the beginning of a long effort at ensuring compliance.

Because of China's size, diversity, and political organization, it is better to think of it as a group of six regions rather than a single country—a grouping of regional markets rather than a single market. There is no one-growth strategy for China. Each region is at a different stage economically and has its own link to other regions as well as links to other parts of the world. Each has its own investment patterns, is taxed differently, and has substantial autonomy in how it is governed. But while each region is separate enough to be considered individually, each is linked at the top to the central government in Beijing.

China has two other important steps to take if the road to economic growth is to be smooth: improving human rights and reforming the legal system. The human rights issue has been a sticking point with the United States because of the Tiananmen Square massacre and the jailing of dissidents as well as China's treatment of Tibet. The U.S. government's decision to award PNTR reflected, in part, the growing importance of China in the global marketplace and the perception that trade with China was too valuable to be jeopardized over a single issue. However, the issue remains delicate both within the United States and between the United States and China.

Meanwhile, China continues to reinvent itself. At the 2002 Communist Party's National Congress, Hu Jintao was selected as General Secretary.[25] But, perhaps more important than his selection was the admission of private entrepreneurs into the Party. This signifies a huge transformation of the Chinese Communist Party from a class party representing workers and peasants into one representing the people as a whole.[26]

Despite these positive changes, the American embassy in China has seen a big jump in complaints from disgruntled U.S. companies fed up with their lack of protection under China's legal system. Outside the major urban areas of Beijing, Shanghai, and Guangzhou, companies are discovering that local protectionism and cronyism make business tough even when they have local partners. Many are finding that a Chinese partner with local political clout can rip off its foreign partner and, when complaints are taken to court, influence courts to rule in their favor. An American manager, a ten-year veteran in China, says that shakedowns by officials have steadily increased, and rampant and blatantly open corruption is now prevalent at all levels. The government office that issues licenses for cars and drivers expects "donations" of gasoline and cash in exchange for prompt service. The Chinese press has to be paid off with lavish meals and cash to attend corporate press conferences. A Mercedes-Benz and $10,000 deposited in a Hong Kong bank is not an unusual payment for connections made or agreements reached in a major

[25]Kojima Akira, "The Capitalist Communists," *Look Japan*, February 2003, p. 22.

[26]"Is the Wakening Giant a Monster—China's Economy," *The Economist*, February 15, 2003, p. 73.

**CROSSING BORDERS 9.5** In Developing Countries, Opportunity Means Creating It

There is an old story about two shoe salesmen from different companies sent to Zimara, an imaginary developing country, scouting for new markets. One cables headquarters, "Coming home tomorrow. No possibilities in Zimara. The natives don't wear shoes." The other cables home, "Fantastic sales opportunity!! Natives are all barefoot! Everyone here needs shoes."

Flexibility, patience, commitment, innovation, the right attitude, and the willingness to go the extra mile will often result in vast rewards in emerging markets. After 13 years of talks (patience), Nestlé was finally invited to help boost milk production in China. When Nestlé opened a powdered milk and baby cereal plant, it faced an inadequate source of milk and an overburdened infrastructure. Local trains and roads made it almost impossible to collect milk and deliver the finished product efficiently. Nestlé's solution was to develop its own infrastructure by weaving a distribution network known as the "milk roads" between 27 villages and the factory collection points (the extra mile). Farmers pushing wheelbarrows, pedaling bicycles, or walking on foot delivered their milk and received payment on the spot, another innovation for China.

Suddenly the farms had an incentive to produce milk, and the district herds grew from 6,000 to 9,000 cows in a matter of months. To train the farms in rudimentary animal health and hygiene, Nestlé hired retired teachers who were paid commissions on all sales to Nestlé (incentive). The result? Business took off. In three years, Nestlé factory production rose from 316 tons of powdered milk and infant formula to 10,000 tons. Capacity has tripled with the addition of two factories.

Seventeen years after talks began, Nestlé's $200 million sales were just barely profitable. However, a year later they had risen to $250 million (patience). Nestlé has exclusive rights to sell the output of its factories throughout China for 15 years (reward), and now sales of milk in China are more than $1 billion.

Sources: Carla Rapoport, "Nestle's Brand Building Machine," *Fortune*, September 19, 1994, pp. 147–156; Mark L. Clifford, Dexter Roberts, and Sherrie E. Zhan, "Penetrating Difficult Markets," *World Trade*, January 2000; and Kathy Chen, "New Craze Seizes China's Consumers: A Glass of Milk," *Wall Street Journal*, February 28, 2003, p. A1.

contractual deal. It is estimated that such "gifts" to Chinese officials account for up to 5 percent of operating costs for large Hong Kong companies. Such practices are difficult to deal with, but they are part of the current business culture confronting companies that want to participate in the growth of the largest of all the BEMs.[27] Despite the problems, China is working to build a commercial legal system and to reform current practices.

Actually there are two Chinas—one a maddening, bureaucratic, bottomless money pit, the other an enormous emerging market.[28] There is the old China, where holdovers of the Communist Party's planning apparatus heap demands on multinational corporations, especially in politically important sectors such as autos,[29] chemicals, and telecom equipment. Companies are shaken down by local officials, whipsawed by policy swings, railroaded into bad partnerships, and squeezed for technology. But there is also a new, market-driven China that is quickly emerging. Consumer areas, from fast food to shampoo, are now wide open.[30] Even in tightly guarded sectors, the barriers to entry are eroding as provincial authorities, rival ministries, and even the military challenge the power of Beijing's technocrats.

No industry better illustrates the changing rules than information technology. Chinese planners once limited imports of PCs and software[31] to promote homegrown industries,

[27]"The Honeycomb of Corruption," *The Economist*, April 8, 2000, p. 47.

[28]Gabriel Kahn, "Coke Works Harder at Being the Real Thing in Hinterland," *Wall Street Journal*, November 26, 2002, p. B1.

[29]Michael Dorgan, "An Emerging Auto Market: Great Leap of China Growing Incomes, Falling Car Prices Create Excitement," *Detroit Free Press*, March 13, 2003, p. 1.

[30]Leslie Chang, "Western Stores Woo Chinese Wallets," *Wall Street Journal*, November 26, 2002, p. B1.

[31]Matt Pottinger, "Software Firms Face Setbacks in China," *Wall Street Journal*, May 7, 2003, p. B5.

but the Chinese preferred smuggled imports to the local manufacturers. Beijing eventually loosened the restraints, and Microsoft is now the dominant PC operating system and the PC market is a stronghold of U.S. brands. A market whose modernization plan calls for imports of equipment and technology of over $100 billion per year, with infrastructure expenditures amounting to $250 billion through the remainder of the decade, is worth the effort. China is now the second biggest market for personal computers, following only the United States.[32]

In the long run the economic strength of China will not be as an exporting machine but as a vast market.[33] The economic strength of the United States comes from its resources, productivity, and vast internal market that drives its economy. China's future potential might better be compared with America's economy, which is driven by domestic demand, than with Japan's, driven by exports. China is neither an economic paradise nor an economic wasteland, but a relatively poor nation going through a painfully awkward transformation from a socialist market system to a hybrid socialist/free market system, not yet complete and with the rules of the game still being written.

**Hong Kong.**   After 155 years of British rule, Hong Kong reverted to China in 1997 when it became a special administrative region (SAR) of the People's Republic of China. The Basic Law of the Hong Kong SAR forms the legal basis for China's "one country, two systems" agreement that guarantees Hong Kong a high degree of autonomy. The social and economic systems, lifestyle, and rights and freedoms enjoyed by the people of Hong Kong prior to the turnover were to remain unchanged for at least 50 years. The Hong Kong government negotiates bilateral agreements (then "confirmed" by Beijing) and makes major economic decisions on its own.[34] The central government in Beijing is responsible only for foreign affairs and defense of the SAR.

The Hong Kong dollar continues to be freely convertible, and foreign exchange, gold, and securities markets continue to operate as before. Hong Kong is a free society with legally protected rights. The Hong Kong SAR government continues to pursue a generally noninterventionist approach to economic policy that stresses the predominant role of the private sector. The first test came when the Hong Kong financial markets had a meltdown in 1997 that reverberated around the financial world and directly threatened the mainland's interests. Beijing's officials kept silent; when they said anything, they expressed confidence in the ability of Hong Kong authorities to solve their own problems.

The decision to let Hong Kong handle the crisis on its own is considered strong evidence that the relationship is working for the best for both sides, considering that China has so much riding on Hong Kong. Among other things, Hong Kong is the largest investor in the mainland, investing more than $100 billion over the last few years for factories and infrastructure. The Hong Kong stock market is the primary source of capital for some of China's largest state-owned enterprises. China Telcom, for example, recently raised $4 billion in an initial public offering.

Most business problems that have arisen stem from fundamental concepts such as clear rules and transparent dealings that are not understood the same way on the mainland as they are in Hong Kong. Many thought the territory's laissez-faire ways, exuberant capitalism, and gung-ho spirit would prove unbearable for Beijing's heavy-handed communist leaders but, except for changes in tone and emphasis, even opponents of communist rule concede that Beijing is honoring the "one country, two systems" arrangement.

The keys to Hong Kong's economic success—its free market philosophy, entrepreneurial drive, absence of trade barriers, well-established rule of law, low and predictable taxes, transparent regulations, and complete freedom of capital movement—all remain intact.

---

[32]"China Overtakes Japan as Second Biggest PC Market," *Reuters*, January 24, 2003.

[33]Ben Dolven, "Into China's New Frontier," *Wall Street Journal*, February 20, 2003, p. A10.

[34]Indeed, Hong Kong negotiates with China over trade as well. See Keith Bradsher, "Hong Kong and China Near Pact on Trade," *New York Times*, June 10, 2003, p. 1.

**Taiwan.**   The presidential victory of longtime Taiwan opposition leader and independence advocate Chen Shui-bian fanned fears in Beijing that the island, which it regards as part of China, would finally declare independence from the mainland. However, Chen quickly assuaged those fears when he promised not to formally declare independence unless China attacked Taiwan. Mainland–Taiwan economic ties are approaching a crossroads as both countries enter the World Trade Organization. As both sides implement WTO provisions, they will have to end many restrictions and implement direct trade. Not that they have not been trading. Taiwanese companies invested about $40 billion in China, and about 250,000 Taiwanese-run factories are responsible for about 12 percent of China's exports. Estimates of real trade are even higher if activities conducted through Hong Kong front companies are considered.

It is best to wrap future talks on the One China debate inside a bundle of more concrete issues, such as establishing the "three direct links"—in transportation, trade and communications. The "three direct links" issue must be faced because each country has joined the WTO and the rules insist that members should communicate over trade disputes and other issues. Trade fits well with both countries' needs. Taiwanese companies face rising costs at home; China offers a nearly limitless pool of cheap labor and engineering talent. Taiwan's tech powerhouses also crave access to China's market.

For Beijing, the Taiwanese companies provide plentiful jobs at a time when bloated state enterprises are laying off millions. They also bring the latest technology and management systems,[35] which China needs as it joins the WTO. In any case, Taiwan continues to stand tall in the East Asian economy—in fact, beginning in 2004 the tallest building in the world will be in Taipei, its capital.[36]

**India.**   The wave of change that has been washing away restricted trade, controlled economies, closed markets, and hostility to foreign investment in most developing countries has finally reached India. Since its independence in 1950, the world's largest democracy had set a poor example as a model for economic growth for other developing countries and was among the last of the economically important developing nations to throw off traditional insular policies. As a consequence, India's growth had been constrained and shaped by policies of import substitution and an aversion to free markets. While other Asian countries were wooing foreign capital, India was doing its best to keep it out. Multinational corporations, seen as vanguards of a new colonialism, were shunned. Aside from textiles, Indian industrial products found few markets abroad other than in the former Soviet Union and Eastern Europe.

Now, however, times have changed and India has embarked on the most profound transformation since it won political independence from Britain. A five-point agenda that includes improving the investment climate; developing a comprehensive WTO strategy; reforming agriculture, food processing, and small-scale industry; eliminating red tape; and instituting better corporate governance has been announced. Steps already taken include the following:

- Privatizing state-owned companies as opposed to merely selling shares in them. The government is now willing to reduce its take below 51 percent and to give management control to so-called strategic investors.

- Recasting the telecom sector's regulatory authority and demolishing the monopolies enjoyed by state-owned companies.

- Signing a trade agreement with the United States to lift all quantitative restrictions on imports by 2001.

- Maintaining the momentum in reform of the petroleum sector.

---

[35]Jason Dean, "Taiwan—Made-to-Order Chip Champ," *Far Eastern Economic Review*, January 2, 2003, pp. 82–83.

[36]Jason Dean, "Tallest Tower Rises in Taiwan Capital," *Wall Street Journal*, June 11, 2003, p. B5F.

- Planning the opening of domestic long-distance phone services, housing, and real estate and retail-trading sectors to foreign direct investment.

Leaders have quietly distanced themselves from campaign rhetoric that advocated "computer chips and not potato chips" in foreign investment and a "*swadeshi*" (made in India) economy. The new direction promises to adjust the philosophy of self-sufficiency that had been taken to extremes and to open India to world markets. India now has the look and feel of the next China or Latin America.

There are still problems facing foreign investors and Indian reformers, however. Although India has overthrown the restrictions of earlier governments, reforms meet resistance from bureaucrats, union members, and farmers, as well as from some industrialists who have lived comfortably behind protective tariff walls that excluded competition. Socialism is not dead in the minds of many in India, and religious, ethnic, and other political passions flare easily.[37]

For a number of reasons, India still presents a difficult business environment. Tariffs are well above those of developing world norms, although they have been slashed to a maximum of 65 percent from 400 percent. Inadequate protection of intellectual property rights remains a serious concern. The antibusiness attitudes of India's federal and state bureaucracies continue to hinder potential investors and plague their routine operations. Policymakers have dragged their feet on selling money-losing state-owned enterprises, making labor laws flexible, and deregulating banking.

In addition, widespread corruption and a deeply ingrained system of bribery make every transaction complicated and expensive. One noted authority on India declared that corrupt practices are not the quaint custom of *baksheesh* but pervasive, systematic, structured, and degraded corruption running from the bottom to the top of the political order. Nevertheless, a survey of U.S. manufacturers shows that 95 percent of respondents with Indian operations plan on expanding and none say they are leaving. They are hooked on the country's cheap, qualified labor and the potential of a massive market.

Despite these uncertainties, being included among the BEMs reflects the potential of India's market.[38] With a population now over 1 billion, India is second in size only to China, and both contain enormous low-cost labor pools. India has a middle class numbering some 250 million, about the population of the United States. Among its middle class are large numbers of college graduates, 40 percent of whom have degrees in science and engineering. India has a diverse industrial base and is developing as a center for computer software. India may be on the threshold of an information technology boom. After establishing a reputation among foreign corporations by debugging computer networks in time for Y2K, Indian companies now supply everything from animation work to browsers used on new-generation wireless phones to e-commerce websites. As discussed earlier, India has been an exporter of technical talent to the U.S. Silicon Valley and now many of these individuals are returning to establish IT companies of their own.

India has the capacity to be one of the more prosperous nations in Asia if allowed to develop and live up to its potential. Some worry, however, that the opportunity could be lost if reforms don't soon reach a critical mass—that point when reforms take on a life of their own and thus become irreversible.

## Newest Emerging Markets

The United States' decision to lift the embargo against Vietnam and the United Nations' lifting of the embargo against South Africa have resulted in the rapid expansion of these economies. Because of their growth and potential, the U.S. Department of Commerce has designated both as BEMs.

Vietnam's economy and infrastructure were in a shambles after 20 years of socialism and years of war, but this country of over 70 million is poised for significant growth. A bilateral trade agreement between the United States and Vietnam led to NTR status for

---

[37]Tim Sullivan, "India's Leader in a Beef over Dietary Insult," *Los Angeles Times*, April 6, 2003, p. A20.

[38]Cris Prystay, "Companies Market to India's Have-Littles," *Wall Street Journal*, June 5, 2003, p. B1.

**CROSSING BORDERS 9.6** The Planting Season—Plant Now, Sow Later

The NEC executive turned the radio on to hear that China was considering a new tax on exports. Just what it needed, another tax. NEC's $200 million joint venture was already riddled with unstable power supplies, export quotas, duties on imported equipment, and meddlesome politicians. To get the agreement to build a joint venture chip plant, it had invested $200 million at 29 percent interest. Along with the money, NEC handed over state-of-the-art 0.5- to 0.35-micron process technology. That enabled China to turn out its first 8-inch logic and memory chips in 1999.

Why do people put up with all this aggravation just to get into China? Because they are afraid not to. Industrializing at incredible speed, China (including Hong Kong) has passed Taiwan to become Asia's top semiconductor market after Japan. A market research firm figures that the chip market in China is worth $5.6 billion and is growing at over 30 percent per year.

"Long term China will become a huge market and you can't wait until it is too late to get involved." As the NEC executive speaks, he jots down the three characters that form the Chinese phrase "old friends." The point is clear: The Chinese will remember those who helped them industrialize in the early days.

The automobile industry faces the same kinds of problems, which have caused some to leave China and others to scale back. However, those who continue to invest do so with the view that the risks of not being in China are greater than the risks of being in China. Indeed, the more than seven million passenger cars in China now include an increasing percentage of Bentleys and other luxury cars. As one economic forecaster warns: "You are investing for 2010 and beyond." Doing business in China can be a headache, but no pain, no gain.

Sources: Neil Weinberg, "Planting Season," *Forbes*, October 20, 1997, p. 112; and Peter Landers, "Long Hard Road," *Far Eastern Economic Review*, April 8, 1999; Ben Dolven, "The Drivers' Seat Is More Lavish as Bentley Buyers Grow in China," *Wall Street Journal*, June 11, 2003, p. B5A.

Vietnam and will lower tariffs[39] on Vietnamese exports to the United States from an average of 40 percent to less than 3 percent. For example, Vietnamese coffee is now in almost every pantry in America, and their new competitiveness has caused prices to sharply decline on the world market.[40] If Vietnam follows the same pattern of development as other Southeast Asian countries, it could become another Asian Tiger. Many of the ingredients are there: The population is educated and highly motivated, and the government is committed to economic growth. There are some factors that are a drag on development, including poor infrastructure, minimal industrial base, and a lack of capital and technology, which must come primarily from outside the country. Most of the capital and technology are being supplied by three of the Asian Tigers—Taiwan, Hong Kong, and South Korea. U.S. companies are beginning to make investments now that the embargo is lifted.

South Africa's economic growth has increased significantly now that apartheid is officially over and the United Nations has lifted the economic embargo that isolated that nation from much of the industrialized world. Unlike Vietnam, South Africa has an industrial base that will help propel it into rapid economic growth, with the possibility of doubling its GNP in as few as ten years. The South African market also has a developed infrastructure—airports, railways, highways, telecommunications—that makes it important as a base for serving nearby African markets too small to be considered individually but viable when coupled with South Africa.

Upbeat economic predictions, a stable sociopolitical environment, and reinforced vigor of the South African government in addressing the issues of privatization and deregulation[41] while maintaining the long-term goal of making the country more investor friendly

---

[39]Trade disputes still surface—Reginald Chua and Margot Cohen, "Vietnamese Tiger Growls Again, Investors Want Change of Stripes," *Wall Street Journal*, March 13, 2003, p. A10.

[40]Nicholas Stein, "Crisis in a Coffee Cup," *Fortune*, December 9, 2002, pp. 203–218.

[41]Nicole Itano, "After Industry Protests, South Africa Softens Mining Law," *New York Times*, May 1, 2003, p. W1.

**Exhibit 9.11**   Living Standards in Selected Countries

| Country | Households (millions) | Persons per Household | Color TV (per 100 households) | Passenger Car (per 100 households) | Refrigerator (per 100 households) | Shower (per 100 households) |
|---|---|---|---|---|---|---|
| Brazil | 51 | 3.4 | 86 | 45 | 83 | 75 |
| Chile | 4 | 3.9 | 61 | 45 | 63 | 88 |
| Colombia | 10 | 4.2 | 86 | 34 | 67 | 97 |
| Peru | 6 | 4.7 | 48 | 18 | 46 | 60 |
| Azerbaijan | 2 | 5.2 | 55 | 21 | 56 | 64 |
| China | 358 | 3.6 | 45 | 3 | 6 | 42 |
| Hong Kong | 2 | 3.3 | 99 | 74 | 96 | 98 |
| India | 175 | 5.9 | 32 | 1 | 13 | 41 |
| Indonesia | 55 | 4.0 | 49 | 4 | 26 | 46 |
| Japan | 48 | 2.6 | 99 | 81 | 97 | 100 |
| Kazakhstan | 4 | 4.1 | 58 | 29 | 80 | 66 |
| Malaysia | 5 | 4.5 | 90 | 64 | 97 | 99 |
| Pakistan | 22 | 7.6 | 36 | 5 | 17 | 64 |
| Philippines | 16 | 4.9 | 65 | 8 | 41 | 83 |
| Singapore | 1 | 3.5 | 99 | 41 | 99 | 100 |
| South Korea | 15 | 3.3 | 93 | 44 | 97 | 95 |
| Taiwan | 7 | 3.3 | 99 | 51 | 99 | 98 |
| Thailand | 16 | 3.9 | 83 | 36 | 69 | 64 |
| Vietnam | 16 | 5.1 | 37 | 2 | 18 | 36 |
| United States | 106 | 2.6 | 99 | 93 | 100 | 99 |

Source: Euromonitor, 2003.

bode well for U.S. businesses seeking trading, investment, and joint venture opportunities in South Africa. The country has a fair-sized domestic market of nearly $200 billion with significant growth potential and is increasingly becoming freemarket oriented. It has yet to develop to its full potential, however, because of years of isolation, former inward-looking trade and investment policies, a low savings rate, and a largely unskilled labor force with attendant low productivity.

Vietnam[42] and South Africa have the potential of becoming the newest emerging markets, but their future development will depend on government action and external investment by other governments and multinational firms. In varying degrees, foreign investors are leading the way by making sizable investments.

## Strategic Implications for Marketing

Surfacing in the emerging markets described earlier is a vast population whose expanding incomes are propelling them beyond a subsistence level to being viable consumers. As a country develops, incomes change, population concentrations shift, expectations for a better life adjust to higher standards, new infrastructures evolve, and social capital investments are made (see Exhibit 9.11). Market behavior changes and eventually groups of consumers with common tastes and needs (i.e., market segments) arise.[43]

When incomes rise, new demand is generated at all income levels for everything from soap to automobiles. Officially, per capita income in China is under $1000 a year. But nearly every independent study by academics and multilateral agencies puts incomes, adjusted for black market activity and purchasing power parity, at three or four times that level. Further, large households can translate into higher disposable incomes. Young working people in Asia and Latin American usually live at home until they marry. With

[42]Dana James, "Back to Vietnam," *Marketing News,* May 13, 2003, p. 1.

[43]Peter G.P. Walters and Saeed Samiee, "Marketing Strategy in Emerging Markets: the Case of China," *Journal of International Marketing,* 2003, 11(1), pp. 97–106.

**Exhibit 9.12** Consumption Patterns in Selected Countries (Percentage of Household Expenditures)

| Country | Food | Alcohol | Tobacco | Clothing | Housing | Health/ Medical | Transpor- tation | Communi- cation | Education and Leisure |
|---|---|---|---|---|---|---|---|---|---|
| United States | 7.1% | 1.2% | 1.0% | 4.7% | 14.7% | 17.6% | 11.5% | 2.3% | 11.6% |
| Mexico | 24.0 | 2.5 | 0.6 | 5.0 | 12.4 | 4.3 | 13.9 | 1.7 | 6.1 |
| Azerbaijan | 52.8 | 0.9 | 2.0 | 4.3 | 7.1 | 4.2 | 11.7 | 1.2 | 2.8 |
| India | 46.0 | 0.9 | 3.1 | 5.1 | 6.9 | 4.3 | 12.7 | 0.6 | 3.5 |
| Malaysia | 21.9 | 0.6 | 2.0 | 3.4 | 18.8 | 2.2 | 15.7 | 2.9 | 5.8 |
| Singapore | 11.6 | 0.5 | 1.1 | 4.4 | 16.1 | 2.5 | 17.9 | 2.6 | 10.7 |
| Thailand | 26.6 | 2.6 | 1.8 | 12.1 | 7.0 | 6.2 | 11.3 | 1.7 | 7.1 |
| Algeria | 37.1 | 0.5 | 2.5 | 5.1 | 15.9 | 4.2 | 11.1 | 2.9 | 4.3 |
| South Africa | 20.7 | 7.0 | 2.0 | 4.9 | 9.9 | 7.1 | 13.9 | 2.5 | 6.6 |

Source: Euromonitor, 2003.

no rent to pay, they have more discretionary income and can contribute to household purchasing power. Countries with low per capita incomes are potential markets for a large variety of goods; consumers show remarkable resourcefulness in finding ways to buy what really matters to them. In the United States, the first satellite dishes sprang up in the poorest parts of Appalachia. Similarly, the poorest slums of Calcutta are home to 70,000 VCRs, and in Mexico, homes with color televisions outnumber those with running water.

As incomes rise to middle-class range, demand for more costly goods increases for everything from disposable diapers to automobiles. Incomes for the middle class in emerging markets are less than those in the United States, but spending patterns are different, so the middle class has more to spend than comparable income levels in the United States would indicate. For example, members of the middle class in emerging markets do not own two automobiles and suburban homes, and health care and housing in some cases are subsidized, freeing income to spend on refrigerators, TVs, radios, better clothing, and special treats. Exhibit 9.12 illustrates the percentage of household income spent on various classes of goods and services. More household money goes for food in emerging markets than in developed markets, but the next category of high expenditure[44] for emerging and developed countries alike is appliances and other durable goods. Spending by the new rich, however, is a different story. The new rich want to display their new status; they want to wear status symbols such as Rado watches, the high-end Swiss watch that costs more than $1,000.

A London securities firm says that a person earning $250 annually in a developing country can afford Gillette razors, and at $1,000, he or she can become a Sony television owner. A Nissan or Volkswagen could be possible with a $10,000 income. Whirlpool estimates that in Eastern Europe a family with an annual income of $1,000 can afford a refrigerator, and with $2,000 they can buy an automatic washer as well. Estimates are that a sustainable growth in the car market will occur in China when average annual income of $5,000 is achieved. Even though that will not likely happen until 2010, one million cars are forecast to be sold in 2005—that makes the Chinese market as large as all of South Asia combined.

Recognizing the growth in Asia, Whirlpool invested $265 million to buy controlling interest in four competitors in China and two in India. The attraction is expanding incomes and low appliance ownership rates. Fewer than 10 percent of Chinese households have air conditioners, microwave ovens, or washers. At the same time, incomes are reaching levels where demand for such appliances will grow.

One analyst suggests that as a country passes the $5,000 per capita GNP level, people become more brand conscious and forgo many local brands to seek out foreign brands

---

[44]Manjeet Kripalani and Mark L. Clifford, "Finally, Coke Gets it Right ... in India," *BusinessWeek*, February 10, 2003, p. 47.

they recognize. At $10,000, they join those with similar incomes who are exposed to the same global information sources. They join the "$10,000 Club" of consumers with homogeneous demands who share a common knowledge of products and brands. They become global consumers. If a company fails to appreciate the strategic implications of the $10,000 Club, it will miss the opportunity to participate in the world's fastest-growing global consumer segment. There are now over one billion people in the world whose income is $10,000 or better. In Asia alone, Singapore's average income is over $27,000, Hong Kong's is at $25,000, and Taiwan's is just over $12,000.[45] Companies that look for commonalities among this 700 million will find a growing market for global brands.

Markets are changing rapidly, and in many countries there are identifiable market segments with similar consumption patterns across countries. Emerging markets will be the growth areas of the twenty-first century.

## Summary

The ever-expanding involvement in world trade of more and more people with varying needs and wants will test old trading patterns and alliances. The foreign marketer of today and tomorrow must be able to react to market changes rapidly and to anticipate new trends within constantly evolving market segments that may not have existed as recently as last year. Many of today's market facts will likely be tomorrow's historical myths.

Along with dramatic shifts in global politics, the increasing scope and level of technical and economic growth have enabled many nations to advance their standards of living by as much as two centuries in a matter of decades. As nations develop their productive capacity, all segments of their economies will feel the pressure to improve. The impact of these political, social, and economic trends will continue to be felt throughout the world, resulting in significant changes in marketing practices. Further, the impact of information technology will speed the economic growth in every country. Marketers must focus on devising marketing plans designed to respond fully to each level of economic development. China and Russia continue to undergo rapid political and economic changes that have brought about the opening of most socialist-bloc countries to foreign direct investments and international trade. And though big emerging markets present special problems, they are promising markets for a broad range of products now and in the future. Emerging markets create new marketing opportunities for MNCs as new market segments evolve.

## Questions

1. Define the following terms:

   economic development, 245
   stage of economic
     development, 245
   NICs, 246
   infrastructure, 251
   economic dualism, 254
   BEMs, 258

2. Is it possible for an economy to experience economic growth as measured by total GNP without a commensurate rise in the standard of living? Discuss fully.

3. Why do technical assistance program by more affluent nations typically ignore the distribution problem or relegate it to a minor role in development planning? Explain.

4. Discuss each of the stages of evolution in the marketing process. Illustrate each stage with a particular country.

5. As a country progresses from one economic stage to another, what in general are the marketing effects?

6. Locate a country in the agricultural and raw materials stage of economic development and discuss what changes will occur in marketing when it passes to a manufacturing stage.

7. What are the consequences of each stage of marketing development on the potential for industrial goods within a country? For consumer goods?

8. Discuss the significance of economic development to international marketing. Why is the knowledge of economic development important in assessing the world-marketing environment? Discuss.

9. The Internet accelerates the process of economic growth. Discuss.

10. Discuss the impact of the IT revolution on the poorest countries.

11. Select one country in each of the five stages of economic development. For each country, outline the basic existing marketing institutions and show how their stages of development differ. Explain why.

12. Why should a foreign marketer study economic development? Discuss.

13. The infrastructure is important to the economic growth of an economy. Comment.

14. What are the objectives of economically developing countries? How do these objectives relate to marketing? Comment.

15. Using the list of NIC growth factors, evaluate India and China as to their prospects for rapid growth. Which factors will be problems for India? For China?

---

[45]World Bank and Euromonitor, 2003.

16. What is marketing's role in economic development? Discuss marketing's contributions to economic development.

17. Discuss the economic and trade importance of the big emerging markets.

18. What are the traits of those countries considered big emerging markets? Discuss.

19. Discuss how the economic growth of BEMs is analogous to the situation after World War II.

20. Discuss the problems a marketer might encounter when considering the Marxist-socialist countries as a market.

21. One of the ramifications of emerging markets is the creation of a middle class. Discuss.

22. The needs and wants of a market and the ability to satisfy them are the result of the three-way interaction of the economy, culture, and the marketing efforts of businesses. Comment.

23. Discuss the strategic implications of marketing in India.

24. "Too much emphasis is usually laid—by Chinese policymakers as well as by foreign businessmen—on China's strength as an export machine. China is so big that its economic potential might more usefully be compared with continental America's." Discuss fully.

# CHAPTER 10

# multinational market regions and market groups

# Global Perspective

## MIGHT FREE TRADE BRING PEACE TO THE MIDDLE EAST?

The nearly complete destruction of the continental European economies by World War II seriously endangered the stability of Europe's social and political institutions. Its leaders knew that to rebuild from the ruins it was essential to form new kinds of international institutions to ensure prosperity, stability, and peace in the region. The first of these was the European Coal and Steel Community established in 1952 to integrate the coal and steel industries of France, West Germany, Italy, Belgium, The Netherlands, and Luxembourg. Fifty years later, based on the success of this first small experiment in economic interdependence, we now see the European Union with 15 member nations and 13 candidate countries set to join during the next few years. The economies have burgeoned, but more importantly peace has persisted.

Might such an approach work in the war-torn Middle East? Let's consider the possibilities and potential of a Middle Eastern Union. The crux of the problem is Jerusalem. The holy Old City is a matter of faith to so many people. For Christians it is sacred because of its associations with Christ. For Jews it has served as the center for their people—not only in a national way, but more importantly, in a religious sense. For Muslims only Mecca and Medina are more important spiritual places. And the fighting over the land that contains the Old City appears to be perpetual.

Jerusalem can be a primary part of the solution. But we must look beyond current violence. We must imagine a safe, prosperous, and peaceful place. Imagine an international shrine. Perhaps the Old City would be administered by Buddhists or Norwegians or the United Nations. Israel would have its grand capital to the west, in the New City, and the Palestinians to the east a bit.

Religious tourism would feed the economies in both countries, as well as in the surrounding area. Imagine the possibilities! In 2000, before the most recent insanity of violence, tourism brought in $3.2 billion in revenues for Israel. Compare that with Disneyland in Orange County, California. That park's yearly 10 million visitors spend about $100 each on tickets, food, and souvenirs. Add in the transportation, hotel, and restaurant revenues appreciated in the neighborhood, and that's more than a couple of billion dollars a year coming to the city of Anaheim.

The Church of the Holy Sepulcher (built over the tomb of Jesus) would draw Christians. The Wailing Wall is a special place for Jews. Muslims would flock to the Dome of the Rock (Mohammed was carried by the angel Gabriel for a visit to Heaven after praying at the Rock). The most enlightened tourists would visit all three. Disney might consult on the queuing problems. And outside of the Old City are Bethlehem, Nazareth, Jericho, the Sea of Galilee, the Dead Sea and Red Sea, to name only the more obvious attractions just in Israel. We're talking $10 to 20 billion in annual revenues if things are done right—that's about 10 to 15 percent of the current GDP of Israel.

To the east the new Hijaz Railway Corp. is already working on a line connecting Iran and Jordan via Syria, and is talking about lines connecting Iraq, Turkey, and Europe as well—all for the sake of religious tourism. Indeed, the line's original purpose was taking pilgrims to Medina from Damascus; that was before Lawrence of Arabia severed it for carrying arms and troops during World War I. The current company executives reckon the two-day trip from Tehran to Amman will cost only about $30, and the Shiite Muslims of Iran will flock to their holy sights in the area. Why not run the line all the way to east Jerusalem?

How about Jerusalem as the site for the 2020 Olympic games? That's another $5 billion in revenues. And ignoring the dollars for a moment, please consider the sentiments associated with "the 2020 Jerusalem Games" juxtaposed with the disaster of Munich in 1972. And ignoring the dollars for another moment, imagine the spiritual splendor for so many millions visiting the sources of their faith, treading some of the original paths of David, Jesus, and Mohammed.

This little fantasy presumes a peaceful political division of Israel and Palestine along the lines reaffirmed in the Oslo Accords. It presumes a dropping of all commercial boycotts in the region. It presumes that Palestinians won't have to risk being shot while "hopping the fence" to work in Israel. It presumes that companies like Nestlé will be able to integrate the operations of their complementary plants in the area. It presumes that the United States and other countries will send to the region legions of tourists rather than boatloads of weapons. It presumes an open, international, and most importantly, a whole Old City of Jerusalem. And it presumes free trade and travel among all nations in the region allowing all to prosper in new ways.

Finally, Pulitzer Prize winner Jared Diamond points out that historically the Middle East was referred to as the Fertile Crescent; it was the cradle of civilization. It became so very long ago because of innovation and trade in the region. One can only imagine what free trade in the area would produce now?

Source: Excerpted from John L. Graham, "Trade Brings Peace," a paper delivered at the Global Ethics and Religion Forum; Clare Hall, Cambridge University conference, *War and Reconciliation: Perspectives of the World Religions,* May 26, 2003 in Cambridge, England; and Jared Diamond, "The Erosion of Civilization," *Los Angeles Times,* June 15, 2003, p. M1.

Following the success of the aforementioned European Steel and Coal Community, a global economic revolution began in 1958 when the European Economic Community was ratified and Europe took the step that would ultimately lead to the present-day European Union (EU). Until then, skeptics predicted that the experiment would never work and that the alliance would fall apart quickly. It was not until the single market was established that the United States, Japan, and other countries gave serious thought to creating other alliances. The creation of common markets, coupled with the trend away from planned economies to the free market system in Latin America, Asia, and eventually the former USSR, created fertile ground that sparked the drive to establish trade alliances and free markets the world over. Nation after nation embraced the free market system, implementing reforms in their economic and political systems with the desire to be part of a multinational market region in the evolving global marketplace. Traditions that are centuries old are being altered, issues that cannot be resolved by decree are being negotiated to an acceptable solution, governments and financial systems are restructuring, and companies are being reshaped to meet new competition and trade patterns.

The evolution and growth of **multinational market regions**—those groups of countries that seek mutual economic benefit from reducing interregional trade and tariff barriers—are the most important global trends today. Organizational form varies widely among market regions, but the universal goal of multinational cooperation is economic benefit for the participants. Political and social benefits sometimes accrue, but the dominant motive for affiliation is economic. The world is awash in economic cooperative agreements as countries look for economic alliances to expand access to free markets.

Regional economic cooperative agreements have been around since the end of World War II. The most successful one has been the European Community (EC), the world's largest multinational market region and foremost example of economic cooperation. Multinational market groups form large markets that provide potentially significant market opportunities for international business. As it became apparent in the late 1980s that the EC was to achieve its long-term goal of a single European market, a renewed interest in economic cooperation followed, with the creation of several new alliances. The North American Free Trade Agreement (NAFTA) and Mercosur (Southern Cone Common Market) in the Americas, and the Association of Southeast Asian Nations (ASEAN) and Asia-Pacific Economic Cooperation (APEC) in the Asian-Pacific Rim are all relatively new or reenergized associations that are gaining strength and importance as multinational market regions.

Along with the growing trend of economic cooperation, there is concern about the effect of such cooperation on global competition. Governments and businesses worry that the European Economic Area (EEA), North American Free Trade Agreement (NAFTA), and other cooperative trade groups will become regional trading blocs without trade restrictions internally but with borders protected from outsiders. It is too early to determine to what extent trading groups will close their borders to outsiders, but whatever the future, global companies face a richer and more intense competitive environment.

Three global regions—Europe, the Americas, and the Asian-Pacific Rim—are involved in forging a new economic order for trade and development that will dominate world markets for years to come. Kenichi Ohmae's book *Triad Power* points out that the global companies that will be Triad powers must have significant market positions in each of the Triad regions.[1] At the economic center of each Triad region will be an economic industrial power: In the European Triad, it is the European Union; in the American Triad, it is the United States; in the Asian Triad, it is Japan.

## La Raison d'Etre

Successful economic union requires favorable economic, political, cultural, and geographic factors as a basis for success. Major flaws in any one factor can destroy a union unless the other factors provide sufficient strength to overcome the weaknesses. In general,

---

[1]Kenichi Omae, *Triad Power,* (New York: Free Press, 1985), p. 220.

the advantages of economic union must be clear-cut and significant, and the benefits must greatly outweigh the disadvantages before nations forgo any part of their sovereignty. Many of the associations formed in Africa and Latin America have had little impact because there were not sufficient perceived benefits to offset the partial loss of sovereignty.

In the past, a strong threat to the economic or political security of a nation was the impetus for cooperation. The cooperative agreements among European countries that preceded the EC had their roots in the need for economic redevelopment after World War II, the belief that economic integration created peace between[2] and within nations,[3] and the political concern for the perceived threat of communism. Many felt that if Europe was to survive there had to be economic unity; the agreements made then formed the groundwork for the European Community. The more recent creation of multinational market groups has been driven by the fear that not to be part of a vital regional market group is to be left on the sidelines of the global economic boom of the twenty-first century.

## Economic Factors

Every type of economic union shares the development and enlargement of market opportunities as a basic orientation; usually, markets are enlarged through preferential tariff treatment for participating members or common tariff barriers against outsiders, or both. Enlarged, protected markets stimulate internal economic development by providing ensured outlets and preferential treatment for goods produced within the customs union, and consumers benefit from lower internal tariff barriers among the participating countries. In many cases, external as well as internal barriers are reduced because of the greater economic security afforded domestic producers by the enlarged market.

Nations with complementary economic bases are least likely to encounter frictions in the development and operation of a common market unit. However, for an economic union to survive, it must have agreements and mechanisms in place to settle economic disputes. In addition, the total benefit of economic integration must outweigh individual differences that are sure to arise as member countries adjust to new trade relationships. The European Community included countries with diverse economies, distinctive monetary systems, developed agricultural bases, and different natural resources. It is significant that most of the problems encountered by the EC arose over agriculture and monetary policy. In the early days of the European Community, agricultural disputes were common. The British attempted to keep French poultry out of the British market, France banned Italian wine, and the Irish banned eggs and poultry from other member countries. In all cases, the reason given was health and safety, but the probable motive was the continuation of the age-old policy of market protection. Such skirmishes are not unusual but they do test the strength of the economic union. In the case of the EC, the European Commission was the agency used to settle disputes and charge the countries that violated EC regulations.

The demise of the Latin American Free Trade Association (LAFTA) was the result of economically stronger members not allowing for the needs of the weaker ones. Many of the less well-known attempts at common markets have languished because of economic incompatibility that could not be resolved and the uncertainty of future economic advantage.[4]

## Political Factors

Political amenability among countries is another basic requisite for development of a supranational market arrangement. Participating countries must have comparable

---

[2]By far the strongest evidence for the trade-causes-peace notion is that provided by Solomon W. Polachek, "Why Democracies Cooperate More and Fight Less: the Relationship between International Trade and Cooperation," *Review of International Economics,* 1997, 5(3), pp. 295–309; additional evidence is supplied at www.cpbp.org, click on Peace Monitor, then Countries; and Jonathan Schell, *The Unconquerable World* (New York: Metropolitan Books, 2003).

[3]New study of the causes of civil wars supports their belief—see Paul Collier, "The Market for Civil War," *Foreign Policy,* May/June 2003, pp. 38–45.

[4]For more detail regarding economic advantages created by regional integration, see Maurice Schiff and Won Chang, "Market Presence, Contestability, and the Terms-of-Trade Effects of Regional Integration," *Journal of International Economics,* May 2003, p. 161–175.

The geographic proximity allows Mexicans from Baja California to attend Padres' baseball games in close-by San Diego. The team maintains this successful store just across the border in Plaza Rio shopping center in Tijuana. And, of course, historically Padre Junipero Serra had visited both places in the late 1700s while establishing the chain of missions in old Spanish California.

aspirations and general compatibility before surrendering any part of their national sovereignty.[5] State sovereignty is one of the most cherished possessions of any nation and is relinquished only for a promise of significant improvement of the national position through cooperation.[6]

Economic considerations provide the basic catalyst for the formation of a customs union group, but political elements are equally important. The uniting of the original European Community countries was partially a response to the outside threat of the Soviet Union's great political and economic power; the countries of Western Europe were willing to settle their family squabbles to present a unified front to the Russian bear. The communist threat no longer exists, but the importance of political unity to fully achieve all the benefits of economic integration has driven EC countries to form the European Union.

**Geographic Proximity**   Although it is not absolutely imperative that cooperating members of a customs union have geographic proximity, such closeness does facilitate the functioning of a common market.[7] Transportation networks (basic to any marketing system) are likely to be interrelated and well developed when countries are close together. Issues of immigration, legal and illegal, also promote closer economic integration between close neighbors.[8] One of the first major strengths of the European Community was its transportation network; the opening of the tunnel between England and France further bound this common market. Countries that are widely separated geographically have major barriers to overcome in attempting economic fusion. However, with increasing efficiencies in communication and transportation the importance of such factors is waning.[9]

**Cultural Factors**   Cultural similarity eases the shock of economic cooperation with other countries. The more similar the culture, the more likely a market is to succeed because members understand the outlook and viewpoints of their colleagues. Although there is great cultural diversity in the European Union, key members share a long-established Christian heritage and are commonly aware of being European. Language, as a part of culture, has not created as much a barrier for European Union countries as was expected. Nearly every educated European can do business in at least two or three languages, so the linguistic diversity of several major languages did not impede trade.

## Patterns of Multinational Cooperation   Multinational market groups take several forms, varying significantly in the degree of cooperation, dependence, and interrelationship among participating nations. There are five fundamental groupings for regional economic integration, ranging from regional cooperation for development, which requires the least amount of integration, to the ultimate integration of political union.

**Regional Cooperation Groups.**   The most basic economic integration and cooperation is the *regional cooperation for development (RCD)*. In the RCD arrangement,

[5]"Poland and the EU, Back into the Fold," *The Economist*, June 14, 2003, pp. 45–46.

[6]Paul Magnusson, "The Highest Court You've Ever Heard Of, Do NAFTA Judges Have Too Much Authority?" *BusinessWeek*, April 1, 2003, pp. 76–77.

[7]Sebastian Edwards, "How Chile Can Make the Most of Its U.S. Trade Deal," *The Wall Street Journal*, January 3, 2003, p. A11.

[8]"Half an Enchilada—Mexico's Relationship with the United States," *The Economist*, January 25, 2003, p. 42.

[9]Scott Miller, "Lamy Makes Case for WTO's Way," *The Wall Street Journal*, March 20, 2003, p. A1.

# CROSSING BORDERS 10.1   Free Trade Means Losing Jobs—or Does It?

"Is Your Job Next?" "Euro-skeptics Think the European Union Is Hostile to Free Markets." These and comparable headlines reflect the fears many have about free trade and multinational associations like the North American Free Trade Agreement (NAFTA), the European Community (EC), and other trade alliances among nations. Concerns range from jobs being exported to other countries to companies being closed out of once open, lucrative markets. In short, many fear that free trade will not live up to its promises of open markets, market growth, lower prices, more trade, and more jobs. Big multinational companies will not be hurt; the small company and the worker will suffer the brunt of free trade.

Since most trade alliances are still works in progress, it is much too early to make a definitive evaluation of their success or failure. However, consider the following "textbook examples" of how it is supposed to work.

Federal Express is a good example of how companies benefit from the growth in trade. Prior to NAFTA, FedEx could only service Mexico with one daily flight in and out of Mexico City. Today, it flies three large-capacity planes daily, six times per week, in and out of Mexico City, Guadalajara, and Monterrey.

"Prior to NAFTA, the Mexican market was effectively shut to companies like ours because of high tariffs and import licenses," says the CEO of Quaker Fabric, a Massachusetts textile manufacturer. "NAFTA has reduced those obstacles and our sales to Mexico have grown sharply. Quaker's exports to our NAFTA partners now account for 8 percent to 10 percent of our business, worth $25 to $30 million a year." Without NAFTA, Quaker would probably have relocated to Mexico, or an even lower-wage country. NAFTA's rules of origin encourage the use of U.S. fabric and cloth in products made in Mexico for export. The increase in apparel imports from Mexico has come largely at the expense of Asian producers who do not use U.S. fabrics.

Yes, international business decisions can and do affect domestic jobs, but domestic business decisions also affect the job market. It is inherent in the course of commerce. When the meatpacking industry moved to the epicenter of the cattle market in the rural areas in Nebraska and Colorado, jobs were also lost. Fortunately for those displaced by NAFTA, the government will provide federal aid to help offset job losses.

Exports by small companies created thousands of new jobs in the last decade, many of which are a result of sales to new markets created by free trade and of products in markets where you would least expect sales. A Vermont company sells cheddar cheese in the village of Cheddar in southwest England. In France, imports of mozzarella cheese have tripled to 315,172 pounds from 92,568 pounds in six months. Poppers, maker of frozen appetizers such as mozzarella sticks and onion rings, exported 3.2 million pounds of appetizers to Europe in 1996, up from 800,000 pounds a year earlier.

Ten years ago, a Cape Cod, Massachusetts, entrepreneur and his wife began a small business making kettle-fried chips. Today, they are growing at 100 percent per year, selling in markets in Europe, South America, and Canada. Their Cape Cod Potato Chips are displayed among nearly 100 other stands hawking American food at the Salon International de l'Alimentation, one of the largest international food trade shows.

These are just a few examples of what is happening all over the United States. Some companies are moving offshore to Mexico and jobs are lost. In other cases, exports to Mexico and Canada are increasing and thus creating new jobs. It is much too early to gauge the success or failure of NAFTA, but as you explore the issues in this chapter, consider the consequences if the United States were not an active member of viable multinational trade regions.

Sources: Helene Cooper and Scott Kilman, "Exotic Tastes: Trade Wars Aside, U.S. and Europe Buy More of Each Other's Food," *The Wall Street Journal*, November 11, 1997, p. A1; Jon Jeter, "Some Initial Losses Followed Free Trade Pact's Passage but Exports Are Now on the Rise," *Washington Post*, November 29, 1997, p. A6; David Wernick, "Next Generation NAFTA," *Latin America Trade Finance*, July 2000, p. 8; and Pete Engardio, Aaron Bernstein, Manjeet Kripalani, "Is Your Job Next, the New Global Job Shift," *BusinessWeek*, February 3, 2003, pp. 45–51.

governments agree to participate jointly to develop basic industries beneficial to each economy. Each country makes an advance commitment to participate in the financing of a new joint venture and to purchase a specified share of the output of the venture. An example is the project between Colombia and Venezuela to build a hydroelectric generating plant on the Orinoco River. They shared jointly in construction costs and they share the electricity produced.

**Free Trade Area.**   A **free trade area** (**FTA**) requires more cooperation and integration than the RCD. It is an agreement between two or more countries to reduce or eliminate customs duties and nontariff trade barriers among partner countries while members maintain individual tariff schedules for external countries. Essentially, an FTA provides its members with a mass market without barriers to impede the flow of goods and services. The United States has free trade agreements with Canada and Mexico (NAFTA) and separately with Israel.

**Customs Union.**   A **customs union** represents the next stage in economic cooperation. It enjoys the free trade area's reduced or eliminated internal tariffs and adds a common external tariff on products imported from countries outside the union. The customs union is a logical stage of cooperation in the transition from an FTA to a common market. The European Community was a customs union before becoming a common market. Customs unions exist between France and Monaco, Italy and San Marino, and Switzerland and Liechtenstein, to name some examples.

**Common Market.**   A **common market** agreement eliminates all tariffs and other restrictions on internal trade, adopts a set of common external tariffs, and removes all restrictions on the free flow of capital and labor among member nations. Thus a common market is a common marketplace for goods as well as for services (including labor) and for capital. It is a unified economy and lacks only political unity to become a political union. The Treaty of Rome, which established the European Economic Community (EEC) in 1957, called for common external tariffs and the gradual elimination of intramarket tariffs, quotas, and other trade barriers. The treaty also called for elimination of restrictions on the movement of services, labor, and capital; prohibition of cartels; coordinated monetary and fiscal policies; common agricultural policies; use of common investment funds for regional industrial development; and similar rules for wage and welfare payments. The EEC existed until the Maastricht Treaty created the European Union, an extension of the EEC into a political union.

Latin America boasts three common markets: the Central American Common Market (CACM), the Andean Common Market, and the Southern Cone Common Market (**Mercosur**). The three have roughly similar goals and seek eventual full economic integration.

**Political Union.**   **Political union** is the most fully integrated form of regional cooperation. It involves complete political and economic integration, either voluntary or enforced. The most notable enforced political union was the Council for Mutual Economic Assistance (COMECON), a centrally controlled group of countries organized by the USSR. With the dissolution of the USSR and the independence of Eastern Europe, COMECON was disbanded.

A *commonwealth* of nations is a voluntary organization providing for the loosest possible relationship that can be classified as economic integration. The British Commonwealth comprises Britain and countries formerly part of the British Empire. Its members recognize the British monarch as their symbolic head, although Britain has no political authority over any commonwealth country. Its member states had received preferential tariffs when trading with Great Britain, but when Britain joined the European Community, all preferential tariffs were abandoned. A commonwealth can best be described as the weakest of political unions and is mostly based on economic history and a sense of tradition. Heads of state meet every three years to discuss trade and political issues they jointly face, and compliance with any decisions or directives issued is voluntary.

Two new political unions came into existence in the 1990s: the Commonwealth of Independent States (CIS), made up of the republics of the former USSR, and the European Union (EU). The European Union was created when the 12 nations of the European Community ratified the **Maastricht Treaty**. The members committed themselves to economic and political integration. The treaty allows for the free movement of goods, persons, services, and capital throughout the member states; a common currency; common foreign and security policies, including defense; a common justice system; and cooperation between police and other authorities on crime, terrorism, and immigration issues.

Although not all the provisions of the treaty have been universally accepted,[10] each year the EU members become more closely tied economically and politically.[11] Most recently The Economic and Monetary Union has been put in place and all participating members share a common currency.

## Global Markets and Multinational Market Groups

The globalization of markets, the restructuring of Eastern Europe into independent market-driven economies, the dissolution of the Soviet Union into independent states, the worldwide trend toward economic cooperation, and enhanced global competition make it important that market potential be viewed in the context of regions of the world rather than country by country. Formal economic cooperation agreements such as the EC are the most notable examples of multinational market groups, but many new coalitions are forming, old ones are being reenergized, and the possibility of many new cooperative arrangements is on the horizon.

This section presents basic information and data on markets and market groups in Europe, the Americas, Africa, Asia, and the Middle East. Existing economic cooperation agreements within each of these regions are reviewed. The reader must appreciate that the status of cooperative agreements and alliances among nations is extremely fluid in some parts of the world. Many are fragile and may cease to exist or may restructure into a totally different form. It will probably take several decades for many of the new trading alliances that are now forming to stabilize into semipermanent groups.

## Europe

The European Union is the focus of the European region of the first Triad. Within Europe, every type of multinational market grouping exists. The European Community, European Union, European Economic Area, and the European Free Trade Association are the most established cooperative groups (see Exhibit 10.1 and Exhibit 10.2).

Of escalating economic importance are the fledgling capitalist economies of Eastern Europe and the three Baltic states that gained independence from the USSR just prior to its breakup. Key issues center on their economic development and eventual economic alliance with the EU. Also within the European region is the Commonwealth of Independent States. New and untested, this coalition of 12 former USSR republics may or may not survive in its present form to take its place among the other multinational market groups.

### European Community

Of all the multinational market groups, none has been more secure in its cooperation or more important economically than the European Community. From its beginning, it has made progress toward achieving the goal of complete economic integration and, ultimately, political union. However, many people, including Europeans, had little hope for the success of the European Economic Community, or the European Common Market as it is often called, because of the problems created by integration and the level of national sovereignty that would be conceded to the community. After all, there were 1,000 years of economic separatism to overcome and the European Common Market is quite heterogeneous. There are language differences, individual national interests, political differences, and centuries-old restrictions designed to protect local national markets.

Historically, standards have been used to effectively limit market access. Germany protected its beer market from the rest of Europe with a purity law requiring beer sold in Germany to be brewed only from water, hops, malt, and yeast. Italy protected its pasta market by requiring that pasta be made only from durum wheat. Incidentally, the European Court of Justice has struck down both the beer and pasta regulations as trade violations. Such restrictive standards kept competing products, whether from other European countries or elsewhere, out of their respective markets. Skeptics, doubtful that such cultural, legal,

---

[10]A. S. Byatt, "What is a European," *New York Times Magazine,* October 13, 2002, p. 46.

[11]"All Aboard the Euro Train!" *The Economist,* April 5, 2003, p. 50.

**Exhibit 10.1**   European Market Regions

| Association | Member | Population (millions) | GDP* (billions) | GDP* per Capita | Imports of Goods and Services (billions) | Exports of Goods and Services (billions) |
|---|---|---|---|---|---|---|
| **European Union (EU)** | | | | | | |
| | Belgium | 1.03 | $ 321.1 | $31,218 | $233.7 | $251.5 |
| | Denmark | 5.4 | 207.5 | 38,710 | 83.8 | 92.6 |
| | Germany | 82.3 | 2,701.6 | 32,813 | 850.9 | 941.6 |
| | Greece | 10.6 | 144.8 | 13,669 | 46.6 | 34.8 |
| | Spain | 41.1 | 723.5 | 17,595 | 237.0 | 221.9 |
| | France | 59.2 | 1,804.9 | 30,492 | 483.0 | 815.7 |
| | Ireland | 3.8 | 112.9 | 29,401 | 100.3 | 120.1 |
| | Italy | 57.0 | 1,225.3 | 21,144 | 347.3 | 370.7 |
| | Luxembourg | 0.4 | 24.9 | 56,382 | 30.9 | 35.2 |
| | Netherlands | 16.0 | 502.5 | 31,333 | 310.9 | 339.2 |
| | Austria | 8.1 | 269.8 | 33,172 | 310.9 | 339.2 |
| | Portugal | 10.0 | 131.4 | 13,109 | 59.9 | 46.7 |
| | Finland | 5.2 | 166.7 | 32,121 | 57.8 | 79.0 |
| | Sweden | 8.9 | 281.3 | 31,627 | 116.5 | 143.7 |
| | United Kingdom | 58.8 | 1,334.6 | 22,697 | 534.6 | 455.1 |
| **EU Candidate Countries** | | | | | | |
| | Bulgaria | 7.9 | 13.1 | 1,630 | 10.8 | 8.5 |
| | Czech Republic | 10.3 | 57.1 | 5,583 | 51.1 | 46.1 |
| | Estonia | 1.4 | 6.4 | 4,707 | 7.5 | 6.6 |
| | Cyprus | 0.8 | 57.1 | 14,592 | — | — |
| | Latvia | 2.4 | 6.6 | 2,816 | 4.2 | 3.7 |
| | Lithuania | 3.5 | 8.0 | 2,308 | 7.3 | 5.6 |
| | Hungary | 10.2 | 56.4 | 5,540 | 38.0 | 36.6 |
| | Malta | 0.4 | 4.0 | 10,098 | — | — |
| | Poland | 38.6 | 143.6 | 3,716 | 56.5 | 54.1 |
| | Romania | 22.4 | 31.2 | 1,393 | 20.1 | 14.5 |
| | Slovenia | 2.0 | 23.9 | 11,984 | 15.5 | 14.6 |
| | Slovak Republic | 5.4 | 23.8 | 4,405 | 19.6 | 18.6 |
| | Turkey | 68.5 | 190.3 | 2,873 | 56.5 | 65.2 |
| **European Free Trade Area (EFTA)** | | | | | | |
| | Iceland | 0.3 | 9.0 | 32,060 | 3.7 | 3.5 |
| | Liechtenstein | 0.03 | — | — | — | — |
| | Norway | 4.5 | 172.8 | 38,298 | 61.5 | 68.5 |
| | Switzerland | 7.2 | 340.3 | 47,064 | 135.6 | 147.8 |

*Constant 1995 dollars.

Source: World Bank, 2003. Copyright 2003 by TRANSACTION PUBS. Reproduced with permission of TRANSACTION PUBS via Copyright Clearance Center.

and social differences could ever be overcome, held little hope for a unified Europe. Their skepticism has proved wrong. Today, many marvel at how far the European Economic Community has come. Although complete integration has not been fully achieved, a review of the structure of the EC, its authority over member states, the Single European Act, the European Economic Area, the Maastricht Treaty, and the Amsterdam Treaty will show why the final outcome of full economic and political integration seems certain.

**The Single European Act.**   Exhibit 10.3 illustrates the evolution of the EU from its beginnings after World War II to today. The **Single European Act** (1987) was the agreement designed to finally remove all barriers to trade and make the European Community a single internal market. The ultimate goal of the Treaty of Rome (1957), the agreement that founded the EC, was economic and political union, a United States of Europe. The Single European Act moved the EC one step closer to the goal of economic integration.

**Exhibit 10.2**

The European Economic Area: EU, EFTA, and Associates

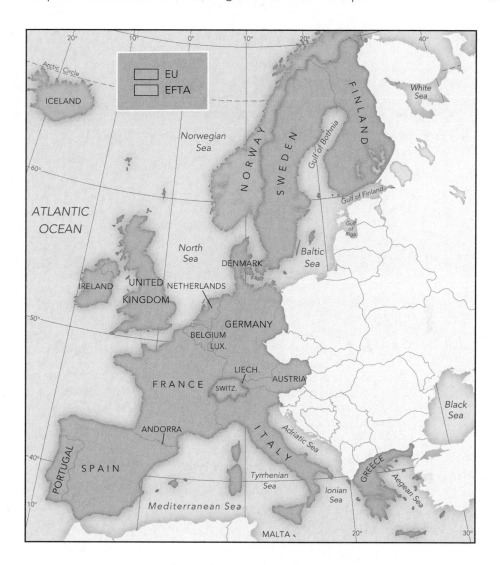

The European Commission, the EC's executive body, began the process toward total unification with a white paper outlining almost 300 pieces of legislation designed to remove physical, technical, and fiscal barriers between member states. The white paper was incorporated into the Single European Act, providing for the elimination of internal border controls with corresponding strengthening of external border controls, the unification of technical regulations on product standards, procedures to bring national value-added and excise tax systems among member countries closer together, and free migration of the population. Implementation of this series of economic changes began in 1992 and will continue into the foreseeable future.

In addition to dismantling the existing barriers, the Single European Act proposed a wide range of new commercial policies, including single European standards, one of the more difficult and time-consuming goals to achieve. Technical standards for electrical products are a good example of how overwhelming the task of achieving universal standards is for the EC. There are 29 types of electrical outlets, 10 types of plugs, and 12 types of cords used by EC member countries. The estimated cost for all EC countries to change wiring systems and electrical standards to a single European standard is 90 billion euros, or about 95 billion U.S. dollars. Because of the time it will take to achieve uniform Euro-standards for health, safety, technical, and other areas, the Single European Act provides for a policy of harmonization and mutual recognition.

Under *harmonization,* the most essential requirements for protection of health, safety, the environment, and product standards are established. Once all members meet these

**Exhibit 10.3**

From the European Coal and Steel Community to Monetary Union

Source: "Chronology of the EU," www.europa.eu.int/ (select Abc). Reprinted with permission from the European Communities.

| 1951 | Treaty of Paris | European Coal and Steel Community (ECSC) (Founding members are Belgium, France, Germany, Italy, Luxembourg, and the Netherlands). |
| --- | --- | --- |
| 1957 | Treaty of Rome | Blueprint, European Economic Community (EEC). |
| 1958 | European Economic Community | Ratified by ECSC founding members. Common Market is established. |
| 1960 | European Free Trade Association | Established by Austria, Denmark, Norway, Portugal, Sweden, Switzerland, and United Kingdom. |
| 1973 | Expansion | Denmark, Ireland, and United Kingdom join EEC. |
| 1979 | European monetary system | The European Currency Unit (ECU) is created. All members except the UK agree to maintain their exchange rates within specific margins. |
| 1981 | Expansion | Greece joins EEC. |
| 1985 | 1992 Single Market Program | White paper for action introduced to European Parliament. |
| 1986 | Expansion | Spain and Portugal join EEC. |
| 1987 | Single European Act | Ratified, with full implementation by 1992. |
| 1992 | Treaty on European Union | Also known as Maastricht Treaty. Blueprint for Economic and Monetary Union (EMU). |
| 1993 | Europe 1992 | Single European Act in force (January 1, 1993). |
| 1993 | European Union | Treaty on European Union (Maastricht Treaty) in force, with monetary union by 1999. |
| 1994 | European Economic Area | The EEA was formed with EU members and Norway and Iceland. |
| 1995 | Expansion | Austria, Finland, and Sweden join EU. |
| 1997 | Amsterdam Treaty | Established procedures for expansion to Central and Eastern Europe. |
| 1999 | Monetary union | Conversion rates are fixed, and euro used by banking and finance industry. Consumer prices are quoted in local currency and in euros. |
| 2002 | Banknotes and coins | Circulation of euro banknotes and coins begins January 1, and legal status of national banknotes and coins cancelled July 1, 2002. |

EC-wide essential requirements (i.e., harmonization), each member state will be expected to recognize each other's national standards for nonessential characteristics (i.e., *mutual recognition*). In other words, all member countries must adopt the same essential requirements as a base but also accept any different national standards as adequate.

Mutual recognition extends beyond technical or health standards and includes mutual recognition for marketing practices as well. The European Court of Justice (ECJ) interpreted Article 30, which establishes the principle of mutual recognition, to mean that a product put on sale legally in one member state should be available for sale in the same way in all others. The ECJ's landmark decision involved Germany's ban on the sale of Cassis de Dijon, a French liqueur. Germany claimed that selling the low-alcohol drink would encourage alcohol consumption, considered by authorities to be unhealthy. The Court of Justice rejected the argument, ruling that the restriction represented a nontariff barrier outlawed by Article 30. In other words, once Cassis de Dijon was legally sold in France, Germany was obligated, under mutual recognition, to allow it in Germany.

When all the directives are fully implemented, such artificial barriers to trade will be done away with. However, there are still problems to be resolved. Food definition problems in particular have impeded progress in guaranteeing free circulation of food products within the Community. For example, several EC member states maintain different definitions of yogurt, so an EC standard has yet to be established. The French insist that anything called yogurt must contain live cultures; thus, they prohibited the sale of a Dutch product under the name yogurt because it did not contain live cultures, as does the French product. Until a standard for yogurt is established, mutual recognition will not work as

Each month the European Parliament meets for three weeks here in Brussels, Belgium, and then moves for one week to meet in Strasbourg, France. The inconvenience of the fourth week move was a concession to French pride. Or, perhaps the cheese is better there?

intended. There are similar problems elsewhere, especially in the area of health, but the policy of harmonization and mutual recognition will, when fully implemented, eliminate national standards as a barrier to trade.

Among the first and most welcome reforms were the single customs document that replaced the 70 forms originally required for transborder shipments to member countries, the elimination of cabotage rules (which kept a trucker from returning with a loaded truck after delivery), and the creation of EC-wide transport licensing. More than 60,000 customs and tax formalities previously imposed at country borders were eliminated. These changes alone were estimated to reduce distribution costs 50 percent for companies doing cross-border business in the EC.

A survey showed that there was considerable benefit from the program over a five-year period. Up to 900,000 jobs were created, and the gross domestic product of the EU is between 1.1 percent and 1.5 percent higher than it would have been without the effects of the Single European Act. Additionally, price differentials between member states narrowed somewhat. Prior to 1992, the average price differential for consumer goods was 22.5 percent and for services was 33.7 percent, but it has since fallen to 19.6 percent and 28.6 percent, respectively, and is expected to fall further as integration continues.

Although several member states are not fully implementing all the measures, they are making progress. The proportion of directives not yet implemented in all 15 member states has fallen dramatically from 26.7 percent to 12.6 percent. Taxation is one of the areas where implementation lags and reform continues to be necessary. Value-added and registration taxes for automobiles, for example, range from 15 percent in Luxembourg to 218 percent in Denmark. A midsize Mercedes in Haderslev, Denmark, costs $90,000, nearly triple the amount you would pay in Flensburg, Germany, just 30 miles south. A Honda Civic costs the British consumer 89 percent more than it costs Continental customers. Scotch in Sweden has an $18 tax, nine times the amount levied in Italy. The EU finance ministers addressed these issues and made some progress, even though tax-raising ability is a sacred power of the nation-state. The full implementation of the legislation is expected to take several years. Even though all proposals have not been met, the program for unification has built up a pace that cannot be reversed.

**EC Institutions.**   The European Community's institutions form a federal pattern with executive, parliamentary, and judicial branches: the European Commission, the Council of Ministers, the European Parliament, and the Court of Justice. Their decision-making processes have legal status and extensive powers in fields covered by common policies.

The European Community uses three legal instruments: (1) regulations binding the member states directly and having the same strength as national laws; (2) directives also binding the member states but allowing them to choose the means of execution; and (3) decisions addressed to a government, an enterprise, or an individual, binding the parties named. Over the years, the Community has gained an increasing amount of authority over its member states.

The European Commission initiates policy and supervises its observance by member states, and it proposes and supervises execution of laws and policies. Commission members act only in the interest of the EC, and their responsibilities are to ensure that the EC rules and the principles of the common market are respected.

The Council of Ministers is the decision-making body of the EC; it is the council's responsibility to debate and decide which proposals of the Single European Act to accept as binding on EC members. The council can enact into law all proposals by majority vote except for changes in tax rates on products and services, which require unanimous vote. The council, for example, drafted the Maastricht Treaty, which was presented to member states for ratification.

The European Parliament originally had only a consultative role that passed on most Community legislation. It can now amend and adopt legislation, although it does not have the power to initiate legislation. It also has extensive budgetary powers that allow it to be involved in major EC expenditures.

The European Court of Justice is the Community's Supreme Court. It is responsible for challenging any measures incompatible with the Treaty of Rome and for passing judgment, at the request of a national court, on interpretation or validity of points of EC law. The court's decisions are final and cannot be appealed in national courts. For example, Estée Lauder Companies appealed to the ECJ to overrule a German court's decision to prohibit it from selling its product Clinique. The German court had ruled that the name could mislead German consumers by implying medical treatment. The ECJ pointed out that Clinique is sold in other member states without confusing the consumer and ruled in favor of Estée Lauder. This was a landmark case because many member countries had similar laws that were in essence nontariff trade barriers designed to protect their individual markets. If the German court ruling against Estée Lauder had stood, it would have been difficult for companies to market their products across borders in an identical manner. This is but one example of the ECJ's power in the EC and its role in eliminating nontariff trade barriers.

**European Free Trade Association and European Economic Area.**   Britain, not wanting to join the EEC, conceived the European Free Trade Association for those European nations not willing to join the EEC but wanting to participate in a free trade area. Britain and other EFTA countries later became members of the European Community in 1973. When Austria, Finland, and Sweden joined the EC in 1995 (see Exhibit 10.2) only Iceland, Liechtenstein, Norway, and Switzerland remained in EFTA. EFTA will most probably dissolve as its members join either the EEA or the EU.

Because of the success of the EC and concern that they might be left out of the massive European market, five members of the European Free Trade Association elected to join the 12 members of the EC in 1994 to form the European Economic Area, a single market with free movement of goods, services, and capital. The EFTA countries joining the EEA adopted most of the EC's competition rules and agreed to implement EC rules on company law; however, they maintain their domestic farm policies. The EEA is governed by a special Council of Ministers composed of representatives from EEA member nations.

**European Union**   The final step in the European Community's march to union was ratification of the Maastricht Treaty (1992). The treaty provided for the Economic and Monetary Union (**EMU**) and European Union.[12] The treaty touched on all the missing links needed for a truly European political union, including foreign policy. Because procedures on how foreign

[12]See www.europa.eu.int/abc-en.htm.

## CROSSING BORDERS 10.2  There Are Myths and Then There Are Euromyths

The Austrians feared the EU would force them to eat chocolate made with blood. The French worried about EU plans to ban certain maggots as bait because they suffer *"le stresse"* on a fishing hook. Italians complained about a fanciful plan to paint all taxis white. Others feared the EU would require nudity on beaches. Trendy Italian chefs cried foul when they heard that their cherished wood-burning ovens were to be banned. Brussels sprouted an edict on sexual harassment that struck down Valentine's Day cards. Then the EU wanted to do away with Britain's beloved double-decker buses and pull-chain toilets and classify carrots as fruit. In addition, Brussels outlawed asymmetrical Christmas trees and pronounced that donkeys must wear diapers. By the time EU packaging rules criminalized the curved cucumber, it was clear that the Eurocrats had clearly lost their senses.

"There Is No Absurdity of Which the European Community Is Not Capable," "The Whole Thing Has Turned into a Mad, Bureaucratic Alice in Wonderland Crossed with Kafka," blared the headlines. Yet what is really Kafkaesque is that each of these stories has only a remote relationship to reality. The EU calls them "Euromyths."

The EU didn't actually ban skiing when snow is less than 20 centimeters deep—but the European Parliament did raise the possibility of such a prohibition. Brussels didn't require donkeys to wear diapers on Euro-beaches, but it won't award its Blue Flag to beaches that admit the animals.

Curved cucumbers aren't banned, just classified differently for packaging reasons. The guidelines lay down a "maximum height of arc, 10 mm per 10 cm length of cucumber." The official EU justification is that "if you have straight cucumbers, it's possible to know how many you are getting in a box." As for symmetrical Christmas trees, a trade association, not the EU, proposed something like this. Carrots *are* classified as fruit, which allows the Portuguese to continue their practice of making carrot jam.

Some myths are completely fanciful, like the one about the EU banning square gin bottles; this started as an April Fool's joke in the *Times*. Also in this category is the Valentine's Day warning that the sending of unwanted cards could qualify as sexual harassment under EU law; it was meant to be tongue in cheek.

At the extremes are stories likening those implementing European child safety standards to Nazi collaborators (*The Mirror*) or suggesting that EU grants have funded IRA arms bunkers (*Daily Mail*). Both demonstrate nothing more than paranoia.

The EU has therefore hired grown men and women to spend their days reassuring an alarmed public that the EU has no plans to do away with paperboys, small bananas, knotty oak trees, saucy postcards, and any pizza that isn't 11 inches in diameter. Additionally, the European Commission publishes *Press Watch* to address press bias.

Sources: Dana Milbank, "Will Unified Europe Put Mules in Diapers and Ban Mini-Pizza?" *The Wall Street Journal*, June 22, 1995, p.1; Peter Popham and Scott Hughes, "Could This Banana Be Straighter?" *Independent* (London), February 2, 1996, p.4; "Addressing the Bias," *Press Watch—the European Union*, April 2000, www.cec.org.uk/pubs/prwatch/pw00/pw0009.htm; and Andrew Grice, "Paranoid British Press Is Full of Jingoistic Rubbish," *Independent News*, April 12, 2000.

---

policy and social legislation decisions are to be made are so complex, another round of negotiations that was concluded in the Amsterdam Treaty (1997) was necessary. Initially, there was considerable doubt about the viability of a European Union. Surrendering more sovereignty beyond that already relinquished with the provisions of the Single European Act seemed too extreme for many. There was concern that a monetary union would move monetary policy away from the individual countries to a central power. And even more sovereignty would be lost as the Court of Justice gained more power over business transactions. However, within months of the ratification of the treaty, the EU was expanded to include Austria, Finland, and Sweden. Norway voted not to join the EU but remains as a member of the European Free Trade Area. Much of the concern persists even as the Economic and Monetary Union is put into place.

**Economic and Monetary Union.**   The EMU, a provision of the Maastricht Treaty, established the parameters of the creation of a common currency for the EU, the *euro*, and established a timetable for its implementation. In 2002, a central bank was established, conversion rates were fixed, circulation of euro banknotes and coins was completed

**Exhibit 10.4**
The Euro

Source: Euro, www.europa.eu.int/
euro. Reprinted with permission from
the European Communities.

**Notes.** There are seven euro notes in different colors and sizes, denominated in 500, 200, 100, 50, 20, 10 and 5 euros. The designs symbolize Europe's architectural heritage, with windows and gateways on the front side as symbols of the spirit of openness and cooperation in the EU. The reverse side features a bridge from a particular age, a metaphor for communication among the people of Europe and the rest of the world.

**Coins.** There are eight euro coins, denominated in 2 and 1 euros, then 50, 20, 10, 5, 2, and 1 cent. Every coin will carry a common European face—a map of the European Union against a background of transverse lines to which are attached the stars of the European flag. On the obverse, each member state will decorate the coins with their own motifs, for example, the King of Spain or some national hero. Regardless of the motif, every coin can be used and will have the same value in all 11 member states.

**Sign.** The graphic symbol for the euro was inspired by the Greek letter epsilon, in reference to the cradle of European civilization and to the first letter of the word *Europe*. It looks like an *E* with two clearly marked, horizontal parallel lines across it. The parallel lines are meant to symbolize the stability of the euro. The official abbreviation is "EUR."

It took some selling for the Greeks to adopt the euro instead of the 2500-year-old drachma. The truck seen here in Athens Syntagma Square was equipped with video projectors and euro information stands and traveled to 40 Greek towns, informing folks about the new currency. (© AFP/CORBIS)

(see Exhibit 10.4), and the legal tender status of participating members' banknotes and coins was cancelled. To participate, members must meet strict limits on several financial and economic criteria, including a member's national deficit, debt, and inflation. The 12 member states switching to the euro beginning in January 1, 2001, were Austria, Belgium, Finland, France, Germany, Greece, Ireland, Italy, Luxembourg, Netherlands, Portugal, and Spain. Denmark voted in 2000 not to join the monetary union, leaving Britain[13] and Sweden still undecided. Denmark's rejection strengthened the anti-euro groups and means that there will be several years before the euro zone is expanded any further. Denmark's rejection of the euro has serious implications for the broader debate on the EU's future. Anti-euro advocates relied more on fears of a "European super state" and local interference from Brussels than on economic arguments when pushing for rejection.

Predictions of the impact of the euro range from its high costs and economic and political risk to its positive long-term impact. It is considered to be one of the most important economic events in postwar European history[14] and one that will have a positive long-term impact, albeit a negative effect on economic growth in the short run. The cost for changing over to euros will be high for members as well as companies. As an example of the cost a company will incur to convert to euros, Philips, the Dutch-based MNC, has 35 groups involving about 250 people under a steering committee of 35 senior managers working to convert all intracompany transactions to euros. All EU-based companies are converting as Philips is doing, and companies operating in the EU are converting prices, billing, and so forth because the euro will be the currency of the realm.

**Treaty of Amsterdam.**   The **Treaty of Amsterdam**, concluded in 1997, addressed some of the issues left undone in the Maastricht Treaty. It identifies the priority measures needed to bring the single market fully into effect and to lay a solid foundation for both the single currency and the enlargement into Central and Eastern Europe. The treaty's four objectives are to place employment and citizens' rights at the heart of the

---

[13]"Britain and the Euro, What a Pity, What a Relief," *The Economist,* June 14, 2003, p. 46.

[14]David McHugh, "Year after Switch, Euro Struggles with Image Problems," *Oregonian,* January 1, 2003, p. D1.

## CROSSING BORDERS 10.3  Death of the Drachma

Having officially joined the European Union on Jan. 1, Greece began phasing out the drachma, Europe's oldest currency and the survivor of some 2,500 years of war and economic turmoil. Below, highlights from its storied history.—MEGAN JOHNSTON

Source: March 2001 *Money.* Used by permission of *Money Magazine.*

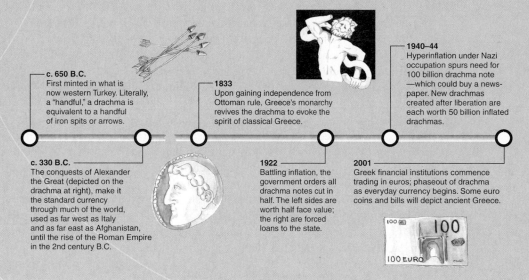

**c. 650 B.C.**
First minted in what is now western Turkey. Literally, a "handful," a drachma is equivalent to a handful of iron spits or arrows.

**c. 330 B.C.**
The conquests of Alexander the Great (depicted on the drachma at right), make it the standard currency through much of the world, used as far west as Italy and as far east as Afghanistan, until the rise of the Roman Empire in the 2nd century B.C.

**1833**
Upon gaining independence from Ottoman rule, Greece's monarchy revives the drachma to evoke the spirit of classical Greece.

**1922**
Battling inflation, the government orders all drachma notes cut in half. The left sides are worth half face value; the right are forced loans to the state.

**1940–44**
Hyperinflation under Nazi occupation spurs need for 100 billion drachma note—which could buy a newspaper. New drachmas created after liberation are each worth 50 billion inflated drachmas.

**2001**
Greek financial institutions commence trading in euros; phaseout of drachma as everyday currency begins. Some euro coins and bills will depict ancient Greece.

Union, to sweep away the last remaining obstacles to freedom of movement and strengthen security, to give Europe a stronger voice in world affairs, and to make the union's institutional structure more efficient with a view to enlarging the Union.

The original 40-year-old operating rules of the EC were proving to be inadequate in dealing with the problems that confront the EU today. Expansion beyond its present 15 members, managing the conversion to the euro and EMU, and speaking with one voice on foreign policy that directly affects the European continent are all issues that require greater agreement among members and thus more responsibility and authority for the institutions of the EU.[15] The Amsterdam Treaty increases the authority of the institutions of the EU and is designed to accommodate the changes brought about by the monetary union and the admission of new members.[16]

**Expansion of the European Union.**   The process of enlargement is the most important item on the EU's agenda. Much progress has been made in the negotiations with the 13 front-runners for membership,[17] but the impact on the EU's legislative structure must be addressed before expansion is complete. The original target date for admission of the first ten, 2004, was pushed back in the estimation of many to 2006 at the earliest. One of the main preoccupations is the prospect of illegal immigrants from former Soviet states surging across poorly guarded borders of the candidate states and making their way further west within the EU. The EU is demanding that borders be sealed, but the candidate states are reluctant to jeopardize relations with neighboring communities.[18] Further, the

---

[15]Alison Hardie, "Blair Hints at New Role as EU President," *The Scotsman,* April 23, 2003, p. 4.

[16]John Andrews, "Agenda 2003," *Europe,* December–January 2003, pp. 14–17.

[17]David Holley, "Accord Reached on 10-Nation Expansion of the European Union," *Los Angeles Times,* December 14, 2002, p. A3.

[18]David Fairlamb and Rick Butler, "Will Poland Turn Its Back on EU Membership?" *BusinessWeek,* May 26, 2003, p. 60.

EU fears a flood of cheap labor even if the borders are closed; it wants a long transition period before freedom of movement of labor, whereas the applicants say their citizens should be allowed to work anywhere in the EU after they are members.

Aside from the border issue, other difficult areas of negotiation are agriculture, human rights issues, and financial considerations. The applicant countries are eager to see their farming communities integrated into the EU's Common Agricultural Policy from the first day of entry, but the EU negotiators want to stagger the process over several years. The delays have caused consternation on both sides because there is fear that both sides will lose interest in enlargement and that many of the reforms in the candidate countries will be slowed. These issues must be negotiated to the satisfaction of both sides before expansion is undertaken. Regarding human rights, Turkey's legislature has made several recent changes in laws affecting its racial minority Kurds and freedom of the press to come into compliance with EU requirements.[19] All ten newcomers will have to meet stiff economic[20] and currency stability criteria as well.[21]

A more serious issue facing the EU is the impact that admitting 6 or more members would have on the internal legislative process. Institutions designed for the founding EU members would simply collapse under the weight of adding 6 or more members to the existing 15. The legislative process, particularly the voting system, is already cumbersome with only 15 member states; with expansion to 20 and then 25 or more it would all but grind to a halt. An intergovernmental conference was held in Nice, France, to address institutional issues necessary to keep the EU workable with more members.

Intergovernmental conferences are extremely important; they are the only means of amending the 1957 Treaty of Rome, which governs all of the Union's activities. Any proposed amendment must be referred to a conference for unanimous agreement; its recommendations are then put to a summit meeting of EU heads of state and government. If approved there, all the member states and the European Parliament must then ratify them.

## Strategic Implications for Marketing in Europe

The complexion of the entire world marketplace was changed significantly by the coalition of nations into multinational market groups. To international business firms, multinational groups spell opportunity in bold letters through access to greatly enlarged markets with reduced or abolished country-by-country tariff barriers and restrictions. Production, financing, labor, and marketing decisions are affected by the remapping of the world into market groups.

World competition will intensify as businesses become stronger and more experienced in dealing with large market groups. European and non-European multinationals are preparing to deal with the changes in competition in a fully integrated Europe. In an integrated Europe, U.S. multinationals may have an initial advantage over expanded European firms because U.S. businesses are more experienced in marketing to large, diverse markets and are accustomed to looking at Europe as one market. U.S. firms do not carry the cumbersome baggage of multiple national organizations dealing in many currencies, with differentiated pricing and administration, with which most EU firms must contend. The advantage, however, is only temporary as mergers, acquisitions, and joint ventures consolidate operations of European firms in anticipation of the benefits of a single European market. Individual national markets will still confront international managers with the same problems of language, customs, and instability, even though they are packaged under the umbrella of a common market. However, as barriers come down and multi-country markets are treated as one common market, a global market will be one notch closer to reality.

Regulation of business activities has intensified throughout multinational market groups; each group now has management and administrative bodies specifically concerned

---

[19]Amberin Zaman, "Turkey Passes More Reforms in Quest for EU Membership," *Los Angeles Times*, June 20, 2003, p. A3 (agrees to human rights reforms).

[20]James Mehring, "High Hurdles for New EU Members to Clear," *BusinessWeek*, May 5, 2003, p. 26.

[21]"Not So Easy to Join," *The Economist*, May 24, 2003, p. 40.

with business. In the process of structuring markets, rules and regulations common to the group are often more sophisticated than those of the individual countries. Despite the problems and complexities of dealing with the new markets, the overriding message to the astute international marketer continues to be opportunity and profit potential.

**Opportunities.**   Economic integration creates large mass markets for the marketer. Many national markets, too small to bother with individually, take on new dimensions and significance when combined with markets from cooperating countries. Large markets are particularly important to businesses accustomed to mass production and mass distribution because of the economies of scale and marketing efficiencies that can be achieved. In highly competitive markets, the benefits derived from enhanced efficiencies are often passed along as lower prices that lead to increased purchasing power.

Most multinational groups have coordinated programs to foster economic growth as part of their cooperative effort. Such programs work to the advantage of marketers by increasing purchasing power, improving regional infrastructure, and fostering economic development. Despite the problems that are sure to occur because of integration, the economic benefits from free trade can be enormous.

Major savings will result from the billions of dollars now spent in developing different versions of products to meet a hodgepodge of national standards. Philips and other European companies invested a total of $20 billion to develop a common switching system for Europe's ten different telephone networks. This compares with the $3 billion spent in the United States for a common system and $1.5 billion in Japan for a single system.

**Market Barriers.**   The initial aim of a multinational market is to protect businesses that operate within its borders. An expressed goal is to give an advantage to the companies within the market in their dealings with other countries of the market group. Analysis of the interregional and international trade patterns of the market groups indicates that such goals have been achieved. Intra-EU imports now account for 67.9 percent of total manufacturing imports compared with 61.2 percent before the 1992 program began. Intra-EU service imports also increased somewhat, from 49.6 percent of the total to 50 percent. This increase of trade among the member states was not at the expense of third countries.

Companies willing to invest in production facilities in multinational markets may benefit from protectionist measures because these companies become a part of the market. Exporters, however, are in a considerably weaker position. This prospect confronts many U.S. exporters who face the possible need to invest in Europe to protect their export markets in the European Union. The major problem for small companies may be adjusting to the EU standards. A company selling in one or two EU member countries and meeting standards there may find itself in a situation of having to change standards or be closed out when an EU-wide standard is adopted.

A manufacturer of hoses used to hook up deep-fat fryers and other gas appliances to gas outlets faced such a problem when one of its largest customers informed the company that McDonald's was told it could no longer use their hoses in its British restaurants. The same thing happened in EuroDisney. Unfortunately, when the common standards were written, only large MNCs and European firms participated, so they had the advantage of setting standards to their benefit. The small company has only one choice: Change or leave. In this particular case, it appears that competitors are working to keep the company out of the market. There are, however, enough questions about threaded fittings and compatibility that the company is working with individual countries to gain entrance to their markets—just like it was before a single market existed.

The prospect of Europe as one unified internal market has many countries concerned about the EU becoming Fortress Europe—free trade within but highly protectionist to all others. Only when the EU has adjusted to the euro and its new directives and focuses more on external trade will it be apparent if issues of protectionism arise.

**Reciprocity.**   Reciprocity is an important part of the trade policy of a unified Europe. If a country does not open its markets to an EU firm, it cannot expect to have access to the EU market. Europeans see reciprocity as a fair and equitable way of allowing foreign

The hammer and sickle logo of the old USSR has been replaced by signs of free enterprise in Russia. Here in the main shopping district of St. Petersburg Nike Sport is prominent along with the Coca-Cola advertising.

companies to participate in the European market without erecting trade barriers, while at the same time giving Europeans equal access to foreign markets.

**Marketing Mix Implications**  Companies are adjusting their marketing mix strategies to reflect anticipated market differences in a single European market. In the past, companies often charged different prices in different European markets. Nontariff barriers between member states supported price differentials and kept lower-priced products from entering those markets where higher prices were charged. Colgate-Palmolive Company has adapted its Colgate toothpaste into a single formula for sale across Europe at one price. Before changing its pricing practices, Colgate sold its toothpaste at different prices in different markets.

Beddedas Shower Gel is priced in the middle of the market in Germany and as a high-priced product in the United Kingdom. As long as products from lower-priced markets could not move to higher-priced markets, such differential price schemes worked. Now, however, under the EC rules, companies cannot prevent the free movement of goods, and parallel imports from lower-priced markets to higher-priced markets are more apt to occur. Price standardization among country markets will be one of the necessary changes to avoid the problem of parallel imports. With the adoption of the euro, price differentials are much easier to spot. And from the consumer's viewpoint, it will be easier to search for brand-name products at the best bargains. Further, the euro will make marketing on the Internet a much simpler task for the European firm than it presently is. On balance, a single currency will make competition in Europe a lot fairer and also a lot tougher.

In addition to initiating uniform pricing policies, companies are reducing the number of brands they produce to focus advertising and promotion efforts. For example, Nestlé's current three brands of yogurt in the EU will be reduced to a single brand. Unilever began to winnow its 1,600 brands down to focus on 400 core brands. They plan to develop master brands in certain markets such as the EU and to market others globally. A major benefit from an integrated Europe is competition at the retail level. Europe lacks an integrated and competitive distribution system that would support small and midsize outlets. The elimination of borders could result in increased competition among retailers and the creation of Europe-wide distribution channels.

## The Commonwealth of Independent States

Europe has two other trade groups that emerged after the dissolution of the USSR: the Commonwealth of Independent States (CIS) and the Central European Free Trade Area (CEFTA). The series of events after the aborted coup against Mikhail Gorbachev led to the complete dissolution of the USSR. The first to declare independence were the Baltic states, which quickly gained recognition by several Western nations. The remaining 12 republics of the former USSR, collectively known as the Newly Independent States (NIS), regrouped into the Commonwealth of Independent States (see Exhibit 10.5).

The CIS is a loose economic and political alliance with open borders but no central government (see Exhibit 10.6). The main provisions of the commonwealth agreement are to repeal all Soviet laws and assume the powers of the old regimes; launch radical economic reforms, including freeing most prices; keep the ruble, but allow new currencies; establish a European Community–style free trade association; create joint control of nuclear weapons; and fulfill all Soviet foreign treaties and debt obligations.

The 12 members of the CIS share a common history of central planning, and their close cooperation could make the change to a market economy less painful, but differences over economic policy, currency reform, and control of the military may break them apart. How the CIS will be organized and what its ultimate importance will be is anyone's guess.

The three Slavic republics of Russia, Ukraine, and Belarus have interests and history in common, as do the five Central Asian republics. But the ties between these two core groups of the CIS are tenuous and stem mainly from their former Soviet membership.

**Exhibit 10.5**   The Newly Independent States

The CIS is by no means coming apart, although it has not solidified to the point of having a stable membership and purpose. Under Vladimir Putin,[22] Russia shows renewed interest in the CIS, and a free trade zone, which Russia had blocked since the CIS was created, may become a reality.

Of all the former republics, Azerbaijan, Georgia, and Armenia have done the best economically since leaving the former USSR. After the USSR collapsed, their economies had all imploded to less than half their peak size during Soviet days. Now, however, they are showing sustained signs of commercial renewal[23]—and multinational icons like Intel

---

[22]Michael Wines, "Russia: Putin Backs Belarus Union," *New York Times,* January 21, 2003, p. 5.

[23]Dean Kuipers, "The Russians Are Coming," *Los Angeles Times,* February 5, 2003, p. E3.

**Exhibit 10.6**   Commonwealth of Independent States (CIS)

| Country | Population (millions) | GDP* (billions) | GDP* per Capita | Imports of Goods and Services (billions) | Exports of Goods and Services (billions) |
|---|---|---|---|---|---|
| Russia | 144.8 | $377.6 | $2,609 | $87.4 | $109.1 |
| Ukraine | 49.1 | 48.4 | 986 | 29.2 | 31.6 |
| Belarus | 10.0 | 14.9 | 1,493 | 9.7 | 9.3 |
| Armenia | 3.1 | 4.1 | 1,068 | 2.1 | 1.1 |
| Moldova | 4.3 | 2.9 | 678 | 3.3 | 2.0 |
| Azerbaijan | 8.1 | 3.7 | 460 | 2.8 | 0.9 |
| Uzbekistan | 25.1 | 12.8 | 512 | 3.2 | 3.2 |
| Turkmenistan | 5.3 | 8.6 | 1,587 | 2.8 | 2.8 |
| Tajikistan | 6.2 | 2.6 | 420 | — | — |
| Kazakhstan | 14.9 | 25.5 | 1,712 | 10.2 | 9.3 |
| Kyrgystan | 5.0 | 2.1 | 417 | 0.5 | 0.5 |
| Georgia | 5.2 | 2.6 | 499 | 1.5 | 1.0 |

*Constant 1995 dollars.

are pouring investment into the area.[24] Despite Russia's economic problems, all members of the CIS have had economic growth, and inflation was held between a high of 5.9 percent for Tajikistan and a low of 0.2 percent for Kazakhstan.[25]

**Central European Free Trade Area**

The newest free trade area in Europe is the six-member Central European Free Trade Area (CEFTA), organized in 1993 by Poland, Hungary, Slovakia, and the Czech Republic and later joined by Slovenia and Romania. Initially, import duties were removed from 60 percent of items, and there was a commitment to abolish all duties and quotas within five years. Unlike the CIS, CEFTA was successful in its plan to remove barriers to trade. Since 1996, approximately 80 percent of industrial exports among CEFTA members were duty free, and in 1997 all tariffs were abolished.

Economically, CEFTA has been a success story. Tariff reductions are on schedule and there was growth in the gross domestic product (GDP), falling unemployment, and a slowdown of inflationary trends for all members of the association. Since all six member states requested admission to the EU, CEFTA really serves as a vehicle to get their economies to a level that allows accession to the EU.

## The Americas

The Americas,[26] the second Triad region, have as their center the United States. Within the Americas, the United States, Canada, Central America, and South America are natural if sometimes contentious trading partners. As in Europe, the Americas are engaged in all sorts of economic cooperative agreements, with NAFTA being the most significant and Mercosur gaining in importance.

**North American Free Trade Agreement**

Preceding the creation of the North American Free Trade Agreement (NAFTA),[27] the United States and Canada had the world's largest bilateral trade agreement; each was the other's largest trading partner. Despite this unique commercial relationship, tariff and other trade barriers hindered even greater commercial activity. To further support trade activity, the two countries established the **United States–Canada Free Trade Agreement** (CFTA), designed to eliminate all trade barriers between the two countries. The CFTA created a single, continental commercial market for all goods and most services. The agreement between the United States and Canada was not a customs union like the European Community; no economic or political union of any kind was involved. It provided only for the elimination of tariffs and other trade barriers.

Shortly after both countries ratified the CFTA, Mexico announced that it would seek free trade with the United States. Mexico's overtures were answered positively by the United States, and talks on a U.S.–Mexico free trade area began. Mexico and the United States were strong trading partners for decades, but Mexico had never officially expressed an interest in a free trade agreement until the President of Mexico, Carlos Salinas de Gortari, announced that Mexico would seek such an agreement with the United States and Canada.

Despite the disparity between Mexico's economy and the economies of the other two countries, there were sound reasons for such an alliance. Canada is a sophisticated industrial economy, resource rich, but with a small population and domestic market. Mexico, on the other hand, desperately needs investment, technology, exports, and other economic reinforcement to spur its economy. Even though Mexico has an abundance of oil and a rapidly growing population, the number of new workers is increasing faster than its economy can create new jobs. The United States needs resources (especially oil) and, of

[24]Andy Reinhardt and Paul Starobin, "Intel Inside—Russia That Is," *BusinessWeek,* June 23, 2003, p. 48.

[25]Sabrina Tavernise, "Buying on Credit is the Latest Rage in Russia," *New York Times,* January 20, 2003, p. 1.

[26]For a comprehensive list of all trade agreements in the Americas, with links to specific documents, visit www.sice.oas.org and select Trade Agreements.

[27]The following website provides information on both NAFTA and FTAA: www.mac.doc.gov.

## CROSSING BORDERS 10.4  Americans Obey European Rules

Americans may not realize it, but rules governing the food they eat, the software they use, and the cars they drive increasingly are set by the European Union. The EU regulates more frequently and more rigorously than the United States, especially when it comes to consumer protection. So even though the American market is bigger, the EU, as the jurisdiction with the tougher rules, tends to call the shots for the world's farmers and manufacturers.

Because of the EU, Microsoft Corp. modified contracts with software makers and Internet service providers to give consumers a wider choice of technologies, and McDonald's Corp. stopped giving soft plastic toys with its Happy Meals. Twenty years ago, if you designed something to U.S. standards you could pretty much sell it all over the world. Carrier air conditioners are redesigned to comply with pending European recycling rules, which are tougher than U.S. standards. The EU initiative requires electrical-equipment makers to eschew certain hard-to-recycle plastics and chemicals, such as brominated flame retardants. For many of GE's businesses, ranging from light bulbs to plastics, "almost 99 percent" of new regulations will come from the EU over time, says GE's chief executive.

Regulators on both sides of the Atlantic are trying to figure out how to protect consumers' online privacy. But while the U.S. has mostly promoted industry self-regulation, the EU, in October 1998, laid down the law: Europe's residents have the right to know what data is collected about them online, and to get that information changed, if it is inaccurate, or force the collector to delete it. The EU threatened to cut off trans-Atlantic e-mail traffic if U.S. companies failed to guarantee those rights. But during the past two years, voluntary agreements to abide by the EU rules have been signed by 176 companies, ranging from film manufacturer Eastman Kodak Co. to chewing-gum maker Wm. Wrigley Jr. Co. As global businesses, they didn't want to go to the expense of creating special websites or data-processing procedures just for Europeans. "There's only one program of privacy protection at Microsoft," and its Europe's, says Microsoft's director of corporate privacy.

Another EU initiative targets automakers. A preliminary agreement between the European Commission and automakers in Europe, the U.S., and Japan would require car hoods and bumpers to be redesigned so they would cause fewer injuries in accidents with pedestrians. Metal "bull bars"—the protruding curved pipes that help make the fronts of many sport-utility vehicles look rugged—would be banned on any new vehicles sold in Europe, because the rigid bars could make the vehicles more deadly if they struck a pedestrian. Automakers signed the deal because they figured it would be less onerous than binding legislation. The executive director of safety for General Motors Corp., says the bumper rule could force GM to retool its Corvette factory because the cost of designing and using special parts for the European market would be hard to justify.

U.S. farmers cater to European tastes, too. Although the U.S. Food and Drug Administration approved the use of most genetically modified crops in human food, the EU placed strict limits on which genetically modified seeds can be planted and how they can be used. What causes trouble for American farmers is the EU's labeling requirements for food containing even one percent of a genetically modified ingredient. Thus some U.S. food processors won't buy genetically modified corn or soybeans because they sell their products internationally, and it isn't practical to make special non-genetically modified batches just for Europe. Some food processors won't even buy conventional grain from farmers who also plant GMO varieties. Worried about trade with Europe, the Illinois Department of Agriculture last year asked farmers not to plant a Monsanto Co. corn that isn't approved in the EU. Kraft Foods Inc. says it won't use genetically modified vegetable oil in the Toblerone chocolate and Milka candy bars that it exports from Europe to 150 other countries, including the United States. Most recently the U.S. government has tired of the "food fight" and decided to sue the EU over what it sees as breaches of WTO rules.

Source: Brandon Mitchener, "Increasingly, Rules of Global Economy Are Set in Brussels" *The Wall Street Journal*, April 23, 2002, p. A1; and "Genetic Food Fight," *The Wall Street Journal*, May 15, 2003, p. A16. Copyright 2003 by Dow Jones & Co. Inc. Reproduced with permission of Dow Jones & Co. Inc. via Copyright Clearance Center.

course, markets. The three need each other to compete more effectively in world markets, and they need mutual assurances that their already dominant trading positions in each other's markets are safe from protection pressures. When NAFTA was ratified and became effective in 1994, a single market of 360 million people with a $10 trillion GDP emerged.

## Exhibit 10.7   Key Provisions of NAFTA*

**Market access**

Within 10 years of implementation, all tariffs will be eliminated on North American industrial products traded between Canada, Mexico, and the United States. All trade between Canada and the United States not already duty free will be duty free as provided for in CFTA. Mexico will immediately eliminate tariffs on nearly 50 percent of all industrial goods imported from the United States, and remaining tariffs will be phased out entirely within 15 years.

**Nontariff barriers**

In addition to elimination of tariffs, Mexico will eliminate nontariff barriers and other trade-distorting restrictions. U.S. exporters will benefit immediately from the removal of most import licenses that have acted as quotas, essentially limiting the importation of products into the Mexican market. NAFTA also eliminates a host of other Mexican barriers, such as local-content, local-production, and export-performance requirements that have limited U.S. exports.

**Rules of origin**

NAFTA reduces tariffs only for goods made in North America. Tough rules of origin will determine whether goods qualify for preferential tariff treatment under NAFTA. Rules of origin are designed to prevent free riders from benefiting through minor processing or transshipment of non-NAFTA goods. For example, Japan could not assemble autos in Mexico and avoid U.S. or Canadian tariffs and quotas unless the auto had a specific percentage of Mexican (i.e., North American) content. For goods to be traded duty free, they must contain substantial (62.5 percent) North American content. Because NAFTA rules of origin have been strengthened, clarified, and simplified over those contained in the U.S.-Canada Free Trade Agreement, they supersede the CFTA rules.

**Customs administration**

Under NAFTA, Canada, Mexico, and the United States have agreed to implement uniform customs procedures and regulations. Uniform procedures ensure that exporters who market their products in more than one NAFTA country will not have to adapt to multiple customs procedures. Most procedures governing rules-of-origin documentation, recordkeeping, and verification will be the same for all three NAFTA countries. In addition, the three will issue advanced rulings, on request, on whether or not a product

qualifies for tariff preference under the NAFTA rules of origin.

**Investment**

NAFTA will eliminate investment conditions that restrict the trade of goods and services to Mexico. Among conditions eliminated are the requirements that foreign investors export a given level or percentage of goods or services, use domestic goods or services, transfer technology to competitors, or limit imports to a certain percentage of exports.

**Services**

NAFTA establishes the first comprehensive set of principles governing services trade. U.S. and Canadian financial institutions are permitted to open wholly owned subsidiaries in Mexico, and all restrictions on the services they offer will be lifted. NAFTA opens Mexico's market for international truck, bus, and rail transport and eliminates the requirement to hand off cargo to a Mexican vehicle upon entry into Mexico, saving U.S. industry both time and money. U.S. truck and bus companies will have the right to use their own drivers and equipment for cross-border cargo shipment and passenger service with Mexico.

**Intellectual property**

NAFTA will provide the highest standards of protection of intellectual property available in any bilateral or international agreement. The agreement covers patents, trademarks, copyrights, trade secrets, semiconductor integrated circuits, and copyrights for North American movies, computer software, and records.

**Government procurement**

NAFTA guarantees businesses fair and open competition for procurement in North America through transparent and predictable procurement procedures. In Mexico, PEMEX (the national oil company), CFE (the national electric company), and other government-owned enterprises will be open to U.S. and Canadian suppliers.

**Standards**

NAFTA prohibits the use of standards and technical regulations used as obstacles to trade. However, NAFTA provisions do not require the United States or Canada to lower existing health, environmental, or safety regulations, nor does NAFTA require the importation of products that fail to meet each country's health and safety standards.

*A complete description of NAFTA provisions can be found at www.mac.doc.gov/nafta/3001.htm.

NAFTA requires the three countries to remove all tariffs[28] and barriers to trade over 15 years, but each country will have its own tariff arrangements with nonmember countries. All changes already occurring under CFTA will stand and be built on under NAFTA. Some of the key provisions of the agreement can be found in Exhibit 10.7.

[28]Carol J. Williams, "Farmers in Mexico Fear End of Tariffs," *Los Angeles Times*, January 1, 2003, p. A3.

**NAFTA** is a comprehensive trade agreement that addresses, and in most cases improves, all aspects of doing business within North America. The elimination of trade and investment barriers among Canada, Mexico, and the United States creates one of the largest and richest markets in the world. Cross-border cooperation seems to be ameliorating other longstanding areas of conflict such as legal and illegal immigration.[29] NAFTA paved the way for Wal-Mart to move into Mexico[30] and Mexican supermarket giant, Gigante, to move into the United States.[31] Other cross-border services are also thriving, including entertainment[32] and healthcare.[33]

NAFTA has its detractors, and it is safe to say that there has been constant turmoil since its inception. Mexico had a serious financial crisis that led to the devaluation of the peso, and the expansion of NAFTA became a political hot potato in the United States when it was severely politicized during the 1996 presidential election. Unfortunately, all the candidates presented a distorted picture. Opponents painted a picture of economic doom. One candidate claimed that NAFTA would produce a "giant sucking sound" of jobs running from the United States to Mexico. Proponents created an equally distorted picture of economic bliss. Neither side presented a factual picture. First, it was much too early to estimate accurately the effect of NAFTA; second, it was expected that jobs would be lost and companies displaced in the short run. Misinformation prevailed and the general public turned sour on NAFTA. With public opinion turning against the expansion of NAFTA to Chile, the next stage in the agreement, it became obvious that a request for fast-track authorization was in jeopardy; the Clinton administration lost interest, and NAFTA progress languished. While none of its members advocated disbanding NAFTA, it did appear that the U.S. administration had directed its attention elsewhere and did not follow through to the second stage—expansion beyond Mexico.

Depending on who you ask, NAFTA has been a "wash," a costly creator of deep U.S. trade deficits[34] and job losses, or a success.[35] A survey taken three years after its beginning revealed that 67 percent of Mexicans surveyed believed that Mexico had had little or no success with NAFTA. In another study, 57 percent of U.S. citizens said they were against any new trade pacts with Latin American countries. Our own quick look at the consequences of NAFTA suggest that unemployment has declined, GDP per capita, foreign direct investment inflows, and exports have risen for all three countries in the 10 years since passage.[36]

U.S. and foreign investors with apparel and footwear factories in Asia have been encouraged to relocate their production operations to Mexico. For example, Victoria's Secret lingerie chain opened a new manufacturing plant near Mexico City. The company previously used contractors in Asia for its lingerie line. Even with wages in Mexico three times the monthly wages in Sri Lanka, the company will still come out ahead because it is cheaper and faster to move goods from Mexico City to the United States than from Colombo—the time it takes to make a sample can be cut from weeks to days. Further, there are no tariffs on Mexican goods, whereas Sri Lanka goods carry a 19 percent duty.

---

[29]Eduardo Porter, "Mexico Woos Its Citizens Living in the U.S.," *The Wall Street Journal,* October 24, 2002, p. B1.

[30]Traci Carl, "Wal-Mart Waves Its Retail Magic Wand Overseas," *Oregonian,* March 30, 2003, p. D1.

[31]Tiffany Montgomery, "Gigante's Big Steps," *Orange County Register,* September 10, 2002, p. B1; and Denise Bonilla, "Latino Market Arrives with Giant Aspirations—Once Shunned by City Officials, Gigante Gets Warm Welcome in Anaheim," *Los Angeles Times,* May 7, 2003, p. B6.

[32]"The Mexicans are Coming, Americans Take to Mexico's Movies," *The Economist,* October 5, 2002, p. 35.

[33]Jennifer Mena, "Cross-Border Health Coverage," *Los Angeles Times,* July 29, 2002, p. B1.

[34]Christopher J. Chipello, "NAFTA's Benefits to Firms in Canada May Top Those for Mexico," *Wall Street Journal,* February 23, 2003, p. A2.

[35]David T. Griswold, "NAFTA at 10," *World Trade,* March 2003, p. 10; and Julie Demers, "Learning from NAFTA," *CMA Management,* April 2003, pp. 48–50.

[36]World Bank statistics, 2003.

Mexico's apparel exports to the United States have tripled to $3.3 billion since NAFTA began. Last year Mexico surpassed Hong Kong and China to become the United States' top source of imported apparel. This is a great boon for U.S. fabric and yarn makers. In years past they supplied only minuscule amounts of fabric to the vertically integrated Asian apparel markets; now they supply 70 percent of the raw material going to Mexican sewing shops.

Total foreign direct investment in Mexico has averaged $11 billion a year since 1995 as companies from all over the world poured money into auto and electronics plants, telecommunications, petrochemicals, and a host of other areas. A large chunk of investment is earmarked for factories that will use Mexico as an export platform for the rest of North America, and increasingly the rest of Latin America.

The investment boom in Mexico has been a major source of new demand for U.S. manufacturers of capital goods. The largest post-NAFTA gains in U.S. exports to Mexico have been in such high-technology manufacturing sectors as industrial machinery, transportation and electronic equipment, plastics, rubber, fabricated metal products, and chemicals.

Job losses have not been as drastic as once feared, in part because companies such as Lucent Technologies have established *maquiladora* plants in anticipation of the benefits from NAFTA. The plants have been buying more components from U.S. suppliers while cutting back on Asian sources. Miles Press, a $2 million maker of directory cards, saw orders from Lucent grow 20 percent in just a few months. Berg Electronics, a $700 million component maker, expects to triple sales to Lucent's Guadalajara plant next year. This ripple effect has generated U.S. service-sector jobs as well. Fisher Price shifted toy production for the U.S. market from Hong Kong to a plant in Monterrey. Celadon Trucking Services, which moves goods produced for Fisher Price from Mexico to the United States, has added 800 new U.S. drivers to the payroll.

For Valley Drive Systems, manufacturer of automobile front-wheel-drive assemblies, NAFTA has been a success. Because Canadian tariffs on its products were lowered, Valley Drive products are now competitive with those from Taiwan. The company made its first-ever exports in 1996 and now exports 17 percent of its products.

NAFTA is a work in progress. It is too early to pass judgment; after all, the EC has been in existence for more than 40 years and has had its ups and downs. NAFTA is a mere babe in arms in comparison. What is happening is that economic relationships among the three countries are becoming more intense each day, for the most part quietly and profitably. In short, it will take at least 10 to 15 years for an objective evaluation of NAFTA to be possible.

During the protracted economic slump following the dot.com bust in the United States, *maquiladora* plants have been closing at an alarming rate. The manufacturing is migrating to other low-paying countries such as China,[37] Guatemala, and Vietnam.[38] However, the firms operating in Tijuana and other border cities are responding with investments in technology and increased marketing efforts.[39]

**Southern Cone Free Trade Area (Mercosur)**

Mercosur[40] is the second-largest common-market agreement in Latin America after NAFTA. The Treaty of Asunción, which provided the legal basis for Mercosur, was signed in 1991 and formally inaugurated in 1995. The treaty calls for a common market that would eventually allow for the free movement of goods, capital, labor, and services among the member countries, with a uniform external tariff. Because there was concern among Mercosur members about sacrificing sovereign control over taxes and other policy matters, the agreement envisioned no central institutions similar to those of the European Common Market institutions.

[37]Geri Smith, "Wasting Away: Despite SARS, Mexico Is Still Losing Export Ground to China," *BusinessWeek,* June 2, 2003, pp. 42–44.

[38]Geri Smith, "The Decline of the *Maquiladora*," *BusinessWeek,* April 29, 2003, p. 59.

[39]Evelyn Iritani and Richard Bourdreaux, "Mexico's Factories Shift Gears to Survive," *Los Angeles Times,* January 5, 2003, p. C1.

[40]See www.guia-mercosur.com/main.htm.

Since its inception, Mercosur has become the most influential and successful free trade area in South America. With the addition of Bolivia and Chile in 1996, Mercosur became a market of 220 million people with a combined GDP of nearly $1 trillion and is the third largest free trade area in the world. Mercosur has demonstrated greater success than many observers expected. The success can be attributed to the willingness of the region's governments to confront some very tough issues caused by dissimilar economic policies related to the automobile and textile trade and to modify antiquated border customs procedures that initially created a bottleneck to smooth border crossings. The lack of surface and transportation infrastructure to facilitate trade and communications is a lingering problem that is being addressed at the highest levels.

Mercosur has pursued agreements aggressively with other countries and trading groups.[41] For example, there are concrete negotiations under way to create a free trade program with Mexico, talks with Canada regarding a free trade agreement, and talks between Chile and Mercosur aimed at gradual and reciprocal trade liberalization.

In addition, negotiations are well under way for a free trade agreement between the EU and Mercosur, the first region-to-region free trade accord. A framework agreement was signed in 1995, and the long-term objective is to reach convergence in all areas by 2005: cooperation, trade, market access, intellectual property, and political dialogue. The two blocs propose the largest free trade area in the world. The advantages of the accord to Mercosur will mainly come from lifting trade barriers on agricultural and agro-industrial products, which account for the lion's share of Mercosur exports to Europe. However, that will also be a major stumbling block if the EU is unwilling to open its highly protected agricultural sector to Brazilian and Argentine imports. Nevertheless, one official of the EU indicated that the EU was already in the process of reforming its Common Agricultural Policy. Although negotiations will not be easy, Mercosur and the EU should be able to reach an accord. As we shall see in the next section, Mercosur has assumed the leadership in setting the agenda for the creation of a free trade area of the Americas or, more likely, a South American Free Trade Area (SAFTA).

## Latin American Economic Cooperation

Besides the better-known NAFTA and Mercosur, there are other Latin American market groups (Exhibit 10.8) that have had varying degrees of success. Plagued with tremendous foreign debt, protectionist economic systems, triple-digit inflation, state ownership of basic industries, and over-regulation of industry, most Latin American countries were in a perpetual state of economic chaos. Under these conditions there was not much trade or integration among member countries. But, as discussed earlier, sparked by the success of Mercosur and NAFTA, there is a wave of genuine optimism in Latin America about the economic miracle under way spurred by political and economic reforms from the tip of Argentina to the Rio Grande. Coupled with these market-oriented reforms is a desire to improve trade among neighboring countries by reviving older agreements or forming new ones. In fact, many of the trade groups are seeking ties to Mercosur or the European Union, or both.

Keeping track of all the proposed free trade areas in Latin America is a major endeavor, because almost every country has either signed some type of trade agreement or is involved in negotiations. In addition to new trade agreements, many of the trade accords that have been in existence for decades moved from a moribund to an active state. For example, the first and most ambitious, the Latin American Free Trade Association (LAFTA) gave way to the Latin American Integration Association (LAIA), with new rules of organization that revitalized that group.

**Latin American Integration Association.**   The long-term goal of the LAIA, better known by its Spanish acronym, ALADI, is a gradual and progressive establishment of a Latin American common market. One of the more important aspects of LAIA that differs from LAFTA, its predecessor, is differential treatment of member countries according to their level of economic development. Over the years, negotiations among

---

[41]Terry Wade, "Latin Trade Bloc Flexes Muscles," *The Wall Street Journal,* June 16, 2003, p. A13.

**Exhibit 10.8**  Market Regions of the Americas

| Association | Member | Population (millions) | GDP* (billions) | GDP* per Capita | Imports of Goods and Services (billions) | Exports of Goods and Services (billions) |
|---|---|---|---|---|---|---|
| **North American Fair Trade (NAFT)** | | | | | | |
| | United States | 285.3 | $9,013.9 | $31,592 | $1,560.3 | $1,148.0 |
| | Mexico | 99.4 | 371.7 | 3,739 | 188.0 | 158.5 |
| | Canada | 31.1 | 717.4 | 23,080 | 278.9 | 313.1 |
| **Central American Common Market (CACM)** | | | | | | |
| | Guatemala | 11.7 | 18.2 | 1,554 | 5.5 | 3.7 |
| | Costa Rica | 3.9 | 15.1 | 3,900 | 6.8 | 7.9 |
| | El Salvador | 6.4 | 11.2 | 1,757 | 5.2 | 4.3 |
| | Nicaragua | 5.2 | 2.1 | 437 | 1.9 | 0.8 |
| | Honduras | 6.6 | 4.7 | 711 | 2.3 | 1.9 |
| **Caribbean Community and Common Market (CARICOM)** | | | | | | |
| | Antigua and Barbuda | 0.1 | 0.6 | 9,015 | 0.5 | 0.4 |
| | Barbados | 0.3 | 2.3 | 8,610 | 1.2 | 1.1 |
| | Belize | 0.2 | 0.8 | 3,189 | 0.6 | 0.4 |
| | Dominica | 0.1 | 0.2 | 3,291 | 0.2 | 0.1 |
| | Grenada | 0.1 | 0.4 | 3,579 | 0.3 | 0.2 |
| | Guyana | 0.8 | 0.7 | 942 | 0.8 | 0.7 |
| | Haiti | 8.1 | 2.9 | 354 | 1.0 | 0.5 |
| | Jamaica | 2.6 | 5.6 | 2,171 | 3.0 | 2.7 |
| | Montserrat St. Kitts-Nevis | — | 0.3 | 6,535 | 0.2 | 0.1 |
| | St. Lucia | 0.2 | 0.6 | 3,771 | 0.4 | 0.3 |
| | Surinam | 0.4 | 0.4 | 1,036 | 0.1 | 0.1 |
| | Trinidad-Tobago | 1.3 | 7.3 | 5,553 | 4.4 | 4.0 |
| **Latin American Integration Association (LAIA)** | | | | | | |
| | Argentina | 37.5 | 280.0 | 7,468 | 32.0 | 34.7 |
| | Bolivia | 8.5 | 8.0 | 944 | 2.2 | 1.7 |
| | Brazil | 172.4 | 798.8 | 4,633 | 79.9 | 86.0 |
| | Chile | 15.4 | 83,0 | 5,385 | 24.2 | 32.5 |
| | Colombia | 43.0 | 98.0 | 2,277 | 18.4 | 18.8 |
| | Ecuador | 12.9 | 19.0 | 1,478 | 5.4 | 5.8 |
| | Mexico | as above | — | | — | |
| | Paraguay | 5.4 | 9.6 | 1,703 | 2.5 | 1.2 |
| | Peru | 26.3 | 60.1 | 2,311 | 10.0 | 10.8 |
| | Uruguay | 3.4 | 19.7 | 5,870 | 4.1 | 3.9 |
| | Venezuela | 24.6 | 81.9 | 3,326 | 23.7 | 24.8 |

*Constant 1995 dollars.

Source: World Bank, 2003. Copyright 2003 by TRANSACTION PUBS. Reproduced with permission of TRANSACTION PUBS via Copyright Clearance Center.

member countries lowered duties on selected products and eased trade tensions over quotas, local-content requirements, import licenses, and other trade barriers. An important feature of LAIA is the provision that permits members to establish bilateral trade agreements among member countries. It is under this proviso that trade agreements are developed among LAIA members.

**Caribbean Community and Common Market (CARICOM).**   The success of the Caribbean Free Trade Association led to the creation of the Caribbean Community and

Common Market. CARICOM member countries continue in their efforts to achieve true regional integration. The group has worked toward a single-market economy, and in 2000 established the CSME (CARICOM Single Market and Economy) with the goal of a common currency for all members. The introduction of a common external tariff structure was a major step toward that goal, but there is some unease as to whether the CSME will actually come into full existence in 2001, the date set for its implementation. CARICOM continues to seek stronger ties with other groups in Latin America and has signed a trade agreement with Cuba.

## NAFTA to FTAA or SAFTA?

Initially NAFTA was envisioned as the blueprint for a free trade area extending from Alaska to Argentina. The first new country to enter the NAFTA fold was to be Chile,[42] then membership was to extend south until there was a Free Trade Area of the Americas (FTAA)[43] by 2005. The question now is whether there will be an FTAA or whether there will be a tri-country NAFTA in the north and a South American Free Trade Area (SAFTA) led by Brazil and the other member states of Mercosur in the south. The answer to this question rests in part with the issue of fast-track legislation and the policies of the Bush administration. Although the Clinton administration was successful in gaining legislation to create NAFTA, its policies toward Latin America and NAFTA drifted aimlessly afterward. As discussed earlier, NAFTA was severely politicized during the 1996 presidential elections, and the perceived lack of interest on the part of the United States created doubt among Latin American leaders about the sincerity of U.S. leadership. Although NAFTA remains a solid tri-country free trade area, it may or may not become a part of a larger trade area of the Americas.

Regrettably, the United States may have lost its leadership role in the creation of a broader and more inclusive Americas trade area. At the time of the 1994 Miami summit for the Free Trade Area of the Americas, the United States' leadership was unquestioned. Today, Brazil-led Mercosur is providing the leadership for the creation of the FTAA. The United States' declining influence was apparent in a 1997 presummit meeting of the various working groups, where support for the U.S. blueprint to build an FTAA was only lukewarm. The U.S. plan was seen as a threat to Brazil's burgeoning regional status; as a consequence, Brazil was pushing its own plan, which differed in timing and process from that of the United States. The question of how to proceed toward a free trade area for the Western Hemisphere was seen as a clash between the two largest economies in the Americas, Brazil and the United States.

The first confrontation was over two issues: the timing of tariff reductions and a single binding agreement versus a series of separate agreements. Brazil, speaking on behalf of its Mercosur partners, favored a gradual buildup to talks on tariffs using a three-stage approach. Step one would involve negotiations over what it called business facilitation and deregulation. Step two would involve embarking on negotiations on trade-related rules such as dispute settlement and rules of origin. Step three would involve beginning talks on tariffs. The United States, backed by Canada, wanted to start negotiations on all the issues immediately after the Santiago summit in 1998, with all tariff reductions in place by 2005.

Another cause for agitation between the United States and the rest of Latin America is the United States' insistence that FTAA be used as the basis for a wide-ranging agreement on hemispheric issues such as security, drug trafficking, the environment, and labor issues. Brazil takes a much narrower approach, believing the accords should be limited to trade only. Brazil's response was that the United States "will have to stop using trade as an instrument of political pressure" if it expects to secure the fast-growing Latin American market through the FTAA.

---

[42]Evelyn Iritani, "U.S. and Chile Sign Free Trade Agreement to Reduce Tariffs and Other Barriers," *Los Angeles Times,* June 7, 2003, p. C1.

[43]See www.ftaa.org.

Linking foreign trade with foreign policy is a tactic for which Latin America has continuously faulted the United States. A recent example cited by Brazil was the politically motivated trade sanction against Argentina in which 300 Argentine products were pulled out of a system of preferences that had been operating since 1974, a measure that increased the price of exports from Argentina to the United States by more than $260 million annually. Washington said the measure was punishment for unsatisfactory protection of intellectual rights in Argentina. Colombia also has been sanctioned for dumping its flower exports and therefore pays the maximum 76 percent tariff; Ecuador has seen restrictions imposed on its bananas, and Brazil is facing problems on textile imports, orange juice, and other agricultural produce.

Brazil convened the first Latin American summit of 12 heads of state in 2000 to discuss economic integration and other issues. The first steps were taken toward the creation of a South American trade bloc by setting goals to integrate the continent's economies via a network of highways, bridges, and river transportation and telecommunications systems. The goal was a continent-wide trade bloc that would give the region greater bargaining power in negotiations leading up to the creation of the U.S. sponsored FTAA. Brazil wants to slow the process of establishing the FTAA until the regional trade blocs have time to solidify and merge into a South American–wide bloc capable of competing on a hemispheric scale.

One of the results of the South American summit was the Declaration of Brasilia, which pledged to unite South America's two main trade blocs into a single free trade zone with 340 million consumers and an economic output of $13 trillion. The president of Venezuela said the region would be "wiped off the map" if it did not unite before the creation in 2005 of an FTAA.

Not to be an active participant in the FTAA and not to be able to influence the final architecture of the FTAA could be a blow to the U.S. economy and trade. As a market for U.S. goods, the Western Hemisphere is nearly twice as large as the European Union and nearly 50 percent larger than Asia. Moreover, between 1960 and 1996 U.S. goods exports globally increased 57 percent, but U.S. exports to Latin America (excluding Mexico) increased by 110 percent. If these trends were to continue, Latin America alone could exceed Japan and Western Europe combined as an export market for U.S. goods by 2010.

With or without U.S. influence, FTAA continues to evolve, but it may evolve into a South American Free Trade Area with Mercosur at the center providing the necessary drive. Mercosur's negotiations with Canada are going smoothly because Canadian business supports the FTAA and the Canadian government is a strong champion of liberalized trade. Negotiations under way with Europe and the rest of South America also seem positive. Other countries are getting involved with their own negotiations; a meeting with the Pacific Economic Cooperation Council (PECC) was organized by Chile to discuss establishing a partnership between Pacific Asia (East Asia, Australia, and New Zealand) and Latin America. Chile was praised as performing a laudable role as the gateway for Pacific Asia into Latin America. Within the Americas, Chile has established separate free trade links with Mexico and Canada and has associate membership in Mercosur.

One of the objectives in the creation of NAFTA was to expand throughout the Americas and build a unified free trade area to preclude a piecemeal and complex system of conflicting bilateral and multilateral agreements among nations in the Americas—a situation that could lead to disastrous trade wars. Unfortunately, the direction Latin America seems to be heading is the very situation that NAFTA was intended to avoid. For example, between 1992 and 1997, Latin America and Asia signed 20 new trade agreements that excluded the United States. Further, there has been a proliferation of subregional trade pacts. Mexico, for example, has signed trade treaties with Chile, Costa Rica, Bolivia, Colombia, Venezuela, Nicaragua, and Uruguay, and it is negotiating with several Central American countries as well as Israel and Japan. While the United States has remained on the sidelines, the EU is expanding into Central Europe and the Americas, and APEC continues its expansion to include other areas of Asia and possibly even China.

Fast-track authorization was granted to the Bush administration and talks are ongoing with Latin American trading partners. Mexico's President Fox and President Bush appear to be strong advocates of NAFTA expansion, as is Canada. Initial reports of the 2001 summit of the Americas in Quebec indicate that President Bush will push for FTAA by 2005 but the question remains whether the president can obtain approval from Congress. The expansion depends on the dedication and foresight of the United States and the other countries in establishing an FTAA. It is critical for the United States to look beyond five or even ten years and consider the economic and political impact of a trading world dominated by trading blocs, a process that is well under way. The ultimate question is, Can the United States afford to stand alone in NAFTA while the remainder of the trading world is organized in an expanded EU, SAFTA, and an Asian Free Trade Area?

## Asian-Pacific Rim

Countries in the Asian-Pacific Rim constitute the third Triad region. Japan is at the center of this Triad region, which also includes many of the world's newly industrialized countries (NICs) whose early economic growth depended on exports to U.S. markets. Now, after decades of depending on the United States and Europe for technology and markets, countries in the Asian-Pacific Rim are preparing for the next economic leap driven by trade, investment, and technology aided by others in the region. Though few in number, trade agreements among some of the Asian NICs are seen as movement toward a regionwide, intra-Asian trade area, with Japan at the center of this activity.

Although the United States is Japan's single largest trading partner, markets in China and Southeast Asia are increasingly more important in Japanese corporate strategy for trade and direct investment. Once a source of inexpensive labor for products shipped to Japan or to third markets, these countries are now seen as viable markets. Further, Japanese investment across a number of manufacturing industries is geared toward serving local customers and building sophisticated local production and supplier networks.

Present trade agreements include one multinational trade group, the Association of Southeast Asian Nations (ASEAN), which is evolving into the ASEAN Free Trade Area (**AFTA**); **ASEAN+3**, a forum for ASEAN ministers plus ministers from China, Japan, and South Korea; and the Asia-Pacific Economic Cooperation (**APEC**), a forum that meets annually to discuss regional economic development and cooperation.

## Association of Southeast Asian Nations

The primary multinational trade group in Asia is ASEAN.[44] The goals of the group are economic integration and cooperation through complementary industry programs; preferential trading, including reduced tariff and nontariff barriers; guaranteed member access to markets throughout the region; and harmonized investment incentives. Like all multinational market groups, ASEAN has experienced problems and false starts in attempting to unify the combined economies of its member nations. Most of the early economic growth came from trade outside the ASEAN group. Similarities in the kinds of products they had to export, in their natural resources, and other national assets hampered earlier attempts at intra-ASEAN trade. The steps countries took to expand and diversify their industrial base in order to foster intraregional trade when ASEAN was first created have resulted in the fastest-growing economies in the region and an increase in trade among members (see Exhibit 10.9).

Four major events account for the vigorous economic growth of the ASEAN countries and their transformation from cheap-labor havens to industrialized nations: (1) the ASEAN governments' commitment to deregulation, liberalization, and privatization of their economies; (2) the decision to shift their economies from commodity-based to manufacturing-based; (3) the decision to specialize in manufacturing components in which they have a comparative advantage (this created more diversity in their industrial output and increased opportunities for trade); and (4) Japan's emergence as a major provider of technology and capital necessary to upgrade manufacturing capability and develop new industries.

Although there has never been an attempt to duplicate the supranational government of the European Union, each year the group becomes more interrelated. ASEAN Vision 2020 is the most outward-looking commitment to regional goals ever accepted by the

[44]See www.aseansec.org.

**Exhibit 10.9**   Far Eastern Market Group

| Association | Member | Population (millions) | GDP* (billions) | GDP* per Capita | Imports of Goods and Services (billions) | Exports of Goods and Services (billions) |
|---|---|---|---|---|---|---|
| **ASEAN Free Trade Area (AFTA)** | | | | | | |
| | Brunei | 0.3 | $  5.7 | $17,650 | $  — | $  — |
| | Cambodia | 12.3 | 3.9 | 317 | 2.3 | 2.3 |
| | Indonesia | 209.0 | 216.2 | 1,034 | 50.4 | 60.2 |
| | Laos | 5.4 | 2.5 | 465 | — | — |
| | Malaysia | 23.8 | 112.1 | 4,708 | 98.7 | 117.6 |
| | Myanmar | 48.3 | — | — | — | — |
| | Philippines | 78.3 | 91.1 | 1,165 | 37.6 | 34.0 |
| | Singapore | 4.1 | 112.0 | 27,118 | — | — |
| | Thailand | 61.2 | 174.6 | 2,853 | 72.7 | 94.6 |
| | Vietnam | 79.5 | 31.0 | 390 | 15.3 | 10.6 |
| **Plus Three** | | | | | | |
| | China | 1,271.8 | 1,117.2 | 878 | 371.4 | 457.4 |
| | Japan | 127.0 | 5,647.7 | 44,458 | 487.6 | 591.9 |
| | South Korea | 47.3 | 639.2 | 13,502 | 213.8 | 320.9 |

*Constant 1995 dollars.

Source: World Bank, 2003. Copyright 2003 by TRANSACTION PUBS. Reproduced with permission of TRANSACTION PUBS via Copyright Clearance Center.

group. Among the targets that will lead to further integration is the commitment to implement fully and as rapidly as possible the ASEAN Free Trade Area.

Just as was the case in the EU, businesses are drafting plans for operation within a free trade area. The ability to sell in an entire region without differing tariff and nontariff barriers is one of the important changes that will affect many parts of the marketing mix. Distribution can be centralized at the most cost-effective point rather than having distribution points dictated by tariff restrictions. Some standardization of branding is necessary because large customers buy at the regional level rather than bit by bit at the country level. Pricing can be more consistent, which helps reduce the smuggling and parallel importing that occur when there are major price differentials among countries because of different tariff schedules. In essence, marketing can become more regionally and centrally managed.

One result of the Asian financial crisis of 1997 to 1998 was the creation of ASEAN+3 (ASEAN plus China, Japan, and South Korea) to deal with trade and monetary issues facing Asia. Most of East Asia felt that they were both let down and put upon by the West, who they felt created much of the problem by pulling out in the midst of the crisis. It was felt that the leading financial powers either declined to take part in the rescue operations, as the United States did in Thailand, or that they proposed unattainable solutions. The result was the creation of ASEAN+3, consisting of the foreign and finance ministers of each country, who meet annually after ASEAN meetings. Their first meeting was devoted to devising a system whereby the member countries share foreign exchange reserves to defend their currencies against future attack. Although still only tentative, there was also discussion among the members of ASEAN+3 of creating a common market and even a single currency or, perhaps, a new Asian entity encompassing both Northeast and Southeast Asia. Closer links between Southeast Asia and Northeast Asia are seen as a step toward strengthening Asia's role in the global economy and creating of a global three-bloc configuration.

**Asia-Pacific Economic Cooperation**

The other important grouping that encompasses the Asian-Pacific Rim is the Asia-Pacific Economic Cooperation.[45] Formed in 1989, APEC provides a formal structure for the major governments of the region, including the United States and Canada, to discuss

[45]See www.apec.org.

their mutual interests in open trade and economic collaboration. APEC is a unique forum that has evolved into the primary regional vehicle for promoting trade liberalization and economic cooperation. APEC includes all the major economies of the region and the most dynamic, fastest-growing economies in the world. APEC has as its common goal a commitment to open trade, to increase economic collaboration, to sustain regional growth and development, to strengthen the multilateral trading system, and to reduce barriers to investment and trade without detriment to other economies.

Representatives from APEC member nations meet annually to discuss issues confronting the group, to propose solutions to problems arising from the growing interdependence among their economies, and to continue their quest for ways to lower barriers to trade. Although APEC is still far from being a free trade area, each meeting seems to advance it another step in that direction, notwithstanding the objections of some members.

## Africa

Africa's multinational market development activities can be characterized as a great deal of activity but little progress. Including bilateral agreements, an estimated 200 economic arrangements exist between African countries (Exhibit 10.10). Despite the large number and assortment of paper organizations, there is little actual economic integration because of the political instability that has characterized Africa in recent decades[46] and the unstable economic base on which Africa has had to build. The United Nations Economic Commission for Africa (ECA) has held numerous conferences but has been hampered by governmental inexperience, undeveloped resources, labor problems, and chronic product shortages.

The Economic Community of West African States (ECOWAS) and the Southern African Development Community (SADC) are the two most active regional cooperative groups. A 15-nation group, ECOWAS has an aggregate gross domestic product of more than $57.9 billion and is striving to achieve full economic integration. The twentieth ECOWAS summit in 1997 approved a plan to accelerate subregional economic integration and development, with emphasis on their full commitment to regional monetary integration and the eventual adoption of a single West African currency. Unfortunately, ECOWAS continues to be plagued with financial problems, conflict within the group, and inactivity on the part of some members. After 25 years, the ECOWAS treaty and its much-defined objectives and the way they are to be achieved over a 15-year period in three stages languishes; nothing has been achieved and free trade remains a deferred dream.

---

[46]"Peacekeeping in Congo: Is Protection a Mirage?" *The Economist,* June 14, 2003, pp. 43–44.

The HIV/AIDS epidemic and the associated poverty prevents sub-Saharan Africa from participating in the economic development associated with the global economy. There appears no end in sight to the misery for the millions living there. Protestors march to the U.S. Embassy in Pretoria, South Africa. *(AP/Wide World Photos)*

**Exhibit 10.10**     African Market Groups (continued on next page)

| Association | Member | Population (millions) | GDP* (billions) | GDP* per Capita | Imports of Goods and Services (billions) | Exports of Goods and Services (billions) |
|---|---|---|---|---|---|---|
| **Afro-Malagasy Economic Union** | | | | | | |
| | Benin | 6.4 | $ 2.7 | 424 | $ 0.8 | $ 0.6 |
| | Burkina Faso | 11.6 | 2.9 | 250 | 0.7 | 0.4 |
| | Cameroon | 15.2 | 10.6 | 696 | 3.3 | 3.1 |
| | Central African Republic | 3.8 | 1.3 | 339 | — | — |
| | Chad | 52.4 | 1.8 | 230 | 1.2 | 0.2 |
| | Congo | 16.4 | 4.5 | 85 | 3.3 | 2.6 |
| | Cote d'Ivoire | 1.3 | 11.7 | 715 | 3.7 | 4.3 |
| | Gabon | 11.1 | 5.5 | 4,379 | 2.0 | 2.6 |
| | Mali | 2.7 | 3.2 | 292 | 1.3 | 1.1 |
| | Mauritania | 2.7 | 1.4 | 502 | 0.7 | 0.6 |
| | Niger | 11.2 | 2.3 | 208 | 0.4 | 0.4 |
| | Senegal | 9.8 | 6.1 | 629 | 2.4 | 2.1 |
| | Togo | 4.7 | 1.5 | 322 | 0.7 | 0.4 |
| **East African Customs Union** | | | | | | |
| | Ethiopia | 54.8 | 7.9 | 121 | 2.1 | 1.3 |
| | Kenya | 30.7 | 10.0 | 325 | 3.8 | 3.3 |
| | Sudan | 31.7 | 10.4 | 328 | — | — |
| | Tanzania | 34.4 | 6.8 | 197 | 2.2 | 1.5 |
| | Uganda | 22.8 | 8.1 | 355 | 2.3 | 1.3 |
| | Zambia | 10.3 | 4.2 | 405 | 1.5 | 1.9 |
| **Union of Arab Maghreb** | | | | | | |
| | Algeria | 30.8 | 49.4 | 1,616 | 12.6 | 14.8 |
| | Libya | 5.4 | — | — | — | — |
| | Tunisia | 9.7 | 24.8 | 2,562 | 12.5 | 11.7 |
| | Morocco | 29.2 | 41.9 | 1,436 | 16.3 | 12.1 |
| | Mauritania | as above | — | — | — | — |
| **Economic Community of West African States** | | | | | | |
| | Benin | as above | — | — | — | — |

The Southern African Development Community is the most advanced and viable of Africa's regional organizations. Its 14 members encompass a landmass of 6.6 million square kilometers containing abundant natural resources and a population of over 199 million. South Africa, the region's dominant economy, has a GDP of $176 billion and accounts for 76.8 percent of SADC market share. After years of negotiations, 11 members of SADC approved a free trade agreement aimed at phasing out a minimum of 85 percent of tariffs within eight years, and all tariffs by the end of 2012.

## Middle East

The Middle East has been less aggressive in the formation of successfully functioning multinational market groups. The Arab Common Market has set goals for free internal trade but has not succeeded. The aim is to integrate the economies of the 22 Arab countries, but before that will be feasible, a long history of border disputes and persisting ideological differences must be overcome. The idea is still alive, however, and is a topic of discussion whenever Arab foreign ministers meet. The Arab Gulf states, Egypt, and Morocco are focusing on the proposed establishment of an Arab Free Trade Area by 2007. This proposal may become a reality because several Arab nations now have bilateral free trade zones, and

| | | | | | |
|---|---|---|---|---|---|
| Burkina Faso | as above | — | — | — | — |
| Cape Verde | 0.4 | 0.7 | 1,550 | 0.4 | 0.2 |
| Cote d'Ivoire | as above | — | — | — | — |
| Gambia | 1.3 | 0.5 | 382 | 0.4 | 0.3 |
| Ghana | 19.7 | 8.3 | 421 | 3.9 | 2.9 |
| Guinea | 7.6 | 4.7 | 613 | 1.0 | 1.0 |
| Guinea-Bissau | 1.2 | 0.3 | 206 | 0.1 | 0.1 |
| Liberia | 3.2 | 0.6 | 196 | — | — |
| Mali | as above | — | — | — | — |
| Mauritania | as above | — | — | — | — |
| Niger | as above | — | — | — | — |
| Nigeria | 1129.9 | 33.4 | 257 | 21.5 | 13.5 |
| Senegal | as above | — | — | — | — |
| Sierra Leone | 5.1 | 0.8 | 158 | 0.1 | 0.0 |
| Togo | 4.7 | — | — | — | — |
| **Southern African Development Community** | | | | | |
| Angola | 13.5 | 7.1 | 525 | — | — |
| Botswana | 1.7 | 7.0 | 4,130 | 3.1 | 3.5 |
| Congo | as above | — | — | — | — |
| Lesotho | 2.1 | 1.2 | 563 | 1.0 | 0.4 |
| Namibia | 1.8 | 4.3 | 2,383 | 2.5 | 2.0 |
| Malawi | 10.5 | 1.7 | 163 | 0.7 | 0.5 |
| Mauritius | 1.2 | 5.2 | 4,352 | 3.3 | 3.0 |
| Mozambique | 18.1 | 3.9 | 213 | 1.7 | 1.1 |
| Seychelles | 0.1 | 0.5 | 5,939 | 0.6 | 0.5 |
| S. Africa | 43.2 | 175.9 | 4,068 | 42.0 | 46.2 |
| Swaziland | 1.1 | 1.6 | 1,529 | 1.3 | 1.1 |
| Tanzania | as above | — | — | — | — |
| Zambia | 10.3 | — | — | — | — |
| Zimbabwe | 12.8 | 7.2 | 559 | 3.0 | 3.0 |

*Constant 1995 dollars.

Source: World Bank, 2003. Copyright 2003 by TRANSACTION PUBS. Reproduced with permission of TRANSACTION PUBS via Copyright Clearance Center.

one report indicated that many Arab countries are refurbishing their economic infrastructures to prepare for membership.

Iran, Pakistan, and Turkey, formerly the Regional Cooperation for Development (RCD), have renamed their regional group the Economic Cooperation Organization (ECO). Since reorganizing, Afghanistan and six of the Newly Independent States were accepted into the ECO. Impressive strides in developing basic industrial production were being made when the RCD was first organized, but the revolution in Iran ended any economic activity. ECO has as its primary goal the development of its infrastructure in order to pave the way for regional cooperation. Unfortunately, trade volume among ECO members constitutes only 7 percent of their total trade. However, a recent announcement from ECO indicated that there has been an agreement to reduce tariff and nontariff barriers to boost trade.

The other activity in the region, led by Iran, is the creation of the Organization of the Islamic Conference (OIC), a common market composed of Islamic countries. A preferential tariff system among the member states of the OIC and the expansion of commercial services in insurance, transport, and transit shipping are among the issues to be debated at the next conference of Islamic countries. The OIC represents 60 countries and over 650 million Muslims worldwide. The member countries' vast natural resources, substantial capital, and cheap labor force are seen as the strengths of the OIC.

# Regional Trading Groups and Emerging Markets

There are two opposing views regarding the direction of global trade in the future. One view suggests that the world is dividing into major regional trading groups such as the European Union, NAFTA, and the

ASEAN Free Trade Area that are now and will continue to be the major markets of the future. The other view is that global economic power may be shifting away from the traditional industrialized markets to the developing world and its emerging markets.

Those who support the first view see the world divided into three regional Triads centered on a major industrialized power: the United States in the Americas, the EU in Europe, and Japan in Asia. Further, these trading blocs will lead the industrialized world into a more protectionist period that excludes countries not aligned with a trade group. Speculation is that until the member countries of the EU adjust to a new internal competitive environment there will be a strong tendency to "keep the EU for Europeans." It is also conceivable that the United States and an expanded NAFTA will become more protective of markets in the Americas, and that Japan and ASEAN will dominate Asian markets. Further, it is natural for the dominant countries in each of the regions to focus more of their economic trade within their respective areas. This suggests that these three Triads will dominate trade patterns. Should such a scenario develop, those countries not tied economically to one of these trading blocs will be denied access to markets, capital, and technology, and, thus, to economic growth.

Those who hold the second view see the focus of international trade shifting away from the mature economies of the United States, Europe, and Japan and toward the emerging markets. The most important argument given in support of this view is that developed countries have mature, stable markets dominated by global companies. Thus their economies will grow more slowly than emerging markets and offer less opportunity for new trade. Conversely, enormous demand will be created as emerging economies continue the rate of economic development experienced over the last decade. These emerging economies will need highways, communications networks, utilities, factories, and the other capital goods necessary for industrialization. And as their economies continue to prosper, consumer goods will be needed to satisfy the demands of a newly affluent consumer market. Rather than international trade being driven by the major industrialized countries, emerging economies may be the engine for global market growth. Many experts predict that over the next 50 years the majority of global economic growth will be in the developing world, principally in those countries identified as emerging markets. While most of the immediate growth will be accounted for by 10 countries now on the threshold of expansion, many of the 120 other developing countries in Europe, Latin America, and Asia are awakening to the desire for economic development and industrialization and may soon be among the future emerging markets.

A shift in global demand may already be occurring. For example, during the last decade the U.S. share of exports going to industrialized countries remained flat, while the share of exports going to emerging markets increased for that same period. A similar pattern has occurred in Japan: In 1988, Japan exported more than 5 percent more to the United States than to Asia, but nearly a decade later, Japan exported nearly 40 percent more to Asia than it did to the United States.

In reality, both views may be too extreme. What is more likely to occur is that global economic growth will be spurred by both the creation of regional trade groups and the desire for economic growth in the developing world. The future may be as much about sharing in the enormous projected growth of the emerging markets as it is about sharing markets of the industrialized world. It is very likely that the competitive battleground of the future will encompass both the industrialized world and emerging markets. Competitive rivals will be Japan, Europe, and the United States as well as several of the NICs. All the players are in place. Only time will tell which direction global trade will take.

## Summary

The experiences of the multinational market groups developed since World War II point out both the successes and the hazards such groups encounter. The various attempts at economic cooperation represent varying degrees of success and failure, but almost without regard to their degree of success, the economic market groups have created great excitement among marketers.

Economic benefits possible through cooperation relate to more efficient marketing and production. Marketing efficiency is effected through the development of mass markets, encouragement of competition, the improvement of personal income, and various psychological market factors. Production efficiency derives from specialization, mass production for mass markets, and the free movement of the factors of production. Economic integration also tends to foster political harmony among the countries involved; such harmony leads to stability, which is beneficial to the marketer.

The marketing implications of multinational market groups may be studied from the viewpoint of firms located inside the market or of firms located outside, which wish to sell to the markets. For each viewpoint the problems and opportunities are somewhat different; regardless of the location of the marketer, however, multinational market groups provide great opportunity for the creative marketer who wishes to expand volume. Market groupings make it economically feasible to enter new markets and to employ new marketing strategies that could not be applied to the smaller markets represented by individual countries. At the same time, market groupings intensify competition by protectionism within a market group but may foster greater protectionism between regional markets. Since there is little question that future global markets will revolve around regional superpowers, tomorrow's marketers must concern themselves with positioning in these trade groupings in order to keep the door open to opportunity. Mercosur and ASEAN+3, for example, suggest the growing importance of economic cooperation and integration. Such developments will continue to confront the international marketer by providing continually growing market opportunities and challenges.

## Questions

1. Define the following terms:

   | | |
   |---|---|
   | multinational market region, 278 | EMU, 288 |
   | | Treaty of Amsterdam, 290 |
   | free trade area, 282 | United States–Canada |
   | customs union, 282 | Free Trade Agreement, 296 |
   | common market, 282 | NAFTA, 299 |
   | Mercosur, 282 | AFTA, 305 |
   | political union, 282 | ASEAN+3, 305 |
   | Maastricht Treaty, 282 | APEC, 305 |
   | Single European Act, 284 | |

2. Elaborate on the problems and benefits that multinational market groups represent for international marketers.

3. Explain the political role of multinational market groups.

4. Identify the factors on which one may judge the potential success or failure of a multinational market group.

5. Explain the marketing implications of the factors contributing to the successful development of a multinational market group.

6. Imagine that the United States was composed of many separate countries with individual trade barriers. What marketing effect might be visualized?

7. Discuss the possible types of arrangements for regional economic integration.

8. Differentiate between a free trade area and a common market. Explain the marketing implications of the differences.

9. It seems obvious that the founders of the European Community intended it to be a truly common market, so much so that economic integration must be supplemented by political integration to accomplish these objectives. Discuss.

10. The European Commission, the Council of Ministers, and the Court of Justice of the EC have gained power in the last decade. Comment.

11. Select any three countries that might have some logical basis for establishing a multinational market organization and illustrate their compatibility as a regional trade group. Identify the various problems that would be encountered in forming multinational market groups of such countries.

12. U.S. exports to the European Community are expected to decline in future years. What marketing actions might a company take to counteract such changes?

13. "Because they are dynamic and because they have great growth possibilities, the multinational markets are likely to be especially rough and tumble for the external business." Discuss.

14. Differentiate between a customs union and a political union.

15. Why have African nations had such difficulty in forming effective economic unions?

16. Discuss the implications of the European Union's decision to admit Eastern European nations to the group.

17. Discuss the consequences to the United States of not being a part of SAFTA.

18. Discuss the strategic marketing implications of NAFTA.

19. How is the concept of reciprocity linked to protectionism?

20. Visit the Web pages for NAFTA (www.mac.doc.gov/nafta/nafta2.htm) and Mercosur (www.mercosur.com/ or www.mercosur.org/english/) and locate each group's rules of origin. Which group has the most liberal rules of origin? Why is there a difference?

21. Using the factors that serve as the basis for success of an economic union (political, economic, social, and geographic), evaluate the potential success of the EC, NAFTA, AFTA, and Mercosur.

22. For each regional trade group—EC, NAFTA, AFTA, ASEAN+3 and Mercosur—cite which of the factors for success are the strongest and which are the weakest. Discuss each factor.

23. What is the motive behind ASEAN+3 and what are the probable implications for global trade?

24. NAFTA has been in existence for several years—how has it done? Read Exhibit 10.5, which discusses the initial provisions of the agreement, and, using the Internet, evaluate how well the provisions have been met.

# Global Marketing Management:
## PLANNING AND ORGANIZATION

**CHAPTER 11**

## CHAPTER LEARNING OBJECTIVES

What you should learn from chapter 11:

- How global marketing management differs from international marketing management

- The increasing importance of international strategic alliances

- The need for planning to achieve company goals

- The important factors for each alternative market-entry strategy

# Global Perspective

## GLOBAL GATEWAYS

With their domestic market crowded with competitors, Yahoo!, Lycos, America Online (AOL), and others are rushing to establish their brands in Europe, Asia, and Latin America before local competitors can create dominant franchises of their own.

Recently, Lycos Europe, a joint venture between Lycos Inc. and Germany's Bertelsmann AG, had its initial public offering on Germany's Neuer Markt. Many more such offerings are expected because U.S. Web executives and investors believe that the Internet will continue to grow faster abroad than at home. The United States share of Internet users fell from 42 percent in 1997 to 28 percent in 2001.

The battle has been hottest in Europe among the portals that serve as starting points for Web surfers looking for news, shopping, and search services. Yahoo! and Lycos each operate about two dozen foreign portals, most with native-language news, shopping links, and other content custom tailored to the local population. Lycos's German site features tips on brewing beer at home and a program for calculating auto speeding fines. Yahoo's Singapore site offers real-time information on haze and smog in Southeast Asia. AOL has about a dozen international ventures, and Excite,

the portal arm of At Home Corporation, has nine international partners.

The top U.S. players face tough home-grown competitors, who often have a better sense of local culture and Internet styles. In many countries, the dominant telephone companies offer portals, giving them a big leg up because customers are automatically sent to their home pages when they log on. Germany's leading portal, T-Online, is run by Deutsche Telekom. In France, No. 1 Wanadoo is operated by France Telecom.

U.S. portals risk being viewed as digital colonists trying to flex their muscles around the world, according to industry analysts. Many advise that American companies hoping to set up shop abroad are better served by forming partnerships with local outfits that understand the culture.

Source: Jon G. Auerbach, Bernard Wysocki Jr., and Neal E. Boudette, "For U.S. Internet Portals, the Next Big Battleground is Overseas," *Wall Street Journal,* March 23, 2000, p. B1; Stephanic Gruner, "Arrendo: Net Is Here to Stay," *Wall Street Journal Europe,* March 1, 2001, p. 21; World Bank, 2003; and Daekwan Kim, "The Internationalization of U.S. Portals: Does It Fit the Model of Internationalization?" *Marketing Intelligence & Planning,* 21(1), 2003, pp. 23–36.

The competition among soft drink bottlers in India is fierce. Here Coke and Pepsi combine to ruin the view of the Taj Mahal. Notice how the red of Coke stands out among its competitors in the picture. Of course, now Coca-Cola has purchased Thums Up, a prominent local brand—this is a strategy the company is applying around the world. But the red is a substantial competitive advantage on both store shelves and in outdoor advertising of the sort common in India and other developing countries. We're not sure who borrowed the "monsoon/thunder" slogan from whom.

Confronted with increasing global competition for expanding markets, multinational companies are changing their marketing strategies and altering their organizational structures.[1] Their goals are to enhance their competitiveness and to ensure proper positioning in order to capitalize on opportunities in the global marketplace.

A recent study of North American and European corporations indicated that nearly 75 percent of the companies are revamping their business processes, that most have formalized strategic-planning programs, and that the need to stay cost competitive was considered to be the most important external issue affecting their marketing strategies. Change is not limited to the giant multinationals but includes midsize and small firms as well.

In fact, the flexibility of a smaller company may enable it to reflect the demands of global markets and redefine its programs more quickly than larger multinationals. Acquiring a global perspective is easy, but the execution requires planning, organization, and a willingness to try new approaches—from engaging in collaborative relationships to redefining the scope of company operations.

---

[1]Perhaps the most interesting strategic event of the year is China's Legend Group's plan to attack Dell's and Hewlett-Packard's hold on the personal computer market in the United States. This will be interesting to watch. See Rebecca Buckman, "Computer Giant in China Sets Sights on U.S.," *Wall Street Journal,* June 19, 2003, p. B1.

This chapter discusses global marketing management, competition in the global marketplace, strategic planning, and alternative market-entry strategies. It also identifies the elements that contribute to an effective international or global organization.

## Global Marketing Management: An Old Debate and a New View    In the 1970s the argument was framed as "standardization vs. adaptation." In the 1980s it was "globalization vs. localization," and in the 1990s it was "global integration vs. local responsiveness."[2] The fundamental question was whether the global homogenization of consumer tastes allowed global standardization of the marketing mix. The Internet revolution of the 1990s with its unprecedented global reach added a new twist to the old debate.

Even today, some companies are answering "global" as the way to go. For example, executives at Twix Cookie Bars recently tried out their first global campaign with a new global advertising agency, Grey Worldwide. With analysis, perhaps a global campaign does make sense for Twix. But look at the companies that are going in the other direction. Levi's jeans faded globally in recent years. Ford chose to keep acquired nameplates such as Mazda, Jaguar, and Volvo. And perhaps the most global company of all, Coca-Cola, is peddling two brands in India—Coke and Thums Up. Coke's new CEO Douglas Daft, an Australian, explains, "Coke has had to come to terms with a conflicting reality. In many parts of the world, consumers have become pickier, more penny-wise, or a little more nationalistic, and they are spending more of their money on local drinks whose flavors are not part of the Coca-Cola lineup."[3]

Part of this trend back toward localization (if you wish to call it that, and Douglas Daft does: "Think local, act local") is caused by the new efficiencies of customization made possible by the Internet and increasingly flexible manufacturing processes. Indeed, a good example of the new "mass customization" is Dell Computer Corporation, which maintains no inventory and builds each computer to order.[4] Also crucial has been the apparent rejection of the logic of globalism by trade unionists, environmentalists, and consumers so well demonstrated in Seattle during the World Trade Organization meetings in 2000. While there is a growing body of empirical research illustrating the risks and difficulties of global standardization,[5] contrary results also appear in the literature.[6] Finally, prominent among firms' standardization strategies is Mattel's recently successful globalization of blonde Barbie.[7] We think a better approach is that of Disney with their more culturally diverse line of "Disney Princesses" including Mulan (Chinese) and Jasmine (Arabic).[8] No matter who wins this battle of the new "toy soldiers," the question will still not be settled.

Indeed, the debate itself is a wonderful example of the ethnocentrism of American managers and academics alike. That is, from the European or even the Japanese perspective, markets are by definition international, and the special requirements of the huge American market must be considered from the beginning. Only in America can international market requirements be an afterthought.

---

[2]Masaaki Kotabe, "Contemporary Research Trends in International Marketing: The 1990s," Chapter 17 in Alan Rugman and Thomas L. Brewer (eds.), *Oxford Handbook of International Business* (Oxford: Oxford University Press, 2001).

[3]Rance Crain, "Agencies Press Get-Global Plans but Clients Face Local Realities," *Advertising Age,* February 14, 2000, p. 32.

[4]Terril Yue Jones, "Dell Advancing to the Championship Round," *Los Angeles Times,* June 1, 2003, p. C1.

[5]Carl Arthur Solbert, "The Perennial Issue of Adaptation or Standardization of International Marketing Communication: Organizational Contingencies and Performance," *Journal of International Marketing,* 10(3), 2002, pp. 1–21.

[6]Aref A. Alashban, Linda A. Hayes, George M. Zinkhan, and Anne L. Balazs, "International Brand-Name Standardization/Adaptation: Antecedents and Consequences," *Journal of International Marketing,* 10(3), 2002, pp. 22–48.

[7]Lisa Bannon and Carlta Vitzthum, "One-Toy-Fits-All: How Industry Learned to Love the Global Kid," *Wall Street Journal,* April 29, 2003, p. A1.

[8]"A Challenge to Barbie," *The Economist,* April 19, 2003, p. 66.

Items in the Disney Princess collection are on display at the Licensing International show at New York's Javits Convention Center. It will be interesting to see how the ethnic breadth of the Disney line competes with the narrowness of the global Barbie line. (*AP/Wide World Photos*)

Moreover, as the information explosion allows marketers to segment markets ever more finely, it is only the manufacturing or finance managers in companies who argue for standardization for the sake of economies of scale. From the marketing perspective customization is always best. The ideal market segment size, if customer satisfaction is the goal, is *one*. According to one expert, "Forward-looking, proactive firms have the ability and willingness . . . to accomplish both tasks [standardization and localization] simultaneously."[9]

We believe things are actually simpler than that. As global markets continue to homogenize and diversify simultaneously, the best companies will avoid the trap of focusing on *country* as the primary segmentation variable.[10] Other segmentation variables are often more important—for example, climate, language group, media habits, age, or income. The makers of Twix apparently think that media habits (that is, MTV viewership) supercede country, according to their latest segmentation scheme. Sumner Redstone, CEO of Viacom, concurs regarding media-based segmentation: "With media splintering into smaller and smaller communities of interest, it will become more and more important to reach those audiences wherever [whichever country] they may be. Today, media companies are increasingly delivering their content over a variety of platforms: broadcast—both TV and radio—and cable, online and print, big screen and video. And advertisers are using the same variety of platforms to reach their desired audience."[11] Finally, perhaps a few famous Italian brands are the best examples: Bruno Magli shoes, Gucci leather goods, and Ferrari cars sell to the highest income segments globally. Indeed, for all three companies their U.S. sales are greater than their Italian sales.

In the twenty-first century, standardization versus adaptation is simply not the right question to ask.[12] Marketers will rightly always argue for the latter. Rather, the crucial question facing international marketers is what are the most efficient ways to segment

[9]Kotabe, "Contemporary Research Trends in International Marketing," 2001. Also consistent are the findings of Shouming Zou and S. Tamer Cavusgil, "The GMS: A Broad Conceptualization of Global Marketing Strategy and Its Effect on Firm Performance," *Journal of Marketing,* October 2002, 66(4), pp. 40–57.

[10]Jagdish N. Sheth and Atul Parvatiyar, "The Antecedents and Consequences of Integrated Global Marketing," *International Marketing Review,* 18(1), 2001, pp. 16–29.

[11]Sumner M. Redstone, "The ABCs of Success in the 21st Century," *Executive Speeches,* June/July 2000, 14(6), pp. 30–34.

[12]Panjak Ghemawat, "Semiglobalization and International Business Strategy," *Journal of International Business Studies,* 2003, 34, pp. 138–152.

markets. Country has been the most obvious segmentation variable, particularly for Americans. But as better communication systems continue to dissolve national borders, other dimensions of global markets are growing in salience.

**The Nestlé Way: Evolution Not Revolution**

Nestlé certainly wasn't bothered by the debate on standardization versus adaptation. Nestlé was international almost from its start in 1866 as a maker of infant formula. By 1920, the company was producing in Brazil, Australia, and the United States, and exporting to Hong Kong. Today it sells more than 8,500 products produced in 489 factories in 193 countries. Nestlé is the world's biggest marketer of infant formula, powdered milk, instant coffee, chocolate, soups, and mineral water. It ranks second in ice cream, and in cereals it ties Ralston Purina and trails only Kellogg Company. Its products are sold in the most upscale supermarkets in Beverly Hills, California, and in huts in Nigeria, where women sell Nestlé bouillon cubes alongside homegrown tomatoes and onions. Although the company has no sales agents in North Korea, its products somehow find their way into stores there, too.

The "Nestlé way" is to dominate its markets.[13] Its overall strategy can be summarized in four points: (1) Think and plan long term, (2) decentralize, (3) stick to what you know, and (4) adapt to local tastes. To see how Nestlé operates, consider its approach to Poland, one of the largest markets of the former Soviet bloc. Company executives decided at the outset that it would take too long to build plants and create brand awareness. Instead, the company pursued acquisitions and followed a strategy of "evolution not revolution." It purchased Goplana, Poland's second best-selling chocolate maker (it bid for the No. 1 company but lost out), and carefully adjusted the end product via small changes every two months over a two-year period until it measured up to Nestlé's standards and was a recognizable Nestlé brand. These efforts, along with all-out marketing, put the company within striking distance of the market leader, Wedel. Nestlé also purchased a milk operation and, as it did in Mexico, India, and elsewhere, sent technicians into the field to help Polish farmers improve the quality and quantity of the milk it buys through better feeds and improved sanitation.

Nestlé's efforts in the Middle East are much longer term. The area currently represents only about 2 percent of the company's worldwide sales, and individually, the markets are relatively small. Further, regional conflicts preclude most trade among the countries. Nevertheless, Nestlé anticipates that hostility will someday subside, and when that happens the company will be ready to sell throughout the entire region. Nestlé set up a network of factories in five countries that can someday supply the entire region with different products. The company makes ice cream in Dubai, and soups and cereals in Saudi Arabia. The Egyptian factory makes yogurt and bouillon, while Turkey produces chocolate. And a factory in Syria makes ketchup, a malted-chocolate energy food, instant noodles, and other products. If the obstacles between the countries come down, Nestlé will have a network of plants ready to provide a complete line to market in all the countries. In the meantime, factories produce and sell mostly in the countries in which they are located.

For many companies such a long-term strategy would not be profitable, but it works for Nestlé because the company relies on local ingredients and markets products that consumers can afford. The tomatoes and wheat used in the Syrian factory, for example, are major local agricultural products. Even if Syrian restrictions on trade remain, there are 14 million people to buy ketchup, noodles, and other products the company produces there. In all five countries and on all brands sold by Nestlé, the Nestlé name and the bird-in-a-nest trademark appear on every product.

Nestlé bills itself as "the only company that is truly dedicated to providing a complete range of food products to meet the needs and tastes of people from around the world, each hour of their day, throughout their entire lives."

---

[13]David Phillips, "Sitting Pretty," *Dairy Foods,* March 2003, pp. 20–27; and Paul Rodgers, "The Top 100 Global Confectionary Companies," *Candy Industry,* January 2003, pp. 35–39.

## CROSSING BORDERS 11.1   Swedish Takeout

Fifty years ago in the woods of southern Sweden, a minor revolution took place that has since changed the concept of retailing and created a mass market in a category where none previously existed. The catalyst of the change was and is IKEA, the Swedish furniture retailer and distributor that virtually invented the idea of self-service, takeout furniture. IKEA sells high-quality, reasonably priced, and innovatively designed furniture and home furnishings for a global marketplace.

The name was registered in Agunnaryd, Sweden, in 1943 by Ingvar Kamprad—the IK in the company's name. He entered the furniture market in 1950, and the first catalog was published in 1951. The first store didn't open until 1958 in Almhult. It became so incredibly popular that a year later the store had to add a restaurant for people who were traveling long distances to get there.

IKEA entered the United States in 1985. Although IKEA is global, most of the action takes place in Europe, with about 85 percent of the firm's $7 billion in sales. Nearly one-quarter of that comes from stores in Germany, while NAFTA units account for about $1 billion.

One reason for the relatively slow growth in the United States is that its stores are franchised by Netherlands-based Inter IKEA Systems, which carefully scrutinizes potential franchisees—individuals or companies—for strong financial backing and a proven record in retailing. The IKEA Group, based in Denmark, is a group of private companies owned by a charitable foundation in the Netherlands; they operate more than 100 stores. The Group also develops, purchases, distributes, and sells IKEA products, which are available only in company stores. The items are purchased from more than 2,400 suppliers in 65 countries and shipped through 14 distribution centers.

Low price is built into the company's lines. Even catalog prices are guaranteed not to increase for one year. The drive to produce affordable products inadvertently put IKEA at the forefront of the environmental movement several decades ago. In addition to lowering costs, minimization of materials and packing addressed natural resource issues. Environmentalism remains an integral operational issue at IKEA. Even the company's catalog is completely recyclable and produced digitally rather than on film.

On the day that Russia's first IKEA store opened in 2000, the wait to get in was an hour. Highway traffic backed up for miles. More than 40,000 people crammed into the place, picking clean sections of the warehouse. The store still pulls in more than 100,000 customers per week. IKEA has big plans for Russia. Company officials dream of placing IKEA's simple shelves, kitchens, bathrooms, and bedrooms in millions of Russian apartments that haven't been remodeled since the Soviet days.

Source: Michael Friedman, Len Lewis, Richard Turcsik, Barry Janoff, and Jenny Summerour, "Profiles in Excellence," *Progressive Grocer,* April 2000, pp. 22–48; Colin McMahon, "Russians Flock to IKEA as Store Battles Moscow," *Chicago Tribune,* May 17, 2000; Katarina Kling and Ingela Goteman, "IKEA CEO Anders Dahlvig on International Growth and IKEA's Unique Corporate Culture and Brand Identity," *Academy of Management Executive,* February 2003, pp. 31–37.

## Benefits of Global Marketing

When large market segments can be identified, economies of scale in production and marketing can be important competitive advantages for global companies. As a case in point, Black & Decker Manufacturing Company—makers of electrical hand tools, appliances, and other consumer products—realized significant production cost savings when it adopted a pan-European strategy. It was able to reduce not only the number of motor sizes for the European market from 260 to 8 but also reduce 15 different models to 8. Similarly, Ford estimates that by unifying product development, purchasing, and supply activities across several countries it can save up to $3 billion a year.

Transfer of experience and know-how across countries through improved coordination and integration of marketing activities is also cited as a benefit of global operations. Global diversity in marketing talent leads to new approaches across markets. Unilever successfully introduced two global brands originally developed by two subsidiaries. Its South African subsidiary developed Impulse body spray, and a European branch developed a detergent that cleaned effectively in European hard water. Aluminum Company of America's (Alcoa) joint venture partner in Japan produced aluminum sheets so perfect that U.S. workers, when shown samples, accused the company of hand-selecting the samples. Line workers were sent to the Japanese plant to learn the techniques, which were then transferred to the U.S. operations. Because of the benefits of such transfers of knowledge, Alcoa has changed its practice of sending managers overseas to "keep an eye on things" to sending line workers and managers to foreign locations to seek out new techniques and processes.

Marketing globally also ensures that marketers have access to the toughest customers. For example, in many product and service categories the Japanese consumer has been the hardest to please; the demanding customers are the reason that the highest-quality products and services often emanate from that country. Competing for Japanese customers provides firms with the best testing ground for high-quality products and services.

Diversity of markets served carries with it additional financial benefits. Spreading the portfolio of markets served brings an important stability of revenues and operations to many global companies. Companies with global marketing operations suffered less during the Asian market downturn of the late 1990s than did firms specializing in the area. Firms that market globally also are able to take advantages of changing financial circumstances in other ways as well. For example, as tax and tariff rates ebb and flow around the world, the most global companies are able to leverage the associated complexity to their advantage.[14]

## A Balanced Approach to Global Marketing Strategy—3M Corporation

3M Corporation's decision to reorganize into a global company illustrates the benefits cited previously. In the early 1980s, 3M Corporation faced mounting competition in its major markets for its magnetic audio and video products. Once the traditional leader in North America and Europe, 3M had lost significant market share in those markets; in Japan, it lagged behind competitors by a significant margin. 3M's approach had been to treat country markets as different segments, with no uniformity in packaging across country markets and little coordination and communication among subsidiary personnel. A study revealed a proliferation of brands with homogeneous packaging, which contributed to consumers' inability to distinguish one product from another. Further, a careful analysis of consumer preferences confirmed that trends in the marketplace were consistent across national boundaries, allowing for the development of a distinctive and consistent image for 3M products on a global basis.

3M then developed a global strategy and introduced a global brand identity and packaging for the entire line of magnetic media products. The package was designed to communicate the Scotch-3M brand quality to a variety of markets. It was fashioned to be used for all the division's products (the firm's first uniform package) and in all markets (packages had differed from country to country). To communicate the design change to consumers, 3M launched a major global advertising campaign for the new logo. Because both print and television advertisements heavily emphasized the logo, the ads were easier to adapt to different country markets. Foreign-language versions of the commercial were produced in Japanese, German, Spanish, and Italian, and theme music was tailored to reflect national taste. In addition, packaging and advertising standardization mechanisms to improve communication and coordination between the parent and foreign subsidiaries were set in place.

The result of this global effort was that 3M achieved its goals in all three major markets;[15] it recovered the lead in Europe and North America and dramatically increased its market share in Japan. In addition to boosting volume and market share, the program helped reduce the cost of marketing through the use of a unified packaging system. Global marketing also made a marked difference in accelerating product launch on a global scale. For example, a high-grade super-VHS videotape was introduced in Japan in one month, in the United States three months later, and in Europe just six months after its introduction in

---

[14]Michael Bowe and James W. Dean, "International Financial Management and Multinational Enterprises," Chapter 20 in Alan Rugman and Thomas L. Brewer (eds.), *Oxford Handbook of International Business* (Oxford: Oxford University Press, 2001).

[15]"3M Profits, Sales Rise in Response to Weaker Dollar," *Los Angeles Times,* April 22, 2003, p. C3.

## CROSSING BORDERS 11.2  There Was a Guy Riding a Bike and Talking on His Cell Phone

Bikers with cell phones are not an uncommon sight on streets throughout China—the problem for Lucent was how to get a piece of the action. As Aaron Fisher, general manager of wireless products for Lucent Microelectronics, explains, "There are a lot of screwdriver joint ventures in China, where a cell phone maker parachutes in a bag of parts and all the locals do is screw it together and ship it. There's no buildup of manufacturing know-how. The Chinese government is favoring companies that are doing more." There lay Lucent's chance, since "favoring" means choosing who does and who doesn't get a license to market cell phones in the country.

As a first step Lucent acquired more talent. In 1998 it bought Optima, a specialist in cell phone software based in Munich, Germany, for $65 million. Next it put together a team of Chinese nationals, including some working for other parts of its parent company, Lucent Technologies, which has six joint ventures, two wholly owned operations, and a new research center in China. The team then began approaching Chinese manufactur-

ing companies with an offer they found hard to refuse: Let us put you in the cell phone business.

Lucent offered a basic design and production know-how for a phone circuit board with—no surprise—a three-piece Lucent chip. Most important, the circuit board met requirements for approval worldwide as a GSM phone. GSM, or Global System for Mobile Communications, is the most widely used cell phone technology in China as well as Europe. Admonished not to change a thing in the basic design, the Chinese company was free to dream up its own exterior plastic case, display, and keypad. Using Optima software, it could program the phone with special features: a visual display with Chinese characters, and, when keys are touched, notes from the Chinese musical scale, which differs from the Western one.

Source: Philip Siekman, "The Secret of U.S. Exports: Great Products," *Fortune*, January 1, 2000, pp. 154–164; "Lucent Technologies Solves USB Bandwidth Bottleneck," *M2 Presswire*, May 23, 2000; and "Lucent to Open Research Center in China," *New York Times*, June 6, 2003, p. 4.

Japan. In the past, it would have been impossible to get effective media coverage and introduce a new 3M product in all its markets in such a short time.

## Planning for Global Markets

Planning is a systematized way of relating to the future. It is an attempt to manage the effects of external, uncontrollable factors on the firm's strengths, weaknesses, objectives, and goals to attain a desired end. Further, it is a commitment of resources to a country market to achieve specific goals. In other words, planning is the job of making things happen that might not otherwise occur.

Is there a difference between planning for a domestic company and for an international company? The principles of planning are not in themselves different, but the intricacies of the operating environments of the multinational corporation (i.e., host country, home, and corporate environments), its organizational structure, and the task of controlling a multicountry operation create differences in the complexity and process of international planning.

Planning allows for rapid growth of the international function, changing markets, increasing competition, and the turbulent challenges of different national markets. The plan must blend the changing parameters of external country environments with corporate objectives and capabilities to develop a sound, workable marketing program. A strategic plan commits corporate resources to products and markets to increase competitiveness and profits.

Planning relates to the formulation of goals and methods of accomplishing them, so it is both a process and a philosophy. Structurally, planning may be viewed as corporate, strategic, or tactical. International **corporate planning** is essentially long term, incorporating generalized goals for the enterprise as a whole. **Strategic planning** is conducted at the highest levels of management and deals with products, capital, and research, and long- and short-term goals of the company. **Tactical planning**, or market planning, pertains to specific actions and to the allocation of resources used to implement strategic planning goals in specific markets. Tactical plans are made at the local level and address marketing and advertising questions.

A major advantage to a multinational corporation (MNC) involved in planning is the discipline imposed by the process. An international marketer who has gone through the planning process has a framework for analyzing marketing problems and opportunities and a basis for coordinating information from different country markets. The process of planning may be as important as the plan itself because it forces decision makers to examine all factors that affect the success of a marketing program and involves those who will be responsible for its implementation. Another key to successful planning is evaluating company objectives, including management's commitment and philosophical orientation to international business. Finally, the planning process is a primary medium of organizational learning.

## Company Objectives and Resources

Evaluation of a company's objectives and resources is crucial in all stages of planning for international operations. Each new market can require a complete evaluation, including existing commitments, relative to the parent company's objectives and resources. As markets grow increasingly competitive, as companies find new opportunities, and as the cost of entering foreign markets increases, companies need such planning.

Defining objectives clarifies the orientation of the domestic and international divisions, permitting consistent policies. The lack of well-defined objectives has found companies rushing into promising foreign markets only to find activities that conflict with or detract from the companies' primary objectives.

Foreign market opportunities do not always parallel corporate objectives; it may be necessary to change the objectives, alter the scale of international plans, or abandon them. One market may offer immediate profit but have a poor long-term outlook, while another may offer the reverse.[16] Only when corporate objectives are clear can such differences be reconciled effectively.

## International Commitment

The planning approach taken by an international firm affects the degree of internationalization to which management is philosophically committed. Such commitment affects the specific international strategies and decisions of the firm. After company objectives have been identified, management needs to determine whether it is prepared to make the level of commitment required for successful international operations—commitment in terms of dollars to be invested, personnel for managing the international organization, and determination to stay in the market long enough to realize a return on these investments.

The degree of commitment to an international marketing cause reflects the extent of a company's involvement. A company uncertain of its prospects is likely to enter a market timidly, using inefficient marketing methods, channels, or organizational forms, thus setting the stage for the failure of a venture that might have succeeded with full commitment and support by the parent company. Any long-term marketing plan should be fully supported by senior management and have realistic time goals set for sales growth. Occasionally, casual market entry is successful, but more often than not, market success requires long-term commitment.

## The Planning Process

Whether a company is marketing in several countries or is entering a foreign market for the first time, planning is essential to success. The first-time foreign marketer must decide what products to develop, in which markets, and with what level of resource commitment. For the company that is already committed, the key decisions involve allocating effort and resources among countries and product(s), deciding on new markets to develop or old ones to withdraw from, and determining which products to develop or drop.

---

[16]Farok J. Contractor, Sumit K. Kundu, and Chin-Chun Hsu, "A Three-Stage Theory of International Expansion: the Link between Multinationality and Performance in the Service Sector," *Journal of International Business Studies,* 2003, 34, pp. 5–18.

**Exhibit 11.1**   International Planning Process

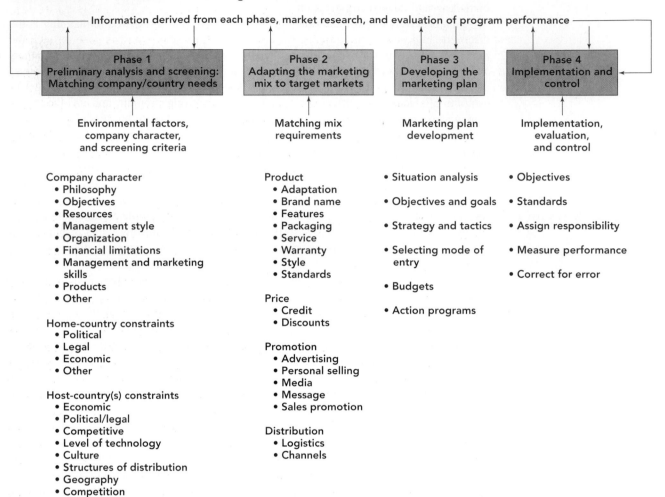

Guidelines and systematic procedures are necessary for evaluating international opportunities and risks and for developing strategic plans to take advantage of such opportunities. The process illustrated in Exhibit 11.1 offers a systematic guide to planning for the multinational firm operating in several countries.

**Phase 1: Preliminary Analysis and Screening—Matching Company and Country Needs.** Whether a company is new to international marketing or heavily involved, an evaluation of potential markets is the first step in the planning process. A critical first step in the international planning process is deciding in which existing country market to make a market investment. A company's strengths and weaknesses, products, philosophies, and objectives must be matched with a country's constraining factors and market potential. In the first part of the planning process, countries are analyzed and screened to eliminate those that do not offer sufficient potential for further consideration. Emerging markets pose a special problem because many have inadequate marketing infrastructures, distribution channels are underdeveloped, and income level and distribution vary among countries.

The next step is to establish screening criteria against which prospective countries can be evaluated. These criteria are ascertained by an analysis of company objectives, resources, and other corporate capabilities and limitations. It is important to determine the reasons for entering a foreign market and the returns expected from such an investment. A company's commitment to international business and its objectives for going international are important in establishing evaluation criteria. Minimum market potential, minimum profit, return on investment, acceptable competitive levels,[17] standards of political stability, acceptable legal requirements, and other measures appropriate for the company's products are examples of the evaluation criteria to be established.

After evaluation criteria are set, a complete analysis of the environment within which a company plans to operate is made. The environment consists of the uncontrollable elements discussed earlier and includes both home-country and host-country restraints, marketing objectives, and any other company limitations or strengths that exist at the beginning of each planning period. Although an understanding of uncontrollable environments is important in domestic market planning, the task is more complex in foreign marketing because each country under consideration presents the foreign marketer with a different set of unfamiliar environmental constraints. It is this stage in the planning process that more than anything else distinguishes international from domestic marketing planning.

The results of Phase 1 provide the marketer with the basic information necessary to evaluate the potential of a proposed country market, identify problems that would eliminate the country from further consideration, identify environmental elements that need further analysis, determine which part of the marketing mix can be standardized and which part of and how the marketing mix must be adapted to meet local market needs, and develop and implement a marketing action plan.

Information generated in Phase 1 helps companies avoid the kinds of mistakes that plagued Radio Shack Corporation, a leading merchandiser of consumer electronic equipment in the United States, when it first went international. Radio Shack's early attempts at international marketing in Western Europe resulted in a series of costly mistakes that could have been avoided had it properly analyzed the uncontrollable elements of the countries targeted for its first attempt at multinational marketing. The company staged its first Christmas promotion for December 25 in Holland, unaware that the Dutch celebrate St. Nicholas Day and give gifts on December 6. Furthermore, legal problems in various countries interfered with some of their plans; they were unaware that most European countries have laws prohibiting the sale of citizen-band radios, one of the company's most lucrative U.S. products and one they expected to sell in Europe. German courts promptly stopped a free flashlight promotion in German stores because giveaways violate German sales laws. In Belgium, the company overlooked a law requiring a government tax stamp on all window signs, and poorly selected store sites resulted in many of the new stores closing shortly after opening.

With the analysis in Phase 1 completed, the decision maker faces the more specific task of selecting country target markets and segments, identifying problems and opportunities in these markets, and beginning the process of creating marketing programs.

**Phase 2: Adapting the Marketing Mix to Target Markets.** A more detailed examination of the components of the marketing mix is the purpose of Phase 2. When target markets are selected, the market mix must be evaluated in light of the data generated in Phase 1. Incorrect decisions at this point lead to products inappropriate for the intended market or to costly mistakes in pricing, advertising, and promotion. The primary goal of Phase 2 is to decide on a marketing mix adjusted to the cultural constraints imposed by the uncontrollable elements of the environment that effectively achieves corporate objectives and goals.[18]

The process used by the Nestlé Company is an example of the type of analysis done in Phase 2. Each product manager has a country fact book that includes much of the information suggested in Phase 1. The country fact book analyzes in detail a variety of culturally related questions. In Germany, the product manager for coffee must furnish

---

[17]Andreas F. Grein, C. Samuel Craig, and Hirokazu Takada, "Integration and Responsiveness: Marketing Strategies of Japanese and European Automobile Manufacturers," *Journal of International Marketing,* 2001, 9(2), pp. 19–50.

[18]Gerald Albaum and David K. Tse, "Adaptation of International Marketing Strategy Components, Competitive Advantage, and Firm Performance: A Study of Hong Kong Exporters," *Journal of International Marketing,* 2001, 9(4), pp. 59–81.

Given all the tea in China, it's particularly amazing that now you can buy a mocha frappuccino in the Forbidden City in Beijing. The yellow roof symbolizes imperial grounds, but we don't think the Emperor had grounds of the coffee sort in mind when he built the place in the 1400s. China joining the WTO has opened up the market in new ways to franchisers from around the world. However, the store opened in 2000 to strong protests by the local media.

answers to a number of questions. How does a German rank coffee in the hierarchy of consumer products? Is Germany a high or a low per capita consumption market? (These facts alone can be of enormous consequence. In Sweden the annual per capita consumption of coffee is 6.4 kilograms, whereas in Japan it's 0.8!) How is coffee used—in bean form, ground, or powdered? If it is ground, how is it brewed? Which coffee is preferred—Brazilian Santos blended with Colombian coffee, or robusta from the Ivory Coast? Is it roasted? Do the people prefer dark roasted or blonde coffee? (The color of Nestlé's soluble coffee must resemble as closely as possible the color of the coffee consumed in the country.)

As a result of the answers to these and other questions, Nestlé produces 200 types of instant coffee, from the dark robust espresso preferred in Latin countries to the lighter blends popular in the United States. Almost $50 million a year is spent in four research laboratories around the world experimenting with new shadings in color, aroma, and flavor. Do the Germans drink coffee after lunch or with their breakfast? Do they take it black or with cream or milk? Do they drink coffee in the evening? Do they sweeten it? (In France, the answers are clear: In the morning, coffee with milk; at noon, black coffee—that is, two totally different coffees.) At what age do people begin drinking coffee? Is it a traditional beverage, as in France; is it a form of rebellion among the young, as in England, where coffee drinking has been taken up in defiance of tea-drinking parents; or is it a gift, as in Japan? There is a coffee boom in tea-drinking Japan, where Nescafé is considered a luxury gift item; instead of chocolates and flowers, Nescafé is toted in fancy containers to dinners and birthday parties. With such depth of information, the product manager can evaluate the marketing mix in terms of the information in the country fact book.

Phase 2 also permits the marketer to determine possibilities for applying marketing tactics across national markets.[19] The search for similar segments across countries can often lead to opportunities for economies of scale in marketing programs. This was the case for Nestlé when research revealed that young coffee drinkers in England and Japan had identical motivations. As a result, Nestlé now uses principally the same message in both markets.

Frequently, the results of the analysis in Phase 2 indicate that the marketing mix would require such drastic adaptation that a decision not to enter a particular market is made. For example, a product may need to be reduced in physical size to fit the needs of the market, but the additional manufacturing cost of a smaller size may be too high to justify market entry. Also, the price required to be profitable might be too high for a majority of the market to afford. If there is no way to reduce the price, sales potential at the higher price may be too low to justify entry.

The answers to three major questions are generated in Phase 2:

1. Are there identifiable market segments that allow for common marketing mix tactics across countries?

2. Which cultural/environmental adaptations are necessary for successful acceptance of the marketing mix?

3. Will adaptation costs allow profitable market entry?

Based on the results in Phase 2, a second screening of countries may take place, with some countries dropped from further consideration. The next phase in the planning process is development of a marketing plan.

---

[19]Daaekwan Kim, "The Internationalization of U.S. Internet Portals: Does It Fit the Process Model of Internationalization?" *Marketing Intelligence & Planning,* 21(1), 2003, pp. 23–36.

**Phase 3: Developing the Marketing Plan.**  At this stage of the planning process, a marketing plan is developed for the target market—whether it is a single country or a global market segment. The marketing plan begins with a situation analysis and culminates in the selection of an entry mode and a specific action program for the market. The specific plan establishes what is to be done, by whom, how it is to be done, and when. Included are budgets and sales and profit expectations. Just as in Phase 2, a decision not to enter a specific market may be made if it is determined that company marketing objectives and goals cannot be met.

**Phase 4: Implementation and Control.**  A "go" decision in Phase 3 triggers implementation of specific plans and anticipation of successful marketing. However, the planning process does not end at this point. All marketing plans require coordination and control during the period of implementation. Many businesses do not control marketing plans as thoroughly as they could even though continuous monitoring and control could increase their success. An evaluation and control system requires performance-objective action, that is, bringing the plan back on track should standards of performance fall short. A global orientation facilitates the difficult but extremely important management tasks of coordinating and controlling the complexities of international marketing.

Although the model is presented as a series of sequential phases, the planning process is a dynamic, continuous set of interacting variables with information continuously building among phases. The phases outline a crucial path to be followed for effective, systematic planning.

Utilizing a planning process encourages the decision maker to consider all variables that affect the success of a company's plan. Furthermore, it provides the basis for viewing all country markets and their interrelationships as an integrated global unit. By following the guidelines presented in Part VI of this text, "The Country Notebook—A Guide for Developing a Marketing Plan," the international marketer can put the strategic planning process into operation.

As a company expands into more foreign markets with several products, it becomes more difficult to efficiently manage all products across all markets. Marketing planning helps the marketer focus on all the variables to be considered for successful global marketing. With the information developed in the planning process and a country market selected, the decision regarding the entry mode can be made. The choice of mode of entry is one of the more critical decisions for the firm because the choice will define the firm's operations and affect all future decisions in that market.

## Alternative Market-Entry Strategies

When a company makes the commitment to go international, it must choose an entry strategy. This decision should reflect an analysis of market characteristics (such as potential sales, strategic importance, cultural differences,[20] and country restrictions[21]) and company capabilities[22] and characteristics,[23] including the degree of near-market knowledge,[24] marketing involvement, and commitment that management is prepared to make. Even so, many firms simply imitate others in the industry or

[20]Keith D. Brouthers, "Institutional, Cultural, and Transaction Cost Influences on Entry Mode Choice and Performance," *Journal of International Business Studies,* 2002, 33(2), pp. 203–231.

[21]Shih-Fen S. Chen and Jean-Francois Hennart, "Japanese Investors' Choice of Joint Ventures Versus Wholly-Owned Subsidiaries in the U.S.: The Role of Market Barriers and Firm Capabilities," *Journal of International Business Studies,* 2002, 33(1), pp. 1–18.

[22]M. Krishna Erramilli, Sanjeev Agarwal, and Chekitan S. Dev, "Choice Between Non-Equity Entry Modes: An Organizational Capability Perspective," *Journal of International Business Studies,* 2002, 33(2), pp. 223–242.

[23]Pol Herrmann and Deepak K. Datta, "CEO Successor Characteristics and the Choice of Foreign Market Entry Mode: An Empirical Study," *Journal of International Business Studies,* 2002, 33(3), pp. 551–569.

[24]Debanjan Mitra and Peter N. Golder, "Whose Culture Matters? Near-Market Knowledge and Its Impact on Foreign Market Entry Timing," *Journal of Marketing Research,* August 2002, 39(3), pp. 350–365.

**Exhibit 11.2**
Alternative Market-Entry Strategies

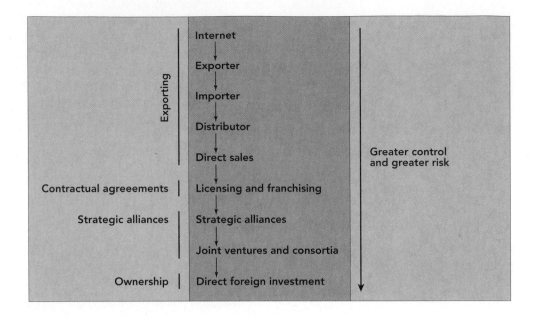

repeat their own successful entry strategies[25]—this is not what we recommend. The approach to foreign marketing can range from minimal investment with infrequent and indirect exporting and little thought given to market development, to large investments of capital and management in an effort to capture and maintain a permanent, specific share of world markets. Depending on the firm's objectives and market characteristics, either approach can be profitable.

Companies most often begin with modest export involvement. As sales revenues grow the firms often proceed through the series of steps listed in Exhibit 11.2.[26] Also, experience in larger numbers of foreign markets can increase the number of entry strategies used. In fact, a company in various country markets may employ a variety of entry modes because each country market poses a different set of conditions. For example, JLG Industries in Pennsylvania makes self-propelled aerial work platforms and sells them all over the world. The firm actually manufactured in Scotland and Australia beginning in the 1970s, but was forced to close the plants in 1991. However, the company's international sales have burgeoned again. The growth in European business is allowing for a simplification of distribution channels there involving elimination of middlemen; dealerships have been purchased in Germany, Norway, Sweden, and the United Kingdom. JLG set up dealership joint ventures in Thailand and Brazil, and sales are brisk despite economic problems in those countries. The company also established sales and service businesses from scratch in Scotland, Italy, and South Africa.

A company has four different modes of foreign market entry from which to select: exporting, contractual agreements, strategic alliances, and direct foreign investment. The different modes of entry can be further classified on the basis of the equity or nonequity requirements of each mode.[27] The amount of equity required by the company to use different modes affects the risk, return, and control that it will have in each mode. For example, indirect exporting requires no equity investment and thus has a low risk, low rate of return, and little control, whereas direct foreign investment requires the most equity of

[25]Jane W. Lu, "Intra- and Inter-Organizational Imitative Behavior: Institutional Influences on Japanese Firms' Entry Mode Choice," *Journal of International Business Studies,* 2002, 33(1), pp. 19–37.

[26]Mauro F. Guillen, "Experience, Imitation, and the Sequence of Foreign Entry: Wholly Owned and Joint-Venture Manufacturing by South Korean Firms and Business Groups in China, 1987–1995," *Journal of International Business Studies,* 2003, 34(2), pp. 185–198.

[27]Vibha Gaba, Yigang Pan, and Gerardo R. Ungson, "Timing of Entry in International Markets: An Empirical Study of U.S. Fortune 500 Firms in China," *Journal of International Business Studies,* 2002, 33(1), pp. 39–55.

the four modes and creates the greatest risk, while offering the most control. Although direct foreign investment is the riskiest of the four modes, it has the potential for the highest return and affords the greatest control over all activities.

**Exporting**

Exporting can be either direct or indirect. With **direct exporting** the company sells to a customer in another country. This is the most common approach employed by companies taking their first international step because the risks of financial loss can be minimized. In contrast, **indirect exporting** usually means that the company sells to a buyer (importer or distributor) in the home country who in turn exports the product. Customers include large retailers such as Wal-Mart or Sears, wholesale supply houses, trading companies, and others that buy to supply customers abroad.

Early motives for exporting often are to skim the cream from the market or gain business to absorb overhead. Early involvement may be opportunistic and come in the form of an inquiry from a foreign customer or initiatives from an importer in the foreign market. Such is the case with Pilsner Urquell, the revered Czech beer, which for many years has sold in the United States through Guinness Bass Import Corporation (GBIC). However, in early 2000 the Czech firm severed its relationship with the importer because it wasn't getting the attention of the other imported beers in GBIC's portfolio. The firm is now establishing its own sales force of two dozen to handle five key metropolitan areas in the United States. Prices are being reduced and a global media plan is being developed with a British ad agency. The firm may import other brands from the Czech parent as well.

Exporting is also a common approach for mature international companies. Some of America's largest companies engage in exporting as their major market-entry method. (Boeing is the best example, as America's largest exporter.) The mechanics of exporting and the different middlemen available to facilitate the exporting process are discussed in detail in Chapters 14 and 15.

**The Internet.**   The Internet is becoming increasingly important as a foreign market entry method. Initially, Internet marketing focused on domestic sales. However, a surprisingly large number of companies started receiving orders from customers in other countries, resulting in the concept of international Internet marketing (IIM). Picture-Phone Direct, a mail-order reseller of desktop video-conferencing equipment, posted its catalog on the Internet expecting to concentrate on the northeastern United States. To their surprise, PicturePhone's sales staff received orders from Israel, Portugal, and Germany.

Other companies have had similar experiences and are actively designing Internet catalogs targeting specific countries with multilingual websites. Dell Computer Corporation expanded its strategy of selling computers over the Internet to foreign sites as well. Dell began selling computers via the Internet to Malaysia, Australia, Hong Kong, New Zealand, Singapore, Taiwan, and other Asian countries through a "virtual store" on the Internet. The same selling mode was launched in Europe.

Amazon.com jumped into the IIM game with both feet. They hired a top Apple Computer executive to manage their fast-growing international business. Just 15 months after setting up book and CD e-tailing sites in Germany and the United Kingdom, the new overseas Amazon websites surged to become the most heavily trafficked commercial venues in both markets. Among the companies with the most profitable e-tailing businesses are former catalog companies such as Lands' End and L.L. Bean. However, Lands' End's successes in foreign markets were tainted by recent problems in Germany. German law bans "advertising gimmicks"—and that's what regulators there call Lands' End's "unconditional lifetime guarantee." The firm took the dispute all the way to the German supreme court and lost.[28] Moreover, the uncertainty swirling around the EU's approach to taxing Internet sales is great cause for concern.

---

[28]Neal E. Boudette, "German Shoppers May Get 'Sale Freedom'—Pressure Mounts to Soften a Strict Law of Competition," *Wall Street Journal,* January 23, 2002, p. B7D.

As discussed in Chapter 2, the full impact of the Internet on international marketing is yet to be determined. However, IIM should not be overlooked as an alternative market-entry strategy by the small or large company. Coupled with the international scope of credit card companies such as MasterCard and Visa and international delivery services such as UPS and Federal Express, deliveries to foreign countries can be relatively effortless.

**Direct Sales.** Particularly for high technology and big ticket industrial products a direct sales force may be required in a foreign country. This may mean establishing an office with local and/or expatriate managers and staff depending of course on the size of the market and potential sales revenues. Sales Management is one of the topics covered in detail in Chapter 17.

## Contractual Agreements

*Contractual agreements* are long-term, nonequity associations between a company and another in a foreign market. Contractual agreements generally involve the transfer of technology, processes, trademarks, or human skills. In short, they serve as a means of transfer of knowledge rather than equity.

**Licensing.** A means of establishing a foothold in foreign markets without large capital outlays is **licensing**. Patent rights, trademark rights, and the rights to use technological processes are granted in foreign licensing. It is a favorite strategy for small and medium-sized companies, although it is by no means limited to such companies. Common examples of industries that use licensing arrangements in foreign markets are television programming[29] and pharmaceuticals.[30] Not many confine their foreign operations to licensing alone; it is generally viewed as a supplement to exporting or manufacturing, rather than the only means of entry into foreign markets. The advantages of licensing are most apparent when capital is scarce, import restrictions forbid other means of entry, a country is sensitive to foreign ownership, or it is necessary to protect patents and trademarks against cancellation for nonuse. The risks of licensing are choosing the wrong partner, quality and other production problems, payment problems, contract enforcement, and loss of marketing control.

Although licensing may be the least profitable way of entering a market, the risks and headaches are fewer than for direct investments. It is a legitimate means of capitalizing on intellectual property in a foreign market, and such agreements can also benefit the economies of target countries. Licensing takes several forms. Licenses may be granted for production processes, for the use of a trade name, or for the distribution of imported products. Licenses may be closely controlled or be autonomous, and they permit expansion without great capital or personnel commitment if licensees have the requisite capabilities. Not all experiences with licensing are successful because of the burden of finding, supervising, and inspiring licensees.

**Franchising.** **Franchising** is a rapidly growing form of licensing in which the franchisor provides a standard package of products, systems, and management services, and the franchisee provides market knowledge, capital, and personal involvement in management. The combination of skills permits flexibility in dealing with local market conditions and yet provides the parent firm with a reasonable degree of control. The franchisor can follow through on marketing of the products to the point of final sale. It is an important form of vertical market integration. Potentially, the franchise system provides an effective blending of skill centralization and operational decentralization; it is an increasingly important form of international marketing. In some cases franchising is having a profound effect on traditional businesses. For example, in England, it is estimated that annual franchised sales of fast foods are nearly $2 billion, which accounts for 30 percent of all foods eaten outside the home.

---

[29]Daisy Whitney, "U.S. Syndicators Struggle Overseas," *Advertising Age,* January 20, 2003, p. 24.

[30]Prabuddha Ganguli, "Global Pharmaceutical Industry: Intellectual Wealth and Asset Protection," *International Journal of Technology Management,* 2003, 25(3,4), pp. 284–313.

## CROSSING BORDERS 11.3  The Men Who Would Be Pizza Kings

"All the water served in the restaurant has been passed by the manager" states the message at the bottom of a menu in a Delhi eatery. Pizza menus won't boast of such startling messages, but you'll see eye-catching entries all the same—chatpata chana masala, a chettinad, or a chicken tikka.

In more senses than one, pizza outlets are set to mushroom all over India. The wait for pizza lovers in places like Surat, Kochi, and Bhubaneshwar is finally over. Domino's, the home delivery specialist, and Pizza Hut have plans to significantly increase the number of their restaurants. Chennai-based Pizza Corner, having established itself in the south, has now boldly ventured into the north—it already opened three outlets in Delhi and is planning to increase the number to eight.

While Domino's is trying to dish out a pizza for every ethnic group, Pizza Hut is trying to expose Indians to the pizza's Chinese cousin. It came up with the "Oriental," which has hot Chinese sauce, spring onions, and sesame seeds as its toppings. It was developed based on the Indian fondness for Chinese food. This is not to say that Pizza Hut does not pay heed to the spice-soaked Indian version. Apart from the Oriental, it is also dishing out a spicy paneer tikka pizza. Milk shakes are also on the menu. Most recently an Indian dairy company was eating market share in both pizzas and ice cream. Things are quickly getting interesting there. And in spite of Kipling's prophesy that the two streams shall never meet, the Indianization of the pizza is truly here.

Source: Smita Tripathi, "Butter Chicken Pizza in Ludhiana," *Business Standard*, June 17, 2000, p. 2; Rahul Chandawarkar, "Collegians Mix Money with Study Material," *Times of India*, June 22, 2000; and Saritha Rai, "Battling to Satisfy India's Taste for Ice Cream," *New York Times*, August 20, 2002, p. W1.

Prior to 1970, international franchising was not a major activity. A survey by the International Franchising Association revealed that only 14 percent of its member firms had franchises outside of the United States, and the majority of those were in Canada. Now more than 30,000 franchises of U.S. firms are located in countries throughout the world. Franchises include soft drinks, motels (including membership "organizations" like Best Western International), retailing, fast foods, car rentals, automotive services, recreational services, and a variety of business services from print shops to sign shops. Canada[31] is the dominant market for U.S. franchisors, with Japan and the United Kingdom second and third in importance. The Asia-Pacific Rim has seen rapid growth as companies look to Asia for future expansion.

Despite temporary setbacks during the global economic downturn right after the turn of the millennium,[32] franchising is still expected to be the fastest-growing market-entry strategy. Franchises were often among the first types of foreign retail business to open in the emerging market economies of Eastern Europe, the former republics of Russia, and China. McDonald's is in Moscow (their first store seated 700 inside and had 27 cash registers), and Kentucky Fried Chicken is in China (the Beijing KFC store has the highest sales volume of any KFC store in the world). The same factors that spurred the growth of franchising in the U.S. domestic economy led to its growth in foreign markets. Franchising is an attractive form of corporate organization for companies wishing to expand quickly with low capital investment. The franchising system combines the knowledge of the franchisor with the local knowledge and entrepreneurial spirit of the franchisee. Foreign laws and regulations are friendlier toward franchising because it tends to foster local ownership, operations, and employment.

Two types of franchise agreements are used by franchising firms—master franchise and licensing—either of which can have a country's government as one partner. The master franchise is the most inclusive agreement and the method used in more than half of the international franchises. The *master franchise* gives the franchisee the rights to a specific

---

[31]Mary E. Tomzack, "The ABCs of Cross-Border Franchising," *Franchising World*, April 2003, pp. 18–20.

[32]Philip F. Zeidman, "The Global Brand: Asset or Liability?" *Franchising World*, May/June 2003, p. 4.

area (many are for an entire country), with the authority to sell or establish subfranchises. The McDonald's franchise in Moscow is a master agreement owned by a Canadian firm and its partner, the Moscow City Council Department of Food Services.

Licensing a local franchisee the right to use a product, good, service, trademark, patent, or other asset for a fee is a second type of franchise arrangement. Coca-Cola Company licenses local bottlers in an area or region to manufacture and market Coca-Cola using syrup sold by Coca-Cola. Rental-car companies often enter a foreign market by licensing a local franchisee to operate a rental system under the trademark of the parent company.

Lil' Orbits, a Minneapolis-based company that sells donut-making equipment and ingredients to entrepreneurs, is an example of how a small company can use licensing and franchising to enter a foreign market.[33] Lil' Orbits sells a donut maker that turns out 1.5-inch donuts while the customer waits. The typical buyer in the United States buys equipment and mix directly from the company without royalties or franchise fees. The buyer has a small shop or kiosk and sells donuts by the dozen for takeout or individually along with a beverage.

Successful in the United States, Lil' Orbits ran an advertisement in *Commercial News USA,* a magazine showcasing products and services in foreign countries, that attracted 400 inquiries. Pleased with the response, the company set up an international franchise operation based on royalties and franchise fees. Now a network of international franchised distributors markets the machines and ingredients to potential vendors. The distributors pay Lil' Orbits a franchise fee and buy machines and ingredients directly from Lil' Orbits or from one of the licensed blenders worldwide, from which Lil' Orbits receives a royalty. This entry strategy enabled the company to enter foreign markets with minimal capital investment outside the home country. The company has 20,000 franchised dealers in 78 countries. About 60 percent of the company's business is international.

Although franchising enables a company to expand quickly with minimal capital, there are costs associated with servicing franchisees. For example, to accommodate different tastes around the world, Lil' Orbits developed a more pastry-like, less-sweet mix than that used in the United States. Other cultural differences had to be met as well. For example, customers in France and Belgium could not pronounce the trade name, Lil' Orbits, so Orbie is used instead. Toppings also had to be adjusted to accommodate different tastes. Cinnamon sugar is the most widely accepted topping, but in China, cinnamon is considered a medicine, so only sugar is used. In the Mediterranean region, the Greeks like honey, and chocolate sauce is popular in Spain. Powdered sugar is more popular than granulated sugar in France, where the donuts are eaten in cornucopia cups instead of on plates. Other donut-making companies watched Lil' Orbit's international successes with great interest. It will be interesting to see if the hugely successful American firm Krispy Kreme (already in Canada, Australia, and the United Kingdom)[34] will follow Japan's Mister Donut franchises into big new international markets like China. Yum!

## Strategic International Alliances

A **strategic international alliance (SIA)** is a business relationship established by two or more companies to cooperate out of mutual need and to share risk in achieving a common objective. Strategic alliances grew in importance over the last few decades as a competitive strategy in global marketing management. SIAs are sought as a way to shore up weaknesses and increase competitive strengths. Opportunities for rapid expansion into new markets, access to new technology, more efficient production and marketing costs, strategic competitive moves, and access to additional sources of capital are motives for engaging in strategic international alliances. Finally, there is some evidence that SIAs often contribute nicely to profits.[35]

[33]Rob Turner, "Coping Mechanism," *Fortune,* February 17, 2003, p. 153.

[34]Tania Mason, "Krispy Kreme Plans UK Doughnut Stores Debut," *Marketing,* May 15, 2003, p. 6.

[35]Africa Arino, "Measures of Strategic Alliance Performance: An Analysis of Construct Validity," *Journal of International Business Studies,* 2003, 34(1), pp. 66–79.

In the Wings strategic alliance, U.S. based Northwest Airlines and Dutch KLM share several aspects of their operations including ticketing and reservations, catering, cargo, and airport slots. As the global airline industry consolidates after September 11th, more strategic partnerships are being formed.

Perhaps the most visible SIAs are now in the airlines industry. American Airlines, Cathay Pacific, British Airways, Canadian Airlines, Aer Lingus, and Quantas are partners in the Oneworld alliance, which integrates schedules and mileage programs. Competing with Oneworld are the Star (led by United and Lufthansa) and Wings (led by Northwestern and KLM). These kinds of strategic international alliances imply that there is a common objective; that one partner's weakness is offset by the other's strength; that reaching the objective alone would be too costly, take too much time, or be too risky; and that together their respective strengths make possible what otherwise would be unattainable. For example, during the recent turmoil in the global airline industry Star Alliance began moving in the direction of buying aircraft, this being a new strategic innovation.[36]

In short, an SIA is a synergistic relationship established to achieve a common goal in which both parties benefit.

An SIA with multiple objectives involves C-Itoh (Japan), Tyson Foods (United States), and Provemex (Mexico). It is an alliance that processes Japanese-style *yakatori* (bits of marinated and grilled chicken on a bamboo stick) for export to Japan and other Asian countries. Each company had a goal and made a contribution to the alliance. C-Itoh's goal was to find a lower-cost supply of *yakatori;* because it is so labor intensive, it was becoming increasingly costly and noncompetitive to produce in Japan. C-Itoh's contribution was access to its distribution system and markets throughout Japan and Asia. Tyson's goal was new markets for its dark chicken meat, a by-product of demand for mostly white meat in the U.S. market. Tyson exported some of its excess dark meat to Asia and knew that C-Itoh wanted to expand its supplier base. But Tyson faced the same high labor costs as C-Itoh. Provemex, the link that made it all work, had as its goal expansion beyond raising and slaughtering chickens into higher value-added products for international markets. Provemex's contribution was to provide highly cost-competitive labor.

Through the alliance, they all benefited. Provemex acquired the know-how to debone the dark meat used in *yakatori* and was able to vertically integrate its operations and secure a foothold in a lucrative export market. Tyson earned more from the sale of surplus chicken legs than was previously possible and gained an increased share of the Asian market. C-Itoh had a steady supply of competitively priced *yakatori* for its vast distribution and marketing network. This is a collaborative relationship: Three companies with individual strengths created a successful alliance in which each contributes and each benefits.

Many companies also are entering SIAs to be in a strategic position to be competitive and to benefit from the expected growth in the single European market. As a case in point, when General Mills wanted a share of the rapidly growing breakfast-cereal market in Europe, it joined with Nestlé to create Cereal Partners Worldwide. The European cereal market was projected to be worth hundreds of millions of dollars as health-conscious Europeans changed their breakfast diet from eggs and bacon to dry cereal. General Mills's main U.S. competitor, Kellogg, has been in Europe since 1920 and controls about half of the market.

It would have been extremely costly for General Mills to enter the market from scratch. Although the cereal business uses cheap commodities as its raw materials, it is both capital and marketing intensive; sales volume must be high before profits develop. Only recently did Kellogg earn significant profit in Europe. For General Mills to reach its goal alone would require a manufacturing base and a massive sales force. Further, Kellogg's stranglehold on supermarkets would be difficult for an unknown to breach easily. The solution was a joint venture with Nestlé. Nestlé had everything General Mills

---

[36]Daniel Michaels and J. Lynn Lunsford, "Airlines Move Toward Buying Planes Jointly," *Wall Street Journal,* May 20, 2003, p. A3.

**Exhibit 11.3**   Building Strategic Alliances

| Primary Relationship Activity | Typical Actions, Interactions, Activities | Key Relationship Skill |
|---|---|---|
| Dating | Senior executives leveraging personal networks<br>Wondering how to respond to inquiries<br>Wondering how to seek out possibilities | Good radar; good relationship self-awareness |
| Imaging | Seeing the reality in possibilities<br>Creating a shared vision from being together<br>Involving trusted senior managers | Creating intimacy |
| Initiating | Bringing key executives into action<br>Creating trust through face-to-face time | Trust building |
| Interfacing | Facilitating the creating of personal relationships at many levels<br>Traveling to partner facilities and engaging in technical conversations<br>Blending social and business time | Partnering |
| Committing | Demonstrating that managers are fully committed to the alliance and each other<br>Managing the conflict inherent in making hard choices<br>Accepting the reality of the alliance and its relationships | Commitment |
| Fine-tuning | Relying on mature and established relationships<br>Facilitating interaction and relationships with future successors | Growing *with* another |

Source: Adapted from Robert E. Spekman, Lynn A. Isabella, with Thomas C. MacAvoy, *Alliance Competence* (New York: Wiley, 2000), p. 81. Copyright © 2000, John Wiley & Sons, Inc. This material is used by permission of John Wiley & Sons, Inc.

lacked—a well-known brand name, a network of plants, and a powerful distribution system—except for the one thing that General Mills could provide: strong cereal brands.

The deal was mutually beneficial. General Mills provided the knowledge in cereal technology, including some of its proprietary manufacturing equipment, its stable of proven brands, and its knack for pitching these products to consumers.[37] Nestlé provided its name on the box, access to retailers, and production capacity that could be converted to making General Mills' cereals. In time, Cereal Partners Worldwide intends to extend its marketing effort beyond Europe. In Asia, Africa, and Latin America, Cereal Partners Worldwide will have an important advantage over the competition because Nestlé is a dominant food producer.

As international strategic alliances grow in importance, more emphasis is placed on a systematic approach to forming them. Most experts in the field agree that following the steps outlined in Exhibit 11.3 leads to successful, high-performance strategic alliances.[38] Of course, in international business there are no guarantees. And a key activity in all the steps outlined in the Exhibit is international negotiation, which is the subject of Chapter 19.

**International Joint Ventures.**   International joint ventures (IJVs) as a means of foreign market entry have accelerated sharply since the 1970s. Besides serving as a means of lessening political and economic risks by the amount of the partner's contribution to the venture, IJVs provide a less risky way to enter markets that pose legal and cultural barriers than would be the case in an acquisition of an existing company.

---

[37]Patricia Callahan, "Freeze-Dried Berries Heat Up Cereal Duel," *Wall Street Journal,* May 15, 2003, p. B2.
[38]Robert E. Spekman, Lynn A. Isabella with Thomas C. MacAvoy, *Alliance Competence* (New York: Wiley, 2000).

A **joint venture (JV)** is differentiated from other types of strategic alliances or collaborative relationships in that a joint venture is a partnership of two or more participating companies that join forces to create a separate legal entity. Joint ventures are different from minority holdings by an MNC in a local firm.

Four factors are associated with joint ventures: (1) JVs are established, separate, legal entities; (2) they acknowledge intent by the partners to share in the management of the JV; (3) they are partnerships between legally incorporated entities such as companies, chartered organizations, or governments, and not between individuals; and (4) equity positions are held by each of the partners.

IJVs can be hard to manage.[39] Choice of partners[40] and the qualities of the relationships[41] between the executives are important factors leading to success. Even so, nearly all companies active in world trade participate in at least one international joint venture somewhere; many companies have dozens of joint ventures. A recent Conference Board study indicated that 40 percent of Fortune 500 companies were engaged in one or more international joint ventures. Particularly in telecommunications and Internet markets, joint ventures are increasingly favored. For example, Excite At Home established joint venture relationships in Belgium, the Netherlands, Germany, Australia, and Japan.

In the Asia-Pacific Rim, where U.S. companies face unfamiliar legal and cultural barriers, joint ventures are preferred to buying existing businesses.[42] Local partners can often lead the way through legal mazes and provide the outsider with help in understanding cultural nuances. A joint venture can be attractive to an international marketer when it enables a company to utilize the specialized skills of a local partner, when it allows the marketer to gain access to a partner's local distribution system, when a company seeks to enter a market where wholly owned activities are prohibited, when it provides access to markets protected by tariffs or quotas, and when the firm lacks the capital or personnel capabilities to expand its international activities.

In China, a country considered to be among the riskiest in Asia, there have been more than 50,000 joint ventures established in the 20 years since the government began allowing IJVs there. Among the many reasons IJVs are so popular is that they offer a way of getting around high Chinese tariffs, allowing a company to gain a competitive price advantage over imports. Manufacturing locally with a Chinese partner rather than importing bypasses China's high tariffs. (The tariff has been as high as 200 percent on automobiles, 150 percent on cosmetics, and an average of 75 percent on miscellaneous products.) Manufacturing locally with a Chinese partner rather than importing achieves additional savings as a result of low-cost Chinese labor. Many Western brands are manufactured and marketed in China at prices that would not be possible if the products were imported.

**Consortia.** *Consortia* are similar to joint ventures and could be classified as such except for two unique characteristics: (1) They typically involve a large number of participants, and (2) they frequently operate in a country or market in which none of the participants is currently active. Consortia are developed to pool financial and managerial resources and to lessen risks. Often, huge construction projects are built under a consortium arrangement in which major contractors with different specialties form a separate company specifically to negotiate for and produce one job. One firm usually acts as the lead firm, or the newly formed corporation may exist quite independently of its originators.

---

[39]Yan Zhang and Nandini Rajagopalan, "Inter-Partner Credible Threat in International Joint Ventures: An Infinitely Repeated Prisoner's Dilemma Model," *Journal of International Business Studies,* 2002, 33(3), pp. 457–478; and Vijay Pothukuchi, Fariborz Damanpour, Jaepil Choi, Chao C. Chen, and Seung Ho Park, "National and Organizational Differences and International Joint Venture Performance, *Journal of International Business Studies,* 2002, 33(2), pp. 243–265.

[40]Peter Leung-Kwong Wong and Paul Ellis, "Social Ties and Partner Identification in Sino-Hong Kong International Joint Ventures," *Journal of International Business Studies,* 2002, 33(2) pp. 267–289.

[41]Steven C. Currall and Andrew C. Inkpen, "A Multilevel Approach to Trust in Joint Ventures," *Journal of International Business Studies,* 2003, 33(3), pp. 479–495.

[42]Thomas Crampton, "AOL Modifies Its China Strategy," *International Herald Tribune,* May 28, 2003, p. 11.

**CROSSING BORDERS 11.4** The Consortium Goes Corporate—Bad News for Boeing?

The partners in Airbus Industrie jacked up the competitive pressure on Boeing by turning their consortium into a corporation and officially starting to sell the A380 superjumbo jet. The announcement by the consortium companies came only hours before three of them launched the initial public offering of their merged company, the European Aeronautic Defence & Space Company (EADS), through which they planned to raise 3.5 billion euros.

Airbus was run by four companies—one French, one Spanish, one German, and one British. The four built planes as allied but independent companies and marketed them through their Airbus Industrie joint venture. Under the new agreement, they combined all their individual Airbus production assets and the joint venture (EADS) into a new French-registered company, the working name of which is Airbus Integrated Company (AIC).

The partners said that creating the AIC was a prerequisite to launching the 550-seat A380. Developing the jet, which would be the world's largest passenger plane, would cost $12 billion, and the partners said that the complex consortium structure was too inefficient to support such a large project.

The A380 drew interest and orders from at least eight airlines, among them Quantas, Singapore Airlines, and Air France. The superjumbo jet will compete with Boeing's 400+-seat 747 jumbo jets, a major source of profit for the Chicago company because it had a monopoly on building the biggest jets. The consolidation of Airbus should make it more nimble and profitable as well as help it compete against Boeing. The A380 project should break even within ten years on sales of 250 planes. They already have booked orders for half that number.

Source: Daniel Michaels, "It's Official: Airbus Will Become a Company and Market A380 Jet," *Wall Street Journal Europe*, June 26, 2000, p. 6; Stanley Holmes, "Boeing is Choking on Airbus' Fumes," *BusinessWeek*, June 30, 2003, p. 50. Copyright 2000 by Dow Jones & Co. Inc. Reproduced with permission of Dow Jones & Co. Inc. via Copyright Clearance Center.

Without doubt the most prominent international consortium has been Airbus, Boeing's European competitor in the global commercial aircraft market.[43] Airbus Industrie was originally formed when four major European aerospace firms agreed to work together to build commercial airliners. The four partners are France's Aerospatiale Matra, Germany's Dasa aerospace unit of DaimlerChrysler, Britian's BAE Systems, and Spain's Construcciones. In 2000 the four agreed to transform the consortium into a global company to achieve operations efficiencies that would allow it to compete better against Boeing. Meanwhile, Boeing is joining together with its own consortium to develop new 7E7 aircraft.[44]

Sematech, the other candidate for most prominent consortium, was originally an exclusively American operation. Sematech is an R&D consortium formed in Austin, Texas, during the 1980s to regain America's lead in semiconductor development and sales from Japan. Members included firms such as IBM, Intel, Texas Instruments, Motorola, and Hewlett-Packard. However, at the turn of the millennium even Sematech went international. Several of the founding American companies left and were replaced by firms from Taiwan, Korea, Germany, and the Netherlands (still none from Japan). The firm is also broadening its own investment portfolio to include a greater variety of international companies.

It should be noted that all such international contractual agreements can run into problems. Ford and Nissan launched a joint venture minivan in 1992 called the Mercury Villager/Nissan Quest. The car was mildly successful in the U.S. market, but in 2002 the joint venture stopped producing the cars—that's two years earlier than the original contract called for. Now that Nissan is controlled by French automaker Renault, it produced its own minivan for 2003 for sale in the United States. When General Motors formed a joint venture with Daewoo, its purpose was to achieve a significant position in the Asian car market. Instead, Daewoo used the alliance to enhance its own automobile technology, and by the time the partnership was terminated GM had created a new global competitor for itself.

---

[43]Stanley Holmes, "Will This Idea Really Fly?" *BusinessWeek*, June 23, 2003, pp. 34–35.
[44]"Boeing Says Japanese Firms to Take Stake in Plane," *Los Angeles Times*, June 16, 2003, p. C5.

Recently Nestlé was involved in a particularly ugly dissolution dispute with Dabur India. The Swiss firm owned 60 percent and the Indian firm 40 percent of a joint venture biscuit company, Excelcia Foods. Following months of acrimony, in March of 2000 Dabur filed a petition with the Indian government accusing Nestlé of indulging in oppression of the minority shareholder and of mismanaging the joint venture company. In particular, Dabur alleged that Nestlé was purposefully running Excelcia into bankruptcy so that Nestlé could wriggle out of its "non-compete obligations and go after the India biscuit market using another brand." Nestlé countered that the problem had more to do with the partners' inability to agree on a mutually acceptable business plan. In June of that year the dispute was settled out of court by Nestlé buying Dabur's 40 percent interest, shortly after which Excelcia was closed in lieu of restructuring.

**Direct Foreign Investment**

A fourth means of foreign market development and entry is *direct foreign investment,* that is, investment within a foreign country. Companies may manufacture locally to capitalize on low-cost labor, to avoid high import taxes, to reduce the high costs of transportation to market, to gain access to raw materials, or as a means of gaining market entry. Firms may either invest in or buy[45] local companies or establish new operations facilities.[46]

The growth of free trade areas that are tariff free among members but have a common tariff for nonmembers creates an opportunity that can be capitalized on by direct investment. Similar to its Japanese competitors, Korea's Samsung invested some $500 million to build television tube plants in Tijuana, Mexico, to feed the already huge NAFTA TV industry centered there. Kyocera Corporation, a Japanese high-tech company, bought Qualcomm's wireless consumer phone business as a means of fast entry into the American market. Finally, Nestlé is building a new milk factory in Thailand to serve the ASEAN Free Trade Area.

A hallmark of global companies today is the establishment of manufacturing operations throughout the world.[47] This is a trend that will increase as barriers to free trade are eliminated and companies can locate manufacturing wherever it is most cost effective.

The selection of an entry mode and partners[48] are critical decisions because the nature of the firm's operations in the country market is affected by and depends on the choices made. It affects the future decisions because each mode entails an accompanying level of resource commitment, and it is difficult to change from one entry mode to another without considerable loss of time and money.

# Organizing for Global Competition

An international marketing plan should optimize the resources committed to company objectives. The organizational plan includes the type of organizational arrangements to be used, and the scope and location of responsibility. Because organizations need to reflect a wide range of company-specific characteristics—such as size, the level of policy decisions, length of chain of command, staff support, source of natural and personnel resources, degree of control, centralization, and type or level of marketing involvement—it is difficult to devise a standard organizational structure. Many ambitious multinational plans meet with less than full success because of confused lines of authority, poor communications, and lack of cooperation between headquarters and subsidiary organizations.

---

[45]Michael Shari, "Unilever Indonesia," *BusinessWeek Online,* March 19, 2003.

[46]John O'Dell, "Along for the Ride," *Los Angeles Times,* June 15, 2003, p. C1.

[47]John A. Doukas and L.H.P. Lang, "Foreign Direct Investment, Diversification, and Firm Performance," *Journal of International Business Studies,* 2003, 34(2), pp. 153–172.

[48]Carlos M. Rodriquez and David T. Wilson, "Relationship Bonding and Trust as a Foundation for Commitment in U.S.–Mexican Strategic Alliances: A Structural Equation Modeling Approach," *Journal of International Marketing,* 2002, 10(4), pp. 53–76.

**Exhibit 11.4**   Schematic Marketing Organization Plan Combining Product, Geographic, and Functional Approaches

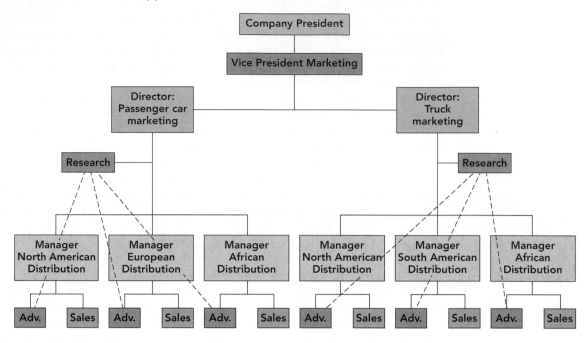

An organizational structure that effectively integrates domestic and international marketing activities is not yet devised.[49] Companies face the need to maximize the international potential of their products and services without diluting their domestic marketing efforts. Companies are usually structured around one of three alternatives: (1) global product divisions responsible for product sales throughout the world; (2) geographical divisions responsible for all products and functions within a given geographical area; or (3) a matrix organization consisting of either of these arrangements with centralized sales and marketing run by a centralized functional staff, or a combination of area operations and global product management.

Companies that adopt the global product division structure are generally experiencing rapid growth and have broad, diverse product lines. Geographic structures work best when a close relationship with national and local governments is important.

The matrix form—the most extensive of the three organizational structures—is popular with companies as they reorganize for global competition. A matrix structure permits management to respond to the conflicts that arise between functional activity, product, and geography. It is designed to encourage sharing of experience, resources, expertise, technology, and information among global business units. At its core is better decision making, in which multiple points of view affecting functional activity, product, and geography are examined and shared. A matrix organization can also better accommodate customers who themselves have global operations and global requirements.

A company may be organized by product lines but have geographical subdivisions under the product categories. Both may be supplemented by functional staff support. Exhibit 11.4 shows such a combination. Modifications of this basic arrangement are used by a majority of large companies doing business internationally.

---

[49]Kelly Hewett and William O. Beardon, "Dependence, Trust, and Relational Behavior on the Part of Foreign Subsidiary Marketing Operations: Implications for Managing Global Marketing Operations," *Journal of Marketing,* October 2001, 65(4), pp. 51–66.

The turbulence of global markets requires flexible organizational structures.[50] Forty-three large U.S. companies studied indicated that they planned a total of 137 organizational changes for their international operations over a five-year period. Included were such changes as centralizing international decision making, creating global divisions, forming centers of excellence, and establishing international business units. Bausch & Lomb, one of the companies in the study, revamped its international organizational structure; it collapsed its international division into a worldwide system of three regions and set up business management committees to oversee global marketing and manufacturing strategies for four major product lines. Bausch & Lomb's goal was to better coordinate central activities without losing touch at the local level. "Global coordination is essential," according to the company's CEO, "but in a way that maintains the integrity of the foreign subsidiaries." More recently, General Motors dramatically revamped its global strategies through its network of strategic alliances.

To the extent that there is a trend, two factors seem to be sought, regardless of the organizational structure: a single locus for direction and control and the creation of a simple line organization that is based on a more decentralized network of local companies.

## Locus of Decision

Considerations of where decisions will be made, by whom, and by which method constitute a major element of organizational strategy. Management policy must be explicit about which decisions are to be made at corporate headquarters, which at international headquarters, which at regional levels, and which at national or even local levels. Most companies also limit the amount of money to be spent at each level. Decision levels for determination of policy, strategy, and tactical decisions must be established. Tactical decisions normally should be made at the lowest possible level, without country-by-country duplication. This guideline requires American headquarters managers to trust the expertise of their local managers.

## Centralized versus Decentralized Organizations

An infinite number of organizational patterns for the headquarters activities of multinational firms exist, but most fit into one of three categories: centralized, regionalized, or decentralized organizations. The fact that all of the systems are used indicates that each has certain advantages and disadvantages. The chief advantages of centralization are the availability of experts at one location, the ability to exercise a high degree of control on both the planning and implementation phases, and the centralization of all records and information.

Some companies affect extreme decentralization by selecting competent managers and giving them full responsibility for national or regional operations. These executives are in direct day-to-day contact with the market but lack a broad company view, which can mean partial loss of control for the parent company.

Multinationals are constantly seeking the "right" organizational structure that will provide them with flexibility, an ability to respond to local needs, and worldwide control over far-flung business units. No single traditional organizational plan is adequate for today's global enterprise seeking to combine the economies of scale of a global company with the flexibility and marketing knowledge of a local company. Companies are experimenting with several different organizational schemes, but greater centralization of decisions is common to all.

In many cases, whether a company's formal organizational structure is centralized or decentralized, the informal organization reflects some aspect of all organizational systems. This is especially true relative to the locus of decision making. Studies show that even though product decisions may be highly centralized, subsidiaries may have a substantial amount of local influence in pricing, advertising, and distribution decisions. If a product is culturally sensitive, the decisions are more apt to be decentralized.

[50]Brian Bremmer, "Nomura's Comeback CEO Junichi Ujiie Has Succeeded in Grabbing Back M&A Business from Foreigners," *BusinessWeek,* April 7, 2003, p. 80.

# Summary

Expanding markets around the world have increased competition for all levels of international marketing. To keep abreast of the competition and maintain a viable position for increasingly competitive markets, a global perspective is necessary. Global competition also requires quality products designed to meet ever-changing customer needs and rapidly advancing technology. Cost containment, customer satisfaction, and a greater number of players mean that every opportunity to refine international business practices must be examined in light of company goals. Collaborative relationships, strategic international alliances, strategic planning, and alternative market-entry strategies are important avenues to global marketing that must be implemented in the planning and organization of global marketing management.

# Questions

1. Define the following terms:

   corporate planning, 320
   strategic planning, 320
   tactical planning, 320
   direct exporting, 327
   indirect exporting, 327
   licensing, 328
   franchising, 328
   strategic international alliance
       (SIA), 330
   joint venture (JV), 333

2. Define strategic planning. How does strategic planning for international marketing differ from domestic marketing?

3. Discuss the effect of shorter product life cycles on a company's planning process.

4. What is the importance of collaborative relationships to competition?

5. In Phases 1 and 2 of the international planning process, countries may be dropped from further consideration as potential markets. Discuss some of the conditions that may exist in a country that would lead a marketer to exclude a country in each phase.

6. Assume that you are the director of international marketing for a company producing refrigerators. Select one country in Latin America and one in Europe and develop screening criteria to use in evaluating the two countries. Make any additional assumptions that are necessary about your company.

7. "The dichotomy typically drawn between export marketing and overseas marketing is partly fictional; from a marketing standpoint, they are but alternative methods of capitalizing on foreign market opportunities." Discuss.

8. How will entry into a developed foreign market differ from entry into a relatively untapped market?

9. Why do companies change their organizations when they go from being an international to a global company?

10. Formulate a general rule for deciding where international business decisions should be made.

11. Explain the popularity of joint ventures.

12. Compare the organizational implications of joint ventures versus licensing.

13. Visit the websites of Maytag Corporation (www.maytag.com/) and the Whirlpool Corporation (www.whirlpool.com/), both appliance manufacturers in the United States. Search their sites and compare their international involvement. How would you classify each—as exporter, international, or global?

14. Using the sources in Question 13, list the different entry modes each company uses.

15. Visit the Nestlé Corporation website (www.nestle.com/) and the Unilever website (www.unilever.com/). Compare their strategies toward international markets. In what ways (besides product categories) do they differ in their international marketing?

# products and services for consumers

**CHAPTER 12**

## CHAPTER LEARNING OBJECTIVES

What you should learn from Chapter 12:

- The importance of offering a product suitable for
the intended market

- The importance of quality and how quality is defined

- Country-of-origin effects on product image

- Physical, mandatory, and cultural requirements for
product adaptation

- The need to view all attributes of a product in order
to overcome resistance to acceptance

# Global Perspective

## HONG KONG—DISNEY ROLLS THE DICE AGAIN

With the opening of Disneyland in Anaheim in 1955 the notion of the modern theme park was born. The combination of the rides, various other attractions, and the Disney characters has remained irresistible. Tokyo Disneyland also proved to be a big success, making modest money for Disney through licensing and major money for their Japanese partners. Three-quarters of the visitors at the Tokyo park are repeat visitors, the best kind.

Then came EuroDisney. Dissatisfied with the ownership arrangements at the Tokyo park, the EuroDisney deal was structured much differently. Disney negotiated a much greater ownership stake in the park and adjacent hotel and restaurant facilities. Along with the greater control and potential profits came a higher level of risk.

Even before the park's grand opening ceremony in 1992, protestors decried Disney's "assault" on the French culture. The location was also a mistake—the Mediterranean climate of the alternative Barcelona site not chosen seemed much more attractive on chill winter days in France. Managing both a multicultural workforce and clientele proved daunting. For example, what language was most appropriate for the Pirates of the Caribbean attraction—French or English? Neither attendance nor consumer purchases targets were achieved during the early years: Both were off by about 10 percent. By the summer of 1994 EuroDisney had lost some $900 million. Real consideration was given to closing the park.

A Saudi prince provided a crucial cash injection that allowed for a temporary financial restructuring and a general reorganization, including a new French CEO and a new name, Paris Disneyland. The Paris park returned to profitability and attendance increased. However, the temporary holiday on royalties, management fees, and leases is now expired and profits are dipping again. Disney's response was to expand with a second "Disney Studios" theme park and an adjacent retail and office complex at the Paris location.

In 2006, Hong Kong Disneyland is expected to open for business. The Hong Kong government is providing the bulk of the investment for the project (almost 80 percent of the $3 billion needed). As in Europe, the clientele will be culturally diverse, even though primarily Chinese. Performances will be done in Cantonese (the local dialect), Mandarin (the national language), and English. Disney also inked a new joint venture agreement for online delivery of entertainment services to customers in China. Indeed, it will be quite interesting to follow Mickey's international adventures in the new millennium!

Sources: www.disney.go.com; "Disney to Build Hong Kong Theme Park; Euro Disney's Profit Slumped," Dow Jones News Service, November 2, 1999; "California Southland Focus, Chase to Help Fund Disney Hong Kong Park," *Los Angeles Times,* August 18, 2000, p. C-2; and Richard Verrier, "Disney Theme Parks Chief Trying to Put a Little Magic in Marketing," *Los Angeles Time,* January 31, 2003, p. C1.

The opportunities and challenges for international marketers of consumer goods and services today have never been greater or more diverse. New consumers are springing up in emerging markets in Eastern Europe, the Commonwealth of Independent States, China and other Asian countries, India, Latin America—in short, globally. Although some of these emerging markets have little purchasing power today, they promise to be huge markets in the future. In the more mature markets of the industrialized world, opportunity and challenge also abound as consumers' tastes become more sophisticated and complex and as increases in purchasing power provide them with the means of satisfying new demands.

As described in the Global Perspective, Disney is the archetypal American exporter for global consumer markets. The distinction between products and services for such companies means little. Their videotapes are *products,* whereas cinema performances of the same movies are *services.* Consumers at the theme parks (including foreign tourists at domestic sites) pay around $40 to get in the gate, but they also spend about the same amount on hats, T-shirts, and meals while there. And the movies, of course, help sell the park tickets and the associated toys and clothing. Indeed, this lack of distinction between products and services led to the invention of new terms encompassing both products and services, such as *market offerings*[1] and *business-to-consumer marketing.* However, the governmental agencies that keep track of international trade still maintain the questionable product/service distinction, and thus so do we in this chapter and the next.[2] The reader should also note that when it comes to U.S. exports targeting consumers, the totals are about evenly split among the three major categories of durable goods (such as cars and computers), nondurable goods (mainly food, drugs, toys), and services (for example, tourism and telecommunications).

Never has the question "Which products/services should we sell?" been more critical than it is today. For the company with a domestic market extension orientation like Ben & Jerry's Ice Cream, the answer generally is "Whatever we are selling at home." The company with a multidomestic market orientation develops different products and services to fit the uniqueness of each country market; the global company ignores frontiers and seeks commonalities in needs among sets of country markets and responds with global market offerings.

The trend for larger firms is toward becoming global in orientation and strategy. However, product adaptation is as important a task in a smaller firm's marketing effort as it is for global companies. As competition for world markets intensifies and as market preferences become more global, selling what is produced for the domestic market in the same manner as it is sold at home proves to be increasingly less effective. Some products cannot be sold at all in foreign markets without modification; others may be sold as is, but their acceptance is greatly enhanced when tailored specifically to market needs. In a competitive struggle, quality products and services that meet the needs and wants of consumers at an affordable price should be the goal of any marketing firm.

## Quality

Global competition is placing new emphasis on some basic tenets of business. It is shortening product life cycles and focusing on the importance of quality, competitive prices, and innovative products. The power in the marketplace is shifting from a seller's market to customers, who have more choices because there are more companies competing for their attention. More competition, more choices, puts more power in the hands of the customer, and that, of course, drives the need for quality. Gone are the days when the customer's

---

[1]For example, Philip Kotler, *Marketing Management,* 11th edition (Upper Saddle River, NJ: Prentice Hall, 2002).

[2]We hope that it is obvious that many of the points we make regarding the development of consumer products are pertinent to consumer services as well, and vice versa. Of course, some distinctions are still substantive. These are focused on in the section of the chapter entitled Marketing Consumer Services Globally.

knowledge was limited to one or at best just a few different products. Today the customer knows what is best, cheapest, and highest quality. It is the customer who defines quality in terms of his or her needs and resources. For example, cell phones that don't roam don't sell in Japan at any price, but in China they sell very well. Just ask the folks at UTStarcom, a California firm that will soon be selling in India and Vietnam, as well as China.[3]

American products have always been among the world's best, but competition is challenging us to make even better products. In most global markets the cost and quality of a product are among the most important criteria by which purchases are made. For consumer and industrial products alike, the reason often given for preferring one brand over another is better quality at a competitive price. Quality, as a competitive tool, is not new to the business world, but many believe that it is the deciding factor in world markets. However, we must be clear about what we mean by quality.

## Quality Defined

**Quality** can be defined on two dimensions: market-perceived quality and performance quality. Both are important concepts, but consumer perception of a quality product often has more to do with market-perceived quality[4] than performance quality. The relationship of quality conformance to customer satisfaction is analogous to an airline's delivery of quality. If viewed internally from the firm's perspective (performance quality), an airline has achieved quality conformance with a safe flight and landing. But because the consumer expects performance quality to be a given, quality to the consumer is more than compliance (a safe flight and landing). Rather, cost, timely service, frequency of flights, comfortable seating, and performance of airline personnel from check-in to baggage claim are all part of the customer's experience that is perceived as being of good or poor quality. Considering the number of air miles flown daily, the airline industry is approaching zero defects in quality conformance, yet who will say that customer satisfaction is anywhere near perfection? These market-perceived quality attributes are embedded in the total product, that is, the physical or core product and all the additional features the consumer expects.

In a competitive marketplace where the market has choices, most consumers expect performance quality to be a given. Naturally, if the product does not perform up to standards it will be rejected.[5] When there are alternative products, all of which meet performance quality standards, the product chosen is the one that meets market-perceived quality attributes. Interestingly, China's leading refrigerator maker recognized the importance of these market-perceived quality attributes when it adopted a technology that enabled it to let consumers choose from 20 different colors and textures for door handles and moldings. For example, a consumer can design an off-white refrigerator with green marble handles and moldings. Why is this important? Because it lets consumers "update the living rooms" where most of the refrigerators are parked. The company's motive was

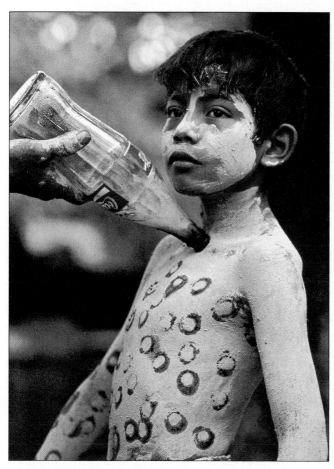

Products are not used in the same ways in all markets. Here a boy in an eastern Mexican village is prepared for a "Jaguar dance" to bring rain. Clay, ashes, and the globally ubiquitous Coke bottle make for the best cat costumes. (© *Kenneth Garrett/National Geographic Image Collection*)

---

[3]Peter Burrows, "Ringing off the Hook in China," *BusinessWeek,* June 9, 2003, pp. 80–81.

[4]There is much evidence that perceptions of quality vary across cultures. For example, see Terrence Witkowski and Mary Wolfinbarger, "Comparative Service Quality: German and American Ratings of Five Different Service Settings," *Journal of Business Research,* November 2002, pp. 875–881.

[5]Gail Edmonsdson, Christopher Palmeri, Brian Grow, and Christine Tierney, "BMW, Will Panke's High-Speed Approach Hurt the Brand?" *BusinessWeek,* June 9, 2003, pp. 57–60.

**CROSSING BORDERS 12.1** The Quality of Food Is a Matter of Taste

Food preferences not only vary across countries, but within them as well. For example many Vietnamese still must eat whatever they can lay their hands on. Pet birds and dogs are kept indoors to save them from the cooking pot. In 1998, the government tried to reduce the consumption of snakes and cats by banning their sale since the exploding rat population was damaging crops. Instead, peasants simply took to eating rats as well. The dwindling number of rats, in turn, has caused an explosion in the numbers of another tasty treat: snails.

Meanwhile, in nearby Ho Chi Minh city, the country's commercial capital, a recent survey found that 12.5 percent of children were obese—and the figure is rising. Local restaurants vie with one another in expense and luxury. Hoang Khai, a local businessman, recalls how his family always celebrated at home when he was young, because there was nowhere to go out. He decided to

change all that, by plowing the returns from his textile business into a restaurant lavish enough to suit the city's business elite. The result is *Au Manoir de Khai*, a colonial villa smothered in gilt and silk where a meal with imported wine can set you back more than most Vietnamese earn in a year.

One wonders how ice cream from Fugetsudo, a small confectionary shop in northern Japan, would sell in either neighborhood in Vietnam? You can get fish, seal slug, whale meat, turtle, or cedar chip flavored ice cream there. His competition sells pickled-orchid, chicken-wing, shrimp, eel, and short-necked clam flavors. Yum!

Sources: "Eating Out in Vietman," *The Economist*, December 21, 2002, pp. 49–50; and Phred Dvorak, "Something Fishy Is Going On In Japan In the Ice-Cream Biz," *Wall Street Journal*, September 4, 2002, p. 1.

simple: It positioned its product for competition from multinational brands by giving the consumer another expression of quality.

Quality is also measured in many industries by objective third parties. In the United States, JD Power and Associates expanded its auto quality ratings based on consumer surveys to other areas, such as computers. Customer satisfaction indexes developed first in Sweden are now being used to measure customer satisfaction across a wide variety of consumer products and services.[6] Finally, the U.S. Department of Commerce annually recognizes American firms for the quality of their international offerings—the Ritz Carlton Hotel chain won the prestigious award twice.

**Maintaining Quality**

Maintaining performance quality is critical,[7] but frequently a product that leaves the factory at performance quality is damaged as it passes through the distribution chain. This is a special problem for many global brands for which production is distant from the market and/or control of the product is lost because of the distribution system within the market. When Mars Company's Snickers and other Western confectioneries were first introduced to Russia, they were a big hit. Foreign brands such as Mars, Toblerone, Waldbaur, and Cadbury were the top brands—indeed, only one Russian brand placed in the top ten. But within five years the Russian brands had retaken eight of the top spots, and only one U.S. brand, Mars's Dove bars, was in the top ten.

What happened? A combination of factors caused the decline. Russia's Red October Chocolate Factory got its act together, modernized its packaging, product mix, and equipment, and set out to capture the market. Performance quality was also an issue. When

---

[6]Claes Fornell, Michael D. Johnson, Eugene W. Anderson, Jaesung Cha, and Barbara Everitt Bryant, "The American Consumer Satisfaction Index: Nature, Purpose, and Findings," *Journal of Marketing*, October 1996, 60(4), pp. 35–46; and Jon E. Hilsenrath, "Satisfaction Theory: Mixed Yield—Professor's Portfolio Shows Strategy Linking Returns to Reputation Isn't Perfect," *Wall Street Journal*, February 19, 2003, p. A2.

[7]Duncan I. Simester, John R. Hauser, Birger Wernerfelt, and Roland T. Rust, "Implementing Quality Improvement Programs Designed to Enhance Customer Satisfaction: Quasi-Experiments in the United States and Spain," *Journal of Marketing Research*, February 2000, 37, pp. 102–112.

the Russian market opened to outside trade, foreign companies anxious to get into the market dumped surplus out-of-date and poor-quality products. In other cases, chocolates were smuggled in and sold on street corners and were often mishandled in the process. By the time they made it to consumers, the chocolates were likely to be misshapen or discolored—poor quality compared with Russia's Red October chocolate.

Market-perceived quality was also an issue. Russian chocolate has a different taste because of its formulation—more cocoa and chocolate liqueur are used than in Western brands, which makes it grittier. Thus, the Red October brand appeals more to Russian taste even though it is generally priced above Western brands. As evinced by this example, quality is not just desirable, it is essential for success in today's competitive global market, and the decision to standardize or adapt a product is crucial in delivering quality.

## Physical or Mandatory Requirements and Adaptation

A product may have to change in a number of ways to meet the physical or mandatory requirements of a new market, ranging from simple package changes to total redesign of the physical core product. In many countries the term product **homologation** is used to describe the changes mandated by local product and service standards. A recent study reaffirmed the often-reported finding that mandatory adaptations were more frequently the reason for product adaptation than adapting for cultural reasons.

Some changes are obvious with relatively little analysis; a cursory examination of a country uncovers the need to rewire electrical goods for a different voltage system, simplify a product when the local level of technology is not high, or print multilingual labels where required by law. Electrolux, for example, offers a cold-wash-only washing machine in Asian countries where electric power is expensive or scarce. Other necessary changes may surface only after careful study of an intended market.

Legal, economic, political, technological, and climatic requirements of the local marketplace often dictate product adaptation. During a period in India when the government was very against foreign investment, Pepsi-Cola changed its product name to Lehar-Pepsi (in Hindi, *lehar* means "wave") to gain as much local support as possible. The name returned to Pepsi-Cola when the political climate turned favorable. Laws that vary among countries usually set specific package sizes and safety and quality standards. The European Union bans products with forms of genetically modified food content.[8] The World Health Organization is beginning to regulate the marketing of high carcinogen American cigarettes.[9] But most interestingly, videogame content is regulated around the world according to violence levels and sexual content.[10] To make a purchase more affordable in low-income countries, the number of units per package may be reduced from the typical quantities offered in high-income countries. Razor blades, cigarettes, chewing gum, and other multiple-pack items are often sold singly or two to a pack instead of the more customary 10 or 20. Cheetos, a product of PepsiCo's Frito-Lay, is packaged in 15-gram boxes in China so it can be priced at 1 yuan, about 12 cents. At this price, even children with little spending money can afford cheetos.

Changes may also have to be made to accommodate climatic differences.[11] General Motors of Canada, for example, experienced major problems with several thousand Chevrolet automobiles shipped to a Mideast country; it was quickly discovered they were unfit for the hot, dusty climate. Supplementary air filters and different clutches had to be added to adjust for the problem. Similarly, crackers must be packaged in tins for humid areas.

The less economically developed a market is, the greater degree of change a product may need for acceptance. One study found that only one in ten products could be

---

[8]Lizette Alvarez, "Consumers in Europe Resist Gene-Altered Foods," *New York Times,* February 11, 2003, p. A3.

[9]Myron Levin, "Study Shows More Carcinogens in Marlboros Than Non-U.S. Brands," *Los Angeles Times,* May 30, 2003, p. C3.

[10]Alex Pham and Scott Sandell, "In Germany, Video Games Showing Frontal Nudity Are OK, but Blood Is Verboten," *Los Angeles Times,* June 9, 2003, p. C1.

[11]Philip M. Parker and Nader T. Tavossoli, "Homeostasis and Consumer Behavior across Cultures," *International Journal of Research in Marketing,* March 2000, 17(1), pp. 33–53.

**CROSSING BORDERS 12.2** In Germany, Video Games Showing Frontal Nudity Are OK, but Blood Is Verboten

Video game heroine Lara Croft is an adrenaline junkie unafraid of getting bloody. But in Germany, the buxom starlet of the "Tomb Raiders" series doesn't bleed—even if she's being mauled by a tiger.

Although the $25-billion video game industry is global, the games themselves aren't. They reflect the distinct cultures and traditions of different markets, and game publishers carefully tweak their titles and other details to tone down offensive materials. And "offensive" varies from country to country.

Red blood in a game sold in the United States turns green in Australia. A topless character in a European title acquires a bikini in the United States. Human enemies in an American game are changed into robots in Germany. Violent sex scenes in a Japanese game disappear in the American version.

Of all countries, Germany is one of the trickiest to tackle, publishers say. The country spent five decades developing one of the world's strictest decency standards for virtually all media, from books and comics to music and games.

If a game features blood splatterings, decapitations, or death cries, it runs the risk of being placed on a government list known as "the index." Being indexed means it can't be sold to anyone under 18, displayed in stores or advertised on television, in newspapers, or in magazines. Games containing pornography or glorifications of war, Nazism, and racial hatred face the same fate.

The scariest part of this story is not the games themselves, but the newest use of them as political tools. One game indexed in Germany involves a prisoner of war camp for Turkish detainees. On the other side, Hizbollah, the terrorist organization best known for killing 240 American marines in Lebanon in 1983, also published a new "click-and-kill" game. When are such games more than just entertainment?

Sources: A. Phan, S. Sandell. "Germany, Video Games Showing Frontal Nudity Are OK, but Blood Is *Verboten*", *Los Angeles Times*, June 9, 2003, p. C1; and "Jihad in Cyperspace—Hizbollah's New Video Game," *The Economist*, March 15, 2003, p. 42.

marketed in developing countries without modification of some sort. Because most products sold abroad by international companies originate in home markets and most require some form of modification, companies need a systematic process to identify products that need adaptation.

## Green Marketing and Product Development

A quality issue of growing importance the world over, especially in Europe and the United States, is green marketing. Europe is at the forefront of the "green movement," with strong public opinion and specific legislation favoring environmentally friendly marketing and products. **Green marketing** is a term used to identify concern with the environmental consequences of a variety of marketing activities. In the United States, Japanese car manufacturers are taking advantage of their gas-guzzling American cousins as consumers become more concerned about the environmental effects of SUVs like the General Motors Hummer.[12] The European Commission passed legislation to control all kinds of packaging waste throughout the European Community. Two critical issues that affect product development are the control of the packaging component of solid waste and consumer demand for environmentally friendly products.

The European Commission (EC) issued guidelines for eco-labeling that became operational in 1992. Under the directive, a product is evaluated on all significant environmental effects throughout its life cycle, from manufacturing to disposal—a cradle-to-grave approach. A detergent formulated to be biodegradable and nonpolluting would be judged friendlier than a detergent whose formulation would be harmful when discharged into the environment. Aerosol propellants that do not deplete the ozone layer are another

---

[12]David Welch and Kathleen Kerwin, "Detroit Is Wrecking Its SUV Edge," *BusinessWeek*, March 3, 2003, p. 42.

example of environmentally friendly products. No country's laws yet require products to carry an eco-label to be sold, however. The designation that a product is "environmentally friendly" is voluntary, and environmental success depends on the consumer selecting the eco-friendly product.

Since the introduction of the eco-label idea, Hoover washing machines are the only products that gained approval for the eco-label. Interestingly enough, the benefits of winning the symbol resulted in Hoover trebling its market share in Germany and doubling its share of the premium sector of the U.K. washing-machine market. The approval process seems to be deterring many European manufacturers, many of whom are using their own, unofficial symbols. The National Consumer Council, a consumer watchdog group, reports that many consumers are so confused and cynical about the myriad symbols that they are giving up altogether on trying to compare the green credentials of similar products.

Laws that mandate systems to control solid waste, while voluntary in one sense, do carry penalties. The EC law requires that packaging material through all levels of distribution, from the manufacturer to the consumer, be recycled or reused. Currently, between 50 percent and 65 percent of the weight of the packaging must be recovered, and between 25 percent and 45 percent of the weight of the totality of packaging materials contained in packaging waste are recycled.

Each level of the distribution chain is responsible for returning all packaging, packing, and other waste materials up the chain. The biggest problem is with the packaging the customer takes home; by law the retailer must take back all packaging from the customer if no central recycling locations are available. For the manufacturer's product to participate in direct collection and not have to be returned to the retailer for recycling, the manufacturer must guarantee financial support for curbside or central collection of all materials. The growing public and political pressure to control solid waste is a strong incentive for compliance.

Although the packaging and solid waste rules are burdensome, there are successful cases of not only meeting local standards but also being able to transfer this approach to other markets. Procter & Gamble's international operations integrated global environmental concerns as a response to increasing demands in Germany. It introduced Lenor, a fabric softener in a superconcentrated form, and sold it in a plastic refill pouch that reduced packaging by 85 percent. This move increased brand sales by 12 percent and helped set a positive tone with government regulators and activists. The success of Lenor was transferred to the United States, where P&G faced similar environmental pressures. A superconcentrated Downy, the U.S. brand of fabric softener, was repackaged in refill pouches that reduced package size by 75 percent, thereby costing consumers less and actually increasing Downy market share. The global marketer should not view green marketing as a European problem; concern for the environment is worldwide and similar legislation is sure to surface elsewhere. This is another example of the need to adapt products for global marketing.

## Products and Culture

To appreciate the complexity of standardized versus adapted products, one needs to understand how cultural influences are interwoven with the perceived value and importance a market places on a product. A product is more than a physical item: It is a bundle of satisfactions (or *utilities*) that the buyer receives. These include its form, taste, color, odor, and texture; how it functions in use; the package; the label; the warranty; manufacturer's and retailer's servicing; the confidence or prestige enjoyed by the brand; the manufacturer's reputation; the country of origin; and any other symbolic utility received from the possession or use of the goods. In short, the market relates to more than a product's physical form and primary function. The values and customs within a culture confer much of the importance of these other benefits. In other words, a product is the sum of the physical and psychological satisfactions it provides the user.

A product's physical attributes generally are required to create its primary function. The primary function of an automobile, for example, is to move passengers from point A to point B. This ability requires a motor, transmission, and other physical features to achieve its primary purpose. The physical features or primary function of an automobile is generally in demand in all cultures where there is a desire to move from one point to another other than by foot or animal power. Few changes to the physical attributes of a product are required when moving from one culture to another. However, an automobile has a bundle of psychological features that are as important in providing consumer satisfaction as its physical features. Within a specific culture, other automobile features (color, size, design, brand name, price) have little to do with its primary function—the movement from point A to B—but do add value to the satisfaction received.

The meaning and value imputed to the psychological attributes of a product can vary among cultures and are perceived as negative or positive. To maximize the bundle of satisfactions received and to create positive product attributes rather than negative ones, adaptation of the nonphysical features of a product may be necessary. Coca-Cola, frequently touted as a global product, found it had to change Diet Coke to Coke Light when it was introduced in Japan. Japanese women do not like to admit to dieting, and further, the idea of diet implies sickness or medicine. So instead of emphasizing weight loss, "figure maintenance" is stressed. Anti-American sentiment is also causing Coke problems with Muslim consumers. Three new competitors popped up recently—Mecca Cola, Muslim Up, and Arab Cola. McDonald's is also responding to such problems with their new McArabia sandwich.[13]

Adaptation may require changes of any one or all of the psychological aspects of a product. A close study of the meaning of a product shows to what extent the culture determines an individual's perception of what a product is and what satisfaction that product provides.

The adoption of some products by consumers can be affected as much by how the product concept conforms with norms, values, and behavior patterns as by its physical or mechanical attributes. For example, only recently did Japanese consumers take an interest in dishwashers—they simply didn't have room in the kitchen. However, very compact designs by Mitsubishi, Toto (a Japanese toilet company), and others are making new inroads into Japanese kitchens. A novelty always comes up against a closely integrated cultural pattern, and it is primarily this that determines whether, when, how, and in what form it gets adopted. Some financial services are difficult to introduce into Muslim countries because the pious have claimed they promoted usury and gambling, both explicitly forbidden in the Koran.[14] The Japanese have always found all body jewelry repugnant. The Scots decidedly resist pork and all its associated products, apparently from long ago when such taboos were founded on fundamentalist interpretations of the Bible. Filter cigarettes have failed in at least one Asian country because a very low life expectancy hardly places many people in the age bracket most prone to fears of lung cancer—even supposing that they shared Western attitudes about death.

When analyzing a product for a second market, the extent of adaptation required depends on cultural differences in product use and perception between the market the product was originally developed for and the new market. The greater these cultural differences between the two markets, the greater the extent of adaptation that may be necessary.

An example of this rule of thumb involves an undisputed American leader in cake mixes, which tacitly admitted failure in the English market by closing down operations after five unsuccessful years. Taking its most successful mixes in the U.S. market, the company introduced them into the British market. Considerable amounts of time, money, and effort were expended to introduce its variety of cake mixes to this new market. Hindsight provides several probable causes for the company's failure. Traditionalism was certainly among the most important. The British eat most of their cake with tea instead of dinner and have always preferred dry sponge cake, which is easy to handle; the fancy, iced cakes favored in the United States were the type introduced. Fancy iced cakes are

---

[13]John Tabliabue, "U.S. Brands Abroad Are Feeling Global Tension," *New York Times*, March 15, 2003, p. C3.

[14]Jerry Useem, "Banking on Allah," *Fortune*, June 10, 2002, pp. 155–160.

accepted in Britain, but they are considered extra special and are purchased from a bakery or made with much effort and care at home. The company introduced what it thought to be an easy cake mix. This easy cake mix was considered a slight to domestic prowess. Homemakers felt guilty about not even cracking an egg, and there was suspicion that dried eggs and milk were not as good as fresh ones. Therefore, when the occasion called for a fancy cake, an easy cake mix was simply not good enough.

Ironically, this same company faced almost identical problems, which they eventually overcame, when introducing new easy cake mixes in the U.S. market. There was initial concern about the quality of mixes and the resulting effect on the homemaker's reputation as a baker. Even today there remains the feeling that "scratch" cakes are of special quality and significance and should be made for extra-important occasions. This feeling persists in spite of the fact that the uniform quality of results from almost all mixes and the wide variety of flavors certainly equal, if not exceed, the ability of most to bake from scratch.

Such a cultural phenomenon apparently exists in other cultures as well. When instant cake mixes were introduced in Japan, the consumers' response was less than enthusiastic. Not only do Japanese reserve cakes for special occasions, but they prefer the cakes to be beautifully wrapped and purchased in pastry shops. The acceptance of instant cakes was further complicated by another cultural difference: Many Japanese homes do not have ovens. An interesting sidebar to this example is the company's attempt to correct for that problem by developing a cake mix that could be cooked in a rice cooker, which all Japanese homes have. The problem with that idea was that in a Japanese kitchen rice and the manner in which it is cooked has strong cultural overtones, and to use the rice cooker to cook something other than rice is a real taboo.

Examples are typically given about cultures other than American, but the need for cultural adaptation is often necessary when a foreign company markets a product in the United States. A major Japanese cosmetics company, Shiseido, attempted to break into the U.S. cosmetic market with the same products sold in Japan. After introducing them in more than 800 U.S. stores, the company realized that American taste in cosmetics is very different from Japanese. The problem was that Shiseido's makeup required a time-consuming series of steps, a point that does not bother Japanese women. Success was attained after designing a new line of cosmetics as easy to use as American products.

The problems of adapting a product to sell abroad are similar to those associated with the introduction of a new product at home. Products are not measured solely by their physical specifications. The nature of the new product is in what it does to and for the customer—to habits, tastes, and patterns of life. The problems illustrated in the cake mix example have little to do with the physical product or the user's ability to make effective use of it, but more with the fact that acceptance and use of the cake mixes would have required upsetting behavior patterns considered correct or ideal.

What significance, outside its intended use, might a product have in a different culture? When product acceptance requires changes in patterns of life, habits, or tastes, the understanding of new ideas, the acceptance of the difficult to believe, or the acquisition of completely new tastes or habits, special emphasis must be used to overcome natural resistance to change.

Finally, there are some interesting surprises in the area of adaptation. The most recent example is Harry Potter. About 20 percent of the sales of his newest adventure book in Japan are in English. Japanese consumers are looking for ways to augment English lessons and the books and associated audiotapes fill that particular need quite well. For them Potter is not just entertainment, it's education.[15]

**Innovative Products and Adaptation**

An important first step in adapting a product to a foreign market is to determine the degree of newness as perceived by the intended market. How people react to newness and how new a product is to a market must be understood. In evaluating the newness of

---

[15]"Potter's Japanese Adventure," *The Economist*, February 16, 2002, p. 39.

a product, the international marketer must be aware that many products successful in the United States, having reached the maturity or even decline stage in their life cycles, may be perceived as new in another country or culture and thus must be treated as innovations. From a sociological viewpoint, any idea perceived as new by a group of people is an **innovation**.

Whether or not a group accepts an innovation, and the time it takes to do so, depends on the product's characteristics. Products new to a social system are innovations, and knowledge about the **product diffusion** (i.e., the process by which innovation spreads) of innovation is helpful in developing a successful product strategy. Sony's marketing strategies for the U.S. introduction of its PlayStation 2 were well informed by its wild successes achieved six months earlier during the product's introduction in Japan. Conversely, mid-1990s dips in Japanese sales of Apple computers were preceded by dips in Apple's home U.S. market.[16] Marketing strategies can guide and control to a considerable extent the rate and extent of new product diffusion because successful new product diffusion depends on the ability to communicate relevant product information and new product attributes.

A critical factor in the newness of a product is its effect on established patterns of consumption and behavior. In the preceding cake mix example, the fancy, iced cake mix was a product that required both acceptance of the "difficult to believe," that is, that dried eggs and milk are as good in cake as the fresh products, and the acquisition of new ideas, that is, that easy-to-bake fancy cakes are not a slight to one's domestic integrity. In this case, the product directly affected two important aspects of consumer behavior, and the product innovation met with sufficient resistance to convince the company to leave the market. Had the company studied the target market before introducing the product, perhaps it could have avoided the failure.

Another U.S. cake mix company entered the British market but carefully eliminated most of the newness of the product. Instead of introducing the most popular American cake mixes, the company asked 500 British housewives to bake their favorite cake. Since the majority baked a simple, very popular dry sponge cake, the company brought to the market a similar easy mix. The sponge cake mix represented familiar tastes and habits that could be translated into a convenience item and did not infringe on the emotional aspects of preparing a fancy product for special occasions. Consequently, after a short period of time, the second company's product gained 30 to 35 percent of the British cake mix market. After the idea of a mix for sponge cake was acceptable, the introduction of other flavors became easier.

The goal of a foreign marketer is to gain product acceptance by the largest number of consumers in the market in the shortest span of time. However, as discussed in Chapter 4 and as many of the examples cited have illustrated, new products are not always readily accepted by a culture; indeed, they often meet resistance. Although they may ultimately be accepted, the time it takes for a culture to learn new ways, to learn to accept a new product, is of critical importance to the marketer because planning reflects a time frame for investment and profitability. If a marketer invests with the expectation that a venture will break even in three years and it takes seven to gain profitable volume, the effort may have to be prematurely abandoned. The question comes to mind of whether the probable rate of acceptance can be predicted before committing resources and, more critically, if the probable rate of acceptance is too slow, whether it can be accelerated. In both cases, the answer is a qualified yes. Answers to these questions come from examining the work done in diffusion research—research on the process by which innovations spread to the members of a social system.

## Diffusion of Innovations

Everett Rogers notes that "crucial elements in the diffusion of new ideas are (1) an innovation, (2) which is communicated through certain channels, (3) over time, (4) among

[16]Joel West, *Standards Competition and Apple Computers,* unpublished doctoral dissertation, Graduate School of Management, University of California, Irvine, 2000.

the members of a social system."[17] Rogers continues with the statement that it is the element of time that differentiates diffusion from other types of communications research. The goals of the diffusion researcher and the marketer are to shorten the time lag between introduction of an idea or product and its widespread adoption.

Rogers and others[18] give ample evidence of the fact that product innovations have a varying rate of acceptance. Some diffuse from introduction to widespread use in a few years; others take decades. Patterns of alcoholic beverage consumption are seen to be converging across Europe only when a 50-year time frame is considered. Microwave ovens, introduced in the United States initially in the 1950s, took nearly 20 years to become widespread; the contraceptive pill was introduced during that same period and gained acceptance in a few years. In the field of education, modern math took only five years to diffuse through U.S. schools, whereas the idea of kindergartens took nearly 50 years to gain total acceptance. A growing body of evidence suggests that the understanding of diffusion theory may provide ways in which the process of diffusion can be accelerated. Knowledge of this process may provide the foreign marketer with the ability to assess the time it takes for a product to diffuse—before it is necessary to make a financial commitment. It also focuses the marketer's attention on features of a product that provoke resistance, thereby providing an opportunity to minimize resistance and hasten product acceptance.

At least three extraneous variables affect the rate of diffusion of an object: the degree of perceived newness, the perceived attributes of the innovation, and the method used to communicate the idea. Each variable has a bearing on consumer reaction to a new product and the time needed for acceptance. An understanding of these variables can produce better product strategies for the international marketer.

The more innovative a product is perceived to be, the more difficult it is to gain market acceptance. However, the perception of innovation can often be changed if the marketer understands the perceptual framework of the consumer. This certainly proved to be the case with the fast global diffusion of Internet usage, e-tailing, and health- and beauty-related products and services.

Analyzing the five characteristics of an innovation can assist in determining the rate of acceptance or resistance of the market to a product. A product's (1) *relative advantage* (the perceived marginal value of the new product relative to the old); (2) *compatibility* (its compatibility with acceptable behavior, norms, values, and so forth); (3) *complexity* (the degree of complexity associated with product use); (4) *trialability* (the degree of economic and/or social risk associated with product use); and (5) *observability* (the ease with which the product benefits can be communicated) affect the degree of its acceptance or resistance. In general, it can be postulated that the rate of diffusion is positively related to relative advantage, compatibility, trialability, and observability, but negatively related to complexity.

By analyzing a product within these five dimensions, a marketer can often uncover perceptions held by the market that if left unchanged would slow product acceptance. Conversely, if these perceptions are identified and changed, the marketer may be able to accelerate product acceptance.

The evaluator must remember that it is the perception of product characteristics by the potential adopter, not the marketer, that is crucial to the evaluation. A market analyst's self-reference criterion (SRC) may cause a perceptual bias when interpreting the characteristics of a product. Thus instead of evaluating product characteristics from the foreign user's frame of reference, the marketer might analyze them from his or her frame of reference, leading to a misinterpretation of the product's cultural importance.

After the analysis is made, some of the perceived newness or causes for resistance can be minimized through adroit marketing. The more congruent that product perceptions are

---

[17]Everett M. Rogers, *Diffusion of Innovations,* 5th edition (New York: Free Press, 2003). This is a book that should be read by anyone responsible for product development and brand management, domestic or international.

[18]Marnik G. Dekimpe, Philip M. Parker, and Miklos Sarvary, "Global Diffusion and Technological Innovations: A Couple-Hazard Approach," *Journal of Marketing Research,* February 2000, 38, pp. 47–59.

**CROSSING BORDERS 12.3**  So This Is What Is Called an Innovation—
                             But Does It Flush?

An American diplomat was at a dinner party in a Japanese home when he excused himself to go to the bathroom. He completed his errand, stood up, and realized he didn't have a clue about how to flush the toilet.

The diplomat spoke Japanese, but he was still baffled by the colorful array of buttons on the complicated keypad on the toilet. This super-high-tech toilet had a control panel that looked like the cockpit of a plane. So he just started pushing.

He hit the noisemaker button that makes a flushing sound to mask any noise you might be making in the bathroom. He hit the button that starts the blow dryer for your bottom. Then he hit the bidet button and watched helplessly as a little plastic arm, sort of a squirt gun shaped like a toothbrush, appeared from the back of the bowl and began shooting a stream of warm water across the room and onto the mirror.

And that's how one of America's promising young Foreign Service officers ended up frantically wiping down a Japanese bathroom with a wad of toilet paper.

Other buttons he could have tried automatically open and close the lid: The button for men lifts the lid and seat; the button for women lifts the lid only. Some toilets even have a handheld remote control, sort of a clicker for the loo.

What confounded this diplomat was one of Japan's recent additions to the bathroom: the Toto "Washlit," a toilet of the future sold for $2,000 to $4,000, depending on the number of functional features. The company sells about $400 million annually of these technological wonders and successfully entered the U.S. market with a less-complicated, less-expensive model—it features only the seat warmer, bottom washer, and deodorizing fan for $400—they call it a Niagra!

Sources: Mary Jordan and Kevin Sullivan, "But Do They Flush?" *Washington Post*, May 15, 1997, p. 1; Anthony Paul, "Made in Japan, the Country's R&D Labs Are Busy Inventing the 21st Century," *Fortune*, December 6, 1999, pp. 190–202; and Robert P. Mader, "Toilet Test Results Clash," *Contractor*, December 2002, p. 7.

with current cultural values, the less resistance there will be and the more rapid product diffusion or acceptance will be.

**Production of Innovations**

Some consideration must be given to the inventiveness of companies and countries.[19] For example, it is no surprise that most of the new ideas associated with the Internet are being produced in the United States. The 143 million American users of the Internet far outnumber the 56 million Japanese users.[20] Similarly, America wins the overall R&D expenditure contest. Expenditures are about the same across OECD countries at about 2 to 3 percent of GDP, so America's large economy supports twice the R&D spending as does Japan, for example. This spending yields about three times the U.S. patents granted to American firms versus Japanese firms. Most interestingly, the Japanese government diagnosed the problem as a lack of business training. Their engineers are not versed in marketing and entrepreneurship and American-style educational programs are being created at a record pace to fill the gap.[21] Many Japanese firms also take advantage of American innovativeness by establishing design centers in the United States—most notable are the plethora of auto design centers in southern California. At the same time American automobile firms established design centers in Europe. Recent studies show that innovativeness varies across cultures[22] and companies are placing design centers worldwide. Indeed, the Ford Taurus, the car that saved Ford in the 1980s, was a European design.

---

[19]Anyone interested in a wonderful book on this topic should read the Pulitzer Prize winning *Guns, Germs, and Steel—the Fates of Human Societies* by Jared Diamond (New York: Norton, 1999).

[20]World Bank, 2003.

[21]"Redesigned, Japan's Best Engineers Are Having to Learn about Business," *The Economist*, June 14, 2003, p. 64.

[22]James T. Simpson and Christine Kollmannsberger, "New Product Development in German and US Technology Firms," *European Journal of Innovation Management*, 2002, 5(4), pp. 194–207.

The Japanese and the Dutch are the world's champions in toilet innovations. Japan's abundance of water has allowed the culture to focus on cleanliness, frequent bathing, and high-tech bathrooms. Thus, Matsushita's toilet reads your body weight, temperature, and blood pressure. Soon you will also be able to get a readout on glucose and protein levels in your urine! The Dutch are also worried about plumbing— much of their country is below sea level. Sphinx in Maastricht produces a urinal for women and a fly imbedded in the porcelain for their men's urinal. The latter reduces maintenance costs as the company's research has shown that most men will aim for the fly which is strategically placed to minimize splash. Either Dutch innovation can be seen in Schiphol Airport outside of Amsterdam. *(top: © Michael Edrington/The Image Works)*

While increasing numbers of Japanese at the largest and most diversified firms are going back to business school, their Korean conglomerate competitors are leveraging their vertical integration more successfully at the lower end of the consumer electronics business. Samsung created a number of very successful innovations by tying together product development teams across semiconductors, telecom, digital appliance, and digital media units.[23]

## Analyzing Product Components for Adaptation

A product is multidimensional, and the sum of all its features determines the bundle of satisfactions (utilities) received by the consumer. To identify all the possible ways a product may be adapted to a new market, it

---

[23]Cliff Edwards, Moon Ihlwan, and Pete Engardio, "The Samsung Way," *BusinessWeek*, June 16, 2003, pp. 56–61.

**Exhibit 12.1**
Product Component
Model

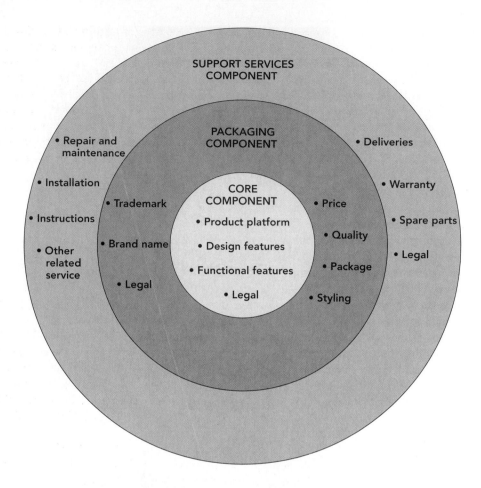

helps to separate its many dimensions into three distinct components as illustrated in Exhibit 12.1, the **Product Component Model**. By using this model, the impact of the cultural, physical, and mandatory factors (discussed previously) that affect a market's acceptance of a product can be focused on the core component, packaging component, and support services component. These components include all a product's tangible and intangible elements and provide the bundle of utilities the market receives from use of the product.

## Core Component

The *core component* consists of the physical product—the platform that contains the essential technology—and all its design and functional features. It is on the product platform that product variations can be added or deleted to satisfy local differences. Major adjustments in the platform aspect of the core component may be costly because a change in the platform can affect product processes and thus require additional capital investment. However, alterations in design, functional features, flavors, color, and other aspects can be made to adapt the product to cultural variations. In Japan, Nestlé originally sold the same kind of corn flakes it sells in the United States, but Japanese children ate them mostly as snacks instead of for breakfast. To move their product into the larger breakfast market, Nestlé reformulated its cereals to more closely fit Japanese taste. The Japanese traditionally eat fish and rice for breakfast, so Nestlé developed cereals with familiar tastes—seaweed, carrots and zucchini, and coconuts and papaya. The result was a 12 percent share of the growing breakfast-cereal market.

For the Brazilian market, where fresh orange juice is plentiful, General Foods changed the flavor of its presweetened powdered juice substitute, Tang, from the traditional orange to passion fruit and other flavors. Changing flavor or fragrance is often necessary to bring a product in line with what is expected in a culture. Household cleansers with the traditional pine odor and hints of ammonia or chlorine popular in U.S. markets were not successful when introduced in Japan. Many Japanese sleep on the floor on futons with their heads close to the surface they have cleaned, so a citrus fragrance is more pleasing.

Rubbermaid could have avoided missteps in introducing its line of baby furniture in Europe with modest changes in the core component. Its colors were not tailored to European tastes, but worst of all, its child's bed didn't fit European-made mattresses!

Functional features can be added or eliminated depending on the market. In markets where hot water is not commonly available, washing machines have heaters as a functional feature. In other markets, automatic soap and bleach dispensers may be eliminated to cut costs or to minimize repair problems. Additional changes may be necessary to meet safety and electrical standards or other mandatory (homologation) requirements. The physical product and all its functional features should be examined as potential candidates for adaptation.

## Packaging Component

The *packaging component* includes style features, packaging, labeling, trademarks, brand name, quality, price, and all other aspects of a product's package. Apple Computer found this out the hard way when it first entered the Japanese market. Some of its Macintosh computers were returned unused after customers found the wrapping on the instruction manual damaged! As with the core component, the importance of each of the elements in the eyes of the consumer depends on the need that the product is designed to serve.

Packaging components frequently require both discretionary and mandatory changes. For example, some countries require labels to be printed in more than one language, while others forbid the use of any foreign language. Several countries are now requiring country-of-origin labeling for food products. Elements in the packaging component may incorporate symbols that convey an unintended meaning and thus must be changed. One company's red-circle trademark was popular in some countries but was rejected in parts of Asia, where it conjured up images of the Japanese flag. Yellow flowers used in another company trademark were rejected in Mexico, where a yellow flower symbolizes death or disrespect.

A well-known baby-food producer that introduced small jars of baby food in Africa complete with labels featuring a picture of a baby experienced the classic example of misinterpreted symbols: The company was absolutely horrified to find that consumers thought the jars contained ground-up babies. In China, although not a problem of literacy per se, Brugel, a German children's cereal brand that features cartoon drawings of dogs, cats, birds, monkeys, and other animals on the package, was located in the pet foods section of a supermarket. The label had no Chinese, and store personnel were unfamiliar with the product. It is easy to forget that in low-literacy countries, pictures and symbols are taken quite literally as instructions and information.

Package size and price have an important relationship in poor countries. Companies find that they must package in small units to bring the price in line with spending norms. Unilever makes its Sunsilk brand shampoo affordable in India by packaging it in tiny plastic bags, enough for one shampoo.

Care must be taken to ensure that corporate trademarks and other parts of the packaging component do not have unacceptable symbolic meanings. Particular attention should be given to translations of brand names and colors used in packaging. When Ford tried to sell its Pinto automobile in Brazil, it quickly found out that the car model's name translated to "tiny male genitals." White, the color for purity in Western countries, is the color for mourning in others. In China, P&G packaged diapers in a pink wrapper. Consumers shunned the pink package—pink symbolized a girl, and in a country with a one-child-per-family rule where males are preferred, you do not want anyone to think you have a girl, even if you do.

There are countless reasons why a company might need to adapt a product's package. In some countries, laws stipulate specific bottle, can, and package sizes and measurement units. If a country uses the metric system, it will probably require that weights and measurements conform to the metric system. Such descriptive words as "giant" or "jumbo" on a package or label may be illegal. High humidity or the need for long shelf life because of extended distribution systems may dictate extra-heavy packaging for some products. As is frequently mentioned, Japanese attitudes about quality include the packaging of a product. A poorly packaged product conveys an

# CROSSING BORDERS 12.4 "Happy End" Toilet Paper—Well, at Least It's Descriptive!

Not all brand names travel well, and some, like the German brand mentioned in the title, will never see the light of day as a global brand. But it is probably better than the Danish brand of toilet paper named Krapp. The point is that brand names that mean absolutely nothing in the home market can carry totally different meanings elsewhere. Here are a few other brand names that must be changed if they come to the U.S. market: Some of these brand names have no meaning in English, but phonetically they sound like a word we know—which is often the problem with brand names when they travel the globe.

*Alu-Fanny:* French foil wrap

*Atum Bom:* Portuguese tuna

*Crapsy Fruit:* French cereal

*Kack:* Danish sweets

*Mukk:* Italian yogurt

*Kum Onit:* German pencil sharpeners

*Pocari Sweat:* Japanese soft drink

*Plopp:* Scandinavian chocolate

*Poo:* Argentine curry powder

*Pschitt:* French lemonade

*Collon Bisquits:* Dutch chocolate cookie

*Fart:* Polish cleanser

*Bimbo:* the most popular brand of bread in Spain and Mexico

Sources: "But Will It Sell in Tulsa?" *Newsweek,* March 17, 1997, p. 8; and "The Battle for Identity in the Face of International Branding," *Brand Strategy,* September 19, 1997, p. 23; and student contributions, 2004.

impression of poor quality to the Japanese. It is also important to determine if the packaging has other uses in the market. Lever Brothers sells Lux soap in stylish boxes in Japan because more than half of all soap cakes there are purchased during the two gift-giving seasons. Size of the package is also a factor that may make a difference to success in Japan. Soft drinks are sold in smaller-size cans than in the United States to accommodate the smaller Japanese hand. In Japan, most food is sold fresh or in clear packaging, while cans are considered dirty. So when Campbell introduced soups to the Japanese market, it decided to go with a cleaner, more expensive pop-top opener.

Labeling laws vary from country to country and do not seem to follow any predictable pattern. In Saudi Arabia, for example, product names must be specific. "Hot Chili" will not do; it must be "Spiced Hot Chili." Prices are required to be printed on the labels in Venezuela, but in Chile it is illegal to put prices on labels or in any way suggest retail prices. Coca-Cola ran into a legal problem in Brazil with its Diet Coke. Brazilian law interprets *diet* to have medicinal qualities. Under the law, producers must give the daily recommended consumption on the labels of all medicines. Coca-Cola had to get special approval to get around this restriction. Until recently in China, Western products could be labeled in a foreign language with only a small temporary Chinese label affixed somewhere on the package. Under the new Chinese labeling law, however, food products must have their name, contents, and other specifics listed clearly in Chinese printed directly on the package—no temporary labels are allowed.

Labeling laws create a special problem for companies selling products in various markets with different labeling laws and small initial demand in each. In China, for example, there is a demand for American- and European-style snack foods even though the demand is not well developed at this time. The expense of labeling specially to meet Chinese law often makes market entry cost prohibitive. Forward-thinking manufacturers with wide distribution in Asia are adopting packaging standards comparable to those required in the European Union, by providing standard information in several different languages on the same package. A template is designed with a space on the label reserved for locally required content, which can be inserted depending on the destination of a given production batch.

Marketers must examine each of the elements of the packaging component to be certain that this part of the product conveys the appropriate meaning and value to a new market. Otherwise they may be caught short, as was the U.S. soft-drink company that incorporated six-pointed stars as decoration on its package labels. Only when investigating weak sales did they find they had inadvertently offended some of their Arab customers who interpreted the stars as symbolizing pro-Israeli sentiments.

The most controversial labeling and product contents issue of all regards genetically modified (GM) foods, or what the critics are calling "Frankenfood." The disputes, primarily with the European Union, have huge implications for American firms, which lead the world in this technology. Japan, Australia, and New Zealand are adopting labeling requirements, and other countries are implementing bans and boycotts. And the problem has now spread to the United States itself, with government considering new labeling laws for domestic GM foods and products.

## Support Services Component

The *support services* component includes repair and maintenance, instructions, installation, warranties, deliveries, and the availability of spare parts. Many otherwise successful marketing programs ultimately failed because little attention was given to this product component. Repair and maintenance are especially difficult problems in developing countries. In the United States, a consumer has the option of company service as well as a score of competitive service retailers ready to repair and maintain anything from automobiles to lawn mowers. Equally available are repair parts from company-owned or licensed outlets or the local hardware store. Consumers in a developing country and in many developed countries may not have even one of the possibilities for repair and maintenance available in the United States.

In some countries, the concept of routine maintenance or preventive maintenance is not a part of the culture. As a result, products may need to be adjusted to require less-frequent maintenance, and special attention must be given to features that may be taken for granted in the United States.

Literacy rates and educational levels of a country may require a firm to change a product's instructions. A simple term in one country may be incomprehensible in another. In rural Africa, for example, consumers had trouble understanding that Vaseline Intensive Care lotion is absorbed into the skin. *Absorbed* was changed to *soaks into,* and the confusion was eliminated. The Brazilians successfully overcame the low literacy and technical skills of users of the sophisticated military tanks it sells to Third World countries. The manufacturers include videocassette players and videotapes with detailed repair instructions as part of the standard instruction package. They also minimize spare parts problems by using standardized, off-the-shelf parts available throughout the world. And, of course, other kinds of cultural preferences come into play even in service manuals. For example, Japanese consumers actually read software manuals, some even find them entertaining, and the manuals often include cartoon characters and such.[24]

Although it may seem obvious to translate all instructions into the language of the market, many firms overlook such a basic point. "Do Not Step Here," "Danger," or "Use No Oil" have little meaning to an Arab unfamiliar with the English language. And, now marketers are facing a new challenge of this sort. The costs of a customer service call center in the Philippines or India can be ten percent of those in Omaha, Nebraska. Companies around the world, like Delta Airlines and General Electric, are flooding such English-speaking countries with call center business.[25] Despite the fluent English of these new, less-expensive employees, all the cross-cultural problems of angry American consumers "talking" to service representatives halfway around the world do crop up. Investments in training are key if the cost savings are to make up for the quality of services provide.

---

[24]Michelle Delio, "Read the F***ing Story, Then RTFM," *wired.com,* June 4, 2002.

[25]Pete Engardio, Aaron Bernstein, and Manjeet Kripalani, "Is Your Job Next," *BusinessWeek,* February 3, 2003, pp. 50–60.

## CROSSING BORDERS 12.5 So Your Computer Isn't Working?

Most people have two options when the desk beast starts acting up. Call the service center or read the manual. Both are becoming cross-cultural activities. With increasing frequency service call centers are being staffed by folks in the Philippines, India, and other developing countries where English is commonly spoken. The savings for the companies can be in the 90 percent range. But, for consumers it was tough enough bridging the technician/lay gap. Now a cross-cultural layer is being added to the interaction.

At least many manufacturers are getting better at adapting user manuals. In some countries the manuals are treasured for their entertainment value. Mike Adams of Arial Global Reach, a translation and marketing firm, explains, "Japanese people really enjoy reading documentation, but that's because Japanese documentation is actually fun to look at." Japanese manuals are often jazzed up with creative cartoons. Even program interfaces are animated. Microsoft's much-maligned Clippy the Paperclip is replaced in Japan with an animated dolphin. "And even highly technical Japanese engineers don't feel at all childish when they view or interact with these animations."

Put those cute characters in manuals in countries other than Japan and the customer will doubt the seriousness of the firm. Mark Katib, general manager of Middle East Translation Services, says most customers in that part of the world, as do Americans, prefer uncluttered, nontechnical explanations. He spends most of his time making sure that information is presented in an acceptable manner, not offending one people's beliefs.

Apparently you cannot give an Italian a command such as "never do this." The consequences for that kind of language are calls from Italians who broke their machines by doing exactly "this." Instead, Italian manuals must use less-demanding language like "you might consider . . . ."

The Germans reject manuals with imbedded humor. Hungarians like to fix things themselves, so their manuals are more like machine shop guides. Finally, one software maker that developed a WAN (wide area network) used a flowing stream of text, "WAN WAN WAN WAN" on the package. To the Japanese that's the sound a dog makes, and in Japan no one would buy a product advertising itself by a barking dog.

The main point here is that "technobabble" is hard to translate in any language.

Sources: Michelle Delio, "Read the F***ing Story, then RTFM," *Wired News* (www.wired.com), June 4, 2002; and Pete Engardio, Aaron Bernstein, and Manjeet Kripalani, "Is Your Job Next?" *BusinessWeek*, February 3, 2003, pp. 50–60.

---

The Product Component Model can be a useful guide in examining adaptation requirements of products destined for foreign markets. A product should be carefully evaluated on each of the three components for mandatory and discretionary changes that may be needed.

## Marketing Consumer Services Globally

As mentioned at the beginning of the chapter, much of the advice regarding adapting products for international consumer markets also applies to adapting services. Moreover, some services are closely associated with products. Good examples are the support services just described or the customer services associated with the delivery of a Big Mac to a consumer in Moscow. However, many consumer services are distinguished by four unique characteristics—intangibility, inseparability, heterogeneity, and perishability—and thus require special consideration.[26]

Products are often classified as tangible, whereas services are *intangible*. Automobiles, computers, and furniture are examples of products that have a physical presence; they are things or objects that can be stored and possessed, and their intrinsic value is embedded within their physical presence. Insurance, dry cleaning, hotel accommodations, and airline passenger or freight service are intangible and have intrinsic value resulting from a process, a performance, or an occurrence that only exists while it is being created.

---

[26]Valarie A. Zeithaml and Mary Jo Bitner, *Services Marketing,* 3rd edition (New York: McGraw-Hill, 2002).

The intangibility of services results in characteristics unique to a service: It is *inseparable* in that its creation cannot be separated from its consumption; it is *heterogeneous* in that it is individually produced and is thus virtually unique; it is *perishable* in that once created it cannot be stored but must be consumed simultaneously with its creation. Contrast these characteristics with a tangible product that can be produced in one location and consumed elsewhere, that can be standardized, whose quality assurance can be determined and maintained over time, and that can be produced and stored in anticipation of fluctuations in demand.

As is true for many tangible products, a service can be marketed both as an industrial (business-to-business) or a consumer service, depending on the motive of, and use by, the purchaser. For example, travel agents and airlines sell industrial or business services to a businessperson and a consumer service to a tourist. Financial services, hotels, insurance, legal services, and others may each be classified as either a business or consumer service. As one would suspect, the unique characteristics of services result in differences in the marketing of services and the marketing of consumer products.

## Services Opportunities in Global Markets

International tourism is by far the largest services export of the United States, ranking behind only capital goods and industrial supplies when all exports are counted. Spending by foreign tourists visiting American destinations such as Orlando or Anaheim is roughly double that spent by foreign airlines on Boeing's commercial jets. Worldwide tourists spent some $3.5 trillion last year,[27] and an agency of the United Nations projects that number will grow to four times that by 2020. The industry employs some 200 million people all around the world. That same agency predicts that China will be the most popular destination in the next century, followed by the United States, France, Spain, Hong Kong, Italy, Britain, Mexico, Russia, and the Czech Republic. Currently, France, Spain, the U.S., Italy, and China are numbers one through five in that order. Most tourists will be, as they are today, Germans, Japanese, and Americans; Chinese will be the fourth largest group. Currently, Japanese tourists contribute the most to U.S. tourism income, at some $20 billion. SARS and the conflicts[28] in the Middle East have had their temporary impacts on otherwise viable tourist destinations. But, overall the business is still expected to grow at its traditionally brisk pace.[29]

The dramatic growth in tourism prompted American firms and institutions to respond by developing new travel services. For example, the Four Seasons Hotel in Philadelphia offers a two-day package including local concerts and museum visits. In addition to its attractions for kids, Orlando, Florida, now sells its Opera Company with performances by Domingo, Sills, and Pavarotti. The cities of Phoenix, Las Vegas, and San Diego have formed a consortium and put together a $500,000 marketing budget specifically appealing to foreign visitors to stop at all three destinations in one trip. Even the smallest hotels are finding a global clientele on the Internet.

Other top consumer services exports include transportation, financial services, education, telecommunications, entertainment, information, and health care, in that order. Consider the following examples of each:

- American airlines are falling all over themselves to capture greater shares of the fast-expanding Latin American travel market through investments in local carriers.

- Insurance sales are also burgeoning in Latin America, with joint ventures between local and global firms making the most progress.

- Financial services in China are undergoing a revolution with new services being offered at an incredible pace—new sources of investor information[30] and

---

[27]Rana Foroohar, "Travel Forecast: Clearing?" *Newsweek,* May 26, 2003, pp. 40–46.

[28]"Airlines Grounded by War," *International Herald Tribune,* March 24, 2003, p. 10.

[29]Arundhati Parmar, "New Ads and Marketing Up Tourism to Mexico," *Marketing News,* April 14, 2003, pp. 8–9.

[30]"Bush Telegraph, How an American Woman Is Filling China's Financial-Information Gap," *The Economist,* May 24, 2003, p. 77.

National Cash Register ATMs popping up everywhere. Poles are just getting acquainted with ATMs as well.

- Merrill Lynch is going after the investment-trust business that took off after Japan allowed brokers and banks to enter that business for the first time in 1998.

- A half a million foreign students (63,000 from China[31]) spend some $7 billion a year in tuition to attend American universities and colleges.[32]

- Currently, phone rates in markets such as Germany, Italy, and Spain are so high that American companies cannot maintain toll-free information hotlines or solicit phone order catalog sales. Other telecommunications markets are deregulating, creating opportunities for foreign firms. Wireless communications are taking Japan and Europe by storm.

- *Xena, Hercules,* and comparably "dumbed-down" (i.e., heavy on action, violence, and sex) video-game heroes are conquering electronic screens worldwide. Even movies on Pearl Harbor are successfully being exhibited in Japan.[33]

- Cable TV is exploding in Latin America.

- The latest Gallup poll in China indicates that 43 percent of Beijing residents are aware of the Internet.

- Sporting events are being sold all over the world—American football in Scotland, American baseball in Mexico, and professional soccer in China.[34]

- Finally, not only are foreigners coming to the United States for healthcare services in fast-growing numbers,[35] but North American firms are building hospitals abroad as well. Recently two infants, one from Sweden and one from Japan, received heart transplants at Loma Linda Hospital in California—laws in both their countries prohibit such life-saving operations. Beijing Toronto International Hospital will soon open its doors for some 250 Chinese patients; the services include a 24-hour satellite link for consultations with Toronto.

## Barriers to Entering Global Markets for Consumer Services

Most other services—automobile rentals, airline services, entertainment, hotels, and tourism, to name a few—require production and consumption to occur almost simultaneously; thus, exporting is not a viable entry method for them. The vast majority of services (some 85 percent) enter foreign markets by licensing, franchising, or direct investment. Four kinds of barriers face consumer services marketers in this growing sector of the global marketplace: protectionism, controls on transborder data flows, protection of intellectual property, and cultural requirements for adaptation.

**Protectionism.**   The European Union is making modest progress toward establishing a single market for services. However, it is not clear exactly how foreign service providers will be treated as unification proceeds. Reciprocity and harmonization, key concepts in the Single European Act, possibly will be used to curtail the entrance of some service industries into Europe. The U.S. film and entertainment industry is a particularly difficult sector, although Vivendi's (a French company) recent purchase of Universal Studios makes things a bit more interesting. A directive regarding transfrontier television broadcasting created a quota for European programs, requiring EU member states to ensure that at least 50 percent of entertainment air time is devoted to "European works." The EU argues that this set-aside for domestic programming is

[31]Kimberly Song, "Learning Business on the Fly," *Asian Wall Street Journal,* March 21, 2003, p. A11.

[32]"Student Visas—Chillier on Campus?" *The Economist,* November 24, 2001, pp. 31–32.

[33]Mark Magnier, "Japan Moviegoers Giving 'Pearl Harbor' a Boost," *Los Angeles Times,* July 19, 2001, p. C1.

[34]Robert Hardman, "Eating Barbecued Bat in a Pounds 33-a-Night Room—the Sad World of Gazza in China," *Daily Mail,* March 1, 2003, p. 93.

[35]Jennier Mena, "Cross-Border Health Coverage," *Los Angeles Times,* July 29, 2002.

## CROSSING BORDERS 12.6 Homecare Isn't Home Decorating!

Can U.S.-based home healthcare companies expand their services beyond U.S. borders? There are a number of reasons why this might not be a viable idea. First, home healthcare was invented in the United States in response to an aging population and double-digit healthcare inflation in the 1980s, which gave rise to cost-containment pressures from the government and managed-care payers. The level of home healthcare sophistication in the United States significantly lowered hospital lengths of stay and provided an alternative to hospital admissions, resulting in significant cost savings. In Western Europe, however, homecare is viewed as a lower level of care and is not accepted as clinically viable for pediatric, oncologic, or medically complex patients with comorbidities. Hence, there is a general reluctance to discharge to the home.

Second, exporters of home healthcare are thwarted by the lack of trained clinicians to deliver the care and of sales representatives to communicate the viability of homecare. In the United Kingdom, homecare is often confused with "home decorating." Third, there are tech-nological barriers to homecare stemming from electrical incompatibility. In many instances, home medical equipment and diagnostic instruments were designed to meet U.S. specifications, thus making them inoperable in the rest of the world. And finally, medieval traditions stemming from feudal guilds and aristocracies prevent modern companies from utilizing existing distribution systems. For example, in the United Kingdom the royal postal service cannot be used for the distribution of medications.

Even with these challenges, Western Europe, Asia, and Canada are primary expansion markets for U.S.-based homecare in the next several decades. Moreover, the national healthcare services in these areas of the world are looking for alternatives to institutional care for their expanding elderly population to avoid bankrupting the national coffers.

Sources: Sarah Ladd Eames, Executive Vice President, Transworld Healthcare, 2001; and Livio Di Matteo and Rosanna Di Matteo, "Public Homecare Expenditures in Canada," *Canadian Public Policy*, September 2001, pp. 313–333. Used by permission of Canadian Public Policy.

---

necessary to preserve Europe's cultural identity. The consequences for the U.S. film industry are significant, since over 40 percent of U.S. film industry profits come from foreign revenues.

**Restrictions on Transborder Data Flows.**   There is intense concern about how to deal with the relatively new "problem" of transborder data transfers. The European Commission is concerned that data on individuals (such as income, spending preferences, debt repayment histories, medical conditions, and employment data) are being collected, manipulated, and transferred between companies with little regard to the privacy of the affected individuals. A proposed directive by the Commission would require the consent of the individual before data are collected or processed. A wide range of U.S. service companies would be affected by such a directive—insurance underwriters, banks, credit reporting firms, direct marketing companies, and tour operators are a few examples. The directive would have broad effects on data processing and data analysis firms because it would prevent a firm from transferring information electronically to the United States for computer processing if it concerned individual European consumers. Hidden in all the laws and directives are the unstated motives of most countries: a desire to inhibit the activities of multinationals and to protect local industry. As the global data transmission business continues to explode into the next century, regulators will focus increased attention in that direction.

**Protection of Intellectual Property.**   An important form of competition that is difficult to combat arises from pirated trademarks, processes, copyrights, and patents. Computer design and software, trademarks, brand names, and other intellectual properties are easy to duplicate and difficult to protect. The protection of intellectual property rights is a major problem in the services industries. Countries seldom have adequate, if any, legislation, and any laws they do have are extremely difficult to enforce. The Trade-Related Intellectual Property Rights (TRIPs) part of the GATT agreement obligates all members to provide strong protection for copyright and related rights, patents, trademarks, trade

## CROSSING BORDERS 12.7  Just To Go To School

Koffi Annan, the secretary-general of the United Nations, did it; so did Vicente Fox of Mexico, Jacques Chirac of France, and King Abdullah of Jordan. All of them went to "college" in America (the French president enhanced his experience with a job scooping ice cream). Moreover, one-third of U.S. Nobel Prize winners were foreign born. But, as the war for talent gives way to the war against terrorism, the welcome America extends to foreigners on its campuses is becoming much more guarded.

Last year, nearly 600,000 foreign students were enrolled at American universities and colleges. According to the Institute of International Education (IIE), about half came from Asia, mainly China and India. Fewer than 7 percent came from the Middle East. Students account for under 2 percent of all nonimmigrant visas (though they have the right to stay for much longer than tourists). They spend $11 billion a year on tuition and living expenses, helping to make higher education America's fifth-largest service export. And, as any visit to a Silicon Valley start-up reveals, they bring huge talent to the American economy.

Until September 11, the chief complaint was that America did not fully exploit this human capital. Like other countries, it limits the amount of time foreign students can work in the country after they graduate. The IIE frets that America's share of the foreign-student market dropped from 40 percent to under 30 percent in the past decade. It blames not only higher university fees in the United States and greater competition from Europe and Australia, but also America's cumbersome visa process.

For college students from mostly Muslim Malaysia it used to take about two weeks to get a student visa, but last year twenty Malay freshmen waited six months. They missed the fall semester. Undergraduate applications are declining nationwide. White House Science Advisor John H. Marburber III argues that the delays do not reflect policies to exclude. However, Representative Dana Rohrbacher (R-Calif.) says that the appropriate objective is "to reduce the need to attract such a high percentage of foreign students."

Sources: "Student Visas: Chillier on Campus," *The Economist,* November 24, 2001, pp. 31–32; and Catherine Arnst, "How the War on Terror is Damaging the Brain Pool," *BusinessWeek,* May 19, 2003, pp. 72–73.

---

secrets, industrial designs, geographic indications, and layout designs for integrated circuits. The TRIPs agreement is helpful, but the key issue is that enforcement is very difficult without the full cooperation of host countries. The situation in China was particularly bad because that country was not actively combating piracy of intellectual property. The annual cost of pirated software, CDs, books, and movies in China alone is estimated to be more than $1 billion. Worldwide, industry estimates are that U.S. companies lose $60 billion annually on piracy of all types of intellectual property. Because it is so easy to duplicate software, electronically recorded music, and movies, pirated copies often are available within a few days of their release. In Thailand, for example, illegal copies of movies are available within ten days of their release in the United States. In Russia, pirated movies are sometimes available before their (legal) U.S. debut!

**Cultural Barriers and Adaptation.**   Because trade in services more frequently involves people-to-people contact, culture plays a much bigger role in services than in merchandise trade. Examples are many: Eastern Europeans are perplexed by Western expectations that unhappy workers put on a "happy face" when dealing with customers. But McDonald's requires Polish employees to smile whenever they interact with customers. Such a requirement strikes many employees as artificial and insincere. The company learned to encourage managers in Poland to probe employee problems and to assign troubled workers to the kitchen rather than to the food counter. Japanese Internet purchasers often prefer to pay in cash and in person rather than trust the Internet transaction or pay high credit card fees.

As another example, notice if the Japanese student sitting next to you in class ever verbally disagrees with your instructor. Classroom interactions vary substantially around the world. Students in Japan listen to lectures, take notes, and ask questions only after class, if then. In Japan the idea of grading class participation is nonsense. Conversely, because Spaniards are used to large undergraduate classes (hundreds rather than dozens), they tend to talk to their friends even when the instructor is talking. Likewise, health-care delivery systems and doctor-patient interactions reflect cultural differences. Americans ask questions and get second opinions. Innovative healthcare services are developed on the basis of extensive marketing research. However, in Japan the social hierarchy is reflected heavily in the patients' deference to their doctors. While Japanese patient compliance is excellent and longevity is the best in the world, the healthcare system there is relatively unresponsive to the expressed concerns of consumers.

Japanese also tend to take a few long vacations—seven to ten days is the norm. Thus, vacation packages designed for them are packed with activities. Phoenix, Las Vegas, and San Diego or Rome, Geneva, Paris, and London in ten days makes sense to them. The Four Seasons Hotel chain provides special pillows, kimonos, slippers, and teas for Japanese guests. Virgin Atlantic Airways and other long-haul carriers now have interactive screens available for each passenger, allowing viewing of Japanese (or American, French, etc.) movies and TV.

Managing a global services workforce is certainly no simple task. Just ask the folks at UPS. Some of the surprises UPS ran into included indignation in France when drivers were told they couldn't have wine with lunch, protests in Britain when drivers' dogs were banned from delivery trucks, dismay in Spain when it was found that the brown UPS trucks resembled the local hearses, and shock in Germany when brown shirts were required for the first time since 1945.

And, while tips of 10 to 15 percent are an important part of services workers' incentives in the United States, this is not the case in Germany, where tips are rounded to the nearest deutsche mark, or in China, where they are considered an insult. Thus, closer management of service personnel is required in those countries to maintain high levels of customer satisfaction.

Clearly, opportunities for the marketing of consumer services will continue to grow in the twenty-first century. International marketers will have to be quite creative in responding to the legal and cultural challenges of delivering high-quality services in foreign markets and to foreign customers at domestic locales.

## Brands in International Markets

Hand in hand with global products and services are global brands. A **global brand** is defined as the worldwide use of a name, term, sign, symbol (visual and/or auditory[36]), design, or combination thereof intended to identify goods or services of one seller and to differentiate them from those of competitors. Much like the experience with global products, there is no single answer to the question of whether or not to establish global brands. There is, however, little question of the importance of a brand name. Exhibit 12.2 lists the estimated worth (equity) of the 20 top global brands.[37] And, as indicated in previous chapters, protecting brand names is also a big business.[38]

A successful brand is the most valuable resource a company has. The brand name encompasses the years of advertising, good will, quality evaluation, product experience, and other beneficial attributes the market associates with the product. Brand image is at the very core of business identity and strategy. Customers everywhere respond to images, myths, and metaphors that help them define their personal and national identities within a global context of world culture and product benefits.[39] Global brands play

---

[36]Nader T. Tavassoli and Jin K. Han, "Auditory and Visual Brand Identifiers in Chinese and English," *Journal of International Marketing,* November 2002, 10(2), pp. 13–28.

[37]Gerry Khermouch, "The Best Global Brands," *BusinessWeek,* August 5, 2002, pp. 92–99.

[38]Kate Gillespie, Kishore Krishna, and Susan Jarvis, "Protecting Global Brands: Toward a Global Norm," *Journal of International Marketing,* November 2002, 10(2), pp. 99–112; and Karbey Leggett, "GM Says New Chinese Subcompact Looks Awfully Similar to a Car It Plans to Sell There Shortly," *Wall Street Journal,* June 19, 2003, p. B1.

[39]Douglas B. Holt, "What Becomes an Icon Most?" *Harvard Business Review,* March 2003, pp. 43–49.

**Exhibit 12.2**    Top 20 Global Brands

| Rank | Brand | 2002 Brand Value (billions) | Country of Ownership | Description/Recent Events |
|---|---|---|---|---|
| 1. | Coca-Cola | $69.6 | United States | Still the best brand by far. Growth in the developing world offset 50-50 new products like Diet Coke with Lemon. |
| 2. | Microsoft | 64.1 | United States | Its name is still dragged through the courtroom, but the biggest challenge is stagnant PC purchases. |
| 3. | IBM | 51.2 | United States | Good thing Big Blue was rebuilt on services, which remains the most promising segment for tech spending. |
| 4. | GE | 41.3 | United States | The retirement of Jack Welch and angst over corporate America took a toll on the GE name. |
| 5. | Intel | 30.9 | United States | "Intel inside" put it on the map, but now the brand faces tough competition and sluggish PC sales. |
| 6. | Nokia | 20.0 | Finland | Still the cell-phone brand of choice among consumers, but overall sales of mobile handsets are weak. |
| 7. | Disney | 29.3 | United States | Even monster hit *Monsters Inc.* couldn't compensate for a post-September 11 falloff at theme parks. |
| 8. | McDonald's | 26.4 | United States | Who remembers mad cow disease? Global expansion is spotty as negative PR fades. |
| 9. | Marlboro | 24.2 | United States | The iconic brand uses fine extensions and merchandising clout to overcome court challenges and skyrocketing price of cigs. |
| 10. | Mercedes | 21.0 | Germany | The leading luxury car brand, but its low-end models suffered from poor reviews. |
| 11. | Ford | 20.4 | United States | At least Ford admitted to pursuing strategies that were "poorly conceived or poorly timed." But where's the fix? |
| 12. | Toyota | 19.5 | Japan | Cruising along after capturing broad midmarket appeal in the United States, including new SUVs and pickups. |
| 13. | Citibank | 18.1 | United States | A slowing U.S. economy and a hit from the Enron fiasco hurt both results and image. |
| 14. | Hewlett-Packard | 16.8 | United States | More and more its printers are commodities. Bickering during the Compaq merger also didn't boost HPs image. |
| 15. | American Express | 16.3 | United States | Wary U.S. consumers, penny-pinching corporations, and white-hot competition in credit cards made it a tough year for the prestigious brand. |
| 16. | Cisco | 16.2 | United States | The popping of the Internet bubble and the plunge in telecom spending drew down brand value. |
| 17. | AT&T | 16.1 | United States | Nobody loves telecom these days. But at least it's faring better than WorldCom. |
| 18. | Honda | 15.1 | Japan | Solid, dependable, and nurturing a growing reputation for earth friendly "hybrid" technology. |
| 19. | Gillette | 15.0 | United States | The King of Blades is still gaining share, as higher marketing boosts the premium Mach 3 and Venus razors. |
| 20. | BMW | 14.4 | Germany | Bold new design—from the space-age 7-series sedan to the athletic X5 SUV—helped BMW boost sales and profit margins. |

Source: Interbrand Corp., J.P.Morgan Chase & Co., *BusinessWeek*, 2002.

Copying is the highest form of flattery? Not so in the car business. The new *QQ* model from Chinese company Chery (left) resembles the *Matiz* or *Spark* from GM's Daewoo (right) perhaps a bit too much. (© *KEVIN LEE/BLOOMBERG NEWS/Landov*)

an important role in that process. The value of Kodak, Sony, Coca-Cola, McDonald's, Toyota, and Marlboro is indisputable. One estimate of the value of Coca-Cola, the world's most valuable brand, places it at over $70 billion and growing. In fact, one authority speculates that brands are so valuable that companies will soon include a "statement of value" addendum to their balance sheets to include intangibles such as the value of their brands.

**Global Brands**   Naturally, companies with such strong brands strive to use those brands globally. In fact, it appears that even perceived "globalness" leads to increases in sales.[40] The Internet and other technologies are accelerating the pace of the globalization of brands.[41] Even for products that must be adapted to local market conditions, a global brand can be successfully used with careful consideration.[42] Heinz produces a multitude of products that are sold under the Heinz brand all over the world. Many are also adapted to local tastes. In the United Kingdom, for example, Heinz Baked Beans Pizza (available with cheese or sausage) was a runaway hit, selling over 2.5 million pizzas in the first six months after its introduction. In the British market, Heinz's brand of baked beans is one of the more popular products. The British consumer eats an average of 16 cans annually, for a sales total of $1.5 billion a year. The company realizes that consumers in other countries are unlikely to rush to stores for bean pizzas, but the idea could lead to the creation of products more suited to other cultures and markets.

Ideally a global brand gives a company a uniform worldwide image that enhances efficiency and cost savings when introducing other products associated with the brand name,[43] but not all companies believe a single global approach is the best. Indeed, we

[40]Jan-Benedict E.M. Steenkamp, Rajeev Batra, and Dana L. Alden, "How Perceived Brand Globalness Creates Brand Value," *Journal of International Business Studies,* 2003, 34, pp. 53–65.

[41]April Wright, "Technology as an Enabler of the Global Branding of Retail Financial Services," *Journal of International Marketing,* November 2002, 10(2), pp. 83–98.

[42]Shi Zhang and Bernd H. Schmitt, "Creating Local Brands in Multilingual International Markets," *Journal of Marketing Research,* August 2001, 38, pp. 313–325; Brand Name Translation: Language Constraints, Product Attributes, and Consumer Perceptions in East and Southeast Asia," *Journal of International Marketing,* November 2002, 10(2), pp. 29–45; and Giana M. Eckhardt and Michael J. Houston, "Cultural Paradoxes Reflected in Brand Meaning: McDonald's in Shanghai, China," *Journal of International Marketing*, November 2002, 10(2), pp. 68–82.

[43]Susan P. Douglas, C. Samuel Craig, and Edwin J. Nijssen, "Integrating Branding Strategy across Markets: Building International Brand Architecture," *Journal of International Marketing,* 2001, 9(2), pp. 97–114.

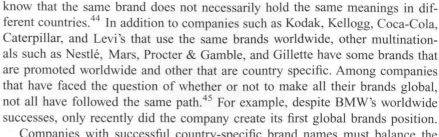

Caterpillar shoes and clothing—apparently Norwegian consumers like the industrial strength of this brand.

know that the same brand does not necessarily hold the same meanings in different countries.[44] In addition to companies such as Kodak, Kellogg, Coca-Cola, Caterpillar, and Levi's that use the same brands worldwide, other multinationals such as Nestlé, Mars, Procter & Gamble, and Gillette have some brands that are promoted worldwide and other that are country specific. Among companies that have faced the question of whether or not to make all their brands global, not all have followed the same path.[45] For example, despite BMW's worldwide successes, only recently did the company create its first global brands position.

Companies with successful country-specific brand names must balance the benefits of a global brand against the risk of losing the benefits of an established brand. And some brand names simply do not translate.[46] The cost of reestablishing the same level of brand preference and market share for the global brand that the local brand has must be offset against the long-term cost savings and benefits of having only one brand name worldwide. In those markets where the global brand is unknown, many companies are buying local brands of products that consumers want and revamping, repackaging, and finally relaunching them with a new image. Unilever purchased a local brand of washing powder, Biopan, that had a 9 percent share of the market in Hungary; after relaunching, market share rose to about 25 percent.

When Mars, a U.S. company that includes candy and pet food among its product lines, adopted a global strategy, it brought all its products under a global brand, even those with strong local brand names. In Britain, the largest candy market in Europe, M&Ms were sold as Treets and Snickers candy was sold under the name Marathon to avoid association with *knickers,* the British word for women's underpants. To bring the two candy products under the global umbrella, Mars returned the candies to their original names. The pet food division adopted Whiskas and Sheba for cat foods and Pedigree for dog food as the global brand name replacing KalKan. To support this global division that accounts for over $4 billion annually, Mars also developed a website for the pet food brands. The site (www.petcat.com) functions as a "global infrastructure" that can be customized locally by any Pedigree Petfoods branch worldwide. For instance, Pedigree offices can localize languages and information on subjects such as veterinarians and cat-owner gatherings.

## National Brands

A different strategy is followed by the Nestlé Company, which has a stable of global and country-specific national brands in its product line. The Nestlé name itself is promoted globally, but its global brand expansion strategy is two-pronged. In some markets it acquires well-established national brands when it can and builds on their strengths—there are 7,000 local brands in its family of brands. In other markets where there are no strong brands to be local, people to be regional, and technology to be global. It does, however, own some of the world's largest global brands; Nescafé is but one.

Unilever is another company that follows a similar strategy of a mix of national and global brands. In Poland, Unilever introduced its Omo brand detergent (sold in many other countries), but it also purchased a local brand, Pollena 2000. Despite a strong

[44]Ming H. Hsieh, "Identifying Brand Image Dimensionality and Measuring the Degree of Brand Globalization: A Cross-National Study," *Journal of International Marketing,* November 2002, 10(2), pp. 46–67.

[45]Prominent among those arguing against global brands are David A. Aaker and Erich Joachimsthaler, "The Lure of Global Branding," *Harvard Business Review,* November-December 1999; and Aysegul Ozsomer and Gregory E. Prussia, "Competing Perspectives in International Strategy: Contingency and Process Models," *Journal of International Marketing,* January 1, 2000, pp. 27–50. For an interesting view of the arguments for and against globalization of brands see Anand P. Raman, "The Global Face Off," *Harvard Business Review,* June 2003, pp. 35–46.

[46]June Francis, Janet P.Y. Lam, and Jan Walls, "The Impact of Linguistic Differences on International Brand Name Standardization: A Comparison of English and Chinese Brand Names of Fortune 500 Companies," *Journal of International Marketing,* 2002, 10(1), pp. 98–116.

introduction of two competing brands, Omo by Unilever and Ariel by Procter & Gamble, a refurbished Pollena 2000 had the largest market share a year later. Unilever's explanation was that East European consumers are leery of new brands; they want brands that are affordable and in keeping with their own tastes and values. Pollena 2000 is successful not just because it is cheaper but because it chimes with local values.

Multinationals must also consider rises in nationalistic pride that occur in some countries and their impact on brands. In India, for example, Unilever considers it critical that its brands, such as Surf detergent and Lux and Lifebuoy soaps, are viewed as Indian brands. Just as is the case with products, the answer to the question of when to go global with a brand is, "It depends—the market dictates." Use global brands where possible and national brands where necessary.

## Country-of-Origin Effect and Global Brands

As discussed earlier, brands are used as external cues to taste, design, performance, quality, value, prestige, and so forth. In other words, the consumer associates the value of the product with the brand. The brand can convey either a positive or a negative message about the product to the consumer and is affected by past advertising and promotion, product reputation, and product evaluation and experience. In short, many factors affect brand image. One factor that is of great concern to multinational companies that manufacture worldwide is the country-of-origin effect on the market's perception of the product.

*Country-of-origin effect (COE)* can be defined as any influence that the country of manufacture, assembly, or design has on a consumer's positive or negative perception of a product. A company competing in global markets today manufactures products worldwide; when the customer becomes aware of the country of origin, there is the possibility that the place of manufacture will affect product or brand image.[47]

The country, the type of product, and the image of the company and its brands all influence whether the country of origin will engender a positive or negative reaction. A variety of generalizations can be made about country-of-origin effects on products and brands. Consumers tend to have stereotypes about products and countries that are formed by experience, hearsay, and myth. Following are some of the more frequently cited generalizations.

Consumers have broad but somewhat vague stereotypes about specific countries and specific product categories that they judge "best": English tea, French perfume, Chinese silk, Italian leather, Japanese electronics, Jamaican rum, and so on. Stereotyping of this nature is typically product specific and may not extend to other categories of products from these countries.

The importance of these types of stereotypes was emphasized recently as a result of a change in U.S. law that requires any cloth "substantially altered" (woven, for instance) in another country to identify that country on its label. Designer labels such as Ferragamo, Gucci, and Versace are affected in that they now must include on the label "Made in China" because the silk comes from China. The lure to pay $195 and up for scarves "Made in Italy" by Ferragamo loses some of its appeal when accompanied with a "Made in China" label. As one buyer commented, "I don't care if the scarves are made in China as long as it doesn't say so on the label." The irony is that 95 percent of all silk comes from China, which has the reputation for the finest silk but also a reputation of producing cheap scarves. The "best" scarves are made in France or Italy by one of the *haute couture* designers.

Ethnocentrism can also have country-of-origin effects; feelings of national pride—the "buy American" effect, for example—can influence attitudes toward foreign products. Honda, which manufactures one of its models almost entirely in the United States,

---

[47]Svein Ottar Olsen and Ulf H. Olsson, "Multientity Scaling and the Consistency of Country-of-Origin Attitudes," *Journal of International Business Studies,* 2002, 33(1), pp. 149–167; Jill Gabrielle Klein, "Us Versus Them, or Us Versus Everyone? Delineating Consumer Aversion to Foreign Goods," *Journal of International Business Studies,* 2002, 33(2), pp. 345–363.

**Enjoy the Flag Sweater from sea to shining sea.** This tidy crew features a stylized version of Old Glory across the chest – a great way to display your pride in the Stars and Stripes. It layers easily over your favorite shirt or tee. And rib knitting at the cuffs and bottom helps it keep its shape. 100% combed cotton. Machine wash, lay flat to dry. Made in USA or imported. *Colors below.*

Men's Regular M-XXL.          8222-9324    49.00
Women's Regular S-XL.         8223-032X    49.00

Dark Indigo Heather          Pale Chambray Heather          Tan Heather

Lands' End manages the sticky country-of-origin problem with their American flag sweater by offering it in their catalog as "Made in USA or imported." *(2003 © Lands' End, Inc. Used with permission.)*

recognizes this phenomenon and points out how many component parts are made in America in some of its advertisements. On the other hand, others have a stereotype of Japan as producing the "best" automobiles. A recent study found that U.S. automobile producers may suffer comparatively tarnished images regardless of whether they actually produce superior products.

Countries are also stereotyped on the basis of whether they are industrialized, in the process of industrializing, or developing. These stereotypes are less product specific; they are more a perception of the quality of goods and services in general produced within the country. Industrialized countries have the highest quality image, and there is generally a bias against products from developing countries.

In Russia, for example, the world is divided into two kinds of products: "ours" and "imported." Russians prefer fresh, homegrown food products but imported clothing and manufactured items. Companies hoping to win loyalty by producing in Russia have been unhappily surprised. Consumers remain cool toward locally produced Polaroid cameras and Philips irons. On the other hand, computers produced across the border in Finland are considered high quality. For Russians, country of origin is more important than brand name as an indicator of quality. South Korean electronics manufacturers have difficulty convincing Russians that their products are as good as Japanese ones. Goods produced in Malaysia, Hong Kong, or Thailand are more suspect still. Eastern Europe is considered adequate for clothing, but poor for food or durables. Turkey and China are at the bottom of the heap.

One might generalize that the more technical the product, the less positive is the perception of one manufactured in a less developed or newly industrializing country. There is also the tendency to favor foreign-made products over domestic-made in less developed countries. Foreign products do not fare equally well because consumers in developing countries have stereotypes about the quality of foreign-made products even from industrialized countries. A survey of consumers in the Czech Republic found that 72 percent of Japanese products were considered to be of the highest quality, German goods followed with 51 percent, Swiss goods with 48 percent, Czech goods with 32 percent, and, last, the United States with 29 percent.

One final generalization about COE involves fads that often surround products from particular countries or regions in the world. These fads are most often product specific and generally involve goods that are themselves faddish in nature. European consumers' affection for American products is quite fickle. The affinity for Jeep Cherokees, Budweiser beer, and Bose sound systems of the 1990s faded to an outright rejection of American brands as a protest of American political policies. Likewise, in the 1970s and 1980s there was a backlash against anything American, but in the 1990s American was in. In China, anything Western seems to be the fad. If it is Western it is in demand, even at prices three and four times higher than domestic products. In most cases such fads wane after a few years as some new fad takes over.

There are exceptions to the generalizations presented here, but it is important to recognize that country of origin can affect a product or brand's image. Further, not every consumer is sensitive to a product's country of origin. A finding in a recent study suggested that more knowledgeable consumers are more sensitive to a product's COE than those less knowledgeable. Another study report that COE varies across consumer groups. Japanese were found to be move sensitive than American consumers.[48] The multinational company needs to take these factors into consideration in product development and

---

[48]Zeynep Gurhan-Canli and Durariraj Maheswaran, "Cultural Variations in Country of Origin Effects," *Journal of Marketing Research,* August 2000, 37, pp. 309–317.

marketing strategy because a negative country stereotype can be detrimental to a product's success unless overcome with effective marketing.

After the market gains experience with a product, negative stereotypes can be overcome. Nothing would seem less plausible than selling chopsticks made in Chile to Japan, but it happened. It took years for a Chilean company to overcome doubts about the quality of its product, but persistence, invitations to Japanese to visit the Chilean poplar forests that provided the wood for the chopsticks, and a quality product finally overcame doubt; now the company cannot meet the demand for chopsticks.

Country stereotyping can be overcome with good marketing. The image of Korean electronics improved substantially in the United States once the market gained positive experience with Korean brands. All of this stresses the importance of building strong global brands like Sony, General Electric, and Levi's. Brands effectively advertised and products properly positioned can help ameliorate a less-than-positive country stereotype.

## Private Brands

Private brands owned by retailers are growing as challenges to manufacturers' brands, whether global or country specific. In the food-retailing sector in Britain and many European countries, private labels owned by national retailers increasingly confront manufacturers' brands. From blackberry jam and vacuum-cleaner bags to smoked salmon and sun-dried tomatoes, private-label products dominate grocery stores in Britain and in many of the hypermarkets of Europe. Private brands captured nearly 30 percent of the British and Swiss markets and more than 20 percent of the French and German markets. In some European markets, private-label market share doubled in just the past five years.

Sainsbury, one of Britain's largest grocery retailers with 420 stores, reserves the best shelf space for its own brands. A typical Sainsbury store has about 16,000 products, of which 8,000 are Sainsbury labels. Their labels account for two-thirds of store sales. The company avidly develops new products, launching 1,400 to 1,500 new private-label items each year, and weeds out hundreds of others no longer popular. It launched its own Novon brand laundry detergent; in the first year, its sales climbed past Procter & Gamble's and Unilever's top brands to make it the top-selling detergent in Sainsbury stores and the second-best seller nationally, with a 30 percent market share. The 15 percent margin on private labels claimed by chains such as Sainsbury helps to explain why their operating profit margins are as high as 8 percent, or eight times the profit margins of their U.S. counterparts.

As it stands now, private labels are formidable competitors. They provide the retailer with high margins; they receive preferential shelf space and strong in-store promotion; and, perhaps most important for consumer appeal, they are quality products at low prices. Contrast that with manufacturers' brands, which traditionally are premium priced and offer the retailer lower margins than they get from private labels.

To maintain market share, global brands need to be priced competitively and provide real consumer value. Global marketers must examine the adequacy of their brand strategies in light of such competition. This may make the cost and efficiency benefits of global brands even more appealing.

# Summary

The growing globalization of markets that gives rise to standardization must be balanced with the continuing need to assess all markets for those differences that might require adaptation for successful acceptance. The premise that global communications and other worldwide socializing forces have fostered a homogenization of tastes, needs, and values in a significant sector of the population across all cultures is difficult to deny. However, more than one authority notes that in spite of the forces of homogenization, consumers also see the world of global symbols, company images, and product choice through the lens of their own local culture and its stage of development and market sophistication. Each product must be viewed in light of how it is perceived by each culture with which it comes in contact. What is acceptable and comfortable within one group may be radically new and resisted within others, depending on the experiences and perceptions of each group. Understanding that an established product in one culture may be considered an innovation in another is critical in planning and developing consumer products for foreign markets. Analyzing a product as an innovation and using the Product Component Model may provide the marketer with important leads for adaptation.

# Questions

1. Define the following terms:

   quality, 343

   homologation, 345

   green marketing, 346

   innovation, 350

   product diffusion, 350

   Product Component Model, 354

   global brand, 363

2. Debate the issue of global versus adapted products for the international marketer.

3. Define the country-of-origin effect and give examples.

4. The text discusses stereotypes, ethnocentrism, degree of economic development, and fads as the basis for generalizations about country-of-origin effect on product perception. Explain each and give an example.

5. Discuss product alternatives and the three marketing strategies: domestic market extension, multidomestic markets, and global market strategies.

6. Discuss the different promotional/product strategies available to an international marketer.

7. Assume you are deciding to "go international." Outline the steps you would take to help you decide on a product line.

8. Products can be adapted physically and culturally for foreign markets. Discuss.

9. What are the three major components of a product? Discuss their importance to product adaptation.

10. How can knowledge of the diffusion of innovations help a product manager plan international investments?

11. Old products (that is, old in the U.S. market) may be innovations in a foreign market. Discuss fully.

12. "If the product sells in Dallas, it will sell in Tokyo or Berlin." Comment.

13. How can a country with a per capita GNP of $100 be a potential market for consumer goods? What kinds of goods would probably be in demand? Discuss.

14. Discuss the characteristics of an innovation that can account for differential diffusion rates.

15. Give an example of how a foreign marketer can use knowledge of the characteristics of innovations in product adaptation decisions.

16. Discuss "environmentally friendly" products and product development.

# products and services for businesses

**CHAPTER 13**

## CHAPTER LEARNING OBJECTIVES

What you should learn from Chapter 13:

- The importance of derived demand in industrial markets

- How demand is affected by technology

- Characteristics of an industrial product

- The importance of ISO 9000 certification

- The growth of business services and nuances of their marketing

- The importance of trade shows in promoting industrial goods

- The importance of relationship marketing for industrial products and services

# Global Perspective

## INTEL, THE BOOM AND THE INESCAPABLE BUST

This is what we wrote here in the 1999 edition of this book:

*Fortune's* cover story, "Intel, Andy Grove's Amazing Profit Machine—and His Plan for Five More Years of Explosive Growth" is capped only by *Time's* Man of the Year story, "Intel's Andy Grove, His Microchips Have Changed the World—and Its Economy." 1997 was the eighth consecutive year of record revenue ($25.1 billion) and earnings ($6.5 billion) for the company Grove helped found. Yet at the beginning of 1998 the real question was, Will the world change Intel? Judging from Intel's own forecasts for a flat first quarter in 1998, Chairman of the Board Grove and his associates were concerned that the financial meltdown in Asian markets would affect Intel's plans for "five more years of explosive growth." Some 30 percent of the firm's record 1997 revenues came from Asian markets. Indeed, one pundit had earlier predicted, "I see no clear technology threats. The biggest long-term threat to Intel is that the market growth slows." Others warned there's something wrong out there: computer-industry overcapacity.

Actually Intel had an even longer list of threats all posted as a disclaimer to its published forecast: "Other factors that could cause actual results to differ materially are the following: business and economic conditions, and growth in the computing industry in various geographic regions; changes in customer order patterns, including changes in customer and channel inventory levels, and seasonal PC buying patterns; changes in the mixes of microprocessor types and speeds, motherboards, purchased components and other products; competitive factors, such as rival chip architectures and manufacturing technologies, competing software-compatible microprocessors and acceptance of new products in specific market segments; pricing pressures; changes in end users' preferences; risk of inventory obsolescence and variations in inventory valuation;

timing of software industry product introductions; continued success in technological advances, including development, implementation and initial production of new strategic products and processes in a cost-effective manner; execution of manufacturing ramp; excess storage of manufacturing capacity; the ability to successfully integrate any acquired businesses, enter new market segments and manage growth of such businesses; unanticipated costs or other adverse effects associated with processors and other products containing errata; risks associated with foreign operations; litigation involving intellectual property and consumer issues; and other risk factors listed from time to time in the company's SEC reports."

*Time's* Man of the Year had a lot to worry about—most of all that industrial market booms are always followed by busts. Will the rise truly last five more years?

How is it that the brilliant Mr. Grove didn't see the inescapable bust coming? Hadn't he been in this cyclic business from the beginning? His boom did last another 3.5 years beyond his 1997 prediction, not five. And the bust was an ugly thing. Sales revenues declined by more than 20 percent during 2001; the stock price crashed from a high of $75 a share to below $20, shedding 80 percent of the company's value along the way, and 11,000 layoffs were announced. Ouch!

The lesson here is a simple one. In industrial markets, including the global ones, what goes up must come down!

Sources: Adapted from David Kirkpatrick, "Intel Andy Grove's Amazing Profit Machine—and His Plan for Five More Years of Explosive Growth," *Fortune,* February 17, 1997, pp. 60–75; "Man of the Year," *Time,* January 5, 1998, pp. 46-99; Peter Burrow, Gary McWilliams, Paul C. Judge, and Roger O. Crockett, "There's Something Wrong Out There," *Business Week,* December 29, 1997, pp. 38–49; Julie Creswell, "Are Chips About To Dip?" *Fortune,* May 12, 2003, p. 160–162.

**Exhibit 13.1**    Major Categories U.S. Exports*

| Category | Percentage |
|---|---|
| **Services Total** | **29.6** |
| Travel (hotels, etc) | 9.0 |
| Transportation (fares, freight, and port services) | 7.8 |
| Commercial, professional, and technical services (advertising, accounting, legal, construction, engineering) | 1.8 |
| Financial services (banking and insurance) | 1.6 |
| Education and training services (mostly foreign student tuition) | 1.0 |
| Entertainment (movies, books, records) | 0.8 |
| Other categories (telecommunications, information, health care) | 7.6 |
| **Merchandise Total** | **70.4** |
| Foods, feeds, and beverages (wheat, fruit, meat) | 5.1 |
| Industrial supplies (crude oil, plastics, chemicals, metals) | 15.9 |
| Capital goods (construction equipment, aircraft, computers, telecommunications) | 29.4 |
| Automotive vehicles, engines, and parts | 8.0 |
| Consumer goods (pharmaceuticals, tobacco, toys, clothing) | 8.5 |
| Other categories | 3.3 |

*The United States exports approximately $1 trillion worth of services and goods each year. Services exports are the more understated, so these percentages are only reasonable approximations of the importance of each category listed. Each U.S. Commerce Department category comprises many kinds of products or services, including (but certainly not limited to) those listed in parentheses.

Source: U.S. Department of Commerce, www.doc.gov. 2004.

While everyone is familiar with most of the consumer brands described in Chapter 12, sales of such products and services do not constitute the majority of export sales for industrialized countries. Take the United States, for example. As can be seen in Exhibit 13.1, the main product the country sells for international consumption is *technology*. This is reflected in categories such as capital goods and industrial supplies, which together account for some 47 percent of all U.S. exports of goods and services.[1] Technology exports are represented by both the smallest and the largest products—semiconductors and commercial aircraft, the latter prominently including America's export champions, Boeing's 747s. The two most valuable companies in the world at this writing—Microsoft and General Electric[2]—are both sellers of high-technology industrial products.

The issues of standardization versus adaptation discussed in Chapter 12 have less relevance to marketing industrial goods than consumer goods because there are more similarities in marketing products and services to businesses across country markets than there are differences. The inherent nature of industrial goods and the sameness in motives and behavior among business customers create a market where product and marketing mix standardization are commonplace. Photocopy machines are sold in Belarus for the same reasons as in the United States: to make photocopies. Some minor modification may be necessary to accommodate different electrical power supplies or paper size but, basically, photocopy machines are standardized across markets, as are the vast majority of industrial goods. For industrial products that are basically custom made (specialized steel, customized machine tools, and so on), adaptation takes place for domestic as well as foreign markets.

Two basic factors account for greater market similarities among industrial goods customers than among consumer goods customers. First is the inherent nature of the product: Industrial products and services are used in the process of creating other goods and services; consumer goods are in their final form and are consumed by individuals. Second,

---

[1]Internet jargon seems to be morphing the manager's lexicon toward B2B and B2C distinctions (that is, business-to-business and business-to-consumer) and away from the traditional industrial and consumer goods distinctions. International trade statistics, categories, and descriptors haven't kept up with these changes. Consequently, we use the adjectives *industrial* and *business-to-business* interchangeably in this book.

[2]See "Forbes 500," March 28, 2003, www.forbes.com.

**CROSSING BORDERS 13.1** Trade Statistics Don't Tell the Whole Story

One reason U.S. manufacturers don't trumpet their export successes is that large companies no longer distinguish carefully between sales to Texas and to Thailand. The totals could be discerned, but why bother? It's one world, after all. Besides, it's incredibly complicated in some cases to determine the net contribution a manufacturer makes to the U.S. balance of trade. Lucent Technologies' Microelectronics Group, which exports half of what it makes to customers in Europe and Asia, is an extreme example. A wafer of Lucent's integrated circuits is often designed at its laboratories in Ascot, England, made in its plants in Pennsylvania or Florida, then shipped to Bangkok to be tested, diced, and packaged. After that the finished chips might move on to Germany to be used by Siemens in telecommunications equipment that, in turn, is shipped to BellSouth and installed in Charlotte, North Carolina.

Source: Philip Siekman, "Industrial Management & Technology/Export Winners," *Fortune*, January 10, 2000, pp. 154–163.

the motive or intent of the user differs: Industrial consumers are seeking profit, whereas the ultimate consumer is seeking satisfaction. These factors are manifest in specific buying patterns and demand characteristics, and in a special emphasis on relationship marketing as a competitive tool. Whether a company is marketing at home or abroad, the differences between business-to-business and consumer markets merit special consideration.

Along with industrial goods, business services are a highly competitive growth market seeking quality and value. Manufactured products generally come to mind when we think of international trade. Yet the most rapidly growing sector of U.S. international trade today consists of business services—accounting, advertising, banking, consulting, construction, hotels, insurance, law, transportation, and travel sold by U.S. firms in global markets. The intangibility of services creates a set of unique problems to which the service provider must respond. A further complication is a lack of uniform laws that regulate market entry. Protectionism, although prevalent for industrial goods, can be much more pronounced for the service provider.

This chapter discusses the special problems in marketing goods and services to businesses internationally, the increased competition and demand for quality in those goods and services, and the implications for the global marketer.

## Demand in Global Business-to-Business Markets

Gauging demand in industrial markets can involve some huge bets. Shanghai's new 19-mile, $1.2 billion bullet train is one example. The product of a Sino-German joint venture, it is really a prototype for fast things to come in mass transit-dependent China.[3] A bigger bet that went bad was Iridium LLC—their 72-satellite, $5 billion communications system may be in orbit but they can't sell the associated phones. They badly miscalculated demand for their approach to global telecommunications, and the entire system is currently in disuse and is now classified by investors as space refuse. Three factors seem to affect the demand in international industrial markets differently than in consumer markets. First, demand in industrial markets is by nature more volatile. Second, stages of industrial and economic development affect demand for industrial products. Finally, the level of technology of products and services makes their sale more appropriate for some countries than others.

### The Volatility of Industrial Demand

There are numerous reasons why consumer products firms market internationally— exposure to more-demanding customers, keeping up with the competition, extending product life cycles, and growing sales and profits, to name a few. For firms producing products and services for industrial markets there is an additional crucial reason for venturing

---

[3]Ching-Ching Ni, "Shanghai Rising with a Bullet," *Los Angeles Times*, January 1, 2003, p. A3.

Servers are sold to companies, thus the demand for them is more volatile than the demand for personal computers being sold to individual consumers. Here Microsoft acknowledges the technology bust of 2000 in its ads for servers in both the U.S. and Japan. In both countries, the pressure is on CIOs to "do more with less." Both executives face "larger projects" and "shrinking budgets." The American executive is working late; everyone else has gone home. The focus on the Japanese individual executive may look odd to older, more collectivistic Japanese managers. However, Microsoft is acknowledging that things are changing in Japan—particularly information technology decisions are more focused and less consensus-oriented. Younger Japanese will like the independence reflected in the image. Finally, do you think it's a coincidence that both executives are standing near windows? *(top: Courtesy Microsoft Corporation. Photographer: Kiran Masters; bottom: Courtesy Microsoft Corporation. Photographer: Tadayuki Minamoto; Talent: Takushi Yasumoto; CD/AD: Jun Asano; CW: Kenichi Okubo)*

abroad: dampening the natural volatility of industrial markets.[4] Indeed, perhaps the single most important difference between consumer and industrial marketing is the huge, cyclical swings in demand inherent in the latter.[5] It is true that demand for consumer durables such as cars, furniture, or home computers can be quite volatile. In industrial markets, however, two other factors come into play that exacerbate both the ups and downs in demand: Professional buyers tend to act in concert, and derived demand accelerates changes in markets.

Purchasing agents at large personal computer manufacturers such as IBM, Apple, Acer, Samsung, and Toshiba are responsible for obtaining component parts for their firms

---

[4]"The CEMEX Way," *The Economist,* June 16, 2001, pp. 75–76.

[5]Russ Arensman, "When Slower is Better," *Electronic Business,* March 2003, pp. 52–57.

**Exhibit 13.2** Derived Demand Example

| Time Period | Consumer Demand for Premolded Fiberglass Shower Stalls | | | Number of Machines in Use to Produce the Shower Stalls | | | Demand for the Machines | | |
|---|---|---|---|---|---|---|---|---|---|
| Year | Previous Year | Current Year | Net Change | Previous Year | Current Year | Net Change | Replacement | New | Total |
| 1 | 100,000 | 100,000 | — | 500 | 500 | — | 50 | — | 50 |
| 2 | 100,000 | 110,000 | +10,000 | 500 | 550 | +50 | 50 | 50 | 100 |
| 3 | 110,000 | 115,000 | +5,000 | 550 | 575 | +25 | 50 | 25 | 75 |
| 4 | 115,000 | 118,000 | +3,000 | 575 | 590 | +15 | 50 | 15 | 65 |
| 5 | 118,000 | 100,000 | −18,000 | 590 | 500 | −90 | — | −40 | −40 |
| 6 | 100,000 | 100,000 | — | 500 | 500 | — | 10 | — | 10 |

Source: Adapted from R. L. Vaile, E. T. Grether, and R. Cox, *Marketing in the American Economy* (New York: Ronald Press, 1952), p. 16. Appears in Robert W. Haas, *Business Marketing*, 6th edition (Cincinnati, OH: Southwestern, 1995), p. 115.

as cheaply as possible and in a timely manner. They monitor demand for PCs and prices of components such as microprocessors or disk drives, and changes in either customer markets or supplier prices directly affect their ordering. Declines in PC demand or supplier prices can cause these professionals to slam on the brakes in their buying; in the latter case they wait for further price cuts. And because the purchasing agents at all the PC companies, here and abroad, are monitoring the same data, they all brake (or accelerate) simultaneously. Consumers monitor markets as well, but not nearly to the same degree. Purchases of cola, clothing, and cars tend to be steadier.

For managers selling capital equipment and big-ticket industrial services, understanding the concept of derived demand[6] is absolutely fundamental to their success. **Derived demand** can be defined as demand dependent on another source. Thus the demand for Boeing 747s is derived from the worldwide consumer demand for air travel services, and the demand for Fluor Daniel's global construction and engineering services to design and build oil refineries in China is derived from Chinese consumers' demands for gasoline. Minor changes in consumer demand mean major changes in the related industrial demand. In the example in Exhibit 13.2, a 10 percent increase in consumer demand for shower stalls in year 2 translates into a 100 percent increase in demand for the machines to make shower stalls. The 15 percent decline in consumer demand in year 5 results in a complete shutdown of demand for shower-stall-making machines. For Boeing the September 11 terrorist attacks, the continuing threat of more of the same, and the subsequent armed conflicts in the Middle East have combined to dramatically reduce air travel (both vacation and commercial) worldwide, which in turn caused cancellations of orders for aircraft. Moreover, the airlines are not just canceling orders, they're mothballing parts of their current fleets. During August 2003 there were 310 jetliners stored in a Mojave Desert facility awaiting demand to pick up again.[7] The commercial aircraft industry has always been and will continue to be one of the most volatile of all.

Industrial firms can take several measures to manage this inherent volatility, such as maintaining broad product lines, raising prices faster and reducing advertising expenditures during booms, ignoring market share as a strategic goal, eschewing layoffs,[8] and focusing on stability. For most American firms, where corporate cultures emphasize beating competitors, such stabilizing measures are usually given only lip service. Conversely,

[6]David Moschella, "Spotting the Signs of an IT Recovery," *Computerworld,* August 27, 2001, p. 25.
[7]Edward Wong, "Airlines' Unwanted Fleet Grows in the Desert," *New York Times,* June 7, 2003, p. C1.
[8]Southwest Airlines management, different from almost all their competitors, has avoided layoffs during the recent bust in the industry. Refusing to make layoffs has been a founding principle of the organization. "Southwest Airlines Traffic Rises," *Wall Street Journal,* June 4, 2003, p. B4.

German and Japanese firms value employees and stability more highly and are generally better at managing volatility in markets.[9]

Some U.S. companies, such as Microsoft, and especially General Electric,[10] have been quite good at spreading their portfolio of markets served. Late-1990s declines in Asian markets were somewhat offset by strong American markets, just as late-1980s increases in Japanese demand offset declines in the United States. Indeed, one of the strange disadvantages of having the previously command economies go private is their integration into the global market. That is, prior to the breakup of the USSR, Soviets bought industrial products according to a national five-year plan that often had little to do with markets outside of the communist bloc. Their off-cycle ordering tended to dampen demand volatility for companies able to sell there. Now privately held Russian manufacturers watch and react to world markets just as their counterparts do all over the globe. The increasing globalization of markets will tend to increase the volatility in industrial markets as purchasing agents around the world act with even greater simultaneity. Managing this inherent volatility will necessarily affect all aspects of the marketing mix, including product/service development.

## Stages of Economic Development

Perhaps the most significant environmental factor affecting the international market for industrial goods and services is the degree of industrialization. Although generalizing about countries is almost always imprudent, the degree of economic development can be used as a rough measure of a country's industrial market. Please recall Rostow's[11] five-stage model of economic development presented in Chapter 9; demand for industrial products and services can be classified correspondingly.

**Stage 1** (*the traditional society*). The important industrial demand is associated with natural resources extraction—think parts of Africa and the Middle East.

**Stage 2** (*preconditions for takeoff*). Manufacturing is beginning. Primary needs are related to infrastructure development—for example, telecommunications, construction, and power generation equipment and expertise. Vietnam would fit this category.

**Stage 3** (*take-off*). Manufacturing of both semidurable and nondurable consumer goods begins. Goods demanded relate to equipment and supplies to support manufacturing. Russian and Eastern European countries fit this category.

**Stage 4** (*drive to maturity*). These are industrialized economies such as Korea or the Czech Republic. Their focus is more on low-cost manufacturing of a variety of consumer and some industrial goods. They buy from all categories of industrial products and services.

**Stage 5** (*the age of mass consumption*). These are countries where design activities are going on and manufacturing techniques are developing, and they are mostly services economies. Japan and Germany are obvious examples of countries that purchase the highest technology products and services mostly from other Stage 5 suppliers, and consumer products from Stage 3 and 4 countries.

## Technology and Market Demand

Another important approach to grouping countries is on the basis of their ability to benefit from and use technology, particularly now that countries are using technology as economic leverage to leap several stages of economic development in a very short time. Perhaps the best indicator of this dimension of development is the quality of the educational

[9]Cathy Anterasian, John L. Graham, and R. Bruce Money, "Are American Managers Superstitious about Market Share?" *Sloan Management Review,* Summer 1996, pp. 667–77; and John L. Graham, "Culture and Human Resources Management," Chapter 18 in Alan Rugman and Thomas L. Brewer (eds.), *The Oxford Handbook of International Business* (Oxford: Oxford University Press, 2001).

[10]Stanley Holmes, GE: Little Engines that Could," *BusinessWeek,* January 20, 2003, pp. 62–63; and Paul Meller, "Europe Extends Deadline on GE's Finnish Deal," *New York Times,* May 13, 2003, p. W7.

[11]Walt W. Rostow, *The Stages of Economic Growth,* 2nd edition (London: Cambridge University Press, 1971).

system. Despite relatively low levels of per capita GDP, many countries (e.g., China, the Czech Republic, and Russia) place great emphasis on education, which affords them the potential to leverage the technology that is transferred.

Not only is technology the key to economic growth, but for many products it is also the competitive edge in today's global markets. As precision robots and digital control systems take over the factory floor, manufacturing is becoming more science oriented and access to inexpensive labor and raw materials is becoming less important. The ability to develop the latest information technology and to benefit from its application is a critical factor in the international competitiveness of managers, countries, and companies. Three interrelated trends spur demand for technologically advanced products: (1) expanding economic and industrial growth in Asia, particularly China and India; (2) the disintegration of the Soviet empire; and (3) the privatization of government-owned industries worldwide.

Beginning with Japan, many Asian countries have been in a state of rapid economic growth over the last 25 years. Although this growth recently slowed, the long-term outlook for these countries remains excellent. Japan is the most advanced industrialized country in the region, whereas South Korea, Hong Kong, Singapore, and Taiwan (the Four Tigers) successfully moved from being cheap labor sources to becoming industrialized nations. The Southeast Asian countries of Malaysia, Thailand, Indonesia, and the Philippines are exporters of manufactured products to Japan and the United States now, and after they overcome current financial problems they will continue to gear up for greater industrialization. Countries at each of the first three levels of industrial development demand technologically advanced products for further industrialization that will enable them to compete in global markets.

As a market economy develops in the Newly Independent States (former republics of the USSR) and other Eastern European countries, new privately owned businesses will create a demand for the latest technology to revitalize and expand manufacturing facilities. The BEMs (big emerging markets) discussed in Chapter 9 are estimated to account for more than $1.5 trillion of trade by 2010. These countries will demand the latest technology to expand their industrial bases and build modern infrastructures.

Concurrent with the fall of communism that fueled the rush to privatization in Eastern Europe, Latin Americans began to dismantle their state-run industries in hopes of reviving their economies. Mexico, Argentina, and Venezuela are leading the rest of Latin America in privatizing state-owned businesses. The move to privatization will create enormous demand for industrial goods as new owners invest heavily in the latest technology. Telmex, a $4 billion joint venture between Southwestern Bell, France Telecom, and Teléfonos de Mexico, is investing hundreds of millions of dollars to bring the Mexican telephone system up to the most advanced standards. Telmex is only one of scores of new privatized companies from Poland to Paraguay that are creating a mass market for the most advanced technology.

The return to economic growth in Asia, the creation of market economies in Eastern Europe and the republics of the former Soviet Union, and the privatization of state-owned enterprises in Latin America and elsewhere will create an expanding demand, particularly for industrial goods and business services, well into the twenty-first century. The competition to meet this global demand will be stiff; the companies with the competitive edge will be those whose products are technologically advanced, of the highest quality, and accompanied by world-class service.

## Quality and Global Standards

As discussed in Chapter 12, the concept of quality encompasses many factors, and the perception of quality rests solely with the customer. The level of technology reflected in the product, compliance with standards that reflect customer needs, support services and follow-through, and the price relative to competitive products are all part of a customer's evaluation and perception of quality. As noted, these requirements are different for consumers versus industrial customers because of differing end uses. The factors themselves also differ among industrial goods customers because their needs are varied.

Business-to-business marketers frequently misinterpret the concept of quality. Good quality as interpreted by a highly industrialized market is not the same as that interpreted by standards of a less-industrialized nation. For example, an African government was buying hand-operated dusters for farmers to distribute pesticides in cotton fields. The duster supplied was a finely machined device requiring regular oiling and good care. But the fact that this duster turned more easily than any other on the market was relatively unimportant to the farmers. Furthermore, the requirement for careful oiling and care simply meant that in a relatively short time of inadequate care the machines froze up and broke. The result? The local government went back to an older type of French duster that was heavy, turned with difficulty, and gave a poorer distribution of dust, but which lasted longer because it required less care and lubrication. In this situation, the French machine possessed more relevant quality features and therefore, in marketing terms, possessed the higher quality.

Likewise, when commercial jet aircraft were first developed, European and American designs differed substantially. For example, American manufacturers built the engines slung below the wings whereas the British competitor built the engines into the wings. The American design made for easier access and saved on repair and servicing costs, and the British design reduced aerodynamic drag and saved on fuel costs. Both designs were "high quality" for their respective markets. At the time labor was relatively expensive in the United States and fuel was relatively expensive in the United Kingdom.

## Quality Is Defined by the Buyer

One important dimension of quality is how well a product meets the specific needs of the buyer.[12] When a product falls short of performance expectations, its poor quality is readily apparent. However, it is less apparent but nonetheless true that a product that exceeds performance expectations is also of poor quality. A product whose design exceeds the wants of the buyer's intended use generally has a higher price that reflects the extra capacity. Quality for many goods is assessed in terms of fulfilling specific expectations—no more and no less. Thus a product that produces 20,000 units per hour when the buyer needs one that produces only 5,000 units per hour is not a quality product, in that the extra capacity is unnecessary to meet the buyer's use expectations. This is one of the key issues facing personal computer makers. Many business buyers are asking the question, "Do we really need the latest $1,000 PC for everyone?" And more and more often the answer is no, the $500 machines will do just fine.

This **price–quality relationship** is an important factor in marketing in developing economies, especially those in the first three stages of economic development described earlier. Standard quality requirements of industrial products sold in the U.S. market that command commensurately higher prices may be completely out of line for the needs of the less-developed markets of the world. Labor-saving features are of little importance when time has limited value and labor is plentiful. Also of lesser value is the ability of machinery to hold close tolerances where people are not quality-control conscious, where large production runs do not exist, and where the wages of skillful workers justify selective fits in assembly and repair work. Features that a buyer does not want or cannot effectively use do not enhance a product's quality rating.

This does not mean quality is unimportant or that the latest technology is not sought in developing markets. Rather, it means that those markets require products designed to meet their specific needs, not products designed for different uses and expectations, especially if the additional features result in higher prices. This attitude was reflected in a study of purchasing behavior of Chinese import managers, who ranked product quality first, followed in importance by price. Timely delivery was third and product style/features ranked 11th out of 17 variables studied. Hence, a product whose design reflects the needs and expectations of the buyer—no more, no less—is a quality product.

---

[12]Wolfgang Ulaga and Samir Chacour, "Measuring Customer-Perceived Value in Business Markets: A Prerequisite for Marketing Strategy Development and Implementation," *Industrial Marketing Management*, August 2001, 30(6), pp. 525–540.

## CROSSING BORDERS 13.2   Your Hoses Are a Threat to Public Security!

Universal standards made life miserable for Evan Segal. He is president of Dormont Manufacturing Company, which makes hoses that hook up deep-fat fryers and the like to gas outlets and which once sold these hoses throughout Europe. Then one day one of his top customers, Frymaster Corporation of Shreveport, Louisiana, called to alert him that McDonald's was being told it could no longer use his hoses in its British restaurants. Similar problems popped up elsewhere, including EuroDisney outside Paris; shortly before the theme park opened, French inspectors demanded that Dormont's hoses be replaced with French-approved equipment.

The disparate national standards stemmed from the fact that the hoses are crucial to safe operation of gas appliances and thus fell under the product-safety provisions, allowing each country to set its own standards. In Dormont's case, the specifications were written by committees often dominated by domestic European producers. They spell out minutiae of each country's acceptable gas hose design—such as the color of plastic coating or how the end pieces should be attached to the rest of the hose.

Mr. Segal thought he made a major breakthrough when the British Standards Institute, one of the European agencies that test equipment and hand out approvals, issued Dormont a certificate authorizing the company to paste a seal of approval on its products signifying that the hoses conformed with European Union rules for gas appliances, enabling the company to sell them throughout the region. But the victory was short-lived. A miffed German competitor fired off a formal complaint to the European Commission, the EU's Brussels-based executive body. Commission officials familiar with the case say the rival argued that the British office erred because hoses are not really part of a gas appliance. The approval was withdrawn.

Source: Timothy Aeppel, "Europe's Unity Undoes a U.S. Exporter," *Wall Street Journal,* April 1, 1996, p. B1; and Brandon Mitchener, "Standard Bearers: Increasingly, Rules of Global Economy are Set in Brussels," *Wall Street Journal,* April 23, 2002, p. A1. Copyright 1996 by Dow Jones & Co. Inc. Reproduced with permission of Dow Jones & Co. Inc. via Copyright Clearance Center.

The design of a product must be viewed from all aspects of use. Extreme variations in climate create problems in designing equipment that is universally operable. Products that function effectively in Western Europe may require major design changes to operate as well in the hot, dry Sahara region or the humid, tropical rain forests of Latin America. Trucks designed to travel the superhighways of the United States almost surely will experience operational difficulties in the mountainous regions of Latin America on roads that often barely resemble Jeep trails. Manufacturers must consider many variations in making products that will be functional in far-flung markets.

In light of today's competition, a company must consider the nature of its market and the adequacy of the design of its products. Effective competition in global markets means that over-engineered and overpriced products must give way to products that meet the specifications of the customer at competitive prices. Success lies in offering products that fit a customer's needs—technologically advanced for some and less sophisticated for others, but all of high quality. To be competitive in today's global markets, the concept of total quality management (TQM)[13] must be a part of all MNCs' management strategy, and TQM starts with talking to customers.[14] Indeed, more and more frequently industrial customers, including foreign ones, are directly involved in all aspects of the product development process, from generating new ideas to prototype testing.

**Universal Standards**   A lack of universal standards is another problem in international sales of industrial products. The United States has two major areas of concern in this regard for the industrial goods exporter: a lack of common standards for manufacturing highly specialized

---

[13]Juan A. Magana-Campos and Elaine Aspinwall, "Comparative Study of Western and Japanese Improvement Systems," *TQM & Business Excellence,* June 2003, 14(4), pp. 423–436.

[14]Ching-Chow Yang, "The Establishment of a TQM System for the Health Care Industry," *TQM Magazine,* 2003, 15(2), pp. 93–98.

## CROSSING BORDERS 13.3 Yes, Opinions Do Differ about the Metric System

In Canada, feelings about the metric system run high, as shown by the following newspaper column:

A generation has not passed since Canada's traditional system of weights and measures was suppressed by bureaucratic edict, in a direct assault on the public will. Countless millions have since been spent—most of it imposed in costs to industry, but millions more taxed to feed Ottawa's metric police and propaganda machine. And after years of the most audacious brainwashing campaign ever attempted on our nation's children, this alien system has made some progress. I said "alien" not because metric is French, but because it is inhuman.

The metric system was originally imposed on France by the blood-soaked operatives of the Revolutionary Terror. It was then dragged across Europe by the armies of Napoleon. It met popular resistance wherever it appeared, and everywhere that resistance was quelled by force.

Yet to this day, in France, as in our old monarchist citadel of Quebec, there are workmen calculating in *pieds* (feet) and *pouces* (inches), in *livres* (pounds) and *onces* (ounces)—quietly, beyond the reach of the metric police and their informers. These are masons and carpenters and the like. Their eyes are wistful and they smile to themselves.

Ten is the magical number of tyranny. It can be halved only once, and can never go into thirds. It allows the deceptive ease of calculating in decimal places, such that when right we only approximately hit the boat, but when wrong we land in another ocean.

In America, metric boosters insist that the switch is happening, but in stealthy ways. More than 2,000 American businesses use the metric system in research, development, and marketing, according to the U.S. Metric Association, a California advocacy group. All of Eastman Kodak's product development is done in the metric system; Procter & Gamble's Scope mouthwash is sold in incremental liter bottles. The reason is financial. Making deals in pounds isn't easy when you're negotiating with someone who speaks in grams

Britain duly converted to the metric system, selling its gasoline in liters and, more recently, its supermarket goods in grams. But small shopkeepers remained exempt until January 1, 2000. It was then that the new government regulations took effect, requiring every seller of loose goods—things like fruits, vegetables, carpets, window shades, loose candy, and meat—to begin selling in metric units.

The point, of course, was to harmonize with the rest of the European Union, a concept that is dear to the government of Prime Minister Tony Blair. But a healthy percentage of the country's 96,000 small shopkeepers do not feel much like harmonizing, especially not with the Germans and the French.

Sources: David Warren, "Ten: The Magical Number of Tyranny," *National Post* (Montreal), July 8, 2000, p. A14; Reed Tucker, "Why Don't We Use the Metric System?" *Fortune*, May 29, 2000, p. 56; and Sarah Lyall, "Shopkeepers Dragging Their Feet on Metric Switch," *New York Times*, July 20, 2000, p. 4.

equipment such as machine tools and computers; and the use of the inch-pound, or English, system of measurement. Conflicting standards are encountered in test methods for materials and equipment, quality control systems, and machine specifications. In the telecommunications industry, the vast differences in standards among countries create enormous problems for expansion of that industry.

Efforts are being made through international organizations to create international standards. For example, the International Electrotechnical Commission is concerned with standard specifications for electrical equipment for machine tools. The search has also been engaged for ways in which an international roaming umbrella can be established for wireless communications. The U.S. Department of Commerce participates in programs to promote U.S. standards and is active in the development of the Global Harmonization Task Force, an international effort to harmonize standards for several industry sectors. The U.S. Trade Representative participates in negotiations to harmonize standards as well. Recently a key agreement was signed with the European Union to mutually recognize one another's standards in six sectors. The agreements eliminate the need for double testing (once each on both sides of the Atlantic) and address inspection or certification in telecommunications, medical devices, electromagnetic compatibility, electrical safety, recreation craft, and pharmaceuticals. The agreements cover approximately $50 billion in two-way trade and are expected to equal a 2 percent to 3 percent drop in tariffs.

In addition to industry and international organizations setting standards, countries often have standards for products entering their markets. Saudi Arabia is setting standards for everything from light bulbs to lemon juice, and it asked its trading partners for help. The standards, the first in Arabic, will most likely be adopted by the entire Arab world. Most countries sent representatives to participate in the standard setting. For example, New Zealand sent a representative to help write the standards for the shelf life of lamb. Unfortunately, the United States failed to send a representative until late in the discussions, and thus many of the hundreds of standards written favor Japanese and European products. Also, Saudi Arabia adopted the new European standard for utility equipment. The cost in lost sales to just two Saudi cities by just one U.S. company, Westinghouse, could be from $15 million to $20 million for U.S.-standard distribution transformers. Increasingly, American firms are waking up to the necessity of participating in such standards discussions early on.

In the United States, conversion to the metric system and acceptance of international standards are slow.[15] Congress and industry dragged their feet for fear conversion would be too costly. But the cost will come from *not* adopting the metric system; the General Electric Company had a shipment of electrical goods turned back from a Saudi port because its connecting cords were six feet long instead of the required standard of two meters.

As foreign customers using the metric system account for more and more American industrial sales, the cost of delaying standardization mounts. Measurement-sensitive products account for one-half to two-thirds of U.S. exports, and if the European Union bars nonmetric imports, as expected, many U.S. products will lose access to that market just as the EU is on the threshold of major economic expansion. About half of U.S. exports are covered by the EU's new standards program.

To spur U.S. industry into action, the Department of Commerce indicated that accepting the metric system will not be mandatory unless you want to sell something to the U.S. government; all U.S. government purchases will be conducted exclusively in metric. All federal buildings are now being designed with metric specifications, and highway construction funded by Washington uses metric units. Because the U.S. government is the nation's largest customer, this directive may be successful in converting U.S. business to the metric system. The Defense Department now requires metric for all new weapons systems, as well.

Despite the edicts from Washington, the National Aeronautics and Space Administration (NASA), which presides over some of the most advanced technology in the world, resists metrification. The $100 billion-plus[16] space station now being built will contain some metric parts, but most of the major components are made in the United States and will be based on inches and pounds. NASA's excuse is that it was too far into the design and production to switch. Unfortunately, the space station is supposed to be an international effort with Russia as one of the partners, and this decision creates large problems for systems integration. Worse yet, the cause of the 1999 failure of the $125 million Mars Climate Orbiter was a mix-up between metric and English measurement systems.[17] It is hard to believe that the only two countries not officially on the metric system are Myanmar and the United States. It is becoming increasingly evident that the United States must change or be left behind.

---

[15]"Pounded by the Metric System," *Wall Street Journal,* May 1, 2001, p. A27. Metrification has met resistance in other countries as well, such as Canada (see David Warren, "Ten: The Magical Number of Tyrrany, *National Post* [Montreal], July 8, 2000, p. A14) and England (see Sarah Lyall, "Shopkeepers Dragging Their Feet on Metric Switch," *New York Times,* July 20, 2000, p. 4).

[16]The original cost estimate was $16 billion. Nick Anderson and David Holley, "International Space Station Proves a Diplomatic Success, if Nothing Else," *Los Angeles Times,* May 3, 2003, p. A16.

[17]Andrew Murr, "Final Answer: It Crashed: A Simple Fix Might Have Prevented the Latest Mars Failure," *Newsweek,* March 10, 2000, p. 46.

## ISO 9000 Certification: An International Standard of Quality

With quality becoming the cornerstone of global competition, companies are requiring ensurance of standard conformance from suppliers just as their customers are requiring the same from them. ISO 9000 certification was also found to positively affect the performance[18] and stock prices[19] of firms.

**ISO 9000s,** a series of five international industrial standards (ISO 9000–9004) originally designed by the International Organization for Standardization in Geneva to meet the need for product quality assurances in purchasing agreements, are becoming a quality assurance certification program with competitive and legal ramifications when doing business in the European Union and elsewhere.[20] The original ISO 9000 system was promulgated in 1994. In 2000 the system was streamlined, as it will be again in 2006.

ISO 9000 concerns the registration and certification of a manufacturer's quality system. It is a certification of the existence of a quality control system a company has in place to ensure it can meet published quality standards. ISO 9000 standards do not apply to specific products. They relate to generic system standards that enable a company, through a mix of internal and external audits, to provide assurance that it has a quality control system. It is a certification of the production process only, and does not guarantee that a manufacturer produces a "quality" product or service. The series describes three quality system models, defines quality concepts, and gives guidelines for using international standards in quality systems.

The Japanese manufacturer is quite proud of the ISO quality ratings for its plant in San Jose, Costa Rica.

To receive ISO 9000 certification,[21] a company requests a certifying body (a third party authorized to provide an ISO 9000 audit) to conduct a registration assessment—that is, an audit of the key business processes of a company. The assessor will ask questions about everything from blueprints to sales calls to filing. Does the supplier meet promised delivery dates? and Is there evidence of customer satisfaction? are two of the questions asked and the issues explored. The object is to develop a comprehensive plan to ensure that minute details are not overlooked. The assessor helps management create a quality manual that will be made available to customers wishing to verify the organization's reliability. When accreditation is granted the company receives certification. A complete assessment for recertification is done every four years, with intermediate evaluations during the four-year period.

Although ISO 9000 is generally voluntary, except for certain regulated products, the EU Product Liability Directive puts pressure on all companies to become certified. The directive holds that a manufacturer, including an exporter, will be liable, regardless of fault or negligence, if a person is harmed by a product that fails because of a faulty component. Thus customers in the EU need to be assured that the components of their products are free of defects or deficiencies. A manufacturer with a well-documented quality system will be better able to prove that products are defect free and thus minimize liability claims.

A strong level of interest in ISO 9000 is driven more by marketplace requirements than by government regulations, and ISO 9000 is now an important competitive marketing tool in Europe. As the market demands quality and more companies adopt some form of TQM,

---

[18]Mile Terziovski, Damien Power, and Amrik S. Sohal, "The Longitudinal Effects of the ISO 9000 Certification Process on Business Performance," *European Journal of Operational Research,* May 1, 2003, pp. 580–595.

[19]Muli Rajan and Nabil Tamimi, "Payoff to ISO 9000 Registration," *Journal of Investing,* Spring 2003, 12(1), pp. 71–77.

[20]Brandon Mitchener, "Standard Bearers: Increasingly, Rules of Global Economy Are Set in Brussels," *Wall Street Journal,* April 23, 2003, p A1.

[21]Tammy Landon, "13 Steps to Certification in Less Than a Year," *Quality Progress,* March 2003, 36(3), pp. 32–41.

**CROSSING BORDERS 13.4** Garbage Collection an International Service? Perhaps!

Having persuaded hundreds of local governments in the United States to contract out street cleaning and trash collection, WMX Technologies is collecting trash, cleaning streets, and constructing sanitary landfills in 20 countries, including Argentina, New Zealand, and Saudi Arabia. It also has a 15-year contract to run a hazardous-waste treatment plant that will process all of Hong Kong's industrial and chemical waste.

Even the French are handling British trash. Sita Group, a subsidiary of Suez Lyonnaise des Eaux, recently won a 25-year contract for waste collection in Surrey, England. With Surrey's population of around 1 million creating 500,000 tons of waste per year, the contract is worth some 1.5 billion euros. At the same time, Sita Group sold its subsidiaries in Australia and New Zealand to Waste Management of Houston, Texas.

More recently, because of financial problems at home Waste Management began to shed its foreign acquisitions. The firm is even having trouble in close-by Mexico. Mexico is creating mountains of trash and industrial waste that it cannot safely manage, which should be a great opportunity for American waste management expertise and technology. However, of all the American firms that rushed into the market right after the NAFTA signing, few are left, and even those few have scaled back operations.

Problems are the lack of clear rules, bureaucratic snafus, and unanticipated political opposition to new dumps. One of the biggest U.S. firms, Waste Management, is selling its share of Mexico's leading waste hauler and seeking a $60 million judgment against the Mexican government for breaking NAFTA obligations to protect American businesses. Other U.S. firms filed similar suits. Mexican governmental officials fault the companies. At least now with NAFTA, the American firms can seek redress in a systematic and transparent way. Many on both sides of the border await the outcomes.

Sources: Joel Millman, "Waste Management Concerns Get Trashed in Mexico," *Wall Street Journal,* May 26, 1999, p. A17; and "Waste Management CEO Says Sale of International Units Imminent," *Dow Jones Business News,* January 25, 2000; and Ryan Starr, "The Ugly Duckling," *Canadian Business,* April 14, 2003, pp. 71–72.

manufacturers are increasingly requiring ISO 9000 registration of their suppliers. Companies manufacturing parts and components in China are quickly discovering that ISO 9000 certification is a virtual necessity, and the Japanese construction industry now requires ISO 9000 as part of the government procurement process. More and more buyers, particularly those in Europe, are refusing to buy from manufacturers without internationally recognized third-party proof of their quality capabilities. ISO 9000 may also be used to serve as a means of differentiating "classes" of suppliers, particularly in high-tech areas where high product reliability is crucial. In other words, if two suppliers are competing for the same contract, the one with ISO 9000 registration may have a competitive edge.

Although more countries (now more than 100) and companies continue to adopt ISO 9000 standards, many have complaints about the system and its spread. For example, 39 electronics companies battled against special Japanese software criteria for ISO 9000. Electronics companies also protested against the establishment of a new ISO Health and Safety Standard. Still others are calling for more comprehensive international standards along the lines of America's Malcolm Baldrige Award, which considers seven criteria—leadership, strategic planning, customer and market focus, information and analysis, human resource development, management, and business results. The telecommunications industry recently promulgated an industry-specific TL 9000 certification program that combines aspects of ISO 9000 and several other international quality standards.

Perhaps the most pertinent kind of quality standard is now being developed by the University of Michigan Business School and the American Society for Quality Control.[22] Using survey methods, their American Customer Satisfaction Index (ACSI) measures

[22]Claes Fornell, Michael D. Johnson, Eugene W. Anderson, Jaesung Cha, and Barbara Everitt Bryant, "The American Consumer Index: Nature, Purpose, and Findings," *Journal of Marketing,* October 1996, 60(4), pp. 35–46; and www.asq.org and www.theasci.org.

customers' satisfaction and perceptions of quality of a representative sample of America's goods and services. The approach was actually developed in Sweden and is now being considered in other European countries. The appeal of the ACSI approach is its focus on results, that is, quality as perceived by product and service users. So far the ACSI approach is applied only in consumer product and service contexts; however, the fundamental notion that customers are the best judges of quality is certainly applicable to international business-to-business marketing settings as well. Individual industrial marketing firms are seeking even better ways to implement quality improvement programs.[23]

## Business Services

For many industrial products the revenues from associated services exceed the revenues from the products.[24] Perhaps the most obvious case is cellular phones, in which the physical product is practically given away to gain the phone services contract. Or consider how inexpensive printers may seem until the costs of operation (i.e., ink cartridges) are considered. Indeed, for many capital equipment manufacturers the margins on after-sale services (i.e., maintenance contracts, overhauls, repairs, and replacement parts) are much higher than the margins on the machinery itself. Further, when companies lease capital equipment to customers, the distinction between products and services almost disappears completely. When a business customer leases a truck, is it purchasing a vehicle or transportation services?

Businesses also buy a variety of services that are not associated with products. Professional services are purchased from advertising and legal agencies, transportation and insurance companies, oil field services,[25] banks, and healthcare providers to name only a few. Both categories of business services are discussed in this section.

## After-Sale Services

Effective competition abroad not only requires proper product design but effective service, prompt deliveries, and the ability to furnish spare and replacement parts without delay.[26] For example, GE Medical Systems provides a wide range of after-sale services for hospitals that buy MRIs and other equipment—training, information technologies, associated healthcare services, and parts and accessories.[27] In the highly competitive European Union it is imperative to give the same kind of service a domestic company or EU company can give. One U.S. export management firm warned that U.S. businesses may be too apathetic about Europe, treating it as a subsidiary market not worthy of "spending time to develop." It cites the case of an American firm with a $3 million potential sale in Europe that did not even give engineering support to its representatives although the same sale in the United States would have brought out "all the troops."

For many technical products, the willingness of the seller to provide installation and training may be the deciding factor for the buyers in accepting one company's product over another's. South Korean and other Asian businesspeople are frank in admitting they prefer to buy from American firms but that Japanese firms often get the business because of outstanding after-sales service. Frequently heard tales of conflicts between U.S. and foreign firms over assistance expected from the seller are indicative of the problems of after-sales service and support. A South Korean executive's experiences with an American engineer and some Japanese engineers typify the situation. The Korean electronic firm purchased semiconductor-chip-making equipment for a plant expansion. The American engineer was slow in completing the installation; he stopped work at five o'clock and would not work on weekends. The Japanese, installing other equipment, understood

[23]Duncan I. Simester, John R. Hauser, Birger Wernerfelt, and Roland T. Rust, "Implementing Quality Improvement Programs Designed to Enhance Customer Satisfaction: Quasi-Experiments in the United States and Spain," *Journal of Marketing Research,* February 2000, 37, pp. 102–112.

[24]Jim Carbone, "Who Will Survive?" *Purchasing,* May 15, 2003, pp. 33–42.

[25]"Industry Trends," *Oil & Gas Journal*, May 19, 2003, p. 7.

[26]John Conley, "What Happened to Customer Service?" *Risk Management,* April 2003, pp. 22–26.

[27]See apps.gemedicalsystems.com/apps2/accessories/catalog.jhtml.

the urgency of getting the factory up and running; without being asked they worked day and night until the job was finished.

Unfortunately this is not an isolated case. In another example, Hyundai Motor Company bought two multimillion-dollar presses to stamp body parts for cars. The presses arrived late, even more time was required to set up the machines, and Hyundai had to pay the Americans extra to get the machines to work correctly. Such problems translate into lost business for U.S. firms. Samsung Electronics Company, Korea's largest chip maker, used U.S. equipment for 75 percent of its first memory-chip plant; when it outfitted its most recent chip plant, it bought 75 percent of the equipment from Japan. Of course, not all American companies have such problems. Indeed, in India Intel recently opened a data center comprising an Internet server farm of hundreds of servers. Already customers in many countries connect and store their servers and have them serviced by Intel at such centers.

Customer training is rapidly becoming a major after-sales service when selling technical products in countries that demand the latest technology but do not always have trained personnel. China demands the most advanced technical equipment but frequently has untrained people responsible for products they do not understand. Heavy emphasis on training programs and self-teaching materials to help overcome the common lack of skills to operate technical equipment is a necessary part of the after-sales service package in much of the developing world. Although McDonald's Hamburger University may be the most famous international customer training center, industrial sellers may soon catch up. Cisco Systems, collaborating with the government and a university in Singapore, recently established the first Cisco Academy Training Centre to serve that region of the world, and Intel is establishing e-Business Solutions Centers in five European countries.

A recent study of international users of heavy construction equipment revealed that, next to the manufacturer's reputation, quick delivery of replacement parts was of major importance in purchasing construction equipment. Furthermore, 70 percent of those questioned indicated they bought parts not made by the original manufacturer of the equipment because of the difficulty of getting original parts. Smaller importers complain of U.S. exporting firms not responding to orders or responding only after extensive delay. It appears that the importance of timely availability of spare parts to sustain a market is forgotten by some American exporters. When companies are responsive, the rewards are significant. U.S. chemical production equipment manufacturers dominate sales in Mexico because, according to the International Trade Administration, they deliver quickly. The ready availability of parts and services provided by U.S. marketers can give them a competitive edge.

Some international marketers also may be forgoing the opportunity of participating in a lucrative aftermarket. Certain kinds of machine tools use up to five times their original value in replacement parts during an average life span and thus represent an even greater market. One international machine tool company capitalized on the need for direct service and available parts by changing its distribution system from "normal" to one of stressing rapid service and readily available parts. Instead of selling through independent distributors, as do most machine tool manufacturers in foreign markets, this company established a series of company stores and service centers similar to those found in the United States. The company can render service through its system of local stores, whereas most competitors must dispatch service people from their home-based factories. The service people are kept on tap for rapid service calls in each of its network of local stores, and each store keeps a large stock of standard parts available for immediate delivery. The net result of meeting industrial needs quickly is keeping the company among the top suppliers in foreign sales of machine tools.

International small-package door-to-door express air services and international toll-free telephone service helped speed the delivery of parts and made after-sales technical service almost instantly available. Amdahl, the giant mainframe computer maker, uses air shipments almost exclusively for cutting inventory costs and ensuring premium customer service, which is crucial to competing against larger rivals. With increasing frequency, electronics, auto parts, and machine parts sent by air are a formidable weapon

**Exhibit 13.3**

Expansion of U.S. Law
Firms in Selected Cities
Worldwide

Source: *National Law Journal* "Top
250 Report," 2003.

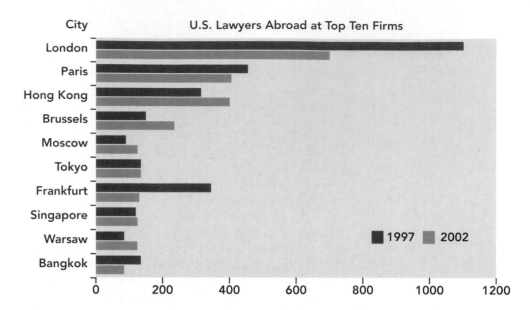

in cutting costs and boosting competitiveness. Technical advice is only a toll-free call away, and parts are air-expressed immediately to the customer. Not only does this approach improve service standards, but it also is often more cost-effective than maintaining an office in a country, even though foreign-language speakers must be hired to answer calls.

After-sales services are not only crucial in building strong customer loyalty and the all-important reputation that leads to sales at other companies, but are also almost always more profitable than the actual sale of the machinery or product.

**Other Business
Services**

Trade creates demands for international services. Most U.S. business services companies enter international markets to service their U.S. clients abroad. Accounting and advertising firms were among the earlier companies to establish branches or acquire local affiliations abroad to serve their U.S. multinational clients. Hotels and auto-rental agencies followed the business traveler abroad. Most recently, healthcare services providers are following firms abroad—Blue Cross is now selling HMO services to American companies operating in Mexico. Once established, many of these **client followers**, as one researcher refers to them, expand their client base to include local companies as well. As global markets grow, creating greater demand for business services, service companies become international market seekers. Indeed, notice in Exhibit 13.3 how American law firms expanded overseas in recent years.[28]

As mentioned in Chapter 12, the mode of entry for most consumer services firms is licensing, franchising, or direct investment. This is so because of the inseparability of the creation and consumption of the services. However, because some business services have intrinsic value that can be embodied in some tangible form (such as a blueprint or architectural design), they can be produced in one country and exported to another. Data processing and data analysis services are good examples. The analysis or processing is completed on a computer located in the United States, and the output (the service) is transmitted via satellite to a distant customer. Architecture and engineering consulting services are exportable when the consultant travels to the client's site and later returns home to write and submit a report or a design.

Business services firms face most of the same constraints and problems confronting merchandise traders. Protectionism is the most serious threat to the continued expansion of international services trade. The growth of international services was so rapid during

---

[28]Mary K. Pratt, "International Fare: Lawyers Find Reach Expands Abroad," *Boston Business Journal*, March 10, 2003, p. 1.

the last decade it drew the attention of local companies, governments, and researchers.[29] As a result, direct and indirect trade barriers were imposed to restrict foreign companies from domestic markets. Every reason, from the protection of infant industries to national security, was used to justify some of the restrictive practices. A list of more than 2,000 instances of barriers to the free flow of services among nations was recently compiled by the U.S. government. In response to the threat of increasing restriction, the United States successfully negotiated to open business services markets through both NAFTA and GATT.

Until the GATT and NAFTA agreements, there were few international rules of fair play governing trade in services. Service companies faced a complex group of national regulations that impeded the movement of people and technology from country to country. The United States and other industrialized nations want their banks, insurance companies, construction firms, and other business service providers to be allowed to move people, capital, and technology around the globe unimpeded. Restrictions designed to protect local markets range from not being allowed to do business in a country to requirements that all foreign professionals pass certification exams in the local language before being permitted to practice. In Argentina, for example, an accountant must have the equivalent of a high school education in Argentinean geography and history before being permitted to audit the books of a multinational company's branch in Buenos Aires.

Restrictions on cross-border data flows are potentially the most damaging to both the communications industry and other MNCs that rely on data transfers across borders to conduct business. Some countries impose tariffs on the transmission of data, and many others are passing laws forcing companies to open their computer files to inspection by government agencies or are tightly controlling transmission domestically. Most countries have a variety of laws to deal with the processing and electronic transmission of data across borders. In many cases, concern stems from not understanding how best to tax cross-border data flows.

As mentioned earlier, competition in all sectors of the services industry is increasing as host-country markets are invaded by many foreign firms. The practice of following a client into foreign markets and then expanding into international markets is not restricted to U.S. firms. Service firms from Germany, Britain, Japan, and other countries follow their clients into foreign markets and then expand to include local business as well. Telecommunications, advertising, and construction are U.S. services that face major competition, not only from European and Japanese companies but also from representatives of Brazil, India, and other parts of the world.

Clearly opportunities for the marketing of business services will continue to grow well into the twenty-first century. International marketers must be quite creative in responding to the legal and cultural challenges of delivering high-quality business services in foreign markets and to foreign customers.

## Trade Shows: A Crucial Part of Business-to-Business Marketing

The promotional problems encountered by foreign industrial marketers are little different from the problems faced by domestic marketers. Until recently there was a paucity of specialized advertising media in many countries.[30] In the last decade, however, specialized industrial media were developed to provide the industrial marketer with a means of communicating with potential customers, especially in Western Europe and to some extent in Eastern Europe, the Commonwealth of Independent States (CIS), and Asia.

---

[29]Farok J. Contractor, Sumit K. Kundu, and Chin-Chun Hsu, "A Three-Stage Theory of International Expansion: The Link between Multinationality and Performance in the Service Sector," *Journal of International Business Studies,* 2003, 34, pp. 5–19.

[30]Of course, it should be noted that some industrial companies still use nonspecialized media building brand awareness at all levels. Perhaps the best example is Intel's sponsorship of the official website of the Tour de France in 2002.

So you want to buy a jet fighter? How about kicking the tires of one at the Paris Airshow, the world's biggest aerospace trade show. (© AFP/CORBIS)

In addition to advertising in print media and reaching industrial customers through catalogs, websites,[31] and direct mail, the trade show or trade fair is the primary vehicle for doing business in many foreign countries. As part of its international promotion activities, the U.S. Department of Commerce sponsors trade fairs in many cities around the world. Additionally, there are annual trade shows sponsored by local governments in most countries. African countries, for example, host more than 70 industry-specific trade shows.

Trade shows serve as the most important vehicles for selling products, reaching prospective customers, contacting and evaluating potential agents and distributors, and marketing in most countries. Although important in the United States, they serve a much more important role in other countries. They were at the center of commerce in Europe for centuries and are where most prospects are found. European trade shows attract high-level decision makers who are not attending just to see the latest products but are there to buy. Preshow promotional expenditures are often used in Europe to set formal appointments. The importance of trade shows to Europeans is reflected in the percentage of their media budget spent on participating in trade events and how they spend those dollars. On average, Europeans spend 22 percent of their total annual media budget on trade events, whereas American firms typically spend less than 5 percent. Europeans tend not to spend money on circus-like promotions, gimmicks, and such; rather, they focus on providing an environment for in-depth dealings. More than 2,000 major trade shows are held worldwide every year. The Hanover Industry Fair (Germany), the largest trade fair in the world, has nearly 6,000 exhibitors who show a wide range of industrial products to 600,000 visitors.

Trade shows provide the facilities for a manufacturer to exhibit and demonstrate products to potential users and to view competitors' products. They are an opportunity to create sales and establish relationships with agents, distributors, franchisees,[32] and suppliers that can lead to more-permanent distribution channels in foreign markets. In fact, a trade show may be the only way to reach some prospects. Trade show experts estimate that 80 to 85 percent of the people seen on a trade show floor never have a salesperson call on them. Several websites now specialize in virtual trade shows. They often include multimedia and elaborate product display booths that can be virtually toured. Some of these virtual trade shows last only a few days during an associated actual trade show.

The number and variety of trade shows is such that almost any target market in any given country can be found through this medium. Most remarkable is the recent Medical Expo in Havana—the first trade show to be sanctioned by both the U.S. and Cuban governments in more than four decades.[33] Over 8,000 Cuban doctors, nurses, technicians, and hospital administrators attended. This initial event was followed in 2002 with a major food products trade show in Havana.[34] In Eastern Europe, fairs and exhibitions offer

[31]For illustrative examples of the burgeoning information available to industrial customers on websites, see www.caterpillar.com, www.fluor.com, www.hewlett-packard.com, and www.qualcom.com.

[32]Brad Fishman, "International Trade Shows: The Smartest Ticket for Overseas Research," *Franchising World,* April 2003, pp. 25–26.

[33]Mark Fineman, "U.S. Medical Expo in Cuba Fuels Hope for Healthy Ties," *Los Angeles Times,* January 26, 2000, p. A1.

[34]Paul Richter, "Cuba Trade Show Kicks Off with a Hearty Welcome from Castro," *Los Angeles Times,* September 27, 2002, p. A3.

## CROSSING BORDERS 13.5 No More Aching Feet, but What about the 15-Ton Russian Tank?

During April 2000, the first stand-alone virtual trade show was staged by ISP Virtual Show. It was aimed at an appropriate audience—Internet service providers (ISPs). The address was (and will be) ISPVirtualShow.com. Technology for the show was provided by iTradeFair.com, a website worth the visit.

According to the promoters, "The advantages of a virtual trade show far outweigh those of the physical model. Exhibitors (booths start at $1,995) and attendees (tickets are $99) from all over the world will now be able to exhibit and attend direct from their desktops. There are endless benefits of a virtual show; including massive reductions in costs—both in exhibiting and manpower terms, savings on booth space and buildings, accommodations, flights, expenses, the obligatory bar bills and costs of time spent out of the office."

The virtual trade show offers a fresh alternative to the traditional model. Using advanced technology, anyone anywhere in the world can visit the virtual show and access information in his or her own language—making language barriers a thing of the past. Also, if attendees and exhibitors would like to continue a discussion offline, clocks displaying times from all over the world make scheduling easy. Finally, weary executives attending the same trade shows year in, year out will no longer suffer aching feet, hot stuffy rooms without air conditioning, and overpriced, plastic food.

Although this pitch sounds great, the authors of this book believe that an aspect of real trade shows that the virtual ones miss is the face-to-face contact and the all-important interpersonal relationship building that goes on over drinks or during those plastic meals. And there is no virtual way to achieve the same effect as a Russian software developer who recently displayed a 15-ton Russian tank in his booth at Comtek Trade Show in Moscow. We shall see how this new promotional medium evolves.

Sources: "ISP Virtual Show: World's First Virtual Trade Show," *M2 Presswire*, October 26, 1999; and Jeanette Borzo, "Moscow's Comtek Trade Show Confronts Internet Challenge," Dow Jones News Service, April 19, 2000.

companies the opportunity to meet new customers, including private traders, young entrepreneurs, and representatives of non-state organizations. The exhibitions in countries such as Russia and Poland offer a cost-effective way of reaching a large number of customers who might otherwise be difficult to target through individual sales calls. Specialized fairs in individual sectors such as computers, the automotive industry, fashion, and home furnishings regularly take place.

In difficult economic and/or political circumstances online trade shows become a useful, but obviously less than adequate substitute.[35] A good example of the kinds of services being developed can be found at www.itradefair.com and Crossing Borders 13.5. During the weakened global economy at the turn of the century slimmer travel budgets and SARS scares dramatically reduced attendance, and even forced cancellations, of traditionally popular international trade fairs.[36] Political conflicts between the EU and the United States over Middle East policies resulted in the U.S. Department of Defense discouraging American attendance at the 2003 Paris Air Show.[37] Top American executives at Boeing, Lockheed, and the like dutifully stayed away. Exhibit space declined by 5 percent and orders announced dropped from $45 billion in 2001 to $32 billion.[38] It is hard to estimate what the costs in terms of international orders are for firms such as Boeing when their top executives cannot mix with potential customers at such a crucial event. We do know that Airbus inked orders for dozens of commercial aircraft from customers

[35]Jennifer Saranow, "The Show Goes On: Online Trade Shows Offer Low-Cost, Flexible Alternatives for Organizers, Especially in These Days of Tight Travel Budgets," *Wall Street Journal*, April 28, 2003, p R4.

[36]James Zoltak, "AEE Confab Cancelled Due to SARS," *Amusement Business*, April 28, 2003, p. 1.

[37]Daniel Michaels, "Paris Air Show May Sputter—Economic, Political Factors Stifle Aerospace Industry," *Wall Street Journal*, June 13, 2003, p. B4.

[38]"Plane Makers Land Fewer Deals at Paris Air Show," *Los Angeles Times*, June 23, 2003, p. C3.

in Qatar and the Arab Emirates. Not even the best online trade show imaginable can make up for this apparent step backwards in international trade and cooperation.[39]

# Relationship Marketing in Business-to-Business Contexts

The characteristics that define the uniqueness of industrial products and services lead naturally to **relationship marketing**.[40] The long-term relationships with customers that define relationship marketing fit the characteristics inherent in industrial products and are a viable strategy for business-to-business marketing. The first and foremost characteristic of industrial goods markets is the motive of the buyer: to make a profit. Industrial products fit into a business or manufacturing process, and their contributions will be judged on how well they contribute to that process. In order for an industrial marketer to fulfill the needs of a customer, the marketer must understand those needs as they exist today and how they will change as the buyer strives to compete in global markets that call for long-term relationships.

The industrial customer's needs in global markets are continuously changing, and suppliers' offerings must also continue to change. The need for the latest technology means that it is not a matter of selling the right product the first time but rather of continuously changing the product to keep it right over time. The objective of relationship marketing is to make the relationship an important attribute of the transaction, thus differentiating oneself from competitors. It shifts the focus away from price to service and long-term benefits. The reward is loyal customers that translate into substantial long-term profits.

Focusing on long-term relationship building is especially important in most international markets where culture dictates stronger ties between people and companies. Particularly in countries with relationship-oriented cultures such as those in Latin America or Asia,[41] trust is a crucial aspect of commercial relationships. Constant and close communication with customers is the single most important source of information about the development of new industrial products and services. Indeed, in a recent survey of Japanese professional buyers a key choice criterion for suppliers was a trait they called "caring" (those who defer to requests without argument and recognize that in return buyers will care for the long-term interests of sellers). Longer-term and more communication-rich relationships are keys to success in international industrial markets.

As in all areas of international business, the Internet is facilitating relationship building and maintenance in new ways.[42] Cisco Systems is a leader in this area; it not only supplies the hardware that allows B2B commerce to work, but its relationship management practices and process also serve as models for the industry. Cisco's international customers can visit its website to check out product specs and make their orders. That information is then routed on the Internet through Cisco to its suppliers. A full 65 percent of the orders move directly from the supplier to the customer—Cisco never touches them. Things are built only after they are ordered; thus little, if any, inventory is kept in warehouses. Based on Cisco's success, businesses around the world are beginning to reorganize themselves accordingly.

IBM of Brazil stresses stronger ties with its customers by offering planning seminars that address corporate strategies, competition, quality, and how to identify marketing

---

[39]Information about trade shows is available from the following sources: the U.S. Trade Information Center's *Export Promotion Calendar,* which lists dates and locations of trade shows worldwide; *Europe Trade Fairs,* which lists European shows, including the U.S. Department of Commerce sponsored shows; *Trade Shows Worldwide* (published by Gale Research), a comprehensive listing of more than 6,000 trade shows worldwide; and *International Trade Fairs and Conferences* (published by Co-Mar Management Services), which lists 5,000 trade shows worldwide.

[40]Jagdish Sheth and Atul Parvatiyar, "Evolving Relationship Marketing into a Discipline," *Journal of Relationship Marketing,* 2002, 1(1), pp. 3–16.

[41]Alfred Wong, Dean Tjosvold, and Zhang Pengzhu, "Commitment and Conflict Management for Relational Marketing in China," *Journal of Technology Management,* 2002, 24(1), pp. 88–105.

[42]Sheena Leek, Peter W. Turnbull, and Peter Naude, "How Is Information Technology Affecting Business Relationships? Results from a U.K. Survey," *Industrial Marketing Management,* February 2003, 32(2), pp. 119–126.

# solar Turbines inc.
## A Global industrial marketer

With more than 80 percent of its sales outside the United States, Solar Turbines Inc. is the most global subsidiary of one of America's most global companies. About half of Caterpillar's 2003 sales of $21 billion were to customers outside the United States, making the parent corporation one of the country's leading exporters. Pictured here is work on the world's largest earthmoving project, the Three Gorges Dam site in China.

Solar® industrial gas turbines are used by customers in 86 countries worldwide, in the oil and gas industries, electrical power generation, and marine propulsion. Solar promotes its products on the Internet (see www.solarturbines.com) and in brochures and print media around the world, as represented below:

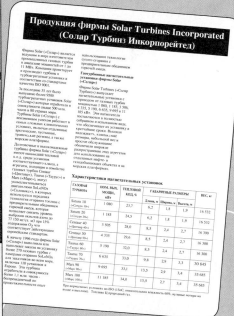

An ad appearing in a French trade publication. It emphasizes the energy-saving and low-pollution attributes of the products. Notice the Caterpillar yellow in the logo and the phone number for the European subsidiary offices.

The compact size makes Solar gas turbines ideally suited for offshore oil applications in places like the North Sea, the Gulf of Mexico, and offshore Malaysia and Latin America.

A Russian language brochure. The former Soviet Union and now the Russian oil and gas industry has remained an important customer for Solar for more than 20 years.

(Courtesy Solar Turbines Inc.)

# the project team

**The Customer** is involved as a vital member of the Project Team from the initial inquiry to final acceptance. The Customer works with and issues project specifications to our . . .

**Sales Engineer**, who maintains initial Customer contact, prompts analysis of Customer needs, submits a comprehensive proposal to the Customer, monitors execution of the order, and submits the order to the assigned . . .

**Application Engineer**, who is responsible for determining the best product match for Customer requirements and recommending alternative approaches as appropriate. The Application Engineer works closely with . . .

**Engineering and Control Systems**, who design gas turbines, gas compressors, and controls and customize gas turbine packages for the customers based on proven designs.

Solar Turbines sells its products and services through Project Teams that include both customer personnel and vendors. In this particular case, Solar has followed ENRON, its American customer, around the world, supplying equipment and services for ENRON's global ventures.

Personal selling is the most important aspect of the promotions mix for industrial companies like Solar. In addition to calling on clients directly, sales engineers attend key trade shows around the world, such as this one in Amsterdam.

**Project Manager** handles all aspects of the order, maintains liaison with the Customer, controls documentation, arranges quality audits, and is responsible for on-time shipment and scheduling equipment commissioning at the Customer site.

**Manufacturing Technicians** produce, assemble, and test industrial gas turbines and turbomachinery packages designed to meet specific Customer needs. Manufacturing also arranges shipment of equipment to the Customer site where . . .

**Customer Services** handles installation and start-up of the turbomachinery, trains personnel, and provides a wide range of vital services to support Customer and operating requirements.

**Suppliers** are a critical element of all project teams; they provide materials and components that must meet Solar's demanding Quality Standards.

The Venezuelan offshore oil and gas platform pictured here is about a $40 million project for Solar; it includes four sets of turbomachinery. Close coordination among customer, subcontractors, and Solar is required from initial designs through powering up the facility.

**(Courtesy Solar Turbines Inc.)**

Solar's sales and services efforts don't stop when the machine has been turned on. After-sales services (maintenance contracts, overhaul, and spare parts) often account for a third of some industrial manufacturers' revenues, and Solar is no exception to that rule. Pictured are company overhaul operations in Indonesia.

# solar's marketing affiliates

Solar sells and distributes its products through a variety of kinds of affiliates around the world. Most firms would prefer to keep things simple—direct sales worldwide. However, Solar has learned to be flexible and makes distribution decisions based on the level of business and local regulations.

Solar has packaging agreements with three Japanese companies, including Mitsui Zosen, Niigata, and Yanmar. The one pictured, Yanmar, buys the turbine engines from Solar, then packages them with generators to suit Japanese regulations and customer specifications.

Delcom is Solar's distributor in Malaysia. Almost all the manufacturing is done in the United States and Delcom's principal role is marketing in Southeast Asia. Pictured is Delcom's booth at a Malay trade show.

Solar has a variety of sales and manufacturing operations and affiliations in Mexico, including a maquiladora plant in Tijuana, offices in Mexico City, and a technology-sharing agreement with Turbinas Solar. The last facility is located in Veracruz and is pictured above.

Solar has also signed long-term alliance agreements with some of its major customers like Shell Oil. Pictured here are the Solar and Shell executives who worked on the agreement and then signed it at Solar's San Diego headquarters.

(Courtesy Solar Turbines Inc.)

opportunities. One of these seminars showed a food import-export firm how it could increase efficiency by decentralizing its computer facilities to better serve its customers. The company's computers were centralized at headquarters, while branches took orders manually and mailed them to the home office for processing and invoicing. It took several days before the customer's order was entered, which added several days to delivery time. The seminar helped the company realize it could streamline its order processing by installing branch-office terminals that were connected to computers at the food company's headquarters. A customer could then place an order and receive an invoice on the spot, shortening the delivery time by several days or weeks. Helping clients or suppliers identify problems and their solutions also helps IBM sell equipment to the attending companies. Not all participants who attend the 30 different seminars offered annually become IBM customers, but the seminars create a continuing relationship with potential customers.

## Summary

Industrial (business-to-business) marketing requires close attention to the exact needs of customers. Basic differences across various markets are less than for consumer goods, but the motives behind purchases differ enough to require a special approach. Global competition has risen to the point that industrial goods marketers must pay close attention to the level of economic and technological development of each market to determine the buyer's assessment of quality. Companies that adapt their products to these needs are the ones that should be the most effective in the marketplace.

The demand for products and services in business-to-business markets is by nature more volatile than in most consumer markets.

The demand also varies by level of economic development and the quality of educational systems across countries. Ultimately, product or service quality is defined by customers, but global quality standards such as ISO 9000 are being developed that provide information about companies' attention to matters of quality. After-sale services are a hugely important aspect of industrial sales. The demand for other kinds of business services (e.g., banking, legal services, advertising) is burgeoning around the world. Trade shows are an especially important promotional medium in business-to-business marketing.

## Questions

1. Define the following terms:

   derived demand, 377                    client followers, 388
   price–quality relationship, 380    relationship marketing, 392
   ISO 9000, 384

2. What are the differences between consumer and industrial goods and what are the implications for international marketing?

3. Discuss how the various stages of economic development affect the demand for industrial goods.

4. "Industrialization is typically a national issue, and industrial goods are the fodder for industrial growth." Comment.

5. "The adequacy of a product must be considered in relation to the general environment within which it will be operated rather than solely on the basis of technical efficiency." Discuss the implications of this statement.

6. Why hasn't the United States been more helpful in setting universal standards for industrial equipment? Do you feel that the argument is economically sound? Discuss.

7. What roles do service, replacement parts, and standards play in competition in foreign marketing? Illustrate.

8. Discuss the role industrial trade fairs play in international marketing of industrial goods.

9. Describe the reasons an MNC might seek an ISO 9000 certification.

10. What ISO 9000 legal requirements are imposed on products sold in the EU? Discuss.

11. Discuss the competitive consequences of being ISO 9000 certified.

12. Discuss how the characteristics that define the uniqueness of industrial products lead naturally to relationship marketing. Give some examples.

13. Discuss some of the more pertinent problems in pricing industrial goods.

14. What is the price–quality relationship? How does this affect a U.S. firm's comparative position in world markets?

15. Select several countries, each at a different stage of economic development, and illustrate how the stage affects demand for industrial goods.

16. England has almost completed the process of shifting from the inch-pound system to the metric system. What effect do you think this will have on the traditional U.S. reluctance to make such a change? Discuss the economic implications of such a move.

17. Discuss the importance of international business services to total U.S. export trade. How do most U.S. service companies become international?

18. Discuss the international market environment for business services.

# international marketing channels

## CHAPTER LEARNING OBJECTIVES

What you should learn from Chapter 14:

- The variety of distribution channels and how they affect cost and efficiency in marketing

- The Japanese distribution structure and what it means to Japanese customers and to competing importers of goods

- How distribution patterns affect the various aspects of international marketing

- The growing importance of e-commerce as a distribution alternative

- The functions, advantages, and disadvantages of various kinds of middlemen

- The importance of middlemen to a product's success and the importance of selecting and maintaining middlemen

# Global Perspective

## 500 MILLION STICKS OF DOUBLEMINT TODAY—BILLIONS TOMORROW

Outside a corner candy stand in Shanghai, 10-year-old Zhang Xiaomei folds a piece of Wrigley's Doublemint gum into her mouth—one of 500 million sticks the Wm. Wrigley Jr. Company will sell in China this year. To reach the flimsy blue plywood stand that serves this customer in pigtails, the minty stick traveled a thousand miles by truck, rusting freighter, tricycle cart, and bicycle—and it is still freshly soft and sugar-dusted at the time it is sold. That's something of a wonder given the daunting scale and obstacles in the world's largest developing country.

Mastering the distribution system is the single most important challenge of China's economic revolution. The task facing every consumer products company trying to reach the giant Chinese market is how to get the product to the consumer at a convenient location, in salable condition, properly displayed, and aggressively sold. That, at least, is the ideal.

Western goods can effectively reach only about 200 million of China's 1.2 billion people today. But the number of accessible Chinese consumers is increasing rapidly as companies become more adept at meeting the challenges of navigating where roads are poor, rivers are jammed, and railways are clogged.

Finding reliable distributors, usually by word of mouth, is the first challenge, but seldom the last. Distributors are mainly state owned and have little incentive to position a brand, let alone an understanding of how to do so. Market coverage, maintaining product quality, and effective presentation at the point of sale are Wrigley's goals. Wrigley wants its gum consumed within eight months of manufacture; otherwise, the gum dries out or sugar bleeds through the packaging.

Let's follow the route taken by Zhang Xiaomei's stick of Doublemint from a factory in Guangzhou on the southern coast of China to a corner stand in Shanghai. The gum is shipped to Shanghai from Guangzhou on a coastal freighter. But off the coast of Zhejiang province, a marine patrol seizes the ship; along with 960,000 packs of gum, the ship is loaded with smuggled cars. The gum and other cargo are seized by customs, while Wrigley waits and frets the whole time about aging. Finally, the gum is released and loaded onto a truck at the Shanghai port, only to face a complicated bribe-strewn journey through the distribution system on its way to market. Wrigley-hired trucks are often stopped not only by bandits but also by provincial gendarmes demanding exorbitant fees before they let the vehicles pass.

After the gum gets into Shanghai, Wrigley loses control. Distribution now depends on one of the firms spun off from China's once-mighty state-owned trading companies. Wholesalers in China do not do much delivering; instead, like Wrigley wholesaler Chen Tuping, they wait in their warehouses for buyers to arrive.

So, how does that stick of gum get to Zhang Xiaomei? Wrigley's legwork, that's how. Teams of Wrigley representatives walk the streets, talking to shop owners, handing out free Wrigley posters and plastic display stands. Among the targets is Xu Meili, who runs a booth at the Beautiful & Rich Wholesale Market. After a successful sales call, she begins to stock Wrigley's gum, which she fetches with a tricycle cart from Mr. Chen, the wholesaler, or one of his competitors.

Wrigley salesmen continue visiting small kiosks, like the blue plywood stand in Shanghai. Inside the stand, a young woman who calls herself Little Yan naps on her folded arms between sales. When stocks run low, she rides her bike the few blocks to Ms. Xu's booth to buy more gum or candy. All of this just to get Zhang Xiaomei a stick of gum.

"The margin isn't great," says Wrigley's international business chief. But for now, he says, the company is content to build market share. He adds: "We're a very patient company." To quote a statement on distribution from Wrigley's website, "The modest price of chewing gum means almost everybody can afford to buy it." The global market for gum is vast and Wrigley seeks markets in every country it can enter, even where consumers don't yet chew gum. For example, Wrigley recently invested in new plants in India, where only a very small number of Indians use chewing gum. But with a population almost as large as China's, it means big growth if only a small percentage of the almost one billion people buy the product. Wrigley's global distribution strategy is to ensure that everyone in the world can get gum wherever and whenever he or she wants.

Effort pays off—Doublemint chewing gum has a 91 percent market share in China.

Sources: Craig S. Smith, "Doublemint in China: Distribution Isn't Double the Fun," *Wall Street Journal,* December 5, 1995, p. B1; "The Story of Chewing Gum: Channels of Distribution," www.wrigley.com; and David Shook, "Wrigley: Solid Growth by Gum," *BusinessWeek Online,* April 11, 2003.

If marketing goals are to be achieved, a product must be made accessible to the target market at an affordable price. Getting the product to the target market can be a costly process if inadequacies within the distribution structure cannot be overcome. Forging an aggressive and reliable channel of distribution may be the most critical and challenging[1] task facing the international marketer. Moreover, some argue that meeting such challenges is a key catalyst to economic development.[2]

Each market contains a distribution network with many channel choices whose structures are unique and, in the short run, fixed. In some markets the distribution structure is multilayered, complex, inefficient, even strange,[3] and often difficult for new marketers to penetrate; in others, there are few specialized middlemen except in major urban areas; and in yet others, there is a dynamic mixture of traditional and new, evolving distribution systems available on a global scale.[4] Regardless of the predominating distribution structure, competitive advantage resides with the marketer best able to build the most efficient channel from among the alternatives available.

This chapter discusses the basic points involved in making channel decisions: channel structures; distribution patterns; available alternative middlemen; factors affecting choice of channels; and locating, selecting, motivating, and terminating middlemen.

# Channel-of-Distribution Structures

In every country and in every market, urban or rural, rich or poor, all consumer and industrial products eventually go through a distribution process. The **distribution process** includes the physical handling and distribution of goods, the passage of ownership (title), and—most important from the standpoint of marketing strategy—the buying and selling negotiations between producers and middlemen and between middlemen and customers.

A host of policy and strategic channel-selection issues confronts the international marketing manager. These issues are not in themselves very different from those encountered in domestic distribution, but the resolution of the issues differs because of different channel alternatives and market patterns.

Each country market has a **distribution structure** through which goods pass from producer to user. Within this structure are a variety of middlemen whose customary functions, activities, and services reflect existing competition, market characteristics, tradition, and economic development.

In short, the behavior of channel members is the result of the interactions between the cultural environment and the marketing process. Channel structures range from those with little developed marketing infrastructure such as those found in many emerging markets to the highly complex, multilayered system found in Japan.

## Import-Oriented Distribution Structure

Traditional channels in developing countries evolved from economies with a strong dependence on imported manufactured goods. In an *import-oriented* or *traditional distribution structure,* an importer controls a fixed supply of goods and the marketing system develops around the philosophy of selling a limited supply of goods at high prices to a small number of affluent customers. In the resulting seller's market, market penetration and mass distribution are not necessary because demand exceeds supply and, in most cases, the customer seeks the supply from a limited number of middlemen.

This configuration affects the development of intermediaries and their functions. Distribution systems are local rather than national in scope, and the relationship between the

---

[1]Indeed, David Ford argues that this challenge hasn't abated with new technologies, etc. See "Distribution, Internationalization and Networks: Solving Old Problems, Learning New Things, and Forgetting Most of Them," *International Marketing Review,* 2002, 19(2-3), pp. 225–235.

[2]Paul Ellis, "Are International Trade Intermediaries Catalysts in Economic Development? A New Research Agenda," *Journal of International Marketing,* 2003, 11(1), pp. 73–96.

[3]See www3.tky.ne.jp/~edjacob/vending.html for a look at some strange vending machines.

[4]Sarah McBride, "Kia's Audacious Sorento Plan," *Wall Street Journal,* April 4, 2003, p. A12.

They're in China, but they aren't Peking ducks. The birds are for sale in Guangzhou's free market, the first farmers' market to be opened in China after the Cultural Revolution. This was the place where free enterprise found its rebirth. Every kind of food is for sale here—from ducks to dogs, from scorpions to dried lizards on sticks.

importer and any middleman in the marketplace is considerably different from that found in a mass-marketing system. The idea of a channel as a chain of intermediaries performing specific activities and each selling to a smaller unit beneath it until the chain reaches the ultimate consumer is not common in an import-oriented system.[5]

Because the importer-wholesaler traditionally performs most marketing functions, independent agencies that provide advertising, marketing research, warehousing and storage, transportation, financing, and other facilitating functions found in a developed, mature marketing infrastructure are nonexistent or underdeveloped. Thus few independent agencies to support a fully integrated distribution system develop.

Contrast this with the distribution philosophy of mass consumption that prevails in the United States and other industrialized nations. In these markets, one supplier does not dominate supply, supply can be increased or decreased within a given range, and profit maximization occurs at or near production capacity. Generally a buyer's market exists and the producer strives to penetrate the market and push goods out to the consumer, resulting in a highly developed channel structure that includes a variety of intermediaries, many of which are unknown in developing markets.

Obviously, few countries fit the import-oriented model today, although the channel structure for chewing gum illustrated in the Global Perspective comes closest to describing a traditional import-oriented structure. As China develops economically, its market system and distribution structure evolves as well. As already discussed, economic development is uneven, and various parts of an economy may be at different stages of development. Channel structures in countries that historically evolved from an import-oriented base usually have vestiges of their beginnings reflected in a less than fully integrated system. At the other extreme is the Japanese distribution system with multiple layers of specialized middlemen.

## Japanese Distribution Structure

Distribution in Japan has long been considered the most effective nontariff barrier to the Japanese market.[6] Even though the market is becoming more open as many traditional modes of operation are eroding in the face of competition from foreign marketers, it still serves as an excellent case study for the pervasive impact culture plays on economic institutions such as national distribution systems. The Japanese distribution structure is different enough from its U.S. or European counterparts that it should be carefully studied by anyone contemplating entry. The Japanese system has four distinguishing features: (1) a structure dominated by many small middlemen dealing with many small retailers, (2) channel control by manufacturers, (3) a business philosophy shaped by a unique culture,[7] and (4) laws that protect the foundation of the system—the small retailer.

**High Density of Middlemen.** The density of middlemen, retailers, and wholesalers in the Japanese market is unparalleled in any Western industrialized country. The traditional Japanese structure serves consumers who make small, frequent purchases at small, conveniently located stores. An equal density of wholesalers supports the high density of small stores with small inventories. It is not unusual for consumer goods to go through

[5]Some progress is being made in e-commerce in some of the least developed countries. See William Wresh, "Initial e-Commerce Efforts in Nine Least Developed Countries," *Journal of Global Information Management,* April–June 2003, pp. 67–78.

[6]For a detailed study on this subject, see Frank Alpert, Michael Kamins, Tokoaki Sakano, Naoto Onzo, and John L. Graham, "Retail Buyer Decision Making in Japan: What U.S. Sellers Need to Know," *International Business Review,* 1997, 6(2), pp. 91–104.

[7]Keysuk Kim and Changho Oh, "On Distributor Commitment in Marketing Channels for Industrial Products: Contrast between the United States and Japan," *Journal of International Marketing,* 2002, 10(1), pp. 72–97.

**Exhibit 14.1**   Comparison of Distribution Channels between the United States and Japan

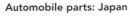

Automobile parts: Japan

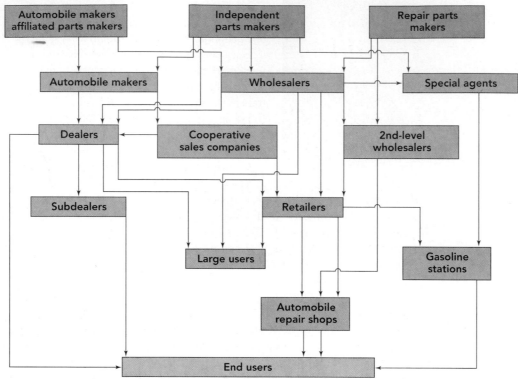

Automobile parts: United States

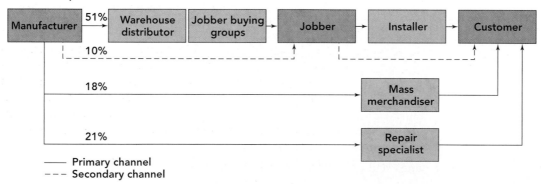

—— Primary channel
--- Secondary channel

three or four intermediaries before reaching the consumer—producer to primary, secondary, regional, and local wholesaler, and finally to retailer to consumer. Exhibit 14.1 illustrates the contrast between shorter U.S. channels and the long Japanese channels.

Although other countries have large numbers of small retail stores, the major difference between small stores (nine or fewer employees) in Japan and the United States is the percentage of total retail sales accounted for by small retailers. In Japan, small stores (95.1 percent of all retail food stores) account for 57.7 percent of retail food sales; in the United States, small stores (69.8 percent of all retail food stores) generate 19.2 percent of food sales. A disproportionate percentage of nonfood sales are made in small stores in Japan as well. In the United States, small stores (81.6 percent of all stores) sell 32.9 percent of nonfood items; in Japan, small stores (94.1 percent of all stores) sell 50.4 percent. Such differences are also reflected in Exhibit 14.2. Notice the American emphasis on supermarkets, discount food stores, and department stores versus the Japanese prevalence of independent groceries and bakers.

**Exhibit 14.2**
Retail Structure in Three
Countries

Source: Euromonitor, 2003.

| | Retail Outlets (000s) | | |
|---|---|---|---|
| | **Germany** | **Japan** | **United States** |
| **Food Stores** | | | |
| Supermarkets | 9.0 | 15.0 | 43.7 |
| Hypermarkets | 2.3 | 1.5 | 3.1 |
| Discounters | 15.4 | 1.0 | 29.1 |
| Independent Grocers | 34.2 | 62.0 | 9.7 |
| Bakers | 47.2 | 74.7 | 2.8 |
| Butchers | 44.3 | 16.4 | 8.0 |
| Fishmongers | 27.1 | 27.0 | 1.6 |
| Green Grocers | 16.1 | 27.7 | 3.3 |
| **Nonfood Stores** | | | |
| Booksellers | 25.6 | 37.0 | 12.7 |
| Chemists | 39.4 | 83.3 | 47.4 |
| Department Stores | 1.2 | 0.3 | 13.5 |
| Electronics, computers | 30.6 | 61.9 | 30.3 |
| Home furnishings | 11.7 | 38.7 | 28.2 |
| Sporting goods | 8.3 | 19.3 | 23.2 |
| Toy shops | 3.6 | 12.1 | 18.0 |

As we shall see in a later section, profound changes in retailing are occurring in Japan. Although it is still accurate to describe the Japanese market as having a high density of middlemen, the number of small stores is declining and they are being replaced by larger discount and specialty stores. The number of retail stores is down more than 10 percent since 1998, and the number of retail stores with a staff of four or fewer dropped more than 15 percent. These small stores serve an important role for Japanese consumers. High population density, the tradition of frequent trips to the store, an emphasis on service, freshness, and quality, and wholesalers who provide financial assistance, frequent deliveries of small lots, and other benefits combine to support the high number of small stores.

**Channel Control.**   Manufacturers depend on wholesalers for a multitude of services to other members of the distribution network. Financing, physical distribution, warehousing, inventory, promotion, and payment collection are provided to other channel members by wholesalers. The system works because wholesalers and all other middlemen downstream are tied to manufacturers by a set of practices and incentives designed to ensure strong marketing support for their products and to exclude rival competitors from the channel. Wholesalers typically act as agent middlemen and extend the manufacturer's control through the channel to the retail level.

Control is maintained through the following elements:

**1. Inventory financing.** Sales are made on consignment with credits extending for several months.

**2. Cumulative rebates.** Rebates are given annually for any number of reasons, including quantity purchases, early payments, achieving sales targets, performing services, maintaining specific inventory levels, participating in sales promotions, remaining loyal to suppliers, maintaining manufacturer's price policies, cooperating, and contributing to overall success.

**3. Merchandise returns.** All unsold merchandise may be returned to the manufacturer.

**4. Promotional support.** Intermediaries receive a host of displays, advertising layouts, management education programs, in-store demonstrations, and other dealer aids that strengthen the relationship between the middleman and the manufacturer.

**Business Philosophy.**   Coupled with the close economic ties and dependency created by trade customs and the long structure of Japanese distribution channels is a relationship-oriented business philosophy that emphasizes loyalty, harmony, and friendship. The value system supports long-term dealer/supplier relationships that are difficult to change as long as each party perceives economic advantage. The traditional partner, the insider, generally has the advantage.

A general lack of price competition, the provision of costly services, and other inefficiencies render the cost of Japanese consumer goods among the highest in the world. Indeed, when you just compare paychecks at current exchange rates (that is, GDP per capita), Japanese at $44,458 outearn Americans at $31,592. However, if you take into consideration what those paychecks will buy (that is, GDP per capita at purchase price parity [PPP]), then Americans at $34,320 do better than Japanese at $25,130.[8] Such prices create a perfect climate for discounting, which is beginning to be a major factor. The Japanese consumer contributes to the continuation of the traditional nature of the distribution system through frequent buying trips, small purchases, favoring personal service over price, and a proclivity for loyalty to brands perceived to be of high quality. Additionally, Japanese law gives the small retailer enormous advantage over the development of larger stores and competition. All these factors support the continued viability of small stores and the established system, although changing attitudes among many Japanese consumers are beginning to weaken the hold traditional retailing has on the market.

**Large-Scale Retail Store Law and Its Successor.**   Competition from large retail stores had been almost totally controlled by *Daitenho*—the Large-Scale Retail Store Law. Designed to protect small retailers from large intruders into their markets, the law required that any store larger than 5,382 square feet (500 square meters) must obtain approval from the prefecture government to be "built, expanded, stay open later in the evening, or change the days of the month they must remain closed." All proposals for new "large" stores were first judged by the Ministry of International Trade and Industry (MITI). Then, if all local retailers *unanimously* agreed to the plan, it was swiftly approved. However, without approval at the prefecture level the plan was returned for clarification and modification, a process that could take several years (ten years was not unheard of) for approval. Designed to protect small retailers against competition from large stores, the law was imposed against both domestic and foreign companies. It took ten years for one of Japan's largest supermarket chains to get clearance for a new site. Toys "R" Us[9] fought rules and regulations for over three years before it gained approval for a store. Besides the *Daitenho,* there were myriad licensing rules. One investigation of retail stores uncovered many different laws, each requiring a separate license to open a full-service store.

Businesspeople in Japan and the United States see the Japanese distribution system as a major nontariff barrier, and Japanese see it as a major roadblock to improvement of the Japanese standard of living. However, pressure from the United States and the Structural Impediments Initiative (SII) negotiations to pry open new markets for American companies resulted in large cracks in the system. The most recent is the **Large-Scale Retail Store Location Act** of June 2000, which replaced the Large-Scale Retail Store Law.

The new law takes MITI out of the approval process. Under the new law, restrictions on the opening of large retailers near smaller shops are relaxed and the restriction on the number of days stores must be closed is abolished. However, local government has the authority to block construction if it thinks the new project will exacerbate pollution, traffic congestion, or noise. There is concern that the real impact of the new law depends on how it is interpreted by local governments. It remains to be seen whether they will use environmental protection as an excuse to limit new store openings and thus be more restrictive rather than less restrictive.

---

[8]Euromonitor, 2003.

[9]Lisa Bannon and Carlta Vizthum, "Small World: One-Toy-Fits-All: How Industry Learned to Love the Global Kid," *Wall Street Journal,* April 29, 2003, p. A1.

## CROSSING BORDERS 14.1  Mitsukoshi Department Store, Established 1611—But Will It Be There in 2011?

Japanese department stores have a long history in Japanese retailing; indeed, Mitsukoshi department store, the epitome of Japanese retailing, began as a dry goods store in 1611. Department stores were Japan's first big corporations, which created Japan's first banks. Those banks in turn spawned the *keiretsu* system of corporate family groups that drove Japan's transformation into an economic power. But are their days numbered?

To visit a Japanese department store is to get a glimpse of Japanese life. In the basements and sub-basements, food abounds, with everything from crunchy Japanese pickles to delicate French pastry and soft-colored, seasonally changing forms of Japanese candies. Besides the traditional floors for women's and men's apparel and furniture, most stores have a floor devoted to kimonos and related accessories and another floor dedicated to children's needs and wants. On the roof there may be miniature open-air amusement parks for children.

But wait, there's more. Department stores are not merely content to dazzle with variety, delight with imaginative displays, and accept large amounts of yen for clothes and vegetables. They also seek to serve up a bit of culture. Somewhere between the floors of clothing and the roof, it is likely that you will find a banquet hall, an art gallery, an exhibition hall, and one or two floors of restaurants serving everything from *doria* (creamy rice with cheese) to tempura. Department stores aim to be "total life-style enterprises," says one manager. "We try to be all-inclusive, with art, culture, shopping, and fashion. We stress the philosophy of *i-shoku-ju,* the three big factors in life: what you wear, what you eat, and how you live."

Two kinds of stores dominate Japanese retailing: giant department stores like Mitsukoshi and small neighborhood shops, both kept alive by a complex distribution system that translates into high prices for the Japanese consumer. In exchange for high prices,

the Japanese consumer gets variety, services, and, what may be unique to Japanese department stores, cultural enlightenment.

But there are winds of change. Department stores' sales fell for 45 straight months from 1992 to late 1995. There was a slight increase prior to a sales tax increase, but a downward trend started by mid-1997. The Japanese like the amenities of department stores, but they are beginning to take notice of the wave of "new" discount stores that are challenging the traditional retail system by offering quality products at sharply reduced prices. Aoyama Trading Company, which opened a discount men's suit store in the heart of Ginza, where Tokyo's most prestigious department stores are located, may be the future. The owner says he can sell suits for two-thirds the department store price by purchasing directly from manufacturers. Fast Retailing Company, which operates the spectacularly successful Uni-Qlo clothing brand stores, took a Gap-like approach to clothes by selling simple and casual wear. Many people weave through its aisles to pay rock-bottom prices. Another omen may be Toys "R" Us, which opened 100 discount toy stores by 2000 and is now the largest toy retailer in Japan. Department store response was to discount toy prices, for the first time, by as much as 30 percent. As one discounter after another "cherry picks" item after item to discount, can department stores continue to be "total life-style enterprises"? Will there be a Mitsukoshi, as we know it today, in 2011?

Sources: Virginia Kouyoumdjian, "Retailing in Japan: The U.S. Revolution," *American Chamber of Commerce in Japan Journal,* www.accj.or.jp (September 1997); "Tokyo Department Store Sales Slip 0.6% in April," Kyodo World News Service, May 16, 2000; "Japanese Retailers Still Struggling to Make a Sale," Reuters, May 24, 2000; and Fred Crawford, "Business without Borders," *Chain Store Age,* December 2001, p. 86–96.

**Changes in the Japanese Distribution System.**  SII and deregulation caused changes in Japanese distribution practices, but it will ultimately be those merchants challenging the traditional ways by giving the consumer quality products at competitive, fair prices that will bring about the demise of the traditional distribution system. Specialty discounters are sprouting up everywhere, and entrepreneurs are slashing prices by buying direct and avoiding the distribution system altogether. For example, Kojima, a consumer electronics discounter, practices what it calls "global purchasing" and buys merchandise anywhere in the world as cheaply as possible. Kojima's tie with General Electric enables it to offer a 410-liter GE refrigerator for $640, down from the typical price of $1,925, and to reduce the 550-liter model from $3,462 to $1,585.

The "new" retailers are relatively small and account for no more than 5 percent of retail sales, compared with 14 percent for all specialty discounters in the United States. But the impact extends beyond their share of market because they are forcing the system to change.[10] Traditional retailers are modifying marketing and sales strategies in response to the new competition as well so as to take advantage of changing Japanese lifestyles. There are also indications that some wholesalers are modernizing and consolidating operations as more retailers demand to buy direct from the manufacturer or from the largest wholesalers. The process is slow because the characteristics of the distribution system are deeply rooted in the cultural history of Japan. However, the long supply chain consisting of many layers of middlemen in Japan is vulnerable to the efficiencies that business-to-business (B2B) commerce provides. Because the Internet allows suppliers and retailers to seek the cheapest price in the global market, it will be harder for the many Japanese middlemen to maintain the control they had.

Similarly, traditional Japanese retailing is slowly giving ground to specialty stores, supermarkets, discounters, and convenience stores. Fast Retailing, a casual-clothing retailer, features good clothes at bargain prices. The store can sell cheaply without lowering quality because it shuns the traditional middlemen and designs its own clothes and sources them directly from factories in China. In 12 months, Fast Retailing's sales jumped by a third to $927 million, just as Japanese retail sales showed their thirty-sixth consecutive monthly drop.

*Konbini,* as convenience stores are called in Japan, are among those retailers bringing about a revolution in Japanese retailing. Besides the traditional array of convenience goods, *konbini* are adding an Internet feature whereby customers can pay bills, bank, or purchase travel packages, music, and merchandise on in-store terminals or over the Internet at home. Seven-Eleven Japan, with 8,000 outlets, has a joint venture with  www.7dream.com. Instead of offering door-to-door delivery, 7dream wants to lure customers to the nearest 7-Eleven store to pay and pick up purchases. What seemed to be an impenetrable tradition-bound distribution system just a few years ago now is on the verge of radical change. Japanese retailing is following a direction similar to that of the United States decades earlier and may not be recognizable in a decade or two.

## Trends: From Traditional to Modern Channel Structures

Today, few countries are so sufficiently isolated that they are unaffected by global economic and political changes. These currents of change are altering all levels of the economic fabric, including the distribution structure. Traditional channel structures are giving way to new forms, new alliances, and new processes—some more slowly than others, but all are changing.[11] Pressures for change in a country come from within and without. Multinational marketers are seeking ways to profitably tap market segments that are served by costly, traditional distribution systems. Direct marketing, door-to-door selling, hypermarkets, discount houses, shopping malls, catalog selling, the Internet, and other distribution methods are being introduced in an attempt to provide efficient distribution channels.

Some important trends in distribution will eventually lead to greater commonality than disparity among middlemen in different countries. Wal-Mart, for example, is expanding all over the world—from Mexico to Brazil and from Europe to Asia. Avon is expanding into Eastern Europe; Mary Kay Cosmetics and Amway into China; and L.L. Bean and Lands' End made successful entry into the Japanese market. The effect of all these intrusions into the traditional distribution systems is change that will make discounting, self-service, supermarkets, mass merchandising and e-commerce concepts common all over the world, and that elevates the competitive climate to a level not known before.

[10]Adrian Slywotzky and Richard Wise, "An Unfinished Revolution," *Sloan Management Review,* Spring 2003, pp. 94–95.

[11]"When You Can't Sell the Goods, Sell the Shop; Retailing," *The Economist,* January 18, 2003, pp. 61–61.

## CROSSING BORDERS 14.2  Big-Box Cookie-Cutter Stores Don't Always Work

Wal-Mart, JCPenney, and Office Depot are all going global with their successful U.S. operating strategy. Friendly service, low prices, extensive variety, and apples-to-appliance offerings—all hallmarks of such stores—make tradition-bound retail foreign markets look ripe to pick with their poor service, high prices, and limited products. Counting on their tremendous buying power and operating efficiency to enable them to lower prices, such large retailers went global. But not all is the same the world over. Adaptation is still important, and many had to adapt their operating strategy to accommodate cultural and business differences. Growth strategies must be supported by three foundations: (1) The retailer must offer a competitively superior product as defined by local customers, (2) the retailer must be able to develop superior economies across the value chain that delivers the product to the local consumer, and (3) global retailers must be able to execute in the local environment.

Consider, for example, some of the problems U.S. retailers had when building their global strategies on these three pillars.

- In fashion and clothing markets, personal taste is critically important in the buying decision. Distinctions in culture, climate, and even physiology demand that products be tailored to each market. Tight skirts, blouses, and any other article that tightly hugs the female silhouette are sure sellers in Southern Europe and are sure losers in the north. Dutch women bicycle to work, so tight skirts are out. French men insist that trousers be suitable for cuffs; German men cannot be bothered with cuffs. Rayon and other artificial fabrics are impossible to sell in Germany, but next door in Holland artificial fabrics are popular because they are much cheaper.

- The best-selling children's lines in northern Europe don't have a significant following in France; the French dress their children as little adults, not as kids. One of the best sellers is a downsized version of a women's clothing line for girls.

- The lack of sunshine in Northern Europe means that lime green fashions don't sell well there;

consumers sense that the color leaves a rather sickly impression. But in the south, lime green looks great with a St. Tropez tan.

- Operational costs vary too. Costs in the United States, where the minimum wage is $5.15 per hour, are dramatically different than in France, where the minimum wage is over $10.00, including employer social charges. As a consequence, Toys "R" Us was forced to adapt its operating structure in France, where it uses one-third fewer employees per store than it does in the United States.

- The image of Sam Walton's English setter on packages of its private-label dog food, Ol' Roy, was replaced with a terrier after Wal-Mart's German executives explained that terriers are popular in Germany, while setters aren't familiar.

- JCPenney is closing its five home-furnishing stores in Japan, in part because so many products, from curtains to bed sheets, had to be made differently there.

- Office Depot closed its U.S.-style cookie-cutter stores in Japan and reopened stores one-third the size of the larger ones. Customers were put off by the warehouse-like atmosphere and confused by the English-language signs. The new stores have signs in Japanese and are stocked with office products more familiar to Japanese and purchased locally, such as two-ring loose-leaf binders rather than the typical three-ring binders sold in the United States.

- After initially doing well, Starbucks in no longer making a profit in Japan. It appears to be a matter of taste. One consumer reports, "The coffee tastes artificial."

Sources: Ernest Beck and Emily Nelson, "As Wal-Mart Invades Europe, Rivals Rush to Match Its Formula," *Wall Street Journal*, October 6, 1999; John C. Koopman, "Successful Global Retailers: A Rare Breed," *Canadian Manager*, April 2000, p. 22; Yumiko Ono, "U.S. Superstores Find Japanese Are a Hard Sell," *Wall Street Journal*, February 14, 2000, p. C1; and Stanley Holmes, Irene M. Kunii, Jack Ewing, Kerry Capell, "For Starbucks, There's No Place Like Home," *BusinessWeek*, June 9, 2003, p. 48.

As U.S. retailers invade Europe, staid nationally based retailers are merging with former competitors and companies from other countries to form Europeanwide enterprises. Carrefour, a French global marketer, merged with Promodes, one of its fierce French competitors, to create, in the words of its CEO, "a worldwide retail leader." The U.K. supermarket giant Sainsbury entered an alliance with Esselunga of Italy (supermarkets),

Docks de France (hypermarkets, supermarkets, and discount stores), and Belgium's Delhaize (supermarkets). The alliance provides the four companies the opportunity to pool their experience and buying power to better face growing competition and opportunity afforded by the single European market and the euro.

While European retailers see a unified Europe as an opportunity for pan-European expansion, foreign retailers are attracted by the high margins and prices. Costco, the U.S.-based warehouse retailer, saw the high gross margins that British supermarkets command (7 to 8 percent compared with 2.5 to 3.0 percent in the United States) as an opportunity. Costco prices will be 10 to 20 percent cheaper than rival local retailers.

Expansion outside of the home country, as well as new types of retailing, is occurring throughout Europe. El Corte Inglés, Spain's largest department store chain, is not only moving into Portugal and other European countries but was also one of the first retailers to offer a virtual supermarket on the Internet (www.elcorteingles.es) and to sponsor two 24-hour home shopping channels in Spain. It may very well be that the Internet will be the most important trend affecting distribution.

One of Wal-Mart's strengths is its internal Internet-based system, which makes its transactions with suppliers more efficient and lowers its cost of operations. Indeed, it is buying ailing retailers around the world with the intention of "saving them" with its distribution technologies.[12] This same type of system is available on the Internet for both business-to-business and business-to-consumer transactions. For example, General Motors, Ford Motor Company, and DaimlerChrysler created a single online site called Covisint (www.covisint.com) for purchasing automotive parts from suppliers, which is expected to save the companies millions of dollars. A typical purchase order costs Ford $150, whereas a real-time order via Covisint costs about $15. Sears Roebuck and Carrefour of France created GlobalNetXchange (www.gnx.com), a retail exchange that allows retailers and their suppliers to conduct transactions online. Any company with a Web browser can access the exchange to buy, sell, trade, or auction goods and services. Described as "one of the most dramatic changes in consumer-products distribution of the decade," the exchange is expected to lower costs for both buyer and supplier. As more such exchanges evolve, one can only speculate about the impact on traditional channel middlemen.

We have already seen the impact on traditional retailing within the last few years caused by e-commerce retailers such as Amazon.com,[13] Dell Computer, e-Toys, eBay, and others—all of which are expanding globally. Most brick-and-mortar retailers are experimenting with or have fully developed websites, some of which are merely extensions of their regular stores, allowing them to extend their reach globally. L.L. Bean, Eddie Bauer, and Lands' End are a few examples.

One of the most challenging aspects of Web sales is delivery of goods. As discussed earlier, one of the innovative features of the 7dream program at 7-Eleven stores in Japan is the use of convenience stores for pick-up points for Web orders. It worked so well in Japan that Ito-Yokado Corporation, owner of Seven-Eleven Japan and 72 percent of the U.S. chain, is exporting the idea to U.S. stores. In the Dallas–Fort Worth area, 250 stores installed ATM-like machines tied into a delivery and payment system that promises to make 7-Elevens a depot for e-commerce. FedEx, UPS, and other package delivery services that are the backbone of e-commerce delivery in the United States are offering similar services for foreign customers of U.S. e-commerce companies as well as for foreign-based e-commerce companies. When goods cross borders, UPS and others offer seamless shipments, including customs and brokerage. Most of these service companies are established in Europe and Japan and are building networks in Latin America and China.

The impact of these and other trends will change traditional distribution and marketing systems. While this latest retailing revolution is in flux, new retailing and middlemen

[12]Deborah Ball and Ann Zimmerman, "Wal-Mart's Offer for Safeway Comes with Risks Built In," *Wall Street Journal,* January 15, 2003, p. B12.

[13]Jeffrey A. Trachtenberg, Charles Goldsmith, and Cris Prystay, "Stores, Families Strategize to Meet Harry Potter," *Wall Street Journal,* June 18, 2003, p. B1.

Now that Russians can own their homes, they're spending fast in home improvement stores like this one in St. Petersburg. In English it would be called "Super Home."

systems will be invented, and established companies will experiment, seeking ways to maintain their competitive edge. These changes will resonate throughout the distribution chain before new concepts are established and the system stabilizes. Not since the upheaval that occurred in U.S. distribution after World War II that ultimately led to the "big box" type of retailer has there been such potential for change in distribution systems. This time, however, such change will not be limited mostly to the United States—it will be worldwide. Competition will translate efficiencies into lower consumer prices and force distribution to become even more innovative.

## Distribution Patterns

Even though patterns of distribution are in a state of change and new patterns are developing, international marketers need a general awareness of the traditional distribution base. The "traditional" system will not change overnight, and vestiges of it will remain for years to come. Nearly every international firm is forced by the structure of the market to use at least some middlemen in the distribution arrangement. It is all too easy to conclude that, because the structural arrangements of foreign and domestic distribution seem alike, foreign channels are the same as or similar to domestic channels of the same name. This is misleading. Only when the varied intricacies of actual distribution patterns are understood can the complexity of the distribution task be appreciated. The following description should convey a sense of the variety of distribution patterns.

### General Patterns

Generalizing about internal distribution channel patterns of various countries is almost as difficult as generalizing about behavior patterns of people. Despite similarities, marketing channels are not the same throughout the world. Marketing methods taken for granted in the United States are rare in many countries.

**Middlemen Services.** The service attitudes of people in trade vary sharply at both the retail and wholesale levels from country to country. In Egypt, for example, the primary purpose of the simple trading system is to handle the physical distribution of available goods. On the other hand, when margins are low and there is a continuing battle for customer preference, both wholesalers and retailers try to offer extra services to make their goods attractive to consumers. When middlemen are disinterested in promoting or selling individual items of merchandise, the manufacturer must provide adequate inducement to the middlemen or undertake much of the promotion and selling effort. Such is the case in China, where wholesalers see their function as storing the goods and waiting for their customers to come to them. Exhibit 14.2 gives an idea of the relative importance of different types of middlemen in the United States, Germany, and Japan.

**Line Breadth.**    Every nation has a distinct pattern relative to the breadth of line carried by wholesalers and retailers. The distribution system of some countries is characterized by middlemen who carry or can get everything; in others, every middleman is a specialist dealing only in extremely narrow lines. Government regulations in some countries limit the breadth of line that can be carried by middlemen, and licensing requirements to handle certain merchandise are not uncommon.

**Costs and Margins.**    Cost levels and middleman margins vary widely from country to country, depending on the level of competition, services offered, efficiencies or inefficiencies of scale, and geographic and turnover factors related to market size, purchasing power, tradition, and other basic determinants. In India, competition in large cities is so intense that costs are low and margins thin; in rural areas, however, the lack of capital has permitted the few traders with capital to gain monopolies, with consequent high prices and wide margins.

**Channel Length.**    Some correlation may be found between the stage of economic development and the length of marketing channels. In every country, channels are likely to be shorter for industrial goods and high-priced consumer goods than for low-priced products. In general, there is an inverse relationship between channel length and the size of the purchase. Combination wholesaler-retailers or semi-wholesalers exist in many countries, adding one or two links to the length of the distribution chain. In China, for example, the traditional distribution system for over-the-counter drugs consists of large local wholesalers divided into three levels. First-level wholesalers supply drugs to major cities such as Beijing and Shanghai. The second level services medium-sized cities, and the third level distributes to counties and cities with 100,000 people or less. It can be profitable for a company to sell directly to the two top-level wholesalers and have them sell to the third level, which is so small that it would be unprofitable for the company to seek out.

**Nonexistent Channels.**    One of the things companies discover about international channel-of-distribution patterns is that in many countries adequate market coverage through a simple channel of distribution is nearly impossible.[14] In many instances, appropriate channels do not exist; in others, parts of a channel system are available but other parts are not. In Peru, for example, the informal distribution network accounts for almost a quarter of all retail cash sales. The ubiquitous street markets and ambulatory sellers offer far wider market penetration than formal distribution companies. Further, their prices are generally lower than traditional retailers, partly because of lower overhead costs compared with the higher costs generated by the overextended formal distribution chain of the traditional retailer. Thus several distinct distribution channels are necessary to reach different segments of a market; channels suitable for distribution in urban areas seldom provide adequate rural coverage.

**Blocked Channels.**    International marketers may be blocked from using the channel of their choice. Blockage can result from competitors' already-established lines in the various channels or from trade associations or cartels having closed certain channels. The classic example of blocked channels is Japan, as discussed earlier, but it is by no means the only example. In China FedEx and DHL[15] initially ran into the Chinese government's own mail service as a "blocking" competitor.[16]

Associations of middlemen sometimes restrict the number of distribution alternatives available to a producer. Druggists in many countries inhibit distribution of a wide range of goods through any retail outlets except drugstores. The drugstores, in turn, are supplied

---

[14]Harry Maurer, "Where Coke Is It—If the Trucks Get Through," *BusinessWeek,* September 24, 2001, pp. 20E1–2.

[15]Lara Wozniak, "DHL and FedEx Race to Integrate China," *Far Eastern Economic Review,* February 27, 2003, pp. 42–44.

[16]Charles Hutzler and Scott Neuman, "Express-Mail Firms Get Unlikely Ally in China—As Beijing Restricts Access, One Ministry Protests," *Wall Street Journal,* May 13, 2002, p. A13.

PEMEX (Petróleos Mexicanos), the Mexican national oil company, will not let foreign firms compete there. However, in Malaysia a Mobil station sits right across the boulevard from a government-owned PETRONAS (Petroliam Nasional) station.

by a relatively small number of wholesalers who have long-established relationships with their suppliers. Thus through a combination of competition and association, a producer may be kept out of the market completely. In the United Kingdom, simple magnifying reading glasses that can be purchased in a dozen different types of stores in the United States can only be purchased by prescription through registered optical stores, which are controlled by a few large companies.

**Stocking.**   The high cost of credit, the danger of loss through inflation, a lack of capital, and other concerns cause foreign middlemen in many countries to limit inventories. This often results in out-of-stock conditions and sales lost to competitors. Physical distribution lags intensify the problem so that in many cases the manufacturer must provide local warehousing or extend long credit to encourage middlemen to carry large inventories. Often large inventories are out of the question for small stores with limited floor space. Considerable ingenuity, assistance, and perhaps pressure are required to induce middlemen in most countries to carry adequate or even minimal inventories. BMW took a unique step to alleviate this problem in Germany. They encourage their customers to pick up their new cars at the factory by providing an amusement park for the kids adjacent to the plant.[17]

**Power and Competition.**   Distribution power tends to concentrate in countries where a few large wholesalers distribute to a mass of small middlemen. Large wholesalers generally finance middlemen downstream. The strong allegiance they command from their customers enables them to effectively block existing channels and force an outsider to rely on less effective and more costly distribution.

**Retail Patterns**   Retailing shows even greater diversity in its structure than does wholesaling. In Italy and Morocco, retailing is composed largely of specialty houses that carry narrow lines, whereas in Finland most retailers carry a more general line of merchandise. Retail size is represented at one end by Japan's giant department store, Mitsukoshi, which reportedly enjoys the patronage of more than 100,000 customers every day, and at the other extreme by the market of Ibadan, Nigeria, where some 3,000 one- or two-person stalls serve not many more customers.

---

[17]Carol J. Williams, "German Car Buyers' Favorite Pickup," *Los Angeles Times,* April 16, 2002, p. A1.

**Exhibit 14.3**
Retail Structure in
Selected Countries

Source: Euromonitor, World
Bank 2003.

| Country | All Retailers (000) | People Served per Retailer | Internet Users (per 1000) |
|---|---|---|---|
| United States | 702 | 395 | 501 |
| Canada | 112 | 276 | 434 |
| Argentina | 296 | 127 | 88 |
| Germany | 410 | 200 | 374 |
| Poland | 390 | 99 | 98 |
| Israel | 53 | 119 | 281 |
| South Africa | 93 | 482 | 71 |
| China | 21,188 | 61 | 11 |
| Japan | 1,202 | 106 | 440 |
| Australia | 93 | 208 | 371 |

**Size Patterns.**   The extremes in size in retailing are similar to those that predominate in wholesaling. Exhibit 14.3 dramatically illustrates some of the variations in size and number of retailers per person that exist in some countries. The retail structure and the problems it engenders cause real difficulties for the international marketing firm selling consumer goods. Large dominant retailers can be sold direct, but there is no adequate way to directly reach small retailers who, in the aggregate, handle a great volume of sales. In Italy, official figures show there are 865,000 retail stores, or one store for every 66 Italians. Of the 340,000 food stores, fewer than 1,500 can be classified as large. Thus middlemen are a critical factor in adequate distribution in Italy.

Underdeveloped countries present similar problems. Among the large supermarket chains in South Africa there is considerable concentration. One thousand of the country's 31,000 stores control 60 percent of all grocery sales, leaving the remaining 40 percent of sales to be spread among 30,000 stores. It may be difficult to reach the 40 percent of the market served by those 30,000 stores. In black communities in particular, retailing is on a small scale—cigarettes are often sold singly, and the entire fruit inventory may consist of four apples in a bowl.

Retailing around the world was in a state of active ferment for several years. The rate of change is directly related to the stage and speed of economic development, and even the least-developed countries are experiencing dramatic changes. Supermarkets of one variety or another are blossoming in developed and underdeveloped countries alike. Discount houses that sell everything from powdered milk and canned chili to Korean TVs and VCRs are thriving and expanding worldwide.

**Direct Marketing.**   Selling directly to the consumer through the mail, by telephone, or door-to-door is often the approach of choice in markets with insufficient or underdeveloped distribution systems.[18] The approach, of course, also works well in the most affluent markets.[19] Amway, operating in 42 foreign countries,[20] successfully expanded into Latin America and Asia with its method of direct marketing.[21] Companies that enlist individuals to sell their products are proving to be especially popular in Eastern Europe and other countries, where many people are looking for ways to become entrepreneurs. In the Czech Republic, for example, Amway Corporation signed up 25,000 Czechs as distributors and sold 40,000 starter kits at $83 each in its first two weeks of business. Avon is another American company that is expanding dramatically overseas.[22]

[18]Miriam Jordon, "Knock, Knock: In Brazil, an Army of Underemployed Goes Door-to-Door," *Wall Street Journal,* February 19, 2003, p. A1.

[19]Lorna Tan, "100,000 People Here Are in Multi-Level Marketing," *Straits Times,* April 5, 2003, p. C1.

[20]Thomas A. Foster, "Amway's Dutch Gateway to European Success," *Logistics Management,* May 2003, 42(5), pp. E65–E67.

[21]Leslie Chang, "Amway in China, Once Barred, Now Booming," *Wall Street Journal,* March 12, 2003, p. B1.

[22]"Avon Products Inc.: Earnings Forecast Is Raised On International Performance," *Wall Street Journal,* March 31, 2003, p. B4.

## CROSSING BORDERS 14.3 It Depends on What "Not Satisfied" Means

Amway's policy is that dissatisfied customers can get a full refund at any time, no questions asked—even if the returned bottles are empty. This refund policy is a courtesy to customers and testament that the company stands behind its products, and it is the same all over the world. But such capitalistic concepts are somewhat unfamiliar in China.

The best game in town for months among the rising ranks of Shanghai's entrepreneurs was an $84 investment for a box of soaps and cosmetics that they could sell as Amway distributors. Word of this no-lose proposition quickly spread, with some people repackaging the soap, selling it, and then turning in the containers for a refund. Others dispensed with selling altogether and scoured garbage bins instead—showing up at Amway's Shanghai offices with bags full of bottles to be redeemed.

One salesman got nearly $10,000 for eight sacks full of all kinds of empty Amway containers. And at least one barbershop started using Amway shampoos for free and returning each empty bottle for a full refund. In a few weeks refunds were totaling more than $100,000 a day. "Perhaps we were too lenient," said Amway's

Shanghai chief. Amway changed the policy, only to have hundreds of angry Amway distributors descend on the company's offices to complain that they were cheated out of their money. Amway called a press conference to explain that it wasn't changing its refund policy, simply raising the standard for what is deemed dissatisfaction. If someone returns half a bottle, fine, but for empties Amway announced it would check records to see if the person had a pattern of return.

But the company didn't anticipate the unusual sense of entitlement it engendered in China. The satisfaction-guaranteed policy didn't spell out specifically what dissatisfaction meant, something people in the Western world understood. "We thought that it would be understood here, too." The change in policy left some people dissatisfied. One distributor protested, "Don't open a company if you can't afford losses."

Source: Craig S. Smith, "Distribution Remains the Key Problem for Market Makers," *Business China*, May 13, 1996, p. 4; and "In China, Some Distributors Have Really Cleaned Up with Amway," *Wall Street Journal*, August 4, 1997, p. B1; and Leslie Chang, "Amway in China, Once Barred, Now Booming," *Wall Street Journal*, March 12, 2003, B1.

Direct sales through catalogs are a successful way to enter foreign markets. In Japan, it is an important way to break the trade barrier imposed by the Japanese distribution system. For example, a U.S. mail-order company, Shop America, teamed up with Seven-Eleven Japan to distribute catalogs in its 4,000 stores. Shop America sells items such as compact discs, Canon cameras, and Rolex watches for 30 to 50 percent less than Tokyo stores; a Canon Autoboy camera sells for $260 in Tokyo and $180 in the Shop America catalog.

Many catalog companies are finding they need to open telephone service centers in a country to accommodate customers with questions or problems. Hanna Andersson, for example, received complaints that it was too difficult to get questions answered and to place orders by telephone, so it opened a service center with 24 telephone operators to assist customers who generate over $5 million in sales annually. Many catalog companies also have active websites that augment their catalog sales.

**Resistance to Change.**   Efforts to improve the efficiency of the distribution system, new types of middlemen, and other attempts to change traditional ways are typically viewed as threatening and are thus resisted.[23] A classic example is restructuring of the film distribution business being caused by the fast-changing technologies of digitization and piracy.[24] Laws abound that protect the entrenched in their positions. In Italy, a new retail outlet must obtain a license from a municipal board composed of local tradespeople. In a two-year period, some 200 applications were made and only 10 new licenses granted. Opposition to retail innovation is everywhere, yet in the face of all

---

[23]Dan Bilefsky, "A New Facet of Diamond Industry: Indians," *Wall Street Journal*, May 27, 2003, p. B1.
[24]"Hollywood Blockbusters Mutating," *The Economist*, April 26, 2003, p. 55.

**Exhibit 14.4**
International Channel-
of-Distribution Alternatives

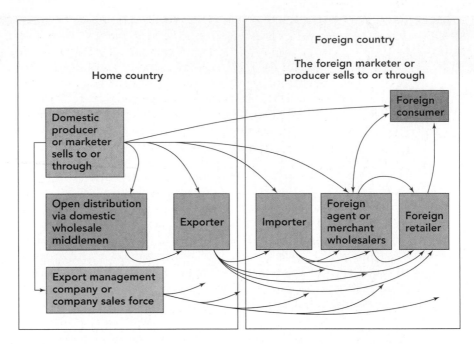

the restrictions and hindrances, self-service, discount merchandising, liberal store hours, and large-scale merchandising continue to grow because they offer the consumer convenience and a broad range of quality product brands at advantageous prices. Ultimately the consumer does prevail.

## Alternative Middleman Choices

A marketer's options range from assuming the entire distribution activity (by establishing its own subsidiaries and marketing directly to the end user) to depending on intermediaries for distribution of the product. Channel selection must be given considerable thought because once initiated it is difficult to change, and if it proves inappropriate, future growth of market share may be affected.

The channel process includes all activities, beginning with the manufacturer and ending with the final consumer. This means the seller must exert influence over two sets of channels: one in the home country and one in the foreign-market country. Exhibit 14.4 shows some of the possible channel-of-distribution alternatives. The arrows show those to whom the producer and each of the middlemen might sell. In the home country, the seller must have an organization (generally the international marketing division of a company) to deal with channel members needed to move goods between countries. In the foreign market, the seller must supervise the channels that supply the product to the end user. Ideally, the company wants to control or be directly involved in the process through the various channel members to the final user. To do less may result in unsatisfactory distribution and the failure of marketing objectives. In practice, however, such involvement throughout the channel process is not always practical or cost effective. Consequently, selection of channel members and effective controls are high priorities in establishing the distribution process.

After the marketer clarifies company objectives and policies, the next step is the selection of specific intermediaries needed to develop a channel. External middlemen are differentiated on whether or not they take title to the goods: **Agent middlemen** represent the principal rather than themselves, whereas **merchant middlemen** take title to the goods and buy and sell on their own account. The distinction between agent and merchant middlemen is important because a manufacturer's control of the distribution process is affected by who has title to the goods in the channel.

Agent middlemen work on commission and arrange for sales in the foreign country but do not take title to the merchandise. By using agents, the manufacturer assumes trading risk but maintains the right to establish policy guidelines and prices and to require its agents to provide sales records and customer information.

Merchant middlemen actually take title to manufacturers' goods and assume the trading risks, so they tend to be less controllable than agent middlemen. Merchant middlemen provide a variety of import and export wholesaling functions involved in purchasing for their own account and selling in other countries. Because merchant middlemen primarily are concerned with sales and profit margins on their merchandise, they are frequently criticized for not representing the best interests of a manufacturer. Unless they have a franchise or a strong and profitable brand, merchant middlemen seek goods from any source and are likely to have low brand loyalty. Ease of contact, minimized credit risk, and elimination of all merchandise handling outside the United States are some of the advantages of using merchant middlemen.

Middlemen are not clear-cut, precise, easily defined entities. It is exceptional to find a firm that represents one of the pure types identified here. Thus intimate knowledge of middlemen functions is especially important in international activity because misleading titles can fool a marketer unable to look beyond mere names. What are the functions of a British middleman called a stockist, or one called an exporter or importer? One exporter may, in fact, be an agent middleman, whereas another is a merchant. Many, if not most, international middlemen wear several hats and can be clearly identified only in the context of their relationship with a specific firm.

Only by analyzing middlemen functions in skeletal simplicity can the nature of the channels be determined. Three alternatives are presented: first, middlemen physically located in the manufacturer's home country; next, middlemen located in foreign countries; and finally, government-affiliated middlemen.

## Home-Country Middlemen

**Home-country middlemen**, or *domestic middlemen,* located in the producing firm's country, provide marketing services from a domestic base. By selecting domestic middlemen as intermediaries in the distribution processes, companies relegate foreign-market distribution to others. Domestic middlemen offer many advantages for companies with small international sales volume, those inexperienced with foreign markets, those not wanting to become immediately involved with the complexities of international marketing, and those wanting to sell abroad with minimum financial and management commitment. A major trade-off when using home-country middlemen is limited control over the entire process. Domestic middlemen are most likely to be used when the marketer is uncertain or desires to minimize financial and management investment. A brief discussion of the more frequently used types of domestic middlemen follows.

**Manufacturers' Retail Stores.**   An important channel of distribution for a large number of manufacturers is the owned, or perhaps franchised,[25] retail store. Disney, Benetton,[26] and many of the classic Italian luxury goods makers take this approach.[27]

**Global Retailers.**   As global retailers like Ikea,[28] Costco, Sears Roebuck, Toys "R" Us, and Wal-Mart[29] expand their global coverage, they are becoming major domestic middlemen for international markets.[30] Wal-Mart, with 1,028 stores in nine foreign markets, is an attractive entry point to international markets for U.S. suppliers. Wal-Mart offers an effective way to enter international markets with a minimum of experience. For example, Pacific Connections, a California manufacturer of handbags with $70 million in sales, ventured into overseas markets in Argentina, Brazil, Canada, and Mexico through

---

[25]McDonald's also fits this description. Robert Baker, "Are the Golden Arches That Tarnished?" *BusinessWeek,* April 14, 2003, p. 91.

[26]Gail Edmondson, "Has Benetton Stopped Unraveling?" *BusinessWeek,* June 30, 2003, p. 76.

[27]Cecilie Rohwedder, "Viva la Differenza, Pursuing Jaded Jet-Setters, High-End Brands Now Strive to Vary Stores, Merchandise," *Wall Street Journal,* January 29, 2003, p. B1.

[28]"To Russian, with Love: The Multinational's Song," *BusinessWeek,* September 16, 2002, pp. 44–45.

[29]"Sales Abroad Boost Wal-Mart," *Los Angeles Times,* February 10, 2003, p. C3.

[30]Peter Gwynne, "The Myth of Globalization?" *Sloan Management Review,* winter 2003, 44(2), p. 11.

Remember for a moment the scene in the Pixar movie *Monsters Inc.*—millions of doors on conveyor belts. That scene is reminiscent of the inside of the Nike's European distribution center in Laakdal, Belgium. The shoes come from a variety of Asian low-cost manufacturers and arrive at the center via Rotterdam and Antwerp and the adjacent canal. Twelve thousand people work at the heavily automated facility where 8 million pairs of shoes are sorted and then shipped to customers all over the continent via truck. Even as sales grow the company will not need to expand the center because the trend is for the factories to ship directly to the major European retailers including the Nike Sport in St. Petersburg pictured in Chapter 10.

its ties to Wal-Mart. Likewise, with easing trade restrictions such as NAFTA, new global retailers are being created—Gigante from Mexico is a good example of this trend.[31]

**Export Management Companies.** The *export management company (EMC)* is an important middleman for firms with relatively small international volume or for those unwilling to involve their own personnel in the international function.[32] EMCs range in size from 1 person upward to 100 and handle about 10 percent of the manufactured goods exported. An example of an EMC is a Washington, D.C.–based company that has exclusive agreements with ten U.S. manufacturers of orthopedic equipment and markets these products on a worldwide basis.

Typically, the EMC becomes an integral part of the marketing operations of its client companies. Working under the names of the manufacturers, the EMC functions as a low-cost, independent marketing department with direct responsibility to the parent firm. The working relationship is so close that customers are often unaware they are not dealing directly with the export department of the company (see Exhibit 14.5).

The export management company may take full or partial responsibility for promotion of the goods, credit arrangements, physical handling, market research, and information on financial, patent, and licensing matters. An EMC's specialization in a given field often makes it possible to offer a level of service that could not be attained by the manufacturer without years of groundwork. Traditionally, the EMC works on commission, although an increasing number are buying products on their own account.

**Exhibit 14.5**
How Does an EMC
Operate?

Source: "The Export Management
Company," U.S. Department of
Commerce, Washington, D.C.

Most export management companies offer a wide range of services and assistance, including the following:

Researching foreign markets for a client's products. Traveling overseas to determine the best method of distributing the product. Appointing distributors or commission representative as needed in individual foreign countries, frequently within an already existing overseas network created for similiar goods. Exhibiting the client's products at international trade shows, such as U.S. Department of Commerce–sponsored commercial exhibitions at trade fairs and U.S. Export Development Offices around the world.

Handling the routine details in getting the product to the foreign customer—export declarations, shipping and customs documentation, insurance, banking, and instructions for special export packing and marking.

Granting the customary finance terms to the trade abroad and assuring payment to the manufacturer of the product.

Preparing advertising and sales literature in cooperation with the manufacturer and adapting it to overseas requirements for use in personal contacts with foreign buyers.

Corresponding in the necessary foreign languages.

Making sure that goods being shipped are suitable for local conditions and meet overseas legal and trade norms, including labeling, packaging, purity, and electrical characteristics. Advising on overseas patent and trademark protection requirements.

[31]Denise Bonilla, "Latino Market Arrives with Giant Aspirations," *Los Angeles Times,* May 7, 2003, p. B3.
[32]Courtney Fingar, "The ABCs of EMCs," *Global Business,* May 2001, pp. 51–56.

Two of the chief advantages of EMCs are minimum investment on the part of the company to get into international markets, and no commitment of company personnel or major expenditure of managerial effort. The result, in effect, is an extension of the market for the firm with negligible financial or personnel commitments.

The major disadvantage is that EMCs can seldom afford to make the kind of market investment needed to establish deep distribution for products because they must have immediate sales payout to survive. Such a situation does not offer the market advantages gained by a company that can afford to use company personnel. Carefully selected EMCs can do an excellent job, but the manufacturer must remember that the EMC depends on sales volume for compensation and probably will not push the manufacturer's line if it is spread too thinly, generates too small a volume from a given principal, or cannot operate profitably in the short run. In such cases the EMC becomes an order taker and not the desired substitute for an international marketing department.

**Trading Companies.**   Trading companies have a long and honorable history as important intermediaries in the development of trade between nations. **Trading companies** accumulate, transport, and distribute goods from many countries. In concept, the trading company has changed little in hundreds of years.

The British firm Gray MacKenzie and Company is typical of companies operating in the Middle East. It has some 70 salespeople and handles consumer products ranging from toiletries to outboard motors and Scotch whiskey. The key advantage to this type of trading company is that it covers the entire Middle East.

Large, established trading companies generally are located in developed countries; they sell manufactured goods to developing countries and buy raw materials and unprocessed goods. Japanese trading companies *(sogo shosha)*[33] date back to the early 1700s and operate both as importers and exporters. Some 300 are engaged in foreign and domestic trade through 2,000 branch offices outside Japan and handle over $1 trillion in trading volume annually. Japanese trading companies account for 61 percent of all Japanese imports and 39 percent of all exports, or about one-fifth of Japan's entire GDP.

For companies seeking entrance into the complicated Japanese distribution system, the Japanese trading company offers one of the easiest routes to success. The omnipresent trading companies virtually control distribution through all levels of channels in Japan. Because trading companies may control many of the distributors and maintain broad distribution channels, they provide the best means for intensive coverage of the market.

**U.S. Export Trading Companies.**   The **Export Trading Company (ETC) Act** allows producers of similar products to form export trading companies. A major goal of the ETC Act was to increase U.S. exports by encouraging more efficient export trade services to producers and suppliers in order to improve the availability of trade finance and to remove antitrust disincentives to export activities. By providing U.S. businesses with an opportunity to obtain antitrust preclearance for specified export activities, the ETC Act created a more favorable environment for the formation of joint export ventures. Through such joint ventures, U.S. firms can take advantage of economies of scale, spread risk, and pool their expertise. In addition, through joint selling arrangements, domestic competitors can avoid interfirm rivalry in foreign markets. Prior to the passage of the ETC Act, competing companies could not engage in joint exporting efforts without possible violation of antitrust provisions. The other important provision of the ETC Act is to permit bank holding companies to own ETCs.

Immediately after passage of the ETC Act, several major companies (General Electric, Sears Roebuck, Kmart, and others) announced the development of export trading companies. In most cases, these export firms did not require the protection of the ETC Act since they initially operated independently of other enterprises. They provided international sales for U.S. companies to a limited extent, but primarily they operated as trading companies for their own products. To date, many of the trading companies

---

[33]Dominic Jones, "Developing the Service Front," *Trade Finance,* April 2003, pp. 24–26.

Recall that the Japanese are the world-champion fish consumers at nearly 60 kg per person per year—see Exhibit 4.2. Consequently, just as world prices for cut flowers are set at the Aalsmeer Flower Auction in the Netherlands, world prices for fish are set at the Tsukigi fish market in Tokyo. A big fresh bluefin tuna caught in the Atlantic, iced and shipped by air to Tokyo, can bring $10,000 at auction, and then be shipped by air back to Boston for hungry sushi consumers.

established after passage of the ETC Act have closed their doors or are languishing.

**Complementary Marketers.**   Companies with marketing facilities or contacts in different countries with excess marketing capacity or a desire for a broader product line sometimes take on additional lines for international distribution; although the formal name for such activities is **complementary marketing**, it is commonly called *piggybacking*. General Electric Company has been distributing merchandise from other suppliers for many years. It accepts products that are noncompetitive but complementary and that add to the basic distribution strength of the company itself.

Most piggyback arrangements are undertaken when a firm wants to fill out its product line or keep its seasonal distribution channels functioning throughout the year. Companies may work either on an agency or merchant basis, but the greatest volume of piggyback business is handled on an ownership (merchant) purchase-and-resale arrangement. The selection process for new products for piggyback distribution determines whether (1) the product relates to the product line and contributes to it, (2) the product fits the sales and distribution channel presently employed, (3) there is an adequate margin to make the undertaking worthwhile, and (4) the product will find market acceptance and profitable volume. If these requirements are met, piggybacking can be a logical way of increasing volume and profit for both the carrier and the piggybacker.

**Manufacturer's Export Agent.**   The *manufacturer's export agent (MEA)* is an individual agent middleman or an agent middleman firm providing a selling service for manufacturers. Unlike the EMC, the MEA does not serve as the producer's export department but has a short-term relationship, covers only one or two markets, and operates on a straight commission basis. Another principal difference is that MEAs do business in their own names rather than in the name of the client. Within a limited scope of operation, the MEAs provide services similar to those of the EMC.

**Home-Country Brokers.**   The term *broker* is a catchall for a variety of middlemen performing low-cost agent services. The term is typically applied to import-export brokers who provide the intermediary function of bringing buyers and sellers together and who do not have a continuing relationship with their clients. Most brokers specialize in one or more commodities, for which they maintain contact with major producers and purchasers throughout the world.

**Buying Offices.**   A variety of agent middlemen may be classified simply as buyers or buyers for export. Their common denominator is a primary function of seeking and purchasing merchandise on request from principals; as such, they do not provide a selling service. In fact, their chief emphasis is on flexibility and the ability to find merchandise from any source. They do not often become involved in continuing relationships with domestic suppliers and do not provide a continuing source of representation.

**Selling Groups.**   Several types of arrangements have developed in which various manufacturers or producers cooperate in a joint attempt to sell their merchandise abroad. This may take the form of complementary exporting or of selling to a combined business such as a Webb-Pomerene export association. Both are considered agency arrangements when the exporting is done on a fee or commission basis.

**Webb-Pomerene Export Associations.** *Webb-Pomerene export associations (WPEAs)* are another major form of group exporting. The Webb-Pomerene Act of 1918 made it possible for American business firms to join forces in export activities without being subject to the Sherman Antitrust Act. WPEAs cannot participate in cartels or other international agreements that would reduce competition in the United States, but can offer four major benefits: (1) reduction of export costs, (2) demand expansion through promotion, (3) trade barrier reductions, and (4) improvement of trade terms through bilateral bargaining. Additionally, WPEAs set prices, standardize products, and arrange for disposal of surplus products. Although they account for less than 5 percent of U.S. exports, WPEAs include some of America's blue-chip companies in agricultural products, chemicals and raw materials, forest products, pulp and paper, textiles, rubber products, motion pictures, and television.

**Foreign Sales Corporation.** A *foreign sales corporation (FSC)* is a sales corporation set up in a foreign country or U.S. possession that can obtain a corporate tax exemption on a portion of the earnings generated by the sale or lease of export property. Manufacturers and export groups can form FSCs. An FSC can function as a principal, buying and selling for its own account, or as a commissioned agent. It can be related to a manufacturing parent or can be an independent merchant or broker. The WTO in 2003 ruled FSCs to be in violation of international trade rules, thus starting a major trade dispute with the European Union.[34]

**Export Merchants.** *Export merchants* are essentially domestic merchants operating in foreign markets. As such, they operate much like the domestic wholesaler. Specifically, they purchase goods from a large number of manufacturers, ship them to foreign countries, and take full responsibility for their marketing. Sometimes they utilize their own organizations, but more commonly they sell through middlemen. They may carry competing lines, have full control over prices, and maintain little loyalty to suppliers, although they continue to handle products as long as they are profitable. Canadian wholesalers selling low cost pharmaceuticals to American consumers is an increasingly important, albeit controversial, example.[35]

**Export Jobbers.** *Export jobbers* deal mostly in commodities; they do not take physical possession of goods but assume responsibility for arranging transportation. Because they work on a job-lot basis, they do not provide a particularly attractive distribution alternative for most producers.

Exhibit 14.6 summarizes information pertaining to the major kinds of domestic middlemen operating in foreign markets.[36] No attempt is made to generalize about rates of commission, markup, or pay because many factors influence compensation. Services offered or demanded, market structure, volume, and product type are some of the key determinants. The data represent the predominant patterns of operations; however, individual middlemen of a given type may vary in their operations.

**Foreign-Country Middlemen**

The variety of agent and merchant middlemen in most countries is similar to that in the United States. International marketers seeking greater control over the distribution process may elect to deal directly with middlemen in the foreign market. They gain the advantage of shorter channels and deal with middlemen in constant contact with the market.

Using foreign-country middlemen moves the manufacturer closer to the market and involves the company more closely with problems of language, physical distribution, communications, and financing. Foreign middlemen may be agents or merchants, they may be associated with the parent company to varying degrees, or they may be temporarily

[34]Lawrence B. Lindsey, "How to Start a Trade War," *Wall Street Journal,* June 25, 2003, p. A12.

[35]John Dorschner, "GlaxoSmithKline Discusses Decision to Stop Supplying Some Canadian Wholesalers," *Miami Herald,* March 1, 2003.

[36]See George I. Balabanis, "Factors Affecting Export Intermediaries' Services Offerings: The British Example," *Journal of International Business Studies,* 2000, 31(1), pp. 83–94.

# Exhibit 14.6

Characteristics of Domestic Middlemen Serving Overseas Markets

| Type of Duties | Agent | | | | | Merchant | | | | |
|---|---|---|---|---|---|---|---|---|---|---|
| | EMC | MEA | Broker | Buying Offices | Selling Groups | Norazi | Export Merchant | Export Jobber | Importers and Trading Companies | Complementary Marketers |
| Take title | No* | No | No | No | No | Yes | Yes | Yes | Yes | Yes |
| Take possession | Yes | Yes | No | Yes | Yes | Yes | Yes | No | Yes | Yes |
| Continuing relationship | Yes | Yes | No | Yes | Yes | No | No | Yes | Yes | Yes |
| Share of foreign output | All | All | Any | Small | All | Small | Any | Small | Any | Most |
| Degree of control by principal | Fair | Fair | Nil | Nil | Good | Nil | None | None | Nil | Fair |
| Price authority | Advisory | Advisory | Yes (at market level) | Yes (to buy) | Advisory | Yes | Yes | Yes | No | Some |
| Represent buyer or seller | Seller | Seller | Either | Buyer | Seller | Both | Self | Self | Self | Self |
| Number of principals | Few to many | Few to many | Many | Small | Few | Several per transaction | Many sources | Many sources | Many sources | One per product |
| Arrange shipping | Yes | Yes | Not usually | Yes | Yes | Yes | Yes | Yes | Yes | Yes |
| Type of goods | Manufactured goods and commodities | Staples and commodities | Staples and commodities | Staples and commodities | Complementary to their own lines | Contraband | Manufactured goods | Bulky and raw materials | Manufactured goods | Complementary to line |
| Breadth of line | specialty to wide | All types of staples | All types of staples | Retail goods | Narrow | n.a. | Broad | Broad | Broad | Narrow |
| Handle competitive lines | No | No | Yes | Yes—utilizes many sources | No | Yes | Yes | Yes | Yes | No |
| Extend to promotion and selling effort | Good | Good | One shot | n.a. | Good | Nil | Nil | Nil | Good | Good |
| Extend credit to principal | Occasionally | Occasionally | Seldom | Seldom | Seldom | No | Occasionally | Seldom | Seldom | Seldom |
| Market information | Fair | Fair | Price and market conditions | For principal, not for manufacturer | Good | No | Nil | Nil | Fair | Good |

Note: n.a. = not available.

*The EMC may take title and thus become a merchant middleman.

hired for special purposes. Some of the more important foreign-country middlemen are manufacturer's representatives and foreign distributors.

**Manufacturer's Representatives.**  *Manufacturer's representatives* are agent middlemen who take responsibility for a producer's goods in a city, regional market area, entire country, or several adjacent countries. When responsible for an entire country, the middleman is often called a *sole agent.* As in the United States, the well-chosen, well-motivated, well-controlled manufacturer's representative can provide excellent market coverage for the manufacturer in certain circumstances. The manufacturer's representative is widely used in distribution of industrial goods overseas and is an excellent representative for any type of manufactured consumer goods.

Foreign manufacturer's representatives have a variety of titles, including sales agent, resident sales agent, exclusive agent, commission agent, and indent agent. They take no credit, exchange, or market risk but deal strictly as field sales representatives. They do not arrange for shipping or for handling and usually do not take physical possession. Manufacturers who wish the type of control and intensive market coverage their own sales force would afford, but who cannot field one, may find the manufacturer's representative a satisfactory choice.

**Distributors.**  A *foreign distributor* is a merchant middleman. This intermediary often has exclusive sales rights in a specific country and works in close cooperation with the manufacturer. The distributor has a relatively high degree of dependence on the supplier companies, and arrangements are likely to be on a long-run, continuous basis. Working through distributors permits the manufacturer a reasonable degree of control over prices, promotional effort, inventories, servicing, and other distribution functions. If a line is profitable for distributors, they can be depended on to handle it in a manner closely approximating the desires of the manufacturer.[37]

**Foreign-Country Brokers.**  Like the export broker discussed in an earlier section, *foreign-country brokers* are agents who deal largely in commodities and food products. The foreign brokers are typically part of small brokerage firms operating in one country or in a few contiguous countries. Their strength is in having good continuing relationships with customers and providing speedy market coverage at a low cost. Atypical, but still part of this category, are art auction houses such as those in China[38] and in the Netherlands. At the latter you can spend $85,000,000 for Rembrandt if you can spare the change.[39]

**Managing Agents and Compradors.**  A *managing agent* conducts business within a foreign nation under an exclusive contract arrangement with the parent company. The managing agent in some cases invests in the operation and in most instances operates under a contract with the parent company. Compensation is usually on the basis of cost plus a specified percentage of the profits of the managed company. In some countries, managing agents may be called *compradors* and there are some differences in duties performed (see Exhibit 14.7).

**Dealers.**  Generally speaking, anyone who has a continuing relationship with a supplier in buying and selling goods is considered a dealer. More specifically, **dealers** are middlemen selling industrial goods or durable consumer goods direct to customers; they are the last step in the channel of distribution. Dealers have continuing, close working relationships with their suppliers and exclusive selling rights for their producer's products within a given geographic area. Finally, they derive a large portion of their sales volume from the products of a single supplier firm.

Some of the best examples of dealer operations include Massey Ferguson, with a vast, worldwide network of dealers, and Caterpillar Tractor Company, with dealers in every major city of the world.

---

[37]Matthew Smith, "Distributed Near You," *Asia Inc,* May 2003, pp. 24–25.

[38]Karen Mazurkewich, "Auction House in China Bets on Western Art," *Wall Street Journal,* October 24, 2002, p. B1.

[39]The European Fine Arts Fair (TEFAF) is in Maastricht every spring. "A Taste of Money," *Go Dutch,* March 2003, pp, 44–45.

# Exhibit 14.7
Characteristics of Foreign-Country Middlemen

| Type of Duties | Agent | | | | Merchant | | | |
|---|---|---|---|---|---|---|---|---|
| | Broker | Manufacturer's Representative | Managing Agent | Comprador | Distributor | Dealer | Import Jobber | Wholesaler and Retailer |
| Take title | No | No | No | No | Yes | Yes | Yes | Yes |
| Take possession | No | Seldom | Seldom | Yes | Yes | Yes | Yes | Yes |
| Continuing relationship | No | Often | With buyer, not seller | Yes | Yes | Yes | No | Usually not |
| Share of foreign output | Small | All or part for one area | n.a. | All, for one area | All, for certain countries | Assignment area | Small | Very small |
| Degree of control by principal | Low | Fair | None | Fair | High | High | Low | Nil |
| Price authority | Nil | Nil | Nil | Partial | Partial | Partial | Full | Full |
| Represent buyer or seller | Either | Seller | Buyer | Seller | Seller | Seller | Self | Self |
| Number of principals | Many | Few | Many | Few | Small | Few major | Many | Many |
| Arrange shipping | No | No | No | No | No | No | No | No |
| Type of goods | Commodity and food | Manufactured goods | All types | Manufactured goods | Manufactured goods | Manufactured goods | Manufactured goods | Manufactured consumer goods |
| Breadth of line | Broad | Allied lines | Broad | Varies | Narrow to broad | Narrow | Narrow to broad | Narrow to broad |
| Handle competitive lines | Yes | No | Yes | No | No | No | Yes | Yes |
| Extent of promotion and selling effort | Nil | Fair | Nil | Fair | Fair | Good | Nil | Nil usually |
| Extend credit to principal | No | No | No | Sometimes | Sometimes | No | No | No |
| Market information | Nil | Good | Nil | Good | Fair | Good | Nil | Nil |

Note: n.a. = not available.

**Import Jobbers, Wholesalers, and Retailers.**  **Import jobbers** purcha:
directly from the manufacturer and sell to wholesalers and retailers and to indus
tomers. Large and small wholesalers and retailers engage in direct importing for their own
outlets and for redistribution to smaller middlemen. The combination retailer-wholesaler
is more important in foreign countries than in the United States. It is not uncommon to
find large retailers wholesaling goods to local shops and dealers. Exhibit 14.7 summarizes the characteristics of foreign-country middlemen.

**Government-
Affiliated
Middlemen**

Marketers must deal with governments in every country of the world. Products, services,
and commodities for the government's own use are always procured through government
purchasing offices at federal, regional, and local levels. In the Netherlands, the state's
purchasing office deals with more than 10,000 suppliers in 20 countries. About one-third
of the products purchased by that agency are produced outside the Netherlands.

## Factors Affecting Choice of Channels

The international marketer needs a clear understanding
of market characteristics and must have established operating policies before beginning the
selection of channel middlemen. The following points should be addressed prior to the selection process.

1. Identify specific target markets within and across countries.
2. Specify marketing goals in terms of volume, market share, and profit margin
   requirements.
3. Specify financial and personnel commitments to the development of international
   distribution.
4. Identify control, length of channels, terms of sale, and channel ownership.

Once these points are established, selecting among alternative middlemen choices to
forge the best channel can begin. Marketers must get their goods into the hands of consumers and must choose between handling all distribution or turning part or all of it over
to various middlemen.[40] **Distribution channels** vary depending on target market size,
competition, and available distribution intermediaries.

Key elements in distribution decisions include the functions performed by middlemen
(and the effectiveness with which each is performed), the cost of their services, their
availability, and the extent of control that the manufacturer can exert over middlemen
activities.

Although the overall marketing strategy of the firm must embody the company's profit
goals in the short and long run, channel strategy itself is considered to have six specific
strategic goals. These goals can be characterized as the six Cs of channel strategy: cost,
capital, control, coverage, character, and continuity.

In forging the overall channel-of-distribution strategy, each of the six Cs must be considered in building an economical, effective distribution organization within the long-range
channel policies of the company. It should also be noted that many firms use multiple or
hybrid[41] channels of distribution because of the tradeoffs associated with any one
option.[42] Indeed, both Dell[43] selling computers at kiosks inside Japan's Jusco supermarkets and Toys "R" Us[44] selling toys in food stores are good examples.

---

[40]Alex Rialp, Catherine Axxin, and Sharon Tach, "Exploring Channel Internalization among Spanish
Exporters," *International Marketing Review,* 2002, 19(2-3), pp. 133–155.

[41]Mika Gabrielsson, V.H.Manek Kirpalani, and Reijo Luostarinen, "Multiple Channel Strategies in the
European Personal Computer Industry," *Journal of International Marketing,* 2002, 10(3), pp. 73–95.

[42]Rod B. McNaughton, "The Use of Multiple Export Channels by Small Knowledge-Intensive Firms,"
*International Marketing Review,* 2002, 19(2-3), pp. 190–203.

[43]Gary McWilliams and Ann Zimmerman, "Dell Plans to Peddle PCs Inside Sears, Other Large Chains,"
*Wall Street Journal,* January 30, 2003, p. B1.

[44]"Toys "R" Us to Set up Shop in Albertson's," *Los Angeles Times,* June 4, 2003, p. C3.

**Cost**

There are two kinds of channel cost: (1) the capital or investment cost of developing the channel and (2) the continuing cost of maintaining it. The latter can be in the form of direct expenditure for the maintenance of the company's selling force or in the form of margins, markup, or commissions of various middlemen handling the goods. Marketing costs (a substantial part of which is channel cost) must be considered as the entire difference between the factory price of the goods and the price the customer ultimately pays for the merchandise. The costs of middlemen include transporting and storing the goods, breaking bulk, providing credit, and local advertising, sales representation, and negotiations.

Despite the old truism that you can eliminate middlemen but you cannot eliminate their functions or cost, creative, efficient marketing does permit channel cost savings in many circumstances. Some marketers found, in fact, that they can reduce cost by eliminating inefficient middlemen and thus shortening the channel. Mexico's largest producer of radio and television sets built annual sales of $36 million on its ability to sell goods at a low price because it eliminated middlemen, established its own wholesalers, and kept margins low. Conversely, many firms accustomed to using their own sales forces in large-volume domestic markets found they must lengthen channels of distribution to keep costs in line with foreign markets.

**Capital Requirements**

The financial ramifications of a distribution policy are often overlooked. Critical elements are capital requirements and cash-flow patterns associated with using a particular type of middleman. Maximum investment is usually required when a company establishes its own internal channels, that is, its own sales force. Use of distributors or dealers may lessen the capital investment, but manufacturers often must provide initial inventories on consignment, loans, floor plans, or other arrangements. Coca-Cola initially invested in China with majority partners that met most of the capital requirements. However, Coca-Cola soon realized that it could not depend on its local majority partners to distribute its product aggressively in the highly competitive, market-share-driven business of carbonated beverages. To assume more control of distribution, it had to assume management control, and that meant greater capital investment from Coca-Cola. One of the highest costs of doing business in China is the capital required to maintain effective distribution.

**Control**

The more involved a company is with the distribution, the more control it exerts. A company's own sales force affords the most control, but often at a cost that is not practical. Each type of channel arrangement provides a different level of control;[45] as channels grow longer, the ability to control price, volume, promotion, and type of outlets diminishes. If a company cannot sell directly to the end user or final retailer, an important selection criterion for middlemen should be the amount of control the marketer can maintain.[46]

**Coverage**

Another major goal is full-market coverage to gain the optimum volume of sales obtainable in each market, secure a reasonable market share, and attain satisfactory market penetration. Coverage may be assessed by geographic or market segments, or both. Adequate market coverage may require changes in distribution systems from country to country or time to time. Coverage is difficult to develop both in highly developed areas and in sparse markets—the former because of heavy competition and the latter because of inadequate channels.

Many companies do not attempt full-market coverage but seek significant penetration in major population centers. In some countries, two or three cities constitute the

[45]Daniel C. Bello, Cristian Chelariu, and Li Zhang, "The Antecedents and Performance Consequences of Relationalism in Export Distribution Channels," *Journal of Business Research,* January 2003, 56(1), pp. 1–16.

[46]Michael Harvey and Milorad M. Novicevic, "Selecting Marketing Managers to Effectively Control Global Channels of Distribution," *International Marketing Review,* 2002, 19(4-5), pp. 525–544.

You can buy just about anything at Stockmann's Department Store in Helsinki—men's and women's fashions, hardware (hammers, etc.) and software, bakery goods and garden supplies, fillet of reindeer and furniture, televisions—yes, everything from Audi A3s to artichokes. They even have cold storage services for your mink. But, Stockmann's doesn't stock Samsung cell phones. The Korean company hasn't yet penetrated Nokia's home market.

majority of the national buying power. For instance, 60 percent of the Japanese population lives in the Tokyo-Nagoya-Osaka market area, which essentially functions as one massive city.

At the other extreme are many developing countries with a paucity of specialized middlemen except in major urban areas. Those that do exist are often small, with traditionally high margins. In China, for example, the often-quoted one-billion-person market is, in reality, confined to fewer than 25 to 30 percent of the population of the most affluent cities. Even as personal income increases in China, distribution inadequacies limit marketers in reaching all those who have adequate incomes. In both extremes, the difficulty of developing an efficient channel from existing middlemen plus the high cost of distribution may nullify efficiencies achieved in other parts of the marketing mix.

To achieve coverage, a company may have to use many different channels—its own sales force in one country, manufacturers' agents in another, and merchant wholesalers in still another.

**Character**   The channel-of-distribution system selected must fit the character of the company and the markets in which it is doing business. Some obvious product requirements, often the first considered, relate to perishability or bulk of the product, complexity of sale, sales service required, and value of the product.

Channel commanders must be aware that channel patterns change; they cannot assume that once a channel is developed to fit the character of both company and market, no more need be done.

Great Britain, for example, has epitomized distribution through specialty-type middlemen, distributors, wholesalers, and retailers; in fact, all middlemen have traditionally worked within narrow product specialty areas. In recent years, however, there was a trend toward broader lines, conglomerate merchandising, and mass marketing. The firm that neglects the growth of self-service, scrambled merchandising, or discounting may find it has lost large segments of its market because its channels no longer reflect the character of the market.

**Continuity**   Channels of distribution often pose longevity problems. Most agent middlemen firms tend to be small institutions. When one individual retires or moves out of a line of business, the company may find it has lost its distribution in that area. Wholesalers and especially retailers are not noted for their continuity in business either. Most middlemen have little loyalty to their vendors. They handle brands in good times when the line is making money, but quickly reject such products within a season or a year if they fail to produce during that period. Distributors and dealers are probably the most loyal middlemen, but even with them, manufacturers must attempt to build brand loyalty downstream in a channel lest middlemen shift allegiance to other companies or other inducements.

## Locating, Selecting, and Motivating Channel Members

The actual process of building channels for international distribution is seldom easy, and many companies are stopped in their efforts to develop international markets by their inability to construct a satisfactory system of channels.

Construction of the middleman network includes seeking out potential middlemen, selecting those who fit the company's requirements, and establishing working relationships with them. In international marketing, the channel-building process is hardly routine. The closer the company wants to get to the consumer in its channel contact, the larger the sales force required. If a company is content with finding an exclusive importer or selling agent for a given country, channel building may not be too difficult; however, if it goes down to the level of subwholesaler or retailer, it is taking on a tremendous task and must have an internal staff capable of supporting such an effort.

## Locating Middlemen

The search for prospective middlemen should begin with study of the market and determination of criteria for evaluating middlemen servicing that market. The checklist of criteria differs according to the type of middlemen being used and the nature of their relationship with the company. Basically, such lists are built around four subject areas: productivity or volume, financial strength, managerial stability and capability, and the nature and reputation of the business. Emphasis is usually placed on either the actual or potential productivity of the middleman.

The major problems are locating information to aid in the selection and choice of specific middlemen, and discovering middlemen available to handle one's merchandise. Firms seeking overseas representation should compile a list of middlemen from such sources as the following: the U.S. Department of Commerce; commercially published directories; foreign consulates; chamber-of-commerce groups located abroad; other manufacturers producing similar but noncompetitive goods; middlemen associations; business publications; management consultants; carriers—particularly airlines; and Internet-based services such as Unibex, a global technology services provider. Unibex provides a platform for small- to medium-size companies and larger enterprises to collaborate in business-to-business commerce.

## Selecting Middlemen

Finding prospective middlemen is less a problem than determining which of them can perform satisfactorily. Low volume or low potential volume hampers most prospects, many are underfinanced, and some simply cannot be trusted.[47] In many cases, when a manufacturer is not well known abroad, the reputation of the middleman becomes the reputation of the manufacturer, so a poor choice at this point can be devastating.

**Screening.**    The screening and selection process itself should include the following actions: an exploratory letter including product information and distributor requirements in the native language sent to each prospective middleman; a follow-up to the best respondents for more specific information concerning lines handled, territory covered, size of firm, number of salespeople, and other background information; check of credit and references from other clients and customers of the prospective middleman; and if possible, a personal check of the most promising firms. It is easier to obtain financial information on prospective middlemen via such Internet companies as Unibex, which provides access to Dun & Bradstreet and other client information resources.

Experienced exporters suggest that the only way to select a middleman is to go personally to the country and talk to ultimate users of your product to find who they consider to be the best distributors. Visit each possible middleman before selecting the one to represent you; look for one with a key person who will take the new product to his or her heart and make it a personal objective to make the sale of that line a success. Further, exporters stress that if you cannot sign one of the two or three customer-recommended distributors, it might be better not to have a distributor in that country because having a worthless one costs you time and money every year and may cut you out when you finally find a good one.

**The Agreement.**    Once a potential middleman is found and evaluated, there remains the task of detailing the arrangements with that middleman. So far the company is in a buying position; now it must shift into a selling and negotiating position to convince the middleman to handle the goods and accept a distribution agreement that is workable for the company. Agreements must spell out specific responsibilities of the manufacturer and the middleman, including an annual sales minimum. The sales minimum serves as a basis for evaluation of the distributor; failure to meet sales minimums may give the exporter the right of termination.

---

[47]"Global Pitfalls," *Sales and Marketing.Com*, April 9, 2003.

Some experienced exporters recommend that initial contracts be signed for one year only. If the first year's performance is satisfactory, they should be reviewed for renewal for a longer period. This permits easier termination, and more important, after a year of working together in the market, a more workable arrangement generally can be reached.

## Motivating Middlemen

The level of distribution and the importance of the individual middleman to the company determine the activities undertaken to keep the middleman motivated. On all levels there is a clear correlation between the middleman's motivation and sales volume. Motivational techniques that can be employed to maintain middleman interest and support for the product may be grouped into five categories: financial rewards, psychological rewards, communications, company support, and corporate rapport.

Obviously, financial rewards must be adequate for any middleman to carry and promote a company's products. Margins or commissions must be set to meet the needs of the middleman and may vary according to the volume of sales and the level of services offered. Without a combination of adequate margin and adequate volume, a middleman cannot afford to give much attention to a product.

Being human, middlemen and their salespeople respond to psychological rewards and recognition of their efforts. A trip to the United States or to the parent company's home or regional office is a great honor. Publicity in company media and local newspapers also builds esteem and involvement among foreign middlemen.

In all instances, the company should maintain a continuing flow of communication in the form of letters, newsletters, and periodicals to all its middlemen. The more personal these are, the better. One study of exporters indicated that the more intense the contact between the manufacturer and the distributor, the better the performance from the distributor. More and better contact naturally leads to less conflict and a smoother working relationship.

Finally, considerable attention must be paid to the establishment of close rapport between the company and its middlemen. In addition to methods noted earlier, a company should be certain that the conflicts that arise are handled skillfully and diplomatically. Bear in mind that all over the world business is a personal and vital thing to the people involved.

## Terminating Middlemen

When middlemen do not perform up to standards or when market situations change, requiring a company to restructure its distribution, it may be necessary to terminate relationships. In the United States, it is usually a simple action regardless of the type of middlemen; they are simply dismissed. However, in other parts of the world, the middleman often has some legal protection that makes termination difficult. In Colombia, for example, if you terminate an agent, you are required to pay 10 percent of the agent's average annual compensation, multiplied by the number of years the agent served, as a final settlement.

Competent legal advice is vital when entering distribution contracts with middlemen. But as many experienced international marketers know, the best rule is to avoid the need to terminate distributors by screening all prospective middlemen carefully. A poorly chosen distributor may not only fail to live up to expectations but may also adversely affect future business and prospects in the country.

## Controlling Middlemen

The extreme length of channels typically used in international distribution makes control of middlemen especially important. Marketing objectives must be spelled out both internally and to middlemen as explicitly as possible. Standards of performance should include sales volume objective, market share in each market, inventory turnover ratio, number of accounts per area, growth objective, price stability objective, and quality of publicity. Cultural differences enter into all these areas of management.[48]

Control over the system and control over middlemen are necessary in international business. The first relates to control over the distribution network. This implies overall controls

---

[48]Jody Evans, Felix T. Mavondo, "Psychic Distance and Organizational Performance: An Empirical Examination of International Retailing Operations," *Journal of International Business Studies,* 2002, 33(3), pp. 515–532.

for the entire system to be certain the product is flowing through desired middlemen. Some manufacturers lost control through "secondary wholesaling" or parallel imports.[49] A company's goods intended for one country are sometimes diverted through distributors to another country, where they compete with existing retail or wholesale organizations.

The second type of control is at the middleman level. When possible, the parent company should know (and to a certain degree control) the activities of middlemen in respect to their volume of sales, market coverage, services offered, prices, advertising, payment of bills, and even profit. Quotas, reports, and personal visits by company representatives can be effective in managing middleman activities at any level of the channel.

## The Internet

The Internet is an important distribution method for multinational companies and a source of products for businesses and consumers. Computer hardware and software companies and book and music retailers were the early e-marketers to use this method of distribution and marketing. More recently there was an expansion of other types of retailing and business-to-business (B2B) services into e-commerce. Technically, e-commerce is a form of direct selling; however, because of its newness and the unique issues associated with this form of distribution, it is important to differentiate it from other types of direct marketing.

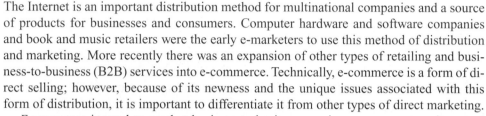

*E-commerce* is used to market business-to-business services, consumer services, and consumer and industrial products via the World Wide Web. It involves the direct marketing from a manufacturer, retailer, service provider, or some other intermediary to a final user. Some examples of e-marketers with an international presence are Dell Computer Corporation (www.dell.com), which generates nearly 50 percent of its total sales, an average of about $69 million a day, online, and Cisco Systems (www. cisco.com), which generates more than $1 billion in sales annually. Cisco's website appears in 14 languages and has country-specific content for 49 nations. Gateway has global sites in Japan, France, the Netherlands, Germany, Sweden, Australia, the United Kingdom, and the United States, to name a few (www.gateway.com). Sun Microsystems and its after-marketing company, SunExpress, have local-language information on more than 3,500 aftermarket products. SunPlaza enables visitors in North America, Europe, and Japan to get information online on products and services and to place orders directly in their native languages.

Besides consumer goods companies such as Lands' End, Levi, Nike, and others, many smaller and less well-known companies have established a presence on the Internet beyond their traditional markets. An Internet customer from the Netherlands can purchase a pair of brake levers for his mountain bike from California-based Price Point. He pays $130 instead of the $190 that the same items would cost in a local bike store.

For a Spanish shopper in Pamplona, buying sheet music used to mean a 400-kilometer trip to Madrid. Now he crosses the Atlantic to shop—and the journey takes less time than a trip to the corner store. Via the Internet he can buy directly from specialized stores and high-volume discounters in New York, London, and almost anywhere else.

E-commerce is more developed in the United States than the rest of the world partly because of the vast number of people who own personal computers and because of the much lower cost of access to the Internet than found elsewhere. See Exhibit 14.3. Besides language, legal, and cultural differences, the cost of local phone calls (which are charged by the minute in most European countries) initially discouraged extensive use and contributed to slower Internet adoption in Europe. However, according to some estimates Europeans actually spent more on e-commerce in 2002 than Americans, both at about $15.8 billion.[50]

---

[49]See the discussion of parallel imports in Chapter 18.

[50]Such estimates vary considerable and must be taken with a grain of salt. These numbers come from "Europeans Outspend Americans," *Time,* December 23, 2002, p. A3. In "Santa's Little Helper," *The Economist,* December 4, 2002, p. 1, lower estimates are attributed to Forrester Research: $7.6 billion for Europeans and $9.5 billion for Americans. One thing is certain, Europeans and others outside of North America are adopting the Internet at a much faster rate as American usage is nearing saturation.

# CROSSING BORDERS 14.4  No More Roses for My Miami Broker

Eight out of ten flowers you buy this year will come from Colombia, our nation's leading supplier of cut flowers. Colombia's cut-flower industry now amounts to $580 million in exports annually. The majority of the flowers coming to the United States arrive in Miami aboard jets, bound for Miami flower brokers who then hold them on consignment until U.S. wholesalers and retailers negotiate on price and place orders. Growers often financed the supply chain and had no idea what a shipment would bring until sales were negotiated in Miami by brokers who charged an average of 15 percent for their services. That was the situation until the creation of the Flower Purchase Network (FPN) and its Floraplex website (www.floraplex.com), the first electronic marketplace where flower growers, wholesalers, retailers, and consumers can meet online to conduct e-business.

FPN allows buyers to negotiate directly with the growers; the FPN system provides growers an opportunity to expand their markets and increase profits quickly and efficiently. Users can buy from Holland, Africa, and Israel with service through the Dutch auctions (refer back to Chapter 4, page 100), and from South and North America with service through self-provided logistics providers. Floraplex members who utilize the Marketplace receive all their invoices, orders, sales history, purchase history, and more by using the one-stop account summary page. This seamless link between buyer and seller means sellers can negotiate directly with buyers while simultaneously reducing the cost of middlemen. Floraplex applies a 3 percent to 8 percent service fee for system usage, depending on volume, whereas Miami brokers charge an average of 15 percent commission.

FPN, owned by World Commerce Online, handles roughly one million stems of flowers per week and actively trades flowers on six continents—and that's after being on the Web for less than a year. The next Web launch will be Freshplex, designed to do for the entire produce industry what Floraplex is doing for the flower industry.

Sources: "Colombia's Hope: Less Coca, More Carnations," *Christian Science Monitor*, March 24, 2000; Floraplex home page, www.floraplex.com; Mike Candelaria, "Changing the Way the Fresh-Cut Flower Industry Does Business," *Latin Trade*, June 2000; and T. Christian Miller, "Everything Is Coming up Roses for Colombia's Flower Industry," *Los Angeles Times*, February 14, 2003, p. A3.

The largest B2B players today are U.S.-based brick-and-mortar companies that generate a significant percentage of revenue internationally from sales via the Internet. Global B2B commerce is forecasted to reach $4 billion in the United States in 2006 and surpass $9 trillion worldwide.[51] The expansion of B2B transactions will be fueled by growth in industrial inputs, such as steel, chemicals, and car components; transactions by smaller firms; and an increased number of business services offered over the Internet.

Small and middle-sized firms are expected to generate substantial growth in Internet transactions, as well as to pool their purchases through various Internet exchanges for everything from telephone services and office furniture to electricity. Although each order is individually small, such purchases combined account for 30 to 60 percent of firms' total nonlabor costs and are usually bought inefficiently and expensively. Reduced prices by bulk buying through an online intermediary and the savings resulting from placing and processing orders online, which is much cheaper and faster than the traditional way, could reduce costs by 10 to 20 percent. One study estimates that if all small and medium-sized firms in Britain used the Internet to buy indirect inputs, they could save up to $36 billion a year.

Services, the third engine for growth, are ideally suited for international sales via the Internet. All types of services—banking, education, consulting, retailing, gambling—can be marketed through a website that is globally accessible. As outsourcing of traditional in-house tasks such as inventory management, quality control, and accounting, secretarial, translation, and legal services has become more popular among companies, the Internet providers of these services have grown both in the United States and internationally.

---

[51]"Marketing Factbook," *Marketing News*, July 8, 2003, p. 14.

B2B enables companies to cut costs in three ways. First, it reduces procurement costs, making it easier to find the cheapest supplier, and it cuts the cost of processing the transactions. Estimates are that a firm's possible savings from purchasing over the Internet vary from 2 percent in the coal industry to up to 40 percent in electronic components. British Telecom claims that procuring goods and services online will reduce the average cost of processing a transaction by 90 percent and reduce the direct costs of goods and services it purchases by 11 percent. The Ford, GM, and DaimlerChrysler exchange network for buying components from suppliers could reduce the cost of making a car by as much as 14 percent. Second, it allows better supply-chain management. For example, 75 percent of all Cisco orders now occur online, up from 4 percent in 1996. This connection to the supply chain allowed Cisco to reduce order cycle time from up to 8 weeks to 1 to 3 weeks, and to increase customer satisfaction as well.

And third, it makes possible tighter inventory control. With Wal-Mart's direct Internet links between its inventory control system and its suppliers, each sale automatically triggers a replenishment request. Fewer out-of-stock situations, the ability to make rapid inventory adjustments, and reduced ordering and processing costs made Wal-Mart one of the industry's most efficient companies.

The worldwide potential for firms operating on the Internet is extraordinary, but only if they are positioned properly. The World Wide Web, as a market, is rapidly moving through the stage where the novelty of buying on the Web is giving way to a more sophisticated customer who has more and constantly improving websites to choose from. In short, Web merchants are facing more competition, and Web customers have more choice. This means that if a company is going to be successful in this new era of marketing, the basics of good marketing cannot be overlooked. For example, Forrester Research discovered that nearly half the international orders received by U.S. companies go unfilled even though a typical U.S. company can expect 30 percent of its Web traffic to come from foreign countries and 10 percent of its orders to come from abroad.

By its very nature e-commerce has some unique issues that must be addressed if a domestic e-vendor expects to be a viable player in the international cybermarketplace. International legal issues were discussed in Chapter 7.[52] Many other issues arise because the host-country intermediary who would ordinarily be involved in international marketing is eliminated. An important advantage of selling direct is that total costs can be lowered so that the final price overseas is considerably less than it would have been through a local-country middleman. However, such activities as translating prospective customer inquiries and orders into English and replying in the customer's language, traditionally done by a local distributor, must be done by someone. When intermediaries are eliminated, someone, either the seller or the buyer, must assume the functions they performed. Consequently, an e-vendor must be concerned with the following issues.

**1. Culture.** The preceding chapters on culture should not be overlooked when doing business over the Web. The website and the product must be culturally neutral or adapted to fit the uniqueness of a market, because culture does matter. In Japan, the pickiness of Japanese consumers about what they buy and their reluctance to deal with merchants at a distance must be addressed when marketing on the Web. Even a Japanese-language site can offend Japanese sensibilities. As one e-commerce consultant warns, in a product description, you wouldn't say "Don't turn the knob left," because that's too direct. Instead, you would say something like: "It would be much better to turn the knob to the right." To many Europeans, American sites come off as having too many bells and whistles because European sites are more consumer oriented. The different cultural reactions to color can be a potential problem for websites designed for global markets. While red may be highly regarded in China or associated with love in the United States, in Spain it is associated with socialism. The point is that when designing a website, culture cannot be forgotten.

---

[52]Matthew Newman, "E-Commerce: The Rules—So Many Countries, So Many Laws," *Wall Street Journal,* April 28, 2003, p. R8.

**CROSSING BORDERS 14.5** Shatner Will Fly in Japan; Priceline May Not

Some concepts work better in certain countries than in others. Think of warm beer in England, frog's legs in France, and lederhosen in Germany. So when Priceline announced it was partnering with Softbank on a name-your-own-price service in Japan—offering airfare and hotel rooms initially, and possibly other products after that—we had some questions. First off, how will that Uber-American style of bargain bidding fare in the Land of the Rising Sun? How will Priceline tailor its site to a Japanese audience? For an early take, we talked to Japanese business expert Terri Morrison, co-author of *Kiss, Bow, or Shake Hands: How to Do Business in 60 Countries.* She raised a few issues that Priceline executives may want to think about:

*Website design:* "Well, [Priceline] should consider the fact that the Japanese read from right to left—that's a big one."

*Profit margins:* "The Japanese are really tough negotiators, and they'll do really thorough research to figure out exactly what they should pay for an item. It's not like in America. Priceline may not get very good margins with the Japanese."

*The strict no-cancellations policy:* "Contracts [in Japan] are not perceived as final agreements. Traditionally, if either party has remorse, there are renegotiations."

*The one-hour acceptance or rejection of bids:* "It's a culture where people generally don't like to make snap decisions."

*Bargain hunting:* "In Japan talking about the price of something is very gauche. It's not that Japanese won't negotiate fiercely, but would they admit to doing so? That could be seen as tacky."

*Customer service:* "At times you may need to pretend you are sure that your Japanese colleague or friend has understood you, even if you know this is not the case. This is important for maintaining a good relationship."

*Giveaways:* "In Japan, avoid giving gifts with an even number of components, such as an even number of flowers in a bouquet. Four is an especially inauspicious number; never give four of anything."

*William Shatner:* "They'll definitely know him over there. I don't know if those ads with that beat poetry he does will fly . . . maybe he could do karaoke."

Source: Lee Clifford, "Shatner Will Fly in Japan; Priceline May Not" *Fortune,* October 2, 2000, p. 66. Michael J. Mandel, "The Internet Economy: The World's Next Growth Engine," *Business Week,* October 4, 1999; and Tim Nudd, "More for Trekkies," *Adweek,* October 21, 2002, p. 38.

2. **Adaptation.** Ideally, a website should be translated into the languages of the target markets. This may not be financially feasible for some companies, but at least the most important pages of the site should be translated. Simple translation of important pages is only a stopgap, however. If companies are making a long-term commitment to sales in another country, Web pages should be designed (in all senses of the term—color, use features, etc.) for that market. One researcher suggests that if a website does not have at least multiple languages, a company is losing sales. It is the company's responsibility to bridge the language and cultural gap; the customer will not bother—he or she will simply go to a site that speaks his or her language. As discussed earlier, culture does count, and as competition increases, a country-specific website may make the difference between success and failure.[53]

3. **Local contact.** Companies fully committed to foreign markets are creating virtual offices abroad; they buy server space and create mirror sites, whereby a company has a voicemail or fax contact point in key markets. Foreign customers are more likely to visit sites in their own country and in the local language. In Japan, where consumers seem particularly concerned about the ability to easily return goods, companies may have outlets where merchandise can be returned and picked up. These so-called click-and-mortar models have gained a large following.

---

[53]Patrick Y.K. Chau, Melissa Cole, Anne P. Massey, Mitzi Montoya-Weiss, and Robert O'Keefe, "Cultural Differences in the On-Line Behavior of Consumers," *Communications of the ACM,* 2002, 45(10), pp. 138–143.

**4. Payment.** The consumer should be able to use a credit card number—either by e-mail (from a secure page on the website), by fax, or over the phone.

**5. Delivery.** For companies operating in the United States, surface postal delivery of small parcels is most cost effective but takes the longest time. For more rapid but more expensive deliveries, Federal Express, United Parcel Service, and other private delivery services provide delivery worldwide. For example, Tom Clancy's bestseller *Executive Orders,* shipped express to Paris from Seattle-based Amazon.com, would cost a reader $55.52. The same book delivered in four to ten weeks via surface mail costs $25.52, which is a substantial savings over the cost of the book in a Paris bookstore, where it sells for $35.38.

Once sufficient volume in a country or region is attained, container shipments to free trade zones or bonded warehouses can be used for distribution of individual orders via local delivery services within the region. These same locations can also be used for such after-sale services as spare parts, defective product returns, and supplies. Companies such as FedEx, UPS, and similar small-package delivery services also have overseas storage and fulfillment centers for individual orders that e-commerce companies can use to provide faster and less costly in-country delivery.

**6. Promotion.** Although the Web is a means of promotion, if you are engaging in e-commerce you also need to advertise your presence and the products or services offered. The old adage "Build a better mouse trap and the world will beat a path to your door" does not work for e-commerce, just as it does not work with other products unless you tell your target market about the availability of the "better mouse trap." How do you attract visitors from other countries to your website? The same way you would at home—except in the local language. Search engine registration, press releases, local newsgroups and forums, mutual links, and banner advertising are the traditional methods. A website should be seen as a retail store, with the only difference between it and a physical store being that the customer arrives over the Internet instead of on foot.

When discussing the Internet and international channels of distribution, the question of how traditional channels will be changed by the Internet must be considered. Already, comparison shopping across the Continent via the Internet is wrenching apart commercial patterns cobbled together over centuries. Before the Internet, Europeans rarely

A FedEx employee checks cargo being loaded at the Roissy airport north of Paris near its European dispatch center. More than 1000 employees there move more than 500 tons of parcels each day. Notice the white arrow imbedded in the company's logo between the E and the x—FedEx means motion. *(© AFP/CORBIS)*

shopped across borders, and car companies, exempt from EU antitrust laws in distribution, offered cars at price differentials of up to 40 percent. The Internet blew this system apart and allows the European customer to shop easily for the best price.

Not only will the traditional channels change, but also the Internet, which is still evolving. Much of what is standard practice today may well be obsolete tomorrow as new means of data transmission are achieved, costs of accessing the Web decrease, and new e-commerce models are invented. The Web is rapidly growing and changing as it grows.

## Summary

From the foregoing discussion, it is evident that the international marketer has a broad range of alternatives for developing an economical, efficient, high-volume international distribution system. To the uninitiated, however, the variety may be overwhelming.

Careful analysis of the functions performed suggests more similarity than difference between international and domestic distribution systems; in both cases the three primary alternatives are using agent middlemen, merchant middlemen, or government-affiliated middlemen. In many instances, all three types of middlemen are employed on the international scene, and channel structure may vary from nation to nation or from continent to

continent. The neophyte company in international marketing can gain strength from the knowledge that information and advice are available relative to the structuring of international distribution systems and that many well-developed and capable middleman firms exist for the international distribution of goods. Although international middlemen are more numerous, more reliable, and more sophisticated within the past decade, traditional channels are being challenged by the Internet, which is rapidly becoming an important alternative channel to many market segments. Such growth and development offer an ever-wider range of possibilities for entering foreign markets.

## Questions

1. Define the following terms:

   distribution process, 400
   distribution structure, 400
   Large-Scale Retail Store
     Location Act, 404
   agent middlemen, 414
   merchant middlemen, 414
   home-country middlemen, 415
   trading companies, 417

   Export Trading Company
     Act, 417
   complementary marketing,
     418
   dealers, 421
   import jobbers, 423
   distribution channels, 423

2. Discuss the distinguishing features of the Japanese distribution system.

3. Discuss the ways Japanese manufacturers control the distribution process from manufacturer to retailer.

4. Describe Japan's Large-Scale Retail Store Law and discuss how the Structural Impediments Initiative (SII) is bringing about change in Japanese retailing.

5. "Japanese retailing may be going through a change similar to that which occurred in the United States after World War II." Discuss and give examples.

6. Discuss how the globalization of markets, especially Europe after 1992, affects retail distribution.

7. To what extent, and in what ways, do the functions of domestic middlemen differ from those of their foreign counterparts?

8. Why is the EMC sometimes called an independent export department?

9. Discuss how physical distribution relates to channel policy and how they affect one another.

10. Explain how and why distribution channels are affected, as they are when the stage of development of an economy improves.

11. In what circumstances is the use of an EMC logical?

12. In which circumstances are trading companies likely to be used?

13. How is distribution-channel structure affected by increasing emphasis on the government as a customer and by the existence of state trading agencies?

14. Review the key variables that affect the marketer's choice of distribution channels.

15. Account, as best you can, for the differences in channel patterns that might be encountered in a highly developed country and an underdeveloped country.

16. One of the first things companies discover about international patterns of channels of distribution is that in most countries it is nearly impossible to gain adequate market coverage through a simple channel-of-distribution plan. Discuss.

17. Discuss the various methods of overcoming blocked channels.

18. What strategy might be employed to distribute goods effectively in the dichotomous small/large middleman pattern, which characterizes merchant middlemen in most countries?

19. Discuss the economic implications of assessing termination penalties or restricting the termination of middlemen. Do you foresee such restrictions in the United States?

20. Discuss why Japanese distribution channels can be the epitome of blocked channels.

21. What are the two most important provisions of the Export Trading Company Act?

# Exporting and Logistics:
## SPECIAL ISSUES FOR BUSINESS

CHAPTER 15

## CHAPTER LEARNING OBJECTIVES

What you should learn from Chapter 15:

- How the U.S. government helps exporters

- The additional steps necessary to move goods across country borders

- How various import restrictions are used politically

- Means of reducing import taxes to remain competitive

- The main instruments of foreign commercial payments

- The mechanics of export documents and their importance

- The logistics and problems of the physical movement of goods

# Global Perspective

## AN EXPORT SALE: FROM TRADE SHOW TO INSTALLATION

### February 3: The Trade Show and the Order

This account of the sale of paper-converting machinery, called a case maker, between Austin Inc., a New Hampshire–based manufacturer, and China Books, a Chinese book publisher, details the steps of an international export sale. The story begins in Germany at DRUPA, the largest trade show in the world for the printing and paper market. Mr. Kang, a representative for China Books, approaches Austin's booth and thinks, "Well, it took a week to find the Americans' booth, but watching their machines run has made it easier to see which equipment serves us best." Kang also muses that it was nice to meet the people who actually design and build the machine and to see the solid relationship with their Far Eastern sales agent. Kang likes the equipment and signs an order for $500,000, which stipulates a 15 percent deposit ($75,000) and the pledge of a letter of credit for the rest.

### March 3: The Financing

Once Mr. Kang returns home he applies for financing and an import license. The import license requirements make the whole deal a chicken-and-egg situation. Kang can't complete the financing until he gets the import license, and once he gets the license, he has a specified time in which to complete the transaction.

### July 3: Import License and the Letter of Credit

Four months later, Mr. Kang finally gets the import license. Because it is only good for six months, he must be careful that the letter of credit's latest ship and expiry dates are within the effective time of the import permit. He applies for financing and the letter of credit.

In the United States, Mr. Roberts, Austin's controller, is concerned about the sale to China Books. "It's been more than four months since the sales department sent a copy of the signed order, and yet the company still hasn't received the 15 percent deposit," Roberts thinks. "Until they send the money, the customer isn't really committed. Nevertheless, the general manager has decided to release a stock machine to the manufacturing department to begin the necessary adaptations that the Chinese buyer wants. If the company doesn't begin work now, the equipment will not be ready as promised on the order. If this customer doesn't come through, the company will be stuck with a product finished to China Books' specifications and no cash."

Over the past four months there was a flurry of fax messages between Austin and China Books. Before the instructions for the letter of credit can be completed, details on the proposed shipment dates (before December 31), terms of sale (CIF—cost, insurance, and freight), and lists of Export-Import (Ex-Im) Bank facilities from the trade resource center in Portsmouth, New Hampshire (China Books wants to finance part of the cost of the purchase with an Ex-Im Bank–guaranteed loan), must be confirmed by both parties.

Roberts chooses CIF as the terms of sale so his company can select its regular freight forwarder to handle all the details. This is the company's first sale to China, so CIF gives Roberts some peace of mind—he won't have to rely on unknown people to collect on the letter of credit. It also means Austin controls selection of the shipping carrier and presumably will get the best shipping rate.

In addition, China Books was able to use one of the banks on the Ex-Im Bank list so the financing should go smoothly, and Roberts is satisfied that China Books will qualify for a loan.

### August 1: Closing the Deal

The bank just called Mr. Kang with loan approval. "Now I've got to get wire instructions for the letter of credit and send the 15 percent deposit. They said delivery this December. I'll put down December 31 as the latest shipment date, with an expiry of January 31."

Roberts receives the request for wire instructions from Kang. "It will probably take about three weeks for everything to clear the bank," he thinks. "But the wire instructions must go out now since nothing can be shipped until the original letter of credit is received." Shipping had advised Roberts that shipping the machinery through Montreal could avoid some stiff harbor maintenance fees that shipping out of New York would entail. Thus when Roberts sends the wire instructions to Kang, he asks the Chinese buyer to permit shipment through Montreal.

### September 4: Production and Shipment

Mr. Kang thinks to himself, "This faxing across the world is awkward but more efficient than telephoning, because while I'm writing in mid-morning, they're going to bed. Now we just need to wait for the machine to get here." Kang begins planning for the integration of the new case maker into China Book's production line, and realizes they need to add a counter stacker option to the machine. The extra $20,000 should be worth the plant efficiency that will be gained. Mr. Kang starts to call the bank to have the counter stacker added to the letter of credit but hesitates and thinks, "I'm sick of bank rhetoric, so we'll just wire them the additional funds before shipment. The amendment to the letter of credit will cost too much time and money."

Because a lot rides on this order, Mr. Kang decides he will schedule a trip to New Hampshire for the final acceptance test. He wants to be sure the machine will handle the paper stock the company uses. No one wants the machine to be delivered and then find out it won't work the way they expect. Too many complications arise if the equipment is paid for and delivered and it needs major adjustments.

Back in New Hampshire, Roberts is checking details to make sure the case maker will be shipped on time. "Things are getting hectic—so much to do, so little time. If they expect to ship this year, the customer must accept the machine by December 16. That gives us a week to break it down and skid it (bolt the machine to a wooden pallet) and a week to get it on a boat. We have very little room for error because of the holidays. Besides, the customer wants special packing in desiccant because of climatic conditions. So we'll need to send the shipment to a packing specialist before it goes to port."

## November 1: Letter of Credit

Roberts sends the original letter of credit to his freight forwarder by second-day air and includes the bank invoice forms and marine insurance certificate.

## December 2: Final Inspection and Shipping Schedules

In China, Kang thinks, "Roberts faxed me possible vessel dates. They're going for Friday, December 20, out of Montreal, and I'm booked to be in New Hampshire December 11–15. The vessel arrives in Shanghai January 25. That would be just right. I hope they'll be ready for the test run because our material will be a challenge for them to run."

Meanwhile, Roberts is thinking, "I'm glad our general manager decided to release the case maker as a stock machine during the DRUPA show. He OK'd it because the China Books deal looked firm. We'd never be able to ship it this year otherwise. Kang seems like a decent person—very bright. They got their material here two weeks ago for us to try, and since then manufacturing has been working hard trying to meet their specs. I hope we have a good week."

## December 13: The Test Run

"The machine looks impressive," Kang observes after he watches the test run take place. "But I'm not convinced we can run a consistent 120 per minute. I insisted we come in tomorrow for one more demo. They're close, so if they don't quite do it, I won't pay the installation bill until we're comfortable with production at our plant. Besides, Roberts told me the boat would probably leave late, so they have a little extra time to get the container to the pier."

A second test run takes place the next day. Kang asks for a few minor adjustments but is otherwise satisfied that China Books will get consistently good production from Austin's case maker.

In his office, Roberts wonders why all foreign shipments seem to occur at year-end. "Cheryl at Fast Forwarder (Austin's freight forwarder) said we should be ready first thing on Monday, December 16, if we want to get the container on board for a December 31 sailing. Since nothing happens during the last week of the year, it needs to be there this Friday morning to be processed by the line. The steamship companies will probably start the holidays at noon on the 24th. Red alert! Call Cheryl immediately and tell her the 40-footer (container) must have a wooden floor—with no room for surprises!"

## January 2: It's on the Way

Kang is ecstatic. "Roberts just faxed me the ocean bill of lading. The case maker was on board the vessel *Tiger Shark* December 31, with an estimated arrival in Shanghai on January 30. They just made it!"

## Analysis

Although this scenario may seem staggering, it is not intended to overwhelm you or make you wary of exporting. The point is that there are specific export mechanics that occur when goods are shipped from one country to another, and although they may be tedious, you cannot escape them. The good news is that assistance is available for the exporter from government and private sources. This scenario occurred prior to widespread use of the Internet, and many of the steps can either be completed on the Internet or sped up by using the Internet but not eliminated. According to one source, a bank's role in handling the risks in shipping and paying for goods has not changed much since the seventeenth century. What has changed is technology. Banks are adapting their trade finance to the electronic age. Instead of faxes, telegraph, and postal service as used in the Global Perspective, many banks take a direct feed from a client's purchase-order system, extract the data and use it to create a letter of credit, and provide real-time information on transaction status.

For example, Bank One offers an Internet-based tool for creating, modifying, and sending letters of credit and collections. And in the future, banks will act as a hub to all parties involved in transactions—buyer, seller, bank, carrier, freight forwarder, insurance company and customs authorities. The rules and regulations remain the same but the process is expedited. Such are the benefits of the Internet. As you read this chapter, identify each of the places in this scenario where the Internet could be used to expedite the process.

Sources: Robert R. Costa, "Tales of Foreign Sales," *Financial Executive*, January–February 1997, pp. 43–46 and Steve Marlin, "Banks Link Their Trade Platforms with the International Movement of Goods," *Information Week*, May 12, 2003, p. 48.

**Exhibit 15.1**
The Exporting Process

| Leaving the Exporting Country | Physical Distribution | Entering the Importing Country |
|---|---|---|
| **Licenses** | International shipping and logistics | Tariffs, taxes |
| General | Packing | **Nontariff barriers** |
| Validated | Insurance | Standards |
| **Documentation** | | Inspection |
| Export declaration | | Documentation |
| Commercial invoice | | Quotas |
| Bill of lading | | Fees |
| Consular invoice | | Licenses |
| Special certificates | | Special certificates |
| Other documents | | Exchange permits |
| | | Other barriers |

Exporting is an integral part of all international business, whether the company is large or small, or whether it markets in one country or is a global marketer. Goods manufactured in one country and destined for another must be moved across borders to enter the distribution system of the target market.

Most countries control the movement of goods crossing their borders, whether leaving (exports) or entering (imports). Export and import documents, tariffs, quotas, and other barriers to the free flow of goods between independent sovereignties are requirements that must be met by either the exporter or importer, or both.[1]

In addition to selecting a target market, designing an appropriate product, establishing a price, planning a promotional program, and selecting a distribution channel, the international marketer must meet the legal requirements involved in moving goods from one country to another. The exporting process (see Exhibit 15.1) includes the licenses and documentation necessary to leave the country, an international carrier to transport the goods, and fulfillment of the import requirements necessary to get the shipment legally into another country.

Firms often have staff experienced in dealing with export mechanics, but when confronted with unfamiliar situations or a task that is too burdensome, there are agencies, government and private, available to provide expert assistance.[2] More and more, companies are finding it cost effective to outsource many of the exporting activities. In those cases where it is done in-house, much of the mechanics necessary for exporting can be completed via the Internet. These mechanics of exporting are sometimes considered the essence of foreign marketing; however, while their importance cannot be minimized, they should not be seen as the primary task of international marketing but as a necessary step in completing the process of marketing.

There are many reasons why countries impose some form of regulation and restriction on the exporting and importing of goods. **Export regulations** may be designed to conserve scarce goods for home consumption or to control the flow of strategic goods to actual or potential enemies. **Import regulations** may be imposed to protect health, conserve foreign exchange, serve as economic reprisals, protect home industry, or provide revenue in the form of tariffs. To comply with various regulations, the exporter may have to acquire export licenses or permits from the home country and ascertain that the potential customer has the necessary permits for importing the goods. The rules and regulations that cover the exportation and importation of goods and their payment, and the physical movement of those goods between countries, are the special concerns of this chapter.

[1]For a comprehensive review of trade barriers see "2003 National Trade Estimate Report on Foreign Trade Barriers," see www.ustr.gov/reports.

[2]Comprehensive coverage of the mechanics of exporting can be found in the following: U.S. Department of Commerce, *A Basic Guide to Exporting, 3rd edition,* Alexandra Woznick (Navato, CA, World Trade Press, 2000).

# Export Restrictions

Although the United States requires no formal or special license to engage in exporting as a business, permission or a license to export may be required for certain commodities and certain destinations. Export licensing controls apply to exports of commodities and technical data from the United States; re-exports of U.S.-origin commodities and technical data from a foreign destination to another foreign destination; U.S.-origin parts and components used in foreign countries to manufacture foreign products for exports; and, in some cases, foreign products made from U.S.-origin technical data. Most items requiring special permission or a license for exportation are under the control of the Bureau of Industry and Security (BIS)[3] of the Department of Commerce.[4]

The volume of exports and the number of companies exporting from the United States have grown spectacularly over the last decade. In an effort to alleviate many of the problems and confusions of exporting and to expedite the process, the Department of Commerce published a revised set of export regulations known as the **Export Administration Regulations (EAR)**. They are intended to speed up the process of granting export licenses by removing a large number of items from specific export license control and by concentrating licensing on a very specific list of items, most of which affect either national security, nuclear nonproliferation, terrorism, or chemical and biological weapons. Along with these changes comes a substantial increase in responsibility on the part of the exporter since the exporter must now ensure that Export Administration Regulations are not violated.

The export control provisions of the Export Administration Regulations are intended to serve the national security, foreign policy, and nonproliferation interests of the United States and, in some cases, to carry out its international obligations.[5] The EAR also includes some export controls to protect the United States from the adverse impact of the unrestricted export of commodities in short supply, such as Western cedar. Items that do not require a license for a specific destination can be shipped with the notation NLR (no license required) on the Shipper's Export Declaration.

## Determining Export Requirements

The first step when complying with export licensing regulations is to determine the appropriate license for your product. Products exported from the United States require either a general or a validated export license, depending on the product, where it is going, the end use, and the final user. The *general license* permits exportation of certain products that are not subject to EAR control with nothing more than a declaration of the type of product, its value, and its destination. The *validated license,* issued only on formal application, is a specific document authorizing exportation within specific limitations designated under the EAR.

The responsibility of determining if a license is required rests with the exporter. The steps necessary to determine the type of license required and/or if an item can be shipped are as follows:

- The exporter is responsible for selecting the proper classification number known as the **Export Control Classification Number (ECCN)** for the item to be exported. TheECCN leads to a description in the **Commerce Control List (CCL)**, which indicates the exportability status of the item.

- The exporter must decide from the CCL if there are end-use restrictions on the items, such as uses in nuclear, chemical, and biological weapons. The exporter must also determine if the product has a dual use, that is, can it be used both in commercial and restricted applications.

- The exporter is responsible for determining the ultimate end customer and ultimate end uses of the product, regardless of the initial buyer. This step includes

---

[3]Formally known as the Bureau of Export Administration (BXA)

[4]"BIS Norms Now Cover 24 More Import Items," *The Economic Times,* April 19, 2003.

[5]For a primer on Commerce Department export controls, see "Introduction to Commerce Department Export Controls," May 8, 2003. See www.bis.doc.gov and select Export Control basics.

carefully screening end users and end uses of the product to determine if the final destination of the product is to an unapproved user or for an unapproved use. U.S. law requires firms to avoid shipments if the firm has knowledge that customers will use its products for illegal purposes or resell the product to unauthorized end users.

For purposes of illustration, suppose you are an exporter of shotguns and you are beginning the process of fulfilling orders from Argentina (20-inch barrel shotguns), Australia (23-inch and 26-inch barrels), and Sudan (26-inch barrels).[6]

The first step is to determine the proper Export Control Classification Number (ECCN) for the commodity to be exported. Each ECCN consists of five characters that identify its category, product group, type of control, and country group level. There are three general ways to determine a product's ECCN:

- If you are the exporter of the product but not its manufacturer, you can contact the manufacturer or developer to see if they already have an ECCN.

- Compare the general characteristics of the product to the Commerce Control List and find the most appropriate product category. Once the category is identified, you go through the entire category and identify the appropriate ECCN by determining the product's particular functions.

- Request a classification from the BIS. The request must include the end use, end user, and/or destination. The BIS will advise you whether a license is required or likely to be granted for a particular transaction. This type of request is known as an *advisory opinion*. An advisory opinion does not bind the BIS to issuing a license in the future, since government policies may change before a license is actually granted.

Once the proper ECCN is obtained (in this illustration 0A984, see Exhibit 15.2), the second step is to locate the number in the Commerce Control List. Consulting the (CCL)

---

[6]This is an abbreviated example intended to illustrate the general idea of the steps necessary to determine licensing requirements.

**Exhibit 15.2**

Illustration Commerce Control List Requirements for ECCN 0A984

Source: Abstracted from Export Administration Regulations Database, Bureau of Industry and Security, www.bis.doc.gov.

**0A984** Shotguns, barrel length 18 inches (45.72 cm) or over; buckshot shotgun shells; except equipment used exclusively to treat or tranquilize animals, and except arms designed solely for signal, flare, or saluting use; and parts, n.e.s.

**License Requirements**

*Reason for Control:* CC, FC, UN

| Control(s) | Country Chart |
|---|---|
| FC applies to firearms | FC Column 1 |
| CC 1 applies to shotguns with a barrel length greater than or equal to 18 in. (45.72 cm), but less than 24 in. (60.96 cm) or buckshot, shotgun shells controlled by this entry, regardless of end-user. | CC Column 1 |
| CC 2 applies to shotguns with a barrel length greater than or equal to 24 in. (60.96 cm), regardless of end-user. | CC Column 2 |
| CC 3 applies to shotguns with a barrel length greater than or equal to 24 in. (60.96 cm) if for sale or resale to police or law enforcement. | CC Column 3 |
| UN applies to UN sanctions that ban shipments of all firearms, regardless of type, to countries listed. | Rwanda; Serbia and Montenegro (formerly Yugoslavia) |

**List of Items Controlled**

Unit: $ value

*Related Controls:* this entry does not control shotguns with a barrel length of less than 18 inches (45.72 cm). These items are subject to the export licensing authority of the Department of State.

## Exhibit 15.3   Commerce Country Chart: Reasons for Control (Selected Countries)

| Country | Chemical & Biological Weapons | | | Nuclear Nonproliferation | | National Security | | Missile Tech | Regional Stability | | Firearms Convention | Crime Control | | | Anti-Terrorism | |
|---|---|---|---|---|---|---|---|---|---|---|---|---|---|---|---|---|
| | CB 1 | CB 2 | CB 3 | NP 1 | NP 2 | NS 1 | NS 2 | MT 1 | RS 1 | RS 2 | FC 1 | CC 1 | CC 2 | CC 3 | AT 1 | AT 2 |
| Albania | x* | x | | x | | x | x | x | x | x | | x | x | | | |
| Argentina | x | | | | | x | x | x | x | x | x | x | | x | | |
| Australia | x | | | | | x | | x | x | | | | | | | |
| Canada | x | | | | | | | | | | x | | | | | |
| China | x | x | x | x | | x | x | x | x | x | | x | | x | | |
| France | x | | | | | x | | x | x | | | | | | | |
| India | x | x | x | x | x | x | x | x | x | x | | x | | x | | |
| Mexico | x | x | | x | | x | x | x | x | x | x | x | | x | | |
| Sudan | x | x | | x | | x | x | x | x | x | | x | | x | x | x |
| Syria | x | x | x | x | | x | x | x | x | x | | x | | x | x | |

*x = special license required.

Source: Abstracted from Commerce Country Chart, www.bxa.doc.gov. Under *Rules, Regulations and Lists* select *Go Direct to the Regs* and then select *part name, 738spir*, June 20, 2000.

for shotguns (see Exhibit 15.2), the description shows that the reasons for control are Crime Control (CC), Firearms Convention (FC), and UN sanctions (UN) and that there are different restrictions depending on the length of the shotgun barrel.

The third step is to consult the **Commerce Country Chart (CCC)** (Exhibit 15.3), which helps you determine, based on the reason(s) for control associated with your item, if you need a license to export or re-export your item to a particular destination. In combination with the Commodity Control List, the CCC allows you to determine whether a license is required for items on the CCL exported to any country in the world.

In checking the CCC (Exhibit 15.3), you find Argentina, Australia, and Sudan all listed. Looking at the Crime Control and Firearms Convention columns and referencing the product description in the Commodity Control List, you see that the Argentine order for shotguns with 20-inch barrels falls into CC Column 1 and FC Column 1, where the x indicates that the order cannot be shipped without a special license. The Australian orders for 23-inch and 26-inch shotguns (CC Columns 1 and 2) do not require special licenses.

Finally, an examination of the Sudanese order for 26-inch shotguns reveals in CC Column 2 that the product can be exported without a special license; however, CC Column 3 indicates that if the guns are for sale or resale to police or law enforcement, a special license is required. Because you are not sure if the shotguns are to be resold, more information will be needed before the order can be processed. If you determine that the guns will not be resold to police or law enforcement, they can be shipped without special license; otherwise, a license must be obtained before the shipment can take place.

But the challenge is not yet over. An exporter also must establish that the end user is not listed in the List of Denied Persons,[7] which lists those denied export privileges; no shipments may be made to any person or company on the denied persons list. In addition to checking the denial list, the exporter needs to make a general check to be sure there are no indications that the end-user's intentions will lead to an unauthorized use of the product.

Unfortunately, you cannot always rely on the buyer's word. Sun Microsystems sold one of its supercomputers to a Hong Kong firm that claimed the computer was destined for a scientific institute near Beijing, an authorized sale. A trace of the final destination revealed that the computer was at a military research facility in China, an unauthorized end use and end user. Because Sun Microsystems monitored the sale and reported the diversion, there were no legal consequences. Negotiations between China and the U.S.

---

[7]A database of all prohibited parties can be found on the "Prohibited Parties Database" which, in addition to the Denied Persons List, includes Debarred Parties, Entity List and Specially Designated Nationals, Terrorists, Narcotics Traffickers, Blocked Persons, and Vessels, all of whom must be screened before completing an export order. The list of denied persons can be found at www.bsi.doc.gov and select Denied Persons List under Rules, Regulations and Lists.

Chinese air force officers undergo a training session on the latest command center instruments at a training school in Beijing. China successfully test-fired a new type of long-range ground-to-ground missile within its territory as tensions between China and Taiwan intensified after Taiwan's president declared that relations between Taipei and Beijing should be regarded as "special state-to-state relations." Much of the electronic technology used in long-range missiles is dual-use; that is, the technology can be used for both non-military and military applications. It is the exporter's responsibility to assure that the final user of restricted dual-use products complies with exports restrictions. (© *Roger Ressmeyer/CORBIS*)

government resulted in the return of the computer to Sun Microsystems. To be alert to possible problems like the one Sun faced, the Export Administration Regulations suggest looking for red flags (Exhibit 15.4). which may give a clue that your customer is planning an unlawful diversion.

## Exhibit 15.4
Red Flags

Source: www.bxa.doc.gov and select *Red Flags*.

The exporter has an important role to play in preventing exports and reexports that might be contrary to the national security and foreign policy interests of the United States and to ensure that the shipment is not in violation of Bureau of Export Administration regulations. To assist in determining the motives of a buyer, the BXA proposes these indicators as possible signs that a customer is planning an unlawful diversion:

1. The customer or purchasing agent is reluctant to offer information about the end use of a product.
2. The product's capabilities do not fit the buyer's line of business; for example, a small bakery places an order for several sophisticated lasers.
3. The product ordered is incompatible with the technical level of the country to which the product is being shipped. For example, semiconductor-manufacturing equipment would be of little use in a country without an electronics industry.
4. The customer has little or no business background.
5. The customer is willing to pay cash for a very expensive item when the terms of the sale call for financing.
6. The customer is unfamiliar with the product's performance characteristics but still wants the product.
7. The customer declines routine installation, training, or maintenance services.
8. Delivery dates are vague, or deliveries are planned for out-of-the-way destinations.
9. A freight-forwarding firm is listed as the product's final destination.
10. The shipping route is abnormal for the product and destination.
11. Packaging is inconsistent with the stated method of shipment or destination.
12. When questioned, the buyer is evasive or unclear about whether the purchased product is for domestic use, export, or reexport.

**Exhibit 15.5**
Examples of Violations
and Penalties of BIS
Export Controls

Sources: "Case Histories for Calendar
Year 2000," "Three-Year Denial of
Export Privileges Imposed," and, U.S.
Department of Justice, 2003, *Bureau
of Industry and Security,* U.S.
Department of Commerce News
Releases, www.bis.doc.gov.

| | |
|---|---|
| **Export License Requirements** | Frank Curic, of Bosnia and Herzegovina, was placed on the Denial of Export Privileges list for three years. BIS charged Curic tried to export a Mossberg shotgun by concealing it in a vehicle that he was shipping from the United States; the export of the vehicle was authorized under a license exception which required that the vehicle not contain personal belongings. The export of shotguns of 18 inches or longer is subject to licensing under EAR regulations to support the U.S. foreign policy of promoting the observance of human rights. |
| **Antiboycott Provisions** | The Commerce Department imposed a $105,000 civil penalty on Kenclaire Electrical Agencies for 11 violations of the antiboycott provisions of EAR. On each occasion Kenclaire failed to delete, reject, amend, or otherwise take exception to the following language contained in the 11 orders from Saudi Arabia: "No items or the components thereof made by the manufacturer covered and banned under the Arab Boycott Rules shall be sold to the Buyer. Seller shall be fully responsible to replace all such items at no cost to the Buyer. Seller shall be further responsible to pay for all penalties and expenses for defying the Arab Boycott Laws"* |
| **Duel Use Products** | Bushnell Corporation, which does business as Worldwide Sports & Recreation, pleaded guilty to conspiracy and violation of export regulations. For a period of two years, over 500 Night Ranger night vision devices were shipped to Japan and 14 other countries without the required export license. U.S. Attorney warned that "distributors of equipment with potential military use must be vigilant about compliance with export restrictions. . . . Willful blindness and deliberate ignorance of the law is not an excuse when national security is at issue." Under a plea agreement, Bushnell agreed to pay a criminal fine of $650,000 and receive 5 years of corporate probation. |

*This or a similar statement must be rejected, deleted, or amended or a shipper is in violation.

As is true of all the export mechanics that an exporter encounters, the details of exporting must be followed to the letter. Good record keeping verifying the steps undertaken in establishing the proper ECCN and in evaluating the intentions of end users and end uses is important should a disagreement arise between the exporter and the Bureau of Industry and Security. Penalties can entail denial of export privileges or fines, or both. For example, a five-year denial of export privileges was imposed on a resident of Pittsfield, Massachusetts, based on his conviction for illegally exporting 150 riot shields to Romania without the required export license. At the time of the shipment, the riot shields were controlled for export worldwide for foreign policy reasons. See Exhibit 15.5 for examples of violations and penalties.

## ELAIN, STELA, ERIC, and SNAP

Although the procedure for acquiring an export license may seem tedious on first reading, there are four electronic services designed to cut through the paperwork and time necessary to acquire export licenses.

- First, **ELAIN** (Export License Application and Information Network) enables exporters that have authorization to submit license applications via the Internet for all commodities except supercomputers to all free-world destinations. When approved, licensing decisions are conveyed back to the exporters via the Internet.

- Second, **STELA** (System for Tracking Export License Applications) an automated voice-response system for tracking applications, can be accessed using a touch-tone phone. It provides applicants with the status of their license and classification applications and is available 24 hours a day, seven days a week. STELA can give exporters authority to ship their goods for those licenses approved without conditions.

- Third, **ERIC** (Electronic Request for Item Classification), a supplementary service to ELAIN, allows an exporter to submit commodity classification requests via the Internet to the Bureau of Export administration.

- Fourth, **SNAP** (Simplified Network Application Process), an alternative to paper license submissions, enables an exporter to submit export and reexport applications, high-performance computer notices, and commodity classification requests via the Internet. Acknowledgments of submissions will be received the same day, and electronic facsimiles of export licenses and other validations can be obtained online. SNAP is one of the changes made by the Department of Commerce to move it from being a paper-based bureaucracy to an all-digital department.

## Import Restrictions

When an exporter plans a sale to a foreign buyer, it is necessary to examine the export restrictions of the home country as well as the import restrictions and regulations of the importing country.[8] Although the responsibility of import restrictions may rest with the importer, the exporter does not want to ship goods until it is certain that all import regulations of the destination country are met. Goods arriving without proper documentation can be denied entry and returned to the shipper.[9]

Besides import tariffs, many other trade restrictions are imposed by foreign countries. A few examples from the 30 basic barriers to exporting considered important by *Business International* include import licenses, quotas, and other quantitative restrictions; currency restrictions and allocation of exchange at unfavorable rates on payments for imports; devaluation; prohibitive prior import deposits, prohibition of collection-basis sales, and insistence on cash letters of credit; arbitrarily short periods in which to apply for import licenses; and delays resulting from pressure on overworked officials or from competitors' influence on susceptible officials.[10]

Trading with the European Union from outside the Union or within member states, an exporter continues to be confronted with market barriers that are not yet eliminated.[11] One study of 20,000 EC exporting firms indicated that the most troublesome barriers were administrative roadblocks, border-crossing delays, and capital controls. The French government imposed one such barrier against Japanese VCRs. All Japanese VCRs were directed to land only at one port, where only one inspector was employed; hence, just 10 to 12 VCRs could enter France each day. Generally such barriers are challenged and ultimately dropped. As the EU becomes a single market, many of the barriers that exist among member countries will be eliminated, although not as rapidly as some expect. The single European market will no doubt make trade easier among its member countries.

The most frequently encountered trade restrictions, besides tariffs, are such nontariff barriers (NTBs) as exchange permits, quotas, import licenses, boycotts, standards, and voluntary agreements.

## Tariffs

Recall that tariffs are the taxes or customs duties levied against goods imported from another country. All countries have tariffs for the purpose of raising revenue and protecting home industries from competition with foreign-produced goods. Tariff rates are based on value or quantity or a combination of both. In the United States, for example, the types of customs duties used are classified as follows: (1) *ad valorem duties,* which are based on a percentage of the determined value of the imported goods; (2) *specific duties,* a stipulated amount per unit weight or some other measure of quantity; and (3) a *compound duty,* which combines both specific and ad valorem taxes on a particular

---

[8]"Vietnam: Trade Regulations," *Economist Intelligence Unit,* May 12, 2003.

[9]"Exporters Face 142 Import Restrictions Overseas," *The Korea Times,* February 2, 2003.

[10]Martin Crutsinger, "U.S. Releases Trade Barriers Review," *AP Online,* May 1, 2003.

[11]Robin Munro, "IKEA Fights Plan to Hike Import Tariff," *The Moscow Times,* March 6, 2003.

## CROSSING BORDERS 15.1 You Don't Look Like a Mexican Peanut to Me!

The U.S. government is serious about its import restrictions, especially on agricultural products. It doesn't look kindly, for example, on peanuts from China being shipped as Mexican peanuts. But how do you tell where peanuts, orange juice, and other agricultural products come from? With an "inductively coupled plasma mass spectrometer," that's how.

The U.S. Customs Service uses such a machine to determine whether a peanut headed for Safeway matches a peanut grown in Mexico or Georgia. It's a little like DNA testing for plants. While the machine can't tell exactly whether the peanuts come from a specific country, it can tell if the peanuts in a sample match a sample of peanuts known to come from a specific country. This process began about 10 years ago with the analyzing of frozen orange juice. Since frozen

orange juice from different countries has different tariff schedules, transshipment through a lower-tariff country can make a big difference in tariffs paid.

In a little over a year, with the help of the machine, U.S. Customs was able to build a case of "dumping" against Chinese garlic, an illegal transshipment case against Argentine peanuts, and a case against a California coffee distributor who was adulterating Hawaiian Kona coffee with cheaper Central American beans and selling the result as pure Kona.

Source: Guy Gugliotta, "High-Tech Trade Enforcement Tracks Peanuts Across Borders," *Washington Post,* December 4, 1997, p. A21, and Bob Dart, "U. S. Takes Aim at Peanut Traffickers: High-tech Equipment Is Helping to Detect Illegal Over-the-Border Shipments: Undercutting NAFTA," *The Atlanta Journal and Constitution,* December 9, 1997, p A12.

item, that is, a tax per pound plus a percentage of value. Because tariffs frequently change, published tariff schedules for every country are available to the exporter on a current basis.[12]

### Exchange Permits

Especially troublesome to exporters are exchange restrictions placed on the flow of currency by some foreign countries. To conserve scarce foreign exchange and alleviate balance-of-payment difficulties, many countries impose restrictions on the amount of their currency they will exchange for the currency of another country—in effect, they ration the amount of currency available to pay for imports. Exchange controls may be applied in general to all commodities, or a country may employ a system of multiple exchange rates based on the type of import. Essential products might have a very favorable exchange rate, while nonessentials or luxuries would have a less favorable rate of exchange. South Africa, for example, has a two-tier system for foreign exchange: Commercial Rand and Financial Rand. At times, countries may not issue any exchange permits for certain classes of commodities.

In countries that use exchange controls, the usual procedure is for the importer to apply to the control agency of the importing country for an import permit; if the control agency approves the request, an import license is issued. On presentation to the proper government agency, the import license can be used to have local currency exchanged for the currency of the seller.

Receiving an import license, or even an exchange permit, however, is not a guarantee that a seller can exchange local currency for the currency of the seller. If local currency is in short supply—a chronic problem in some countries—other means of acquiring home-country currency are necessary. For example, in a transaction between the government of Colombia and a U.S. truck manufacturer, there was a scarcity of U.S. currency to exchange for the 1,000 vehicles Colombia wanted to purchase. The problem was solved through a series of exchanges. Colombia had a surplus of coffee that the truck manufacturer accepted and traded in Europe for sugar; the sugar was traded for pig iron, and finally the pig iron was traded for U.S. dollars.

[12]The entire Harmonized Tariff Schedule of the U.S. can be downloaded, or accessed via an interactive tariff database, at USITC: www.usitc.gov, select Harmonized Tariff Schedule.

## CROSSING BORDERS 15.2 Major Smuggling Ring Busted—A Sweet Deal

The United States maintains an artificial price for sugar to protect the cane and beet sugar industry. This feat is accomplished by placing a quota on sugar imports. The amount of sugar imported annually is determined by estimating the annual consumption less estimated U.S. production. In 1999 consumption was 10.2 tons, production was 8.4 tons thus the quota for that year was 1.8 tons. This held U.S. domestic raw sugar prices to 22.07 cents per pound compared with 7.05 cents on the world market. Under this scenario if you could figure a way to buy sugar at 7 cents on the world market and sell it at 22 cents in the United States, you could make a pot full of money—but then there is that nasty quota standing in the way. Well there may be a way around those quotas if we read the law carefully.

Eureka! After a careful reading of the categories of sugar and derivatives covered by the sugar quota, an enterprising importer spotted a category not included in the quota, a gooey brown sugar-based molasses that is good for little more than animal feed. The Customs Department was contacted about the molasses product and agreed that it was not covered by the sugar restrictions, and gave its explicit approval to import the mixture without paying high tariffs. The company built a processing plant in Canada to turn Brazilian sugar into the molasses and a refinery across the border in Michigan to reverse the process and produce precisely the sort of sugar syrup covered by the tariffs. It then sold it to their usual customers: big makers of ice cream, confectionery and breakfast cereals.

All went well until the ever-vigilant sugar lobby put pressure on prominent politicians from sugar producing states to stop those "smugglers"—causing Customs to reverse itself. Alarmed that it might see its tariffs rise by some 7,000 percent, the company challenged the decision in the Court of International Trade (CIT). The court sided with the firm, dismissing the government's action as "arbitrary, capricious, and abuse of discretion," citing the precedent that products are classified according to the way they are imported, not their ultimate use. More pointedly, the court maintained that an importer had the right to design products specifically to get a lower duty. An internal memo from the agency said that under long-standing policy, it didn't matter what happened to a product after it was across the border. The fact that, after importation, the product may be processed causing it to compete directly with sugar subject to the quota is not relevant to classification.

The agency has always tolerated a certain amount of tariff engineering. The judge said that carmakers routinely import parts they later assemble in the United States in order to avoid high tariffs. The judge noted that even when pearls are imported with holes already drilled in them ready for stringing, customs classifies them as pearls, not jewelry which carries a higher tax rate.

A month after the ruling, the litigators began an appeal to Congress to change the definition of the sugar syrup to one of ultimate use, rather than what it is when imported. This would make the customs ruling and the court case irrelevant. It would also put the company out of business. But until the law is rewritten, truckloads of molasses goop cross the border into the United States to become clear sugar syrup that is used, among other things, as a coating for your breakfast cereal.

Sources: "United States: Sugar Protectionism, *The Economist*, April 22, 2000; and Bill Walsh, "Smart or Smuggling?" *The Times-Picayune*, April 30, 2000, p. F9.

This somewhat complicated but effective countertrade transaction is not uncommon. As will be discussed in Chapter 18, countertrade deals are often a result of the inability to convert local currency into home-country currency or of the refusal of a government to issue foreign exchange.

**Quotas**   Countries may also impose limitations on the quantity of certain goods imported during a specific period. These quotas may be applied to imports from specific countries or from all foreign sources in general. The United States, for example, has specific quotas for importing sugar, wheat, cotton, tobacco, textiles, and peanuts; in the case of some of these items, there also are limitations on the amount imported from specific countries. The most important reasons to set quotas are to protect domestic industry and to conserve foreign exchange. Some importing countries also set quotas to ensure an equitable distribution of a major market among friendly countries.

**Import Licenses**   As a means of regulating the flow of exchange and the quantity of a particular imported commodity, countries often require import licenses. The fundamental difference between quotas and import licenses as a means of controlling imports is the greater flexibility of import licenses over quotas. Quotas permit importing until the quota is filled; licensing limits quantities on a case-by-case basis.

**Standards**

Like many nontariff barriers, standards have legitimacy. Health standards, safety standards, and product quality standards are necessary to protect the consuming public, and imported goods are required to comply with local laws. Unfortunately, standards can also be used to slow down or restrict the procedures for importing to the point that the additional time and cost required to comply become, in effect, trade restrictions.

Safety standards are a good example. Most countries have safety standards for electrical appliances and require that imported electrical products meet local standards. However, safety standards can be escalated to the level of an absolute trade barrier by manipulating the procedures used to determine if products meet the standards. The simplest process is for the importing nation to accept the safety standard verification used by the exporting country, such as Underwriters Laboratories (UL) in the United States. If the product is certified for sale in the United States, and if U.S. standards are the same as the importing country's, then U.S. standards and certification are accepted and no further testing is necessary. Most countries not interested in using standards as a trade barrier follow such a practice.

The extreme situation occurs when the importing nation does not accept the same certification procedure required by the exporting nation and demands all testing be done in the importing country. Even more restrictive is the requirement that each item be tested instead of accepting batch testing. When such is the case, the effect is the same as a boycott. Until recently, Japan required all electrical consumer products to be tested in Japan or tested in the United States by Japanese officials. Japan now accepts the UL's safety tests except for medical supplies and agricultural products which still must be tested in Japan.

**Boycotts**

A boycott is an absolute restriction against trade with a country, or trade of specific goods. American firms must honor boycotts sanctioned by the U.S. government; however, a U.S. company participating in an unauthorized boycott could be fined for violating the U.S. antiboycott law. For example, U.S. companies are prohibited from participating in the Arab League boycott on trade with Israel. U.S. law forbids U.S. firms to comply with such unauthorized boycotts. If an American firm refuses to trade with Israel in order to do business with an Arab nation, or in any other way participates in the Arab League boycott, it faces stiff fines. Boycotts are the most restrictive NTB because they ban all trade, whereas other types of restrictions permit some trade.

**Voluntary Restrictions**

Foreign restrictions of all kinds abound, and the United States can be counted among those governments using restrictions. For over a decade, U.S. government officials have been arranging "voluntary" agreements with the Japanese steel and automobile industries to limit sales to the United States. Japan entered these voluntary agreements under the implied threat that if it did not voluntarily restrict the export of automobiles or steel to an agreed limit, the United States might impose even harsher restrictions, including additional import duties. Similar negotiations with the governments of major textile producers have limited textile imports as well. It is estimated that the cost of tariffs, quotas, and voluntary agreements on all fibers is as much as $40 billion at the retail level. This works out to be a hidden tax of almost $500 a year for every American family.

**Other Restrictions**

Restrictions may be imposed on imports of harmful products, drugs, medicines, and immoral products and literature. Products must also comply with government standards set for health, sanitation, packaging, and labeling. For example, in the Netherlands all imported hen and duck eggs must be marked in indelible ink with the country of origin; in Spain, imported condensed milk must be labeled to show fat content if it is less than 8 percent fat; and in the European Community, strict import controls have been placed on beef and beef products imported from the United Kingdom because of mad cow disease. Add to this list all genetically modified foods, which are meeting stiff opposition from the EU as well as activists around the world.

Failure to comply with regulations can result in severe fines and penalties. Because requirements vary for each country and change frequently, regulations for all countries must be consulted individually and on a current basis. *Overseas Business Reports,* issued periodically by the Department of Commerce, provides the foreign marketer with the most recent foreign trade regulations of each country as well as U.S. regulations regarding each country.

Although sanitation certificates, content labeling, and other such regulations serve a legitimate purpose, countries can effectively limit imports by using such restrictions as additional trade barriers. Most of the economically developed world encourages foreign trade and works through the World Trade Organization (WTO) to reduce tariffs and nontariff barriers to a reasonable rate. Yet in times of economic recession, countries revert to a protectionist philosophy and seek ways to restrict the importing of goods. Nontariff barriers have become one of the most potent ways for a country to restrict trade. The elimination of nontariff barriers has been a major concern of GATT negotiations in both the Tokyo and Uruguay Rounds and continues with the WTO.

# Terms of Sale

**Terms of sale**, or *trade terms,* differ somewhat in international marketing from those used in the United States. In U.S. domestic trade, it is customary to ship FOB (free on board, meaning that the price is established at the door of the factory), freight collect, prepaid, or COD (cash, or collect, on delivery). International trade terms often sound similar to those used in domestic business but generally have different meanings. International terms indicate how buyer and seller divide risks and obligations and, therefore, the costs of specific kinds of international trade transactions. When quoting prices, it is important to make them meaningful. The most commonly used international trade terms include the following.[13]

- **CIF** (cost, insurance, freight) to a named overseas port of import. A CIF quote is more meaningful to the overseas buyer because it includes the costs of goods, insurance, and all transportation and miscellaneous charges to the named place of debarkation.

- **C&F** (cost and freight) to a named overseas port. The price includes the cost of the goods and transportation costs to the named place of debarkation. The cost of insurance is borne by the buyer.

- **FAS** (free alongside) at a named U.S. port of export. The price includes cost of goods and charges for delivery of the goods alongside the shipping vessel. The buyer is responsible for the cost of loading onto the vessel, transportation, and insurance.

- **FOB** (free on board) at a named inland point, at a named port of exportation, or at a named vessel and port of export. The price includes the cost of the goods and delivery to the place named.

- **EX** (named port of origin). The price quoted covers costs only at the point of origin (example, EX Factory). All other charges are the buyer's concern.

A complete list of terms and their definitions can be found in *Incoterms,* a booklet published by the International Chamber of Commerce.[14] It is important for the exporter to understand exactly the meanings of terms used in quotations. A simple misunderstanding regarding delivery terms may prevent the exporter from meeting contractual obligations or make that person responsible for shipping costs he or she did not intend to incur. Exhibit 15.6 indicates who is responsible for a variety of costs under various terms.

---

[13]"Exporting to Europe: ME Survey Reveals 57% of U.S. Exporters Use 6 Terms," *Managing Exports,* April 1, 2003.

[14]A list of *Incoterms* can be found at www.iccbooks.com.

**Exhibit 15.6** Who's Responsible for Costs under Various Terms?

| Cost Items/Terms | FOB, Inland Carries at Factory | FOB Inland Carrier at Point of Shipment | FAS, Vessel or Plane at Port of Shipment | CIF, at Port of of Destination |
|---|---|---|---|---|
| Export packing* | Buyer | Seller | Seller | Seller |
| Inland freight | Buyer | Seller | Seller | Seller |
| Port charges | Buyer | Buyer | Seller | Seller |
| Forwarder's fee | Buyer | Buyer | Buyer | Seller |
| Consular fee | Buyer | Buyer | Buyer | Buyer[†] |
| Loading on vessel or plane | Buyer | Buyer | Buyer | Seller |
| Ocean freight | Buyer | Buyer | Buyer | Seller |
| Cargo insurance | Buyer | Buyer | Buyer | Seller |
| Customs duties | Buyer | Buyer | Buyer | Buyer |
| Ownership of goods passes | When goods on board an inland ocean carrier (truck, rail, etc.) or in hands of inland carrier | When goods unloaded by inland carrier | When goods alongside carrier, in hands of air or ocean carrier | When goods on board air or carrier at port of shipment |

*Who absorbs export packing? This charge should be clearly agreed on. Charges are sometimes controversial.

[†]The seller has responsibility to arrange for consular invoices (and other documents requested by buyer's government). According to official definitions, the buyer pays fees, but sometimes as a matter of practice, the seller includes fees in quotations.

# Getting Paid: Foreign Commercial Payments

The sale of goods in other countries is further complicated by additional risks encountered when dealing with foreign customers. Risks from inadequate credit reports on customers, problems of currency exchange controls, distance, and different legal systems, and the cost and difficulty of collecting delinquent accounts require a different emphasis on payment systems.[15] In U.S. domestic trade, the typical payment procedure for established customers is an **open account**—that is, the goods are delivered and the customer is billed on an end-of-the-month basis. However, the most frequently used term of payment in foreign commercial transactions for both export and import sales is a letter of credit, followed closely in importance by commercial dollar drafts or bills of exchange drawn by the seller on the buyer. Internationally, open accounts are reserved for well-established customers, and cash in advance is required of only the poorest credit risks or when the character of the merchandise is such that not fulfilling the terms of the contract may result in heavy loss. Because of the time required for shipment of goods from one country to another, advance payment of cash is an unusually costly burden for a potential customer and places the seller at a definite competitive disadvantage.

Terms of sales are typically arranged between the buyer and seller at the time of the sale. The type of merchandise, amount of money involved, business custom, credit rating of the buyer, country of the buyer, and whether the buyer is a new or old customer must be considered in establishing the terms of sale. The five basic payment arrangements—letters of credit, bills of exchange, cash in advance, open accounts, and forfaiting—are discussed in this section.

## Letters of Credit

Export **letters of credit** opened in favor of the seller by the buyer handle most American exports. Letters of credit shift the buyer's credit risk to the bank issuing the letter of credit. When a letter of credit is used, the seller ordinarily can draw a draft against the bank issuing the credit and receive dollars by presenting proper shipping documents. Except for cash in advance, letters of credit afford the greatest degree of protection for the seller.

The procedure for a letter of credit begins with completion of the contract. (See Exhibit 15.7 for the steps in a letter-of-credit transaction.) Then the buyer goes to a local

[15]Martin Posner, "Exports: Opportunities and Risks," *Credit Management*, April 2003, p. 18.

**Exhibit 15.7**   A Letter-of-Credit Transaction

Here is what typically happens when payment is made by an irrevocable letter of credit confirmed by a U.S. bank. Follow the steps in the illustration below.

1. Exporter and customer agree on terms of sale.
2. Buyer requests its foreign bank to open a letter of credit.
3. The buyer's bank prepares an irrevocable letter of credit (LC), including all instructions, and sends the irrevocable letter of credit to a U.S. bank.
4. The U.S. bank prepares a letter of confirmation and letter of credit and sends to seller.
5. Seller reviews LC. If acceptable, arranges with freight forwarder to deliver goods to designated port of entry.
6. The goods are loaded and shipped.
7. At the same time the forwarder completes the necessary documents and sends documents to the seller.
8. Seller presents documents, indicating full compliance, to the U.S. bank.
9. The U.S. bank reviews the documents. If they are in order, issues seller a check for amount of sale.
10. The documents are airmailed to the buyer's bank for review.
11. If documents are in compliance, the bank sends documents to buyer.
12. To claim goods, buyer presents documents to customs broker.
13. Goods are released to buyer.

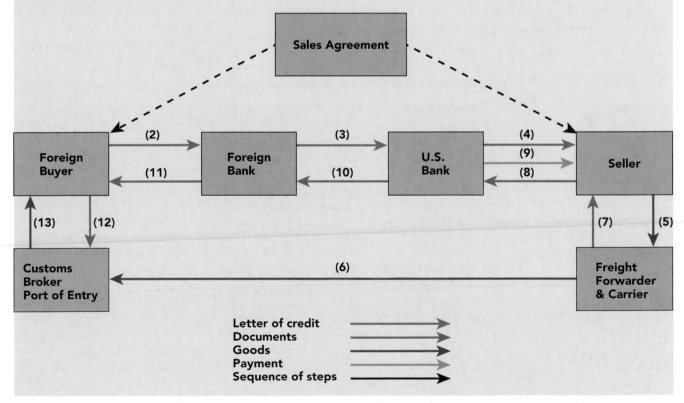

Source: Based on "A Basic Guide to Exporting," U.S. Department of Commerce, International Trade Administration, Washington, D.C.

bank and arranges for the issuance of a letter of credit; the buyer's bank then notifies its correspondent bank in the seller's country that the letter has been issued. After meeting the requirements set forth in the letter of credit, the seller can draw a draft against the credit (in effect, the bank issuing the letter) for payment for the goods. The precise conditions of the letter of credit are detailed in it and usually also require presentation of certain documents along with the draft before the correspondent bank will honor it. The documents usually required are a commercial invoice, a consular invoice (when requested), a clean bill of lading, and an insurance policy or certificate.

Letters of credit can be revocable or irrevocable. An *irrevocable letter of credit* means that once the seller has accepted the credit, the buyer cannot alter it in any way without permission of the seller. Added protection is gained if the buyer is required to confirm the letter of credit through a U.S. bank. This irrevocable, confirmed letter of credit means that a U.S. bank accepts responsibility to pay regardless of the financial situation of the buyer or foreign bank. From the seller's viewpoint, this eliminates the foreign political risk and replaces the commercial risk of the buyer's bank with that of the confirming bank. The confirming bank assures payment against a confirmed letter of credit. As soon as the documents are presented to the bank, the seller receives payment.

The international department of a major U.S. bank cautions that a letter of credit is not a guarantee of payment to the seller. Rather, payment is tendered only if the seller complies exactly with the terms of the letter of credit. Since all letters of credit must be exact in their terms and considerations, it is important for the exporter to check the terms of the letter carefully to be certain that all necessary documents have been acquired and properly completed. Some of the discrepancies found in documents that cause delay in honoring drafts or letters of credit include the following:

- Insurance defects such as inadequate coverage, no endorsement or countersignature, and a dating later than the bill of lading
- Bill-of-lading defects such as the bill lacking an "on board" endorsement or signature of carrier, missing an endorsement, or failing to specify prepaid freight
- Letter-of-credit defects such as an expired letter or one that is exceeded by the invoice figure, or one including unauthorized charges or disproportionate charges
- Invoice defects such as missing signatures or failure to designate terms of shipment (C&F, CIF, FAS) as stipulated in the letter of credit
- Documents that are missing, stalemated, or inaccurate

As illustrated in the Global Perspective at the beginning of this chapter, the process of getting a letter of credit can takes days, if not weeks.[16] Fortunately, this process is being shortened considerably as financial institutions provide letters of credit on the Internet. As one example, AVG Letter of Credit Management LLC, uses eTrade Finance Platform (eTFP), an e-commerce trade transaction system that enables exporters, importers, freight forwarders, carriers, and trade banks to initiate and complete trade transactions over the Internet. The company advertises that the efficiencies afforded by the Internet makes it possible to lower the cost of an export Letter of Credit from $500 to $25.[17]

## Bills of Exchange

Another important form of international commercial payment is **bills of exchange** drawn by sellers on foreign buyers. In letters of credit, the credit of one or more banks is involved, but with bills of exchange (also known as *dollar drafts*), the seller assumes all risk until the actual dollars are received. The typical procedure is for the seller to draw a draft on the buyer and present this with the necessary documents to the seller's bank for collection. The documents required are principally the same as for letters of credit. On receipt of the draft, the U.S. bank forwards it with the necessary documents to a correspondent bank in the buyer's country; the buyer is then presented with the draft for acceptance and immediate or later payment. With acceptance of the draft, the buyer receives the properly endorsed bill of lading that is used to acquire the goods from the carrier.

Bills of exchange or dollar drafts can have one of three time periods—sight, arrival, or date. A *sight draft* requires acceptance and payment on presentation of the draft and often before arrival of the goods. An *arrival draft* requires payment be made on arrival of the goods. Unlike the other two, a *date draft* has an exact date for payment and in no way is affected by the movement of the goods. Time designations may be placed on sight

[16]John L. Amos, Rowena Gates, and Gen. Merril A. McPeak, USAF (Ret.), "New Thoughts on Documenting Trade," *World Trade,* November 1, 2002.

[17]"New Web Technology Reduces LC Costs Under e-UCP Rules, *Managing Exports,* May 2003.

and arrival drafts to stipulate a fixed number of days after acceptance when the obligation must be paid. Usually this period is 30 to 120 days, thus providing a means of extending credit to the foreign buyer.

Dollar drafts have advantages for the seller because an accepted draft frequently can be discounted at a bank for immediate payment. Banks, however, usually discount drafts only with recourse; that is, if the buyer does not honor the draft, the bank returns it to the seller for payment. An accepted draft is firmer evidence in the case of default and subsequent litigation than an open account would be.

## Cash in Advance

The volume of international business handled on a cash-in-advance basis is not large. Cash places unpopular burdens on the customer and typically is used when credit is doubtful, when exchange restrictions within the country of destination are such that the return of funds from abroad may be delayed for an unreasonable period, or when the American exporter for any reason is unwilling to sell on credit terms. Although full payment in advance is employed infrequently, partial payment (from 25 to 50 percent) in advance is not unusual when the character of the merchandise is such that an incomplete contract can result in heavy loss. For example, complicated machinery or equipment manufactured to specification or special design would necessitate advance payment, which would be, in fact, a nonrefundable deposit.

## Open Accounts

Sales on open accounts are not generally made in foreign trade except to customers of long standing with excellent credit reputations or to a subsidiary or branch of the exporter. Open accounts obviously leave sellers in a position where most of the problems of international commercial finance work to their disadvantage. It is generally recommended that sales on open accounts not be made when it is the practice of the trade to use some other method, when special merchandise is ordered, when shipping is hazardous, when the country of the importer imposes difficult exchange restrictions, or when political unrest requires additional caution.

## Forfaiting

Inconvertible currencies and cash-short customers can kill an international sale if the seller cannot offer long-term financing. Unless the company has large cash reserves to finance its customers, a deal may be lost. **Forfaiting** is a financing technique for such a situation.

The basic idea of a forfaiting transaction is fairly simple. The seller makes a one-time arrangement with a bank or other financial institution to take over responsibility for collecting the account receivable. The exporter offers a long financing term to its buyer, but intends to sell its account receivable, at a discount, for immediate cash. The forfaiter buys the debt, typically a promissory note or bill of exchange, on a nonrecourse basis. Once the exporter sells the paper, the forfaiter assumes the risk of collecting the importer's payments. The forfaiting institution also assumes any political risk present in the importer's country.[18]

While forfaiting is similar to factoring, it is not the same. In *factoring* a company has an ongoing relationship with a bank that routinely buys its short-term accounts receivable at a discount—in other words, the bank acts as a collections department for its client. In forfaiting, however, the seller makes a one-time arrangement with a bank to buy a specific account receivable.

## Export Documents

Each export shipment involves many documents to satisfy government regulations controlling exporting as well as to meet requirements for international commercial payment transactions. The most frequently required documents are export declarations, consular invoices or certificates of origin, bills of lading, commercial invoices, and insurance certificates. Additional documents such as import licenses, export licenses, packing lists, and inspection certificates for agricultural products are often necessary.

[18]For more information about forfaiting, visit www.afia-forfaiting.org.

**Exhibit 15.8**
Principal Export
Documents

Source: Department of Commerce.

**Export Documents** Presented at the port of exit, includes the names and addresses of the principals involved, the destination of the goods, a full description of the goods, and their declared value.

**Consular Invoice or Certificate of Origin** Some countries require consular invoices obtained from the country's consulate and returned with two to eight copies in the language of the country, along with copies of other required documents (e.g., import license, commercial invoice, and/or bill of lading), before certification is granted. Preparation of the document should be handled with extreme care because fines are levied for any errors uncovered. In most countries, the fine is shared with whoever finds the errors, so few go undetected.

**Bill of Lading** The bill of lading is the most important document required for establishing legal ownership and facilitating financial transactions. It serves the following purposes: (1) as a contract for shipment between the carrier and shipper, (2) as a receipt from the carrier for shipment, and (3) as a certificate of ownership or title to the goods.

**Commercial Invoice** Every international transaction requires a commercial invoice, that is, a bill or statement for the goods sold. This document often serves several purposes; some countries require a copy for customs clearance, and it is one of the financial documents required in international commercial payments.

**Insurance Policy or Certificate** The insurance policy or certificate of insurance is considered a key document in export trade.

**Licenses** Export or import licenses are additional documents frequently required in export trade. In those cases where import licenses are required by the country of entry, a copy of the license or license number is usually required to obtain a consular invoice. Whenever a commodity requires an export license, it must be obtained before an export declaration can be properly certified.

**Other Documents** Sanitary and health inspection certificates attesting to the absence of disease and pests may be required for certain agricultural products before a country allows goods to enter its borders. Packing lists with correct weights are also required in some cases.

The paperwork involved in successfully completing a transaction is considered by many to be the greatest of all nontariff trade barriers. There are 125 different documents in regular or special use in more than 1,000 different forms. A single shipment may require over 50 documents and involve as many as 28 different parties and government agencies, or require as few as five. Luckily, there is software available that takes some of the burden out of this task. In one such program, the export information is entered once and the program automatically completes more than two dozen standard export forms, which can then be either printed or e-mailed to freight forwarders, customs brokers, or customers.

Although the preparation of documents can be handled routinely, their importance should not be minimized; incomplete or improperly prepared documents lead to delays in shipment. For example, a Mexican Customs official noticed that a certain piece of documentation out of all the paperwork required for a complete trainload of containers lacked a required signature, just one signature. The officer held the train up for almost two days until every container was unloaded and opened to verify that the contents matched the contents listed on the manifest.[19] In some countries, there could have been penalties, fines, or even confiscation of the goods as a result of errors in documentation.

**Export documents** are the result of requirements imposed by the exporting government, of requirements set by commercial procedures established in foreign trade, and, in some cases, of the supporting import documents required by the importing government. See Exhibit 15.8 for descriptions of the principal export documents.

---

[19]Michael D. White, *International Marketing Blunders* (Novato, CA, World Trade Press, 2002), p. 80.

## Packing and Marking

In addition to completing all documentation, special packing and marking requirements must be considered for shipments destined to be transported over water, subject to excessive handling, or destined for parts of the world with extreme climates or unprotected outdoor storage. Packing that is adequate for domestic shipments often falls short for goods subject to the conditions mentioned. Protection against rough handling, moisture, temperature extremes, and pilferage may require heavy crating, which increases total packing costs as well as freight rates because of increased weight and size. Because some countries determine import duties on gross weight, packing can add a significant amount to import fees. To avoid the extremes of too much or too little packing, the marketer should consult export brokers, export freight forwarders, or other specialists.

All countries regulate the marking of imported goods and containers, and noncompliance can result in severe penalties. Recently announced Peruvian regulations require all imported foreign products to bear a brand name, country of origin, and an expiration date clearly inscribed on the product. In the case of imported wearing apparel, shoes, electric appliances, automotive parts, liquors, and soft drinks, the name and tax identity card number of the importer must also be added. Peruvian customs refuse clearance to foreign products not fulfilling these requirements, and the importer must reship the goods within 60 days of the customs appraisal date or they are seized and auctioned as abandoned goods. Further, goods already in Peru must meet the provisions of the decree or be subject to public auction.

The exporter must be careful that all marking on the container conforms exactly to the data on the export documents because customs officials often interpret discrepancies as an attempt to defraud. A basic source of information for American exporters is the Department of Commerce pamphlet series entitled *Preparing Shipment to [Country]*, which details the necessary export documents and pertinent U.S. and foreign government regulations for labeling, marking, packing, and customs procedures.

## Customs-Privileged Facilities

To facilitate export trade, countries designate areas within their borders as **customs-privileged facilities**, that is, areas where goods can be imported for storage and/or processing with tariffs and quota limits postponed until the products leave the designated areas. Foreign trade zones (also known as free trade zones), free ports, and in-bond arrangements are all types of customs-privileged facilities that countries use to promote foreign trade.[20]

### Foreign Trade Zones

The number of countries with **foreign-trade zones** (FTZs)[21] has increased as trade liberalization has spread through Africa, Latin America, Eastern Europe, and other parts of Europe and Asia. Most FTZs function in a similar manner regardless of the host country.

In the United States, FTZs extend their services to thousands of firms engaged in a spectrum of international trade-related activities ranging from distribution to assembly and manufacturing. More than 150 foreign trade zones are located throughout the United States, including New York, New Orleans, San Francisco, Seattle, Toledo, Honolulu, Mayaques (Puerto Rico), Kansas City, Little Rock, and Sault St. Marie. Goods subject to U.S. custom duties and quota restrictions can be landed in these zones for storage or such processing as repackaging, cleaning, and grading before being brought into the United States or reexported to another country. Merchandise can be held in an FTZ even if it is subject to U.S. quota restrictions. When a particular quota opens up, the merchandise may then be immediately shipped into the United States. Merchandise subject to quotas may also be substantially transformed within a zone into articles that are not covered by quotas, and then shipped into the United States free of quota restrictions.[22]

---

[20]Japan's version of the FTZ is called a foreign access zone (FAZ). It operates much like an FTZ. A complete description can be found on the JETRO website www.jetro.go.jp (search for FAZ).

[21]For a review of FTZs, see www.ia.ita.doc.gov/ftzpage.

[22]For a detailed discussion of FTZs, see Ian MacLeod, "How Foreign Trade Zones Can Help You Export," *Export America,* June 2000, p. 12.

## CROSSING BORDERS 15.3  Underwear, Outwear, and Pointed Ears—What Do They Have in Common?

What do underwear, outerwear, and pointed ears have in common? Quotas, that's what! Call the first one The Madonna Effect. Madonna, the voluptuous pop star, affected the interpretation of outerwear/underwear when the ever-vigilant U.S. Customs Service stopped a shipment of 880 bustiers at the U.S. border. The problem was quota and tariff violations. The shipper classified them as underwear, which comes into the United States without quota and tariff. Outerwear imports, however, have a quota and the Customs official classified the fashion item inspired by Madonna as "outerwear" and demanded the appropriate quota certificates.

"It was definitely outerwear. I've seen it; and I've seen the girls wearing it, and they're wearing it as outerwear." It took the importer three weeks to obtain sufficient outerwear quota allowances to cover the shipment; by that time, several retailers had canceled their orders.

Call the second The Vulcan Effect. EU officials applied the Vulcan death grip to Star Trek hero Spock. Likenesses of the pointed-eared Spock and other "nonhuman creatures" fell victim to an EU quota on dolls made in China. The EU Council of Ministers slapped a quota equivalent to $81.7 million on nonhuman dolls from China—but it left human dolls alone.

British customs officials are in the unusual position of debating each doll's humanity. They have blacklisted teddy bears but cleared Batman and Robin. And although they have turned away Spock because of his Vulcan origins, they have admitted Star Trek's Captain Kirk. The Official Fan Club for Star Trek said the customs officials "ought to cut Spock some slack" because his mother, Amanda, was human. But Britain's customs office said, "We see no reason to change our interpretation. You don't find a human with ears that size."

Sources: Abstracted from Rosalind Resnick, "Busting Out of Tariff Quotas," *North American International Business* (now published as *International Business*), February 1991, p. 10; and Dana Milbank, "British Customs Officials Consider Mr. Spock Dolls to Be Illegal Aliens," *The Wall Street Journal*, August 2, 1994, p. B1.

In situations in which goods are imported into the United States to be combined with American-made goods and reexported, the importer or exporter can avoid payment of U.S. import duties on the foreign portion and eliminate the complications of applying for a *drawback*, that is, a request for a refund from the government of 99 percent of the duties paid on imports later reexported. Other benefits for companies utilizing foreign trade zones include lower insurance costs due to the greater security required in FTZs; more working capital, since duties are deferred until goods leave the zone; the opportunity to stockpile products when quotas are filled or while waiting for ideal market conditions; significant savings on goods or materials rejected, damaged, or scrapped, for which no duties are assessed; and exemption from paying duties on labor and overhead costs incurred in an FTZ, which are excluded in determining the value of the goods.[23]

**Offshore Assembly (Maquiladoras)**

**Maquiladoras**, *in-bond companies,* or *twin plants* are names given to a special type of customs-privileged facility that originated in Mexico in the early 1970s.[24] This type of facility has since expanded to other countries with abundant, low-cost labor. Even though in-bond operations vary from country to country, the original arrangement between Mexico and the United States remains the most typical. In 1971, the Mexican and U.S. governments established an in-bond program that created a favorable opportunity for U.S. companies to use low-cost Mexican labor.

The Mexican government allows U.S. processing, packaging, assembling, and/or repair plants located in the in-bond area to import parts and processed materials without import taxes, provided the finished products are reexported to the United States or to another foreign country. In turn, the U.S. government permits the reimportation of the packaged,

---

[23]See Chapter 18 for a discussion of using FTZs to help reduce price escalation.

[24]For a detailed explanation of maquiladoras, visit the U.S Treasury Department's site at www.itds. treas.gov/maquiladora.html.

processed, assembled, or repaired goods with a reasonably low import tariff applied only to the value added while in Mexico. Originally goods processed in maquiladoras could not be sold in Mexico without first being shipped back to the United States and reimported at regular Mexican tariffs. However, Mexican law was changed to allow maquiladoras, with special permission, the right to sell a maximum of 50 percent of their products in Mexico if they use some Mexican-made components.

As a result of NAFTA, there are some changes in the rules governing maquiladoras. Preferential tariff treatment and all export performance requirements (for example, trade and foreign exchange balancing) were eliminated for NAFTA countries. Also 100 percent of all maquiladora-manufactured goods can be sold in Mexico versus the 50 percent permitted prior to NAFTA.[25]

More than 2,600 companies participate in the maquiladoras program, with finished products valued at more than $30 billion annually. Although still dominated by U.S. companies, the maquiladoras are no longer only American. Heavy investments are pouring in from Asia and Europe, spurring expansion at close to 7 percent annually. Products made in maquiladoras include electronics, healthcare items, automotive parts, furniture, clothing, and toys. In most in-bond arrangements, special trade privileges are also part of the process. The maquiladoras arrangement is becoming more cost efficient for many companies that previously operated in Asia as Asian wage rates increase. Higher costs in Mexico are offset by the wage increases in Asia and increased shipping costs from Asia to the United States rather than from Mexico.

## Logistics

When a company is primarily an exporter from a single country to a single market, the typical approach to the physical movement of goods is the selection of a dependable mode of transportation that ensures safe arrival of the goods within a reasonable time for a reasonable carrier cost.[26] As a company becomes global, such a solution to the movement of products could prove costly and highly inefficient for seller and buyer.[27] As some global marketers say, the hardest part is not making the sale but getting the correct quantity of the product to customers in the required time frame at a cost that leaves enough margins for a profit.

At some point in the growth and expansion of an international firm, costs other than transportation are such that an optimal cost solution to the physical movement of goods cannot be achieved without thinking of the physical distribution process as an integrated system. When an international marketer begins producing and selling in more than one country and becomes a global marketer, it is time to consider the concept of **logistics management**, that is, a total systems approach to management of the distribution process that includes all activities involved in physically moving raw material, in-process inventory, and finished goods inventory from the point of origin to the point of use or consumption.[28]

## Interdependence of Physical Distribution Activities

A **physical distribution system** involves more than the physical movement of goods. It includes location of plants and warehousing (storage), transportation mode, inventory quantities, and packing. The concept of physical distribution takes into account the interdependence of the costs of each activity; a decision involving one activity affects the cost and efficiency of one or all others. In fact, because of their interdependence, there are an infinite number of "total costs" for the sum of each of the different activity costs. (*Total cost* of the system is defined as the sum of the costs of all these activities.)

The idea of interdependence can be illustrated by the classic example of airfreight. Exhibit 15.9 is an illustration of an actual company's costs of shipping 44,000 peripheral

[25]See "Maquiladoras," www.itds.treas.gov/maquiladora.html, 2002.

[26]Douglas J. Coates, "International Logistics," *World Trade,* March 2003, p. 28.

[27]"Motorola's Asian Logistics Center Starts Building," *Asiainfo Services,* December 23, 2002.

[28]An excellent source on this subject is Donald F. Wood et al., *International Logistics,* 2nd Edition (New York, NY: Amacom, American Management Association, 2002).

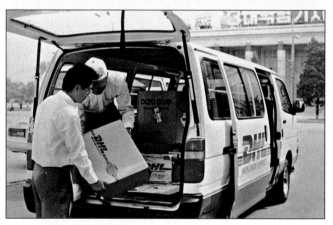

Getting the product to market can mean multi-transportation modes ranging from a floating market in Thailand, cargo containers and shipping, to DHL Worldwide Express delivery service in North Korea. *(left: Jean-Marc Truchet/Getty Images; right top: © Macduff Everton/CORBIS; right bottom: AP/Wide World Photos)*

boards worth $7.7 million from a Singapore plant to the U.S. West Coast using two modes of transportation—ocean freight and the seemingly more expensive airfreight. When considering only rates for transportation and carrying costs for inventory in transit, air transportation costs were approximately $57,000 higher than ocean freight. But notice that when total costs are calculated, airfreight was actually less costly than ocean freight because of other costs involved in the total physical distribution system.

To offset the slower ocean freight and the possibility of unforeseen delays and to ensure prompt customer delivery schedules, the company had to continuously maintain 30 days of inventory in Singapore and another 30 days' inventory at the company's distribution centers. The costs of financing 60 days of inventory and of additional warehousing at both points—that is, real physical distribution costs—would result in the cost of ocean freight exceeding air by more than $75,000. There may even be additional costs associated with ocean freight—for example, higher damage rate, higher insurance, and higher packing rates for ocean freight.

Substantial savings can result from systematic examination of logistics costs and the calculation of total physical distribution costs. Amdahl, the computer manufacturer, was able to trim more than $50 million from its logistics costs, shrinking spending to 5 percent of sales from 8.5 percent, while improving customer service. The beauty of such savings is that they go right to the bottom line.

Another example involves a large multinational firm with facilities and customers the world over. This firm shipped parts from its U.S. Midwest plant to the nearest East Coast

**Exhibit 15.9**

Real Physical Distribution Costs between Air and Ocean Freight— Singapore to the United States

Source: Adapted from "Air and Adaptec's Competitive Strategy," *International Business*, September 1993, p. 44.

In this example, 44,000 peripheral boards worth $7.7 million are shipped from a Singapore plant to the U.S. West Coast. Cost of capital to finance inventories is 10 percent annually or $2,109 per day to finance $7.7 million.

|  | **Ocean** | **Air** |
|---|---|---|
| Transport costs | $ 31,790 (in transit 21 days) | $127,160 (in transit 3 days) |
| In-transit inventory financing costs | $ 44,289 | $   6,328 |
| Total transportation costs | $ 76,179 | $133,488 |
| Warehousing inventory costs, Singapore and U.S. | (60 days @ $2,109 per day) $126,540 | |
| Warehouse rent | $   6,500 | |
| Real physical distribution costs | $209,219 | $133,488 |

port, then by water route around the Cape of Good Hope (Africa), and finally to its plants in Asia, taking 14 weeks. Substantial inventory was maintained in Asia as a safeguard against uncertain water-borne deliveries. The transportation carrier costs were the least expensive available; however, delivery delays and unreliable service caused the firm to make emergency air shipments to keep production lines going. As a result, air shipment costs rose to 70 percent of the total transport bill. An analysis of the problem in the physical distribution system showed that using higher-cost motor carriers could lower costs by trucking the parts to West Coast ports, then shipping them to Asia by sea. Transit time was reduced, delivery reliability improved, inventory quantities in Asia lowered, and emergency air shipments eliminated. The new distribution system produced annual savings of $60,000.

Although a cost difference will not always be the case, the examples serve to illustrate the interdependence of the various activities in the physical distribution mix and the total cost. A change of transportation mode can effect a change in packaging and handling, inventory costs, warehousing time and cost, and delivery charges.

The concept behind physical distribution is the achievement of the optimum (lowest) system cost consistent with the customer service objectives of the firm. If the activities in the physical distribution system are viewed separately, without consideration of their interdependence, the final cost of distribution may be higher than the lowest possible cost (optimum cost) and the quality of service may be adversely affected. Additional variables and costs that are interdependent and must be included in the total physical distribution decision heighten the distribution problems confronting the international marketer. As the international firm broadens the scope of its operations, the additional variables and costs become more crucial in their effect on the efficiency of the distribution system.

One of the major benefits of the European Community's unification is the elimination of transportation barriers among member countries. Instead of approaching Europe on a country-by-country basis, a centralized logistics network can be developed.[29] The trend in Europe is toward pan-European distribution centers. Studies indicate that companies operating in Europe may be able to cut 20 warehousing locations to 3 and maintain the same level of customer service. A German white goods manufacturer was able to reduce its European warehouses from 39 to 10, as well as improve its distribution and enhance customer service. By cutting the number of warehouses, it reduced total distribution and warehousing costs, brought down staff numbers, held fewer items of stock, provided greater access to regional markets, made better use of transport networks, and improved service to customers, all with a 21 percent reduction of total logistics costs.

---

[29]Karen E. Thuermer, "Europe Logistics: Fit To Be Tied," *Global Business*, March 2000, p. 52

**Benefits of a Physical Distribution System**

There are more benefits to a system of physical distribution than cost advantages. An effective physical distribution system can result in optimal inventory levels and, in multiplant operations, optimal production capacity, both of which can maximize the use of working capital. In making plant-location decisions, a company with a physical distribution system can readily assess operating costs of alternative locations to serve various markets.

A physical distribution system may also result in better (more dependable) delivery service to the market; when production occurs at different locations, companies are able to determine quickly the most economical source for a particular customer. As companies expand into multinational markets and source these markets from multinational production facilities, they are increasingly confronted with cost variables that make it imperative to employ a total systems approach to the management of the distribution process to achieve efficient operation. Finally, a physical distribution system can render the natural obstructions created by geography less economically critical for the multinational marketer. Getting the product to market can mean multitransportation modes, such as canal boats in China, pedal power in Vietnam, and speed trains in Japan or Europe.

**Export Shipping and Warehousing**

Whenever and however title to goods is transferred, those goods must be transported. Shipping goods to another country presents some important differences from shipping to a domestic site. The goods can be out of the shipper's control for longer periods of time than in domestic distribution, more shipping and collections documents are required, packing must be suitable, and shipping insurance coverage is necessarily more extensive. The task is to match each order of goods to the shipping modes best suited for swift, safe, and economical delivery. Ocean shipping, airfreight, air express, and parcel post are all possibilities. Ocean shipping is usually the least expensive and most frequently used method for heavy bulk shipment. For certain categories of goods, airfreight can be the most economical and certainly the speediest.

Shipping costs are an important factor in a product's price in export marketing, and the transportation mode must be selected in terms of the total impact on cost. One estimate is that logistics account for between 19 and 23 percent of the total cost of a finished product sold internationally. One of the important innovations in ocean shipping in reducing or controlling the high cost of transportation is the use of containerization. Containerized shipments, in place of the traditional bulk handling of full loads or break-bulk operations, have resulted in intermodal transport between inland points, reduced costs, reduction in losses from pilferage and damage, and simplified handling of international shipments.

With increased use of containerization, rail container service developed in many countries to provide the international shipper with door-to-door movement of goods under seal, originating and terminating inland. This eliminates several loadings, unloadings, and changes of carriers and reduces costs substantially. Unfortunately, such savings are not always possible for all types of cargo.

For many commodities of high unit value and low weight and volume, international airfreight has become important. Airfreight has shown the fastest growth rate for freight transportation even though it accounts for only a fraction of total international shipments. Although airfreight can cost two to five times the surface charges for general cargo, some cost reduction is realized through reduced packing requirements, paperwork, insurance, and the cost of money tied up in inventory. Although usually not enough to offset the higher rates charged for airfreight, it can, as illustrated in Exhibit 15.9, be a justifiable alternative if the commodity has high unit value or high inventory costs, or if there is concern with delivery time. Many products moving to foreign markets meet these criteria.

In the last decade there has been continuous improvement in the services available to the international shipper both in the home market and abroad. *Intermodal services,*[30] a

---

[30]Helen L. Richardson, "Intermodal Update," *World Trade,* May 17, 2003.

**CROSSING BORDERS 15.4**  If the Shoe Fits, Wear It . . . or Abandon It

Pilferage and theft are ongoing problems in shipping. These problems are constantly being addressed with different security strategies. Using containers for shipping is one of the more successful strategies, but containers also can be stolen. Such was the case in Los Angeles when thieves cut through security fencing at a major container terminal, drove a truck tractor into the area, and broke open a few containers until they found one with sports shoes that sell for $140 a pair in retail stores. They hooked up the container and drove out with their booty.

But the police had the last laugh. A week later they found the container abandoned with its cargo intact. The U.S.-based shoe importer routinely ships all its left shoes in one container and all its right shoes in another. The thieves had stolen the container with left shoes.

Source: Adapted from John Davies, "Sneaking Up on Security," *International Business*, February 1997, p. 18.

transportation system that unites various modes of transportation into one seamless movement of goods from factory to the customer's port of entry, have become more efficient as deregulation allows the coupling of various modes of transportation. In addition, intermodal marketing companies (IMC) evolved to broker transportation services so that an exporter can make one transaction with an IMC that takes care of the movement of goods from factory to customer, rivaling the simplicity of single-mode freight transportation. The IMC stitches together each of the transportation modes involved in freight movements, which may involve as many as four separate transportation modes. All of this can be done within guaranteed time frames, with 98 percent on-time performance schedules more the norm than the exception. As one logistics specialist commented, "no matter how fast or timely the ship carrying a 45-foot container from Shenzhen to Long Beach, it is the speed and dependability of the whole pipeline—the underlying modes and logistics functions to achieve the door-to-door requirements of the shipper that matters."[31]

Intermodal services in other parts of the world are not as advanced as in the United States. Europe comes the closest to providing similar services; however, deregulation and barriers that existed before unification are not yet completely eliminated. Unlike truck transportation, Europe's 26 railways did not capitalize on the removal of borders in Europe's single market. Progress is being made as railroads are beginning to restructure, and a pan-European intermodal marketing company similar to those in the United States is formed. Before long it will be possible to extend the services in the United States to European customers so that one transaction can be made to ensure freight delivery from a factory in the United States to a final customer in Europe. Such services are now becoming available in Asia and Latin America as improvements in transportation services are made in both areas.

Rail transportation between the United States and Mexico improved with investments by Kansas City Southern and Union Pacific that created a direct route from Chicago to Mexico City. Further, with the proposed merger between Canadian National and Burlington Northern Santa Fe, there will be a North American rail line from Canada into Mexico. U.S. railroad companies' investments in Brazil, New Zealand, and Britain call for major investments in the improvement of these rail systems. Moving goods rapidly and on a timely schedule is more important today than ever before, and the improvement of rail systems and the development of intermodal systems will go a long way toward making that possible.

Another innovation in transportation and logistics is the service provided by companies such as United Parcel Service (UPS), Federal Express (FedEx), and others. Besides

---

[31]J. Douglas Coates, "International Logistics," *World Trade*, March 1, 2003, p. 28.

Two giant pandas, four-year-old male Le Le and two-year-old female Ya Ye, are being loaded onto the Panda Express, a FedEx plane, that is airlifting them from China to the Memphis, Tennessee, zoo for a ten-year visit. Whether it's pandas, time-sensitive deliveries, or cost-saving solutions, FedEx delivers high-value shipments door-to-door to as many as 210 countries. *(AP/Wide World Photos)*

providing air-express service for packages, these companies are offering complete logistics management services for their clients—truly door-to-door delivery around the world.

This service includes delivery as well as support services. For example, FedEx provides total logistics support. It will take a manufacturer's product, warehouse it and keep inventory, provide all the labor and technology, and move it throughout the world. FedEx can warehouse a computer system made in Malaysia, move it to Japan to be coupled with components from Taiwan, and then deliver a completed product to the final destination in yet another country. One client's experience illustrates how such a service can improve a company's distribution costs and service. The computer parts repair center of this company moved into a FedEx Express Distribution Center in Japan and was able to cut average total turnaround time from 45 days to 5 days and at less cost. FedEx took over storage, control, and shipment of the parts using its own networks and aircraft. UPS offers similar services, including local parts stocking and defective return services in Europe, the Pacific Rim, and the Americas.

Distribution and its costs are an important part of every international transaction. Cheap labor may make Chinese clothing competitive in the United States, but if delays in shipment tie up working capital and cause winter coats to arrive in April, the advantage may be lost. Similarly, production machinery disabled for lack of a part can affect cost throughout the system, all of which may be avoided with a viable logistics system.

The globalization of marketing and manufacturing, in which component parts are made in several countries, assembled in some others, and serviced the world over, puts tremendous pressure on a company's ability to physically move goods. A narrow solution to physical movement of goods is the selection of transportation; a broader application is the concept of logistics management or physical distribution. When broad product assortment is valued by customers, holding a great number of products or component parts in inventory increases the costs of the supplier.[32] Although it is possible to reduce need for warehousing with direct deliveries from manufacturers, the value of direct deliveries is diminished when orders are received in several shipments and at different times. One solution to this problem is **merge-in-transit**, a distribution method in which goods shipped from several supply locations are consolidated into one final customer

---

[32]Ephraim Schwartz, "Skipping Steps," *InfoWorld,* February 5, 2001, p. 1B.

delivery point while they are in transit and then shipped as a unit to the customer.[33] As distribution systems become more complex and costly, merge-in-transit is one system designed to increase customer value and decrease distribution costs.

## Foreign Freight Forwarder

The *foreign freight forwarder,* licensed by the Federal Maritime Commission, arranges for the shipment of goods as the agent for an exporter. The forwarder is an indispensable agent for an exporting firm that cannot afford an in-house specialist to handle paperwork and other export trade mechanics.[34]

Even in large companies with active export departments capable of handling documentation, a forwarder is useful as a shipment coordinator at the port of export or at the destination port. Besides arranging for complete shipping documentation, the full-service foreign freight forwarder provides information and advice on routing and scheduling, rates and related charges, consular and licensing requirements, labeling requirements, and export restrictions. Further, the agent offers shipping insurance, warehouse storage, packing and containerization, and ocean cargo or airfreight space.

An astute freight forwarder will also double-check all assumptions made on the export declaration, such as commodity classifications, and will check the list of denied parties and end uses. Both large and small shippers find freight forwarders' wide range of services useful and well worth the fees normally charged. In fact, for many shipments, forwarders can save on freight charges because they can consolidate shipments into larger, more economical quantities. Although there are many forwarders available, more and more companies are using those that have joined alliances with shippers and become part of the larger multifaceted integrators discussed earlier. Experienced exporters regard the foreign freight forwarder as an important addition to in-house specialists.

## The 24-Hour Rule and Logistics

The Cargo and Container Security Initiative, **24-Hour Rule**, is one of the U.S. government's increased efforts to enhance security. With 5.7 million containers entering U.S. seaports each year, it is critically important to guard against terrorists using shipping containers to sneak deadly weapons into the country.[35]

The 24-Hour Rule requires sea carriers and NVOCC (Non-Vessel Operating Common Carriers)[36] to provide U.S. Customs with detailed descriptions (manifests) of the contents of containers bound for the United States 24 hours before a container is loaded on board a vessel. The rule allows U.S. Customs officers time to analyze the container content information and identify potential terrorist threats before the U.S.-bound container is loaded at a foreign port rather than after it arrives at a U.S. port. Cargo manifests must use precise terms as part of the 24-Hour Rule; "Freight-All-Kinds," "Said-To-Contain," or "General Merchandise," descriptions often used in the past, are no longer acceptable.[37] If there is any discrepancy in the manifest and if it is not presented 24 hours before loading, the shipment can be denied loading and entry into a U.S. port. Whenever an "invalid" cargo description is used, a "Do Not Load" message will be posted and loading denied.[38]

Cargo bound for a foreign port to be loaded on a vessel with cargo bound for the United States must also have a valid manifest presented within the 24-Hour Rule or it will not be allowed to be shipped.[39] A violation of the 24-Hour Rule may prevent the vessel from loading cargo or from unloading any cargo even if the violation applies to

---

[33]Mikko Karkkainen, Timo Ala-Risku, and Jan Holmstrom, "Increasing Customer Value and Decreasing Distribution Costs With Merge-in-Transit," *International Journal of Physical Distribution and Logistics Management,* vol. 33 number 2, 2003, p. 132.

[34]Helen L. Richardson, "A Shift in Freight Forwarding," *World Trade,* February 1, 2003.

[35]Jeannine Aversa, "Sea Containers Barred From Ships to U.S.," *AP News Service,* February 13, 2003.

[36]Trucks, railroads, and other non-ocean carriers.

[37]"Customs Issues 'No-Load' Directives on the 24-Hour Rule," *Customs & Border Protection,* U.S. Department of Homeland Security, www.cbp.gov, February 13, 2003.

[38]"Strict Enforcement of Notice for US-bound Cargo," *Business Times (Malaysia),* January 27, 2003.

[39]"Frequently Asked Questions: 24-Hour Advance Vessel Manifest Rule," *Customs & Border Protection,* U.S. Department of Homeland Security, www.cbp.gov, May 5, 2003.

only one container.[40] Trucking companies are also bound by the 24-Hour Rule and are expected to provide a manifest 4 hours before trucks are loaded with products entering the United States and 24 hours in advance when leaving the United States.[41]

In an effort to safeguard food against bio-terrorism, prior notice to the FDA of all food being imported or offered for import into the U.SA must be submitted no later than noon on the day before the articles will arrive at the U.S. border. Food offered for import with no prior notice or inadequate prior notice will be refused admission.[42] Similar rules apply to drugs and medical devices.

Ports have become the gatekeepers for the entire supply chain, preventing illegal entry of terrorists and weapons of mass destruction. They are expected to accomplish this without interruption of service and without additional cost to the shipper.[43] However, many believe that these rules may cause a significant slowdown in global trade. At this time, there have been several "Do Not Load" messages issued but few significant delays, i.e., more than an hour or two. However, the 24-Hour Rule has not been in place long and the full impact is not yet known.[44]

## Role of the Internet in International Logistics

As discussed previously, the essence of international logistics is to integrate all the steps necessary to physically move goods from supplier to manufacturer to customer. This means that a logistics system has to deal with an often disparate set of agents and activities—carriers, warehouses, export regulations, import regulations, customs agents, freight forwarders and so on—each of which must be accessed individually by the logistics manager. The goals are multidimensional and include cost minimization, increased levels of service, improved communication among customers or suppliers, and increased flexibility in terms of delivery and response time. The ability of firms to achieve these goals was limited until recently because existing communication and knowledge links did not bring together all of the players in the process. The advent of the Internet allowed communication with the participants in real time via a single connection point.

As illustrated in Crossing Borders 15.5, integrated software application systems like NextLinx[45] in conjunction with the Internet have made it possible for large companies such as Cisco Systems to manage their imports and exports more efficiently. Such software capabilities also made it possible for companies such as UPS, FedEx, and DHL to integrate their core services with other service providers to offer a fully integrated logistics system to customers.

The huge surge in demand for business-to-consumer and business-to-business delivery of everything from dime-a-dozen doilies to computer components worth tens of thousands of dollars has spawned the concept of the *integrator*,[46] that is, a system or company that integrates the entire process of importing or exporting, including order management, payment processing, warehousing, transportation, delivery, and post-transaction management of returns, repairs, and customer service at one location.

United States Customs officer helps direct the use of a mobile gamma ray scanner to reveal the contents of a steel-shipping container, one of the 20 million closed containers that carry cargo into the U.S. each year. The device, used to help reveal nuclear, biological, or chemical threats inside, is one of more than 100 gamma and x-ray inspection devices deployed at major ports and border crossings into the U.S. (AP/Wide World Photos)

[40]"Severe Penalty for Violation of U.S. Customs Rule," *Business Times (Malaysia)*, February 17, 2003.

[41]"Cargo-Reporting Rules Seen As Crippling Transport Firms, Fear Anti-terrorist Measure," *The Washington Times*, January 18, 2003.

[42]"Pre-Importation Notification of Food Products," *Online News Letter*, www.aeilogistics.com, March 27, 2003.

[43]Kimball Payne, "Security Will Narrow Expected Port Bottlenecks," *Daily Press*, May 21, 2003.

[44]Jeffrey Sparshott, "Companies Involved in Global Trade Face Possible Security-Related Slowdown," *The Washington Times*, March 21, 2003.

[45]See "NextLinx-Trade Collaborator: Software for Import and Export" at www.nextlinx.com/trd_col.html.

[46]Jatin S. Bains, "Demand Chain Logistics," *World Trade*, September, 2002.

## CROSSING BORDERS 15.5  NextLinx: Revolutionizing Logistics

E-commerce hype says the world is your marketplace once the website goes live. But not until the complex, and often byzantine, customs rules and import/export regulations are dealt with. One software company, NextLinx, provides an import, export, and logistics software application that has at its core a database of relevant import/export regulations and logistics information. NextLinx lets companies and their customers navigate the maze of country-specific regulations that can determine final pricing for a transaction and whether the buyer is permitted to purchase the goods. The system delivers real-time trade regulation information during a purchase. So the buyer of 100 widgets who lives in Europe might pull up all the relevant tax and duties information, shipping options, and delivery times for the order.

According to research, 85 percent of firms can't or won't fill international orders because of the complexities of shipping across borders. And those who can are shipping to only a few countries in Europe and Asia where they can deliver from local warehouses. "We don't ship globally today, and we have no future plans to do so. The taxes and tariffs make it so we can't give accurate cost data to the customer when ordering goods," said one electronics manufacturer. "So they're quoted one price for the product, but by the time it would ship to them, there would be several back-end charges the buyer didn't expect. As a result, customers often return the products."

Companies traditionally used customs agents and freight forwarders, as well as internal staff to manage imports and exports. People want improved cycle times and a manual operation is too slow, so one of the rationales is to make the process quicker and bulletproof. One solution is NextLinx Global Trade Suite, which acts like a virtual customs broker, international trade lawyer, and logistics expert all rolled into one.

NextLinx calculates on the fly the total cost of delivering goods to the buyer's door, along with providing relevant information to the buyer. One hundred templates of various international trade documents needed to facilitate import/export clearance are contained in the system. During the transaction, the logistics component of the application offers shipping options, electronically books shipping space, and tracks shipping status. It accomplishes this with several specific applications.

- Calculates the duty, VAT, Excise, and Other Governmental Charges based on invoice values.
- Screens for Denied Parties and list of embargoed countries.
- Checks export/import licensing requirements.
- Creates the necessary export, import, and commercial documentation. It fills out defined documents and relays them to the requesting party.
- Calculates the total landed costs of any shipment going from one country to another including freight, customs duties, port charges, insurance, and third party fees.

NextLinx then sends the crucial global commerce data straight to customers' browsers while they are making their buying decisions. It simplifies and automates the export process, helping organizations expand e-Commerce beyond the national borders.

Managers at Cisco Systems say using NextLinx helped keep the total number of employees clearing international exports down to four, at a time when total revenue is approaching $18 billion. Twice a day, a Cisco analyst reviews reports generated by NextLinx's applications to see if any international orders for any of the company's 60,000 products needs any special regulatory treatment before shipping. Less than 1 percent of the transactions require any additional licensing information.

Sources: "Global Knowledge," "Global Trade Applications," "Global Markets," and "White Paper," www.NextLinx.com, John Berry, "NextLinx Helps Sites Sell Globally," *InternetWeek*, June 5, 2000, p. 41.

Such a system provides market efficiencies and enables global economies of scale between thousands of shippers, receivers, carriers, freight forwarders, and third-party logistics providers (3PL), e-marketplaces, vertical portals, and transportation exchanges not possible just a few years ago. Once connected, participants can conduct paperless business transactions with all other network members without having to master and manage individual data translations and integration points. Further, they can communicate with the other participants in real time via a single connection point, monitoring the performance of both inbound and outbound logistics activities.[47] Exporters are able to determine in advance exactly how expensive it will be to move a shipment through a particular foreign customs authority. Users are able to calculate add-on costs, enabling them to make critical marketing decisions about where to target their sales to avoid unprofitable deals. In some countries, a single order for $27 worth of compact discs can be increased by as much as $268 in transport and customs charges by the time it reaches a customer's hand.

When a computer manufacturer must coordinate supply chains that reach into China and Malaysia and Mexico and Portugal, software such as that provided by NextLinx, Descartes,[48] and others is used to fully automate its supply chain systems. Trucks, ships, trains, and planes cannot be made to travel much faster than they presently do; thus, any additional speed must come from better logistics management. An automated supply chain system can cut the time needed for deliveries from the Far East to warehouses in the United Kingdom from months to just 25 days.

For companies not wishing to maintain a fully automated supply chain system in-house, third-party logistics providers, or integrators such as UPS Logistics Group can process and store all inventory and then ship it within two hours to the precise location within a plant where it is needed.[49] They can also handle such tasks as customs clearance and return and repair of certain merchandise. Manufacturers can shift their supply chain structures much more rapidly and with less pain than is the case with vertically integrated operations.

By providing inventory management, order fulfillment, and collections, integrators can assist e-commerce customers to more quickly enter new markets without having to invest in warehousing and distribution centers. The scramble is on to be able to fulfill orders that come from anywhere in the world without having to set up significant operations in such markets.[50] The less onerous the process of moving products across a particular border, the easier it becomes for manufacturers to set up where it makes sense for business. Speed is perhaps the most essential goal for any manufacturer looking to develop a twenty-first-century supply chain.

## Summary

An awareness of the mechanics of export trade is indispensable to the foreign marketer who engages in exporting goods from one country to another. Although most marketing techniques are open to interpretation and creative application, the mechanics of exporting are very exact; there is little room for interpretation or improvisation with the requirements of export licenses, quotas, tariffs, export documents, packing, marking, and the various uses of commercial payments. The very nature of the regulations and restrictions surrounding importing and exporting can lead to frequent and rapid change. In handling the mechanics of export trade successfully, the manufacturer must keep abreast of all foreign and domestic changes in requirements and regulations pertaining to the product involved. For firms unable to maintain their own export staffs, foreign-freight forwarders can handle many details for a nominal fee.

With paperwork completed, the physical movement of goods must be considered. Transportation mode affects total product cost because of the varying requirements of packing, inventory levels, time requirements, perishability, unit cost, damage and pilfering losses, and customer service. Transportation for each product must be assessed in view of the interdependent nature of all these factors. To ensure optimal distribution at minimal cost, a physical distribution system determines everything from plant location to final customer delivery in terms of the most efficient use of capital investment, resources, production, inventory, packing, and transportation.

[47]"3PLs Stay Strong," *Modern Materials Handling,* May 2003, p. 1.

[48]For more information on these two software applications, visit www.nextlinx.com and www.descartes.com.

[49]"3PL Providers Work to Close the Gap," *Logistics Management & Distribution Report,* February 2003, p. E64.

[50]Richard Armstrong, "Searching For a Global 3PL," *World Trade,* September, 2002.

# Questions

1. Define and show the significance to international marketing of the following terms:

   | | |
   |---|---|
   | export regulations, 437 | open account, 448 |
   | import regulations, 437 | letters of credit, 448 |
   | Export Administration Regulations (EAR), 438 | bills of exchange, 450 |
   | | forfaiting, 451 |
   | Export Control Classification Number (ECCN), 438 | export documents, 452 |
   | | customs-privileged facilities, 453 |
   | Commerce Control List (CCL), 438 | |
   | | foreign-trade zone, 453 |
   | Commerce Country Chart (CCC), 440 | maquiladoras, 454 |
   | | logistics management, 455 |
   | ELAIN, 442 | physical distribution system, 455 |
   | STELA, 442 | |
   | ERIC, 443 | merge-in-transit, 460 |
   | SNAP, 443 | 24-Hour Rule, 461 |
   | terms of sale, 447 | |

2. Explain the reasoning behind the various regulations and restrictions imposed on the exportation and importation of goods.

3. What determines the type of license needed for exportation? Discuss.

4. Discuss the most frequently encountered trade restrictions.

5. What is the purpose of an import license? Discuss.

6. Explain foreign-trade zones and illustrate how an exporter may use them. How do foreign-trade zones differ from bonded warehouses?

7. How do in-bond areas differ from foreign-trade zones? How would an international marketer use an in-bond area?

8. Explain each of the following export documents:

   a. Bill of lading

   b. Consular invoice

   c. Commercial invoice

   d. Insurance certificate

9. Why would an exporter use the services of a foreign-freight forwarder? Discuss.

10. Besides cost advantages, what are the other benefits of an effective physical distribution system?

11. Explain how merge-in-transit can be beneficial to all parties in the distribution process.

12. Discuss customs-privileged facilities. How are they used?

13. Why would a company engage the services of an intermodal transportation service instead of performing activities inhouse?

14. You are the manager of a small company that manufactures and sells various types of personal restraints (for example, handcuffs and leg irons) that you sell to law enforcement agencies, private security companies, and novelty stores. You receive a large order from an importer in Madrid. You have never done business with this importer although you have previously sold your product in Spain. Do you need a special export license? Outline the steps you would take to ensure that your transaction is legal. (Note: The solution to this problem cannot be completely answered from information in the text. Additional information needs to be obtained from sources on the Internet.)

15. You are the sales manager of a small company with sales in the United States. About 30 percent of your business is mail order and the remainder is from your two retail stores. You recently created an e-store on the Web and a few days later received an order from a potential customer from a city near Paris, France. The shipping charges listed on the Web are all for locations in the United States. You don't want to lose this $350 order. You know you can use the postal service but the customer indicated she wanted the item in about a week. Air Express seems logical but how much will it cost? Consult both the FedEx homepage (www.fedex. com) and the UPS homepage (www.ups.com) to get some estimates on shipping costs. Here are some details you will need: value $350; total weight of the package, 2.5 pounds; package dimensions, 4 inches high by 6 inches wide; U.S. Zip Code, 97035; and French Zip Code, 91400. (Note: It's not fair to call UPS or FedEx—use the Internet.)

16. Based on the information collected in Question 15, how practical would it be to encourage foreign sales? Your average order ranges from about $250 to $800. All prices are quoted plus shipping and handling. You handle a fairly exclusive line of Southwestern Indian jewelry that sells for about 15 to 20 percent higher in Europe than in the United States. The products are lightweight and high in value.

## CHAPTER LEARNING OBJECTIVES

What you should learn from Chapter 16:

- Local market characteristics that affect the advertising and promotion of products

- The strengths and weaknesses of sales promotion and public relations in global marketing

- When global advertising is most effective; when modified advertising is necessary

- The effects of a single European market on advertising

- The effect of limited media, excessive media, and government regulations on advertising and promotion budgets

- The communication process and advertising misfires

# Global Perspective

## BARBIE VERSUS MULAN

For years, Barbie dolls sold in Japan looked different from their U.S. counterparts. They had Asian facial features, black hair, and Japanese-inspired fashions. Then, about three years ago, Mattel Inc. conducted consumer research around the world and learned something surprising: The original Barbie, with her yellow hair and blue eyes, played as well in Hong Kong as it did in Hollywood. Girls didn't care if Barbie didn't look like them. "It's all about fantasies and hair," says Peter Broegger, general manager of Mattel's Asian operations. "Blonde Barbie sells just as well in Asia as in the U.S."

Major toy makers are rethinking one of the basic tenets of their $55 billion global industry—that children in different countries want different playthings. The implications are significant for both kids and companies. In the past, giants such as Mattel, Hasbro Inc., and Lego Co. produced toys and gear in a variety of styles. Increasingly, they are designing and marketing one version worldwide. This has led to a series of massive merchandise blitzkriegs, with companies deluging boys and girls around the globe simultaneously with identical dolls, cars, and gadgets.

For example, Mattel's Rapunzel Barbie, whose ankle-length blonde locks cascade down her pink ball gown, was released on the same day last fall in 59 countries including the United States—the company's biggest product launch ever. Since then, Rapunzel Barbie and related merchandise generated $200 million in global sales, nearly half of that outside the United States. Mattel no longer makes Asian-featured Barbies.

Two recent developments are changing kids' tastes. One is the rapid worldwide expansion of cable and satellite TV channels, which along with movies and the Internet expose millions of kids to the same popular icons. For example, Walt Disney Co. now operates 24 Disney-branded cable and satellite channels in 67 countries outside the United States—up from zero eight years ago. The other development is the widening international reach of retailing giants such as Wal-Mart Stores Inc., Toys "R" Us Inc. and Carrefour SA, which between them opened 2,300 stores outside their home markets. Increasingly, the mass retailers enter into exclusive deals with toy and consumer-products companies, allowing them to stage huge, coordinated promotional campaigns.

For example, when Rapunzel Barbie debuted in October, Wal-Mart stores in South Korea and China hired local women to dress up like the doll and greet children as they entered. At the same time, the Mattel TV ad campaign was broadcast around the world in 15-, 20-, and 30-second spots—in 35 different languages. Mattel's Barbie website, which has eight language options, featured Rapunzel stories and games. A computer-animated movie called "Barbie as Rapunzel" was broadcast on TV and released on video and DVD around the world, and shown in some theaters overseas.

In Madrid, the launch was accompanied by a "premiere" of the movie and special promotions of hair-comb sets and other accessories at Carrefour stores across Spain. After experiencing the premiere, the kids could and did buy the dolls. For some parents this meant Christmas shopping later in the year at the often frenetic Toys "R" Us in Madrid for stuffed dragons from the movie, or a Barbie laptop computer, a Barbie kitchen set, a Barbie travel van, and a host of other Barbie gadgets and accessories.

Some toys, games, and animated characters don't cross national boundaries. German children, for example, rarely play with action figures. According to the NPD Group, which tracks toy sales, action figures last year made up just 1 percent of the German toy market, compared with 5 percent of the U.S. and 6 percent of the U.K. toy markets. American kids want Nascar toy cars, while European kids want Formula One models. Cheerleader-themed anything is irrelevant outside the United States. And few American companies sell toys in the Islamic world. Mattel, the world's largest toy company, has no plans to do so.

Perhaps Disney's Jasmine will sell well there, although she's actually inappropriately dressed for many of Islamic faith. Jasmine is just one of the new series of "Princess" dolls aimed directly at Barbie's dominance of the doll category. Snow White, Pocahontas, and Mulan are others in the band. Their diversity may have broader appeal. Disney uses pink in the packaging and Mattel objects. Disney is also mindful of the fashion-conscious Barbie's critics. Disney Princess is more about tiaras and wands rather than handbags and high heels. Where Barbie is more a role model, and therefore objectionable to parents, Disney is putting their emphasis on the fantasy. Too bad someone isn't emphasizing education.

Sources: Lisa Bannon and Carlta Vitshum, "One-Toy-Fits-All: How Industry Learned to Love the Global Kid," *Wall Street Journal*, April 29, 2003, p. A1; and "A Challenge to Barbie, Toy Franchises," *The Economist*, April 19, 2003, p. 66.

**Integrated marketing communications** (IMC) are composed of advertising, sales promotions, trade shows, personal selling, direct selling, and public relations—almost all are included in the Barbie campaign described in the Global Perspective. Indeed, even the *Wall Street Journal* story itself was most likely prompted by a company press release. All these mutually reinforcing elements of the promotional mix have as their common objective the successful sale of a product or service. In many markets the availability of appropriate communication channels to customers can determine entry decisions. For example, most toy manufacturers would agree that toys cannot be marketed profitably in countries without commercial television advertising directed toward children. Thus product and service development must be informed by research regarding the availability of communication channels. Once a market offering is developed to meet target market needs, intended customers must be informed of the offering's value and availability. Often different messages are appropriate for different communications channels, and vice versa.

For most companies, advertising and personal selling are the major components in the marketing communications mix. In this chapter the other elements of IMC not covered in previous chapters are briefly discussed first. The goal of most companies is to achieve the synergies possible when sales promotions, public relations efforts, and advertising are used in concert. However, the primary focus of this chapter is on international advertising. The topic of the next chapter is global sales management.

# Sales Promotions in International Markets

**Sales promotions** are marketing activities that stimulate consumer purchases and improve retailer or middlemen effectiveness and cooperation. Cents off, in-store demonstrations, samples, coupons, gifts, product tie-ins, contests, sweepstakes, sponsorship of special events such as concerts and fairs (even donut parades), and point-of-purchase displays are types of sales promotion devices designed to supplement advertising and personal selling in the promotional mix. The Rapunzel Barbie movie premiere is too.

Sales promotions are short-term efforts directed to the consumer or retailer to achieve such specific objectives as consumer-product trial or immediate purchase, consumer introduction to the store, gaining retail point-of-purchase displays, encouraging stores to stock the product, and supporting and augmenting advertising and personal sales efforts. For example, Procter & Gamble's introduction of Ariel detergent in Egypt included the "Ariel Road Show," a puppet show (not the Little Mermaid!) that was taken to local markets in villages, where more than half of all Egyptians still live. The show drew huge crowds, entertained people, told about Ariel's better performance without the use of additives, and sold the brand through a distribution van at a nominal discount. Besides creating brand awareness for Ariel, the road show helped overcome the reluctance of the rural retailers to handle the premium-priced Ariel. Our favorite example in this genre is the Simpson's international festival sponsored by Fox in Hollywood. Spain's Simpson trivia champion competed against 11 other global contestants in the "Bart Bowl World Finals."[1]

In markets where the consumer is hard to reach because of media limitations, the percentage of the promotional budget allocated to sales promotions may need to be increased. In some less-developed countries, sales promotions constitute the major portion of the promotional effort in rural and less-accessible parts of the market. In parts of Latin America, a portion of the advertising-sales budget for both Pepsi-Cola and Coca-Cola is spent on carnival trucks, which make frequent trips to outlying villages to promote their products. When a carnival truck makes a stop in a village, it may show a movie or provide some other kind of entertainment; the price of admission is an unopened bottle of the product purchased from the local retailer. The unopened bottle is to be exchanged for a cold bottle plus a coupon for another bottle. This promotional effort

---

[1]Jordan Raphael, "Simpson's Fanfest Attracts International Set," *Los Angeles Times*, October 31, 2000, p. F3.

These vehicular ads make an effective advertising medium even in a dense London fog. Because most London cabs are black, the Snickers ad catches the eye immediately.

tends to stimulate sales and encourages local retailers, who are given prior notice of the carnival truck's arrival, to stock the product. Nearly 100 percent coverage of retailers in the village is achieved with this type of promotion. In other situations, village stores may be given free samples, have the outsides of their stores painted, or receive clock signs in attempts to promote sales.

An especially effective promotional tool when the product concept is new or has a very small market share is product sampling. Nestlé Baby Foods faced such a problem in France in its attempt to gain share from Gerber, the leader. The company combined sampling with a novel sales promotion program to gain brand recognition and to build goodwill. Since most French take off for a long vacation in the summertime, piling the whole family into the car and staying at well-maintained campgrounds, Nestlé provided rest-stop structures along the highway where parents could feed and change their babies. Sparkling clean *Le Relais Bébés* are located along main travel routes. Sixty-four hostesses at these rest stops welcome 120,000 baby visits and dispense 600,000 samples of baby food each year. There are free disposable diapers, a changing table, and high chairs for the babies to sit in while dining.

As is true in advertising, the success of a promotion may depend on local adaptation. Further, research shows that responses to promotions can vary across promotional types[2] and cultures. Major constraints are imposed by local laws, which may not permit premiums or free gifts to be given. Some countries' laws control the amount of discount given at retail, others require permits for all sales promotions, and in at least one country, no competitor is permitted to spend more on a sales promotion than any other company selling the product. Effective sales promotions can enhance the advertising and personal selling efforts and, in some instances, may be effective substitutes when environmental constraints prevent full utilization of advertising.

## International Public Relations

Creating good relationships with the popular press and other media to help companies communicate messages to their publics—customers, the general public, and governmental regulators—is the role of **public relations** (PR).[3] The job consists of not only encouraging the press to cover positive stories[4] about companies (as in the Barbie story), but also of managing unfavorable rumors, stories, and events. Regarding the latter, the distinction between advertising and public relations is an issue now considered by the United States Supreme Court. Nike was criticized for using "sweatshop" labor

---

[2]Lenard C. Huff and Dana L. Alden, "A Model of Managerial Response to Sales Promotions: A Four-Country Analysis," *Journal of Global Marketing,* 2000, 13(3), pp. 7–28.

[3]The story about how the Mayo brothers traveled the world makes for an interesting example of early, and quite effective public relations. See Misty Hathaway and Kent Seltman, "International Market Research at the Mayo Clinic," *Marketing Health Services,* Winter 2001, pp. 18–23.

[4]"Selling the Concept [of corporate social responsibility]," *Business Europe,* July 24, 2002, p. 3. We like their advice, "avoid greenwashing."

# CROSSING BORDERS 16.1  PR in the PRC

In 1999 an industry was born in China when the Ministry of Labor and Social Security recognized public relations as a profession. These excerpts from the *China Daily* illustrate how institutions evolve in emerging economies:

More laws are needed to regulate China's fledgling public relations profession, an industry leader said yesterday in Beijing. "To seize the enormous business opportunities promised by China's upcoming entry in the World Trade Organization, we need specific laws to regulate the market, curb malpractice and promote competency of local PR firms," said Li Yue, vice-director of the China International Public Relations Association. Her comments were made during a national symposium on public relations, also know as PR.

Symposium delegates said they were concerned about the disorder in the PR industry and the frequent personnel changes in PR firms. They urged the passage of more laws to put an end to what many consider to be the chaos in the profession. Industry insiders cited a limited talent pool, cut-throat price wars, and low professional standards as the industry's major problems.

In the 1980s, most Chinese people would think of reception girls, lavish banquets, and the use of connections when public relations were mentioned. Now, public relations firms are seen as helping their clients gain better name recognition of their companies. They also manage corporate images.

To help the industry develop, the Labor and Social Security Ministry this year instituted a nationwide qualifying exam for PR professionals. In 1999, the industry reported a total business volume of $120 million, while employing 3,000 people.

Source: "China: More Regulation of PR Sought," *China Daily*, January 20, 2000, p. 3. "PRW: The Top European PR Consultancies 2000," *PR Week*, June 23, 2000, p. 7.

in Asia and responded to critics with paid advertising. The Court decided that freedom of speech issues did not pertain to the ads, and the associated civil suit against the firm for false advertising could go forward. Indeed, it appears that Nike exacerbated and extended the problem, from a public relations standpoint, by taking the case all the way to the Supreme Court.[5]

The importance of public relations in international marketing is perhaps best demonstrated by the Bridgestone/Firestone Tires safety recall disaster of 2000. The Japanese company was blamed for more than 100 deaths in the United States because of its defective tires. True to form in such corporate disasters, the Japanese CEO of the American subsidiary "declared his full and personal responsibility" for the deaths at a U.S. Senate hearing. Such an approach is good public relations in Japan. However, in Washington the senators were not interested in apologies. Moreover, the company blamed its customer, Ford Motor Company, for the problems as well, accusing Ford of telling customers to underinflate the tires for a smoother ride. The problem spread to other markets—Saudi Arabia banned imports of vehicles equipped with Firestone tires. Unbelievably, the company's response to the Saudi action was to denounce it as a violation of WTO agreements. The global impact of this product-quality and public relations disaster is certain to be great and long lasting. Perhaps the company would have been better off promoting its ISO 9000 rating—refer back to the picture in Chapter 13 on page 384.[6]

Public relations firms' billings in the international arena have been growing at double-digit rates for some years. Handling such international PR problems as global workplace standards is big business for companies serving corporate clients such as Mattel Toys, McDonald's, and of course Nike. Fast growth is also being fueled by the expanding international communications industry. New companies need public relations consultation for "building an international profile," as the marketing manager of VDSL Systems explained when hiring MCC, a prominent British firm. Surprising growth is occurring in emerging markets like Russia as well. The industry itself is experiencing a wave of mergers and

---

[5]Stanley Holmes, "Free Speech or False Advertising," *BusinessWeek*, April 28, 2003, pp. 69–70.

[6]Robert C. Wilson, "ISO and PR," *Pollution Engineering*, July 2002, pp. 44–45.

takeovers, including the blending of the largest international advertising agencies and the most well-established PR firms.

Corporate sponsorships might be classified as an aspect of public relations, although their connections to advertising are also manifest. The tobacco companies are particularly creative at using sports event sponsorships in avoiding countries' advertising regulations associated with more traditional media. Other prominent examples are Coca-Cola's sponsorship of European football (soccer) matches or Ford's sponsorship of the Australian Open tennis tournament. McDonald's executed a huge international IMC campaign surrounding its sponsorship of the 2000 Sydney Olympics. Included were Olympic-themed food promotions, packaging, and in-store signs, TV and print ads, and Web chats with superstar athletes such as American basketball player Grant Hill. In addition to the various promotions targeting the 43 million daily customers in their 27,000 restaurants around the world, the firm targeted the athletes themselves. As the official restaurant partner, McDonald's got to operate seven restaurants in Sydney, including the two serving the Olympic Village. During the three weeks of the Olympic Games nearly 1.5 million burgers were served to the athletes, officials, coaches, media staffers, and spectators. Similarly, one of the more innovative sponsorship arrangements was Intel's agreement with the Tour de France to support the official Tour website, www.letour.com. Of course, all these aspects of IMC work best when coordinated and reinforced with a consistent advertising campaign, the topic covered in the rest of the chapter.

# International Advertising

At the turn of the century growth in global advertising expenditures has slowed with the global economy. Most estimates of total expenditures for 2003 are in the neighborhood of $400 to $500 billion.[7] A four percent annual growth rate is predicted through 2006, but that of course depends on a resurgence of growth in the general global economy. In this difficult global economic environment the advertising industry continues to undergo substantial restructuring.[8] Global mass media advertising is a powerful tool for cultural change,[9] and as such it receives continuing scrutiny by a wide variety of institutions. Even so, most scholars agree that we are just beginning to understand some of the key issues involved in international advertising.[10]

Exhibits 16.1 and 16.2 illustrate the biggest companies and product categories for international advertising. While the automotive companies dominate the lists, Proctor & Gamble was the global champion of spending. Also, notice the lack of growth across many of the categories and companies. We also broke out the spending patterns for two emerging markets in Exhibits 16.3a and b. Demonstrated is a key difference in stage of development between China and Russia. Whereas the latter is dominated by foreign food firms, China is creating it's own home-grown brands of pharmaceuticals. Judging the relative progress of the two countries on this single criterion, China looks like it is farther up the ladder of economic development.

Of all the elements of the marketing mix, decisions involving advertising are those most often affected by cultural differences among country markets. Consumers respond in terms of their culture, its style, feelings, value systems, attitudes, beliefs, and perceptions. Because advertising's function is to interpret or translate the qualities of products and services in terms of consumer needs, wants, desires, and aspirations, the emotional appeals, symbols, persuasive approaches, and other characteristics of an advertisement must coincide with cultural norms if the ad is to be effective.

[7] www.medialifemagazine.com, 2003.

[8] "Carving Up Cordiant," *The Economist,* June 21, 2003, p. 61.

[9] Lalita A. Manrai, Dana-Nicoleta Lascu, Ajay K. Manrai, and Harold W. Babb, "A Cross-Cultural Comparison of Style in Eastern European Emerging Markets," *International Marketing Review,* 2001, 18(3), pp. 270–285.

[10] Charles R. Taylor, "What is Wrong with International Advertising Research?" *Journal of Advertising Research,* November–December 2002, 42(6), pp. 48–54.

**Exhibit 16.1**   Top 20 Global Advertisers ($ millions)*

| 2001 | 2000 | Advertiser | Headquarters | 2001 | Percent Change |
|------|------|------------|--------------|------|----------------|
| 1 | 2 | Procter & Gamble Co. | Cincinnati | $3,820.2 | 6.6 |
| 2 | 1 | General Motors Corp. | Detroit | 3,028.9 | –20.1 |
| 3 | 3 | Unilever | London/Rotterdam | 3,005.5 | 2.6 |
| 4 | 6 | Ford Motor Co. | Dearborn, MI | 2,309.0 | 3.0 |
| 5 | 5 | Toyota Motor Corp. | Toyota City, Japan | 2,213.3 | –3.1 |
| 6 | 8 | AOL Time Warner | New York | 2,099.8 | 9.5 |
| 7 | 4 | Philip Morris Cos. | New York | 1,934.6 | –19.0 |
| 8 | 7 | DaimlerChrysler | Stuttgart | 1,835.3 | –12.4 |
| 9 | 9 | Nestlé | Vevey, Switzerland | 1,798.5 | 3.2 |
| 10 | 10 | Volkswagen | Wolfsburg, Germany | 1,574.1 | –2.0 |
| 11 | 13 | Honda Motor Co. | Tokyo | 1,426.0 | 5.6 |
| 12 | 11 | McDonald's Corp. | Oak Brook, IL | 1,405.3 | –3.6 |
| 13 | 14 | Coca-Cola Co. | Atlanta | 1,402.4 | 6.5 |
| 13 | 12 | L'Oreal | Paris | 1,348.8 | –2.1 |
| 15 | 16 | Walt Disney Co. | Burbank, CA | 1,260.4 | –1.6 |
| 16 | 18 | Johnson & Johnson | New Brunswick, NJ | 1,227.3 | –0.4 |
| 17 | 17 | Nissan Motor Co. | Tokyo | 1,224.0 | –3.8 |
| 18 | 15 | Sony Corp. | Tokyo | 1,218.9 | –4.9 |
| 19 | 20 | GlaxoSmithKline | Greenford, Middlesex, U.K. | 1,130.1 | 6.0 |
| 20 | 21 | PepsiCo | Purchase, NY | 1,025.8 | 8.3 |

*Figures are U.S. dollars in millions and are *Advertising Age* estimates.

Source: "Special Report Global Marketers," *Advertising Age,* Supplement to the Ad Age Special Report, November 11, 2002. Copyright, Crain Communications Inc. 2002.

Reconciling an international advertising campaign with the cultural uniqueness of markets is the challenge confronting the international or global marketer. The basic framework and concepts of international advertising are essentially the same wherever used. Seven steps are involved:

1. Perform marketing research.
2. Specify the goals of the communication.
3. Develop the most effective message(s) for the market segments selected.
4. Select effective media.
5. Compose and secure a budget.

**Exhibit 16.2**

Top 100 Advertiser's Global Spending by Category ($ millions)

Source: "Special Report Global Marketers," *Advertising Age,* Supplement to the Ad Age Special Report, November 11, 2002. Copyright, Crain Communications Inc. 2002.

| Category | 2001 | Percent Change from 2000 | Percent Total |
|----------|------|--------------------------|---------------|
| Automotive | $19,334.4 | –3.3 | 27.3 |
| Food | 11,220.7 | –6.9 | 15.8 |
| Personal care | 10,300.2 | 5.2 | 14.5 |
| Electronics, computers | 6,557.5 | –8.0 | 9.2 |
| Media and entertainment | 6,285.4 | 3.2 | 8.9 |
| Pharmaceuticals | 5,655.8 | 3.6 | 8.0 |
| Fast food | 2,989.4 | –2.3 | 4.2 |
| Household cleaners | 2,203.5 | 6.6 | 3.1 |
| Telecommunications | 1,733.0 | –19.7 | 2.4 |
| Financial services, credit | 1,156.3 | –14.8 | 1.6 |
| Retail | 987.3 | –6.4 | 1.4 |
| Beer, wine and liquor | 951.3 | 1.5 | 1.3 |
| Toys | 529.2 | –12.2 | 0.7 |
| Photo film | 490.4 | 4.9 | 0.7 |
| Miscellaneous | 556.3 | –10.7 | 0.8 |

**Exhibit 16.3a**
Russia's Top Ten
Advertisers ($ millions)

Source: "Special Report Global
Marketers," *Advertising Age*,
Supplement to the Ad Age Special
Report, November 11, 2002.
Copyright, Crain Communications Inc.
2002.

| Advertiser | 2001 | Percent Change from 2000 |
|---|---|---|
| Procter & Gamble Co | $105.32 | 22.4 |
| Nestlé | 61.19 | 48.7 |
| Mars Inc. | 54.85 | 25.4 |
| Unilever | 50.44 | 51.0 |
| PepsiCo | 45.88 | 62.2 |
| Wm. Wrigley Jr. Co. | 42.80 | −3.7 |
| Danone Group | 38.08 | 227.9 |
| Wimm-Bill-Dann | 35.53 | 46.0 |
| Henkel | 31.23 | 328.9 |
| Coca-Cola Co. | 23.88 | 48.5 |

**Exhibit 16.3b**
China's Top Ten
Advertisers ($ millions)

Source: "Special Report Global
Marketers," *Advertising Age*,
Supplement to the Ad Age Special
Report, November 11, 2002.
Copyright, Crain Communications Inc.
2002.

| Advertiser | 2001 | Percent Change from 2000 |
|---|---|---|
| Procter & Gamble Co | $102.45 | 114.9 |
| Taita Pharmaceutical | 56.54 | 98.6 |
| Diaopai | 55.41 | 153.4 |
| Naobaijin Pharmaceutical | 52.66 | −15.6 |
| Changjia | 50.96 | 240.4 |
| Medical Treatment Information | 50.54 | 9.1 |
| Sanjing Pharmaceutical | 44.85 | −38.5 |
| Hutong Pharmaceutical | 42.68 | NA |
| Danwang Pharmaceutical | 41.91 | NA |
| Neptunus | 37.52 | 2305.5 |

6. Execute the campaign.

7. Evaluate the campaign relative to the goals specified.

Of these seven steps, developing messages almost always represents the most daunting task for international marketing managers, so that topic is emphasized here. Nuances of international media are then discussed. Advertising agencies are ordinarily involved in all seven steps and are the subject of a separate section. Finally, the chapter closes with a discussion of broader issues of governmental controls on advertising.

## Advertising Strategy and Goals

The goals of advertising around the world vary substantially. For example, Chinese manufacturers are establishing new brands as their economy expands;[11] Unilever is introducing a new product-line extension, Dove Shampoo, in East Asian markets;[12] and, Russia's airline Aeroflot is seeking to upgrade its quality image.[13] All these marketing problems require careful marketing research and thoughtful and creative advertising campaigns in country, regional, and global markets, respectively.

[Intense competition for world markets and the increasing sophistication of foreign consumers led to a need for more sophisticated advertising strategies.] Increased costs, problems of coordinating advertising programs in multiple countries, and a desire for a broader company or product image caused multinational companies (MNCs) to seek greater control and efficiency without sacrificing local responsiveness. In the quest for more effective and responsive promotion programs, the policies covering centralized or

---

[11]Michael T. Ewing, Julie Napoli, Leyland Pitt, and Alistair Watts, "On the Renaissance of Chinese Brands," *International Journal of Advertising,* 2002, 21(2), pp. 197–217.

[12]Normandy Madden, "Dove Shampoo Cleans up with New O&M Campaign," *AdAgeGlobal,* May 2002, pp. 17–18.

[13]Alexey Komarov, "Aeroflot Toes Tight Fiscal Line As It Targets Fleet Upgrades," *Aviation Week,* August 6, 2001, pp. 53–54.

decentralized authority,[14] use of single or multiple foreign or domestic agencies, appropriation and allocation procedures, copy, media, and research are being examined. More multinational companies are managing the balance between standardization[15] of advertising themes and customization.[16] And recently, as described in Chapter 12, more companies are favoring the latter.[17]

A case in point is the Gillette Company, which sells 800 products in more than 200 countries. Gillette has a consistent worldwide image as a masculine, sports-oriented company, but its products have no such consistent image. Its razors, blades, toiletries, and cosmetics are known by many names. Trac II blades in the United States are more widely known worldwide as G-II, and Atra blades are called Contour in Europe and Asia. Silkience hair conditioner is known as Soyance in France, Sientel in Italy, and Silkience in Germany. Whether or not global brand names could be chosen for Gillette's many existing products is speculative. However, Gillette's current corporate philosophy of globalization provides for an umbrella statement, "Gillette, the Best a Man Can Get," in all advertisements for men's toiletries products in the hope of providing some common image.

A similar situation exists for Unilever, which sells a cleaning liquid called Vif in Switzerland, Viss in Germany, Jif in Britain and Greece, and Cif in France. This situation is a result of Unilever marketing separately to each of these countries. At this point, it would be difficult for Gillette or Unilever to standardize their brand names because each brand is established in its market. Nortel Networks used a "local heroes" approach in its international advertising. The company picks local celebrities to pitch standardized messages across national markets for their telecommunications services.

In many cases standardized products may be marketed globally. But because of differences in cultures, they still require a different advertising appeal in different markets.[18] For instance, Ford's advertising varies by nation because of language and societal nuances. Ford advertises the affordability of its Escort in the United States, where the car is seen as entry level. But in India, Ford launched the Escort as a premium car. "It's not unusual to see an Escort with a chauffeur there," said a Ford executive.

Finally, many companies are using market-segment strategies that ignore national boundaries—business buyers or high-income consumers across the globe are often targeted, for example.[19] Others are proposing newer global market segments defined by "consumer cultures" related to shared sets of consumption-related symbols—convenience, youth, America, internationalism, and humanitarianism are examples. Other more traditional segments are product and region related; those are discussed next.

## Product Attribute and Benefit Segmentation

As discussed in the chapters on product and services development (Chapters 12 and 13), a market offering really is a bundle of satisfactions the buyer receives. This package of satisfactions or utilities includes the primary function of the product or service along with many other benefits imputed by the values and customs of the culture. Different cultures often seek the same value or benefits from the primary function of a product; for example, the ability of an automobile to get from point A to point B, a camera to take a picture, or a wristwatch to tell time. But while usually agreeing on the benefit of

---

[14]Carl Solberg, "The Perennial Issue of Adaptation or Standardization of International Marketing Communications: Organizational Contingencies and Performance," *Journal of International Marketing,* 10(3), pp. 1–21.

[15]Michael Laroche, V.H. Kirpalani, Frank Pons, and Lianxi Zhou, "A Model of Advertising Standardization in Multinational Companies," *Journal of International Business Studies,* 2001, 32(2), pp. 249–266.

[16]Ali Kanso, Richard Alan Nelson, "Advertising Localization Overshadows Standardization," *Journal of Advertising Research,* January–February 2002, 42(1), pp. 79–89.

[17]Claudia Eller and Lorenza Munoz, "The Plot Thickens in Foreign Markes," *Los Angeles Times,* October 6, 2002, p. 1.

[18]Cris Prystay, "Selling to Singapore's Teens is Tricky," *Wall Street Journal*, October 4, 2002, p. B2.

[19]Greg Harris and Suleiman Attour, "The International Advertising Practices of Multinational Companies: A Content Analysis Study," *European Journal of Marketing,* 2003, 37(1-2), pp. 154–168.

the primary function of a product, other features and psychological attributes of the item can have significant differences.

Consider the different market-perceived needs for a camera. In the United States, excellent pictures with easy, foolproof operation are expected by most of the market; in Germany and Japan, a camera must take excellent pictures, but the camera must also be state of the art in design. In Africa, where penetration of cameras is less than 20 percent of the households, the concept of picture taking must be sold. In all three markets, excellent pictures are expected (i.e., the primary function of a camera is demanded), but the additional utility or satisfaction derived from a camera differs among cultures. There are many products that produce such different expectations beyond the common benefit sought by all.

Dannon's brand of yogurt promotes itself as the brand that understands the relationship between health and food, but it communicates the message differently depending on the market.[20] In the United States, where Dannon yogurt is seen as a healthy, vibrant food, the brand celebrates its indulgent side. In France, however, Dannon was seen as too pleasure oriented. Therefore, Dannon created the Institute of Health, a real research center dedicated to food and education. The end result is the same message but communicated differently—a careful balance of health and pleasure.

The Blue Diamond Growers Association's advertising of almonds is an excellent example of the fact that some products are best advertised only on a local basis. Blue Diamond had a very successful ad campaign in the United States showing almond growers knee-deep in almonds while pleading with the audience, "A can a week, that's all we ask." The objective of the campaign was to change the perception of almonds as a special-occasion treat to an everyday snack food. The ad was a success; in addition to helping change the perception of almonds as a snack food, it received millions of dollars worth of free publicity for Blue Diamond from regional and national news media. The successful U.S. ad was tested in Canada for possible use outside the United States. The Canadian reaction was vastly different; to them, the whole idea was just too silly. And further, Canadians prefer to buy products from Canadian farmers, not American farmers. This led to the decision to study each market closely and design an advertisement for each country market. The only similarity between commercials airing in markets in New York, Tokyo, Moscow, Toronto, or Stockholm is the Blue Diamond logo.

In Japan, the Blue Diamond brand of almonds was an unknown commodity until Blue Diamond launched its campaign of exotic new almond-based products that catered to local tastes. Such things as almond tofu, almond miso soup, and Clamond—a nutritional snack concocted from a mixture of dried small sardines and slivered almonds—were featured in magazine ads and in promotional cooking demonstrations. Television ads featured educational messages on how to use almonds in cooking, their nutritional value, the versatility of almonds as a snack, and the California mystique and health benefits of almonds. As a result, Japan is now the Association's largest importer of almonds.

In Korea, the emphasis was on almonds and the West. Commercials featured swaying palms, beach scenes, and a guitar-playing crooner singing "Blue Diamond" to the tune of "Blue Hawaii." And so it goes in the 94 countries where Blue Diamond sells its almonds. Blue Diamond assumes that no two markets will react the same, that each has its own set of differences—be they "cultural, religious, ethnic, dietary, or otherwise"— and that each will require a different marketing approach, a different strategy. The wisdom of adapting its product advertising for each market is difficult to question since two-thirds of all Blue Diamond's sales are outside the United States.

**Regional Segmentation**   The emergence of pan-European communications media is enticing many companies to push the balance toward more standardized promotional efforts. As media coverage across Europe expands, it will become more common for markets to be exposed to

---

[20]Jae H. Pae, Saeed Samiee, and Susan Tai, "Global Advertising Strategy: The Moderating Role of Brand Familiarity and Execution Style," *International Marketing Review,* 2002, 19(2-3), pp. 176–189.

MICROSOFT annually spends approximately three-fourths of a billion dollars on its global advertising. The company has 75 subsidiaries around the world. The management processes used to develop the "Windows XP" campaign are instructive.

Things begin with marketing research in individual countries regarding key market segments, most attractive product features, and potential themes. The data collected by the international subsidiaries are then sent to McCann-Erickson's San Francisco offices for the development of a set of universal themes. McCann-Erickson Worldwide has more than 200 offices in 111 countries and is ideally suited for global clients such as Microsoft, Coca-Cola, DuPont, and Lucent Technologies. The San Francisco office is closest to Redmond, Washington, where Microsoft is headquartered, and, of course, it is also adjacent to the Silicon Valley.

The agency sends the appropriate core concepts, video footage, photographic layouts, and copy themes that comprise the set of universal materials. Then, in cooperation with their local agencies, managers at each subsidiary choose the most appropriate materials for their particular consumers and markets. The most customization is required in Brazil, China, India, and Russia—all are plagued by major piracy problems. Also, since Japan is the firm's second largest market behind only the U.S., executives there are given more freedom to adapt to local requirements and tastes.

"yes you can." has been used in magazines in the U.S. Photography and file sharing features are emphasized. *(Courtesy Microsoft Corporation. Photographer: Laura Greenfield)*

"you can do as you wish." is the theme promoted in China. A variety of applications ranging from music to instant messaging to office uses are mentioned in the copy. *(Courtesy Microsoft Corporation. Photographer: Laura Greenfield)*

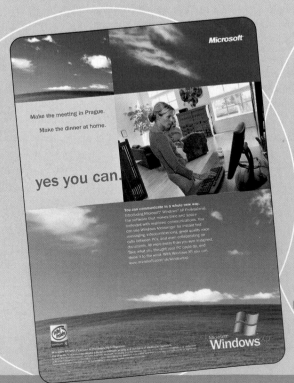

"yes you can." has also been used in the United Kingdom. But, here the emphasis is on office-in-the-home applications. *(Courtesy Microsoft Corporation. Photographer: Laura Greenfield)*

*"Surprenez-vous."* (*"Surprise your-self."*) apparently appeals to French consumers. Again the photo and video production and file sharing features are emphasized. (*Courtesy Microsoft Corporation. Photographer: Laura Greenfield*)

*"Alles wird leichter."* (*"Everything will be easier."*) focuses on the office features for the German market. Themes of security, reliability, and services are key. (*Courtesy Microsoft Corporation. Photographer: Laura Greenfield*)

*"yes you can."* even kiss your boyfriend using XP in Japan. Compared to the other countries, even the U.S., the Japanese copy is quite distinctive—explaining that XP allows face-to-face communications via your computer monitor. Almost everything is included—facial expressions, tone of voice, and gestures can be seen. (*Courtesy Microsoft Corporation. Photographer: Takashi Honma; CD/CW: Isamu Nakamura [McCann-Tokyo]; AD: Ryoko Shinbo [McCann-Tokyo]*)

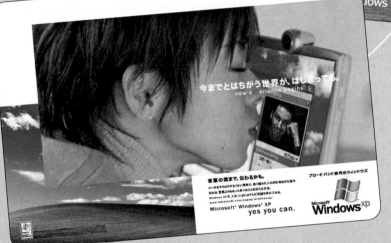

Finally, the skyline of the XP campaign can be seen amongst the skyline of Shanghai, suggesting the variety of outdoor media used by Microsoft around the world. (© Reuters NewMedia Inc./CORBIS)

The translations are done locally, so for example, the copy is different between Mexico and Spain. As can be seen in the ads displayed, a variety of themes and media (print and outdoor) are used across countries. And, in any one country, several themes and media may be used, particularly in the larger, more diverse markets.

Finally, the executions are then tested in each market and adjustments are made. This global approach makes sense for Microsoft because the product, its uses, and its market share are virtually the same across markets. This integrated approach has saved some $30 million in man-hours and production costs over previous similar campaigns.

**(Courtesy Microsoft Corporation)**

multiple messages and brands of the same product. To avoid the confusion that results when a market is exposed to multiple brand names and advertising messages, as well as for reasons of efficiency, companies strive for harmony in brand names, advertising, and promotions across Europe.

Mars, the candy company, traditionally used several brand names for the same product but found it necessary to select a single name to achieve uniformity in its standardized advertising campaigns. As a result, a candy bar sold in some parts of Europe under the brand name Raider was changed to Twix, the name used in the United States and the United Kingdom.

IBM gradually created a pan-European promotional strategy by moving away from campaigns individually tailored for each European country. Broadcast and print advertisements for its personal computers feature an identical image with text that is translated into local languages. To ensure uniformity in its promotional materials, IBM developed a manual to provide step-by-step instructions on how to achieve a common theme in the design of all the company's product and service brochures. An important reason for uniform promotional packaging across country markets is cost savings. In IBM's case, one set of European ads versus one set for each country for one of its personal computers saved an estimated $2 million. The company also estimates that a completely unified European advertising strategy will result in stretching its $150 million European budget by an extra 15 to 20 percent.

Along with changes in behavior patterns, legal restrictions are slowly being eliminated, and viable market segments across country markets are emerging. Although Europe will never be a single homogenous market for every product, that does not mean that companies should shun the idea of developing Europeanwide promotional programs. A pan-European promotional strategy would mean identifying a market segment across all European countries and designing a promotional concept appealing to market segment similarities. IBM and Mars candy are good examples of this strategy.

With a common language (Brazil being the one exception), Latin America also lends itself to regionwide promotion programs. Eveready Battery successfully developed a 16-country campaign with one message instead of the patchwork of messages that previously existed. Cable and satellite TV channels also provide regionwide media. For example, HBO promotes American cable-TV hit *Six Feet Under* using a pan-Asian campaign.[21]

# The Message: Creative Challenges

**Global Advertising and the Communications Process**

International communications may fail for a variety of reasons: A message may not get through because of media inadequacy, the message may be received by the intended audience but not be understood because of different cultural interpretations, or the message may reach the intended audience and be understood but have no effect because the marketer did not correctly assess the needs and wants or the thinking processes[22] of the target market.

The effectiveness of promotional strategy can be jeopardized by so many factors that a marketer must be certain no controllable influences are overlooked. Those international executives who understand the communications process are better equipped to manage the diversity they face in developing an international promotional program.

In the international communications process, each of the seven identifiable steps can ultimately affect the accuracy of the process. As illustrated in Exhibit 16.4, the process consists of the following:

---

[21]Magz Osborne, "HBO Highlights Quirky Humor in Pan-Asian Ads For TV hit *Six Feet Under,*" *AdAgeGlobal,* October 18, 2002.

[22]Jennifer Aaker, "Accessibility or Diagnosticity? Disentangling the Influence of Culture on Persuasion Processes and Attitudes," *Journal of Consumer Research,* March 2000, 26(4), pp. 340–357.

**Exhibit 16.4**
The International
Communications Process

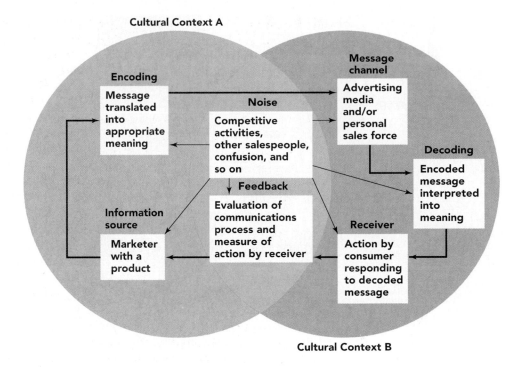

1. **An information source.** An international marketing executive with a product message to communicate.

2. **Encoding.** The message from the source converted into effective symbolism for transmission to a receiver.

3. **A message channel.** The sales force and/or advertising media that convey the encoded message to the intended receiver.

4. **Decoding.** The interpretation by the receiver of the symbolism transmitted from the information source.

5. **Receiver.** Consumer action by those who receive the message and are the target for the thought transmitted.

6. **Feedback.** Information about the effectiveness of the message that flows from the receiver (the intended target) back to the information source for evaluation of the effectiveness of the process.

7. **Noise.** Uncontrollable and unpredictable influences such as competitive activities and confusion that detract from the process and affect any or all of the other six steps.

Unfortunately, the process is not as simple as just sending a message via a medium to a receiver and being certain that the intended message sent is the same one perceived by the receiver. In Exhibit 16.4, the communications-process steps are encased in Cultural Context A and Cultural Context B to illustrate the influences complicating the process when the message is encoded in one culture and decoded in another. If not properly considered, the different cultural contexts can increase the probability of misunderstandings. Research in the area suggests that effective communication demands the existence of a "psychological overlap" between the sender and the receiver; otherwise, a message falling outside the receiver's perceptual field may transmit an unintended meaning. It is in this area that even the most experienced companies make blunders.

Most promotional misfires or mistakes in international marketing are attributable to one or several of these steps not properly reflecting cultural influences or to a general lack of knowledge about the target market. Referring to Exhibit 16.4, the information source is a marketer with a product to sell to a specific target market. The product

City streets in Singapore are alive with advertising. California Fitness Centers in Southeast Asia are owned by America's 24-hour Fitness Centers. Obviously the image of "bodyland" southern California sells well around the world. However, there's an interesting irony in that brand name for Muslim customers. The word *California* first appears in the eleventh-century epic poem *The Song of Roland;* there it literally means the "caliph's domain"—the Caliph of Baghdad ruled the Islamic Empire then. The Spaniards who named California in the early 1500s thought they were in Asia!

message to be conveyed should reflect the needs and wants of the target market; however, often the actual market needs and the marketer's perception of them do not coincide. This is especially true when the marketer relies more on the self-reference criterion (SRC) than on effective research. It can never be assumed that "if it sells well in one country, it will sell in another." For instance, bicycles designed and sold in the United States to consumers fulfilling recreational exercise needs are not sold as effectively for the same reason in a market where the primary use of the bicycle is transportation. Cavity-reducing fluoride toothpaste sells well in the United States, where healthy teeth are perceived as important, but has limited appeal in markets such as Great Britain and the French areas of Canada, where the reason for buying toothpaste is breath control. From the onset of the communications process, if basic needs are incorrectly defined, communications fail because an incorrect or meaningless message is received even though the remaining steps in the process are executed properly.

The encoding step causes problems even with a "proper" message. At this step such factors as color,[23] timing, values,[24] beliefs,[25] humor,[26] tastes, and appropriateness of spokespersons can cause the international marketer to symbolize the message incorrectly. For example, the marketer wants the product to convey coolness so the color green is used; however, people in the tropics might decode green as dangerous or associate it with disease. Another example of the encoding process misfiring was a perfume presented against a backdrop of rain that, for Europeans, symbolized a clean, cool, refreshing image, but to Africans was a symbol of fertility. The ad prompted many viewers to ask if the perfume was effective against infertility. David Beckham may be a wonderful spokesperson in most of the world, but in the United States even the greatest soccer players get little recognition—that is, his fame will not be encoded.[27]

Problems of literacy, media availability, and types of media create problems in the communications process at the encoding step. Message channels must be carefully selected if an encoded message is to reach the consumer. Errors such as using television as a medium when only a small percentage of an intended market is exposed to TV, or using print media for a channel of communications when the majority of the intended users cannot read or do not read the language in the medium, are examples of ineffective media channel selection in the communications process.

Decoding problems are generally created by improper encoding, which caused such errors as Pepsi's "Come Alive" slogan being decoded as "Come out of the grave." Chevrolet's brand name for the Nova model (which means new star) was decoded into Spanish as No Va!, meaning "it doesn't go." In another misstep, a translation that was

[23]Thomas J. Madden, Kelly Hewett, Martin S. Roth, "Managing Images in Different Cultures: A Cross-National Study of Color Meanings and Preferences," *Journal of International Marketing,* 2000, 8(4), pp. 108–121.

[24]Cheng Lu Wang and Allan K.K. Chan, "A Content Analysis of Connectedness vs. Separateness Themes Used in U.S. and PRC Print Advertisements," *International Marketing Review,* 2001, 18(2), pp. 145–160.

[25]Mark Magnier, "Japan Moviegoers Giving 'Pearl Harbor' a Boost," *Los Angeles Times,* July 19, 2001, p C1.

[26]Erin White, "Europeans Take a Satirical Jab at the U.S.," *Wall Street Journal,* April 28, 2003, p. B1.

[27]Erin White and Maureen Tkacik, "Spend It Like Beckham," *Wall Street Journal,* June 19, 2003, p. B1.

## CROSSING BORDERS 16.2   Arnold Terminates Site Leaking Foreign TV Ads

It's hard to say no to Arnold Schwarzenegger, or so a Victoria-based website has learned. The site, dedicated to showing celebrities pitching products to Japanese audiences, was forced to terminate an overseas commercial featuring the brawny movie star.

The three co-founders of the parody Internet site decided to say *hasta la vista* to the ad, never meant for release in North America, after receiving a cease-and-desist order from lawyers in Tokyo threatening legal action.

But the publicity surrounding the Web video of Mr. Schwarzenegger, the star of action movies including *The Terminator*, resulted in an unprecedented number of visits to the Gaijin a Go-Go Café site set up by the small Canadian Web company Zero One Design. "I don't understand what all the hubbub is about," Jonathan Lathigee, the site's 26-year-old

co-founder, said. "We were a little blown away by all the attention."

The commercial at the center of the controversy was made for DirecTV, a Japanese satellite TV channel that broadcasts U.S. movies and programs. It shows Mr. Schwarzenegger playing several characters, including a reporter and a politician, and revisits his famous *Terminator* role.

The website at www.gaijinagogo.com downloads Japanese commercials featuring U.S. celebrities such as Demi Moore, Keanu Reeves, and Leonardo DiCaprio, who hawk everything from whisky to beauty cream in lucrative overseas commercials not meant for North American audiences.

Source: Kim Lunman, "Arnold Terminates Site Leaking Foreign TV Ads," *Globe Mail*, August 11, 2000, p. A3. Reprinted with Permission from The Globe and Mail.

Spend it like Beckham—in addition to Vodafone and Nike on his jersey, David Beckham, here in his Manchester United red, also represents Pepsi, Adidas, Castrol, Upper Deck, Marks & Spencer, Police, Meiji, Tokyo Beauty Center, etc., etc., etc. Most recently the Spanish soccer power Real Madrid spent $40 million buying Mr. Beckham's contract from his British home team. One disadvantage of the move south—the white jersey of the Spanish team won't catch the eye as did the Manchester United red. (© AFP/CORBIS)

supposed to be decoded as "hydraulic ram" was instead decoded as "wet sheep." In a Nigerian ad, a platinum blonde sitting next to the driver of a Renault was intended to enhance the image of the automobile. However, the model was perceived as not respectable and so created a feeling of shame. An ad used for Eveready Energizer batteries with the Energizer bunny was seen by Hungarian consumers as touting a bunny toy, not a battery.

Decoding errors may also occur accidentally. Such was the case with Colgate-Palmolive's selection of the brand name Cue for toothpaste. The brand name was not intended to have any symbolism; nevertheless, it was decoded by the French into a pornographic word. In some cases, the intended symbolism has no meaning to the decoder. In an ad transferred from the United States, the irony of tough-guy actor Tom Selleck standing atop a mountain with a steaming mug of Lipton tea was lost on Eastern Europeans.

Errors at the receiver end of the process generally result from a combination of factors: an improper message resulting from incorrect knowledge of use patterns, poor encoding producing a meaningless message, poor media selection that does not get the message to the receiver, or inaccurate decoding by the receiver so that the message is garbled or incorrect. Even bad luck comes into play. French's mustard was boycotted (along with French wines, fries, etc.) by Americans when the Paris government did not go along with the attack in Iraq in 2003. This was so, even though the brand name had nothing to do with the country—the American company founder's name was Robert T. French.[28]

---

[28]Floyd Norris, "It's French's Mustard. What's in a Name these Days?" *International Herald Tribune*, March 29, 2003, p. 13.

Notice the Coke advantage at work—the red contrasts with the outdoor environment while the Cristal aqua blends more with the blue sky. Cristal is a popular brand of bottled water actually owned by Coca-Cola and sold here in the Yucatan Peninsula in Mexico. The Coke ads are emblazoned on a café in the central plaza of Canas, Costa Rica.

Finally, the feedback step of the communications process is important as a check on the effectiveness of the other steps. Companies that do not measure their communications efforts are apt to allow errors of source, encoding, media selection, decoding, or receiver to continue longer than necessary. In fact, a proper feedback system (ad testing) allows a company to correct errors before substantial damage occurs.

In addition to the problems inherent in the steps outlined, the effectiveness of the international communications process can be impaired by noise. **Noise** comprises all other external influences, such as competitive advertising, other sales personnel, and confusion at the receiving end, that can detract from the ultimate effectiveness of the communication. Noise is a disruptive force interfering with the process at any step and is frequently beyond the control of the sender or the receiver. As Exhibit 16.4 illustrates with the overlapping cultural contexts, noise can emanate from activity in either culture or be caused by the influences of the overlapping of the cultural contexts.

The model's significance is that one or all steps in the process, cultural factors,[29] or the marketer's SRC can affect the ultimate success of the communication. For example, the message, encoding, media, and the intended receiver can be designed perfectly but the inability of the receiver to decode may render the final message inoperative. In developing advertising messages, the international marketer can effectively use this model as a guide to help ensure that all potential constraints and problems are considered so that the final communication received and the action taken correspond with the intent of the source.

The growing intensity of international competition, coupled with the complexity of multinational marketing, demands that the international advertiser function at the highest creative level. The creative task is made more daunting by other kinds of barriers to effective communications—legal, linguistic, cultural, media, production, and cost considerations.

**Legal Constraints**    Laws that control comparative advertising vary from country to country in Europe. In Germany, it is illegal to use any comparative terminology; you can be sued by a competitor if you do. Belgium and Luxembourg explicitly ban comparative advertising, whereas it is clearly authorized in the United Kingdom, Ireland, Spain, and Portugal. The directive covering comparative advertising allows implicit comparisons that do not name competitors, but bans explicit comparisons between named products. The European

[29]Donnel A. Briley and Robert S. Wyer Jr., "The Effect of Group Membership Salience on the Avoidance of Negative Outcomes: Implications for Social and Consumer Research," *Journal of Consumer Research,* December 2002, 29(3), pp. 400–415.

Commission issued several directives to harmonize the laws governing advertising. However, member states are given substantial latitude to cover issues under their jurisdiction. Many fear that if the laws are not harmonized, member states may close their borders to advertising that does not respect their national rules.

Comparative advertising is heavily regulated in other parts of the world, as well. In Asia, an advertisement showing chimps choosing Pepsi over Coke was banned from most satellite television; the phrase "the leading cola" was accepted only in the Philippines. An Indian court ordered Lever to cease claiming that its New Pepsodent toothpaste was "102% better" than the leading brand. Colgate, the leading brand, was never mentioned in the advertisement, although a model was shown mouthing the word "Colgate" and the image was accompanied by a "ting" sound recognized in all Colgate ads as the ring of confidence. Banning explicit comparisons rules out an effective advertising approach heavily used by U.S. companies at home and in other countries where it is permitted.

A variety of restrictions on advertising of specific products exists around the world. Advertising of pharmaceuticals is restricted in many countries. For example, critics in Canada complain that laws there haven't been revised in 50 years and are rendered obsolete by the advent of TV and more recently the Internet. Toy, tobacco, and liquor advertising is restricted in numerous countries. The French government until recently forbade TV ads for retailers, publishing, cinema, and the press.[30]

Advertising on television is strictly controlled in many countries.[31] In Kuwait, the government-controlled TV network allows only 32 minutes of advertising per day, in the evening. Commercials are controlled to exclude superlative descriptions, indecent words, fearful or shocking shots, indecent clothing or dancing, contests, hatred or revenge shots, ethnic derision,[32] and attacks on competition. Russian law forbids subliminal advertising, but it is still prevalent because enforcement resources are lacking.[33] Regulations regarding levels of violence in ads also vary around the world, as a division of Mitsubishi recently discovered in Spain.[34]

There is some softening of country laws against accessibility to broadcast media. Australia ended a ban on cable television spots, and Malaysia is considering changing the rules to allow foreign commercials to air on newly legalized satellite signals. However, with rare exceptions, all commercials on Malaysian television still must be made in Malaysia.

Companies that rely on television infomercials and television shopping are restricted by the limitations placed on the length and number of television commercials permitted when their programs are classified as advertisements. The levels of restrictions in the European Community vary widely, from no advertising on the BBC in the United Kingdom to member states that limit advertising to a maximum of 15 percent of programming daily. The Television without Frontiers directive permits stricter or more detailed rules to the broadcasters under jurisdiction of each member state. In Germany, for example, commercials must be spaced at least 20 minutes apart and total ad time may not exceed 12 minutes per hour. Commercial stations in the United Kingdom are limited to 7 minutes per hour.

Internet services are especially vulnerable as EU member states decide which area of regulation should apply to these services. Barriers to pan-European services will arise if

---

[30]Lawrence T. Speer, "France Launches Study of Outdated TV Ad Ban for Retail, Publishing, Cinema, Press," *AdAgeGlobal,* October 18, 2002.

[31]Sunil Erevelles, Fred Morgan, Ilkim Buke, and Rachel Nguyen, "Advertising Strategy in China: An Analysis of Cultural and Regulatory Factors," *Journal of International Consumer Marketing,* 2002, 15(1), pp. 91–123.

[32]Arundhati Parmar, "Objections to Indian Ad Not Taken Lightly," *Marketing News,* June 9, 2003, p. 4.

[33]Robyn Dixon, "Abusing the Power of Suggestion in Russian Ads," *Los Angeles Times,* August 25, 2002, p. A5.

[34]Ivan Castono, "Mitsubishi To Appeal Court Ruling on 'Violent' Ad," *AdAgeGlobal,* October 18, 2002.

## CROSSING BORDERS 16.3  Joe Canuck Bashes America

Standing foursquare in front of a screen flashing Canadian symbols—beavers, Ottawa's Peace Tower, the Maple Leaf flag—an average Joe Canuck in a check flannel shirt rips into American misperceptions about his country.

"I have a prime minister, not a president. I speak English or French, not American," he says, voice swelling with emotion. "And I pronounce it 'about,' not 'aboot.'"

"I believe in peacekeeping, not policing; diversity, not assimilation," he goes on in the 60-second television spot as the national icons loom over his shoulder. "And that the beaver is a proud and noble animal."

Strangely, in a country known for its aversion to the sort of rah-rah jingoism associated with its southern neighbor, this nationalistic tirade became an overnight sensation: taped and shown in bars, filling megascreens at hockey games, performed live in movie theaters.

Stranger still is the revved-up public reaction the ad is evoking in this notoriously reticent land: wild cheers, stamping feet, frantic flag waving, and fists punching the air. And perhaps strangest of all, the spot is not the cunning propaganda of some ultrapatriot cabal, but a commercial for Molson Canadian beer.

The irony—the director of the commercial is an American, Kevin Donovan. Perhaps they'll make him an honorary Canuck!

Source: Colin Nickerson, "Anti-U.S. Beer Ad Is so Canada," *Orange County Register*, April 15, 2000, p. 29 and 42. Reproduced with permission of Globe Newspaper Co. (MA) via Copyright Clearance Center; Paula Lyon Andruss, "Understanding Canada," *Marketing News*, March 15, 2001, pp. 1 and 11. Used by permission of American Marketing Association.

some member states opt to apply television-broadcasting rules to the Internet while other countries apply print-media advertising rules. The good news is that the EU is addressing the issue of regulation of activities on the Internet. Although most of the attention will be focused on domain names and Internet addresses, the Commission does recognize that online activities will be severely hampered if subject to fragmented regulation.

Some countries have special taxes that apply to advertising, which might restrict creative freedom in media selection. The tax structure in Austria best illustrates how advertising taxation can distort media choice by changing the cost ratios of various media: In federal states, with the exception of Bergenland and Tyrol, there is a 10 percent tax on ad insertions; for posters, there is a 10 to 30 percent tax according to state and municipality. Radio advertising carries a 10 percent tax, except in Tyrol, where it is 20 percent. In Salzburg, Steiermark, Karnten, and Voralbert, there is no tax. There is a uniform tax of 10 percent throughout the country on television ads. Cinema advertising has a 10 percent tax in Vienna, 20 percent in Bergenland, and 30 percent in Steiermark. There is no cinema tax in the other federal states.

## Linguistic Limitations

Language is one of the major barriers to effective communication through advertising.[35] The problem involves different languages of different countries, different languages or dialects within one country, and the subtler problems of linguistic nuance and vernacular.[36] For many countries language is a matter of cultural pride and preservation—France is the best example, of course.[37]

Careless handling of language creates problems in all countries.[38] Some examples suffice. Chrysler Corporation was nearly laughed out of Spain when it translated its U.S. theme that advertised "Dart Is Power." To the Spanish, the phrase implied that buyers

---

[35]Shi Zhang and Bernd H. Schmitt, "Creating Local Brands in Multilingual International Markets," *Journal of Marketing Research*, August 2001, 38, pp. 313–325.

[36]Roger Harris, "Firm Can Translate All Words Foreign to You," *Ventura County Star*, November 4, 2002, p. C1.

[37]Paul Johnson, "Current Events," *Forbes*, June 10, 2002, p. 13; Clifford Krauss, "Quebec Seeking To End Its Old Cultural Divide," *New York Times*, April 13, 2003, p. A12.

[38]See www.engrish.com for a wide range of (mostly) humorous translation problems related to the use of English for Japanese products, signage, etc.

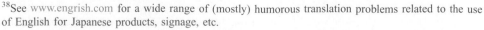

sought but lacked sexual vigor. The Bacardi Company concocted a fruity bitters with a made-up name, Pavane, suggestive of French chic. Bacardi wanted to sell the drink in Germany, but Pavane is perilously close to *pavian,* which means "baboon." A company marketing tomato paste in the Middle East found that in Arabic the phrase "tomato paste" translates as "tomato glue." In Spanish-speaking countries you need to be careful of words that have different meanings in the different countries. The word *ball* translates in Spanish as *bola,* which means ball in one country, revolution in another, a lie or fabrication in another, and is an obscenity in yet another.

Tropicana brand orange juice was advertised as *jugo de China* in Puerto Rico, but when transported to Miami's Cuban community, it failed. To the Puerto Rican, *China* translated into *orange,* but to the Cuban it was China the country—and the Cubans were not in the market for Chinese juice. One Middle East advertisement featured an automobile's new suspension system that, in translation, said the car was "suspended from the ceiling." Since there are at least 30 dialects among Arab countries, there is ample room for error. What may appear as the most obvious translation can come out wrong. For example, "a whole new range of products" in a German advertisement came out as "a whole new stove of products."

Language raises innumerable barriers that impede effective, idiomatic translation and thereby hamper communication. This is especially apparent in advertising materials and on the Internet.[39] Abstraction, terse writing, and word economy, the most effective tools of the advertiser, pose problems for translators. Communication is impeded by the great diversity of cultural heritage and education that exists within countries and which causes varying interpretations of even single sentences and simple concepts. Some companies tried to solve the translation problem by hiring foreign translators who live in the United States. This often is not satisfactory because both the language and the translator change, so the expatriate in the United States is out of touch after a few years. Everyday words have different meanings in different cultures. Even pronunciation[40] causes problems: Wrigley had trouble selling its Spearmint gum in Germany until it changed the spelling to Speermint.

In addition to translation challenges, low literacy in many countries seriously impedes communications and calls for greater creativity and use of verbal media. Multiple languages within a country or advertising area pose another problem for the advertiser. Even a tiny country such as Switzerland has four separate languages. The melting-pot character of the Israeli population accounts for some 50 languages. A Jerusalem commentator says that even though Hebrew "has become a negotiable instrument of daily speech, this has yet to be converted into advertising idiom." Advertising communications must be perfect, and linguistic differences at all levels cause problems. In-country testing with the target consumer group is the only way to avoid such problems.

**Cultural Diversity**

The problems associated with communicating to people in diverse cultures present one of the great creative challenges in advertising.[41] One advertising executive puts it bluntly: "International advertising is almost uniformly dreadful mostly because people don't understand language and culture." Communication is more difficult because cultural factors largely determine the way various phenomena are perceived.[42] If the perceptual framework is different, perception of the message itself differs.[43]

---

[39]Clyde A. Warden, Mengkuan Lai, and Wann-Yih Wu, "How Worldwide is Marketing Communication on the World Wide Web," *Journal of Advertising Research,* September–October 2002, 42(5), pp. 72–84.

[40]Nicholas Kristof, "Fizzling on a $250,000 Stage," *Oregonian,* April 8, 2003, p. C7.

[41]Gillian Rice and Mohammed Al-Mossawi, "The Implications for Islam for Advertising Messages: The Middle Eastern Context," *Journal of Euro-Marketing,* 2002, 11(3), pp. 71–96.

[42]"AFLAC Tames Its Duck for Japanese Market," *Los Angeles Times,* May 13, 2003, p. C7.

[43]Some of the most important work being done in the area of culture and advertising is represented by Jennifer Aaker's and Patti Williams' "Empathy and Pride: The Influence of Emotional Appeals across Cultures," *Journal of Consumer Research,* December 1998, 25, pp. 241–261.

Knowledge of cultural diversity must encompass the total advertising project.[44] General Mills had two problems with one product. When it introduced instant cake mixes in the United States and England, it had the problem of overcoming the homemaker's guilt feelings. When General Mills introduced instant cake mixes in Japan, the problem changed. Cakes were not commonly eaten in Japan, so there was no guilt feeling, but the homemaker was concerned about failing. She wanted the cake mix as complete as possible. In testing TV commercials promoting the notion that making a cake is as easy as making rice, General Mills learned it was offending the Japanese homemaker, who believes the preparation of rice requires great skill.

Existing perceptions based on tradition and heritages are often hard to overcome. For example, marketing researchers in Hong Kong found that cheese is associated with *Yeung-Yen* (foreigners) and rejected by some Chinese. The concept of cooling and heating the body is important in Chinese thinking—malted milk is considered heating, whereas fresh milk is cooling; brandy is sustaining, whiskey harmful.

Procter & Gamble's initial advertisement for Pampers brand diapers failed because of cultural differences between the United States and Japan. A U.S. commercial that showed an animated stork delivering Pampers diapers to homes was dubbed into Japanese with the U.S. package replaced by the Japanese package and was put on the air. To P&G's dismay the advertisement failed to build the market. Some belated consumer research revealed that consumers were confused about why this bird was delivering disposable diapers. According to Japanese folklore, giant peaches that float on the river bring babies to deserving parents, not storks.

In addition to concerns with differences among nations, advertisers find subcultures within a country require attention as well. In Hong Kong there are ten different patterns of breakfast eating. The youth of a country almost always constitute a different consuming culture from the older people, and urban dwellers differ significantly from rural dwellers. Besides these differences, there is the problem of changing traditions. In all countries, people of all ages, urban or rural, cling to their heritage to a certain degree but are willing to change some areas of behavior. A few years ago, it was unthinkable to try to market coffee in Japan, but it has become the fashionable drink for younger people and urban dwellers who like to think of themselves as European and sophisticated. Coffee drinking in Japan was introduced with instant coffee, and only recently has Starbucks entered the market with mixed success.

## Media Limitations

Media are discussed at length later, so here we note only that limitations on creative strategy imposed by media may diminish the role of advertising in the promotional program and may force marketers to emphasize other elements of the promotional mix. A marketer's creativity is certainly challenged when a television commercial is limited to ten showings a year with no two exposures closer than ten days, as is the case in Italy. Creative advertisers in some countries even developed their own media for overcoming media limitations. In some African countries, advertisers run boats up and down the rivers playing popular music and broadcasting commercials into rural areas as they travel.

## Production and Cost Limitations

Creativity is especially important when a budget is small or where there are severe production limitations, such as poor-quality printing and a lack of high-grade paper. For example, the poor quality of high-circulation glossy magazines and other quality publications in Eastern Europe caused Colgate-Palmolive to depart from its customary heavy use of print media in the West for other media. Newsprint is of such low quality in China that a color ad used by Kodak in the West is not an option.

Kodak's solution was to print a single-sheet color insert as a newspaper supplement. The necessity for low-cost reproduction in small markets poses another problem in many countries. For example, hand-painted billboards must be used instead of printed sheets

---

[44]Radka Koudelova and Jeryl Whitelock, "A Cross-Cultural Analysis of Television Advertising in the U.K. and the Czech Republic," *International Marketing Review,* 2001, 18(3), pp. 286–300.

**CROSSING BORDERS 16.4** Objections to Indian Ad Not Taken Lightly

*A financially strapped father laments his fate, saying, "Kaash agar mera beta hota," ("If I only had a son") while his dark-skinned, plain Jane daughter looks on, helpless and demoralized because she can't bear the financial responsibility of her family. Fast-forward and plain Jane is transformed into a gorgeous light-skinned woman through the use of a "fairness cream." Now clad in a miniskirt, the woman is a successful flight attendant and can take her father to dine at a five-star hotel. She's happy and so is her father.*

All's well that ends well—except not so for Hindustan Lever Ltd. (HLL). The company, a subsidiary of Unilever, launched this television campaign to promote its Fair & Lovely fairness cream in India. It withdrew the campaign two months later amid severe criticism for its portrayal of women. The incident underscores the changing social mores in India and highlights tensions between the government, consumer groups, and the industry regulatory agencies.

While tanning is the rage in Western countries, skin lightening treatments have been historically popular in Asia. The Japanese market for such products is estimated to be around $6 billion and in India about $150 million.

It may be safe for the skin, but not for society, says the All India Women's Democratic Association. Three things were objectionable about the campaign to the group. It was racist, it promoted the son preference, and it was insulting to working women. A government ministry found the ads to be in violation of the Cable and Television Act of 1995, which in part forbids ads that, "deride any race, caste, color, creed, and nationality." Industry regulators agreed and pressured the company to stop airing the ad. The company admitted no wrong, but complied.

If you haven't already, for an interesting discussion you might juxtapose this grim tale to our story about Barbie in the Global Perspectives at the start of the chapter. If you think that the $55-billion-global-toy, $100-billion-global-cosmetics, and the $500-billion-advertising industries are unrelated, you need to go back and re-read Chapter 4. And finally you might want to consider how different cultures solve the "problem" of the appearance of women by juxtaposing the global expenditures on cosmetics and on burkas. Unfortunately, Euromonitor doesn't provide an estimate of the latter.

Source: Arundhati Parmar, "Objections to Indian Ad Not Taken Lightly," *Marketing News*, June 9, 2003, pp. 4–5. Used by permission of American Marketing Association.

because the limited number of billboards does not warrant the production of printed sheets. In Egypt, static-filled television and poor-quality billboards led companies such as Coca-Cola and Nestlé to place their advertisements on the sails of feluccas, boats that sail along the Nile. Feluccas, with their triangle sails, have been used to transport goods since the time of the pharaohs and serve as an effective alternative to attract attention to company names and logos.

# Media Planning and Analysis

**Tactical Considerations**
Although nearly every sizable nation essentially has the same kinds of media, there are a number of specific considerations, problems, and differences encountered from one nation to another. In international advertising, an advertiser must consider the availability, cost, coverage, and appropriateness of the media. For example, billboard ads next to highways cannot include paragraphs of text. Moreover, recent research demonstrated that media effectiveness varies across cultures and product types. Local variations and lack of market data require added attention. Major multinationals are beginning to recognize the importance of planning communications channels as media companies continue to rationalize and evolve. Indeed, media giants such as Disney and AOL Time Warner cover an increasingly broad spectrum of the electronic media, necessitating that MNCs rethink relationships with media service providers.

Imagine the ingenuity required of advertisers confronted with these situations:

- In Brazil, TV commercials are sandwiched together in a string of 10 to 50 commercials within one station break.

- National coverage in many countries means using as many as 40 to 50 different media.

- Specialized media reach small segments of the market only. In the Netherlands, there are Catholic, Protestant, socialist, neutral, and other specialized broadcasting systems.

- In Germany, TV scheduling for an entire year must be arranged by August 30 of the preceding year, with no guarantee that commercials intended for summer viewing will not be run in the middle of winter.

- In Vietnam, advertising in newspapers and magazines is limited to 10 percent of space, and to 5 percent of time, or three minutes an hour, on radio and TV.

**Availability.**   One of the contrasts of international advertising is that some countries have too few advertising media and others have too many. In some countries, certain advertising media are forbidden by government edict to accept some advertising materials. Such restrictions are most prevalent in radio and television broadcasting. In many countries there are too few magazines and newspapers to run all the advertising offered to them. Conversely, some nations segment the market with so many newspapers that the advertiser cannot gain effective coverage at a reasonable cost. One head of an Italian advertising agency commented about his country: "One fundamental rule. You cannot buy what you want." Please compare media coverage across several countries in Exhibit 16.5.

In China the only national TV station, CCTV, has one channel that must be aired by the country's 27 provincial/municipal stations. Recently CCTV auctioned off the most popular break between the early evening news and weather; a secured year-long, daily five-second billboard ad in this break went for $38.5 million. For this price, advertisers are assured of good coverage—over 70 percent of households have TV sets. One of the other options for advertisers is with the 2,828 TV stations that provide only local coverage.

**Cost.**   Media prices are susceptible to negotiation in most countries. Agency space discounts are often split with the client to bring down the cost of media. The advertiser may find that the cost of reaching a prospect through advertising depends on the agent's bargaining ability. The per-contract cost varies widely from country to country. One study showed that the cost of reaching one thousand readers in 11 different European countries ranged from $1.58 in Belgium to $5.91 in Italy; in women's service magazines, the page cost per thousand circulation ranged from $2.51 in Denmark to $10.87 in Germany. Shortages of advertising time on commercial television in some markets have caused substantial price increases. In Britain, prices escalate on a bidding system. They do not have fixed rate cards; instead, there is a preempt system in which advertisers willing to pay a higher rate can bump already-scheduled spots.

**Exhibit 16.5**   Media Penetration in Selected Countries (per 1000 persons)

| Country | Color TV | Cable TV | Satellite TV | Telephone Lines | Internet Users | Newspapers (per day) |
|---|---|---|---|---|---|---|
| United States | 842 | 268 | 64 | 703 | 501 | 153 |
| Canada | 666 | 294 | 68 | 709 | 434 | 236 |
| Argentina | 265 | 176 | 34 | 210 | 88 | 96 |
| Germany | 605 | 252 | 172 | 634 | 374 | 388 |
| Poland | 411 | 108 | 150 | 333 | 98 | 194 |
| Israel | 359 | 190 | 75 | 508 | 281 | 250 |
| South Africa | 216 | 58 | 36 | 124 | 71 | 31 |
| China | 165 | 49 | 8 | 142 | 11 | 49 |
| Japan | 701 | 140 | 102 | 590 | 440 | 462 |
| Australia | 617 | 74 | 78 | 526 | 371 | 241 |

Source: Euromonitor, World Bank 2003. Reproduced with permission of Transaction Pubs via Copyright Clearance Center.

**Coverage.**   Closely akin to the cost dilemma is the problem of coverage. Two points are particularly important: One relates to the difficulty of reaching certain sectors of the population with advertising, and the other to the lack of information on coverage. In many world marketplaces, a wide variety of media must be used to reach the majority of the markets. In some countries, large numbers of separate media have divided markets into uneconomical advertising segments. With some exceptions, a majority of the population of less-developed countries cannot be reached readily through the medium of advertising. In India, video vans are used to reach India's rural population with 30-minute infomercials extolling the virtues of a product. Consumer goods companies deploy vans year-round except in the monsoon season. Colgate hires 85 vans at a time and sends them to villages that research shows to be promising.

Because of the lack of adequate coverage by any single medium in Eastern European countries, it is necessary for companies to resort to a multimedia approach. In the Czech Republic, for example, TV advertising rates are high, and the lack of available prime-time spots forced companies to use billboard advertising. In Slovenia the availability of adequate media is such a problem that companies resort to some unique approaches to get their messages out. For example, in the summer lasers are used to project images onto clouds above major cities. Cement-mixers are used as moving billboards where Kodak ads have appeared. On the positive side, crime is so low that products can be displayed in free-standing glass cabinets on sidewalks; Bosch Siemens (Germany) and Kodak have both used this method.

**Lack of Market Data.**   Verification of circulation or coverage figures is a difficult task. Even though many countries have organizations similar to the Audit Bureau of Circulation in the United States, the accuracy of circulation and audience data are uncertain. For example, the president of the Mexican National Advertisers Association charged that newspaper circulation figures are grossly exaggerated. He suggested that as a rule, agencies should divide these figures in two and take the result with a grain of salt. The situation in China is no better; surveys of habits and market penetration are available only for the cities of Beijing, Shanghai, and Guangzhou. Radio and television audiences are always difficult to measure, but at least in most countries, geographic coverage is known. Research data are becoming more reliable as advertisers and agencies demand better-quality data.

Even where advertising coverage can be measured with some accuracy, there are questions about the composition of the market reached. Lack of available market data seems to characterize most international markets; advertisers need information on income, age, and geographic distribution, but such basic data seem chronically elusive except in the largest markets. Even the attractiveness of global television (satellite broadcasts) is diminished somewhat because of the lack of media research available.

**Specific Media Information**

An attempt to evaluate specific characteristics of each medium is beyond the scope of this discussion. Furthermore, such information would quickly become outdated because of the rapid changes in the international advertising media field. It may be interesting, however, to examine some of the unique international characteristics of various advertising media. In most instances, the major implications of each variation may be discerned from the data presented.

**Newspapers.**   The newspaper industry is suffering in some countries from lack of competition and choking because of it in others. Most U.S. cities have just one or two major daily newspapers, but in many countries, there are so many newspapers that an advertiser has trouble achieving even partial market coverage. Uruguay, population 3 million, has 21 daily newspapers with a combined circulation of 553,000. Turkey has 380 newspapers, and an advertiser must consider the political position of each newspaper so that the product's reputation is not harmed through affiliation with unpopular positions. Japan has only 5 national daily newspapers, and the complications of producing a Japanese-language newspaper are such that they each contain just 16 to 20 pages. Connections are necessary to buy advertising space; *Asahi,* Japan's largest newspaper, has been known to turn down over a million dollars a month in advertising revenue.

In many countries there is a long time lag before an advertisement can be run in a newspaper. In India and Indonesia, paper shortages delay publication of ads for up to six months. Furthermore, because of equipment limitations, most newspapers cannot be made larger to accommodate the increase in advertising demand. Indeed, Nike may be wishing this were so in the United States, now that the Supreme Court has ruled against it.

Separation between editorial and advertising content in newspapers provides another basis for contrast on the international scene. In some countries, it is possible to buy editorial space for advertising and promotional purposes; the news columns are for sale to anyone who has the price. Because there is no indication that the space is paid for, it is impossible to tell exactly how much advertising appears in a given newspaper.

**Magazines.** The use of foreign national consumer magazines by international advertisers is notably low for many reasons. Few magazines have a large circulation or provide dependable circulation figures. Technical magazines are used rather extensively to promote export goods but, as with newspapers, paper shortages cause placement problems. Media planners are often faced with the largest magazines accepting up to twice as many advertisements as they have space to run them in—then the magazines decide what advertisements will go in just before going to press by means of a raffle.

Such local practices may be key factors favoring the growth of so-called international media that attempt to serve many nations. Increasingly, U.S. publications are publishing overseas editions. *Reader's Digest International* added a new Russian-language edition to its more than 20 other language editions. Other American print media available in international editions range from *Playboy* to *Scientific American,* and even include the *National Enquirer,* recently introduced to the United Kingdom. Advertisers have three new magazines through which to reach women in China: Hachette Filipachi Presse, the French publisher, is expanding Chinese-language editions of *Elle,* a fashion magazine; *Woman's Day* is aimed at China's "busy modern" woman; and *L'Evenement Sportif* is a sports magazine. These media offer alternatives for multinationals as well as for local advertisers.

**Radio and Television.** Possibly because of their inherent entertainment value, radio and television are major communications media in most nations. Most populous areas have television broadcasting facilities. In some markets, such as Japan, television is almost a national obsession and thus finds tremendous audiences for its advertisers. In China, virtually all homes in major cities have a television and most adults view television and listen to radio daily. Radio is relegated to a subordinate position in the media race in countries where television facilities are well developed. In many countries, however, radio is a particularly important and vital advertising medium when it is the only one reaching large segments of the population.

Television and radio advertising availability varies between countries. Three patterns are discernible: competitive commercial broadcasting, commercial monopolies, and noncommercial broadcasting. Countries with free competitive commercial radio and television normally encourage competition and have minimal broadcast regulations. Elsewhere, local or national monopolies are granted by the government, and individual stations or networks may then accept radio or TV commercials according to rules established by the government. In some countries, commercial monopolies may accept all the advertising they wish; in others, only spot advertising is permissible and programs may not be sponsored. Live commercials are not permitted in some countries; in still others, commercial stations must compete for audiences against the government's noncommercial broadcasting network.

Some countries do not permit any commercial radio or television, but several of the traditional noncommercial countries changed their policies in recent years because television production is so expensive. Until recently, France limited commercials to a daily total of 18 minutes, but now has extended the time limit to 12 minutes per hour per TV channel. South Korea has two television companies, both government owned, which broadcast only a few hours a day. They do not broadcast from midnight to 6 A.M. and they usually cannot broadcast between 10 A.M. and 5:30 P.M. on weekdays. Commercials

## CROSSING BORDERS 16.5 Advertising Themes That Work in Japan, Including a Polite Duck

*Respect for tradition:* Mercedes ads stress that it was the first to manufacture passenger cars.

*Mutual dependence:* Shiseido ads emphasize the partnership (with their beauty consultants) involved in achieving beauty.

*Harmony with nature:* Toyotas are shown in front of Mt. Fuji.

*Use of seasons:* Commercials are often set in and products are often used in specific seasons only.

*Newness and evolution:* Products are shown to evolve from the current environment slowly.

*Distinctive use of celebrities, including* gaijin *(foreigners):* A recent study showed that 63 percent of all Japanese commercials featured hired celebrities. See Crossing Borders 16.2 for more details.

*Aging of society:* Seniors are featured often.

*Changing families:* The changing role of fathers—more time spent at home—is a common theme.

*Generation gaps and individualism:* Younger characters are shown as more individualistic.

*Self-effacing humor:* A dented Pepsi can was used in an ad to demonstrate its deference to more-popular Coke.

*Polite ducks:* The AFLAC duck is going to Japan, but with a softer quack. Instead of the American version's abrasive quack, the Japanese actor portrays the duck with a more soothing tone. "The Japanese culture does not like being yelled at," says the AFLAC spokeswoman. About 70 percent of the firm's international revenues come from Japan, some $8 billion last year. Although this campaign is the first to be shot specifically for Japan, the Japanese have met the duck before. In 2001 the company used dubbed voices of American ads.

Sources: George Fields, Hotaka Katahira, and Jerry Wind, *Leveraging Japan, Marketing to the New Asia* (San Francisco: Jossey-Bass, 2000); and "AFLAC Tames Its Duck for Japanese Market," *Los Angeles Times*, May 13, 2003, p. C7.

are limited to 8 percent of airtime and are shown in clusters at the beginning and end of programs. One advertiser remarked, "We are forced to buy what we don't want to buy just to get on."

Lack of reliable audience data is another major problem in international marketing via radio and television. Measurement of radio and television audiences is always a precarious business, even with highly developed techniques. In most countries, audience size is either not audited or the existing auditing associations are ineffective. Despite the paucity of audience data, many advertisers use radio and television extensively. Advertisers justify their inclusion in the media schedule on the inherent logic favoring the use of these media, or defend their use on the basis of sales results.

**Satellite and Cable TV.** Of increasing importance in TV advertising is the growth and development of satellite TV broadcasting.[45] Sky Channel, a United Kingdom–based commercial satellite television station, beams its programs and advertising into most of Europe to cable TV subscribers. The technology that permits households to receive broadcasts directly from the satellite via a dish the size of a dinner plate costing about $350 is adding greater coverage and the ability to reach all of Europe with a single message. The expansion of TV coverage will challenge the creativity of advertisers and put greater emphasis on global standardized messages. For a comparison of penetration rates by cable and satellite TV and the Internet in the several countries, see Exhibit 16.5.

Advertisers and governments are both concerned about the impact of satellite TV. Governments are concerned because they fear further loss of control over their airwaves and the spread of "American cultural imperialism." European television programming includes such U.S. shows as *Roseanne. Wheel of Fortune* is the most popular foreign show in the United Kingdom and in France, where both the U.S. and French versions

---

[45]"African Media, Watching You, Africa," *The Economist,* June 21, 2003, pp. 60–61.

Given the ubiquitous Guinness advertising in Dublin, it's not surprising that Irish livers need assurance. Ireland is behind only the Czech Republic when it comes to per capita consumption of beer. Actually, Royal Liver Assurance is a British pension/insurance company with offices in Dublin (it was established in the 1850s as the Liverpool Liver Burial Society). "Hurling" is a rather brutal form of field hockey popular in Ireland. The Irish government does recognize the causal effects of advertising on consumption—beer ads are not allowed on radio or TV before sports programs and may not be shown more than once per night on any one channel. See www.eurocare.org/profiles/irelnatpol.htm for more on the consumption of alcohol in Ireland.

are shown. U.S. imports are so popular in France and Germany that officials fear low-brow U.S. game shows, sitcoms, and soap operas will crush domestic producers. This battle even reached political levels associated with differences in worldviews represented in the news. France is investing in developing, not surprisingly, a French language "CNN." Al-Jazeera, initially subsidized by Qatar government loans, is currently struggling to break even. Even so, it is the now widely recognized Arabic "CNN," and is commensurately influential in the Middle East.[46]

Parts of Asia and Latin America receive TV broadcasts from satellite television networks. Univision and Televisa are two Latin American satellite television networks broadcasting via a series of affiliate stations in each country to most of the Spanish-speaking world, including the United States. *Sabado Gigante,* a popular Spanish-language program broadcast by Univision, is seen by tens of millions of viewers in 16 countries. Star TV, a new pan-Asian satellite television network, has a potential audience of 2.7 billion people living in 38 countries from Egypt through India to Japan, and from the Soviet Far East to Indonesia. Star TV was the first to broadcast across Asia but was quickly joined by ESPN and CNN. The first Asian 24-hour all-sports channel was followed by MTV Asia and a Mandarin Chinese–language channel that delivers dramas, comedies, movies, and financial news aimed at the millions of overseas Chinese living throughout Asia. Programs are delivered through cable networks but can be received through private satellite dishes.

One of the drawbacks of satellites is also their strength, that is, their ability to span a wide geographical region covering many different country markets. That means a single message is broadcast throughout a wide area. This may not be desirable for some products; further, with cultural differences such as language, preferences, and so on, a single message may not be as effective. PVI (Princeton Video Imaging) is an innovation

---

[46]"Television in the Arab World, All That Jazeera," *The Economist,* June 21, 2003, p. 60.

that will make regional advertising in diverse cultures easier than it presently is when using cable or satellite television. PVI allows ESPN, which offers this service, to fill visual real estate—blank walls, streets, stadium sidings—with computer-generated visuals that look like they belong in the scene. For instance, if you are watching the "street luge" during ESPN's X-games, you will see the racers appear to pass a billboard advertising Adidas shoes that really is not there. That billboard can say one thing in Holland and quite another in Cameroon. And if you are watching in Portland, Oregon, where Adidas might not advertise, you will see the scene as it really appears—without the billboard. These commercials can play in different languages, in different countries, and even under different brand names.

Most satellite technology involves some government regulation. Singapore, Taiwan, and Malaysia prohibit selling satellite dishes, and the Japanese government prevents domestic cable companies from rebroadcasting from foreign satellites. Such restrictions seldom work for long, however. In Taiwan, there are an estimated 1.5 million dishes in use and numerous illicit cable operators. Through one technology or another, Asian households will be open to the same kind of viewing choice Americans are accustomed to and the advertising that it brings with it.

**Direct Mail.**   Direct mail is a viable medium in an increasing number of countries.[47] It is especially important when other media are not available. As is often the case in international marketing, even such a fundamental medium is subject to some odd and novel quirks. For example, in Chile, direct mail is virtually eliminated as an effective medium because the sender pays only part of the mailing fee; the letter carrier must collect additional postage for every item delivered. Obviously, advertisers cannot afford to alienate customers by forcing them to pay for unsolicited advertisements. Despite some limitations with direct mail, many companies find it a meaningful way to reach their markets. The Reader's Digest Association used direct mail advertising in Mexico to successfully market its magazines.

In Southeast Asian markets, where print media are scarce, direct mail is considered one of the most effective ways to reach those responsible for making industrial goods purchases, even though accurate mailing lists are a problem in Asia as well as in other parts of the world. In fact, some companies build their own databases for direct mail. Industrial advertisers are heavy mail users and rely on catalogs and sales sheets to generate large volumes of international business. Even in Japan, where media availability is not a problem, direct mail is successfully used by marketers such as Nestlé Japan and Dell Computer. To promote its Buitoni fresh chilled pasta, Nestlé is using a 12-page color direct mail booklet of recipes, including Japanese-style versions of Italian favorites.

In Russia, the volume of direct mail has gone from just over 150,000 letters per month to over 500,000 per month in one year. Although small by U.S. standards, the response rate to direct mailings is as high as 10 to 20 percent, compared with only 3 to 4 percent or less in the United States. One suggestion as to why it works so well is that Russians are flattered by the attention—needless to say, that will probably change as the medium grows.

**The Internet.**   Though still evolving, the Internet is emerging as a viable medium for advertising and should be included as one of the media in a company's possible media mix.[48] Its use in business-to-business communications and promotion via catalogs and product descriptions is rapidly gaining in popularity. Because a large number of businesses have access to the Internet, the Internet can reach a large portion of the business-to-business market.

Although limited in its penetration of households, the Internet is used by a growing number of companies as an advertising medium for consumer goods. Many consumer

---

[47]Geoffrey A. Fowler, "Junk Mailers Discover Asia Is Close to Heaven," *Wall Street Journal,* March 5, 2003, p. B1.

[48]Wenyu Dou, Ulrik Nielsen, and Chee Ming Tan, "Using Corporate Websites for Export Marketing," *Journal of Advertising Research,* September-October 2002, 42(5), pp. 105–115.

goods companies have e-stores, and others use the Internet as an advertising medium to stimulate sales in retail outlets. Waterford Crystal of Ireland has set up its website specifically to drive store traffic. The aim is to promote its products and to attract people into stores that sell Waterford crystal. Sites list and display almost the entire catalog of the Waterford collection, while stores like Bloomingdale's that stock Waterford support the promotional effort by also advertising on the Internet.

For consumer products, the major limitation of the Internet is coverage (see Exhibit 16.5). In the United States growing numbers of households have access to a computer, but there are fewer in other countries. However, the growing number of Internet households accessible outside the United States generally constitutes a younger, better-educated market segment with higher than average incomes. For many companies, that group is an important market niche. Furthermore, this limitation is only temporary as new technology allows access to the Internet via television and as lower prices for personal computers expand the household base.

As the Internet continues to grow and countries begin to assert control over what is now a medium with few restrictions, increasingly limitations will be set. Besides control of undesirable information, issues such as pay-per-view,[49] taxes, unfair competition, import duties, and privacy are being addressed all over the world. In Australia, local retailers are calling for changes in laws because of loss of trade to the Internet; under current law Internet purchases do not carry regular import duties. The Internet industry is lobbying for a global understanding on regulation to avoid a crazy quilt of confusing and contradictory rules.

Another limitation that needs to be addressed soon is the competition for Web surfers. The sheer proliferation of the number of websites makes it increasingly difficult for a customer to stumble across a particular page. Search engines are now crucial directors of Web surfers' attention. Also, serious Internet advertisers or e-marketers need to be more effective in communicating the existence of their Internet sites via other advertising media. Some companies are coupling their traditional television spots with a website; IBM, Swatch Watches, AT&T, and Samsung electronics are among those going for a one-two punch of on-air and online presences. TV spots are used to raise brand awareness of product regionally and to promote the company's website. Additionally, a company can buy ad banners on the Web that will lead enthusiastic consumers to the company's site, which also promotes the product. Some TV networks offer a package deal: a TV spot and ad banners on the network's website. For example, the EBN (European Business News) channel offers a cross-media program that includes TV spots and the advertiser's ad banner on the EB Interactive page for $15,000 a quarter.

The online advertising business itself—for example, a banner ad for Amazon.com placed on a *Wall Street Journal* website—has come into its own. The industry is now conducting international festivals annually in Cannes, France. In 2003 over $8 billion was spent worldwide on online ads; continued dramatic growth is forecasted. Of course, the creative possibilities (with global reach, hyperlinks, and such) are endless.

**Other Media.**   Restrictions on traditional media or their availability cause advertisers to use lesser media to solve particular local-country problems. The cinema is an important medium in many countries, as are billboards and other forms of outside advertising. Billboards are especially useful in countries with high illiteracy rates. Hong Kong is clearly the neon capital of the world with Tokyo's Ginza and New York's Times Square running close behind.[50] Indeed, perhaps the most interesting "billboard" was the Pizza Hut logo that appeared on the side of a Russian Proton rocket launched to carry parts of the international space station into orbit—can extraterrestrials read?

[49]Ashutosh Prasad, Vijay Mahajan, and Bart Bronnenberg, "Advertising versus Pay-Per-View in Electronic Media," *International Journal of Research in Marketing,* March 2003, 20(1), pp. 13–30.

[50]Geoffrey Fowler, "Changing the Neon Guard on Hong Kong's Night Skyline," *Wall Street Journal,* January 29, 2003, p. B1.

Two novel media here: (1) Not only do the Russians sell space for tourists on their rockets, they also sell advertising space! (2) Japanese beverage company Suntory promotes their products with "Monitor Man" during a football match at National Stadium. "Monitor Man" puts on a LCD display showing ads for Pepsi and other products and walks around the stadium. The job requires some muscle as the equipment weighs about 15 pounds. All this is perhaps purposely reminiscent of the Simpson's "Duff Man." Ohhh yaaaa! *(left: AP/Wide World Photos; right: Tatsuyuki Tayama/Fujifotos/The Image Works)*

In Haiti, sound trucks equipped with powerful loudspeakers provide an effective and widespread advertising medium. Private contractors own the equipment and sell advertising space much as a radio station would. This medium overcomes the problems of illiteracy, lack of radio and television set ownership, and limited print media circulation. In Ukraine, where the postal service is unreliable, businesses found that the most effective form of direct business-to-business advertising is direct faxing.

In Spain, a new medium includes private cars that are painted with advertisements for products and serve as moving billboards as they travel around. This system, called *Publicoche* (derived from the words *publicidad,* meaning advertising, and *coche,* meaning car), has 75 cars in Madrid. Car owners are paid $230 a month and must submit their profession and "normal" weekly driving patterns. Advertisers pay a basic cost of $29,000 per car per month, and can select the type and color of car they are interested in and which owners are most suited to the campaign based on their driving patterns.

## Campaign Execution and Advertising Agencies

The development of advertising campaigns and their execution are managed by advertising agencies. Just as manufacturing firms are international, so too are U.S., Japanese,[51] and European advertising agencies expanding internationally to provide sophisticated agency assistance worldwide. See Exhibit 16.6 for a listing of the largest international advertising agencies. Local agencies also expanded as the demand for advertising services by MNCs developed. Thus the international marketer has a variety of alternatives available. In most commercially significant countries, an advertiser has the opportunity to employ a local domestic agency, its company-owned agency, or one of the multinational advertising agencies with local branches. There are strengths and weaknesses associated with each. The discussion regarding firm and agency

[51]Erin White, "Dentsu Has a Global Appetite But Faces a Pared-Down Menu," *Wall Street Journal,* April 17, 2003, p. B7.

**Exhibit 16.6**   World's Top 10 Advertising Agency Organizations

| 2002 | Agency | Headquarters | Global Expenditures 2002 | Percent Change from 2001 | U.S. only Expenditures 2002 | Percent Change from 2001 |
|------|--------|-------------|---------|---------|---------|---------|
| 1. | Omnicom Group | New York | $7,536.3 | 9.4 | $4,284.6 | 15.3 |
| 2. | Interpublic Group of Cos. | New York | 6,203.6 | −8.7 | 3,491.1 | 10.0 |
| 3. | WPP Group | London | 5,781 | −0.3 | 2,448.2 | −3.7 |
| 4. | Publicis Groupe | Paris | 2,711.9 | 24.3 | 1,179.9 | 27.2 |
| 5. | Dentsu | Tokyo | 2,060.9 | −8.0 | 44.5 | 37.5 |
| 6. | Havas | Suresnes, France | 1,841.6 | −9.8 | 804.5 | −8.4 |
| 7. | Grey Global Group | New York | 1,199.7 | −1.4 | 520.5 | 3.0 |
| 8. | Hakuhodo | Tokyo | 860.8 | −1.1 | 1.3 | 14.8 |
| 9. | Cordiant Communications Group | London | 788.5 | −9.6 | 227.2 | 17.2 |
| 10. | Asatsu-DK | Tokyo | 339.5 | 15.1 | 3.8 | 18.8 |

Source: "Special Report Global Marketers," *AdvertisingAge*, Supplement to the Ad Age Special Report, November 11, 2002. Copyright, Crain Communications Inc. 2002.

relations in Chapter 8 on page 234 and Exhibit 8.3 are quite pertinent here. Moreover, the agency/company relationships can be quite complicated and fragile in the international context—Ford and Disneyland Paris recently changed agencies, for example.

A local domestic agency may provide a company with the best cultural interpretation in situations where local modification is sought, but the level of sophistication can be weak. Moreover, the cross-cultural communication between the foreign client and the local agency can also be problematic. However, the local agency may have the best feel for the market, especially if the multinational agency has little experience in the market. Eastern Europe has been a problem for multinational agencies that are not completely attuned to the market. In Hungary, a U.S. baby-care company advertisement of bath soap showing a woman holding her baby hardly seemed risqué. But where Westerners saw a young mother, scandalized Hungarians saw an unwed mother. The model was wearing a ring on her left hand; Hungarians wear wedding bands on the right hand. It was obvious to viewers that this woman wearing a ring on her left hand was telling everybody in Hungary she wasn't married. This is a mistake a local agency would not have made. Finally, in some emerging markets like Vietnam, local laws require a local partner.

The best compromise is the multinational agency with local branches because it has the sophistication of a major agency with local representation. Further, the multinational agency with local branches is better able to provide a coordinated worldwide advertising campaign. This is especially important for firms doing business in Europe. With the interest in global or standardized advertising, many agencies expanded to provide worldwide representation. Many companies with a global orientation employ one, or perhaps two, agencies to represent them worldwide.

Compensation arrangements for advertising agencies throughout the world are based on the U.S. system of 15 percent commissions. However, agency commission patterns throughout the world are not as consistent as they are in the United States; in some countries, agency commissions vary from medium to medium. Companies are moving from the commission system to a reward-by-results system, which details remuneration terms at the outset. If sales rise, the agency should be rewarded accordingly. This method of sharing in the gains or losses of profits generated by the advertising is gaining in popularity and may become the standard. Services provided by advertising agencies also vary greatly, but few foreign agencies offer the full services found in U.S. agencies.

Even a sophisticated business function such as advertising may find it is involved in unique practices. In some parts of the world, advertisers often pay for the promotion with the product advertised rather than with cash. Kickbacks on agency commissions are

## CROSSING BORDERS 16.6 Subliminal Advertising in Russia

Deep within a Russian television advertisement for a local beer, Klinskoye, lurked a split-second message for another thirst quencher: Pepsi. An image of Palmolive Fruit Essentials soap was there and gone in the blink of an eye on the NTV television network. Young viewers of Russian MTV unconsciously absorbed marketing messages for Secret deodorant, the New Musical Express newspaper, and the Red Hot Chili Peppers album, "By The Way."

In fact, according to Russian scientists, subliminal television advertising, although illegal in Russia, is strewn across the airwaves. Russian television stations insist they have no way of knowing whether video material provided by advertising agencies contains subliminal messages. Advertising firms and the companies whose products appear in subliminal messages deny any involvement. Such advertising is also outlawed in the United States, but the majority of marketing researchers deny its potency anyway.

"There are very many cases. I'm surprised by the quantity," said Svetlana Nemtsova, deputy director-general of the All Russian Research Institute for TV and Radio Broadcasting, a state agency. "There are channels that are impossible to watch," she said, referring to the amount of subliminal advertising broadcast. "There are channels that don't overdo it, and there are also channels that don't do it at all." She declined to describe the list of offenders.

But time is running out for them. Nemtsova and other Russian scientists at the broadcasting institute have developed equipment to trace subliminal messages that will constantly monitor Russian TV airwaves.

Finally, did you notice the three subliminal messages imbedded in the text on pages 100–101, 376, and 432? (1) The layout about Dutch flowers is arranged as a flower with the pictures as petals. (2) The "windows" in the Microsoft server ads—an executive at the company tells us that this is a mere coincidence. (3) We already mentioned the arrow the firm purposely imbedded in the FedEx logo to connote motion. Have you noticed any other examples in the book?

Source: Robyn Dixon, "Abusing the Power of Suggestion in Russian Ads," *Los Angeles Times*, August 25, 2002, p. A5.

prevalent in some parts of the world and account in part for the low profitability of international advertising agencies. In Mexico, India, and Greece, the advertiser returns half the media commissions to the agencies. In many developing countries, long-term credit is used to attract clients.

## International Control of Advertising: Broader Issues

In a previous section specific legal restrictions on advertising were presented. Here broader issues related to the past, present, and future of the international regulation of advertising are considered.

Consumer criticisms of advertising are not a phenomenon of the U.S. market only. Consumer concern with the standards and believability of advertising may have spread around the world more swiftly than have many marketing techniques. A study of a representative sample of European consumers indicated that only half of them believed advertisements gave consumers any useful information. Six of ten believed that advertising meant higher prices (if a product is heavily advertised, it often sells for more than brands that are seldom or never advertised); nearly eight of ten believed advertising often made them buy things they did not really need, and that ads often were deceptive about product quality. In Hong Kong, Colombia, and Brazil, advertising fared much better than in Europe. The non-Europeans praised advertising as a way to obtain valuable information about products; most Brazilians consider ads entertaining and enjoyable.

European Union officials are establishing directives to provide controls on advertising as cable and satellite broadcasting expands. Deception in advertising is a thorny issue since most member countries have different interpretations of what constitutes a misleading advertisement. Demands for regulation of advertising aimed at young consumers is a trend appearing in both industrialized and developing countries.

Decency and the blatant use of sex in advertisements also are receiving public attention. One of the problems in controlling decency and sex in ads is the cultural variations found around the world. An ad perfectly acceptable to a Westerner may be very offensive to someone from the Mideast, or, for that matter, another Westerner. Standards for appropriate behavior as depicted in advertisements vary from culture to culture. Regardless of these variations, there is growing concern about decency, sex, and ads that demean women and men. International advertising associations are striving to forestall laws by imposing self-regulation, but it may be too late; some countries are passing laws that define acceptable standards.

The difficulty that business has with self-regulation and restrictive laws is that sex can be powerful in some types of advertisements. European advertisements for Häagen-Dazs, a premium U.S. ice cream marketer, and LapPower, a Swedish laptop computer company, received criticism for being too sexy. Häagen-Dazs's ad showed a couple, in various stages of undress, in an embrace feeding ice cream to one another. Some British editorial writers and radio commentators were outraged. One commented that "the ad was the most blatant and inappropriate use of sex as a sales aid." The ad for LapPower personal computers that the Stockholm Business Council on Ethics condemned featured the co-owner of the company with an "inviting smile and provocative demeanor displayed." (She was bending over a LapPower computer in a low-cut dress.) The bottom line for both these companies was increased sales. In Britain, ice cream sales soared after the "Dedicated to Pleasure" ads appeared, and in Sweden, the co-owner stated, "Sales are increasing daily." Whether laws are passed or the industry polices itself, there is an international concern about advertising and its effect on people's behavior.

Advertising regulations are not limited to Europe; there is an enhanced awareness of the expansion of mass communications and the perceived need to effect greater control in developing countries as well. Malaysia consistently regulates TV advertising to control the effect of the "excesses of Western ways." The government became so concerned that it will not allow "Western cultural images" to appear in TV commercials. No bare shoulders or exposed armpits are allowed, nor are touching or kissing, sexy clothing, or blue jeans. These are just a few of the prohibitions spelled out in a 41-page advertising code that the Malaysian government has been adding to for more than ten years.

The assault on advertising and promotion of tobacco products is escalating.[52] In the United States the tobacco firms agreed to curtail promotion as part of government-supported class-action lawsuits. The European Union Parliament approved larger health warnings on cigarette packs. Most significantly, the World Health Organization (WHO) launched a global campaign against the tobacco industry. Dr. Gro Harlen Brundtland, director-general of the WHO, explains, "Tobacco is a communicable disease—it's communicated through advertising, marketing, and making smoking appear admirable and glamorous." A worldwide ban of tobacco advertising is just one of the stated goals of the new WHO action.

Product placement within TV programming is another area of advertising receiving the attention of regulators. In the United States complaints have been aired regarding cigarette smoking in movies and TV. The product placements avoid some of the regulations in markets like China, where ad time is limited. Because these practices are new to China, the growth rate has been initially dramatic. It will be interesting to follow how product placement advertising is regulated as the practice proliferates.

The advertising industry is sufficiently concerned with the negative attitudes and skepticism of consumers and governments and with the poor practices of some advertisers that the International Advertising Association and other national and international industry groups have developed a variety of self-regulating codes. Sponsors of these codes feel that unless the advertisers themselves come up with an effective framework for control, governments will intervene. This threat of government intervention spurred interest groups in Europe to develop codes to ensure that the majority of ads conform to standards set for "honesty, truth, and decency." In those countries where the credibility of advertising is questioned and in those where the consumerism movement exists, the creativity of the advertiser is challenged. The most egregious control, however, may be in Myanmar (formerly Burma), where each medium has its own censorship board that

[52]"Puffed Up or Stubbed Out," *The Economist*, May 24, 2003, p. 66.

passes judgment on any advertising even before it is submitted for approval by the Ministry of Information. There is even a censorship board for calendars. Content restrictions are centered on any references to the government or military, other political matters, religious themes, or images deemed degrading to traditional culture.

In many countries, there is a feeling that advertising, and especially TV advertising, is too powerful and persuades consumers to buy what they do not need, an issue that has been debated in the United States for many years. South Korea, for example, has threatened to ban advertising of bottled water because the commercials may arouse public mistrust of tap water!

## Summary

An integrated marketing communications (IMC) program includes coordination among advertising, sales management, public relations, sales promotions, and direct marketing. Global marketers face unique legal, language, media, and production limitations in every market. These must be considered when designing an IMC program. During the late 1990s many large firms moved toward an advertising strategy of standardization. However, more recently even the most multinational companies changed emphasis to strategies based on national, subcultural, demographic, or other market segments.

The major problem facing international advertisers is designing the best messages for each market served. The potential for cross-cultural misunderstandings is great in both public relations and in the various advertising media. The availability and quality of advertising media also vary substantially around the world. Marketers may be unable to profitably enter markets for lack of appropriate advertising media—for example, some products require the availability of TV.

Advances in communication technologies (particularly the Internet) are causing dramatic changes in the structure of the international advertising and communications industries. New problems are also being posed for government regulators as well. Despite these challenges the industry is experiencing dramatic growth as new media are developed and as new markets open to commercial advertising.

## Questions

1. Define the following terms:

   integrated marketing  
   communications, 468  
   sales promotions, 468  
   public relations, 469  
   noise, 482

2. "Perhaps advertising is the side of international marketing with the greatest similarities from country to country throughout the world. Paradoxically, despite its many similarities, it may also be credited with the greatest number of unique problems in international marketing." Discuss.

3. Someone once commented that advertising is America's greatest export. Discuss.

4. With satellite TV able to reach many countries, discuss how a company can use satellite TV and deal effectively with different languages, different cultures, and different legal systems.

5. Outline some of the major problems confronting an international advertiser.

6. Defend either side of the proposition that advertising can be standardized for all countries.

7. Review the basic areas of advertising regulation. Are such regulations purely foreign phenomena?

8. How can advertisers overcome the problems of low literacy in their markets?

9. What special media problems confront the international advertiser?

10. After reading the section in this chapter on direct mail, develop guidelines to be used by a company when developing a direct mail program.

11. Will the ability to broadcast advertisements over TV satellites increase or decrease the need for standardization of advertisements? What are the problems associated with satellite broadcasting? Comment.

12. "In many world marketplaces, a wide variety of media must be used to reach the majority of the market." Explain.

13. Cinema advertising is unimportant in the United States but a major medium in such countries as Austria. Why?

14. "Foreign newspapers cannot be considered homogeneous advertising entities." Elaborate.

15. Borrow a foreign magazine from the library. Compare the foreign advertising with that in an American magazine.

16. What is sales promotion and how is it used in international marketing?

17. Show how the communications process can help an international marketer avoid problems in international advertising.

18. Take each of the steps of the communications process and give an example of how cultural differences can affect the final message perceived.

19. Discuss the problems created because the communications process is initiated in one cultural context and ends in another.

20. What is the importance of feedback in the communications process? Of noise?

# personal selling and sales management

**CHAPTER 17**

## CHAPTER LEARNING OBJECTIVES

What you should learn from Chapter 17:

- The role of interpersonal selling in international marketing

- The considerations in designing an international sales force

- The steps to recruiting three types of international sales people

- Selection criteria for international sales and marketing positions

- The special training needs of international personnel

- Motivation techniques for international sales representatives

- How to design compensation systems for an international sales force

- How to prepare Americans for foreign assignments

- The changing profile of the global sales and marketing manager

# Global Perspective

## INTERNATIONAL ASSIGNMENTS ARE GLAMOROUS, RIGHT?

"Glamorous" is probably not the adjective the following executives would use.

> The problem as I see it with the company's talk about international managers is that they were just paying lip service to it. When I applied for the posting to Malaysia they gave me all this stuff about the assignment being a really good career move and how I'd gain this valuable international experience and so on. And don't get me wrong, we really enjoyed the posting. We loved the people and the culture and the lifestyle and when it came back to returning home, we weren't really all that keen. . . . The problem was that while I had been away, the company had undergone a wholesale restructuring. . . . This meant that when I got back, my job had been effectively eliminated.

> We have been in the United States for eleven months and I reckon it will be another six to twelve months before my wife and the kids are really settled here. I'm still learning new stuff every day at work and it has taken a long time to get used to American ways of doing things. . . . I mean if the company said, "Oh, we want you to move to South Africa in a year's time," I would really dig my heels in because it was initially very disruptive for my wife when she first came here.

And "glamorous" would not be on the tip of these expatriate spouses' tongues either:

> I found I haven't adapted to Spanish hours. I find it a continual problem because the 2–5 P.M. siesta closure is really awkward. I always find myself where I have to remind myself that from 2–5 I have a blank period that I can't do anything. . . . We started adjusting to the eating schedule. Whether we like it or not, we eat a lot later.

> Well, we went down to Club Med for a vacation and the French were all topless and my 8-year-old son didn't say anything but my 4-year-old daughter now refuses to wear a top. I will not let her get away with it back in the U.S.

> We've been really fortunate we haven't had to use health care services here. . . . The thought of going to, needing to go to a doctor is scary because for me it would have to be someone English speaking or I wouldn't, you know, feel comfortable.

Given these kinds of problems, is that international sales position being offered to you as attractive as it looks? Will it really help your career?

Sources: Nick Forster, "The Myth of the 'International Manager,'" *International Journal of Resource Management,* February 2000, 11(1), pp. 126–142; and Mary C. Gilly, Lisa Penaloza, and Kenneth M. Kambara, "The Role of Consumption in Expatriate Adjustment and Satisfaction," working paper, Graduate School of Management, University of California, Irvine, 2004.

The salesperson is a company's most direct tie to the customer; in the eyes of most customers, the salesperson is the company. As presenter of company offerings and gatherer of customer information, the sales representative is the final link in the culmination of a company's marketing and sales effort.

Growing global competition coupled with the dynamic and complex nature of international business increases both the need and the means for closer ties with both customers and suppliers. Relationship marketing, built on effective communications between the seller and buyer, focuses on building long-term alliances rather than treating each sale as a one-time event. Advances in information technology are allowing for increasingly higher levels of coordination across advertising, marketing research,[1] and personal selling efforts, yielding new roles and functions in customer relationship management (CRM).[2] Similarly, such advances are changing the nature of personal selling and sales management, leading some to forecast substantial reductions in field sales efforts.[3]

In this ever-changing environment of international business, the tasks of designing, building, training, motivating, and compensating an international sales group generate unique problems at every stage of management and development. This chapter discusses the alternatives and problems of managing sales and marketing personnel in foreign countries. Indeed, these problems are among the most difficult facing international marketers. In one survey of CEOs and other top executives, the respondents identified "establishing sales and distribution networks" and "cultural differences" as major difficulties in international sales and operations.[4]

## Designing the Sales Force

The first step in managing a sales force is its design. Based on analyses of current and potential customers, the selling environment,[5] competition, and the firm's resources and capabilities, decisions must be made regarding the numbers, characteristics, and assignments of sales personnel. All these design decisions are made more challenging by the wide variety of pertinent conditions and circumstances in international markets. Moreover, the globalization of markets and customers, as illustrated by the IBM—Ford story in Crossing Borders 17.1, makes the job of international sales manager quite interesting.

---

[1]Milton Liebman does a great job of describing the latest usage of competitive information systems in pharmaceutical sales. See "Competitive Edge," *Medical Marketing & Media*, February 1, 2003, pp. 36–39.

[2]J. Sairamesh, R. Mohan, M. Kumar, C. Bender, "A Platform for Business-to-Business Sell-Side, Private Exchanges and Marketplaces," *IBM Systems Journal*, January 1, 2002, p. 242–249; "Imperbel Increases Customer Retention [Across Europe] with New Stayinfront CRM Platform," *M2 Presswire*, March 17, 2003; European sales representatives use PDA-based information. See "PepsiCo France Selects WebForceCG, Dendrite's New Sales Channel Management Suite for Consumer Goods Industry," *M2 Presswire*, March 31, 2003.

[3]Erika Rasmussen, "Going Global with CRM," *Sales & Marketing Management*, March 2000, pp. 96–98; David J. Cichelli, "Sales Compensation and the E-World," *ACA News*, March 2000, pp. 42–45; and "Accelerated Business Activity Propels Dendrite's Growth in European Market," *M2 Presswire*, February 28, 2003.

[4]Dennis J. Aigner, "The 2003 Orange County Executive Survey," University of California, Irvine, 2003, p. 28. Despite the obvious importance of international sales management and personal selling there exists a paucity of systematic research to support decision making in the area. International topics are generally ignored in most sales management texts and in the academic literature. See Maasaki Kotabe, "Contemporary Research Trends in International Marketing," in Alan M. Rugman and Thomas L. Brewer (eds.), *The Oxford Handbook of International Business* (Oxford: Oxford University Press, 2001). Moreover, the trajectory of work in the area is downward. We did find one book entitled *Discover Your Sales Strengths: How the World's Greatest Salespeople Develop Winning Careers* (by Benson Smith and Tony Rutigliano, New York: Warner Business Books, 2003), but no mention was made of international issues within.

[5]Many firms downsized and reorganized their global sales forces in response to the general persistent economic downturn of the early 2000s. See Jake Keaveny, "Citigroup Global Equities Review May Mean Job Cuts," *Reuters English News Service*, April 7, 2003.

# CROSSING BORDERS 17.1   Sales Force Management and Global Customers

Did IBM really need a new sales compensation plan? For proof, just ask Kevin Tucker. Tucker, an IBM global account manager dedicated to Ford Motor Company, closed a $7 million sale with the automotive giant's European operations. Ford wanted Tucker and his team of IBM representatives to install networking systems in its engineering facilities. The systems would run the applications that design the company's automobiles.

Ford's installation required help from an IBM sales executive in Germany, the project's headquarters. So Tucker, whose office sits in Ford's Dearborn, Michigan, headquarters, sent an e-mail requesting the executive's assistance. And that's when things turned ugly. Although the rep in Germany didn't turn his back on the project, his initial reaction was less than enthusiastic. Ford wanted the systems installed throughout Europe, yet the compensation plan for IBM's Germany-based reps rewarded only the systems that were installed in that country. With 80 percent of the work scheduled outside of Germany, the executive was left wondering: Where's the payoff? Tucker and other IBM sales incentive managers wasted three weeks discussing ways to maximize the rep's incentive. Energy that could have been focused on the customer was wasted on a pay plan. "Ford was world-centric, we were country-centric," Tucker says. "The team in Germany was asking, 'Kevin, how can you make us whole?'"

They weren't the only salespeople asking that question at IBM. Tucker's predicament represents just one of many problems that were rooted in IBM's "$72 billion" sales incentive plan—a plan that had been obviously put on the back burner as the company giant tinkered with its vision.

Bob Wylie, manager of incentive strategies for IBM Canada, says, "There was the attitude that if it's outside my territory and outside my measurements, I don't get paid for it, and I don't get involved. What's in my pay plan defines what I do." Not the best setup for a company that operates in 165 countries.

Apparently, IBM solved many of these problems. Ford signed contracts for more than $300 million with IBM to create almost all of the car company's software, including Internet and e-commerce applications in Europe and North America. Details about IBM's new sales compensation program are provided later in this chapter.

Source: Michele Marchetti, "Gamble: IBM Replaced Its Outdated Compensation Plan with a Worldwide Framework. Is It Paying Off?" *Sales & Marketing Management*, July 1996, pp. 65–69; "Ford Motor and IBM," *Wall Street Journal Europe*, January 13, 1999, p. UK5A; William M. Bulkeley, "IBM and Dassault Capture Software Job from EDS," *Wall Street Journal*, February 6, 2003, p. B5.

---

As described in previous chapters, distribution strategies often vary from country to country. Some markets may require a direct sales force, whereas others may not. How customers are approached can differ as well. For example, banks are placing sales representatives in Russian appliance stores to sell credit, a new concept there.[6] The hard sell that may work in some countries can be inappropriate in others.[7] Automobiles were sold door to door in Japan for years, and only recently have stocks been sold over the Internet in Europe. More than 100,000 of Singapore's 6 million inhabitants are involved in home product sales and other forms of multilevel marketing.[8] The size of accounts certainly makes a difference as well—notice in Crossing Borders 17.1 that an IBM sales representative works inside Ford. Selling high-technology products may allow for the greater use of American expatriates, whereas selling consulting services tends to require more participation by native sales representatives. Selling in information-oriented cultures such as Germany may also allow for greater use of expatriates. However, relationship-oriented countries such as Japan require the most complete local knowledge possessed

---

[6]Sabrina Tavernise, "Buying on Credit Is the Latest Rage in Russia," *New York Times*, January 20, 2003, p. 1.

[7]Janet Matthews, "China, Insurance Pitching for Business," *China Economic Review*, January 14, 2003, pp. 15–17; and Raymond Ma, "Aggressive Mortgage Salesmen Pose Possible Risk for Home Buyers," *South China Morning Post*, February 20, 2003, p. 9.

[8]Lorna Tan, "100,000 People Here Are in Multilevel Marketing," *Straits Times*, April 5, 2003.

only by natives. Writing about Japan, two international marketing experts agree: "Personal selling as a rule has to be localized for even the most global of corporations and industries."[9]

After decisions are made about how many expatriates, local nationals, or third-country nationals a particular market requires, then more intricate aspects of design can be started, such as territory allocation and customer call plans. Many of the most advanced operations research tools developed in the United States can be applied in foreign markets, with appropriate adaptation of inputs, of course. For example, one company provided tools to help international firms create balanced territories and find optimal locations for sales offices in Canada, Mexico, and Australia.[10] However, the use of such high-tech resource allocation tools requires intricate knowledge of not only geographical details but also appropriate call routines. Many things can differ across cultures—length of sales cycles, the kinds of customer relationships, and the kinds of interactions with customers. Indeed, more than one study has identified substantial differences in the importance of referrals in the sales of industrial services in Japan vis-à-vis the United States.[11] The implications are that in Japan sales calls must be made not only on customers, but also on the key people, such as bankers, in the all-important referral networks.

# Recruiting Marketing and Sales Personnel

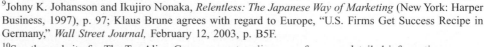

The number of marketing management personnel from the home country assigned to foreign countries varies according to the size of the operation and the availability of qualified locals. Increasingly, the number of U.S. home-country nationals (expatriates) assigned to foreign posts is smaller as the pool of trained, experienced locals grows.[12]

The largest personnel requirement abroad for most companies is the sales force, recruited from three sources: expatriates, local nationals, and third-country nationals. A company's staffing pattern may include all three types in any single foreign operation, depending on qualifications, availability, and a company's needs. Sales and marketing executives can be recruited via the traditional media of advertising (including newspapers, magazines, job fairs, and the Internet), employment agencies or executive search firms,[13] and the all-important personal referrals. The last source is crucial in many foreign countries, particularly the relationship-oriented ones.

## Expatriates

The number of companies relying on expatriate personnel is declining as the volume of world trade increases and as more companies use locals to fill marketing positions. However, when products are highly technical, or when selling requires an extensive background of information and applications, an **expatriate** sales force remains the best choice. The expatriate salesperson may have the advantages of greater technical training, better knowledge of the company and its product line, and proven dependability. Because they are not locals, expatriates sometimes add to the prestige of the product line in the eyes of foreign customers. And perhaps most important, expatriates usually are able to effectively communicate with and influence headquarters personnel.

[9]Johny K. Johansson and Ikujiro Nonaka, *Relentless: The Japanese Way of Marketing* (New York: Harper Business, 1997), p. 97; Klaus Brune agrees with regard to Europe, "U.S. Firms Get Success Recipe in Germany," *Wall Street Journal*, February 12, 2003, p. B5F.

[10]See the website for The TerrAlign Group, www.terralign.com, for more detailed information.

[11]R. Bruce Money, Mary C. Gilly, and John L. Graham, "National Culture and Referral Behavior in the Purchase of Industrial Services in the United States and Japan," *Journal of Marketing*, October 1998, 62(4), pp. 76–87; and Chanthika Pornpitakpan, "Trade in Thailand: A Three-Way Cultural Comparison," *Business Horizons*, March–April 2000, pp. 61–70.

[12]An interesting sign of the shrinking expatriate populations is the demise of the only English-language paper sold in Mexico City. See Reed Johnson, "English Paper in Mexico Folds," *Los Angeles Times*, January 17, 2003, p. A3.

[13]The largest international executive search firm is Korn/Ferry International (www.kornferry.com).

The chief disadvantages of an expatriate sales force are the high cost, cultural and legal barriers, and the limited number of high-caliber personnel willing to live abroad for extended periods. Companies in the United States are finding it difficult to persuade outstanding employees to take overseas posts. Employees are reluctant to go abroad for many reasons: Some find it difficult to uproot families for a two- or three-year assignment, increasing numbers of dual-career couples often require finding suitable jobs for spouses, and many executives believe such assignments impede their subsequent promotions at home. Recall the comments of the executives in the Global Perspective. The loss of visibility at corporate headquarters plus the belief that "out of sight is out of mind" are major reasons for the reluctance to accept a foreign assignment. Companies with well-planned career development programs have the least difficulty. Indeed, the best international companies make it crystal clear that a ticket to top management is an overseas stint. Korn/Ferry International reports in its most recent survey of 75 senior executives from around the world that "international experience" is the attribute identified as second most important for CEOs—experience in marketing and finance positions were first and third, respectively.[14]

Expatriates commit to foreign assignments for varying lengths of time, from a few weeks or months to a lifetime. Some expatriates have one-time assignments (which may last for years), after which they are returned to the parent company; others are essentially professional expatriates, working abroad in country after country. Still another expatriate assignment is a career-long assignment to a given country or region; this is likely to lead to assimilation of the expatriate into the foreign culture to such an extent that the person may more closely resemble a local than an expatriate. Because expatriate marketing personnel are likely to cost substantially more than locals, a company must be certain of their effectiveness.

More and more American companies are taking advantage of American employees who are fluent in languages other than English. For example, many U.S. citizens speak Spanish as their first language. The large number of Puerto Ricans working for American multinationals in places like Mexico City is well documented. Recent immigrants and their sons and daughters that learn their parents' languages and about their native cultures will continue to be invaluable assets for firms wishing to enter such markets. Certainly ethnic Chinese- and Vietnamese-Americans are serving as cultural bridges for commerce with those two nations. Indeed, throughout history patterns of commerce have always followed paths of immigration.

## Virtual Expatriates

The Internet and other advances in communications technologies, along with the growing reluctance of executives to move abroad, are creating a new breed of expatriate, the virtual one. According to a PricewaterhouseCoopers survey of 270 organizations, there is a substantial increase in shorter-term, commuter, and virtual assignments since 1997. Virtual expatriates manage operations in other countries but don't move there. They stay in hotels, make long visits, and maintain their families at home. Some spend up to 75 percent of their working time traveling. None leave home without the ubiquitous laptop and cell phone.

Close contact with subordinates and customers is, of course, tougher for virtual expatriates. Moreover, the travel can be a killer—that is, foreign bugs are often more virulent and easier to catch on long international flights (indeed, one doctor calls airplanes "germ tubes"), living in hotels is lonely, and crime against expatriates and travelers in foreign cities is a real hazard.[15] Indeed, one website provides a measure of the comparative risks of violence across a number of countries—see Exhibit 17.1. However, virtual expatriates' families don't have to be uprooted, and executives can stay in closer touch with the home office. Finally, from the firm's perspective a virtual assignment may be the only option and often a good way to avoid the extra expenses of an actual executive move.

[14]See "Marketing Is Fastest Route to the Executive Suite," Korn/Ferry International, www.kornferry.com (2000).

[15]See the UCIrvine Citizen Peacebuilding Program website for more details about global violence (www.cpbp.org).

**Exhibit 17.1**  Risks of Violence in the International Marketplace

The best source of information we can find on comparative violence levels across countries is the World Health Organization (WHO) Mortality Statistics. The agency collects data from 69 countries on causes of death. Among the more than 100 causes listed, three are pertinent: "Homicide and injury purposely inflicted by other persons," "Other violence," and "Other external causes." We add these three numbers together and combine them with the WHO Estimated Mortality Coverage (Table 4) data to produce the "Deaths by Violence" statistics reported below.

| Rank | Country | Deaths by Violence per 100,000 | Rank | Country | Deaths by Violence per 100,000 |
|---|---|---|---|---|---|
| 1 | Norway | 1.2 | 36 | Albania | 6.2 |
| 2 | Spain | 1.3 | 37 | U.K. (Scotland) | 7.0 |
| 3 | Greece | 1.4 | 38 | Slovenia | 7.1 |
| 4 | Netherlands | 1.7 | 38 | Switzerland | 7.1 |
| 5 | Austria | 1.7 | 40 | Cuba | 7.6 |
| 6 | New Zealand | 2.0 | 41 | United States | 7.9 |
| 6 | Japan | 2.0 | 42 | Poland | 8.1 |
| 8 | Australia | 2.1 | 43 | Israel | 8.3 |
| 9 | Luxembourg | 2.3 | 44 | Costa Rica | 8.5 |
| 10 | Ireland | 2.5 | 45 | Singapore | 8.7 |
| 11 | Iceland | 2.6 | 46 | Tajikistan | 9.0 |
| 12 | Malta | 2.7 | 47 | Azerbaijan | 9.1 |
| 12 | Canada | 2.7 | 48 | Uzbekistan | 9.2 |
| 14 | Italy | 2.8 | 49 | Thailand | 10.2 |
| 15 | Yugoslav Republic | 3.0 | 50 | Turkmenistan | 10.6 |
| 16 | Mauritius | 3.1 | 51 | Mexico | 13.6 |
| 17 | U.K. (Northern Ireland) | 3.4 | 52 | Armenia | 15.1 |
| 18 | Kuwait | 3.8 | 53 | Portugal | 15.6 |
| 19 | Germany | 3.9 | 54 | Argentina | 16.8 |
| 20 | Hungary | 4.0 | 55 | Lithuania | 19.1 |
| 20 | France | 4.0 | 56 | Chile | 19.6 |
| 22 | U.K. (England, Wales) | 4.2 | 57 | Kyrgyzstan | 22.0 |
| 23 | Croatia | 4.4 | 58 | Brazil | 22.4 |
| 24 | San Marino | 4.5 | 59 | Georgia | 22.5 |
| 25 | U.K. | 4.6 | 60 | Latvia | 22.9 |
| 26 | Czech Republic | 4.7 | 61 | Belize | 23.5 |
| 26 | Belgium | 4.7 | 62 | Estonia | 24.8 |
| 26 | Sweden | 4.7 | 63 | Republic of Moldova | 25.1 |
| 29 | Romania | 5.0 | 64 | Belarus | 31.3 |
| 30 | Finland | 5.1 | 65 | Kazakhstan | 36.1 |
| 31 | Slovakia | 5.5 | 66 | Ukraine | 36.3 |
| 31 | Denmark | 5.5 | 67 | Venezuela | 45.5 |
| 33 | Republic of Korea | 5.7 | 68 | Philippines | 58.1 |
| 34 | Bulgaria | 5.9 | 69 | Russian Federation | 77.4 |
| 35 | Uruguay | 6.0 | | | |

Source: Peace Monitor (www.cpbp.org, click on Peace Monitor).

**Local Nationals**  The historical preference for expatriate managers and salespeople from the home country is giving way to a preference for **local nationals**. At the sales level, the picture is clearly biased in favor of local nationals because they transcend both cultural and legal barriers. More knowledgeable about a country's business structure than an expatriate would be, local salespeople are better able to lead a company through the maze of unfamiliar distribution systems and referral networks. Furthermore, in some places there are now pools of qualified foreign personnel available that cost less to maintain than a staff of expatriates.[16]

---

[16]Michael Shari, "Unilever Indonesia, Using All the Levers," *BusinessWeek Online*, March 19, 2003.

A worker cleans an American Airlines plane detained at San Jose International Airport after a nonstop flight from Tokyo in which several passengers complained of symptoms similar to SARS, or Severe Acute Respiratory Syndrome. Officials found no threat after isolating passengers and crew for two hours. International travel can be a lot of work! (© David Paul Morris/Getty Images)

In Europe and Asia, many local nationals have MBA degrees earned in the United States; thus, a firm gets the cultural knowledge of the local meshed with an understanding of U.S. business management systems. Although expatriates' salaries may be no more than those of their national counterparts, the total cost of keeping comparable groups of expatriates in a country can be considerably higher (often three times the expense) because of special cost-of-living benefits, moving expenses, taxes, and other costs associated with keeping an expatriate abroad. As can be seen in Exhibit 17.2, only four of the most expensive cities in the world are in the United States.

The main disadvantage of hiring local nationals is the tendency of headquarters personnel to ignore their advice. Although most foreign nationals are careful to keep relationships at the home office warm, their influence is often reduced by their limited English communication skills and lack of understanding of how home-office politics influence decision making. Another key disadvantage can be their lack of availability; one CEO of a consulting firm that specializes in recruiting managers in China reports

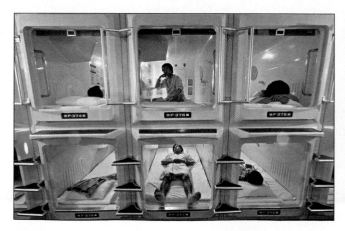

Locals hit the road. Japanese salesmen saving on expenses in this "capsule hotel" in Osaka. Meanwhile, the Avon Lady calls on a customer in rural Brazil. (left: © Roger Ressmeyer/CORBIS; right: © John Maier, Jr./The Image Works)

## CROSSING BORDERS 17.2  The New Risks of International Travel

It's bad enough that sleep becomes a luxury because of jet lag. Your yawns at important meetings aren't the only dangers. Personal safety can also be a consideration for international sales representatives and expatriates. The U.S. State Department has long issued warnings for travelers (www.travel.state.gov). Here's a recent one:

Nigeria—Exercise extreme caution. Avoid demonstrations against U.S. policies. Visitors may be victims of armed robberies. Possible shakedowns at checkpoints.

The new terrorism yields advice like the following:

Stay in establishments that don't necessarily attract Americans. In planning for a recent trip to London, for example, a software executive changed her reservation from a Holiday Inn to a small place outside the city.

And then there's SARS (Severe Acute Respiratory Syndrome). The deaths are tragic and the macroeconomic effects are huge on the affected areas and companies. In the first affected places the economists knocked a percentage point off annual growth rates. Cathay Pacific, Singapore Air, and Qantas grounded 40 percent of their flights. But the inconvenience for sales representatives is more than just a bother. Here's one person's account from Hong Kong:

The Amoy Plaza shopping mall is brightly lit but deserted. A big Kentucky Fried Chicken restaurant in the center is cordoned off with tape. Out back, men in protective suits are spraying each other with disinfectant. In front, almost everybody on the sidewalk is wearing a surgical mask.

This is a city living in fear. You can see it in people's eyes when somebody starts coughing on the bus or in the elevator. Nobody is prepared to risk their health and the health of their family and colleagues to be polite. Change seats or get off on the next floor, that's the best policy.

The biggest complaints come from those who have to travel for work. On the plane you sit helplessly breathing recirculated air that could be laden with the mystery virus. And then at your destination you will be shunned like a leper.

Finally, there's the ill-omened irony of the Tourist Boards' public relations slogan issued right before the SARS outbreak—Hong Kong will take your breath away!

Sources: Pete Engardio, Mark L. Clifford, Michael Shari, "Epidemics and Economics," *BusinessWeek*, April 28, 2003, pp. 44–45; Anne Field, "Low-Profile Traveling," *BusinessWeek*, April 7, 2003; Hugo Restall, "My Mask Fatigue," *Wall Street Journal*, April 11, 2003; and "Perspectives," *Newsweek*, April 21, 2003, p. 19.

that ten openings exist for every one qualified applicant. Moreover, although in the United States it is common practice to hire away experienced salespeople from competitors,[17] suppliers, or vendors, the same approach will not work in other countries. In places like Japan, employees are much more loyal to their companies and therefore are difficult to lure away even for big money. College recruits can also be hard to hire in Japan because

**Exhibit 17.2**

The 20 Most Expensive Cities to Live in on the Planet (in order)

| | |
|---|---|
| Osaka/Kobe | Tel Aviv |
| Tokyo | Beijing |
| Hong Kong | Geneva |
| Libreville | Chicago |
| Oslo | Paris |
| London | San Francisco |
| New York | Los Angeles |
| Zurich | Shanghai |
| Singapore | Guangzhou |
| Taipei | Copenhagen |

Source: The Economist Intelligence Unit, March 2001 (www.eiu.com). The cities are listed in order; Osaka/Kobe is the most expensive and Copenhagen the least.

---

[17] Andy Cohen, "Seizing the Moment: AT&T Has the Opportunity of a Lifetime," *Sales & Marketing Management*, January 1, 2003, pp. 22–24.

## CROSSING BORDERS 17.3  Avon Calling—or Not?

In a gold-mining town near an Amazon tributary, Maria de Fatima Nascimento ambles among mud shacks hawking Honesty and Care Deeply, two beauty products by Avon. She is part of a several-thousand-member Avon army that travels via foot, kayak, riverboat, and small plane through the Amazon basin. Latin America accounts for 35 percent of Avon's total sales, and its success can be attributed to the company's willingness to adapt to local conditions. Cash payments aren't required; many Brazilian customers barter for products with fruit, eggs, flour, or wood. Two-dozen eggs buys a Bart Simpson roll-on deodorant, and miners pay from 1 to 4 grams of gold powder or nuggets for fragrances like Sweet Crystal Splash. "Ladies of the evening," who regard the cosmetics as a cost of doing business, are some of Nascimento's better customers. But then, so are miners. One commented, "It's worth 1½ grams of gold to smell nice."

Despite the success of the Bart Simpson roll-on in some parts of the world, Avon is not rolling along in the old-fashioned way in others. In 1998 at least ten people were killed in China during antigovernment rioting in

several cities. Many of the rioters were from among the country's 200,000 Avon Ladies. The Chinese government had banned direct selling, complaining in a directive that such practices spawn "weird cults, triads, superstitious groups, and hooliganism." Worse yet, the authorities criticized meetings of direct marketers that involved singing, chanting, and inspirational sermons. *The Peoples' Daily* once even complained that the direct sales encouraged "excessive hugging"!

The latest and perhaps most serious threat to the 2.6 million Avon Ladies working worldwide in 135 countries is the Internet. Many fret that Avon.com may replace "Ding dong, it's Avon calling." But, no matter what, Avon's international sales keep rolling along.

Sources: "Avon Calling near the Amazon," *U.S. News & World Report*, October 25, 1994, pp. 16–17; Andrew Higgins, "Avon Calling? Not in China," *The Guardian*, May 1, 1998, p. 18; and Kate Quill, "Ding Dong, Gone . . . Farewell Avon Lady?" *Times* (London), February 7, 2000, p. 7; Miriam Jordon, "Knock Knock, In Brazil an Army of Underemployed Goes Door-to-Door," *Wall Street Journal*, February 19, 2003, p. A1.

the smartest students are heavily recruited by the largest Japanese firms. Smaller firms and foreign firms are seen in Japan as much more risky employment opportunities.

One other consideration makes recruiting of local nationals as sales representatives more difficult in many foreign countries. We all know about Americans' aversion to being a "salesman." Personal selling is often derided as a career and represented in a negative light in American media—Arthur Miller's *Death of a Salesman* is of course the best example. Despite the bad press, however, personal selling is the most common job in the United States. Indeed, the United States is described as "a nation of salesmen."[18] But as negatively as the selling profession is viewed in the United States, in many other countries it's viewed in even worse ways. Particularly in the more relationship-oriented cultures such as France, Mexico, and Japan, sales representatives tend to be on the bottom rung of the social ladder. Thus it can be very difficult to recruit the brightest people to fill sales positions in foreign operations.

**Third-Country Nationals**

The internationalization of business has created a pool of third-country nationals (**TCNs**), expatriates from their own countries working for a foreign company in a third country. TCNs are a group whose nationality has little to do with where they work or for whom. An example would be a German working in Argentina for a U.S. company. Historically, there were few expatriates or TCNs who spent the majority of their careers abroad, but now a truly "global executive" has begun to emerge. The recently appointed chairman of a division of a major Netherlands company is a Norwegian who gained that post after stints in the United States, where he was the U.S. subsidiary's chairman, and in Brazil, where he held the position of general manager. At one time, Burroughs Corporation's Italian subsidiary was run by a Frenchman, the Swiss subsidiary by a Dane, the German

---

[18]See Earl Shorris's excellent and still pertinent book, *A Nation of Salesmen* (New York: Norton, 1994).

subsidiary by an Englishman, the French subsidiary by a Swiss, the Venezuelan subsidiary by an Argentinean, and the Danish subsidiary by a Dutchman.

American companies often seek TCNs from other English-speaking countries to avoid the double taxation costs of their American managers. Americans working in Spain, for example, must pay both Spanish and U.S. income taxes, and most American firms' compensation packages for expatriates are adjusted accordingly. So, given the same pay and benefits, it is cheaper for an American firm to post a British executive in Spain than an American.

Overall, the development of TCN executives reflects not only a growing internationalization of business but also an acknowledgment that personal skills and motivations are not the exclusive property of one nation. TCNs often are sought because they speak several languages and know an industry or foreign country well. More and more companies feel that talent should flow to opportunity regardless of one's home country.

**Host-Country Restrictions**     The host government's attitudes toward foreign workers often complicate selecting expatriate U.S. nationals instead of locals. Concerns about foreign corporate domination, local unemployment, and other issues cause some countries to restrict the number of nonnationals allowed to work within the country. Most countries have specific rules limiting work permits for foreigners to positions that cannot be filled by a national. Further, the law often limits such permits to periods just long enough to train a local for a specific position. Such restrictions mean that MNCs have fewer opportunities for sending home-country personnel to management positions abroad.

In earlier years, personnel gained foreign-country experience by being sent to lower management positions to gain the necessary training before eventually assuming top-level foreign assignments. Most countries, including the United States, control the number of foreigners allowed to work or train within their borders. Since September 11, 2001, U.S. immigration authorities have clamped down even harder on the issuance of all kinds of work visas.[19]

# Selecting Sales and Marketing Personnel

To select personnel for international marketing positions effectively, management must define precisely what is expected of its people. A formal job description can aid management in expressing long-range needs as well as current needs. In addition to descriptions for each marketing position, the criteria should include special requirements indigenous to various countries.

People operating in the home country need only the attributes of effective salespersons, whereas a transnational manager can require skills and attitudes that would challenge a diplomat. International personnel requirements vary considerably. However, some basic requisites leading to effective performance should be considered because effective executives and salespeople, regardless of what foreign country they are operating in, share certain personal characteristics, skills, and orientations.

*Maturity* is a prime requisite for expatriate and third-country personnel. Managers and sales personnel working abroad typically must work more independently than their domestic counterparts. The company must have confidence in their ability to make decisions and commitments without constant recourse to the home office or they cannot be individually effective.

International personnel require a kind of *emotional stability* not demanded in domestic positions. Regardless of location, these people are living in cultures dissimilar to their own; to some extent they are always under scrutiny and always aware that they are official representatives of the company abroad. They need sensitivity to behavioral variations in different countries, but they cannot be so hypersensitive that their behavior is adversely affected.

Managers or salespeople operating in foreign countries need considerable *breadth of knowledge* of many subjects both on and off the job. The ability to speak one or more other languages is always preferable.

---

[19]Bernard Wysocki, Jr., "Foreign Scientists Are Being Stranded by War on Terror," *Wall Street Journal*, January 20, 2003, p. A1.

The marketer who expects to be effective in the international marketplace needs to have a *positive outlook* on an international assignment. People who do not like what they are doing and where they are doing it stand little chance of success, particularly in a foreign country. Failures usually are the result of overselling the assignment, showing the bright side of the picture, and not warning about the bleak side.

An international salesperson must have a high level of *flexibility,* whether working in a foreign country or at home. Expatriates working in a foreign country must be particularly sensitive to the habits of the market; those working at home for a foreign company must adapt to the requirements and ways of the parent company.

Successful adaptation in international affairs is based on a combination of attitude and effort. A careful study of the customs of the market country should be initiated before the marketer arrives and should be continued as long as there are facets of the culture that are not clear. One useful approach is to listen to the advice of national and foreign businesspeople operating in that country. *Cultural empathy* is clearly a part of the basic orientation because it is unlikely that anyone can be effective if antagonistic or confused about the environment.

Finally, international sales and marketing personnel must be *energetic* and *enjoy travel.* Many international sales representatives spend about two-thirds of their nights in hotel rooms around the world. Going through the long lines of customs and immigration after a 15-hour flight requires a certain kind of stamina not commonly encountered. Some even argue that frequent long flights can damage your health. Even the seductive lights of Paris nights fade after the fifth business trip there.

Most of these traits can be assessed during interviews and perhaps during role-playing exercises. Paper-and-pencil ability tests, biographical information, and reference checks are of secondary importance. Indeed, as previously mentioned, in many countries referrals are the best way to recruit managers and sales representatives, making reference checks during evaluation and selection processes irrelevant.

There is also evidence that some traits that make for successful sales representatives in the United States may not be important in other countries. In one study sales

International sales is hard work. A typical week for this Canadian executive looks like this: Leaves Singapore with the flu. Arrives home in Toronto to discover that a frozen pipe has burst. Immediately boards a plane for a two-day trip to Chicago. Back to Toronto. On to Detroit, battling jet lag and the flu. Back to Toronto, running through the Detroit airport "like O.J. in the Hertz commercial" and throwing his briefcase into a closing door. Takes a brief break in flooded house before boarding another plane to China. Reports having woken up in a plane and asked his seatmate where they were landing. Seventeen flights in two weeks left him a bit confused. (© *David McIntyre/Black Star*)

representatives in the electronics industries in Japan and the United States were compared. For the American representatives, pay and education were both found to be positively related to performance and job satisfaction. In Japan they were not. That is, the Americans who cared more about money and were more educated tended to perform better in and be more satisfied with their sales jobs. Conversely, the Japanese sales representatives tended to be more satisfied with their jobs when their values were consistent with those of their company.[20] The few systematic studies in this area suggest that selection criteria must be localized, and American management practices must be adapted to foreign markets.

Selection mistakes are costly. When an expatriate assignment does not work out, hundreds of thousands of dollars are wasted in expenses and lost time. Getting the right person to handle the job is also important in the selection of locals to work for foreign companies within their home country. Most developing countries and many European countries have stringent laws protecting workers' rights. These laws are specific as to penalties for the dismissal of employees. Perhaps Venezuela has the most stringent dismissal legislation: With more than three months of service in the same firm, a worker gets severance pay amounting to one month's pay at severance notice plus 15 days' pay for every month of service exceeding eight months plus an additional 15 days' pay for each year employed. Further, after an employee is dismissed, the law requires that person be replaced within 30 days at the same salary. Colombia and Brazil have similar laws that make employee dismissal a high-cost proposition.

Finally, there is new evidence that a manager's culture affects such personnel decisions. In a new line of international sales management research, one study reports "that managers given an identical [personnel selection] problem do not make the same decisions nor do they value the criteria often used in recruitment and promotion decisions equally. For example, we found that Austrian and German managers are more likely to hire compatriots than Italian managers."[21] Thus we are just scratching the surface of a variety of issues in the area of international sales management research.

## Training for International Marketing

The nature of a training program depends largely on whether expatriate or local personnel are being trained for overseas positions. Training for the expatriates focuses on the customs and the special foreign sales problems that will be encountered, whereas local personnel require greater emphasis on the company, its products, technical information, and selling methods. In training either type of personnel, the sales training activity is burdened with problems stemming from long-established behavior and attitudes. Local personnel, for instance, cling to habits continually reinforced by local culture. Nowhere is the problem greater than in China or Russia, where the legacy of the communist tradition lingers. The attitude that whether you work hard or not, you get the same rewards must be changed if training is going to stick. Expatriates are also captives of their own habits and patterns. Before any training can be effective, open-minded attitudes must be established (see Exhibit 17.3).

Continual training may be more important in foreign markets than in domestic ones because of the lack of routine contact with the parent company and its marketing personnel. In addition, training of foreign employees must be tailored to the recipients' ways of learning and communicating. For example, the Dilbert cartoon characters theme that worked so well in ethics training courses with a company's American employees did not translate well in many of its foreign offices.

---

[20]R. Bruce Money and John L. Graham, "Sales Performance, Pay, and Job Satisfaction: Tests of a Model Using Data Collected in the U.S. and Japan," *Journal of International Business Studies*, 1999, 30(1), pp. 149–172.

[21]Dominique Rouzies, Michael Segalla, and Barton A. Weitz, "Cultural Impact on European Staffing Decisions in Sales Management," *International Journal of Research in Marketing*, March 2003, 20(1), pp. 67–85.

**Exhibit 17.3**    Personal Selling Tips, from Brussels to Bangkok

The best training programs are much more than just a list of tips. But a quick read of such tips provides a glimpse of the cultural variation facing sales representatives around the globe.

Belgium—Be able to identify the decision makers. In Flanders (Dutch-speaking region) group decisions are common, but in Wallonia (French-speaking region) the highest-level execs have the final say.

China—Expect to continue negotiations after a deal is inked. To Chinese, signing a contract is just the beginning of the business relationship; therefore, they expect both sides to continue working together to fix problems that arise.

Colombia—Business counterparts want to get to know you personally and form a strong friendship with you. Be sure not to change reps in midstream, because often a switch puts an end to negotiations.

Germany—Be prepared with data and empirical evidence that supports your sales proposition. German business-people are unimpressed by flashy advertising and brochures, so keep them serious and detailed, with unexaggerated information.

India—Make sure your schedule remains flexible. Indians are more casual about time and punctuality. Because of India's rigid hierarchy, decisions are made only by the highest-level boss.

Mexico—When planning a meeting, breakfast and lunch are preferable. Take your time and cultivate relationships with business contacts. Those relationships are generally considered more important than professional experience.

Peru—Peruvians relate to individuals and not corporate entities. Establish personal rapport and don't switch your representative in the middle of negotiations.

Russia—Your first meeting will be just a formality. Your Russian counterparts will take this time to judge your credibility, so it's best to be warm and approachable.

Scotland—Scottish people tend to be soft-spoken and private. It takes time to build relationships, but business counterparts seem friendlier after bonds are established. (By the way, Scotch is a drink, not a nationality—it's Scottish.)

South Korea—Status is important. Make sure your business card clearly indicates your title. Don't send a rep to meet with a Korean executive of higher status—it could be viewed as disrespectful.

Thailand—The Thai culture emphasizes nonconflict, so don't make assertive demands when making sales pitches.

 Source: *Sales & Marketing Management* publishes these tips regularly in its magazine and on its website (www.salesandmarketing.com).

One aspect of training is frequently overlooked: Home-office personnel dealing with international marketing operations need training designed to make them responsive to the needs of the foreign operations. In most companies, the requisite sensitivities are expected to be developed by osmosis in the process of dealing with foreign affairs. However, the best companies provide home-office personnel with cross-cultural training and send them abroad periodically to increase their awareness of the problems of the foreign operations.

The Internet now makes some kinds of sales training much more efficient. Users can study text on-screen and participate in interactive assessment tests. Sun Microsystems estimates that its use of the Internet can shorten training cycles by as much as 75 percent. And in some parts of the world where telecommunications facilities are more limited, CD-ROM approaches are quite successful. Lockheed-Martin uses an interactive CD-ROM–based system to train its employees worldwide on the nuances of the Foreign Corrupt Practices Act and associated corporate policies and ethics.

## Motivating Sales Personnel

Motivation is especially complicated because the firm is dealing with different cultures, different sources, and different philosophies.[22] Marketing is a business function requiring high motivation regardless of the location of the practitioner. Marketing managers and sales managers typically work hard, travel extensively, and have day-to-day challenges. Selling is hard, competitive work wherever undertaken, and a constant flow of inspiration is needed to keep personnel functioning at an optimal level. National differences must always be considered in motivating the marketing force.[23] In one study, sales

---

[22]James P. Neelankavil, Anil Mathur, and Yong Zang, "Determinants of Managerial Performance: A Cross-Cultural Comparison of the Perceptions of Middle-Level Managers in Four Countries," *Journal of International Business Studies*, 2000, 31(1), pp. 121–140.

[23]Sales Strategies Across the Globe," *Sales & Marketing Management*, April 1, 2003, p 19.

## Exhibit 17.4

Salespeople's Distribution of 100 Points among Rewards in Terms of Their Importance

Source: R. Bruce Money and John L. Graham, "Salesperson Performance, Pay, and Job Satisfaction: Tests of a Model Using Data Collected in the U.S. and Japan," *Journal of International Business Studies*, 1999.

| Rewards | Relative Importance (mean) | |
| --- | --- | --- |
| | Japanese | Americans |
| Job security | 18.5 | 17.6 |
| Promotion | 13.7 | 14.9 |
| Merit increase in pay | 24.7 | 26.2 |
| Feeling of worthwhile accomplishment | 18.5 | 18.2 |
| Social recognition (sales club awards) | 8.1 | 5.2 |
| Personal growth and development | 16.6 | 17.8 |

Part of the corporate culture (some say peer pressure) that motivates Japanese sales representatives is the morning calisthenics. (© Tom Wagner/CORBIS SABA)

representatives in comparable Japanese and American sales organizations were asked to allocate 100 points across an array of potential rewards from work.[24] As shown in Exhibit 17.4, the results were surprisingly similar. The only real difference between the two groups was in Social Recognition, which, predictably, the Japanese rated as more important. However, the authors of the study concluded that although individual values for rewards may be similar, the social and competitive contexts still require different motivational systems.

Because the cultural differences reviewed in this and earlier chapters affect the motivational patterns of a sales force, a manager must be extremely sensitive to the personal behavior patterns of employees.[25] Individual incentives that work effectively in the United States[26] can fail completely in other cultures. For example, with Japan's emphasis on paternalism and collectivism and its system of lifetime employment and seniority, motivation through individual incentive does not work well because Japanese employees seem to derive the greatest satisfaction from being comfortable members of a group. Thus an offer of an individual financial reward for outstanding individual effort could be turned down because an employee would prefer not to appear different from peers and possibly attract their resentment. Japanese bonus systems are therefore based on group effort, and individual commission systems are quite rare. Japanese sales representatives are more motivated by the social pressure of their peers than the prospect of making more money based on individual effort. Likewise, compensation packages in Eastern European countries typically involve a substantially greater emphasis on base pay than in the United States, and performance-based incentives are less effective. Although some point out that motivational practices are changing even in Japan, such patterns do not change very quickly or without substantial efforts.

Communications are also important in maintaining high levels of motivation; foreign managers need to know that the home office is interested in their operations, and, in turn, they want to know what is happening in the parent country. Everyone performs better when well informed. However, differences in languages, culture, and communication styles[27] can make mutual understanding between managers and sales representatives more difficult.

---

[24]Money and Graham, "Sales Performance . . .", 1999.

[25]Shahid N. Bhuian and Bulent Manguc, "An Extension and Evaluation of Job Characteristics, Organizational Commitment, and Job Satisfaction in Expatriate, Guest Worker, Sales Setting," *Personal Selling & Sales Management*, 22(1), Winter 2002, pp. 1–11.

[26]Some argue "commission-centric" compensation schemes can misfire in the U.S. as well. See Jennifer Gilbert, "A Matter of Trust . . . In the Aftermath of Corporate Scandals," *Sales & Marketing Management*, March 1, 2003, pp. 30–33.

[27]Alma Mintu-Wimsatt and Julie B. Gassenheimer, "The Moderating Effects of Cultural Context in Buyer-Seller Negotiation," *Journal of Personal Selling and Sales Management*, Winter 2000, 20(1), pp. 1–9.

**CROSSING BORDERS 17.4** How Important Are Those Meetings?

In Japan, they're very important. A former American sales manager tells this story:

> I worked as general manager of the Japanese subsidiary of an American medical equipment company. Our office was in downtown Tokyo, which made for a two-hour commute for most of our salesmen. Rather than have them come into the office before beginning sales calls everyday, I instructed them to go to their appointments directly from home and to come to the office only for a weekly sales meeting. Although this was a common way for a U.S. sales force to operate, it was a disaster in Japan. Sales fell, as did morale. I quickly changed the policy and had everyone come to the office every day. Sales immediately climbed as the salesmen reinforced their group identity.

Now contrast that with how sales representatives are managed at Hewlett-Packard in the United States, as described by one of its sales executives: "We're really looking at this issue of work/family balance. If someone wants to work at home, they can, and we'll outfit their home offices at our expense, provided they have a good reason to want to work at home. If you want to drive productivity, getting people's work lives and home lives in balance is key."

Sam Palmisano, IBM's new CEO, puts it even more strongly, "To win, our players have to be on the field. We can't win the game in the locker room. . . . We want our people on the field in front of the customers, not in conference rooms talking to their managers or other staff organizations." At IBM a new corporate policy limits sales meeting to one per week.

Or consider the following statement from IBM's employment website: "Because when you walk through the door at IBM, you're going to be presented not just with attractive compensation, but also with educational reimbursement plans, flexible work schedules, global opportunities, activities, clubs, child care options—to help you learn, play, and work the way you want. After all, it's about time. How do you want to spend yours"?

Sources: Clyde V. Prestowitz, *Trading Places—How We Are Giving Away Our Future to Japan and How to Reclaim It* (New York: Basic Books, 1989); and Geoffrey Brewer et al., "The Top (25 Best Sales Forces in the U.S.)," *Sales & Marketing Management,* November 1, 1996, p. 38; Erin Strout, "Blue Skies Ahead?" *Sales & Marketing Management,* March 1, 2003, pp. 24–26 and www1.ibm.com/employment/reason/reason_22.html (April 2003).

Because promotion and the opportunity to improve status are important motivators, a company needs to make clear the opportunities for growth within the firm. In truly global firms, foreign nationals can aspire to the highest positions in the firm. Likewise, one of the greatest fears of expatriate managers, which can be easily allayed, is that they will be forgotten by the home office. Blending company sales objectives and the personal objectives of the salespeople and other employees is a task worthy of the most skilled manager. The U.S. manager must be constantly aware that many of the techniques used to motivate U.S. personnel and their responses to these techniques are based on the seven basic cultural premises discussed in Chapter 5. Therefore, each method used to motivate a foreigner should be examined for cultural compatibility.

## Designing Compensation Systems

**For Expatriates**  Developing an equitable and functional compensation plan that combines balance, consistent motivation, and flexibility is extremely challenging in international operations. This is especially true when a company operates in a number of countries, when it has individuals who work in a number of countries, or when the sales force is composed of expatriate and local personnel. Fringe benefits play a major role in many countries. Those working in high-tax countries prefer liberal expense accounts and fringe benefits that are nontaxable instead of direct income subject to high taxes. Fringe-benefit costs are high in Europe, ranging from 35 to 60 percent of salary.

Pay can be a significant factor in making it difficult for a person to be repatriated. Often those returning home realize they have been making considerably more money with a lower cost of living in the overseas market; returning to the home country means a cut in pay and a cut in standard of living.

Conglomerate operations that include domestic and foreign personnel cause the greatest problems in compensation planning.[28] Expatriates tend to compare their compensation with what they would have received at the home office during the same time, and local personnel and expatriate personnel are likely to compare notes on salary. Although any differences in the compensation level may easily and logically be explained, the group receiving the lower amount almost always feels aggrieved and mistreated.

Short-term assignments for expatriates further complicate the compensation issue, particularly when the short-term assignments extend into a longer time. In general, short-term assignments involve payments of overseas premiums (sometimes called **separation allowances** if the family does not go along), all excess expenses, and allowances for tax differentials. Longer assignments can include home-leave benefits or travel allowances for the spouse.

Besides rewarding an individual's contribution to the firm, a compensation program can be used effectively to recruit, develop, motivate, or retain personnel. Most recommendations for developing a compensation program suggest that a program focus on whichever one of these purposes fits the needs of a particular situation. If all four purposes are targeted, it can result in unwieldy programs that become completely unmanageable. International compensation programs also provide additional payments for hardship locations and special inducements to reluctant personnel to accept overseas employment and to remain in the position.

## For a Global Sales Force

Compensation plans of American companies vary substantially around the globe, reflecting the economic and cultural differences in the diverse markets served. As reflected in Exhibit 17.5, some experts feel compensation plans in Japan and Southern Europe are most different from the standard U.S. approach. Those same experts believe that generally compensation schemes around the world are becoming more similar to the U.S. system with its emphasis on commissions based on individual performance. However, the data in Exhibit 17.5 still reflect the locations of the larger differences.[29]

One company went to great lengths to homogenize its worldwide compensation scheme. Beginning in 1996 IBM rolled out what is perhaps the most global approach to compensating a worldwide sales force.[30] The main features of that plan, which applies to 140,000 sales executives in 165 countries, are presented in Exhibit 17.6. The plan was developed in response to "global" complaints from sales representatives that the old plan was confusing and did not provide for work done outside one's territory (such as in the scenario presented in Crossing Borders 17.1), and that it therefore did not promote cross-border teamwork. IBM sales incentive managers from North America, Latin America, Asia Pacific, and Europe worked together with consultants on the design for some nine months. At first glance it may appear that IBM is making the cardinal error of trying to force a plan developed centrally onto sales offices literally spread around the world and across diverse cultures; however, the compensation plan still allows substantial latitude for local managers. Compensation managers in each country determine the frequency of incentive payouts and the split between base and incentive pay, while following a global

---

[28]For a still excellent discussion of the problems of constructing a compensation plan for expatriates, nationals, and third-country nationals, see Michael Harvey, "Empirical Evidence of Recurring International Compensation Problems," *Journal of International Business Studies,* 4th Quarter, 1993, pp. 785–799. Chao C. Chen, Jaepil Choi, and Shu-Chen Chi, "Making Justice Sense of Local-Expatriate Compensation Disparity," *Academy of Management Journal,* 45(4), August 2002, pp. 807–817; Anna Healy Fenton, "Expats Get Seven Times the Perks of Local Workers," *South China Morning Post,* February 7, 2003, p. 5.

[29]Personal interview with David J. Cichelli, Vice President, Alexander Group, on May 7, 2003.

[30]Michele Marchetti, "Gamble: IBM Replaces Its Outdated Compensation Plan with a World Wide Framework. Will It Pay Off?" *Sales & Marketing Management,* July 1996, pp. 65–69. IBM continues to globalize its sales management practices. See Erin Strout, "Blue Skies Ahead? IBM Is Transforming the Way Its Sales Force Does Business," *Sales & Marketing Management,* March 1, 2003, pp. 24–27.

**Exhibit 17.5**   Global Similarity to U.S. Compensation Plans

| Countries/Regions | | Degree of Plan Similarity with the United States | | | | | |
|---|---|---|---|---|---|---|---|
| | | Eligibility | Performance Measures | Weighting | Plan Mechanics | Mix/ Leverage | Payout Frequency |
| Europe | United Kingdom | | | | | | |
| | Scandinavia | | | | | | |
| | France | | | | | | |
| | Germany | | | | | | |
| | Spain/Italy | | | | | | |
| Southeast Asia | Hong Kong | | | | | | |
| | Korea | | | | | | |
| | Taiwan | | | | | | |
| | Malaysia | | | | | | |
| | Indonesia | | | | | | |
| | (Singapore) | | | | | | |
| | Australia | | | | | | |
| Japan | | | | | | | |
| Canada | | | | | | | |
| South America | | | | | | | |

☐ Similar      ☐ Varies      ☐ Dissimilar

**Data represent multiple client projects conducted by The Alexander Group Inc. for primarily high-technology industry sales organizations.**

Source: David G. Schick and David J. Cichelli, "Developing Incentive Compensation Strategies in a Global Sales Environment," *ACA Journal*, Autumn 1996; updated based on interview with David J. Cichelli, Vice President of the Alexander Group, in May 2003.

scheme of performance measures. Thus the system allows for a high incentive component in countries like the United States and high base-salary components in countries like Japan.

Perhaps the most valuable information gained during IBM's process of revamping its sales compensation scheme was the following list of the "do's and don'ts" of global compensation:[31]

1. Do involve representatives from key countries.
2. Do allow local managers to decide the mix between base and incentive pay.
3. Do use consistent performance measures (results paid for) and emphasis on each measure.
4. Do allow local countries flexibility in implementations.
5. Do use consistent communication and training themes worldwide.
6. Don't design the plan centrally and dictate to local offices.
7. Don't create a similar framework for jobs with different responsibilities.
8. Don't require consistency on every performance measure within the incentive plan.
9. Don't assume cultural differences can be managed through the incentive plan.
10. Don't proceed without the support of senior sales executives worldwide.

[31]Ibid.

**Exhibit 17.6**
A Compensation Blueprint: How IBM Pays 140,000 Sales Executives Worldwide

Source: Adapted from Michele Marchetti, "Gamble: IBM Replaces Its Outdated Compensation Plan with a World Wide Framework. Will It Pay Off?" *Sales and Marketing Management*, July 1996, pp. 65–69.

| Total Compensation | | Plan Components | Payout Frequency | Pay Measurements | Number of Measurements Used to Calculate |
|---|---|---|---|---|---|
| **Benefits** | | | | | |
| **Variable Pay** → | | **Corporate Objectives** | **Annually** | **Bonus payment (based on)** • **Profit** • **Customer satisfaction** | **2** |
| **Incentive Compensation** → | | **Teamwork** | **Monthly** | **20% of incentive compensation** • **Work team performance** • **Industry performance** | **2** |
| | | **Personal Contribution** | **Quarterly** | **60% of incentive compensation** • **Growth** • **Solutions** • **Channels/partners** • **Profit contribution** | **1–2** |
| | | **Challenges/ Contests** | **As earned** | **20% of incentive compensation** • **National** • **Local** | **1–4** |
| **Recognition** | | | | | |
| **Base Salary** | | | | | |

# Evaluating and Controlling Sales Representatives

Evaluation and control of sales representatives in the United States is a relatively simple task. In many sales jobs, emphasis is placed on individual performance, which can easily be measured by sales revenues generated (often compared with past performance, forecasts, or quotas). In short, a good sales representative produces big numbers. However, in many countries the evaluation problem is more complex, particularly in relationship-oriented cultures, where teamwork is favored over individual effort. Performance measures require closer observation and may include the opinions of customers, peers, and supervisors. Of course, on the other hand, managers of sales forces operating in relationship-oriented cultures may see measures of individual performance as relatively unimportant.

One study comparing American and Japanese sales representatives' performance illustrates such differences.[32] Supervisors' ratings of the representatives on identical performance scales were used in both countries. The distribution of performance of the Japanese was statistically normal—a few high performers, a few low, but most in the middle. The American distribution was different—a few high, most in the middle, but almost no low performers. In the United States, poor performers either quit (because they are not making any money) or they are fired. In Japan the poor performers stay with the company and are seldom fired. Thus sales managers in Japan have a problem their American counterparts do not: how to motivate poor performers. Indeed, sales management textbooks in the United States usually include material on how to deal with "plateaued" salespeople, but say little about poor performers because the latter are not a problem.

The primary control tool used by American sales managers is the incentive system. Because of the Internet and fax machines, more American sales representatives operate out of offices in their homes and see supervisors infrequently. Organizations have become quite flat and spans of control increasingly broad in recent years. However, in many other countries spans of control can be quite narrow by American standards—even in Australia and particularly in Japan. In the latter country, supervisors spend much more time with fewer subordinates. Corporate culture and frequent interactions with peers and supervisors are the means of motivation and control of sales representatives in relationship-oriented cultures like Japan.

---

[32]Money and Graham, "Salesperson Performance," 1999.

# Preparing U.S. Personnel for Foreign Assignments

Estimates of the annual cost of sending and supporting a manager and his or her family in a foreign assignment range from 150 to 400 percent of base salary. The cost in money (some estimates are in the $300,000 to $600,00 range) and morale increases substantially if the expatriate requests a return home before completing the normal tour of duty (a normal stay is two to four years). In addition, if repatriation into domestic operations is not successful and the employee leaves the company, an indeterminately high cost in low morale and loss of experienced personnel results. To reduce these problems, international personnel management has increased planning for expatriate personnel to move abroad, remain abroad, and then return to the home country. The planning process must begin prior to the selection of those who go abroad and extend to their specific assignments after returning home. Selection, training, compensation, and career development policies (including repatriation) should reflect the unique problems of managing the expatriate.

Besides the job-related criteria for a specific position, the typical candidate for an international assignment is married, has two school-aged children, is expected to stay overseas three years, and has the potential for promotion into higher management levels. These characteristics of the typical expatriate are the basis of most of the difficulties associated with getting the best-qualified personnel to go overseas, keeping them there, and assimilating them on their return.

## Overcoming Reluctance to Accept a Foreign Assignment

Concerns for career and family are the most frequently mentioned reasons for a manager to refuse a foreign assignment. The most important career-related reservation is the fear that a two- or three-year absence will adversely affect opportunities for advancement. This "out of sight, out of mind" fear (as exemplified in the opening Global Perspective) is closely linked to the problems of repatriation. Without evidence of advance planning to protect career development, better-qualified and ambitious personnel may decline the offer to go abroad. However, if candidates for expatriate assignments are picked thoughtfully, returned to the home office at the right moment, and rewarded for good performance with subsequent promotions at home, companies find recruiting of executives for international assignments eased.

Even though the career development question may be adequately answered with proper planning, concern for family may interfere with many accepting an assignment abroad. Initially, most potential candidates are worried about uprooting a family and settling into a strange environment. Questions about the education of the children, isolation from family and friends, proper health care, and, in some countries, the potential for violence reflect the misgivings a family faces when relocating to a foreign country. Special compensation packages are the typical way to deal with this problem. A hardship allowance, allowances to cover special educational requirements that frequently include private schools, housing allowances, and extended all-expense-paid vacations are part of compensation packages designed to overcome family-related problems with an overseas assignment. Ironically, the solution to one problem creates a later problem when that family returns to the United States and must give up those extra compensation benefits used to induce them to accept the position.

## Reducing the Rate of Early Returns

After the employee and family accept the assignment abroad, the next problem is keeping them there for the assigned time. The attrition rate of those selected for overseas positions can be very high, although some studies suggest it is declining overall.[33] One firm with a hospital management contract experienced an annualized failure rate of 20 percent—not high when compared with the construction contractor who started out in Saudi Arabia with 155 Americans and was down to 65 after only two months.

The most important reasons a growing number of companies are including an evaluation of an employee's family among selection criteria are the high cost of sending an expatriate

---

[33]Gary S. Insch and John D. Daniels, "Causes and Consequences of Declining Early Departure from Foreign Assignments," *Business Horizons*, November–December, 45(6), pp. 39–48, 2003.

American expatriates flock to stores like this one in Amsterdam. Inside you'll find not only books in English, but also Kraft macaroni and cheese, Bisquick, and other hard-to-find-in-Europe staples of the American diet.

abroad and increasing evidence that unsuccessful family adjustment is the single most important reason for expatriate dissatisfaction and the resultant request for return home. In fact, a study of personnel directors of over 300 international firms found that the inability of the manager's spouse to adjust to a different physical or cultural environment was the primary reason for an expatriate's failure to function effectively in a foreign assignment. One researcher estimated that 75 percent of families sent to a foreign post experience adjustment problems with children or have marital discord. One executive suggests that there is so much pressure on the family that if there are any cracks in the marriage and you want to save it, think long and hard about taking a foreign assignment.

Dissatisfaction is caused by the stress and trauma of adjusting to new and often strange cultures. The employee has less trouble adjusting than family members; a company's expatriate moves in a familiar environment even abroad and is often isolated from the cultural differences that create problems for the rest of the family. And about half of American expatriate employees receive cross-cultural training before the trip—much more often than their families.[34] Family members have far greater daily exposure to the new culture but are often not given assistance in adjusting. New consumption patterns must be learned, from grocery shopping to seeking healthcare services.[35] Family members frequently cannot be employed and, in many cultures, female members of the family face severe social restrictions. In Saudi Arabia, for example, the woman's role is strictly dictated. In one situation, a woman's hemline offended a religious official who, in protest, sprayed black paint on her legs. In short, the greater problems of culture shock befall the family. Certainly any recruiting and selection procedure should include an evaluation of the family's ability to adjust.

Families with the potential and the personality traits that would enable them to adjust to a different environment may still become dissatisfied with living abroad if they are not properly prepared for the new assignment. More and more companies realize the need for cross-cultural training to prepare families for their new homes. One- to two-day briefings to two- to three-week intensive programs that include all members of the family are provided to assist assimilation into new cultures. Language training, films, discussions, and lectures on cultural differences, potential problems, and stress areas in adjusting to a new way of life are provided to minimize the frustration of the initial cultural shock. This cultural training helps a family anticipate problems and eases adjustment. After the family is abroad, some companies even provide a local ombudsman (someone experienced in the country) to whom members can take their problems and get immediate assistance. Although the cost of preparing a family for an overseas assignment may appear high, it must be weighed against estimates that the measurable cost of prematurely returned families could cover cross-cultural training for 300 to 500 families. Companies that do not prepare employees and their families for culture shock have the highest incidence of premature return to the United States.

### Successful Expatriate Repatriation

A Conference Board study reported that many firms have sophisticated plans for executives going overseas but few have comprehensive programs to deal with the return home. Many have noted that too often repatriated workers are a valuable resource neglected or wasted by inexperienced U.S. management.[36]

[34]Visit www.natwestoffshore.com for a quick view of the kinds of services provided by expatriate preparation companies.

[35]Mary C. Gilly, Lisa Penaloza, and Kenneth M. Kambara, "The Role of Consumption in Expatriate Adjustment and Satisfaction," working paper, Graduate School of Management, University of California, Irvine, 2004.

[36]Joann S. Lublin, "Making the Transition Back to Local Work After an Overseas Job," *Wall Street Journal*, April 1, 2003, p. B1.

Low morale and a growing rate of attrition among returning expatriates have many causes. Some complaints and problems are family related, while others are career related. The family-related problems generally deal with financial and lifestyle readjustments. Some expatriates find that, in spite of higher compensation programs, their net worths have not increased, and the inflation of intervening years makes it impossible to buy a home comparable to the one they sold on leaving. The hardship compensation programs used to induce the executive to go abroad also create readjustment problems on the return home. Such compensation benefits frequently permitted the family to live at a much higher level abroad than at home (for example, yard boys, chauffeurs, domestic help, and so forth). Because most compensation benefits are withdrawn when employees return to the home country, their standard of living decreases and they must readjust. Unfortunately, little can be done to ameliorate these kinds of problems short of transferring the managers to other foreign locations. Current thinking suggests that the problem of dissatisfaction with compensation and benefits upon return can be lessened by reducing benefits when overseas. Rather than provide the family abroad with hardship payments, some companies are considering reducing payments on the premise that the assignment abroad is an integral requirement for growth, development, and advancement within the firm.

Family dissatisfaction, which causes stress within the family on returning home, is not as severe a problem as career-related complaints. A returning expatriate's dissatisfaction with the perceived future is usually the reason many resign their positions after returning to the United States. The problem is not unique to U.S. citizens; Japanese companies have similar difficulties with their personnel. The most frequently heard complaint involves the lack of a detailed plan for the expatriate's career when returning home. New home-country assignments are frequently mundane and do not reflect the experience gained or the challenges met during foreign assignment. Some feel their time out of the mainstream of corporate affairs made them technically obsolete and thus ineffective in competing immediately on return. Finally, there is some loss of status requiring ego adjustment when an executive returns home.

Companies with the least amount of returnee attrition differ from those with the highest attrition in one significant way: personal career planning for the expatriate.[37] This planning begins with the decision to send the person abroad. The initial transfer abroad should be made in the context of a long-term company career plan. Under these circumstances, the individual knows not only the importance of the foreign assignment but also when to expect to return and at what level. Near the end of the foreign assignment, the process for repatriation is begun. The critical aspect of the return home is to keep the executive completely informed regarding such matters as the proposed return time, new assignment and an indication of whether it is interim or permanent, new responsibilities, and future prospects. In short, returnees should know where they are going and what they will be doing next month and several years ahead.

A report on what MNCs are doing to improve the reentry process suggests five steps:

1. Commit to reassigning expatriates to meaningful positions.

2. Create a mentor program. Mentors are typically senior executives who monitor company activities, keep the expatriate informed on company activities, and act as liaison between the expatriate and various headquarters departments.

3. Offer a written job guarantee stating what the company is obligated to do for the expatriate on return.

4. Keep the expatriate in touch with headquarters through periodic briefings and headquarters visits.

5. Prepare the expatriate and family for repatriation when a return date is set.

---

[37]Aimin Yan, Guorong Zhu, and Douglas T. Hall, "International Assignments for Career Building," *Academy of Management Review*, 27(3), July 2002, pp. 373–391.

Some believe the importance of preparing the employee and family for culture shock upon return is on a par with preparation for going abroad.

## Developing Cultural Awareness

Many businesses focus on the functional skills needed in international marketing, overlooking the importance of cultural knowledge. Just as the idea "if a product sells well in Dallas it will sell well in Hong Kong" is risky, so is the idea that "a manager who excels in Dallas will excel in Hong Kong." Most expatriate failures are not caused by lack of management or technical skills but rather by lack of an understanding of cultural differences and their effect on management skills. As the world becomes more interdependent and as companies depend more on foreign earnings, there is a growing need for companies to develop cultural awareness among those posted abroad.

Just as someone can achieve good social skills (i.e., an ability to remain poised and be in control under all social situations), so too can good cultural skills be developed. These skills serve a similar function in varying cultural situations; they provide the individual with the ability to relate to a different culture even when the individual is unfamiliar with the details of that particular culture. Cultural skills can be learned just as social skills can be learned. People with cultural skills can:

- Communicate respect and convey verbally and nonverbally a positive regard and sincere interest in people and their culture.
- Tolerate ambiguity and cope with cultural differences and the frustration that frequently develops when things are different and circumstances change.
- Display empathy by understanding other people's needs and differences from their point of view.
- Remain nonjudgmental about the behavior of others, particularly with reference to their own value standards.
- Recognize and control the self-reference criteria, that is, recognize their own culture and values as an influence on their perceptions, evaluations, and judgment in a situation.
- Laugh things off—a good sense of humor helps when frustration levels rise and things do not work as planned.

## The Changing Profile of the Global Manager

Until recently the road to the top was well marked. Surveys of chief executives consistently reported that more than three-quarters had finance, manufacturing, or marketing backgrounds. As the post–World War II period of growing markets and domestic-only competition fades, however, so too does the narrow one-company, one-industry chief executive. In the new millennium increasing international competition, the globalization of companies, technology, demographic shifts, and the speed of overall change will govern the choice of company leaders. It will be difficult for a single-discipline individual to reach the top in the future.

The executive recently picked to head Procter & Gamble's U.S. operations is a good example of the effect globalization is having on businesses and the importance of experience, whether in Japan, Europe, or elsewhere. The head of all P&G's U.S. business was born in the Netherlands, received an MBA from Rotterdam's Eramus University, then rose through P&G's marketing ranks in Holland, the United States, and Austria. After proving his mettle in Japan, he moved to P&G's Cincinnati, Ohio, headquarters to direct its push into East Asia, and then to his new position. Speculation is that if he succeeds in the United States, as he did in Japan, he will be a major contender for the top position at P&G.

Fewer companies today limit their search for senior-level executive talent to their home countries. Coca-Cola's former CEO, who began his ascent to the top in his native Cuba, and the former IBM vice chairman, a Swiss national who rose through the ranks in Europe, are two prominent examples of individuals who rose to the top of firms outside their home countries.

## CROSSING BORDERS 17.5   Iberia Grinds Airbus and Boeing

The principal characters were (1) Spain's Iberia Airlines CFO, Enrique Dupuy de Lome, (2) Boeing's top salesman (American), Toby Bright, and (3) Airbus' top salesman, John Leahy (American). In the crashed commercial jet market of 2003 the two Americans were fighting fiercely for the Spaniard's business.

And Señor Dupuy was having a great time, "Everything [in the negotiations] has been structured to maintain tension up to the last minute." The Americans were sweating. The order was for 12 wide-body jets for a total price of about $2 billion.

Leahy thought he had the inside edge, being the European supplier. But Dupuy put the heat on him by shopping for used 747s in Singapore. Terrorism threats, the war in Iraq, and SARS were killing air travel markets, and the airlines were grounding older jets with higher operating costs. Next Dupuy had to woo a skeptical Toby Bright into the game, and he succeeded in doing so over an expensive dinner in London.

Mr. Leahy not only sell jets, he also spends most of his time sitting in one—about 220 days each year. During the negotiations he made several trips from Airbus headquarters in Toulouse, France, to Madrid only to sit long hours into the night arguing with the Iberia team about the number of seats you can fit into a Boeing 777. Iberia argued they could put 30 more seats in the Boeing than the Airbus A340.

Meanwhile Dupuy used another lever on Leahy. Back in 1995 Leahy had conceded an asset-value guarantee to Iberia to consummate another 18-jet sale. That previous guarantee was haunting Leahy now as Dupuy threatened to make Airbus buy back the older planes at a high, promised price if he didn't cut prices further. Moreover, a new internal analysis by Iberia staff members favored the Boeing jets over the Airbus.

Señor Dupuy continued to keep all three options on the table. He interrupted a skiing vacation with his family in the Pyrenees for a four-hour lunch with Leahy. Then he flew to Seattle to further encourage Bright. And he kept talking about the Singapore Airlines 747s. As the global airline market sank deeper, both the companies cut prices further. Dupuy was enjoying himself immensely.

The deal clincher was a phone conversation between the CEOs of Iberia and Airbus. The two Europeans made what Boeing's Toby Bright criticized as the "easiest decision." John Leahy had won the day? However, Iberia's news release crowed about Airbus's new price guarantees, and Dupuy bragged he had won "extraordinary conditions." Personal selling is tough business, even when you win!

Sources: Daniel Michaels, "In Clandestine World of Airplane Contracts, An Inside Look at a Deal," *Wall Street Journal Europe*, March 10, 2003, p. A1; Daniel Michaels and J. Lynn Lunsford, "Airbus Could Overtake Boeing," *Wall Street Journal Europe*, January 14, 2003, p. A5.

Some companies, such as Colgate-Palmolive, believe that it is important to have international assignments early in a person's career, and international training is an integral part of their entry-level development programs. Colgate recruits its future managers from the world's best colleges and business schools. Acceptance is highly competitive, and successful applicants have a BA or MBA with proven leadership skills, fluency in at least one language besides English, and some experience living abroad. A typical recruit might be a U.S. citizen who has spent a year studying in another country, or a national of another country who was educated in the United States.

Trainees begin their careers in a two-year, entry-level, total-immersion program that consists of stints in various Colgate departments. A typical rotation includes time in the finance, manufacturing, and marketing departments and an in-depth exposure to the company's marketing system. During that phase, trainees are rotated through the firm's ad agency, marketing research, and product management departments and then work seven months as field salespeople. At least once during the two years, trainees accompany their mentors on business trips to a foreign subsidiary. The company's goal is to develop in their trainees the skills they need to become effective marketing managers, domestically or globally.

On completion of the program, trainees can expect a foreign posting, either immediately after graduation or soon after an assignment in the United States. The first positions are not in London or Paris, as many might hope, but in developing countries such as Brazil, the Philippines, or maybe Zambia. Because international sales are so important to Colgate (60 percent of its total revenues are generated abroad), a manager might not return to the United States after the first foreign assignment but rather move from one overseas post to another, developing into a career internationalist, which could open to a CEO position.

Companies whose foreign receipts make up a substantial portion of their earnings, and who see themselves as global companies rather than as domestic companies doing business in foreign markets, are the most active in making the foreign experience an integrated part of a successful corporate career. Indeed, for many companies a key threshold seems to be that when overseas revenues surpass domestic revenues, then the best people in the company want to work on international accounts. Such a global orientation then begins to permeate the entire organization—from personnel policies to marketing and business strategies. Such was the case with Gillette, which in the early 1990s made a significant recruitment and management-development decision when it decided to develop managers internally. Gillette's international human resources department implemented its international-trainee program, designed to supply a steady stream of managerial talent from within its own ranks. Trainees are recruited from all over the world, and when their training is complete they return to their home countries to become part of Gillette's global management team.

## Foreign Language Skills

Reviews are mixed on the importance of a second language for a career in international business. There are those whose attitude about another language is summed up in the statement that "the language of international business is English." Others feel that even if you speak one or two languages, you may not be needed in a country whose language you speak. So, is language important or not?

Proponents of language skills argue that learning a language improves cultural understanding and business relationships. Others point out that to be taken seriously in the business community, the expatriate must be at least conversational in the host language. Particularly when it comes to selling in foreign countries, languages are important. Says a Dutch sales training expert, "People expect to buy from sales reps they can relate to, and who understand their language and culture. They're often cold toward Americans trying to sell them products."

Some recruiters want candidates who speak at least one foreign language, even if the language will not be needed in a particular job. Having learned a second language is a strong signal to the recruiter that the candidate is willing to get involved in someone else's culture.

Though most companies offer short, intensive language-training courses for managers being sent abroad, many are making stronger efforts to recruit people who are bilingual or multilingual. According to the director of personnel at Coca-Cola, when his department searches its database for people to fill overseas posts, the first choice is often someone who speaks more than one language.

The authors feel strongly that language skills are of great importance; if you want to be a major player in international business in the future, learn to speak other languages or you might not make it—your competition will be those European students described in Crossing Borders 17.6. There is a joke that foreigners tell about language skills. It goes something like this: What do you call a person who speaks three or more languages? Multilingual. What do you call a person who speaks two languages? Bilingual. What do you call a person who speaks only one language? An American! Maybe the rest of the world knows something we don't.[38]

---

[38]Thane Peterson, "The Importance of Being Multilingual," *BusinessWeek Online*, September 6, 2002.

**CROSSING BORDERS 17.6** A Look into the Future: Tomorrow's International
Leaders? An Education for the Twenty-First Century

A school supported by the European Union teaches Britons, French, Germans, Dutch, and others to be future Europeans. The European School in a suburb of Brussels has students from 12 nations who come to be educated for life and work, not as products of motherland or fatherland but as Europeans. The EU runs ten European Schools in Western Europe, enrolling 17,000 students from kindergarten to grade 12. Graduates emerge superbly educated, usually trilingual, and very, very European.

The schools are a linguistic and cultural mélange. There are native speakers of 36 different languages represented in one school alone. Each year students take fewer and fewer classes in their native tongue. Early on, usually in first grade, they begin a second language, known as the "working language," which must be English, French, or German. A third language is introduced in the seventh year, and a fourth may be started in the ninth.

By the time students reach year 11, they are taking history, geography, economics, advanced math, music, art, and gym in the working language. When the students are in groups talking, they are constantly switching languages to "whatever works."

Besides language, students learn history, politics, literature, and music from the perspective of all the European countries—in short, European cultures. The curriculum is designed to teach the French, German, Briton, and other nationalities to be future Europeans.

This same approach is being taken at the MBA level as well. The well-respected European School of Management has campuses in several different cities— Berlin, Paris, Oxford, and Madrid. Students spend part of their time in each of the campuses. American MBA programs are beginning to imitate such programs. The University of Chicago School of Business now has campuses in Barcelona, Spain, and Singapore. The Fuqua School at Duke offers a unique executive MBA program involving travel to several foreign countries and a substantial percentage of teaching delivered interactively over the Internet. This last program attracts students from all over the world who are willing to pay six-figure tuition.

Sources: Glynn Mapes, "Polyglot Students Are Weaned Early off Mother Tongue," *Wall Street Journal*, March 6, 1990, p. A1. Reprinted by permission of *The Wall Street Journal*, © 1990 Dow Jones & Company, Inc. All Rights Reserved Worldwide; Kevin Cape, "Tips on Choosing the Right One, International Schools," *International Herald Tribune*, January 25, 2003, p. 7; and Victoria Griffith, "A Degree that Bridges the World," *Financial Times*, March 10, 2003, p. 13.

## Summary

An effective international sales force constitutes one of the international marketer's greatest concerns. The company's sales force represents the major alternative method of organizing a company for foreign distribution and, as such, is on the front line of a marketing organization.

The role of marketers in both domestic and foreign markets is rapidly changing, along with the composition of international managerial and sales forces. Such forces have many unique requirements that are being filled by expatriates, locals, third-country nationals, or a combination of the three. In recent years, the pattern of development was to place more emphasis on local personnel operating in their own lands. This, in turn, highlighted the importance of adapting U.S. managerial techniques to local needs.

The development of an effective marketing organization calls for careful recruiting, selecting, training, motivating, and compensating of expatriate personnel and their families to ensure maximization of a company's return on its personnel expenditures. The most practical method of maintaining an efficient international sales and marketing force is careful, concerted planning at all stages of career development.

## Questions

1. Define the following terms:

   expatriate, 504          TCNs, 509
   local nationals, 506     separation allowance, 516

2. Why may it be difficult to adhere to set job criteria in selecting foreign personnel? What compensating actions might be necessary?

3. Why does a global sales force cause special compensation problems? Suggest some alternative solutions.

4. Under which circumstances should expatriate salespeople be utilized?

5. Discuss the problems that might be encountered in having an expatriate sales manager supervising foreign salespeople.

6. "To some extent, the exigencies of the personnel situation will dictate the approach to the overseas sales organization." Discuss.

7. How do legal factors affect international sales management?

8. How does the sales force relate to company organization? To channels of distribution?

9. "It is costly to maintain an international sales force." Comment.

10. Adaptability and maturity are traits needed by all salespeople. Why should they be singled out as especially important for international salespeople?

11. Can a person develop good cultural skills? Discuss.

12. Describe the attributes of a person with good cultural skills.

13. Interview a local company that has a foreign sales operation. Draw an organizational chart for the sales function and explain why that particular structure was used by that company.

14. Evaluate the three major sources of multinational personnel.

15. Which factors complicate the task of motivating the foreign sales force?

16. Why do companies include an evaluation of an employee's family among selection criteria for an expatriate assignment?

17. "Concerns for career and family are the most frequently mentioned reasons for a manager to refuse a foreign assignment." Why?

18. Discuss and give examples of why returning U.S. expatriates are often dissatisfied. How can these problems be overcome?

19. If "the language of international business is English," why is it important to develop a skill in a foreign language? Discuss.

20. The global manager of 2020 will have to meet many new challenges. Draw up a sample résumé for someone who could be considered for a top-level executive position in a global firm.

# pricing for international markets

## CHAPTER 18

## CHAPTER LEARNING OBJECTIVES

What you should learn from Chapter 18:

- Components of pricing as competitive tools in international marketing

- The pricing pitfalls directly related to international marketing

- How to control pricing in parallel imports or gray markets

- Price escalation and how to minimize its effect

- Countertrading and its place in international marketing practices

- The mechanics of price quotations

# Global Perspective

## THE PRICE WAR

The battle between Procter & Gamble and Kimberly-Clark is bringing Pampers and Huggies, respectively, to places they have never been, forcing down diaper prices worldwide and expanding the global market for disposable diapers. A battle in Brazil between the two giants gives an interesting glimpse of the global markets of tomorrow. Disposable diapers are still considered a luxury by the vast majority of Brazil's 160 million people whose average annual income is under $4,000. Before P&G and Kimberly arrived, rich and poor alike generally made do with cloth or nothing at all. The disposables that were available were expensive, bulky, and leaky.

When less than 5 percent of the Brazilian mass market used disposable diapers, P&G launched Pampers Uni, a no-frills, unisex diaper. Before Uni, it cost more to pay for disposable diapers than to pay for a maid to wash the cloth ones. The introduction of the relatively cheap, high-quality Uni fundamentally changed the economics of the diaper market for most middle-class Brazilians.

The plan was to put such nonessentials as disposable diapers within the reach of millions of Brazilians for the first time. At the same time, the Brazilian economy was on the upswing—inflation had subsided and overnight the purchasing power of the poor increased by 20 percent. Low-priced products flew off the shelves. P&G had to truck in diapers from Argentina as it struggled to open new production lines.

But the good days didn't last. Kimberly-Clark entered the market and began importing Huggies from Argentina. With the help of a Unilever unit as its Brazilian distributor, Kimberly gained immediate distribution across the country and quickly made deep inroads into the market. Unilever agreed to work with Kimberly-Clark because its archrival in soap was P&G just as Kimberly-Clark's archrival in diapers was P&G. The two companies had earlier entered into a global alliance to look for win-win situations where it was in both their best interests to partner and help each other, from a competitive standpoint, against the dominant P&G. The Brazilian market was the perfect case for cooperation.

With Unilever's help, Kimberly "push girls" invaded markets to demonstrate the diaper's absorption. Sales rose rapidly and began to exceed production. To gain more product, Kimberly formed an alliance with Kenko do Brazil, P&G's largest home-grown rival, and created the "Monica" brand. "Monica's Gang," a comic strip similar to "Peanuts" in the United States, sells four million copies monthly. São Paulo malls were crowded with thousands of kids waiting to get an Easter photo taken with actors in Monica suits, an honor that required the purchase of three packs of diapers. Monica diapers were a big hit, and Kimberly became number one in the Brazilian market.

It was a tough blow to P&G. The company had devoted an entire page of its annual report to how Pampers Uni had tripled its market share in Brazil, helping P&G "retain the number one position in a market that has grown fivefold." Now it suddenly found itself on the defensive. First it cut prices, a step P&G loathes. "Price cutting is like violence: No one wins," says the head of its Brazilian operation. Then it broadened its product range, rolling out an up-market diaper called Super-Seca, priced 25 percent higher than Pampers Uni. Later, in a flanking move, it also unveiled Confort-Seca, a bikini-style diaper originally developed for Thailand and priced 10 to 15 percent lower than the already-inexpensive Uni.

Kimberly fired back, matching the price cut and then introducing a cheaper version of Monica called Tippy Basic. Four weeks later P&G cut prices another 10 percent on Super-Seca and Confort-Seca. Despite the price cuts, the two brands were still relatively expensive; then a wave of really cheap diapers arrived. Carrefour, a French retailer that is now Brazil's biggest supermarket chain, sells crudely made Bye-Bye Pipi diapers from Mexico. Despite their inferior quality, the cheap imports pulled down diaper prices across the board.

Although both U.S. giants are taking hits on price, they also are pouring millions into advertising and direct marketing. The pitches filter down to include an aisle in a supermarket on the outskirts of São Paulo where a Kimberly representative tries to explain to a grandmother cradling a package of Puppet, the cheapest brand in the store, that with diapers, like most products, you get what you pay for. First, he touts the merits of Kimberly's top-of-the-line Huggies and then, getting nowhere, tries to sell her on the cheaper Monica. Both are superior diapers that last for hours and don't leak, he says. The grandmother isn't swayed. "My grandson needs frequent changes," she says, heading for the checkout counter with Puppet in hand.

As the companies took turns slashing prices to capture new customers, prices fell more than 60 percent between 1990 and 2000. Since P&G and Kimberly landed in Brazil the market for disposable diapers increased from 1.4 billion units in 1995 to 4 billion units in 2000, and the market is still growing.

The real war started when lower prices became so attractive that consumers who otherwise could not afford diapers came into the market. As prices continued to drop, the market grew; that attracted more producers, which were mostly small, local Brazilian companies that offered even lower-priced competitive diapers. One such company, Mili saw its market share increase from 4.8 percent in 1999 to 16.2 percent in 2002. What accounts for growth of these smaller companies? One analyst suggests that the multinationals are too sophisticated, and thus, too expensive for the Brazilian market. "Smaller companies are just supplying what consumers need at a price they can afford." But it also can be said that as prices drop, products become more attractive to a larger segment of the total market.

Sources: Raju Narisetti and Jonathan Friedland, "Disposable Income: Diaper Wars of P&G and Kimberly-Clark Now Heat Up in Brazil," *The Wall Street Journal,* June 4, 1997, p. A1; "Brazil: Procter & Gamble Increased Market Share," *SABI* (South American Business Information), May 31, 2000: "Mili Threatens Kimberly Clark," *South American Business Information,* December 17, 2002; and "Inexpensive Diapers a Problem for Large Manufacturers," *South American Business Information,* June 19, 2002. For more information, see Kimberly-Clark's website at www.kimberly-clark.com, and Procter & Gamble's at www.pg.com.

Setting the right price for a product can be the key to success or failure. Even when the international marketer produces the right product, promotes it correctly, and initiates the proper channel of distribution, the effort fails if the product is not properly priced. Although the quality of U.S. products is widely recognized in global markets, foreign buyers, like domestic buyers, balance quality and price in their purchase decisions. A product's price must reflect the quality and value the consumer perceives in the product. Of all the tasks facing the international marketer, determining what price to charge is one of the most difficult. It is further complicated when the company sells its product to customers in different country markets.

As the globalization of world markets continues, competition intensifies among multinational and home-based companies. All are seeking a solid competitive position so they can prosper as markets reach full potential. The competition for the diaper market between Kimberly-Clark, P&G, and the smaller companies illustrates how price becomes increasingly important as a competitive tool and how price competition changes the structure of a market. Whether exporting or managing overseas operations, the manager's responsibility is to set and control the actual price of goods in different markets in which different sets of variables are found: different tariffs, costs, attitudes, competition, currency fluctuations, and methods of price quotation.

This chapter focuses on the basic pricing policy questions that arise from the special cost, market, and competitive factors found in foreign markets. A discussion of price escalation and its control and factors associated with price setting and leasing is followed by a discussion of the use of countertrade as a pricing tool and a review of the mechanics of international price quotation.

## Pricing Policy

Active marketing in several countries compounds the number of pricing problems and variables relating to price policy. Unless a firm has a clearly thought-out, explicitly defined price policy, expediency rather than design establishes prices. The country in which business is being conducted, the type of product, variations in competitive conditions, and other strategic factors affect pricing activity. Price and terms of sale cannot be based on domestic criteria alone.

### Pricing Objectives

In general, price decisions are viewed two ways: pricing as an active instrument of accomplishing marketing objectives, or pricing as a static element in a business decision. If prices are viewed as an active instrument, the company uses price to achieve a specific objective, whether a targeted return on profit, a targeted market share, or some other specific goal.[1] The company that follows the second approach, pricing as a static element, probably exports only excess inventory, places a low priority on foreign business,

---

[1] S. Tamer Cavusgil, Kwog Chan, and Chun Zhang, "Strategic Orientations in Export Pricing: A Clustering Approach to Create Firm Taxonomies," *Journal of International Marketing,* 11 (1), 2003, p. 47.

and views its export sales as passive contributions to sales volume. When U.S. and Canadian international businesses were asked to rate, on a scale of 1 to 5, several factors important in price setting, total profits received an average rating of 4.7, followed by return on investment (4.41), market share (4.13), and total sales volume (4.06). Liquidity ranked the lowest (2.19).

The more control a company has over the final selling price of a product, the better it is able to achieve its marketing goals. However, it is not always possible to control end prices. The broader the product line and the larger the number of countries involved, the more complex the process of controlling prices to the end user.[2]

## Parallel Imports

Besides having to meet price competition country by country and product by product, companies have to guard against competition with their own subsidiaries or branches. Because of the different prices possible in different country markets, a product sold in one country may be exported to another and undercut the prices charged in that country. For example, to meet economic conditions and local competition, an American pharmaceutical company might sell its drugs in a developing country at a low price and then discover that these discounted drugs are being exported to a third country, where, as parallel imports, they are in direct competition with the same product sold for higher prices by the same firm.

**Parallel imports** develop when importers buy products from distributors in one country and sell them in another to distributors who are not part of the manufacturer's regular distribution system. This practice is lucrative when wide margins exist between prices for the same products in different countries. A variety of conditions can create a profitable opportunity for a parallel market.

Restrictions brought about by import quotas and high tariffs also can lead to parallel imports and make illegal imports attractive. India has a three-tier duty structure on computer parts ranging from 50 to 80 percent on imports. As a result, estimates are that as much as 35 percent of India's domestic computer hardware sales are accounted for by the gray market.

The possibility of a parallel market occurs whenever price differences are greater than the cost of transportation between two markets. In Europe, because of different taxes and competitive price structures, prices for the same product vary between countries. When this occurs, it is not unusual for companies to find themselves competing in one country with their own products imported from another European country at lower prices. Pharmaceutical companies face this problem in Italy, Greece, and Spain because of price caps imposed on prescription drugs in those countries. For example, the ulcer drug Losec sells for only $18 in Spain but goes for $39 in Germany. The heart drug Plavix costs $55 in France and sells for $79 in London. Presumably such price differentials were to cease when all restrictions to trade were eliminated in the European Union and in most cases this is true. However, the EC does not prevent countries from controlling drug prices as part of their national health plans.[3]

The drug industry tried to stop parallel trade in Europe but was overruled by European authorities. This time they are trying a different approach, restricting supplies of their products to meet only local demand, according to formulas based on prior demand and anticipated growth. The idea is that a country should receive just enough of a drug for its citizens. Wholesalers that order more with the intention of shipping the drugs to higher-priced markets would not have enough to do so. A number of major pharmaceutical companies imposed similar restrictions. The companies say these measures are intended to streamline distribution, help prevent medicine shortages, and curtail excess inventory while distributors claim the strategy is aimed at thwarting cross-border drug

---

[2]Matthew B. Meyers and Michael Harvey, "The Value of Pricing Control in Export Channels: A Governance Perspective," *Journal of International Marketing* 9 (4), 2001, p. 1.

[3]Vanessa Fuhrmans and Scott Hensley, "Drug Makers Try to Curtail Cheap Imports," *The Wall Street Journal,* April 11, 2002, A1.

## CROSSING BORDERS 18.1    How Do Levi's 501s Get to International Markets?

Levi Strauss sells in international markets—how else would 501 jeans get to market? The answer is via the gray market, or "diverters." Diverters are enterprising people who legally buy 501s at retail prices, usually during sales, and then resell them to foreign buyers. It is estimated that Levi Strauss sells millions of dollars of Levi's abroad at discount prices—all authorized sales. U.S. retail prices for Levi's 501s are $30 to $40 a pair; in Germany, they are sold to authorized wholesalers for about $40, and authorized retailers sell them at about $80. The difference of $40 or so makes it economically possible for a diverter to buy 501s in the United States and sell them to unauthorized dealers who then sell them for $60 to $70, undercutting authorized German retailers. Similar practices happen around the world. How do diverters work?

Here is an example of what is repeated in city after city all over the United States. "They come into a store in groups and buy every pair of Levi's 501 jeans they can," says one store manager. He has seen two or three vans full of people come to the store when there is a sale and buy the six-pair-a-day limit, returning day after day until the sale is over. In another retail chain store, where a similar thing was happening, a month-long storewide sale was stopped, at the behest of Levi's, after only two weeks. The Levi's are then channeled to a diverter, who exports them to unauthorized buyers throughout the world. Many eventually end up in discount stores and are sold at discounted prices relative to those distributed through approved channels. This is but one way diverters acquire merchandise. Another is for wholesalers to buy quantities in excess of their needs and then divert the excess to foreign buyers.

These practices are feasible because of the lower markups and prices of U.S. and other retailers compared with the higher costs and the resulting higher markups and prices that retailers charge in many other countries (Levi's has a higher wholesale price for foreign sales than for domestic sales).

Retail prices in the United States are often more competitive than in other countries where, historically, price competition is not as fierce. For example, besides Levi's 501s, which sell for $73 in Britain versus $45 in the United States, a Mariah Carey CD costs $23 versus $16, and Windows operating system is $243 versus $118. Some, but not all, of the price differences can be attributed to price escalation—that is, tariffs, shipping, and other costs associated with exporting—but that portion of the difference attributable to higher margins creates an opportunity for profitable diverting.

In an attempt to stop discount stores not in the manufacturer's official distribution channel from selling "unauthorized Levi's," Tesco, a U.K. supermarket chain, was sued by Levi-Strauss & Company. After a four-year court battle, Levi won when a London judge ruled that the supermarket had been selling Levi's illegally. However, Tesco, Costco, Wal-Mart, and other mass retailers cater to a vast market interested in value priced, quality products—a market Levi's misses if their products are not sold there. Consequently, Levi's developed a Signature line for Tesco that sells for about £25 a pair—£20 less than ordinary Levi's. It seems the old adage, "If you can't beat them, join them," applies.

Sources: Jim Hill, "Flight of the 501s," *Oregonian*, June 27, 1993, p. G1; "Diversion!" *Journal of Commerce*, June 26, 2000, p. WP; Jean Eaglesham and Deborah Hargreaves, "Court Left To Iron Out Brand Import Wrinkle: Levi's v. Tesco," *National Post*, January 24, 2001, p. C3; "Levi's Win In Court," *Daily Record*, August 1, 2002; and, "Levi Plans Tesco Line," *The Mirror*, April 25, 2003, p. 4.

---

trading. The fact is, "half of all demand in Britain of several products is being met by imports from low-priced countries" and companies are attempting to curtail parallel imports.

Gray market pharmaceutical sales from Canada to the United States are estimated to be about $427 million annually. That is not a large amount when compared with the $135 billion U.S. drug market, but it can be substantial for specific drugs like Paxil, Zyban, and Viagra. Although it is against U.S. law to import prescription drugs from a foreign country, including Canada, a person can travel to Canada or Mexico to make purchases or can buy over the Internet. Technically, buying over the Internet and having the drugs mailed to the United States is illegal. However, the government has taken a relatively lax view toward such purchases, provided the supply does not exceed 90 days. Thanks to the low value of the Canadian dollar and government price caps on drugs, an American can often save 50 percent to 70 percent by ordering from the 70 or more Internet pharmacies operating across Canada.

Naturally, drug companies that are hit the hardest want to put a stop to the traffic. Glaxo SmithKline, the prescription drug maker, asked all Canadian pharmacies and wholesalers to "self-certify" that they are not exporting its drugs outside Canada. Those who fail to comply have their Glaxo supplies cut off—"Glaxo products are approved by Health Canada for sale in Canada only." Some feel that this move will not solve the problem even if Glaxo is able to stop Canadian sales since there are other markets, like Australia or Ireland, where Americans are able to find less expensive drugs. The Internet trade will be hard to shut down as long as there are large price differentials among markets.[4]

**Exclusive distribution,** a practice often used by companies to maintain high retail margins in order to encourage retailers to provide extra service to customers, to stock large assortments, or to maintain the exclusive-quality image of a product, can create a favorable condition for parallel importing. Perfume and designer brands such as Gucci and Cartier are especially prone to gray markets. To maintain the image of quality and exclusivity, prices for such products traditionally include high profit margins at each level of distribution; characteristically, there are differential prices among markets and limited quantities of product, and distribution is restricted to upscale retailers. Wholesale prices for exclusive brands of fragrances are often 25 percent more in the United States than wholesale prices in other countries. These are ideal conditions for a lucrative gray market for unauthorized dealers in other countries who buy more than they need at wholesale prices lower than U.S. wholesalers pay. They then sell the excess at a profit to unauthorized U.S. retailers, but at a price lower than the retailer would have to pay to an authorized U.S. distributor.

The high-priced designer sportswear industry is also vulnerable to such practices. Nike, Adidas, and Calvin Klein were incensed to find their products being sold in one of Britain's leading supermarket chains, Tesco. Nike's Air Max Metallic trainers, which are priced at £120 ($196) in sports shops, could be purchased at Tesco for £50 ($80). Tesco had bought £8 million in Nike sportswear from overstocked wholesalers in the United States. To prevent parallel markets from developing when such marketing and pricing strategies are used, companies must maintain strong control over distribution and prices (see Exhibit 18.1).

Companies that are serious about restricting the gray market must establish and monitor controls that effectively police distribution channels. In some countries they may get help from the courts. A Taiwan court ruled that two companies that were buying Coca-Cola in the United States and shipping it to Taiwan were violating the trademark rights of both the Coca-Cola Company and its sole Taiwan licensee. The violators were prohibited from importing, displaying, or selling products bearing the Coca-Cola trademark. In other countries, the courts have not always come down on the side of the trademark owner. The reasoning is that after the trademarked item is sold, the owner's rights to control the trademarked item are lost. In a similar situation in Canada, the courts did not side with the Canadian exporter who was buying 50,000 cases of Coke a week and shipping them to Hong Kong and Japan. The exporter paid $4.25 a case plus shipping of $1.00 a case and sold them at $6.00, a nifty profit of 75 cents a case. Coca-Cola sued, but the court ruled that the product was bought and sold legally.

Where differences in prices between markets occur, the Internet makes it easy for individuals to participate in the gray market. Music CDs are especially vulnerable because of price differentials. Six foreign-owned record companies that maintain high prices through limited distribution dominate the Australian market and create a situation ripe for the gray market. CDs retail there for an average of $24 but can be purchased for about 25 to 30 percent less from the many e-stores on the Internet. It is estimated that CDs purchased directly from the United States over the Internet have led to a 5 percent fall in Australian retail sales. In the United Kingdom, gray-market CDs come from Italy, where they are about 50 percent cheaper and account for between 15 and 20 percent of sales in some releases. Sony believes that over 100,000 copies of one of Celine Dion's

---

[4]Joel Baglole, "Glaxo Tries New Tack on Cheap Canadian Drugs," *The Wall Street Journal,* January 22, 2003, p. D2.

**Exhibit 18.1**

How Gray-Market Goods End Up in U.S. Stores

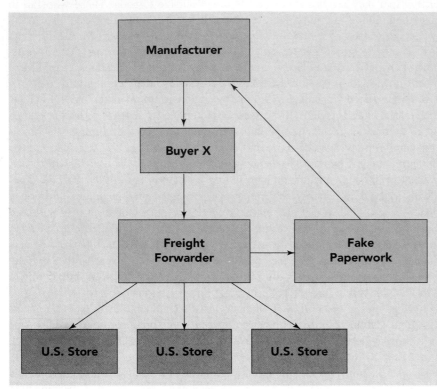

1. A major manufacturer agrees to sell its products, at a price competitive for an overseas market, to "Buyer X" who promises to sell the products overseas.

2. The manufacturer ships the goods to Buyer X.

3. Buyer X has a local freight forwarder at the port take possession of the goods.

4. Instead of shipping the goods to their supposed destination, the freight forwarder (at the behest of Buyer X) sends them to smaller distributors and discount outlets in the U.S.

5. The freight forwarder sends a bogus bill of lading to the manufacturer, so the company believes the goods have been sold overseas.

best-selling albums sold in the United Kingdom were from parallel imports. The Internet truly is a global price equalizer.

Parallel imports can do long-term damage in the market for trademarked products. Customers who unknowingly buy unauthorized imports are not sure of the quality of the item they buy, of warranty support, or of authorized service or replacement parts. Purchasers of computers, for example, may not be able to get parts because authorized dealers have no obligation to service these computers. In the case of software, the buyer may be buying counterfeit product and will not be authorized for technical support. Further, when a product fails, the consumer blames the owner of the trademark, and the quality image of the product is sullied.

With global brands and the euro making price comparison easier and the Internet facilitating purchasing, it is increasingly more difficult to differentiate prices among European markets. Companies must either harmonize prices among member states or contend with parallel imports where there are profitable differences in selling prices. Brand harmonization and price harmonization must be addressed simultaneously.

## Approaches to International Pricing

Whether the orientation is toward control over end prices or over net prices, company policy relates to the net price received. Cost and market considerations are important; a company cannot sell goods below cost of production and remain in business, nor can it sell goods at a price unacceptable in the marketplace. Firms unfamiliar with overseas marketing and firms producing industrial goods orient their pricing solely on a cost basis. Firms that employ pricing as part of the strategic mix,[5] however,

[5]For an insightful discussion of factors that influence international pricing, see Marios Theodosiou and Constantine S. Katsikeas, "Factors Influencing the Degree of International Pricing Strategy Standardization of Multinational Corporations," *Journal of International Marketing* 9 (3) 2001, p. 1.

are aware of such alternatives as market segmentation from country to country or market to market, competitive pricing in the marketplace, and other market-oriented pricing factors.

**Full-Cost versus Variable-Cost Pricing**

Firms that orient their price thinking around cost must determine whether to use variable cost or full cost in pricing their goods. In **variable-cost pricing**, the firm is concerned only with the marginal or incremental cost of producing goods to be sold in overseas markets. Such firms regard foreign sales as bonus sales and assume that any return over their variable cost makes a contribution to net profit. These firms may be able to price most competitively in foreign markets, but because they are selling products abroad at lower net prices than they are selling them in the domestic market, they may be subject to charges of dumping. In that case, they open themselves to antidumping tariffs or penalties that take away from their competitive advantage. Nevertheless, variable-cost (or *marginal*-cost) pricing is a practical approach to pricing when a company has high fixed costs and unused production capacity. Any contribution to fixed cost after variable costs are covered is profit to the company.

On the other hand, companies following the **full-cost pricing** philosophy insist that no unit of a similar product is different from any other unit in terms of cost and that each unit must bear its full share of the total fixed and variable cost.[6] This approach is suitable when a company has high variable costs relative to its fixed costs. In such cases, prices are often set on a cost-plus basis, that is, total costs plus a profit margin. Both variable-cost and full-cost policies are followed by international marketers.

**Skimming versus Penetration Pricing**

Firms must also decide when to follow a skimming or a penetration pricing policy. Traditionally, the decision of which policy to follow depends on the level of competition, the innovativeness of the product, and market characteristics.

A company uses **skimming** when the objective is to reach a segment of the market that is relatively price insensitive and thus willing to pay a premium price for the value received. If limited supply exists, a company may follow a skimming approach in order to maximize revenue and to match demand to supply. When a company is the only seller of a new or innovative product, a skimming price may be used to maximize profits until competition forces a lower price. Skimming often is used in those markets where there are only two income levels: the wealthy and the poor. Costs prohibit setting a price that is attractive to the lower-income market, so the marketer charges a premium price and directs the product to the high-income, relatively price-insensitive segment. Apparently this was the policy of Johnson & Johnson's pricing of diapers in Brazil before the arrival of P&G. Today such opportunities are fading away as the disparity in income levels is giving way to growing middle-income market segments. The existence of larger markets attracts competition and, as is often the case, the emergence of multiple product lines, thus leading to price competition.

A *penetration pricing policy* is used to stimulate market growth and capture market share by deliberately offering products at low prices. Penetration pricing most often is used to acquire and hold share of market as a competitive maneuver. However, in country markets experiencing rapid and sustained economic growth, and where large shares of the population are moving into middle-income classes, penetration pricing may be used to stimulate market growth even with minimum competition. Penetration pricing may be a more profitable strategy than skimming if it maximizes revenues and builds market share as a base for the competition that is sure to come.

Regardless of the formal pricing policies and strategies a company uses, it must be remembered that the market sets the effective price for a product. Said another way, the price must be set at a point at which the consumer perceives value received, and the price must be within reach of the target market. As a consequence, many products are sold in

---

[6]For a research report on cost variables that influence price strategy, see Mary Anne Raymond, John F. Tanner Jr., and Joghoon Kim, "Cost Complexity of Pricing Decisions for Exporters in Developing and Emerging Markets," *Journal of International Marketing* 9 (3) 2001, p. 19.

## CROSSING BORDERS 18.2 Don't Squeeze the Charmin, Mr. Whipple— Or Change the Color

The British pay twice as much as the Germans and the French, and nearly two-and-a-half times as much as Americans, for a standard four-roll pack of toilet paper. Why? Is it price gouging, the impact of the euro, the relative value of the English pound, or just culture?

The answer is rather simple: British consumers insist on a softer, more luxurious texture than their less discriminating continental and American cousins. British toilet paper is four grams heavier per square meter because it contains more fiber than European tissues. Extensive consumer testing has established that British consumers are not willing to be fobbed off with anything less.

Another factor distinguishes the British preference for a special toilet paper roll. Go to any supermarket and you will be confronted by an extraordinary choice of more than 50 colors, sizes, and brands. Honeysuckle, warm pink, summer peach, pearl white, meadow green, breeze blue, and magnolia are just some of the shades offered. The reason for this variety apparently is that the British shopper insists that toilet paper match the color scheme of the bathroom. On the continent, consumers settle happily for white, with pink thrown in as a wild alternative.

Procter & Gamble captured 10 percent of the market in less than five months after offering a stronger Charmin, but it may have gone too far. There were complaints that the "wet strength" of Charmin was unsuitable for U.K. toilets. The U.K. sewage system could handle Charmin alone, but the issue was whether the system would get clogged if several rival tissues adopted the stronger tissue. Procter & Gamble agreed to halve the strength of its Charmin toilet tissue, but will the price come down?

Sources: "Going Soft," *Economist,* March 4, 2000; and "P&G Unblocks Sewage Row with Toilet Paper Revamp," *Reuters,* May 10, 2000, and Tom Bawden, "P&G Agrees to Modigy Charman After Conceding Blockage Threat," *Marketing Week (UK),* May 11, 2000, p. 7.

very small units in some markets in order to bring the unit price within reach of the target market. Warner-Lambert's launch of its five-unit pack of Bubbaloo bubble gum in Brazil failed—even though bubble gum represents over 72 percent of the overall gum sector—because it was priced above the target market. A relaunch of a single-unit "pillow" pack brought the price within range and enabled the brand to quickly gain a respectable market share.

As a country's economy grows and there is a more equitable distribution of wealth, multiple income levels develop, distinct market segments emerge, and multiple price levels and price/quality perceptions increase in importance. As an example, the market for electronic consumer goods in China changed in just a few years. Instead of a market for imported high-priced and high-quality electronic goods aimed at the new rich, and cheaper, poorer-quality Chinese-made goods for the rest of the market, a multitiered market reflecting the growth of personal income emerged.

Sony of Japan, the leading foreign seller of the high-priced consumer electronic goods, was upstaged in the Chinese market when Aiwa, a competitor, recognized the emergence of a new middle tier market for good-quality, modestly priced electronic goods. As part of a global strategy focused on slim margins and high turnover, Aiwa of Korea began selling hi-fi systems at prices closer to Chinese brands than to Sony's. Aiwa's product quality was not far behind that of Sony and was better than top Chinese brands, and the product resembled Sony's high-end systems. Aiwa's recognition of a new market segment and its ability to tap into it resulted in a huge increase in overall demand for Aiwa products.

Similarly, Mattel was successful in selling its Barbie dolls to the upper-end market in much of the world for years. However, sales of new product extensions such as the Holiday Barbie that were highly successful in the United States did not generate enough foreign sales to justify their marketing abroad. Simply adapting U.S. products for foreign markets resulted in overpriced merchandise in some market segments. The company estimates that the potential for Barbie in lower-priced market segments is $2 billion. To

## CROSSING BORDERS 18.3   Thunderbird: The American Classic

Tariff structures in a country can lead to some peculiar opportunities for products; in some situations, they can even dictate taste. In Kuala Lumpur, Malaysia, Ms. Muthu, on her way to a party, stops by a premier supermarket for a favorite California wine to help ring in the New Year. She heads straight for the Thunderbird and Night Train Express, cheap fortified apple wines often associated with skid-row drinking in the United States. "We like the taste of it" as well as the low price, she says.

Thunderbird, which promotes itself as "The American Classic," and Night Train Express don't have much of an image problem in Kuala Lumpur. They are prominently displayed in upscale department stores and at some of the toniest supermarkets in this affluent capital. "They sell like hot cakes," says the liquor department head. Night Train Express (label instructions: serve very cold) was such a hot seller that the store ran out of

stock in the crucial days before the long New Year's holiday weekend.

The popularity of these two wines shows how a tariff system can help dictate taste. Malaysia's bureaucrats decided years ago that so-called beverage wines—those made from fruit other than grapes—should be taxed at a significantly lower rate than grape wines. As a result, cheap table wine, until recently, sold at more than twice the price of Thunderbird, which retails for less than $5. Night Train Express is a little more expensive. Obviously, the wine market in Kuala Lumpur has little understanding of the nuances of wine, and that makes price differences critical.

Source: Adapted from Dan Biers, "What's a Malaysian's Favorite Whine? The Store's All Out of Thunderbird," *The Wall Street Journal*, January 8, 1996, p. A9. Copyright 1996 by Dow Jones & Co. Inc. Reproduced with permission of Dow Jones & Co. Inc. via Copyright Clearance Center.

capture that market, along with brand extensions of a collector Barbie, Mattel will introduce lower-priced dolls in a line called "Global Friends," which features a different doll for each major global city.

Pricing decisions that were appropriate when companies directed their marketing efforts toward single market segments will give way to more sophisticated practices. As

Chinese wait to enter Beijing's first Wal-Mart outlet. Thousands crowded the Sam's Club store on the far western edge of Beijing as the world's biggest retailer made its first foray into a major Chinese city. Wal-Mart has more than 20 stores elsewhere in China; their first was opened in 1996. The low-price-for-good-quality strategy of Wal-Mart and other mass retailers such as Costco and Carrefour, the French supermarket chain, have resulted in lowering retail prices in China, Japan, and other Asian countries they have entered. *(AP/Wide World Photos)*

incomes rise in many foreign markets, the pricing environment a company encounters will be similar to that in the United States. As countries prosper and incomes become more equitably distributed, multiple market segments develop. As these segments emerge, Wal-Mart, Carrefour, and other mass retailers enter the market to offer price-conscious customers good value at affordable prices. This scenario repeats itself in country after country. Within these markets an effective pricing strategy becomes crucial.

# Price Escalation

People traveling abroad often are surprised to find goods that are relatively inexpensive in their home country priced outrageously high in other countries. Because of the natural tendency to assume that such prices are a result of profiteering, manufacturers often resolve to begin exporting to crack these new, profitable foreign markets only to find that, in most cases, the higher prices reflect the higher costs of exporting. A case in point is the pacemaker for heart patients that sells for $2,100 in the United States. Tariffs and the Japanese distribution system add substantially to the final price in Japan. Beginning with the import tariff, each time the pacemaker changes hands an additional cost is incurred. First, the product passes through the hands of an importer, then to the company with primary responsibility for sales and service, then to a secondary or even a tertiary local distributor, and finally to the hospital. Markups at each level result in the $2,100 pacemaker selling for over $4,000 in Japan. Inflation results in price escalation, one of the major pricing obstacles facing the MNC marketer. This is true not only for technical products like the pacemaker, but also for such products as crude oil, soft drinks, and beer. Estimates are that if tariffs and trade barriers on these products were abolished, the consumer would enjoy savings of 6.57 trillion yen.[7]

## Costs of Exporting

Excess profits exist in some international markets, but generally the cause of the disproportionate difference in price between the exporting country and the importing country, here termed **price escalation**, is the added costs incurred as a result of exporting products from one country to another. Specifically, the term relates to situations in which ultimate prices are raised by shipping costs, insurance, packing, tariffs, longer channels of distribution, larger middlemen margins, special taxes, administrative costs, and exchange rate fluctuations. The majority of these costs arise as a direct result of moving goods across borders from one country to another and often combine to escalate the final price to a level considerably higher than in the domestic market.

## Taxes, Tariffs, and Administrative Costs

"Nothing is surer than death and taxes" has a particularly familiar ring to the ears of the international trader because taxes include tariffs, and tariffs are one of the most pervasive features of international trading. Taxes and tariffs affect the ultimate consumer price for a product; in most instances, the consumer bears the burden of both. Sometimes, however, consumers benefit when manufacturers selling goods in foreign countries reduce their net return in order to gain access to a foreign market. Absorbed or passed on, taxes and tariffs must be considered by the international businessperson.

A tariff, or duty, is a special form of taxation. Like other forms of taxes, a tariff may be levied for the purpose of protecting a market or for increasing government revenue. A tariff is a fee charged when goods are brought into a country from another country. Recall from Chapter 15 that the level of tariff is typically expressed as the rate of duty and may be levied as specific, ad valorem, or compound. A specific duty is a flat charge per physical unit imported, such as 15 cents per bushel of rye. Ad valorem duties are levied as a percentage of the value of the goods imported, such as 20 percent of the value of imported watches. Compound duties include both a specific and an ad valorem charge, such as $1 per camera plus 10 percent of its value. Tariffs and other forms of import taxes serve to discriminate against all foreign goods.

---

[7]"Trade Barriers Cost Cosumers Over ¥6 trillion: UFJ Institute," *Nikkei Report,* March 29, 2003.

Fees for import certificates or for other administrative processing can assume such levels that they are, in fact, import taxes. Many countries have purchase or excise taxes, which apply to various categories of goods; value-added or turnover taxes, which apply as the product goes through a channel of distribution; and retail sales taxes.[8] Such taxes increase the end price of goods but, in general, do not discriminate against foreign goods. Tariffs are the primary discriminatory tax that must be taken into account in reckoning with foreign competition.

In addition to taxes and tariffs, there are a variety of administrative costs directly associated with exporting and importing a product. Export and import licenses, other documents, and the physical arrangements for getting the product from port of entry to the buyer's location mean additional costs. Although such costs are relatively small, they add to the overall cost of exporting.[9]

## Inflation

In countries with rapid inflation or exchange variation, the selling price must be related to the cost of goods sold and the cost of replacing the items.[10] Goods often are sold below their cost of replacement plus overhead, and sometimes are sold below replacement cost. In these instances, the company would be better off not to sell the products at all. When payment is likely to be delayed for several months or is worked out on a long-term contract, inflationary factors must be figured into the price. Inflation and lack of control over price were instrumental in the unsuccessful new-product launch in Brazil by the H. J. Heinz Company; after only two years they withdrew from the market. Misunderstandings with the local partner resulted in a new fruit-based drink being sold to retailers on consignment; that is, they did not pay until the product was sold. Faced with a rate of inflation of over 300 percent, just a week's delay in payment eroded profit margins substantially. Soaring inflation in many developing countries (Latin America in particular) makes widespread price controls a constant threat.

Because inflation and price controls imposed by a country are beyond the control of companies, they use a variety of techniques to inflate the selling price to compensate for inflation pressure and price controls. They may charge for extra services, inflate costs in transfer pricing, or break up products into components and price each component separately.

Inflation causes consumer prices to escalate and the consumer is faced with rising prices that eventually exclude many consumers from the market. On the other hand, deflation results in decreasing prices creating a positive result for consumers, but both put pressure to lower costs on everyone in the supply chain.

## Deflation

The Japanese economy has been in a deflationary spiral for a number of years. In a country better known for $10 melons and $100 steaks, McDonald's now sells hamburgers for 52 cents, down from $1.09, a flat screen 32-inch color television is down from $4000 to $2400,[11] and clothing stores compete to sell fleece jackets for $8, down from $25 two years earlier.[12] Prices have dropped to a point that consumer prices are similar to those they previously found only on overseas shopping trips. The high prices prevalent in Japan before deflation allowed substantial margins for everyone in the distribution chain. As prices continued to drop over several years, those less able to adjust costs to allow some margin with deflated prices, fell by the way side. Entirely new retail categories—100-yen discount shops, clothing chains selling low-cost imported products from China, and warehouse-style department stores are

[8]Nathan Trautwein and Shoab Malak, "Reducing the VAT Cost of Imports," *World Trade,* October 1, 2002.

[9]To get some idea of the types of trade barriers facing an exporter, read "USTR Lists Barriers to U.S. Trade, Focusing on Agriculture," *State Department Press Releases and Documents,* April 2003.

[10]Frederik Balfour, "Sinking Prices Ought To Be A Blessing, Right?" *Business Week,* July 29, 2002.

[11]Brian Bremner and Irene M. Kunii, "Deflation Nation," *Business Week,* May 26, 2003.

[12]At least one exception in Japan is Louis Vuitton brand of hand bags, leather, and other luxury goods that has managed to raise prices twice in one year despite Japan's severe deflation. See Philippe Ries, "French Luxury Goods Hold Their Own in Japan Despite Euro's Rise," *Agence France-Presse,* March 2, 2003.

now the norm. Sales at discount stores grew by 78 percent from 1995 to 2000. Discounting is the way to prosper in Japan, which again helps fuel deflation. While those in the distribution chain adjusted to a different competitive environment or gave up, Japanese consumers were reveling in their newfound spending power. Japanese tourists used to travel to the United States to buy things at much cheaper prices, but, as one consumer commented, "Nowadays, I feel prices in Japan are going down and America is no longer cheaper." When she used to bring back suitcases of bargains on trips to the United States, on her last trip she returned from a two-week vacation and limited her purchases to one fanny pack.[13]

In a deflationary market, it is essential for a company to keep prices low and raise brand value to win the trust of consumers.[14] Whether deflation or inflation, an exporter must emphasize controlling price escalation.

## Exchange Rate Fluctuations

At one time, world trade contracts could be easily written because payment was specified in a relatively stable currency. The American dollar was the standard and all transactions could be related to the dollar. Now that all major currencies are floating freely relative to one another, no one is quite sure of the future value of any currency. Increasingly, companies are insisting that transactions be written in terms of the vendor company's national currency, and forward hedging is becoming more common. If exchange rates are not carefully considered in long-term contracts, companies find themselves unwittingly giving 15 to 20 percent discounts. The added cost incurred by exchange rate fluctuations on a day-to-day basis must be considered, especially where there is a significant time lapse between signing the order and delivery of the goods. Exchange rate differentials mount up. Whereas Hewlett-Packard gained nearly half a million dollars additional profit through exchange rate fluctuations in one year, Nestlé lost a million dollars in six months. Other companies lost or gained even larger amounts.

Shoppers look at stacks of discount clothing jutting out on a sidewalk to attract potential buyers at Tokyo's Sugamo shopping district. With the stock market plunging to 16-year lows, talk of deflationary dangers, and a morass of confusion in its political leadership, Japan appears to be headed toward a serious economic crisis. The central bank played down the possibility of deflation, saying that falling prices show the market is finally opening up to competition. However, consumer prices have fallen so precipitously that most believe that Japan's economy is experiencing serious deflation. (*AP/Wide World Photos*)

**Varying Currency Values** In addition to risks from exchange rate variations, other risks result from the changing values of a country's currency relative to other currencies. Consider the situation in Germany for a purchaser of U.S. manufactured goods from mid-2001 to mid-2003. During this period, the value of the U.S. dollar relative to the euro went from a strong position ($1 U.S. to €1.8315) in mid-2001 to a weaker position in mid-2003 ($1 U.S. to €0.8499). A strong dollar produces price resistance because it takes a larger quantity of local currency to buy a U.S. dollar. Conversely, when the U.S. dollar is weak, demand for U.S. goods increases because fewer units of local currency are needed to buy a U.S. dollar. The weaker U.S. dollar, compared with most of the world's stronger currencies, that existed in mid-2003 stimulated exports from the United States. Consequently, when the dollar strengthens U.S. exports will soften.

When the value of the dollar is weak relative to the buyer's currency (i.e., it takes fewer units of the foreign currency to buy a dollar), companies generally employ cost-plus pricing. To remain price competitive when the dollar is strong (i.e., when it takes more units of the foreign currency to buy a dollar), companies must find ways to offset the higher price caused by currency values. When

---

[13]James Brooke, "Japanese Consumers Revel in Deflation's Silver Lining," *New York Times,* December 7, 2001.

[14]Kenichi Murakami, "Nippon Lever Gains Ground Through Focus On Strong Brands," *Nikkei Report,* April 15, 2003.

## Exhibit 18.2
Export Strategies Under Varying Currency Conditions

| When Domestic Currency Is WEAK ... | When Domestic Currency Is STRONG ... |
|---|---|
| Stress price benefits | Engage in nonprice competition by improving quality, delivery, and aftersale service |
| Expand product line and add more-costly features | Improve productivity and engage in vigorous cost reduction |
| Shift sourcing and manufacturing to domestic market | Shift sourcing and manufacturing overseas |
| Exploit export opportunities in all markets | Give priority to exports to relatively strong-currency countries |
| Conduct conventional cash-for-goods trade | Deal in countertrade with weak-currency countries |
| Use full-costing approach, but use marginal-cost pricing to penetrate new/competitive makets | Trim profit margins and use marginal-cost pricing |
| Speed repatriation of foreign-earned income and collections | Keep the foreign-earned income in host country and slow collections |
| Minimize expenditures in local, host-country currency | Maximize expenditures in local, host country currency |
| Buy needed services (advertising, insurance, transportation, etc.) in domestic market | Buy needed services abroad and pay for them in local currencies |
| Minimize local borrowing | Borrow money needed for expansion in local market |
| Bill foreign customers in domestic currency | Bill foreign customers in their own currency |

Source: S. Tamer Cavugil, "Unraveling the Mystique of Export Pricing," Chapter 71 in Sidney J. Levy, George R. Frerichs, and Howard L. Gordon (eds.), *The Dartnell Marketing Manager's Handbook* (Chicago: Dartnell Corporation 1994), Figure 2, p. 1362. Reprinted with permission of Dartnell Corporation. All rights reserved.

the rupee in India depreciated significantly against the U.S. dollar, PC manufacturers faced a serious pricing problem. Because the manufacturers depended on imported components, their option was to absorb the increased cost or raise the price of PCs. Exhibit 18.2 focuses on the different price strategies a company might use under a weak or strong domestic currency. U.S. companies marketing in those countries with strong currencies have a choice between lowering prices even further and thereby expanding their market share, or maintaining prices and accumulating larger profits.

Currency exchange rate swings are considered by many global companies to be a major pricing problem. Because the benefits of a weaker dollar are generally transitory, firms need to take a proactive stance one way or the other. For a company with long-range plans calling for continued operation in foreign markets, yet wanting to remain price competitive, price strategies need to reflect variations in currency values.

Innumerable cost variables can be identified depending on the market, the product, and the situation. The cost, for example, of reaching a market with relatively small potential may be high. High operating costs of small specialty stores like those in Mexico and Thailand lead to high retail prices. Intense competition in certain world markets raises the cost or lowers the margins available to world business. Even small things like payoffs to local officials can introduce unexpected costs to the unwary entrepreneur. Only experience in a given marketplace provides the basis for compensating for cost differences in different markets. With experience, a firm that prices on a cost basis operates in a realm of reasonably measurable factors.

## Middleman and Transportation Costs

Channel length and marketing patterns vary widely, but in most countries channels are longer and middleman margins higher than is customary in the United States. The diversity of channels used to reach markets and the lack of standardized middleman markups leave many producers unaware of the ultimate price of a product.

Besides channel diversity, the fully integrated marketer operating abroad faces various unanticipated costs because marketing and distribution channel infrastructures are underdeveloped in many countries. The marketer can also incur added expenses for warehousing and handling of small shipments and may need to bear increased financing costs when dealing with under-financed middlemen.

A woman looks at a poster offering a half-priced bacon and lettuce hamburger, reduced from USD $3.20 to $1.60 during a monthly discount at a McDonald's restaurant in downtown Tokyo. McDonald's Japan announced that they would reduce the price of their hamburgers by 30 percent for a month to return to their customers the profit they made by the strong yen against the U.S. dollars in importing the raw materials from abroad. McDonald's move creates goodwill among its customers at a time when they are forced to lower prices to "hike" sales in an economy that is suffering a major downturn. This is a good example of how differences in the value of currencies can be positive for a company, as in this case, or negative when the value of the dollar is much stronger than the local currency. (AP/Wide World Photos)

Because no convenient source of data on middleman costs is available, the international marketer must rely on experience and marketing research to ascertain middleman costs. The Campbell Soup Company found its middleman and physical distribution costs in the United Kingdom to be 30 percent higher than in the United States. Extra costs were incurred because soup was purchased in small quantities—small English grocers typically purchase 24-can cases of assorted soups (each case being hand-packed for shipment). In the United States, typical purchase units are 48-can cases of one soup purchased by the dozens, hundreds, or carloads. The purchase habits in Europe forced the company into an extra wholesale level in its channel to facilitate handling small orders.

Exporting also incurs increased transportation costs when moving goods from one country to another. If the goods go over water, there are additional costs for insurance, packing, and handling not generally added to locally produced goods. Such costs add yet another burden because import tariffs in many countries are based on the landed cost, which includes transportation, insurance, and shipping charges. These costs add to the inflation of the final price. The next section details how a reasonable price in the home market may more than double in the foreign market.

## Sample Effects of Price Escalation

Exhibit 18.3 illustrates some of the effects the factors discussed previously may have on the end price of a consumer item. Because costs and tariffs vary so widely from country to country, a hypothetical but realistic example is used. It assumes that a constant net price is received by the manufacturer, that all domestic transportation costs are absorbed by the various middlemen and reflected in their margins, and that the foreign middlemen have the same margins as the domestic middlemen. In some instances, foreign middlemen margins are lower, but it is equally probable that these margins could be greater. In fact, in many instances, middlemen use higher wholesale and retail margins for foreign goods than for similar domestic goods.

Notice that the retail prices in Exhibit 18.3 range widely, illustrating the difficulty of price control by manufacturers in overseas retail markets. No matter how much the manufacturer may wish to market a product in a foreign country for a price equivalent to $10 U.S., there is little opportunity for such control. Even assuming the most optimistic conditions for Foreign Example 1, the producer would need to cut net by more than one-third to absorb freight and tariff costs if the goods are to be priced the same in both foreign and domestic markets. Price escalation is everywhere: A man's dress shirt that sells for $40 in the United States retails for $80 in Caracas. A $20 U.S. electric can opener is priced in Milan at $70; a $35 U.S.-made automatic toaster is priced at $80 in France. The Cadillac Catera, which sells in the United States for $30,000, sells for $46,644 in Switzerland.

Japanese wholesale store manager of meat market in Tokyo arranges packs of beef imported from Australia. Earlier in the day, the government said Japan plans to raise its tariff on refrigerated beef imports to 50 percent from 38.5 percent, following a spike in imports. The price tag reads: Premium beef, sirloin steak from Australia @ 258 yen (U.S. $2.20) per 100 grams. Tariffs are one of the main causes of price escalation for imported products. (AP/Wide World Photos)

Unless some of the costs that create price escalation can be reduced, the marketer is faced with a price that may confine sales to a limited segment of wealthy, price-insensitive customers. In many markets, buyers have less purchasing power than in the United States and can be easily priced out of the market. Further, when price escalation is set in motion it can spiral upward quickly. When the price to middlemen is high and turnover is low, they may insist on higher margins to defray their costs, which, of course, raises the price even higher. Unless price escalation can be reduced, marketers find that the only buyers left are the wealthier ones. If marketers are to compete successfully in the growth of

**Exhibit 18.3**
Sample Causes and Effects of Price Escalation

| | Domestic Example | Foreign Example 1: Assuming the Same Channels with Wholesaler Importing Directly | Foreign Example 2: Importer and Same Margins and Channels | Foreign Example 3: Same as 2 but with 10 Percent Cumulative Turnover Tax | |
|---|---|---|---|---|---|
| Manufacturing net | $ 5.00 | $ 5.00 | $ 5.00 | $ 5.00 | |
| Transport, CIF | n.a. | 6.10 | 6.10 | 6.10 | |
| Tariff (20 percent CIF value) | n.a. | 1.22 | 1.22 | 1.22 | |
| Importer pays | n.a. | n.a. | 7.32 | 7.32 | |
| Importer margin when sold to wholesaler (25 percent) on cost | n.a. | n.a. | 1.83 | 1.83 +0.73 | turnover tax |
| Wholesaler pays landed cost | 5.00 | 7.32 | 9.15 | 9.88 | |
| Wholesaler margin (33⅓ percent on cost) | 1.67 | 2.44 | 3.05 | 3.29 +0.99 | turnover tax |
| Retailer pays | 6.67 | 9.76 | 12.20 | 14.16 | |
| Retail margin (50 percent on cost) | 3.34 | 4.88 | 6.10 | 7.08 +1.42 | turnover |
| Retail price | $10.01 | $14.64 | $18.30 | $22.66 | tax |

Notes: All figures in U.S. dollars; CIF = cost, insurance, and freight; n.a.= not applicable. The exhibit assumes that all domestic transportation costs are absorbed by the middleman. Transportation, tariffs, and middleman margins vary from country to country, but for purposes of comparison, only a few of the possible variations are shown.

markets around the world, cost containment must be among their highest priorities. If costs can be reduced anywhere along the chain from manufacturer's cost to retailer markups, price escalation will be reduced. A discussion of some of the approaches to lessening price escalation follows.

## Approaches to Lessening Price Escalation
Three methods used to reduce costs and lower price escalation are lowering cost of goods, lowering tariffs, and lowering distribution costs.

**Lowering Cost of Goods**   If the manufacturer's price can be lowered, the effect is felt throughout the chain. One of the important reasons for manufacturing in a third country is an attempt to reduce manufacturing costs and thus price escalation. The impact can be profound if you consider that the hourly cost of skilled labor in a Mexican maquiladora is less than $3 an hour including benefits, compared with more than $10 in the United States.

In comparing the costs of manufacturing microwave ovens in the United States and in Korea, the General Electric Company found substantial differences. A typical microwave oven cost GE $218 to manufacture compared with $155 for Samsung, a Korean manufacturer. A breakdown of costs revealed that assembly labor cost GE $8 per oven, and Samsung only 63 cents. Perhaps the most disturbing finding for GE was that Korean laborers delivered more for less cost: GE produced four units per person whereas the Korean company produced nine.

Although Korea remains an important offshore manufacturing location, China is emerging as a global manufacturing powerhouse[15] backed by an inexpensive labor force, rapidly improving production quality, new sources of capital, a more dynamic private

---

[15]Jerry J. Jasinowski, "Made In China, New Trade Strategies a must Made in China," *The Washington Times,* May 20, 2003.

sector, and a deliberately undervalued currency.[16] China supplies a growing range of products to the global marketplace. Japan, the land of zero-defect quality control, is increasingly happy with the competence of Chinese workers. Star Manufacturing, a Japanese precision machine tool manufacturing company, moved 30 percent of its production to China because China's cheap labor and cheap resources reduce production cost by 20 percent.[17]

Eliminating costly functional features or even lowering overall product quality is another method of minimizing price escalation. For U.S.-manufactured products, the quality and additional features required for the more developed home market may not be necessary in countries without the same level of development or consumer demand. In the price war between P&G and Kimberly-Clark in Brazil, the quality of the product was lowered in order to lower the price. Remember that the grandmother in the grocery store chose the poorest-quality and the lowest-priced brand of diaper. Similarly, functional features on washing machines made for the United States, such as automatic bleach and soap dispensers, thermostats to provide four different levels of water temperature, controls to vary water volume, and bells to ring at appropriate times, may be unnecessary for many foreign markets. Eliminating them means lower manufacturing costs and thus a corresponding reduction in price escalation. Lowering manufacturing costs can often have a double benefit: The lower price to the buyer may also mean lower tariffs, since most tariffs are levied on an ad valorem basis.

## Lowering Tariffs

When tariffs account for a large part of price escalation, as they often do, companies seek ways to lower the rate. Some products can be reclassified into a different, and lower, customs classification. An American company selling data communications equipment in Australia faced a 25 percent tariff that affected the price competitiveness of its products. It persuaded the Australian government to change the classification for the type of products the company sells from "computer equipment" (25 percent tariff) to "telecommunication equipment" (3 percent tariff). Like many products, this company's products could be legally classified under either category. One complaint against customs agents in Russia is the arbitrary way in which they often classify products. Russian customs, for instance, insists on classifying Johnson & Johnson's 2 in 1 Shower Gel as a cosmetic with a 20 percent tariff rather than as a soap substitute, which the company considers it, at a 15 percent tariff.

How a product is classified is often a judgment call. The difference between an item being classified as jewelry or art means paying no tariff for art or a 26 percent tariff for jewelry. For example, a U.S. customs inspector could not decide whether to classify a $2.7 million Fabergé egg as art or jewelry. The difference was zero tariff versus $700,000. An experienced freight forwarder/customs broker saved the day by persuading the customs agent that the Fabergé egg was a piece of art. Because the classification of products varies among countries, a thorough investigation of tariff schedules and classification criteria can result in a lower tariff. See Crossing Borders 18.4 for some examples of various tariff rules in the United States.

Besides having a product reclassified into a lower tariff category, it may be possible to modify a product to qualify for a lower tariff rate within a tariff classification. In the footwear industry, the difference between "foxing" and "foxlike" on athletic shoes makes a substantial difference in the tariff levied. To protect the domestic footwear industry from an onslaught of cheap sneakers from the Far East, the tariff schedules state that any canvas or vinyl shoe with a foxing band (a tape band attached at the sole and overlapping the shoe's upper by more than ¼ inch) be assessed at a higher duty rate. As a result, manufacturers design shoes so that the sole does not overlap the upper by more than ¼ inch.

---

[16]"Researcher: China Enjoys Comparative Advantage in Labor Cost," *Xinhua News Agency,* November 17, 2002.

[17]Irene M. Kuni, "Asia's Future: Matsushita's Payoff," *Business Week International,* October 22, 2001, p. 56.

**CROSSING BORDERS 18.4** What Does It Mean To Be Human?—5.2 Percent, That's What

"What does it mean to be human?" asked Judge Barzilay in her chambers at the U.S. Court of International Trade. At the heart of the problem were some 60 little plastic figures of Marvel Enterprises' X-Men and other comic figures.

Marvel subsidiary Toy Biz Inc. sought to have its heroes from a range of comic characters declared nonhuman. At the time, tariffs were higher on dolls (12 percent) than toys (6.8 percent). According to the U.S. tariff code, human figures are dolls, whereas figures representing animals or "creatures," such as monsters and robots, are deemed toys.

Thus began the great debate over the figures' true being. Barbie is a doll. Pooh Bear's a toy. That much is easy. But what about Wolverine, the muscular X-Man with the metal claws that jut out from his fists? Wolverine has known many forms in his more than 40 years as a Marvel character. But is he human? Or is Kraven human, a famed hunter, who once vanquished Spiderman, thanks in part to the strength gained from drinking secret jungle elixirs.

Toy Biz argued that the figures "stand as potent witnesses for their status as nonhuman creatures." How could they be humans if they possessed "tentacles, claws, wings, or robotic limbs?" The U.S. Customs Service argument was that each figure had a "distinctive individual personality." Some were Russians, Japanese, black, white, women, even handicapped. The government insisted, Wolverine was simply "a man with prosthetic hands."

To weigh the question, Judge Barzilay sat down with a sheaf of opposing legal briefs and more than 60 action figures, including Wolverine, Storm, Rogue, Kraven, and Bonebreaker. Judge Barzilay described in her ruling how she subjected many of the figures to "comprehensive examinations." At times, that included "the need to remove the clothes of the figure." The X-Men, oddly, gave her the least trouble. They are mutants, she declared, who "use their extraordinary and unnatural powers on the side of good or evil." Thus the X-Men are "something other than human." Tougher for the Judge were figures from the Fantastic Four and Spiderman series. After careful examination and thought, the judge found Kraven exhibited "highly exaggerated muscle tone in arms and legs." He wore a "lion's mane-like vest." Both features helped relegate him to the netherworld of robots, monsters, and devils. Case closed.

Toy Biz Inc. was elated but the fans were incensed—no way are X-Men mere creatures. "Marvel's superheroes are supposed to be as human as you or I. They live in New York. They have families and go to work. And now they're no longer human?" The current author of Marvel's "Uncanny X-Men" comic-book series is also incredulous. He has worked hard for a year, he says, to emphasize the X-Men's humanity, to show "that they're just another strand in the evolutionary chain." "Don't fret, Marvel fans, a decision that the X-Men figures indeed do have 'nonhuman' characteristics further proves our characters have special, out-of-this world powers."

Although this scenario may seem trivial, it highlights just how arbitrary tariff classification can be. It pays to argue your case if you believe a product can be classified at a lower rate. For every $100,000 of plastic figures Toy Biz imports, the reclassification saves them $5,200. Not a bad day's work considering the hundreds of thousands of dollars worth of figures the company imports annually. Not to mention the undisclosed sum Toy Biz can recoup for years of overpaid tariffs.

Source: Adapted from Niel King Jr., "Is Wolverine Human? A Judge Answers No; Fans Howl in Protest," *The Wall Street Journal*, January 20, 2003; Larry Williams, "X-Men Not Human? That's Inhumane," *South Florida Sun-Sentinel*, May 6, 2003; and Stanford W. Carpenter, "Man or Mutant? A Matter of Import," *The Baltimore Sun*, May 26, 2003, p. 13A.

If the overlap exceed ¼ inch, the shoe is classified as having a foxing band; less than ¼ inch, a foxlike band. A shoe with a foxing band is taxed 48 percent and one with a foxlike band (¼ inch or less overlap) is taxed a mere 6 percent.

There are often differential rates between fully assembled, ready-to-use products and those requiring some assembly, further processing, the addition of locally manufactured component parts, or other processing that adds value to the product and can be performed within the foreign country. For example, a ready-to-operate piece of machinery with a 20 percent tariff may be subject to only a 12 percent tariff when imported unassembled. An even lower tariff may apply when the product is assembled in the country and some local content is added.

Repackaging also may help to lower tariffs. Tequila entering the United States in containers of one gallon or less carries a duty of $2.27 per proof gallon; larger containers are assessed at only $1.25. If the cost of rebottling is less than $1.02 per proof gallon,

## CROSSING BORDERS 18.5   When Is a Car a Truck and a Daily Planner a Diary? When the U.S. Customs Service Says So

How an import is classified can mean a big difference in the tariffs paid. But it is not always apparent how a product should be classified, at least to the U.S. Customs Service. Here are two cases.

U.S. Customs Service classified multipurpose vehicles as trucks, that is, vehicles designed to transport cargo or other goods. Trucks pay a 25 percent tariff, whereas passenger vehicles pay only a 2.5 percent tariff. The two-door Nissan Pathfinder was initially classified as a truck rather than as a passenger vehicle, but Nissan challenged the classification. The Justice Department argued that the Pathfinder was built with the same structural design as the Nissan pickup truck despite all the options added later in production, and should therefore be considered a truck for tariff purposes. The court said that doesn't matter; it's how the vehicle is used that counts. The judge declared that the

Pathfinder "virtually shouts to the consumer, 'I am a car, not a truck!'" The ruling means a $225 savings for every $1,000 the consumer spends on a Pathfinder.

The Mead Corporation imports what they consider to be a loose-leaf daily planner that contains a section for daily notes, phone numbers, and addresses. Customs classified the planners as "Bound Diaries" on which a 4 percent duty applies. Mead challenged the decision and contended that the product should be classified as a daily planner on which there is no duty. The U.S. Supreme Court ruled in favor of Mead.

Sources: "Nissan Wins U.S. Customs Suit," *Associated Press,* September 9, 1994; "U.S. High Court: No Deference to Customs on Tariffs," *Reuters News Service,* June 18, 2001; R. G. Edmonson, "Importers Laud Mead Ruling,"*The Journal of Commerce,* June 19, 2001; and, "Mead Hails Tariff Ruling by High Court," *Associated Press,* June 19, 2001.

and it probably would be, considerable savings could result. As will be discussed shortly, one of the more important activities in foreign trade zones is the assembly of imported goods, using local and frequently lower-cost labor.

**Lowering Distribution Costs**

Shorter channels can help keep prices under control. Designing a channel that has fewer middlemen may lower distribution costs by reducing or eliminating middleman markup. Besides eliminating markups, fewer middlemen may mean lower overall taxes. Some countries levy a value-added tax on goods as they pass through channels. Goods are taxed each time they change hands. The tax may be cumulative or noncumulative. A cumulative value-added tax is based on total selling price and is assessed every time the goods change hands. Obviously, in countries where value-added tax is cumulative, tax alone provides a special incentive for developing short distribution channels. Where that is achieved, tax is paid only on the difference between the middleman's cost and the selling price. While many manufacturers had to cut prices in the wake of Japan's deflation, Louis Vuitton, a maker of branded boutique goods, was able to increase prices instead. A solid brand name and direct distribution permitted Vuitton's price strategy. Vuitton's leather monogrammed bags are now Japanese buyers' "daily necessity" and Vuitton distributes directly and fixes its own prices.[18]

**Using Foreign Trade Zones to Lessen Price Escalation**

Some countries have established foreign or free trade zones (FTZs) or free ports to facilitate international trade.[19] There are more than 300 of these facilities in operation throughout the world where imported goods can be stored or processed. As free trade policies in Africa, Latin America, Eastern Europe, and other developing regions expand, there has been an equally rapid expansion in the creation and use of foreign trade zones.[20] Recall from Chapter 15 that in a free port or FTZ, payment of import duties is postponed until the product leaves the FTZ area and enters the country. An FTZ is, in essence, a tax-free

---

[18]Philippe Ries, "French Luxury Goods Hold Their Own in Japan Despite Euro's Rise," *Agence France-Presse,* March 2, 2003.

[19]"Mauritius Freeport Has Many Incentives," *Africa News Service,* October 1, 2002.

[20]"Two Free Trade Zones Picked," *The Korea Times,* November 11, 2002.

An actor portraying Wolverine, an X-Men fictional character from Marvel Enterprises. A tariff classification issue arose when the company declared the imported toy characters as nonhuman toys and the U.S. Customs said that they were human figure dolls—tariffs on dolls at that time were 12 percent versus 6 percent for toys. U.S. Customs alleged that the X-Men figures were human figures and thus should be classified as dolls and were not figures featuring animals or creatures, which would mean that they could be classified as toys. Product classifications are critical when tariffs are determined. See Crossing Borders 18.4 for more details on this case. (20th Century Fox/Marvel Entertainment Group/The Kobal Collection/Dory, Attila)

enclave and not considered part of the country as far as import regulations are concerned. When an item leaves an FTZ and is imported officially into the host country of the FTZ, all duties and regulations are imposed.

Utilizing FTZs can to some extent control price escalation resulting from the layers of taxes, duties, surcharges, freight charges, and so forth. Foreign trade zones permit many of these added charges to be avoided, reduced, or deferred so that the final price is more competitive. One of the more important benefits of the FTZ in controlling prices is the exemption from duties on labor and overhead costs incurred in the FTZ in assessing the value of goods.

By shipping unassembled goods to an FTZ in an importing country, a marketer can lower costs in a variety of ways:

- Tariffs may be lower because duties are typically assessed at a lower rate for unassembled versus assembled goods.

- If labor costs are lower in the importing country, substantial savings may be realized in the final product cost.

- Ocean transportation rates are affected by weight and volume; thus, unassembled goods may qualify for lower freight rates.

- If local content, such as packaging or component parts, can be used in the final assembly, there may be a further reduction of tariffs.

All in all, a foreign or free trade zone is an important method for controlling price escalation. Incidentally, all the advantages offered by an FTZ for an exporter are also advantages for an importer. U.S. importers use over 100 FTZs in the United States to help lower their costs of imported goods. See Exhibit 18.4 for illustrations of how FTZs are used.

## Exhibit 18.4
How Are Foreign Trade Zones Used?

There are more than 100 foreign trade zones (FTZs) in the United States, and FTZs exist in many other countries as well. Companies use them to postpone the payment of tariffs on products while they are in the FTZ. Here are some examples of how FTZs in the United States are used.

- A Japanese firm assembles motorcycles, jet skis, and three-wheel all-terrain vehicles for import as well as for export to Canada, Latin America, and Europe.

- A U.S. manufacturer of window shades and miniblinds imports and stores fabric from Holland in an FTZ, thereby postponing a 17 percent tariff until the fabric leaves the FTZ.

- A manufacturer of hair dryers stores its product in an FTZ, which it uses as its main distribution center for products manufactured in Asia.

- A European-based medical supply company manufactures kidney dialysis machines and sterile tubing using raw materials from Germany and U.S. labor. It then exports 30 percent of its products to Scandinavian countries.

- A Canadian company assembles electronic teaching machines using cabinets from Italy; electronics from Taiwan, Korea, and Japan; and labor from the United States, for export to Colombia and Peru.

In all these examples, tariffs are postponed until the products leave the FTZ and enter the United States. Further, in most situations the tariff is at the lower rate for component parts and raw materials versus the higher rate that would be charged if products were imported directly as finished goods. If the finished products are not imported into the United States from the FTZ but are shipped to another country, no U.S. tariffs apply.

Sources: Lewis E. Leibowitz, "An Overview of Foreign Trade Zones," *Europe*, Winter-Spring 1987, p. 12; "Cheap Imports," *International Business*, March 1993, pp. 98–100; and "Free-Trade Zones: Global Overview and Future Prospects," http://www.stat-usa.gov.

**Dumping**    A logical outgrowth of a market policy in international business is goods priced competitively at widely differing prices in various markets. Marginal (variable) cost pricing, as discussed earlier, is a way prices can be reduced to stay within a competitive price range. The market and economic logic of such pricing policies can hardly be disputed, but the practices often are classified as dumping and are subject to severe penalties and fines. Various economists define **dumping** differently. One approach classifies international shipments as dumped if the products are sold below their cost of production. The other approach characterizes dumping as selling goods in a foreign market below the price of the same goods in the home market.

World Trade Organization (WTO) rules allow for the imposition of a dumping duty when goods are sold at a price lower than the normal export price or less than the cost in the country of origin, increased by a reasonable amount for the cost of sales and profits, when this is likely to be prejudicial to the economic activity of the importing country. A **countervailing duty** or *minimum access volume (MAV),* which restricts the amount a country will import, may be imposed on foreign goods benefiting from subsidies whether in production, export, or transportation.

For countervailing duties to be invoked, it must be shown that prices are lower in the importing country than in the exporting country and that producers in the importing country are being directly harmed by the dumping. A report by the U.S. Department of Agriculture indicated that levels of dumping by the United States hover around 40 percent for wheat, between 25 percent and 30 percent for corn and levels for soybeans have risen steadily over the past four years, to nearly 30 percent. These percentages, for example, mean that wheat is selling up to 40 percent below their cost of production. For cotton, the level of dumping for 2001 rose to a remarkable 57 percent, and for rice it has stabilized at around 20 percent. The study indicated that these commodities are being dumped onto international markets by the United States in violation of World Trade Organization (WTO) rules. The report found that after many years of accepting agricultural dumping, a few countries have begun to respond with investigation into whether some U.S. agricultural exports are dumped. Brazil is considering a case against U.S. cotton before the WTO. In 2001, Canada briefly imposed both countervailing and antidumping duties on U.S. corn imports.[21]

Dumping is rarely an issue when world markets are strong. In the 1980s and 1990s dumping became a major issue for a large number of industries when excess production capacity relative to home-country demand caused many companies to price their goods on a marginal-cost basis. In a classic case of dumping, prices are maintained in the home-country market and reduced in foreign markets.

Today, tighter government enforcement of dumping legislation is causing international marketers to seek new routes around such legislation. Assembly in the importing country is a way companies attempt to lower prices and avoid dumping charges. However, these *screwdriver plants,* as they are often called, are subject to dumping charges if the price differentials reflect more than the cost savings that result from assembly in the importing country. Another subterfuge is to alter the product so that the technical description fits a lower duty category. To circumvent a 16.9 percent countervailing duty imposed on Chinese gas-filled, nonrefillable pocket flint lighters, the manufacturer attached a useless valve to the lighters so that they fell under the "nondisposable" category, thus avoiding the duty. Countries do see through many such subterfuges and impose taxes. For example, the EC imposed a $27 to $58 dumping duty per unit on a Japanese firm that assembled and sold electronic typewriters in the EC. The firm was charged with valuing imported parts for assembly below cost.

The U.S. market is currently more sensitive to dumping than in the recent past. In fact, the Uruguay Round of the GATT included a section on antidumping that grew out of U.S. insistence on stricter controls on dumping of foreign goods in the United States

[21]"U.S. Exports Farm Products at Below the Cost of Production," *Africa News Service,* February 11, 2003

at prices below those charged at home. Changes in U.S. law enhanced the authority of the Commerce Department to prevent circumvention of antidumping duties and countervailing duties that have been imposed on a country for dumping. The United States and the European Union have been the most ardent users of antidumping duties. A question asked by many, are dumping charges just a cover for protectionism?[22] Previously, when an order was issued to apply antidumping and countervailing duties on products, companies charged with the violation would get around the order by slightly altering the product or by doing minor assembly in the United States or a third country. This created the illusion of a different product not subject to the antidumping order. The new authority of the Department of Commerce closes many such loopholes.

## Leasing in International Markets

An important selling technique to alleviate high prices and capital shortages for capital equipment is the leasing system. The concept of equipment leasing is increasingly important as a means of selling capital equipment in overseas markets. In fact, it is estimated that $50 billion worth (original cost) of U.S.-made and foreign-made equipment is on lease in Western Europe.[23]

The system of leasing used by industrial exporters is similar to the typical lease contracts used in the United States. Terms of the leases usually run one to five years, with payments made monthly or annually; included in the rental fee are servicing, repairs, and spare parts. Just as contracts for domestic and overseas leasing arrangements are similar, so are the basic motivations and the shortcomings. For example:

- Leasing opens the door to a large segment of nominally financed foreign firms that can be sold on a lease option but might be unable to buy for cash.
- Leasing can ease the problems of selling new, experimental equipment, because less risk is involved for the users.
- Leasing helps guarantee better maintenance and service on overseas equipment.
- Equipment leased and in use helps to sell other companies in that country.
- Lease revenue tends to be more stable over a period of time than direct sales would be.

The disadvantages or shortcomings take on an international flavor. Besides the inherent disadvantages of leasing, some problems are compounded by international relationships. In a country beset with inflation, lease contracts that include maintenance and supply parts (as most do) can lead to heavy losses toward the end of the contract period. Further, countries where leasing is most attractive are those where spiraling inflation is most likely to occur. The added problems of currency devaluation, expropriation, or other political risks are operative longer than if the sale of the same equipment is made outright. In light of these perils, there is greater risk in leasing than in outright sale; however, there is a definite trend toward increased use of this method of selling internationally.

## Countertrade as a Pricing Tool

**Countertrade** is a pricing tool that every international marketer must be ready to use, and the willingness to accept a countertrade often gives the company a competitive advantage. The challenges of countertrade must be viewed from the same perspective as all other variations in international trade. Marketers must be aware of which markets require countertrades just as they must be aware of social customs and legal requirements. Assessing this factor along with all other market factors enhances a marketer's competitive position.

One of the earliest barter arrangements occurred between Russia and PepsiCo before the ruble was convertible and before most companies were trading with Russia. PepsiCo

[22]"The Dumping Dilemma; Rising Protectionism," *Finance and Economics*, June 1, 2002, p. 91.

[23]Richard Barovick, "Export Leasing," *World Trade,* May 7, 2003.

wanted to beat Coca-Cola into the Russian market. The only way possible was for them to accept vodka (sold under the brand name Stolichnaya) from Russia and bottled wines (sold under the brand name of Premiat) from Romania to finance Pepsi-Cola bottling plants in those countries. From all indications, this was a very profitable arrangement for Russia, Romania, and PepsiCo. PepsiCo continues to use countertrade to expand its bottling plants. In a recent agreement between PepsiCo and Ukraine, Pepsi agreed to market $1 billion worth of Ukrainian-made commercial ships over an eight-year period. Some of the proceeds from the ship sales will be reinvested in the shipbuilding venture, and some will be used to buy soft-drink equipment and build five Pepsi bottling plants in Ukraine. PepsiCo dominates the cola market in Russia and all the former republics of the USSR, in part because of its exclusive countertrade agreement with Russia that locked Coca-Cola out of the Russian cola market for more than 12 years. After the USSR was dismembered, the Russian economy crashed and most of the Russian payment system broke down into barter operations. Truck loads of aspirin were swapped by one company which was then traded for poultry, which in turn was bartered for lumber, in turn to be exchanged for X-ray equipment from Kazakhstan—all to settle debts. Many of these transactions involved regional electricity companies that were owed money by virtually everyone.[24]

Although cash may be the preferred method of payment, countertrades are an important part of trade with Eastern Europe, the Newly Independent States, China, and, to a varying degree, some Latin American and African nations. Barter or countertrades constitute between 20 and 40 percent of all transactions in the economies of the former Soviet bloc. Corporate debts to suppliers, payment and services, even taxes—all have a noncash component or are entirely bartered. Many of these countries constantly face a shortage of hard currencies with which to trade and thus resort to countertrades when possible. A recent purchase of 48 F-16 Falcons from Lockheed Martin was pegged at $3.5 billion. The financial package included soft loans and a massive offset program—purchases from Polish manufacturers that more than erased the costs of the deal in foreign exchange.[25] With an economy short of hard currency, Russia is offering a wide range of products in barter for commodities they need. For example, their expertise in space technology is offered for Malaysian palm oil and rubber, and military equipment, in exchange for crude palm oil from Indonesia. Exhibit 18.5 illustrates the many reasons countries demand countertrades. Today an international company must include in its market-pricing tool kit some understanding of countertrading.

## Types of Countertrade

Countertrade includes four distinct transactions: barter, compensation deals, counterpurchase, and buy-back. **Barter** is the direct exchange of goods between two parties in a transaction. For example, the Malaysian government bought 20 diesel-electric locomotives from General Electric. Officials of the government said that GE will be paid with palm oil to be supplied by a plantation company. The company will supply about 200,000 metric tons of palm oil over a period of 30 months.[26] This was GE's first barter deal for palm oil and palm products, although its division GE Trading has several other countertrade agreements worldwide. No money changed hands, nor were any third parties involved. Obviously, in a barter transaction, the seller must be able to dispose of the goods at a net price equal to the expected selling price in a regular, for-cash transaction. Further, during the negotiation stage of a barter deal, the seller must know the market and the price for the items offered in trade. In the General Electrical example, palm oil has an established price and a global market for palm oil and palm products. But not all bartered goods have an organized market and products can range from hams to iron pellets, mineral water, furniture, or olive oil—all somewhat more difficult to price and to find customers.

---

[24]Martin R. Snyder, "Doing Business in Russia Again?" *The Moscow Times,* January 9, 2002.

[25]Sam Vaknin, "Analysis: Poland's Offset Deal," *United Press International,* December 30, 2002.

[26]"Malaysia's Government to Buy Locomotives From GE For $65 million," *Dow Jones International News,* October 1, 2001.

**Exhibit 18.5**
Why Purchasers Impose Countertrade

*To preserve hard currency.* Countries with nonconvertible currencies look to countertrade as a way of guaranteeing that hard currency expenditures (for foreign imports) are offset by hard currency (generated by the foreign party's obligation to purchase domestic goods).

*To improve balance of trade.* Nations whose exports have not kept pace with imports increasingly rely on countertrade as a means to balance bilateral trade ledgers.

*To gain access to new markets.* As a nonmarket or developing country increases its production of exportable goods, it often lacks a sophisticated marketing channel to sell the goods to the West for hard currency. By imposing countertrade demands, foreign trade organizations utilize the marketing organizations and expertise of Western companies to market their goods for them.

*To upgrade manufacturing capabilities.* By entering compensation arrangements under which foreign (usually Western) firms provide plant and equipment and buy back resultant products, the trade organizations of less-developed countries can enlist Western technical cooperation in upgrading industrial facilities.

*To maintain prices of export goods.* Countertrade can be used as a means to dispose of goods at prices that the market would not bear under cash-for-goods terms. Although the Western seller absorbs the added cost by inflating the price of the original sale, the nominal price of the counterpurchased goods is maintained, and the seller need not concede what the value of the goods would be in the world supply-and-demand market. Conversely, if the world price for a commodity is artificially high, such as the price for crude oil, a country can barter its oil for Western goods (e.g., weapons) so that the real "price" the Western partner pays is below the world price.

*To force reinvestment of proceeds from weapons deals.* Many Arab countries require that a portion of proceeds from weapons purchases be reinvested in facilities designated by the buyer—everything from pipelines to hotels and sugar mills.

Source: Leo G. B. Welt, "Countertrade? Better Than No Trade," *Export Today*, Spring 1985, p. 54; and Anne Marie Squeo and Daniel Pearl, "The Big Sell: How a Gulf Sheikdom Landed Its Sweet Deal with Lockheed Martin," *The Wall Street Journal*, April 20, 2000.

Barter may also be used to reduce a country's foreign debt. To save foreign exchange reserves, the Philippine government offered some creditors canned tuna to repay part of a state-owned $4-billion debt. If tuna is not enough, coconut oil and a seaweed extract, carrageen, used as an additive in foods, toothpaste, cosmetics, and ice cream were offered. The seaweed and tuna exporters will be paid with pesos so no currency leaves the country.[27]

**Compensation deals** involve payment in goods and in cash. A seller delivers lathes to a buyer in Venezuela and receives 70 percent of the payment in convertible currency and 30 percent in tanned hides and wool. In an actual deal, General Motors Corporation sold $12 million worth of locomotives and diesel engines to Yugoslavia and took cash and $4 million in Yugoslavian cutting tools as payment. McDonnell Douglas agreed to a compensation deal with Thailand for eight top-of-the-range F/A-18 strike aircraft. Thailand agreed to pay $578 million of the total cost in cash, and McDonnell Douglas agreed to accept $93 million in a mixed bag of goods including Thai rubber, ceramics, furniture, frozen chicken, and canned fruit. In a move to reduce its current account deficit, the Thai government requires that 20 to 50 percent of the value of large contracts be paid for in raw and processed agricultural goods.

An advantage of a compensation deal over barter is the immediate cash settlement of a portion of the bill; the remainder of the cash is generated after successful sale of the goods received. If the company has a use for the goods received, the process is relatively simple and uncomplicated. On the other hand, if the seller has to rely on a third party to find a buyer, the cost involved must be anticipated in the original compensation negotiation if the net proceeds to the seller are to equal the market price.

**Counterpurchase**, or *offset trade*, is probably the most frequently used type of countertrade. For this trade, the seller agrees to sell a product at a set price to a buyer and receives payment in cash. However, two contracts are negotiated. The first contract is contingent on a second contract that is an agreement by the original seller to buy goods

---

[27]Rosemarie Francisco, "High Foreign Debt and Looking for Ways To Pay It Off? Try Offering Tuna Instead. Or Seaweed," *Reuters*, February 21, 2002.

from the buyer for the total monetary amount involved in the first contract or for a set percentage of that amount.[28] This arrangement provides the seller with more flexibility than the compensation deal because there is generally a time period—6 to 12 months or longer—for completion of the second contract. During the time that markets are sought for the goods in the second contract, the seller has received full payment for the original sale. Further, the goods to be purchased in the second contract are generally of greater variety than those offered in a compensation deal. Even greater flexibility is offered when the second contract is nonspecific; that is, the books on sales and purchases need to be cleared only at certain intervals. The seller is obligated to generate enough purchases to keep the books balanced or clear between purchases and sales.

Offset trades are becoming more prevalent among economically weak countries. Several variations of a counterpurchase or offset have developed to make it more economical for the selling company. For example, the Lockheed Martin Corporation entered into an offset trade with the United Arab Emirates (UAE) in a $6.4 billion deal for 80 F-16 fighter planes called Desert Falcons. Lockheed agreed to make a $160 million cash investment in a gas pipeline running from Qatar to UAE industrial projects and then on to Pakistan. The UAE requires that some of the proceeds from weapon sales be reinvested in the UAE. Such offsets are a common feature of arms deals, in which sellers build facilities ranging from hotels to sugar mills at the request of the buyer.

McDonnell Douglas actively engages in all types of countertrades. A $100 million sale of DC-9s to Yugoslavia required McDonnell Douglas to sell or buy $25 million in Yugoslavian goods. Some of its commitment to Yugoslavia was settled by buying Yugoslavian equipment for its own use, but it also sold items such as hams, iron castings, rubber bumper guards, and transmission towers to others. McDonnell Douglas held showings for department store buyers to sell glassware and leather goods to fulfill its counterpurchase agreement. Twice a year, company officials meet to claim credits for sales and clear the books in fulfillment of the company's counterpurchase agreements.

**Product buy-back agreement** is the fourth type of countertrade transaction. This type of agreement is made when the sale involves goods or services that produce other goods and services, that is, production plant, production equipment, or technology. The buy-back agreement usually involves one of two situations: The seller agrees to accept as partial payment a certain portion of the output, or the seller receives full price initially but agrees to buy back a certain portion of the output. One U.S. farm equipment manufacturer sold a tractor plant to Poland and was paid part in hard currency and the balance in Polish-built tractors. In another situation, General Motors built an auto manufacturing plant in Brazil and was paid under normal terms but agreed to the purchase of resulting output when the new facilities came online. Levi Strauss took Hungarian blue jeans, which it sells abroad, in exchange for setting up a jeans factory near Budapest.

An interesting buy-back arrangement was agreed on between the Rice Growers Association of California (RGAC) and the Philippine government. The RGAC will invest in Philippine farmlands and bring new technologies to enhance local rice production. In return, the RGAC will import rice and other food products in payment. A major drawback to product buy-back agreements comes when the seller finds that the products bought back are in competition with its own similarly produced goods. On the other hand, some find that a product buy-back agreement provides them with a supplemental source in areas of the world where there is demand but where they have no available supply.

## Problems of Countertrading

The crucial problem confronting a seller in a countertrade negotiation is determining the value of and potential demand for the goods offered. Frequently there is inadequate time to conduct a market analysis; in fact, it is not unusual to have sales negotiations almost completed before countertrade is introduced as a requirement in the transaction.

---

[28]Paul Cuckoo, "Airbus Dangles $500 Million Offset Bait for IA Order," *The Economic Times*, February 6, 2003.

Although such problems are difficult to deal with, they can be minimized with proper preparation. In most cases where losses occurred in countertrades, the seller was unprepared to negotiate in anything other than cash. Some preliminary research should be done in anticipation of being confronted with a countertrade proposal. Countries with a history of countertrading are identified easily, and the products most likely to be offered in a countertrade often can be ascertained. For a company trading with developing countries, these facts and some background on handling countertrades should be a part of every pricing tool kit. Once goods are acquired, they can be passed along to institutions that assist companies in selling bartered goods.[29]

*Barter houses* specialize in trading goods acquired through barter arrangements and are the primary outside source of aid for companies beset by the uncertainty of a countertrade. Although barter houses, most of which are found in Europe, can find a market for bartered goods, it requires time, which puts a financial strain on a company because capital is tied up longer than in normal transactions.

In the United States, there are companies that assist with bartered goods and their financing. Citibank has created a countertrade department to allow the bank to act as a consultant as well as to provide financing for countertrades. It is estimated that there are now about 500 barter exchange houses in the United States, many of which are accessible on the Internet. Some companies with a high volume of barter have their own in-house trading groups to manage countertrades. The 3M Company (Minnesota Mining and Manufacturing), for example, has a wholly owned division, 3M Global Trading (www.3m.com/globaltrading), which offers its services to smaller companies.

## The Internet and Countertrade

The Internet may become the most important venue for countertrade activities. Finding markets for bartered merchandise and determining market price are two of the major problems with countertrades. Several barter houses have Internet auction sites, and a number of Internet exchanges are expanding to include global barter.

Some speculate that the Internet may become the vehicle for an immense online electronic barter economy, to complement and expand the offline barter exchanges that take place now. In short, some type of electronic trade dollar would replace national currencies in international trade transactions. This would make international business considerably easier for many countries because it would lessen the need to acquire sufficient U.S. currency or other hard currency to complete a sale or purchase.[30]

TradeBanc, a market-making service, introduced a computerized technology that enables members of trade exchanges to trade directly, online, with members of other trade exchanges anywhere in the world, as long as their barter company is a TradeBanc affiliate (www.tradebanc.com/home.taf). The medium of exchange could be the Universal Currency proposed by the International Reciprocal Trade Association (IRTA), (www.irta.com) an association of trade exchanges with members including Russia, Iceland, Germany, Chile, Turkey, Australia, and the United States. The IRTA proposed to establish and operate a Universal Currency Clearinghouse, which would enable trade exchange members to easily trade with one another by using this special currency. When the system is in full swing all goods and services from all the participating affiliates would be housed in a single database. The transactions would be cleared by the local exchanges, and settlement would be made using IRTA's Universal Currency, which could be used to purchase anything from airline tickets to potatoes.[31]

## Proactive Countertrade Strategy

Currently most companies have a reactive strategy; that is, they use countertrade when they believe it is the only way to make a sale. Even when these companies include countertrade as a permanent feature of their operations, they use it to react to a sales demand

---

[29]David Hew, "Time for Asia To Cash In On Countertrade," *Business Times (Singapore),* September 4, 2002.

[30]Bob Meyer, "The Original Meaning of Trade Meets the Future in Barter," *World Trade,* January 2000, p. 46.

[31]You may want to visit American Countertrade Association (www.countertrade.org) for a detailed discussion of the services offered a countertrader.

rather than using countertrade as an aggressive marketing tool for expansion. Some authorities suggest, however, that companies should have a defined countertrade strategy as part of their marketing strategy rather than be caught unprepared when confronted with a countertrade proposition.

A proactive countertrade strategy is the most effective strategy for global companies that market to exchange-poor countries. Economic development plans in Eastern European countries, the Commonwealth of Independent States (CIS), and much of Latin America will put unusual stress on their ability to generate sufficient capital to finance their growth. Further, as countries encounter financial crises such as in Latin America in 1996 and Asia in 1998, countertrade becomes especially important as a means of exchange. To be competitive, companies must be willing to include some countertraded goods in their market planning. Companies with a proactive strategy make a commitment to use countertrade aggressively as a marketing and pricing tool. They see countertrades as an opportunity to expand markets rather than as an inconvenient reaction to market demands.

Successful countertrade transactions require that the marketer accurately establish the market value of the goods being offered and dispose of the bartered goods once they are received. Most unsuccessful countertrades result from not properly resolving one or both of these factors.

In short, unsuccessful countertrades are generally the result of inadequate planning and preparation. One experienced countertrader suggests answering the following questions before entering into a countertrade agreement: (1) Is there a ready market for the goods bartered? (2) Is the quality of the goods offered consistent and acceptable? (3) Is an expert needed to handle the negotiations? (4) Is the contract price sufficient to cover the cost of barter and net the desired revenue?

Capital-poor countries striving to industrialize account for much of the future demand for goods. Indonesia, for instance, requires any foreign purchase exceeding $500 million to have a portion in a countertrade.[32] Companies not prepared to seek this business with a proactive countertrade strategy will miss important market opportunities.[33]

## Transfer Pricing Strategy

As companies increase the number of worldwide subsidiaries, joint ventures, company-owned distributing systems, and other marketing arrangements, the price charged to different affiliates becomes a preeminent question. Prices of goods transferred from a company's operations or sales units in one country to its units elsewhere, known as *intracompany pricing* or **transfer pricing**, may be adjusted to enhance the ultimate profit of the company as a whole. The benefits are as follows:

- Lowering duty costs by shipping goods into high-tariff countries at minimal transfer prices so that duty base and duty are low.

- Reducing income taxes in high-tax countries by overpricing goods transferred to units in such countries; profits are eliminated and shifted to low-tax countries. Such profit shifting may also be used for "dressing up" financial statements by increasing reported profits in countries where borrowing and other financing are undertaken.

- Facilitating dividend repatriation when dividend repatriation is curtailed by government policy. Invisible income may be taken out in the form of high prices for products or components shipped to units in that country.

Government authorities have not overlooked the tax and financial manipulation possibilities of transfer pricing.[34] Transfer pricing can be used to hide subsidiary profits and to escape foreign-market taxes. Intracompany pricing is managed in such a way that profit

---

[32]"House Wants Tanjung Jati B Project Restarted," *Jakarta Pose,* February 20, 2003.

[33]For a primer on countertrade covering everything about countertrade from the types of trades to the risks, see Dan West, "Countertrade," *Business Credit,* April 2002, p. 48.

[34]Susan C. Borkowski, "Transfer Pricing Documentation and Penalties: How Much Is Enough?" *International Tax Journal,* Spring 2003, p. 31.

is taken in the country with the lowest tax rate. For example, a foreign manufacturer makes a VCR for $50 and sells it to its U.S. subsidiary for $150. The U.S. subsidiary sells it to a retailer for $200, but spends $50 on advertising and shipping so that it shows no profit and pays no U.S. taxes. Meanwhile, the parent company makes a $100 gross margin on each unit and pays at a lower tax rate in the home country. If the tax rate were lower in the country where the subsidiary resides, the profit would be taken in the foreign country and no profit taken in the home country.[35]

When customs and tax regimes are high, there is a strong incentive to trim fiscal liabilities by adjusting the transaction value of goods and services between subsidiaries. Pricing low cuts exposure to import duties; declaring a higher value raises deductible costs and thereby lightens the corporate tax burden. The key is to strike the right balance that maximizes savings overall.

The overall objectives of the intracompany pricing system include maximizing profits for the corporation as a whole; facilitating parent-company control; and offering management at all levels, both in the product divisions and in the international divisions, an adequate basis for maintaining, developing, and receiving credit for their own profitability. Transfer prices that are too low are unsatisfactory to the product divisions because their overall results look poor; prices that are too high make the international operations look bad and limit the effectiveness of foreign managers.

An intracompany pricing system should use sound accounting techniques and be defensible to the tax authorities of the countries involved. All of these factors argue against a single uniform price or even a uniform pricing system for all international operations. Four arrangements for pricing goods for intracompany transfer are as follows:

1. Sales at the local manufacturing cost plus a standard markup
2. Sales at the cost of the most efficient producer in the company plus a standard markup
3. Sales at negotiated prices
4. Arm's-length sales using the same prices as quoted to independent customers

Of the four, the arm's-length transfer is most acceptable to tax authorities and most likely to be acceptable to foreign divisions, but the appropriate basis for intracompany transfers depends on the nature of the subsidiaries and market conditions.

Although the practices described in this section are not necessarily improper, they are being scrutinized more closely by both home and host countries concerned about the loss of potential tax revenues from foreign firms doing business in their countries as well as domestic firms underreporting foreign earnings.[36] The U.S. government is paying particular attention to transfer pricing in tax audits, as are other countries. This led to what some describe as a "tax war" between the United States and Japan over transfer pricing by its MNCs, with each country bringing charges against foreign MNCs for underpayment of taxes because of transfer pricing practices. For example, the United States claimed that Nissan U.S. had inflated the prices it paid to its parent for finished cars it was importing to lower U.S. taxes. As a result, the United States levied a hefty multimillion-dollar tax penalty against Nissan. Japan retaliated by hitting Coca-Cola with a $145 million tax deficiency charge.

Governments are seeking tax revenues from their domestic MNCs as well. Prior to PepsiCo's decision to spin off its restaurant division into a separate company, the IRS charged PepsiCo $800 million after an audit of its foreign operations of Taco Bell, Pizza Hut, and Kentucky Fried Chicken indicated an underreporting of profits of their foreign operations. Penalties can be as high as 40 percent of the amount underreported. The only

---

[35]For a detailed report on transfer pricing methods and their importance to an MNC with divisions located in different countries, see Thomas H. Stevenson and David W. E. Cabell, "Integrating Transfer Pricing Policy and Activity-Based Costing," *Journal of International Marketing* 10 (4) 2002, p. 77.

[36]Jim Abrams, "Study Shows Corporations Manipulate Export-Import Prices to Avoid Taxes," *Associated Press,* November 4, 2002.

certain way to avoid such penalties is to enter an **Advanced Pricing Agreement** (APA) with the IRS. An APA is an agreement between the IRS and a taxpayer on transfer pricing methods that will be applied to some or all of a taxpayer's transactions with affiliates. Such agreements generally apply for up to five years and offer better protection against penalties than other methods. Otherwise, once the IRS charges underreporting, the burden of proof that a transfer price was fair rests with the company.[37]

## Price Quotations

In quoting the price of goods for international sale, a contract may include specific elements affecting the price, such as credit, sales terms, and transportation. Parties to the transaction must be certain that the quotation settled on appropriately locates responsibility for the goods during transportation and spells out who pays transportation charges and from what point. Price quotations must also specify the currency to be used, credit terms, and the type of documentation required. Finally, the price quotation and contract should define quantity and quality. A quantity definition might be necessary because different countries use different units of measurement. In specifying a ton, for example, the contract should identify it as a metric or an English ton, and as a long or short ton. Quality specifications can also be misunderstood if not completely spelled out. Furthermore, there should be complete agreement on quality standards to be used in evaluating the product. For example, "customary merchantable quality" may be clearly understood among U.S. customers but have a completely different interpretation in another country. The international trader must review all terms of the contract; failure to do so may have the effect of modifying prices even though such a change was not intended.

## Administered Pricing

**Administered pricing** is an attempt to establish prices for an entire market. Such prices may be arranged through the cooperation of competitors, through national, state, or local governments, or by international agreement. The legality of administered pricing arrangements of various kinds differs from country to country and from time to time. A country may condone price fixing for foreign markets but condemn it for the domestic market, for instance.

In general, the end goal of all administered pricing activities is to reduce the impact of price competition or eliminate it. Price fixing by business is not viewed as an acceptable practice (at least in the domestic market), but when governments enter the field of price administration, they presume to do it for the general welfare to lessen the effects of "destructive" competition.

The point at which competition becomes destructive depends largely on the country in question. To the Japanese, excessive competition is any competition in the home market that disturbs the existing balance of trade or gives rise to market disruptions. Few countries apply more rigorous standards in judging competition as excessive than Japan, but no country favors or permits totally free competition. Economists, the traditional champions of pure competition, acknowledge that perfect competition is unlikely and agree that some form of workable competition must be developed.

The pervasiveness of price-fixing attempts in business is reflected by the diversity of the language of administered prices; pricing arrangements are known as agreements, arrangements, combines, conspiracies, cartels, communities of profit, profit pools, licensing, trade associations, price leadership, customary pricing, or informal interfirm agreements. The arrangements themselves vary from the completely informal, with no spoken or acknowledged agreement, to highly formalized and structured arrangements. Any type of price-fixing arrangement can be adapted to international business, but of all the forms mentioned, cartels are the most directly associated with international marketing.

---

[37]Hema Ramakrishnan and Shaji Vikraman, "Transfer Pricing Norms May Not Be Eased Yet," *The Economic Times,* February 18, 2003.

**Cartels**  A **cartel** exists when various companies producing similar products or services work together to control markets for the types of goods and services they produce. The cartel association may use formal agreements to set prices, establish levels of production and sales for the participating companies, allocate market territories, and even redistribute profits. In some instances, the cartel organization itself takes over the entire selling function, sells the goods of all the producers, and distributes the profits.

The economic role of cartels is highly debatable, but their proponents argue that they eliminate cutthroat competition and rationalize business, permitting greater technical progress and lower prices to consumers. However, in the view of most experts, it is doubtful that the consumer benefits very often from cartels.

The Organization of Petroleum Exporting Countries (OPEC) is probably the best-known international cartel. Its power in controlling the price of oil resulted from the percentage of oil production it controlled. In the early 1970s, when OPEC members provided the industrial world with 67 percent of its oil, OPEC was able to quadruple the price of oil. The sudden rise in price from $10 or $12 a barrel to $50 or more a barrel was a primary factor in throwing the world into a major recession. In 2000, OPEC members lowered production, and oil prices rose from $10 to over $30, creating a dramatic increase in U.S. gasoline prices. Non-OPEC oil-exporting countries benefit from the price increases while net importers of foreign oil face economic repercussions.

One important aspect of cartels is their inability to maintain control for indefinite periods. Greed by cartel members and other problems generally weaken the control of the cartel. OPEC members tend to maintain a solid front until one decides to increase supply, and then others rapidly follow suit. In the short run, however, OPEC can affect global prices.

A lesser-known cartel, but one that directly impacts international trade, is the shipping cartel that exists among the world's shipping companies. Every two weeks about 20 shipping-line managers gather for their usual meeting to set rates on tens of billions of dollars of cargo. They do not refer to themselves as a cartel but rather operate under such innocuous names as "The Trans-Atlantic Conference Agreement," (www.tacaconf.com). Regardless of the name, they set the rates on about 70 percent of the cargo shipped between the United States and Northern Europe. Shipping between

The DeBeers company is one of the world's largest cartels and, for all practical purposes, it controls most of the world's diamonds and thus is able to maintain artificially high prices for diamonds. One of the ways in which it maintains control is illustrated by a recent agreement with Russia's diamond monopoly where DeBeers will buy at least $550 million in rough gem diamonds from Russia, or about half of the country's annual output. By controlling supply from Russia, the second largest producers of diamonds, the South African cartel can keep prices high. (© Susan Van Etten/Photo Edit)

the United States and Latin American ports and between the United States and Asian ports also is affected by shipping cartels. Not all shipping lines are members of cartels, but a large number are; thus they have a definite impact on shipping. Although legal, shipping cartels are coming under scrutiny by the U.S. Congress, and new regulations may soon be passed.

Another cartel is the diamond cartel controlled by DeBeers. For more than a century, DeBeers smoothly manipulated the diamond market by keeping a tight control over world supply. The company mines about half the world's diamonds and takes in another 25 percent through contracts with other mining companies. In an attempt to control the other 25 percent, De Beers runs an "outside buying office" where it spends millions buying up diamonds to protect prices.[38] The company controls most of the world's trade in rough gems and uses its market power to keep prices high.[39]

The legality of cartels at present is not clearly defined. Domestic cartelization is illegal in the United States, and the European Community also has provisions for controlling cartels. The United States does permit firms to take cartel-like actions in foreign markets, although it does not allow foreign-market cartels if the results have an adverse impact on the U.S. economy. Archer Daniels Midland Company, the U.S. agribusiness giant, was fined $205 million for its role in fixing prices for two food additives, lysine and citric acid. German, Japanese, Swiss, and Korean firms were also involved in the cartel. The group agreed on prices to charge and then allocated the share of the world market each company would get down to the tenth of a decimal point. At the end of the year, any company that sold more than its allotted share was required to purchase in the following year the excess from a co-conspirator that had not reached its volume allocation target.

Although the EC member countries have a long history of tolerating price fixing, the European Commission is beginning to crack down on cartels in the shipping, automobile, and cement industries, among others.[40] The unified market and the single currency have prompted the move. As countries open to free trade, powerful cartels that artificially raise prices and limit consumer choice are coming under closer scrutiny. However, the EC trustbusters are fighting tradition—since the trade guilds of the Middle Ages, cozy cooperation has been the norm. In each European country, companies banded together to control prices within the country and to keep competition out.[41]

## Government-Influenced Pricing

Companies doing business in foreign countries encounter a number of different types of government price setting. To control prices, governments may establish margins, set prices and floors or ceilings, restrict price changes, compete in the market, grant subsidies, and act as a purchasing monopsony or selling monopoly. The government may also influence prices by permitting, or even encouraging, businesses to collude in setting manipulative prices.

The Japanese government traditionally has encouraged a variety of government-influenced price-setting schemes, However, in a spirit of deregulation that is gradually moving through Japan, Japan's Ministry of Health and Welfare will soon abolish regulation of business hours and price setting for such businesses as barbershops, beauty parlors, and laundries. Under the current practice, 17 sanitation-related businesses can establish such price-setting schemes, which are exempt from the Japanese Anti-Trust Law.

Governments of producing and consuming countries play an ever-increasing role in the establishment of international prices for certain basic commodities. There is, for example, an international coffee agreement, an international cocoa agreement, and an

[38]Peter Verburg, "Diamond Cartels Are Forever," *Canadian Business,* July 10, 2000, p. 135.

[39]Linda Wertheimer Siegel, "Critics Believe DeBeers Manipulates the Market to Keep Diamonds High," *All Things Considered (NPR),* November 11, 2001.

[40]"Competition: Commission Fines 18 Firms More Than Euro 160 Million for Cartel Behaviour," *European Report,* December 21, 2002.

[41]Brandon Mitchener and James Kanter, "EU Fines Producers of Beer, Citric Acid for Price-Fixing," *The Wall Street Journal,* December 6, 2001, p. 4.

international sugar agreement. And the world price of wheat has long been at least partially determined by negotiations between national governments.

Despite the pressures of business, government, and international price agreements, most marketers still have wide latitude in their pricing decisions for most products and markets.

## Summary

Pricing is one of the most complicated decision areas encountered by international marketers. Rather than deal with one set of market conditions, one group of competitors, one set of cost factors, and one set of government regulations, international marketers must take all these factors into account, not only for each country in which they are operating, but often for each market within a country. Market prices at the consumer level are much more difficult to control in international than in domestic marketing, but the international marketer must still approach the pricing task on a basis of established objectives and policy, leaving enough flexibility for tactical price movements. Controlling costs that lead to price escalation when exporting products from one country to another is one of the most challenging pricing tasks facing the exporter. Some of the flexibility in pricing is reduced by the growth of the Internet, which has a tendency to equalize price differentials between country markets.

The continuing growth of Third World markets coupled with their lack of investment capital has increased the importance of countertrades for most marketers, making countertrading an important tool to include in pricing policy. The Internet is evolving to include countertrades, which will help eliminate some of the problems associated with this practice.

Pricing in the international marketplace requires a combination of intimate knowledge of market costs and regulations, an awareness of possible countertrade deals, infinite patience for detail, and a shrewd sense of market strategy.

## Questions

1. Define the following terms:

   | | |
   |---|---|
   | parallel imports, 531 | compensation deal, 551 |
   | exclusive distribution, 533 | counterpurchase, 551 |
   | variable-cost pricing, 535 | product buy-back |
   | full-cost pricing, 535 |   agreement, 552 |
   | skimming, 535 | transfer pricing, 554 |
   | price escalation, 538 | Advanced Pricing |
   | dumping, 548 |   Agreement, 556 |
   | countervailing duty, 548 | administered pricing, 556 |
   | countertrade, 549 | cartel, 557 |
   | barter, 550 | |

2. Discuss the causes of and solutions for parallel imports and their effect on price.

3. Why is it so difficult to control consumer prices when selling overseas?

4. Explain the concept of price escalation and tell why it can mislead an international marketer.

5. What are the causes of price escalation? Do they differ for exports and goods produced and sold in a foreign country?

6. Why is it seldom feasible for a company to absorb the high cost of international transportation and reduce the net price received?

7. Price escalation is a major pricing problem for the international marketer. How can this problem be counteracted? Discuss.

8. Changing currency values have an impact on export strategies. Discuss.

9. "Regardless of the strategic factors involved and the company's orientation to market pricing, every price must be set with cost considerations in mind." Discuss.

10. "Price fixing by business is not generally viewed as an acceptable practice (at least in the domestic market), but when governments enter the field of price administration, they presume to do it for the general welfare to lessen the effects of 'destructive' competition." Discuss.

11. Do value-added taxes discriminate against imported goods?

12. Explain specific tariffs, ad valorem tariffs, and compound tariffs.

13. Suggest an approach a marketer may follow in adjusting prices to accommodate exchange rate fluctuations.

14. Explain the effects of indirect competition and how they may be overcome.

15. Why has dumping become such an issue in recent years?

16. Cartels seem to rise, phoenix-like, after they have been destroyed. Why are they so appealing to business?

17. Discuss the different pricing problems that result from inflation versus deflation in a country.

18. Discuss the various ways in which governments set prices. Why do they engage in such activities?

19. Discuss the alternative objectives possible in setting prices for intracompany sales.

20. Why do governments so carefully scrutinize intracompany pricing arrangements?

21. Why are costs so difficult to assess in marketing internationally?

22. Discuss why countertrading is on the increase.

23. Discuss the major problems facing a company that is countertrading.

24. If a country you are trading with has a shortage of hard currency, how should you prepare to negotiate price?

25. Of the four types of countertrades discussed in the text, which is the most beneficial to the seller? Explain.

26. Why should a "knowledge of countertrades be part of an international marketer's pricing toolkit"? Discuss.

27. Discuss the various reasons purchasers impose countertrade obligations on buyers.

28. Discuss how FTZs can be used to help reduce price escalation.

29. Why is a proactive countertrade policy good business in some countries?

30. Differentiate between proactive and reactive countertrade policies.

31. One free trade zone is ZFM of Montevideo. Visit www.zfm.com and discuss how it might be used to help solve the price escalation problem of a product being exported from the United States to one of the Mercosur countries.

32. Select, "What are FTZs" and "What are benefits of FTZs" from the Web page of the National Association of Foreign Trade Zones www.naftz.org and visit the home page of a FTZ in McAllen, Texas, www.medc.org, on the border between the United States and Mexico. How does the description of this FTZ differ from the discussion in the text? Discuss how an exporter from the United States could use this FTZ to lower distribution costs.

33. Visit Global Trading (a division of 3M) at www.mmm.com/globaltrading/edge.html and select The Competitive Edge and Who We Are. Then write a short report on how Global Trading could assist a small company that anticipates having merchandise from a countertrade.

En los negocios no se consigue
lo que se merece, se consigue
lo que se negocia.

*...más que nunca, la gente d...*

# negotiating with international customers, partners, and regulators

## CHAPTER OUTLINE

## CHAPTER LEARNING OBJECTIVES

What you should learn from Chapter 19:

- The problems associated with cultural stereotypes

- How culture influences behaviors at the negotiation table

- Common kinds of problems that crop up during international business negotiations

- The similarities and differences in communication behaviors in several countries

- How differences in values and thinking processes affect international negotiations

- The important factors in selecting a negotiation team

- How to prepare for international negotiations

- Managing all aspects of the negotiation process

- The importance of follow-up communications and procedures

# PART FIVE

# Global Perspective

## A JAPANESE *AISATSU*

It is not so much that speaking only English is a disadvantage in international business. Instead, it's more that being bilingual is a huge advantage. Observations from sitting in on an *aisatsu* (a meeting or formal greeting for high-level executives typical in Japan) involving the president of a large Japanese industrial distributor and the marketing vice president of an American machinery manufacturer are instructive. The two companies were trying to reach an agreement on a long-term partnership in Japan.

Business cards were exchanged and formal introductions made. Even though the president spoke and understood English, one of his three subordinates acted as an interpreter for the Japanese president. The president asked everyone to be seated. The interpreter sat on a stool between the two senior executives. The general attitude between the parties was friendly but polite. Tea and a Japanese orange drink were served.

The Japanese president controlled the interaction completely, asking questions of all Americans through the interpreter. Attention of all the participants was given to each speaker in turn. After this initial round of questions for all the Americans, the Japanese president focused on developing a conversation with the American vice president. During this interaction an interesting pattern of nonverbal behaviors developed. The Japanese president would ask a question in Japanese. The interpreter then translated the question for the American vice president. While the interpreter spoke, the American's attention (gaze direction) was given to the interpreter. However, the Japanese president's gaze direction was at the American. Thus the Japanese president could carefully and unobtrusively observe the American's facial expressions and nonverbal responses. Conversely, when the American spoke the Japanese president had twice the response time. Because the latter understood English, he could formulate his responses during the translation process.

What is this extra response time worth in a strategic conversation? What is it worth to be able to carefully observe the nonverbal responses of your top-level counterpart in a high-stakes business negotiation?

Source: James Day Hodgson, Yoshihiro Sano, and John L. Graham, *Doing Business with the New Japan* (Boulder, CO: Rowman & Littlefield, 2000).

I (John Graham) had been in China a couple of weeks. I was tired. The fog had delayed my flight from Xian to Shanghai by four hours. I was standing in a long line at the counter to check in *again*. I started chatting with the older chap in line ahead of me. Juhani Kari introduced himself as a Finnish sales manager at ABB. He asked me what I did for a living. I responded, "I teach international business." He replied, "There is no such thing as international business. There's only interpersonal business." A wise man, indeed!

Face-to-face negotiations are an omnipresent activity in international commerce.[1] Once global marketing strategies are formulated, once marketing research is conducted to support those strategies, and once product/service, pricing, promotion, and place decisions are made, then the focus of managers turns to implementation of the plans. In international business such plans are almost always implemented through face-to-face negotiations with business partners and customers from foreign countries. The sales of goods and services, the management of distribution channels, the contracting for marketing research and advertising services, licensing and franchise agreements, and strategic alliances all require managers from different cultures to sit and talk with one another to exchange ideas and express needs and preferences.

Executives must also negotiate with representatives of foreign governments who might approve a variety of their marketing actions or in fact be the actual ultimate customer for goods and services. In many countries governmental officials may also be joint venture partners, and in some cases vendors. For example, negotiations for the television broadcast rights for the 2008 Summer Olympics in Beijing, China, included NBC, the International Olympic Committee, and Chinese governmental officials. Some of these negotiations can become quite complex, involving several governments, companies, and cultures.[2] Good examples are the European and North American talks regarding taxing the Internet,[3] the ongoing interactions regarding global environmental issues,[4] or the ongoing WTO negotiations begun in Doha, Qatar in 2001.[5] All these activities demand a new kind of "business diplomacy."

One authority on international joint ventures suggests that a crucial aspect of all international commercial relationships is the negotiation of the original agreement. The seeds of success or failure often are sown at the negotiation table, *vis-à-vis* (face-to-face), where not only are financial and legal details agreed to, but perhaps more important, the

---

[1]Several excellent books have been published on the topic of international business negotiations. Among them are Camille Schuster and Michael Copeland, *Global Business, Planning for Sales and Negotiations* (Fort Worth, TX: Dryden, 1996); Robert T. Moran and William G. Stripp, *Dynamics of Successful International Business Negotiations* (Houston: Gulf, 1991); Pervez Ghauri and Jean-Claude Usunier (eds.), *International Business Negotiations* (Oxford: Pergamon, 1996); Donald W. Hendon, Rebecca Angeles Henden, and Paul Herbig, *Cross-Cultural Business Negotiations* (Westport, CT: Quorum, 1996); Sheida Hodge, *Global Smarts* (New York: Wiley, 2000); and Jeanne M. Brett, *Negotiating Globally* (San Francisco: Jossey-Bass, 2001). Additionally, Roy J. Lewicki, David M. Saunders, and John W. Minton's *Negotiation: Readings, Exercises, and Cases,* 3rd edition (Boston: Irwin/McGraw-Hill, 1999) is an important book on the broader topic of business negotiations. The material from this chapter draws extensively on John L. Graham, "Vis-á-Vis International Business Negotiations," Chapter 3, pp. 69–91, in the Ghauri and Usunier book; James Day Hodgson, Yoshihiro Sano, and John L. Graham, *Doing Business with the New Japan* (Boulder, CO: Rowman & Littlefield, 2000); and John L. Graham, "Culture and Human Resources Management," in Alan M. Rugman and Thomas L. Brewer (eds.), *The Oxford Handbook of International Business* (Oxford: Oxford University Press, 2001), pp. 503–536.

[2]R. Bruce Money provides an interesting theoretical perspective on the topic in "International Multilateral Negotiations and Social Networks," *Journal of International Business Studies,* 1998, 29(4), pp. 695–710. Lively anecdotes are included in Jiang Feng, "Courting the Olympics: Beijing's Other Face," *The Asian Wall Street Journal,* February 26, 2001, p.6; and Ashling O'Connor, "After 54 Years, the Olympic Clock is Ticking," *Times of London,* February 10, 2003, p. 35.

[3]Michail Geist, "Fairness Says It's Time to Tax Goods Sold Online," *Toronto Star,* March 24, 2003, p. D03.

[4]Katherine Q. Seelye, "Politics and the Economy: The Environment," *New York Times,* January 9, 2003, p. 24.

[5]Paul Mannusson, "A Man of Many Missions," *Business Week,* March 31, 2003, p. 94; and Elizabeth Price, "USTR offers WTO Expanded Access to U.S. Services Markets," *Dow Jones International News,* March 31, 2003.

ambiance of cooperation is established. Indeed, the legal details and the structure of international business ventures are almost always modified over time, usually through negotiations. But the atmosphere of cooperation initially established face-to-face at the negotiation table persists—or the venture fails.

Business negotiations between business partners from the same country can be difficult. The added complication of cross-cultural communication can turn an already daunting task into an impossible one.[6] On the other hand, if cultural differences are considered, often-times wonderful business agreements can be made that lead to long-term, profitable relationships across borders. The purpose of this final chapter is to help prepare managers for the challenges and opportunities of international business negotiations. To do this, we discuss the dangers of stereotypes, the impact of culture on negotiation behavior, and the implications of cultural differences for managers and negotiators.

## The Dangers of Stereotypes

The images of John Wayne, the cowboy, and the samurai, the fierce warrior, often are used as cultural stereotypes in discussions of international business negotiations.[7] There is almost always a grain of truth to such representations—an American cowboy kind of competitiveness versus a samurai kind of organizational (company) loyalty.

---

[6]James K. Sebenius, "The Hidden Challenge of Cross-Border Negotiations," *Harvard Business Review,* March-April, 2002, pp. 76–82.

[7]Nurit Zaidman discusses how stereotypes are formed in "Stereotypes of International Managers: Content and Impact on Business Interactions," *Group & Organizational Management,* March 1, 2000, pp. 45–54.

The Europeans stereotype themselves. This postcard can be purchased at the European Parliament gift store in Brussels. Of course, not all Dutch are cheap, there are sober Irish, etc., etc., etc. (© J N Hughes-Wilson)

One Dutch expert on international business negotiations argues, "The best negotiators are the Japanese because they will spend days trying to get to know their opponents. The worst are Americans because they think everything works in foreign countries as it does in the USA."[8] There are, of course, many Americans who are excellent international negotiators and some Japanese who are ineffective. The point is that negotiations are not conducted between national stereotypes; negotiations are conducted between people, and cultural factors often make huge differences.

Recall our discussion on the cultural diversity within countries from Chapter 4 and consider its relevance to negotiation. For example, we might expect substantial differences in negotiation styles between English-speaking and French-speaking Canadians. The genteel style of talk prevalent in the American Deep South is quite different from the faster speech patterns and pushiness more common in places like New York City. Experts tell us that negotiation styles differ across genders in America as well. Still others tell us that the urbane negotiation behaviors of Japanese bankers are very different from the relative aggressiveness of those in the retail industry in that country. Finally, age and experience can also make important differences. The older Chinese executive with no experience dealing with foreigners is apt to behave quite differently from her young assistant with undergraduate and MBA degrees from American universities.

The focus of this chapter is culture's influence on international negotiation behavior. However, it should be clearly understood that individual personalities and backgrounds also heavily influence behavior at the negotiation table—and it is the manager's responsibility to consider these factors. Remember: Companies and countries do not negotiate—people do. Consider the culture of your customers and business partners, but treat them as individuals.

## The Pervasive Impact of Culture on Negotiation Behavior

The primary purpose of this section is to demonstrate the extent of cultural differences in negotiation styles and how these differences can cause problems in international business negotiations. The material in this section is based on a systematic study of the topic over the last two decades in which the negotiation styles of more than 1,000 businesspeople in 16 countries (19 cultures) were considered.[9] The countries studied were Japan, Korea, Taiwan, China (Tianjin, Guangzhou, and Hong Kong), the Philippines, Russia, Norway, the Czech Republic, Germany, France, the United Kingdom, Spain, Brazil, Mexico, Canada (English-speaking and French-speaking), and the United States. The countries were chosen because they constitute America's most important present and future trading partners.

Looking broadly across the several cultures, two important lessons stand out. The first is that regional generalizations very often are not correct.[10] For example, Japanese and

---

[8]Samfrits Le Poole comments on the American stereotype in "John Wayne Goes to Brussels," in Roy J. Lewicki, Joseph A. Litterer, David M. Saunders, and John W. Minton (eds.), *Negotiation: Readings, Exercises, and Cases,* 2nd edition (Burr Ridge, IL: Irwin, 1993). The quote is from the Spanish newspaper *Expansion,* November 29, 1991, p. 41.

[9]The following institutions and people have provided crucial support for the research upon which this material is based: U.S. Department of Education; Toyota Motor Sales USA, Inc.; Solar Turbines, Inc. (a division of Caterpillar Tractors Co.); the Faculty Research and Innovation Fund and the International Business Educational Research (IBEAR) Program at the University of Southern California; Ford Motor Company; The Marketing Science Institute; Madrid Business School; and Professors Nancy J. Adler (McGill University), Nigel Campbell (Manchester Business School), A. Gabriel Esteban (University of Houston, Victoria), Leonid I. Evenko (Russian Academy of the National Economy), Richard H. Holton (University of California, Berkeley), Alain Jolibert (Université des Sciences Sociales de Grenoble), Dong Ki Kim (Korea University), C. Y. Lin (National Sun-Yat Sen University), Hans-Gunther Meissner (Dortmund University), Alena Ockova (Czech Management Center), Sara Tang (Mass Transit Railway Corporation, Hong Kong), Kam-hon Lee (The Chinese University of Hong Kong), and Theodore Schwarz (Monterrey Institute of Technology).

[10]Rohit Deshpande and John Farley, "High Performance Firms in a Complex New China: A Tale of Six Cities," *Journal of Global Marketing,* 2002, 16(1-2), pp. 207–209.

Korean negotiation styles are quite similar in some ways, but in other ways they could not be more different. The second lesson learned from this study is that Japan is an exceptional place: On almost every dimension of negotiation style considered, the Japanese are on or near the end of the scale. Sometimes, Americans are on the other end. But actually, most of the time Americans are somewhere in the middle. The reader will see this evinced in the data presented in this section. The Japanese approach, however, is most distinct, even *sui generis.*

Cultural differences cause four kinds of problems in international business negotiations, at the levels of:[11]

1.  Language

2.  Nonverbal behaviors

3.  Values

4.  Thinking and decision-making processes

The order is important; the problems lower on the list are more serious because they are more subtle. For example, two negotiators would notice immediately if one were speaking Japanese and the other German. The solution to the problem may be as simple as hiring an interpreter or talking in a common third language, or it may be as difficult as learning a language. Regardless of the solution, the problem is obvious. Cultural differences in nonverbal behaviors, on the other hand, are almost always hidden below our awareness. That is to say, in a face-to-face negotiation participants nonverbally—and more subtly—give off and take in a great deal of information.[12] Some experts argue that this information is more important than verbal information. Almost all this signaling goes on below our levels of consciousness. When the nonverbal signals from foreign partners are different, negotiators are most apt to misinterpret them without even being conscious of the mistake. For example, when a French client consistently interrupts, Americans tend to feel uncomfortable without noticing exactly why. In this manner, interpersonal friction often colors business relationships, goes undetected, and, consequently, goes uncorrected. Differences in values and thinking and decision-making processes are hidden even deeper and therefore are even harder to cure. We discuss these differences here, starting with language and nonverbal behaviors.

### Differences in Language and Nonverbal Behaviors

Americans are clearly near the bottom of the languages skills list,[13] although Australians assert that Australians are even worse. It should be added, however, that American undergrads recently have begun to see the light and are flocking to language classes and study abroad programs. Unfortunately, foreign language teaching resources in the United States are inadequate to satisfy the increasing demand. In contrast, the Czechs are now throwing away a hard-earned competitive advantage: Young Czechs will not take Russian anymore. It is easy to understand why, but the result will be a generation of Czechs who cannot leverage their geographic advantage because they will not be able to speak to their neighbors to the east.

The language advantages of the Japanese executive in the description of the *aisatsu* that opened the chapter were quite clear. However, the most common complaint heard from American managers regards foreign clients and partners breaking into side conversations in their native languages. At best, it is seen as impolite, and quite often American negotiators are likely to attribute something sinister to the content of the foreign talk— "They're plotting or telling secrets."

[11]For additional details see John L. Graham, "Culture and Human Resources Management," in Alan M. Rugman and Thomas L. Brewer (eds.), *The Oxford Handbook of International Business* (Oxford: Oxford University Press, 2001), pp. 503–536.

[12]Thomas V. Leigh and John O. Sommers, "An Initial Evaluation of Industrial Buyers' Impressions of Salespersons' Nonverbal Cues," *Journal of Personal Selling & Sales Management,* January 1, 2002, pp. 41–53.

[13]Thane Peterson, "The Importance of Being Multilingual," *Business Week Online,* September 6, 2002.

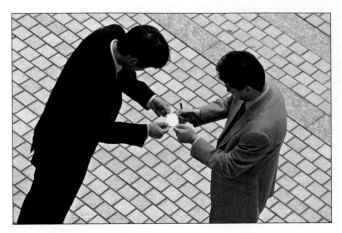

Japanese negotiators exchange business cards at the front end of a meeting. Even more important than the nonverbal demonstration of respect in the "little ritual" is the all-important information about the relative status of the negotiators clearly communicated by job title and company. Japanese executives literally do not know how to talk to one another until the status relationship is determined, because proper use of the language depends on knowledge of the relative status of the negotiators. (© *Photodisc*)

This is a frequent American mistake. The usual purpose of such side conversations is to straighten out a translation problem. For instance, one Korean may lean over to another and ask, "What'd he say?" Or the side conversation can regard a disagreement among the foreign team members. Both circumstances should be seen as positive signs by Americans—that is, getting translations straight enhances the efficiency of the interactions, and concessions often follow internal disagreements. But because most Americans speak only one language, neither circumstance is appreciated. By the way, people from other countries are advised to give Americans a brief explanation of the content of their first few side conversations to assuage the sinister attributions.

Data from simulated negotiations are also informative. In our study, the verbal behaviors of negotiators in 14 of the cultures (six negotiators in each of the 14 groups) were videotaped. The numbers in the body of Exhibit 19.1 represent the percentages of statements that were classified into each category listed. That is, 7 percent of the statements made by Japanese negotiators were classified as promises, 4 percent as threats, 7 percent as recommendations, and so on. The verbal bargaining behaviors used by the negotiators during the simulations proved to be surprisingly similar across cultures. Negotiations in all 14 cultures studied were composed primarily of information-exchange tactics—questions and self-disclosures. Note that the Japanese appear on the low end of the continuum of self-disclosures. Their 34 percent (along with the Spaniards and the English-speaking Canadians) was the lowest across all 14 groups, suggesting that they are the most reticent about giving information. Overall, however, the verbal tactics used were surprisingly similar across the diverse cultures.

Exhibit 19.2 provides analyses of some linguistic aspects and nonverbal behaviors for the 14 videotaped groups. Although these efforts merely scratch the surface of these kinds of behavioral analyses, they still provide indications of substantial cultural differences.[14] Note that, once again, the Japanese are at or next to the end of the continuum on almost every dimension of the behaviors listed. Their facial gazing and touching are the least among the 14 groups. Only the Northern Chinese used the word *no* less frequently, and only the Russians used more silent periods than did the Japanese.

A broader examination of the data in Exhibits 19.1 and 19.2 reveals a more meaningful conclusion: The variation across cultures is greater when comparing linguistic aspects of language and nonverbal behaviors than when the verbal content of negotiations is considered. For example, notice the great differences between Japanese and Brazilians in Exhibit 19.1 vis-à-vis Exhibit 19.2.

Following are further descriptions of the distinctive aspects of each of the 14 cultural groups videotaped. Certainly, conclusions about the individual cultures cannot be drawn from an analysis of only six business people in each culture, but the suggested cultural differences are worthwhile to consider briefly.

**Japan.**  Consistent with most descriptions of Japanese negotiation behavior, the results of this analysis suggest their style of interaction is among the least aggressive (or most polite). Threats, commands, and warnings appear to be de-emphasized in favor of the more positive promises, recommendations, and commitments. Particularly indicative of their polite conversational style was their infrequent use of *no* and *you* and facial gazing, as well as more frequent silent periods.

**Korea.**  Perhaps one of the more interesting aspects of the analysis is the contrast of the Asian styles of negotiations. Non-Asians often generalize about the Orient; the findings

[14]Thomas W. Leigh and John O. Summers, "An Initial Evaluation of Industrial Buyers' Impressions of Salespersons' Nonverbal Cues," *Journal of Personal Selling & Sales Management*, Winter 2002, pp. 41–53.

## Exhibit 19.1
Verbal Negotiation Tactics (The "What" of Communications)

**Cultures (in each group, n = 6)**

| Bargaining Behaviors and Definitions | JPN | KOR | TWN | CHN* | RUSS | GRM | UK | FRN | SPN | BRZ | MEX | FCAN | ECAN | USA |
|---|---|---|---|---|---|---|---|---|---|---|---|---|---|---|
| **Promise.** A statement in which the source indicated its intention to provide the target with a reinforcing consequence, which source anticipates target will evaluate as pleasant, positive, or rewarding. | 7† | 4 | 9 | 6 | 5 | 7 | 11 | 5 | 11 | 3 | 7 | 8 | 6 | 8 |
| **Threat.** Same as promise, except that the reinforcing consequences are thought to be noxious, unpleasant, or punishing. | 4 | 2 | 2 | 1 | 3 | 3 | 3 | 5 | 2 | 2 | 1 | 3 | 0 | 4 |
| **Recommendation.** A statement in which the source predicts that a pleasant environmental consequence will occur to the target. Its occurrence is not under source's control. | 7 | 1 | 5 | 2 | 4 | 5 | 6 | 3 | 4 | 5 | 8 | 5 | 4 | 4 |
| **Warning.** Same as recommendation, except that the consequences are thought to be unpleasant. | 2 | 0 | 3 | 1 | 0 | 1 | 1 | 3 | 1 | 1 | 2 | 5 | 0 | 1 |
| **Reward.** A statement by the source that is thought to create pleasant consequences for the target. | 1 | 3 | 2 | 1 | 3 | 4 | 5 | 3 | 3 | 2 | 1 | 1 | 3 | 2 |
| **Punishment.** Same as reward, except that the consequences are thought to be unpleasant. | 1 | 5 | 1 | 0 | 1 | 2 | 0 | 3 | 2 | 3 | 0 | 2 | 1 | 3 |
| **Positive normative appeal.** A statement in which the source indicates that the target's past, present, or future behavior was or will be in conformity with social norms. | 1 | 1 | 0 | 1 | 0 | 0 | 0 | 0 | 0 | 0 | 0 | 1 | 0 | 1 |
| **Negative normative appeal.** Same as positive normative appeal except that the target's behavior is in violation of social norms. | 3 | 2 | 1 | 0 | 0 | 1 | 1 | 0 | 1 | 1 | 1 | 2 | 1 | 1 |
| **Commitment.** A statement by the source to the effect that its future bids will not go below or above a certain level. | 15 | 13 | 9 | 10 | 11 | 9 | 13 | 10 | 9 | 8 | 9 | 8 | 14 | 13 |
| **Self-disclosure.** A statement in which the source reveals information about itself. | 34 | 36 | 42 | 36 | 40 | 47 | 39 | 42 | 34 | 39 | 38 | 42 | 34 | 36 |
| **Question.** A statement in which the source asks the target to reveal information about itself. | 20 | 21 | 14 | 34 | 27 | 11 | 15 | 18 | 17 | 22 | 27 | 19 | 26 | 20 |
| **Command.** A statement in which the source suggests that the target perform a certain behavior. | 8 | 13 | 11 | 7 | 7 | 12 | 9 | 9 | 17 | 14 | 7 | 5 | 10 | 6 |

*Northern China (Tianjin and environs).

†Read "7 percent of the statements made by Japanese negotiators were promises."

Source: Reprinted from Hodgson, Sano, and Graham, 2000.

**Exhibit 19.2**
Linguistic Aspects of Language and Nonverbal Behaviors ("How" Things Are Said)

| Bargaining Behaviors (per 30 minutes) | Cultures (in each group, n = 6) | | | | | | | | | | | | | |
| --- | --- | --- | --- | --- | --- | --- | --- | --- | --- | --- | --- | --- | --- | --- |
| | JPN | KOR | TWN | CHN* | RUSS | GRM | UK | FRN | SPN | BRZ | MEX | FCAN | ECAN | USA |
| **Structural Aspects** | | | | | | | | | | | | | | |
| **"No's."** The number of times the word no was used by each negotiator. | 1.9 | 7.4 | 5.9 | 1.5 | 2.3 | 6.7 | 5.4 | 11.3 | 23.2 | 41.9 | 4.5 | 7.0 | 10.1 | 4.5 |
| **"You's."** The number of times the word you was used by each negotiator. | 31.5 | 34.2 | 36.6 | 26.8 | 23.6 | 39.7 | 54.8 | 70.2 | 73.3 | 90.4 | 56.3 | 72.4 | 64.4 | 54.1 |
| **Nonverbal Behavior** | | | | | | | | | | | | | | |
| **Silent periods.** The number of conversational gaps of ten seconds or longer. | 2.5 | 0 | 0 | 2.3 | 3.7 | 0 | 2.5 | 1.0 | 0 | 0 | 1.1 | 0.2 | 2.9 | 1.7 |
| **Conversational overlaps.** Number of interruptions. | 6.2 | 22.0 | 12.3 | 17.1 | 13.3 | 20.8 | 5.3 | 20.7 | 28.0 | 14.3 | 10.6 | 24.0 | 17.0 | 5.1 |
| **Facial gazing.** Number of minutes negotiators spent looking at opponent's face. | 3.9 | 9.9 | 19.7 | 11.1 | 8.7 | 10.2 | 9.0 | 16.0 | 13.7 | 15.6 | 14.7 | 18.8 | 10.4 | 10.0 |
| **Touching.** Incidents of bargainers touching one another (not including handshaking). | 0 | 0 | 0 | 0 | 0 | 0 | 0 | 0.1 | 0 | 4.7 | 0 | 0 | 0 | 0 |

*Northern China (Tianjin and environs).

Source: Reprinted from Hodgson, Sano, and Graham, 2000.

**CROSSING BORDERS 19.1** Poker Faces and Botox Injections

We often hear from American executives the complaint that their Japanese counterparts are "hard to read" at the negotiation table, that is, they are "poker faced." However, when we videotape and count negotiators' facial movements (smiles and frowns) we see no differences between Japanese and Americans. It appears that because of differences in the timing and meaning of facial expressions across the two cultures the Americans are unable to intepret the Japanaese facial expressions, so they mistakenly report seeing nothing.

Now it seems that American executives are seeking their own poker-face advantage through the new wonder of science, Botox. Shots of the new drug are being used to freeze and sculpt their faces into "semi-permanent serenity." Says one American executive, "When you look strong and tough and not afraid, people respect you more . . . showing less expression really makes a statement."

Paul Ekman, a University of California psychologist who studies facial expressions, describes this trend as "very scary." Facial expressions have evolved to serve a purpose, to aid in the formation of basic human bonds through subconscious facial movements. Take those away and how can we tell friend or foe, mate or murderer?

And there are other hazards. An overzealous doctor pumped too much Botox into one executive's forehead, causing paralysis in the upper third of her face. Her underlings kept asking whether she was tired or sick. Until the treatment wore off she was forced to avoid any animated conversations inside and outside the company.

Rather than preparing for your international negotiations using Botox, we instead recommend a good book, a nice round of golf, or perhaps a good old-fashioned facial!

Sources: James D. Hodgson, Yoshihiro Sano, and John L. Graham, *Doing Business with the New Japan* (Bolder, CO: Rowman & Littlefield, 2000); and Suein L. Hwang, "Some Type A Staffers Dress for Success with a Shot of Botox," *Wall Street Journal*, June 31, 2002, p. B1.

demonstrate, however, that this is a mistake. Korean negotiators used considerably more punishments and commands than did the Japanese. Koreans used the word *no* and interrupted more than three times as frequently as the Japanese. Moreover, no silent periods occurred between Korean negotiators.

**China (Northern).** The behaviors of the negotiators from Northern China (i.e., in and around Tianjin) were most remarkable in the emphasis on asking questions (34 percent). Indeed, 70 percent of the statements made by the Chinese negotiators were classified as information-exchange tactics. Other aspects of their behavior were quite similar to the Japanese, particularly the use of *no* and *you* and silent periods.[15]

**Taiwan.** The behavior of the businesspeople in Taiwan was quite different from that in China and Japan but similar to that in Korea. The Chinese on Taiwan were exceptional in the time of facial gazing—on the average, almost 20 of 30 minutes. They asked fewer questions and provided more information (self-disclosures) than did any of the other Asian groups.

**Russia.** The Russians' style was quite different from that of any other European group, and, indeed, was quite similar in many respects to the style of the Japanese. They used *no* and *you* infrequently and used the most silent periods of any group. Only the Japanese did less facial gazing, and only the Chinese asked a greater percentage of questions.

**Germany.** The behaviors of the Germans are difficult to characterize because they fell toward the center of almost all the continua. However, the Germans were exceptional in

---

[15]There is a burgeoning literature on negotiations with Chinese. See Catherine H. Tinsley and Jeanne M. Brett, "Managing Workplace Conflict in the U.S. and Hong Kong," *Organizational Behavior and Human Decision Process*, forthcoming; Pervez Ghauri and Tony Fang, "Negotiating with the Chinese: A Socio-Cultural Analysis," *Journal of World Business*, September 22, 2001, pp. 303–312; and Vivian C. Sheer and Ling Chen, "Successful Sino-Western Business Negotitation: Participants' Accounts of National and Professional Cultures," *Journal of Business Communication*, January 1, 2003, pp. 50–64.

the high percentage of self-disclosures (47 percent) and the low percentage of questions (11 percent).

**United Kingdom.**  The behaviors of the British negotiators were remarkably similar to those of the Americans in all respects.

**Spain.**  *Diga* is perhaps a good metaphor for the Spanish approach to negotiations evinced in our data. When you make a phone call in Madrid, the usual greeting on the other end is not *hola* ("hello") but is, instead, *diga* ("speak"). It is not surprising, then, that the Spaniards in the videotaped negotiations likewise used the highest percentage of commands (17 percent) of any of the groups and gave comparatively little information (self-disclosures, only 34 percent). Moreover, they interrupted one another more frequently than any other group, and they used the terms *no* and *you* very frequently.

**France.**  The style of the French negotiators was perhaps the most aggressive of all the groups. In particular, they used the highest percentage of threats and warnings (together, 8 percent). They also used interruptions, facial gazing, and *no* and *you* very frequently compared with the other groups, and one of the French negotiators touched his partner on the arm during the simulation.

**Brazil.**  The Brazilian businesspeople, like the French and Spanish, were quite aggressive. They used the second-highest percentage of commands of all the groups. On average, the Brazilians said the word *no* 42 times, *you* 90 times, and touched one another on the arm about 5 times during 30 minutes of negotiation. Facial gazing was also high.

**Mexico.**  The patterns of Mexican behavior in our negotiations are good reminders of the dangers of regional or language-group generalizations.[16] Both verbal and nonverbal behaviors were quite different than those of their Latin American (Brazilian) or continental (Spanish) cousins. Indeed, Mexicans answer the telephone with the much less demanding *bueno* (short for "good day"). In many respects, the Mexican behavior was very similar to that of the negotiators from the United States.

**French-Speaking Canada.**  The French-speaking Canadians behaved quite similarly to their continental cousins. Like the negotiators from France, they too used high percentages of threats and warnings, and even more interruptions and eye contact. Such an aggressive interaction style would not mix well with some of the more low-key styles of some of the Asian groups or with English speakers, including English-speaking Canadians.

**English-Speaking Canada.**  The Canadians who speak English as their first language used the lowest percentage of aggressive persuasive tactics (threats, warnings, and punishments totaled only 1 percent) of all 14 groups. Perhaps, as communications researchers suggest, such stylistic differences are the seeds of interethnic discord as witnessed in Canada over the years. With respect to international negotiations, the English-speaking Canadians used noticeably more interruptions and *no*'s than negotiators from either of Canada's major trading partners, the United States and Japan.

**United States.**  Like the Germans and the British, the Americans fell in the middle of most continua. They did interrupt one another less frequently than all the others, but that was their sole distinction.

These differences across the cultures are quite complex, and this material by itself should not be used to predict the behaviors of foreign counterparts. Instead, great care should be taken with respect to the aforementioned dangers of stereotypes. The key here is to be aware of these kinds of differences so that the Japanese silence, the Brazilian "no, no, no . . .," or the French threat are not misinterpreted.

---

[16]T. Lenartowicz and J.P. Johnson, "A Cross-National Assessment of the Values of Latin American Managers: Contrasting Hues or Shades of Gray?" *Journal of International Business Studies,* May 2003, 34(3), pp. 266–281.

## Differences in Values

Four values—objectivity, competitiveness, equality, and punctuality—that are held strongly and deeply by most Americans seem to frequently cause misunderstandings and bad feelings in international business negotiations.

**Objectivity.** "Americans make decisions based upon the bottom line and on cold, hard facts." "Americans don't play favorites." "Economics and performance count, not people." "Business is business." Such statements well reflect American notions of the importance of objectivity.

The single most important book on the topic of negotiation, *Getting to Yes*,[17] is highly recommended for both American and foreign readers. The latter will learn not only about negotiations but, perhaps more important, about how Americans think about negotiations. The authors are quite emphatic about "separating the people from the problem," and they state, "Every negotiator has two kinds of interests: in the substance and in the relationship." This advice is probably quite worthwhile in the United States or perhaps in Germany, but in most places in the world such advice is nonsense. In most places in the world, particularly in relationship-oriented cultures, personalities and substance are not separate issues and cannot be made so.

For example, consider how important nepotism is in Chinese or Hispanic cultures. Experts tell us that businesses don't grow beyond the bounds and bonds of tight family control in the burgeoning "Chinese Commonwealth." Things work the same way in Spain, Mexico, and the Philippines by nature. And, just as naturally, negotiators from such countries not only will take things personally but will be personally affected by negotiation outcomes. What happens to them at the negotiation table will affect the business relationship regardless of the economics involved.

**Competitiveness and Equality.** Simulated negotiations can be viewed as a kind of experimental economics wherein the values of each participating cultural group are roughly reflected in the economic outcomes. The simple simulation used in our studies represented the essence of commercial negotiations—it had both competitive and cooperative aspects. At least 40 businesspeople from each culture played the same buyer-seller game, negotiating over the prices of three products. Depending on the agreement reached, the "negotiation pie" could be made larger through cooperation (as high as $10,400 in joint profits) before it was divided between the buyer and seller. The results are summarized in Exhibit 19.3.

---

[17]Roger Fisher, William Ury, and Bruce Patton, *Getting to Yes: Negotiating Agreement without Giving In* (New York: Penguin, 1991).

**Exhibit 19.3**
Cultural Differences in Competitiveness and Equality

Based upon at least 40 business people in each cultural group. Source: Reprinted from Hodgson, Sano, and Graham, 2000.

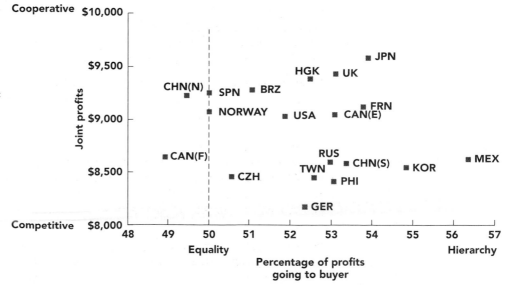

The Japanese were the champions at making the pie big. Their joint profits in the simulation were the highest (at $9,590) among the 18 cultural groups involved. The American pie was more average sized (at $9,030), but at least it was divided relatively equitably (51.8 percent of the profits went to the buyers). Conversely, the Japanese (and others) split their pies in strange ways, with buyers making higher percentages of the profits (53.8 percent). The implications of these simulated business negotiations are completely consistent with the comments of other authors and the adage that in Japan the buyer is "kinger." By nature, Americans have little understanding of the Japanese practice of giving complete deference to the needs and wishes of buyers. That is not the way things work in America. American sellers tend to treat American buyers more as equals, and the egalitarian values of American society support this behavior. Moreover, most Americans will, by nature, treat Japanese buyers more frequently as equals. Likewise, American buyers will generally not "take care of" American sellers or Japanese sellers. The American emphasis on competition and individualism represented in these findings is quite consistent with the work of Geert Hofstede[18] detailed in Chapter 4, which indicated that Americans scored the highest among all the cultural groups on the individualism (versus collectivism) scale. Moreover, values for individualism/collectivism have been shown to directly influence negotiation behaviors in several other countries.[19]

Finally, not only do Japanese buyers achieve higher results than Americans buyers, but compared with American sellers ($4,350), Japanese sellers also get more of the commercial pie ($4,430) as well. Interestingly, when shown these results, Americans in executive seminars still often prefer the American seller's role. In other words, even though the American sellers make lower profits than the Japanese, many American managers apparently prefer lower profits if those profits are yielded from a more equal split of the joint profits.

**Time.**   "Just make them wait." Everyone else in the world knows that no negotiation tactic is more useful with Americans, because no one places more value on time, no one has less patience when things slow down, and no one looks at their wristwatches more than Americans do. The material from Chapter 5 on P-time versus M-time is quite pertinent here. Edward T. Hall[20] in his seminal writing is best at explaining how the passage of time is viewed differently across cultures and how these differences most often hurt Americans.

Even Americans try to manipulate time to their advantage, however. As a case in point, Solar Turbines Incorporated (a division of Caterpillar) once sold $34 million worth of industrial gas turbines and compressors for a Russian natural gas pipeline project. Both parties agreed that final negotiations would be held in a neutral location, the south of France. In previous negotiations, the Russians had been tough but reasonable. But in Nice, the Russians were not nice. They became tougher and, in fact, completely unreasonable, according to the Solar executives involved.

It took a couple of discouraging days before the Americans diagnosed the problem, but once they did, a crucial call was made back to headquarters in San Diego. Why had the Russians turned so cold? They were enjoying the warm weather in Nice and weren't interested in making a quick deal and heading back to Moscow! The call to California was the key event in this negotiation. Solar's headquarters people in San Diego were sophisticated enough to allow their negotiators to take their time. From that point on, the routine of the negotiations changed to brief, 45-minute meetings in the mornings, with afternoons at the golf course, beach, or hotel, making calls and doing paperwork. Finally, during the fourth week, the Russians began to make concessions and to ask for longer meetings. Why? They could not go back to Moscow after four weeks on the

---

[18]Geert Hofstede, *Cultures Consequences* (2nd edition, Thousand Oaks, CA: Sage, 2001).

[19]John L. Graham, "Culture's Influence on Business Negotiations: An Application of Hofstede's and Rokeach's Ideas," in Farok J. Contractor and Peter Lorange (eds.), *Cooperative Strategies and Alliances* (Amsterdam: Pergamon, 2002), pp. 461–492. Also, see Roy J. Lewicki, David M. Saunders, and John W. Minton, *Essentials of Negotiation* (2nd edition, Boston: McGraw-Hill, 2001).

[20]Edward T. Hall, "The Silent Language in Overseas Business," *Harvard Business Review,* May-June, 1960, pp. 87–96.

**CROSSING BORDERS 19.2**   A Russian and an Indonesian Manager Talk about Negotiations

The new Russian business managers are traders. Many got their start in the black markets of the old Soviet system. They will promise you the world, but these promises often lack substance. Although they are inexperienced in Western business practices, they are often very shrewd negotiators. In many instances, the stubborn Russian negotiator gets the best of his Western counterpart who is in a rush to close the deal.

However, those who live in Russia and get used to the Russian bargaining techniques often come to enjoy the intricacies of negotiating there. Formalized games of power politics and posturing can provide hours of enjoyment for the entire office staff. To negotiate successfully in Russia, you must be thick-skinned, bullheaded, and warmhearted. And always remember that Russians are the world's greatest chess players.

—*Marina Volobueva*

I grew up outside my native Indonesia but went back to do an internship in the family business. One day I had the privilege of accompanying my father during a fairly important negotiation. We met first for lunch, but we never discussed the business deal at all. Instead, the person my father was meeting spent the entire time asking questions about my education in the United States. Apparently he intended to send his son to school there. After spending what seemed to me two unproductive hours, we agreed to play golf that Saturday morning. Afterward, my father told me that most important business deals take place on the golf course. That Saturday, we met on the course, but it was not until the tenth hole that they finally got around to discussing business. After the game was over, they agreed to meet again at the office to finish up the details of the deal.

—*Aidil A. Madjid*

Source: Reprinted with permission from Sheida Hodge, *Global Smarts* (New York: Wiley, 2000), pp. 191 and 196. This material used by permission of John Wiley & Sons, Inc.

Mediterranean without a signed contract. This strategic reversal of the time pressure yielded a wonderful contract for Solar.

**Differences in Thinking and Decision-Making Processes**

When faced with a complex negotiation task, most Westerners (notice the generalization here) divide the large task up into a series of smaller tasks. Issues such as prices, delivery, warranty, and service contracts may be settled one issue at a time, with the final agreement being the sum of the sequence of smaller agreements. In Asia, however, a different approach is more often taken wherein all the issues are discussed at once, in no apparent order, and concessions are made on all issues at the end of the discussion. The Western sequential approach and the Eastern holistic approach do not mix well.[21]

That is, American managers often report great difficulties in measuring progress in Japan. After all, in America, you are half done when half the issues are settled. But in Japan, nothing seems to get settled. Then, surprise, you are done. Often, Americans make unnecessary concessions right before agreements are announced by the Japanese. For example, one American department store buyer traveling to Japan to buy six different consumer products for his chain lamented that negotiations for his first purchase took an entire week. In the United States, such a purchase would be consummated in an afternoon. So, by his calculations, he expected to have to spend six weeks in Japan to complete his purchases. He considered raising his purchase prices to try to move things along faster. But before he was able to make such a concession, the Japanese quickly agreed on the other five products in just three days. This particular businessman was, by his own admission, lucky in his first encounter with Japanese bargainers.

---

[21]Other East-West differences in thinking are studied in detail in Joel Brockner, Ya-Ru Chen, Elizabeth A. Mannix, Kwok Leung, and Daniel P. Skarlicki, "Culture and Procedural Fairness: When the Effects of What You Do Depend on How You Do It," *Administrative Science Quarterly*, March 1, 2000, pp. 138–157. Most important is Richard E. Nisbett, *The Geography of Thought, How Asians and Westerners Think Differently . . . and Why* (New York: Free Press, 2003).

This American businessman's near blunder reflects more than just a difference in decision-making style. To Americans, a business negotiation is a problem-solving activity, the best deal for both parties being the solution. To a Japanese businessperson, on the other hand, a business negotiation is a time to develop a business relationship with the goal of long-term mutual benefit. The economic issues are the context, not the content, of the talks. Thus, settling any one issue really is not that important. Such details will take care of themselves once a viable, harmonious business relationship is established. And as happened in the case of our retail goods buyer, once the relationship was established—signaled by the first agreement—the other "details" were settled quickly.

American bargainers should anticipate such a holistic approach and be prepared to discuss all issues simultaneously and in an apparently haphazard order. Progress in the talks should not be measured by how many issues have been settled. Rather, Americans must try to gauge the quality of the business relationship. Important signals of progress can be the following:

- Higher-level foreigners being included in the discussions
- Their questions beginning to focus on specific areas of the deal
- A softening of their attitudes and position on some of the issues—"Let us take some time to study this issue"
- At the negotiation table, increased talk among themselves in their own language, which may often mean they're trying to decide something
- Increased bargaining and use of the lower-level, informal, and other channels of communication

## Implications for Managers and Negotiators

Considering all the potential problems in cross-cultural negotiations, particularly when you mix managers from relationship-oriented cultures with those from information-oriented ones, it is a wonder that any international business gets done at all. Obviously, the economic imperatives of global trade make much of it happen despite the potential pitfalls. But an appreciation of cultural differences can lead to even better international commercial transactions—it is not just business deals but highly profitable business relationships that are the real goal of international business negotiations.

Four steps lead to more efficient and effective international business negotiations. They are as follows: (1) selection of the appropriate negotiation team;[22] (2) management of preliminaries, including training, preparations, and manipulation of negotiation settings; (3) management of the process of negotiations, that is, what happens at the negotiation table; and (4) appropriate follow-up procedures and practices. Each is discussed in this section.

### Negotiation Teams

One reason for global business successes is the large numbers of skillful international negotiators. These are the managers who live in foreign countries and speak foreign languages. In many cases, they are immigrants to the United States or have been immersed in foreign cultures in other capacities (Peace Corps volunteers and Mormon missionaries are common examples). More business schools are beginning to reemphasize language training and visits abroad. Indeed, it is interesting to note that the original Harvard Business School catalog of 1908–1909 listed German, French, and Spanish correspondence within its curriculum.

The selection criteria for international marketing and sales personnel previously detailed in Chapter 17 are applicable in selecting negotiators as well. Traits such as maturity, emotional stability, breadth of knowledge, optimism, flexibility, empathy, and stamina are all important, not only for marketing executives involved in international negotiations, but also for the technical experts who often accompany and support them. In studies conducted at Ford Motor Company and AT&T, three additional traits were found

---

[22]Leonidas C. Leonidou, Constantine S. Katsikeas, and John Hadjimarcou, "Building Successful Export Business Relationships," *Journal of International Marketing*, January 1, 2002, pp. 96–101.

Women can get the job done. Here Chile's Foreign Minister, Maria Soledad Alvear, at a news conference with U.S. Trade Representative Robert Zoellick discusses the free trade pact between the two nations. Zoellick was preceded in his job by two American women, both quite successful in opening up foreign markets. Indeed, Charlene Barshefsky earned the nickname "Velvet Crowbar" from her Asian counterparts while she served as USTR during President Clinton's second term. *(AP/Wide World Photos)*

to be important predictors of negotiator success with international clients and partners: willingness to use team assistance, listening skill, and influence at headquarters.

Willingness to use team assistance is particularly important for American negotiators. Because of a cultural heritage of independence and individualism, Americans often make the mistake of going it alone against greater numbers of foreigners. One American sitting across the negotiation table from three or four Chinese negotiators is unfortunately an all too common sight. The number of brains in the room does make a difference. Moreover, business negotiations are social processes, and the social reality is that a larger number of nodding heads can exercise greater influence than even the best arguments. It is also much easier to gather detailed information when teams are negotiating rather than individuals. For example, the Japanese are quite good at bringing along junior executives for the dual purposes of careful note taking and training via observation. Compensation schemes that overly emphasize individual performance can also get in the way of team negotiating—a negotiation team requires a split commission, which many Americans naturally eschew. Finally, negotiators may have to request the accompaniment of senior executives to better match up with client's and partner's negotiation teams. Particularly in relationship-oriented cultures, rank speaks quite loudly in both persuasion and the demonstration of interest in the business relationship.

The single most important activity of negotiations is listening. The negotiator's primary job is collecting information with the goal of enhancing creativity. This may mean assigning one team member the sole responsibility of taking careful notes and not worrying about speaking during the meetings. This may also mean that knowing the language of clients and partners will be crucial for the most complete understanding of their needs and preferences. The importance of listening skills in international business negotiations cannot be overstated.

Bringing along a senior executive is important because influence at headquarters is crucial to success. Many experienced international negotiators argue that half the negotiation is with headquarters. The representatives' lament goes something like this, "The better I understand my customer, the tougher time I have with headquarters." Of course, this misery associated with boundary-spanning roles is precisely why international negotiators and sales executives make so much money.

Finally, it is also important to reiterate a point made in Chapter 5: Gender should not be used as a selection criterion for international negotiation teams. This is so despite the great differences in the roles of women across cultures. Even in countries where women do not participate in management, American women negotiators are treated as foreigners first. For obvious reasons it may not be appropriate for women managers to participate in some forms of business entertainment—common baths in locker rooms at Japanese golf course club houses, for example. However, it is still important for women executives to establish personal rapport at restaurants and other informal settings. Indeed, one expert on cross-gender communication suggests that women may actually have some advantages in international negotiations:

> In general, women are more comfortable talking one-on-one. The situation of speaking up in a meeting is a lot closer to boys' experience of using language to establish their position in a large group than it is to girls' experience using language to maintain intimacy. That's something that can be exploited. Don't wait for the meeting; try to make your point in advance, one-to-one. This is what the Japanese do, and in many ways American women's style is a lot closer to the Japanese style than to American men's.[23]

[23]Deborah Tannen, *You Just Don't Understand: Men and Women in Conversation* (New York: William Morrow, 1990).

## Negotiation Preliminaries

Many companies in the United States provide employees with negotiations training. For example, through his training programs, Chester Karrass[24] has taught more people (some 400,000) to negotiate than any other purveyor of the service[25]—see his ads in almost all in-flight magazines of domestic American air carriers. However, very few companies provide training for negotiations with managers from other countries. Even more surprising is the lack of cultural content in the training of the government's diplomats. Instead, in most schools of diplomacy the curricula cover language skills, social and diplomatic skills, and knowledge specific to the diplomatic profession, including diplomatic history and international relations, law, economics, politics, international organizations, and foreign policies. Cultural differences in negotiation and communication styles are seldom considered.

Things are different at Ford Motor Company. Ford does more business with Japanese companies than any other firm. Ford owns 33 percent of Mazda, it built a successful minivan with Nissan, and it buys and sells component parts and completed cars from and to Japanese companies. But perhaps the best measure of Ford's Japanese business is the 8,000 or so U.S.-to-Japan round-trip airline tickets the company buys annually. Ford has made a large investment in training its managers with Japanese responsibilities. Over 2,000 of its executives have attended a three-day program on Japanese history and culture and the company's Japanese business strategies. Further, more than 1,000 Ford managers who work face-to-face with Japanese have attended a three-day program entitled "Managing Negotiations: Japan" (MNJ). The MNJ program includes negotiation simulations with videotape feedback, lectures with cultural differences demonstrated via videotapes of Japanese/American interactions, and rehearsals of upcoming negotiations. The company has also conducted similar programs on Korea and the People's Republic of China.

**En los negocios no se consigue lo que se merece, se consigue lo que se negocia.**

*Ahora, más que nunca, la gente de éxito acude a Karrass.*

La revista **Forbes** lo dijo en pocas palabras: "Claro, hay docenas de tipos -demasiados -que corren de acá para allá dando cursos, pero la lista de clientes de Karrass es de otra casta: Mobil, General Motors, Ford, IBM, General Electric, Arco, Shell, ITT, Phillips Petroleum, -9 de las 15 empresas más grandes de los Estados Unidos -y 140 más." Añadió **Forbes:**
Kaiser Aluminum & Chemical, que gastó en el transcurso de varios años, cerca de $15,000 dólares en cursos de Karrass, pidió que sus empleados identificaran ahorros específicos logrados al negociar mejor. El total sumó millones de dólares. Un ejecutivo de ventas de Boeing dijo lo mismo acerca de una sola negociación en el Medio Oriente. En General Electric, reconocida por sus programas internos de capacitación, el 90 por ciento de los empleados se

*Dr. Chester L. Karrass*

**Continúa** en la siguiente página

Through his books and training courses, Chester Karrass has taught more people to negotiate than anyone else on earth. His firm offers seminars in dozens of countries and advertises in in-flight magazines here in Spanish. *(Copyrighted and used by permission of KARRASS, LTD. Beverly Hills, California)*

In addition to MNJ, the broader Japan training efforts at Ford must be credited for their successes in Japan. Certainly, MNJ alumni can be seen exercising influence across and up the ranks regarding Japanese relationships. But the organizational awareness of the cultural dimensions of the Japanese business system was quickly raised as well by their broader, three-day program on Japanese business strategies. Remember the story about the Russians in Nice? Two critical events took place. First, the Solar Turbines negotiators diagnosed the problem. Second, and equally important, their California superiors appreciated the problem and approved the investments in time and money to outwait the Russians. So it is that the Ford programs have targeted not only the negotiators working directly with the Japanese but also their managers who spend most of their time in the

[24]See Karrass's website for information regarding his programs: www.karrass.com. Other websites providing information about publically offered training programs and information on international negotiation styles are www.pon.harvard.edu, www.usip.org, www.iimcr.org, www.executiveplanet.com, www.etiquetteintl.com. See Marisa Mohd Isa, "Learning the Art of Refined Behavior," *New Straits Times,* March 17, 2003, p. 23.

[25]Lee Edison provides an interesting description of what he calls "The Negotiation Industry," in an article he wrote in *Across the Board,* April 2000, 37(4), pp. 14–20. Other commentators on training for international business negotiators are Yeang Soo Ching, "Putting a Human Face on Globalization," *New Straits Times,* January 16, 2000, p. 10; A. J. Vogl, "Negotiation: The Advanced Course," *Across the Board,* April 1, 2000, p. 21; and R. V. Veera, "MIT Preparing Students for New Millennium," *New Straits Times,* July 21, 2002, p. 5.

**CROSSING BORDERS 19.3** Ford Trains Executives for Negotiations with Japanese

"Proactive and direct" is the approach Ford uses to develop competence in employees who interact with the Japanese. This occurs through a variety of practices, including programs that help Ford personnel better understand the Japanese culture and negotiating practices, and by encouraging the study of the spoken language. By designing training that highlights both the pitfalls and the opportunities in negotiations, Ford increases the chance "to expand the negotiation pie."

The key personnel on our minivan team attended one of the first sessions of the Managing Negotiations: Japan's (MNJ) program at the Ford Executive Development Center. Its negotiations with the Nissan team improved immediately. But perhaps the best measure of the usefulness of the MNJ program is the success of the Nissan joint venture product itself. Reflected in the Villager/Quest are countless hours of effective face-to-face meetings with Ford's Japanese partners.

Not everyone negotiating outside the United States has the advantages of in-house training. However, many sources of information are available—books (particularly, on Japan), periodicals, and colleagues with first-hand experience. To succeed, I believe negotiators have to be truly interested in and challenged by the international negotiating environment. Structuring negotiations to achieve win-win results and building a long-term relationship take thoughtful attention and commitment.

*—Joe Gilmore*
(Ford executive in charge of the minivan project with Nissan)

Source: James Day Hodgson, Yoshihiro Sano, and John L. Graham, *Doing Business with the New Japan* (Boulder, CO: Rowman & Littlefield, 2000), p. 81. Used by permission of Rowman & Littlefield.

company's Detroit headquarters. Negotiators need information specific to the cultures in which they work. Just as critical, their managers back in the United States need a basic awareness and appreciation for the importance of culture in international business so that they will be more apt to listen to the "odd-sounding" recommendations coming from their people in Moscow, Rio, or Tokyo.

Any experienced business negotiator will tell you that there is never enough time to get ready. Given the time constraints of international negotiations, preparations must be accomplished efficiently—the homework must be done before the bargaining begins. We recommend the following checklist to ensure proper preparation and planning for international negotiations:

1. Assessment of the situation and the people
2. Facts to confirm during the negotiation
3. Agenda
4. Best alternative to a negotiated agreement (BATNA)[26]
5. Concession strategies
6. Team assignments

Preparation and planning skill is at the top of almost everyone's list of negotiator traits, yet it seems many Americans are still planning strategies during over-ocean flights when they should be trying to rest. Quick wits are important in business negotiations, and arduous travel schedules and jet lag dull even the sharpest minds. Obviously, information about the other side's goals and preferences should be sought ahead of time. Also important are clear directions from headquarters and detailed information about market conditions.

---

[26]The most instructive story we have ever seen regarding how to build one's BATNA is found in Daniel Michael, "In Clandestine World of Airplane Contracts, An Inside Look at a Deal," *Wall Street Journal*, March 10, 2003, p. A1. It is a must-read for anyone interested in the topic of international business negotiations.

Different negotiation settings have different advantages and disadvantages. Of course, teleconferencing saves money, but meetings tend to be rushed. Golf course negotiations are perhaps the most leisurely, but thoughtful responses are more likely as golfers can consider reactions to statements made at the tee as they chase down their errant shots. E-mail also allows for thoughtful reactions in a similar way. Here an executive "negotiates" a putt at China's first golf course, the Chuan Shan Hot Spring Golf Club. *(left: © Charles Gupton/CORBIS; right: Macduff Everton/CORBIS)*

No matter how thorough the preliminary research, negotiators should always make a list of key facts to reconfirm at the negotiation table. Information gathered about foreign customers and markets almost always includes errors, and things can change during those long airline flights. Next, anticipate that managers from other cultures may put less emphasis on a detailed agenda, but it still makes sense to have one to propose and help organize the meetings.

The most important idea in *Getting to Yes* is the notion of the *best alternative to a negotiated agreement* (**BATNA**).[27] This is how power in negotiations is best measured. Even the smallest companies can possess great power in negotiations if they have many good alternatives and their large-company counterparts do not. It is also important to plan out and write down concession strategies. Concessions can often snowball, and writing them down ahead of time helps negotiators keep them under control.

Finally, specific team assignments should be made clear—who handles technical details, who takes notes, who plays the tough guy, who does most of the talking for the group, and so forth. Also, in relationship-oriented cultures selection of intermediaries and the seniority of negotiators are crucial considerations.

There are at least seven aspects of the negotiation setting that should be manipulated ahead of time if possible:

1. Location
2. Physical arrangements
3. Number of parties
4. Number of participants
5. Audiences (news media, competitors, fellow vendors, etc.)
6. Communications channels
7. Time limits

Location speaks loudly about power relations. Traveling to a negotiating counterpart's home turf is a big disadvantage, and not just because of the costs of travel in money and fatigue. A neutral location may be preferred—indeed, many trans-Pacific business negotiations are conducted in Hawaii. The weather and golf are nice and the jet lag is about

---

[27]Fisher, Ury, and Patton, *Getting to Yes,* 1991.

equal. Location is also an important consideration because it may determine legal juris-diction if disputes arise. If you must travel to your negotiating counterpart's city, then a useful tactic is to invite clients or partners to work in a meeting room at your hotel. You can certainly get more done if they are away from the distractions of their offices.

Physical arrangements can affect cooperativeness in subtle ways. In high-context cultures the physical arrangements of rooms can be quite a source of embarrassment and irritation if handled improperly. To the detriment of their foreign business relationships, Americans tend to be casual about such arrangements. Furthermore, views about who should attend negotiations vary across cultures. Americans tend to want to get everyone together to "hammer out an agreement" even if opinions and positions are divergent. Japanese prefer to talk to everyone separately, then, once everyone agrees, to schedule more inclusive meetings. Russians tend toward a cumulative approach, meeting with one party and reaching an agreement, then both parties calling on a third party, and so on. In addition, the importance of not being outnumbered in international business negotiations has already been mentioned.

Audiences can have crucial influences on negotiation processes. Purchasing executives at PetroBras, the Brazilian national oil company, are well known for putting competitive bidders in rooms adjacent to one another to increase competitive pressures on both vendors. Likewise, news leaks to the press played a crucial role in pushing along the negotiations between General Motors and Toyota regarding a joint venture production agreement.

As electronic media become more available, efficient,[28] and sometimes necessary (e.g., the war in Iraq or the SARS[29] outbreak mentioned in Chapter 17), more business can be conducted without face-to-face communication. However, Americans should recognize that their counterparts in many other countries do not necessarily share their attraction to the Internet[30] and teleconferencing.[31] Indeed, recent research shows that when using e-mail trust is harder to build[32] and in Hong Kong businesspeople tend to negotiate more competitively than in face-to-face settings.[33] So, a conversation over a long dinner may actually be the most efficient way to communicate with clients and partners in places like Mexico, Malaysia, and China.

Finally, it is important to manipulate time limits. Recall the example about the Russians and Americans in Nice. The patience of the home office may be indispensable, and major differences in time orientation should be planned for when business negotiations are conducted in most other countries.

## At the Negotiation Table

The most difficult aspect of international business negotiations is the actual conduct of the face-to-face meeting. Assuming that the best representatives are chosen, and assuming those representatives are well prepared and that situational factors are manipulated in one's favor, things can still go sour at the negotiation table. Obviously, if these other preliminaries are not managed properly, things will go wrong during the meetings. Even with great care and attention to preliminary details, managing the dynamics of the negotiation process is almost always the greatest challenge facing Americans seeking to do business in other countries.

---

[28]J. Sairamesh, R. Mohan, M. Kumar, and C. Bender, "A Platform for Business-to-Business Sell-Side, Private Exchanges and Marketplaces," *IBM Systems Journal,* January 1, 2002, pp. 242–248.

[29]Joseph Menn, Charles Ornstein, and Tim Reiterman, "Jet Detained on Mystery Illness Fears," *Los Angeles Times,* April 2, 2003, pp. B1 and B10.

[30]Jan M. Uljn, Andreas Lincke, and Yunus Karakaya, "Non-Face-to-Face International Business Negotiation: How Is National Culture Reflected in this Medium?" *IEEE Transactions on Professional Communication,* June 2001, 44(2), pp. 126–137.

[31]Tim Ambler and Chris Styles, *The Silk Road to International Marketing* (London: Financial Times and Prentice Hall, 2000).

[32]Charles E. Naquin and Gaylen D. Paulson, "Online Bargaining and Interpersonal Trust," *Journal of Applied Psychology,* 88(1), 2003, pp. 113–120.

[33]Guang Yang, *The Impact of Computer Mediated Communication on the Processes and Outcomes of Buyer-Seller Negotiations,* unpublished doctoral dissertation, University of California, Irvine, 2003.

## CROSSING BORDERS 19.4  The Digital Impact on International Negotiations

All in all, e-commerce is good for global marketing. It allows domestic firms to internationalize more quickly and at less cost. It allows international firms to communicate internally and externally with greater efficiency. Fax replaced telex, which, in turn, replaced the telegram. But e-mail is only partly replacing mail, fax, and phone. It is better seen as a different, more informal medium than fax and more convenient than phone. For networking purposes, e-mail is easily copied and relayed, though excess should be avoided. Many of us have learned to screen out e-mails addressed to multiple recipients.

Above all, e-mail can nurture, but not create, the long-term relationships so crucial to international marketing. The decision by Boeing to enter into an auto-mated relationship with Dell was not made by two machines, but by personal contact between executives on both sides. The success of the P&G/Wal-Mart relationship rests with the personal relationships and interactions between P&G's key account team and Wal-Mart's buyers. Although non-Thais can learn a great deal about Thailand from the Internet, they can never really understand Thai customers, the way they do business and their feelings toward products, unless they interact directly. Understanding culture requires personal experiential learning, the wellspring of social information.

Source: Reprinted with permission from Tim Ambler and Chris Styles, *The Silk Road to International Marketing* (London: The Financial Times/Prentice Hall, 2000). Reprinted by permission of Pearson Education, Inc. Upper Saddle River, NJ.

Going into a business negotiation, most people have expectations about the "proper" or normal process of such a meeting.[34] Based on these expectations, progress is measured and appropriate bargaining strategies are selected. That is, things may be done differently in the latter stages of a negotiation than they were in the earlier. Higher-risk strategies may be used to conclude talks—as in the final two minutes of a close soccer match. But all such decisions about strategy are made relative to perceptions of progress through an expected course of events.

Differences in the expectations held by parties from different cultures are one of the major difficulties in any international business negotiation. Before these differences are discussed, however, it is important to point out similarities. Everywhere around the world we have found that business negotiations proceed through four stages:

1. Nontask sounding
2. Task-related exchange of information
3. Persuasion
4. Concessions and agreement

The first stage, nontask sounding, includes all those activities that might be described as establishing a rapport or getting to know one another, but it does not include information related to the "business" of the meeting. The information exchanged in the second stage of business negotiations regards the parties' needs and preferences. The third stage, persuasion, involves the parties' attempts to modify one another's needs and preferences through the use of various persuasive tactics. The final stage of business negotiations involves the consummation of an agreement, which is often the summation of a series of concessions or smaller agreements.

Despite the consistency of this process across diverse cultures, the content and duration of the four stages differ substantially. For example, Exhibit 19.4 details procedural differences in Japan and the United States, as well as differences in language, nonverbal behavior, and values.

---

[34]Sometimes these expectations are referred to as "the spirit of the deal" or the "social contract." See Ron S. Fortgang, David A. Lax, and James K. Sebenius, "Negotiating the Spirit of the Deal," *Harvard Business Review,* January-February 2003, pp. 66–74.

## Exhibit 19.4
Summary of Japanese and American Business Negotiation Styles

| Category | Japanese | Americans |
|---|---|---|
| Language | Most Japanese executives understand English, although interpreters are often used. | Americans have less time to formulate answers and observe Japanese nonverbal responses because of a lack of knowledge of Japanese. |
| Nonverbal behaviors | The Japanese interpersonal communication style includes less eye contact, fewer negative facial expressions, and more periods of silence. | American businesspeople tend to "fill" silent periods with arguments or concessions. |
| Values | Indirectness and face saving are important. Vertical buyer/seller relationships, with sellers depending on goodwill of buyers (*amae*), is typical. | Speaking one's mind is important. Buyer/seller relationships are horizontal. |

**Four Stages of Business Negotiations**

| | | |
|---|---|---|
| 1. Nontask sounding | Considerable time and expense devoted to such efforts is the practice in Japan. | Very short periods are typical. |
| 2. Task-related exchange of information | This is the most important step—high first offers with long explanations and in-depth clarifications. | Information is given briefly and directly. "Fair" first offers are more typical. |
| 3. Persuasion | Persuasion is accomplished primarily behind the scenes. Vertical status relations dictate bargaining outcomes. | The most important step: Minds are changed at the negotiation table and aggressive persuasive tactics are often used. |
| 4. Concessions and agreement | Concessions are made only toward the end of negotiations—a holistic approach to decision making. Progress is difficult to measure for Americans. | Concessions and commitments are made throughout—a sequential approach to decision making. |

Source: James Day Hodgson, Yoshihiro Sano, and John L. Graham, *Doing Business with the New Japan* (Boulder, CO: Rowman & Littlefield, 2000), p. 45. Used by permission of Rowman & Littlefield.

**Nontask Sounding.**   Americans always discuss topics other than business at the negotiation table (for example, the weather, family, sports, politics, and business conditions in general), but not for long. Usually the discussion is moved to the specific business at hand after five to ten minutes. Such preliminary talk, known as **nontask sounding**, is much more than just friendly or polite; it helps negotiators learn how the other side feels that particular day. During nontask sounding one can determine if a client's attention is focused on business or distracted by other matters, personal or professional.

Learning about a client's background and interests also provides important cues about appropriate communication styles. To the extent that people's backgrounds are similar, communication can be more efficient. Engineers can use technical jargon when talking to other engineers. Sports enthusiasts can use sports analogies. Those with children can compare the cash drain of "putting a kid through college," and so on.

During these initial stages of conversation, judgments, too, are made about the "kind" of person(s) with whom one is dealing: Can this person be trusted? Will he be reliable? How much power does she have in her organization? All such judgments are made before business discussions ever begin.

There is a definite purpose to these preliminary nontask discussions. Although most people are often unaware of it, such time almost always is used to size up one's clients. Depending on the results of this process, proposals and arguments are formed using different jargon and analogies. Or it may be decided not to discuss business at all if clients are distracted by other personal matters or if the other people seem untrustworthy. All this sounds like a lot to accomplish in five to ten minutes, but that's how long it usually takes in the information-oriented United States. This is not the case in other relationship-oriented countries like China or Brazil; the goals of the nontask sounding are identical, but the time spent is much, much longer.

In the United States, firms resort to the legal system and their lawyers when they've made a bad deal because of a mistake in sizing up a customer or vendor. In most other countries the legal system cannot be depended upon for such purposes. Instead, executives in places like Korea and Egypt spend substantial time and effort in nontask sounding so that problems do not develop later. Americans need to reconsider, from the foreigner's perspective, the importance of this first stage of negotiations if they hope to succeed in Seoul or Cairo.

**Task-Related Information Exchange.**    Only when nontask sounding is complete and a trusting personal relationship is established should business be introduced. American executives are advised to let the foreign counterpart decide when such substantive negotiations should begin, that is, to let them bring up business.

A **task-related information exchange** implies a two-way communication process. However, observations suggest that when Americans meet executives from some cultures across the negotiation table, the information flow is unidirectional. Japanese, Chinese, and Russian negotiators all appear to ask "thousands" of questions and to give little feedback. The barrage of questions severely tests American negotiators' patience, and the lack of feedback causes them great anxiety. Both can add up to much longer stays in these countries, which means higher travel expenses.

Certainly it is an excellent negotiation tactic to "drain" information from one's negotiation counterparts. But the oft-reported behaviors of Chinese, Japanese, and Russians may not necessarily represent a sophisticated negotiation ploy. Indeed, reference to Exhibit 19.2 provides some hints that differences in conversational styles—silent periods occurred more frequently in negotiations in all three cultures—may be part of the explanation. Indeed, in careful studies of conversational patterns of Americans negotiating with Japanese, the Americans seem to fill the silent periods and do most of the talking. These results suggest that American negotiators must take special care to keep their mouths shut and let foreign counterparts give them information.

Exchanging information across language barriers can be quite difficult as well. Most of us understand about 80 to 90 percent of what our same-culture spouses or roommates say—that means 10 to 20 percent is misunderstood or misheard. That latter percentage goes up dramatically when someone is speaking a second language, no matter the fluency levels or length of acquaintance. And when the second language capability is limited, entire conversations may be totally misunderstood. Using multiple communication channels during presentations—writing, exhibits, speaking, repetition—works to minimize the inevitable errors.

In many cultures negative feedback is very difficult to obtain. In high-context cultures such as Mexico and Japan, speakers are reluctant to voice objections lest they damage the all-important personal relationships. Some languages themselves are by nature indirect and indefinite. English is relatively clear, but translations from languages like Japanese can leave much to be understood. In more collectivistic cultures like China, negotiators may be reluctant to speak for the decision-making group they represent, or they may not even know how the group feels about a particular proposal. All such problems suggest the importance of having natives of customer countries on your negotiation team and of spending extra time in business and informal entertainment settings trying to understand better the information provided by foreign clients and partners. Conversely, low-context German executives often complain that American presentations include too much

# CROSSING BORDERS 19.5 Fishing for Business in Brazil

How important is nontask sounding? Consider this description about an American banker's meeting in Brazil, as told by an observer.

Introductions were made. The talk began with the usual "How do you like Rio?" questions—Have you been to Ipanema, Copacabana, Corcovado, etc? There was also talk about the flight down from New York. After about five minutes of this chatting, the senior American quite conspicuously glanced at his watch, and then asked his client what he knew about the bank's new services.

"A little," responded the Brazilian. The senior American whipped a brochure out of his briefcase, opened it on the desk in front of the client, and began his sales pitch.

After about three minutes of "fewer forms, electronic transfers, and reducing accounts receivables," the Brazilian jumped back in, "Yes, that should make us more competitive . . . and competition is important here in Brazil. In fact, have you been following the World Cup *fútbol* (soccer) matches recently? Great games." And so the reel began to whir, paying out that monofilament line, right there in that hot high-rise office.

After a few minutes' dissertation on the local *fútbol* teams, Pélé, and why *fútbol* isn't popular in the United States, the American started to try to crank the Brazilian back in. The first signal was the long look at his watch, then the interruption, "Perhaps we can get back to the new services we have to offer."

The Brazilian did get reeled back into the subject of the sale for a couple of minutes, but then the reel started to sing again. This time he went from efficient banking transactions to the nuances of the Brazilian financial system to the Brazilian economy. Pretty soon we were all talking about the world economy and making predictions about the U.S. presidential elections.

Another look at his Rolex, and the American started this little "sport fishing" ritual all over again. From my perspective (I wasn't investing time and money toward the success of this activity), this all seemed pretty funny. Every time the American VP looked at his watch during the next 45 minutes, I had to bite my cheeks to keep from laughing out loud. He never did get to page two of his brochure. The Brazilian just wasn't interested in talking business with someone he didn't know pretty well.

Source: Reprinted from John L. Graham, *International Business Negotiations*, copyright 1996, pp. 69–91, with permission from Elsevier Science; also see Philip R. Harris and Robert T. Moran, *Managing Cultural Differences* (Houston: Gulf Publishing, 2000).

"fluff"—they are interested in copious information only, not the hyperbole and hedges so common in American speech. Negative feedback from Germans can seem brutally frank to higher-context Americans.

A final point of potential conflict in information exchange has to do with first offers. Price padding varies across cultures, and Americans' first offers tend to come in relatively close to what they really want. "A million dollars is the goal, let's start at $1.2 million" seems about right to most Americans. Implicit in such a first offer is the hope that things will get done quickly. Americans do not expect to move far from first offers. Negotiators in many other countries do not share the goal of finishing quickly, however. In places like China, Brazil, or Spain, the expectation is for a relatively longer period of haggling, and first offers are more aggressive to reflect these expectations. "If the goal is one million, we better start at two," makes sense there. Americans react to such aggressive first offers in one of two ways: They either laugh or get mad. And when foreign counterparts' second offers reflect deep discounts, Americans' ire increases.

A good example of this problem regards an American CEO shopping for a European plant site. When he selected a $20 million plot in Ireland, the Spanish real estate developer he had visited earlier telephoned wondering why the American had not asked for a lower price for the Madrid site before choosing Dublin. He told the Spaniard that his first offer "wasn't even in the ball park." He wasn't laughing when the Spaniard then offered to beat the Irish price. In fact, the American executive was quite mad. A potentially good deal was forgone because of different expectations about first offers. Yes, numbers were exchanged, but information was not. Aggressive first offers made by foreigners should be met with questions, not anger.

**Persuasion.**   In Japan, a clear separation does not exist between task-related information exchange and persuasion. The two stages tend to blend together as each side defines and refines its needs and preferences. Much time is spent in the task-related exchange of information, leaving little to "argue" about during the persuasion stage. Conversely, Americans tend to lay their cards on the table and hurry through the information exchange to persuasion. After all, the persuasion is the heart of the matter. Why hold a meeting unless someone's mind is to be changed? A key aspect of sales training in the United States is "handling objections." So the goal in information exchange among Americans is to quickly get those objections out in the open so they can be handled.

You want him on your side! Banana salespeople such as this fellow in Agra, India, are known worldwide for their negotiation skills—they're hawking a perishable product that shows the wear. In Japan they even have a negotiation strategy named for them. That is, outrageously high first offers are derogated as "*banana no tataki uri*," the banana sale approach.

This handling can mean providing clients with more information. It can also mean getting mean.[35] As suggested by Exhibit 19.2, Americans make threats and issue warnings in negotiations.[36] They do not use such tactics often, but negotiators in many other cultures use such tactics even less frequently and in different circumstances. For example, notice how infrequently the Mexicans and English-speaking Canadians used threats and warnings in the simulated negotiations. Others have found Filipino and Chinese negotiators to use a less aggressive approach than Americans.[37] Indeed, in Thailand or China the use of such aggressive negotiation tactics can result in the loss of face and the destruction of important personal relationships. Such tough tactics may be used in Japan, but by buyers only and usually only in informal circumstances—not at the formal negotiation table. Americans also get mad during negotiations and express emotions that may be completely inappropriate in foreign countries. Such emotional outbursts may be seen as infantile or even barbaric behavior in places like Hong Kong and Bangkok.

The most powerful persuasive tactic is actually asking more questions. Foreign counterparts can be politely asked to explain why they must have delivery in two months or why they must have a 10 percent discount. Chester Karrass, in his still useful book *The Negotiation Game*,[38] suggests that it is "smart to be a little dumb" in business negotiations. Repeat questions; for example, "I didn't completely understand what you meant—can you please explain that again?" If clients or potential business partners have good answers, then perhaps it is best to compromise on the issue. Often, however, under close and repeated scrutiny their answers are not very good. When their weak position is exposed, they are obliged to concede. Questions can elicit key information, being the most powerful yet passive persuasive device. Indeed, the use of questions is a favored Japanese tactic, one they use with great effect on Americans.

[35]Apparently Australians get angry, too. See Catherine Fox, "Negotiating is an Emotional Business," *Australian Financial Review,* October 1, 2002, p. 66.

[36]For more details see Deborah A. Cai and Edward L. Fink, "Conflict Style Differences Between Individualists and Collectivists," *Communication Monographs,* March 1, 2002, pp. 67–75.

[37]X. Michael Song, Jinhong Xie, and Barbara Dyer, "Antecedents and Consequences of Marketing Managers' Conflict Handling Procedures," *Journal of Marketing,* January 2000, 64, pp. 50–66; and Alma Mintu-Wimsatt and Julie B. Gassenheimer, "The Moderating Effects of Cultural Context in Buyer-Seller Negotiation," *Journal of Personal Selling & Sales Management,* Winter 2000, 20(1), pp. 1–9.

[38]Chester Karrass, *The Negotiation Game* (New York: Crowell, 1970).

Third parties and informal channels of communication are the indispensable media of persuasion in many countries, particularly the more relationship-oriented ones. Meetings in restaurants or meetings with references and mutual friends who originally provided introductions may be used to handle difficult problems with partners in other countries. The value of such informal settings and trusted intermediaries is greatest when problems are emotion laden. They provide a means for simultaneously delivering difficult messages and saving face. Although American managers may eschew such "behind the scenes" approaches, they are standard practice in many countries.

**Concessions and Agreement.**   Comments made previously about the importance of writing down concession-making strategies and understanding differences in decision-making styles—sequential versus holistic—are pertinent here. Americans often make concessions early, expecting foreign counterparts to reciprocate. However, in many cultures no concessions are made until the end of the negotiations. Americans often get frustrated and express anger when foreign clients and partners are simply following a different approach to concession making, one that can also work quite well when both sides understand what is going on.

## After Negotiations

Contracts between American firms are often longer than 100 pages and include carefully worded clauses regarding every aspect of the agreement. American lawyers go to great lengths to protect their companies against all circumstances, contingencies, and actions of the other party. The best contracts are ones written so tightly that the other party would not think of going to court to challenge any provision. The American adversarial system requires such contracts.

In most other countries, particularly the relationship-oriented ones, legal systems are not depended upon to settle disputes. Indeed, the term *disputes* does not reflect how a business relationship should work. Each side should be concerned about mutual benefits of the relationship and therefore should consider the interests of the other. Consequently, in places like Japan written contracts are very short—two to three pages—are purposely loosely written, and primarily contain comments on principles of the relationship. From the Japanese point of view, the American emphasis on tight contracts is tantamount to planning the divorce before the wedding.

Tung Chee Hwa, Chief Executive of the Hong Kong Special Administrative Region, consummated the deal with the Mouse for Asia's new Walt Disney World, scheduled for opening in 2005. (AP/Wide World Photos)

In other relationship-oriented countries, such as China, contracts are more a description of what business partners view their respective responsibilities to be. For complicated business relationships they may be quite long and detailed. However, their purpose is different from the American understanding. When circumstances change, then responsibilities must also be adjusted, despite the provisions of the signed contract. The notion of enforcing a contract in China makes little sense.

Informality being a way of life in the United States, even the largest contracts between companies are often sent through the mail for signature. In America, ceremony is considered a waste of time and money. But when a major agreement is reached with foreign companies, their executives may expect a formal signing ceremony involving CEOs of the respective companies. American companies are wise to accommodate such expectations.

Finally, follow-up communications are an important part of business negotiations with partners and clients from most foreign countries. Particularly in high-context cultures, where personal relationships are crucial, high-level executives must stay in touch with their counterparts. Letters, pictures, and mutual visits remain important long after contracts are signed. Indeed, warm relationships at the top often prove to be the best medicine for any problems that may arise in the future.

# Conclusions

Despite the litany of potential pitfalls facing international negotiators, things are getting better. The stereotypes of American managers as "innocents abroad" or cowboys are becoming less accurate. Likewise, we hope it is obvious that the stereotypes of the reticent Japanese or the pushy Brazilian evinced in the chapter may no longer hold so true. Experience levels are going up worldwide, and individual personalities are important. So you can find talkative Japanese, quiet Brazilians, and effective American negotiators. But culture still does, and always will, count. We hope that it is quickly becoming the natural behavior of American managers to take culture into account.

English author Rudyard Kipling said some one hundred years ago: "Oh, East is East, and West is West, and never the twain shall meet." Since then most have imbued his words with an undeserved pessimism. Some even wrongly say he was wrong.[39] The problem is that not many have bothered to read his entire poem, *The Ballad of East and West:*

> Oh, East is East, and West is West, and never the twain shall meet,
> Till Earth and Sky stand presently at God's great Judgment Seat;
> But there is neither East nor West, border, nor breed, nor birth,
> When two strong men stand face to face, though they come from the ends of the earth!

The poem can stand some editing for these more modern times. It should include the other directions—North is North and South is South. And the last line properly should read, "When two strong *people* stand face to face." But Kipling's positive sentiment remains. Differences between countries and cultures, no matter how difficult, can be worked out when people talk to each other in face-to-face settings. Kipling rightly places the responsibility for international cooperation not on companies or governments, but instead directly on the shoulders of individual managers, present and future, like you. Work hard!

# Summary

Because styles of business negotiations vary substantially around the world, it is important to take cultural differences into account when meeting clients, customers, and business partners across the international negotiation table. In addition to cultural factors, negotiators' personalities and backgrounds also influence their behavior. Great care should be taken to get to know the individuals who represent client and customer companies. Cultural stereotypes can be quite misleading.

Four kinds of problems frequently arise during international business negotiations—problems at the level of language, nonverbal behaviors, values, and thinking and decision-making processes. Foreign language skills are an essential tool of the international negotiator. Nonverbal behaviors vary dramatically across cultures, and because their influence is often below our level of awareness, problems at this level can be quite serious. Whereas most Americans value objectivity, competitiveness, equality, and punctuality, many foreign executives may not. As for thinking and decision making, Western business executives tend to address complex negotiations by breaking deals down into smaller issues and settling them sequentially; in many Eastern cultures a more holistic approach is taken in discussions.

Much care must be taken in selecting negotiation teams to represent companies in meetings with foreigners. Listening skills, influence at headquarters, and a willingness to use team assistance are important negotiator traits. Americans should be careful to try to match foreign negotiation teams in both numbers and seniority. The importance of cross-cultural training and investments in careful preparations cannot be overstated. Situational factors such as the location for meetings and the time allowed must also be carefully considered and managed.

All around the world business negotiations involve four steps: nontask sounding, task-related information exchange, persuasion, and concessions and agreement. The time spent on each step can vary considerably from country to country. Americans spend little time on nontask sounding or getting to know foreign counterparts. Particularly in high-context cultures, it is important to let the customers bring up business when they feel comfortable with the personal relationship. Task-related information goes quickly in the United States as well. In other countries, such as Japan, the most time is spent on the second stage, and careful understandings of partners are focused upon. Persuasion is the most important part of negotiations from the American perspective. Aggressive persuasive tactics (threats and warnings) are used frequently. Such persuasive tactics, although they may work well in some cultures, cause serious problems in others. Finally, because Americans tend to be deal oriented, more care should be taken in follow-up communications with foreign clients and partners who put more emphasis on long-term business relationships.

---

[39]Michael Elliot, "Killing off Kipling," *Newsweek,* December 29, 1997, pp. 52–55.

# Questions

1. Define the following terms:

   BATNA, 580            task-related information
   nontask sounding, 583      exchange, 584

2. Why can cultural stereotypes be dangerous? Give some examples.

3. List three ways that culture influences negotiation behavior.

4. Describe the kinds of problems that usually come up during international business negotiations.

5. Why are foreign language skills important for international negotiators?

6. Describe three cultural differences in nonverbal behaviors and explain how they might cause problems in international business negotiations.

7. Why is time an important consideration in international business negotiations?

8. What can be different about how a Japanese manager might address a complex negotiation compared with an American negotiator?

9. What are the most important considerations in selecting a negotiation team? Give examples.

10. What kinds of training are most useful for international business negotiators?

11. Name three aspects of negotiation situations that might be manipulated before talks begin. Suggest how this might be done.

12. Explain why Americans spend so little time on nontask sounding and Brazilians so much.

13. Why is it difficult to get negative feedback from counterparts in many foreign countries? Give examples.

14. Why won't getting mad work in Mexico or Japan?

15. Why are questions the most useful persuasive tactic?

# country notebook

## THE COUNTRY NOTEBOOK—A GUIDE
## FOR DEVELOPING A MARKETING PLAN

### THE COUNTRY NOTEBOOK OUTLINE

Cultural Analysis

Economic Analysis

Market Audit and Competititve Market Analysis

Preliminary Marketing Plan

The first stage in the planning process is a preliminary country analysis. The marketer needs basic information to evaluate a country market's potential, identify problems that would eliminate a country from further consideration, identify aspects of the country's environment that need further study, evaluate the components of the marketing mix for possible adaptation, and develop a strategic marketing plan. One further use of the information collected in the preliminary analysis is as a basis for a country notebook.

Many companies, large and small, have a *country notebook* for each country in which they do business. The country notebook contains information a marketer should be aware of when making decisions involving a specific country market. As new information is collected, the country notebook is continually updated by the country or product manager. Whenever a marketing decision is made involving a country, the country notebook is the first database consulted. New product introductions, changes in advertising programs, and other marketing program decisions begin with the country notebook. It also serves as a quick introduction for new personnel assuming responsibility for a country market.

This section presents four separate guidelines for collection and analysis of market data and preparation of a country notebook: (1) guideline for cultural analysis, (2) guideline for economic analysis, (3) guideline for market audit and competitive analysis, and (4) guideline for preliminary marketing plan. These guidelines suggest the kinds of information a marketer can gather to enhance planning.

The points in each of the guidelines are general. They are designed to provide direction to areas to explore for relevant data. In each guideline, specific points must be adapted to reflect a company's products. The decision as to the appropriateness of specific data and the depth of coverage depends on company objectives, product characteristics, and the country market. Some points in the guidelines are unimportant for some countries or some products and should be ignored. Preceding chapters of this book provide specific content suggestions for the topics in each guideline.

# I. Cultural Analysis

The data suggested in the cultural analysis include information that helps the marketer make market planning decisions. However, its application extends beyond product and market analysis to being an important source of information for someone interested in understanding business customs and other important cultural features of the country.

The information in this analysis must be more than a collection of facts. Whoever is responsible for the preparation of this material should attempt to interpret the meaning of cultural information. That is, how does the information help in understanding the effect on the market? For example, the fact that almost all the populations of Italy and Mexico are Catholic is an interesting statistic but not nearly as useful as understanding the effect of Catholicism on values, beliefs, and other aspects of market behavior. Furthermore, even though both countries are predominantly Catholic, the influence of their individual and unique interpretation and practice of Catholicism can result in important differences in market behavior.

## Guideline

I. Introduction
   Include short profiles of the company, the product to be exported, and the country with which you wish to trade.
II. Brief discussion of the country's relevant history
III. Geographical setting
   A. Location
   B. Climate
   C. Topography
IV. Social institutions
   A. Family
      1. The nuclear family
      2. The extended family

   3. Dynamics of the family
      a. Parental roles
      b. Marriage and courtship
   4. Female/male roles (changing or static?)
B. Education
   1. The role of education in society
      a. Primary education (quality, levels of development, etc.)
      b. Secondary education (quality, levels of development, etc.)
      c. Higher education (quality, levels of development, etc.)
   2. Literacy rates
C. Political system
   1. Political structure
   2. Political parties
   3. Stability of government
   4. Special taxes
   5. Role of local government
D. Legal system
   1. Organization of the judiciary system
   2. Code, common, socialist, or Islamic-law country?
   3. Participation in patents, trademarks, and other conventions
E. Social organizations
   1. Group behavior
   2. Social classes
   3. Clubs, other organizations
   4. Race, ethnicity, and subcultures
F. Business customs and practices
V. Religion and aesthetics
   A. Religion and other belief systems
      1. Orthodox doctrines and structures
      2. Relationship with the people
      3. Which religions are prominent?
      4. Membership of each religion
      5. Any powerful or influential cults?
   B. Aesthetics
      1. Visual arts (fine arts, plastics, graphics, public art, colors, etc.)
      2. Music
      3. Drama, ballet, and other performing arts
      4. Folklore and relevant symbols
VI. Living conditions
   A. Diet and nutrition
      1. Meat and vegetable consumption rates
      2. Typical meals
      3. Malnutrition rates
      4. Foods available
   B. Housing
      1. Types of housing available
      2. Do most people own or rent?
      3. Do most people live in one-family dwellings or with other families?
   C. Clothing
      1. National dress
      2. Types of clothing worn at work
   D. Recreation, sports, and other leisure activities
      1. Types available and in demand
      2. Percentage of income spent on such activities
   E. Social security
   F. Health care

    VII. Language
        A. Official language(s)
        B. Spoken versus written language(s)
        C. Dialects
    VIII. Executive summary

        After completing all of the other sections, prepare a *two-page* (maximum length) summary of the major points and place it at the front of the report. The purpose of an executive summary is to give the reader a brief glance at the critical points of your report. Those aspects of the culture a reader should know to do business in the country but would not be expected to know or would find different based on his or her SRC should be included in this summary.

    IX. Sources of information
    X. Appendixes

## II. Economic Analysis

The reader may find the data collected for the economic analysis guideline are more straightforward than for the cultural analysis guideline. There are two broad categories of information in this guideline: general economic data that serve as a basis for an evaluation of the economic soundness of a country, and information on channels of distribution and media availability. As mentioned earlier, the guideline focuses only on broad categories of data and must be adapted to particular company and product needs.

**Guideline**

    I. Introduction
    II. Population
        A. Total
            1. Growth rates
            2. Number of live births
            3. Birthrates
        B. Distribution of population
            1. Age
            2. Sex
            3. Geographic areas (urban, suburban, and rural density and concentration)
            4. Migration rates and patterns
            5. Ethnic groups
    III. Economic statistics and activity
        A. Gross national product (GNP or GDP)
            1. Total
            2. Rate of growth (real GNP or GDP)
        B. Personal income per capita
        C. Average family income
        D. Distribution of wealth
            1. Income classes
            2. Proportion of the population in each class
            3. Is the distribution distorted?
        E. Minerals and resources
        F. Surface transportation
            1. Modes
            2. Availability
            3. Usage rates
            4. Ports
        G. Communication systems
            1. Types
            2. Availability
            3. Usage rates
        H. Working conditions
            1. Employer-employee relations

      2. Employee participation
      3. Salaries and benefits
  I. Principal industries
      1. What proportion of the GNP does each industry contribute?
      2. Ratio of private to publicly owned industries
  J. Foreign investment
      1. Opportunities?
      2. Which industries?
  K. International trade statistics
      1. Major exports
         a. Dollar value
         b. Trends
      2. Major imports
         a. Dollar value
         b. Trends
      3. Balance-of-payments situation
         a. Surplus or deficit?
         b. Recent trends
      4. Exchange rates
         a. Single or multiple exchange rates?
         b. Current rate of exchange
         c. Trends
  L. Trade restrictions
      1. Embargoes
      2. Quotas
      3. Import taxes
      4. Tariffs
      5. Licensing
      6. Customs duties
  M. Extent of economic activity not included in cash income activities
      1. Countertrades
         a. Products generally offered for countertrading
         b. Types of countertrades requested (i.e., barter, counterpurchase, etc.)
      2. Foreign aid received
  N. Labor force
      1. Size
      2. Unemployment rates
  O. Inflation rates
IV. Developments in science and technology
  A. Current technology available (computers, machinery, tools, etc.)
  B. Percentage of GNP invested in research and development
  C. Technological skills of the labor force and general population
V. Channels of distribution (macro analysis)
This section reports data on all channel middlemen available within the market.
Later, you will select a specific channel as part of your distribution strategy.
  A. Retailers
      1. Number of retailers
      2. Typical size of retail outlets
      3. Customary markup for various classes of goods
      4. Methods of operation (cash/credit)
      5. Scale of operation (large/small)
      6. Role of chain stores, department stores, and specialty shops
  B. Wholesale middlemen
      1. Number and size
      2. Customary markup for various classes of goods
      3. Method of operation (cash/credit)

C.  Import/export agents
D.  Warehousing
E.  Penetration of urban and rural markets

VI.  Media

This section reports data on all media available within the country or market. Later, you will select specific media as part of the promotional mix and strategy.

A.  Availability of media
B.  Costs
1.  Television
2.  Radio
3.  Print
4.  Other media (cinema, outdoor, etc.)
C.  Agency assistance
D.  Coverage of various media
E.  Percentage of population reached by each of the media

VII.  Executive summary

After completing the research for this report, prepare a two-page (maximum) summary of the major economic points and place it at the front

VIII.  Sources of information
IX.  Appendixes

# III. Market Audit and Competitive Market Analysis

Of the guidelines presented, this is the most product or brand specific. Information in the other guidelines is general in nature, focusing on product categories, whereas data in this guideline are brand specific and are used to determine competitive market conditions and market potential.

Two different components of the planning process are reflected in this guideline. Information in Parts I and II, Cultural Analysis and Economic Analysis, serve as the basis for an evaluation of the product or brand in a specific country market. Information in this guideline provides an estimate of market potential and an evaluation of the strengths and weaknesses of competitive marketing efforts. The data generated in this step are used to determine the extent of adaptation of the company's marketing mix necessary for successful market entry and to develop the final step, the action plan.

The detailed information needed to complete this guideline is not necessarily available without conducting a thorough marketing research investigation. Thus another purpose of this part of the country notebook is to identify the correct questions to ask in a formal market study.

**Guideline**

I.  Introduction
II.  The product
A.  Evaluate the product as an innovation as it is perceived by the intended market
1.  Relative advantage
2.  Compatibility
3.  Complexity
4.  Trialability
5.  Observability
B.  Major problems and resistances to product acceptance based on the preceding evaluation
III.  The market
A.  Describe the market(s) in which the product is to be sold
1.  Geographical region(s)
2.  Forms of transportation and communication available in that (those) region(s)

  3. Consumer buying habits
   a. Product-use patterns
   b. Product feature preferences
   c. Shopping habits
  4. Distribution of the product
   a. Typical retail outlets
   b. Product sales by other middlemen
  5. Advertising and promotion
   a. Advertising media usually used to reach your target market(s)
   b. Sales promotions customarily used (sampling, coupons, etc.)
  6. Pricing strategy
   a. Customary markups
   b. Types of discounts available
 B. Compare and contrast your product and the competition's product(s)
  1. Competitor's product(s)
   a. Brand name
   b. Features
   c. Package
  2. Competitor's prices
  3. Competitor's promotion and advertising methods
  4. Competitor's distribution channels
 C. Market size
  1. Estimated industry sales for the planning year
  2. Estimated sales for your company for the planning year
 D. Government participation in the marketplace
  1. Agencies that can help you
  2. Regulations you must follow
IV. Executive summary
 Based on your analysis of the market, briefly summarize (two-page maximum) the major problems and opportunities requiring attention in your marketing mix, and place the summary at the front of the report.
V. Sources of information
VI. Appendixes

# IV. Preliminary Marketing Plan
Information gathered in guidelines I through III serves as the basis for developing a marketing plan for your product or brand in a target market. How the problems and opportunities that surfaced in the preceding steps are overcome or exploited to produce maximum sales and profits are presented here. The action plan reflects, in your judgment, the most effective means of marketing your product in a country market. Budgets, expected profits and losses, and additional resources necessary to implement the proposed plan are also presented.

**Guideline**

I. The marketing plan
 A. Marketing objectives
  1. Target market(s) (specific description of the market)
  2. Expected sales 20—
  3. Profit expectations 20—
  4. Market penetration and coverage
 B. Product adaptation or modification—Using the product component model as your guide, indicate how your product can be adapted for the market.
  1. Core component
  2. Packaging component
  3. Support services component

C. Promotion mix
1. Advertising
   a. Objectives
   b. Media mix
   c. Message
   d. Costs
2. Sales promotions
   a. Objectives
   b. Coupons
   c. Premiums
   d. Costs
3. Personal selling
4. Other promotional methods

D. Distribution: From origin to destination
1. Port selection
   a. Origin port
   b. Destination port
2. Mode selection: Advantages/disadvantages of each mode
   a. Railroads
   b. Air carriers
   c. Ocean carriers
   d. Motor carriers
3. Packing
   a. Marking and labeling regulations
   b. Containerization
   c. Costs
4. Documentation required
   a. Bill of lading
   b. Dock receipt
   c. Air bill
   d. Commercial invoice
   e. Pro forma invoice
   f. Shipper's export declaration
   g. Statement of origin
   h. Special documentation
5. Insurance claims
6. Freight forwarder
   If your company does not have a transportation or traffic management department, then consider using a freight forwarder. There are distinct advantages and disadvantages to hiring one.

E. Channels of distribution (micro analysis)
This section presents details about the specific types of distribution in your marketing plan.
1. Retailers
   a. Type and number of retail stores
   b. Retail markups for products in each type of retail store
   c. Methods of operation for each type (cash/credit)
   d. Scale of operation for each type (small/large)
2. Wholesale middlemen
   a. Type and number of wholesale middlemen
   b. Markup for class of products by each type
   c. Methods of operation for each type (cash/credit)
   d. Scale of operation (small/large)
3. Import/export agents

4. Warehousing
   a. Type
   b. Location
F. Price determination
   1. Cost of the shipment of goods
   2. Transportation costs
   3. Handling expenses
      a. Pier charges
      b. Wharfage fees
      c. Loading and unloading charges
   4. Insurance costs
   5. Customs duties
   6. Import taxes and value-added tax
   7. Wholesale and retail markups and discounts
   8. Company's gross margins
   9. Retail price
G. Terms of sale
   1. EX works, FOB, FAS, C&F, CIF
   2. Advantages/disadvantages of each
H. Methods of payment
   1. Cash in advance
   2. Open accounts
   3. Consignment sales
   4. Sight, time, or date drafts
   5. Letters of credit
II. Pro forma financial statements and budgets
   A. Marketing budget
      1. Selling expense
      2. Advertising/promotion expense
      3. Distribution expense
      4. Product cost
      5. Other costs
   B. Pro forma annual profit and loss statement (first year and fifth year)
III. Resource requirements
   A. Finances
   B. Personnel
   C. Production capacity
IV. Executive summary
   After completing the research for this report, prepare a two-page (maximum) summary of the major points of your successful marketing plan, and place it at the front of the report.
V. Sources of information
VI. Appendixes
   The intricacies of international operations and the complexity of the environment within which the international marketer must operate create an extraordinary demand for information. When operating in foreign markets, the need for thorough information as a substitute for uninformed opinion is equally as important as it is in domestic marketing. Sources of information needed to develop the country notebook and answer other marketing questions are discussed in Chapter 8 and its appendix.

## Summary

Market-oriented firms build strategic market plans around company objectives, markets, and the competitive environment. Planning for marketing can be complicated even for one country, but when a company is doing business internationally, the problems are multiplied. Company objectives may vary from market to market and from time to time; the structure of international markets also changes periodically and from country to country; and the competitive, governmental, and economic parameters affecting market planning are in a constant state of flux. These variations require international marketing executives to be specially flexible and creative in their approach to strategic marketing planning.

# cases I

## AN OVERVIEW

**OUTLINE OF CASES**

# CASE 1-1   Starbucks—Going Global Fast

The Starbucks coffee shop on Sixth Avenue and Pine Street in downtown Seattle sits serene and orderly, as unremarkable as any other in the chain bought 15 years ago by entrepreneur Howard Schultz. A little less than three years ago, however, the quiet storefront made front pages around the world. During the World Trade Organization talks in November, 1999, protesters flooded Seattle's streets, and among their targets was Starbucks, a symbol, to them, of free-market capitalism run amok, another multinational out to blanket the earth. Amid the crowds of protesters and riot police were black-masked anarchists who trashed the store, leaving its windows smashed and its tasteful green-and-white decor smelling of tear gas instead of espresso. Says an angry Schultz: "It's hurtful. I think people are ill-informed. It's very difficult to protest against a can of Coke, a bottle of Pepsi, or a can of Folgers. Starbucks is both this ubiquitous brand and a place where you can go and break a window. You can't break a can of Coke."

The store was quickly repaired, and the protesters have scattered to other cities. Yet cup by cup, Starbucks really is caffeinating the world, its green-and-white emblem beckoning to consumers on three continents. In 1999, Starbucks Corp. had 281 stores abroad. Today, it has about 1,200—and it's still in the early stages of a plan to colonize the globe. If the protesters were wrong in their tactics, they weren't wrong about Starbucks' ambitions. They were just early.

The story of how Schultz & Co. transformed a pedestrian commodity into an upscale consumer accessory has a fairy-tale quality. Starbucks has grown from 17 coffee shops in Seattle 15 years ago to 5,689 outlets in 28 countries. Sales have climbed an average of 20 percent annually since the company went public 10 years ago, to $2.6 billion in 2001, while profits bounded ahead an average of 30 percent per year, hitting $181.2 million last year. And the momentum continues. In the first three quarters of this fiscal year, sales climbed 24 percent, year to year, to $2.4 billion, while profits, excluding onetime charges and capital gains, rose 25 percent, to $159.5 million.

Moreover, the Starbucks name and image connect with millions of consumers around the globe. It was one of the fastest-growing brands in a *BusinessWeek* survey of the top 100 global brands published August 5. At a time when one corporate star after another has crashed to earth, brought down by revelations of earnings misstatements, executive greed, or worse, Starbucks hasn't faltered. The company confidently predicts up to 25 percent annual sales and earnings growth this year. On Wall Street, Starbucks is the last great growth story. Its stock, including four splits, has soared more than 2,200 percent over the past decade, surpassing Wal-Mart, General Electric, PepsiCo, Coca-Cola, Microsoft, and IBM in total return. Now at $21, it is hovering near its all-time high of $23 in July, before the overall market drop.

And after a slowdown last fall and winter, when consumers seemed to draw inward after September 11, Starbucks is rocketing ahead once again. Sales in stores open at least 13 months grew by 6 percent in the 43 weeks through July 28, and the company predicts monthly same-store sales gains as high as 7 percent through the end of this fiscal year. That's below the 9 percent growth rate in 2000, but investors seem encouraged. "We're going to see a lot more growth," says Jerome A. Castellini, president of Chicago-based CastleArk Management, which controls about 300,000 Starbucks shares. "The stock is on a run."

But how long can that run last? Already, Schultz's team is hard-pressed to grind out new profits in a home market that is quickly becoming saturated. Amazingly, with 4,247 stores scattered across the United States and Canada, there are still eight states in the United States with no Starbucks stores. Frappuccinofree cities include Butte, Mont., and Fargo, N.D. But big cities, affluent suburbs, and shopping malls are full to the brim. In coffee-crazed Seattle, there is a Starbucks outlet for every 9,400 people, and the company considers that the upper limit of coffee-shop saturation. In Manhattan's 24 square miles, Starbucks has 124 cafes, with four more on the way this year. That's one for every 12,000 people—meaning that there could be room for even more stores. Given such concentration, it is likely to take annual same-store sales increases of 10 percent or more if the company is going to match its historic overall sales growth. That, as they might say at Starbucks, is a tall order to fill.

Indeed, the crowding of so many stores so close together has become a national joke, eliciting quips such as this headline in The Onion, a satirical publication: "A New Starbucks Opens in Restroom of Existing Starbucks." And even the company admits that while its practice of blanketing an area with stores helps achieve market dominance, it can cut sales at existing outlets. "We probably self-cannibalize our stores at a rate of 30 percent a year," Schultz says. Adds Lehman Brothers Inc. analyst Mitchell Speiser: "Starbucks is at a defining point in its growth. It's reaching a level that makes it harder and harder to grow, just due to the law of large numbers."

To duplicate the staggering returns of its first decade, Starbucks has no choice but to export its concept aggressively. Indeed, some analysts give Starbucks only two years at most before it saturates the U.S. market. The chain now operates 1,200 international outlets, from Beijing to Bristol. That leaves plenty of room to grow. Indeed, about 400 of its planned 1,200 new stores this year will be built overseas, representing a 35 percent increase in its foreign base. Starbucks expects to double the number of its stores worldwide, to 10,000 in three years. During the past 12 months, the chain has opened stores in Vienna, Zurich, Madrid, Berlin, and even in far-off Jakarta. Athens comes next. And within the next year, Starbucks plans to move into Mexico and Puerto Rico. But global expansion poses huge risks for Starbucks. For one thing, it makes less money on each overseas store because most of them are operated with local partners. While that makes it easier to start up on foreign turf, it reduces the company's share of the profits to only 20 percent to 50 percent.

Moreover, Starbucks must cope with some predictable challenges of becoming a mature company in the United States. After riding the wave of successful baby boomers through the '90s, the company faces an ominously hostile reception from its future consumers, the twenty- or thirtysomethings of Generation X. Not only are the activists among them turned off by the power and image of the well-known brand, but many others say that Starbucks' latte-sipping sophisticates and piped-in Kenny G music are a real turn-off. They don't feel wanted in a place that sells designer coffee at $3 a cup.

Even the thirst of loyalists for high-price coffee can't be taken for granted. Starbucks' growth over the past decade coincided with a remarkable surge in the economy. Consumer spending has continued strong in the downturn, but if that changes, those $3 lattes might be an easy place for people on a budget to cut back. Starbucks executives insist that won't happen, pointing out that even in the weeks following the terrorist attacks, same-store comparisons stayed positive while those of other retailers skidded.

Starbucks also faces slumping morale and employee burnout among its store managers and its once-cheery army of baristas. Stock options for part-timers in the restaurant business was a Starbucks innovation that once commanded awe and respect from its employees. But now, though employees are still paid better than comparable workers elsewhere—about $7 per hour—many regard the job as just another fast-food gig. Dissatisfaction over odd hours and low pay is affecting the quality of the normally sterling service and even the coffee itself, say some customers and employees. Frustrated store managers among the company's roughly 470 California stores sued Starbucks in 2001 for allegedly refusing to pay legally mandated overtime. Starbucks settled the suit for $18 million this past April, shaving $0.03 per share off an otherwise strong second quarter. However, the heart of the complaint—feeling overworked and underappreciated—doesn't seem to be going away.

To be sure, Starbucks has a lot going for it as it confronts the challenge of maintaining its growth. Nearly free of debt, it fuels expansion with internal cash flow. And Starbucks can maintain a tight grip on its image because stores are company-owned: There are no franchisees to get sloppy about running things. By relying on mystique and word-of-mouth, whether here or overseas, the company saves a bundle on marketing costs. Starbucks spends just $30 million annually on advertising, or roughly 1 percent of revenues, usually just for new flavors of coffee drinks in the summer and product launches, such as its new in-store Web service. Most consumer companies its size shell out upwards of $300 million per year. Moreover, unlike a McDonald's or a Gap Inc., two other retailers that rapidly grew in the United States, Starbucks has no nationwide competitor.

Starbucks also has a well-seasoned management team. Schultz, 49, stepped down as chief executive in 2000 to become chairman and chief global strategist. Orin Smith, 60, the company's numbers-cruncher, is now CEO and in charge of day-to-day operations. The head of North American operations is Howard Behar, 57, a retailing expert who returned last September, two years after retiring. The management trio is known as H20, for Howard, Howard, and Orin.

Schultz remains the heart and soul of the operation. Raised in a Brooklyn public-housing project, he found his way to Starbucks, a tiny chain of Seattle coffee shops, as a marketing executive in the early '80s. The name came about when the original owners looked to Seattle history for inspiration and chose the moniker of an old mining camp: Starbo. Further refinement led to Starbucks, after the first mate in Moby-Dick, which they felt evoked the seafaring romance of the early coffee traders (hence the mermaid logo). Schultz got the idea for the modern Starbucks format while visiting a Milan coffee bar. He bought out his bosses in 1987 and began expanding. Today, Schultz has a net worth of about $700 million, including $400 million of company stock.

Starbucks has come light-years from those humble beginnings, but Schultz and his team still think there's room to grow in the United States—even in communities where the chain already has dozens of stores. Clustering stores increases total revenue and market share, Smith argues, even when individual stores poach on each other's sales. The strategy works, he says, because of Starbucks' size. It is large enough to absorb losses at existing stores as new ones open up, and soon overall sales grow beyond what they would have with just one store. Meanwhile, it's cheaper to deliver to and manage stores located close together. And by clustering, Starbucks can quickly dominate a local market.

The company is still capable of designing and opening a store in 16 weeks or less and recouping the initial investment in three years. The stores may be oases of tranquility, but management's expansion tactics are something else. Take what critics call its "predatory real estate" strategy—paying more than market-rate rents to keep competitors out of a location. David C. Schomer, owner of Espresso Vivace in Seattle's hip Capitol Hill neighborhood, says Starbucks approached his landlord and offered to pay nearly double the rate to put a coffee shop in the same building.

The landlord stuck with Schomer, who says: "It's a little disconcerting to know that someone is willing to pay twice the going rate." Another time, Starbucks and Tully's Coffee Corp., a Seattle-based coffee chain, were competing for a space in the city. Starbucks got the lease but vacated the premises before the term was up. Still, rather than let Tully's get the space, Starbucks decided to pay the rent on the empty store so its competitor could not move in. Schultz makes no apologies for the hardball tactics. "The real estate business in America is a very, very tough game," he says. "It's not for the faint of heart."

Still, the company's strategy could backfire. Not only will neighborhood activists and local businesses increasingly resent the tactics, but customers could also grow annoyed over having fewer choices. Moreover, analysts contend that Starbucks can maintain about 15 percent square-footage growth in the United States—equivalent to 550 new stores—for only about two more years. After that, it will have to depend on overseas growth to maintain annual 20 percent revenue growth.

Starbucks was hoping to make up much of that growth with more sales of food and other noncoffee items, but has stumbled somewhat. In the late '90s, Schultz thought that offering $8 sandwiches, desserts, and CDs in his stores and selling packaged coffee in supermarkets would significantly boost sales. The specialty business now accounts for about 16 percent of sales, but growth has been less than expected. A healthy 19 percent this year, it's still far below the 38 percent growth rate of fiscal 2000. That suggests that while coffee can command high prices in a slump, food—at least at Starbucks—cannot. One of Behar's most important goals is to improve that record. For instance, the company now has a test program of serving hot breakfasts in 20 Seattle stores and may move to expand supermarket sales of whole beans.

What's more important for the bottom line, though, is that Starbucks has proven to be highly innovative in the way it sells its main course: coffee. In 800 locations it has installed automatic espresso machines to speed up service. And in November, it began offering prepaid Starbucks cards, priced from $5 to $500, which clerks swipe through a reader to deduct a sale. That, says the company, cuts transaction times in half. Starbucks has sold $70 million of the cards.

In early August, Starbucks launched Starbucks Express, its boldest experiment yet, which blends java, Web technology, and faster service. At about 60 stores in the Denver area, customers can pre-order and prepay for beverages and pastries via phone or on the Starbucks Express website. They just make the call or click the mouse before arriving at the store, and their beverage will be waiting—with their name printed on the cup. The company will decide in January on a national launch.

And Starbucks is bent on even more fundamental store changes. On August 21, it announced expansion of a high-speed wireless Internet service to about 1,200 Starbucks locations in North America and Europe. Partners in the project—which Starbucks calls the world's largest Wi-Fi network—include Mobile International, a wireless subsidiary of Deutsche Telekom, and Hewlett-Packard. Customers sit in a store and check e-mail, surf the Web, or download multimedia presentations without looking for connections or tripping over cords. They start with 24 hours of free wireless broadband before choosing from a variety of monthly subscription plans.

Starbucks executives hope such innovations will help surmount their toughest challenge in the home market: attracting the next generation of customers. Younger coffee drinkers already feel uncomfortable in the stores. The company knows that because it once had a group of twentysomethings hypnotized for a market study. When their defenses were down, out came the bad news. "They either can't afford to buy coffee at Starbucks, or the only peers they see are those working behind the counter," says Mark Barden, who conducted the research for the Hal Riney & Partners ad agency (now part of Publicis Worldwide) in San Francisco. One of the recurring themes the hypnosis brought out was a sense that "people like me aren't welcome here except to serve the yuppies," he says. Then there are those who just find the whole Starbucks scene a bit pretentious. Katie Kelleher, 22, a Chicago paralegal, is put off by Starbucks' Italian terminology of grande and venti for coffee sizes. She goes to Dunkin' Donuts, saying: "Small, medium, and large is fine for me."

As it expands, Starbucks faces another big risk: that of becoming a far less special place for its employees. For a company modeled around enthusiastic service, that could have dire consequences for both image and sales. During its growth spurt of the mid- to late-1990s, Starbucks had the lowest employee turnover rate of any restaurant or fast-food company, largely thanks to its then unheard-of policy of giving health insurance and modest stock options to part-timers making barely more than minimum wage.

Such perks are no longer enough to keep all the workers happy. Starbucks' pay doesn't come close to matching the workload it requires, complain some staff. Says Carrie Shay, a former store manager in West Hollywood, Calif.: "If I were making a decent living, I'd still be there." Shay, one of the plaintiffs in the suit against the company, says she earned $32,000 a year to run a store with 10 to 15 part-time employees. She hired employees, managed their schedules, and monitored the store's weekly profit-and-loss statement. But she was also expected to put in significant time behind the counter and had to sign an affidavit pledging to work up to 20 hours of overtime a week without extra pay—a requirement the company has dropped since the settlement. Smith says that Starbucks offers better pay, benefits, and training than comparable companies, while it encourages promotions from within.

For sure, employee discontent is far from the image Starbucks wants to project of relaxed workers cheerfully making cappuccinos. But perhaps it is inevitable. The business model calls for lots of low-wage workers. And the more people who are hired as Starbucks expands, the less they are apt to feel connected to the original mission of high service—bantering with customers and treating them like family. Robert J. Thompson, a professor of popular culture at Syracuse University, says of Starbucks: "It's turning out to be one of the great twenty-first century American success stories—complete with all the ambiguities."

Overseas, though, the whole Starbucks package seems new and, to many young people, still very cool. In Vienna, where Starbucks had a gala opening for its first Austrian store last December, Helmut Spudich, a business editor for the paper *Der Standard,* predicted that Starbucks would attract a younger crowd than the established cafes. "The coffeehouses in Vienna are nice, but they are old. Starbucks is considered hip," he says.

But if Starbucks can count on its youth appeal to win a welcome in new markets, such enthusiasm cannot be counted on indefinitely. In Japan, the company beat even its own bullish expectations, growing to 368 stores after opening its first in Tokyo in 1996. Affluent young Japanese women like Anna Kato, a 22-year-old Toyota Motor Corp. worker, loved the place. "I don't care if it costs more, as long as it tastes sweet," she says, sitting in the world's busiest Starbucks, in Tokyo's Shibuya district. Yet same-store sales growth has fallen in the past 10 months in Japan, Starbucks' top foreign market, as rivals offer similar fare. Add to that the depressed economy, and Starbucks Japan seems to be losing steam. Although it forecasts a 30 percent gain in net profit, to $8 million, for the year started in April, on record sales of $516 million, same-store sales are down 14 percent for the year ended in June. Meanwhile in England, Starbucks' second-biggest overseas market, with 310 stores, imitators are popping up left and right to steal market share.

Entering other big markets may be tougher yet. The French seem to be ready for Starbucks' sweeter taste, says Philippe Bloch, cofounder of Columbus Cafe, a Starbucks-like chain. But he wonders if the company can profitably cope with France's arcane regulations and generous labor benefits. And in Italy, the epicenter of European coffee culture, the notion that the locals will abandon their own 200,000 coffee bars en masse for Starbucks strikes many as ludicrous. For one, Italian coffee bars prosper by serving food as well as coffee, an area where Starbucks still struggles. Also, Italian coffee is cheaper than U.S. java and, say Italian purists, much better. Americans pay about $1.50 for an espresso. In northern Italy, the price is 67 cents; in the south, just 55 cents. Schultz insists that Starbucks will eventually come to Italy. It'll have a lot to prove when it does. Carlo Petrini, founder of the antiglobalization movement Slow Food, sniffs that Starbucks' "substances served in styrofoam" won't cut it. The cups are paper, of course. But the skepticism is real.

As Starbucks spreads out, Schultz will have to be increasingly sensitive to those cultural challenges. In December, for instance, he flew to Israel to meet with Foreign Secretary Shimon Peres and other Israeli officials to discuss the Middle East crisis. He won't divulge the nature of his discussions. But subsequently, at a Seattle synagogue, Schultz let the Palestinians have it. With Starbucks outlets already in Kuwait, Lebanon, Oman, Qatar, and Saudi Arabia, he created a mild uproar among Palestinian supporters. Schultz quickly backpedaled, saying that his words were taken out of context and asserting that he is "pro-peace" for both sides.

There are plenty more minefields ahead. So far, the Seattle coffee company has compiled an envious record of growth. But the giddy buzz of that initial expansion is wearing off. Now, Starbucks is waking up to the grand challenges faced by any corporation bent on becoming a global powerhouse.

Profit at Starbucks Coffee Japan fell 70 percent in the first nine months of the year because of growing competition from rival coffee chains. Sales at stores open more than one year fell 16 percent. The firm expects a loss for the full year.

## QUESTIONS

As a guide, use Exhibit 1.3 and its description in Chapter 1, and do the following:

1. Identify the controllable and uncontrollable elements that Starbucks has encountered in entering global markets.

2. What are the major sources of risk facing the company and discuss potential solutions.

3. Critique Starbucks' overall corporate strategy.

4. How might Starbucks improve profitability in Japan? Visit www.starbucks.com for more information.

Sources: Stanley Holmes, Drake Bennett, Kate Carlisle, and Chester Dawson, "Planet Starbucks: To Keep Up the Growth It Must Go Global Quickly," *BusinessWeek*, December 9, 2002, pp. 100–110. Reprinted by permission of *BusinessWeek*; and Ken Belson, "Japan: Starbucks Profit Falls," *New York Times*, February 20, 2003, p. 1.

# CASE I-2 Nestlé: The Infant Formula Controversy

Nestlé Alimentana of Vevey, Switzerland, one of the world's largest food-processing companies with worldwide sales of over $8 billion, has been the subject of an international boycott. For over 20 years, beginning with a Pan American Health Organization allegation, Nestlé has been directly or indirectly charged with involvement in the death of Third World infants. The charges revolve around the sale of infant feeding formula, which allegedly is the cause for mass deaths of babies in the Third World.

In 1974 a British journalist published a report that suggested that powdered-formula manufacturers contributed to the death of Third World infants by hard-selling their products to people incapable of using them properly. The 28-page report accused the industry of encouraging mothers to give up breast feeding and use powdered milk formulas. The report was later published by the Third World Working Group, a lobby in support of less-developed countries. The pamphlet was entitled "Nestlé Kills Babies," and accused Nestlé of unethical and immoral behavior.

Although there are several companies that market infant baby formula internationally, Nestlé received most of the attention. This incident raises several issues important to all multinational companies. Before addressing these issues, let's look more closely at the charges by the Infant Formula Action Coalition and others and the defense by Nestlé.

## THE CHARGES

Most of the charges against infant formulas focus on the issue of whether advertising and marketing of such products have discouraged breast feeding among Third World mothers and have led to misuse of the products, thus contributing to infant malnutrition and death. Following are some of the charges made:

- A Peruvian nurse reported that formula had found its way to Amazon tribes deep in the jungles of northern Peru. There, where the only water comes from a highly contaminated river—which also serves as the local laundry and toilet—formula-fed babies came down with recurring attacks of diarrhea and vomiting.

- Throughout the Third World, many parents dilute the formula to stretch their supply. Some even believe the bottle itself has nutrient qualities and merely fill it with water. The result is extreme malnutrition.

- One doctor reported that in a rural area, one newborn male weighed 7 pounds. At four months of age, he weighed 5 pounds. His sister, aged 18 months, weighed 12 pounds, what one would expect a four-month-old baby to weigh. She later weighed only 8 pounds. The children had never been breast fed, and since birth their diets were basically bottle feeding. For a four-month baby, one can of formula should have lasted just under three days. The mother said that one can lasted two weeks to feed both children.

- In rural Mexico, the Philippines, Central America, and the whole of Africa, there has been a dramatic decrease in the incidence of breast feeding. Critics blame the decline

largely on the intensive advertising and promotion of infant formula. Clever radio jingles extol the wonders of the "white man's powder that will make baby grow and glow." "Milk nurses" visit nursing mothers in hospitals and their homes and provide samples of formula. These activities encourage mothers to give up breast feeding and resort to bottle feeding because it is "the fashionable thing to do or because people are putting it to them that this is the thing to do."

## THE DEFENSE

The following points are made in defense of the marketing of baby formula in Third World countries:

- First, Nestlé argues that the company has never advocated bottle feeding instead of breast feeding. All its products carry a statement that breast feeding is best. The company states that it "believes that breast milk is the best food for infants and encourages breast feeding around the world as it has done for decades." The company offers as support of this statement one of Nestlé's oldest educational booklets on "Infant Feeding and Hygiene," which dates from 1913 and encourages breast feeding.

- However, the company does believe that infant formula has a vital role in proper infant nutrition as a supplement, when the infant needs nutritionally adequate and appropriate foods in addition to breast milk, and as a substitute for breast milk when a mother cannot or chooses not to breast feed. One doctor reports, "Economically deprived and thus dietarily deprived mothers who give their children only breast milk are raising infants whose growth rates begin to slow noticeably at about the age of three months. These mothers then turn to supplemental feedings that are often harmful to children. These include herbal teas and concoctions of rice water or corn water and sweetened, condensed milk. These feedings can also be prepared with contaminated water and are served in unsanitary conditions."

- Mothers in developing nations often have dietary deficiencies. In the Philippines, a mother in a poor family who is nursing a child produces about a pint of milk daily. Mothers in the United States usually produce about a quart of milk each day. For both the Filipino and U.S. mothers, the milk produced is equally nutritious. The problem is that there is less of it for the Filipino baby. If the Filipino mother doesn't augment the child's diet, malnutrition develops.

- Many poor women in the Third World bottle feed because their work schedules in fields or factories will not permit breast feeding. The infant feeding controversy has largely to do with the gradual introduction of weaning foods during the period between three months and two years. The average well-nourished Western woman, weighing 20 to 30 pounds more than most women in less-developed countries, cannot feed only breast milk beyond five or six months. The claim that Third World women can breast feed exclusively for one or two years and have healthy, well-developed children is outrageous. Thus, all children beyond the ages of five to six months require supplemental feeding.

- Weaning foods can be classified as either native cereal gruels of millet or rice, or commercial manufactured milk formula. Traditional native weaning foods are usually made by mixing maize, rice, or millet flours with water and then cooking the mixture. Other weaning foods found in use are crushed crackers, sugar and water, and mashed bananas.

There are two basic dangers to the use of native weaning foods. First, the nutritional quality of the native gruels is low. Second, microbiological contamination of the traditional weaning foods is a certainty in many Third World settings. The millet or the flour is likely to be contaminated, the water used in cooking will most certainly be contaminated, and the cooking containers will be contaminated; therefore, the native gruel, even after it is cooked, is frequently contaminated with colon bacilli, staph, and other dangerous bacteria. Moreover, large batches of gruel are often made and allowed to sit, inviting further contamination.

- Scientists recently compared the microbiological contamination of a local native gruel with ordinary reconstituted milk formula prepared under primitive conditions. They found both were contaminated to similar dangerous levels.
- The real nutritional problem in the Third World is not whether to give infants breast milk or formula, but how to supplement mothers' milk with nutritionally adequate foods when they are needed. Finding adequate locally produced, nutritionally sound supplements to mothers' milk and teaching people how to prepare and use them safely are the issues. Only effective nutrition education along with improved sanitation and good food that people can afford will win the fight against dietary deficiencies in the Third World.

## THE RESOLUTION

In 1974, Nestlé, aware of changing social patterns in the developing world and the increased access to radio and television there, reviewed its marketing practices on a region-by-region basis. As a result, mass media advertising of infant formula began to be phased out immediately in certain markets and, by 1978, was banned worldwide by the company. Nestlé then undertook to carry out more comprehensive health education programs to ensure that an understanding of the proper use of their products reached mothers, particularly in rural areas.

"Nestlé fully supports the WHO [World Health Organization] Code. Nestlé will continue to promote breast feeding and ensure that its marketing practices do not discourage breast feeding anywhere. Our company intends to maintain a constructive dialogue with governments and health professionals in all the countries it serves with the sole purpose of servicing mothers and the health of babies." This quote is from *Nestlé Discusses the Recommended WHO Infant Formula Code.*

In 1977, the Interfaith Center on Corporate Responsibility in New York compiled a case against formula feeding in developing nations, and the Third World Institute launched a boycott against many Nestlé products. Its aim was to halt promotion of infant formulas in the Third World. The Infant Formula Action Coalition (INFACT, successor to the Third World Institute), along with several other world organizations, successfully lobbied the World Health Organization to draft a code to regulate the advertising and marketing of infant formula in the Third World. In 1981, by a vote of 114 to 1 (three countries abstained and the United States was the only dissenting vote), 118 member nations of WHO endorsed a voluntary code. The eight-page code urged a worldwide ban on promotion and advertising of baby formula and called for a halt to distribution of free product samples or gifts to physicians who promoted the use of the formula as a substitute for breast milk.

In May 1981 Nestlé announced it would support the code and waited for individual countries to pass national codes that would then be put into effect. Unfortunately, very few such codes were forthcoming. By the end of 1983, only 25 of the 157 member nations of the WHO had established national codes. Accordingly, Nestlé management determined it would have to apply the code in the absence of national legislation, and in February 1982 it issued instructions to marketing personnel that delineated the company's best understanding of the code and what would have to be done to follow it.

In addition, in May 1982 Nestlé formed the Nestlé Infant Formula Audit Commission (NIFAC), chaired by former Senator Edmund J. Muskie, and asked the commission to review the company's instructions to field personnel to determine if they could be improved to better implement the code. At the same time, Nestlé continued its meetings with WHO and UNICEF (United Nations Children's Fund) to try to obtain the most accurate interpretation of the code. NIFAC recommended several clarifications for the instructions that it believed would better interpret ambiguous areas of the code; in October 1982, Nestlé accepted those recommendations and issued revised instructions to field personnel.

Other issues within the code, such as the question of a warning statement, were still open to debate. Nestlé consulted extensively with WHO before issuing its label warning statement in October 1983, but there was still not universal agreement with it. Acting on WHO recommendations, Nestlé consulted with firms experienced and expert in developing and field testing educational materials, so that it could ensure that those materials met the code.

When the International Nestlé Boycott Committee (INBC) listed its four points of difference with Nestlé, it again became a matter of interpretation of the requirements of the code. Here, meetings held by UNICEF proved invaluable, in that UNICEF agreed to define areas of differing interpretation—in some cases providing definitions contrary to both Nestlé's and INBC's interpretations.

It was the meetings with UNICEF in early 1984 that finally led to a joint statement by Nestlé and INBC on January 25. At that time, INBC announced its suspension of boycott activities, and Nestlé pledged its continued support of the WHO code.

## NESTLÉ SUPPORTS WHO CODE

The company has a strong record of progress and support in implementing the WHO code, including the following:

- Immediate support for the WHO code, May 1981, and testimony to this effect before the U.S. Congress, June 1981.
- Issuance of instructions to all employees, agents, and distributors in February 1982 to implement the code in all Third World countries where Nestlé markets infant formula.
- Establishment of an audit commission, in accordance with Article 11.3 of the WHO code, to ensure the company's

compliance with the code. The commission, headed by Edmund S. Muskie, was composed of eminent clergy and scientists.

- Willingness to meet with concerned church leaders, international bodies, and organization leaders seriously concerned with Nestlé's application of the code.

- Issuance of revised instructions to Nestlé personnel, October 1982, as recommended by the Muskie committee to clarify and give further effect to the code.

- Consultation with WHO, UNICEF, and NIFAC on how to interpret the code and how best to implement specific provisions, including clarification by WHO/UNICEF of the definition of children who need to be fed breast milk substitutes, to aid in determining the need for supplies in hospitals.

## NESTLÉ POLICIES

In the early 1970s Nestlé began to review its infant formula marketing practices on a region-by-region basis. By 1978 the company had stopped all consumer advertising and direct sampling to mothers. Instructions to the field issued in February 1982 and clarified in the revised instructions of October 1982 to adopt articles of the WHO code as Nestlé policy include the following:

- No advertising to the general public
- No sampling to mothers
- No mothercraft workers
- No use of commission/bonus for sales
- No use of infant pictures on labels
- No point-of-sale advertising
- No financial or material inducements to promote products
- No samples to physicians except in three specific situations: a new product, a new product formulation, or a new graduate physician; limited to one or two cans of product
- Limitation of supplies to those requested in writing and fulfilling genuine needs for breast milk substitutes
- A statement of the superiority of breast feeding on all labels/materials
- Labels and educational materials clearly stating the hazards involved in incorrect usage of infant formula, developed in consultation with WHO/UNICEF

Even though Nestlé stopped consumer advertising, it was able to maintain its share of the Third World infant formula market. In 1988 a call to resume the seven-year boycott was made by a group of consumer activist members of the Action for Corporate Accountability. The group claimed that Nestlé was distributing free formula through maternity wards as a promotional tactic that undermined the practice of breast feeding. The group claimed that Nestlé and others, including American Home Products, have continued to dump formula in hospitals and maternity wards and that, as a result, "babies are dying as the companies are violating the WHO resolution." As late as 1997 the Interagency Group on Breastfeeding Monitoring (IGBM) claimed Nestlé continues to systematically violate the WHO code. Nestlé's response to these accusations is included on their website (see www.nestlé.com for details).

The boycott focus is Taster's Choice Instant Coffee, Coffeemate Nondairy Coffee Creamer, Anacin aspirin, and Advil.

Representatives of Nestlé and American Home Products rejected the accusations and said they were complying with World Health Organization and individual national codes on the subject.

## THE NEW TWIST

A new environmental factor has made the entire case more complex: As of 2001 it was believed that some 3.8 million children around the world have contracted the human immunodeficiency virus (HIV) at their mothers' breasts. In affluent countries mothers can be told to bottle feed their children. However, 90 percent of the child infections occur in developing countries. There the problems of bottle feeding remain. Further, in even the most infected areas, 70 percent of the mothers do not carry the virus, and breast feeding is by far the best option. The vast majority of pregnant women in developing countries have no idea whether they are infected or not. One concern is that large numbers of healthy women will switch to the bottle just to be safe. Alternatively, if bottle feeding becomes a badge of HIV infection, mothers may continue breast feeding just to avoid being stigmatized. In Thailand, pregnant women are offered testing, and if found HIV positive, are given free milk powder. But in some African countries, where women get pregnant at three times the Thai rate and HIV infection rates are 25 percent compared with the 2 percent in Thailand, that solution is much less feasible. Finally, the latest medical evidence indicates that extending breastfeeding reduces the risk of breast cancer.

## THE ISSUES

Many issues are raised by this incident and the ongoing swirl of cultural change. How can a company deal with a worldwide boycott of its products? Why did the United States decide not to support the WHO code? Who is correct, WHO or Nestlé? A more important issue concerns the responsibility of an MNC marketing in developing nations. Setting aside the issues for a moment, consider the notion that, whether intentional or not, Nestlé's marketing activities have had an impact on the behavior of many people. In other words, Nestlé is a cultural change agent. When it or any other company successfully introduces new ideas into a culture, the culture changes and those changes can be functional or dysfunctional to established patterns of behavior. The key issue is, What responsibility does the MNC have to the culture when, as a result of its marketing activities, it causes change in that culture? Finally, how might Nestlé now participate in the battle against the spread of HIV and AIDS in developing countries?

## QUESTIONS

1. What are the responsibilities of companies in this or similar situations?

2. What could Nestlé have done to have avoided the accusations of "killing Third World babies" and still market its product?

3. After Nestlé's experience, how do you suggest it, or any other company, can protect itself in the future?

4. Assume you are the one who had to make the final decision on whether or not to promote and market Nestlé's baby formula in Third World countries. Read the section titled "Ethically and

Socially Responsible Decisions" in Chapter 5 (pp. 145–146) as a guide to examine the social responsibility and ethical issues regarding the marketing approach and the promotion used. Were the decisions socially responsible? Were they ethical?

5. What advice would you give to Nestlé now in light of the new problem of HIV infection being spread via mothers' milk?

---

This case is an update of "Nestlé in LDCs," a case written by J. Alex Murray, University of Windsor, Ontario, Canada, and Gregory M. Gazda and Mary J. Molenaar, University of San Diego. The case originally appeared in the fifth edition of this text.

The case draws from the following: "International Code of Marketing of Breastmilk Substitutes" (Geneva: World Health Organization, 1981); *INFACT Newsletter,* Minneapolis, February 1979; John A. Sparks, "The Nestlé Controversy—Anatomy of a Boycott" (Grove City, PA: Public Policy Education Funds); "WHO Drafts a Marketing Code," *World Business Weekly,* January 19, 1981, p. 8; "A Boycott over Infant Formula," *Business Week,* April 23, 1979, p. 137; "The Battle over Bottle-Feeding," *World Press Review,* January 1980, p. 54; "Nestlé and the Role of Infant Formula in Developing Countries: The Resolution of a Conflict" (Nestlé Company, 1985); "The Dilemma of Third World Nutrition" (Nestlé SA, 1985), 20 pp.; Thomas V. Greer, "The Future of the International Code of Marketing of Breastmilk Substitutes: The Socio-Legal Context," *International Marketing Review,* Spring 1984, pp. 33–41; James C. Baker, "The International Infant Formula Controversy: A Dilemma in Corporate Social Responsibility," *Journal of Business Ethics,* 1985, no. 4, pp. 181–190; and Shawn Tully, "Nestlé Shows How to Gobble Markets," *Fortune,* January 16, 1989, p. 75. For a comprehensive and well-balanced review of the infant formula issue, see Thomas V. Greer, "International Infant Formula Marketing: The Debate Continues," *Advances in International Marketing* 1990, 4, pp. 207–225. For a discussion of the HIV complication, see "Back to the Bottle?" *Economist,* February 7, 1998, p. 50; Alix M. Freedman and Steve Stecklow, "Bottled Up: As UNICEF Battles Baby-Formula Makers, African Infants Sicken," *Wall Street Journal,* December 5, 2000; and Rone Tempest, "Mass Breast-Feeding by 1,128 Is Called a Record," *Los Angeles Times,* August 4, 2002, p. B1.

# CASE 1-3 Coke and Pepsi Learn to Compete in India

## THE BEVERAGE BATTLEFIELD

In 2003 Jagdeep Kapoor, chairman of Samsika Marketing Consultants in Mumbai (formerly Bombay), commented that "Coke lost a number of years over errors. But at last it seems to be getting its positioning right." Similarly, Ronald McEachern, PepsiCo's Asia chief, asserted "India is the beverage battlefield for 2003."

The experience of the world's two giant soft drinks companies in India during the 1990s and the beginning of the new millennium was not a happy one, even though the government had opened its doors wide to foreign companies. Both companies experienced a range of unexpected problems and difficult situations that led them to recognize that competing in India requires special knowledge, skills and local expertise. In many ways, Coke and Pepsi managers had to learn the hard way that "what works here" does not always "work there." In spring 2003, Alex von Behr, the president of Coca-Cola India admitted ruefully, "The environment in India is challenging, but we're learning how to crack it."

## THE INDIAN SOFT DRINKS INDUSTRY

In India, over 45 percent of the soft drinks industry in 1993 consisted of small manufacturers. Their combined business was worth $3.2 million dollars. Leading producers included Parle Agro (hereafter "Parle"), Pure Drinks, Modern Foods, and McDowells. They offered carbonated cola drinks, orange, and lemon-lime beverages. Coca-Cola Corporation (hereafter "Coca-Cola") was only a distant memory to most Indians at that time. The company had been present in the Indian market from 1958 until its withdrawal in 1977, following a dispute with the government over its trade secrets. After decades in the market, Coca-Cola chose to leave India rather than cut its equity stake to 40 percent and hand over its secret formula for the syrup.

Following Coca-Cola's departure, Parle became the market leader and established thriving export franchise businesses in Dubai, Kuwait, Saudi Arabia, and Oman in the Gulf, along with Sri Lanka. It set up production in Nepal and Bangladesh, and served distant markets in Tanzania, Britain, the Netherlands, and the United States. Parle invested heavily in image advertising at home, establishing the dominance of its flagship brand, Thums Up.

Thums Up is a brand associated with a "job well done" and personal success. These are persuasive messages for its target market of young people aged 15 to 24. Parle has been careful in the past not to call Thums Up a cola drink, so it has avoided direct comparison with Coke and Pepsi, the world's brand leaders.

The soft drinks market in India is composed of six product segments: cola, "cloudy lemon," orange, "soda" (carbonated water), mango, and "clear lemon," in order of importance. Cloudy lemon and clear lemon together make up the lemon-lime segment. Prior to the arrival of foreign producers in India, the fight for local dominance was between Parle's Thums Up and Pure Drinks' Campa Cola.

In 1988, the industry had experienced a dramatic shakeout following a government warning that BVO, an essential ingredient in locally produced soft drinks, was carcinogenic. Producers either had to resort to using a costly imported substitute, estergum, or

they had to finance their own R&D in order to find a substitute ingredient. Many failed and quickly withdrew from the industry.

Competing with the segment of carbonated soft drinks is another beverage segment composed of noncarbonated fruit drinks. These are a growth industry because Indian consumers perceive fruit drinks to be natural, healthy, and tasty. The leading brand has traditionally been Parle's Frooti, a mango-flavored drink, which was also exported to franchisees in the United States, Britain, Portugal, Spain and Mauritius.

## OPENING UP THE INDIAN MARKET IN 1991

In June 1991, India experienced an economic crisis of exceptional severity, triggered by the rise in imported oil prices following the first Gulf War (after Iraq' a invasion of Kuwait). Foreign exchange reserves fell as nonresident Indians (NRIs) cut back on repatriation of their savings, imports were tightly controlled across all sectors, and industrial production fell while inflation was rising. A new government took office in June 1991 led by Prime Minister Narasimha Rao. Inspired by Finance Minister Dr. Manmohan Singh, the government introduced measures to stabilize the economy in the short term and launched a fundamental restructuring program to ensure medium-term growth. Results were dramatic. By 1994, inflation was halved, exchange reserves were greatly increased, exports were growing, and foreign investors were looking at India, a leading Big Emerging Market, with new eyes.

The turnaround could not be overstated; one commentator said, "India has been in economic depression for so long that everything except the snake-charmers, cows and the Taj Mahal has faded from the memory of the world." For many years, the outside world had viewed the Indian government as unfriendly to foreign investors. Outside investment had been allowed only in high tech sectors and was almost entirely prohibited in consumer goods sectors. The "principle of indigenous availability" had specified that if an item could be obtained anywhere else within the country, imports of similar items were forbidden. As a result of this policy, India became self-reliant in its defense industry, developing both nuclear and space programs. In contrast, Indian consumers had little choice of products or brands, and no guarantees of quality or reliability.

Following liberalization of the Indian economy in 1991 and introduction of the New Industrial Policy intended to dismantle complicated trade rules and regulations, foreign investment increased dramatically. Beneficiary industries included processed foods, software, engineering plastics, electronic equipment, power generation, and petroleum generation. A commentator observed, "In the 1970s and 1980s, it was almost antinational to advocate foreign investment. Today the Prime Minister and Finance Minister are wooing foreign investors."

Foreign companies that had successfully pioneered entry into the Indian market many decades earlier, despite all the stringent rules, quickly increased their equity stakes under the new rules from 40 percent to 51 percent. These long-established companies included global giants such as Unilever, Procter and Gamble, Pfizer, Hoechst, BAT, and Philips (of the Netherlands).

# COCA-COLA AND PEPSICO ENTER THE INDIAN MARKET

Despite its huge population, India had not been considered by foreign beverage producers to be an important market in the past. In addition to the deterrents imposed by the government through its austere trade policies, rules and regulations, local demand for carbonated drinks in India was very low, compared to countries at a similar stage of economic development. In 1989, the average Indian was buying only three bottles a year. This compared to percapita consumption rates of 11 bottles a year in Bangladesh and 13 in Pakistan, India's two neighbors.

## PepsiCo

PepsiCo lodged a joint venture application to enter India in July 1986. It had selected two local partners, Voltas and Punjab Agro. This application was approved under the name "Pepsi Foods Ltd." by the government of Rajiv Gandhi in September 1988. As expected, very stringent conditions were imposed on the venture. Sales of soft drink concentrate to local bottlers could not exceed 25 percent of total sales for the new venture. This limit also included processing of fruits and vegetables by Pepsi Foods Ltd. Robert Beeby, CEO of Pepsi-Cola International, said at that time: "We're willing to go so far with India because we wanted to make sure we get an early entry while the market is developing."

In May 1990, the government mandated that Pepsi Food's products be promoted under the name "Lehar Pepsi" ("lehar" meaning "wave"). Foreign collaboration rules in force at the time prohibited use of foreign brand names on products intended for sale inside India. Other examples of this policy were Maruti Suzuki, Carrier Aircon, L&T Honeywell, Wilkinson's Wiltech, Modi-Champion, and Modi-Xerox.

In keeping with local tastes, Pepsi Foods launched Lehar 7UP in the clear lemon category, along with Lehar Pepsi. Marketing and distribution were focused in the north and west around the major cities of Delhi and Mumbai. An aggressive pricing policy on the one-liter bottles had a severe impact on the local producer, Pure Drinks. The market leader, Parle, preempted any further pricing moves by Pepsi Foods by introducing a new 250-ml. bottle that sold for the same price as its 200-ml. bottle.

Pepsi Foods struggled to fight off local competition from Pure Drinks' Campa Cola, Duke's lemonade, and various brands of Parle. Aware of its difficulties, Pepsi Foods approached Parle in December 1991 to offer an alliance. Parle declined the offer, choosing to stand its ground and continuing to fight to preserve its number one position.

The fight for dominance intensified in 1993 with Pepsi Food's launch of two new brands, Slice and Teem, along with the introduction of fountain sales. At this time, market shares in the cola segment were 60 percent for Parle (down from 70 percent), 26 percent for Pepsi Foods, and 10 percent for Pure Drinks.

## Coca-Cola

In May 1990, Coca-Cola attempted to reenter India by means of a proposed joint venture with a local bottling company owned by the giant Indian conglomerate, Godrej. The government of Rajiv Gandhi turned down this application just as PepsiCo's application was being approved. Undeterred, Coca-Cola made its return to India by joining forces with Britannia Industries India Ltd., a local producer of snack foods. The new venture was called "Britco Foods." In 1993 Coca-Cola filed an application to create a 100 percent-owned soft drinks company, Coca-Cola India.

The arrival of Coca-Cola in the Indian soft drinks industry forced local small producers to consider extreme survival measures. The small Delhi-based company, Pure Drinks, tried to revamp its bottling alliance with Coca-Cola from earlier years, even offering to withdraw its own leading brand, Campa Cola, as an inducement to Coca-Cola. Campa Cola's brand share at the time was 10 percent. However, Coca-Cola had its sights set on a different partner, Parle.

Among local producers, it was believed at that time that Coca-Cola would not take away market share away from local companies because the beverage market was itself growing consistently from year to year. Yet this belief did not stop individual local producers from trying to align themselves with the market leader. Thus, in July 1993, Parle offered to sell Coca-Cola its bottling plants in the four key cities of Delhi, Mumbai, Ahmedabad, and Surat. In addition, Parle offered to sell its leading brands including Thums Up, Limca, Citra, Gold Spot, and Mazaa. It chose to retain ownership only of Frooti and a soda (carbonated water) called Bisleri.

As a result of Parle's offer, two new ventures were set up to bottle and market both companies' products. The marketing venture would provide advertising, media services, and promotional and sales support. Parle's chief, Ramesh Chauhan, was named Chairman and Coca-Cola staffed the Managing Director's position. Parle held 49 percent of the marketing venture but took an equal 50 percent stake in the bottling venture.

# FAST FORWARD TO THE NEW MILLENNIUM

## Seasonal Sales Promotions—the 2000 Navratri Campaign

In India the summer season for soft drink consumption lasts 70–75 days from mid-April to June. During this time, over 50 percent of the year's carbonated beverages are consumed across the country. The second-highest season for consumption lasts only 20–25 days during the cultural festival of Navratri ("Nav" means nine and "ratri" means night). This is a traditional Gujarati festival and it goes on for nine nights in the state of Gujarat, in the western part of India. Mumbai also has a significant Gujarati population that is considered part of the target market for this campaign.

As Sunil Kapoor, Regional Marketing Manager for Coca-Cola India stated, "As part of the 'think local—act local' business plan, we have tried to involve the masses in Gujarat with "Thums Up Toofani Ramjhat": with 20,000 free passes issued, one per Thums Up bottle. ("Toofan" means a thunderstorm and "ramjhat" means "let's dance," so together these words convey the idea of a "fast dance.") There are a number of (retail) on-site activities too, such as the 'buy one—get one free' scheme and lucky draws where one can win a free trip to Goa." (Goa is an independent Portuguese-speaking state on the west coast of India, that is famed for its beaches and tourist resorts.)

For its part, PepsiCo also participates in annual Navratri celebrations through massive sponsorships of "garba" competitions in selected venues in Gujarat. ("Garba" is the name of a dance, which is done by women during the Navratri festival.) In 2000 Deepak Jolly, Executive Vice-President for PepsiCo India, commented: "For the first time, Pepsi has tied up with the Gujarati TV channel, Zee Alpha, to telecast "Navrartri Utsav 2000 at Mumbai" on all nine nights. ("Utsav" means festival.) Then there is the mega offer for the people of Ahmedabad, Baroda, Surat, and Rajkot where every refill of a case of Pepsi 300-ml. bottles will fetch one kilo of Basmati rice free." (These are four cities located in the state of Gujarat. Basmati rice is considered to be a premium quality rice.

After the initial purchase of a 300-ml. bottle, consumers can get refills at reduced rates at select stores.)

During the Navrartri festival, both companies are extremely generous with giveaways in their sales promotions. For example, in 2000 Pepsi Foods offered a free Kit Kat with every 1.5 liter bottle and a Polo (hard candies like "Lifesavers") with each 500-ml. bottle of Pepsi and Mirinda.

### The 2002 Summer TV Campaign

In 2002 Pepsi Foods took the lead in the clear lime category with 7UP leading its category, followed by Coca-Cola's Sprite brand. On March 7, 2002, it launched a new summer campaign for 7UP. This date was chosen to coincide with the India-Zimbabwe One-Day cricket series. The new campaign slogan was "Keep It Cool" to emphasize the product attribute of refreshment.

A nationwide television advertising campaign was designed with the objectives of growing the category and building brand salience. The national campaign was to be reinforced with regionally adapted TV campaigns, outdoor activities, and retail promotions.

PepsiCo's ad spending for 7UP was not comparable to the level invested in its flagship brand, Pepsi-Cola, because the clear lime segment in 2002 was minuscule, accounting for just 4.5 percent of the total carbonated soft drinks market. This was equal to about 250–270 million cases. The cloudy lemon segment is more than twice this size, with 10 percent market share; carbonated orange drinks account for about 15 percent.

7UP was being sold in 250-ml., 300-ml., and 500-ml. bottles, and in 200-ml. bottles in southern states. The industry trend was pushing toward 200-ml. bottles in order to increase frequency of purchase and volume of consumption. Pepsi Foods rolled out its Mirinda Lemon, Apple and Orange in 200-ml. bottles in the Delhi market, following similar market launches in Punjab and Uttar Pradesh in the previous year.

In the past, celebrity actors, Amitabh Bachchan and Govinda who are famous male stars of the Indian movie industry, had endorsed Mirinda Lemon. This world-famous industry is referred to as "Bollywood" (the Hollywood of India based in Bombay).

Both Coca-Cola and PepsiCo routinely keep close track of the success of their seasonal advertising campaigns in India through use of marketing research agencies. Coca-Cola has used ORG-MARG, while Pepsi Foods has worked with IMRB. ORG-MARG uses its weekly "Ad Track" to study spontaneous ad recall among 1,000 male and female respondents aged 12-49 in seventeen cities. IMRB's "Perception Analyzer System" surveys 15 to 30 year olds in four cities. Responses are sought on measures of likeability of the ad and intention to buy.

### Pepsi's Sponsorship of Cricket and Football (Soccer)

After India won an outstanding victory in the 2002 India-England NatWest One Day cricket series finals, PepsiCo launched a new ad campaign featuring the batting sensation, Mohammad Kaif. Although he had been signed up a year earlier, Kaif had not yet figured in Pepsi ads. The spotlight had been on Sachin Tendulkar and Amitabh Bachchan who are famous icons as a cricket player and a movie star, respectively. Sachin Tendulkar is considered to be the best batsman in the history of cricket. He started his international cricket career at the age of 16, and now at age 29 he already figures in the list of top young billionaires in the country! Amitabh Bachchan has the distinction of having being the leading superstar in the Indian movie industry for the last 30 years.

Even now, at 60 years of age he commands the highest name rating any star has ever received in Bollywood.

PepsiCo's line-up of other cricket celebrities includes Saurav Ganguly, Rahul Dravid, Harbhajan Singh, Zaheer Khan, V.V.S. Laxman, and Ajit Agarkar. Saurav Ganguly is presently the captain of the Indian cricket team. All of these players were part of the Indian team for the 2003 World Cup Cricket held in South Africa, where they performed superbly, reaching the finals. They lost to Australia in the finals, but PepsiCo was able to capitalize on the overall team's performance during the month and a half long tournament.

Six months earlier, PepsiCo had taken advantage of World Cup soccer fever in India, featuring football heroes such as Baichung Bhutia in their celebrity and music-related advertising communications. These ads featured football players pitted against Sumo wrestlers. In addition, para football tournaments were held in selected cities.

In 2003, similar sports-themed promotions took place, centered around PepsiCo's sponsorship of the World Cup Series in cricket. During the two months of the Series, a new product, Pepsi Blue, was marketed nationwide. This was positioned as a "limited edition," icy-blue cola sold in 300-ml. returnable glass bottles and 500-ml. plastic bottles. These were priced at 8 rupees (Rs) and Rs. 15 respectively. In addition, commemorative, nonreturnable 250-ml. Pepsi bottles priced at Rs. 12 were introduced. (1 Rupee was equal to US 2.08 cents in 2003).

To consolidate its investment in the 2003 campaign, PepsiCo also featured a music video with other celebrity endorsers including the Bollywood stars Amitabh Bachchan, Kareena Kapoor, Abishek Bachchan (the son of Amitabh Bachchan) and Fardeen Khan, as well as several cricketers. The new music video aired on SET Max which is a satellite channel owned by Sony. This channel is popular among the 15–25 age group, mainly in the northern and western parts of India.

### Coca-Cola's Lifestyle Advertising

In 2002 and 2003, Coca-Cola India used a strategy of "building a connect using the relevant local idioms," according to Rajesh Mani, Regional Marketing Manager. The ad strategy, developed by Orchard Advertising in Bangalore, was based on use of "gaana" music and ballet. ("Gaana" means to sing.)

The first ad execution, called "Bombay Dreams," featured A. R. Rahman, who is a famous music director. This approach was very successful among the target audience of young people, increasing sales by about 50 percent. It also won an Effi Award from the Mumbai Advertising Club. (Note: Even though the name of the city has been officially changed from Bombay to Mumbai, local people still continue to use Bombay.)

2003 saw the launch of a second execution of this regional strategy in Chennai (formerly Madras), called "Chennai Dreams." This ad featured Vijay, a youth icon who is famous as an actor in the regional movies of south India. The campaign targeted consumers in Tamil Nadu located in the southern part of the country. Thomas Xavier, Executive Creative Director of Orchard Advertising, commented that the success of the ad was due to insight into needs of the target market. "We were clear that the need of the hour was not for an ad film, but for a Tamil feature film in 60 seconds."

In 2002 Coca-Cola India worked hard to build up a brand preference for its flagship brand, Coke, among young people in rural target markets. The campaign slogan was "thanda matlab Coca-Cola," (or "cool means Coca-Cola" in Hindi). Coca-Cola India calls its rural youth target market "India B." The prime objective in this market is to grow the generic soft drinks category and to develop brand preference for Coke. The "thanda" ("cold") campaign of 2002 successfully propelled Coke into the number three position in rural markets.

The urban youth target market, known as "India A," includes 18- to 24-year-olds in the major metropolitan areas. In 2003, the urban youth market was targeted with a campaign developed by McCann Erickson. The TV ad ran for 60 seconds and featured actor Vivek Oberoi with Aishwarya Rai. Both are famous as Bollywood movie stars. Aishwarya was the winner of the Miss World crown in 1994 and became an instant hit in Indian movies after she decided on a career of acting.

This ad showed Oberoi trying to hook up with Rai by deliberately leaving his mobile phone in the taxi that she hails, and then calling her. The ad message aimed to emphasize confidence and optimism, and a theme of "seize the day," according to Shripad Nadkarni, Vice-President of Marketing for Coca-Cola India. The 2003 campaign used a variety of media including television, print, outdoor, point-of-sale, restaurant and grocery chains, and local promotional events. "While awareness of soft drinks is high, there is a need to build a deeper brand connect" in urban centers, according to Sharda Agarwal, Director of Marketing for Coca-Cola India. "Vivek Oberoi—who's an up and coming star today, and has a wholesome, energetic image,—will help build a stronger bond with the youth, and make them feel that it is a brand that plays a role in their life, just as much as Levi's or Ray-Ban."

Coca-Cola's specific marketing objectives for 2003 were to grow the per-capita consumption of soft drinks in the rural markets, and to capture a larger share in the urban market from competition and increase the frequency of consumption there, according to Ms. Agarwal. It was expected that a new 'affordability plank' in the advertising strategy, along with introduction of a new 5 Rupee bottle, would help to achieve all of these goals.

### The "Affordability Plank"

In 2003, Coca-Cola India dramatically reduced prices of its soft drinks by 15 percent to 25 percent nationwide, in order to encourage consumption. This followed an earlier regional action in North India that reduced prices by 10–15 percent for its carbonated brands, Coke, Thums Up, Limca, Sprite and Fanta. In other regions such as Rajasthan, western and eastern Uttar Pradesh, and Tamil Nadu, prices were slashed to Rs. 5 for 200-ml. glass bottles and Rs. 8 for 300-ml. bottles from the existing Rs. 7 and Rs.10 price points, respectively.

These price reductions were in keeping with Coca-Cola's goal of enhancing affordability of their products, bringing them within arm's reach of consumers and thereby promoting regular consumption. Given the very low per-capita consumption of soft drinks in India, it was expected that price reductions would expand both the consumer base and the market for soft drinks. PepsiCo was forced to match these price reductions, leading PepsiCo's Asia chief to conclude: "India is the beverage battlefield for 2003."

Another initiative by Coca-Cola was the introduction of a new size, the "Mini." This was expected to increase total volume of sales and account for the major chunk of Coca-Cola's carbonated soft drink sales, according to Rajesh Mani, Regional Marketing Manager for Coca-Cola India.

The price reduction and new production launch were announced together by means of a new television ad campaign for Fanta and Coke in Tamil. Lowe Chennai created the ad concept, with executions by Primary Colors for Fanta and Rajiv Menon Productions for Coke. Both agencies are based in Chennai.

The 30-second Fanta spot featured brand ambassador, actress Simran, well known for her dance sequences in Hindi movies. The ad showed Simran stuck in a traffic jam. Thirsty, she tosses a 5 Rupee coin to a roadside stall and signals to the vendor that she wants a Fanta Mini by pointing to her orange dress. (Fanta is an orangeade drink.) She gets her Fanta and sets off a chain reaction on the crowded street, with everyone from school children to a traditional "nani" mimicking her action. ("Nani" is the Hindi word for grandmother.)

Rajesh Mani commented that the company wanted to make consumers "sit up and take notice." This was accomplished "by using a local star, with local insight, because Tamil Nadu is a big market for Fanta."

## A NEW PRODUCT CATEGORY

In order to encourage growth in demand for bottled beverages in the Indian market, several producers have launched their own brand in a new category, bottled water. This market was valued at 1,000 Crore in 2003. (1 Crore = 10,000,000 Rupees, US$1 = Rs. 48, so 1000 Crore = US$ 0.2083 million.)

Coca-Cola's brand, Kinley, was introduced in 2000. Ogilvy and Mather designed a two-ad television campaign. By 2002 Kinley had achieved a 28 percent market share and was being produced in 15 plants. The biggest of these are located in Mumbai, Delhi, Goa and Bangalore. In 2003 it was planned to double bottling capacity by adding another ten to fifteen production plants. These would be a combination of company-owned plants, franchisee operations, contract packing companies.

The Kinley brand of bottled water sells in various pack sizes: 500 ml., 1 liter, 1.5 liter, 2 liter, 5 liter, 20 liter, and 25 liter. The smallest pack was priced at Rs. 6 for 500-ml., while the 2-liter bottle was Rs. 17.

The current market leader with 40 percent market share is the Bisleri brand, owned by Ramesh Chauhan who is the CEO of Parle. Pepsi Foods' brand is Aquafina with about 11 percent market share. Aquafina is produced in six company-owned or franchised bottling plants in Roha (Maharashtra), Bangalore, Kolkata (formerly Calcutta), and New Delhi. Focusing on metropolitan areas, Pepsi Foods' ad campaign uses both television and outdoor media, and is managed by HTA, Pepsi Foods' agency.

Other competing brands in this segment include Bailley by Parle, Hello by Hello Mineral Waters Pvt. Ltd., Pure Life by Nestlé, and a new brand launched by Indian Railways, called Rail Neer.

## COCA-COLA'S ATTEMPTS TO "CRACK" THE INDIAN MARKET

By 2002, Coca-Cola owned 30 bottling plants, ten franchisees, and held a 56 percent market share of the national soft drink market in India. Yet despite creative and locally responsive marketing efforts and a total investment of some $840 million to build its distribution and manufacturing infrastructure, Coca-Cola had reported losses in India since its return there in 1993. In 2001 the company had written off a loss of $400 million. Total accumulated losses were estimated to be over 2,000 Crore (US$ 0.4166 million).

To make matters worse, in January 2002 the company was ordered by the government to sell to Indian investors 49 percent of Hindustan Coca-Cola Holding Pvt. Ltd. (HCCHPL), the wholly owned holding company for all Coca-Cola operations in India. This move by the government followed action taken by Coca-Cola in 1996 when it had requested and received government permission to increase its investment in the Indian market. Under the new governmental policy passed that same year affecting all new soft drink investments, Coca-Cola had agreed to sell 49 percent of its equity to Indian partners within two years. This time limit had been extended once already, but a request for a second extension to 2007 was turned down on October 3, 2001. Coca-Cola was hoping that by 2007 it would be in a stronger financial position and would receive a better return on its forced disinvestment.

The government's response to the company's second request was that "entry conditions cannot be changed." This response might have been acceptable if investment rules in India were clear and unchanging, but this was not the case during the 1990s when implementation of government rules had been inconsistent. Some companies, like Coca-Cola, were required to reduce their equity in order to allow Indians into the industry. At the same time, other companies—like Philips (of the Netherlands), Carrier (of the United States), and Cadbury-Schweppes (of Britain)—were being allowed to buy back most of their outstanding shares and would likely delist their shares altogether, effectively making their Indian operations wholly-owned subsidiaries. This was the status that Coca-Cola was being forced to give up.

Local market analysts commented that there is no apparent logic behind these government policies, other than to allow local investors to become bargain hunters at the expense of Coca-Cola.

Coca-Cola responded by trying to maintain some control over its operations. It applied for government approval from the Foreign Investment Promotion Board (FIPB) to deny voting rights to its new Indian shareholders. Again the government response was that the company had to abide by the legal provisions that were applicable on the date of its original foreign investment in the country. Since all equities back in 1996–1997 had mandatory voting rights, it was considered normal that Indian shareholders in this case should receive voting rights. The Indian government in May 2002 turned down Coca-Cola's request for a waiver of the disinvestment rule.

Making things even more difficult for Coca-Cola at that time was a change of oversight of the FIPB, from the Ministry of Industry to the Department of Economic Affairs. This change would require Coca-Cola and other foreign companies to build new relationships with bureaucrats, rendering past lobbying efforts useless.

Local business observers faulted Coca-Cola for trying to obtain repeated waivers of the disinvestment rule, pointing to the favorable expectation of an over-subscription for shares in the company's Initial Public Offering. One commentator said "This is in no way a priority industry, and when it (Coca-Cola) was permitted to do business in India, it was with the condition that it will dilute a 49 percent stake after five years. Foreign companies keep on saying that in India promises are not fulfilled. Why doesn't this multinational set an example by fulfilling its own commitment in this particular issue?" Another stated unsympathetically, "They went into this with their eyes open."

The Indian government had originally stipulated the 49 percent disinvestment clause as a condition for its agreement to allow Coca-Cola to buy out local Indian bottlers when the company first entered the market, instead of setting up greenfield bottling plants, as Coca-Cola had initially proposed. In contrast to Coca-Cola,

PepsiCo had entered India in a different year under a different set of rules. Moreover, it was not held to a disinvestment rule because it had opted to set up several greenfield bottling units.

Coca-Cola India initiated its compliance with the government disinvestment rule in February 2003 by following the private placement route. It agreed to place 49 percent of equity from its wholly owned subsidiary Hindustan Coca-Cola Holdings Pvt. Ltd. (HCCHPL) worth $41 million, in its bottling subsidiary Hindustan Coca-Cola Beverages Pvt. Ltd. (HCCBPL). HCCBPL runs the bottling plants originally taken over from local Indian bottlers including Parle. Of the 49 percent equity placed by HCCHPL, 10 percent was placed in Hindustan Coca-Cola Beverages (HCCB), in favor of employee and welfare trusts.

## THE SECOND GULF WAR

During spring 2003, as a result of the attack by the United States and Britain on Iraq, a call was launched by the All-India Anti-Imperialist Forum to boycott purchases of American and British goods. The boycott targeted specifically Pepsi, Coca-Cola, and McDonald's as a protest against the "unjust" war. The Forum's president is Justice V. R. Krishna Iyer, a former judge of the Indian Supreme Court. The Forum's general secretary, S. K. Mukherjee, said "We give a call to all peace-loving people of the world and India to rise up in protest against the imperialist aggression against Iraq. . . ." Within two weeks of the announcement of the boycott, sales of Coke and Pepsi in the southern Indian state of Kerala plummeted 50 percent.

Members of the Forum included more than 250 nongovernmental groups. These went on "shop-to-shop" campaigns to persuade retailers not to stock American products. They visited homes in Kerala presenting the same plea to consumers. Other items on the boycott list included toothpaste, soap, cooking oil, and cosmetics. Retailers feared a public backlash if they stocked items on the boycott list. In place of brand name items, retailers were asked to promote local substitutes such as a herbal product in place of toothpaste and mango juice instead of colas. Sunil Gupta, vice-president of Hindustan Coca-Cola Beverages, commented that this action would hurt not only the Kerala region. "We have one million retail suppliers of our products (in India). In the event of a boycott, it is the Indian economy that will be hit."

## LEARNING SOME HARD LESSONS

In 2002 Coca-Cola's overall sales reached $940 million and company products accounted for more than half the soft drinks market. A three-year cost-cutting program had brought dramatic results, reducing the company's payroll by 23 percent. Eight outdated plants, inherited from the Thums Up purchase, were closed. Local purchasing policies brought savings of 57 percent on import duties. Coca-Cola's well known but poorly supported Thums Up brand was reinvigorated with an infusion of $3.5 million spent on advertising and distribution. Market share for Thums Up that had slipped from more than 60 percent of carbonated beverage sales down to a puny 15 percent was regained. Within a year, Thums Up was back to the number two rank nationwide. Coke still trailed its archrival Pepsi however, with a market share of only 16.5 percent versus 23.5 percent.

Compared with per-capita consumption rates in other Big Emerging Markets, India's rate was still very low in 2003 at seven (8 ounce) servings per person. This compared with 14 in Pakistan,

89 in China, 278 in South Africa, 471 in Brazil, 1,484 in Mexico, and 1, 404 in the domestic U.S. market. Coca-Cola India's Director of Finance, N. Sridhar, stated confidently however, "We have turned a corner." In a similar vein, Jagdeep Kapoor, chairman of Samsika Marketing Consultants in Mumbai, concluded "Coke lost a number of years over errors. But at last it seems to be getting its positioning right."

## QUESTIONS

1. The political environment in India has proven to be critical to company performance for both PepsiCo and Coca-Cola India. What specific aspects of the political environment have played key roles? Could these effects have been anticipated prior to market entry? If not, could developments in the political arena have been handled better by each company?

2. Timing of entry into the Indian market brought different results for PepsiCo and Coca-Cola India. What benefits or disadvantages accrued as a result of earlier or later market entry?

3. The Indian market is enormous in terms of population and geography. How have the two companies responded to the sheer scale of operations in India in terms of product policies, promotional activities, pricing policies, and distribution arrangements?

4. "Global localization" (glocalization) is a policy that both companies have implemented successfully. Give examples for each company from the case.

5. Some analysts consider that Coca-Cola India made mistakes in planning and managing its return to India. Do you agree? What or who do you think was responsible for any mistakes?

6. Which of the two companies do you think has better long-term prospects for success in India?

7. What lessons can each company draw from its Indian experience as it contemplates entry into other Big Emerging Markets?

Dr. Lyn S. Amine, PhD, Professor of Marketing and International Business and Vikas Kumar, International Business and Marketing, ABD Saint Louis University, prepared this case from public sources as a basis for classroom discussion only. It is not intended to illustrate either effective or ineffective handling of administrative problems. Copyright 2003.

Sources: Lyn S. Amine and Deepa Raizada (1995), "Market Entry into the Newly Opened Indian Market: Recent Experiences of US Companies in the Soft Drinks Industry," in *Developments in Marketing Science,* XVIII, proceedings of the annual conference of the Academy of Marketing Science, Roger Gomes, ed., AMS: Coral Gables, FL, 287–292. *Business Week, Business Line, Financial Daily, Fortune, India Express.*

# CASE I-4 Marketing Microwave Ovens to a New Market Segment

You are the Vice President of International Marketing for White Appliances, an international company that manufactures and markets appliances globally. The company has a line of microwave ovens—some manufactured in the U.S. and some in Asia which are exported to the U.S. market and Europe. Your company markets several high-end models in India that are manufactured in the United States. Your presence in the Indian market is limited at this time.

After preliminary analysis, you and your team have come to the conclusion that, besides the market for high-end models, a market for microwave ovens at all price levels exists. Several international companies like Samsung, Whirlpool and LG Electronics India, are entering the market with the idea that demand can be expanded with the right product at the right price. There are, however, several challenges in the Indian market, not the least of which is the consumer's knowledge about microwaves and the manner in which they are perceived as appliances.

In conducting research on the market, your research team put together a summary of comments from consumers and facts about the market that should give you a feel for the market and the kinds of challenges that will have to be dealt with if the market is to grow and if White Appliances is to have a profitable market share.

- Five top consumer durable companies are in the race to sell the oven. But to sell the product, they must first sell the idea. The players don't even agree on the size of the market; fewer still on what the oven will do for the Indian family.

- It may be a convenient and efficient way to cook, but is has been invented with European food in mind. "Only when Indian eating habits change can the microwave ovens market grow in a big way," says one market leader in appliances.

- Some companies disagree with the statement above. Their contention is that all Indian dishes can be prepared in a microwave, people only need to know how to use one.

- Consumer comments were mixed. One housewife commented, "The microwave oven was the first purchase after my wedding. I bought it only because I liked it and I had the money. But I must say its performance surprised me."

- Men no longer have an excuse for not helping in cooking. My husband, who never used to enter the kitchen, now uses the microwave oven to cook routinely.

- Somebody gifted it to me but food doesn't taste the same when cooked in a microwave whatever the company people may claim.

- To the chagrin of microwave oven marketers, the Indian perception of the gadget remains grey. Yet, for the first time in the some seven years that it's been officially around optimism towards the microwave has been on the upswing.

- A microwave oven is beginning to replace the demand for a second television or a bigger refrigerator. The middle-income consumer comes looking for novelty, value and competitive pricing.

- The penetration level of microwave ovens remains shockingly minuscule, under one percent. The top seven cities comprise nearly 70 percent of the market with Delhi and Mumbai (Bombay) recording the highest sales. But the good news is that the microwave is beginning to be seen in smaller towns.

- When asked about the nonurban market, one microwave oven company executive commented, "We know it's an alien concept for the rural consumer, but we want to do our homework now to reap the benefits years later. Once the consumer is convinced a microwave can actually be part of daily cooking, the category will grow immensely."

- Apart from styling and competitive pricing, marketers acknowledge that cracking the mindset that microwaves are not suited to Indian food holds the key to future growth.

- People who own microwaves usually have cooks who may not be using the gadget in any case. Even consumers who own microwave ovens don't use them frequently; usage is confined to cooking western food or reheating.

- With consumers still unclear on how to utilize the microwave oven for their day-to-day cooking, marketers are shifting away from mass marketing to a more direct marketing-oriented approach to create awareness about the benefits of the product.

- The challenge in this category is to get the user to cook in the microwave oven rather than use it as a product for reheating food. Keeping this in mind, companies are expecting an increasing number of sales for microwave ovens to come from the semi-urban/rural markets. We are seeing an increasing number of sales coming from the upcountry markets.

- "Elite fad or smoke-free chullah for low-fat paranthas? Which way will the microwave oven go in the Indian market?" asks one company representative.

- Most agree on a broadly similar strategy to expand the Indian market: product and design innovation to make the microwave suited to Indian cooking; local manufacturing facility to promote innovation while continuing to import high-end models; reduce import content to cut cost; boost volumes; and bring down prices.

- Even as early as 1990, the microwave was touted as a way to cook Indian food. Julie Sahni, the nation's best known authority on Indian cooking, has turned her attention to the microwave. And her new cookbook sets a new threshold for the microwave cook. Simple cooked lentils, spicy dal, even tandoori chicken—with its distinctive reddish color—come steaming from the modern microwave with the spices and scents of an ancient cuisine. Cynics who think microwave cooking is bland and unimaginative will eat their words.

MouthShut.com, India's first, largest, and most comprehensive Person to Person (P2P) Information Exchange with offices in Bombay, India, Vienna, Austria, Virginia, U.S.A., and Dubai, UAE, has posted on its website the results of a customer's review of the LG Robogrill Microwave oven. For the complete review, visit www.mouthshut.com, select Household, then Microwave Ovens, then LG (under brands), and then select model #LGMH-685 HD.

## MARKET DATA

LG Electronics, the category leader, has a 33.5 percent share of the 1.6 lakh[1] units market; its eight models are priced in the range of Rs. 8,500–19,000 with a marked presence in the Indian family size of 28–30 liter.

In the early days, microwave ovens did not figure at all in the consumers purchase list. Kelvinator's Magicook made a high-profile entry some seven years ago. What went wrong, according to the analyst, was the pricing which was nothing less than Rs 20,000 and sizes which were too small to accommodate large Indian vessels.

Efforts to grow the market are concentrated in large urban areas with routine fare such as organizing cookery classes, recipe contests, in-house demos, giving away accessories such as glass bowls, aprons and gloves as freebies and hosting co-promotions.

"To change the way you look, just change the way you cook" was a recent tagline by one of the companies.

What will really spur the category's growth will be a change in eating habits. One company piggybacks on "freshness," a tactic the company adopts for all its product lines.

According to industry projections, the 1.6-lakh unit microwave oven market will cross the two-lakh mark in 2002, with the market growing anywhere between 20 percent and 25 percent.

There is some difference of opinion on the right price for the ovens. For the microwave market to take off its price would have to be below Rs. 7000 says one company. During the time that microwave ovens have been introduced locally prices have been all over the waterfront. For example, one company prices its ovens be-

tween Rs. 7,000 and Rs. 18,000, another between Rs. 12,500 and 15,000 and an oven with grill functions for Rs. 17,900.

From wooing the super mom to courting the single male the journey of microwave ovens has just begun. Once, perceived as a substitute to the OTG (Oven Toaster and Grill), companies with large shares of this segment now are portraying microwaves as more than just a reheating device.

According to one analyst, the product category is going through a transition period and the consumer today is more educated about an OTG than a microwave. The analyst believes there is demand for both microwave and OTG categories.

Microwave companies face a chicken-and-egg question on price and sales. Prices will not come down easily until volumes go up, while volumes depend on prices.

The product is a planned purchase and not an impulse buy. Samsung has set up call centers where the customers can call and get all their queries pertaining to the Samsung Microwave Oven answered.

Though the concept of microwave ovens is western, the fact is that microwave technology today has advanced to a level wherein even complex cooking like Indian cooking is very much possible.

One of the older company marketing managers, who has worked in microwave marketing most of his career, is somewhat skeptical about the prospects of rapid growth of the Indian market. He remarked that the microwave oven first introduced in the U.S. market in about 1950 did not become popular across all market segments until about the mid-1970s. Of course, now almost every household in the U.S. has at least one microwave.

Your task is to develop a strategy to market White Appliance's microwave ovens in India. Include target market(s), microwave oven features, price(s), promotion and distribution in your program. You should also consider both short-term as well as long-term marketing programs. Some of the issues you may want to consider are:

- Indian food preparation versus Western food preparation.
- Values and customs that might affect opinions about microwave ovens.
- The effects of competition in the market.

You may also want to review the Country Notebook: A Plan for Developing a Marketing Plan, p. 591 of the text, for some direction.

---

[1] A lakh is a unit in a traditional number system, still widely used in India. One lakh is equal to 100 thousand. A Crore is also a traditional number system unit and one crore is equal to 10 million.

# cases 2

## THE CULTURAL ENVIRONMENT OF GLOBAL MARKETING

# CASE 2-1 The Not-So-Wonderful World of EuroDisney—Things Are Better Now at Paris Disneyland

## BONJOUR, MICKEY!

In April 1992, EuroDisney SCA opened its doors to European visitors. Located by the river Marne some 20 miles east of Paris, it was designed to be the biggest and most lavish theme park that Walt Disney Company (Disney) had built to date—bigger than Disneyland in Anaheim, California; Disney World in Orlando, Florida; and Tokyo Disneyland in Japan.

Much to Disney management's surprise, Europeans failed to "go goofy" over Mickey, unlike their Japanese counterparts. Between 1990 and early 1992, some 14 million people had visited Tokyo Disneyland, with three-quarters being repeat visitors. A family of four staying overnight at a nearby hotel would easily spend $600 on a visit to the park. In contrast, at EuroDisney, families were reluctant to spend the $280 a day needed to enjoy the attractions of the park, including *les hamburgers* and *les milkshakes.* Staying overnight was out of the question for many because hotel rooms were so high priced. For example, prices ranged from $110 to $380 a night at the Newport Bay Club, the largest of EuroDisney's six new hotels and one of the biggest in Europe. In comparison, a room in a top hotel in Paris cost between $340 and $380 a night.

Financial losses became so massive at EuroDisney that the president had to structure a rescue package to put EuroDisney back on firm financial ground. Many French bankers questioned the initial financing but the Disney response was that their views reflected the cautious, Old World thinking of Europeans who didn't understand U.S.-style free market financing. After some acrimonious dealings with French banks a two-year financial plan was negotiated. Disney management rapidly revised their marketing plan and introduced strategic and tactical changes in the hope of "doing it right" this time.

**A Real Estate Dream Come True**  The Paris location was chosen over 200 other potential sites stretching from Portugal through Spain, France, Italy, and into Greece. Spain thought it had the strongest bid based on its yearlong, temperate, and sunny Mediterranean climate, but insufficient acreage of land was available for development around Barcelona.

In the end, the French government's generous incentives, together with impressive data on regional demographics, swayed Disney management to choose the Paris location. It was calculated that some 310 million people in Europe live within two hours' air travel of EuroDisney, and 17 million could reach the park within two hours by car—better demographics than at any other Disney site. Pessimistic talk about the dismal winter weather of northern France was countered with references to the success of Tokyo Disneyland, where resolute visitors brave cold winds and snow to enjoy their piece of Americana. Furthermore, it was argued, Paris is Europe's most-popular city destination among tourists of all nationalities.

**Spills and Thrills**  Disney had projected that the new theme park would attract 11 million visitors and generate over $100 million in operating earnings during the first year of operation. By summer 1994, EuroDisney had lost more than $900 million since opening. Attendance reached only 9.2 million in 1992, and visitors spent 12 percent less on purchases than the estimated $33 per head.

If tourists were not flocking to taste the thrills of the new EuroDisney, where were they going for their summer vacations in 1992? Ironically enough, an unforeseen combination of transatlantic airfare wars and currency movements resulted in a trip to Disney World in Orlando being cheaper than a trip to Paris, with guaranteed good weather and beautiful Floridian beaches within easy reach.

EuroDisney management took steps to rectify immediate problems in 1992 by cutting rates at two hotels up to 25 percent, introducing some cheaper meals at restaurants, and launching a Paris ad blitz that proclaimed "California is only 20 miles from Paris."

**An American Icon**  One of the most worrying aspects of EuroDisney's first year was that French visitors stayed away; they had been expected to make up 50 percent of the attendance figures. A park services consulting firm framed the problem in these words: "The French see EuroDisney as American imperialism—plastics at its worst." The well-known, sentimental Japanese attachment to Disney characters contrasted starkly with the unexpected and widespread French scorn for American fairy-tale characters. French culture has its own lovable cartoon characters such as Astérix, the helmeted, pint-sized Gallic warrior who has a theme park located near EuroDisney.

Hostility among the French people to the whole "Disney idea" had surfaced early in the planning of the new project. Paris theater director Ariane Mnouchkine became famous for her description of EuroDisney as "a cultural Chernobyl." In fall 1989, during a visit to Paris, French Communists pelted Michael Eisner with eggs. The joke going around at the time was, "For EuroDisney to adapt properly to France, all seven of Snow White's dwarfs should be named Grumpy *(Grincheux).*"

Early advertising by EuroDisney seemed to aggravate local French sentiment by emphasizing glitz and size, rather than the variety of rides and attractions. Committed to maintaining Disney's reputation for quality in everything, more detail was built into EuroDisney. For example, the centerpiece castle in the Magic Kingdom had to be bigger and fancier than in the other parks. Expensive trams were built along a lake to take guests from the hotels to the park, but visitors preferred walking. Total park construction costs were estimated at FFr 14 billion ($2.37 billion) in 1989 but rose by $340 million to FFr 16 billion as a result of all these add-ons. Hotel construction costs alone rose from an estimated FFr 3.4 billion to FFr 5.7 billion.

EuroDisney and Disney managers unhappily succeeded in alienating many of their counterparts in the government, the banks, the ad agencies, and other concerned organizations. A barnstorming, kick-the-door-down attitude seemed to reign among the U.S. decision makers. "They had a formidable image and convinced everyone that if we let them do it their way, we would all have a marvelous adventure." One former Disney executive voiced the opinion, "We were arrogant—it was like 'We're building the Taj Mahal and people will come—on our terms.'"

## STORM CLOUDS AHEAD

Disney and its advisors failed to see signs at the end of the 1980s of the approaching European recession. Other dramatic events included the Gulf War in 1991, which put a heavy brake on vacation travel for the rest of that year. Other external factors that Disney executives have cited are high interest rates and the devaluation of several currencies against the franc. EuroDisney also encountered difficulties with regard to competition—the World's Fair in Seville and the 1992 Olympics in Barcelona were huge attractions for European tourists.

Disney management's conviction that it knew best was demonstrated by its much-trumpeted ban on alcohol in the park. This proved insensitive to the local culture because the French are the world's biggest consumers of wine. To them a meal without *un verre de rouge* is unthinkable. Disney relented. It also had to relax its rules on personal grooming of the projected 12,000 cast members, the park employees. Women were allowed to wear redder nail polish than in the United States, but the taboo on men's facial hair was maintained. "We want the clean-shaven, neat and tidy look," commented the director of Disney University's Paris branch, which trains prospective employees in Disney values and culture. EuroDisney's management did, however, compromise on the question of pets. Special kennels were built to house visitors' animals. The thought of leaving a pet at home during vacation is considered irrational by many French people.

Plans for further development of EuroDisney after 1992 were ambitious. The initial number of hotel rooms was planned to be 5,200, more than in the entire city of Cannes on the Côte d'Azur. Also planned were shopping malls, apartments, golf courses, and vacation homes. EuroDisney would design and build everything itself, with a view to selling at a profit. As a Disney executive commented, "Disney at various points could have had partners to share the risk, or buy the hotels outright. But it didn't want to give up the upside."

"From the time they came on, Disney's Chairman Eisner and President Wells, had never made a single misstep, never a mistake, never a failure," said a former Disney executive. "There was a tendency to believe that everything they touched would be perfect." The incredible growth record fostered this belief. In the seven years before EuroDisney opened, they took the parent company from being a company with $1 billion in revenues to one with $8.5 billion, mainly through internal growth.

### Telling and Selling Fairy Tales

Mistaken assumptions by the Disney management team affected construction design, marketing and pricing policies, and park management, as well as initial financing. Disney executives had been erroneously informed that Europeans don't eat breakfast. Restaurant breakfast service was downsized accordingly, and guess what? "Everybody showed up for breakfast. We were trying to serve 2,500 breakfasts in a 350-seat restaurant [at some of the hotels]. The lines were horrendous. And they didn't just want croissants and coffee, they wanted bacon and eggs."

In contrast to Disney's American parks where visitors typically stay at least three days, EuroDisney is at most a two-day visit. Energetic visitors need even less time. One analyst claimed to have "done" every EuroDisney ride in just five hours. Typically many guests arrive early in the morning, rush to the park, come back to their hotel late at night, and then check out the next morning before heading back to the park.

Vacation customs of Europeans were not taken into consideration. Disney executives had optimistically expected that the arrival of their new theme park would cause French parents to take their children out of school in mid-session for a short break. It did not happen, unless a public holiday occurred over a weekend. Similarly, Disney expected that the American-style short but more frequent family trips would displace the European tradition of a one-month family vacation, usually taken in August. However, French office and factory schedules remained the same, with their emphasis on an August shutdown.

In promoting the new park to visitors, Disney did not stress the entertainment value of a visit to the new theme park; the emphasis was on the size of the park, which "ruined the magic." To counter this, ads were changed to feature Zorro, a French favorite, Mary Poppins, and Aladdin, star of the huge moneymaking movie success. A print ad campaign at that time featured Aladdin, Cinderella's castle, and a little girl being invited to enjoy a "magic vacation," at the kingdom where all dreams come true. Six new attractions were added in 1994, including the Temple of Peril, Storybook Land; and the Nautilus attraction. Donald Duck's birthday was celebrated on June 9—all in hopes of positioning EuroDisney as the No. 1 European destination of short duration, one to three days.

**Tomorrowland**   Faced with falling share prices and crisis talk among shareholders, Disney was forced to step forward in late 1993 to rescue the new park. Disney announced that it would fund EuroDisney until a financial restructuring could be worked out with lenders. However, it was made clear by the parent company, Disney, that it "was not writing a blank check."

In June 1994, EuroDisney received a new lifeline when a member of the Saudi royal family agreed to invest up to $500 million for a 24 percent stake in the park. The prince has an established reputation in world markets as a "bottom-fisher," buying into potentially viable operations during crises when share prices are low. The princes plans included a $100 million convention center at EuroDisney. One of the few pieces of good news about EuroDisney is that its convention business exceeded expectations from the beginning.

## MANAGEMENT AND NAME CHANGES

Frenchman Philippe Bourguignon took over at EuroDisney as CEO in 1993 and has navigated the theme park back to profitability. He was instrumental in the negotiations with the firm's bankers, cutting a deal that he credits largely for bringing the park back into the black.

Perhaps more important to the long-run success of the venture were his changes in marketing. The pan-European approach to marketing was dumped, and national markets were targeted separately. This new localization took into account the differing tourists' habits around the continent. Separate marketing offices were opened in London, Frankfurt, Milan, Brussels, Amsterdam, and Madrid, and each was charged with tailoring advertising and packages to its own market. Prices were cut by 20 percent for park admission and 30 percent for some hotel room rates. Special promotions were also run for the winter months.

The central theme of the new marketing and operations approach is that people visit the park for an "authentic" Disney day out. They may not be completely sure what that means, except that it entails something American. This is reflected in the transformation of the park's name. The "Euro" in EuroDisney was first shrunk in the logo, and the word "land" added. Then in October 1994 the "Euro" was eliminated completely; the park is now called Disneyland Paris.

In 1996 Disneyland Paris became France's most visited tourist attraction, ahead of both the Louvre Art Museum and the Eiffel Tower. 11.7 million visitors (a 9 percent increase from the previous year) allowed the park to report another profitable year.

## THEME PARK EXPANSION IN THE TWENTY-FIRST CENTURY

With the recovery of Disneyland Paris, Disney embarked on an ambitious growth plan. In 2001 the California Adventure Park was added to the Anaheim complex at a cost of $1.4 billion and Walt Disney Studios Theme Park was added to Disneyland Paris. Through agreements with foreign partners, Disney will open Disney-Sea in Tokyo and plans are underway for a theme park in Shanghai that Chinese officials hope will open in time for the 2008 Olympic Games in Beijing and a park in Hong Kong is to open in 2006.

A decade after being slammed for its alleged ignorance of European ways with EuroDisney, Disney is trying to prove it's gotten things right the second time around. The new movie-themed park, Walt Disney Studios, adjacent to Disneyland Paris, is designed to be a tribute to moviemaking—but not just the Hollywood kind. The Walt Disney Studios blend Disney entertainment and attractions with the history and culture of European film since French camera-makers helped invent the motion picture. The park's general layout is modeled after an old Hollywood studio complex, and some of the rides and shows are near replicas of Disney's first film park, Disney-MGM Studios. Rather than celebrating the history of U.S. Disney characters, the characters in the new theme park speak six different languages. A big stunt show features cars and motorcycles that race through a village modeled after the French resort town of St. Tropez.

Small details reflect the cultural lessons learned. "We made sure that all our food venues have covered seating," recalling that, when EuroDisney first opened, the open-air restaurants offered no protection from the rainy weather that assails the park for long stretches of the year.

On the food front, EuroDisney offered only a French sausage, drawing complaints from the English, Germans, Italians, and everyone else about why their local sausages weren't available. This time around, the park caters to the multiple indigenous cultures throughout Europe—which includes a wider selection of sausages.

Unlike Disney's attitude with their first park in France, "Now we realize that our guests need to be welcomed on the basis of their own culture and travel habits," says Disneyland Paris Chief Executive. Disneyland Paris today is Europe's biggest tourist attraction—even more popular than the Eiffel Tower—a turnaround that showed the park operators' ability to learn from their mistakes.

The root of Disney's problems in EuroDisney may be found in the tremendous success of Japan's Disneyland. The Tokyo Park was a success from the first day and it has been visited by millions of Japanese who wanted to capture what they perceived at the ultimate U.S. entertainment experience.

Disney took the entire U.S. theme park and transplanted it in Japan. It worked because of the Japanese attachment to Disney characters. Schools have field trips to meet Mickey and his friends to the point that the Disney experience has become ingrained in Japanese life. In the book, *Disneyland as Holy Land,* University of Tokyo professor Masako Notoji wrote: "The opening of Tokyo Disneyland was, in retrospect, the greatest cultural event in Japan during the '80s." With such success, is there any wonder that Disney thought they had the right model when they first went to France? The Tokyo Disney constitutes a very rare case in that the number of visitors has not decreased since the opening.

While Disney Japan was a success the company also admitted making a major financial error when the park was launched. It had licensed its name and image to another company that actually owns and operates the park as well as the land where it sits. Disney collects only a small fraction of the revenues that run into hundreds of millions of dollars every year. Since they were not certain of the success of the first international venture, it was the price they were willing to pay; however, it vowed never to repeat that error and to never have its hands tied again. As a consequence, when they began the Paris Park, they were fanatically intent on owning and controlling the park as well as enough adjacent property for its own exclusive hotels—"they were sure they had the right model and they were going to own it all." Thus, they began planning EuroDisney.

## REFERENCES

"An American in Paris," *Business Week,* March 12, 1990, pp. 60–61, 64.

"EuroDisney Tries to End Evil Spell," *Advertising Age,* February 7, 1994, p. 39.

"EuroDisney's Prince Charming?" *Business Week,* June 13, 1994, p. 42.

"The Kingdom inside the Republic (New Management Strategy at Euro-Disney)," *Economist,* April 13, 1996, p. 66.

"The Mouse Isn't Roaring," *Business Week,* August 24, 1992, p. 38.

"Mouse Trap: Fans Like EuroDisney but Its Parent's Goofs Weigh the Park Down," *The Wall Street Journal,* March 10, 1994, p. A12.

"Saudi to Buy as Much as 24% of EuroDisney," *The Wall Street Journal,* June 2, 1994, p. A4.

Wolfson, Bernard J., "The Mouse That Roared Back," *Orange County Register,* April 9, 2000, pp. 1.

Chester Dawson, "Will Tokyo Embrace Another Mouse?" *Business Week,* September 10, 2001.

Paul Herbig, "Disney's Mickey Mouse: N'est Ce Oas..Faux Pas," in Michael D. White, *International Marketing Blunders* (Novato, CA: World Trade Press, 2002), p. 4.

Richard Verrier, "Disney May Add 2nd China Park," *Los Angeles Times,* July 20, 2002, p. C2.

Paulo Prada and Bruce Orwall, "A Certain 'Je Ne Sais Quoi' at Disney's New Park," *The Wall Street Journal,* March 12, 2002, p. B1.

James Zoltak, "Tokyo DisneySea Plans New Attractions," *Amusement Business,* May 26, 2003, p. 1.

Asahi Shimbun, " Tokyo Disney Prospers in Its Own Way," *Asahi Evening News,* April 22, 2003.

"Disney Characters in Europe Will Mark Quebec's National Holiday by Chowing Down on Poutine," *Broadcast News* (Canada), June 24, 2003.

## QUESTIONS

1. What factors contributed to EuroDisney's poor performance during its first year of operation?

2. To what degree do you consider that these factors were (a) foreseeable and (b) controllable by either EuroDisney or the parent company, Disney?

3. What role does ethnocentrism play in the story of EuroDisney's launch?

4. How do you assess the cross-cultural marketing skills of Disney?

5. *a.* Why did success in Tokyo predispose Disney management to be too optimistic in their expectations of success in France? Discuss.

  *b.* Do you think the new theme park would have encountered the same problems if a location in Spain had been selected? Discuss.

6. Now that Disney has succeeded in turning around Disneyland Paris and has begun work on the new Hong Kong and Shanghai locations, where and when should it go next? Assume you are a consultant hired to give Disney advice on the issue of where and when to go next. Pick three locations and select the one you think will be the best new location for "Disneyland *X*." Discuss.

7. Given your choice of local *X* for the newest Disneyland, what are the operational implications of the history of EuroDisney for the new park?

Professor Lyn S. Amine prepared this case with graduate student Carolyn A. Tochtrop, Saint Louis University, Saint Louis, Missouri, as a basis for class discussion rather than to illustrate either effective or ineffective handling of a situation. The original case appearing in the 11th edition has been edited and updated to reflect recent developments.

# CASE 2-2 Cultural Norms, *Fair & Lovely*, and Advertising

*Fair and Lovely,* a branded product of Hindustan Lever, LTD (HLL), is touted as a cosmetic that lightens skin color. On its website (www.hll.com) the company calls its product, "the miracle worker," which is "proven to deliver one to three shades of change." While tanning is a rage in Western countries, skin lightening treatments are popular in Asia.

According to industry sources, the top-selling skin lightening cream in India is *Fair & Lovely* from Hindustan Lever, followed by CavinKare's *Fairever* brand. HLL's *Fair & Lovely* brand was the undisputed monarch of the market with a 90 percent share until CavinKare Ltd (CKL) launched *Fairever*. In just two years, the *Fairever* brand gained an impressive 15 percent market share. HLL's share of market for the *Fair & Lovely* line generates about $60 million annually. The product sells for about 23 rupees ($0.29) for a 25-gram tube of cream.

The rapid growth of CavinKare's *Fairever* (www.cavinkare.com) brand prompted HLL to increase their advertising effort and to launch a series of ads depicting a "fairer girl gets the boy theme." One advertisement featured a financially strapped father lamenting his fate, saying, "If only I had a son." While his dark-skinned daughter looks on, helpless and demoralized because she can't bear the financial responsibility of her family. Fast-forward and plain Jane has been transformed into a gorgeous light-skinned woman through the use of a "fairness cream," *Fair & Lovely.* Now clad in a miniskirt, the woman is a successful flight attendant and can take her father to dine at a five-star hotel. She's happy and so is her father.

In another ad, two attractive young women are sitting in a bedroom; one has a boyfriend and, consequently, is happy. The darker-skinned woman, lacking a boyfriend, is not happy. Her friend's advice? Use a bar of soap to wash away the dark skin that's keeping men from flocking to her.

HLL's series of ads provoked CavinKare Ltd to counter with an ad that takes a dig at HLL's *Fair & Lovely* ad. CavinKare's ad has a father-daughter duo as the protagonists, with the father shown encouraging the daughter to be an achiever irrespective of her complexion. CavinKare maintained that the objective of its new commercial is not to take a dig at *Fair & Lovely* but to "reinforce *Fairever's* positioning."

"We have noticed attempts by *Fair & Lovely* to blur our positioning by changing its communication platform from "wanting to get married" to "achievement," the principal *Fairever* theme. Since we don't have the spending power to match HLL, a tactical way for us to respond is to reinforce our brand positioning and "the commercial will be aired until the company's 'objective' is achieved," a CavinKare official said.

Skin color is a powerful theme in India as well as much of Asia where a lighter color represents a higher status. While Americans and Europeans flock to tanning salons, many across Asia seek ways to have "fair" complexions. Culturally, fair skin is associated with positive values that relate to class and beauty. One Indian lady commented that when she was growing up, her mother forbade her to go outdoors. She was not trying to keep her daughter out of trouble but was trying to keep her skin from getting dark.

Brahmins, the priestly caste at the top of the social hierarchy, are considered fair because they traditionally stayed inside, poring over books. The undercaste at the bottom of the ladder are regarded as the darkest people because they customarily worked in the searing sun. Ancient Hindu scriptures and modern poetry eulogize women endowed with skin made out of white marble.

Skin color is closely identified with caste and is laden with symbolism. Pursue any of the "grooms" and "brides wanted" ads in newspapers or on the web that families use to arrange suitable alliances and you will see that most potential grooms and their families are looking for "fair" brides; some are progressive enough to invite responses from women belonging to a different caste. These ads, hundreds of which appear in India's daily newspapers, reflect attempts to solicit individuals with the appropriate religion, caste, regional ancestry, professional and educational qualifications, and frequently, skin color. Even in the growing numbers of ads that announce "caste no bar," the adjective "fair" regularly precedes professional qualifications.

Bollywood (India's Hollywood) glorifies conventions on beauty by always casting a fair-skinned actress in the role of heroine, surrounded by darkest extras. Women want to use whiteners because it is "aspirational," like losing weight.

Even the gods supposedly lament their dark complexion—Krishna sings plaintively, "Radha kyoon gori, main kyoon kala? (Why is Radha so fair when I'm dark?)"—a skin deficient in melanin (the pigment that determines the skin's brown color) is an ancient predilection. More than 3,500 years ago, Charaka, the famous sage, wrote about herbs that could help make the skin fair.

Indian dermatologists maintain that fairness products cannot truly work as they only reach the upper layers of the skin and so do not affect melanin production. Nevertheless, "hope springs eternal" and for some *Fair & Lovely* is a "miracle worker." "The last time I went to my parents' home, I got compliments on my fair skin from everyone," one user gushes. But for others, only disappointment. One 26-year-old working woman has been a regular user for the past eight years but to no avail. "I should have turned into Snow White by now but my skin is still the same wheatish color."

The number of Indians of the opinion that lighter skin is more beautiful may be shrinking. Sumit Isralni, a 22-year-old hair designer in his father's salon, thinks things have changed in the last two years, at least in India's most cosmopolitan cities, Delhi, Mumbai and Bangalore. Women now "prefer their own complexion, their natural way" Isralni says; he prefers a more "Indian beauty" himself. "I won't judge my wife on how fair her complexion is." Sunita Gupta, a beautician in the same salon, is more critical. "It's just foolishness!" she exclaimed. The premise of the ads that women could not become airline attendants if they are dark-skinned was wrong, she said. "Nowadays people like black beauty." It is a truism that women, especially in the tropics, desire to be a shade fairer no matter what their skin color. Although, unlike the approach used in India, advertisements elsewhere usually show how to use the product and how it works.

HLL launched their television ad campaign to promote *Fair & Lovely* in December 2001 and withdrew it in February 2003, amid severe criticism for its portrayal of women. Activists argued that one of the messages the company sends through its "air hostess" demonstrating the preference for a son who would be able to take on the financial responsibility for his parents—is especially harmful in a country such as India where gender discrimination is rampant. Another offense is perpetuating a culture of discrimination in a society where "fair" is synonymous with "beautiful." AIDWA (All India Democratic Women's Association) lodged a complaint in March and April 2002 with HLL about their offensive ads but Hindustan Lever failed to respond.

The women's association then appealed to the National Human Rights Commission alleging that the ad demeaned women. AIDWA objected to three things: (1) the ads were racist, (2) they were promoting son preference, and (3) they were insulting to working women. "The way they portrayed the young woman who, after using *Fair & Lovely,* became attractive and therefore lands a job suggested that the main qualification for a woman to get a job is the way she looks." The Human Rights Commission passed AIDWA's complaints on to the Ministry of Information and Broadcasting which said the campaign violated the Cable and Television Networks Act of 1995—provisions in the Act state that no advertisement shall be permitted which "derides any race, caste, color, creed and nationality" and that "Women must not be portrayed in a manner that emphasized passive, submissive qualities and encourages them to play a subordinate secondary role in the family and society." The government issued notices of the complaints to HLL. After a year-long campaign led by the AIDWA, Hindustan Lever Limited discontinued two of its television advertisements for *Fair & Lovely* fairness cold cream in March 2003.

Shortly after pulling its ads off the air, and, coincidentally, on International Women's Day, HLL launched its "Fair & Lovely Foundation," vowing to "encourage economic empowerment of women across India" by providing resources in education and business. Millions of women "who, though immensely talented and capable, need a guiding hand to help them take the leap forward." Presumably into a fairer future.

HLL sponsored career fairs in over 20 cities across the country offering counseling in as many as 110 careers. It supported 100 rural scholarships for women students passing their tenth grade, a professional course for aspiring beauticians, and a three-month Home Healthcare Nursing Assistant's course catering to young women between the ages 18 and 30. According to HLL, The Fair & Lovely Academy for Home Care Nursing Assistants offers a unique training opportunity for young women who possess no entry level skills and, therefore, are not employable in the new economy job market. Fair & Lovely Foundation plans to serve as a catalyst for the economic empowerment for women across India. The Fair & Lovely Foundation will showcase the achievements of these women not only to honor them, but also to set an example for several other women to follow.

Here are a few facts about HLL taken from www.hll.com.

Lever Limited is India's largest Packaged Mass Consumption Goods company. We are leaders in Home and Personal Care Products and Food and Beverages including such products as Ponds and Pepsodent.

We seek to "meet everyday needs to people everywhere to anticipate the aspirations of our consumers and customers and to respond creatively and competitively with branded products and services which raise the quality of life." It is this purpose which inspires us to build brands.

Over the past 70 years, we have introduced about 110 brands.

Fair & Lovely has been specially designed and proven to deliver one to three shades of change in most people. Also its sunscreen system is specially optimized for Indian skin. Indian skin unlike Caucasian skin tends to 'tan' rather than 'burn' and, hence, requires a different combination of UVA & UVB sunscreens.

The fairness cream is marketed in over 38 countries through HLL Exports and local Unilever companies and is the largest selling skin lightening cream in the world. The brand today offers a substantive range of products to consumers including Fair & Lovely Fairness Reviving Lotion, Fair & Lovely Fairness Cold Cream and Fair & Lovely Fairness Soap.

Some information on CavinKare taken from www.cavinkare. com:

"We shall achieve growth by continuously offering unique products and services that would give customers utmost satisfaction and thereby be a role model."

**Goal**

In fifteen years (2012) we will be a hundred times our current turnover.

**Values and Beliefs of CavinKare**

*Integrity*   The company values honesty and truthfulness above everything else in all its interactions. Our thoughts, words and actions shall be the same. We shall try our utmost to fulfill promises and honor commitments.

*Fairness*   The company shall be fair in all its dealings with people inside and outside. We will follow rules, norms and procedures not only in letter but in spirit as well; we will show common decency in all our dealings with people; we will not exploit undue advantages; we will respect the rights of others.

*Excellence*   The company values highly all efforts that lead to high standards in everyday work and results. We shall attempt to be the best-in-class in anything we choose to work on. We shall encourage any individual or collective effort in promoting excellence.

*Innovation*   The company values innovative thinking, innovative approaches and innovative solutions in our regular work life. We will always look for better ways of doing things; we will seek new ideas to solve problems; we will experiment with new concepts, ideas and solutions.

*Openness*   The company believes that openness to new ideas, thoughts and opinions makes relationships stronger and productive, we shall listen to others; we shall openly discuss among colleagues all that is appropriate; we shall welcome ideas from everywhere.

*Trust*   The company believes that trust is an important ingredient for effective functioning within the organization and with the outside world. While we shall protect our legitimate business interests, we would also approach the people, issues and associations with straightforwardness, optimism and positive outlook.

*Stretch*   The company believes that people have infinite potential. We have an extraordinary capability to exert and extend the limits of the possible. We shall aim for stretch goals, ambitious targets and ever-receding horizons.

## QUESTIONS

1. Is it ethical to sell a product that is, at best, only mildly effective? Discuss.

2. Is it ethical to exploit cultural norms and values to promote a product? Discuss.

3. Is the advertising of *Fair & Lovely* demeaning to women or is it portraying a product not too dissimilar to cosmetics in general?

4. Will HLL's Fair & Lovely Foundation counter charges made by AIDWA? Discuss.

5. In light of AIDWA's charges, how would you suggest *Fair & Lovely* promote their product? Discuss. Would your response be different if *Fairever* continues to use "fairness" as a theme of their promotion? Discuss.

6. Propose a promotion/marketing program that will counter all the arguments and charges against *Fair & Lovely* and be an effective program.

7. Based on CavinKare's statement of Values and Beliefs, how would you evaluate CavinKaire's advertising/marketing programs?

Sources: Nicole Leistikow, "Indian Women Criticize 'Fair & Lovely' Ideal," *Women's eNews,* April 28, 2003; Shuchi Sinha, "Skin Care: Fair & Growing," *India Today,* December 4, 2000, p. 48; Ratna Bhushan, "CavinKare Changes Tack to Challenge HLL Strategy," *Business Line (The Hindu),* July 10, 2002; Arundhati Parmar, "Objections to Indian Ad Not Taken Lightly," *Marketing News,* June 9, 2003, p. 4; "Fair & Lovely Launches Foundation to Promote Economic Empowerment of Women," *Press Release, Fair & Lovely Foundation* (www.hll.com and search for foundation), March 11, 2003; Cavinkare Changes Tack to Challenge HLL Strategy," *Indian Business Insight,* July 10, 2002; Shunu Sen, "A Fair Way of Advertising," *Business Line (The Hindu),* August 1, 2002; "Ad Nauseam," *The Statesman-Asia Africa Intelligence Wire,* March 9, 2002; Rina Chandran, "All For Self-Control," *Business Line (The Hindu),* April 24, 2003; Miriam Jordan, "Creams for a Lighter Skin Capture the Asian Market, Especially in India, as a Cultural Virtue," *International Herald Tribune,* May 24, 1998; Simon Robinson and Peter Hawthorne, "Color Blindness: Obsessed with Fair Skin, Many African Women Are Using Dangerous Lighteners," *Time,* July 30, 2001; Khozem Merchant and Edward Luce, "Not So Fair and Lovely," *Financial Times,* March 19, 2003; and Bhanu Pande and Seema Shukla, "Big Brother Is Watching," *The Economic Times,* May 9, 2003.

# CASE 2-3 Starnes-Brenner Machine Tool Company: To Bribe or Not to Bribe?

The Starnes-Brenner Machine Tool Company of Iowa City, Iowa, has a small one-man sales office headed by Frank Rothe in Latino, a major Latin American country. Frank has been in Latino for about 10 years and is retiring this year; his replacement is Bill Hunsaker, one of Starnes-Brenner's top salespeople. Both will be in Latino for about eight months, during which time Frank will show Bill the ropes, introduce him to their principal customers, and, in general, prepare him to take over.

Frank has been very successful as a foreign representative in spite of his unique style and, at times, complete refusal to follow company policy when it doesn't suit him. The company hasn't really done much about his method of operation, although from time to time he has angered some top company people. As President Jack McCaughey, who retired a couple of years ago, once remarked to a vice president who was complaining about Frank, "If he's making money—and he is (more than any of the other foreign offices)—then leave the guy alone." When McCaughey retired, the new chief immediately instituted organizational changes that gave more emphasis to the overseas operations, moving the company toward a truly worldwide operation into which a loner like Frank would probably not fit. In fact, one of the key reasons for selecting Bill as Frank's replacement, besides Bill's record as a top salesperson, is Bill's capacity to be an organization man. He understands the need for coordination among operations and will cooperate with the home office so that the Latino office can be expanded and brought into the mainstream.

The company knows there is much to be learned from Frank, and Bill's job is to learn everything possible. The company certainly doesn't want to continue some of Frank's practices, but much of his knowledge is vital for continued, smooth operation. Today, Starnes-Brenner's foreign sales account for about 25 percent of the company's total profits, compared with about 5 percent only 10 years ago.

The company is actually changing character, from being principally an exporter, without any real concern for continuous foreign market representation, to having worldwide operations, where the foreign divisions are part of the total effort rather than a stepchild operation. In fact, Latino is one of the last operational divisions to be assimilated into the new organization. Rather than try to change Frank, the company has been waiting for him to retire before making any significant adjustments in their Latino operations.

Bill Hunsaker is 36 years old, with a wife and three children; he is a very good salesperson and administrator, although he has had no foreign experience. He has the reputation of being fair, honest, and a straight shooter. Some back at the home office see his assignment as part of a grooming job for a top position, perhaps eventually the presidency. The Hunsakers are now settled in their new home after having been in Latino for about two weeks. Today is Bill's first day on the job.

When Bill arrived at the office, Frank was on his way to a local factory to inspect some Starnes-Brenner machines that had to have some adjustments made before being acceptable to the Latino government agency buying them. Bill joined Frank for the plant visit. Later, after the visit, we join the two at lunch.

Bill, tasting some chili, remarks, "Boy! This certainly isn't like the chili we have in America."

"No, it isn't, and there's another difference, too. The Latinos are Americans and nothing angers a Latino more than to have a 'Gringo' refer to the United States as *America* as if to say that Latino isn't part of America also. The Latinos rightly consider their country as part of America (take a look at the map), and people from the United States are North Americans at best. So, for future reference, refer to home either as the United States, States, or North America, but, for gosh sakes, not just America. Not to change the subject, Bill, but could you see that any change had been made in those S-27s from the standard model?"

"No, they looked like the standard. Was there something out of whack when they arrived?"

"No, I couldn't see any problem—I suspect this is the best piece of sophisticated bribe taking I've come across yet. Most of the time the Latinos are more 'honest' about their *mordidas* than this."

"What's a *mordida*?" Bill asks.

"You know, *kumshaw, dash, bustarella, mordida;* they are all the same: a little grease to expedite the action. *Mordida* is the local word for a slight offering or, if you prefer, bribe," says Frank.

Bill quizzically responds, "Do we pay bribes to get sales?"

"Oh, it depends on the situation, but it's certainly something you have to be prepared to deal with." Boy, what a greenhorn, Frank thinks to himself, as he continues, "Here's the story. When the S-27s arrived last January, we began uncrating them and right away the *jefe* engineer (a government official)—*jefe,* that's the head man in charge—began extra-careful examination and declared there was a vital defect in the machines; he claimed the machinery would be dangerous and thus unacceptable if it wasn't corrected. I looked it over but couldn't see anything wrong, so I agreed to have our staff engineer check all the machines and correct any flaws that might exist. Well, the *jefe* said there wasn't enough time to wait for an engineer to come from the States, that the machines could be adjusted locally, and we could pay him and he would make all the necessary arrangements. So, what do you do? No adjustment his way and there would be an order cancelled; and, maybe there was something out of line, those things have been known to happen. But for the life of me, I can't see that anything had been done since the machines were supposedly fixed. So, let's face it, we just paid a bribe, and a pretty darn big bribe at that—about $1,200 per machine. What makes it so aggravating is that that's the second one I've had to pay on this shipment."

"The second?" asks Bill.

"Yeah, at the border, when we were transferring the machines to Latino trucks, it was hot and they were moving slow as molasses. It took them over an hour to transfer one machine to a Latino truck and we had ten others to go. It seemed that every time I spoke to the dock boss about speeding things up, they just got slower. Finally, out of desperation, I slipped him a fistful of pesos and, sure enough, in the next three hours they had the whole thing loaded. Just one of the local customs of doing business. Generally, though, it comes at the lower level where wages don't cover living expenses too well."

There is a pause and Bill asks, "What does that do to our profits?"

"Runs them down, of course, but I look at it as just one of the many costs of doing business—I do my best not to pay, but when I have to, I do."

Hesitantly, Bill replies, "I don't like it, Frank. We've got good products, they're priced right, we give good service, and keep plenty of spare parts in the country, so why should we have to pay bribes? It's just no way to do business. You've already had to pay two bribes on one shipment; if you keep it up, the word's going to get around and you'll be paying at every level. Then all the profit goes out the window—you know, once you start, where do you stop? Besides that, where do we stand legally? The Foreign Bribery Act makes paying bribes like you've just paid illegal. I'd say the best policy is to never start: You might lose a few sales, but let it be known that there are no bribes; we sell the best, service the best at fair prices, and that's all."

"You mean the Foreign Corrupt Practices Act, don't you?" Frank asks, and continues, in an I'm-not-really-so-out-of-touch tone of voice, "Haven't some of the provisions of the Foreign Corrupt Practices Act been softened somewhat?"

"Yes, you're right, the provisions on paying a *mordida* or grease have been softened, but paying the government official is still illegal, softening or not," replies Bill.

Oh boy! Frank thinks to himself as he replies, "Look, what I did was just peanuts as far as the Foreign Corrupt Practices Act goes. The people we pay off are small, and, granted we give good service, but we've only been doing it for the last year or so. Before that I never knew when I was going to have equipment to sell. In fact, we only had products when there were surpluses stateside. I had to pay the right people to get sales, and besides, you're not back in the States any longer. Things are just done different here. You follow that policy and I guarantee that you'll have fewer sales because our competitors from Germany, Italy, and Japan will pay. Look, Bill, everybody does it here; it's a way of life, and the costs are generally reflected in the markup and overhead. There is even a code of behavior involved. We're not actually encouraging it to spread, just perpetuating an accepted way of doing business."

Patiently and slightly condescendingly, Bill replies, "I know, Frank, but wrong is wrong and we want to operate differently now. We hope to set up an operation here on a continuous basis; we plan to operate in Latino just like we do in the United States. Really expand our operation and make a long-range market commitment, grow with the country! And one of the first things we must avoid is unethical . . ."

Frank interrupts, "But really, is it unethical? Everybody does it, the Latinos even pay *mordidas* to other Latinos; it's a fact of life—is it really unethical? I think that the circumstances that exist in a country justify and dictate the behavior. Remember, man, 'When in Rome, do as the Romans do.'"

Almost shouting, Bill blurts out, "I can't buy that. We know that our management practices and relationships are our strongest point. Really, all we have to differentiate us from the rest of our competition, Latino and others, is that we are better managed and, as far as I'm concerned, graft and other unethical behavior have got to be cut out to create a healthy industry. In the long run, it should strengthen our position. We can't build our futures on illegal and unethical practices."

Frank angrily replies, "Look, it's done in the States all the time. What about the big dinners, drinks, and all the other hanky-panky that goes on? Not to mention PACs' [Political Action Committee] payments to congressmen, and all those high speaking fees certain congressmen get from special interests. How many congressmen have gone to jail or lost reelection on those kinds of things? What is that, if it isn't *mordida* the North American way? The only difference is that instead of cash only, in the United States we pay in merchandise and cash."

"That's really not the same and you know it. Besides, we certainly get a lot of business transacted during those dinners even if we are paying the bill."

"Bull, the only difference is that here bribes go on in the open; they don't hide it or dress it in foolish ritual that fools no one. It goes on in the United States and everyone denies the existence of it. That's all the difference—in the United States we're just more hypocritical about it all."

"Look," Frank continues, almost shouting, "we are getting off on the wrong foot and we've got eight months to work together. Just keep your eyes and mind open and let's talk about it again in a couple of months when you've seen how the whole country operates; perhaps then you won't be so quick to judge it absolutely wrong."

Frank, lowering his voice, says thoughtfully, "I know it's hard to take; probably the most disturbing problem in underdeveloped countries is the matter of graft. And, frankly, we don't do much advance preparation so we can deal firmly with it. It bothered me at first; but then I figured it makes its economic contribution, too, since the payoff is as much a part of the economic process as a payroll. What's our real economic role, anyway, besides making a profit, of course? Are we developers of wealth, helping to push the country to greater economic growth, or are we missionaries? Or should we be both? I really don't know, but I don't think we can be both simultaneously, and my feeling is that, as the company prospers, as higher salaries are paid, and better standards of living are reached, we'll see better ethics. Until then, we've got to operate or leave, and if you are going to win the opposition over, you'd better join them and change them from within, not fight them."

Before Bill could reply, a Latino friend of Frank's joined them and they changed the topic of conversation.

## QUESTIONS

1. Is what Frank did ethical? By whose ethics—those of Latino or the United States?

2. Are Frank's two different payments legal under the Foreign Corrupt Practices Act as amended by the Omnibus Trade and Competitiveness Act of 1988?

3. Identify the types of payments made in the case; that is, are they lubrication, extortion, or subornation?

4. Frank seemed to imply that there is a similarity between what he was doing and what happens in the United States. Is there any difference? Explain.

5. Are there any legal differences between the money paid to the dockworkers and the money paid the *jefe* (government official)? Any ethical differences?

6. Frank's attitude seems to imply that a foreigner must comply with all local customs, but some would say that one of the contributions made by U.S. firms is to change local ways of doing business. Who is right?

7. Should Frank's behavior have been any different had this not been a government contract?

8. If Frank shouldn't have paid the bribe, what should he have done, and what might have been the consequences?

9. What are the company interests in this problem?

10. Explain how this may be a good example of the SRC (self-reference criterion) at work.

11. Do you think Bill will make the grade in Latino? Why? What will it take?

12. How can an overseas manager be prepared to face this problem?

# CASE 2—4 Ethics and Airbus

In September last year, a fraud squad, led by Jean-Claude Van Espen, a Belgian magistrate, raided Airbus's headquarters in Toulouse. "They wanted to check whether there was possible falsification of documents, bribery or other infractions as part of the sale of Airbus aircraft to Sabena," says Mr. Van Espen's spokesman. The team of 20 Belgian and French investigators interviewed several Airbus employees during its three-day stay in Toulouse and carted away boxes of documents.

In November 1997 Sabena had approved an order for 17 Airbus A320s (narrow-bodied aircraft) which it did not need. Even more oddly, it had doubled the order at the last minute to 34, a move which helped trigger the airline's collapse four years later.

Though nominally controlled by the Belgian government, Sabena was run by the parent company of Swissair, SAirGroup, which had owned a stake of 49.5 percent since 1995 and which also went bust in 2001. A former Sabena manager, who arrived after the Airbus order was placed, says that the planes were not needed: "It was a fatal business decision." A Belgian parliamentary commission's recent report confirms that the Airbus order was a big cause of Sabena's collapse.

Mr. Van Espen's separate criminal investigation is continuing. According to the report, it started in October 2001 after Philippe Doyen, then a Sabena employee, lodged a complaint. Among other things, he suggested to Mr. Van Espen that he interview Peter Gysel, a former Swissair employee now working at Airbus, who put together Sabena's deal with Airbus. Mr. Gysel denies any impropriety. The former Sabena manager says: "I never got the slightest whiff that the decision was driven by kickbacks, side-payments and so on. But I cannot rule anything out." Neither does Mr. Van Espen.

Today airlines are ordering about 400 aircraft a year. But in good times 800 planes, worth around $60 billion, are sold a year. In the past ten years Airbus (originally a consortium, now owned 80 percent by EADS and 20 percent by BAE Systems) has caught up with Boeing, which had enjoyed two-thirds of the market since its 747 jumbo-jet entered commercial service in 1970.

Many aircraft are no doubt bought and sold in entirely conventional ways. But many are not. After all, lots of airlines are still state-owned and not subject to normal business rules. Commission payments (licit or illicit) on multimillion-dollar aircraft deals increase the capital cost of aircraft, which are therefore subject to higher depreciation or operating-lease charges, or both. But these extra costs are barely discernible in the pool of red ink created by the carriers' perennial losses.

Aircraft purchases drag on for years, as airlines play Boeing and Airbus off against each other. Especially in a buyer's market, deep discounts are common, performance guarantees are demanding and manufacturers have to offer all sorts of sweeteners (for instance, aircraft trade-ins, or unusual guarantees) to persuade an airline to switch to their aircraft.

Unsurprisingly, given the regulated nature of international air travel, politics plays a part. For instance, no sooner had Air Mauritius bought Airbus A340S in 1994 than it obtained an upgrade from Paris Orly to Charles de Gaulle airport, which is Air France's main base with better onward connections.

Aircraft purchases have long been associated with controversy. In the 1970s, when Lockheed was still making civil jets, it was caught bribing Japanese officials to buy its L1011 wide-bodied airliner. A Japanese prime minister was later charged and convicted in 1983 for taking a bribe. Prince Bernhard of the Netherlands was also disgraced for his involvement with Lockheed. This scandal led in 1977 to Congress passing the Foreign Corrupt Practices Act (FCPA), which forbids American companies, their officers or their representatives from bribing foreign officials.

Critics (including this newspaper) have often pointed out that American firms can side-step the FCPA by using foreign subsidiaries and nationals to pay bribes. Boeing says that its policy is to adhere to the spirit and letter of the FCPA, that its systems of controls ensure employees comply with this policy, and that no Boeing employee has been charged under the FCPA. In 1982 Boeing pleaded guilty to false statements about commissions on the sale of commercial aircraft prior to 1977. Boeing also says that there have been public hearings in the Bahamas over allegations of bribery in the 1990 sale of deHavilland aircraft to Bahamas Air, during Boeing's ownership of deHavilland.

Airbus has not been subject to such constraints. France ratified an OECD convention to outlaw bribery of foreign public officials in 2000. Until then the government even permitted French companies tax deductions for giving bribes.

For years, as they steadily lost market share to the European challenger, the Americans have been outspokenly critical of Airbus. In the 1980s the beef was the huge subsidies that European governments poured into the industry. Now that Airbus repays such launch aid, that is less relevant, especially as Boeing receives indirect subsidies through America's defense budget and space program.

But the American government has also spoken out on the subject of bribery. Two years ago Grant Aldonas, an under-secretary for international trade, told a congressional committee: "Unfortunately this [aircraft manufacturing] is an industry where foreign corruption has a real impact . . . this sector has been especially vulnerable to trade distortions involving bribery of foreign public officials."

According to a European Parliament report, published in 2001, America's National Security Agency (NSA) intercepted faxes and phone calls between Airbus, Saudi Arabian Airlines, and the Saudi government in early 1994. The NSA found that Airbus agents were offering bribes to a Saudi official to secure a lion's share for Airbus in modernizing Saudi Arabian Airlines' fleet. The planes were in a $6 billion deal that Edouard Balladur, France's then prime minister, had hoped to clinch on a visit to see King Fahd in January 1994. He went home empty-handed.

James Woolsey, then director of the Central Intelligence Agency, recounted in a newspaper article in 2000 how the American government typically reacted to intelligence of this sort. "When we have caught you [Europeans] . . . we go to the government you're bribing and tell its officials that we don't take kindly to such corruption," he wrote. Apparently this (and a direct sales pitch from Bill Clinton to King Fahd) swung the aircraft part of the deal Boeing's and McDonnell-Douglas's way.

# KUWAITI KICKBACKS?

Not even the NSA, however, knows about everything in the air-craft-manufacturing industry as it actually happens. Consider the history of an Airbus order placed by Kuwait Airways Corporation (KAC), another state-owned airline.

In November 1995, Reuters reported that Kuwaiti prosecutors had questioned Bader Mallalah, KAC's then chief financial officer, over allegations of embezzlement made against him by KAC. The firm's chairman, Ahmed al Mishari, had suspended Dr. Mallalah from his job the previous month. But KAC had trumped up the allegations against Dr. Mallalah to put the lid on a story of corruption in which its then chairman was himself involved.

That story began exactly five years earlier in Cairo, where KAC had set up temporary headquarters after Iraq's invasion of Kuwait in August 1990. Most of its planes would inevitably be lost or damaged, so Mr. al Mishari was planning a shiny new post-war fleet. Naturally, both Boeing and Airbus were asked to tender. Both firms expected politics to play a part in KAC's choice, especially after an American-led coalition had liberated Kuwait.

Shortly after the liberation of Kuwait, Boeing and KAC met in London. One person present says Mr. al Mishari gave the impression that the order would be Boeing's. After all, until then, American companies had won most of the large reconstruction contracts from a grateful government.

Airbus hoped otherwise. In 1991, shortly before the Paris Air Show, Jean Pierson, the then boss of Airbus, met Mr. al Mishari at the Churchill Hotel in London. The two talked in private for part of the time, so what they discussed is not known. Two clear inferences can, however, be drawn from subsequent events: Mr. al Mishari promised the order to Airbus; and Mr. Pierson pressed for an announcement at the imminent air show.

As substantial public funds were involved, KAC was supposed to follow formal process in Kuwait before placing the order. This included approvals from the Ministry of Finance and the public-spending watchdog. None of these approvals was sought before the air show. In June 1991, at the show, Mr. al Mishari stunned Kuwaiti officials and Boeing, when he announced a firm order for 15 Airbus aircraft, worth $1.1 billion, and options for nine more, worth up to $900 million. A delighted Mr. Pierson trumpeted the deal as Airbus's first single order for all its aircraft types.

Most unusually, Boeing was not asked for its "best and final" offer, according to a former KAC employee. Boeing's response to the announcement was to offer generous discounts to KAC—so that its package was around $100 million cheaper than its rival's—but it was too late. The upshot of a meeting in the summer of 1991 between the boss of Boeing Commercial, furious American officials, and the Crown Prince of Kuwait was a messy compromise. KAC would order the engines for the Airbuses from General Electric; Boeing would receive an order for two wide-bodied planes as a sop; and the firm order for 15 Airbus aircraft would go ahead provided that KAC bought from Boeing in the future.

This left Mr. al Mishari in a rather awkward spot. KAC had an option to buy nine more aircraft from Airbus. An airline is usually able to walk away from an option deal if it forfeits the modest deposit paid. But this case was far from normal. The company that was to take up the option was not KAC itself but a subsidiary, Aviation Lease and Finance Company (ALAFCO), which Mr. al Mishari had set up in Bermuda in September 1992. ALAFCO was to buy the aircraft and lease them to KAC. In late 1992 Mr. al

Mishari confirmed to Mr. Pierson that ALAFCO would buy the nine planes and sent off a $2.5 million deposit. By buying the planes through ALAFCO, Mr. al Mishari intended to bypass formal governmental approval.

There was more to the deal. Airbus chipped in a total of $450,000 between 1992 and 1994 to help with the costs of setting up and running ALAFCO. On December 15, 1992 ALAFCO appointed a part-time commercial adviser, Mohamed Habib El Fekih, a Tunisian national. His day job was then as head of sales in the Middle East—for Airbus. Under his ALAFCO contract of employment, a copy of which *The Economist* has and which was to run for three years from January 1993, Mr. El Fekih received $5,000 a month, and $80,000 in back pay for "services" rendered to ALAFCO from February 1, 1990—31 months before ALAFCO'S incorporation—to December 31, 1992. The $5,000 was paid each month from ALAFCO's account number 201-901-04 at the Commercial Bank of Kuwait in New York to Mr. El Fekih's personal account (number 0000003930B) at Credit Lyonnais's branch in Blagnac, France, where Airbus is based on the outskirts of Toulouse.

By 1993 three of the nine aircraft under option, all cargo planes, were nearly ready for delivery. However, Dr. Mallalah, who was also ALAFCO's chief executive, insisted that the transaction be subject to formal procedure in Kuwait. This meant competitive tenders from Airbus and Boeing. Unsurprisingly, Airbus, with inside knowledge from its two-hatted vice-president, Mr. El Fekih, was able to match exactly offers from Boeing, after Boeing came in over $50 million cheaper. With nothing to choose between the offers, ALAFCO selected Airbus, on the grounds that KAC's fleet now comprised predominantly Airbus aircraft.

The deal sailed through KAC's board and the Ministry of Finance. However, Dr. Mallalah provided Kuwait's public-spending watchdog with full details of ALAFCO's order for the cargo planes. It refused to sanction the deal. Consultants concluded in early 1995 that the purchase of the cargo aircraft was not justified. The Ministry of Finance told KAC not to proceed. After Dr. Mallalah submitted a report to KAC's board on the affair, Mr. El Fekih resigned from ALAFCO in March 1995.

Mr. El Fekih says that he acted in an honest way; Mr. Pierson approved his ALAFCO contract, as did the boards of KAC and ALAFCO; his ALAFCO contract had nothing to do with the sale of Airbus to KAC; KAC cancelled its option; ALAFCO never bought any Airbus aircraft; he acted as a consultant to help set up ALAFCO as an aircraft-financing company; and he declared his earnings to the taxman. Airbus says that it offers this sort of support to customers, when asked. The present owners of the ALAFCO business confirm that ALAFCO bought three Airbus aircraft.

Of the other six aircraft under option, three were not converted into firm orders. Two Airbus A320s were leased to Shorouk Air in Egypt. This joint-venture between KAC and EgyptAir was specifically set up to find a home for them, but is being liquidated because of massive losses. Kuwait's Ministry of Finance leased another.

Mr. al Mishari, sacked as the chairman of KAC in 1999 after spending almost his entire career with the airline, owns a shopping complex in the Salmiya district of Kuwait, which local wags have dubbed the "Airbus Centre." Mr. al Mishari, whose family is wealthy, suffered financial problems when the Kuwaiti stock market collapsed in the early 1980s. Mr. al Mishari declines to comment, as does KAC.

It is not irrelevant to ask if the price of the Airbus aircraft was inflated to allow for kickbacks. No evidence of graft has ever come to light. However, no policeman, in Kuwait (or elsewhere), has looked for any.

## INDIA INK

What about cases where police have carried out investigations? In March 1990 India's Central Bureau of Investigation (CBI) filed a first information report (FIR). It was investigating allegations that Airbus had bribed highly placed public servants and others to induce Indian Airlines (IA) to order its aircraft.

In March 1986 state-owned IA had ordered 19 Airbus A320s, worth $952 million, with an option for 12 more, later exercised. This was despite the fact that, when IA set up a committee in 1983 to recommend replacement aircraft for its aging Boeing fleet, the A320 was not considered—it had not then been launched or flown. With approval from the Indian government, IA had in July 1984 paid Boeing a deposit for 12 Boeing 757s, large narrow-bodied aircraft.

Several civil servants and IA officials were named in the FIR. One name not on the list was that of Rajiv Gandhi, India's prime minister in 1984–89, who was killed in a bomb explosion in May 1991.

How has the CBI's investigation progressed in the intervening 13 years? Hardly at all, despite the hounding on public-interest grounds of the CBI in Delhi's High Court since 1998 by B.L. Wadehra, an anticorruption lawyer based in Delhi. *The Economist* has examined the publicly available court documents—the CBI's status reports on its investigation are secret—from Mr. Wadehra's litigation.

These papers allege, first, that in October 1984, weeks before Mr. Gandhi, a former pilot, succeeded his mother, IA received an offer from Airbus for A320 aircraft, a smaller and less expensive plane than Boeing's 757. It required urgent attention. Second, that in November, the aviation ministry gave IA just three days to appraise the offer for Mr. Gandhi's office.

Much later, in 1990, *Indian Express,* an Indian newspaper, reported a leaked manuscript note which showed that Mr. Gandhi had decided at a meeting on August 2, 1985 that IA "should go in for Airbus A320 aircraft."

Mr. Gandhi's correspondence file on the deal mysteriously vanished. The court papers show that civil servants reconstructed 29 pages of the missing file for the CBI by obtaining copy correspondence from government departments. Remarkably, this task took seven years—and even then the reconstruction was only partial.

After the green light from Mr. Gandhi, approvals from IA and government bodies were a formality. For instance, the IA board approved the Airbus order at a meeting on August 30, 1985, which started at noon. The quality of the analysis presented to the board on the competing offers was pitiful. The board considered only one criterion—comparative fuel efficiency. Even for that, the data were incomplete. The A320 with the engine chosen by IA had yet to be tried and tested anywhere; provisional data only were included in the report for Boeing 737s "since no technical data supplied by the company."

But Boeing had not been asked for any. This was because two hours before the board meeting, at 9:50 AM, IA's managing director, who is named in the FIR as an alleged recipient of kickbacks, received a letter from Richard Elliott, then Boeing's regional sales director. Boeing offered to supply up to 35 of its 737 aircraft, its narrow-bodied rival to the A320, with a discount of $5 million per plane. This would reduce IA's investment in new planes by $140

million, stated Mr. Elliott. IA's board brushed the offer aside on the grounds that "if Boeing was [sic] too serious . . . they [sic] could have made the offer earlier."

The Delhi court has a withering opinion of the help Airbus has given the CBI. It allowed Mr. Wadehra to add Airbus's Indian subsidiary to his action on the grounds that Airbus in France was not cooperating. Airbus told Mr. Wadehra that French law forbade it from answering his questions. "[Airbus] sells its aircraft on their merits," the firm insisted.

The court has castigated the CBI for its dilatory approach. It took the Indian authorities until 1995 to contact Airbus for information, only to be told that such requests should be routed through the French government. The CBI told Mr. Wadehra, despite trying Interpol and diplomatic channels, it was not getting any help from the French government. The French embassy in Delhi in effect told Mr. Wadehra to get lost when he wrote to ask why France was not cooperating.

Mr. Wadehra's case is now topical. This is because in March last year, IA's board approved an order for 43 Airbus planes, worth around $2 billion. The order now needs government approval. However, in September 2000, the Delhi court ruled that the Indian government should not approve further purchases from Airbus until the CBI had obtained the information it wanted from the French.

The upshot of the IA story is that no serious attempt has been made to establish whether or not Airbus paid kickbacks to Mr. Gandhi and associates. The CBI has not answered our written questions.

## MOUNTIES AND BANKS

But there are police forces which have shown rather more resolve and initiative than the CBI. One important case establishes that Airbus has paid "commissions" to individuals hiding behind shell companies in jurisdictions where ownership of companies is not a matter of public record, and where strict bank secrecy applies.

Airbus's first big sale in North America was a $1.5 billion deal, signed in 1988, to sell 34 aircraft to the then state-owned Air Canada. The middleman was Karlheinz Schreiber, a German-Canadian with connections to politicians in Germany and Canada. Mr. Schreiber emerged as a figure in the financing scandal that engulfed Germany's Christian Democrat party and its top politician, Helmut Kohl, a former chancellor, in the late 1990s.

In August 1999 the Royal Canadian Mounted Police, acting on a German arrest warrant, nabbed Mr. Schreiber. In 2000, Mr. Schreiber was charged in Germany with tax evasion on money he had received for the Airbus transaction and other deals. The *Suddeutsche Zeitung,* a German daily, has supplied a copy of Mr. Schreiber's indictment to *The Economist*. According to this document, Airbus signed a consultancy contract (amended four times) with International Aircraft Leasing (IAL) in March 1985. IAL, which was to help with the Air Canada deal, was a shell company based in Vaduz, Liechtenstein, and a subsidiary of another Liechtenstein-registered shell, Kensington Anstalt.

According to the indictment, between September 30, 1988 and October 21, 1993 (i.e., as Air Canada took delivery of Airbus planes), Airbus paid a total of $22,540,000 in "commissions" to IAL. $10,867,000 was paid into IAL's account number 235.972.037 at the Verwaltungs-und Privat-Bank in Vaduz and $11,673,000 into IAL's account number 18.679.4 at Swiss Bank Corporation (SBC) in Zurich. During extradition proceedings against Mr. Schreiber in

1999, Airbus admitted to these payments. In October 2000 Mr. Schreiber won a suspension of execution of his case.

The court ruled that IAL belonged to Mr. Schreiber, but also that, to the extent that Mr. Schreiber had paid out the Airbus "commissions" as Schmiergelder ("grease monies"), these payments could be tax deductible. Mr. Schreiber's German tax lawyer later told the court: "Schmiergelder were not openly paid to the 'greased' person by [Airbus]. It was through third persons to make reception anonymous and the Schmiergelder unrecognisable as such."

So who got the commissions? After years of police investigations in at least five jurisdictions, it is still not clear. According to *The Last Amigo,* a well-researched book on the affair by Harvey Cashore and Stevie Cameron, both Canadian journalists, a lot was withdrawn in cash. Mr. Cashore, a producer on "the fifth estate," Canadian Broadcasting Corporation's main investigative program, says that Mr. Schreiber's bank records and diaries showed that he usually followed a simple formula for dividing up the money: half for Canadians and half for Europeans.

The book alleges that there may have been a smaller scam within the bigger scam: an Airbus employee may have got some of the money. Some of the money was transferred into subaccounts at SBC in Zurich. One of the subaccounts, code-named "Stewardess," received as much as one-eighth of the commissions. The book suggests that this account was intended for Stuart Iddles, Airbus's senior vice-president from 1986 to 1994.

Mr. Iddles's wife bought Casa Las Estacas, a luxurious beach-front villa in Puerto Vallarta, Mexico, in September 1992. Documents in *The Economist*'s possession show the price was $1.5 million. According to a person involved in the deal, the money was wired from account number 154963-01-10 in the name of the Ciclon Foundation at the Zurich branch of Lloyds, a British bank. Mrs. Iddles confirms that she bought the villa in 1992, but says she has not the "foggiest idea" how much it cost, or which bank the money came from. Mr. Iddles has denied any impropriety. Airbus says it has not been indicted in any jurisdiction over the Air Canada deal, or over any other sales. It adds that no investigator has found unethical behaviour on its part.

## SYRIAN SCANDALS

Only one case of Airbus's colluding with a middleman apparently to bribe officials to buy its aircraft has led to convictions. According to Syria's state news agency, three people were sentenced in Syria in October 2001 to 22 years imprisonment each (later reduced to ten years) for "serious irregularities" in connection with state-owned Syrianair's order for six Airbus A320s in 1996. The court also imposed a fine on the three of $268 million. They were a former minister for economic affairs, a former transport minister, and Munir Abu Khaddur, the middleman. Mr. Khaddur was sentenced in absentia, and is reportedly living in Spain. The court found that the men had forced the airline to buy the planes, worth $240 million, and as a result Syrianair had incurred "big financial losses."

The only inferences to be drawn are: either there was a miscarriage of justice; or bribes were paid. If the latter, the news agency did not release details of how much the men embezzled. Quite why bribes would have been necessary is puzzling. Because America deems Syria to be a sponsor of terrorism, Boeing has long been prohibited from exporting there. The Syrian government declines to comment.

The result of our investigations into instances of corruption or alleged corruption by Airbus suggests that Mr. Van Espen will have a very long haul as he tries to establish whether "commissions" influenced Sabena's decision to buy Airbuses. The order for the 34 A320s could be viewed as incompetence. But nobody can predict the results of Mr. Van Espen's inquiry.

The parliamentary report says Sabena's board received some lacunary information that was misleading. The choice of Airbus supposedly meant Sabena was confident of strong sales growth. Yet a month after the order was placed, SAirGroup's chief executive, who also sat on Sabena's board, said: "We're now in the last year or years of the boom in air travel." (We do not mean to imply by inference that the chief executive was corrupt.)

Most of what is recounted in this article happened before Airbus's present top management team arrived, before it was established as a proper company, and before France adopted the OECD convention on bribery.

No one doubts the company's ability to compete across the whole product range with Boeing. By the time next week's Paris Air Show is over, Airbus will probably be well ahead of its rival in market share, thanks to an attractive range of planes. But if charges of corruption involving Airbus were to emerge from Mr. Van Espen's investigation of Sabena, that would deal the company's reputation a severe blow.

## QUESTIONS

1. In each of the cases described above, who benefits and who suffers from the alleged ethical and legal lapses of Airbus?

2. How should the public relations staff at Airbus respond to this article appearing in *The Economist*?

3. What steps might Boeing take to defend itself from this sort of competition?

4. Do you think that Boeing and Airbus behave differently in marketing their aircraft around the globe? How and why?

5. Had France adopted the OECD convention on bribery ahead of these transactions, would the firm's behavior have differed? Why?

Source: "Airbus's Secret Past—Aircraft and Bribery," *The Economist*, June 14, 2003, pp. 55–58.

# CASE 2-5 Coping with Corruption in Trading with China

Corruption is on the rise in China, where the country's press frequently has detailed cases of corruption and of campaigns to crack down on it. The articles primarily have focused on domestic economic crimes among Chinese citizens, and on local officials who have been fired or assessed other penalties. Indeed, China has been rated by Transparency International as number 59 of the 102 countries the German organization rates on its "Corruption Perception Index."[1] Finland is rated the least corrupt at number 1, the United States at 16, and Bangladesh the most corrupt at number 102.

Corruption's long arm now is reaching out to touch China's foreign business community. Traders, trade consultants, and analysts have said that foreign firms are vulnerable to a variety of corrupt practices. Although some of these firms said they had no experience with corruption in the People's Republic of China (PRC), the majority said they increasingly were asked to make payments to improve business, engage in black-market trade of import and export licenses, bribe officials to push goods through customs or the Commodity Inspection Bureau, or engage in collusion to beat the system. The Hong Kong Independent Commission Against Corruption reports that outright bribes as well as gifts or payment to establish *guanxi,* or "connections," average 3 to 5 percent of operating costs in the PRC, or $3 billion to $5 billion of the $100 billion of foreign investments that have been made there. The most common corrupt practices confronting foreign companies in China are examined here.

## PAYING TO IMPROVE BUSINESS

Foreign traders make several types of payments to facilitate sales in China. The most common methods used are trips abroad. Chinese officials, who rarely have a chance to visit overseas, often prefer foreign travel to cash or gifts. (This was especially true when few PRC officials had been abroad.) As a result, traders report that dangling foreign trips in front of their PRC clients has become a regular part of negotiating large trade deals that involve products with a technological component. "Foreign travel is always the first inducement we offer," said an executive involved in machinery trade. In most cases, traders built these costs into the product's sale price. Some trips are "reasonable and bona fide expenditures directly related to the promotion, demonstration, or explanation of products and services, or the execution of a contract with a foreign government agency." But other trips, when officials on foreign junkets are offered large per diems and aren't invited specifically to gain technical knowledge, may be another matter.

Foreign travel isn't always an inducement—it also can be extorted. In one case, a PRC bank branch refused to issue a letter of credit for a machinery import deal. The Chinese customer suggested that the foreign trader invite the bank official on an overseas inspection tour. Once the invitation was extended, the bank issued the letter of credit.

## ANGLING FOR CASH

MNCs also are asked sometimes to sponsor overseas education for children of trading officials. One person told a Chinese source that an MNC paid for that individual's U.S. $1,500-a-month apartment, as well as a car, university education, and expenses.

Firms find direct requests for cash payments—undeniably illegal—the most difficult. One well-placed source said that a major trader, eager for buyers in the face of an international market glut, had fallen into regularly paying large kickbacks into the Honduran, U.S., and Swiss accounts of officials at a PRC foreign trade corporation.

Refusing to make payments may not only hurt sales, it can also be terrifying. A U.S. firm was one of several bidders for a large sale; a Chinese official demanded the MNC pay a 3 percent kickback. When the company representative refused, the official threatened: "You had better not say anything about this. You still have to do business in China, and stay in hotels here." Not surprisingly, the U.S. company lost the deal.

Traders of certain commodities may be tempted to purchase on the black market those import and export licenses that are difficult to obtain legally. A fairly disorganized underground market, for instance, exists for licenses to export China-made garments to the United States.

Some branches of the Commodity Inspection Bureau (CIB) also have posed problems for some traders. Abuses have emerged in the CIB since it started inspecting imports in 1987. A Japanese company, for instance, informed CIB officials of its intention to bring heavy industrial items into China—items that had met Japanese and U.S. standards. The officials responded that they planned to dismantle the products on arrival for inspection purposes. The problem was resolved only after the firm invited the officials to visit Japan.

Some traders get around such problems by purchasing inspection certificates on the black market. According to press accounts, these forms, complete with signatures and seals, can be bought for roughly U.S. $200.

Some claim that, for the appropriate compensation, customs officials in a southern province are very willing to reduce the dutiable value of imports as much as 50 percent. Because the savings can far exceed transport costs, some imports that would logically enter China through a northern port are redirected through the southern province.

## QUESTIONS

1. List all the different types of bribes, payments, or favors represented in this case and say why each is either legal or illegal.

2. For those practices that you say are illegal, classify each as lubrication, extortion, or subornation, and tell why.

3. Which of the payments, favors, or bribes are illegal under the Foreign Corrupt Practices Act (FCPA)?

4. Assuming that the FCPA did not exist, what is the ethical response to each of the payments, favors, or bribes you have

---

[1]See www.transparency.org for more details about their 2002 index.

identified? Read the section titled "Ethically and Socially Responsible Decisions" in Chapter 5 as a guide to assist you in your decision.

5. Now that the OECD has approved an FCPA-like treaty to ban commercial bribery by firms in member countries, do you think bribery will become less prevalent in markets like China?

6. List alternatives to paying bribes in international markets and discuss the pluses and minuses of each.

# CASE 2−6 When International Buyers and Sellers Disagree

No matter what line of business you're in, you can't escape sex. That may have been one conclusion drawn by an American exporter of meat products after a dispute with a German customer over a shipment of pork livers. Here's how the disagreement came about.

The American exporter was contracted to ship "30,000 lbs. of freshly frozen U.S. pork livers, customary merchantable quality, first rate brands." The shipment had been prepared to meet the exacting standards of the American market, so the exporter expected the transaction to be completed without any problem. But when the livers arrived in Germany, the purchaser raised an objection: "We ordered pork livers of customary merchantable quality—what you sent us consisted of 40 percent sow livers."

"Who cares about the sex of the pig the liver came from?" the exporter asked.

"We do," the German replied. "Here in Germany we don't pass off spongy sow livers as the firmer livers of male pigs. This shipment wasn't merchantable at the price we expected to charge. The only way we were able to dispose of the meat without a total loss was to reduce the price. You owe us a price allowance of $1,000."

The American refused to reduce the price. The determined resistance may have been partly in reaction to the implied insult to the taste of the American consumer. "If pork livers, whatever the sex of the animal, are palatable to Americans, they ought to be good enough for anyone," the American thought.

It looked as if the buyer and seller could never agree on eating habits.

## QUESTIONS

1. In this dispute which country's law would apply, that of the United States or of Germany?

2. If the case were tried in U.S. courts, who do you think would win? In German courts? Why?

3. Draw up a brief agreement that would have eliminated the following problems before they could occur.

   a. Whose law applies

   b. Whether the case should be tried in U.S. or German courts

   c. The difference in opinion as to "customary merchantable quality"

4. Discuss how SRC may be at work in this case.

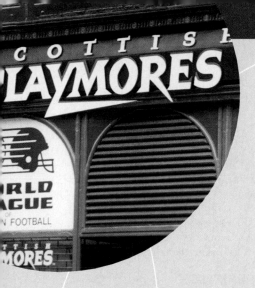

# cases 3

## ASSESSING GLOBAL MARKET OPPORTUNITIES

### OUTLINE OF CASES

# CASE 3—1 *Krispy Kreme Doughnuts Going Global?*

The American doughnut was born in 1847, so the lore goes, when a Maine seaman urged his mother to shove a fork through the center of her "fried cakes." That solved the problem of the cakes' soggy middle and created the doughnut's trademark hole.

Today, perhaps the most celebrated of the sweet treats are those fried up by *Krispy Kreme Doughnuts* Inc., whose hot "original glazed" doughnuts have earned a cult-like following. With virtually no advertising, but an uncanny knack for creating free publicity through the media, the company keeps racking up double-digit gains in sales and profit.

Skeptics keep trying to poke holes in the Krispy Kreme mystique—questioning whether the company can maintain its remarkable growth. Some analysts believe its growth rates already are beginning to ease. They also contend that the company's stock remains too rich for most tastes. Their argument appears to hold some water. Krispy Kreme's stock, after skyrocketing at first, trades for less than it did two years ago despite the company's consistent growth record. But the company is unmoved by the pessimists and has no intention of scaling back its aggressive expansion plans, which include Southern California.

"We may be in the first or second inning of our market penetration opportunities around the world, including the United States," said Scott Livengood, Krispy Kreme's chairman and chief executive. With 288 stores in 38 states and Canada, Krispy Kreme is starting to expand into smaller U.S. cities and other foreign markets. It sees potential for hundreds of additional stores worldwide.

In Southern California, where the company started with its La Habra store in 1999, it now has 22 locations employing 1,300 people. And more are on the horizon. "We'd expect to build as many as 50 stores over the next five years in Southern California," said Richard Reinis, chief executive of Great Circle Family Foods, a Los Angeles company formed to be Krispy Kreme's Southern California franchisee. Among the target locations: Santa Monica, Newport Beach, Laguna Beach and La Jolla.

The company also is thinking of building a West Coast distribution plant, possibly in California, within three years. Krispy Kreme is a story some have found too good to be true ever since the company went public three years ago. Yet the stalwart reputation of the doughnuts—abetted by media that pump up every new store opening as a local sensation—helps maintain the company's prosperity.

As Starbucks Corp. did with coffee shops, Krispy Kreme has transformed a commodity product into a branded specialty with devoted fans. And despite the hand-wringing about its outlook, the company's total stock market value is $2 billion. That means each of its stores, which range in size from 800 to 5,000 square feet, is worth nearly $7 million.

Krispy Kreme was started 66 years ago in Winston-Salem, N.C., where it still has its headquarters. Its doughnuts were mainly a Southern treat until the 1990s, when the company began expanding north and west. The chain's reputation preceded it everywhere. People would camp out for hours, even days, to be first in line to taste a Krispy Kreme at a new location and watch the doughnuts being made.

The media loved "the hubbub," as one Krispy Kreme executive calls it, and they helped the company burst onto the national stage. It was advertising that money couldn't buy, not that Krispy Kreme would anyway. The company doesn't spend a dime on advertising. Instead, everyone at Krispy Kreme from Livengood on down deftly encourages its loyalists to keep the buzz alive.

## SHARING THE 'EXPERIENCE'

Making a 50-cent Krispy Kreme doughnut is "almost hypnotic," Livengood (rhymes with "drive-in-good") rhapsodized in his deep, steady voice. There's "the animation and the giving birth," he said, "the theater aspect of it" and the way it forms "a relationship that is emotional." What some might think of as a mere tasty mixture of dough and sugar, Livengood considers "almost as a member of the family." To him and his customers, a Krispy Kreme isn't just something to chow down with coffee, it's an "experience."

Investors had quite the experience in mid-2000, when the company first sold its stock to the public. Wall Street was left slack-jawed as the shares soared like those of the dot-com companies of the time—before the crash. Its stock rose more than sevenfold after going public at $5.25 a share (adjusting for splits since then). Livengood & Co. were under pressure to keep delivering big gains in sales and profit, and they didn't disappoint. Quarter after quarter, Krispy Kreme has posted double-digit growth.

It's not just expansion that's pushing the growth, either. The chain's same-store sales—those of stores open at least a year, and a key measure of customer loyalty—also have climbed by double digits for 13 straight quarters. The company owns 104 of its stores; the rest are owned by franchisees, some of which have Krispy Kreme as an equity partner. The company sells its doughnut mix, doughnut-making equipment, coffee and other supplies to the franchisees.

Its systemwide sales, including company-owned and franchise stores, are expected to top $1 billion for the first time this year. Sales for Krispy Kreme alone totaled $492 million in its fiscal year ended Feb. 2, up 25 percent from the previous year. In its fiscal first quarter ended May 4, Krispy Kreme's profit soared 48 percent from a year earlier, and the company nudged up its earnings estimate for the full fiscal year, to 90 cents a share. Krispy Kreme's stock has gained 10 percent since the results were announced May 28. The stock closed Friday at $35.05 a share, down $1.40 on the New York Stock Exchange.

That means investors are paying about 39 times this year's expected earnings per share to own Krispy Kreme—much more than they're paying for General Electric Co. or Cisco Systems Inc. At one time, Krispy Kreme's price-to-earnings multiple topped 50. But even today's price is too high for some analysts, no matter the emotional attachment customers have to the doughnuts.

## RISING ANALYST CONCERN

Consider: In the first quarter, Krispy Kreme's systemwide sales jumped a stout 24 percent from a year earlier. But analyst John Ivankoe of J.P. Morgan Securities and others on Wall Street had expected at least a 28 percent gain, and it was the third straight quarter that the company's growth, though robust, fell short of forecasts.

"We are nervous given the continued shortfall" and a lofty P/E ratio, which "limit our enthusiasm for the stock in the near term," Ivankoe said in a report after the earnings came out. He rates the shares "neutral." So Krispy Kreme remains a favorite of "short sellers," traders who bet on stock prices falling. About 15 percent of its shares outstanding are sold short.

In the first quarter, it was "demonstrably clear that sales were below plan," and "there's been a steady deceleration in revenues," asserted David Rocker, managing partner of Rocker Partners, a New York hedge fund that is shorting the stock. Yet others, such as analyst David Geraty of RBC Capital Markets, are still recommending the shares. Krispy Kreme has "a 60-year-old brand, a loyal customer base and is in the infancy of growth," and that high P/E is "well-deserved," he said in a report last month.

Indeed, Krispy Kreme remains a pipsqueak compared with the nation's largest doughnut chain, Dunkin' Donuts, a subsidiary of British spirits maker Allied Domecq that has 5,400 locations in 32 countries. Although some debate its worth, the company is resolute about expansion. It is mapping plans to open stores in Australia, New Zealand, Britain, Mexico and Japan. In each locale, they'll pose the same question that's always been asked: Will this Southern-based doughnut sell here? "I have a healthy anxiety about every time we've gone into a new region," Livengood said. "It's not a lack of confidence, just a healthy fear."

Southern California was no exception. "We'd been warned" that Krispy Kreme might flop in the region, if for no other reason than 1,350 doughnut shops already battle it out in the market, said Reinis, the Krispy Kreme franchisee. "But we believed we had a better doughnut at a competitive price."

Those rivals include Winchell's Donut House, the West Coast's largest doughnut chain with 200 stores, most of them in California. Winchell's, a Santa Ana–based unit of Canada's Shato Holdings Ltd., quickly upgraded its product line to meet the challenge. Mom-and-pop operators, many of them Cambodian immigrants, also braced for the Krispy Kreme onslaught.

## SMALL IN THE SOUTHLAND

For all its exposure, Krispy Kreme accounts for less than 2 percent of Southern California doughnut shops. Yes, fans will drive out of their way to reach the nearest store, yet many consumers choose convenience and buy doughnuts from nearby vendors. In any case, "I don't think we're in competition with the mom-and-pop shops because they're serving other things than doughnuts," such as pastries and various drinks, Reinis said. Krispy Kreme, he said, focuses on selling doughnuts by the dozen, for about $5.99.

The main customers are the "office heroes, soccer moms and church socials" buying Krispy Kremes by the box, he said. Although the chain doesn't advertise, it does promote like heck. It routinely gives away doughnuts in marketing drives, peddles them in supermarkets such as Albertson's to create brand awareness and operates Krispy Kreme stands at Dodger Stadium. Now the company is aiming to develop smaller stores in cities such as San Francisco and New York, where real estate is at a premium.

That will keep Livengood's healthy fear alive. But, "to my absolute delight, it seems like every time we've moved into a new region, things have gone better than ever," he said. Will that hold true in say, Tokyo or London? "My instincts are it will continue," he said. "We know the buzz has already begun."

Finally, some retailing industry analysts are concerned: Wall Street has been little satisfied with the retailing industry's current return in recent years, instead choosing to reward the kind of capital appreciation promised by growth companies. The pressure to deliver double-digit earnings growth has caused many retailers to fall into the trap of opening more and more stores. Retail critics charge that CEOs have gotten caught up in the earnings guidance game and have pushed the envelope too far when it comes to adding square footage in an attempt to sustain growth and meet analysts' expectations. The pressure that the markets put on retail companies to hit earnings targets quarter after quarter and to buttress growth with new store openings is unrealistic, particularly in today's anemic economy. The focus for the next 12 months needs to be on bottom-line rather than top-line growth. Weaker competitors have been weeded out in many segments, making it tough for the remaining players—most of which are strong companies—to add market share and keep layering on double-digit EPS growth. While retail CEOs concede that Wall Street's pressure to grow is intense, many assume total responsibility for managing analysts' expectations and keeping the urge to chase short-term growth maneuvers at bay. It is up to the CEO to make analysts understand a company's long-term strategy.

## QUESTIONS

1. Where should Krispy Kreme go next? List the next ten countries they should enter in order of most viable. What criteria did you use to compose your list?

2. Visit their website and critique their approach to marketing their franchises. Also, visit Dunkin' Donuts' website.

3. How might Japan be different from the United States when it comes to doughnut demand? How might London differ from Southern California?

4. Critique Krispy Kreme's current growth plans.

Sources: James F. Peltz, "Full of Holes? Some Doubt Krispy Kreme's Growth Prospects," *Los Angeles Times,* June 8, 2003, p. C1. Used by permission of Tribune Media Services; and Susan Reda, "Feeding Wall Street's Growth Sharks," *Stores,* January 2003, p. 28–32.

# CASE 3-2 International Marketing Research at the Mayo Clinic

Mayo Clinic has a long international history and has been providing care to international patients since its inception. Despite its history and reputation, however, the marketing staff continues to monitor the international market to gauge the level of awareness, reputation, and attractiveness of Mayo Clinic around the world. Here's a look at how one institution has used word-of-mouth marketing to maintain its global reputation.

Marketing, as most formally defined, has historically not been a critical factor in delivering patients to Mayo Clinic. Indeed, the marketing department at Mayo Clinic has existed for only the past 15 years, and patients have been coming to us for care for more than a century. We like to believe the marketing department provides valuable information to physicians and their support staff, information that helps them deliver better care, highlights their patients' wants and needs, and educates them as to what's going on in the marketplace.

In reality, however, it's the providers themselves—the doctors, nurses, receptionists, and all the rest of the allied health staff—who bring in business by creating positive experiences for patients. Patients who leave Mayo Clinic highly satisfied with their care will return to their communities in the United States and elsewhere and say good things about us to their family and friends. And these family members and friends in turn travel to Mayo Clinic when they need tertiary or quaternary medical care. While we in marketing strive to provide excellent internal support, we know that it's the doctors and other care providers who have created and maintained a brand of health care excellence.

Despite the hype surrounding what has been presented as the highly lucrative international marketplace, "international" is not something new at Mayo Clinic. We know from experience and research that "international" is a part of who we are, as well as part of how the market defines us. Nearly 100 years ago, our founders, a family of physicians named "Mayo," created an international legacy by traveling around the world to compare notes and surgical approaches with physicians across the globe. In some cases, they even returned with international patients who were in need of additional expertise. As in so many other areas of our medical practice, we continue in their traditions.

In recent years, however, we've begun to more thoroughly study our international patient population in particular and the international marketplace in general. Our studies fall into a few categories and grow in number in proportion to our understanding (or perhaps our greater understanding of how much we don't know) of the international marketplace.

First of all, we track our international patient trends rather carefully. This seems like an obvious place to start. But as in most data tracking, the value of the concept is significantly more straightforward than the logistics of acquiring consistently reliable data. Internal data systems must be coordinated—a significant undertaking for any institution, and particularly hard, we believe, when dealing with a large and complicated infrastructure. To give a simple example, data fields must be made uniform—not just on one data system, but on all of them. Rather than a free-text field, for example, that allows a registrant to enter Venzuela, or Venosuela,

or Vensuala, or maybe even Venezuela, we push for a pre-defined field that gives us standardized information.

We monitor our international data by the quarter, carefully watching trends over time by country or region, tracking significant changes in volume, hospitalization rates, and percentage of new patients out of any given market. We know, for example, that we have between 9,000 and 10,000 patients, depending on the year, coming to us from more than 160 different countries annually. Some are third-generation patients—maybe their grandfather was cured here in the 1930s—and others are brand new. Some are our neighbors in Ontario or Monterrey; others come all the way from Indonesia. We know that some markets are significantly less predictable than others, and some countries deliver more "new" patients than others. We probe further to figure out why.

Second, we conduct research with our internal salespeople—the physicians and their support staff who deliver care to our international patients. Through carefully moderated focus groups, we identify the things that are going smoothly as well as the barriers to providing excellent care. And where appropriate, we make recommendations for change.

Third, just as with our U.S.-based patients, we conduct both quantitative and qualitative research in the international marketplace. This includes research with our patients, international physicians, and international health care consumers, designed to help us understand why people choose to leave their own communities for health care, why some of them come to Mayo Clinic, and why others do not. We work hard to understand how health care decisions are made, so we can better assist decision makers, physicians, and their staff in providing care. We position ourselves to perhaps offer counsel on where to best expend valuable institutional resources, both human and financial.

## GLOBAL MARKET RESEARCH

The marketing department conducts periodic and ongoing patient satisfaction studies with our international patients, measuring their assessment of various aspects of the care we provide. To date, we have surveyed nearly 1,500 patients in 20 countries, in four different languages. As any market researcher knows, sound patient satisfaction research requires great attention to detail to ensure reliable data. We find, not surprisingly, that international data collection offers significant additional challenges:

*The quality of our own data.* The name and address fields designed for clean U.S. addresses often are not sufficient to hold reliable international detail. If we want to do it right, we must manually "clean" thousands of patient records before fielding our studies.

*Varying quality of international postal and telecommunications infrastructure.* This variance can create significant problems for either phone or mail surveys; consequently, international studies take a lot more time than U.S.-based studies and require much more patience.

**Exhibit 1**

Which was most important in your decision to choose Mayo Clinic?

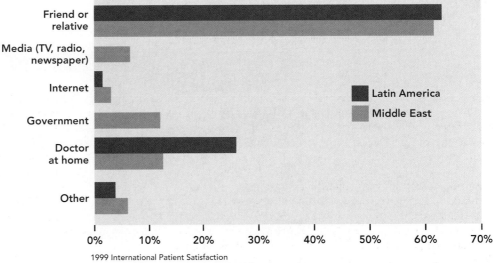

1999 International Patient Satisfaction
*N* = 331 Middle Eastern patients; 755 Latin American patients

*Cultural dynamics.* In some countries, individuals may be suspicious of an international call; in others, they may spend a lot of time outside of their homes. In still others, a nonfamily "gatekeeper" must be diplomatically convinced to transfer the call to the targeted respondents. These cultural dynamics pose further delays and require special sensitivities.

*High standards for quality.* Our own standards for quality compel us to maintain high quality language- and culture-specific fielding of our various research projects. These studies, whether managed internally or through an external vendor, require more oversight than we are accustomed to with U.S.-based research.

Despite these challenges, however, this international research has taught us a lot. International patient satisfaction studies demonstrate that the key driver of our patients' satisfaction seems to hold across borders. This is excellent care—manifested by listening, explaining, and thoroughness on the part of Mayo Clinic physicians. Other factors in the health care experience are important—for example, quality of language interpretation and waiting times—but they don't consistently correlate with overall satisfaction.

The power of word of mouth is also confirmed in the international marketplace. Most of our international patients indicate that friends or relatives provided their most important influence in choosing Mayo Clinic. This finding reminds us of our most powerful marketing "tool"—satisfied patients who say good things about Mayo Clinic and influence others' health care decisions. Exhibit 1 indicates the factors influencing choice of Mayo Clinic by patients from Latin America and the Middle East.

We conducted formal focus groups with international patients and non-patients in six cities around the world, probing to learn more about how those populations make health care decisions, and whether the process is the same or different from U.S. health care consumers. As it turns out, for most aspects of decision making, the process is very similar to that of U.S. consumers. However, for a few others the process is quite different.

The areas where we've found the most difference across borders relate to the role of health insurance. We've been involved in three cosponsored international research projects that have taught us some good lessons and demonstrated that international health

care insurance is as different from that in the United States as it is across countries and regions. Furthermore, many assumptions we take for granted in the U.S. market—for example, name recognition—simply don't hold in certain international markets. Exhibit 2 is a graph of responses from a satisfaction study of our patients from Latin America and the Middle East, showing the different history of Mayo Clinic brand awareness in those regions

We weren't surprised to learn that Mayo Clinic awareness among our patients was much more recent in the Middle East than in Latin America. From other studies, however, we have learned that awareness among nonpatients—even those who have purchased health insurance policies that offer them Mayo Clinic care as a benefit—is not as strong.

The international health care insurance market is expanding rapidly, and many providers view this expansion as a significant opportunity to glean additional patients from outside the United States. Commercial and noncommercial contracts comprise a significant body of business in U.S. health care. If this business could be expanded to provide patients from markets outside the United States, all the better. We know, however, that health care systems vary significantly from country to country, and knowledge and use of health insurance vary even more. To study these differences in detail, we cosponsored two quantitative studies of health care insurance policyholders—in particular, holders of policies that offer some degree of coverage for care at Mayo Clinic.

The first study consisted of face-to-face interviews with 400 policyholders in a particular country and delivered a great deal of information regarding policyholders' preferences, health care behavior, and demographics. In this country, as throughout most of the world, the public health care system exists as a universal "safety net" for all citizens. Even in markets where the private insurance market has expanded, the public system continues to offer care for all citizens. This means that if a private insurance policy does not offer adequate coverage, especially for high-cost procedures, the public system is used to reduce the consumer's financial burden.

The private policy might cover, for example, access to primary and secondary care at private rather than public clinics as well as the price of a private room, or the option of receiving care at a more upscale facility. But for high-cost, life-threatening proce-

## Exhibit 2
How long ago did you first hear of Mayo Clinic?

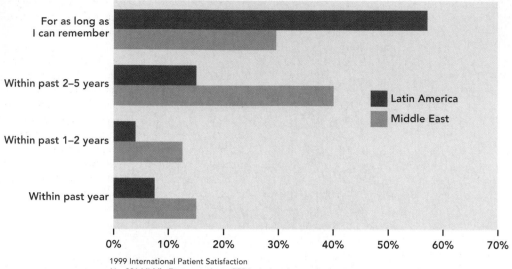

1999 International Patient Satisfaction
N = 331 Middle Eastern patients; 755 Latin American patients

dures, the co-pay or deductible for having these procedures conducted exclusively in the private sector remains significant. The end result, of course, is that the lower cost procedures are transferred to the private system, while the higher cost procedures remain in the public safety net. The implication for U.S. tertiary providers is that, while private insurance might reduce some of the financial risk for traveling out of country for care, in many cases the risk is not completely eliminated. Therefore, the policies might not deliver the volume of patients initially anticipated.

Other factors, such as a lack of brand awareness and limited perceived need for U.S. medical care, may be impediments to attracting patients in the international health care insurance market. In our first study, when we probed for brand awareness among those 400 consumers who had purchased a health insurance policy touting Mayo Clinic coverage as a benefit, we discovered no unaided recall

of that coverage as a benefit of the policy. (See Exhibit 3.) In an aided list, Mayo Clinic coverage was ranked as the least important benefit of the policy, on a par with eyeglass coverage at the bottom of the list.

Furthermore, when we asked policyholders to name a leading medical center in the United States, most (72 percent) didn't know a single one. Twenty-five percent (25 percent) named Mayo Clinic, and the other 2 percent named other U.S. medical centers. We were not particularly surprised that citizens in the studied country were not familiar with Mayo Clinic. However, we were surprised that policyholders who had purchased an insurance product that very publicly advertised the Mayo Clinic benefit were unable to name Mayo Clinic as a leading U.S. medical center.

As it turned out, many of these policyholders had no intention of leaving their home country for medical care. They were buying

## Exhibit 3
Recall of plan benefits (unaided)

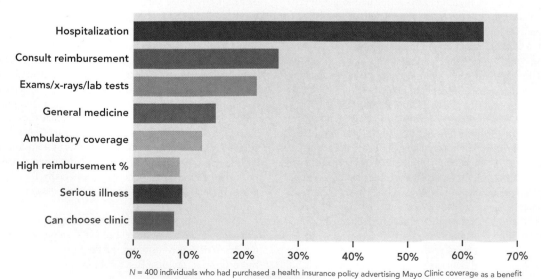

N = 400 individuals who had purchased a health insurance policy advertising Mayo Clinic coverage as a benefit

insurance to facilitate care in the more desirable private system. Furthermore, most felt that the health care in their own country was very good and that there would be little if any reason to ever leave home to obtain care elsewhere. We've encountered this phenomenon repeatedly in our research with U.S. patients. Most believe in the abilities of their own doctor and feel very confident about medical care in their own community. Even though "quality" may be regionally or culturally defined, almost everyone considers his or her doctor to be a good one.

A second cosponsored study consisted of 353 telephone interviews with individuals who had purchased a health care insurance policy specifically for international coverage. Once again, confidence in local care was very high—in fact, significantly higher than in the country of our first study. Nonetheless, this group of individuals had purchased a product that offered them coverage for medical care outside their home country, should they decide it was necessary or appropriate. In this study, our aided brand recognition among policyholders was higher than in the first; when asked directly whether they'd heard of Mayo Clinic, 75 percent responded affirmatively. But when asked unaided to name the best medical centers in the United States, the vast majority (nearly 70 percent) of policyholders indicated they didn't know. And while the majority had heard of Mayo Clinic, fewer than 10 percent were aware of any benefit of their health insurance policy that related to Mayo Clinic.

In both of these studies, we learned substantially more about the nature of international insurance agreements, policyholders' wants and needs, and their disposition toward traveling out of country for medical care. But we also learned that the knowledge of our brand is limited outside the United States and that a high number of policyholders does not necessarily translate into a high number of patients. Our research has taught us to be more selective, to be cautious in expending significant resources to pursue insurance arrangements, and to conduct further research to expand our understanding.

## THE FUTURE

We anticipate that "international" will continue to be part of who we are at Mayo Clinic. Our doctors, hailing from all corners of the globe, will continue to collaborate with their colleagues around the world. Mayo Clinic researchers will conduct clinical trials in collaboration with researchers on many continents. Our students and residents will continue to offer us rich diversity, as Mayo international alumni now number 1,500, representing 67 countries. But most important, Mayo Clinic will strive to provide the best medical care possible to those patients around the world who need us the most.

To support that mission, those of us in "marketing" will continue to support our medical staff by studying our patients' wants, needs, preferences, and behavior patterns, and learning all that we can about the ever-changing, rich and diverse worldwide health care market. In the end, outstanding medical care and sensitive service to patients and families will be our most productive marketing strategy, because it creates positive word-of-mouth about something very important—health care. As the stories of satisfied patients churn—sometimes for decades—in the minds of their friends and family, Mayo Clinic remains an option if they ever need the care we offer.

## QUESTION

1. Assume you are the new marketing vice president at the Mayo Clinic. The CEO and the board have decided to expand their international sales revenues by 100 percent over the next five years. Write a memo to your staff outlining the marketing research that will be needed to support such a strategy. Be specific about sources of secondary data and the best places and media for gathering primary data. Also, be specific about the best methods to use.

---

Source: Misty Hathaway and Kent Seltman, "International Marketing Research at the Mayo Clinic," *Marketing Health Services,* Winter 2001, 21(4), pp. 18–23. Used with permission of American Marketing Association.

# CASE 3–3 Swifter, Higher, Stronger, Dearer

Television and sport are perfect partners. Each has made the other richer. But is the alliance really so good for sport?

Back in 1948, the BBC, Britain's public broadcasting corporation, took a fateful decision. It paid a princely £15,000 (£27,000 in today's money) for the right to telecast the Olympic Games to a domestic audience. It was the first time a television network had paid the International Olympic Committee (IOC, the body that runs the Games) for the privilege. But not the last. The rights to the 1996 Summer Olympics, which opened in Atlanta on July 19, 1996, raised $900 million from broadcasters round the world. And the American television rights to the Olympiads up to and including 2008 have been bought by America's NBC network for an amazing $3.6 billion (see Exhibit 1).

The Olympics are only one of the sporting properties that have become hugely valuable to broadcasters. Sport takes up a growing share of screen time (as those who are bored by it know all too well). When you consider the popularity of the world's great tournaments, that is hardly surprising. *Sportsfests* generate audiences beyond the wildest dreams of television companies for anything else. According to Nielsen Media Research, the number of Americans watching the Super Bowl, the main annual football championship, averaged 94 million. The top eight television programs in America are all sporting events. Some 3 billion people watched some part of the 2000 Olympiad—over half of mankind.

The reason television companies love sport is not merely that billions want to tele-gawk at ever-more-wonderful sporting feats. Sport also has a special quality that makes it unlike almost any other sort of television program: immediacy. Miss seeing a particular episode of, say, *ER,* and you can always catch the repeat and

enjoy it just as much. Miss seeing your team beat hell out of its biggest rival, and the replay will leave you cold. "A live sporting event loses almost all its value as the final whistle goes," says Steve Barnett, author of a British book on sport. The desire to watch sport when it is happening, not hours afterward, is universal: A study in South Korea by Spectrum, a British consultancy, found that live games get 30 percent of the audience while recordings get less than 5 percent.

This combination of popularity and immediacy has created a symbiotic relationship between sport and television in which each is changing the other. As Stephen Wenn, of Canada's Wilfrid Laurier University, puts it, television and the money it brings have had an enormous impact on the Olympic Games, including on the timing of events and their location. For instance, an Asian Olympics poses a problem for American networks: Viewers learn the results on the morning news.

The money that television has brought into professional basketball has put some of the top players among the world's highest-paid entertainers: A few are getting multiyear contracts worth over $100 million. Rugby has begun to be reorganized to make it more television friendly; other sports will follow. And, though soccer and American football draw the largest audiences, television has also promoted the popularity of sports that stir more local passions: rugby league in Australia, cricket in India, table tennis in China, snooker in Britain.

What is less often realized is that sport is also changing television. To assuage the hunger for sports, new channels are being launched at a tremendous pace. In America, ESPN, a cable network owned by Capital Cities/ABC, started a 24-hour sports news network in 1997;

## Exhibit 1
Chariots for Hire: Olympic Broadcast Rights Fees,* $bn (world totals)

Source: International Olympic Committee. Used by permission of the International Olympic Committee.

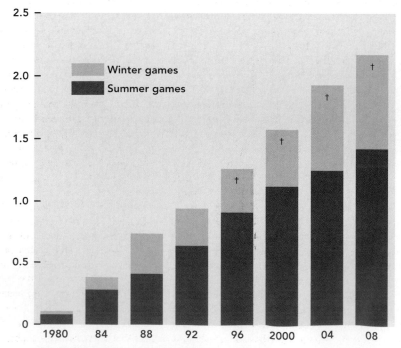

* Rights for 2000 to 2008 Games negotiated to 2012.
† Two years earlier

in Britain, BSkyB, a satellite broadcaster partly owned by Rupert Murdoch, has three sports channels. Because people seem more willing to pay to watch sport on television than to pay for any other kind of programming, sport has become an essential part of the business strategy of television empire-builders such as Mr. Murdoch. Nobody in the world understands the use of sports as a bait for viewers better than he.

In particular, sport suggests an answer to one of the big problems that will face television companies in the future: How can viewers, comfortable with their old analog sets, be persuaded to part with the hefty price of a new digital set and a subscription to an untried service? The answer is to create an exclusive chance to watch a desirable event, or to use the hundreds of channels that digital television provides to offer more variety of sports coverage than analog television can offer. This ploy is not new. "Radio broadcasts of boxing were once used to promote the sale of radios, and baseball to persuade people to buy television sets," points out Richard Burton, a sports marketing specialist at the Lundquist College of Business at Oregon University. In the next few years, the main new outlet for sports programs will be digital television.

## GOING FOR GOLD

To understand how these multiple effects have come about, go back to those vast sums that television companies are willing to pay. In America, according to Neal Weinstock of Weinstock Media Analysis, total spending on sports rights by television companies is about $2 billion a year. Easily the most valuable rights are for American football. One of the biggest sporting coups in the United States was the purchase by Fox, owned by Mr. Murdoch's News Corporation, of the rights to four years of National Football League games for $1.6 billion, snatching them from CBS. Rights for baseball, basketball, and ice hockey are also in the billion-dollar range.

Americans are rare in following four main sports rather than one. America is also uncommon in having no publicly owned networks. As a result, bidding wars in other countries, though just as fierce as in America, are different in two ways: They are often fought between public broadcasters and new upstarts, many of them pay channels, and they are usually about soccer.

Nothing better illustrates the change taking place in the market for soccer rights than the vast deal struck in 1997 by Kirch, a German group owned by a secretive Bavarian media mogul. The group spent $2.2 billion for the world's biggest soccer-broadcasting rights: to show the finals of the World Cup in 2002 and 2006 outside America. That is over six times more than the amount paid for the rights to the World Cups of 1990, 1994, and 1998.

Such vast bids gobble up a huge slice of a television company's budget. In America, reckons London Economics, a British consultancy, sport accounts for around 15 percent of all television-program spending. For some television companies, the share is much larger. BSkyB spends £100 million ($155 million) a year on sports, about a third of its programming budget.

This seems to pose a threat to public broadcasting, for, in any bidding war outside America, public broadcasting companies are generally the losers. A consortium of mainly public broadcasters bought the rights to the 1990 to 1998 World Cups for a total of $344 million. This time around, the consortium raised its bid to around $1.8 billion, and still lost. Public broadcasters often do not have the money to compete. In Britain, the BBC spends about 4 percent of its program budget on sport in a non-Olympic year, about £15 million a year less than BSkyB.

The problem is that the value of sport to viewers ("consumer surplus," as economists would put it) is much larger than the value of most other sorts of programming. Public broadcasters have no way to benefit from the extra value that a big sporting event offers viewers. But with subscription television and with pay TV, where viewers are charged for each event, the television company will directly collect the value viewers put on being able to watch.

Because of this, many people (especially in Europe) worry that popular sports will increasingly be available only on subscription television, which could, they fear, erode the popular support upon which public broadcasters depend. In practice, these worries seem excessive. Although far more sport will be shown on subscription television, especially outside America's vast advertising market, the most popular events are likely to remain freely available for many years to come, for two reasons.

First, those who own the rights to sporting events are rarely just profit-maximizers: They also have an interest in keeping the appeal of their sport as broad as possible. They may therefore refuse to sell to the highest bidder. For example, the IOC turned down a $2 billion bid from Mr. Murdoch's News Corporation for the European broadcasting rights to the Olympic Games between 2000 and 2008 in favor of a lower bid from a group of public broadcasters. Sometimes, as with the sale of World Cup rights to Kirch, the sellers may stipulate that the games be aired on "free" television.

Second, the economics of televising sport means that the biggest revenues are not necessarily earned by tying up exclusive rights. Steven Bornstein, the boss of ESPN, argues that exclusive deals to big events are "not in our long-term commercial interest." Because showing sport on "free" television maximizes the audience, some advertisers will be willing to pay a huge premium for the big occasion. So will sponsors who want their names to be seen emblazoned on players' shirts or on billboards around the field.

It is not only a matter of audience size. Sport is also the most efficient way to reach one of the world's most desirable audiences from an advertiser's point of view: young men with cash to spend. Although the biggest audiences of young men are watching general television, sporting events draw the highest concentrations. Thus, advertisers of products such as beer, cars, and sports shoes can pay mainly for the people they most want to attract.

There are other ways in which sport can be indirectly useful to the networks. A slot in a summer game is a wonderful opportunity to promote a coming autumn show. A popular game wipes out the audience share of the competition. And owning the rights to an event allows a network plenty of scope to entertain corporate grandees who may then become advertisers.

For the moment, though, advertising revenue is the main recompense that television companies get for their huge investments in sport. Overall, according to *Broadcasting & Cable,* a trade magazine, sport generated $3.5 billion, or 10 percent, of total television advertising revenues in America last year. The biggest purchasers of sports rights by far in America are the national networks. NBC alone holds more big sports rights than any other body has held in the history of television. It can, obviously, recoup some of the bill by selling advertising: For a 30-second slot during the Super Bowl, NBC asked for $1.2 million.

Such deals, however, usually benefit the networks indirectly rather than directly. The Super Bowl is a rarity: It has usually made a profit for the network that airs it. "Apart from the Super Bowl, the World Series and probably the current Olympics, the big sports don't usually make money for the networks," says Arthur Gruen of Wilkowsky Gruen, a media consultancy. "But they are a boon for their affiliate stations, which can sell their advertising slots for two or three times as much as other slots." Although Fox lost money on its NFL purchase, it won the loyalty of affiliate stations (especially important for a new network) and made a splash.

Almost everywhere else, the biggest growth in revenues from showing sports will increasingly come from subscriptions or pay-per-view arrangements. The versatility and huge capacity of digital broadcasting make it possible to give subscribers all sorts of new and lucrative services.

In America, DirectTV and Primestar, two digital satellite broadcasters, have been tempting subscribers with packages of sporting events from distant parts of the country. "They have been creating season tickets for all the main events, costing $100–150 per season per sport," says John Mansell, a senior analyst with Paul Kagan, a California consultancy. In Germany, DF1, a satellite company jointly owned by Kirch and BSkyB, has the rights to show Formula One motor racing. It allows viewers to choose to follow particular teams, so that Ferrari fanatics can follow their drivers, and to select different camera angles.

In Italy, Telepiu, which launched digital satellite television in 1997, offers viewers a package in September that allows them to buy a season ticket to live matches played by one or more teams in the top Italian soccer leagues. The system's "electronic turnstile" is so sophisticated that it can shut off reception for subscribers living in the catchment area for a home game, to assuage clubs' worries that they will lose revenue from supporters at the gate. In fact, top Italian clubs usually have to lock out their fanatical subscribers to avoid overcapacity.

Most skillful of all at using sports rights to generate subscription revenue is BSkyB. It signed an exclusive contract with the English Premier League that has been the foundation of its success. Some of those who know BSkyB well argue that £5 billion of the business's remarkable capital value of £8 billion is attributable to the profitability of its soccer rights.

## WINNER TAKE ALL

Just as the purchase of sporting rights enriches television companies, so their sale has transformed the finances of the sports lucky enough to be popular with viewers. On the whole, the biggest beneficiaries have not been the clubs and bodies that run sports, but the players. In the same way as rising revenues from films are promptly dissipated in vast salaries to stars in Hollywood, so in sport the money coming in from television soon flows out in heftier payments to players.

In America, the market for sportsmen is well developed and the cost of players tends to rise with the total revenues of the main sporting organizations. Elsewhere, the market is newer and so a bigger slice of the revenues tends to stick to the television companies. "The big difference between sports and movies is the operating margins," says Chris Akers, chairman of Caspian, a British media group, and an old hand at rights negotiations. "Hollywood majors have per-subscriber deals. No sports federation has yet done such a deal."

Guided by the likes of Mr. Akers, they soon will. Telepiu's latest three-year soccer contract gives the television firm enough revenue to cover its basic costs, guarantees the soccer league a minimum sum, and then splits the takings down the middle. In Britain, BSkyB is locked in dispute with the Premier League over the terms of the second half of its rights deal: Should the league then be able to opt for half the revenue from each subscriber on top of or instead of a fixed hunk of net profits?

The logical next step would be for some clubs or leagues to set up their own pay-television systems, distributing their games directly by satellite or cable. A few people in British soccer are starting to look with interest at America's local sports networks, such as the successful Madison Square Garden cable network, and to wonder whether Europe might move the same way.

If it does, not all teams will benefit equally. In America, football has an elaborate scheme to spread revenues from national television across teams. But in other sports, including baseball, the wealth and size of a team's local market mean large differences in rights from local television. The New York Yankees make almost $50 million a year from local television rights, says Brian Schechter, a Canadian media analyst. At the other end of the scale, the Kansas City Royals make $4 million to $5 million a year.

Not all players benefit equally, either. Television has brought to sport the "winner-take-all" phenomenon. It does not cost substantially more to stage a televised championship game than a run-of-the-week, untelevised match. But the size of the audience, and therefore the revenue generated, may be hugely different. As a result, players good enough to be in the top games will earn vastly more than those slightly less good, who play to smaller crowds.

## THE REFEREE'S WHISTLE

The lure of money is already altering sport and will change it more. Increasingly, games will be reorganized to turn them into better television. British rugby-union officials are squabbling over the spoils from television rights. Rugby league, whose audiences had been dwindling, won a contract worth £87 million over five years from BSkyB earlier this year in exchange for switching its games from winter to summer. Purists were aghast.

Other reorganizations for the benefit of television will surely come. Mr. Murdoch wants to build a rugby superleague, allowing the best teams around the world to play each other. A European superleague for soccer is possible. "At the moment, Manchester United plays AC Milan every 25 years: it's a joke," complains one enthusiast.

Sports traditionalists resist changing their ways for the likes of Mr. Murdoch. So far, the big sporting bodies have generally held out against selling exclusive pay-television rights to their crown jewels, and have sometimes deliberately favored public broadcasters. Regulators have helped them, intervening in some countries to limit exclusive deals with pay-television groups. Britain passed a law to stop subscription channels tying up exclusive rights to some big events, such as the Wimbledon tennis championship. In Australia, a court threw out News Corporation's attempt to build a rugby superleague as the lynchpin of its pay-television strategy.

The real monopolists are not the media companies, however, but the teams. Television companies can play off seven or eight Hollywood studios against each other. But most countries have only one national soccer league, and a public that loves soccer above all other sports. In the long run, the players and clubs hold most of the cards. The television companies are more likely to be their servants than their masters.

## QUESTIONS

1. The following are the prices paid for the American television broadcasting rights of the summer Olympics since 1980: Moscow—NBC agreed to pay $85 million; 1984 in Los Angeles—ABC paid $225 million; 1988 in Seoul—NBC paid

$300 million; 1992 in Barcelona—NBC paid $401 million; 1996 through 2008—NBC will pay $3.6 billion; 2010—NBC will pay $820 million; 2012—NBC will pay $1.18 billion. You have been charged with the responsibility of determining the IOC and local Olympic Committee's asking prices for the 2012 television broadcast rights for five different markets: Japan, China, Australia, the European Union, and Brazil. Determine a price for each and justify your decisions.

2. Your instructor may assign you to represent either the IOC or any one of the television networks in each of the five countries that have been asked to bid for the broadcast rights for the 2012 Games. Prepare to negotiate prices and other organizational details.

3. The World Football League (WFL), a joint venture between the National Football League (NFL) and Fox Television (owned by Rupert Murdoch's News Corporation), has offered you the Edinburgh, Scotland, Claymores franchise. Your Scottish Claymores, should you choose to invest, will be playing against the other five WFL teams from London, Barcelona, Amsterdam, Frankfurt, and Dusseldorf. What would you be willing to pay for the Claymores? The interested investor will note that a previous incarnation of the WFL with three teams in Europe and seven in the United States folded in its second season in 1992 having lost $50 million.

Sources: Adapted from *The Economist,* July 20, 1996, pp. 17–19. Also see Mark Hyman, "The Jets: Worth a Gazillion?" *Business Week,* December 6, 1999, pp. 99–100; Mark Hyman, "Putting the Squeeze on the Media," *Business Week,* December 11, 2000, p. 75; www.worldleague.com/claymores/; and Alan Abrahamson, "NBC Wins Rights to 2010, 2012 Olympics," *Los Angeles Times,* June 7, 2003, p. C1.

# cases 4

## DEVELOPING GLOBAL MARKETING STRATEGIES

# CASE 4–1 Boeing's Product Development Stumble

When Boeing publicly unveiled an artist's rendering of the Sonic Cruiser 21 months ago, the company bragged that its new plane "will change the way the world flies." Capable of transporting 225 passengers at close to the speed of sound, the Sonic Cruiser is the first original jetliner design in 50 years. It looks like nothing else in the skies today. Protruding behind the cockpit are two small wings, known as canards. A large delta wing in the rear replaces the usual swept-back appendages. A pair of powerful engines is mounted in back too, and completing the Star Trek look are two vertical fins that are used in place of the conventional tail and rudder. If anything could lift air travel from mass to class, this was going to be it.

But the Sonic Cruiser won't be taking off after all. The problem is, no one seems to want to buy the plane. Not a single airline has stepped up to say that the time saved by flying so fast is worth the higher price, greater fuel costs, and schedule disruption. So Boeing is backing away from the project, laying the blame on a weak market and shifting customer preferences. An official announcement is expected as soon as year-end.

In place of the Sonic Cruiser, Boeing likely will offer a far more conventional plane, one that will cost less to build, require fewer changes in service procedures, and burn up to 20 percent less fuel. Like every other commercial jetliner (except the money-losing SST), the new model will be a linear descendant of the B-47 that first flew after World War II. In other words, it won't have rocket-ship styling or sound-barrier speed, but it will be much more marketable in today's awful business conditions. Boeing blandly calls it the "super-efficient airplane."

In interviews in mid-November, top Boeing executives insisted they were still trying to make up their minds about which plane to build. "The process of getting to a new airplane is a tortuous road," says chairman and CEO Phil Condit. "By the end of the year we will have arrived at a decision about where we think we ought to go." In fact, the decision has already been made. While Condit and others believe that some airline travelers are willing to pay a premium for better service—an argument for the Sonic Cruiser—they concede that airlines have never been in such bad shape financially. It is clear that customers will opt for the more economical plane. "With the slowing global economy and the terrorist overhang, the airlines clearly need to simplify their fleet," says Alan Mulally, the head of Boeing's Commercial Airplanes. "Their cost structure just leads them to something that will improve operating efficiency."

Scrapping, or at least delaying, the Sonic Cruiser may be a no-brainer from a business standpoint, but it could turn out to be a public-relations disaster. After all, it was Boeing that created heightened expectations for the plane in the first place, then failed to dampen them when it became clear that the plane was simply unsalable. Worse, the Sonic Cruiser will go down as yet another failed airplane for a company that has had its share of them lately—notably the Joint Strike Fighter and the 747X super-jumbo—raising suspicions that Boeing has lost both its courage and its touch. And perhaps most significant, it will be a huge boost for archrival Airbus, which has been raining on the Sonic Cruiser's parade from the start.

The questions surrounding the ambitious project aren't likely to die along with the airplane. Was the Sonic Cruiser ever seriously intended for production, or was it partly a paper plane aimed at keeping Airbus off balance? If it was for real, why didn't Boeing grasp its shortcomings more quickly? And why has the company kept the project alive for the past several months when it was clear that the futuristic plane was on life support?

The delay is especially odd given Condit's efforts to inject business discipline into commercial aviation and insulate the rest of the company from that sector's ups and downs. Since taking over in 1996, the down-to-earth Condit has strengthened Boeing's investments in military aircraft, missile systems, and space-related businesses like the space shuttle. In 2001 he moved Boeing's corporate headquarters to Chicago to get it out from the shadow of the plane-building business in Seattle. The upshot is that in 2003, commercial planes will account for less than half of Boeing's revenue, versus 75 percent in 1996.

The downturn in air travel is taking its toll on the company nonetheless, and most analysts don't expect an immediate upturn. Used to building up to 48 airplanes a month, Boeing is now assembling fewer than 24. So after record profits in the past two years, Boeing's per-share earnings are expected to fall more than 20 percent for 2002 and another 20 percent-plus in 2003. Even a war with Iraq won't help Boeing's sales of big-ticket defense systems, says Condit.

## Exhibit 1
### Boeing's 2003 Product Line

| Model | Seating Capacity | Range (miles) | 2003 Price ($ millions) |
|---|---|---|---|
| 717-200 (formerly MD-95) | 106 | 1800 | 35.0–39.5 |
| 737-600 | 126 | 2600 | 40.5–49.0 |
| 737-900 | 189 | 3100 | 60.0–68.5 |
| 747-400 | 420 | 8300 | 183.0–211.0 |
| 757-200 | 194 | 4500 | 72.5–80.5 |
| 757-300 | 290 | 4000 | 81.0–89.5 |
| 767-400ER | 269 | 7000 | 125.5–138.5 |
| 777-300 | 328 | 8300 | 177.0–203.5 |

Despite initial cheers from aviation experts, the Sonic Cruiser turned out to be the wrong plane at the wrong time. World air traffic has fallen nearly 11 percent in the past two years, and the airlines are expected to lose nearly $10 billion in 2002 after dropping $12 billion in 2001. Airlines everywhere are in disarray as the future of air travel turns into a tug of war between traditional, full-service, hub-and-spoke carriers and upstart, no-frills, point-to-point airlines. "Airlines have no choice but to reinvent themselves," says Nicole Piasecki, Boeing's vice president for strategy.

The Sonic Cruiser might have only added to the industry's problems. Its shape, speed, and cost would require air carriers to do everything from rewriting their schedules to overhauling their maintenance and service procedures. At the same time they would be forced to sell more full-priced fares to pay higher operating costs at a time when business and leisure travelers want bargain rates. For all its glamour, the plane just never seemed to make much business sense. Says equity analyst Nicolas Owens of Morningstar: "I think if Boeing built this thing, it would have become its Vietnam."

Even its birth was star-crossed. Boeing announced plans for the plane on March 29, 2001, the same day that it acknowledged canceling development of a larger version of the venerable 747, known as the 747X, which was to compete with Airbus's super-jumbo A380—a plane that will carry 25 percent more passengers than the 747 and is scheduled for delivery to airlines in 2005. The timing immediately suggested to some that the Sonic Cruiser news was released as much to take the sting out of the 747X failure as to launch a genuinely viable program. In the months to come Boeing would admit that it had announced the plane up to two years earlier than planned because it was ready to show the plane to customers and knew the news would leak out.

As theater, though, the announcement was a smash. Shaped like an arrow, the Sonic Cruiser was going to be plenty fast—up to Mach 0.98, or about 650 miles per hour. That would make it 15 percent to 20 percent faster than every other airliner in service except the Concorde SST, which flies at Mach 2. In both mission and appearance, it was about as far from the chunky, double-deck A380 as any plane could be, and it made a forceful statement about Boeing's product philosophy: Smaller planes flying point to point—that is, from one city to another—would be more valuable than giant carriers busing passengers between congested hubs.

Airline executives rushed to endorse the new plane. CEO Don Carty of American Airlines was quoted as saying, "We obviously see a use for that airplane. It can radically change our business productivity." An ebullient Richard Branson of Virgin Atlantic declared he wanted to order as many as six of the first planes. Airbus, meanwhile, publicly disparaged the project in what would turn out to be a long-running critique. Senior vice president John Leahy said his company had already looked at a similar concept and found that it would cost too much more to operate than a conventional plane. He was right, of course, but it would be months before Boeing's customers—faced with shrinking numbers of air travelers—would reach a similar conclusion.

Boeing had been planning the plane for years. As early as 1995 a working group—consisting of researchers in materials, design, engineering, and manufacturing—began exploring new flying concepts. Initially known as the Airplane Creation Process Strategy team, it was renamed 20XX and charged with finding advanced technologies to design and build airplanes. Four years later a team of about a dozen engineers began work on a new airplane concept, and by fall 2000 they had developed a design that looked very much like the Sonic Cruiser. The new plane was code-named Project Glacier.

Early in 2001, Alan Mulally traveled around the world talking to international air carriers about what new planes Boeing should add to its product line. He mentioned several options, including the 747X. But Mulally really got the airlines' attention when he said Boeing could develop a plane that flew as fast as Mach 0.98 and wouldn't consume any more fuel than an existing airliner. The plane would allow full-fare-paying business travelers, for whom time is more important than money, to cut an hour off a six-hour flight to Europe or two hours from a trip to Asia. At the same time it would enable airlines to squeeze extra daily flights out of their fleet. If the Sonic Cruiser shaved two hours from a 13-hour flight from New York to Tokyo, it could be turned around and flown home the same day, thus making a roundtrip in 24 hours.

Through spring 2001, Boeing continued to feed anticipation of the new airplane. General Electric, Pratt & Whitney, and Rolls-Royce got to work on the new-generation engines that would be required to propel it. At the Paris Air Show in June, a Boeing supplier predicted that more than 500 Sonic Cruisers could be sold in the next ten to 15 years. Mulally did him one better. He declared that with all of the short- and long-range derivatives, Sonic Cruiser sales could reach several thousand airplanes in the next two decades. Airbus's Leahy, meanwhile, gave Boeing another public poke by declaring that the new plane would be neither as fast nor as efficient as Boeing claimed.

By the summer Boeing completed what would be the first of four rounds of meetings with potential airline customers, which were clamoring for a new plane. Engineers tinkered with the initial design. Having discarded the traditional airliner shape, all but unchanged for five decades, they conducted studies to determine the best location for the landing gear and engine air inlets to limit the chances of damage from foreign objects. They also discovered that the position of the canards would hinder the location of loading ramps and made plans to move them.

Meanwhile, weak economic conditions around the world had already begun to depress airline travel, and after Sept. 11 it collapsed entirely. Almost overnight airlines doubled the number of planes put in mothballs, from 1,000 to nearly 2,000—more than 12 percent of the world's fleet. Mulally announced that as many as 30,000 Boeing employees at Commercial Airplanes might lose their jobs by the end of 2002 because of canceled or rescheduled orders.

Yet Boeing pushed ahead with the Sonic Cruiser. It completed the first round of wind tunnel tests and released new details about the materials—carbon fiber composites and titanium—that would be used in place of aluminum to reduce weight and thus fuel consumption.

By the end of 2001 the first signs of doubt about the project began to creep into Boeing's public statements. Executives acknowledged the existence of another new airplane, code-named Project Yellowstone, that was being developed alongside Sonic Cruiser. It would be the same size—about 225 seats—and would also be built of lightweight composites. But since it would fly at only Mach 0.8 to 0.9, it would burn up to 20 percent less fuel and make less noise. Originally designed simply to demonstrate the effect of Sonic Cruiser technology on a conventional design, it would quickly assume a life of its own. Yellowstone was the ultimate low-cost spread, designed to be cheap rather than fast.

In February development of both planes was consolidated under one man, Walt Gillette, a veteran aerodynamic engineer. Gillette, 61, had been involved in every new Boeing airliner since the 747, including the ill-fated 747X program, and he was very conscious of the possibility of failure. He keeps a chart in his office to remind visitors that new-airliner programs sank manufacturers like de Havilland and Lockheed. By contrast Boeing had successfully developed ten planes in a row going back to 1958, and he was determined to keep the streak intact. "Going ten for 11," said Gillette, "isn't acceptable."

In February and March, Boeing conducted a second round of private meetings with nearly two dozen customers. They got their first look at Project Yellowstone, now called the super-efficient airplane, just as they were beginning to have second thoughts about the Sonic Cruiser. It was now clear that the Sonic Cruiser would throw flight schedules into disarray. Planes leaving Asia for London would arrive at Heathrow several hours before the 5 A.M. curfew was lifted. Passengers flying overnight from New York to Europe would get an hour less sleep on what was already a short flight. Meanwhile a report asserted that Boeing was being forced to assume premium ticket prices to offset the higher cost of operating the Sonic Cruiser. An unnamed airline executive was quoted as being skeptical that the time savings offered by the plane would be worth the extra cost.

By April, Boeing was still having problems developing its business case for the Sonic Cruiser; strategist Piasecki said one might not be completed for another nine months. After more than a year of work the company still hadn't figured out how much value the airlines would place on extra speed.

At the Farnborough Air Show in England in July, yellow caution flags began flying all over the Boeing chalet. With the third round of customer meetings completed, a Boeing executive admitted that potential buyers were confused about whether they wanted the plane and that Boeing wouldn't proceed unless the project "makes sense." Other executives conceded that there had been less interest in the Sonic Cruiser since Sept. 11, and that greater attention was being paid to alternative designs. Gillette raised the possibility that the super-efficient plane might be launched together with the Sonic Cruiser "if sufficient market interest continues." It wasn't much of a vote of confidence.

In fact the market wasn't much interested in spending money on anything—old or new—at that point. Boeing disclosed that because of rescheduled or canceled orders, it now expected to deliver no more than 285 new airplanes in 2003, down from the 527 that went to customers in 2000. Since government-subsidized Airbus was scheduled to deliver 300 planes, it would pass Boeing for the first time and attain the position of industry leader.

One by one, potential customers began nervously backpedaling. Singapore Airlines' chief, who once foresaw "very big demand" for the Sonic Cruiser, reportedly shook his head when its name was mentioned. A Cathay Pacific executive said a cheaper plane "may be a better road to go down." Branson ignored the Sonic Cruiser entirely and declared that the Airbus A380 was the wave of the future. There were other concerns besides cost. A Japan Airlines executive worried about ground safety because one of those short fins might interfere with a passenger jetway.

In response Boeing did a little backpedaling of its own. Gillette publicly revealed that Boeing had been working on the superefficient airplane before the Sonic Cruiser but hadn't told customers about it until the second round of meetings. He insisted that the Sonic Cruiser was still his first priority but said that the most important thing was to build the right plane. "We have never gotten it wrong," he said. "I do not intend to get it wrong on the last airplane I get to do." Airbus was waiting to pounce. Chairman Noel Foregard needled Boeing: "We think airlines expect cheap and clean airplanes, and now our competitor is saying the same."

By autumn Boeing began to sound as if the decision on the Sonic Cruiser had been taken out of its hands. Gillette said Boeing would do what the marketplace wanted because "the market was in charge." CEO Condit declared that the Sonic Cruiser and the super-efficient airplane were in a horse race and that the company would pick one or the other. Boeing was sounding less like the pioneering company that had pushed ahead with the 747 on the basis of a single order and more like Procter & Gamble test-marketing a new detergent.

Despite all the bad news, Gillette continued development work back in Seattle. He completed a second round of wind tunnel tests and a fourth round of customer meetings. Boeing ran more analyses to determine how airlines could best utilize the faster plane in their service networks, but the results were only preliminary and required more study. The numbers continued to elude its analysts. CFO Michael Sears conceded, "We're having a problem with the business case." At the end of October, Boeing invited customers to Seattle to discuss the plane for a fifth time, this time in a group meeting. Some Boeing executives were already talking about the plane in the past tense. "If we hear interest in a more efficient airplane, it doesn't mean there will never be a Sonic Cruiser," said one.

The decision to halt development of the Sonic Cruiser, which could come on the eve of the 100th anniversary of the first manned flight, would mark another important date in the history of the Jet Age. Henceforth progress will be measured in tiny steps rather than giant leaps. Instead of higher and faster, the mantra for the future will be leaner and cheaper. A big part of the change will be driven by Boeing, where Condit believes that enhancing shareholder value takes precedence over exploring the wild blue yonder. Says analyst Richard Aboulafia of Teal Group consultants in Washington, D.C.: "The good old days of betting the company on a new airplane have been torpedoed by the capital markets. Airlines today don't want anything but commodities, and everything is replacement technology."

## Exhibit 2
Forecasted Demand for New Airplane Deliveries, 1997–2008

Source: Alex Taylor III, "Canceled: Boeing's Amazing Sonic Cruiser," *Fortune*, December 9, 2002, pp. 169–176. © 2002 Time Inc. All rights reserved. Reprinted by permission of Time Inc.

| Number of Airplanes | | | | |
| --- | --- | --- | --- | --- |
| | Single Aisle | Intermediate Twin Aisle | 747 and Larger | Total |
| North America | 1933 | 452 | 76 | 2461 |
| Europe | 1542 | 373 | 151 | 2066 |
| Asia Pacific | 923 | 625 | 196 | 1744 |
| Rest of world | 774 | 243 | 40 | 1057 |
| Totals | 5172 | 1693 | 463 | 7328 |

For Boeing, canceling the project is clearly the right business decision but will deal another blow to company morale. Employees were badly shaken when hijackers turned four Boeing airplanes into weapons and flew them into the World Trade Center and the Pentagon. Retirement funds have been hard hit by Boeing stock, down nearly 40 percent from its year's high. Both inside and outside the company, many will conclude that by failing to produce the Sonic Cruiser, the company has abandoned its historical mission to build "the next great flying machine."

Having failed to build its radical new plane, Boeing now must scramble to remain competitive. With Airbus preoccupied with getting its A380 ready for delivery, Boeing has a chance to pile up orders for the super-efficient airplane and tighten its grip on the point-to-point airliner market. But to capitalize on that opportunity, it will have to move more quickly than it has in the recent past. The airliner business may only be a two-horse race, but Boeing is running second for the first time in its history—and the Sonic Cruiser has cost it lots of precious time.

## QUESTIONS

1. Comment on Boeing's overall product development strategy.

2. What aspect of marketing research is missing from this story?

3. Fast forward to 2006 and let's assume the global economy is growing nicely again. Does this new design make sense in that scenario?

4. What routes would be most likely to adopt such an innovation?

5. Aside from Airbus, who else is competition for this high-speed jet liner?

6. How might Boeing share some of the great risks inherent in such a major product development venture?

# CASE 4-2 Tambrands: Overcoming Cultural Resistance

Tampax, Tambrands's only product, is the best-selling tampon in the world with 44 percent of the global market. North America and Europe account for 90 percent of those sales. The company saw earnings drop 12 percent to $82.8 million on revenues of $662 million in 1996. The stakes are high for Tambrands because tampons are basically all it sells, and in the United States, which currently generates 45 percent of Tambrands's sales, the company is mired in competition with such rivals as Playtex Products and Kimberly-Clark. What's more, new users are hard to get because 70 percent of women already use tampons.

In the overseas market, Tambrands officials talk glowingly of a huge opportunity. Only 100 million of the 1.7 billion eligible women in the world currently use tampons. In planning for expansion into a global market, Tambrands divided the world into three clusters, based not on geography, but on how resistant women are to using tampons. The goal is to market to each cluster in a similar way.

Most women in Cluster 1, including the United States, the United Kingdom, and Australia, already use tampons and may feel they know all they need to know about the product. In Cluster 2, which includes countries such as France, Israel, and South Africa, about 50 percent of women use tampons. Some concerns about virginity remain and tampons are often considered unnatural products that block the flow. Tambrands enlists gynecologists' endorsements to stress scientific research on tampons. Potentially the most lucrative group—but infinitely more challenging—is Cluster 3 which includes countries like Brazil, China, and Russia. There, along with tackling the virginity issue, Tambrands must also tell women how to use a tampon without making them feel uneasy. While the advertising messages differ widely from country to country, Tambrands is also trying to create a more consistent image for its Tampax tampons. The ads in each country show consecutive shots of women standing outside declaring the tampon message, some clutching a blue box of Tampax. They end with the same tagline, "Tampax. Women Know." While marketing consultants say Tambrands's strategy is a step in the right direction, some caution that tampons are one of the most difficult products to market worldwide.

"The greatest challenge in the global expansion of tampons is to address the religious and cultural mores that suggest that insertion is fundamentally prohibited by culture," says the managing director of a consulting company. "The third market [Cluster 3] looks like the great frontier of tampons, but it could be the seductive noose of the global expansion objective."

A Tambrands spokeswoman says the company is aware that even within Cluster 3, cultural and religious barriers vary. While the company's sales are increasing in some countries like Russia, Tambrands isn't targeting Muslim countries, she says. As Tambrands gears up for international expansion, it is also increasing ad spending in its mainstay U.S. market. Its new focus in the United States—encouraging women to use tampons overnight. Using the Cluster 1 approach of pitching to an already educated and jaded audience, a new ad tries to tease women with a provocative question, "Should I sleep with it, or not?"

The company's new global campaign for Tampax is a big shift from most feminine protection product ads, which often show frisky women dressed in white pants biking or turning cartwheels, while discreetly pushing messages of comfort. The new campaign features local women talking frankly about what had been a taboo subject in many countries. A recent Brazilian ad shows a close-up of a tampon while the narrator chirps, "It's sleek, smooth, and really comfortable to use."

For years Tambrands has faced a delicate hurdle selling Tampax tampons in Brazil because many young women fear they'll lose their virginity if they use a tampon. When they go to the beach in tiny bikinis, tampons aren't their choice. Instead, hordes of women use pads and gingerly wrap a sweater around their waist. Now, the No. 1 tampon maker hopes a bold new ad campaign will help change the mind-set of Brazilian women. "Of course, you're not going to lose your virginity," reassures one cheerful Brazilian woman in a new television ad. Tambrands's risky new ads are just part of a high-stakes campaign to expand into overseas markets where it has long faced cultural and religious sensitivities. The new ads feature local women being surprisingly blunt about such a personal product. In China, another challenging market for Tambrands, a new ad shows a Chinese woman inserting a tampon into a test tube filled with blue water. "No worries about leakage," declares another.

"In any country, there are boundaries of acceptable talk. We want to go just to the left of that," says the creative director of the New York advertising agency that is creating Tambrands's $65 million ad campaign worldwide. "We want them to think they have not heard frankness like this before." The agency planned to launch new Tampax ads in 26 foreign countries and the United States. However, being a single-product company, it is a risky proposition for Tambrands to engage in a global campaign and to build a global distribution network all at the same time.

Tambrands concluded that the company could not continue to be profitable if its major market was the United States and that to launch a global marketing program was too risky to do alone. The company approached Procter & Gamble about a buyout, and the two announced a $1.85 billion deal. The move puts Procter back in the tampon business for the first time since its Rely brand was pulled in 1980 after two dozen women who used tampons died from toxic shock syndrome. Procter plans to sell Tampax as a complement to its existing feminine-hygiene products, particularly in Asia and Latin America. P&G, known for its innovation in such mundane daily goods as disposable diapers and detergent, has grown in recent years by acquiring products and marketing them internationally. "Becoming part of P&G—a world-class company with global marketing and distribution capabilities—will accelerate the global growth of Tampax and enable the brand to achieve its full potential. This will allow us to take the expertise we've gained in the feminine protection business and apply it to a new market with Tampax." Market analysts applauded the deal. "P&G has the worldwide distribution that Tampax so desperately needs," said a stock market analyst. "Tambrands didn't have the infrastructure to tap into growth in the developing countries and P&G does."

P&G's efforts to build on Tambrands earlier marketing overseas have met with failure. The company abandoned its marketing in Brazil as too expensive and slow-growing, despite the promise the country initially seemed to offer with its beach culture and mostly urban population. The company also had dispatched marketers to southern India and Nanjing, China, but decided it couldn't justify the cost of expanding those tests. Most competitors, such as Playtex Products Inc. and Kimberly-Clark Corp., have basically written off creating new tampon markets as not worth the investment.

Regrouping and looking to build a marketing model that it could export to the rest of the globe, P&G began studying cities in Mexico. It figured Monterrey, an industrial hub of four million people—with 1.2 million women as its target customers—was a prime test spot. Research and focus groups of Mexican women led P&G to develop a new approach based on education.

"Everywhere we go, women say 'this is not for senoritas,'" says Silvia Davila, P&G's marketing director for Tampax Latin America. They're using the Spanish word for unmarried women as a modest expression for young virgins. This concern crops up in countries that are predominantly Catholic, executives say. In Italy, for instance, just 4 percent of women use tampons. P&G is finding that in countries where school health education is limited, that concept is difficult to overcome. P&G marketers say they often find open boxes of tampons in stores—a sign, P&G says, that women were curious about the product but unsure as to how it worked.

Hanging out in blue jeans and tank tops and sipping Diet Pepsi on a recent afternoon, Sandra Trevino and her friends seem very much in tune with American culture. But the young women are getting a lesson in Ms. Trevino's living room on how to use a product that is commonplace in the United States—and is a mystery to them.

"We're giving you the opportunity to live differently 'those days' of the month," Karla Romero tells the group. She holds up a chart of the female body, then passes out samples to the 10 women. Tampons will bring freedom and discretion, Ms. Romero says. "For me, it's the best thing that ever happened." A few of the women giggle. Ms. Romero is on the front lines of a marketing campaign for one of the world's most in-the-closet products. Procter & Gamble Co. pays Ms. Romero to give a primer on tampons in gatherings that resemble Tupperware parties.

Ms. Romero and other counselors run through a slide show about the stages of puberty. She pours blue liquid through a stand-up model of a woman's reproductive tract so the girls can see what happens inside their bodies when they have their periods. They see the tampon absorb the blue fluid. Ms. Romero points to the hymen on the model and explains they won't lose their virginity with a tampon. Still, when Maria brought home a sample from another session a few months ago, "my mother said don't use them," she reported. While the 18-year-old can be rebellious—she wears a tiny tank top, heavy-blue eye shadow, and three gold studs in each ear—she shares her mother's doubts. "You can lose your virginity. The norm here is to marry as a virgin," she says.

In addition to in-home demonstrations, counselors, in navy pantsuits or doctor's white coats embroidered with the Tampax logo, speak in stores, schools and gyms, anywhere women gather. One counselor met with 40 late-shift women workers in a cookie factory at midnight.

Counselors are taught to approach the subject in a dignified and sensitive manner. For example, they avoid using the word "tampon," which is too close to the Spanish word tampone, meaning plug. P&G calls its product an "internal absorbent" or simply Tampax.

Early results indicate its investment is paying off. Though tampons currently account for just 4 percent of the total Mexican market for feminine-protection products, that is up from 2 percent before the program. Tampax sales have tripled in the past 12 months.

Based on the success in Mexico, P&G picked Venezuela to be its next market because it's relatively small—23 million people—and its population is mostly urban. P&G gathered women in Caracas for focus groups where they expressed some cultural similarities with their Mexican counterparts, emphasizing the sanctity of virginity. But the tropical weather fostered some promising differences, too. There's a party culture where women seem comfortable with their bodies in skimpy skirts and clingy pants.

This attitude led P&G marketers to conclude that Tampax advertising could be racier in Venezuela. One slogan, though, misfires. On a list of common misconceptions headed by "will I lose my virginity?" P&G wrote, "La Ignorancia es la madre de todo los mitos," which translates as "ignorance is the mother of all myths." Focus groups were offended. "In a Latin culture, ignorance and mother don't go together." The title was scrapped.

In the end, they unveiled ads like, "Es Tiempo De Cambiar Las Reglas," for billboards, buses and magazines. The company knows that Venezuan women will catch the pun: "reglas" is the slang they use for their period, but the ad also translates as "It's time to change the rules."

P&G's advertising for Tampax has met with criticism and ridicule. For example, during the election of Russian President Putin, and as a response to the question why he turned down free radio and television time, he was quoted as saying that "he won't be marketed like Tampax or Snickers."

P&G has always been an early and aggressive adopter of new media, dating back to radio and television. Continuing in this vein, Procter & Gamble is stepping up its Internet activity to use the Web as a marketing medium. P&G's idea is to attract consumers to interactive sites that will be of interest to particular target groups, with the hope of developing deeper relationships with consumers. Its first step was to launch a website for teenage girls with information on puberty and relationships, promoting products such as Clearasil, Sunny Delight, and Tampax. The website, www.beinggirl.com, was designed with the help of an advisory board of teenage girls. Visit Tampax's website at www.tampax.com for some examples of their Web advertising in various countries. Procter & Gamble can be found at www.pg.com.

## QUESTIONS

1. Evaluate the wisdom of Tambrands becoming part of Procter & Gamble.

2. Tambrands indicated that the goal of its global advertising plan was to "market to each cluster in a similar way." Discuss this goal. Should P&G continue with Tambrand's original goal adapted to the new educational program? Why? Why not?

3. For each of the three clusters identified by Tambrands, identify the cultural resistance that must be overcome. Suggest possible approaches to overcoming the resistance you identify.

4. In reference to the approaches you identified in Question 3, is there an approach that can be used to reach the goal of "marketing to each cluster in a similar way"?

5. P&G is marketing in Venezuela with their "Mexican" model. Would that work in Brazil as well? Discuss.

Sources: Yumiko Ono, "Tambrands Ads Aim to Overcome Cultural and Religious Obstacles," *Wall Street Journal*, March 17, 1997, p. B8; Sharon Walsh, "Procter & Gamble Bids to Acquire Tambrands; Deal Could Expand Global Sales of Tampax," *Washington Post*, April 10, 1997, p. C01; Ed Shelton, "P&G to Seek Web Friends," *The European*, November 16, 1998, p. 18; Emily Nelson and Miriam Jordan "Sensitive Export: Seeking New Markets For Tampons, P&G Faces Cultural Barriers," *The Wall Street Journal* December 8, 2000, p.A1; Liane Hansen, "Election Campaign of Russian Acting President, Vladimir Putin," *Weekend Edition Sunday (NPR)*, March 12, 2000; and, "It's Hard to Market the Unmentionable," *Marketing Week*, March 13, 2002, p. 19.

# CASE 4—3 Iberia Airlines Builds a BATNA

MADRID—One day last April, two model airplanes landed in the offices of Iberia Airlines.

They weren't toys. The Spanish carrier was shopping for new jetliners, and the models were calling cards from Boeing Co. and Airbus, the world's only two producers of big commercial aircraft.

It was the first encounter in what would become a months-long dogfight between the two aviation titans—and Iberia was planning to clean up.

Airbus and Boeing may own the jetliner market, with its projected sales of more than $1 trillion in the next 20 years, but right now they don't control it. The crisis in the air-travel industry makes the two manufacturers desperate to nail down orders. So they have grown increasingly dependent on airlines, engine suppliers and aircraft financiers for convoluted deals.

Once the underdog, Airbus has closed the gap from just four years ago—when Boeing built 620 planes to Airbus's 294—and this year the European plane maker expects to overtake its U.S. rival. For Boeing, Iberia was a chance to stem the tide. For Airbus, Iberia was crucial turf to defend.

Iberia and a few other airlines are financially healthy enough to be able to order new planes these days, and they are all driving hard bargains. Enrique Dupuy de Lome, Iberia's chief financial officer and the man who led its search for widebody jets, meant from the start to run a real horse race. "Everything has been structured to maintain tension up to the last 15 minutes," he said.

Throughout the competition, the participants at Iberia, Boeing and Airbus gave *The Wall Street Journal* detailed briefings on the pitches, meetings and deliberations. The result is a rarity for the secretive world of aircraft orders: an inside look at an all-out sales derby with globetrotting executives, huge price tags and tortuous negotiations over everything from seats to maintenance and cabin-noise levels. The rivals' offers were so close that on the final day of haggling, Iberia stood ready with multiple press releases and extracted last-minute concessions in a phone call between the airline's chairman and the winning bidder.

By that point, both suitors felt like they'd been through the wringer. "With 200 airlines and only two plane makers, you'd think we'd get a little more respect," said John Leahy, Airbus's top salesman.

Airbus, a division of European Aeronautic Defense & Space Co., reckoned it had a big edge. It had sold Iberia more than 100 planes since 1997. Mr. Leahy thought last summer that he might even bag the contract with minimal competition. In June he had clinched a separate deal with Iberia for three new Airbus A340 widebodies.

But Mr. Dupuy made Mr. Leahy fight for the order—and so enticed Boeing to compete more aggressively. Then, "just to make things interesting," Mr. Dupuy said, he upped the pressure by going shopping for secondhand airplanes. These are spilling onto the market at cut-rate prices as the airline industry's problems force carriers to ground older jets with their higher operating costs.

Iberia is one of the industry's few highly profitable carriers, thanks to a thorough restructuring before the national carrier was privatized in early 2001. The world's No. 18 in passenger traffic,

with a fleet of 145 planes, it has benefited by flying few routes to North America, where air travel is in tatters, and by dominating the large Latin American market.

The Spanish carrier was looking to replace six Boeing 747-200 jumbo jets more than 20 years old. It wanted as many as 12 new planes to complete a 10-year modernization program for Iberia's long-haul fleet. Based on list prices, the 12-plane order was valued at more than $2 billion.

Iberia's Mr. Dupuy, 45 years old, a soft-spoken career finance man, first needed to woo Boeing to the table. The U.S. producer had last sold Iberia planes in 1995, and since then the carrier had bought so many Airbus jets that Boeing considered not even competing. But in late July, Mr. Dupuy met Toby Bright, Boeing's top salesman for jets. Over dinner in London, according to both men, Mr. Dupuy told Mr. Bright that Iberia truly wanted two suppliers, not just Airbus.

The Boeing sales chief was skeptical, and he recalled thinking at the time, "You're running out of ways to show us." Having worked as Boeing's chief salesman in Europe, Airbus's home turf, he had heard similar lines from customers who eventually bought Airbus planes. So he wondered: "Are we being brought in as a stalking horse?"

Yet replacing Iberia's old 747s with new 777s would be Boeing's last chance for years to win back Iberia. The argument against Boeing was that an all-Airbus fleet would make Iberia's operations simpler and cheaper. Still, going all-Airbus might weaken Iberia's hand in future deals. Airbus would know that the carrier's cost of switching to Boeing would require big investments in parts and pilot training.

In early November, Airbus and Boeing presented initial bids on their latest planes. The four-engine Airbus A340-600 is the longest plane ever built. Boeing's 777-300ER is the biggest twin-engine plane.

The new A340 can fly a bit farther and has more lifting power than the 777. The new Boeing plane is lighter, holds more seats and burns less fuel. The Boeing plane, with a catalog price around $215 million, lists for some $25 million more than the A340.

Mr. Dupuy, whose conference room is decorated with framed awards for innovative aircraft-financing deals, set his own tough terms on price and performance issues including fuel consumption, reliability and resale value. He won't divulge prices, but people in the aviation market familiar with the deal say he demanded discounts exceeding 40 percent.

As negotiations began, Mr. Dupuy told both companies his rule: Whoever hits its target, wins the order. The race was on.

Mr. Bright, who had been appointed Boeing's top airplane salesman in January of 2002, pitched the Boeing 777 as a "revenue machine." He insisted that his plane could earn Iberia about $8,000 more per flight than the A340-600 because it can hold more seats and is cheaper to operate. A burly 50-year-old West Virginian, Mr. Bright joined Boeing out of college as an aerospace designer. He knew the new Airbus would slot easily into Iberia's fleet. But he also felt that Mr. Dupuy's target price undervalued his plane.

At Airbus, Mr. Leahy also fumed at Iberia's pricing demands. A New York City native and the company's highest-ranking American, he pursues one goal: global domination over Boeing. Last year he spent 220 days on sales trips.

To Iberia, he argued that his plane offered a better investment return because the A340 is less expensive to buy and is similar to Iberia's other Airbus planes. From a hodge-podge of 11 models in 1997, Iberia now flies five types, and replacing the old 747s with A340s would trim that to four—offering savings on parts, maintenance and pilot training.

Even before presenting Airbus's offer, Mr. Leahy had flown to Madrid in October to make his case. On Nov. 18, he once again took a chartered plane for the one-hour flight from Airbus headquarters in Toulouse, France, to Madrid. For two hours that evening, he and his team sat with Mr. Dupuy and other Iberia managers around a table in Mr. Dupuy's office, debating how many seats can fit on a 777. Those numbers were crucial to the deal because each seat represents millions of dollars in revenue over the life of a plane but also adds weight and cost.

Boeing had told Iberia that its 777 could hold 30 more seats than the 350 Iberia planned to put on the Airbus plane. Mr. Leahy argued that the Boeing carries at most five more seats. "Get guarantees from Boeing" on the seat count, Mr. Leahy prodded the Iberia managers.

At Boeing, Mr. Bright was eager to soften Iberia's pricing demand. His account manager, Steve Aliment, had already made several visits to pitch the plane, and in late November, Mr. Bright sent him once again to protest that Iberia didn't appreciate the 777's revenue potential. Boeing desperately wanted to avoid competing just on price, so Mr. Bright pushed operating cost and comfort.

On the Airbus side, Mr. Leahy also was feeling pressured because a past sales tactic was coming back to haunt him. In 1995, when Iberia was buying 18 smaller A340s and Mr. Dupuy expressed concern about their future value, Mr. Leahy helped seal the deal by guaranteeing him a minimum resale price, which kicks in after 2005. If Iberia wants to sell them, Airbus must cover any difference between the market price of the used planes and the guaranteed floor price.

The guarantee is one of the tools that Mr. Leahy has used to boost Airbus's share of world sales to about 50 percent today from 20 percent in 1995. Boeing rarely guarantees resale values.

Mr. Dupuy had wanted guarantees because they lower his risk of buying, and thus cut his cost of borrowing. What mattered now was that the guarantees also freed him to sell the planes at a good price. Early in the competition, he suggested to both Airbus and Boeing that he might eventually replace all of Iberia's A340s with Boeings—and potentially stick Airbus with most of the tab.

"If we didn't have the guarantees, the position of Airbus would be very strong," Mr. Dupuy said in an interview. Instead, "we have a powerful bargaining tool on future prices."

On Dec. 4, Mr. Leahy flew again to Madrid to try to persuade Iberia to close a deal by year's end. Running through a presentation in Mr. Dupuy's office, Mr. Leahy and five colleagues ticked off fuel and maintenance costs for their plane. They asserted that passengers prefer the plane because it is quieter than the 777 and has no middle seats in business class.

Mr. Dupuy then rattled Mr. Leahy's cage with a new scenario: Iberia managers would be flying off next week to look at used Boeing 747-400 jumbo jets. Singapore Airlines had stopped flying the planes and was offering to lease them at bargain prices.

Mr. Leahy chided Mr. Dupuy, saying that was "like buying a used car," where a bargain can easily backfire. Mr. Dupuy replied that sometimes buying used makes sense because it offers the flexibility of other options. The message: Iberia could dump its Airbus fleet.

Within Iberia, another debate was ending. Mr. Dupuy heard from his managers the results of a yearlong analysis of the rival planes. The Airbus was cheaper than the Boeing, and the A340's four engines help it operate better in some high-altitude Latin American airports. But Iberia managers had decided they could fit 24 more seats on the Boeing, boosting revenue. And Iberia engineers calculated that the 777 would cost 8 percent less to maintain than the A340. Maintenance on big planes costs at least $3 million a year, so the savings would be huge over the life of a fleet.

Unaware of Iberia's analysis, the Boeing team arrived in Mr. Dupuy's office on the morning of Dec. 11 with three bound selling documents. One contained Boeing's revised offer, titled "Imagine the Possibilities . . . Iberia's 777 Fleet." Knowing Mr. Dupuy as a numbers guy, the Boeing team peppered him with data showing passengers would choose Iberia because they prefer the 777.

Mr. Dupuy told the salesmen their price was still too high.

By mid-December, Iberia chairman Xabier de Irala was getting impatient and wanted a decision by the end of the year. On Dec. 18, Boeing's Mr. Bright flew to Madrid. Over a long lunch, Mr. Dupuy reiterated his price target.

"If that's your number, let's give this up," Mr. Bright said. Talks continued cordially, but the men left doubtful they could close the gap. That Friday, Dec. 20, Mr. Dupuy told Iberia's board that prices from Airbus and Boeing were still too high and he would push the used-plane option harder.

By the start of the year, Airbus's Mr. Leahy, growing frustrated, arranged a Saturday meeting with Mr. Dupuy. On Jan. 4, the Iberia executive interrupted a family skiing holiday in the Pyrenees and drove two hours along winding French roads to meet Mr. Leahy for lunch.

Mr. Leahy spent four hours trying to convince Mr. Dupuy and a colleague that Airbus couldn't offer a better deal. Mr. Dupuy argued that Airbus had just given steep discounts to British airline easyJet, so it should do the same for Iberia. Annoyed, Mr. Leahy said media reports of a 50 percent price cut for easyJet were nonsense.

"You get Boeing to give you a 50 percent discount and I'll send you a bottle of champagne," he told the Iberia executives.

Mr. Bright was frustrated too. In the first week of January, Mr. Dupuy proposed visiting Seattle, where Boeing builds passenger planes. Mr. Bright's reply: If Iberia was unwilling to budge, there was little reason to come. So, when Mr. Dupuy said he would make the 14-hour journey, Mr. Bright was encouraged.

On Jan. 14, Mr. Dupuy and two colleagues arrived in Seattle. In the private dining room of Cascadia, a high-end downtown restaurant, they met for dinner with the Boeing salesmen and Alan Mulally, the chief executive of Boeing's commercial-plane division. Mr. Dupuy was impressed by Mr. Mulally's eagerness and was pleased when he urged Mr. Bright's team to find a way to close the gap.

The next day, the Boeing salesmen offered a new proposal—including a slightly lower price, improved financing and better terms on spare parts, crew training and maintenance support from General Electric Co., maker of the plane's engines.

When Mr. Dupuy left Seattle on Jan. 16, Mr. Bright felt Iberia was relenting a bit on price and that Mr. Dupuy wanted to "find a way to do the deal." Mr. Dupuy was also optimistic about striking a deal with Boeing.

Back in Madrid the next day, he raced off to join Iberia's chairman, Mr. Irala, for a meeting with Mr. Leahy and Airbus President Noel Forgeard. Mr. Irala, a bear of a man who is credited with saving Iberia from bankruptcy eight years ago, told the Airbus executives that Mr. Dupuy's price target remained firm. When the Airbus men relented on a few points, Mr. Irala yielded a bit, too, and spelled out Iberia's remaining targets for Airbus. Mr. Forgeard said a deal looked possible.

As the meeting broke up, Mr. Dupuy was pleased. He felt that Boeing and Airbus were digging deep. And no wonder. The world air-travel market was sinking deeper, and fears of war in Iraq and terrorism had slashed global bookings.

In the next few days, the sales teams from Boeing and Airbus each huddled to refine their offers. Both remained about 10 percent above Mr. Dupuy's price targets. Each called him several times daily, pushing for concessions. Mr. Dupuy didn't budge. On Jan. 23, he told Iberia's board that both companies could do better. The board scheduled a special meeting for the following Thursday, Jan. 30.

Energized by the Seattle meetings, Mr. Bright pushed his team "to go all out to win this bid," and they worked around the clock. Mr. Bright phoned Mr. Dupuy daily from Seattle and occasionally fielded his calls at 3 A.M., Pacific time. By late January, Boeing had cut its price by more than 10 percent after haggling over engine price with GE and financing with leasing firms. The 777 was now less than 3 percent above Mr. Dupuy's target—so close that Mr. Bright asked for a gesture of compromise from Iberia.

Mr. Dupuy was impressed by Boeing's new aggressiveness. But Airbus was also closing the gap so quickly, he said, that he could offer no concessions. To Mr. Leahy, he talked up Boeing's willingness to deal. "I was just talking to Toby . . ." Mr. Dupuy told Mr. Leahy during several conversations, referring to Mr. Bright. Airbus improved its offer further.

On Wednesday, the day before the deadline, Boeing and Airbus were running about even. In Seattle, Mr. Bright threw some clothes in his briefcase and proposed to Mr. Dupuy that he hop on a plane to Madrid. Mr. Dupuy said the choice was his, but what really mattered was the price target. That day, Mr. Dupuy told Messrs. Bright and Leahy that their bosses should call Mr. Irala with any final improvements before the board meeting.

On Thursday morning, Mr. Bright offered to trim Boeing's price further if Mr. Dupuy could guarantee that Boeing would win the deal. "I can't control Forgeard," Mr. Dupuy replied, referring to the Airbus president, who was due to talk soon with Mr. Irala. Mr. Bright made the price cut without the concession.

"You're very close," Mr. Dupuy told him.

Later, Mr. Forgeard got on the phone with Iberia's Mr. Irala, who said he still needed two concessions on the financial terms and economics of the deal. Airbus had already agreed to most of Mr. Dupuy's terms on asset guarantees and, with engine maker Rolls-Royce PLC, agreed to limit Iberia's cost of maintaining the jets. Mr. Forgeard asked if relenting would guarantee Airbus the deal. Mr. Irala replied yes, pending board approval—and looked over with a grin at Mr. Dupuy, who sat nearby with his laptop open. Mr. Forgeard acquiesced. Mr. Dupuy plugged the new numbers in his spreadsheet. Airbus had hit its target.

That evening, Boeing got a call from Iberia saying the airline would soon announce it had agreed to buy nine A340-600s and taken options to buy three more. Hours later, Boeing posted on its website a statement criticizing Iberia's choice as "the easiest decision." Mr. Bright said later that he simply couldn't hit Mr. Dupuy's numbers and "do good business."

In the end, Airbus nosed ahead thanks to its planes' lower price and common design with the rest of Iberia's fleet. By offering guarantees on the planes' future value and maintenance costs, plus attractive financing terms, Airbus edged out Boeing's aggressive package. The deal's final financial terms remain secret.

At Airbus, Mr. Leahy was relieved, but he faced one last slap. Iberia's news release crowed about Airbus's price guarantees on the planes—a detail Mr. Leahy considered confidential. Iberia's Mr. Dupuy said he wasn't rubbing it in. But he had, he boasted, won "extraordinary conditions."

## QUESTIONS

1. Critique the negotiation strategies and tactics of all three key executive involved: Dupuy, Leahy, and Bright.

2. Critique the overall marketing strategies of the two aircraft makers as demonstrated in this case.

3. What were the key factors that ultimately sent the order in Airbus' direction?

4. Assume that Iberia again is on the market for jet liners. How should Bright handle a new inquiry? Be explicit.

Source: Daniel Michaels, "Boeing and Airbus in Dogfight to Meet Stringent Terms of Iberia's Executives," *Wall Street Journal Europe,* March 10, 2003, p. A1. Copyright 2003 by Dow Jones & Co. Inc. Reproduced with permission of Dow Jones & Co. Inc. via Copyright Clearance Center.

# CASE 4−4 Blair Water Purifiers India

"A pity I couldn't have stayed for Diwali," thought Rahul Chatterjee. "But anyway it was great to be back home in Calcutta." The Diwali holiday and its festivities would begin in early November 2000, some two weeks after Chatterjee had returned to the United States. Chatterjee worked as an international market liaison for Blair Company, Inc. This was his eighth year with Blair Company and easily his favorite. "Your challenge will be in moving us from just dabbling in less developed countries [LDCs] to our thriving in them," his boss had said when Chatterjee was promoted to the job last January. Chatterjee had agreed and was thrilled, when asked to visit Bombay and New Delhi in April. His purpose on that trip was to gather background data on the possibility of Blair Company entering the Indian market for home water purification devices. Initial results were encouraging and prompted the second trip.

Chatterjee had used his second trip primarily to study Indian consumers in Calcutta and Bangalore and to gather information on possible competitors. The two cities represented quite different metropolitan areas in terms of location, size, language, and infrastructure—yet both suffered from similar problems in terms of water supplied to their residents. These problems could be found in many LDCs and were favorable to home water purification.

Information gathered on both visits would be used to make a recommendation on market entry and on elements of an entry strategy. Executives at Blair Company would compare Chatterjee's recommendation to those from two other Blair Company liaisons who were focusing their efforts on Argentina, Brazil, and Indonesia.

## INDIAN MARKET FOR HOME WATER FILTRATION AND PURIFICATION

Like most aspects of India, the market for home water filtration and purification took a good deal of effort to understand. Yet despite expending this effort, Chatterjee realized that much remained either unknown or in conflict. For example, the market seemed clearly a mature one, with four or five established Indian competitors fighting for market share. Or was it? Another view portrayed the market as a fragmented one, with no large competitor having a national presence and perhaps 100 small, regional manufacturers each competing in just one or two of India's 25 states. Indeed, the market could be in its early growth stages, as reflected by the large number of product designs, materials, and performances. Perhaps with a next-generation product and a world-class marketing effort, Blair Company could consolidate the market and stimulate tremendous growth—much like the situation in the Indian market for automobiles.

Such uncertainty made it difficult to estimate market potential. However, Chatterjee had collected unit sales estimates for a ten-year period for three similar product categories—vacuum cleaners, sewing machines, and color televisions. In addition, a Delhi-based research firm had provided him with estimates of unit sales for Aquaguard, the best-selling water purifier in several Indian states. Chatterjee had used the data in two forecasting models available at Blair Company along with three subjective scenarios—realistic, optimistic, and pessimistic—to arrive at the estimates and forecasts for water purifiers shown in Exhibit 1. "If anything," Chatterjee had explained to his boss, "my forecasts are conservative because they describe only first-time sales, not any replacement sales over the ten-year forecast horizon." He also pointed out that his forecasts applied only to industry sales in larger urban areas, which was the present industry focus.

One thing that seemed certain was that many Indians felt the need for improved water quality. Folklore, newspapers, consumer activists, and government officials regularly reinforced this need by describing the poor quality of Indian water. Quality suffered particularly during the monsoons because of highly polluted water

## Exhibit 1

Industry Sales Estimates and Forecasts for Water Purifiers in India, 1990–2005 (in thousands)

| Year | Unit Sales Estimates | Unit Sales Forecast Under . . . | | |
|------|------|------|------|------|
| | | Realistic Scenario | Optimistic Scenario | Pessimistic Scenario |
| 1990 | 60 | | | |
| 1991 | 90 | | | |
| 1992 | 150 | | | |
| 1993 | 200 | | | |
| 1994 | 220 | | | |
| 1995 | 240 | | | |
| 1996 | | 250 | 250 | 250 |
| 1997 | | 320 | 370 | 300 |
| 1998 | | 430 | 540 | 400 |
| 1999 | | 570 | 800 | 550 |
| 2000 | | 800 | 1,200 | 750 |
| 2001 | | 1,000 | 1,500 | 850 |
| 2002 | | 1,300 | 1,900 | 900 |
| 2003 | | 1,500 | 2,100 | 750 |
| 2004 | | 1,600 | 2,100 | 580 |
| 2005 | | 1,500 | 1,900 | 420 |

entering treatment plants and because of numerous leaks and unauthorized withdrawals from water systems. Such leaks and withdrawals often polluted clean water after it had left the plants. Politicians running for national, state, and local government offices also reinforced the need for improved water quality through election campaign promises. Governments at these levels set standards for water quality, took measurements at thousands of locations throughout the nation, and advised consumers when water became unsafe.

During periods of poor water quality, many Indian consumers had little choice but to consume the water as they found it. However, better-educated, wealthier, and more health-conscious consumers took steps to safeguard their family's health and often continued these steps year-round. A good estimate of the number of such households, Chatterjee thought, would be around 40 million. These consumers were similar in many respects to consumers in middle-class and upper-middle-class households in the United States and the European Union. They valued comfort and product choice. They saw consumption of material goods as a means to a higher quality of life. They liked foreign brands and would pay a higher price for such brands, as long as purchased products outperformed competing Indian products. Chatterjee had identified as his target market these 40 million households plus those in another 4 million households who had similar values and lifestyles, but as yet took little effort to improve water quality in their homes.

### Traditional Method for Home Water Purification

The traditional method of water purification in the target market relied not on any commercially supplied product but instead on boiling. Each day or several times a day, a cook, maid, or family member would boil two to five liters of water for ten minutes, allow it to cool, and then transfer it to containers for storage (often in a refrigerator). Chatterjee estimated that about 50 percent of the target market used this procedure. Boiling was seen by consumers as inexpensive, effective in terms of eliminating dangerous bacteria, and entrenched in a traditional sense. Many consumers who used this method considered it more effective than any product on the market. However, boiling affected the palatability of water, leaving the purified product somewhat "flat" to the taste. Boiling also was cumbersome, time-consuming, and ineffective in removing physical impurities and unpleasant odors. Consequently, about 10 percent of the target market took a second step by filtering their boiled water through "candle filters" before storage. Many consumers who took this action did so despite knowing that water could become recontaminated during handling and storage.

### Mechanical Methods for Home Water Filtration and Purification

About 40 percent of the target market used a mechanical device to improve their water quality. Half of this group used candle filters, primarily because of their low price and ease of use. The typical candle filter comprised two containers, one resting on top of the other. The upper container held one or more porous ceramic cylinders (candles), which strained the water as gravity drew it into the lower container. Containers were made of plastic, porcelain, or stainless steel and typically stored between 15 and 25 liters of filtered water. Purchase costs depended on materials and capacities, ranging from Rs. 350 for a small plastic model to Rs. 1,100 for a large stainless steel model (35 Indian rupees were equivalent to U.S. $1.00 in 2000). Candle filters were slow, producing 15 liters (one candle) to 45 liters (three candles) of filtered water each 24 hours. To maintain this productivity, candles regularly needed to be removed, cleaned, and boiled for 20 minutes. Most manufacturers recommended that consumers replace candles (Rs. 40 each) either once a year or more frequently, depending on sediment levels.

The other half of this group used water purifiers, devices that were considerably more sophisticated than candle filters. Water purifiers typically employed three water-processing stages. The first removed sediments, the second objectionable odors and colors, and the third harmful bacteria and viruses. Engineers at Blair Company were skeptical that most purifiers claiming the latter benefit actually could deliver on their promise. However, all purifiers did a better job in this respect than candle filters. Candle filters were totally ineffective in eliminating bacteria and viruses (and might even increase this type of contamination), despite advertising claims to the contrary. Water purifiers generally used stainless steel containers and sold at prices ranging from Rs. 2,000 to Rs. 7,000, depending on manufacturers, features, and capacities. Common flow rates were one to two liters of purified water per minute. Simple service activities could be performed on water purifiers by consumers as needed. However, more complicated service required units to be taken to a nearby dealer or required an in-home visit from a skilled technician.

The remaining 10 percent of the target market owned neither a filter nor a purifier and seldom boiled their water. Many consumers in this group were unaware of water problems and thought their water quality acceptable. However, a few consumers in this group refused to pay for products that they believed were mostly ineffective. Overall, Chatterjee believed that only a few consumers in this group could be induced to change their habits and become customers. The most attractive segments consisted of the 90 percent of households in the target market who boiled, boiled and filtered, only filtered, or purified their water.

All segments in the target market showed a good deal of similarity in terms of what they thought important in the purchase of a water purifier. According to Chatterjee's research, the most important factor was product performance in terms of sediment removal, bacteria and virus removal, capacity (either in the form of storage or flow rate), safety, and "footprint" space. Purchase price also was an important concern among consumers who boiled, boiled and filtered, or only filtered their water. The next most important factor was ease of installation and service, with style and appearance rated almost as important. The least important factor was warranty and availability of finance for purchase. Finally, all segments expected a water purifier to be warranted against defective operation for 18 to 24 months and to perform trouble-free for five to ten years.

## FOREIGN INVESTMENT IN INDIA

India appeared attractive to many foreign investors because of government actions begun in the 1980s during the administration of Prime Minister Rajiv Gandhi. The broad label applied to these actions was "liberalization." Liberalization had opened the Indian economy to foreign investors, stemming from recognition that protectionist policies had not worked very well and that Western economies and technologies—seen against the collapse of the Soviet Union—did. Liberalization had meant major changes in approval requirements for new commercial projects, investment policies, taxation procedures, and, most important, attitudes of government officials. These changes had stayed in place through the two national governments that followed Gandhi's assassination.

If Blair Company entered the Indian market, it would do so in one of three ways: joint working arrangement, joint venture company, or acquisition. In a joint working arrangement, Blair Company would supply key purifier components to an Indian company that would manufacture and market the assembled product. License fees would be remitted to Blair Company on a per-unit basis over the term of the agreement (typically five years, with an option to renew for three more). A joint venture agreement would have Blair Company partnering with an existing Indian company expressly for the purpose of manufacturing and marketing water purifiers. Profits from the joint venture operation would be split between the two parties per the agreement, which usually contained a clause describing buy/sell procedures available to the two parties after a minimum time period. An acquisition entry would have Blair Company purchasing an existing Indian company whose operations then would be expanded to include the water purifier. Profits from the acquisition would belong to Blair Company.

Beyond understanding these basic entry possibilities, Chatterjee acknowledged that he was no expert in legal aspects attending the project. However, two days spent with a Calcutta consulting firm had produced the following information. Blair Company must apply for market entry to the Foreign Investment Promotion Board, Secretariat for Industrial Approvals, Ministry of Industries. The proposal would go before the Board for an assessment of the relevant technology and India's need for the technology. If approved by the Board, the proposal then would go to the Reserve Bank of India, Ministry of Finance, for approvals of any royalties and fees, remittances of dividends and interest (if any), repatriations of profits and invested capital, and repayment of foreign loans. Although the process sounded cumbersome and time-consuming, the consultant assured Chatterjee that the government usually would complete its deliberations in less than six months and that his consulting firm could "virtually guarantee" final approval.

Law in India protected trademarks and patents. Trademarks were protected for 7 years and could be renewed on payment of a prescribed fee. Patents lasted for 14 years. On balance, Chatterjee had told his boss that Blair Company would have "no more problem protecting its intellectual property rights in India than in the United States—as long as we stay out of court." Chatterjee went on to explain that litigation in India was expensive and protracted. An appeal process that could extend a case for easily a generation compounded litigation problems. Consequently, many foreign companies preferred arbitration, as India was a party to the Geneva Convention covering Foreign Arbitral Awards.

Foreign companies were taxed on income arising from Indian operations. They also paid taxes on any interest, dividends, and royalties received, and on any capital gains received from a sale of assets. The government offered a wide range of tax concessions to foreign investors, including liberal depreciation allowances and generous deductions. The government offered even more favorable tax treatment if foreign investors would locate in one of India's six free trade zones. Overall, Chatterjee thought that corporate tax rates in India probably were somewhat higher than in the United States. However, so were profits—the average return on assets for all Indian corporations in recent years was almost 18 percent, compared with about 11 percent for U.S. corporations.

Approval by the Reserve Bank of India was needed for repatriation of ordinary profits. However, approval should be obtained easily if Blair Company could show that repatriated profits were being paid out of export earnings of hard currencies. Chatterjee thought that export earnings would not be difficult to realize, given India's extremely low wage rates and its central location to wealthier South Asian countries. "Profit repatriation was really not much of an issue, anyway," he thought. Three years might pass before profits of any magnitude could be realized; at least five years would pass before substantial profits would be available for repatriation. Approval of repatriation by the Reserve Bank might not be required at this time, given liberalization trends. Finally, if repatriation remained difficult, Blair Company could undertake countertrading or other actions to unblock profits.

Overall, investment and trade regulations in India in 2000 meant that business could be conducted much easier than ever before. Hundreds of companies from the European Union, Japan, Korea, and the United States were entering India in all sectors of the country's economy. In the home appliance market, Chatterjee could identify 11 such firms—Carrier, Electrolux, General Electric, Goldstar, Matsushita, Singer, Samsung, Sanyo, Sharp, Toshiba, and Whirlpool. Many of these firms had yet to realize substantial profits, but all saw the promise of a huge market developing over the next few years.

## BLAIR COMPANY

Eugene Blair founded Blair Company in 1975, after he left his position in research and development at Culligan International Company. Blair Company's first product was a desalinator, used by mobile home parks in Florida to remove salts from brackish well water supplied to residents. The product was a huge success, and markets quickly expanded to include nearby municipalities, smaller businesses, hospitals, and bottlers of water for sale to consumers. Geographic markets also expanded, first to other coastal regions near the company's headquarters in Tampa, Florida, and then to desert areas in the southwestern United States. New products were added rapidly as well; by 2000, the product line included desalinators, particle filters, ozonators, ion exchange resins, and purifiers. Industry experts generally regarded the product line as superior in terms of performance and quality, with prices higher than those of many competitors.

Blair Company sales revenues for 2000 would be almost $400 million, with an expected profit close to $50 million. Annual growth in sales revenues averaged 12 percent for the past five years. Blair Company employed over 4,000 people, with 380 having technical backgrounds and responsibilities.

Export sales of desalinators and related products began at Blair Company in 1980. Units were sold first to resorts in Mexico and Belize and later to water bottlers in Germany. Export sales grew rapidly, and Blair Company found it necessary to organize its International Division in 1985. Sales in the International Division also grew rapidly and would reach almost $165 million in 2000. About $75 million would come from countries in Latin and South America, $40 million from Europe (including shipments to Africa), and $50 million from South Asia and Australia. The International Division had sales offices, small assembly areas, and distribution facilities in Frankfurt, Germany; Tokyo, Japan; and Singapore.

The Frankfurt office had been the impetus for development and marketing of Blair Company's first product targeted exclusively to consumer households—a home water filter. Sales engineers at the Frankfurt office began receiving consumer and distributor requests for a home water filter soon after the fall of the Berlin Wall in 1989. By late 1993, two models had been designed in the United States and introduced in Germany (particularly to the eastern regions), Poland, Hungary, Romania, the Czech Republic, and Slovakia.

Blair Company executives watched the success of the two water filters with great interest. The market for clean water in LDCs was huge, profitable, and attractive in a socially responsible sense. However, the quality of water in many LDCs was such that a water filter usually would not be satisfactory. Consequently, in late 1997, executives had directed the development of a water purifier that could be added to the product line. Engineers had given the final design in the project the brand name "Delight." For the time being, Chatterjee and the other market analysts had accepted the name, not knowing if it might infringe on any existing brand in India or in the other countries under study.

## DELIGHT PURIFIER

The Delight purifier used a combination of technologies to remove four types of contaminants found in potable water—sediments, organic and inorganic chemicals, microbials or cysts, and objectionable tastes and odors. The technologies were effective as long as contaminants in the water were present at "reasonable" levels. Engineers at Blair Company had interpreted "reasonable" as levels described in several World Health Organization (WHO) reports on potable water and had combined the technologies to purify water to a level beyond WHO standards. Engineers had repeatedly assured Chatterjee that Delight's design in terms of technologies should not be a concern. Ten units operating in the company's testing laboratory showed no signs of failure or performance deterioration after some 5,000 hours of continuous use. "Still," Chatterjee thought, "we will undertake a good bit of field testing in India before entering. The risks of failure are too large to ignore. And, besides, results of our testing would be useful in convincing consumers and retailers to buy."

Chatterjee and the other market analysts still faced major design issues in configuring technologies into physical products. For example, a "point of entry" design would place the product immediately after water entry to the home, treating all water before it flowed to all water outlets. In contrast, a "point of use" design would place the product on a countertop, wall, or at the end of a faucet and treat only water arriving at that location. Based on cost estimates, designs of competing products, and his understanding of Indian consumers, Chatterjee would direct engineers to proceed only with "point of use" designs for the market.

Other technical details were yet to be worked out. For example, Chatterjee had to provide engineers with suggestions for filter flow rates, storage capacities (if any), unit layout and overall dimensions, plus a number of special features. One such feature was the possibility of a small battery to operate the filter for several hours in case of a power failure (a common occurrence in India and many other LDCs). Another might be one or two "bells or whistles" to tell cooks, maids, and family members that the unit indeed was working properly. Yet another might be an "additive" feature, permitting users to add fluoride, vitamins, or even flavorings to their water.

Chatterjee knew that the Indian market would eventually require a number of models. However, at the outset of market entry, he probably could get by with just two—one with a larger capacity for houses and bungalows and the other a smaller-capacity model for apartments. He thought that model styling and specific appearances should reflect a Western, high-technology school of design in order to distinguish the Delight purifier from competitors' products. To that end, he had instructed a graphics artist to develop two ideas that he had used to gauge consumer reactions on his last visit (see Exhibit 2). Consumers liked both models but preferred the countertop design to the wall-mount design.

## COMPETITORS

Upward of 100 companies competed in the Indian market for home water filters and purifiers. Although information on most of these companies was difficult to obtain, Chatterjee and the Indian research agencies were able to develop descriptions of three major competitors and brief profiles of several others.

**Eureka Forbes**  The most established competitor in the water purifier market was Eureka Forbes, a joint venture company established between Electrolux (Sweden) and Forbes Campbell (India). The company marketed a broad line of "modern, lifestyle products" including water purifiers, vacuum cleaners, and mixers/grinders. The brand name used for its water purifiers was "Aquaguard," a name so well established that many consumers mistakenly used it to refer to other water purifiers or to the entire product category. Aquaguard, with its ten-year market history, was clearly the market leader and came close to being India's only national brand. Eureka Forbes had also recently introduced a second brand of water purifier called "PureSip." The PureSip model was similar to Aquaguard except for its third-stage process, which used a polyiodide resin instead of ultraviolet rays to kill bacteria and viruses. This meant that water from a PureSip purifier could be stored safely for later usage. Also in contrast to Aquaguard, the PureSip model needed no electricity for its operation.

However, the biggest difference between the two products was how they were sold. Aquaguard was sold exclusively by a 2,500-person sales force that called directly on households. In contrast, PureSip was sold by independent dealers of smaller home appliances. Unit prices to consumers for Aquaguard and PureSip in 2000 were approximately Rs. 5,500 and Rs. 2,000, respectively. Chatterjee believed that unit sales of PureSip were much smaller than unit sales for Aquaguard but growing at a much faster rate.

An Aquaguard unit typically was mounted on a kitchen wall, with plumbing required to bring water to the purifier's inlet. A two-meter long power cord was connected to a 230-volt AC electrical outlet—the Indian standard. If the power supply were to drop to 190 volts or lower, the unit would stop functioning. Other limits of the product included a smallish amount of activated carbon, which could eliminate only weak organic odors. It could not remove strong odors or inorganic solutes such as nitrates and iron compounds. The unit's design did not allow for storage of treated water, and its flow rate of one liter per minute seemed slow to some consumers.

Aquaguard's promotion strategy emphasized personal selling. Each salesperson was assigned to a specific neighborhood and was monitored by a group leader who, in turn, was monitored by a supervisor. Each salesperson was expected to canvass his or her neighborhood, select prospective households (e.g., those with annual incomes exceeding Rs. 70,000), demonstrate the product, and make an intensive effort to sell the product. Repeated sales calls helped to educate consumers about their water quality and to reassure them that Aquaguard service was readily available. Television commercials and advertisements in magazines and newspapers supported the personal selling efforts. Chatterjee estimated that Eureka Forbes would spend about Rs. 120 million on all sales activities in 2000, or roughly 11 percent of its sales revenues. He estimated that about Rs. 100 million of the Rs. 120 million would be spent in the form of sales commissions. Chatterjee thought the company's total advertising expenditures for the year would be only about Rs. 1 million.

Eureka Forbes was a formidable competitor. The sales force was huge, highly motivated, and well managed. Moreover, Aquaguard was the first product to enter the water purifier market, and the name had tremendous brand equity. The product itself was probably the weakest strategic component—but it would take much to convince consumers of this. And, while the sales force offered a huge competitive advantage, it represented an enormous

## Exhibit 2
Possible Designs for the Delight Purifier

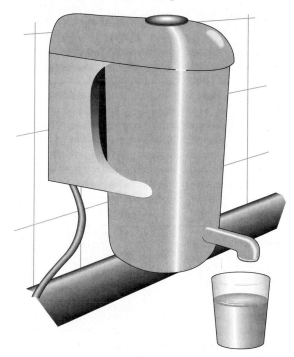

fixed cost and essentially limited sales efforts to large urban areas. More than 80 percent of India's population lived in rural areas, where water quality was even lower.

**Ion Exchange**   Ion Exchange was the premier water treatment company in India, specializing in treatments of water, processed liquids, and wastewater in industrial markets. The company began operations in 1964 as a wholly owned subsidiary of British Permutit. Permutit divested its holdings in 1985, and Ion Exchange became a wholly owned Indian company. The company presently served customers in a diverse group of industries, including nuclear and thermal power stations, fertilizers, petrochemical refineries, textiles, automobiles, and home water purifiers. Its home water purifiers carried the family brand name, Zero-B (Zero-Bacteria).

Zero-B purifiers used a halogenated resin technology as part of a three-stage purification process. The first stage removed suspended impurities via filter pads, the second eliminated bad odors and taste with activated carbon, and the third killed bacteria using trace quantities of polyiodide (iodine). The latter feature was attractive because it helped prevent iodine deficiency diseases and permitted purified water to be stored up to eight hours without fear of recontamination.

The basic purifier product for the home carried the name "Puristore." A Puristore unit typically sat on a kitchen counter near the tap, with no electricity or plumbing hookup needed for its operation. The unit stored 20 liters of purified water. It sold to consumers for Rs. 2,000. Each year the user must replace the halogenated resin at a cost of Rs. 200. Chatterjee estimated that Zero-B had captured about 7 percent of the Indian water purifier market. Probably the biggest reason for the small share was a lack of consumer awareness. Zero-B purifiers had been on the market for less than three years. They were not advertised heavily, nor did they enjoy the sales effort intensity of Aquaguard. Distribution, too, was limited. During Chatterjee's visit, he could find only five dealers in Calcutta carrying Zero-B products and none in Bangalore. Dealers that he contacted were of the opinion that Zero-B's marketing efforts soon would intensify—two had heard rumors that a door-to-door sales force was planned and that consumer advertising was about to begin.

Chatterjee had confirmed the latter point with a visit to a Calcutta advertising agency. A modest number of ten-second TV commercials soon would be aired on Zee TV and DD metro channels. The advertisements would focus on educating consumers with the position, "It is not a filter." Instead, Zero-B is a water purifier and much more effective than a candle filter in preventing health problems. Apart from this advertising effort, the only other form of promotion used was a point-of-sale brochure that dealers could give to prospective customers (see Exhibit 3).

On balance, Chatterjee thought that Ion Exchange could be a major player in the market. The company had over 30 years' experience in the field of water purification and devoted upward of Rs. 10 million each year to corporate research and development. "In fact," he thought, "all Ion Exchange really needs to do is to recognize the market's potential and to make it a priority within the company." However, this might be difficult to do, given the company's prominent emphasis on industrial markets. Chatterjee estimated that Zero-B products would account for less than 2 percent of Ion Exchange's 2000 total sales, estimated at Rs. 1,000 million. He thought the total marketing expenditures for Zero-B would be around Rs. 3 million.

## Exhibit 3
Zero-B's Point-of-Sale Brochure

**Singer**   The newest competitor to enter the Indian water purifier market was Singer India Ltd. Originally, Singer India was a subsidiary of The Singer Company, located in the United States, but a minority share (49 percent) was sold to Indian investors in 1982. The change in ownership had led to construction of manufacturing facilities in India for sewing machines in 1983. The facilities were expanded in 1994 to produce a broad line of home appliances. Sales revenues for 2000 for the entire product line—sewing machines, food processors, irons, mixers, toasters, water heaters, ceiling fans, cooking ranges, and color televisions—would be about Rs. 900 million.

During Chatterjee's time in Calcutta, he had visited a Singer Company showroom on Park Street. Initially he had hoped that Singer might be a suitable partner to manufacture and distribute the Delight purifier. However, much to his surprise, he was told that Singer now had its own brand on the market, "Aquarius." The product was not yet available in Calcutta but was being sold in Bombay and Delhi.

A marketing research agency in Delhi was able to gather some information on the Singer purifier. The product contained nine stages and sold to consumers for Rs. 4,000. It removed sediments, heavy metals, bad tastes, odors, and colors. It also killed bacteria and viruses, fungi, and nematodes. The purifier required water pressure (8 PSI minimum) to operate but needed no electricity. It came in a single countertop model that could be moved from one room to another. Life of the device at a flow rate of 3.8 liters per minute was listed as 40,000 liters—about four to six years of use in the typical Indian household. The product's life could be ex-

tended to 70,000 liters at a somewhat slower flow rate. However, at 70,000 liters, the product must be discarded. The agency reported a heavy advertising blitz accompanying the introduction in Delhi—emphasizing TV and newspaper advertising, plus outdoor and transit advertising as support. All ten Singer showrooms in Delhi offered vivid demonstrations of the product's operation.

Chatterjee had to admit that photos of the Aquarius purifier shown in the Calcutta showroom looked appealing. And a trade article he found had described the product as "state of the art" in comparison to the "primitive" products now on the market. Chatterjee and Blair Company engineers tended to agree—the disinfecting resin used in Aquarius had been developed by the United States government's National Aeronautics and Space Administration (NASA) and was proven to be 100 percent effective against bacteria and viruses. "If only I could have brought a unit back with me," he thought. "We could have some test results and see just how good it is." The trade article also mentioned that Singer hoped to sell 40,000 units over the next two years.

Chatterjee knew that Singer was a well-known and respected brand name in India. Further, Singer's distribution channels were superior to those of any competitor in the market, including those of Eureka Forbes. Most prominent of Singer's three distribution channels were the 210 company-owned showrooms located in major urban areas around the country. Each sold and serviced the entire line of Singer products. Each was very well kept and staffed by knowledgeable personnel. Singer products also were sold throughout India by over 3,000 independent dealers, who received inventory from an estimated 70 Singer-appointed distributors. According to the marketing research agency in Delhi, distributors earned margins of 12 percent of the retail price for Aquarius, while dealers earned margins of 5 percent. Finally, Singer employed over 400 salespeople who sold sewing machines and food processors door to door. Like Eureka Forbes, the direct sales force sold products primarily in large urban markets.

**Other Competitors**   Chatterjee was aware of several other water purifiers on the Indian market. The Delta brand from S & S Industries in Madras seemed a carbon copy of Aquaguard, except for a more eye-pleasing countertop design. According to promotion literature, Delta offered a line of water-related products—purifiers, water softeners, iron removers, desalinators, and ozonators. Another competitor was Alfa Water Purifiers, Bombay. The company offered four purifier models at prices from Rs. 4,300 to Rs. 6,500, depending on capacity. Symphony's Spectrum brand sold well around Bombay at Rs. 4,000 each, but removed only suspended sediments, not heavy metals or bacteria. The Sam Group in Coimbatore recently had launched its Water Doctor purifier at Rs. 5,200. The device used a third-stage ozonator to kill bacteria and viruses and came in two attractive countertop models, with 6- and 12-liter storage. Batliboi was mentioned by the Delhi research agency as yet another competitor, although Chatterjee knew nothing else about the brand. Taken all together, unit sales of all purifiers at these companies plus Zero-B and Singer probably would account for around 60,000 units in 2000. The remaining 190,000 units would be Aquaguards and PureSips.

At least 100 Indian companies made and marketed candle filters. The largest of these probably was Bajaj Electrical Division, whose product line also included water heaters, irons, electric lightbulbs, toasters, mixers, and grillers. Bajaj's candle filters were sold by a large number of dealers who carried the entire product line. Candle filters produced by other manufacturers were sold mostly through dealers who specialized in small household appliances and general hardware. Probably no single manufacturer of candle filters had more than 5 percent of any regional market in the country. No manufacturer attempted to satisfy a national market. Still, the candle filters market deserved serious consideration—perhaps Delight's entry strategy would attempt to "trade up" users of candle filters to a better, safer product.

Finally, Chatterjee knew that sales of almost all purifiers in 2000 in India came from large urban areas. No manufacturer targeted rural or smaller urban areas, and at best, Chatterjee had calculated, existing manufacturers were reaching only 10 to 15 percent of the entire Indian population. An explosion in sales would come if the right product could be sold outside metropolitan areas.

## RECOMMENDATIONS

Chatterjee decided that an Indian market entry for Blair Company was subject to three "givens" as he called them. First, he thought that a strategic focus on rural or smaller urban areas would not be wise, at least at the start. The lack of adequate distribution and communication infrastructure in rural India meant that any market entry would begin with larger Indian cities, most likely on the west coast.

Second, market entry would require manufacturing units in India. Because the cost of skilled labor in India was around Rs. 20 to Rs. 25 per hour (compared with $20 to $25 per hour in the United States), importing complete units was out of the question. However, importing a few key components would be necessary at the start of operation.

Third, Blair Company should find an Indian partner. Chatterjee's visits had produced a number of promising partners: Polar Industries, Calcutta; Milton Plastics, Bombay; Videocon Appliances, Aurangabad; BPL Sanyo Utilities and Appliances, Bangalore; Onida Savak, Delhi; Hawkins India, Bombay; and Voltas, Bombay. All companies manufactured and marketed a line of high-quality household appliances, possessed one or more strong brand names, and had established dealer networks (minimum of 10,000 dealers). All were involved to greater or lesser degrees with international partners. All were medium-sized firms—not too large that a partnership with Blair Company would be one-sided, not too small that they would lack managerial talent and other resources. Finally, all were profitable (15 to 27 percent return on assets in 1998) and looking to grow. However, Chatterjee had no idea if any company would find the Delight purifier and Blair Company attractive or if they might be persuaded to sell part or all of their operations as an acquisition.

### Field Testing and Product Recommendations

The most immediate decision Chatterjee faced was whether or not he should recommend a field test. The test would cost about $25,000, placing 20 units in Indian homes in three cities and monitoring their performance for three to six months. The decision to test really was more than it seemed—Chatterjee's boss had explained that a decision to test was really a decision to enter. It made no sense to spend this kind of time and money if India were not an attractive opportunity. The testing period also would give Blair Company representatives time to identify a suitable Indian company as a licensee, joint venture partner, or acquisition.

Fundamental to market entry was product design. Engineers at Blair Company had taken the position that purification technologies

planned for Delight could be "packaged in almost any fashion as long as we have electricity." Electricity was needed to operate the product's ozonator as well as to indicate to users that the unit was functioning properly (or improperly, as the case might be). Beyond this requirement, anything was possible. Chatterjee thought that a modular approach would be best. The basic module would be a countertop unit much like that shown in Exhibit 2. The module would outperform anything now on the market in terms of flow rate, palatability, durability, and reliability, and would store two liters of purified water. Two additional modules would remove iron, calcium, or other metallic contaminants that were peculiar to particular regions. For example, Calcutta and much of the surrounding area suffered from iron contamination, which no filter or purifier now on the Indian market could remove to a satisfactory level. Water supplies in other areas in the country were known to contain objectionable concentrations of calcium, salt, arsenic, lead, or sulfur. Most Indian consumers would need neither of the additional modules, some would need one or the other, but very few would need both.

### Market Entry and Marketing Planning Recommendations

Assuming that Chatterjee recommended proceeding with the field test, he would need to make a recommendation concerning mode of market entry. In addition, his recommendation should include an outline of a marketing plan.

*Licensee Considerations*   If market entry were in the form of a joint working arrangement with a licensee, Blair Company financial investment would be minimal. Chatterjee thought that Blair Company might risk as little as $30,000 in capital for production facilities and equipment, plus another $5,000 for office facilities and equipment. These investments would be completely offset by the licensee's payment to Blair Company for technology transfer and personnel training. Annual fixed costs to Blair Company should not exceed $40,000 at the outset and would decrease to $15,000 as soon as an Indian national could be hired, trained, and left in charge. Duties of this individual would be to work with Blair Company personnel in the United States and with management at the licensee to see that units were produced per Blair Company's specifications. Apart from this activity, Blair Company would have no control over the licensee's operations. Chatterjee expected that the licensee would pay royalties to Blair Company of about Rs. 280 for each unit sold in the domestic market and Rs. 450 for each unit that was exported. The average royalty probably would be around Rs. 300.

*Joint Venture/Acquisition Considerations*   If entry were in the form of either a joint venture or an acquisition, financial investment and annual fixed costs would be much higher and depend greatly on the scope of operations. Chatterjee had roughed out some estimates for a joint venture entry, based on three levels of scope (see Exhibit 4). His estimates reflected what he thought were reasonable assumptions for all needed investments plus annual fixed expenses for sales activities, general administrative overhead, research and development, insurance, and depreciation. His estimates allowed for the Delight purifier to be sold either through dealers or through a direct, door-to-door sales force. Chatterjee thought that estimates of annual fixed expenses for market entry via acquisition would be identical to those for a joint venture. However, estimates for the investment (purchase) might be considerably higher, the same, or lower. It depended on what was purchased.

**Exhibit 4**
Investments and Fixed
Costs for a Joint Venture
Market Entry

|  | Operational Scope | | |
| --- | --- | --- | --- |
|  | **Two Regions** | **Four Regions** | **National Market** |
| 2000 market potential (units) | 55,000 | 110,000 | 430,000 |
| Initial investment (Rs. 000) | 4,000 | 8,000 | 30,000 |
| Annual fixed overhead expenses (Rs. 000) | | | |
| Using dealer channels | 4,000 | 7,000 | 40,000 |
| Using direct sales force | 7,200 | 14,000 | 88,000 |

Chatterjee's estimates of Delight's unit contribution margins reflected a number of assumptions—expected economies of scale, experience curve effects, costs of Indian labor and raw materials, and competitors' pricing strategies. However, the most important assumption was Delight's pricing strategy. If a skimming strategy was used and the product sold through a dealer channel, the basic module would be priced to dealers at Rs. 5,500 and to consumers at Rs. 5,900. "This would give us about a Rs. 650 unit contribution, once we got production flowing smoothly," he thought. In contrast, if a penetration strategy was used and the product sold through a dealer channel, the basic module would be priced to dealers at Rs. 4,100, to consumers at Rs. 4,400, and yield a unit contribution of Rs. 300. For simplicity's sake, Chatterjee assumed that the two additional modules would be priced to dealers at Rs. 800, to consumers at Rs. 1,000, and would yield a unit contribution of Rs. 100.

To achieve unit contributions of Rs. 650 or Rs. 300, the basic modules would employ different designs. The basic module for the skimming strategy would be noticeably superior, with higher performance and quality, a longer warranty period, more features, and a more attractive appearance than the basic module for the penetration strategy. Positioning, too, most likely would be different. Chatterjee recognized several positioning possibilities: performance and taste, value for the money/low price, safety, health, convenience, attractive styling, avoiding diseases and health-related bills, and superior American technology. The only position he considered "taken" in the market was that occupied by Aquaguard—protect family health and service at your doorstep. While other competitors had claimed certain positions for their products, none

had devoted financial resources of a degree that Delight could not dislodge them. Chatterjee believed that considerable advertising and promotion expenditures would be necessary to communicate Delight's positioning. He would need estimates of these expenditures in his recommendation.

If a direct sales force were employed instead of dealers, Chatterjee thought that prices charged to consumers would not change from those listed previously. However, sales commissions would have to be paid in addition to the fixed costs necessary to maintain and manage the sales force. Under a skimming price strategy, the sales commission would be Rs. 550 per unit and the unit contribution would be Rs. 500. Under a penetration price strategy, the sales commission would be Rs. 400 per unit and the unit contribution would be Rs. 200. These financial estimates, he would explain in his report, would apply to 2001 or 2002, the expected first year of operation.

"If we go ahead with Delight, we'll have to move quickly," thought Chatterjee. "The window of opportunity is open but if Singer's product is as good as they claim, we'll be in for a fight. Still, Aquarius seems vulnerable on the water pressure requirement and on price. We'll need a product category 'killer' to win."

Professor James E. Nelson, University of Colorado at Boulder, wrote this case. He thanks students in the Indian Institute of Management, Calcutta, for their invaluable help in collecting all data needed to write this case. He also thanks Professor Roger Kerin, Southern Methodist University, for his helpful comments in writing this case. The case is intended for educational purposes rather than to illustrate either effective or ineffective decision-making. Some data as well as the identity of the company are disguised. Used with permission.

# CASE 4—5 Sales Negotiations Abroad for MRI Systems

International sales of General Medical's Magnetic Resonance Imaging (MRI) systems have really taken off in recent months. Your representatives are about to conclude important sales contracts with customers in both Tokyo and Rio de Janeiro. Both sets of negotiations require your participation, particularly as final details are worked out. The bids you approved for both customers are identical (see tables). Indeed, both customers had contacted you originally at a medical equipment trade show in Las Vegas, and you had all talked business together over drinks at the conference hotel. You expect your two new customers will be talking together again over the Internet about your products and prices as they had in Las Vegas. The Japanese orders are potentially larger because the doctor you met works in a hospital that has nine other units in the Tokyo/Yokohama area. The Brazilian doctor represents a very large hospital in Rio, which may require more than one unit. Your travel arrangements are now being made. Your local representatives will fill you in on the details. Best of luck!

[*Note:* Your professor will provide you with additional material that you will need to complete this case.]

## Table 1
### Price Quotation

| | |
|---|---|
| Deep Vision 2000 MRI (basic unit) | $1,200,000 |
| Product options | |
| • 2D and 3D time-of-flight (TOF) angiography for capturing fast flow | 150,000 |
| • Flow analysis for quantification of cardiovascular studies | 70,000 |
| • X2001 software package | 20,000 |
| Service contract (2 years normal maintenance, parts, and labor) | 60,000 |
| Total price | $1,500,000 |

## Table 2
### Standard Terms and Conditions

| | |
|---|---|
| Delivery | 6 months |
| Penalty for late delivery | $10,000/month |
| Cancellation charges | 10% of contract price |
| Warranty (for defective machinery) | parts, one year |
| Terms of payment | COD |

# CASE 4-6 National Office Machines—Motivating Japanese Salespeople: Straight Salary or Commission?

National Office Machines of Dayton, Ohio, manufacturers of cash registers, electronic data processing equipment, adding machines, and other small office equipment, has recently entered into a joint venture with Nippon Cash Machines of Tokyo, Japan. Last year, National Office Machines (NOM) had domestic sales of over $1.4 billion and foreign sales of nearly $700 million. Besides in the United States, it operates in most of Western Europe, the Mideast, and some parts of the Far East. In the past, it has had no significant sales or sales force in Japan, although the company was represented there by a small trading company until a few years ago. In the United States, NOM is one of the leaders in the field and is considered to have one of the most successful and aggressive sales forces found in this highly competitive industry.

Nippon Cash Machines (NCM) is an old-line cash register manufacturing company organized in 1882. At one time, Nippon was the major manufacturer of cash register equipment in Japan, but it has been losing ground since 1970 even though it produces perhaps the best cash register in Japan. Last year's sales were 9 billion yen, a 15 percent decrease from sales the prior year. The fact that it produces only cash registers is one of the major problems; the merger with NOM will give them much-needed breadth in product offerings. Another hoped-for strength to be gained from the joint venture is managerial leadership, which is sorely needed.

Fourteen Japanese companies have products that compete with Nippon; other competitors include several foreign giants such as IBM, National Cash Register, and Unisys of the United States, and Sweda Machines of Sweden. Nippon has a small sales force of 21 men, most of whom have been with the company their entire adult careers. These salespeople have been responsible for selling to Japanese trading companies and to a few larger purchasers of equipment.

Part of the joint venture agreement included doubling the sales force within a year, with NOM responsible for hiring and training the new salespeople, who must all be young, college-trained Japanese nationals. The agreement also allowed for U.S. personnel in supervisory positions for an indeterminate period of time and for retaining the current Nippon sales force.

One of the many sales management problems facing the Nippon/American Business Machines Corporation (NABMC, the name of the new joint venture) was which sales compensation plan to use. That is, should it follow the Japanese tradition of straight salary and guaranteed employment until death with no individual incentive program, or the U.S. method (very successful for NOM in the United States) of commissions and various incentives based on sales performance, with the ultimate threat of being fired if sales quotas go continuously unfilled?

The immediate response to the problem might well be one of using the tried-and-true U.S. compensation methods, since they have worked so well in the United States and are perhaps the kind of changes needed and expected from U.S. management. NOM management is convinced that salespeople selling its kinds of products in a competitive market must have strong incentives to produce. In fact, NOM had experimented on a limited basis in the United States with straight salary about ten years ago and it was a bomb. Unfortunately, the problem is considerably more complex than it appears on the surface.

One of the facts to be faced by NOM management is the traditional labor-management relations and employment systems in Japan. The roots of the system go back to Japan's feudal era, when a serf promised a lifetime of service to his lord in exchange for a lifetime of protection. By the start of Japan's industrial revolution in the 1880s, an unskilled worker pledged to remain with a company all his useful life if the employer would teach him the new mechanical arts. The tradition of spending a lifetime with a single employer survives today mainly because most workers like it that way. The very foundations of Japan's management system are based on lifetime employment, promotion through seniority, and single-company unions. There is little chance of being fired, pay raises are regular, and there is a strict order of job-protecting seniority.

Japanese workers at larger companies still are protected from outright dismissal by union contracts and an industrial tradition that some personnel specialists believe has the force of law. Under this tradition, a worker can be dismissed after an initial trial period only for gross cause, such as theft or some other major infraction. As long as the company remains in business, the worker isn't discharged, or even furloughed, simply because there isn't enough work to be done.

Besides the guarantee of employment for life, the typical Japanese worker receives many fringe benefits from the company. Bank loans and mortgages are granted to lifetime employees on the assumption that they will never lose their jobs and therefore the ability to repay. Just how paternalistic the typical Japanese firm can be is illustrated by a statement from the Japanese Ministry of Foreign Affairs that gives the example of A, a male worker who is employed in a fairly representative company in Tokyo.

> To begin with, A lives in a house provided by his company, and the rent he pays is amazingly low when compared with average city rents. The company pays his daily trips between home and factory. A's working hours are from 9 A.M. to 5 P.M. with a break for lunch which he usually takes in the company restaurant at a very cheap price. He often brings home food, clothing, and other miscellaneous articles he has bought at the company store at a discount ranging from 10 percent to 30 percent below city prices. The company store even supplies furniture, refrigerators, and television sets on an installment basis, for which, if necessary, A can obtain a loan from the company almost free of interest.
>
> In case of illness, A is given free medical treatment in the company hospital, and if his indisposition extends over a number of years, the company will continue paying almost his full salary. The company maintains lodges at seaside or mountain resorts where A can spend the holidays or an occasional weekend with the family at moderate prices. . . . It must also be remembered that when A reaches retirement age (usually 55) he will receive a lump-sum

retirement allowance or a pension, either of which will assure him a relatively stable living for the rest of his life.

Even though A is only an example of a typical employee, a salesperson can expect the same treatment. Job security is such an expected part of everyday life that no attempt is made to motivate the Japanese salesperson in the same manner as in the United States; as a consequence, selling traditionally has been primarily an order-taking job. Except for the fact that sales work offers some travel, entry to outside executive offices, the opportunity to entertain, and similar side benefits, it provides a young person with little other incentive to surpass basic quotas and drum up new business. The traditional Japanese bonuses are given twice yearly, can be up to 40 percent of base pay, and are no larger for salespeople than any other functional job in the company.

As a key executive in a Mitsui-affiliated engineering firm put it recently, "The typical salesman in Japan isn't required to have any particular talent." In return for meeting sales quotas, most Japanese salespeople draw a modest monthly salary, sweetened about twice a year by bonuses. Manufacturers of industrial products generally pay no commission or other incentives to boost their businesses.

Besides the problem of motivation, a foreign company faces other different customs when trying to put together and manage a sales force. Class systems and the Japanese distribution system with its penchant for reciprocity put a strain on the creative talents of the best sales managers, as Simmons, the U.S. bedding manufacturer, was quick to learn.

In the field, Simmons found itself stymied by the bewildering realities of Japanese marketing, especially the traditional distribution system that operates on a philosophy of reciprocity that goes beyond mere business to the core of the Japanese character. It's involved with *on,* the notion that regards a favor of any kind as a debt that must be repaid. To wear another's *on* in business and then turn against that person is to lose face, abhorrent to most Japanese. Thus, the owner of large Western-style apartments, hotels, or developments buys his beds from the supplier to whom he owes a favor, no matter what the competition offers.

In small department and other retail stores, where most items are handled on consignment, the bond with the supplier is even stronger. Consequently, all sales outlets are connected in a complicated web that runs from the largest supplier, with a huge national sales force, to the smallest local distributor, with a handful of door-to-door salespeople. The system is self-perpetuating and all but impossible to crack from the outside.

However, there is some change in attitude taking place as both workers and companies start discarding traditions for the job mobility common in the United States. Skilled workers are willing to bargain on the strength of their experience in an open labor market in an effort to get higher wages or better job opportunities; in the United States, it's called shopping around. And a few companies are showing a willingness to lure workers away from other concerns. A number of companies are also plotting how to rid themselves of deadwood workers accumulated as a result of promotions by strict seniority.

Toyo Rayon company, Japan's largest producer of synthetic fibers, started reevaluating all its senior employees every five years with the implied threat that those who don't measure up to the company's expectations have to accept reassignment and possibly demotion; some may even be asked to resign. A chemical engineering and construction firm asked all its employees over 42 to negotiate a new contract with the company every two years. Pay raises and promotions go to those the company wants to keep. For those who

think they are worth more than the company is willing to pay, the company offers retirement with something less than the $30,000 lump-sum payment the average Japanese worker receives at age 55.

More Japanese are seeking jobs with foreign firms as the lifetime-employment ethic slowly changes. The head of student placement at Aoyama Gakuin University reports that each year the number of students seeking jobs with foreign companies increases. Bank of America, Japan Motorola, Imperial Chemical Industries, and American Hospital Supply are just a few of the companies that have been successful in attracting Japanese students. Just a few years ago, all Western companies were places to avoid.

Even those companies that are successful work with a multitude of handicaps. American companies often lack the intricate web of personal connections that their Japanese counterparts rely on when recruiting. Further, American companies have the reputation for being quick to hire and even quicker to fire, whereas Japanese companies still preach the virtues of lifelong job security. Those U.S. companies that are successful are offering big salaries and promises of Western-style autonomy. According to a recent study, 20- to 29-year-old Japanese prefer an employer-changing environment to a single lifetime employer. They complain that the Japanese system is unfair because promotions are based on age and seniority. A young recruit, no matter how able, has to wait for those above him to be promoted before he too can move up. Some feel that if you are really capable, you are better off working with an American company.

Some foreign firms entering Japan have found that their merit-based promotion systems have helped them attract bright young recruits. In fact, a survey done by *Nihon Keizai Shimbun,* Japan's leading business newspaper, found that 80 percent of top managers at 450 major Japanese corporations wanted the seniority promotion system abolished. But, as one Japanese manager commented, "We see more people changing their jobs now, and we read many articles about companies restructuring, but despite this, we won't see major changes coming quickly."

A few U.S. companies operating in Japan are experimenting with incentive plans. Marco and Company, a belting manufacturer and Japanese distributor for Power Packing and Seal Company, was persuaded by Power to set up a travel plan incentive for salespeople who topped their regular sales quotas. Unorthodox as the idea was for Japan, Marco went along. The first year, special one-week trips to Far East holiday spots like Hong Kong, Taiwan, Manila, and Macao were inaugurated. Marco's sales of products jumped 212 percent, and the next year sales were up an additional 60 percent.

IBM also has made a move toward chucking the traditional Japanese sales system (salary plus a bonus but no incentives). For about a year, it has been working with a combination that retains the semiannual bonus while adding commission payments on sales over preset quotas. "It's difficult to apply a straight commission system in selling computers because of the complexities of the product," an IBM Japan official said. "Our salesmen don't get big commissions because other employees would be jealous." To head off possible ill feeling, therefore, some nonselling IBM employees receive monetary incentives.

Most Japanese companies seem reluctant to follow IBM's example because they have doubts about directing older salesmen to go beyond their usual order-taking role. High-pressure tactics are not well accepted here, and sales channels are often pretty well set by custom and long practice (e.g., a manufacturer normally deals with one trading company, which in turn sells only to customers A, B, C, and D). A salesman or trading company, for that matter, is not often encouraged to go after customer Z and get him away from a rival supplier.

**Exhibit 1**
Life Goals

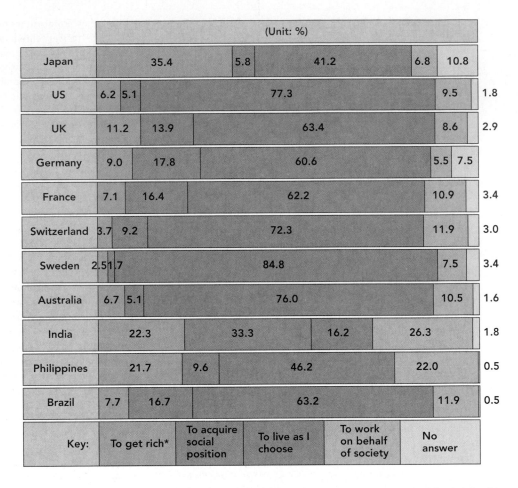

| | (Unit: %) | | | | | |
|---|---|---|---|---|---|---|
| Japan | 35.4 | 5.8 | 41.2 | | 6.8 | 10.8 |
| US | 6.2  5.1 | | 77.3 | | 9.5 | 1.8 |
| UK | 11.2 | 13.9 | 63.4 | | 8.6 | 2.9 |
| Germany | 9.0 | 17.8 | 60.6 | | 5.5  7.5 | |
| France | 7.1 | 16.4 | 62.2 | | 10.9 | 3.4 |
| Switzerland | 3.7  9.2 | | 72.3 | | 11.9 | 3.0 |
| Sweden | 2.5 1.7 | | 84.8 | | 7.5 | 3.4 |
| Australia | 6.7  5.1 | | 76.0 | | 10.5 | 1.6 |
| India | 22.3 | 33.3 | 16.2 | | 26.3 | 1.8 |
| Philippines | 21.7 | 9.6 | 46.2 | | 22.0 | 0.5 |
| Brazil | 7.7 | 16.7 | 63.2 | | 11.9 | 0.5 |
| Key: | To get rich* | To acquire social position | To live as I choose | To work on behalf of society | No answer | |

The Japanese market is becoming more competitive and there is real fear on the part of NOM executives that the traditional system just won't work in a competitive market. On the other hand, the proponents of the incentive system agree that the system really has not been tested over long periods or even adequately in the short term because it has been applied only in a growing market. In other words, was it the incentive system that caused the successes achieved by the companies or was it market growth? Especially there is doubt because other companies following the traditional method of compensation and employee relations also have had sales increases during the same period.

The problem is further complicated for NABMC because it will have both new and old salespeople. The young Japanese seem eager to accept the incentive method, but older ones are hesitant. How do you satisfy both since you must, by agreement, retain all the sales staff?

A study done by the Japanese government on attitudes of youth around the world suggests that younger Japanese may be more receptive to U.S. incentive methods than one would anticipate. In a study done by the Japanese prime minister's office, there were some surprising results when Japanese responses were compared with responses of similar-aged youths from other countries. Exhibit 1 summarizes some of the information gathered on life goals. One point that may be of importance in shedding light on the decision NOM has to make is a comparison of Japanese attitudes with young people in 11 other countries—the Japanese young people are less satisfied with their home life, school, and working situations, and are more passive in their attitudes toward social and political problems. Further, almost a third of those employed said they were dissatisfied with their present jobs primarily because of low income and short

vacations. Asked if they had to choose between a difficult job with responsibility and authority or an easy job without responsibility and authority, 64 percent of the Japanese picked the former, somewhat less than the 70 to 80 percent average in other countries.

Another critical problem lies with the nonsales employees; traditionally, all employees on the same level are treated equally, whether sales, production, or staff. How do you encourage competitive, aggressive salesmanship in a market unfamiliar with such tactics, and how do you compensate salespeople to promote more aggressive selling in the face of tradition-bound practices of paternalistic company behavior?

## QUESTIONS

1. What should NABMC offer—incentives or straight salary? Support your answer.

2. If incentives are out, how do you motivate salespeople and get them to compete aggressively?

3. Design a U.S.-type program for motivation and compensation of salespeople. Point out where difficulties may be encountered with your plan and how the problems are to be overcome.

4. Design a pay system you think would work, satisfying old salespeople, new salespeople, and other employees.

5. Discuss the idea that perhaps the kind of motivation and aggressiveness found in the United States is not necessary in the Japanese market.

6. Develop some principles of motivation that could be applied by an international marketer in other countries.

# CASE 4−7 AIDS, Condoms, and Carnival

Worldwide more than 3 million people died of AIDS in 2002 and more than 40 million are estimated to be living with HIV/AIDS.

## BRAZIL

Half a million Brazilians are infected with the virus that causes acquired immunodeficiency syndrome (AIDS), and millions more are at high risk of contracting the incurable ailment, a federal study reported. The Health Ministry study is Brazil's first official attempt to seek an estimate of the number of residents infected with human immunodeficiency virus (HIV). Many had doubted the government's prior number of 94,997. The report by the National Program for Transmissible Diseases/AIDS said 27 million Brazilians are at high risk to contract AIDS, and another 36 million are considered to be at a medium risk. It said Brazil could have 7.5 million AIDS victims in the next decade.

"If we are going to combat this epidemic, we have to do it now," said Pedro Chequer, a health ministry official. Chequer said the Health Ministry would spend $300 million next year, distributing medicine and 250 million condoms and bringing AIDS awareness campaigns to the urban slums, where the disease is most rampant. Last month, Brazil became one of the few countries to offer a promising AIDS drug free to those who need it. The drug can cost as much as $12,000 a year per patient.

AIDS cases in Brazil have risen so dramatically for married women that the state of São Paulo decided that it must attack a basic cultural practice in Latin America: Their husbands don't practice safe sex. Last month, the government of Brazil's megalopolis started promoting the newly released female condom.

Many of the new AIDS cases in Brazil are married women who have children, according to a report released last month at the Pan-American Conference on AIDS in Lima, Peru. Worldwide, women constitute the fastest-growing group of those diagnosed with HIV. And of the 30.6 million people who are diagnosed with HIV, 90 percent live in poor countries.

One Brazilian mother, Rosana Dolores, knows well why women cannot count on male partners to use condoms. She and her late husband never thought of protecting their future children against AIDS. "We were married. We wanted to have kids," says Mrs. Dolores, both of whose children were born HIV positive. "These days, I would advise young people to always use condoms. But married couples . . . who is going to?"

Brazil, with its 155 million people and the largest population in South America, has the second-highest number of reported HIV infections in the Americas, after the United States, according to a report released by the United Nations agency UNAIDS.

Public health officials say one reason why AIDS prevention efforts have failed is that many Brazilians just don't like condoms. Although use in Brazil has quadrupled in the past six years, it is still the least popular method of birth control—a touchy issue in the predominantly Roman Catholic country. Another reason is that condoms cost about 75 cents each, making them more expensive here than anywhere else in the world, health officials say.

Plus, Latin-style machismo leaves women with little bargaining power. Only 14 percent of Brazilian heterosexual men used condoms last year, according to AIDSCAP, an AIDS prevention program funded by the U.S. Agency for International Development. In other studies, many women said they would not ask their partner to use a condom, even if they knew he was sleeping with others.

"Women are afraid of asking their men to have safe sex, afraid of getting beaten, afraid of losing their economic support," says Guido Carlos Levi, a director at the health department at Emilio Ribas Hospital. "This is not Mexico, but we're quite a machistic society here."

The frequency with which Latin men stray from monogamous relationships has compounded the problem. In studies conducted in Cuba by the Pan American Health Organization, 49 percent of men and 14 percent of women in stable relationships admitted they had had an affair in the past year.

In light of statistics showing AIDS as the number one killer of women of childbearing age in São Paulo state, public health officials here launched a campaign in December promoting the female condom. The hope is that it will help women—especially poor women—protect themselves and their children. But the female condom seemed unlikely to spark a latex revolution when it hit city stores January 1. The price is $2.50 apiece—more than three times the price of most male condoms.

The Family Health Association is asking the government to help subsidize the product and to cut the taxes on condoms that make them out of reach for many poor Brazilians. "We're looking for a pragmatic solution to prevent the transmission of HIV-AIDS," group President Maria Eugenia Lemos Fernandes said. "Studies show there is a high acceptance of this method because it's a product under the control of women."

While 75 percent of the women and 63 percent of the men in a pilot study on the female condom said they approved of the device, many women with AIDS say they would have been no more likely to have used a female condom than a conventional one.

Part of the problem is perception: 80 percent of women and 85 percent of men in Brazil believe they are not at risk of contracting HIV, according to a study conducted by the Civil Society for the Well-Being of the Brazilian Family.

Also at risk are married women, 40 percent of whom undergo sterilization as an affordable way of getting around the Catholic church's condemnation of birth control, health officials noted.

"It's mostly married women who are the victims. You just never think it could be you," says a former hospital administrator who was diagnosed with the virus after her husband had several extramarital affairs. He died two years ago. "I knew everything there was to know about AIDS—I worked in a hospital—but I never suspected he was going out like that. He always denied it," she says.

While HIV is making inroads in rural areas and among teenagers in Brazil, Fernandes says it doesn't have to reach epidemic proportions as in Uganda or Tanzania. "There is a very big window of opportunity here."

Brazil's Health Ministry is adding a new ingredient to the heady mix that makes up the country's annual Carnival—condoms. The ministry will distribute 10 million condoms next month, along with free advice on how to prevent the spread of

AIDS, at places like Rio de Janeiro's sambadrome, where bare-breasted dancing girls attract millions of spectators every year.

"It's considered as a period of increased sexual activity," a spokeswoman at the ministry's AIDS coordination department said on Monday. "The euphoria provoked by Carnival and the excessive consumption of alcohol make it a moment when people are more likely to forget about prevention," she explained.

## INDIA

S. Mani's small barbershop in a southern Indian city looks like any other the world over. It's equipped with all the tools of the trade: scissors, combs, razors—and condoms, too.

A blue box full of free prophylactics stands in plain view of his customers as Mr. Mani trims hair and dispenses advice on safe sex, a new dimension to his 20-year career. "I start by talking about the family and children," Mr. Mani explains, snipping a client's moustache. "Slowly, I get to women, AIDS, and condoms."

Many Indian men are too embarrassed to buy condoms at a drugstore or to talk freely about sex with health counselors and family members. There's one place where they let down their hair: the barbershop. So, the state of Tamil Nadu is training barbers to be frontline soldiers in the fight against AIDS.

Programs like the barber scheme are what make Tamil Nadu, a relatively poor Indian state that's home to 60 million people, a possible model for innovative and cost-effective methods to contain AIDS in the developing world.

Six years after it was first detected in India, the AIDS virus is quickly spreading in the world's second most populous nation. Already, up to 5 million of India's 920 million people are infected with HIV—more than in any other country, according to UNAIDS, the United Nations' AIDS agency.

But faced with more immediate and widespread health woes, such as tuberculosis and malaria, officials in many Indian states are reluctant to make AIDS prevention a priority. And in some states, the acquired immunodeficiency syndrome is regarded as a Western disease of decadence; officials deny that prostitution and drug use even exist in their midst. "Some Indian states are still in total denial or ignorance about the AIDS problem," says Salim Habayeb, a World Bank physician who oversees an $84 million loan to India for AIDS prevention activities.

Tamil Nadu, the state with the third-highest incidence of HIV infection, has been open about its problem. Before turning to barbers for help, Tamil Nadu was the first state to introduce AIDS education in high school and the first to set up a statewide information hotline. Its comprehensive AIDS education program targets the overall population, rather than only high-risk groups.

In the past two years, awareness of AIDS in Tamil Nadu has jumped to 95 percent of those polled, from 64 percent, according to Operations Research Group, an independent survey group. "Just two years ago, it was very difficult to talk about AIDS and the condom," says P. R. Bindhu Madhavan, director of the Tamil Nadu State AIDS Control Society, the autonomous state agency managing the prevention effort.

The AIDS fighters take maximum advantage of the local culture to get the message across. Tamils are among the most ardent moviegoers in this film-crazed country. In the city of Madras, people line up for morning screenings even during weekdays. Half of the state's 630 theaters are paid to screen an AIDS-awareness short before the main feature. The spots are usually melodramatic musicals laced with warnings.

In the countryside, where cinemas are scarce, a movie mobile does the job. The concept mimics that used by multinationals, such as Colgate-Palmolive, for rural advertising. Bright red-and-blue trucks ply the back roads, blaring music from well-known movie soundtracks whose lyrics have been rewritten to address AIDS issues. In villages, hundreds gather for the show, on a screen that pops out of the rear of the truck.

In one six-minute musical, a young husband's infidelity leads to his death from AIDS, the financial ruin of his family, and then the death of his wife, also infected. The couple's toddler is left alone in the world. The heart-rending tale is followed by a brief lecture by an AIDS educator—and the offer of a free pack of condoms and an AIDS brochure.

Tamil Nadu's innovations have met with obstacles. It took several months for state officials to persuade Indian government television, Doordarshan, to broadcast an AIDS commercial featuring the Hindu gods of chastity and death. Even then, Mr. Madhavan says, Doordarshan "wouldn't do it as a social ad, so we have to pay a commercial rate."

Later, the network refused to air a three-minute spot in which a woman urges her husband, a truck driver, to use a condom when he's on the road. Safe infidelity was deemed "inappropriate for Indian living rooms," says Mr. Madhavan. A number of commercial satellite channels have been willing to run the ad.

Tamil Nadu has met little resistance recruiting prostitutes for the cause. For almost a year, 37-year-old prostitute Vasanthi has been distributing condoms to colleagues. With state funding, a nongovernmental agency has trained her to spread the word about AIDS and other sexually transmitted diseases. As an incentive, the state pays participants like Ms. Vasanthi, a mother of three, the equivalent of $14 a month, about what she earns from entertaining a client.

Before Ms. Vasanthi joined the plan, she didn't know that the condom could help prevent HIV infection. These days, if any client refuses to wear a condom, "I kick him out, even if it takes using my shoes," she says. "I'm not flexible about this." More men are also carrying their own condoms, she says.

Thank barbers such as Mr. Mani for that. Especially in blue-collar areas of Madras, men "trim their hair and beard before frequenting a commercial sex worker," says Mr. Madhavan. They can pick up their condom on the way out.

Tamil Nadu launched the barber program in Madras last March. So far, it has enlisted 5,000 barbers, who receive AIDS education at meetings each Tuesday—the barbers' day off. The barbers aren't paid to be AIDS counselors, but they appear to take pride in their new responsibility.

Over the generations, India's barbers have been respected as traditional healers and trusted advisers. "If you want to get to the king's ears, you tell his barber," says Mr. Madhavan, the state AIDS director. Reinforcing the image of barbers as healers, the local trade group is called the Tamil Nadu Medical Barber Association.

"I first talked about AIDS with my barber," says Thiyagrajan, an electrician in his 40s. "I don't have multiple partners, so I don't need a condom, but I take them for my friends."

One recent night, a man in his 30s walked into Aruna Hair Arts, greeted Mr. Swami, then headed out the door with a fistful of condoms scooped from the plastic dispenser. "That's OK," Mr. Swami says approvingly. "He's a regular customer."

A local nongovernmental organization helps barbers replenish condom stocks by providing each shop with self-addressed order forms. But the central government hasn't always been able to meet supply, for reasons ranging from bureaucracy to price disputes with manufacturers.

Tamil Nadu has started sourcing condoms from elsewhere. But they're too expensive to give away. So the next stage of the barber scheme, just under way, is to charge two rupees (six cents) for a two-condom "pleasure pack." The barbers will get a 25 percent commission. Thus far, the only perk of participating has been a free wall calendar listing AIDS prevention tips.

Roughly 30 percent of barbers approached by Tamil Nadu have refused to participate in the AIDS program, fearing that they would alienate customers. But those who take part insist that carrying the AIDS message hasn't hurt business. "We give the message about AIDS, but we still gossip about women," says barber N. V. Durairaj at Rolex Salon.

## LONDON INTERNATIONAL GROUP

London International Group (LIG) is recognized worldwide as a leader in the development of latex and thin-film barrier technologies. The Group has built its success on the development of its core businesses: the Durex family of branded condoms, Regent medical gloves, and Marigold household and industrial gloves. These are supported by a range of noncore health and beauty products.

With operational facilities in over 40 countries, 12 manufacturing plants, either wholly or jointly owned, and an advanced research and development facility based in Cambridge, England, LIG is well placed to expand into the new emerging markets of the world.

Durex is the world's No. one condom brand in terms of quality, safety, and brand awareness. The Durex family of condom brands includes Sheik, Ramses, Hatu, London, Kohinoor, Dua Lima, Androtex, and Avanti. Sold in over 130 countries worldwide and leader in more than 40 markets, Durex is the only global condom brand.

The development of innovative and creative marketing strategies is key to communicating successfully with target audiences. Consumer marketing initiatives remain focused on supporting the globalization of Durex. A series of innovative yet cost-effective projects have been used to communicate the global positioning "Feeling Is Everything" to the target young adult market, securing loyalty.

The Durex Global Survey, together with a unique multimillion-pound global advertising and sponsorship contract with MTV, has successfully emphasized the exciting and modern profile of Durex and presented significant opportunities for local public relations and event sponsorship, especially in emerging markets like Taiwan.

LIG continues to focus on education, using sponsorship of events such as the XI Annual AIDS Conference held in Vancouver and other educational initiatives to convey the safer sex message to governments, opinion formers, and educators worldwide.

## JAPAN

London Okamoto Corporation, the joint venture company between London International Group and Okamoto Industries, announced the Japanese launch in Spring 1998 of Durex Avanti, the world's first polyurethane male condom.

This is the first time an international condom brand will be available in Japan, the world's most valuable condom market, which is estimated to be worth £260 million ($433 million). Durex Avanti has already been successfully launched in the United States and Great Britain, and will be launched in Italy and other selected European countries during the next 12 months.

Durex Avanti condoms are made from Duron, a unique polyurethane material twice as strong as latex, which enables them to be made much thinner than regular latex condoms, thereby increasing sensitivity without compromising safety. In addition, Durex Avanti condoms are able to conduct body heat, creating a more natural feeling, and are the first condoms to be totally odorless, colorless, and suitable for use with oil-based lubricants.

Commenting on the launch, Nick Hodges, chief executive of LIG, said; "Japan is a very important condom market; with oral contraceptives still not publicly available, per capita usage rates for condoms are among the highest in the world. Our joint venture with Okamoto, Japan's leading condom manufacturer, gives us instant access to this strategically important market."

The joint venture with Okamoto, which is the market leader in Japan with a 53 percent share, was established in 1994 with the specific purpose of marketing Durex Avanti. Added Mr. Takehiko Okamoto, president of Okamoto, "We are confident that such an innovative and technically advanced product as Durex Avanti, coupled with our strong market franchise, will find significant consumer appeal in Japan's sophisticated condom market."

Durex Avanti, which is manufactured at LIG's research and development center in Cambridge, England, has taken over ten years to develop and represents an investment by LIG of approximately £15 million.

## QUESTIONS

1. Comment on the Brazilian and Indian governments' strategies for the prevention of AIDS via the marketing of condoms.

2. How is the AIDS problem different in the United States compared with Brazil and India?

3. Would the approaches described in Brazil and India work in the United States? Why or why not?

4. Suggest additional ways that London International Group could promote the prevention of AIDS through the use of condoms worldwide.

Sources: "Half a Million Brazilians Are Infected with the AIDS Virus," *Associated Press,* December 21, 1996; Andrea McDaniels, "Brazil Turns to Women to Stop Dramatic Rise in AIDS Cases. São Paulo Pushes Female Condom to Protect Married Women from Husbands. But Costs of Devices Are High," *Christian Science Monitor,* January 9, 1998, p. 7; "Brazil to Hand out 10 Million Condoms during Carnival," *Chicago Tribune,* January 19, 1998, p. 2; Miriam Jordan, "India Enlists Barbers in the War on AIDS," *Wall Street Journal,* September 24, 1996, p. A18; Caro Ezzzell, "Care for a Dying Continent," *Scientific American,* May 2000, pp. 96–105; and Ginger Thompson, "In Grip of Aids, South Africa Cries for Equity," *New York Times,* p. 4. Also see the websites www.lig.com and www.durex.com.

# CASE 4-8 Making Socially Responsible and Ethical Marketing Decisions: Selling Tobacco to Third World Countries

Strategic decisions move a company toward its stated goals and perceived success. Strategic decisions also reflect the firm's social responsibility and the ethical values on which such decisions are made. They reflect what is considered important and what a company wants to achieve.

Mark Pastin, writing on the function of ethics in business decisions, observes:

> There are fundamental principles, or ground rules, by which organizations act. Like the ground rules of individuals, organizational ground rules determine which actions are possible for the organization and what the actions mean. Buried beneath the charts of organizational responsibility, the arcane strategies, the crunched numbers, and the political intrigue of every firm are sound rules by which the game unfolds.

The following situations reflect different decisions made by multinational firms and governments and also reflect the social responsibility and ethical values underpinning the decisions. Study the following situations in the global cigarette marketplace carefully and assess the ground rules that guided the decisions of firms and governments.

## EXPORTING U.S. CIGARETTE CONSUMPTION

In the United States, 600 billion cigarettes are sold annually, but sales are shrinking rapidly. Unit sales have been dropping at about 1 to 2 percent a year, and sales have been down by almost 5 percent in the last six years. The U.S. Surgeon General's campaign against smoking, higher cigarette taxes, and the concern Americans have about general health have led to the decline in tobacco consumption. Faced with various class-action lawsuits, the success of states in winning lawsuits, and the pending federal legislation, tobacco companies have stepped up their international marketing activities to maintain profits.

Even though companies have agreed to sweeping restrictions in the United States on cigarette marketing and secondhand smoke and to bolder cancer-warning labels, they are fighting as hard as ever in the Third World to convince the media, the public, and policy makers that similar changes are not needed. At seminars in luxury resorts worldwide, tobacco companies invite journalists, all expenses paid, to participate in programs that play down the health risks of smoking. It is hard to gauge the influence of such seminars, but in the Philippines a government plan to reduce smoking by children was "neutralized" by a public relations campaign of cigarette companies to remove "cancer awareness and prevention" as a "key concern." A slant in favor of the tobacco industry's point of view seemed to prevail.

At a time when most industrialized countries are discouraging smoking, the tobacco industry is avidly courting consumers throughout the developing world, using catchy slogans, obvious image campaigns, and single-cigarette sales that fit a hard-pressed customer's budget. The reason is clear: The Third World is an expanding market. As an example, Indonesia's per capita cigarette consumption quadrupled in less than ten years. Increasingly, cigarette advertising on radio and television is being restricted in some countries; however, other means of promotion, especially to young people, are not controlled.

Recently, a major U.S. tobacco company signed a joint venture agreement with the Chinese government to produce cigarettes in China. The $21 million factory will employ 350 people and produce 2.5 billion cigarettes annually when fully operational. China, with more than 300 million smokers, produces and consumes about 1.4 trillion cigarettes per year, more than any other country in the world. The company projects that about 80 percent of the cigarettes produced under the joint venture will be for the domestic market, with the remainder for export.

By using China's low-cost labor, this factory will put cigarettes within easy reach of 1.1 billion consumers. The tobacco company estimates that China has more smokers than the United States has people. Just 1 percent of that 1.4 trillion cigarette market would increase the U.S. tobacco company's overseas sales by 15 percent and would be worth as much as $300 million in added revenue.

American cigarette companies have received a warm welcome in Russia, where at least 50 percent of the people smoke. Consumers are hungry for most things Western, and tobacco taxes are low. Unlike in the United States and other countries that limit or ban cigarette advertising, there are few effective controls on tobacco products in Russia.

## ADVERTISING AND PROMOTIONS

In Gambia, smokers send in cigarette box tops to qualify for a chance to win a new car. In Argentina, smoking commercials fill 20 percent of television advertising time. And in crowded African cities, billboards that link smoking to the good life tower above the sweltering shantytowns. They found such things as baby clothes with cigarette logos, health warnings printed in foreign languages and tobacco-sponsored contests for children. Latin American tobacco consumption rose by more than 24 percent over a ten-year period. In the same period, it rose by 4 percent in North America.

Critics claim that sophisticated promotions in unsophisticated societies entice people who cannot afford the necessities of life to spend money on a luxury—and a dangerous one at that. The sophistication theme runs throughout the smoking ads. In Kinshasa, Zaire, billboards depict a man in a business suit stepping out of a black Mercedes as a chauffeur holds the door. In Nigeria, promotions for Graduate brand cigarettes show a university student in his cap and gown. Those for Gold Leaf cigarettes have a barrister in a white wig and the slogan, "A very important cigarette for very important people." In Kenya, a magazine ad for Embassy cigarettes shows an elegant executive officer with three young men and women equivalent to American yuppies. She said the most disturbing trend in developing countries is marketing that associates tobacco with American affluence and culture. Some women in Africa, in their struggle for women's rights, defiantly smoke cigarettes as a symbol of freedom. Billboards all over Russia feature pictures of skyscrapers and white sandy beaches and slogans like "Total Freedom" or "Rendezvous with America." They aren't advertising foreign travel but American cigarette brands.

Every cigarette manufacturer is in the image business, and tobacco companies say their promotional slant is both reasonable and common. They point out that in the Third World a lot of people cannot understand what is written in the ads anyway, so the ads zero in on the more understandable visual image. "In most of the world, the Marlboro Man isn't just a symbol of the Wild West, he's a symbol of the West." "You can't convince people that all Americans don't smoke." In Africa, some of the most effective advertising includes images of affluent white Americans with recognizable landmarks, such as the New York City skyline, in the background. In much of Africa, children as young as five are used to sell single cigarettes, affordable to other children, to support their own nicotine habits, she said.

The scope of promotional activity is enormous. In Kenya, a major tobacco company is the fourth-largest advertiser. Tobacco-sponsored lotteries bolster sales in some countries by offering as prizes expensive goods that are beyond most people's budgets. Gambia has a population of just 640,000, but a tobacco company lottery attracted 1.5 million entries (each sent in on a cigarette box top) when it raffled off a Renault car.

Evidence is strong that the strategy of tobacco companies has targeted young people as a means of expanding market demand. Report after report reveals that adolescents receive cigarettes free as a means of promoting the product. For example, in Buenos Aires, a Jeep decorated with the yellow Camel logo pulls up in front of a high school. The driver, a blond woman wearing khaki safari gear, begins handing out free cigarettes to 15- and 16-year-olds on lunch recess. Teens visiting the Music Television Network's websites in China, Germany, India, Poland and Latin America were given the chance to click on a banner ad that led them to a questionnaire about their exposure to cigarette ads and other marketing tools in their countries. Some 10,000 teens responded to the banner ads. "In the past week, more than 62 percent of teenagers in these countries have been exposed to tobacco advertising in some form," the 17-year-old SWAT (Students Working Against Tobacco) chairman, told Reuters. "The tobacco companies learned that marketing to teens and kids worked in this country, but since they can't do it here anymore, they've taken what they learned to other countries." At a video arcade in Taipei, free American cigarettes are strewn atop each game. "As long as they're here, I may as well try one," says a high school girl.

In Malaysia, *Gila-Gila,* a comic book popular with elementary school students, carries a Lucky Strike ad. Attractive women in cowboy outfits regularly meet teenagers going to rock concerts or discos in Budapest and hand them Marlboros. Those who accept a light on the spot also receive Marlboro sunglasses.

In Russia, a U.S. cigarette company sponsors disco parties where thousands of young people dance to booming music. Admission is the purchase of one pack of cigarettes. In other cigarette-sponsored parties, attractive women give cigarettes away free.

In many countries, foreign cigarettes have a status image that also encourages smoking. A 26-year-old Chinese man says he switched from a domestic brand to Marlboro because "You feel a higher social position" when you smoke foreign cigarettes. "Smoking is a sign of luxury in Czechoslovakia as well as in Rus-

sia and other Eastern countries," says an executive of a Czech tobacco firm that has a joint venture with a U.S. company. "If I can smoke Marlboro, then I'm a well-to-do man."

The global tobacco companies insist that they are not attempting to recruit new smokers. They say they are only trying to encourage smokers to switch to foreign brands. "The same number of cigarettes are consumed whether American cigarettes or not," was the comment of one executive. Internal corporate documents reveal that British American Tobacco, the world's second-largest multinational tobacco company, secretly encouraged tax evasion and cigarette smuggling for decades in a global effort to secure market share and lure generations of new smokers.

The company vehemently denied the accusations, however, the evidence strongly suggested otherwise. Evidence showed that corporate executives in Britain, the United States, and other locales controlled the volumes, brands, marketing campaigns, timing, and price levels throughout the smuggling distribution networks they exploited. Company officials worked closely with their local agents—giving them perks such as tickets to soccer matches and vacation holidays. Researchers demonstrated that a large percentage of cigarettes were entering the black market by comparing annual global exports with global imports, about one-third of all cigarettes entering international commerce each year could not be accounted for. The industry's sanguine reaction to apparently losing a third of its inventory annually only fueled suspicions that companies knew more than they were willing to admit. "That cannot be happening without the knowledge of the producing companies."

Another source of concern is the tar and nicotine content of cigarettes. A 1979 study found three major U.S. brands with filters had 17 milligrams of tar in the United States, 22.3 in Kenya, 29.7 in Malaysia, and 31.1 in South Africa. Another brand with filters had 19.1 milligrams of tar in the United States, 28.8 in South Africa, and 30.9 in the Philippines.

Although cigarette companies deny they sell higher tar and nicotine cigarettes in the Third World, one British tobacco company does concede that some of its brands sold in developing countries contain more tar and nicotine than those sold in the United States and Europe. This firm leaves the tar- and nicotine-level decisions to its foreign subsidiaries, which tailor their products to local tastes. The firm says that Third World smokers are used to smoking their own locally made product, which might have several times more tar and nicotine.

C. Everett Koop, the retired U.S. Surgeon General, was quoted in a recent news conference as saying "Companies' claims that science cannot say with certainty that tobacco causes cancer were flat-footed lies" and that "sending cigarettes to the Third World was the export of death, disease, and disability." An Oxford University epidemiologist has estimated that, because of increasing tobacco consumption in Asia, the annual worldwide death toll from tobacco-related illnesses will more than triple over the next two decades. He forecasts about 3 million a year to 10 million a year by 2050, a fifth of them in China.

## GOVERNMENT INVOLVEMENT

Third World governments often stand to profit from tobacco sales. Brazil collects 75 percent of the retail price of cigarettes in taxes, some $100 million a month. The Bulgarian state-owned tobacco company, Bulgartabac, contributes almost $30 million in taxes to the government annually. Bulgartabac is a major exporter of cigarettes to Russia, exporting 40,000 tons of cigarettes in 1997.

Tobacco is Zimbabwe's largest cash crop. One news report from a Zimbabwe newspaper reveals strong support for cigarette companies. "Western antitobacco lobbies demonstrate unbelievable hypocrisy," notes one editorial. "It is relatively easy to sit in Washington or London and prattle on about the so-called evils of smoking, but they are far removed from the day-to-day grind of earning a living in the Third World." It goes on to comment that it doesn't dispute the fact that smoking is addictive or that it may cause diseases, but "smoking does not necessarily lead to certain death. Nor is it any more dangerous than other habits." Unfortunately, tobacco smoking has attracted the attention of a particularly "sanctimonious, meddling sector of society. They would do better to keep their opinions to themselves."

Generally, smoking is not a big concern of governments beset by debt, internal conflict, drought, or famine. It is truly tragic, but the worse famine becomes, the more people smoke—just as with war, when people who are worried want to smoke. "In any case," says one representative of an international tobacco company, "People in developing countries don't have a long enough life expectancy to worry about smoking-related problems. You can't turn to a guy who is going to die at age 40 and tell him that he might not live up to 2 years extra at age 70." As for promoting cigarettes in the Third World, "If there is no ban on TV advertising, then you aren't going to be an idiot and impose restrictions on yourself," says the representative, "and likewise, if you get an order and you know that they've got money, no one is going to turn down the business."

Cigarette companies figure China's self-interest will preserve its industry. Tobacco provides huge revenues for Beijing because all tobacco must be sold through the China National Tobacco Company monopoly. Duty on imported cigarettes is nearly 450 percent of their value. Consequently, tobacco is among the central government's biggest source of funding, accounting for more than $6 billion a year in income. China is also a major exporter of tobacco. In 2000, China's exports of tobacco were over $500 million, a substantial increase from a year earlier.

National self-interest is not limited to Third World countries alone. The United States sends mixed signals as well. On the one hand, the State Department sent a directive to all U.S. diplomatic posts in 1998 instructing them not to promote American tobacco products abroad. According to the directive, tobacco would be treated as a danger to health. At the same time, the directive also stated that the government would continue to oppose trade policies abroad that favor local tobacco products over those made in the United States. Unfortunately, even unambiguous directives have not always been followed. In 1994, the administration promised to work toward lowering smoking around the world but worked hand in hand with tobacco companies against an effort by the government of Thailand to require tobacco companies to disclose the ingredients in each brand of cigarettes. In 1994, the ambassador to Romania attended the opening of a new U.S. cigarette company plant and declared, "I'm sure that the splendid products of [company name] will prosper in Romania."

## ASSESSING THE ETHICS OF STRATEGIC DECISIONS

Ethical decision-making is not a simplistic "right" or "wrong" determination. Ethical ground rules are complex, tough to sort out and to prioritize, tough to articulate, and tough to use.

The complexity of ethical decisions is compounded in the international setting, which comprises different cultures, different perspectives of right and wrong, different legal requirements, and different goals. Clearly, when U.S. companies conduct business in an international setting, the ground rules become further complicated by the values, customs, traditions, ethics, and goals of the host countries, which have developed their own ground rules for conducting business.

Three prominent American ethicists have developed a framework to view ethical implications of strategic decisions by American firms. They identify three ethical principles that can guide American managers in assessing the ethical implications of their decisions and the degree to which these decisions reflect these ethical principles or ground rules. They suggest asking, "Is the corporate strategy acceptable according to the following ethical ground rules?"

| *Principles* | *Question* |
| --- | --- |
| Utilitarian ethics (Bentham, Smith) | Does the corporate strategy optimize the "common good" or benefits of all constituencies? |
| Rights of the parties (Kant, Locke) | Does the corporate strategy respect the rights of the individuals involved? |
| Justice or fairness (Aristotle, Rawls) | Does the corporate strategy respect the canons of justice or fairness to all parties? |

These questions can help uncover the ethical ground rules embedded in the tobacco consumption situation described in this case. These questions lead to an ethical analysis of the degree to which this strategy is beneficial or harmful to the parties, and ultimately, whether it is a "right" or "wrong" strategy, or whether the consequences of this strategy are ethical or socially responsible for the parties involved. These ideas are incorporated in the decision tree in Exhibit 1.

Laczniak and Naor discuss the complexity of international ethics or, more precisely, the ethical assumptions that underlie strategic decisions for multinationals.[1] They suggest that multinationals can develop consistency in their policies by using federal law as a baseline for appropriate behavior as well as respect for the host country's general value structure. They conclude with four recommendations for multinationals:

1. Expand codes of ethics to be worldwide in scope.

2. Expressly consider ethical issues when developing worldwide corporate strategies.

3. If the firm encounters major ethical dilemmas, consider withdrawal from the problem market.

4. Develop periodic ethics-impact statements, including impacts on host parties.

---

[1]Gene R. Laczniak and Jacob Naor, "Global Ethics: Wrestling with the Corporate Conscience," *Business*, July–September, 1985.

**Exhibit 1**

A Decision Tree for Incorpoating Ethical and
Social Responsibility Issues into Multinational
Business Decisions

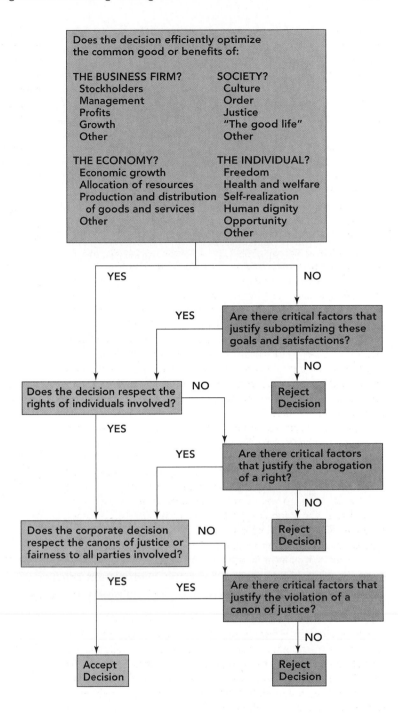

**QUESTIONS**

1. Using the model in Exhibit 1 as a guide, assess the ethical and
   social responsibility implications of the situation described.

2. Can you recommend alternative strategies or solutions to the
   dilemmas confronting the tobacco companies? To governments? What is the price of ethical behavior?

 3. Should the U.S. government support U.S. tobacco company interests abroad? See www.who.int, the World Health Organization website, for more details regarding the current tobacco
   controversy. See also www.getswat.com for a worldwide student initiative against smoking.

# NAME INDEX

# SUBJECT INDEX

## a